# MANAGERIAL ACCOUNTING INFORMATION

## AN INTRODUCTION TO ITS
## CONTENT AND USEFULNESS

A. THOMPSON MONTGOMERY

# MANAGERIAL ACCOUNTING INFORMATION

## AN INTRODUCTION TO ITS CONTENT AND USEFULNESS

ADDISON-WESLEY PUBLISHING COMPANY
Reading, Massachusetts • Menlo Park, California
London • Amsterdam • Don Mills, Ontario • Sydney

Sponsoring editor: William Hamilton
Production editor: Mary Cafarella
Designer: Phil Carver & Friends, Inc.
Illustrator: Richard Morton
Cover design: Richard Hannus

**Library of Congress Cataloging in Publication Data**

Montgomery, A. Thompson
  Managerial accounting information.

  Includes index.
  1. Managerial accounting. 2. Financial statements. 3. Accounting. I. Title
HF5635.M77      657'.3      78-67943
ISBN 0-201-04927-9

*Second printing, August 1980*

ISBN 0-201-04927-9
ABCDEFGHIJ-DO-89876543210

To the one
most deserving,
in long-overdue
recognition

# CONTENTS

# 2
## PLANNING AND CONTROL—AN OVERVIEW 49

Chapter preview; Need for planning and control; Organizations and their
objectives; Role of management: planning, organizing, and controlling;
Three types of management: operating, financial, and tax; Management
by objectives (MBO); Planning horizons; Strategic planning; Intermediate
planning; Budgeting: *sales budget, inventory budget, purchases and
other operating budgets, capital budgets, cash budgets, the master
operating budget and the financial budget, pro-forma financial statements;*
Budgeting objectives; Control: *goal congruence, the organization chart and
responsibility centers;* Control reporting; Role of managerial accounting
and the controller.

Chapter overview 77   New vocabulary and concepts; Review questions;
Mini-cases and questions for discussion; Essential problems; Supplementary problems.

*CHAPTER 2 APPENDIX   FINANCIAL RATIOS AND FINANCING
ACTIVITIES* 85
Financial statement ratios: *position or condition ratios, performance
ratios, investment return ratios;* Financing considerations and activities:
*short-term maintenance of adequate cash, long-term maintenance of
adequate working capital, long-term maintenance of adequate capacity
assets, long-term maintenance of desired capital structure.*

---

## THE PLANNING PROCEDURE AND ITS COMPONENTS
(Chapters 3 through 10) 95

# 3
## REVENUE AND ACTIVITY PLANNING: THE SALES BUDGET 95

Chapter preview; How much business will we do next year? Sales budget
critically important starting point; Steps in preparing the sales budget;
Characteristics of sales demand; Various forecasting approaches; Market-
based (macro) forecasting: *demand curves, sophisticated economic models,
anticipated economic benefits, customer surveys (market research), limitations of market-based forecasts;* Sales-based (micro) forecasts: *extrapolation of past sales experience, projections by the firm's sales personnel,
limitations of sales-based forecasts;* Planning for controllable factors:
*marketing strategy and promotional activities, credit policy, pricing,
special orders and modifications of sales mix;* Forecasting vs. budgeting:
translating forecasts into budgets; Budgets as expectations or motivating
devices; Planning for revenues other than sales; Planning activity in
nonprofit-directed organizations.

# 4
## INVENTORY AND PRODUCTION PLANNING: THE PURCHASES BUDGET

Chapter preview; What must I produce this year? What should I buy and when? *preparing the finished goods inventory budget, preparing the preliminary production schedule, preparing the raw materials inventory budget, preparing the purchases budget;* Inventory objectives; Lead times; Safety stock; ABC inventory control; Economic order quantities.

# 5
## COST BEHAVIOR AND THE PLANNING OF OPERATING COSTS: THE OPERATING BUDGETS

Chapter preview; What will my total operating costs be next year? *preparing the direct labor budget, preparing the manufacturing overhead budget;* Budgeting by responsibility centers; Building the company operating expenditure budget: *manufacturing budget, general selling and administrative budget, operating expenditure budget;* The importance of costs and their proper budgeting and control; Types of costs; Characteristics of costs; Cost behavior: *fixed costs, variable costs, linearity assumptions, mixed costs;* Determining specific cost patterns: *choosing the activity base;* Operating expenditure budgets for nonmanufacturers and nonprofit-directed organizations; Uses of cost information.

# 6
## CONTRIBUTION AND PROFIT PLANNING                                    221

Chapter preview; How can I increase my profitability? *analysis of proposed change in marketing strategy, analysis of proposed special order;* Role of profit; Profit maximization vs. satisfactory profit; Determining a satisfactory profit—the cost of capital; Achieving earnings equivalent to the cost of capital; Common errors in profit planning; Contribution and profitability analysis; Contribution per unit vs. contribution percentage; Some uses of contribution analysis: *breakeven and margin of safety, breakeven sensitivity, profit projections, necessary sales volume; product selection;* Assumptions and limitations of contribution (CVP) analysis; Contribution (CVP) analysis for nonprofit-directed organizations; Contribution and product costing alternatives.

Chapter overview  244   New vocabulary and concepts; Review questions; Mini-cases and questions for discussion; Essential problems; Supplementary problems.

*CHAPTER 6 APPENDIX   PRICING AND PRODUCT MIX   257* Pricing: *importance of pricing decision, economic model of pricing, practical economics of pricing, cost-related pricing, pricing new products, pricing established products, pricing special orders, competitive bids, regulated prices, related pricing issues;* Product mix; Suggestions for further reading.

# 7
## RELEVANT COSTS AND BUSINESS DECISIONS                              265

Chapter preview; Should I make or buy this item? Intermediate planning and decisions involving a segment or portion of the firm's activities; Relevant costs; Avoidable/escapable costs (or revenues); Sunk costs; Opportunity costs; Related fringe costs; Possible related investments; Noninvestment decisions involving only revenues; Noninvestment decisions involving only variable costs; Noninvestment decisions involving uniform flows of expected costs and benefits: *within relevant range and below capacity, within relevant range and at capacity, beyond relevant range, summary of decision rules for even flows;* Noninvestment decisions involving uneven flows of costs and benefits; Review of decision rules; Nonquantified considerations.

Chapter overview  288   New vocabulary and concepts; Review questions; Mini-cases and questions for discussion; Essential problems; Suppletary problems; Suggestions for further reading.

*CHAPTER 7 APPENDIX   REVIEW OF NET PRESENT VALUE (NPV)   299* *Present value of a single receipt (or payment), present value of a stream of receipts (or payments), simplified calculation when payment stream uniform;* Present value review problems.

# 8

## INVESTMENT DECISIONS—THE CAPITAL BUDGET 305

Chapter preview; Which truck should I buy? Characteristics of investment decisions: *resource commitments and risk, focus upon after-tax cash flows;* Investment-related tax considerations: *depreciation tax shield, investment tax credit, netting all tax effects into a single figure, comprehensive example of tax effects;* Alternative approaches to analyzing investment decisions; Acceptability criteria (decision rules) for investment decisions; Techniques of investment decision analysis: *adjustment for uneven lives, using differential cost analysis as a shortcut;* Sample analysis of sophisticated investment problem; Capital rationing; Incorporating provision for risk: *sensitivity analysis;* Providing for inflation; Other considerations; Control over investment decisions; The final capital budget.

Chapter overview 340    New vocabulary and concepts; Review questions; Mini-cases and questions for discussion; Essential problems; Supplementary problems; Suggestions for further reading.

*CHAPTER 8 APPENDIX    REVIEW OF CAPITAL LEASES, LEASE/ BUY DECISIONS, AND INTERNAL RATE OF RETURN    353 Accounting for leased property, the lease-vs.-buy decision, internal rate of return (IRR).*

# 9

## CASH PLANNING—THE CASH BUDGET 359

Chapter preview; Review of previous budgeting steps; Will we have enough cash in January to meet the payroll? Importance of cash management; Overview of cash budgeting process; Budgeting the first quarter: *schedule of receivables collections, schedule of cash from operations;* Completing the preliminary cash budget; Making provisions for adequate cash: *internal sources, external sources;* Providing for use of excess cash; The final cash budget; Appropriate time segments for cash budgeting; Cash budgeting without a formal budgeting and control system; Updating cash budgets throughout the year.

Chapter overview 387    New vocabulary and concepts; Review questions; Mini-cases and questions for discussion; Essential problems; Supplementary problems; Suggestions for further reading.

*CHAPTER 9 APPENDIX    REVIEW OF FUNDS FLOW    400* Various definitions and uses of the term "funds"; Function and information content of funds flow statements; Balanced approach; Funds from operations: *different uses of the term "operations";* Matched pairs; Funds flow statement—working capital only; Funds flow statement—cash only; Cash flow statements and cash budgets.

# 10
## TOTAL RESOURCE PLANNING—THE MASTER BUDGET                417

Chapter preview; What will be my profit and financial position next year? Planning of required resources: *the operating cycle and the need for working capital, requirements for noncurrent assets, appropriate amount of total assets—adequate capitalization, appropriate composition of assets;* Preparing the budgeted balance sheet (asset side): *budgeting cash and marketable securities, budgeting accounts receivable, budgeting inventories, completing the budgeted schedule of cost of goods manufactured, budgeting other working capital requirements, budgeting noncurrent assets;* Preparing the budgeted income statement; Completing the preliminary budgeted balance sheet; Determining need for additional long-term financing; Possible overall budget revision; Completing the master budget; Simplified master budgeting.

*CHAPTER 10 APPENDIX   FINANCING DESIRED RESOURCES*   449
Overview of financing alternatives: *short-term financing, long-term financing—equity financing, long-term financing—debt financing;* Choices between debt and equity financing—financial leverage.

## THE CONTROLLING PROCESS AND DIFFERENT APPROACHES
(Chapters 11 through 15)                                              459

# 11
## BUDGETARY CONTROL THROUGH RESPONSIBILITY CENTERS        459

Chapter preview; How can managers' performance be measured? Control objectives; Elements of control; Role of managerial accounting; Human and organizational motivation and behavior; Relating budgets and performance standards to organizational structure: *patterns of organization, types of responsibility centers;* The control cycle; Objectives of performance reports; Content of performance reports; The control chart; Using control information; Misusing planning and control information.

# 12
## CONTROL OF EXPENDITURE CENTERS—COMPARISON WITH
## THE BUDGET                                                        495

Chapter preview; Measuring expenditure center performance in unplanned situations; Fixed vs. flexible budgets; Performance reporting for expenditure centers: *volume variance, spending variance;* Importance of selecting meaningful activity measure; Segregating fixed and noncontrollable costs; Special considerations related to overhead variances; Budgeting and controlling programmed and nonmanufacturing costs; Budgeting and controlling common costs and service centers: *charging all costs on basis of usage, charging all costs by predetermined formula, artificial profit center with market-based transfer prices, separate budgeting with full-cost usage-based charges, separate budgeting and variable-cost-based usage charges;* Cost allocation for planning and control.

Chapter overview 519    New vocabulary and concepts; Review questions; Mini-cases and questions for discussion; Essential problems; Supplementary problems; Suggestions for further reading.

*CHAPTER 12 APPENDIX    ALLOCATING COSTS TO PRODUCTS AND OVERHEAD VARIANCE ANALYSIS    532*
*Special problems related to service centers;* Overhead variance analysis: *three-way overhead variance analysis.*

# 13
## EXPENDITURE CONTROL AND STANDARD COSTS                    543

Chapter preview; Who is responsible for these variances? Budgeting rates and standards; Setting standards and standard costs: *maintaining or revising standards;* Standard cost variances: *direct material variances, direct labor variances, interdependence and responsibility for variances;* Standards and different cost accounting systems; Standards for overhead; Standards and operating budgets; Standards for nonmanufacturing activities.

Chapter overview 562    New vocabulary and concepts; Review questions; Mini-cases and questions for discussion; Essential problems; Supplementary problems; Suggestions for further reading.

*CHAPTER 13 APPENDIX    REVIEW OF RECORDING PROCEDURES FOR PRODUCT COSTS    573*
*Merchandiser's inventory, retail inventory method, manufacturer's inventories.*

# 14
## CONTROL OF REVENUE, PROFIT, AND INVESTMENT CENTERS    581

Chapter preview; How good a job is the sales vice-president doing? Elements of revenue control: *revenue variance, contribution variance, other sales-related data, revenue reports by responsibility center;* How well is the firm doing overall? Profit centers for control: *transfer prices;* Investment centers; Performance evaluation.

Chapter overview 609    New vocabulary and concepts; Review questions;

# 17

## APPENDIXES

# PREFACE
# FOR INSTRUCTORS

This book is a companion volume to *Financial Accounting Information: An Introduction to Its Preparation and Use.*[1] It is designed for use in a single course devoted to managerial accounting offered at the undergraduate or MBA foundation-course level. Distinct managerial accounting courses have evolved as part of a growing awareness of several interrelated factors:

1. All business majors, and especially nonaccounting majors, need a thorough grounding in managerial accounting tools and concepts.

2. Managerial accounting is quite different and distinct from financial accounting. An inappropriate and potentially confusing impression of its purpose and role is often given when the subject is appended to or even combined in the same course or text with financial accounting.

3. A more balanced coverage of the two areas in separate courses can provide the majority of business majors with adequate basic exposure to both topics.

4. An understanding of cost behavior, relevant costs for decision purposes, and the operations and implications of a budgetary control system is of more importance to the nonaccountant than are the details of a cost accounting system.

5. Future accountants more readily learn cost accounting essentials at the intermediate-course level. Where much cost accounting detail is also included in the introductory course, unnecessary duplication may exist.

6. Future accountants need a more complete exposure to budgeting and control than is generally included in most common intermediate and advanced accounting courses.

---

[1] Reading, Mass.: Addison-Wesley Publishing Company, 1978.

7. Therefore, a managerial accounting course that emphasizes cost attributes, decision making, and budgeting, and that provides minimal exposure to cost accounting, achieves two objectives. First, it provides the majority of business students with the most appropriate emphasis, given their needs. Second, it provides future accountants with both necessary exposure to budgetary control and costs relevant to decision making and also the context for subsequent in-depth study of cost systems.

In the past, many students have found managerial accounting courses confusing and unnecessarily difficult for several reasons:

1. Courses and texts have often been merely a collection of loosely related topics with no obvious unifying objective or purpose. In some instances, continuity and coherence have been attempted by making the course a thinly disguised and watered-down version of an intermediate cost course. In the latter instance, most students who have not identified, and may never identify, with the cost accountant's interests and objectives find their only unifying objective to be "pass this course." Even potential accountants may become disillusioned when not presented with a meaningful, integrated picture of the vital importance and usefulness of accounting information to all levels of business and thus to society.

2. In some courses and texts, new subject matter is first introduced as something to be learned for its supposed intrinsic value. The material is then followed by isolated examples of application and usefulness. The "what" and "how" precede the "why." Today's students are less willing to learn material blindly on the premise that sometime in the future they will (may) find it relevant and useful.

3. Some existing managerial texts assume an unrealistic level of student sophistication. A large number of today's elementary accounting students are almost totally unfamiliar with business objectives, business problems, and the business information needs that managerial accounting serves. Often students are no longer required to take a basic business course as a prerequisite to elementary accounting courses. They may not even perceive lower cost or higher profit to be a desirable objective. Even MBA students taking foundation courses are novices with respect to business practice and terminology. They may be brighter and able to assimilate material more rapidly and in more depth, but they start at the same point as their undergraduate counterparts.

## SPECIAL FEATURES

This text has certain distinctive features intended both to serve the objectives and also to cope with the problems listed above:

• The central unifying focus of this book is upon the budgetary and control process. Integration is accomplished through the use, throughout the text, of the same small manufacturing firm, to which students can readily relate. All major concepts are introduced in the context of serving this one firm's problems.

- The essential elements of cost accounting are all covered in the first chapter and in Chapter 13. The introductory cost chapter may serve as a bridge from financial accounting to managerial accounting (financial accounting is not an essential prerequisite to the use of this text—see below).

- Chapter 2 provides an overview of the entire budgeting and control process, and introduces an eight-chapter section devoted to budgeting and decision making. Following the normal and logical budgeting sequence, the student is involved in each step leading to the final preparation of the master budget in Chapter 10.

- Chapters 11 through 15 are devoted to various aspects of control, and include an entire chapter devoted to control in nonprofit organizations; and Chapters 16 and 17 introduce the price-level issue and more sophisticated quantitative tools.

Following the pattern developed and successfully used in the companion text:

- Students are continuously involved in the learning process. Each chapter leads off with a business problem involving the development and use of managerial accounting information. Students first perceive the need for specific accounting information as a means of solving the problem. The information is then introduced in the context of the desired solution and in terms of general applicability. Students are encouraged to use newly introduced knowledge in the solution of other practical and relevant business (as distinct from accounting) problems.

- Students encounter new accounting topics only as they need them, and the topics are in a logical learning sequence of "building blocks" of progressively greater sophistication.

- The informal and conversational tone throughout the book is less severe and potentially intimidating than in traditional texts, and thus further encourages involvement.

- Coverage is included of some topics often omitted in elementary courses. Exposure to basic economic concepts and to uses of managerial accounting information in finance, marketing, and general management is presented at a simplified level and is designed to heighten the relevance that is the aim of the course. Throughout the text the student is provided with illustrations of the interface between managerial accounting and the other common business core-subject areas.

- Each chapter starts with a preview of material to be covered and its relevance, and concludes with a summary of behavioral skills that the student should have developed in working through the chapter.

• No significant knowledge of business practice or terminology is assumed. Important new common business and managerial accounting terms are italicized when first introduced and then listed for review at the end of each chapter. An extensive glossary of over 1,000 terms is included in an appendix for ready student reference and review.

• Chapter review questions cover all important concepts introduced in the chapter.

• Chapter problems are separately designated as "essential" and "supplementary." The latter category has particular relevance to graduate MBA foundation courses and more rigorous undergraduate courses.

• Complete solutions to all odd-numbered problems are included in an appendix. The student therefore has available, if needed, additional examples of applications in each topic area beyond the minimal samples included with the chapter text material. The student also has the opportunity to solve the odd-numbered problems and have immediate reinforcement, in a manner similar to that in a programmed text.

• Chapters contain mini-cases and questions for class discussion that are designed, particularly for graduate students, to highlight unresolved managerial accounting issues, and to stimulate involved interest beyond material covered in the text.

• Many chapters are divided into a main body and an appendix, to facilitate instructor flexibility in selecting materials and making assignments (see discussion below).

• An overview of essential financial accounting concepts is also included in a text appendix. For students taking managerial accounting without having previously taken a course or courses in financial accounting, this material should be assigned between the Introduction and Chapter 1. Others may use the material for review, or omit it entirely.

## FLEXIBILITY IN USE

A reading of the table of contents will reveal that the coverage of this book is extensive and perhaps greater than that desired by many instructors. Chapters 1 through 6 and 9 through 14 represent the core of the book and are designed for study in the sequence presented. Chapters 7 and 8 may be assigned as a pair in their given position, or between Chapters 10 and 11, or following Chapter 14. Chapters 15, 16, and 17 may be included or omitted, depending upon the aim of a particular course. It is recommended that Chapters 15 and 16 be assigned as related outside reading if they are not to be incorporated in the mainstream of your course.

Appendices provide even greater flexibility. The appendices to Chapters 2 and 9, along with book appendices D and E, are designed to provide or reinforce essential financial accounting concepts. The appendices to Chapters 3 and 5 are provided for those instructors who desire to incorporate least-squares regression analysis. Assigning both has proved to provide needed reinforcement, although the Chapter 5 appendix may stand alone. The Chapter 7 appendix reviewing present value should be assigned to all students not previously familiar with PV calculation who will be required to study Chapters 7 and 8. The appendix to Chapter 13 may be omitted or assigned, depending upon the relative preparer (bookkeeping) emphasis in a course. The remaining chapter appendices (4, 6, 8, 10, 12, 14, 15, and 16) include more sophisticated material related to their respective chapters, and may be included or omitted by instructor choice.

This flexibility makes the book suitable over a range of students from second-semester freshmen at a community college to graduate students. Specific suggested course outlines, including time and emphasis recommendations for each topic, depending upon course length (quarter or semester) and upon level of coverage desired, are included in the Instructor's Manual, together with customary support materials.

## ACKNOWLEDGMENTS

Acknowledgments are so necessary, so deserved, and so numerous. As stated in the companion text, I am indebted to Professors Charles Horngren, Gerald Wentworth, and James Porterfield at Stanford for much needed encouragement and support years ago when I was completing the doctorate. Department chairmen George Stenberg, William Niven, Julien Wade, and Dean Arthur Cunningham at San Francisco State made possible the scheduling opportunity that has allowed me to validate in the classroom the somewhat distinctive approaches in this text.

I am particularly indebted to Professors Lawrence A. Tomassini at the University of Texas at Austin, Doug Johnson at Arizona State University, and Anthony DiFrancesco at San Francisco State University. Each reviewed the first sixteen chapters in detail, and their valuable suggestions have been included. Professors Surendra Mansinghka, W. Gerald Platt, Paul Rech, and Charles Mott, also colleagues at San Francisco State, respectively contributed significantly to the Chapter 10 appendix, to Chapter 15, to Chapter 17, and to the Glossary. The text has also benefited from the many constructive criticisms of hundreds of graduate and undergraduate students at San Francisco State who have used portions of the manuscript over several years. Of course, none of these individuals is responsible for errors or oversights contained herein.

Pat Kennedy typed the many drafts of the entire manuscript. I trust that she will always be sure of my everlasting gratitude.

Once again the team of Bill Hamilton and Mary Cafarella, my editors at Addison-Wesley Publishing Company, somehow managed to convert the manuscript into a printed volume. Their miracles are appreciated.

I will welcome suggestions and comments on this text and the support materials, from both faculty and students.

*San Francisco*                                                                                 A.T.M.
*January, 1979*

# INTRODUCTION
# FOR STUDENTS

## FINANCIAL AND MANAGERIAL ACCOUNTING

This text is designed for your use in a course in managerial accounting. Together with its companion volume, *FINANCIAL ACCOUNTING INFOR-MATION—An Introduction to Its Preparation and Use,*[1] it covers topics commonly included in elementary accounting courses. Financial accounting supplies information to outsiders (creditors and owners) to assist them in making resource allocation decisions among different firms (interfirm resource allocation). In contrast, managerial accounting supplies data to insiders (managers) to facilitate resource allocation decisions within the firm (intrafirm resource allocation).

The inside–outside distinction, while useful, is not totally accurate. Management is also interested in financial statements, for they provide a wrap-up of the year's or period's activities and their effect upon the firm's position. They provide managers with a basis for forecasting as well as with the picture being presented to outsiders. Financial statements are significant to managers both as a planning tool and as the basis upon which their overall performance is evaluated by investors.

Managerial accounting includes some activities that provide information to, and are therefore linked to, financial accounting. Managerial accounting includes three subsystems: cost accounting, budgeting, and budgetary control. On the diagram in Fig. I.1, note carefully the information flows among the several activities.

Note that cost accounting feeds data into the financial accounting system for use in financial statements. Budgets are simply detailed plans for future activities expressed in dollar terms, and cost accounting supplies data on past costs to serve as a basis for predicting future costs. Also, as part of the budgeting or planning process, cost accounting supplies data for specific decisions that may be required covering major resource changes. For example:

- Whether to acquire a new piece of equipment;
- Whether to lease, purchase, or build a needed item;
- Whether to add or discontinue a product or product line, and so forth.

Managing a firm involves both planning and control. For control, management compares actual cost data for a period with planned data for the same period or actual data from previous periods. Budgeting supplies planned data and cost accounting supplies actual data. In Fig. I.1, the territorial boundaries between financial and managerial accounting are obvious. Managerial accounting includes cost accounting, budgeting, and budgetary control.

---

[1]    Addison-Wesley Publishing Company; Reading, Massachusetts; 1978.

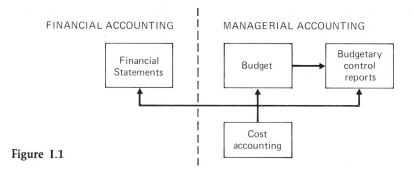

**Figure I.1**

## RELEVANCE OF MANAGERIAL ACCOUNTING

Unless you intend to major in accounting or finance, or to work in these areas, financial accounting knowledge is desirable primarily as the basis for learning those aspects of financial management that are necessary for the survival and success of any business. The study of financial accounting is a desirable, but not absolutely necessary, prerequisite to the study of managerial accounting. If you have not successfully completed a course in financial accounting, or if your exposure is more than six months in the past, you are advised to first review Appendix D at the back of this book **before** starting with Chapter 1.

Managerial accounting involves information and understanding common and necessary to all business careers. Whether you choose public relations, personnel, engineering, marketing, or any other career path apparently unrelated to accounting, you will need to work with costs and budgets. You can benefit by learning how costs are measured, accumulated, and reported by accountants and how budgets are prepared and interpreted. You will need to communicate with accountants concerning these subjects, for you will be evaluated by your superiors in terms of how well you can plan for costs and control them. Somewhat paradoxically, therefore, managerial accounting is often more relevant to nonaccountants than to accountants. Nonaccountants live and work with costs and budgets. Accountants dispassionately observe and report about them.[2]

## MANAGERIAL ACCOUNTING AND THE MANAGEMENT INFORMATION SYSTEM

Another difference between financial and managerial accounting involves agreement on topics covered. The study of financial accounting has been formalized and structured for many years. There is general agreement among

---

[2]    Accountants, of course, are concerned with those costs included in budgets related to their own recording and reporting activities. However, these costs are often a small fraction of total business costs, and cost control is not a primary focus of the accountant's activity.

educators and persons in business with respect to the topics and accounting activities that clearly relate to and should be covered by courses in Financial Accounting. Managerial accounting, on the other hand, is relatively new, and the need for more structured internal information has grown as rapidly as the size of business firms.

Within business organizations, the collection or set of all information produced and exchanged internally is referred to as the *management information system*. Responsibility for the parts of this information system has not developed uniformly among businesses. Within some firms, the managerial accounting territory includes only cost accounting, budgeting, and budgetary control. In others, it also includes material and production control, and even personnel and marketing information-related activities.

In college and university courses, coverage of the management information system is often even more fragmented. Information related to sales forecasting, planning, and control, may be found in both economics and marketing courses. Financial planning and control may be covered in both finance and economics courses. Controls over purchases, personnel, inventory, and production, are often covered in management courses. And many tools and techniques for forecasting and control are incorporated in quantitative methods, management science, information systems, and computer courses. In this book you can learn how these subsystems interface to accomplish the overall control system of the firm. This knowledge can serve as an integrating frame of reference when you proceed through the other more specialized functional courses commonly part of a business-major core.

## MANAGERIAL ACCOUNTING AND GAAP

A further distinction between financial and managerial accounting concerns Generally Accepted Accounting Principles, or GAAP. GAAP circumscribes the measurement and external reporting of financial information. Except for the cost accounting data supplied to financial accounting, GAAP does **not** apply to managerial accounting. Since managerial accounting information is prepared solely for use within the firm, there is no need for its comparison with data of other firms. The only criteria for managerial accounting information (except for the GAAP-related data noted above) are "Does it work for our firm?" "Is it cost-effective or cost-efficient, in that it provides needed information and the benefits derived exceed the cost of the information?"

Fortunately, most firms do not have unique managerial accounting systems. If they did, there would be no common basis for study. Most firms, through experimentation and interchange of ideas, have developed markedly similar systems comprised of elements that have proved to be cost-effective. In this book you can learn about these elements and the most common patterns followed by various cost, budgeting, and control systems.

Interchange of solutions to common managerial accounting problems is facilitated by a professional organization called the National Association of

Accountants (NAA). This organization was formerly known as the National Association of Cost Accountants. Its name now reflects the expanding role and responsibilities of the managerial accountant. The organization publishes *Management Accounting*, a journal that includes articles on solutions to managerial accounting problems and the implications of alternative solutions. The NAA also sponsors continuing education seminars and workshops and, through numerous local chapters, provides for interchange of information among members on an informal basis. In an effort to upgrade the professionalism of managerial accountants, the NAA offers an extensive examination leading to a Certificate in Managerial Accounting or CMA.[3] The CMA exam is similar in intent to the CPA exam, in that it measures professional accounting competence. The CMA exam focuses on the knowledge and skills required by the internal accountant, and the CPA exam focuses on the activities of the independent accountant or external auditor.

## LEARNING ABOUT MANAGERIAL ACCOUNTING

What is your learning objective with respect to managerial accounting? The primary objectives of this text are to assist you to learn how to prepare, read, use, and understand budgets and budget performance reports, and to develop an understanding of what information is and is not contained in budget-related reports. You will have the opportunity to see how your decisions and actions may affect your firm in both the planning and doing stages. A secondary objective is to provide you with a general understanding of cost accounting.

In both areas, particularly in cost accounting, you will need to learn some of the accountant's language and systems. This will enable you to understand what information is and is not included in specific cost or revenue data for a given item or activity or on a particular budget or budget performance report. You can understand how the data are measured and when and where they are reported.

To assist you in identifying new vocabulary, when an important managerial accounting or business term is first introduced it will be printed in *italics*. At the end of each chapter, you will find a list of the important terms introduced in that chapter. As a further aid, an extensive Glossary of common business and accounting vocabulary is included in Appendix B in the back of the book. If the meaning of a word or phrase is not clear to you, use the Glossary. Otherwise, you could misunderstand subsequent material, problems, or examinations using the term.

---

[3]   Note that managerial accounting is such a relatively new field that there is no agreement on even its title—managerial accounting vs. management accounting. Texts in this field are divided. Some are called management accounting and some managerial. Since the management of a firm is interested and involved with all aspects of accounting including financial accounting, the term managerial accounting would appear more appropriate as a description of nonfinancial accounting used by managers.

Future accountants will also need to learn the details of the practices and procedures followed by accountants in recording, summarizing, and reporting cost information. All individuals associated with business need to understand for proper interpretation **what** is included in cost data and what is not included. Accountants must also understand **how** cost data is accumulated and from what sources it is obtained. A brief description of cost-related bookkeeping procedures is included in Appendix E at the back of the book and in the Appendix to Chapter 13.

## PREREQUISITE KNOWLEDGE

Before attempting to learn managerial accounting, you should satisfy yourself that you have adequate prerequisite knowledge. Necessary prerequisite knowledge includes:

1. An ability to deal rapidly and confidently with simple algebra including: simultaneous equations, decimals, fractions, percentages, and square roots (essential).
2. An understanding of basic business practices and of the esssential elements of the financial accounting system (extremely helpful but not essential).
3. An elementary understanding of microeconomics (helpful but not necessary).

## COMMON DIFFICULTIES IN LEARNING ACCOUNTING

(*Note.* If you are familiar with and have used the companion text *FINANCIAL ACCOUNTING INFORMATION—An Introduction to Its Preparation and Use*, you may wish to skip this introductory discussion and proceed to the section entitled "Footnotes." This and other intervening sections are essentially the same as those included in the introduction to the other text.)

Unfortunately, some students, even if they have done well in the introductory financial accounting course, find managerial accounting difficult. You may avoid most difficulties if you are aware of the causes, properly diagnose the problem, and take corrective action. Experience has shown that the following items may be sources of difficulty in many courses and especially in elementary accounting:

**1. Student does not choose to assume personal responsibility for learning.** A text and/or an instructor cannot teach you accounting. They can help you learn accounting once you choose to take responsibility to learn and to put forth whatever effort is necessary.

**2. Student does not have adequate prerequisite knowledge and skills.**   To learn accounting effectively and efficiently, you need three skills. You should have the ability to read the English language carefully and precisely. You should have the ability to deal with simple algebraic concepts. You should have a general understanding of, and ability to conceptualize, common business language and problems. Deficiency in any of these areas will make your learning of accounting more difficult. You should seek the counsel of your instructor if you think you might have problems in these areas.

**3. Student does not choose to devote sufficient time and effort to learning.** Most students find that successful learning of accounting requires an investment of at least six to eight hours per week of intensive outside preparation for the typical course. Some students find that they can read or skim material and do minimum assigned problems in much less time. They fail to use the extra time for mastering vocabulary and concepts and for reinforcement (see items 4 and 5 below). Eventually they discover that many more hours than those previously "saved" are required to catch up. A few find it impossible to catch up.

**4. Student does not choose to thoroughly master new vocabulary and concepts with each chapter before proceeding to the next.**   Each chapter builds upon vocabulary and concepts introduced in previous chapters. To avoid confusion and extra effort, you must master the material in each chapter as assigned and not let yourself fall behind. Chapters in this text contain checklists to test yourself before proceeding. These checklists will be described later in this introduction.

**5. Student does not choose to adequately reinforce his or her new knowledge.** Effective and lasting learning of new knowledge and skill requires reinforcement. Reinforcement involves both repetition and application. The amount of necessary reinforcement varies among students and among different subjects. Each student must provide himself or herself with whatever repetition is necessary. Chapters in this text have cases and problems to provide opportunities for testing and reinforcing new knowledge through application to new situations.

**6. Student does not choose to seek assistance from others when needed.** Students may avoid asking questions of their fellow students or their instructor because they think they will appear stupid. Unless one is truly exceptional, it is difficult to learn all managerial accounting without some assistance. If you share your confusion with your classmates and your instructor, they may help you.

**7. Student does not choose to prepare preperly for accounting examinations.** Most managerial accounting examination questions require precise answers. Correct answers require knowledge of all the vocabulary and concepts related to the item being examined. A general, as distinct from a specific, understanding often will not suffice. Knowing **almost** all of the necessary parts is usually not enough. The missing or unclear part can be vital. Continual review and self-testing in an environment duplicating exam conditions as you proceed through the course will pinpoint problem areas in time for corrective action before formal examinations.

**8. Student chooses to merely memorize vocabulary, concepts, and example problem solutions.**   Some rote memorization of accounting vocabulary and concepts is necessary, but it is not sufficient in learning managerial accounting. To be of value, accounting knowledge must also be generalized so as to be readily applicable to new problem situations.

**9. Student incorrectly identifies the source of his or her difficulty.**   It is important that you properly identify the source of a difficulty. Many students' problems in managerial accounting courses are caused by one or more of these nine items. If you are having trouble and the real source is one or more of these items, deciding merely that the problem is accounting will be counter-productive. Only when the real cause is identified can your difficulty be readily resolved. You should seek assistance from your instructor if you experience difficulty and cannot pinpoint the cause.

## ORGANIZATION OF THIS TEXT

The order of presentation of new material in this text differs from that in many other managerial accounting books. If you should have a friend in another class using a different text, do not fear that you are missing something. You will have covered all of the same important material by the end of the course. You will probably find the sequence in this book easier to grasp.

Research and probably your own past experience have shown that one learns most easily and rapidly when in a problem-solving situation. Learning is more efficient when one experiences a need to learn and an immediate benefit —when one sees the road ahead and is actively involved in the learning process. Each chapter will start with a preview of its coverage: what you can learn. Where practicable, you will then be presented with a user problem situation. The new material that will follow will relate to your understanding and solving of the problem. It will also provide many more tools for solving similar problems. The introductory user problem is designed to give you a context or objective—a reason why—for learning all of the new material.

You can choose to be actively involved in the learning process as you proceed through this book. This choice will allow you to learn managerial accounting most rapidly and efficiently. Alternatively, you can choose to rely on your instructor to induce your involvement. The latter choice will always prove less efficient and often does not work. If you do not become actively involved, you will fail to learn managerial accounting. If you do choose involvement, you will have a successful learning experience.

If you choose to assume responsibility for your learning and make a commitment to active involvement, you will find special opportunities in many chapters. At points where your existing intuitive knowledge can be related to managerial accounting, you will be asked a question before being provided with an explanation. At places where it is important for you to verify the adequacy of your understanding before proceeding, the text will give you a problem and suggest you pause and work out your own solution before reading further. In addition, Appendix C at the back of the book contains solutions to all odd-numbered chapter problems. Chapters themselves contain a minimum of exhibits. To be faced with too many exhibits might be distracting or unnecessary for you. Should you require further examples of a particular application for better understanding, you can use the odd-numbered problems and solutions as additional clarifying exhibits. Also, you can use these problems after you have completed each chapter, to verify and reinforce your understanding of the main ideas (see below).

Also, as you know, new knowledge must be further reinforced and tested before you can be certain that it is mastered. At the end of the chapters, you will find materials intended to provide opportunity for self-checking and reinforcement:

1. *Chapter Overview.* Section reviewing the major new materials in the chapter with which you should be familiar.
2. *New Vocabulary and Concepts.* List of the important new managerial accounting terms and concepts introduced. Definitions of terms may be found in the glossary—Appendix B—at the back of the book. New concepts may be reviewed in the chapter itself.
3. *Review Questions.* Questions designed for you to test your understanding of new major ideas.
4. *Mini-cases and Questions for Discussion.* Brief cases and questions designed to clarify issues and introduce others for your consideration that were not specifically covered in the chapter.
5. *Essential Problems.* Problems designed to provide opportunity for you to demonstrate proper application of the essential ideas already introduced in the text. Solutions to odd-numbered problems are provided in Appendix C at the back of the book.
6. *Supplementary Problems.* Additional problems provided for further reinforcement and for extension of concepts to new or ambiguous situations not specifically covered in the text. Solutions to odd-numbered problems are provided in Appendix C.

The odd-numbered essential and supplementary problems can assist you in a manner similar to that of a programed (self-teaching) text. As in the case of a programed text, the potential benefit results from first attempting problem solutions independently **before** turning to the solutions. If you rely on the solutions before your own analysis is completed, you will preclude the experience of validating (and thus reinforcing) correct learning or, alternatively, identifying areas requiring further study.

You can be sure that you have mastered the essential material in each chapter only when you are confident that you could, if asked:

- Accurately define new vocabulary listed;
- Accurately explain new concepts listed;
- Answer all review questions;
- Intelligently discuss issues related in the mini-cases and questions for discussion;
- Solve all essential problems.

## FOOTNOTES

You will probably notice more footnotes in this book than in other texts with which you are familiar. Don't let yourself be intimidated by footnotes! You will find that, in certain topic areas, you are sufficiently interested to want more precise information, while in others elaboration could be confusing. In this book many footnotes are used to provide such additional precision. This approach is used to separate the less important material from the important main ideas.

Since footnotes are used primarily to provide more precise clarification, they will not be used to provide specific reference to more advanced information sources. Such references are often unused in elementary courses and can prove distracting. Should you desire to explore any topic further, at the end of many chapters you will find suggestions for further reading. Your instructor may also advise you of additional available sources.

## LARGE QUANTITIES OF DATA

Another different feature of this text is that it contains many examples of business reports. These reports are shown completely rather than only in abbreviated or excerpted form. Don't let yourself be intimidated by large quantities of data! You should find it easier to grasp and to remember the significance and usefulness of a specific piece of information in the context of an overall report. It is essential, furthermore, that you learn both where desired information may be located and also how to select specific information from a collection of data. In your future job you will not have a text or an instructor to preselect relevant data for you.

## YEAR DESIGNATIONS

From financial accounting or other business courses you should be aware that any business data or information is relatively worthless unless it is properly labeled or identified. An important part of this required identification is the date or time period reported upon. When actual dates such as January 1, 1975, or April 15, 1997, are used in an illustration, they can prove distracting. A date in the past can trigger memories unrelated to the subject at hand and can also make information appear ancient and possibly obsolete. A date in the future can introduce a feeling of unreality. For these reasons, all dates in this text are shown in the form 19X0, 19X1, 19X2, and so forth. My intention, in using various dates, is to indicate relationships among **any** different sequential years and not to refer to specific years that you may have experienced at the time you read this book.

## SEQUENCING OF SUBJECT MATTER

As described earlier, one of the activities of cost accounting involves supplying information to the financial accounting system related to inventory costs. The activity of measuring and recording inventory costs is common to both financial and managerial accounting. Since this activity is usually not emphasized in financial accounting courses or texts, particularly as it applies to a manufacturer's inventory, it will be covered first in Chapter 1. A brief exposure to this part of cost accounting will also provide you with the opportunity to become familiar with cost data and terminology used in budgeting and control. Chapter 1 will thus serve two purposes:

1. It will complete your general understanding of financial accounting.

2. It will provide a bridge between financial accounting and managerial accounting.

Chapters 2 through 10 will cover various aspects of planning a firm's future activities—budgeting. Chapter 2 provides an overview of the budgeting process. The remaining chapters in this section start with revenue planning; then move into expense planning; then planning for nonroutine activities, including acquisition of capital assets; and will conclude with overall integrated planning in the form of the master budget.

Chapters 11 through 15 will cover different approaches to management control. This section will start with control objectives; then move to expense control; then control of revenues, investments, and profit centers; and will conclude with a brief introduction to control in organizations that are not profit-directed.

Chapters 16 and 17 cover special topics or special considerations related to managerial accounting. Chapter 16 covers some of the problems introduced by inflation and some suggested solutions. Chapter 17 provides a brief introduction to certain more sophisticated quantitative models and tools relevant to managerial accounting.

## YOUR SUGGESTIONS

Obviously the effectiveness of this book for you will depend on factors such as your interest and effort and your classroom experience. It also will depend on how well this book is organized and written for you personally. If you like this text, be sure to tell your instructor. Also, as the author, I am very interested in obtaining your specific comments and suggestions to incorporate in future revised editions. You may forward your ideas directly to the publisher: Addison-Wesley Publishing Company, Reading, Massachusetts 01867; or give them to your instructor for forwarding. Your ideas will be appreciated and considered.

# 1

# COST CONCEPTS, TERMS, AND PRACTICES

CHAPTER PREVIEW

The objective of this chapter is to complete your elementary knowledge of cost determination for inventory and cost of goods sold. It is also intended to make you familiar with various cost classifications and terminology. In this chapter you can:

- Learn the distinction between product and period costs and between direct and indirect costs;
- Become familiar with inventory costs common to all firms and with those peculiar to a manufacturer;
- Learn to distinguish between manufacturing and nonmanufacturing costs;
- Develop an understanding of the three components of manufacturing costs—material, labor, and overhead—and which costs are commonly classified in each of these three categories;
- Learn how and when manufacturing costs are applied to or become part of inventory costs;
- Learn certain methods of accounting for special situations including joint or common costs, spoilage, payroll fringe benefits, idle time, and cost changes over time.

With this knowledge, you will have an adequate picture of cost flows and classifications to enable you to:

- Explore cost behavior and the planning of costs;
- Know cost data that may be available for planning and decision-making purposes;
- Learn further how actual cost information can be included in the control process.

*Note.* If you have not already done so, you should read the Introduction for Students immediately preceding this chapter before continuing.

## MANAGERIAL VS. COST ACCOUNTING

*Managerial accounting* is primarily concerned with the various techniques and systems for planning and controlling a firm's activities, with providing the informational tools with which managers at various levels can manage the firm. Since a significant portion of management activity is devoted to anticipating, minimizing, and controlling costs, the logical starting point in the study of managerial accounting is the study of costs. *Cost accounting* refers to that portion of accounting concerned with the gathering, classifying, recording, summarizing, and reporting of cost information. Cost accountants originally gathered cost information exclusively for proper determination of ending inventory and other nonmonetary assets on the balance sheet, together with cost of goods sold and other expenses on the income statement. With the development of the more structured activities of managerial accounting, and with the increasing use of cost information in decision-making in all functional areas of a business, the role of the cost accountant has expanded. The cost accountant now provides cost data for many activities other than financial accounting. Often cost information is provided:

- To engineering to assist in product design decisions,
- To marketing for use in pricing and marketing strategy decisions,
- To personnel to provide the basis for wage and salary structures and for wage negotiations with unions,
- To operating management for use in the planning and control of current operations, and
- To top management for use in long-range planning.

These different needs for cost information related to managerial planning and control activities often provide the primary demand upon cost accounting. The provision of cost information to the financial accounting system has, in many firms, become a secondary focus or almost a by-product of the cost accounting system.

Throughout most of this book, you will be learning about different demands for and uses of cost information. As a starting point, and as a natural bridge between financial and managerial accounting, you can augment your knowledge of accounting for past costs of inventory on the balance sheet and on the income statement.

## INVENTORY COSTS

For all firms that sell products, knowledge of the cost of these products, whether still in inventory or already sold to customers, is crucial. Product cost information is an essential factor in making pricing decisions. Even though prices may not bear a direct relation to costs, a firm whose prices do not exceed costs will not survive very long. The difference between product cost (of goods sold) on the income statement and sales is defined as gross profit:

$$\text{Gross Profit} = \text{Net sales} - \text{Cost of goods sold}$$

Gross profit represents the amount available to cover all of the firm's operating expenses and, ideally, provide an excess known as income or earnings.

Recall from your study of financial accounting the basic flows of inventory common to all firms; these are shown in Fig. 1.1.

**Figure 1.1**

For a merchandiser (a firm that sells products but does not manufacture them), inventory costs or *product costs* are relatively simple to obtain. A merchandiser's product costs consist solely of the net purchase costs of merchandise acquired. *Net purchases* consist of the cost of gross purchases and transportation (freight) in less any returns and allowances and any purchase discounts taken.

$$
\begin{array}{l}
\quad \text{Gross purchases} \\
+ \text{ Transportation in} \\
- \text{ Purchase returns and allowances} \\
- \text{ Purchase discounts} \\
\hline
= \text{Net purchases}
\end{array}
$$

Assume that, in a given period, a firm had purchased items with a total (gross) invoice cost of \$400,000, and had incurred incoming shipping costs of \$20,000. If items costing \$26,000 had been returned to the supplier as defective, and if purchase discounts of \$4,000 had been taken for prompt payment, net purchases for the period would equal \$390,000. If, during the same period, beginning inventory had amounted to \$130,000 and the cost of ending inventory was determined to be \$135,000, then cost of goods sold would be reported as \$385,000.

A manufacturer has a more difficult problem than a merchandiser in determining product costs. For a manufacturer, net purchases are only part of total product cost. In addition, the costs of transforming the purchased material into finished products (goods) must be included in total product cost. Furthermore, a manufacturer's year-end inventory usually does not consist solely of completed products. Usually raw materials and semifinished products are also on hand.

Exhibits 1.1 and 1.2 illustrate the differences between a merchandiser's and a manufacturer's financial statements. Exhibit 1.1 indicates the balance sheet and income statement differences. Note that the manufacturer's balance sheet includes three separate inventory accounts for items in different stages of completion. And note on the income statement that net purchases is replaced by cost of goods manufactured (or completed and ready to sell).

Exhibit 1.2 illustrates a Schedule of Cost of Goods Manufactured, which is included with the financial statements of a manufacturing firm. Note that such a schedule would be irrelevant for a merchandiser who has only net purchase costs and only one inventory level. Note in Exhibit 1.2 that, in addition to purchase costs, manufacturing costs identified as *direct labor* and *manufacturing overhead* are included in total product cost. These terms will be explained and defined below.

## Exhibit 1.1

### COMPARISON OF CURRENT ASSET BALANCE SHEET DETAIL
### AND
### COST OF GOODS SOLD INCOME STATEMENT DETAIL

| Manufacturer | | | Merchandiser | |
|---|---|---|---|---|
| **Current Assets (Balance Sheet)** | | | **Current Assets (Balance Sheet)** | |
| Cash | | $20,000 | Cash | $ 10,000 |
| Marketable securities | | 10,000 | Marketable securities | 5,000 |
| Accounts receivable (net) | | 60,000 | Accounts receivable (net) | 90,000 |
| Inventories: | | | Merchandise inventory | 135,000 |
| Raw materials | $10,000 | | Supplies | 5,000 |
| Work-in-process | 25,000 | | Prepaid items | 15,000 |
| Finished goods | 45,000 | 80,000 | Total | $260,000 |
| Supplies | | 15,000 | | |
| Prepaid items | | 5,000 | | |
| Total | | $190,000 | | |

| **Cost of Goods Sold (Income Statement)** | | | **Cost of Goods Sold (Income Statement)** | |
|---|---|---|---|---|
| Beginning finished goods inventory | | $ 50,000 | Beginning merchandise inventory | $130,000 |
| Add: Cost of goods manufactured | | 270,000 | Add: Net purchases | 390,000 |
| Goods available for sale | | $320,000 | Goods available for sale | $520,000 |
| Deduct: Ending finished goods inventory | | 45,000 | Deduct: Ending merchandise inventory | 135,000 |
| Cost of goods sold | | $275,000 | Cost of goods sold | $385,000 |

**Exhibit 1.2**
## MANUFACTURER'S SCHEDULE OF COST OF GOODS MANUFACTURED

| | | |
|---|---:|---:|
| Direct materials: | | |
|     Beginning raw materials inventory | $15,000 | |
|     Add: Net purchases | 50,000 | |
|     Total raw materials available | $65,000 | |
|     Deduct: Ending raw materials inventory | 10,000 | |
|     Direct materials used in manufacturing | | $ 55,000 |
| Direct labor | | 70,000 |
| Manufacturing overhead: | | |
|     Indirect materials (supplies) | $13,000 | |
|     Indirect labor | 40,000 | |
|     Supervision | 50,000 | |
|     Utilities | 8,000 | |
|     Insurance | 3,000 | |
|     Property taxes | 6,000 | |
|     Depreciation | 20,000 | |
|     Total overhead costs | | 140,000 |
| Total manufacturing costs | | $265,000 |
| Add: Beginning work-in-process inventory | | 30,000 |
| | | $295,000 |
| Deduct: Ending work-in-process inventory | | 25,000 |
| Cost of goods manufactured | | $270,000 |

## MANUFACTURER MODEL

If you have worked in a manufacturing plant, you probably have the physical reference to readily interpret a schedule of cost of goods manufactured and to visualize the actual material flows described therein. To provide a physical reference for those who do not have such experience, and to provide a common reference for those who do, a model manufacturer will be used. You can more readily grasp and remember managerial concepts and terminology if you immediately relate them to a specific company that you can visualize. For this purpose, throughout most of this text you will be dealing with the Tripper Water Ski Manufacturing Company, Inc. Tripper is a hypothetical manufacturer of water skis, which it advertises and sells nationally. Currently its factory may be assumed to be located in a small midwestern community.

Exhibit 1.3 is the floor plan of Tripper's single-story plant. It provides you with a picture of what you would see if the roof were removed. Note the location and identification of different areas. Also note the arrows indicating flows of materials and products through the plant. Since it will assist you to understand new managerial accounting concepts and terminology if you can readily picture activities and especially flows within a firm, you should carefully go over the following description, constantly referring to the floor plan in Exhibit 1.3.

**Exhibit 1.3**

TRIPPER WATER SKI MANUFACTURING COMPANY
LAYOUT OF FACTORY AND OFFICE BUILDING

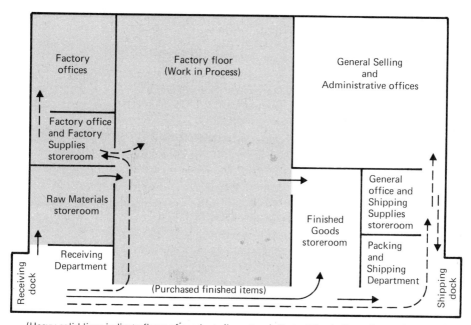

(Heavy solid lines indicate flows of products (inventory). Dotted line indicate flows of supplies.)

Tripper, for simplicity, may be assumed to sell only three products:

Deluxe water skis (manufactured from fiberglass)
Economy water skis (manufactured from wood)
Tow ropes (purchased finished from another supplier)

Finished skis[1] and tow ropes, that are available for sale to customers, are stored in the *finished goods* storeroom.

Tripper purchases, in addition to finished tow ropes and miscellaneous supplies, the following items that are used to make skis:

Wood for the economy skis
Glass cloth and resin for the deluxe fiberglass skis

---

[1]    Tripper sells only slalom or "single" skis. Therefore a sales unit consists of a single slalom ski and **not** a pair of skis.

Completed bindings and directional skegs (fins)[2]
which are attached to skis in the assembly area

Incoming purchases are delivered to the receiving dock and move into the receiving area.

In the receiving area, incoming items are checked to see if they were ordered. If ordered, they are inspected as to quantity and quality; and if satisfactory, are forwarded to appropriate locations. Wood, cloth, resin, bindings, and skegs—*raw materials*—are sent to raw material stores.[3] Completed tow ropes are sent directly to finished goods stores. Factory and factory office supplies go to the factory supplies storeroom. Supplies for the general, sales, and administrative offices and for the shipping department are forwarded to that storeroom.

When production of water skis is scheduled, the ski moulding foreman arranges to obtain necessary raw material from the raw material storeroom and to have it transferred to that portion of the factory floor—the *work-in-process* area—where skis are cut, moulded, and varnished. Bindings and skegs are similarly transferred to the work-in-process area when needed for assembly of the finished skis. When skis are completed they are transferred to finished goods stores. Tripper's factory production workers are divided into two groups, each reporting to a foreman. Workers who make the basic ski report to the moulding foreman. Workers who attach bindings and skegs to skis report to the assembly foreman.

Tripper's cost of tow ropes is merely the net purchase cost of these items, just as if it were a wholesaler or a retailer. It could be calculated by taking the gross invoice (from supplier) cost, adding the cost of transportation (freight) in, and subtracting any purchase returns and any discounts taken. Skis, on the other hand, cost Tripper more than just the net purchase cost of the raw materials. Tripper also has the cost of wages and fringe benefits of production workers –labor costs—and various other factory costs—manufacturing overhead cost. Tripper's cost accountants are concerned with measuring and assigning these costs to those items that are manufactured.

At the end of 19X0, Tripper's management is interested in its *gross profit ratio*. This ratio indicates the relationship of prices and product costs. It can be compared to those of competitive firms and to Tripper's ratio from prior years:

$$\text{Gross profit ratio} = \frac{\text{Gross profit}}{\text{Sales}}.$$

---

[2]     If you are unfamiliar with slalom skis, bindings (not to be confused with boot bindings on snow skis) are like slippers or straps for the feet. They are "foot holders." Skegs are small metal fins or keels attached to the bottom of the ski in the back to provide directional stability.

[3]     The term "raw material" is unfortunate in that it carries the connotation of a natural resource like crude oil or iron ore. In accounting, one firm's finished product becomes another's raw material, as in the case of Tripper's purchased completed bindings and skegs. Raw material merely means items that will be included in the firm's products.

Tripper's management is worried that recent price increases have been insufficient to cover increasing product costs. If this is true, the gross profit ratio will be down in comparison to prior years. You may assume that Tripper's sales for 19X0 totalled $1,123,000. You may also assume that both industry average and prior year's gross profit ratios for Tripper were 0.44, or 44 percent of sales. Therefore, if Tripper's 19X0 cost of goods sold equals approximately $629,000, then its gross profit would be $494,000 and its price and product-cost relationship would be comparable to those for other firms and prior years. Can you determine Tripper's 19X0 cost of goods sold?

## WHAT IS OUR COST OF GOODS SOLD?

For 19X0, Tripper's accountants have accumulated the following data on inventories and costs during the year:

| | | |
|---|---|---|
| Beginning inventories: | Raw materials | $10,000 |
| | Work-in-process | $5,000 |
| | Finished goods | $91,000 |
| Net purchases: | Of raw materials | $100,000 |
| | Of finished goods (tow ropes) | $25,000 |
| Labor hours identified with specific production (direct labor) | | 31,600 hours |
| Other manufacturing costs (factory overhead): | | |
| | Factory supplies used (indirect materials) | $22,400 |
| | Other factory labor (indirect labor) | 23,000 hours |
| | Supervisory salaries (factory) | $65,000 |
| | Utilities (factory) | $18,000 |
| | Insurance on factory building and equipment | $13,000 |
| | Property taxes on factory building and equipment | $17,000 |
| | Depreciation on factory building and equipment | $48,000 |
| Ending inventories: | Raw materials | $14,000 |
| | Work-in-process | $10,000 |
| | Finished goods | $66,000 |
| Labor costs: | Factory direct labor | $6/hour |
| | Factory indirect labor | $5/hour |
| Nonmanufacturing costs (period costs): | | |
| | Office supplies used | $1,000 |
| | General selling and administrative salaries | $325,000 |
| | Utilities (office) | $1,000 |
| | Insurance on office building and equipment | $3,000 |
| | Property taxes on office building and equipment | $6,000 |
| | Depreciation on office building and equipment | $12,000 |
| | Transportation out and other distribution expenses | $7,000 |
| | Advertising, selling commissions, and other marketing expenses | $9,000 |
| | Interest | $14,000 |

**Exhibit 1.4**

TRIPPER WATER SKI MANUFACTURING COMPANY

**Schedule of Cost of Goods Manufactured**
**for Year Ending 12/31/X0**

| | | |
|---|---:|---:|
| Direct materials: | | |
|     Beginning raw materials inventory | $ 10,000 | |
|     Add:  Net purchases during 19X0 | 100,000 | |
|     Total raw materials available | $110,000 | |
|     Deduct:  Raw materials inventory, 12/31/X0 | 14,000 | |
|     Direct materials used in manufacturing | | $ 96,000 |
| Direct labor | | 189,600 |
| Manufacturing overhead: | | |
|     Indirect materials (supplies) | $ 22,400 | |
|     Indirect labor | 115,000 | |
|     Supervision | 65,000 | |
|     Utilities | 18,000 | |
|     Insurance | 13,000 | |
|     Property taxes | 17,000 | |
|     Depreciation | 48,000 | |
|     Actual overhead costs | | 298,400 |
| Total manufacturing costs | | $584,000 |
| Add:  Beginning work-in-process inventory | | 5,000 |
| | | $589,000 |
| Deduct:  Work-in-process inventory 12/31/X0 | | 10,000 |
| Cost of goods manufactured | | $579,000 |

Before proceeding further in this chapter, you should attempt to determine on a separate piece of paper the amount of 19X0 cost of goods sold from the data given above. Use whatever logic you would apply if it were your business and you were aware that GAAP required all manufacturing costs (but only manufacturing costs) to be treated as part of inventory costs. You may wish to follow the format of Exhibits 1.1 and 1.2.

You are correct if you determined that Tripper's accountants would report 19X0 cost of goods sold as $629,000. Nonmanufacturing costs are irrelevant to inventory costs and will appear as separate operating expenses on the 19X0 income statement. Total manufacturing costs incurred during 19X0 amounted to $584,000 ($96,000 material, $189,600 labor, and $298,400 manufacturing overhead). Together with the $5,000 of beginning work-in-process inventory, products costing $589,000 were on the factory floor during the year. With products costing $10,000 only partially completed at year-end, products costing $579,000 were transferred to finished goods and are shown as cost of goods manufactured. Exhibit 1.4 details the various costs included in the $579,000 of cost of goods manufactured. Study this Exhibit until you can visualize in terms of Tripper's layout given in Exhibit 1.3:

- $100,000 of raw material purchases moving through the receiving department into raw materials stores;
- $96,000 of raw material moving onto the factory floor;
- $488,000 of labor and overhead costs incurred;
- $579,000 of finished skis moving into the finished-goods storeroom.

Completing the calculation of 19X0 cost of goods sold is the same as for a merchandiser:

| | |
|---|---:|
| Beginning finished goods inventory | $ 91,000 |
| Purchased finished tow ropes | 25,000 |
| Input from manufacturing | 579,000 |
| Goods available for sale | $695,000 |
| Less:   Ending finished-goods inventory | 66,000 |
| Costs of goods sold | $629,000 |

With sales of $1,123,000 and cost of goods sold of $629,000, Tripper's gross profit ratio is holding at the desired 44 percent.

### Cost Flows Through Inventory Accounts

The same cost flows occurring in the plant, and mirrored on the schedule of cost of goods manufactured and on the income statement, are reflected in the actual accounts themselves. Exhibit 1.5 illustrates these flows in terms of "T"-accounts. If you are not familiar with the T-account and the debit/credit system, you may consider each separate T in this illustration as a storage record with carryover balances and additions on the left side and reductions or transfers to another account shown on the right.[4] Note again how the flows of costs through the accounts may be identified with physical flows through the plant.

## MANUFACTURING AND NONMANUFACTURING COSTS

The cost flows so far discussed have all been so-called *manufacturing costs*. Exhibit 1.3 can also help you visualize the distinction between manufacturing and *nonmanufacturing costs*. Think about Tripper if it were not a manufacturer but instead were merely a wholesaler or retailer of skis. If Tripper were not a manufacturer, all of the shaded areas on Exhibit 1.3 and all of the costs related to these areas would not be needed. The remaining unshaded areas would represent nonmanufacturing cost areas. Nonmanufacturing costs would include:

---

[4]   T-accounts for revenues and equities (not illustrated) would work in the opposite way. Carryover balances and additions would be on the right and subtractions and transfers would be shown on the left.

**Exhibit 1.5**

TRIPPER WATER SKI MANUFACTURING COMPANY

Illustration of Cost Flows Through Manufacturing and Inventory Accounts  During the Year 19X0

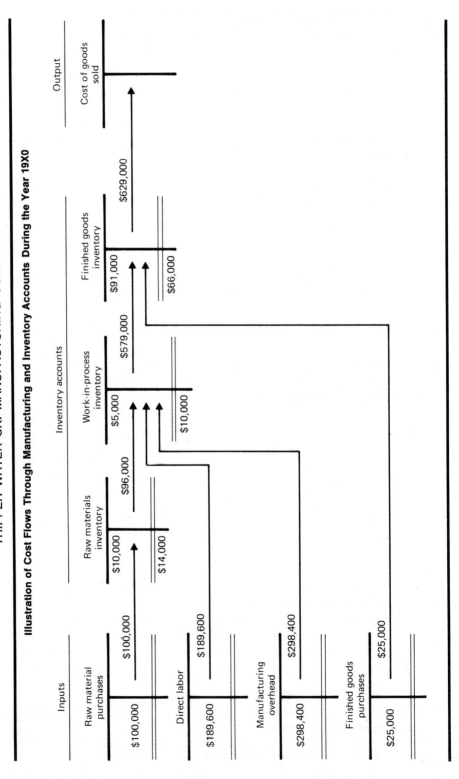

- Costs of purchasing, receiving, and storing merchandise,
- Costs of selling, packaging, and shipping merchandise,
- Accounting costs,
- Design engineering and product development costs,
- Other general administrative costs.

Manufacturing costs associated with the shaded areas on Exhibit 1.3 include all those costs specifically related to and unique to manufacturing. Examples would include:

- The space cost (depreciation, rent, heat, light, power, insurance, and property taxes) for the area devoted to manufacturing;

- Labor cost (wages, salaries, and fringe benefits) of all production/manufacturing employees and supervisory personnel;

- Other factory-related costs including equipment (depreciation or rental), maintenance, supplies, the factory personnel office, the production and material control (scheduling) office, and so forth.

Throughout most of this text, managerial accounting will be discussed for a manufacturer. The reason should be obvious to you. A manufacturer has some of everything to manage. A wholesaler or retailer has only nonmanufacturing costs. When you fully grasp accounting for a manufacturer, you can readily apply the nonmanufacturing portion to other types of businesses.

## PRODUCT COST VS. PERIOD COST

Recall from financial accounting that, on the income statement, the accountant reports the revenue earned in a particular period. He or she attempts to include all expenses that can be associated with obtaining this revenue. One expense that can be readily identified with particular revenue is cost of sales or cost of goods sold.

The term *product cost* refers to those costs that are associated with inventory.[5] In fact product costs may be thought of as inventory costs. There is nothing inherent in a particular cost that makes it a product cost. Product costs are simply those costs that accountants treat or classify as product costs. Remember that, under the financial accounting system, GAAP require that product costs be capitalized into inventory and held as such as an asset on the balance sheet until sale and shipment occurs.[6] Product costs do not normally

---

[5]   Product costs may also be called project costs in construction-related businesses.

[6]   Under percentage-completion accounting, product or project costs may become expenses as a project is partially completed. Also, product costs may be written down prior to sale, to reflect loss of recoverable value under the LOCM rule.

become inventory expenses (cost of goods sold) until they are matched with revenues in the year or period in which the product is sold. The product cost related to certain of Tripper's skis and tow ropes will be reported on the balance sheet as inventory until these same items have been removed from the finished goods storeroom and shipped to customers.

In financial accounting you also learned that many costs cannot readily be traced or matched to the production of specific revenues. These nonproduct costs are therefore treated as expenses in the year or period when incurred. For example, salaries of salespersons and advertising fees are recognized as selling expenses in the same period as incurred; they are not capitalized into an asset account and deferred to future periods. All costs that do not result in objectively measurable assets with future value are expensed in the period in which they occurred and are known as *period costs.*

The distinction between product cost and period cost is helpful in understanding the difference between accounting for wholesalers and retailers as compared to manufacturers. For a merchandiser (wholesaler or retailer), product cost includes only net purchases cost. All other costs are treated as period costs for a merchandiser. For example, space cost (depreciation, rent, taxes, insurance, utilities, and so forth) for all of a merchandiser's buildings would be treated on its income statement as a period cost.

For a manufacturer, product costs would include all manufacturing costs. Only nonmanufacturing costs would be treated as period costs. In the example of the Tripper Company, space costs in proportion to the unshaded area of Exhibit 1.3 would be reported as period costs. Space cost proportionate to the

**Exhibit 1.6**

---

**Listing of Typical Period and Product Costs**

1. President's salary
2. General administrative costs
3. Interest costs
4. Salary of financial vice-president and controller
5. Accounting department costs
6. Salary of sales manager/vice-president for marketing and sales
7. Salaries and other costs of the sales/marketing departments
8. Sales commissions
9. Shipping costs and transportation (freight) out (distribution costs)
10. Product engineering costs
11. Public relations costs
12. All depreciation, rent, insurance, heat, power, light, property taxes (space costs) for nonmanufacturing space and equipment
13. Net purchase costs of merchandise or materials
14. Factory labor costs
15. All costs of factory space and equipment
16. Salaries and other costs of factory supervision
17. Miscellaneous factory supplies

---

shaded area would be included with other manufacturing costs as part of product cost.

To review, Exhibit 1.6 contains a list of the various types of costs found in many firms. Before reading further, you should attempt to select those items that would normally be treated as period costs. Write down the numbers on a separate sheet of paper before proceeding.

You are correct if you identified those costs numbered 1 through 12 on Exhibit 1.6 as usually classified with period costs. Number 13 is the only cost considered a product cost for a wholesaler or a retailer. Numbers 14 through 17 are additional costs unique to a manufacturer, which are also included in product costs.

## DIRECT VS. INDIRECT COSTS

Another cost distinction applicable to all costs but often used only in the context of manufacturing or project costs is between *direct* and *indirect* costs. Direct costs are those costs which **both** can be readily and economically traceable to and identified with a particular activity, and also which a firm's accountant chooses to classify and treat as direct. In most manufacturing situations it is only feasible and economical to separately identify raw material and some production labor as direct costs.

Raw material is defined as material that is actually incorporated in a finished product. However, not all raw material costs may be separately identified by the accountant as *direct material*. For example, in Tripper's case it might be too expensive (for the information benefits derived) to separately identify and record as direct material either the screws used to fasten bindings and skegs to skis or the varnish sprayed on the skis. Screws and varnish might be treated as one of several factory supplies. Only the materials going into the manufacture of the ski itself, bindings, and skegs would then be identified as direct material.

Similarly, not all factory labor and supervision is readily identifiable with and traceable to particular products. To attempt to apportion a foreman's salary depending upon the amount of time spent thinking about production activities related to a particular product could be absurd. Usually factory direct labor includes only the costs of production employees actually working on the product, and then only the costs of their hours actually spent in creating the product, as opposed to other activities such as maintenance, material handling, and so forth. Labor costs for hours worked, but not directly involved in the production of a specific product, such as material-handling labor, are classified as indirect labor. Together with supervision costs, indirect labor is included in manufacturing overhead.

Indirect manufacturing costs include all manufacturing costs that are **not** separately identified and recorded as direct. Usually indirect manufacturing costs include all factory costs other than direct material and direct labor.

## THE COST TRINITY: MATERIAL, LABOR, AND OVERHEAD

Indirect manufacturing costs are generally referred to as manufacturing overhead, or simply overhead.[7] Product costs for a manufacturer therefore consist of a trinity of costs: (direct) material, (direct) labor, and (manufacturing) overhead. The cost accountant will therefore separately accumulate all manufacturing costs in these three categories—direct material, direct labor, and manufacturing overhead. Overhead, as the residual or catchall account, will therefore include all indirect material and indirect labor. In the determination of costs of particular products or projects, the cost accountant will have already identified direct material and direct labor costs. Overhead, on the other hand, is often not readily identifiable with a particular product or project. It must, therefore, periodically be allocated or apportioned to inventory costs.

## WHAT ARE THE UNIT COSTS OF OUR PRODUCTS?

When a firm has several distinct products, determining ending inventory cost and cost of goods sold may not be possible unless costs for each product are separately identifiable.[8] A merchandiser can merely refer to the invoice price of merchandise purchased. But a manufacturer must accumulate manufacturing costs separately for each different product or group of like products. For a manufacturer, each individual product's cost for inventory purposes is the sum of:

- Direct material used in the product,
- Direct labor cost incurred in making the product, and
- A reasonable allocation of total manufacturing overhead.

Unit cost data is perhaps even more important for management decision purposes. In the long run a product's price should at least cover its cost. Therefore, even though prices may not be based on cost, knowledge of a product's cost is an essential component of a pricing decision. Pricing will be discussed further in Chapter 3. Unit cost data, although not necessarily the cost accountant's full-absorption inventory cost, is also valuable in making manufacture-vs.-subcontract or manufacture-vs.-buy decisions. Decisions of this type will be explored in Chapter 7. At this point it is only desirable that you become familiar with the various common systems in use for accumulating unit costs. An understanding of the system used in a specific situation will allow you to know what costs are included and how, in any cost data you may wish to use.

---

[7] Manufacturing overhead is also called: factory burden, burden, factory overhead, factory expense, manufacturing expense, or other similar terms used synonymously.

[8] Retail stores may use the retail method of estimating the cost of ending inventory as a proportion of the selling price of merchandise on hand. The retail inventory method is covered in financial accounting texts.

Two essentially different cost-accumulation systems have evolved. They are known as *process costing* and *job-order costing*. A third system known as *standard costing* may be used as a measurement alternative to either of the first two. The choice of the system to be used in a particular firm will depend upon the characteristics of the manufacturing process being used and upon the characteristics of the firm's product(s). Each of these systems will be introduced below.

## Process Costing

Where a firm is producing a homogeneous product or products over a significant period of time, the simpler system known as process costing would be appropriate. Under process costing, the three manufacturing costs are accumulated during the production period. At the end of the production run or period, total costs incurred, divided by units completed, provide the average cost per unit.[9] An average cost is satisfactory in this situation as all units are homogeneous.

As an example of process costing, assume that Tripper was only manufacturing and selling one model of water ski—the economy model made from wood. Also assume that beginning and ending work-in-process inventory was zero, and that during the period Tripper incurred manufacturing costs as follows: $30,000 material, $20,000 labor, and $40,000 overhead. How much did each water ski cost Tripper if, during the period, it manufactured 4,500 skis? You understand the basic concept of process costing, if you determined that each ski is assigned a cost of $20. Under process costing, unit costs are determined for all products by dividing total manufacturing cost ($90,000) by total completed units (4,500).

An adjustment is required when some units are only partially completed in work-in-process inventory at the beginning or end of a period. Under process costing any partially completed units are translated into equivalent completed units for purposes of calculating unit costs for ending inventory and cost of goods sold. Often *equivalent units* are determined separately for material cost and *conversion costs* (direct labor plus factory overhead), since a partially completed product may already include all of its material cost but only part of its labor and overhead cost. Exhibit 1.7 demonstrates equivalent unit calculation for the Tripper Company, given the following assumptions:

1. During a particular period Tripper was manufacturing only the wooden economy-model ski.

2. Total manufacturing costs (material, labor, and overhead) incurred during the period were $163,100 (material cost $30,800; conversion cost $132,300).

---

[9]    Under process costing, manufacturing overhead is commonly applied at a predetermined rate instead of at actual cost incurred. See discussion of overhead application below.

3. At the end of the period, 5,000 skis had been completed and delivered to finished goods. 600 skis were still in process only two-thirds completed but with all necessary material released to the factory floor.

4. There was no beginning work-in-process inventory.

Exhibit 1.7 indicates a total unit cost of a completed economy ski is $30 ($5.50 material plus $24.50 labor and overhead). Therefore the cost assigned to skis completed and delivered to finished goods would be $150,000 (5,000 × $30). Cost assigned to ending work-in-process inventory would be $13,100 (600 × $5.50 plus 400 × $24.50).

Equivalent unit computations can become more involved when there is beginning inventory and price/cost changes, and when all material is not added at the start of production. These complications are more appropriately covered in intermediate cost accounting texts and courses.

**Exhibit 1.7**
EQUIVALENT UNIT DETERMINATION

|  | Equivalent units | | |
|  | Material component cost | Conversion component cost | Total cost |
| --- | --- | --- | --- |
| 5,000 units to finished goods | 5,000 | 5,000 |  |
| 600 units partially completed | 600 | 400* |  |
| Total equivalent units | 5,600 | 5,400 |  |
| Total costs incurred | $30,800 | $132,300 | $163,100 |
| Cost/equivalent unit | $5.50 | $24.50 | $30.00 |

* 600 units 2/3 complete are the equivalent of 400 completed units with respect to conversion costs.

## Overhead Application

Under some process cost systems, actual overhead incurred may be applied (added) to WIP inventory, as illustrated in the previous simplified examples. Often applying manufacturing overhead at actual cost can be misleading. Since actual overhead costs are usually incurred unevenly, extremely complex accruals would be necessary to achieve a somewhat rational cost allocation during the year. It would not be very meaningful to have a very high overhead charge apply to those items that happen to be manufactured the month property taxes were paid! To avoid the necessity of complex accruals throughout the year, a *predetermined* (average) *overhead rate* is often used.

A predetermined overhead rate essentially involves applying (adding) overhead to inventory on the basis of the amount of overhead that is expected on average throughout the year per unit of expected production or other activity measure. Most commonly an expected activity measure or *activity base* is chosen as some other cost or measure closely correlating with output. Many firms choose direct labor hours or direct labor dollars as the activity base and apply (assign) overhead to WIP inventory proportionally. Total expected overhead is estimated at the beginning of the year. The activity base is also estimated in advance for the year. Total expected overhead divided by total expected activity yields the predetermined rate per unit of activity.

To illustrate the use of a predetermined overhead application rate under process costing, continue with the assumption that Tripper manufactured only economy skis. Suppose the firm believed that direct labor hours were the most reasonable basis for allocating overhead. At the beginning of the year, expected manufacturing overhead is estimated at $150,000. Expected direct labor hours to be incurred are estimated at 30,000 hours.

$$\text{Predetermined overhead rate} = \frac{\text{Estimated total manufacturing overhead}}{\text{Estimated total direct labor hours}}$$

In this example, the overhead rate would be $5 per direct labor hour. Now assume that the following actual data were identified and accumulated during the year:

| | |
|---|---|
| Actual direct material | $ 40,000 |
| Actual direct labor dollars | $100,000 |
| Actual direct labor hours | 24,000 hours |
| Actual manufacturing overhead | $125,000 |
| Equivalent units produced | 8,000 units |

Can you anticipate the accountant's total manufacturing (product) cost applied to inventory and, assuming no beginning WIP inventory, the product cost per unit? Using the predetermined rate, only $120,000 of overhead would be applied to product cost (24,000 hours times $5 per hour). Total manufacturing cost would be $260,000. Product cost per equivalent completed unit would be $32.50.

Note that, whereas actual manufacturing overhead was $125,000, the amount applied to inventory by using the predetermined rate was only $120,000. The $5,000 balance was underapplied or underabsorbed and is known as *underapplied overhead*. The differences between actual and applied or the *accounting variance* could go the other way. If actual overhead were only $110,000 for the year and $120,000 had been applied, there would be $10,000 of *overapplied overhead*.

Accounting variances for overhead (over- or underapplied) are either transferred to cost of goods sold if not material, or allocated between ending inventory and cost of goods sold if material. In this example the $5,000 of underapplied overhead would be charged to or would increase cost of goods sold for the year. In the alternate example, the $10,000 of overapplied overhead would be subtracted from cost of goods sold for the year.

Exhibit 1.8 illustrates cost flows under the process cost system using a predetermined overhead rate. Note, on Exhibit 1.8, that there is only one work-

**Exhibit 1.8**
MANUFACTURING COST FLOWS

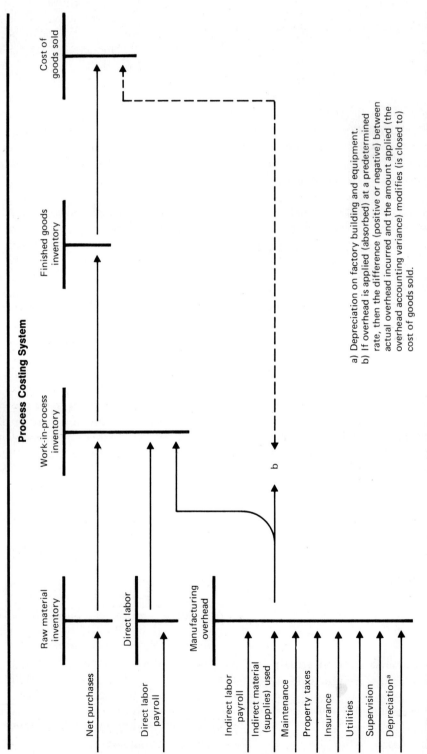

**Process Costing System**

a) Depreciation on factory building and equipment.
b) If overhead is applied (absorbed) at a predetermined rate, then the difference (positive or negative) between actual overhead incurred and the amount applied (the overhead accounting variance) modifies (is closed to) cost of goods sold.

in-process inventory account for all manufacturing activity. Direct material and direct labor are added as used or incurred at actual cost. Overhead is added on the basis of the predetermined rate. The accounting variance (difference between actual incurred and amount applied at the predetermined rate times the actual activity measure) is transferred (closed) to cost of goods sold.

## Job-Order Costing

Process costing is acceptable for homogeneous production, but what can the firm do that produces two or more **non**homogeneous products? In such cases an average cost per unit (say for TV tape recorders and small pocket calculators) would be meaningless, if not ridiculous.

In situations where a firm has many different nonhomogeneous products, the second type of cost system, known as the job-order costing system, is necessary. Under a job-order system, direct material and direct labor costs are identified and accumulated on separate records for each different order or batch of goods produced. Manufacturing overhead is accumulated and totalled for the period, and then allocated among the various orders or batches on the basis of a predetermined overhead rate. Unit costs are then separately determined for each order or batch by dividing total costs applied by total units in the order or batch. Obviously job-order costing is most appropriate for the firm producing many different, one-of-a-kind special orders for customers.

In Tripper's real situation with two nonhomogeneous products, a modified job-order cost system could be used. Direct material and direct labor would be accumulated in two separate work-in-process inventory accounts. In effect, the firm would have just two job orders during the year, one for economy and one for deluxe skis. To illustrate the operation of the job-order system, assume that the predetermined overhead rate for a given year was $5.00 per direct labor hour, as calculated above. Also assume that the following data were accumulated during the year:

| | Economy | Deluxe | Total |
|---|---|---|---|
| Actual direct material | $20,000 | $27,800 | $ 47,800 |
| Actual direct labor hours | 14,000 hrs. | 10,000 hrs. | 24,000 hrs. |
| Actual amount labor dollars | $56,000 | $44,000 | $100,000 |
| Actual manufacturing overhead | — | — | $115,000 |
| Units produced | 5,000 | 3,000 | 8,000 |

Overhead would be applied at the predetermined rate of $5 per actual direct labor hour. $70,000 would be applied to the production of economy skis, and $50,000 to deluxe skis. Product cost of inventory would then be:

| | Economy | Deluxe | Total |
|---|---|---|---|
| Material (applied at actual) | $ 20,000 | $ 27,800 | $ 47,800 |
| Labor (applied at actual) | 56,000 | 44,000 | 100,000 |
| Overhead (applied at predetermined rate) | 70,000 | 50,000 | 120,000 |
| Total costs applied | $146,000 | $121,800 | $267,800 |
| Cost/unit | $29.20 | $40.60 | |

Note that whereas actual manufacturing overhead was only $115,000, the amount applied to inventory by using the predetermined rate was $120,000. The $5,000 difference was overapplied or overabsorbed. In this example the $5,000 accounting variance would be substracted from cost of goods sold for the year. Exhibit 1.9 illustrates the cost flows under a job-order system. Note that separate work-in-process inventory accounts are maintained for each distinct product or job order.

## Standard Costing

The third type of cost system is known as standard costing. Actually standard costing involves a measurement variation applicable to either a process or job-order system, rather than representing a wholly different approach. When a firm uses standard costs under either the process or job-order systems, all three manufacturing cost elements (material, labor, and overhead) are applied to inventory at a standard rate. The standard rates are similar to the predetermined overhead rate previously discussed. They differ in being the result of engineered targets rather than general estimates.

If Tripper were using a standard cost system, it would establish target costs for each product. For example, assume that the standard costs for the recent year were as follows:

|  | Material | Labor | Overhead | Total |
|---|---|---|---|---|
| Economy ski | $5.50 | $ 9.80 | $14.70 | $30 |
| Deluxe ski | 8.70 | 12.50 | 18.80 | 40 |
| Tow rope | 5.00 | None[10] | None[10] | 5 |

Also assume the following data for the period:

| | |
|---|---|
| Beginning and ending raw materials and work-in-process inventories | Zero or Unchanged |
| Tow ropes purchased | 400 units |
| Economy skis completed | 600 units |
| Deluxe skis completed | 500 units |
| Costs incurred: | |
| Material | $10,000 |
| Labor | $12,550 |
| Overhead | $18,500 |
| | $41,000 |

Under a standard cost system, actual costs incurred are not applied/assigned to inventory. Instead costs are applied at standard for the units acquired or produced, as follows:

---

[10]   No conversion cost is applied to tow ropes, because they are a purchased finished product.

**Exhibit 1.9**

MANUFACTURING COST FLOWS

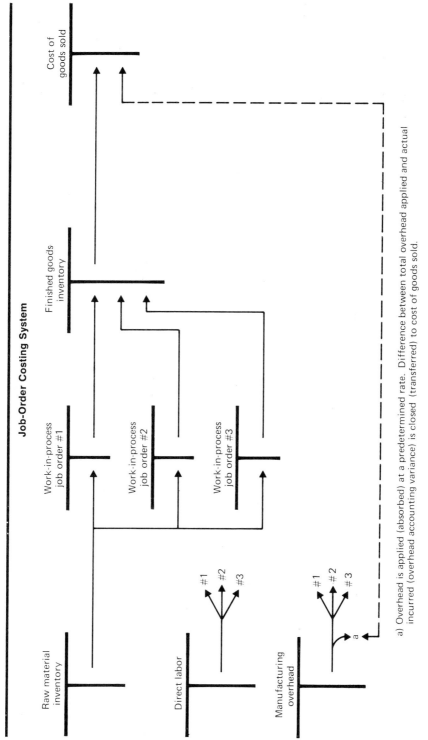

**Job-Order Costing System**

Raw material inventory

Work-in-process job order #1

Work-in-process job order #2

Work-in-process job order #3

Finished goods inventory

Cost of goods sold

Direct labor
#1 #2 #3

Manufacturing overhead
#1 #2 #3
a

a) Overhead is applied (absorbed) at a predetermined rate. Difference between total overhead applied and actual incurred (overhead accounting variance) is closed (transferred) to cost of goods sold.

| | Costs applied/assigned to inventory | | | |
| --- | --- | --- | --- | --- |
| | *Material* | *Labor* | *Overhead* | *Total* |
| Economy skis (Standard × 600) | $3,300 | $ 5,880 | $ 8,820 | $18,220 |
| Deluxe skis (Standard × 500) | 4,350 | 6,250 | 9,400 | 20,000 |
| Tow ropes (Standard × 400) | 2,000 | None | None | 2,000 |
| Total applied | $9,650 | $12,130 | $18,230 | $40,000 |

Note that, in this example, of the $41,000 of actual costs incurred, only $40,000 is assigned (applied) to inventory. The balance of $1,000 is comprised of variances from material, labor, and overhead. These variances or differences between actual and standard are known as accounting variances and are assigned (closed) to cost of goods sold if not material.[11] Exhibit 1.10 illustrates cost flows under a process cost system using standard costing.

Predetermining and then maintaining engineered standards for each item can be costly. Therefore, a standard cost system is often feasible only in those situations where a firm has products that are standardized as to design and manufacture, where they are repeatedly produced in quantity, and where data is available from past production runs. Even though costly to establish and maintain, a standard cost system has distinct advantages in certain situations for use as a management control device. It will therefore be described in more detail in Chapter 13. For now you need only realize that it represents one of three general types of cost systems, and that, under standard costing, products are costed at predetermined standards rather than at actual costs incurred.

## USING COST DATA

Whether costs are accumulated under a process or job-order system, and whether actual or standard costs are used, are both important considerations for a manager using product cost data for decision purposes. Process costs may be more dependable than job-order costs with multiple overhead allocations. Standard costs may be more reliable than actual costs if the standards are not set too high. Under all systems, GAAP requires that all related procurement and production costs be included or absorbed into product cost—so-called *full absorption costing*.

In later chapters dealing with business decisions, you will find that a product's full unit cost for inventory measurement purposes may not be the appropriate measure for use in most business decisions. And you will have the

---

[11]    As for any material (significant) variances arising from the use of a predetermined overhead rate, a standard cost variance that was material would be allocated between ending inventory and cost of goods sold.

**Exhibit 1.10**
MANUFACTURING COST FLOWS

**Process Costing with Standard Costs**

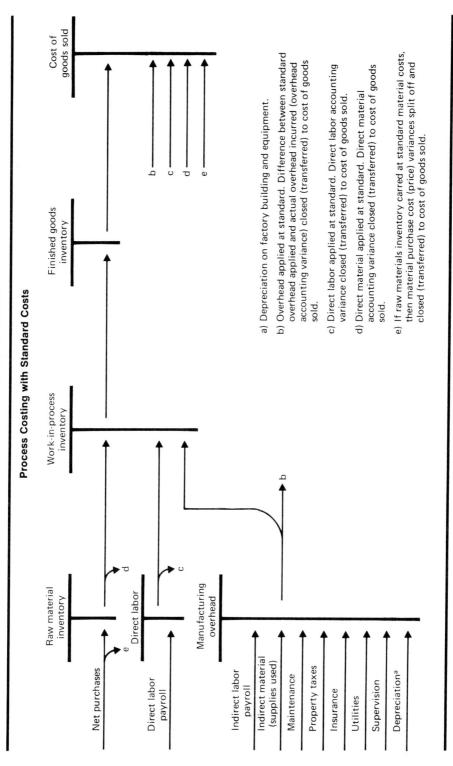

a) Depreciation on factory building and equipment.

b) Overhead applied at standard. Difference between standard overhead applied and actual overhead incurred (overhead accounting variance) closed (transferred) to cost of goods sold.

c) Direct labor applied at standard. Direct labor accounting variance closed (transferred) to cost of goods sold.

d) Direct material applied at standard. Direct material accounting variance closed (transferred) to cost of goods sold.

e) If raw materials inventory carried at standard material costs, then material purchase cost (price) variances split off and closed (transferred) to cost of goods sold.

opportunity to learn which cost components are relevant to specific decisions, and which are not and could result in incorrect decisions if used. You can also become more familiar with various internal cost allocations made by accountants, and with the fact that many such allocations are inherently arbitrary.

Cost allocation represents a significant problem for the cost accountant and for the users of cost accounting data. In addition to allocation of manufacturing overhead, other examples of costs requiring allocation include:

- Space cost, between manufacturing and nonmanufacturing;
- Service center costs (for example, a computer center), between manufacturing and nonmanufacturing;
- Common material costs when two different products are made from a single unit of raw material;
- Common freight-in costs when several different materials are combined in a single shipment.

Problems of cost allocation are beyond the scope of this text. Some are briefly discussed below. Most are covered in detail in cost accounting texts and courses for accounting majors.


## OTHER PARTICULAR COST ACCOUNTING PRACTICES

Before leaving the subject of cost accounting, you should become acquainted with the general approach or approaches commonly used to solve certain problems. You may already have asked yourself one or more of the following questions:

- How is the unit cost determined for a product that is made as part of another product (for example, doughnut holes sold by bakeries)?
- How are costs treated for items that are ruined (spoiled) in the production process?
- What about overtime and fringe-benefit payroll costs? What happens to them?
- How does a manufacturer deal with cost changes such as those resulting from inflation?

As a future user of accounting cost data, you will need to know how these items are included in or excluded from the data you may be using.


### Joint (Common) Costs and By-products

Arbitrary cost allocation is occasionally required with respect to *prime costs*— direct material and direct labor. In some situations two or more products are produced from a single unit of raw material, or from a single unit of partially finished product. When this occurs, the cost accountant must allocate the *joint* or *common cost* to the separate products. Since the separate costs are not directly identifiable or traceable, any allocation or division is purely arbitrary.

Examples of joint costs with which you are familiar include those of crude oil (which is refined into several fuels and chemicals), trees (which are sawed into cut lumber and sawdust), and animals (which are slaughtered and then divided into sides of meat, hides, a tongue, and so forth). Perhaps you can most readily see the joint cost problem in the case of the steer costing $100 which yields one hide, 30 pounds of steaks, 80 pounds of hamburger, and so forth. In this case, what would be the cost of the hamburger?

There are two ways of handling the joint cost dilemma. One is to arbitrarily allocate all costs incurred up to the point of division (known as the *split-off point*). Allocation in such situations is in proportion to the realizable value of separate products, to relative weight or volume, or on some other rational (rationalizable?) basis. The reasoning behind such allocation is simply that significant cost has been incurred that must be included in each product's full cost. To treat all costs up to the split-off point as indirect would be inappropriate and could improperly increase costs (through overhead allocation) of totally unrelated products.

A simple example of a joint cost situation could involve two products both made from a single five-foot length of material. Assume each five-foot length has a purchase cost of $20 and is initially machined with a direct labor cost of $10. It is then cut into one four- and one one-foot pieces. The two pieces are then separately processed into two distinctly different products. One method would be to allocate the prime cost by length.

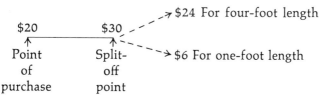

The second alternative is the special case where one product is assigned a cost of zero at the split-off point. In these situations such an item is being treated as a by-product. In the lumber example, it is often appropriate to treat the sawdust as a by-product, which may be subsequently treated with kerosene and compressed into artificial fireplace logs. In costing the artificial logs, cost would be accumulated after the split-off point, assuming that the sawdust was free. Treatment of one product after split-off as a by-product with zero initial cost may be appropriate where the item represents a small physical proportion of the original joint product, or where its future value or usefulness is relatively insignificant.

Managers using cost information must be careful to ascertain whether a joint or common cost situation exists. Sawdust for pressed logs is only "free" and available if the lumber can be profitably sold. And even then it may have alternative value (opportunity cost) as fuel. Usually any cost that is an allocated portion of a common cost may not be "saved" by discontinuing the final product with which it is associated.

## Spoilage

Another troublesome detail in manufacturing accounting concerns what to do with the cost of spoilage that occurs during a production process. Spoilage costs are treated in one of two ways, depending upon whether the spoilage is within the normal amount that may be expected to occur, or abnormal. Normal spoilage is often ignored, with the result that the costs of other units in the process or batch are effectively increased. Abnormal spoilage may be separated from product cost and treated as a period expense.

## Payroll Fringe Benefits, Overtime, and Idle Time

Three specific aspects of labor cost deserve special mention. Payroll fringe benefits are commonly handled by different firms in one of two ways. They may be apportioned between direct and indirect labor, or they may be treated entirely as overhead. If overhead were subsequently allocated on the basis of direct labor dollars, the difference in the final results of the two systems would be minimal. Overtime premium is often charged to overhead rather than to direct labor, since it is not considered an ordinary or routine cost. Also, the cost of a production worker's time spent waiting for machine repair, materials, and so forth, is usually not charged to direct labor. Instead it is assigned to an indirect labor account for the particular activity—material handling, maintenance, idle time, and other similar classifications.

## Accounting for Changes in Costs; LIFO, FIFO, and Average Cost

A final aspect of cost accounting concerns methods of handling cost changes. The term "cost changes" as used herein refers to a "permanent" change resulting from a change in material, processing, or prices as a result of inflation. It is not intended to cover changes resulting from temporary cost overruns (inefficiency) or savings. In financial accounting you learned four common methods used by merchandisers to reflect cost changes in inventory and cost of goods sold. These methods were specific identification, weighted average cost, and the FIFO and LIFO flow assumptions. A manufacturer may use any of the four for finished goods inventory.

GAAP does not require that the same method be used for all levels of inventory. They require only that a particular method, once adopted for a given inventory level, be used consistently. For a manufacturer on a complete job-order costing system, provided lots or batches do not run over many months, the individual lot already provides a modified form of specific identification by lot and weighted average cost per unit. For firms using job-order, standard, or process costing, average cost or FIFO are commonly used for raw materials and work-in-process, with average cost being slightly more popular.

The procedures for handling such cost changes within the accounts are more appropriately covered in cost accounting textbooks and courses.

CHAPTER OVERVIEW

Based on the material contained in this chapter, you should be able to:

- Describe the difference between manufacturing and nonmanufacturing costs and identify the appropriate classification for any particular given cost.
- Describe the difference in the timing of expense recognition between costs that are classified as product costs and those treated as period costs.
- Describe costs typically classified as product costs for a merchandiser and for a manufacturer, and identify those costs for each that are classified as period costs.
- Distinguish between direct and indirect costs in any situation and particularly with reference to a manufacturer's product costs.
- Define and describe the three components of manufacturing costs.
- Describe the flows of costs within a manufacturing firm and explain how and when manufacturing costs become incorporated in inventory cost.
- Explain the difference between process and job-order systems of cost accumulation, and describe those situations where each is appropriate.
- Describe the process of overhead application, using predetermined overhead rates, and explain why such a process might be desirable or necessary.
- Describe, with examples, common alternatives for handling joint or common costs; spoilage costs; overtime, idle-time, and payroll fringe benefits; and permanent cost changes such as those arising from inflation.
- Describe the essential differences of product cost disclosure on the financial statements of a merchandiser and a manufacturer.

## NEW VOCABULARY AND CONCEPTS

| | |
|---|---|
| Managerial accounting | Prime cost |
| Cost Accounting | Period cost |
| Product cost | Direct cost |
| Net purchases | Indirect cost |
| Direct labor | Direct material |
| Manufacturing overhead | Process costing |
| Finished goods | Job-order costing |
| Raw materials | Standard costing |
| Work-in-process | Equivalent units |
| Gross profit ratio | Conversion costs |
| Manufacturing cost | Predetermined overhead rate |
| Nonmanufacturing cost | Activity base |

Underapplied overhead          Full-absorption costing
Accounting variance            Joint (common) cost
Overapplied overhead           Split-off point

- Expense-recognition timing differences between product costs and period costs.
- Allocation/application of indirect (overhead) costs.

## REVIEW QUESTIONS

1. What is the difference between manufacturing and nonmanufacturing cost?
2. Give at least five examples of costs commonly classified as manufacturing costs.
3. Give at least five examples of costs commonly classified as nonmanufacturing costs.
4. What is the difference between product costs and period costs?
5. What costs are commonly classified as product costs for: (a) a merchandiser? (b) a manufacturer?
6. What costs are commonly classified as period costs for: (a) a merchandiser? (b) a manufacturer?
7. What is the difference between direct and indirect costs?
8. What costs are often classified as direct for a manufacturer?
9. What costs are often classified as indirect for a manufacturer?
10. What are indirect manufacturing costs usually called?
11. For a manufacturer, what three types of costs are normally included in the determination of the total cost of each product for inventory measurement purposes?
12. Why must manufacturing overhead usually be allocated to different products? Give examples of overhead allocation/application.
13. What costs are included in raw materials inventory for a manufacturer?
14. What costs are included in work-in-process inventory for a manufacturer?
15. What is the difference between those costs included in finished goods inventory for a merchandiser and those for a manufacturer?
16. a) What is the difference between cost accumulation under a process costing system and under a job-order costing system?
    b) In which situations is each appropriate?
    c) Give examples of cost accumulation under each system.
17. a) What is a predetermined overhead rate?
    b) How is it calculated?
    c) How is it used under either a process or a job-order system?
    d) Is its use necessary under a job-order system? Explain.
18. a) In general, what is a standard cost system?
    b) How do cost standards differ from predetermined overhead rates?
    c) Can standard costs be used with process or job-order systems? Explain.

**19.** a) What is an accounting variance?

b) How might it arise?

c) What is done with it?

**20.** Describe, with examples, two different methods of allocating joint (common) costs.

**21.** a) What are two alternatives for handling spoilage costs?

b) In which circumstances is each appropriate?

**22.** a) How may costs of overtime and payroll fringe benefits for production workers be classified?

b) How will costs of production workers' time not spent on production usually be classified?

**23.** What are the essential differences between the balance sheets and income statements of merchandise firms and those of manufacturers?

## MINI-CASES AND QUESTIONS FOR DISCUSSION

**MC 1.1** John Sweet, an accountant, and Mary Sharp, an operations research specialist, are having an argument over costs. John maintains that full absorption costing (all manufacturing costs included in product cost) is appropriate for inventory cost measurement. "After all," he says, "all manufacturing costs, including all indirect overhead costs, were necessary to produce the product. Without the factory, there would be no product. To disregard any part of overhead makes no more sense than to disregard some portion of direct material or labor."

Mary counters, "Direct costing (only direct manufacturing costs included in product cost) is far more appropriate. The only product costs really added to inventory during the year were material, labor, and any portion of overhead that could be directly attributed to production. The remaining overhead would be there anyway whether you added inventory (made more items than you sold) or not. Indirect overhead is clearly a period cost."

Which is correct? Why might John naturally favor one method and Mary the other? Discuss.

**MC 1.2** In contrast to direct costing, full absorption costing can lead to lower, equal, or greater reported income, depending upon whether production exceeded, was the same as, or was less than sales. Discuss:  a) How and why this could happen? b) Is such a result logical?  c) Wouldn't such a system provide an opportunity for management to manipulate reported income?

**MC 1.3** Opponents of full absorption costing maintain that it is not only inappropriate but is also dangerous. They maintain that, if records are maintained on a full cost basis, managers may inadvertently use such data in their decision-making. Using full product cost as a basis for decisions can lead to incorrect decisions. The indirect portion of cost may be the same regardless of the decision. Discuss.

## ESSENTIAL PROBLEMS

**EP 1.1** Selected cost data for the Curry and Dawson Corporations, both whole-salers, for the year 19X3 are given below in thousands of dollars:

|  | Curry | Dawson |
|---|---|---|
| Beginning merchandise inventory | $ 60 | $ 40 |
| Ending merchandise inventory | 70 | 30 |
| Gross merchandise purchases | 190 | 120 |
| Purchase discounts | 5 | 10 |
| Purchase returns | 10 | 5 |
| Space costs | 20 | 15 |
| Transportation (freight) in | 15 | 5 |
| Wages and salaries | 30 | 25 |

For the Curry Company for 19X3, determine:   a) total products costs incurred during the year;   b) cost of goods sold;   c) operating expenses.

**EP 1.2** Refer to the data given in problem EP 1.1. For the Dawson Company for 19X3, determine:   a) total additional product costs for the year;   b) cost of goods sold;   c) operating expenses.

**EP 1.3** Selected information for the Abco Manufacturing Corporation and for the Berkowitz Company is given below for the month of February, 19X2 (in thousands of dollars):

|  | Abco | Berkowitz |
|---|---|---|
| Beginning inventory: |  |  |
| Finished goods | $ 30 | $ 10 |
| Raw materials | 15 | 5 |
| Work-in-process | 10 | 5 |
| Direct labor | 50 | 5 |
| Ending inventory: |  |  |
| Finished goods | 40 | 10 |
| Raw materials | 10 | 10 |
| Work-in-process | 5 | 15 |
| Indirect labor | 10 | 8 |
| Net purchases—Raw material | 20 | 15 |
| Provision for income taxes | 10 | 5 |
| Salaries: |  |  |
| Administrative and sales | 15 | 10 |
| Factory supervision | 5 | 5 |
| Sales | 160 | 75 |
| Space cost: |  |  |
| Factory | 7 | 5 |
| General and sales offices | 3 | 2 |
| Supplies: |  |  |
| Factory | 3 | 2 |
| General office | 2 | 3 |
| Shipping | 10 | 5 |
| Transportation (freight) out | 5 | 10 |

For Abco for February of 19X2, determine:   a) total manufacturing costs; b) total nonmanufacturing costs.

**EP 1.4** Refer to the data given in Problem EP 1.3. For Berkowitz for February, 19X2, determine. a) total manufacturing costs; b) total nonmanufacturing costs.

**EP 1.5** Refer to the data given in Problem EP 1.3. For Abco for February, 19X2. determine: a) total product costs added to finished goods inventory—cost of goods manufactured; b) total period costs.

**EP 1.6** Refer to the data given in Problem EP 1.3 above. For Berkowitz for February, 19X2, determine: a) total product costs added to finished goods inventory—cost of goods manufactured; b) total period costs.

**EP 1.7** The following data (in tens of thousands of dollars) is selected from the income statements and supporting schedules of eight separate companies, A through H. Complete the missing items for companies A through D.

| | A | B | C | D | E | F | G | H |
|---|---|---|---|---|---|---|---|---|
| Direct materials | 3 | ? | 20 | 15 | 60 | 93 | ? | 5 |
| Direct labor | 4 | 7 | 15 | ? | ? | 60 | 40 | 45 |
| Manufacturing overhead | 8 | 7 | ? | 8 | 26 | ? | 20 | 35 |
| Total manufacturing costs | ? | 20 | ? | 29 | 99 | ? | 73 | ? |
| Beginning work-in-process | 5 | 4 | 4 | ? | ? | 11 | 7 | 9 |
| Ending work-in-process | 6 | ? | 4 | 5 | 6 | 12 | ? | 4 |
| Cost of goods manufactured | ? | 21 | 45 | 28 | 101 | 200 | 71 | ? |
| Beginning finished goods | 3 | ? | 5 | 6 | 9 | 18 | ? | 8 |
| Ending finished goods | ? | 5 | 6 | ? | ? | 19 | 16 | ? |
| Cost of goods sold | 15 | 20 | ? | 30 | 100 | ? | 75 | 90 |

**EP 1.8** Refer to the data given in Problem EP 1.7. Complete the missing items for companies E through H.

**EP 1.9** Refer to the data given in Problem EP 1.3. Prepare for Abco for February, 19X2, a schedule, in good form, of cost of goods manufactured (refer to Exhibit 1.2).

**EP 1.10** Refer to the data given in Problem EP 1.3. Prepare for Berkowitz for February, 19X2, a schedule, in good form, of cost of goods manufactured (refer to Exhibit 1.2).

**EP 1.11** Refer to Problem EP 1.3. Prepare an income statement, in good form, for the Abco Company for February, 19X2.

**EP 1.12** Refer to Problem EP 1.3. Prepare an income statement, in good form, for the Berkowitz Company for February, 19X2.

## SUPPLEMENTARY PROBLEMS

**SP 1.13** During a particular period, a firm incurred the following costs: direct materials $70,000, direct labor $120,000, and manufacturing overhead $230,000. The firm used process costing, applied all costs at actual, and during the period completed 60,000 equivalent units. What was the inventory cost per equivalent unit?

**SP 1.14** During a period, a firm incurred the following costs: direct material $20,000, direct labor $60,000, and manufacturing overhead $100,000. The firm used process costing, applied material and labor at actual, overhead at a predetermined rate of $2 per direct labor dollar, and during the period completed 50,000 equivalent units. What was the inventory cost per equivalent unit?

**SP 1.15** A particular firm manufactured widgets and followed the process costing system. All the material cost in a widget was involved at the start of the production process. Beginning work-in-process inventory was zero. Ending work-in-process inventory consisted of 3,000 units 60 percent complete with respect to conversion cost. During the year 12,000 additional widgets were finished and transferred to finished goods stores. Also, during the year, material costing $33,600 was transferred to work-in-process inventory; and direct labor costs incurred equalled $101,200. Overhead was to be applied at a predetermined rate, $2 per direct labor dollar.

a) What were the equivalent units of production for the period?

b) What was the product cost per unit?

c) What was the dollar cost of ending work-in-process inventory?

d) If beginning finished goods inventory had been zero, and ending finished goods included 2,000 widgets, what amount should be reported as cost of goods sold for the period, not including accounting variances?

**SP 1.16** Assume the same data as in Problem SP 1.15, except:

- Ending work-in-process inventory was 40 percent complete with respect to conversion costs;

- Actual overhead was $210,000;

- Beginning finished goods was $30,000 (1,500 widgets), and the firm followed LIFO for finished goods inventory.

a) What were the equivalent units of production for the period?

b) What was the product cost per unit?

c) What was the dollar cost of ending work-in-process inventory?

d) With ending finished goods inventory at 2,000 units, what figure would appear on the income statement as cost of goods sold (including accounting variances)?

**SP 1.17** Estimated information for the forthcoming period for four different manufacturing firms is as follows:

|                                       | Firm A | Firm B | Firm C | Firm D |
|---------------------------------------|--------|--------|--------|--------|
| Manufacturing overhead                | $ 40,000 | $ 50,000 | $ 60,000 | $ 70,000 |
| Direct labor cost                     | 80,000 | 70,000 | 60,000 | 50,000 |
| Prime cost (material and labor)       | 120,000 | 125,000 | 130,000 | 140,000 |
| Direct labor hours                    | 18,000 | 16,000 | 15,000 | 10,000 |
| Machine hours                         | 19,000 | 18,500 | 18,000 | 17,500 |
| Most appropriate activity base        | Direct labor dollars | Prime dollars | Direct labor hours | Machine hours |

a) Compute the predetermined overhead rate for Firm A.

b) For Firm A, assume actual direct labor cost incurred for the period was $85,000 and actual overhead was $45,000. How much overhead was applied to work-in-process?

c) Under the same assumptions as in (b) above, how much overhead accounting variance will there be? Will it represent over- or underapplied overhead?

d) Compute the predetermined overhead rate for Firm B.

e) For Firm B, assume that actual prime costs incurred were $120,000 and actual overhead was $40,000; how much overhead would be applied to work-in-process?

f) Under the same assumptions as in (e) above, will there be any over- or underapplied overhead? How much?

SP 1.18 Refer to the data given in Problem SP 1.17.

a) Compute the predetermined overhead rates for Firms C and D.

b) Assume that actual direct labor hours were 16,000 for Firm C and that actual machine hours were 17,000 for Firm D. How much overhead would be applied to work-in-process in each firm?

c) In addition to the assumptions in (b) above, also assume that actual overhead incurred was $65,000 for both firms. What will be the amount of overhead variance in each firm, and will it represent over- or underapplied overhead?

SP 1.19 The following data is applicable to the Ashdown Corporation for the year 19X5:

| | |
|---|---|
| Planned total direct labor hours (DLH) for the year (overhead activity base): | 30,000 hrs. |
| Planned total manufacturing overhead for the year: | $120,000 |
| Actual direct material costs incurred for Product A: | $100,000 |
| Actual direct labor hours incurred for Product A: | 10,000 hrs. |
| Actual direct material costs incurred for Product B: | $ 50,000 |
| Actual direct labor hours incurred for Product B: | 25,000 hrs. |
| Actual total manufacturing overhead incurred: | $150,000 |
| Actual units manufactured of Product A: | 100,000 units |
| Actual units manufactured of Product B: | 5,000 units |
| Beginning and ending WIP inventory: | zero |
| Beginning finished goods inventory, Product A (20,000 units): | $ 30,000 |
| Ending finished goods inventory, Product A: | 25,000 units |
| Beginning finished goods inventory, Product B (1,000 units): | $ 50,000 |
| Ending finished goods inventory, Product B: | 800 units |

Ashdown followed a modified job-order cost system and incurred a direct labor cost of $6 per hour. Determine cost of goods sold to appear on the firm's annual income statement, under the following assumptions:

a) The firm used LIFO;

b) The firm used weighted average cost;

c) The firm used FIFO.

**SP 1.20** The following data is applicable to Beck Corporation for the year 19X3:

| | |
|---|---|
| Planned total machine hours for the year: | 130,000 hrs.* |
| Planned total manufacturing overhead for the year: | $260,000 |
| Actual direct material costs incurred for Product X: | $ 50,000 |
| Actual direct labor dollars incurred for Product X: | $100,000 |
| Actual direct material costs incurred for Product Y: | $130,000 |
| Actual direct labor dollars incurred for Product Y: | $ 60,000 |
| Actual total manufacturing overhead incurred: | $230,000 |
| Actual machine hours used for Product X: | 75,000 hrs. |
| Actual machine hours used for Product Y: | 45,000 hrs. |
| Beginning and ending WIP inventory: | zero |
| Beginning finished goods inventory, Product X (12,000 units): | $ 60,000 |
| Ending finished goods inventory, Product X: | 10,000 units |
| Beginning finished goods inventory, Product Y (6,000 units): | $ 36,000 |
| Ending finished goods inventory, Product Y: | 7,000 units |
| Units produced, Product X: | 25,000 units |
| Units produced, Product Y: | 40,000 units |

---

* Overhead activity base.

Assuming Beck used a modified job-order cost system, determine cost of goods sold, to appear on the firm's annual income statement, under the following assumptions:

a) The firm used LIFO;

b) The firm used weighted average cost;

c) The firm used FIFO.


## SUGGESTIONS FOR FURTHER READING

Horngren, Charles T., *Cost Accounting, A Managerial Emphasis*; Fourth Edition (Englewood Cliffs, N. J.: Prentice-Hall, Inc., 1977); Chapters 1, 2, 4, 7, 9, 10, and 17 through 19.

Morse, Wayne J., *Cost Accounting, Processing, Evaluating, and Using Cost Data* (Reading, Mass.: Addison-Wesley Publishing Company, 1978); Chapters 1 through 4 and 14.

# 2

## PLANNING AND CONTROL – AN OVERVIEW

## CHAPTER PREVIEW

The objective of this chapter is to provide you with an overview of the management planning and control process, and show you how managerial accounting and the firm's controller relate to and serve the various activities involved. In this chapter you can:

- Perceive the need for planning and control in both profit-directed and nonprofit-directed organizations;
- Learn of the many similarities between profit-directed and nonprofit-directed organizations and the need of all organizations to have objectives;
- Learn about the management technique known as management by objectives or MBO, and how a firm's budgeting and budgetary control activities are a part of MBO;
- Learn that management activities may be conveniently divided into planning, organizing, and controlling;
- Learn about planning time horizons and the three common types or groups of planning activities—strategic planning, intermediate planning, and budgeting;
- Develop initial familiarity with the kinds of information involved in a budget and the purpose of budgeting;
- Develop an awareness of the need for goal congruence in both planning and plan implementation, and of the need for and usefulness of responsibility centers within an organization;
- Develop an understanding of the meaning and function of control as used in a business management context and of several approaches to control;
- Learn the role of managerial accounting in its relationship to business planning and control;
- Learn of the role of the controller in a business.

With this knowledge you will have adequate perspective to proceed with the subsequent chapters in this book, which cover in more detail the budgeting and controlling elements of managerial accounting. You will be able to relate the subsequent chapters to the overall picture introduced in this chapter.

(*Note.* If you have not recently completed a course in financial accounting, or if your first accounting course(s) heavily emphasized accounting *procedure* (journal entries, trial balances, work sheets, and so forth), you might benefit by first studying the appendix to this chapter before proceeding.)

### NEED FOR PLANNING AND CONTROL

To perceive readily the need for planning and control in an organization, and the various elements involved, you should relate your existing knowledge and what you learn in this course to a specific situation. With this objective you are now asked to assume that you have just inherited the controlling stock of the Tripper Water Ski Company. The stock was bequeathed to you by a distant great-aunt whom you didn't realize even existed, and therefore the whole thing has been a complete surprise. You may assume you have decided to keep the company and be its owner-manager, rather than sell the stock.[1]

One of the first questions you might ask could be, "What should be the objectives or goals of the firm?" "What should the firm be doing; where do I want it to go?" Among many alternatives for consideration would be:

1. Should your objective be to maximize immediate profit, or do you wish to maximize long-term return on your investment?[2]

2. Should you stay exclusively in the water ski business, or should you expand into other activities such as related sporting goods?

3. Within the water ski business, what types of markets do you wish to serve? What type of image do you wish to have for your potential customers? Do you wish to concentrate on the limited market for very high-quality, high-priced skis? Do you wish to aim at a larger market for average-quality, low-price, or discount-price skis? Or do you want to be a broad line supplier with different qualities and prices?

4. Somewhat independent of product/market alternatives, what kind of factory do you wish to operate? Do you wish to operate at the lowest reasonable cost? Or would you prefer to forego some profit and have a more supportive and aesthetically pleasing atmosphere in which you and your employees work?

The above are just some of the hundreds of questions that might come to your mind as alternatives for consideration in planning or deciding upon the goals of the firm. Assume that you have considered all alternatives and have come to the following decisions:

---

[1]    This somewhat extreme fantasy of surprise inheritance will serve you better than assuming you purchased the firm. The purpose of this example is to focus your immediate attention on the decisions you will need to make. In a situation involving purchase, many of these decisions would be made prior to purchase, or be conditioned on the terms of purchase, or would follow purchase. Assuming surprise inheritance, they all come up to be dealt with at once.

[2]    Even though you inherited the firm, you can think of your investment as being the amount of cash you could have received if you sold your inheritance. This cash would be yours, and your decision not to sell may be viewed as having decided to invest this cash in the business.

A) The firm shall stay in the water-ski business for the foreseeable future. It shall broaden its product line to include other water-ski-related items such as flotation belts and jackets.

B) The firm shall concentrate on the middle- and upper-quality portions of the market. It will avoid the "discount" or "lesser-quality" image.

C) The firm shall focus on maximizing long-term return on investment rather than quick or immediate profit. Further, a reasonable share of revenues shall be expended each year to create a more pleasant working and community environment: well decorated and insulated working spaces, landscaped grounds surrounding the building, support of community activities, and so forth.

Towards implementation of these general long-range goals, you might make other specific intermediate-term plans. You might decide to design, develop, and introduce a water-ski belt and a water-ski jacket within the next four years. You might also decide to landscape the surrounding grounds and to pave the employee parking lot within the next two years.

Finally, in the immediate future (within the next year), you might decide to repaint all interior working spaces in decorator colors, and to install comfortable modern employee lounges.

To actually implement and accomplish these plans, you will need the assistance of your employees, and their efforts must be organized. Each member of your organization should know what he or she is expected to do, and each should be aware of the responsibilities that have been assigned to others. You may decide to keep Tripper's existing organization—both individuals and responsibility assignments—at least until you become more familiar with the business, or until circumstances change. But you will need to assign authority and responsibility for the implementation of your specific decisions: new products, landscaping, paving, community contributions, painting, and lounges. You would also be well advised to communicate your new long-term goals to your managers and perhaps to your employees; it is important that they know the firm's goals. With this information, they can make day-to-day decisions in a way that will help the firm move in its chosen direction. Or, if they dislike the firm's goals, they can choose to move to another firm.

In addition to organizing your employees and communicating objectives to them, implementation of your objectives will also require control. You and your managers will need to control the progress of your firm towards its objectives in the same sense that you need to control an automobile to drive from one place to another. You will need to be in control to anticipate or recognize and deal with previously unforeseen events (traffic jams, detours, and so forth). You will also need control to ensure that all members of the organization, who individually have distinct goals, somehow manage to work together towards the firm's goals.

To be able to control, you will require feedback of information. As you proceed, you will need feedback advising you how effectively the organization is achieving or getting close to its objectives. And, in addition, you will need information on how efficiently (most benefit for the least cost) it is performing.

In the general discussion that follows, and in the additional detail in succeeding chapters, you will find it beneficial (gaining easier and more rapid comprehension and more complete retention) if you will pause with each new idea and relate it to something specific within the Tripper Company before proceeding.

## ORGANIZATIONS AND THEIR OBJECTIVES

Business and other institutions in society may be viewed as organizations of people. One of many things that all organizations share or have in common is that they each have objectives or purposes. Business organizations are *profit-directed*, in that one of their major goals (whether or not they are currently profitable) is to earn a profit and maximize the return on the resources invested. Profit-directed organizations or businesses are generally thought of as being in the private sector (private property ownership) of the U.S. economy.

Nonbusiness organizations in the private sector are often called institutions, and are service- rather than profit-oriented. Examples of service organizations that are *nonprofit-directed* may include nongovernmental educational institutions, charitable organizations, hospitals, churches, unions, and so forth. Organizations in the public or governmental sector of the economy are often called governmental institutions or just governments. One of the major objectives of nonprofit-directed service and governmental organizations is to achieve specific service or regulatory goals in an efficient (most benefit for least cost) manner. They are expected to serve the public interest as interpreted by officials, managers, and voters.

In addition to the fact that all organizations are alike in having objectives, they can be observed to share other things:

- They all have managers who attempt to direct the activities of the members of the organization towards its goals.
- They all have an organizational structure, which assigns authority and responsibility to different members. The intention of organization is to ensure that different members achieve different parts of the total goal in an integrated and coordinated manner.
- They all have strategies or policies which communicate their objectives to managers and other members. Such communication is intended both to clarify goals and also to indicate which actions are thought to be appropriate and which inappropriate in the achievement of goals.
- Their managers periodically confer over plans to achieve objectives; and their managers also periodically reevaluate and occasionally modify the objectives themselves.

- Their managers establish control systems intended to ensure that all members' actions serve the organization's objectives within policy constraints.

- Their managers all require information for use in planning and controlling the activities of the members of the organization.

Managerial accounting may be thought of as the system designed to provide information to managers of organizations for use in planning and controlling. Many aspects of planning and controlling are similar among profit-directed and nonprofit-directed organizations. In the first fourteen chapters, the text focuses upon activities in profit-directed businesses. Chapter 15 will provide you with an introduction to those planning and control aspects in nonprofit-directed organizations that differ from those in a business firm.


## ROLE OF MANAGEMENT: PLANNING, ORGANIZING, AND CONTROLLING

From the previous list of characteristics common to all organizations, and from your own intuition in your role as the new owner of the Tripper Company, you may perceive that managers are essentially involved in three distinct activities: planning, organizing, and controlling. Managers must plan what they and the firm intend to achieve: the firm's objectives. They must communicate these objectives to the members of the organization. They must organize their activities, those of their subordinates, and all available resources in a manner best suited to accomplish their objectives. And they then must exercise control, control that is intended to ensure that their own energy and actions and those of their subordinates are directed towards implementation of the organization's objectives.

To experience these various activities in a meaningful and not just an abstract or conceptual context, imagine you are charged with the responsibility (objective) of arranging for the annual picnic for your organization. You would first plan a date, a location, various games, and a menu. You would then organize your membership. You would assign specific responsibilities to various individuals to obtain, bring, and serve specific foods and beverages; to administer various activities (sports, entertainment, and so forth); and to ensure cleanup at the end. You then would be well advised to be there on the picnic day. If you were there, you could see whether everything was proceeding as planned and whether you needed to take corrective action if something was going wrong. Being there (or receiving accurate, timely, feedback information) and seeing that the various activities are proceeding as planned is what is meant by controlling the operation.

## THREE TYPES OF MANAGEMENT: OPERATING, FINANCIAL, AND TAX

In a profit-directed business, planning, organizing, and controlling activities are common to all three types of management. *Operating management* is charged with the responsibility of planning, organizing, and administering (controlling) the resources within the firm to efficiently and effectively accomplish the firm's goals. Operating management is also charged with the responsibility of projecting future resource requirements.

*Financial management*'s job is to maintain solvency (having adequate cash to pay bills when due), to determine the firm's optimal capital structure, and to obtain funds as required in a manner that maintains (over the long run) the desirable capital structure.

*Tax management*'s role is to guide the decisions made by operating and financial managers so as to minimize the firm's tax liability (assuming taxable income to begin with).

$$\underset{\text{management}}{\text{Operating}} + \underset{\text{management}}{\text{Financial}} + \underset{\text{management}}{\text{Tax}} = \underset{\text{management.}}{\text{Total}}$$

## MANAGEMENT BY OBJECTIVES (MBO)

Managers involved in planning, organizing, and controlling at any level within a firm have found they are most effective when both they and their subordinates are completely clear about and take responsibility for specific objectives—where there is clear agreement on objectives. A rapidly developing practice within management involves periodic review and formalization of objectives of all types by written agreement between superior and subordinate. Such agreements can cover anything both parties agree upon as important ranging from changing personal behavior (modification of practices that are counterproductive) to completion of specific projects. (See Fig. 2.1.)

The MBO approach, to be effective, requires not only a planning agreement, but also periodic review and follow-up. Often on an annual or semi-annual basis, the two individuals will set aside time specifically to review achievements and replan (make new agreements) for the following period.

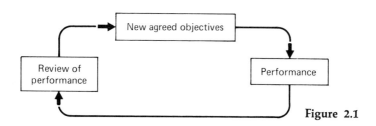

Figure 2.1

You will probably have the opportunity to learn more about the MBO approach in courses devoted to interpersonal management. In this and subsequent chapters, you will have the opportunity to learn how MBO is practiced with respect to the measurable financial (revenue, cost, and investment) objectives of a firm.

## PLANNING HORIZONS

MBO obviously starts with planning. Planning any activity with the intention that it continues forever is often unproductive in a changing world. Instead, most effective planning covers a specific span of time. It is deliberately limited to some finite period in the future. For example, plans might be made for objectives and actions in the long run, over the next 30 or 50 years. Plans might be made over the next five years. Plans might be made for the immediate future, within the next year or an even shorter period. The limit of the planning period is commonly referred to as the *planning horizon*. In learning about planning, it is convenient to group all planning activities into three groups based upon their planning horizons. Planning that is long range, more than five years into the future, is often known as *strategic planning* or *long-range planning*. Planning over a shorter time period, usually two to five years, is commonly called *intermediate planning* or *intermediate-range planning*. Planning for the immediate future, for activities within the next year, is known as *budgeting* or *short-range planning*.

| Budgeting | Intermediate planning | Strategic planning |
|---|---|---|
| Now          1 | 5 | 10–50 |

Planning horizon in years

## STRATEGIC PLANNING

Strategic planning involves determining the long-range objectives of the organization or firm. Strategic planning is essential to provide criteria and guidance for all other management decisions, and particularly for all intermediate and short-range planning. Recall that, as the owner of the Tripper Company, you made certain strategic plans with respect to your firm's future product lines, market segments, and the working environment of the business. A further exploration of strategic planning is beyond the scope of this text. If you are a business major, you will have more detailed exposure to strategic planning in marketing, finance, and industrial relations courses, and also possibly in a business policy or a business core capstone course.

## INTERMEDIATE PLANNING

Intermediate planning involves determining specific objectives for the firm over the next two to five years. Intermediate plans may be thought of as links or bridges partially connecting the planned position of the company at the end of the short-range plan with its long-range or strategic objectives. Strategic plans and policies provide **general** guidelines as to what is to be achieved—in what direction and towards what general long-range goals the company should move. By contrast, intermediate plans or projects are **specific** as to which objectives are to be achieved and by what date. They include measurable results and a target date so that managers may determine specifically whether or not they have been achieved.

Recall that, as owner of the Tripper Company, you established several intermediate plans. You decided to landscape the surrounding grounds and pave the employee's parking lot within the next two years. You also decided to design, develop, and introduce two new products: a ski safety belt and a ski safety jacket. Exhibit 2.1 provides further examples of intermediate objectives you might establish for your company.

In Exhibit 2.1 you may note several common characteristics of intermediate planning objectives. They are realistic and achievable. For instance, marketing and financial objectives would be determined in terms of known market char-

### Exhibit 2.1
### TRIPPER WATER SKI MANUFACTURING COMPANY

**Intermediate-Term Objectives**
**for the Period 19X3–19X7**

MARKETING
1. Sales volume growth of 15 percent per year
2. Market volume of 12 percent by 19X7
3. Introduction of ski belt and ski vest by 19X6

PRODUCTION
1. Redesign factory layout and obtain new equipment so that spoilage and material-handling costs are reduced by 2.3 percent of total manufacturing cost for the year by 19X6
2. Achieve and maintain thereafter an average inventory turnover of 7.5 times per year by 19X7

GENERAL
1. Complete landscaping of grounds and paving of employee parking lot by 19X4

FINANCIAL
1. Achieve receivables turnover of eight times by 19X5 and ten times by 19X7
2. Achieve and maintain a debt ratio of 30 percent by 19X4
3. Maintain a current ratio of at least three to one
4. Obtain earnings before taxes of 12 percent of sales and 19 percent of total assets by 19X5

acteristics and industry averages, respectively; and production and general objectives would result from engineering feasibility studies.

Intermediate planning objectives are specific in nature with a measurable or readily observable indicator as to whether or not they have been achieved. They each have a target date falling within the intermediate planning horizon range. And note that they are **not** specific as to the means with which they are to be accomplished.

By their very nature, most intermediate plans are still objectives where the exact pattern of resource usage in their achievement has not been finalized or committed. It may be impossible, or at least not worth the cost, for management to plan and project in such detail over the two-to-five-year period that it would have a complete plan of both what is to be achieved and exactly how it is to be achieved. Also, intermediate objectives are still subject to modification in response to changes in the forces of competition, legal or physical environment, or to changes in long-range strategies.

Intermediate planning involves detailed evaluation of the costs and benefits of various alternatives under consideration. Chapters 6, 7, and 8 will introduce you to some of the decision-making tools relevant to intermediate planning. Also other business-core courses such as marketing, finance, and production or operations management will build upon and extend your knowledge obtained in these three chapters and enhance your ability to make intelligent intermediate plans.

Regardless of how well made, intermediate-range plans still require implementation or execution. Even though full accomplishment of an intermediate objective may take several years, planned activities for the first and succeeding years of implementation are blended with planning for normal operations. In this way, all short-range planning may fully integrate both normal operations and the short-run implementation of intermediate objectives.


## BUDGETING

Budgeting or short-range planning involves setting objectives for the immediate future—usually for one year. As distinct from intermediate planning, budgeting involves very specific plans or expectations for all activities anticipated during the forthcoming year. These plans are set forth in the budget in terms of not only what will be achieved but exactly how it will be accomplished. Budgets include all anticipated resource inflows: revenues, borrowings, and new owner investments and all expected resource outflows: expenses and owner withdrawals (dividends). Budgets represent firm commitments on the part of managers of their most reasonable plans and expectations of what will occur over the next year. Usually budgets are detailed for portions of the year such as months or quarters. It is not expected that they will be significantly revised except for changes in the actual level of operations or in the event of unforseeable changes in circumstances.

Even though they represent commitments, business budgets must not be confused with governmental budgets. Governmental budgets represent absolute legal ceilings of expenditures beyond which the governmental organization may not go regardless of circumstances. Therefore, a governmental organization may attempt to include in its budget permission to expend funds to cover all possible contingencies. A business budget is usually a plan rather than a ceiling. A business budget[3] is intended to portray reasonably expected events. It is **not** intended to cover contingencies that could not be reasonably forecast or that were not expected to occur.

Whereas strategic planning and intermediate planning are not within the scope of this text, budgeting is one of the important aspects of managerial accounting, and is one of the two major areas upon which this text focuses. Chapters 3 through 10 are all devoted to various aspects of the budgeting process.

## Sales Budget

Exhibit 2.2 illustrates the various steps in the budgeting process. Note that the first step is to determine a *sales* or *revenue* or *activity budget*. Chapter 3 will be devoted entirely to the sales budget as the important first step in the overall budgeting process. Exhibit 2.3 illustrates a sales budget for Tripper for the year 19X1. This budget includes anticipated sales demand for each product in both units and dollars in total and by quarters over the forthcoming year. Many firms find it more desirable to budget by month instead of by quarter, but at this time an illustration of quarterly budgeting will allow you to observe the process without too much detail.[4]

Remember, as you proceed through the next few pages and the next fourteen exhibits, that you are not being asked at this stage to master completely the content of each report that is part of a firm's budget. All of these reports, starting with the sales budget, will be covered in detail in Chapters 3 through 10. At this stage you are expected to become familiar with:

- The various stages in the budgeting process (Exhibit 2.2);
- The titles and a generalized concept of the content of the various budget reports (Exhibits 2.3 through 2.16);
- The types of information flowing between one budget report and the next (to be described below).

---

[3]   In the first fourteen chapters of this text, the word budget by itself will be used to refer to a business budget and not to a budget in a nonprofit-directed or governmental organization.

[4]   Some firms and textbooks include, as part of the sales budget, the plans for anticipated selling and distribution expenses for the period. In this text these selling and distribution expenses will be considered as part of the general, selling, and administrative expense budget (see "other operating budgets" below).

## Exhibit 2.2
### TRIPPER WATER SKI MANUFACTURING COMPANY

**Steps in the Budgeting Process**

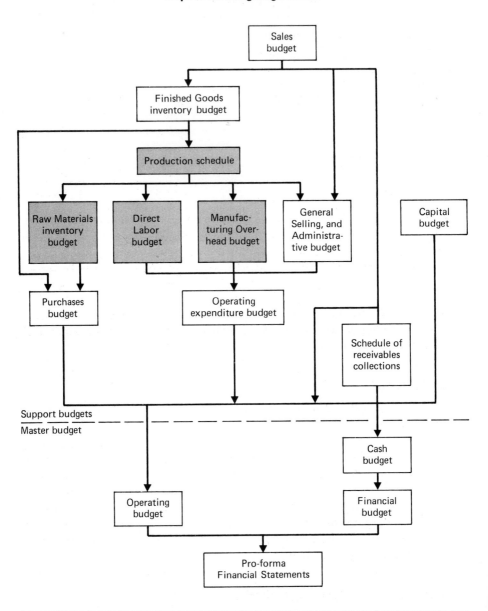

## Exhibit 2.3
## TRIPPER WATER SKI MANUFACTURING COMPANY

**Sales Budget for the Year 19X1**

|  | First quarter | | Second quarter | |
|---|---|---|---|---|
| Products | Units | Dollars | Units | Dollars |
| Economy ski | 2,300 | $115,000 | 4,500 | $225,000 |
| Deluxe ski | 1,200 | 96,000 | 2,700 | 216,000 |
| Tow rope | 1,000 | 10,000 | 2,000 | 20,000 |
| Total | | $221,000 | | $461,000 |
| Percent | | 20.0 | | 40.0 |

|  | Third quarter | | Fourth quarter | | Total year | |
|---|---|---|---|---|---|---|
| Products | Units | Dollars | Units | Dollars | Units | Dollars |
| Economy ski | 3,600 | $180,000 | 1,200 | $ 60,000 | 11,600 | $ 580,000 |
| Deluxe ski | 1,800 | 144,000 | 625 | 50,000 | 6,325 | 506,000 |
| Tow rope | 1,500 | 15,000 | 900 | 9,000 | 5,400 | 54,000 |
| Total | | $339,000 | | $119,000 | | $1,140,000 |
| Percent | | 30.0 | | 10.0 | | 100.0 |

For example, the output of the sales budget (expected sales demand by customers) is the input to the inventory budget (requirements for additional quantities of product).

### Inventory Budget

Once sales demand is projected, it can be compared against anticipated and desired inventory levels to determine necessary production and purchasing. Exhibit 2.4 illustrates an *inventory budget* for 19X1. Note that, on this exhibit, desired ending inventory for each product is combined with anticipated sales to determine necessary goods available for sale. Total requirements are then reduced by anticipated inventory on hand to determine the amount necessary to produce or purchase. You might also note that this budget is prepared in units, and that each quarter's target ending inventory is assumed to be the following quarter's beginning inventory. Chapter 4 discusses inventory planning and control in greater depth.

### Purchases and Other Operating Budgets

With requirements for finished goods established, a *production schedule* can now be determined. Exhibit 2.5 illustrates such a schedule. From the production schedule, final budgets may be prepared for purchases, direct labor, manufacturing overhead, and general selling and administrative expenses. Exhibits 2.6

## Exhibit 2.4
### TRIPPER WATER SKI MANUFACTURING COMPANY

**Finished Goods Inventory Budget (Units) for the year 19X1**

|  | First quarter | Second quarter | Third quarter | Fourth quarter | Year |
|---|---|---|---|---|---|
| **Economy ski** |  |  |  |  |  |
| Sales budget | 2,300 | 4,500 | 3,600 | 1,200 | 11,600 |
| Target inventory* | 2,700 | 2,200 | 700 | 1,500 | 1,500 |
| Total requirements | 5,000 | 6,700 | 4,300 | 2,700 | 13,100 |
| Less: Planned stock** | 1,300 | 2,700 | 2,200 | 700 | 1,300 |
| Necessary acquisitions | 3,700 | 4,000 | 2,100 | 2,000 | 11,800 |
| **Deluxe ski** |  |  |  |  |  |
| Sales budget | 1,200 | 2,700 | 1,800 | 625 | 6,325 |
| Target inventory | 700 | 700 | 700 | 700 | 700 |
| Total requirements | 1,900 | 3,400 | 2,500 | 1,325 | 7,025 |
| Less: Planned stock | 700 | 700 | 700 | 700 | 700 |
| Necessary acquisitions | 1,200 | 2,700 | 1,800 | 625 | 6,325 |
| **Tow rope** |  |  |  |  |  |
| Sales budget | 1,000 | 2,000 | 1,500 | 900 | 5,400 |
| Target inventory | 1,200 | 900 | 500 | 700 | 700 |
| Total requirements | 2,200 | 2,900 | 2,000 | 1,600 | 6,100 |
| Less: Planned stock | 600 | 1,200 | 900 | 500 | 600 |
| Necessary acquisitions | 1,600 | 1,700 | 1,100 | 1,100 | 5,500 |

\* 60% of next 3 months' estimated sales (rounded)    \*\* Target inventory from prior period

## Exhibit 2.5
### TRIPPER WATER SKI MANUFACTURING COMPANY

**Production Schedule (Units to be Manufactured) for the Year 19X1**

|  | First quarter | Second quarter | Third quarter | Fourth quarter | Total year |
|---|---|---|---|---|---|
| **Economy ski** |  |  |  |  |  |
| Requirements[a] | 3,700 | 4,000 | 2,100 | 2,000 | 11,800 |
| From prior quarter[b] | 0 | 300 | 300 | 200 |  |
| Needs, current quarter[b] | 3,700 | 3,700 | 1,800 | 1,800 |  |
| Production orders[c] | 4,000 | 4,000 | 2,000 | 2,000 | 12,000 |
| **Deluxe ski** |  |  |  |  |  |
| Requirements[a] | 1,200 | 2,700 | 1,800 | 625 | 6,325 |
| From prior quarter[b] | 0 | 400 | 900 | 700 |  |
| Needs, current quarter | 1,200 | 2,300 | 900 | 0 |  |
| Production orders | 1,600 | 3,200 | 1,600 | 0 | 6,400 |

(a) From Finished goods inventory budget
(b) From producing more than minimum requirements during previous quarter
(c) Optimal economic lot sizes (quantities) are scheduled. Optimal lot sizes are 2,000 per lot for economy skis and 1,600 per lot for the deluxe ski (see Chapter 4 for discussion of economic lot sizes).

through 2.10 illustrate such budgets. Note that the *purchases budget* includes both raw materials and finished goods. Preparing the purchases budget is also covered in Chapter 4.

Budgets for *direct labor, manufacturing overhead,* and *general selling and administrative expenses* are, of course, dependent upon the volume of work anticipated. This dependency explains why they cannot be established until the anticipated workload has been finalized. In planning expenses, one needs to know about the behavior of different types of costs at different levels of activity (workload). Chapter 5 is devoted to a discussion of cost behavior and to the preparation of *operating budgets* for direct labor, overhead, and general selling and administrative expenses.

**Exhibit 2.6**

TRIPPER WATER SKI MANUFACTURING COMPANY

**Raw Materials Inventory Budget (in units)**
**for the Year 19X1**

| | First quarter | Second quarter | Third quarter | Fourth quarter | Total year |
|---|---|---|---|---|---|
| Wood for economy ski | | | | | |
| Requirements[a] | 4,000 | 4,000 | 2,000 | 2,000 | 12,000 |
| Carryover stock[b] | 2,300 | 300 | 300 | 300 | |
| Needs, current quarter | 1,700 | 3,700 | 1,700 | 1,700 | |
| Scheduled purchases[c] | 2,000 | 4,000 | 2,000 | 2,000 | 10,000 |
| | | | | | |
| Resin and cloth for deluxe ski | | | | | |
| Requirements[a] | 1,600 | 3,200 | 1,600 | 0 | 6,400 |
| Carryover stock[b] | 800 | 200 | 0 | 400 | |
| Needs, current quarter | 800 | 3,000 | 1,600 | 0 | |
| Scheduled purchases[c] | 1,000 | 3,000 | 2,000 | 0 | 6,000 |
| | | | | | |
| Hardware sets for both skis | | | | | |
| Requirements[a] | 5,600 | 7,200 | 3,600 | 2,000 | 18,400 |
| Carryover stock[b] | 1,000 | 400 | 700 | 2,100 | |
| Needs, current quarter | 4,600 | 6,800 | 2,900 | 0 | |
| Scheduled purchases[c] | 5,000 | 7,500 | 5,000 | 0 | 17,500 |

(a) From production schedule
(b) From prior period
(c) Optimal economic order quantities are scheduled. Optimal order quantities are:

|  |  |
|---|---|
| wood | 2,000 units (3 board feet per unit) |
| resin and cloth | 1,000 units |
| hardware | 2,500 units (sets) |

(See Chapter 4 for discussion of economic order quantities.)

**Exhibit 2.7**

TRIPPER WATER SKI MANUFACTURING COMPANY

**Purchases Budget for the Year 19X1**

| Items | First quarter Units* | First quarter Dollars | Second quarter Units* | Second quarter Dollars |
|---|---|---|---|---|
| Wood ($3.00) | 2,000 | $ 6,000 | 4,000 | $12,000 |
| Resin and cloth ($6.20) | 1,000 | 6,200 | 3,000 | 18,600 |
| Hardware sets ($2.50) | 5,000 | 12,500 | 7,500 | 18,750 |
| Tow ropes** ($5.00) | 2,000 | 10,000 | 2,000 | 10,000 |
| Total | | $34,700 | | $59,350 |

| Items | Third quarter Units* | Third quarter Dollars | Fourth quarter Units* | Fourth quarter Dollars | Total year Units | Total year Dollars |
|---|---|---|---|---|---|---|
| Wood ($3.00) | 2,000 | $ 6,000 | 2,000 | $ 6,000 | 10,000 | $ 30,000 |
| Resin and cloth ($6.20) | 2,000 | 12,400 | 0 | 0 | 6,000 | 37,200 |
| Hardware sets ($2.50) | 5,000 | 12,500 | 0 | 0 | 17,500 | 43,750 |
| Tow ropes** ($5.00) | 1,000 | 5,000 | 1,000 | 5,000 | 6,000 | 30,000 |
| Total | | $35,900 | | $11,000 | | $140,950 |

* Planned orders in economic order quantities.
** Purchase orders scheduled in economic order quantities based upon finished goods inventory budget.

**Exhibit 2.8**

TRIPPER WATER SKI MANUFACTURING COMPANY

**Direct Labor Budget for the Year 19X1**

| Products | First quarter Units* | First quarter Dollars | Second quarter Units* | Second quarter Dollars |
|---|---|---|---|---|
| Economy skis | 4,000 | $39,200 | 4,000 | $39,200 |
| Deluxe skis | 1,600 | 20,000 | 3,200 | 40,000 |
| Total | | $59,200 | | $79,200 |

| Products | Third quarter Units* | Third quarter Dollars | Fourth quarter Units* | Fourth quarter Dollars | Total year Units | Total year Dollars |
|---|---|---|---|---|---|---|
| Economy skis | 2,000 | $19,600 | 2,000 | $19,600 | 12,000 | $117,600 |
| Deluxe skis | 1,600 | 20,000 | 0 | 0 | 6,400 | 80,000 |
| Total | | $39,600 | | $19,600 | | $197,600 |

* = Units to be manufactured per production budget in economic lot sizes.

**Exhibit 2.9**

TRIPPER WATER SKI MANUFACTURING COMPANY

**Factory Overhead Budget
for the Year 19X1**

|  | First quarter | Second quarter | Third quarter | Fourth quarter | Total year |
|---|---|---|---|---|---|
| Indirect materials (supplies) | $ 5,850 | $ 7,550 | $ 4,150 | $ 2,450 | $ 20,000 |
| Indirect labor | 34,100 | 44,800 | 23,400 | 12,700 | 115,000 |
| Supervision | 16,250 | 16,250 | 16,250 | 16,250 | 65,000 |
| Utilities | 5,150 | 6,450 | 3,850 | 2,550 | 18.000 |
| Insurance | 12,700 | 0 | 0 | 0 | 12,700 |
| Property taxes | 18,000 | 0 | 0 | 0 | 18,000 |
| Depreciation | 0 | 0 | 0 | 48,000 | 48,000 |
| Total | $92,050 | $75,050 | $47,650 | $81,950 | $296,700 |

**Exhibit 2.10**

TRIPPER WATER SKI MANUFACTURING COMPANY

**General, Selling, and Administrative Expense Budget (in thousands)
for the Year 19X1**

|  | First quarter | Second quarter | Third quarter | Fourth quarter | Total year |
|---|---|---|---|---|---|
| Wages and salaries | $ 82 | $82 | $82 | $82 | $328 |
| Distribution and marketing | 5.5 | 8.5 | 7 | 4 | 25 |
| Insurance | 4 | 0 | 0 | 0 | 4 |
| Interest | 7 | 0 | 7 | 0 | 14 |
| Depreciation | 6 | 0 | 0 | 0 | 6 |
| Property taxes | 0 | 0 | 0 | 12 | 12 |
| Miscellaneous | 1 | 1 | 1 | 1 | 4 |
| Total | $105.5 | $91.5 | $97 | $99 | $393 |

## Capital Budgets

Somewhat distinct from the mainstream of the operating budget process is an activity know as *capital budgeting*. Capital budgets include specific plans for the current year to acquire and/or dispose of major capital assets (fixed assets) by purchase, lease, or construction. Exhibit 2.11 illustrates a capital budget for 19X1. Various aspects of capital budgeting and the decisions involved are introduced in Chapters 6, 7, and 8. As previously mentioned, even though the capital budget just covers the current year, capital asset planning involves investment considerations with planning horizons extending significantly beyond one year. Capital budgeting can therefore be thought of as involving both short-range and intermediate-range planning.

## Exhibit 2.11

### TRIPPER WATER SKI MANUFACTURING COMPANY

**Capital Budget (in thousands) for the Year 19X1**

|  | First quarter | Second quarter | Third quarter | Fourth quarter | Total year |
|---|---|---|---|---|---|
| Acquisitions: |  |  |  |  |  |
| Construct employee lounges | 0 | 0 | $20 | 0 | $20 |
| Paint and decorate lounges | 0 | 0 | 0 | $ 4 | 4 |
| Furniture for lounges | 0 | 0 | 0 | 10 | 10 |
| Total | 0 | 0 | $20 | $14 | $34 |
| *Dispositions:* None |  |  |  |  |  |

## Exhibit 2.12

### TRIPPER WATER SKI MANUFACTURING COMPANY

**Cash Budget for the Year 19X1**

|  | First quarter | Second quarter | Third quarter | Fourth quarter |
|---|---|---|---|---|
| Beginning cash balance | $ 62,910 | $11,460 | $ 14,960 | $11,010 |
| Net cash inflow from operations | (124,450) | 34,900 | 186,850 | 78,450 |
| Capital investments | 0 | 0 | (20,000) | (14,000) |
| Interest | ( 7,000) | 0 | ( 7,000) | 0 |
| Dividends | 0 | 0 | (30,000) | (30,000) |
| Income taxes | ( 10,000) | (11,000) | (11,000) | (11,000) |
| Additional short-term loans | 90,000 | 0 | 0 | 0 |
| Short-term loan repayments, including interest | 0 | (20,400) | (72,800) | 0 |
| Additional investments in marketable securities | 0 | 0 | (50,000) | 0 |
| Proceeds from sale of marketable securities, including interest | 0 | 0 | 0 | 51,500 |
| Budgeted ending cash balance | $ 11,460 | $14,960 | $ 11,010 | $85,960 |

*Note.* Amounts in parentheses are negative or outflows

**Schedule of Cash from Operations**

|  | First quarter | Second quarter | Third quarter | Fourth quarter |
|---|---|---|---|---|
| Cash inflows from operations: |  |  |  |  |
| Receivables collections | $ 160,000 | $340,000 | $400,000 | $230,000 |
| Less:  Cash outflows: |  |  |  |  |
| Purchases | $ 34,700 | $ 59,350 | $ 35,900 | $ 11,000 |
| Other operations* | 249,750 | 245,750 | 177,250 | 140,550 |
| Net cash inflow from operations | $(124,450) | $ 34,900 | $186,850 | $ 78,450 |

* Includes direct labor, manufacturing overhead, and GSA expenditures; excludes interest and depreciation, and allows for payment lag.

## Cash Budgets

Once the capital budget has been completed, data are now available on all anticipated cash receipts (sales budget) and all anticipated cash disbursements (operating budgets and capital budget) for the year. The only cash flows not yet planned involve owner distributions (dividends) and financing plans (new owner investments, obtaining new loans, and retiring old loans). Planning to ensure that adequate cash is on hand at all times to pay bills when due—*cash management*—is critical to the survival of the firm. Exhibit 2.12 illustrates the final *cash budget* for 19X1 recognizing all anticipated cash flows. Chapter 9 covers cash budgeting.

## The Master Operating Budget and The Financial Budget

The operating budgets for various organizational components and the sales budget are combined in an overall master operating budget for the firm. The *master operating budget* contains all anticipated revenues and expenses for the forthcoming period. It can take the form of a projected or pro-forma income statement (see below).

The capital budget and the cash budget, together with planned owner distributions, provide information to financial management as to the possible needs for additional financing, or for additional assets required in the firm's operations. Financing plans (additional owner investment, new long-term debt, debt retirement, and so forth) are set forth in the firm's *financial budget*. The financial budget can take the form of a projected or pro-forma statement of changes in financial position (see below). Chapter 10 covers preparation of the master operating and financial budgets.

## Pro-Forma Financial Statements

The final step in the budgeting process involves preparation of *pro-forma financial statements* for the forthcoming year. The budgeted statement of changes in financial position (SCFP) summarizes all major financial changes expected to occur during the year. The budgeted income statement projects all revenues, expenses, and anticipated earnings. And the budgeted balance sheet indicates the firm's expected financial position at the end of the forthcoming year. Exhibits 2.13 through 2.16 provide examples of pro-forma or budgeted financial statements.

The final all-company budgets are often referred to as the firm's master budget. The master budget is commonly thought of as including:

• The master operating budget,
• The cash budget,
• The financial budget, and
• The pro-forma financial statements.

**Exhibit 2.13**

TRIPPER WATER SKI MANUFACTURING COMPANY

---

**Pro-Forma (Budgeted) SCFP (in thousands)**
**for the Year 19X1**

*Sources:*

| | | |
|---|---|---|
| Net income | $80 | |
| Depreciation | 12 | |
| Funds from operations | $92 | |
| Total sources | | $92 |

*Applications:*

| | | |
|---|---|---|
| Improvement of plant assets | $34 | |
| Dividends | 60 | |
| Total applications | | 94 |
| Net decrease in working capital | | $ 2 |

---

**Exhibit 2.14**

TRIPPER WATER SKI MANUFACTURING COMPANY

---

**Budgeted Schedule of Cost of Goods Manufactured (in thousands)**
**for the Year 19X1**

Direct materials:

| | | |
|---|---|---|
| Beginning raw materials inventory | $ 14 | |
| Add:   Net purchases during 19X1 | 141 | |
| Total raw materials available | $155 | |
| Deduct:   Ending raw materials inventory | 4 | |
| Direct materials used in manufacturing | | $151 |
| Direct labor | | 198 |

Manufacturing overhead:

| | | |
|---|---|---|
| Indirect materials (supplies) | $ 20 | |
| Indirect labor | 115 | |
| Supervision | 65 | |
| Utilities | 18 | |
| Insurance | 13 | |
| Property taxes | 18 | |
| Depreciation | 48 | |
| Total overhead costs | | 297 |
| Total manufacturing costs | | $646 |
| Add:   Beginning work-in-process inventory | | 10 |
| | | $656 |
| Deduct:   Ending work-in-process inventory | | 20 |
| Cost of goods manufactured | | $636 |

## Exhibit 2.15
### TRIPPER WATER SKI MANUFACTURING COMPANY

**Pro-forma (Budgeted) Income Statement (in thousands) for the Year 19X1**

| | | |
|---|---:|---:|
| Sales | | $1,140 |
| Less: Cost of goods sold: | | |
| Beginning finished goods inventory | $ 66 | |
| Cost of goods manufactured | 636 | |
| Purchases of finished goods | 30 | |
| Goods available for sale | $742 | |
| Less: Ending finished goods inventory | 70 | 672 |
| Gross profit | | $ 468 |
| Operating expenses: | | |
| Wages and salaries | $328 | |
| Distribution and marketing | 25 | |
| Insurance | 4 | |
| Interest | 14 | |
| Property taxes | 6 | |
| Depreciation | 12 | |
| Miscellaneous | 4 | 393 |
| Income from operations before taxes | | $ 75 |
| Provision for income taxes | | 35 |
| Net income | | $ 40 |

## Exhibit 2.16
### TRIPPER WATER SKI MANUFACTURING COMPANY

**Pro-Forma (Budgeted) Balance Sheet (in thousands) as of 12/31/X1**

**Assets**

| | | |
|---|---:|---:|
| Cash | | $ 78 |
| Accounts receivable (net) | | 60 |
| Inventories: | | |
| Raw materials | $ 4 | |
| Work-in-process | 20 | |
| Finished goods | 70 | 94 |
| Supplies | | 5 |
| Prepaid items | | 6 |
| Total Current Assets | | $243 |
| Land | | 25 |
| Buildings | | 700 |
| Less: Accumulated depreciation | | (400) |
| Equipment | | 200 |
| Less: Accumulated depreciation | | (100) |
| Office furniture and fixtures | | 50 |
| Less: Accumulated depreciation | | (25) |
| Total Assets | | $693 |

**Equities**

| | |
|---|---:|
| Accounts payable | $ 20 |
| Wages and salaries payable | 29 |
| Interest payable | 7 |
| Taxes payable | 11 |
| Other current liabilities | 6 |
| Total Current Liabilities | $ 73 |
| Long-term debt | 185 |
| Total Liabilities | $258 |
| Stockholders' Equity | |
| Capital stock ($10 par) | $300 |
| Paid-in capital | 50 |
| Retained earnings | 85 |
| Total | $435 |
| Total Equities | $693 |

Chapter 10 covers completion of the master operating budget, the financial budget, and the budgeted financial statements.

To review the budgeting process, and to grasp more firmly the elements of budgeting common to all businesses, turn once more to Exhibit 2.2 illustrating the budget process. Can you visualize what steps would be followed by a merchandiser? If asked, could you prepare a chart similar to Exhibit 2.2 but applicable to a nonmanufacturing firm?

You have a good overall grasp of the budgeting process if you see that a merchandiser's budgeting process would be identical to a manufacturer's with the exception of the boxes shaded in gray on Exhibit 2.2. Only the production schedule, the raw materials inventory budget, the direct labor budget, and the manufacturing overhead budget are unique to a manufacturer. All other steps are common to all business organizations that sell products to customers.

The budgeting process in service organizations is very similar to that for merchandising firms. Since service organizations have no merchandise, no inventory or purchases budgets are required. Exhibit 2.17 illustrates the budgeting steps for a service firm.

## BUDGETING OBJECTIVES

For all businesses, the budgeting process may be viewed as having three objectives:

1. To facilitate MBO. The process of developing budgets focuses the attention of all managers upon objectives and not simply day-to-day problem solving. Budgeting facilitates coordination or *goal congruence* among the plans of various components of the firm. Goal congruence will be discussed below.

2. To facilitate financial management. Budgeting is the source of information for financial management of the firm. Budgets indicate any amounts of additional short- and long-term financing that may be be required. The role of budgets in financial management will be discussed further in Chapter 10.

3. To facilitate control. Budgets provide criteria for the evaluation of future performance in the control process, which will be discussed next.

## CONTROL

Planning without implementation is merely wishful thinking or good intention. To formalize a planning system, as described above, and then not attempt effectively and efficiently to implement the plan would be ridiculously wasteful

**Exhibit 2.17**

**Steps in the Budgeting Process for a Service Firm**

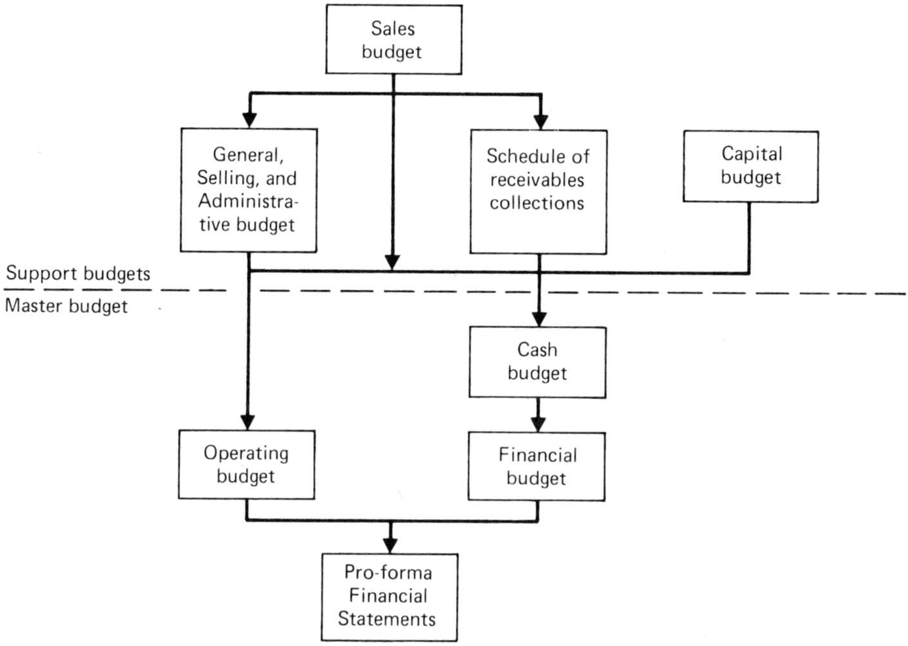

of energy and money. Implementation involves organization and control, and Chapters 11 through 15 cover various considerations and managerial accounting activities related to this process.

## Goal Congruence

One of the primary purposes of organization and control, and also of all planning, is to achieve goal congruence within the organization. Goal congruence simply means that the objectives and actions of all members of an organization are in agreement with or conform to the objectives of the organization. Achieving optimal goal congruence starts with the selection of long-range objectives in the strategic planning process. A firm may have several different strategic objectives that may not be internally consistent without some modification to make them compatible or congruent. For example, for you as the owner of Tripper, to desire both maximum profit and also a more aesthetically supportive work environment than competitively necessary would be inherently contradictory. To make these two goals congruent, they would have to be modified. The profit goal would have to be maximum **after** allowance for the cost of an aesthetically pleasing environment. Similarly, your strategic plan could not both aim at a high-quality, exclusive market image and also at a reputation for the lowest-price discount ski.

Goal congruence is equally applicable among intermediate and strategic objectives. It would not serve your long-range goals of remaining in the water ski business to have an intermediate objective of developing and introducing a line of tennis rackets. And of course, immediate plans—budgets—must be congruent with intermediate and strategic objectives.

The need for goal congruence extends to objectives implementation as well. Even if plans are congruent, their achievement might be difficult or impossible if the goals of managers and employees were too different from those of the firm. In such situations, their actions might work at cross purposes with the firm's objectives. It appears fair to assume that usually the personal goals of managers and especially of employees are not identical with those of the firm's owners. If you worked for General Motors, would all of your personal goals be directed at maximizing the welfare of GM stockholders? Or might you be more interested in personal recognition, power, achievement, and maximizing your personal income and leisure time?

Examples of noncongruent behavior are numerous. An employee might daydream about some enjoyable past or future experience and fail to properly understand an instruction or fail to monitor a process, with resultant destruction of a product or a machine. A manager might build an empire for his or her own ego gratification using resources in a manner not necessary or desirable for the firm's objectives.

A major role of management is to ensure as much congruence between organization plans and the goals of organization members as is feasible. To achieve this goal of congruence, management first organizes managers and employees in a manner intended to facilitate congruent activity. Other actions that enhance congruence will be introduced in subsequent chapters.

### The Organization Chart and Responsibility Centers

All successful firms are organized. Authority and responsibility is apportioned to various subgroups and individuals who focus their energies upon one specified portion of the organization's activities. Often the firm's organization is formalized in the form of an *organization chart*. Exhibit 2.18 provides an organization chart for the Tripper Company.

Note, on Exhibit 2.18, that Tripper is organized into at least 14 distinct *responsibility centers*, excluding the president (you), who has overall responsibility. A responsibility center is a subset or a part of an organization that is given specific authority over, and responsibility for, certain activities. Each center is, therefore, accountable for related costs, revenues, and resources over which it has control. Each responsibility center will usually have its own manager, supervisor, or foreman. Note that, in the Tripper example, each of

**Exhibit 2.18**
## TRIPPER WATER SKI MANUFACTURING COMPANY

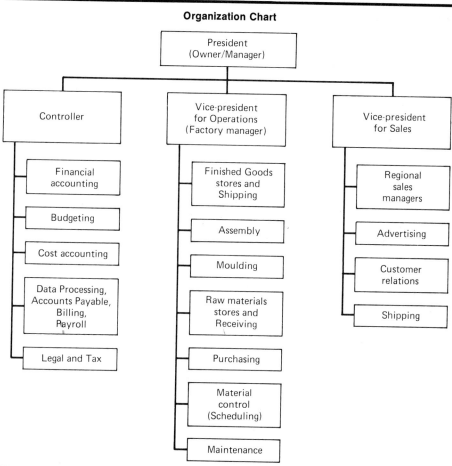

**Organization Chart**

the three top managers is in turn accountable for all responsibility centers under his or her jurisdiction.

Further discussion of organizations, how they facilitate goal congruence, and which are best in specific circumstances, is beyond the scope of this text. Business majors will have an opportunity for further exposure to organizations and their behavior in management courses. For managerial accounting you need only to understand what organizations are, that they involve distinct responsibility centers, and that they provide the structure for budgeting and control activities. In subsequent chapters you will have the opportunity to learn how operating budgets are prepared for each separate responsibility center, and how control is likewise accomplished by responsibility center.

## CONTROL REPORTING

After planning and organizing, the manager must still control the behavior of the members of his organization in an attempt to achieve goal congruence and full implementation of whatever plan has been made. Remember that control is used in the sense of controlling or directing the progress of a moving automobile as if you were the driver. It does not necessarily imply absolute control, as in a dictatorship or a police state.

Control of operations involves four distinct sequential steps:

1. Obtaining feedback information;
2. Determining whether any corrective action is indicated;
3. Determining what corrective action to take;
4. Acting to correct the situation.

The purpose of control feedback information is to tell a manager how well he or she is doing. How effectively are objectives being achieved, and how efficiently are resources being used? For example, for March 19X1, after the actual results of the first quarter's operations were available, you as owner–manager of Tripper, might request and receive a report similar to Exhibit 2.19.[5]

Study Exhibit 2.19 as if you were the owner–manager of the firm. Can you figure out its information content without further explanation? If you received this report, would you feel the company was pretty well in control? What item(s) might you wish to check into during April?

Exhibit 2.19 indicates that the overall company is in control. A 3.4 percent unfavorable difference or variance between plan and actual in final net income is not really significant when it represents only $154 for the entire quarter. Perhaps the only item that might require further investigation and possible action is the $5,494 unfavorable variance in wages and salaries. Suppose from other budget performance information you discovered that this entire variance was in the controller's division. How would you approach your controller? Steps three and four of a manager's control process—determining what corrective action to take and taking the action—are beyond the scope of managerial accounting. These steps involve the techniques of managing people and they are discussed in courses in management, communications, and interpersonal behavior.

Steps one and two—feedback information as an indication of the need for possible action—are intimately related to managerial accounting. Managerial accounting provides managers with the feedback information making possible or facilitating these first two steps in the control process. Chapters 11 through 14 are devoted to managerial accounting's relationship to, and involvement

---

[5]    Budget performance reports for control purposes are normally prepared on a monthly basis. This exhibit of a quarterly report conforms to the quarterly budgeting data offered previously in this chapter for introductory system overview purposes.

**Exhibit 2.19**

TRIPPER WATER SKI MANUFACTURING COMPANY

**Budget Performance Report for Overall Company Operations,
Quarter ending March 31, 19X2**

| | Budget | Actual | Variance Dollars | Variance Percent |
|---|---|---|---|---|
| Sales | $221,000 | $232,400 | $11,400 F* | 5.2 |
| Cost of goods sold | 122,000 | 128,300 | 6,300 U** | 5.2 |
| Gross profit | $ 99,000 | $104,100 | 5,100 F | 5.2 |
| Wages and salaries | 82,000 | 87,494 | 5,494 U | 6.7 |
| Distribution and marketing | 5,500 | 5,300 | 200 F | 3.6 |
| Insurance | 4,000 | 4,000 | 0 | 0 |
| Interest | 0 | 0 | 0 | 0 |
| Property taxes | 0 | 0 | 0 | 0 |
| Depreciation | 0 | 0 | 0 | 0 |
| Miscellaneous | 1,000 | 1,100 | 100 U | 10.0 |
| Income from operations | $ 6,500 | $ 6,206 | 294 U | 4.5 |
| Income taxes | 2,000 | 1,860 | 140 F | 7.0 |
| Net Income | $ 4,500 | $ 4,346 | 154 U | 3.4 |

  * Favorable (F) variance increases income
** Unfavorable (U) variance decreases income

with, the control process. Chapter 11 focuses on the objectives of control and control systems, and discusses various common approaches in different situations. Chapters 12 through 14 provide more detailed information covering certain common alternative control systems.

## ROLE OF MANAGERIAL ACCOUNTING AND THE CONTROLLER

To review, managerial accounting is concerned with supplying information for managers' decisions involving intrafirm resource allocations and for financial managers' decisions regarding the acquisition, retention, and disbursement or use of resources by the firm as a whole. These decisions are conveniently classified by time horizon into strategic, intermediate, and budget categories. Managerial accounting also supplies information for budgetary control.

Remember that managerial accountants do not themselves make the strategic, intermediate, or budget plans, nor do they control the firm's activities.[6] They provide data to top management and other managers who have the individual responsibility for such decisions and actions. Planning and control decisions involve, on the part of managers:

---

[6]    They are, of course, responsible for budgeting and controlling their own activities; and they may also be involved in intermediate or project planning for revised accounting and/or computer information systems.

**Exhibit 2.20**

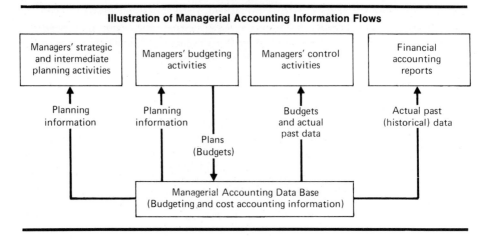

**Illustration of Managerial Accounting Information Flows**

Determining objectives,
Seeking and evaluating alternatives,
Making choices among alternatives,
Communicating these choices.

Choices or decisions with respect to the future always involve risk and uncertainty. It is one of the functions of managerial accounting to develop and maintain a data base of information, and to provide information to decision makers to facilitate their decisions and reduce, if possible, the elements of risk and uncertainty. Exhibit 2.20 illustrates the information flows.

From Exhibit 2.20, you can also see the distinction between managerial accounting information and financial accounting information. Financial accounting information is historical or past-oriented. It pertains to measurements of what has already happened. It is summarized or aggregated for the firm as a whole by type of item or product irrespective of the firm's organization. It is precise and must be measured, classified, and reported following GAAP.

Managerial accounting information is just the opposite. It is future- rather than past-oriented (although past data may be used as a basis for predicting the future or for measuring performance). It concerns what is expected to happen. It is prepared and summarized for each responsibility center, following the firm's organization chart rather than by activity or product. It may be imprecise since it involves projections and is used only for guidance purposes. And most of it is not subject to the constraints of GAAP.[7]

---

[7]    The full-absorption cost requirements of GAAP have acted to constrain the desirable use of direct or variable costing information internally in situations where the firm cannot afford parallel information systems. Much of the pressure for changing GAAP to direct or variable costing (which has produced no noticeable result) has arisen from the desire to use variable costing information internally. With the advent of computers and the relative ease and economy of parallel systems, the pressure may diminish.

Together with financial accounting, managerial accounting is the organizational responsibility of the *controller* or *comptroller*. Exhibit 2.18, the organization chart for the Tripper Company, presents the most common reporting relationships and areas of responsibility for a controller. Usually the controller reports directly to the company president since the controller should have no conflict of interest or loyalty in reporting upon the performance of all segments of the business. In very large organizations, the controller may report to the president through a vice-president for finance.

Usually, as shown on Exhibit 2.18, the controller will have responsibility for financial accounting, cost accounting, budgeting, data processing (computer center), and for tax and legal matters. Normally the controller will be assigned no operating responsibilities. Such assignment could introduce a conflict of interest or lack of objectivity in his reporting on the performance of such a segment.

CHAPTER OVERVIEW

Based on the material contained in this chapter, you should be able to:

- Describe those elements common to all organizations whether profit-directed or nonprofit-directed;
- Describe the only significant difference in the planning of activities between businesses and service organizations in the private sector;
- Describe the general functions and responsibilities that are distinctive to operating management, financial management, and tax management;
- Describe what is meant by MBO and how budgeting and budgetary control relate to MBO;
- Define planning horizons and give examples of different ones;
- Define and give examples of strategic plans and planning alternatives;
- Define and give examples of intermediate plans and planning alternatives;
- Describe budgets, their normal time horizons, and how they otherwise differ from intermediate plans;
- Describe the essential difference between business budgets and governmental budgets;
- Define a master budget and describe the four types of information normally included;
- Describe the sequential steps necessary in the budgeting process for a manufacturer;

- Define goal congruence and describe its relevance to planning and plan implementation;
- Define responsibility centers and relate them to organization charts and their purpose;
- Describe how organization charts and responsibility centers relate to planning and control;
- Describe and give examples of the four sequential steps in any control activity;
- Describe those control steps with which managerial accounting is involved and those with which it is not involved;
- Describe the essential differences between financial accounting data and most managerial accounting data;
- Describe the function or role of a controller and the reporting relationships with which he is often involved.

## NEW VOCABULARY AND CONCEPTS

Profit-directed organizations
Nonprofit-directed organizations
Operating management
Financial management
Tax management
MBO
Planning horizon
Strategic planning/long-range planning
Intermediate-(range) planning
Budgeting/short-range planning
Sales/revenue/activity budget
Inventory budget
Production schedule
Purchases budget
Direct labor budget

Manufacturing overhead budget
General selling and administrative expense budget
Operating budget
Capital budgeting
Capital budget
Master operating budget
Financial budget
Cash management
Cash budget
Master budget
Pro-forma financial statements
Goal congruence
Responsibility center
Controller/comptroller

## REVIEW QUESTIONS

1. What is the primary difference between profit-directed and nonprofit-directed organizations in the private sector?
2. a) What is meant by the term *effective* when used to refer to management? Give examples.
   b) What is meant by the term *efficient* when used to refer to management? Give examples.
3. What are characteristics common to all organizations?

**4.** Describe the three major management activities or roles, and give examples of each.

**5.** Describe three different management activities or responsibility areas within a profit-directed firm, indicating the major objectives of each.

**6.** a) What is MBO?
b) Give several examples of MBO that do not relate to financial objectives.
c) Describe how budgets and budgetary control relate to MBO.

**7.** Define and give examples of planning horizons.

**8.** Describe with examples the three distinct planning horizon categories within a business.

**9.** What are the two essential differences between strategic objectives and inter-mediate-range objectives?

**10.** What are the two essential differences between intermediate-range objectives and budgets?

**11.** What is the essential difference between a business budget and a governmental budget?

**12.** Define, describe the contents of, and indicate the sources of information concerning anticipated activity levels for:
a) Sales budget
b) Inventory budget (finished goods)
c) Production schedule
d) Direct labor budget
e) Manufacturing overhead budget
f) Purchases budget
g) General selling and administrative expense budget
h) Capital budget
i) Cash budget
j) Financial budget
k) Master operating budget
l) Pro-forma financial statements

**13.** a) What is the master budget?
b) What are its four major components?

**14.** a) What is meant by the term *goal congruence?*
b) How does it apply to planning?
c) How does it relate to implementation of plans?

**15.** Describe and explain the purpose of and relationship to budgeting and control of:
a) The organization chart;
b) distinct responsibility centers

**16.** Describe the most common responsibilities and reporting relationships of a firm's controller.

**17.** a) What are the four sequential steps in the control process?
b) With which steps is managerial accounting involved? Explain.
c) With which steps is it not involved? Explain.

**18.** Describe several major differences between managerial accounting information and financial accounting information.

## MINI-CASES AND QUESTIONS FOR DISCUSSION

**MC 2.1** John Thoughtful does not believe that accountants are essentially only scorekeepers and reporters. He reasons as follows:

- Accountants to some extent select the information which they measure and record;
- Accountants determine how they measure the information they choose to record;
- Accountants determine how their data will be summarized, grouped, identified, and reported;
- Managers and executives with responsibility for running the firm, especially in larger firms, are almost totally dependent on the information supplied to them to provide the basis for their decisions;
- Whoever selects and controls information going to managers and executives effectively controls (makes) their decisions;
- Since accountants select and control a large share of data going to managers and executives, they effectively exercise significant control over the decision process and therefore the firm.

What do you think of John's position? Do accountants really effectively manage large segments of a business? If so, are they subject to effective control by owners and creditors? Would such a possibility of "hidden control" be more likely within financial or managerial accounting activities? Discuss.

**MC 2.2** Sally Ashdown is complaining about the budget for her division: "I don't know how **they** can expect me to live within the budget **they** have given me. Those accountants in the budgeting department must be crazy; they don't know what it really takes to run a division like mine."

Who should own (be responsible for) the setting of Sally's budget? Could Sally, in certain circumstances, appropriately really feel this way (as opposed to just complaining)? Would such a feeling be desirable in the overall operation of an effective budget system? What could be done to change Sally's feelings? Discuss.

**MC 2.3** What are the significant differences between financial and managerial accounting, particularly with respect to:

- The objectives of the system?
- Standards constraining the design and operation of the system?
- Timeliness of information for decision purposes?
- Focus of attention with respect to time (past vs. future)?
- Focus of attention with respect to the organization?

Discuss.

**MC 2.4** What are the significant differences between strategic and intermediate planning? Why is articulation between strategic and intermediate planning desirable? Discuss.

**MC 2.5** What are the significant differences between intermediate planning and budgeting? Are they both focused upon the same organizational entity? Is articulation between them desirable? Discuss.

## ESSENTIAL PROBLEMS

**EP 2.1** List in proper sequence the various steps in the budgeting process for a nonmanufacturing (merchandising) firm. For each step, describe its major objectives (informational outputs).

**EP 2.2** List in proper sequence the various steps in the budgeting process for a manufacturing firm. For each step, describe its major objectives (informational outputs).

**EP 2.3**  a) Describe the six major elements making up the master budget.

b) What is the essential information content of each?

c) What is the purpose or function of each?

**EP 2.4**  a) What are the two budgets which somewhat independently are the starting or lead-off points for the budgeting process?

b) Explain why these two budgets are the starting points. What is the information content of each that is subsequently used elsewhere in the budgeting system? Where is this information used?

**EP 2.5** Refer to Exhibits 2.3 through 2.17. For each of the following budgets, describe the informational inputs obtained from a previous budgeting step and how this information is used:

a) Finished goods inventory budget

b) Production schedule

c) Raw materials budget

d) Purchases budget

e) Direct labor budget

f) Factory overhead budget

g) General selling and administrative expense budget

**EP 2.6** Refer to Exhibits 2.3 through 2.17. For each of the following budgets, describe the informational inputs obtained from previous budgets and how this information is used.

a) Cash budget

b) Financial budget and budgeted SCFP

c) Master operating budget and budgeted income statement

d) Budgeted balance sheet

**Exhibit 2.21**

### WILSON COMPANY

---

**Balance Sheets and Income Statements (in thousands of dollars) for the Years 19X6, 19X7, and 19X8**

| Assets | 19X6 | 19X7 | 19X8 |
|---|---|---|---|
| Cash | $ 40 | $ 25 | $ 67 |
| Marketable securities | 5 | 10 | 100 |
| Accounts receivable (net) | 165 | 155 | 145 |
| Inventory: | | | |
| Raw materials | 20 | 20 | 19 |
| Work-in-process | 35 | 30 | 29 |
| Finished goods | 60 | 55 | 49 |
| Prepaid items | 6 | 5 | 7 |
| Total Current Assets | $331 | $300 | $416 |
| Investments and funds | 10 | 20 | 20 |
| Land | 20 | 30 | 50 |
| Fixed assets | 180 | 200 | 300 |
| Less:  Accumulated depreciation | (150) | (160) | (180) |
| Other assets | 10 | 20 | 30 |
| Total Assets | $401 | $410 | $636 |

| Liabilities | | | |
|---|---|---|---|
| Accounts payable | $ 85 | $ 90 | $ 95 |
| Other current liabilities | 73 | 74 | 65 |
| Total Current Liabilities | $158 | $164 | $160 |
| Noncurrent liabilities | 43 | 30 | 100 |
| Total Liabilities | $201 | $194 | $260 |

| Stockholders' Equity | | | |
|---|---|---|---|
| Capital stock | 100 | 100 | 200 |
| Paid-in capital | 50 | 50 | 90 |
| Retained earnings | 50 | 66 | 86 |
| Total Stockholders' Equity | $200 | $216 | $376 |
| Total Equities | $401 | $410 | $636 |

| Income Statement | | | |
|---|---|---|---|
| Sales | $700 | $800 | $900 |
| Cost of goods sold | 455 | 480 | 504 |
| Interest expense | 4 | 3 | 10 |
| Other operating expenses | 208 | 239 | 311 |
| Income from operations before taxes | $ 33 | $ 78 | $ 75 |
| Provision for Income taxes | 13 | 47 | 30 |
| Net Income | $ 20 | $ 31 | $ 45 |

## Exhibit 2.22

## SLATER COMPANY

**Balance Sheets and Income Statements (in thousands of dollars)
for the Years 19X6, 19X7, and 19X8**

| Assets | 19X6 | 19X7 | 19X8 |
|---|---|---|---|
| Cash | $ 25 | $ 20 | $ 30 |
| Marketable securities | 4 | 5 | 0 |
| Accounts receivable (net) | 160 | 140 | 146 |
| Inventory: | | | |
| Raw materials | 8 | 6 | 10 |
| Work-in-process | 16 | 15 | 22 |
| Finished goods | 26 | 25 | 24 |
| Prepaid items | 3 | 2 | 8 |
| Total Current Assets | $242 | $213 | $240 |
| Investments and funds | 0 | 5 | 15 |
| Land | 10 | 10 | 20 |
| Fixed assets | 200 | 200 | 209 |
| Less:  Accumulated depreciation | (50) | (60) | (70) |
| Other assets | 20 | 15 | 10 |
| Total Assets | $422 | $383 | $424 |

| Liabilities | 19X6 | 19X7 | 19X8 |
|---|---|---|---|
| Accounts payable | $100 | $ 90 | $ 80 |
| Other current liabilities | 42 | 28 | 29 |
| Total Current Liabilities | $142 | $118 | $109 |
| Noncurrent liabilities | 111 | 80 | 100 |
| Total Liabilities | $253 | $198 | $209 |

| Stockholders' Equity | 19X6 | 19X7 | 19X8 |
|---|---|---|---|
| Capital stock | 75 | 75 | 75 |
| Paid-in capital | 50 | 50 | 50 |
| Retained earnings | 44 | 60 | 90 |
| Total Stockholders' Equity | $169 | $185 | $215 |
| Total Equities | $422 | $383 | $424 |

| Income Statement | 19X6 | 19X7 | 19X8 |
|---|---|---|---|
| Sales | $550 | $600 | $500 |
| Cost of goods sold | 275 | 240 | 225 |
| Interest expense | 11 | 8 | 10 |
| Other operating expenses | 98 | 252 | 232 |
| Income from operations before  taxes | $166 | $100 | $ 33 |
| Provision for income taxes | 66 | 40 | 13 |
| Net Income | $100 | $ 60 | $ 20 |

## SUPPLEMENTARY PROBLEMS

(The following problems are based on material covered in the chapter appendix.)

**SP 2.7** Refer to Exhibit 2.21. Calculate the following ratios for the Wilson Company for the year 19X7:

    a) Current ratio

    b) Quick ratio

    c) Debt ratio

    d) Receivables turnover

    e) Inventory turnover

    f) Asset turnover

    g) Gross margin (profit) percentage

    h) Operating ratio

    i) Times interest earned

    j) Return on assets employed

    k) Return on owners' investment

**SP 2.8** Refer to Exhibit 2.21. For the Wilson Company for the year 19X8:

    a) Calculate each ratio listed in Problem SP 2.7.

    b) Briefly describe the information content of each ratio.

    c) Compare each ratio to the same ratio for 19X7, and explain whether the 19X8 ratio indicates improvement over 19X7.

**SP 2.9** Refer to Exhibit 2.22. For the Slater Company for the year 19X7, calculate each ratio listed in Problem EP 2.7.

**SP 2.10** Refer to Exhibit 2.22. For the Slater Company for the year 19X8:

    a) Calculate each ratio listed in Problem SP 2.7;

    b) Briefly describe the information content of each ratio;

    c) Compare each ratio to the same ratio for 19X7, and explain whether the 19X8 ratio indicates improvement over 19X7.

CHAPTER 2 APPENDIX

# Financial Ratios and Financing Activities

## FINANCIAL STATEMENT RATIOS

Common ratios obtained from a firm's financial statement data are often insufficiently emphasized in elementary accounting courses. Some instructors in texts minimize or omit ratio analysis as not relevant to a course focused upon the preparation rather than the use of financial statements. Other deemphasize ratios because there is some question as to their usefulness in statement analysis for predicting the future. Regardless of the usefulness of historical ratios as a predictor, there are two uses that are important and relevant for the elementary accounting student:

1. Ratios provide an excellent means to review and reinforce your understanding of the information content of and interrelationships among financial statements.

2. Ratios provide management with an excellent tool to summarize and budget desired financial condition and relationships in the future (see Exhibit 2.1 earlier in this chapter, as an example). They also provide readily measurable criteria against which progress towards these objectives may be measured.

Financial ratios may be conveniently grouped for learning and retention into three sets: ratios that provide information as to a firm's position or condition at a particular point in time, ratios that measure various aspects of a firm's performance over time (regardless of capital invested or its source), and ratios that measure the return on invested capital earned by the firm.

### Position or Condition Ratios

Three ratios are commonly used to summarize a firm's *solvency* and *liquidity*. Solvency, or the ability to meet obligations when due, is critical to the survival of the firm. The two ratios most commonly used to measure solvency are the *current ratio* and the *quick ratio:*

$$\text{Current ratio} = \frac{\text{Total current assets}}{\text{Total current liabilities}};$$

$$\text{Quick ratio} = \frac{\text{Cash, marketable securities, receivables}}{\text{Total current liabilities}[8]}.$$

Note that each is attempting to measure how many times the firm's liquid assets (cash or items that will normally be converted into cash within one year) cover its existing debts, which must be paid within a year. The quick ratio is a more rigorous or severe test in that it ignores inventory, supplies, and prepaid items. There are no absolute good-vs.-bad norms for these ratios applicable to all industries. As a general guideline you might consider current ratios in excess of 2:1, and quick ratios in excess of 1:1, as satisfactory indications of solvency.

Unfortunately, the word "liquidity" is subject to many different interpretations. Liquidity commonly refers to convertibility into cash or the ease with which cash may be obtained through the liquidation of noncash assets. In this text the term will be extended to also cover a firm's ability to raise more cash readily via additional debt. A firm with too much existing debt will find it extremely difficult or costly to borrow more funds if they are needed. The ratio most commonly used to measure potential liquidity is the *debt ratio:*

$$\text{Debt ratio}[9] = \frac{\text{Total liabilities}}{\text{Total equities (Liabilities + Owners' Equity)}}$$

Note that this ratio measures the proportion (or decimal fraction) of debt to total equity, or the proportion of total assets supplied by the creditors. Industry norms for this ratio vary widely. It therefore must be used in the context of a particular industry.[10]

---

[8]    Sometimes the denominator of the quick ratio is restricted to current monetary liabilities, that is, any deferred revenue and estimated warranty repairs are excluded as not normally requiring cash in settlement. Such fine tuning of this ratio usually has little effect, is not commonly used by business, and will be ignored in the balance of this text.

[9]    The debt ratio may sometimes be calculated in three other ways: total liabilities divided by owners' equity, noncurrent liabilities divided by the sum of noncurrent liabilities and owners' equity, or noncurrent liabilities divided by owners' equity. If you are using a debt ratio determined by someone else, you must be sure which formula is being used. In this book the ratio shown above will be used throughout.

[10]    *Key Business Ratios in 125 Lines.* New York: Dun and Bradstreet, Inc.; *Statement Studies,* Robert Morris Associates; and *Quarterly Financial Report for Manufacturing Corporations,* Federal Trade Commission.

## Performance Ratios

There are six commonly used ratios for measuring various aspects of a firm's activities over time. Three of these focus upon asset utilization—*receivables turnover, inventory turnover,* and *asset turnover:*

$$\text{Receivables turnover} = \frac{\text{Sales}^{11}}{\text{Average accounts receivable}};$$

$$\text{Inventory turnover} = \frac{\text{Cost of goods sold}}{\text{Average inventory}};$$

$$\text{Asset turnover} = \frac{\text{Sales}}{\text{Average total assets}}.$$

Receivables turnover measures the average number of times per year the *collection cycle* (sale to receivable to cash) is completed. Receivables turnover is often used to measure the efficiency of the receivables collection process. A high receivables turnover indicates a minimum of resources tied up in carrying customer accounts.

Inventory turnover measures the average number of times the *inventory cycle* (cash to inventory to sale) is completed each year. Inventory turnover used as one indicator of the efficiency of inventory control and inventory management. A higher inventory turnover would mean less inventory investment to generate the same volume of sales.

Asset turnover measures the number of dollars of sales generated per dollar of assets. Asset turnover is a measure of the firm's efficiency in using assets whose sole reason for existence is, after all, to generate revenue.

Note that the denominator of all three turnover ratios represents the **average** asset investment. Since the numerator represents activity over a period of time, it would be inappropriate to compare this to an asset investment at only one point in time. The denominator commonly used in each case is the simple average of assets invested:

$$\text{Simple average asset investment} = \frac{\text{Beginning balance} + \text{ending balance}}{2}.$$

The other three performance ratios relate to operations as reported on the income statement. Two are indicators of profitability and one is a measure of relative safety. The two common profitability indicators are the *gross margin*

---

[11] In theory the numerator should be restricted to credit sales or sales on account. In practice, many firms have an insignificant proportion of cash sales; furthermore, such a breakdown of sales is often not readily available. Total net sales is therefore generally used.

(profit) percentage and the operating ratio:

$$\text{Gross margin (profit) percentage} = \frac{\text{Gross margin (profit)}}{\text{Sales}} \times 100.$$

$$\text{Operating ratio (percentage)}^{12} = \frac{\text{Income from operations before taxes}}{\text{Sales}} \times 100.$$

Note that both ratios measure profit proportions. The gross margin ratio indicates the profit percentage (of sales) available to cover period costs. The operating ratio indicates the profit percentage (of sales) remaining after all product and period costs except for income taxes.

The last common performance ratio is known as *times interest earned:*

$$\text{Times interest earned} = \frac{\text{EBIT}}{\text{Interest expense}}.$$

The numerator *EBIT* represents operating earnings before deductions for either interest expense or income taxes, and the denominator is annual interest charges. The ratio measures the number of times the firm is earning or covering its required fixed interest payments. A high interest earned ratio may indicate less risk of future default on interest obligations.

### Investment Return Ratios

Ultimately the objective of all profit-directed businesses is to earn at least a satisfactory (as good as alternate opportunities of similar risk) return on the capital or assets invested in the firm. There are two commonly used ratios which measure investment return—*return on assets employed* and *return on owners' investment:*

$$\text{Return on assets employed} = \frac{\text{EBIT}}{\text{Average total assets}^{13}};$$

$$\text{Return on owners' investment}^{14} = \frac{\text{Net income}}{\text{Average owners' equity}}.$$

Note that return on assets employed measures the number of dollars earned on each asset dollar invested before these earnings are distributed

---

[12]   Sometimes EBIT (operating earnings before interest and taxes) to sales is used to measure earnings before distribution to creditors, governments, and owners.

[13]   In special cases where a firm has idle assets, or assets being disposed of as part of discounted operations, these will be omitted from the denominator.

[14]   Where a firm has preferred stock outstanding, it is customary to measure return on common stockholders' investment as:

$$\frac{\text{Net income minus preferred dividend}}{\text{Average common stockholder equity}}.$$

among creditors, governments, and owners. The use of EBIT results in a true measure of asset usage efficiency not affected by the relative amount of debt financing in the particular firm or the vagaries of current income taxes. The return on owners' investment is, of course, the final result of all activities—the bottom line. It discloses what the owners have finally made on their investment after all necessary distributions to creditors and governments.

Note again that the denominator of both investment ratios is the average investment over the period. This is necessary, since it is being compared to the numerator, which is a measure of earnings for or during the period.

Return on investment (ROI) measurements are occasionally used to evaluate management's performance. Investors may measure a firm's top management using ROI obtained; and top management may similarly measure the performance of a division manager in a similar manner. Divisional performance measurement is discussed in Chapter 14. At this point you should be aware that:

- ROI does measure the final result of management's performance over a specific period of time, and

- If used as a primary or sole performance measure, ROI can lead to dysfunctional managerial behavior.

When too much emphasis is placed upon current ROI, management may be motivated to inappropriately reduce assets, or to postpone desirable asset acquisitions, to improve the ratio. It is often mistakenly presumed that a manager will strive to improve ROI only through higher earnings (numerator). The quickest and simplest short-term increase in the ROI may be accomplished by reducing the denominator!

## FINANCING CONSIDERATIONS AND ACTIVITIES

Several aspects of a firm's financial management activities are often not covered in financial accounting texts or courses. Although covered in some depth in subsequent courses devoted to finance or financial management, a general understanding of financial management objectives will serve to increase your understanding of one of the major objectives of a firm's budgeting system. In a general sense, as discussed in this chapter, the overall management activities of a firm may be divided into three subsets—operating management, financial management, and tax management. Broadly speaking, operating management can be thought of as concerned with the efficient and effective use of the firm's existing resources. Tax management involves guiding operating and financial decisions so as to minimize taxes payable. Financial management is responsible to see that the firm maintains adequate solvency and liquidity, and obtains, at the least cost, adequate capital (resources) to support its desired level of activity.

Four separate objectives or reponsibilities of financial management are directly served by the budgeting system. These are:

1. Short-term maintenance of adequate cash,

2. Long-term maintenance of adequate working capital,

3. Long-term maintenance of adequate capacity assets,

4. Long-term maintenance of desirable capital structure.


## Short-term Maintenance of Adequate Cash

The primary objective of financial management is to maintain the firm's solvency. Many profitable, growing firms fail because they run out of cash and are unable in the immediate present (short-term) to pay their employees, suppliers, and tax obligations. Short-run cash management is aimed at anticipating such shortages, and at arranging for necessary actions in advance to preclude their occurrence. One of the objectives of the budgeting process is to generate data on expected cash flows (the cash budget) so that action may be taken to maintain solvency. Cash management and cash budgeting will be further discussed in Chapter 9.


## Long-term Maintenance of Adequate Working Capital

A less immediate measure of solvency is the amount of *net working capital* (defined as total current assets minus total current liabilities) in the business.[15] Note that net working capital measures in dollars the same excess of current assets over current liabilities as is measured by the current ratio described earlier. Visualize for a moment any firm's balance sheet and recognize that equities represent sources of assets as well as claims or shares in assets. Equities on a balance sheet disclose the various investors (owners and creditors) who have supplied capital (assets) to the firm. Short-term creditors (current liabilities) supply, often on a non-interest-cost basis, a portion of the current assets in the company. The balance of required current assets—net working capital— plus all necessary noncurrent assets, must come from either long-term creditors or owners:

---

[15]    Many accountants and accounting texts consider the term net working capital redundant, since accountants generally use working capital to mean the difference between current assets and current liabilities. Financial managers and business majors often use working capital to mean only current assets, and net working capital when referring to current assets minus current liabilities. You should therefore be especially careful to ascertain which definition applies whenever you hear or read the term working capital. In this text, to avoid confusion, the term working capital will be used to refer only to current assets and net working capital will refer to the difference between current assets and current liabilities.

$$
\begin{array}{ccc}
\text{Net working capital} & & \text{Noncurrent liabilities} \\
\text{plus} & = & \text{plus} \\
\text{noncurrent assets} & & \text{Owners' Equity}
\end{array}
$$

The above equality may be thought of as illustrating the long-term *capital structure* of the firm. It indicates the amount of assets semipermanently committed to the firm by the long-term investors. Short-term suppliers of credit generally are not interested in financing long-term assets, since such loans would have to be repeatedly extended or refinanced into the future.

Another fact about assets in general and long-term assets in particular should be obvious to you. A certain level or amount of assets is required to provide the financial and physical capacity to conduct a given level or volume of business activity. As the volume of business grows, so must the amount of total assets necessary to support the higher level of business. And assets must come from, or be provided by, someone.

Assume that a firm was comfortably operating near capacity at a sales volume of $600,000, with the following capital structure:

| | | | |
|---|---|---|---|
| Current assets | $100,000 | Current liabilities | $ 50,000 |
| Noncurrent assets | 200,000 | Noncurrent liabilities | 70,000 |
| | | Owners' Equity | 180,000 |
| Total Assets | $300,000 | Total Equities | $300,000 |

Assume it anticipated rapid sales growth, and that it could obtain a volume of $900,000 next year if it could support this higher volume; that is, if it could obtain the necessary additional human, physical, and financial resources to provide 50 percent more capacity. How many more dollars of total assets/capital would be required in the business?

The answer would depend on many detailed factors peculiar to the particular firm. For example:

*Cash:*   More cash would be required but probably not 50 percent more.

*Receivables:*   At least a 50-percent increase in receivables would be required. Possibly more than a 50-percent increase might be expected, since slower-paying, less-select customers may be contributing to the expanded volume.

*Inventory:*   More inventory would be required but, again, probably not a full 50-percent increase.

*Physical capacity assets:*   With the firm presently at capacity, additional capacity of at least 50 percent would be required. Often more than a 50 percent increase might be required, since it is not always possible or desirable to expand physical capacity (new plant and equipment) in increments matching short-run requirements.

For purposes of this illustration, you may make the simple assumption that a 50-percent increase in volume will require a 50-percent increase in total assets; that is, the asset turnover will remain constant.

Where can the firm obtain the needed $150,000? Current creditors will supply a portion of the required additional current assets (inventory and supplies). The balance can **only** come from long-term investors. Even in the unlikely case where short-term creditors provide enough so that the current ratio would remain the same, an additional $25,000 of net working capital would be required to maintain solvency.[16]

In addition to maintaining solvency, another responsibility of financial management is to predict requirements for additional working capital ($25,000, in the example above), and to make arrangements in advance to obtain it from long-term creditors and owners.

### Long-term Maintenance of Adequate Capacity Assets

Noncurrent assets may be thought of as providing the physical capacity to do business. Many noncurrent assets may be either leased or owned, and approaches to making this choice will be discussed in Chapter 7. Other required capacity assets may be sufficiently unique as to not be available on a lease basis. Those necessary noncurrent assets that are to be owned (necessary or economically desirable to own) require capital investment. Yet another part of financial management's responsibility involves encouraging operating management to predict requirements for adequate capacity assets and making advance arrangements to finance these required assets.

Returning to the earlier example, recall that $100,000 of additional noncurrent assets are assumed necessary to support the 50-percent increase in sales volume. Together with $25,000 of additional working capital, long-term financing of $125,000 is required:

| Assets | Projected | Equities | Projected | Present |
|---|---|---|---|---|
| Current assets | $150,000 | Current liabilities | $ 75,000 | $ 50,000 |
| Noncurrent assets | 300,000 | Noncurrent liabilities | | |
| Total Assets | $450,000 | plus Owners' Equity | 375,000 | 250,000 |
| | | Total Equities | $450,000 | $300,000 |

---

[16]   

| | |
|---|---|
| New current asset requirements | = $150,000 |
| Less: Supplies by current creditors assuming maintenance of 2:1 current ratio | = 75,000 |
| New new working capital requirements | = $ 75,000 |
| Less: Existing net working capital | = 50,000 |
| Required additional net working capital | = $ 25,000 |

## Long-term Maintenance of Desired Capital Structure

As mentioned above with reference to the debt ratio, desirable ratios of debt to equity exist for particular firms and particular industries. In addition to obtaining necessary funds, financial management is concerned with their sources. Availability of additional financing through retained earnings, additional long-term debt, and additional owner investment must be considered, together with the long-term maintenance of the desirable debt ratio. These considerations are usually covered in finance or financial management texts and courses within a business major core. At this point it is only important that you have a general understanding of the necessity for these decisions. With such an understanding, you may perceive more clearly the role of managerial accounting, and particularly budgeting, in supplying much of the information required. This role will be further clarified in Chapter 10.

# 3

# REVENUE AND ACTIVITY PLANNING: THE SALES BUDGET

## CHAPTER PREVIEW

The objective of this chapter is to provide you with an introduction to the sales budgeting activity and to how a firm's sales budget may be prepared. In this chapter you can:

- Perceive that the sales budget is the critical starting point of the entire budgeting process.
- Develop an understanding of the characteristics of sales revenue, together with an awareness of how sales result from an interaction among factors within the firm's control and factors over which the firm has little if any control.
- Learn about the various common approaches used to forecast sales revenue.
- Learn how planning for controllable factors is integrated with forecasts of sales demand in preparation of the final sales budget.
- First address the question whether a budget should be a motivating device, a portrayal of reasonable expectations, or both.
- Develop an awareness of the common needs for activity budgeting among all organizations, both profit and nonprofit-directed.

With this knowledge you will have an adequate basic understanding of sales budgets and how they are prepared. You will be in a position to move, in the following chapter, to the next step in the overall budgeting process: inventory budgeting and control. And you will also be able to perceive in detail how the sales and inventory budgets interrelate.

## HOW MUCH BUSINESS WILL WE DO NEXT YEAR?

Perhaps no single piece of information is more important to a manager than the volume of business or activity that can be reasonably expected in the near future. An expected increase in sales provides more potential revenue to support expanded operations and profits. Reasonable expectations of sustained sales volume provide assurance that current activities may continue at near present level. And an expected sales drop at least provides advanced warning of probable need to reduce operations in an orderly and systematic fashion. Planning or budgeting future sales is the first step in the overall budgeting process.

Assume it is early in September of 19X1. As the owner–manager of the Tripper Company, you wish to start the budget process for budgeting 19X2 so that the 19X2 master budget may be completed by the first of December (12/1/X1). Remember from Chapter 2 that the first step is completion of a sales budget (usually by month) for each product.

You have assigned responsibility for preparation of the sales budget to your vice-president for sales, Cherie Carter. Ms. Carter has been sales and marketing manager for five years, and you have found her to be highly competent. Having budgeted with reasonable success in prior years, Ms. Carter has obtained from her marketing assistant and from the company's controller all available relevant information with which to prepare the budget.

So that you may become more personally involved, assume that Ms. Carter has asked you to join her in preparing the sales budget. You know the sales budget must be completed by the end of September if the other budgets and the master budget are to be finished on time. In this example, you will be asked to prepare the sales budget only for the first three months of 19X2 and only for a single product. The remaining nine months, and the other products, would require similar effort. However, working through the first quarter for a single product should be adequate to provide you with an understanding of the sales budgeting process.

In Ms. Carter's file, you find the following documents:

- Original sales budget for 19X1 (current year) by quarter (Exhibit 3.1);
- Actual sales to date for 19X1 by quarter (only two quarters completed) (Exhibit 3.2);
- Original sales budget for 19X1 by month for first quarter (Exhibit 3.3);
- Actual sales during first quarter of 19X1 by month (Exhibit 3.4);
- Market-based forecast for 19X2 by quarter (Exhibit 3.5);
- Sales-based forecast for 19X2 by quarter (Exhibit 3.6).

Before proceeding, you should study these exhibits until you are familiar with the information content/intention (not the specific numbers) of each. The market-based forecast for 19X2 was prepared by Ms. Carter's market research assistant. It is based upon general economic forecasts, and a forecast of total industry demand by the Water Ski Manufacturers' Association, adjusted for Tripper's expected share of the total market. The sales-based forecast for 19X2 is a composite of expected sales and resulting sales quotas for all of the firm's salespersons. It was prepared by individual salespersons in consultation with their immediate supervisors.

### Exhibit 3.1
### TRIPPER WATER SKI MANUFACTURING COMPANY

**Sales Budget for the year 19X1**

| Products | First quarter | | Second quarter | |
|---|---|---|---|---|
| | Units | Dollars | Units | Dollars |
| Economy ski | 2,300 | $115,000 | 4,500 | $225,000 |
| Deluxe ski | 1,200 | 96,000 | 2,700 | 216,000 |
| Tow rope | 1,000 | 10,000 | 2,000 | 20,000 |
| Total | | $221,000 | | $461,000 |
| Percent | | 20.0 | | 40.0 |

| Products | Third quarter | | Fourth quarter | | Total year | |
|---|---|---|---|---|---|---|
| | Units | Dollars | Units | Dollars | Units | Dollars |
| Economy ski | 3,600 | $180,000 | 1,200 | $ 60,000 | 11,600 | $ 580,000 |
| Deluxe ski | 1,800 | 144,000 | 625 | 50,000 | 6,325 | 506,000 |
| Tow rope | 1,500 | 15,000 | 900 | 9,000 | 5,400 | 54,000 |
| Total | | $339,000 | | $119,000 | | $1,140,000 |
| Percent | | 30.0 | | 10.0 | | 100.0 |

### Exhibit 3.2
### TRIPPER WATER SKI MANUFACTURING COMPANY

**Actual Sales for 19X1 by Quarter**

| | First quarter | | Second quarter | | Third quarter | Fourth quarter |
|---|---|---|---|---|---|---|
| | Units | Dollars | Units | Dollars | | |
| Economy skis | 2,420 | $121,000 | 4,750 | $237,500 | Not yet available | Not yet available |
| Deluxe skis | 1,261 | 100,880 | 2,843 | 227,440 | Not yet available | Not yet available |
| Tow ropes | 1,052 | 10,520 | 2,834 | 28,340 | Not yet available | Not yet available |
| Total | | $232,400 | | $493,280 | | |

## Exhibit 3.3
### TRIPPER WATER SKI MANUFACTURING COMPANY

**Sales Budget by Month for First Quarter 19X1**

|  | January Units | January Dollars | February Units | February Dollars |
|---|---|---|---|---|
| Economy skis | 700 | $35,000 | 700 | $35,000 |
| Deluxe skis | 350 | 28,000 | 350 | 28,000 |
| Tow ropes | 300 | 3,000 | 300 | 3,000 |
| Total |  | $66,000 |  | $66,000 |

|  | March Units | March Dollars | Total first quarter Units | Total first quarter Dollars |
|---|---|---|---|---|
| Economy skis | 900 | $45,000 | 2,300 | $115,000 |
| Deluxe skis | 500 | 40,000 | 1,200 | 96,000 |
| Tow ropes | 400 | 4,000 | 1,000 | 10,000 |
| Total |  | $89,000 |  | $221,000 |

## Exhibit 3.4
### TRIPPER WATER SKI MANUFACTURING COMPANY

**Actual Sales, First Quarter 19X1**

|  | January Units | January Dollars | February Units | February Dollars |
|---|---|---|---|---|
| Economy skis | 730 | $36,500 | 740 | $37,000 |
| Deluxe skis | 378 | 30,240 | 379 | 30,320 |
| Tow ropes | 315 | 3,150 | 316 | 3,160 |
| Total |  | $69,890 |  | $70,480 |

|  | March Units | March Dollars | Total first quarter Units | Total first quarter Dollars |
|---|---|---|---|---|
| Economy skis | 950 | $47,500 | 2,420 | $121,000 |
| Deluxe skis | 504 | 40,320 | 1,261 | 100,880 |
| Tow ropes | 421 | 4,210 | 1,052 | 10,520 |
| Total |  | $92,030 |  | $232,400 |

**Exhibit 3.5**

TRIPPER WATER SKI MANUFACTURING COMPANY

**Market-Based Sales Forecast for the Year 19X2**

| | First quarter | | Second quarter | |
|---|---|---|---|---|
| | Units | Dollars | Units | Dollars |
| Economy skis | 2,700 | $135,000 | 5,200 | $260,000 |
| Deluxe skis | 1,450 | 116,000 | 2,840 | 227,200 |
| Tow ropes | 1,250 | 12,500 | 2,400 | 24,000 |
| Total | | $263,500 | | $511,200 |
| Percent | | 20 | | 39 |

| | Third quarter | | Fourth quarter | | Total year | |
|---|---|---|---|---|---|---|
| | Units | Dollars | Units | Dollars | Units | Dollars |
| Economy skis | 4,100 | $205,000 | 1,400 | $ 70,000 | 13,400 | $ 670,000 |
| Deluxe skis | 2,250 | 180,000 | 750 | 60,000 | 7,290 | 583,200 |
| Tow ropes | 1,900 | 19,000 | 650 | 6,500 | 6,200 | 62,000 |
| Total | | $404,000 | | $136,500 | | $1,315,200 |
| Percent | | 31 | | 10 | | 100 |

**Exhibit 3.6**

TRIPPER WATER SKI MANFACTURING COMPANY

**Sales-Based Sales Forecast for the Year 19X2**

| | First quarter | | Second quarter | |
|---|---|---|---|---|
| | Units | Dollars | Units | Dollars |
| Economy skis | 2,400 | $120,000 | 4,800 | $240,000 |
| Deluxe skis | 1,350 | 108,000 | 2,600 | 208,000 |
| Tow ropes | 1,150 | 11,500 | 2,200 | 22,000 |
| Total | | $239,500 | | $470,000 |
| Percent | | 20 | | 39 |

| | Third quarter | | Fourth quarter | | Total year | |
|---|---|---|---|---|---|---|
| | Units | Dollars | Units | Dollars | Units | Dollars |
| Economy skis | 3,800 | $190,000 | 1,300 | $ 65,000 | 12,300 | $ 615,000 |
| Deluxe skis | 2,000 | 160,000 | 700 | 56,000 | 6,650 | 532,000 |
| Tow ropes | 1,750 | 17,500 | 600 | 6,000 | 5,700 | 57,000 |
| Total | | $367,500 | | $ 27,000 | | $1,204,000 |
| Percent | | 31 | | 10 | | 100 |

**Exhibit 3.7**

TRIPPER WATER SKI MANUFACTURING COMPANY

**Data Relevant to Budgeting Economy Skis
for Months of January, February, and March
(Data in Units)**

| | First quarter | Second quarter | Third quarter | Fourth quarter | Total year |
|---|---|---|---|---|---|
| 19X1 Sales budget | 2,300 | 4,500 | 3,600 | 1,200 | 11,600 |
| Percent annual sales | 20 | 39 | 31 | 10 | 100 |
| 19X1 Actual sales | 2,420 | 4,750 | Not yet available | Not yet available | Not yet available |
| 19X2 Market-based forecast | 2,700 | 5,200 | 4,100 | 1,400 | 13,400 |
| Percent annual sales | 20 | 39 | 31 | 10 | |
| 19X2 Sales-based forecast | 2,400 | 4,800 | 3,800 | 1,300 | 12,300 |
| Percent annual sales | 20 | 39 | 31 | 10 | 100 |

| | January | February | March | Total first quarter |
|---|---|---|---|---|
| 19X1 Sales budget | 700 | 700 | 900 | 2,300 |
| Percent of quarter's budget | 30 | 30 | 40 | 100 |
| 19X1 Actual sales | 730 | 740 | 950 | 2,420 |
| Percent of quarter sales | 29 | 31 | 40 | 100 |
| 19X2 Market-based forecast | 800 | 800 | 1,100 | 2,700 |
| Percent of quarter's forecast | 30 | 30 | 40 | 100 |
| 19X2 Sales-based forecast | 730 | 730 | 940 | 2,400 |
| Percent of quarter's forecast | 30 | 30 | 40 | 100 |
| 19X2 Sales budget | ? | ? | ? | ? |

Exhibit 3.7 combines the previous data on a worksheet for the economy model ski for January, February, and March. How would you complete the worksheet by budgeting the three months' sales for 19X2? What steps of further analysis might you undertake? For interest and involvement, you might write down your estimate for each of the three months, before proceeding.

In studying the data in Exhibit 3.7, you might note the following items:

• This year's budget, both forecasts for next year, and this year's sales all agree on the proportion of annual sales to be expected during the first quarter.

• This year's budget appears to have consistently underestimated actual sales. So far, actual sales are running five percent more than budgeted.

- The sales-based forecast for 19X2 projects only a five percent increase over this year's budget. In effect, it is projecting no increase over this year's actual sales rate to date.
- The market-based forecast for 19X2 projects a 15 percent increase over this year's budget or a 10 percent increase over this year's current sales rate.

You may also assume that a study of last year's budgeting files reveals that the 19X1 market-based forecast was overly optimistic by five percent over 19X1 actual sales to date.

Given all this information, it might be reasonable for you to budget economy ski unit sales for the first three months of 19X2 as follows:

|  | January | February | March | Total first quarter |
|---|---|---|---|---|
| Units | 750 | 750 | 1,000 | 2,500 |
| Percent | 30 | 30 | 40 | 100 |

Can you see the logic behind this budget? The market-based forecast for the quarter of 2,700 units represents a 15-percent increase over this year's budget and a 10-percent increase over actual sales. Last year this same forecast proved five-percent overly optimistic. On the other hand, the sales-based forecast projects only a five-percent increase over this year's budget, and sales so far this year are already exceeding budget by five percent. If the sales-based forecast appears five percent too pessimistic, and the market-based one five percent too optimistic, a good guess would be half-way between, or a budget projecting a 10-percent sales increase over last year's budget (five percent over the trend of this year's actual sales). All available information (current year's budget, current year's actual sales, and both forecasts) indicates the same proportion of sales by month within the first quarter:

| | |
|---|---|
| 30 percent, | January |
| 30 percent, | February |
| 40 percent, | March |
| 100 percent, | first quarter |

Allocation of the first quarter's sales by months on a 30/30/40 percent basis therefore appears appropriate. Note also that amounts are rounded to even hundreds for each quarter and to the nearest 10 units for each month. A forecast of 759 units for January would imply unfounded accuracy, and could introduce additional unnecessary detail in the subsequent budgeting stages. Following similar steps for the balance of the year, and for the other two products, will yield the complete 19X2 sales budget, which is illustrated in Exhibit 3.8.

Do you feel let down or disappointed? Did you believe that sales budgeting was somehow more precise and rationally scientific than demonstrated in

**Exhibit 3.8**

TRIPPER WATER SKI MANUFACTURING COMPANY

**Sales Budget for the Year 19X2**

| Percent | | Economy ski | | Deluxe ski | | Tow rope | | Total |
|---|---|---|---|---|---|---|---|---|
| | | Units | Dollars | Units | Dollars | Units | Dollars | Dollars |
| 30 | Jan. | 750 | $ 37,500 | 400 | $ 32,000 | 325 | $ 3,250 | $ 72,750 |
| 30 | Feb. | 750 | 37,500 | 400 | 32,000 | 325 | 3,250 | 72,750 |
| 40 | Mar. | 1,000 | 50,000 | 550 | 44,000 | 450 | 4,500 | 98,500 |
| 100 | 1st qtr. | 2,500 | $125,000 | 1,350 | $108,000 | 1,100 | $11,000 | $ 244,000 |
| 25 | Apr. | 1,250 | $ 62,500 | 750 | $ 60,000 | 550 | $ 5,500 | $ 128,000 |
| 35 | May | 1,750 | 87,500 | 1,050 | 84,000 | 770 | 7,700 | 179,200 |
| 40 | Jun. | 2,000 | 100,000 | 1,200 | 96,000 | 880 | 8,800 | 204,800 |
| 100 | 2nd qtr. | 5,000 | $250,000 | 3,000 | $240,000 | 2,200 | $22,000 | $ 512,000 |
| 50 | Jul. | 2,000 | $100,000 | 1,000 | $ 80,000 | 700 | 7,000 | $ 187,000 |
| 30 | Aug. | 1,200 | 60,000 | 600 | 48,000 | 600 | 6,000 | 114,000 |
| 20 | Sep. | 800 | 40,000 | 400 | 32,000 | 400 | 4,000 | 76,000 |
| 100 | 3rd qtr. | 4,000 | $200,000 | 2,000 | $160,000 | 1,700 | $17,000 | $ 377,000 |
| 50 | Oct. | 650 | $ 32,500 | 350 | $ 28,000 | 400 | 4,000 | $ 64,500 |
| 30 | Nov. | 400 | 20,000 | 200 | 16,000 | 350 | 3,500 | 39,500 |
| 20 | Dec. | 250 | 12,500 | 150 | 12,000 | 250 | 2,500 | 27,000 |
| 100 | 4th qtr. | 1,300 | $ 65,000 | 700 | $ 56,000 | 1,000 | $10,000 | $ 131,000 |
| Total year | | 12,800 | $640,000 | 7,050 | $564,000 | 6,000 | $60,000 | $1,264,000 |

this example? Of all budgeted data, the sales budget is least susceptible to precise projection. As you proceed to general coverage of the various approaches to sales budgeting, remember that, in the last analysis, a sales budget is a calculated guess. Subsequent sections of this chapter are devoted to techniques to improve the accuracy of the guesses or estimates.

## SALES BUDGET CRITICALLY IMPORTANT STARTING POINT

Recall, from the overview of the budgeting process in Chapter 2, that preparation of the sales budget is the starting point of the entire budgeting sequence. It is the sales budget that sets the level of anticipated volume (workload) upon which all activities and expenses in the sales and marketing division are planned (preparation of the selling expense budget will be covered in Chapter 5). It is the sales budget that provides anticipated demand for finished goods inventory which, in turn, provides the basis for all planned manufacturing and purchasing activities. And finally, it is the sales budget that provides the basis for forecasting anticipated cash receipts in the cash budgeting process. To say that sales budgeting is the **critical first step** is perhaps an understatement.

As illustrated in the Tripper Company example, responsibility for sales budgeting generally rests with the vice-president for marketing and sales. In larger firms, large staffs of specialists in economic, market, and sales forecasting are employed for the primary purpose of contributing to the accuracy of the budgeting process. The balance of this chapter will be devoted to a general introduction to the sales budgeting activity. A business major will have an opportunity to acquire more information on this subject in marketing and economics texts and courses.

## STEPS IN PREPARING THE SALES BUDGET

As cited above, perhaps the most difficult item to budget is the volume of anticipated sales. This difficulty results from the simple fact that sales volume is the least controllable part of a business. Sales result from customer demand, and customer demand may be influenced but not completely controlled. If you were to study the sales budgeting activity of an efficient and effective firm, you might conclude that the process can be broken down into four somewhat distinct parts:

1. Identifying factors that influence demand and separating them into two groups: those that are not controllable/influenceable by the firm, and those that are subject to control or influence.
2. Forecasting the noncontrollable factors (such as consumer disposable income) and their effect upon sales.
3. Developing sales goals and planning action with respect to the controllable factors (developing marketing and sales strategy and specific plans).
4. Translating various forecasts, strategies, and plans into expected sales volume: the sales budget.

## CHARACTERISTICS OF SALES DEMAND

Sales or customer demand results from the interaction of controllable and noncontrollable factors. Among those factors which are controlled by the firm and which have an influence on sales demand are the following:

- Selection of desirable markets and appropriate channels of distribution for different products. For Tripper this could involve choosing to focus exclusively on the quality ski market and selling through quality sporting goods and boating outlets rather than by mail order and through discount stores.
- Selection and design of products and services to be offered.

- Pricing—selecting the most desirable price for different products or services. Pricing will be discussed further in the appendix to Chapter 6.
- Promotion—selecting brand names; appropriate packaging; effective and efficient advertising; and selling approaches, aids, and incentives (quotas, commissions, and so forth).

The results of management decisions in each of these areas provide the basis for forecasting both sales demand and future marketing, selling, and distribution expenses.

Some noncontrollable factors which may constrain or limit the effectiveness of controllable activities include:

- The general economic picture, the amount of disposable income in the hands of potential consumers or customers, and the availability of credit (ease of obtaining credit and level of interest rates).
- The state of potential customers' expectations concerning their future income, credit availability, and price changes.
- The activities of competitors.

These and other noncontrollable factors must similarly be anticipated and factored into any sales budget.

## VARIOUS FORECASTING APPROACHES

Many different approaches are used by businesses to forecast sales demand, and many firms use several approaches concurrently. For convenience of understanding, the most common approaches may be thought of as members of one of two possible groups: *market-based (macro) forecasts* or *sales-based (micro) forecasts*.

## MARKET-BASED (MACRO) FORECASTING

Market-based approaches to forecasting focus on identifying various factors exogenous to or outside of the firm and their effect upon sales. Four common market-based forecasting approaches will be discussed briefly below. They involve use of:

1. Demand curves
2. Sophisticated economic models
3. Anticipated economic benefits
4. Customer surveys

### Demand Curves

The simplest approach and the one least relevant to actual practice involves the use of the classical demand curve familiar to economists. A *demand curve* indicates quantities of a given product that will be purchased at various prices.

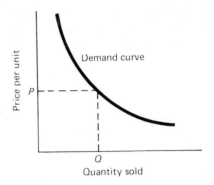

**Figure 3.1**

The curve in Fig. 3.1 assumes *price elasticity;* that is it assumes that lower prices will result in increased quantities sold, and *vice versa*. It reflects the final resolution of all controllable and noncontrollable factors influencing demand.

Controllable efforts on the part of the firm to make the product more attractive such as:

• Increasing quality of product or appearance of quality,

• Improving packaging for product appeal,

• Advertising,

would have the result of shifting the demand curve up and to the right, as shown in Fig. 3.2. The improved demand curve indicates that, at any given price, more items will be sold.

Factors beyond the control of the firm could shift the demand curve for a particular product either way. The demand curve for a consumer product might shift up and to the right (see below) in response to greater disposable income in the hands of consumers as a result of a full employment condition in the economy. Or the demand curve could be shifted in an undesirable direction—down and to the left—by a recession and less disposable income. Successful efforts by a competitor could also result in an undesirable shift down and to the left of the firm's demand curve for a particular product. (See Fig. 3.3.)

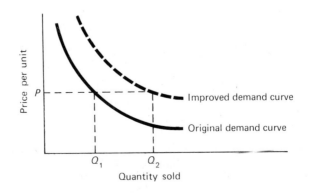

**Figure 3.2**

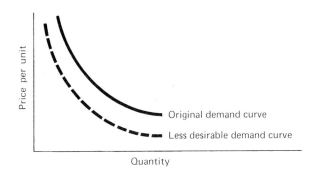

Original demand curve

Less desirable demand curve

**Figure 3.3**

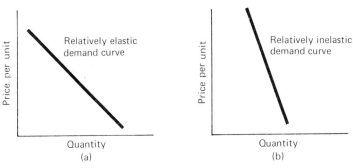

**Figure 3.4**

Although most economists believe a curved demand curve as shown above is most realistic, there exists considerable controversy over whether a straight-line demand curve is not, at least, an adequate approximation. Straight-line demand curves could appear as in Fig. 3.4. In the first example, the straight-line demand curve indicates relatively high elasticity (lower prices yield significantly higher volume, and *vice versa*). In the second example, the demand curve indicates a high degree of inelasticity (sales volume less significantly affected by price changes). The formula for curved demand curves requires mathematical sophistication beyond the level of this book.[1] Since the straight-line curves may be acceptable models, and since the mathematics involved is simpler, straight-line demand curves will be used in the balance of this chapter.

If a firm wanted to use demand curves to facilitate forecasting, it would need to have data, either historical or from surveys (see Customer Surveys, below) indicating quantities demanded at different price levels. With such available data, the firm could derive its demand curve (line) using one of three common techniques of *regression analysis:*

---

[1]   The formula for a curved demand curve may be expressed as:

$$Y = \frac{a}{X} + c$$

where

Y = selling price,          X = quantity,
$a$ = a factor relating to the degree of elasticity,
$c$ = a constant relating to the curve's shape and position.

- Visual fit
- High–low point method
- Least-squares regression analysis

The simplest, and possibly least accurate, technique involves establishing the curve (regression line) by *visual fit*. Following this process you would:

1. Plot the data for various combinations of price and quantity on a graph with price on the y-axis vertical) and quantity on the x-axis (horizontal).

2. Draw a straight line that **best represents** the slope or angle of the curve (where half the dots not exactly on the line are on either side). Note that when one or a few points appear very unusual and far removed from the pattern of the other observations, these unusual items may be ignored.

Exhibit 3.9 illustrates a demand curve (line) drawn by visual fit.

A second method of deriving the demand curve (regression line) is less subject to the possible errors of visually estimating the curve. Two extreme points (demand at a very high price and demand at a very low price) are selected that appear representative and not unusual. The demand curve (regression line) is then drawn through these two points. This approach is known as the *high–low point method*.

The equation for a straight line may be expressed in the form:

$$Y = a \cdot X + b$$

where:

$Y = price,$
$X = quantity,$
$a = $ slope of line,
$b = $ a constant relating to the line's position.

**Exhibit 3.9**

**Illustration of Demand Curve Drawn by Visual Fit**

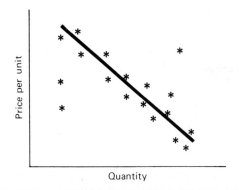

If you knew the slope (*a*) and position (*b*) of the demand curve for a particular product, you could easily forecast the price (*Y*) that would be necessary to sell a desired quantity (*X*), by substituting into the formula for the line. For example, if you knew for a particular product the slope "*a*" equalled minus $0.005^2$ and the position "*b*" was 125, then a quantity of 15,000 units could be sold if the price were $50.

$$Y \text{ (price)} = a \text{ (slope)} \cdot X \text{ (quantity)} + b \text{ (position)},$$
$$Y = -0.005(15{,}000) + 125,$$
$$Y = \$50.$$

Knowing the equation of the demand curve, you could also forecast what quantity would be sold at a particular price. You would merely use a different form of the same equation:

$$X = \frac{Y - b}{a}.$$

Assuming the same slope and position factors per the above, how many units could be sold if the price were dropped to $30?

$$X = \frac{30 - 125}{-0.005},$$

$$X = 19{,}000 \text{ units.}$$

The slope *a* and the position *b* of the demand curve can be obtained by picking two points on the line (for example, the high and the low points). These price–quantity combinations are then each substituted into an equation for a line ($Y = a \cdot X + b$) and the two equations are then solved simultaneously. For example, assume available original data in the above example had included information that:

- At a price of $120, 1,000 units would be sold.
- At a price of $20, 21,000 units would be sold.

Substituting into two equations:

$$\$120 = \phantom{0}1{,}000a + b,$$
$$\$\phantom{0}20 = 21{,}000a + b.$$

Subtracting the second equation from the first:

$$\$100 = -20{,}000a,$$
$$a = -0.005.$$

Substituting $a = -0.005$ in either of the two equations in solving for *b*, you find that $b = \$125$.

---

[2]  Note that the slope is always a decimal fraction, and that a negative slope indicates a line sloping downwards and to the right.

The third and even more accurate method of deriving the demand curve (regression line) from given data is through a process known as least-squares regression analysis. Least-squares regression analysis is covered in the appendix to this chapter. Programs for determining a regression line from given data using the least-squares regression approach are readily available on business school computers and in more sophisticated pocket calculators. Both the visual fit and the high–low-point methods are only crude approximations, and they may be subject to considerable error. For instance, the high and low points chosen may not be representative. With the availability of equipment to quickly and accurately perform more involved computations, regression analysis is best approached by using the more accurate least-squares method.

As you can see from the above example, if a firm could obtain a realistic demand curve for each of its products, forecasting sales would not be difficult. Unfortunately, reasonably accurate demand curves for most products are difficult if not impossible to obtain. Demand curves remain as a simplified economic model with little direct application to the forecasting process. However, the underlying assumptions of the demand curve model involving various elasticities (slopes) of customer demand are very relevant to pricing decisions and will be discussed further in the appendix to Chapter 6. The techniques of obtaining the equation of a line from available data are very useful in the budgeting process as an aid in estimating future costs. You will be using them again in Chapter 5.

## Sophisticated Economic Models

Returning to other approaches to market-based forecasting, with the advent of computers an increasingly popular approach involves the use of *mathematical models*. Following this approach, attempts are made to identify by statistical analysis all the various factors which have significantly influenced past changes in the demand for a product and to identify the relative "strength" of each factor. Such analysis involves use of a mathematical technique known as multiple regression analysis and is beyond the scope of this text. Where such factors can be identified and weighted, they may then be incorporated in a predictive model to generate a sales forecast, given forecasted data for each of the identifiable factors.

Often incorporated in economic sales forecasting models are data relating to *market shares*. In many industries, data are available from trade associations and government agencies on both total past sales and projected future sales of given products. Using such aggregate information together with its own data, an individual firm can determine its own share of the total market. On the basis of its anticipated share of the projected total market, it can forecast its own sales.

Also generally incorporated in forecasting models for sales of a firm's products are general economic forecasts. Economic forecasts cover such items as anticipated employment levels, consumer disposable income, and credit availability. Data are obtainable from government agencies, the larger banks, and from private forecasting firms. A larger firm may also employ its own economists to prepare forecasts specialized to its particular needs. Forecasts of these factors affecting demand may be specifically included in mathematical models or may be less formally used as general guidelines in making sales forecasts.

### Anticipated Economic Benefits

Another forecasting tool less applicable to consumer products involves determination of specific economic benefits of a particular product to its users. If a study can pinpoint substantial economic benefits to particular users resulting from the purchase of a firm's product, and the population of potential users can be readily estimated, then a forecast of potential demand may be prepared. For example, a firm developing a plastic auto bumper that was lightweight, less costly than metal, and otherwise comparable could forecast demand based on known potential customers (auto manufacturers) and their volume plans.

### Customer Surveys (Market Research)

Customer or market surveys, or even test marketing, based on carefully selected samples may also be used. If the sample is selected to be a statistically valid representation of the overall market, survey results can be used as a basis for forecasting sales demand. Note that a survey can focus on demand at a particular price. It can also be designed to obtain different potential price–demand combinations or pairs for use in preparing a projected demand curve as discussed above.

### Limitations of Market-Based Forecasts

Any or all of the approaches cited above and others may be used to prepare forecasts of future sales. However, as the sole basis for sales budgeting, many of the market-based techniques share the following limitations:

1. It is generally difficult to obtain reliable data for particular products, as opposed to product groups.
2. It is often difficult to obtain reliable forecasts by months, as opposed to years or possibly quarters.
3. General economic-based forecasts often cannot provide for any unique aspects of a particular firm's products or distribution system, or for any specific promotional plans related to certain products.

These limitations, although serious, do not negate the value and usefulness of market-based forecasts. They merely act to constrain the usefulness of such forecasts in all situations. Market-based forecasts may be particularly valuable as general guidelines for use in conjunction with sales-based forecasts.

## SALES-BASED (MICRO) FORECASTS

As distinct from market-based forecasts, sales-based or micro forecasts are derived from information internal and peculiar to the firm itself. Sales-based forecasts may be viewed as being one of two types or a combination of both. These two types are extrapolation of past sales experience and projections by the firm's sales personnel.

### Extrapolation of Past Sales Experience

Perhaps the most widely used basis for sales budgeting is a simple extrapolation of past sales experience for each product. Macro-based expectations of a specific rate of sales increase may be factored into established patterns of previous sales experience unique to the firm and its products. In the Tripper example, a general five-percent increase over the recent sales rate (or ten percent over previous budget) was determined to represent an appropriate expectation.

Extrapolation of past sales experience as a tool for sales budget preparation has several distinct advantages:

- Sufficient detail is readily available by product by month.
- Historical sales patterns reflect the uniqueness of the firm's products and distribution channels.
- It is the least costly of all forecasting approaches.

### Projections by the Firm's Sales Personnel

A second sales-based forecast may be prepared independently or in conjunction with the first. Individual salespersons may be asked to project sales in their distinct territories or areas of responsibility. These separate projections are then aggregated into a total company forecast.

Sales projections by individual salespersons have several very positive benefits:

1. They encourage and involve sales personnel in making a commitment to and assuming personal responsibility for the results of their activities on behalf of the company. The value of this action can hardly be overstated. Involving personnel in individual commitments pertaining to their areas of responsibility is the essence of MBO and is essential to the truly successful operation of a budgeting and budgetary control system. This feature should become increasingly apparent as you proceed through all steps of the budgeting and control process.

2. They can incorporate all of the aspects of the firm's situation that are unique to its products, markets, customers, and competitive situation.

3. They may be readily integrated with various approaches adopted by the firm to motivate and control sales. For example, they may be related to the establishment of sales quotas for forthcoming periods and/or incorporated in commission or bonus systems.

**Limitations of Sales-based Forecasts**

Earlier in this chapter, some of the limitations of market-based forecasting were discussed. Can you identify at least two limitations inherent in sales-based forecasts? Take a moment to really think through the issues and come up with a tentative answer. You should find the time well spent, because it should really put you in touch with the inherent difficulties of sales-budgeting in particular and over-all budgeting in general.

Sales-based forecasts may inherently be subject to several limitations:

**1.** Because they are historically based, they may be too heavily influenced by past performance. They may inadequately provide for changing conditions in the forthcoming year. A salesperson could assume that, since a particular customer or territory absorbed 1,000 units of product last year, the same performance would be repeated this year. Such an assumption could be ill-advised if competitive factors are becoming more intense, disposable income is down, or other similar items might realistically lead to lowered expectations.

Conversely, assuming just as much or a little more than last year could ignore very real opportunities for expanded sales volume. Such opportunities could include more favorable external market factors and the potential results of general and specific promotional activities by the firm.

**2.** Related to the first limitation, above, is the fact that sales-based forecasts may be limited by insufficient information. Individual salespersons may be inadequately informed or fail to perceive the consequences of forthcoming company product or promotional changes. They may also be unaware of the full implications of forthcoming changes in the economy or in their firm's competitive situation.

**3.** A third limitation of sales-based forecasts prepared by individual sales personnel is that they involve an inherent or potential conflict of interest or goals. Recall the discussion of goal congruence in Chapter 2. The personal goals of the individual salesperson may be at variance with the company's goal of obtaining an accurate objective forecast. Successful salespersons are often essentially optimistic. Their forecasts may reflect hopes rather than realistic expectations. Or, as is a risk in all budgeting, if individuals know their performances will be evaluated in comparison with the budget, the forecasts may be set at easily obtainable levels. By setting a low target level of performance, an individual practically guarantees in advance the appearance of good performance in the future.

## PLANNING FOR CONTROLLABLE FACTORS

Offsetting some of the limitations of sales-based forecasts are the other portions of sales budgeting activity. In addition to preparing a budget of sales and other revenues over the next period, sales budgeting includes the detailed planning of sales and marketing activities throughout the coming year. These activities relate to the controllable factors cited earlier. The sales-based fore-cast should, and the final sales budget must, follow the sales and marketing planning decisions. Otherwise planned sales will not reflect the intended results of planned actions designed to influence sales. Planning for controllable factors includes:

- Marketing strategy and promotional activities,
- Credit policy,
- Pricing,
- Special orders,
- Modifying product mix to maximize utilization of existing capacity, and
- Budgeting selling expenses for the forthcoming period.

### Marketing Strategy and Promotional Activities

Expected sales should reflect the results of specific planned efforts intended to influence demand in particular markets. Planning activities designed to affect potential customers directly would include product and packaging design or redesign, specific sales promotion activities (coupons, rebates, and so forth), and specific advertising campaigns. Planning activities to influence sales through motivating sales personnel would include sales commissions, sales contests, bonuses, quotas, and so forth.

### Credit Policy

A distinct part of the overall marketing strategy of a firm is its *credit policy*. Generally, the extension of more liberal credit policies to customers will result in increased sales. You have probably experienced, directly or indirectly, the operation of different types of credit policies. Many small restaurants do not extend credit and operate only on a cash basis. Many businesses sell on both a cash and a credit basis, and the growing acceptability of credit cards has multi-plied the number of firms offering such a mixed policy (cash or credit). Many businesses focus their selling efforts around the "buy now, pay later" theme. Some deliberately appeal to the customer who is a poorer credit risk. Others offer credit and provide an incentive for rapid payment through sales discounts.[3]

Whenever a firm extends credit or liberalizes existing credit policies, both revenues and costs increase. Costs of liberalized credit include those costs associated with carrying additional accounts receivable and inventory. Both

---

[3]    Recall, from your study of financial accounting, that sales discounts involve a discount for early payment. Sales terms of 2/10 N30 would offer a two-percent discount from the invoice price if paid within ten days with the full (net) price payable in 30 days.

the costs of the additional investment and related operating costs (billing, collection, purchasing, handling, and storage) are involved with receivables and inventory. And, since not all customers eventually pay their bills, increased losses on bad debts are associated with more liberal credit policies.

The selection of the most desirable credit policy involves comparing the benefits or contribution from changes in sales volume with the associated costs cited above. Detailed approaches to such problems will be covered in Chapter 7. At this point you need only be aware of the interdependence between planned credit policies and expected sales.

## Pricing

Sales demand, as previously discussed in connection with demand curves, can be very elastic. That is, for those products where customers have a sharp image of "the market price," a price higher than market will often drastically reduce sales, and *vice versa*. Many firms go to considerable efforts, via brand names, packaging, advertising, and even product design, to differentiate their products as somewhat better than average in the potential customer's mind. The firm hopes both to reduce relative elasticity and also to make a higher price acceptable. Nevertheless, demand for most products remains relatively elastic, and planned selling price will influence expected sales.

As an example of relative elasticity, think of Tripper's water skis. Suppose the demand curve or demand schedule for the economy ski were as follows:

| Unit price | Annual demand | Total revenue |
|---|---|---|
| $40 | 14,500 | $580,000 |
| 45 | 13,500 | 607,500 |
| 50 | 12,800 | 640,000 |
| 55 | 11,000 | 605,000 |
| 60 | 5,000 | 300,000 |

Note that product differentiation has resulted in an inelastic condition wherein some customers are still willing to buy at a price of $60 whereas, in a more elastic situation, demand could fall to zero above the market price of $50. Conversely, in the only relatively elastic situation, prices below "market" do not result in compensating increases in demand. In the above situation, Tripper's efforts have reduced but not eliminated price elasticity. At an intended price of $50, 12,800 units may be expected to be sold.

Because of price changes, sales budgets are prepared in both dollars and units. Dollar budgets are necessary for subsequent budgeting of receivables investment and cash flow. But unit forecasts are required for budgeting inventory, production, and purchases.

Various approaches to the pricing decision will be covered in the section on pricing included in the appendix to Chapter 6. At this stage it is only important that you recognize planned prices as a potentially significant determinant of forecasted sales.

## Special Orders and Modifications of Sales Mix

Relating to maximizing the use of a firm's existing plant assets are two other marketing-related considerations that are often part of its sales budgeting process. Detailed decision-making techniques applicable to these two areas will be discussed in Chapter 7. Here it is important that you recognize the dimensions of each decision area and its potential effect upon forecasted sales.

Special orders that are, by definition, not part of a firm's standard or regular business can be a mixed blessing. On the one hand, they can provide increased profits and a use for available capacity. On the other, they can interfere with normal production. They also are usually difficult to anticipate or forecast. A firm's policy towards special orders, like its credit policy, can have an influence on expected sales and must be considered in preparing a sales budget.

Another consideration in sales planning involves *product mix*. Product mix refers to the proportions of different products in total sales. Different products may generate more profit than others. When a firm is operating at or near capacity, it might be desirable to focus promotional efforts toward altering the firm's product mix, with the intention of increasing profits within the limits of existing capacity.

A simplified example of the product-mix problem can be seen in the case of the Tripper Company. Suppose Tripper were currently selling 5,000 economy skis and 3,000 deluxe skis per month and was operating at capacity. Assume deluxe skis contributed $20 of profit apiece (for each additional deluxe ski sold, net income increased $20), whereas economy skis contributed only $8 each.[4] Also assume it required twice as much factory capacity to produce a deluxe ski as was required for an economy ski. Should Tripper attempt to push economy skis or deluxe skis harder?

At capacity, one additional deluxe ski produced and sold would require eliminating two economy skis from production and sales. $16 of contribution towards profit from economy skis would be lost and $20 from the deluxe ski added. Obviously, in this example, promotional activities should be focused on expanding deluxe ski sales. Any company plans for alteration of product mix obviously have to be reflected in the final sales budget.

Detailed plans for the ensuing year covering each of the sales-related activities mentioned above are all part of the sales budgeting process. These plans are all reflected in the sales budget for products to be sold. They also are formally detailed on selling expense budgets. Preparation of selling expense budgets will be covered in Chapter 5 after you have developed familiarity with tools for forecasting costs.

---

[4]    How to determine the contribution to profit of a particular item will be covered in detail in Chapter 6.

## FORECASTING VS. BUDGETING: TRANSLATING FORECASTS INTO BUDGETS

As you probably have inferred, forecasts of sales may reflect wishful thinking; or they may reflect undue pessimism. Budgets, as distinct from forecasts, are not intended to reflect unrealistic optimism or pessimism. Budgets are intended to be hardheaded statements of rational and reasonable projections of what is expected to happen, rather than dreams of what might happen. Since sales budgets provide the basis for all other company planning and initial action, they are too important to be allowed to contain the results of inappropriate optimism or pessimism. The last step, therefore, in the sales budgeting process is developing the final sales budget from various forecasts prepared on different bases. Often, as demonstrated earlier with the Tripper example, different forecasts may significantly differ in their predictions for the same future period. Reconciling these disparate anticipations and committing the company to a final sales budget that can be lived with are very much examples of the art of management rather than its science. A commonly used approach involves:

- Starting with one or more sales-based forecasts;
- Comparing totals with market-based forecasts;
- Arriving at a rational figure for budgeted total sales for the period, reflecting the anticipated results of any planned marketing and selling activities not previously incorporated in the forecasts;
- Allocating the total expected sales among future months, based primarily on experience.

The Tripper example at the beginning of this chapter provided an illustration of this process.

## BUDGETS AS EXPECTATIONS OR MOTIVATING DEVICES

An issue common to all budgets and particularly relevant to sales budgets concerns whether budgets should be viewed as statements of reasonable expectations or as motivating devices. Research and your own personal experience has shown that human beings generally will perform to a level set out for them by others, provided it is believable. That is, the individual may not initially expect to achieve that level, but he or she knows or believes that it is achievable. The level or goal is not so far beyond the individual's personal expectations as to appear hopeless or ridiculous. Also, people generally do not perform beyond goals or expectations unless these goals are absurdly low.

Given that individuals behave in this fashion, all employees, managers, and owners of a firm (and the economy through improved productivity) would be better off if each had an objective or goal for the year slightly higher than his or her own level of expectation. Since budgets serve as plans or goals for the forthcoming year, should they be set a little on the high or optimistic side? Or should they reflect what is expected to happen? If budgets are set too optimistically, unneeded production will be scheduled, unneeded resources acquired, and a potentially disrupting cutback in activity will eventually occur. If they are not a little optimistic, the benefit of the increased performance will be lost. Can you clearly see the dilemma?

The ideal answer to this quandary is to define it out of existence. If budgets are established at **reasonably attainable** goals (slightly above each individual's own personal expectations), then they may simultaneously serve as motivating devices and represent projections of expectable results. Managers must be careful to not allow, let alone force, budgets to be set too optimistically. Going too far along the motivation trail can result in backlash or negative reaction and significant unfavorable differences between plans and actual events. Again think of your own experience. If a goal or expectation set for you is too high, you will become discouraged and possibly angry. You then probably will perform at a much lower level than had the goal been lower to begin with.

This problem of expectations vs. motivating goals can be seen clearly with respect to sales quotas or targets. Some firms have even tried establishing motivating sales quotas at a high level, and then secretly budgeted sales at a lower, "more reasonable" level. Usually such experiments do not prove successful if for no other reason than that secrets do not remain secret for very long. Once the inherent dishonesty of such an approach is exposed, the loss of management credibility usually is far more costly than any temporary benefits previously accrued.

In the case of sales quotas, an effective solution is to sometimes set quotas and budgets somewhat higher than initial expectations **openly and in agreement with the sales personnel involved.** Open participation between the individual and the immediate supervisor in the setting of quotas or budgets can have several benefits. Open communication can eliminate the salesperson's possible feeling of need for slack in the quota (a quota set below an attainable amount as insurance that it may be easily met). And both parties can openly take advantage of the motivating force behind slightly optimistic expectations. If the process is handled carefully, the resultant budget will usually turn out to be a reasonable prediction of what will actually occur.

The behavioral implications related to the various approaches to budget setting will be explored further in later chapters. They are introduced here as a reminder that the sales budget covers both controllable and noncontrollable activities. The budget itself can, through controllable activities, have an influence on actual sales results. This extension of significance beyond that of a simple plan should be considered as part of the sales budgeting process. The planning and control of sales revenue and the firm's sales activities have only been briefly introduced in this chapter. You will find them covered more thoroughly in courses and texts in marketing and sales management.

## PLANNING FOR REVENUES OTHER THAN SALES

Although budgeting for sales of goods and services is the major portion of the sales budgeting activity (and why the result is known as the sales budget), to complete the budgeting of inflows from operations, nonsales revenues must also be budgeted. Recall from financial accounting that nonsales revenues can include such things as interest, rent, fees, royalties, dividends on stock investments, and so forth. For cash planning purposes (see Chapter 9), nonsales revenues and their expected times of realization in cash must be budgeted by month over the budget period. Responsibility for budgeting nonsales revenue is often assigned to the controller rather than the sales manager or vice-president for marketing and sales.

## PLANNING ACTIVITY IN NONPROFIT-DIRECTED ORGANIZATIONS

Many nonprofit-directed organizations such as public schools, public universities, charities, and governments obtain no revenue in direct exchange for goods and services provided. Instead, their funds for operations and capital asset acquisitions are derived from tax revenues and/or donations. Nevertheless, these organizations also must budget their activities for forthcoming periods. In such situations, a real problem often exists in relating or measuring outputs (services provided or benefits gained) in relation to a given level of activity or level of expenditure. Often, and traditionally, outputs are not budgeted as such. Instead activity is budgeted solely in terms of inputs or costs to be incurred (payroll, purchases, and so forth). More recently many such organizations are budgeting expenditures in terms of the actual services (outputs) to be provided. This more recent approach is referred to as *program budgeting* and will be covered further in Chapter 15.

Other nonprofit-directed organizations such as publicly owned utilities, publicly and privately owned hospitals, and private schools are involved in providing goods and services to others for a fee. These organizations therefore have revenues that can be budgeted in much the same way as sales are budgeted in a profit-directed firm. Some of these organizations also operate on supplementary funds received from investment (endowment) income and donations. Again these inflows may be budgeted in much the same way as nonsales revenue is budgeted for a business.

Budgeting and control in nonprofit-directed organizations is discussed further in Chapter 15. It is mentioned in this chapter as a reminder that all organizations, both private and public, share similar problems in their common need to budget anticipated levels of activity.

You should note, however, that a significant difference in the focus or intention of budgets exists between those prepared for profit-directed firms and many of those prepared for nonprofit-directed organizations. Business budgets involve plans for future activities expressed in terms of **reasonably**

**expected** outputs (revenues) and inputs (expenditures). Nonbusiness budgets, even though they may be established while taking outputs into consideration (programmed budgeting), are usually expressed solely in terms of inputs or expenditures to be incurred. And these input budgets represent authorizations or ceilings for spending rather than reasonable expectations that may not occur or be exceeded depending on future events.

## CHAPTER OVERVIEW

Based on material contained in this chapter, you should be able to:

- Describe and give examples of the four common steps involved in sales budgeting and how they interrelate;
- Describe the more common controllable factors having a potential influence on sales demand;
- Describe several noncontrollable factors that may influence sales demand;
- Differentiate between market-based (macro) forecasting and sales-based (micro) forecasting;
- Give examples of at least four different forecasting approaches that could be considered market-based;
- Identify three techniques for determining a straight-line demand curve (regression line), given data on various price–quantity combinations, and describe with examples at least two of these techniques;
- Give the equation for a straight line, and describe how the equation for a desired particular line, and especially its slope and position constant, may be determined.
- Give examples of at least two different forecasting approaches that could be considered sales-based;
- Discuss the strengths and limitations of the various forecasting approaches;
- Describe how planning for controllable factors interrelates with the determination of the sales budget;
- Differentiate between a sales forecast and a sales budget;
- Discuss the purpose of budgets and whether they can portray reasonable expectations, or be a motivating device, or both;
- Describe the commonality of activity budgeting among all organizations, and give examples of the manner in which activity budgets may be prepared in nonprofit-directed organizations.

## NEW VOCABULARY AND CONCEPTS

Market-based (macro) forecasts      High–low-point method
Sales-based (micro) forecasts      Mathematical models
Demand curve      Market share
Price elasticity      Credit policy
Regression analysis      Product mix
Visual fit      Program budgeting

- Relative elasticity of sales demand.
- Controllable and noncontrollable factors influencing sales demand.
- Strengths and weaknesses of various market and sales-based forecasting approaches.
- Regression analysis applied to demand curves.
- Budgets as both plans and motivating devices.

## REVIEW QUESTIONS

1. a) What other parts of the overall budgeting process use the outputs of the sales budget as input?
   b) For each such part, explain how the sales budget information is used.
2. What executive/manager is usually responsible for preparing the sales budget?
3. The sales budgeting process can be broken down into four separate activities. Describe these separate activities and how they interrelate.
4. Describe at least four distinct factors that may influence demand for a product or service and that are wholly or partially controllable by the firm.
5. Describe at least three distinct factors that may influence demand for a product or service, and that are **not** controllable to any significant extent by the firm.
6. What are the essential differences between the market-based (macro) and the sales-based (micro) approaches to forecasting sales?
7. Describe at least four approaches to sales forecasting that can be classified as market-based or macro.
8. Describe at least two approaches to sales forecasting that may be used independently or in conjunction with each other and that both can be classified as sales-based or micro.
9. a) What is price elasticity?
   b) What information is provided by a demand curve?
   c) Why do demand curves generally slope down to the right?
10. What is the visual-fit method of constructing a demand curve?
11. a) What is the high–low-point method of constructing a demand curve?
    b) Using the high–low-point method, describe with an example how you would obtain the equation (the slope and position constants) of a particular demand curve (regression line).

c) Given the slope coefficient and the position constant of a demand curve (line), describe how you would determine expected sales quantity given a specific price, and vice versa.

12. What are (a) the advantages and (b) the limitations inherent in using market-based (macro) forecasts as all or part of the sales budgeting process?

13. What are (a) the advantages and (b) the limitations inherent in using sales-based (micro) forecasts as all or part of the sales budgeting process?

14. How can a firm's credit policy influence its sales budget?

15. a) What is the difference between a sales forecast and a sales budget?
    b) Explain in general terms how sales forecasts are translated into sales budgets.

16. Can sales budgets be simultaneously a motivating device and a reasonable forecast of expected performance? Explain your response with examples.


## MINI-CASES AND QUESTIONS FOR DISCUSSION

**MC 3.1** Assume a market situation in which there are only a few sellers (producers), only a few buyers all of whom are knowledgeable, and a product or service that cannot be readily differentiated. What would you expect the relative sensitivity (elasticity) of demand to be for any one seller's product or service? What would you expect to be the individual firm's reaction or method of dealing with this situation? Discuss.

**MC 3.2** In many situations, factors other than or in addition to price significantly influence demand. What are some of these other nonprice factors? Could a demand-type curve be constructed, or at least considered, which would relate costs of such factors ($Y$-axis) to the quantity expected to be sold ($X$-axis)? Discuss.

**MC 3.3** If an individual will perform to a goal set slightly above his or her level of expected performance, doesn't the involvement of the individual in the budget (goal-setting) process tend to eliminate the challenge (motivating) effect? Is there a tradeoff between the possible motivating advantages of an imposed (set by someone else) budget and the advantages of responsibility inherent in a participative (jointly set by individual and his or her supervisor) budget? Discuss.

**MC 3.4** Suppose a particular firm were to establish a sales incentive program with rewards to those salespersons who beat (exceeded) the company's sales budget. Would the objectives of such a program be congruent with the objectives of budgeting?

**MC 3.5** A sales budget set too high could result in excessive costs, employee layoffs, financing difficulties, and reduced profits. A sales budget set too low could also result in excessive costs, financing difficulties, and reduced profits. Are all parts of both of these statements correct? Discuss, giving specific examples.

# ESSENTIAL PROBLEMS

**EP 3.1** The following items are thought to influence the demand for a firm's products:

1. Customer (consumer) income or disposable income,
2. Customer (consumer) expectations of income or disposable income,
3. Demographics (age distribution of customer population),
4. Availability of consumer credit and current level of interest rates,
5. Customer expectations concerning credit availability and interest rates,
6. Availability of directly and indirectly competing products and services,
7. Customer expectations of availability of directly and indirectly competing products and services,
8. Price,
9. Advertising,
10. Direct sales promotion (rebates, coupons, and so forth),
11. Sales personnel (training, commissions, and so forth),
12. Product or service itself (quality, longevity, appearance, and so forth),
13. Availability of product or service (readily available supply),
14. Customer experience with or of product or service,
15. Customer information about product or service from other customers or individuals (word of mouth advertising).

*Required:*

a) Which items are fully controllable by the firm?
b) Which are partially controllable or influenceable by the firm?
c) Which are not controllable/influenceable to any meaningful extent by the firm?

**EP 3.2** Refer to the 15 factors possibly affecting demand listed in problem EP 3.1 above. For each factor **not** controllable/influenceable by the firm, describe how you would expect the demand curve for a product to shift in response to a change in each of these factors taken separately.

**EP 3.3** Refer to the 15 factors possibly affecting demand listed in Problem EP 3.1 above. For each factor over which the firm has control or partial control (influence), describe how a change in each of these factors taken separately might be expected to change the demand curve for a product.

**EP 3.4** Referring to the controllable and partially controllable factors cited in Problem EP 3.3 above, briefly describe with respect to each factor what actions a firm might undertake in an attempt to shift the demand curve up and to the right.

**EP 3.5** A market survey for the Tripper Company resulted in the following data. What would be the potential water ski market in total and by age group?

Distribution of population and water ski demand:

| Age | Population percentage | Demand* |
|-----|----------------------|---------|
| 0–10 | 10 | 3 |
| 10–20 | 20 | 22.5 |
| 20–30 | 25 | 18 |
| 30–40 | 10 | 33 |
| 40–50 | 15 | 15 |
| Over 50 | 20 | 0.75 |

Total population = 200,000,000 persons
Percentage of total market already saturated (individuals already own water skis) = 40 percent

* Note. Demand data is for total market including portion already saturated.

**EP 3.6** Refer to the data in Problem EP 3.5 above. Assume that total industry water ski sales next year would amount to ten percent of the remaining (not yet satisfied/saturated) total demand for new first skis, plus one-percent replacement sales to the saturated market. If Tripper's expected market share was 10.7%, how many skis could it expect to sell next year?

**EP 3.7** As a result of a carefully selected market survey, Tripper has developed the following price/sales demand pairs which it believes valid:

| Price | Quantity |
|-------|----------|
| $36 | 16,000 |
| 43 | 14,000 |
| 53 | 12,000 |
| 59 | 10,000 |
| 69 | 8,000 |
| 76 | 6,000 |

a) Using the high–low-point approach, give the equation for the demand curve (regression line) derived from these data in the form $Y = a \cdot X + b$ with the appropriate values for $a$ and $b$.

b) From this regression line, forecast sales demand at two different prices: $40 and $65.

**EP 3.8** Assume that a firm obtained the following data, from which it wished to construct a demand curve (line):

| Price | Quantity |
|-------|----------|
| $ 5 | 175,000 |
| 10 | 160,000 |
| 15 | 115,000 |
| 20 | 110,000 |
| 25 | 65,000 |
| 30 | 50,000 |

a) Give the equation for the curve (regression line) derived from these data, using the high–low-point method in the form $Y = a \cdot X + b$ with the appropriate values for $a$ and $b$.

b) From this regression line, forecast sales demand at two different prices: $8 and $16.

c) Does the demand curve (line) obtained above indicate that demand is more or less elastic (sensitive to price changes) than that derived in Problem EP 3.7?

EP 3.9  a) Derive a firm's demand curve (line) using the high–low-point method from the price–quantity observations given below (see Problem EP 3.7).

b) Forecast sales demand at prices of $60 and $225.

c) Compare elasticity of demand to the demand curve determined in Problem EP 3.7.

| Price | Quantity |
|---|---|
| $ 50 | 350,000 |
| 100 | 297,000 |
| 150 | 252,000 |
| 200 | 198,000 |
| 250 | 152,000 |
| 300 | 100,000 |

EP 3.10  a) Derive a firm's demand curve (line) using the high–low-point method from the price–quantity observations given below (see problem EP 3.7).

b) Forecast sales demand at prices of $1.75 and $4.50.

c) Compare elasticity of demand to the demand curve in Problem EP 3.9.

| Price | Quantity |
|---|---|
| $ 1 | 175,000 |
| 2 | 156,000 |
| 3 | 130,000 |
| 4 | 96,000 |
| 5 | 72,000 |
| 6 | 50,000 |

EP 3.11  Assume your firm sells two products, P and Q. You have the following information to assist you in budgeting sales in units of P and Q for 19X9:

| | First quarter | Second quarter | Third quarter | Fourth quarter |
|---|---|---|---|---|
| 19X8 budgeted unit sales: | | | | |
| Product P | 1,250 | 2,500 | 3,750 | 5,000 |
| Product Q | 10,200 | 13,600 | 3,400 | 6,800 |
| 19X8 actual unit sales: | | | | |
| Product P | 1,130 | 2,250 | 3,750 | NA |
| Product Q | 9,180 | 12,240 | 3,060 | NA |

|  | First quarter | Second quarter | Third quarter | Fourth quarter |
|---|---|---|---|---|
| 19X9 market-based forecast: |  |  |  |  |
| Product P | 1,310 | 2,630 | 3,940 | 5,240 |
| Product Q | 10,710 | 14,280 | 3,570 | 7,140 |
| 19X9 sales-based forecast: |  |  |  |  |
| Product P | 1,190 | 2,380 | 3,560 | 4,750 |
| Product Q | 9,690 | 12,920 | 3,230 | 6,460 |

Assume 19X9 sales will be distributed as follows:

|  | P | Q |
|---|---|---|
| First quarter | 15% | 30% |
| Second quarter | 25 | 30 |
| Third quarter | 30 | 15 |
| Fourth quarter | 30 | 25 |
| Total year | 100% | 100% |

If you anticipate that total 19X9 sales will be half-way between the market-based and the sales-based projections, and will be distributed in the proportions given above, prepare the 19X9 sales budget in units only for each product.

**EP 3.12** Refer to the unit data in Problem EP 3.11.

a) It appears that 19X8 annual sales will be what percent of the original budget?

b) The 19X9 market-based forecast is what percent of the 19X8 budget?

c) The 19X9 sales-based forecast is what percent of the 19X8 budget?

d) All three projections assume the same distribution of sales within the year by product. What are these common percentage distributions?

e) Do the assumed distributions appear validated by 19X8 actual sales so far? Explain.

f) Assuming 19X9 total annual sales will be 12,000 units of P and 33,000 of Q, and using the distributions identified in (d) above, prepare a sales budget in units only by quarter for both products for 19X9.

## SUPPLEMENTARY PROBLEMS

(*Note.* The following problems employ techniques covered in the chapter appendix.)

**SP 3.13** Refer to the data given in Problem EP 3.7. Using simple regression analysis:

a) Derive the equation for the demand curve (regression line) in the form $Y = a \cdot X + b$ with the appropriate values for $a$ and $b$.

b) Determine the standard error (of estimate) for the above regression line.

**SP 3.14** Refer to the data given in Problem EP 3.8.

    a) Derive the same information as required in Problem SP 3.13 (both parts) above.

    b) Is the regression line derived in this problem a more or less precise forecasting tool than the one obtained in Problem SP 3.13? Explain.

    c) Does the regression line derived in this problem indicate more or less elasticity of demand than the one derived in Problem SP 3.13?

**SP 3.15** Refer to the data given in Problem EP 3.9.

    a) Derive the same information as required in Problem SP 3.13 (both parts).

    b) Is the regression line derived in this problem a more or less precise forecasting tool than the one obtained in Problem SP 3.13? Explain.

    c) Does the regression line derived in this problem indicate more or less elasticity of demand than the one derived in Problem SP 3.13? Explain.

**SP 3.16** Refer to the data given in Problem EP 3.10.

    a) Derive the same information as required in Problem SP 3.13 (both parts).

    b) Is the regression line derived in this problem a more or less reliable forecasting tool than the one obtained in Problem SP 3.15? Explain.

    c) Does the regression line derived in this problem indicate more or less elasticity of demand than the one derived in Problem SP 3:15? Explain.

## SUGGESTIONS FOR FURTHER READING

Butler, W., R. Kavesh, and R. Platt, *Methods and Techniques of Business Forecasting.* Englewood Cliffs, N.J.: Prentice-Hall, Inc., 1974.

Green, Paul E., and Donald S. Tull, *Research for Marketing Decisions*, Second Edition. Englewood Cliffs, N.J.: Prentice-Hall, Inc., 1970; Chapter 16.

Gray, Jack, and Kenneth S. Johnston, *Accounting and Management Action*, Second Edition. New York: McGraw-Hill, 1977; Chapter 6.

Wheelwright, S., and D. Clarke, "Corporate forecasting: Promise and reality," *Harvard Business Review*, November–December 1976.

CHAPTER 3 APPENDIX
# Simple Regression Analysis

There are many instances when a cause-and-effect relationship, or at least a correlation, between two variables may be thought to exist. Two examples would be demand curves discussed in this chapter and cost curves discussed in Chapter 5. In the case of demand curves, a correlation is presumed to exist between the price of a product and the quantity that may be sold by the firm (purchased by customers). In the case of cost curves, a correlation may exist between a particular cost (such as the cost of handling or moving materials within the plant) and the volume of activity (production workload) occurring in the plant.

If a reasonable correlation does exist and the relationship can be established, then a particular sales volume may be predicted for a given price, or a particular level of expected costs may be predicted for a given level of activity (workload). As discussed in this chapter with reference to demand curves, if the relationship between two variables is linear, then it may be expressed or adequately approximated in terms of a straight line. If the relationship is not linear, then only a curved line will adequately express the relationship. Non-linear relationships are beyond the scope of this text.

Where linearity may be assumed, there are three approaches commonly used to establish the *regression line*—the line that expresses the relationship between the variables. The two simplest methods for establishing the regression line are discussed in the main body of this chapter with reference to establishing the price and sales demand or the demand curve (line). These two methods are known as the visual fit and high–low methods, and they will not be covered further in this appendix.

A more sophisticated and reliable method of attempting to establish regression lines is known as *least-squares regression analysis* or simple statistical regression analysis. This method has two distinct advantages over the visual fit or high–low methods. Least-squares regression analysis (or LSRA) results in a line that is the best possible "fit" or correlation for the given data. Secondly, the technique also provides a measure of how well the derived line actually fits the data.

To avoid confusion, the following explanation of LSRA will focus upon attempting to establish a demand curve for a particular product—a predictable relationship between price and sales volume. Remember, as you proceed with

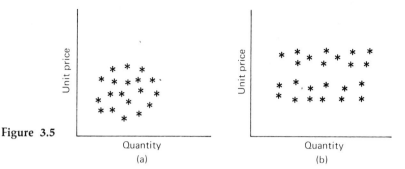

**Figure 3.5**

the following example relating to demand curves, that the same approach may also be used in an attempt to establish cost curves relating cost and volume of activity. LSRA for cost curves will be discussed in the appendix to Chapter 5.

LSRA is not applicable to situations wherein no consistent relationship exists between the variables. For example, if you plotted price and sales demand and came up with either of the pictures shown in Fig. 3.5, you would see that no recognizable pattern or predictable relationship appears to exist. Where there does exist an apparent relationship, as in Fig. 3.6, LSRA may prove a valuable tool.

Several regression lines could be drawn, based on data in Fig. 3.6. Note on Fig. 3.7 that the solid line is a better fit than the dashed line. The distances between each point and the solid line (the errors shown by dotted lines) are less than the distances (errors) from the points to the dotted line. Further, the distances are equal above and below the solid line, whereas more points are above than below the dotted line.

LSRA essentially establishes the regression line that best averages the relationships among the data. The line of *best fit* is defined as the line where both:

- The algebraic sums of the positive and negative (above and below) distances of all points from the line is zero; and

- The squares of the distances (deviations) between all points not falling on the line and the line itself summed is less than a similar sum for any other possible line.

**Figure 3.6**

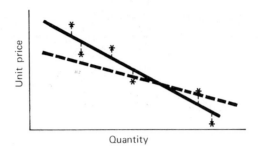

**Figure 3.7**

Quantity

The method is therefore commonly known as the least-squares method.
Two equations are used:

A)
$$\sum XY = b\sum X + a\sum X^2,$$

B)
$$\sum Y = nb + a\sum X,$$
where:[5]

$\sum XY =$ Prices times quantities summed,
$b =$ Constant related to curve's position,
$\sum X =$ Total quantities,
$\sum X^2 =$ Each quantity squared, then all summed,
$a =$ Slope of curve,
$\sum Y =$ Total Prices,
$n =$ Number of observations or price–quantity pairs.

Exhibit 3.10 provides data obtained by the Tripper Company with respect
to recent sales experience for their economy ski. The Exhibit also provides the
results of computations for $XY$, $X^2$, $\sum Y$, $\sum X$, $\sum XY$, $\sum X^2$. Note that each observation or piece of data must be independent of the other (one period's sales do
not affect demand in another period). Also note that different periods must be
chosen so as to avoid different seasonal influences. If this were not done, different sales demand would reflect **both** different prices and different seasons.
A multiple relationship between price, season, and quantity would be reflected
in the data, and LSRA would be inappropriate. Multiple regression analysis
techniques exist for use in such situations, but are beyond the scope of this text.

_____

[5]   For cost curves:

$\sum YX =$ costs times volume summed,
$b =$ total fixed costs,
$\sum X =$ total volume,
$\sum Y =$ total costs,
$n =$ number of observations or cost–volume pairs,
$a =$ variable cost per unit.

**Exhibit 3.10**

TRIPPER WATER SKI MANUFACTURING COMPANY

**Years 19X8 and 19X9**

| Period observed* | Price, Y | Quantity sold/period, X | XY | $X^2$ |
|---|---|---|---|---|
| 1 | $120 | 1,000 | $ 120,000 | 1,000,000 |
| 2 | 100 | 5,500 | 550,000 | 30,250,000 |
| 3 | 75 | 11,000 | 825,000 | 121,000,000 |
| 4 | 50 | 14,000 | 700,000 | 196,000,000 |
| 5 | 40 | 15,500 | 620,000 | 240,250,000 |

Totals:

| | | | | |
|---|---|---|---|---|
| $n$ | 5 | | | |
| $\Sigma Y$ | $385 | | | |
| $\Sigma X$ | | 47,000 | | |
| $\Sigma XY$ | | | $2,815,000 | |
| $\Sigma X^2$ | | | | 588,500,000 |

* Periods are comparable with each other; that is, seasonal demand changes are not responsible for differing price–quantity observations.

Substituting the values determined in Exhibit 3.10 into the LSRA equations (A) and (B) results in:

A) $\qquad 2,815,000 = 47,000b + 588,500,000a,$
B) $\qquad\qquad 385 = 5b + 47,000a.$

These two simultaneous equations are solved for $a$ and $b$, as follows:

*Step 1:* Modify one of the equations so that the coefficient (quantity) of one of the unknowns is exactly the same as the coefficient of the same unknown in the other equation. In this example, equation (B) is multiplied by 9,400 to result in equation $(B_1)$:

$(B_1) \qquad 3,619,000 = 47,000b + 441,800,000a$

*Step 2:* Subtract the modified equation from the other equation and solve for the unknown:

(A) $\qquad 2,815,000 = 47,000b + 588,500,000a$
$(B_1) \qquad 3,619,000 = 47,000b + 441,800,000a$

$(A - B_1) \qquad -804,000 = 146,700,000a$

$$a = \frac{-804,000}{146,700,000},$$

$$a = -0.0055 \text{ (rounded)}.$$

Note that a minus value for *a* indicates that the line slopes down to the right. A lower quantity is associated with a higher price.[6] This slope is expected for demand curves.

*Step 3:* Substitute the value obtained for the one variable from Step 2 above into either of the original equations, and solve for the other variable. In this example, $a = -0.0055$ is substituted into equation (B):

(B)
$$385 = 5b + 47,000(-0.0055),$$
$$385 = 5b - 258.5,$$
$$5b = 643.5,$$
$$b = 128.7.$$

To forecast anticipated unit sales at a particular price, say $60, this price, together with the values for *a* and *b*, would be substituted into the simple equation for a line:

$$Y \text{ (price)} = a \text{ (slope)} \cdot X \text{ (quantity)} + b \text{ (constant)},$$
$$\$60 = -0.0055X + 128.7,$$
$$X = 12,491 \text{ units (rounded)}.$$

The regression line (demand curve) indicates that, at a price of $60, you could predict that 12,491 skis would be sold.

Note that the values obtained by the visual fit and high–low point techniques discussed earlier in the body of this chapter were:

$$a = -0.005,$$
$$b = 125.$$

The values of $-0.0055$ and 128.7 obtained via least-squares regression analysis reflect the greater accuracy of the LSRA method.

The LSRA method provides an additional valuable piece of information not obtainable with either the visual fit or high–low point methods. Suppose your data were highly variable and you arrived at the regression line shown in Fig. 3.8.

Can you see that, even though a line may be the best fit, it may not be a very reliable predictor when a relationship is highly variable? Before using a regression line with some degree of confidence, it is desirable to have a measure of how far the actual observations were from the regression line. The LSRA method allows for measuring this potential error or variance through the use of the *standard error of the estimate*. The higher the standard error, the greater the likelihood of estimating error through using the regression line.

---

[6]   For a cost curve, "*a*" will be a positive amount indicating that the line slopes down to the left. A lower quantity or volume of activity is associated with a lower cost. Such a relationship would be expected for cost curves.

**Figure 3.8**

The standard error (of the estimate) is calculated by means of the following formula:

$$SE = \sqrt{\frac{\Sigma(Y - \overline{Y})^2}{n - 2}}$$

where

$Y$ = observed value of price at a particular quantity,
$\overline{Y}$ = predicted value of price at the same quantity, as obtained from the regression line,
$n$ = number of observations.

Exhibit 3.11 contains the same observations of economy ski sales shown in Exhibit 3.10. Exhibit 3.11 also includes the prices that would have been predicted for (associated with) the actual sales quantities by the regression

**Exhibit 3.11**
### TRIPPER WATER SKI MANUFACTURING COMPANY

**Worksheet for Determining Standard Error of Estimate**

| Period observed | Quantity sold/period, X | Price, Y | Estimated price per regression line, $\overline{Y}$ | $Y - \overline{Y}$ | $(Y - \overline{Y})^2$ |
|---|---|---|---|---|---|
| 1 | 1,000 | $120 | $123.20 | −$3.20 | 10.24 |
| 2 | 5,500 | 100 | 98.45 | +1.55 | 2.40 |
| 3 | 11,000 | 75 | 68.20 | +6.80 | 46.24 |
| 4 | 14,000 | 50 | 51.70 | −1.70 | 2.89 |
| 5 | 15,500 | 40 | 43.45 | −3.45 | 11.90 |

$$\Sigma(Y - \overline{Y})^2 = 73.67$$

line. Substituting the data from Exhibit 3.11 into the formula for the standard error results in:

$$SE = \sqrt{\frac{73.67}{5-2}},$$

$$SE = 4.96.$$

Assuming that any errors that may occur are random or normally distributed, the standard error of $4.96 would indicate that 68.27 percent of the time an actual price should be within plus or minus $4.96 of the price predicted by the regression line (demand curve).

For example, if you were seeking the price at which a quantity of 13,000 skis could be expected to be sold, the demand curve (line) would indicate $57.20.[7] Together with the information about the standard error associated with the line, you would then know that 68.27 percent of the time the price needed to sell this quantity of skis would be between $62.16 and $52.24. Obviously, the smaller the standard error, the more confidently you could predict a relationship using least-squares regression analysis.

Note that, if you are familiar with the statistical concepts of the normal distribution and the standard deviation, the standard error represents one standard deviation. Since two standard deviations cover 95.45 percent of all observations, 95.45 percent of the time 13,000 skis could be expected to be sold at a price between $67.12 and $47.28 ($57.20 plus and minus two standard errors/deviations of $4.96 each). Similarly, since three standard deviations cover 99.73 percent of all observations, 99.73 percent of the time 13,000 skis could be sold at a price between $72.08 and $42.32. Also note that, by reversing the $X$ and $Y$ variables, one can obtain data on the range of quantities associated with a particular price instead of the range of prices associated with a single quantity, as illustrated above.

Simple regression analysis using the least-squares approach is, of course, easier to perform using programmed equipment—computers or hand calculators. If you have access to a computer, you will undoubtedly find that a regression program is available from storage. The supervisor or teaching assistant in your computer lab will be able to assist you. Also, many of the more sophisticated hand calculators designed for business use are programmed for LSRA. The manual accompanying such calculators will describe the procedures for data entry. In either case, use of programmed equipment will save many minutes of otherwise tedious calculations and summarizations.[8]

---

[7]   $Y = aX + b$;   $Y =$ minus 0.005(13,000) plus 128.7;   $Y = \$57.20$.

[8]    Unfortunately, at this writing, most hand calculators that are programmed for easy determination of a least-squares regression line are **not** also programmed to provide the standard error. However, the square-root feature on most calculators makes determination of standard error relatively simple using the approach and formula described above.

# 4

# INVENTORY AND PRODUCTION PLANNING: THE PURCHASES BUDGET

## CHAPTER PREVIEW

The intention of this chapter is to provide you with the opportunity to become familiar with those budgeting steps that involve inventory. You can also become familiar with the issues and techniques involved in unit inventory control (the scheduling of production and purchase orders). In this chapter you can:

- Develop a working understanding of how the purchases budget summarizes planned purchases of raw materials and/or finished goods during the forthcoming year;

- Learn that projected requirements for purchases of finished goods (merchandiser) or for production of finished goods (manufacturer) are developed by combining sales budget data with both anticipated levels of stock on hand and desired inventory levels;

- Become acquainted with a manufacturer's process of production scheduling and with the use of economic manufacturing lot sizes;

- Discover how requirements for raw materials are derived from production schedules, and how these requirements, in turn, generate requirements for purchases of economic order quantities of raw materials;

- Become acquainted with the advantages and disadvantages of maintaining large inventories, and also with the reasoning leading to the use of economic manufacturing lot sizes and purchase order quantities;

- Learn of the significance of lead times to the scheduling and controlling process;

- Become familiar with the function of safety stocks and with the logic behind the ABC approach to inventory planning and control.

In the chapter appendix, you also can learn how to determine the economic order quantity for any particular item.

With this knowledge you will have a working understanding of the preparation of the inventory, production, and purchases budgets, and will be ready to move, in the next chapter, to the subsequent steps in the budgeting process involving the preparation of various operating expenditure budgets for the firm.

# WHAT MUST I PRODUCE THIS YEAR? WHAT SHOULD I BUY AND WHEN?

Remember from Chapter 2 that the budgeting process involves the detailed planning of activities for the forthcoming year. From such plans, a firm can anticipate its cash needs and make advance arrangements to ensure both solvency and adequate long-term financing. Budgets also serve during the forthcoming year to guide the firm's activities and to provide a basis for measuring performance.

For most businesses, the greatest single commitment of current resources or controllable expenditure relates to the acquisition of finished-goods inventory for sale to customers. Only a purely service firm is not vitally concerned with this item. In 1977, the General Motors Corporation reported that approximately 45.3 billion (not million) dollars were involved in the acquisition and sale of inventory. For GM in 1977, cost of goods sold represented approximately 81 percent of sales and almost 91 percent of all reported expenses before income taxes.[1]

Once sales have been budgeted, the next steps in the budgeting process involve planning desired inventory levels and purchases for the forthcoming year. Budgeted inventory levels indicate the level of investment that must be provided in this asset. Budgeted purchases provide the basis for projecting cash needs throughout the year for payments to suppliers. A merchandising firm is concerned only with finished-goods inventory planning since its required inputs to finished-goods inventory represent required purchases. A manufacturer, as first explained in Chapter 2, must be concerned with several additional areas.

To complete the budgeting of inventory levels and purchases, a manufacturer must also plan production of finished goods (and possibly component parts), together with planned work-in-process and raw materials inventory levels. The bulk of a manufacturer's purchases are of raw materials to be used in production. To provide you with the opportunity to become familiar with purchases budgeting for both a merchandiser and a manufacturer, the model Tripper Company is involved in selling both manufactured products (skis) and also purchased finished products (tow ropes).

It is early in October 19X1, and you, as the owner-president of Tripper, have just completed the necessary first step of the budgeting process—the sales budget for 19X2 (Exhibit 3.8 in Chapter 3). Since purchases for Tripper can involve the expenditure of well over $100,000 at the current level of operations, you are very interested in learning the requirements for the forthcoming year, and in assuring yourself that they are developed with reasonable accuracy. Your firm is now in a position to proceed with the next four budgeting

---

[1]    See 1977 Annual Report for General Motors Corporation and Consolidated Subsidiaries, page 16 and 17.

steps involved in completing the purchases budget:

Step 2: Preparation of the finished-goods inventory budget for 19X2.

Step 3: Preparation of the production schedule for 19X2.

Step 4: Preparation of the raw materials inventory budget for 19X2.

Step 5: Preparation of the purchases budget for 19X2.

From the sales budget (Step 1) you have necessary information to project revenues and cash inflows, and these steps will be covered in subsequent chapters. The purchases budget (Step 5) will provide the basis for projecting some of your cash outflows. The production schedule (Step 3) will also serve as a basis for projecting manufacturing costs and cash outflows, and these budgets will be covered in Chapter 5.

Preparation of the inventory, production, and purchases budgets is the responsibility of the vice-president for operations (or in some firms the vice-president for manufacturing). In this chapter you are asked to assume that you are working with the operations vice-president of the Tripper Company, and are responsible for completion of Steps 2 through 5. Specifically, you will be asked to prepare these budgets for the first three months (first quarter) of 19X2. Budgeting a single quarter should serve to provide you with an adequate understanding of these steps in the budgeting process. Budgeting the remaining three quarters of the year will merely be a repetition of the experience of the first quarter, but may involve different quantities, depending upon the seasonality of the business.

You have before you the following past and current budgets:

• Sales Budget for First Quarter of 19X1 (Exhibit 4.1).

• Finished-Goods Inventory Budget for First Quarter of 19X1 (Exhibit 4.2).

• Production Schedule for First Quarter of 19X1 (Exhibit 4.3).

• Raw Materials Inventory Budget for First Quarter of 19X1 (Exhibit 4.4).

• Purchases Budget for First Quarter of 19X1 (Exhibit 4.5).

• Sales Budget for First Quarter of 19X2 (Exhibit 4.6).

Before proceeding, you should study the 19X1 budget exhibits until you can see clearly how a specific sales demand generates a production order and ultimately a purchase order for necessary raw materials.

In studying the 19X1 data and tracing projected customer orders through to necessary purchase orders, you should note the use of *target inventories, economic (manufacturing) lot sizes,* and *economic (purchase) order quantities.* Target inventories result from inventory policy concerning the desirable levels of stock on hand to avoid out-of-stock conditions in case demand exceeds budget or replacement orders are delayed. Target inventories are also referred to as, or can include, *safety stocks,* and will be discussed later in the chapter.

**Exhibit 4.1**
TRIPPER WATER SKI MANUFACTURING COMPANY

**Sales Budget by Month for First Quarter 19X1**

|  | January | | February | | March | | Total first quarter | |
|---|---|---|---|---|---|---|---|---|
|  | Units | Dollars | Units | Dollars | Units | Dollars | Units | Dollars |
| Economy skis | 700 | $35,000 | 700 | $35,000 | 900 | $45,000 | 2,300 | $115,000 |
| Deluxe skis | 350 | 28,000 | 350 | 28,000 | 500 | 40,000 | 1,200 | 96,000 |
| Tow ropes | 300 | 3,000 | 300 | 3,000 | 400 | 4,000 | 1,000 | 10,000 |
| Total | | $66,000 | | $66,000 | | $89,000 | | $221,000 |

**Exhibit 4.2**

TRIPPER WATER SKI MANUFACTURING COMPANY

---

**Finished Goods Inventory Budget (Units) for First Quarter 19X1**

|  | January | February | March | Total first quarter |
|---|---|---|---|---|
| *Economy ski* | | | | |
| Sales budget | 700 | 700 | 900 | 2,300 |
| Target inventory* | 1,635 | 2,160 | 2,700 | 2,700 |
| Total requirements | 2,335 | 2,860 | 3,600 | 5,000 |
| Less:  Planned stock** | 1,300 | 1,635 | 2,160 | 1,300 |
| Necessary acquisitions | 1,035 | 1,225 | 1,440 | 3,700 |
| *Deluxe ski* | | | | |
| Sales budget | 350 | 350 | 500 | 1,200 |
| Target inventory*** | 700 | 700 | 700 | 1,600 |
| Total requirements | 1,050 | 1,050 | 1,200 | 2,800 |
| Less:  Planned stock** | 700 | 700 | 700 | 700 |
| Necessary acquisitions | 350 | 350 | 500 | 2,100 |
| *Tow rope* | | | | |
| Sales budget | 300 | 300 | 400 | 1,000 |
| Target inventory* | 720 | 960 | 1,200 | 1,200 |
| Total requirements | 1,020 | 1,260 | 1,600 | 2,200 |
| Less:  Planned stock** | 600 | 720 | 960 | 600 |
| Necessary acquisitions | 420 | 540 | 640 | 1,600 |

---

\* 60% of next 3 months' expected usage (demand)   \*\* Target inventory from prior period
\*\*\* 700 unit constant amount

**Exhibit 4.3**

TRIPPER WATER SKI MANUFACTURING COMPANY

---

**Production Schedule (Units to be Manufactured) for First Quarter 19X1**

|  | January | February | March | Total first quarter |
|---|---|---|---|---|
| *Economy ski* | | | | |
| Requirements[a] | 1,035 | 1,225 | 1,440 | 3,700 |
| From prior period[b] | 0 | 965 | 1,740 | |
| Current month needs | 1,035 | 260 | 0 | |
| Scheduled production[c] | 2,000 | 2,000 | 0 | 4,000 |
| *Deluxe ski* | | | | |
| Requirements[a] | 350 | 350 | 500 | 1,200 |
| From prior period[b] | 0 | 1,250 | 900 | |
| Current month needs | 350 | 0 | 0 | |
| Scheduled production[c] | 1,600 | 0 | 0 | 1,600 |

---

[a] From finished goods inventory budget
[b] From producing more than minimum requirements in prior period
[c] Production is scheduled in economic lot sizes (quantities)

## Exhibit 4.4
### TRIPPER WATER SKI MANUFACTURING COMPANY

**Raw Materials Inventory Budget (Units)**
**for the First Quarter 19X1**

|  | January | February | March | Total first quarter |
|---|---|---|---|---|
| **Wood (Economy ski)** | | | | |
| Requirements[a] | 2,000 | 2,000 | 0 | 4,000 |
| Carryover stock[b] | 2,300 | 300 | 300 | 2,300 |
| Needed current month | 0 | 1,700 | 0 | |
| Scheduled purchases[c] | 0 | 2,000 | 0 | 2,000 |
| Excess coverage | 300 | 300 | 300 | 300 |
| **Resin and cloth (deluxe ski)** | | | | |
| Requirements[a] | 1,600 | 0 | 0 | 1,600 |
| Carryover stock[b] | 800 | 200 | 200 | 800 |
| Needed current month | 800 | 0 | 0 | |
| Scheduled purchases[c] | 1,000 | 0 | 0 | 1,000 |
| Excess coverage | 200 | 200 | 200 | 200 |
| **Hardware sets (both skis)** | | | | |
| Requirements[a] | 3,600 | 2,000 | 0 | 5,600 |
| Carryover stock[b] | 1,000 | −100 | 400 | 1,000 |
| Needed current month | 2,600 | 2,100 | 0 | |
| Scheduled purchases[c] | 2,500 | 2,500 | 0 | 5,000 |
| Excess coverage | −100 | 400 | 400 | 400 |

[a] From production schedule
[b] From prior month's excess coverage
[c] Purchases are scheduled in economic order quantities

## Exhibit 4.5
### TRIPPER WATER SKI MANUFACTURING COMPANY

**Purchases Budget for First Quarter 19X1**

|  | January | | February | | March | | Total first quarter | |
|---|---|---|---|---|---|---|---|---|
|  | Units | Dollars | Units | Dollars | Units | Dollars | Units | Dollars |
| Wood ($3) | 0 | 0 | 2,000 | $ 6,000 | 0 | 0 | 2,000 | $ 6,000 |
| Resin and cloth ($6.20) | 1,000 | $ 6,200 | 0 | 0 | 0 | 0 | 1,000 | 6,200 |
| Hardware sets ($2.50 | 2.500 | 6,250 | 2,500 | 6,250 | 0 | 0 | 5,000 | 12,500 |
| Tow ropes ($5)* | 1,000 | 5,000 | 0 | 0 | 1,000 | $5,000 | 2,000 | 10,000 |
| Total | | $17,450 | | $12,250 | | $5,000 | | $34,700 |

* Scheduled purchases based on 1,000-unit EOQ and requirements from finished goods inventory budget (Exhibit 4.2).

For reasons covered below, it is often more economical for a firm to re-order items in batches or quantities that may exceed immediate needs. This use of economic order/reorder quantities applies not only to the purchase from suppliers of finished goods and raw materials, but also to quantities of items included in a single production order or run. An economic order quantity applying to production is often termed an economic lot size. At this point you need only observe that Tripper employs target inventories and economic order quantities in inventory scheduling.

In addition to the first six exhibits, you may assume the following information necessary to complete inventory and purchases budgeting for the first quarter of 19X2:

**1.** The 19X2 beginning inventories (and expected 19X1 ending inventories) will be:

|  | Units |
|---|---:|
| Finished economy skis | 1,700 |
| Finished deluxe skis | 775 |
| Tow ropes | 1,200 |
| Work-in-process | Zero |
| Wood (each unit sufficient for one ski) | 300 |
| Resin and cloth (each unit sufficient for one ski) | 400 |
| Hardware sets (bindings and skegs for one ski) | 100 |

**2.** The 19X2 finished goods target inventory policy is to plan to have on hand, as a safety stock, additional items (beyond current month's sales projections) equivalent to the next month's anticipated sales. Note that this represents a change from the 19X1 policy that required a target inventory equivalent to 60 percent of the sum of the next three months' anticipated sales. Target inventories for March are 1,250 for economy skis, 750 for deluxe skis, and 550 for tow ropes. The others may be determined from the data given.

**Exhibit 4.6**

TRIPPER WATER SKI MANUFACTURING COMPANY

**Sales Budget for First Quarter 19X2**

|  | January | | February | | March | | Total first quarter | |
|---|---|---|---|---|---|---|---|---|
|  | Units | Dollars | Units | Dollars | Units | Dollars | Units | Dollars |
| Economy skis | 750 | $37,500 | 750 | $37,500 | 1,000 | $50,000 | 2,500 | $125,000 |
| Deluxe skis | 400 | 32,000 | 400 | 32,000 | 550 | 44,000 | 1,350 | 108,000 |
| Tow ropes | 325 | 3,250 | 325 | 3,250 | 450 | 4,500 | 1,100 | 11,000 |
| Total |  | $72,750 |  | $72,750 |  | $98,500 |  | $244,000 |
| Percent |  | 30 |  | 30 |  | 40 |  | 100 |

**3.** 19X2 economic lot sizes for manufacturing and economic order quantities for purchasing:

|  | ELS/EOQ Units |
| --- | --- |
| Manufacturing economy skis | 2,100 |
| Manufacturing deluxe skis | 1,700 |
| Purchasing wood | 2,100 |
| Purchasing resin and cloth | 1,700 |
| Purchasing hardware sets | 3,800 |
| Purchasing tow ropes | 1,100 |

Note that these quantities represent a change from those used in planning for 19X1. They reflect the increased sales demand anticipated for 19X2. The actual determination of specific economic manufacturing lot sizes and economic purchase order quantities will be discussed later in this chapter. For now you need only understand that, when there is need for more production or purchasing, it should be satisfied with production/purchase orders in these quantities.

**4.** Anticipated costs of items that are purchased from suppliers (unchanged from 19X1):

|  | Costs per unit purchased |
| --- | --- |
| Wood | $3.00 |
| Resin and cloth | 6.20 |
| Hardware sets | 2.50 |
| Tow ropes | 5.00 |

### Preparing the Finished-Goods Inventory Budget

Your first necessary action is to prepare the finished-goods inventory budget for the first quarter of 19X2. For 19X2 you have the following information related to economy skis:

|  | January | February | March | First quarter |
| --- | --- | --- | --- | --- |
| Budgeted sales | 750 | 750 | 1,000 | 2,500 |
| Target inventory | 750 | 1,000 | 1,250 | 1,250 |

Using the 19X1 finished-goods inventory budget as a guide, you should complete the first-quarter 19X2 economy ski budget on a separate piece of paper before proceeding.

Your correct first-quarter budget for economy skis should appear as:

|  | January | February | March | First Quarter |
|---|---|---|---|---|
| Budgeted sales | 750 | 750 | 1,000 | 2,500 |
| Target inventory | 750 | 1,000 | 1,250 | 1,250 |
| Total requirements | 1,500 | 1,750 | 2,250 | 3,750 |
| Less: Planned stock | 1,700 | 950 | 1,000 | 1,700 |
| Necessary acquisitions | 0 | 800 | 1,250 | 2,050 |

Note that planned stock on hand in the current month is normally the same amount as the target inventory from the prior month. The exception occurs when quantities on hand exceed current total requirements (sales plus target inventory for the following month). At the end of January, carryover inventory from the prior year amounted to 200 extra units above January total requirements. Therefore 950 units (750 January target plus 200 excess) were already available in February to meet requirements.

### Exhibit 4.7
### TRIPPER WATER SKI MANUFACTURING COMPANY

#### Finished Goods Inventory Budget (Units) for the First Quarter 19X2

|  | January | February | March | First quarter |
|---|---|---|---|---|
| *Economy skis* | | | | |
| Budgeted sales | 750 | 750 | 1,000 | 2,500 |
| Target inventory* | 750 | 1,000 | 1,250 | 1,250 |
| Total requirements | 1,500 | 1,750 | 2,250 | 3,750 |
| Less: Planned stock | 1,700 | 950 | 1,000 | 1,700 |
| Necessary acquisitions | 0 | 800 | 1,250 | 2,050 |
| *Deluxe skis* | | | | |
| Budgeted sales | 400 | 400 | 550 | 1,350 |
| Target inventory* | 400 | 550 | 750 | 750 |
| Total requirements | 800 | 950 | 1,300 | 2,100 |
| Less: Planned stock | 775 | 400 | 550 | 775 |
| Necessary acquisitions | 25 | 550 | 750 | 1,325 |
| *Tow ropes* | | | | |
| Budgeted sales | 325 | 325 | 450 | 1,100 |
| Target inventory* | 325 | 450 | 550 | 550 |
| Total requirements | 650 | 775 | 1,000 | 1,650 |
| Less: Planned stock | 1,200 | 875 | 550 | 1,200 |
| Necessary acquisitions | 0 | 0 | 450 | 450 |

* Amount of subsequent month's anticipated sales usage

Also note that not all of the amounts shown for the first quarter represent sums of monthly data. Instead they represent amounts that would be used if the firm were budgeting only by quarter and not in detail by month:

$$
\begin{array}{rl}
2{,}500 = & \text{Sum of monthly sales} \\
+1{,}250 = & \text{Target inventory at } \textbf{end of quarter} \\
\hline
3{,}750 = & \text{Total requirements for the quarter} \\
-1{,}700 = & \text{Planned stock at } \textbf{beginning of quarter} \\
\hline
2{,}050 = & \text{Necessary acquisitions}
\end{array}
$$

It will serve to reinforce your learning of the inventory budgeting process if you will first complete, on a separate sheet of paper, the first-quarter 19X2 budgets for deluxe skis and for tow ropes, before proceeding.

You adequately understand the finished-goods inventory budgeting process if your budget is the same as Exhibit 4.7. The completed finished-goods inventory budget determines or establishes both demand on manufacturing (for production of economy and deluxe skis) and also demand on purchasing (for purchase of finished tow ropes).

### Preparing the Preliminary Production Schedule

The third step in the budgeting process for a manufacturer involves establishing the production schedule for the forthcoming year. In the Tripper Company example, you are now asked to prepare, on a separate sheet of paper, such a schedule for the first three months of 19X2. Use the 19X1 schedule (Exhibit 4.3) as a model. Remember you may assume beginning work-in-process inventory of zero units. Also remember that when production is planned, orders of a standard economic lot size (quantity) are scheduled. 19X2 lot sizes are 2,100 units per lot for economy skis and 1,700 units per lot for deluxe skis. You should prepare this simple production schedule to verify your initial understanding of the scheduling process. You should then compare your solution to Exhibit 4.8.

Exhibit 4.8 provides the tentative schedule for all manufacturing to take place in the Tripper factory during the first three months of 19X2. Compare Exhibits 4.3 and 4.8. Note that, in spite of a planned ten-percent increase in 19X2 sales over 19X1, and in spite of slightly larger lot sizes reflecting this increased usage, total planned first-quarter production in 19X2 is significantly below that scheduled for 19X1. Can you explain this apparent paradox?

The source of this temporary reduction in planned manufacturing activity is the change in finished-goods target inventory policy. Remember that, during 19X1, finished-goods target inventories (see discussion of safety stocks later in this chapter) were maintained at 60 percent of the sum of the subsequent three months' anticipated sales. For 19X2 you are budgeting a reduced quantity of target inventory (reduced to next month's anticipated sales). The firm, therefore, started 19X2 with more units on hand than the newly desired minimum inventory. Schedules for additional items are, therefore, reduced while this excess quantity is being "sold off."

Note also on Exhibit 4.8 that no production is being scheduled for March of 19X2. Would you like being a factory employee of the Tripper Company? Would it be intelligent for Tripper to lay off their skilled production workers for the month of March?

**Exhibit 4.8**

TRIPPER WATER SKI MANUFACTURING COMPANY

**Preliminary Production Schedule**
**for First Quarter 19X2**

|  | January | February | March | Total first quarter |
|---|---|---|---|---|
| *Economy ski* |  |  |  |  |
| Requirements | 0 | 800 | 1,250 | 2,050 |
| From prior month | 0 | 0 | 1,300 |  |
| Current month needs | 0 | 800 | 0 |  |
| Scheduled production | 0 | 2,100 | 0 | 2,100 |
| *Deluxe ski* |  |  |  |  |
| Requirements | 25 | 550 | 750 | 1,325 |
| From prior month | 0 | 1,675 | 1,125 |  |
| Current month needs | 25 | 0 | 0 |  |
| Scheduled production | 1,700 | 0 | 0 | 1,700 |

Generally common sense on the part of management (and union pressure) dictates that production schedules be more reasonably balanced throughout the year. Within limits of physical storage and financial capacity, the costs of advancing some production schedules and having additional funds tied up in inventory are often less than the costs of employee ill-will and employee turnover (hiring and training costs). Further exploration of this problem is beyond the scope of this text. It is usually covered in business courses and texts devoted to production or operations management. At this point you need only be aware that a final production schedule is often adjusted to provide more uniform work load throughout the year.

You may have been confused by the separation of the finished-goods budget and the production schedule, and especially by carryover stock of finished items (resulting from scheduling economic lot sizes instead of minimum quantities needed in a particular month) appearing on the production schedule rather than on the inventory budget. This distinction is maintained by many firms to facilitate adjusting the production schedule to actual current demand for finished goods inventory. The budgets could be combined as in the following illustration for deluxe skis:

| | January | February | March | Total first quarter |
|---|---|---|---|---|
| Budgeted sales | 400 | 400 | 550 | 1,350 |
| Target inventory | 400 | 550 | 750 | 750 |
| Total requirements | 800 | 950 | 1,300 | 2,100 |
| Planned stock* | 775 | 2,075 | 1,675 | 775 |
| Necessary acquisitions | 25 | −1,125 | −375 | 1,325 |
| Scheduled orders | 1,700 | 0 | 0 | 1,700 |
| Excess coverage | 1,675 | 1,125 | 375 | 375 |

The separation of the finished-goods inventory budget and the production schedule will be maintained throughout this text in order to focus your attention upon the production schedule as a distinct entity. The combined approach will be illustrated further with the raw-materials inventory budget (below).

Exhibit 4.9 provides the complete finished-goods inventory budget for 19X2. Exhibit 4.10 provides the complete final production schedule for the year after adjustment to provide for balancing of work loads. The final schedule still reflects the extreme seasonality of Tripper's business. Tripper might be well advised to consider expanding its product line to include products with heavy demand during the low months for water skis. Note that, with completion of this schedule, the firm is now in a position to determine its:

> Raw materials requirements and raw materials budget (below)
> Purchases budget (below)
> Direct labor budget (covered in Chapter 5)
> Manufacturing overhead budget (covered in Chapter 5)

## Preparing the Raw-Materials Inventory Budget

Preparing the raw-materials inventory budget is the fourth step in the budgeting process for a manufacturer. For the Tripper Company, you are now asked to prepare, on a separate sheet of paper, such a budget for the first three months of 19X2. Use the 19X1 budget (Exhibit 4.4) as a model. You have been given the following information:

| | Beginning inventory (units) | 19X2 Purchase economic order quantities (units) |
|---|---|---|
| Wood | 300 | 2,100 |
| Resin and cloth | 400 | 1,700 |
| Hardware sets | 100 | 3,800 |

---

* Planned stock equals the sum of prior month's target inventory and any excess coverage.

## Exhibit 4.9

## TRIPPER WATER SKI MANUFACTURING COMPANY

### Finished Goods Inventory Budget (Units)
### for the Year 19X2

| | Budgeted sales | Target inventory | Total require- ments | Less: Planned stock | Necessary acquisitions |
|---|---|---|---|---|---|
| *Economy skis* | | | | | |
| Jan | 750 | 750 | 1,500 | 1,700 | 0 |
| Feb | 750 | 1,000 | 1,750 | 950 | 800 |
| Mar | 1,000 | 1,250 | 2,250 | 1,000 | 1,250 |
| First quarter | 2,500 | 1,250 | 3,750 | 1,700 | 2,050 |
| Apr | 1,250 | 1,750 | 3,000 | 1,250 | 1,750 |
| May | 1,750 | 2,000 | 3,750 | 1,750 | 2,000 |
| Jun | 2,000 | 2,000 | 4,000 | 2,000 | 2,000 |
| Second quarter | 5,000 | 2,000 | 7,000 | 1,250 | 5,750 |
| Jul | 2,000 | 1,200 | 3,200 | 2,000 | 1,200 |
| Aug | 1,200 | 800 | 2,000 | 1,200 | 800 |
| Sep | 800 | 650 | 1,450 | 800 | 650 |
| Third quarter | 4,000 | 650 | 4,650 | 2,000 | 2,650 |
| Oct | 650 | 400 | 1,050 | 650 | 400 |
| Nov | 400 | 250 | 650 | 400 | 250 |
| Dec | 250 | 850 | 1,100 | 250 | 850 |
| Fourth quarter | 1,300 | 850 | 2,150 | 650 | 1,500 |
| Year | 12,800 | | | | 11,950 |
| *Deluxe skis* | | | | | |
| Jan | 400 | 400 | 800 | 775 | 25 |
| Feb | 400 | 550 | 950 | 400 | 550 |
| Mar | 550 | 750 | 1,300 | 550 | 750 |
| First quarter | 1,350 | 750 | 2,100 | 775 | 1,325 |
| Apr | 750 | 1,050 | 1,800 | 750 | 1,050 |
| May | 1,050 | 1,200 | 2,250 | 1,050 | 1,200 |
| Jun | 1,200 | 1,000 | 2,200 | 1,200 | 1,000 |
| Second quarter | 3,000 | 1,000 | 4,000 | 750 | 3,250 |
| Jul | 1,000 | 600 | 1,600 | 1,000 | 600 |
| Aug | 600 | 400 | 1,000 | 600 | 400 |
| Sep | 400 | 350 | 750 | 400 | 350 |
| Third quarter | 2,000 | 350 | 2,350 | 1,000 | 1,350 |
| Oct | 350 | 200 | 550 | 350 | 200 |
| Nov | 200 | 150 | 350 | 200 | 150 |
| Dec | 150 | 450 | 600 | 150 | 450 |
| Fourth quarter | 700 | 450 | 1,150 | 350 | 800 |
| Year | 7,050 | | | | 6,725 |

## Exhibit 4.9 Continued

| | Budgeted sales | Target inventory | Total require- ments | Less: Planned stock | Necessary acquisitions |
|---|---|---|---|---|---|
| *Tow ropes* | | | | | |
| Jan | 325 | 325 | 650 | 1,200 | 0 |
| Feb | 325 | 450 | 775 | 875 | 0 |
| Mar | 450 | 550 | 1,000 | 550 | 450 |
| First quarter | 1,100 | 550 | 1,650 | 1,200 | 450 |
| Apr | 550 | 770 | 1,320 | 550 | 770 |
| May | 770 | 880 | 1,650 | 770 | 880 |
| Jun | 880 | 700 | 1,580 | 880 | 700 |
| Second quarter | 2,200 | 700 | 2,900 | 550 | 2,350 |
| Jul | 700 | 600 | 1,300 | 700 | 600 |
| Aug | 600 | 400 | 1,000 | 600 | 400 |
| Sep | 400 | 400 | 800 | 400 | 400 |
| Third quarter | 1,700 | 400 | 2,100 | 700 | 1,400 |
| Oct | 400 | 350 | 750 | 400 | 350 |
| Nov | 350 | 250 | 600 | 350 | 250 |
| Dec | 250 | 360 | 610 | 250 | 360 |
| Fourth quarter | 1,000 | 360 | 1,360 | 400 | 960 |
| Year | 6,000 | | | | 5,160 |

Also remember that it is necessary to *explode* the requirements for a given production order into its required components (wood or resin, plus cloth and hardware sets). Remember that some components or raw material (hardware sets, in this example) may be used by more than one production item.[2] Finally, since current company target inventory policy for raw materials is zero or none, you may vary purchase order quantities from the EOQ by up to 20 percent in order to achieve this goal. You should prepare this simple raw materials budget to verify your initial understanding of the scheduling process where requirements and covering schedules are combined on the same budget.

Exhibit 4.11 is the completed raw materials inventory budget for the first quarter of 19X2. Note on Exhibits 4.4 and 4.11 that, for both 19X1 and 19X2, Tripper is planning no target inventory or safety stock for raw-material items. A target inventory might be desirable to avoid delays if an additional production order was needed on a rush basis, or to replace materials that might be

---

[2]    More complex products each have a formal list of required components called an engineering bill of material. These lists must be exploded to generate component requirements. In still more involved situations, a bill of material for a finished assembly can explode into both components and subassemblies. Some components and subassemblies may be purchased. Others may be manufactured and will require successive levels of scheduling and exploding requirements until the level of purchased components or raw material is reached for all items.

## Exhibit 4.10

### TRIPPER WATER SKI MANUFACTURING COMPANY

**Final Production Schedule (Units)**
**for the Year 19X2**

|  |  | Requirements | Carryover stock | Current needs | Scheduled production |
|---|---|---|---|---|---|
| *First Quarter* | | | | | |
| Jan | Econ | 0 | 0 | 0 | 0 |
| Feb | Econ | 800 | 0 | 800 | 2,100 |
| Mar | Econ | 1,250 | 1,300 | 0 | 2,100* |
| Jan | Dlx | 25 | 0 | 25 | 1,700 |
| Feb | Dlx | 550 | 1,675 | 0 | 0 |
| Mar | Dlx | 750 | 1,125 | 0 | 0 |
| *Second Quarter* | | | | | |
| Apr | Econ | 1,750 | 2,150 | 0 | 0 |
| May | Econ | 2,000 | 400 | 1,600 | 2,100 |
| Jun | Econ | 2,000 | 500 | 1,500 | 2,100 |
| Apr | Dlx | 1,050 | 375 | 675 | 1,700 |
| May | Dlx | 1,200 | 1,025 | 175 | 1,700 |
| Jun | Dlx | 1,000 | 1,525 | 0 | 0 |
| *Third Quarter* | | | | | |
| Jul | Econ | 1,200 | 600 | 600 | 2,100 |
| Aug | Econ | 800 | 1,500 | 0 | 0 |
| Sep | Econ | 650 | 700 | 0 | 0 |
| Jul | Dlx | 600 | 525 | 75 | 1,700 |
| Aug | Dlx | 400 | 1,625 | 0 | 0 |
| Sep | Dlx | 350 | 1,225 | 0 | 0 |
| *Fourth Quarter* | | | | | |
| Oct | Econ | 400 | 50 | 350 | 2,100 |
| Nov | Econ | 250 | 1,750 | 0 | 0 |
| Dec | Econ | 850 | 1,500 | 0 | 0 |
| Oct | Dlx | 200 | 875 | 0 | 0 |
| Nov | Dlx | 150 | 675 | 0 | 0 |
| Dec | Dlx | 450 | 525 | 0 | 0 |

* Advanced from April to partially balance workload

damaged beyond repair on existing orders in production. Target inventories and safety stocks will be discussed later in this chapter. The Tripper illustration is chosen to familiarize you with scheduling when target inventories are not desired.

Exhibit 4.12 is the complete raw-materials inventory budget for 19X2. Together with requirements for purchased finished products, it provides the basis for preparing the firm's purchases budget.

**Exhibit 4.11**

## TRIPPER WATER SKI MANUFACTURING COMPANY

### Raw Materials Inventory Budget (Units), First Quarter 19X2

|  | January | February | March | Total first quarter |
|---|---|---|---|---|
| *Wood* | | | | |
| Requirements | 0 | 2,100 | 2,100 | 4,200 |
| Carryover stock | 300 | 300 | 0 | 300 |
| Needed, current month | 0 | 1,800 | 2,100 | 3,900 |
| Scheduled purchases | 0 | 1,800[a] | 2,100[a] | 3,900 |
| Excess coverage | 300 | 0 | 0 | 0 |
| *Resin and cloth* | | | | |
| Requirements | 1,700 | 0 | 0 | 1,700 |
| Carryover stock | 400 | 60 | 60 | 400 |
| Needed, current month | 1,300 | 0 | 0 | 1,300 |
| Scheduled purchases | 1,360[b] | 0 | 0 | 1,360 |
| Excess coverage | 60 | 60 | 60 | 60 |
| *Hardware sets* | | | | |
| Requirements | 1,700 | 2,100 | 2,100 | 5,900 |
| Carryover stock | 100 | 2,100 | 0 | 100 |
| Needed, current month | 1,600 | 0 | 2,100 | 5,800 |
| Scheduled purchases | 3,700[c] | 0 | 3,800[c] | 7,500 |
| Excess coverage | 2,100 | 0 | 1,700 | 1,700 |

[a] Economic Order Quantity = 2,100 ± 20 percent
[b] Economic Order Quantity = 1,700 ± 20 percent
[c] Economic Order Quantity = 3,800 ± 20 percent

## Preparing the Purchases Budget

The next logical (fifth) step in the budgeting process is the preparation of the purchases budget. For the Tripper Company you should complete this budget for the first quarter of 19X2. Use the 19X1 budget (Exhibit 4.5) as a model. Remember you are also given the following information:

|  | Unit costs | 19X2 Purchase economic order quantity |
|---|---|---|
| Wood | $3.00 | 2,100 ± 20 percent |
| Resin and cloth | 6.20 | 1,700 ± 20 percent |
| Hardware sets | 2.50 | 3,800 ± 20 percent |
| Tow ropes | 5.00 | 1,000 ± 20 percent |

Compare your solution to the first quarter's data on Exhibit 4.13. Exhibit 4.13 is the completed purchases budget for 19X2. This budget is the first of a series

**Exhibit 4.12**

TRIPPER WATER SKI MANUFACTURING COMPANY

**Raw Materials Inventory Budget (Units)**
**for the Year 19X2**

|  | Requirements | Carryover stock | Current needs | Scheduled purchases |
|---|---|---|---|---|
| *Wood* | | | | |
| Jan | 0 | 300 | 0 | 0 |
| Feb | 2,100 | 300 | 1,800 | 1,800* |
| Mar | 2,100 | 0 | 2,100 | 2,100* |
| Apr | 0 | 0 | 0 | 0 |
| May | 2,100 | 0 | 2,100 | 2,100 |
| Jun | 2,100 | 0 | 2,100 | 2,100 |
| Jul | 2,100 | 0 | 2,100 | 2,100 |
| Aug | 0 | 0 | 0 | 0 |
| Sep | 0 | 0 | 0 | 0 |
| Oct | 2,100 | 0 | 2,100 | 2,100 |
| Nov | 0 | 0 | 0 | 0 |
| Dec | 0 | 0 | 0 | 0 |

* Economic Order Quantity 2,100 ± 20 percent

| | | | | |
|---|---|---|---|---|
| *Resin and cloth* | | | | |
| Jan | 1,700 | 400 | 1,300 | 1,360* |
| Feb | 0 | 60 | 0 | 0 |
| Mar | 0 | 60 | 0 | 0 |
| Apr | 1,700 | 60 | 1,640 | 1,640* |
| May | 1,700 | 0 | 1,700 | 1,700 |
| Jun | 0 | 0 | 0 | 0 |
| Jul | 1,700 | 0 | 1,700 | 1,700 |
| Aug | 0 | 0 | 0 | 0 |
| Sep | 0 | 0 | 0 | 0 |
| Oct | 0 | 0 | 0 | 0 |
| Nov | 0 | 0 | 0 | 0 |
| Dec | 0 | 0 | 0 | 0 |

* Economic Order Quantity = 1,700 ± 20 percent

| | | | | |
|---|---|---|---|---|
| *Hardware sets* | | | | |
| Jan | 1,700 | 100 | 1,600 | 3,700* |
| Feb | 2,100 | 2,100 | 0 | 0 |
| Mar | 2,100 | 0 | 2,100 | 3,800* |
| Apr | 1,700 | 1,700 | 0 | 0 |
| May | 3,800 | 0 | 3,800 | 3,800* |
| Jun | 2,100 | 0 | 2,100 | 3,000* |
| Jul | 3,800 | 900 | 2,900 | 3,000* |
| Aug | 0 | 100 | 0 | 0 |
| Sep | 0 | 100 | 0 | 0 |
| Oct | 2,100 | 100 | 2,000 | 3,000 |
| Nov | 0 | 1,000 | 0 | 0 |
| Dec | 0 | 1,000 | 0 | 0 |

* Economic Order Quantity = 3,800 ± 20 percent

**Exhibit 4.13**

TRIPPER WATER SKI MANUFACTURING COMPANY

Purchases Budget for the Year 19X2

| | Wood | | Resin and cloth | | Hardware sets | | Tow ropes | | Total |
| | Units | Dollars | Units | Dollars | Units | Dollars | Units | Dollars | dollars |
|------|-------|---------|-------|---------|-------|---------|-------|---------|---------|
| Jan | 0 | 0 | 1,360 | $ 8,432 | 3,700 | $ 9,250 | 0 | 0 | $ 17,682 |
| Feb | 1,800 | $ 5,400 | 0 | 0 | 0 | 0 | 0 | 0 | 5,400 |
| Mar | 2,100 | 6,300 | 0 | 0 | 3,800 | 9,500 | 1,220 | $ 6,100 | 21,900 |
| Apr | 0 | 0 | 1,640 | 10,168 | 0 | 0 | 0 | 0 | 10,168 |
| May | 2,100 | 6,300 | 1,700 | 10,540 | 3,800 | 9,500 | 880 | 4,400 | 30,740 |
| Jun | 2,100 | 6,300 | 0 | 0 | 3,000 | 7,500 | 1,300 | 6,500 | 20,300 |
| Jul | 2,100 | 6,300 | 1,700 | 10,540 | 3,000 | 7,500 | 0 | 0 | 24,340 |
| Aug | 0 | 0 | 0 | 0 | 0 | 0 | 800 | 4,000 | 4,000 |
| Sep | 0 | 0 | 0 | 0 | 0 | 0 | 0 | 0 | 0 |
| Oct | 2,100 | 6,300 | 0 | 0 | 3,000 | 7,500 | 960 | 4,800 | 18,600 |
| Nov | 0 | 0 | 0 | 0 | 0 | 0 | 0 | 0 | 0 |
| Dec | 0 | 0 | 0 | 0 | 0 | 0 | 0 | 0 | 0 |
| Total | 12,300 | $36,900 | 6,400 | $39,680 | 20,300 | $50,750 | 5,160 | $25,800 | $153,130 |

to be prepared in subsequent steps which provide information related to expected cash outflows (requirements) by month during the coming year. The purchases budget completes those budgeting steps for the Tripper Company that are relevant to this chapter. You can now proceed to generalize on your knowledge, and to learn about more involved aspects of inventory and production planning that were deliberately excluded from the simplified Tripper example.

## INVENTORY OBJECTIVES

The fact that a firm's inventory (on hand and sold to customers) may represent a most significant cost should be intuitively obvious and be reinforced by the General Motors data cited earlier. Accountants, in recognition of this significance, devote special attention to the measurement and reporting of inventory or product costs, as you have learned in financial accounting and in Chapter 1. But have you ever stopped to really consider such questions as:

1. Why does a firm plan to carry inventory?
2. Can a firm have too little or too much inventory?
3. How can managers determine the best or most desirable level of stock on hand?

It is not difficult to see that a firm dealing in standard (as opposed to special-order) products or merchandise must carry some inventory. Customers are not accustomed to planning and ordering months ahead their needs for standard items. If a supplier is out of stock, the customer will often turn to a competitor; and the particular sale, if not the customer's future business, may be forever lost.

Sometimes overlooked is the cost of carrying **any** inventory. Several costs are involved and will be discussed below. One of the more obvious is the interest cost of money tied up or invested. As of 12/31/77 General Motors reported inventory on hand costing over seven billion dollars. Even assuming a low interest cost of six percent, seven billion dollars of inventory investment would represent an annual interest cost of $420,000,000. If GM could reduce inventory by just ten percent without impairing sales, it could save more than 42 million dollars a year (interest and other costs) and increase its earnings before taxes by this amount.

The dual objectives of inventory planning and control are to have adequate stock on hand and to have a minimum investment in inventory. Achievement of these objectives is complicated by the fact that they conflict. They work against each other, and a desirable trade-off or compromise must be sought.

There are significant advantages to carrying larger inventories, which can be thought of in terms of potential costs savings:

1. There is a lower risk or cost of *stock-out* (being out of stock on hand of a given item). Stock-outs can cause production delays, customer dissatisfaction, and lost sales.
2. There is more flexibility in scheduling production and purchasing to balance work loads.
3. There are fewer costly rush-order crises when sales exceed plan.
4. Larger replacement orders allow for lower ordering cost (paper work, factory setup, transportation) and possible quantity discounts on purchases.

There are significant disadvantages to carrying larger inventories, and these disadvantages represent potential additional costs:

1. Costs of capital (funds) tied up in inventory.
2. Storage or space costs (rent, depreciation, utilities, security, plus insurance and property taxes).
3. Risk (cost) of loss through deterioration and obsolescence.

Essentially, planning inventory levels involves a trade-off or compromise between the costs of having too much inventory and the cost of having too little. This balance is further complicated by the existence of lead times and the costs (personnel and paper work) of planning and controlling inventories.

## LEAD TIMES

The term *lead time* refers to the amount of time between the date on which something is ordered and the date when it is finished and available. In the earlier simplified Tripper Company example, it was assumed that all lead times were zero or, at least, insignificant. If 800 economy skis were needed in finished goods for February sales demand, it was assumed the necessary items could be purchased in February, the skis manufactured in February, and the finished skis available for sale in February. Did you recognize this unrealistic assumption when you were preparing the Tripper budgets above?

Perhaps more realistic assumptions would be that:

1. skis for February sales should arrive in the finished goods storeroom by February 1;
2. a production order of skis would require one month from start to completion in the factory; and
3. materials would require two months from the time the purchase order was placed until they had arrived and passed through necessary inspection.

When would scheduling have to take place in order that the skis would be ready for sale on February 1? You are correct and have a grasp of the lead-time concept if you realized that the scheduling process could take place no

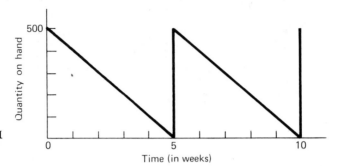

**Figure 4.1**

later than November 1 of the preceding year. The February 19X2 sales budget would generate a production run in January and incoming purchases in December of 19X1. Lead times require that items be ordered before you run out of stock. In effect, to avoid stock-out you must order when the quantity on hand gets down to the level equal to the expected daily (or weekly) usage times the days (or weeks) of reorder lead time. This level is known as the *minimum reorder point*. It can be illustrated as in Fig. 4.1.

In this illustration it is assumed that a reorder quantity of 500 units is in stock, and usage (either by production or in sales to customers) is 100 units per week. If the lead time to reorder was two weeks, what would be the minimum reorder point (quantity)?

Figure 4.2 shows that the minimum reorder point would be 200 units. 200 units with a usage of 100 per week would represent a two-week supply, just enough time for a new order to arrive **provided** there were no delays in reordering and no increase in usage.

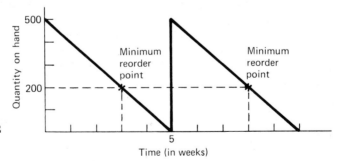

**Figure 4.2**

## SAFETY STOCK

Since reordering delays do occur, and since usage is neither perfectly predictable nor always uniform, a firm may run too great a risk (cost) of stock-out if it operates with minimum reorder points. Most firms will include in their *reorder point* quantity some amount of safety stock. The purpose of safety stock is to provide a cushion or spare amount on hand to cover increased usage and/or normal usage while a reorder is delayed.

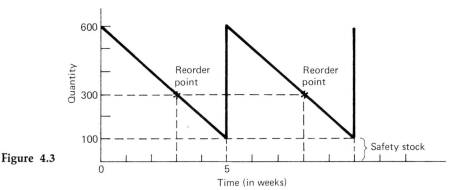

**Figure 4.3**

Figure 4.3 assumes the same conditions as before except that the firm has chosen to maintain a safety stock of 100 units or one week's usage. If there were no unanticipated increases in usage and no reordering delays, the safety stock quantity would never be used.[3] It provides some safety or insurance against stock-out resulting from unanticipated events. The actual reorder point (quantity) would therefore also include the safety stock amount:

Reorder point (quantity) = Minimum reorder point + Safety stock

where

Minimum reorder point = Usage per period × Lead time in period.

Safety stock costs money. Here again the firm is balancing two opposing costs and seeking the minimum total effective cost. Safety stocks generate all of the *inventory-carrying costs* referred to earlier (space costs, insurance costs, tax costs, deterioration and obsolescence costs, and capital costs on funds invested). Many firms find inventory carrying cost totals 25–40 percent of the cost of an item per year! Having no safety stock, on the other hand, can result in stock-out costs (lost sales, customer dissatisfaction, and high costs of rush replacement orders). The effect of these two costs can be visualized as in Fig. 4.4.

Note that the graph in Fig. 4.4 is comparing dollars of cost (vertical axis) to quantities of units carried in safety stock. As the amount of safety stock increases, the probability decreases that an unanticipated demand increase or delayed replacement order will result in stock-out before remedial action can be taken. Costs of stock-out, therefore, decrease with larger and larger safety factors (quantities). At the same time, as safety stocks increase the inventory carrying costs increase, reflecting more inventory on hand. To minimize total costs, the firm should carry a safety factor equal to the quantity SQ corre-

---

[3]   Note that in this hypothetical situation the safety stock **quantity** would not be used. The actual items in safety stock would be replaced with each incoming order (FIFO) to avoid deterioration or spoilage.

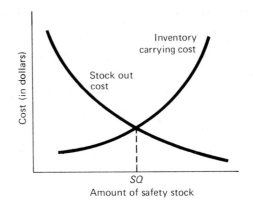

**Figure 4.4**

sponding to the intersection of the two curves. At SQ the sum of the two separate costs is the lowest.

In practice, ideal safety stock quantities (SQ) are difficult to calculate precisely since the risks and cost of stock-outs are hard to pinpoint. Inventory carrying charge will occur with reasonable certainty, but the actual cost of customer dissatisfaction or lost business, even if readily measurable, occurs only if there is a breakdown in the planned reorder system. Statistical models beyond the scope of this text have been developed in an attempt to pinpoint desirable safety stocks. At this stage, you need only understand the function of safety stocks (or target inventories, in the Tripper Company), and the fact that they necessarily and desirably have the effect of reducing inventory turnover.

## ABC INVENTORY CONTROL

Earlier you were reminded that one of the other costs associated with inventory was the cost (personnel and paperwork) of planning and controlling inventory quantities on hand and on order. Given the complexities introduced by lead times, safety stocks, and reorder points, can you imagine for a firm with thousands of parts the costs of keeping records and monitoring every item every day to see if either:

- the reorder point has been reached, or
- usage is changing significantly, and the reorder point requires recalculation?

Even those firms that have unit inventory control on computers find that attempting to devote equal attention to each item may prove both inefficient and too costly.

Fortunately, all items do not cause the same degree of potential difficulty. Studies in numerous firms have discovered a remarkably similar pattern. Often, when all items are ranked in terms of their contribution to overall inventory costs (each item's cost times its annual usage), it will be discovered that:

- Approximately ten percent of all items generate 80 percent of all inventory costs (Group I);
- Another five percent generate 15 percent of inventory costs (Group II);
- The remaining 85 percent of all items together are responsible for only five percent of inventory costs (Group III).

Taking advantage of this phenomenon, most firms concentrate their efforts where the results are most significant. Those few items generating most inventory costs (Group I above) are identified and designated as "A" items. Also identified as **A** items would be any with a very high risk of deterioration or obsolescence (fresh flowers, fad fashion clothing, and so forth), and any with peculiar or difficult storage problems. **A** items are monitored daily or weekly. Little or no safety stocks are planned. Instead, close attention and follow-up more economically minimize stock-outs.

Group II items (above), plus others that represent special situations (such as those with very long lead times), are identified as "B" items. **B** items may be assigned a one month's safety stock, and then may be checked monthly.

The remaining items are classified as "C" items and are relatively uncontrolled. Large safety stocks (sometimes as high as six months' usage) are often more economical than the cost of record keeping and monitoring. Often a crude but effective *bin minimum* or *physical minimum* control system is used. The reorder quantity (including the large safety stock) is physically separated in the storage area. It may even be sealed in a box or bag. When it becomes necessary to use the segregated items, a reorder card is forwarded to inventory control. No other perpetual records need be maintained. In the Tripper Company example, the screws used to attach hardware to skis would probably be treated as factory supplies and controlled on a physical minimum system. Can you see the impracticality of attempting to explode the requirements for a production order of skis to include budgeting for 12 wood screws per ski, or perhaps 14 on the deluxe model?

*ABC inventory control* has been briefly described to help you gain a general understanding of the inventory control process. With such understanding, you can better appreciate the considerations and complexities involved in preparing production schedules and in budgeting for raw materials and purchases. The remaining topic to complete your general understanding relates to economic order quantities.

## ECONOMIC ORDER QUANTITIES

Recall that in budgeting production (shop) orders and purchase orders for Tripper, you were directed to schedule a predetermined quantity, which was often more than the amount immediately required. This reorder quantity (as distinct from reorder point) is commonly referred to as the economic order quantity (EOQ) for purchased items and the economic (manufacturing) lot size (ELS) for manufactured products. The EOQ/ELS concept is the same. The EOQ represents a quantity generating the least total cost for the firm.

Remember that, in the earlier material relating to safety stock, one of the elements of total inventory cost was identified as inventory carrying cost. The concepts of EOQ and safety stock similarly involve consideration of trade-offs of costs, and they both include inventory carrying costs in the trade-off. However, except for also considering inventory carrying cost, **EOQ determination is not related to safety stock.** The EOQ represents the quantity that should be ordered when the reorder point is reached, regardless of whether the reorder point includes any safety stock. Ideally the EOQ will be ordered and received before there is need to use any safety stock quantity.

If the only costs associated with ordering an item were its unit purchase/manufacturing costs and inventory carrying costs, then, to minimize cost, one would never order more than one could use today. However, another cost exists. It is the "order placing," the set-up, or simply the ordering cost.

When a firm is purchasing an item, it has the following costs, which are generally the same **regardless of the size of the order:**

> Locating and contacting supplier
> Making purchase arrangements
> Issuing purchase order
> Following up on order
> Processing receiving record and recording receipt
> Processing invoice and recording liability
> Paying the bill and recording payment

In addition, often a portion of freight-in or transportation charges represents a minimum regardless of order size. The more items in a single order, the less the ordering cost per item. In the case of a manufacturing production (shop) order, the order cost may be very high and may include the cost of setting up tooling in a series of machines in order that they can produce the desired part.

Figure 4.5 shows these two different costs on a per unit basis. Note that EOQ determination involves similar trade-offs to those involved in the determination of safety stock (SQ). The intention of an EOQ is to minimize the sum of ordering costs and inventory carrying costs per unit. The minimal total cost is at the order quantity corresponding to the intersection of the two cost curves.

Note that the upper curve representing the sum of both costs has its lowest point at the intersection quantity. And also note especially that the total cost curve is reasonably flat over a fairly broad range above and below the EOQ point (quantity). This flat shape occurs for many items, and indicates that the EOQ quantity can be adjusted significantly before a substantial cost penalty is incurred. Remember that, in the Tripper example, EOQ quantities for materials were allowed to vary plus or minus 20 percent from the ideal amount.

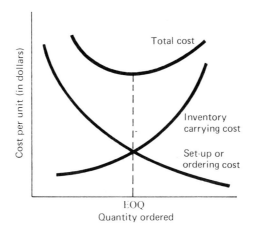

**Figure 4.5**

Since most ELS curves are relatively flat over a certain range, any order quantity within the "ELS Range" is acceptable. Ordering decision rules can then be thought of as:

1. If immediate requirements exceed ELS Range, order requirement;

2. If immediate requirements at or below top of ELS Range, order an amount within the ELS Range that will minimize the number of separate orders taking into account present and future requirements.

Exhibit 4.12 and the solution to Essential Problem EP 4.5 (p. A-90) demonstrate ordering within the ELS Range so as to minimize total orders.

The procedures for calculating the EOQ/ELS amount for a specific item are discussed in the appendix to this chapter. The significance of EOQ/ELS to your understanding of budgeting involves simply the reason for its existence and the fact that, like safety stock, it contributes to a basic average level of inventory that must be anticipated and provided for in the overall budgeting process.

---

## CHAPTER OVERVIEW

Based on the material covered in this chapter, you should now be able to:

• Describe the purpose or intent of budgeting inventory and purchases,

• Contrast the necessary steps leading to a purchases budget for a merchandiser as compared to that for a manufacturer,

• Prepare a finished-goods inventory budget given a sales budget and information on target inventory (safety stock) and beginning inventory,

• Prepare a production schedule given a finished-goods inventory budget and information on lead times and economic lot sizes,

- Prepare a raw materials inventory budget given a final production schedule, bills of material on all items scheduled, lead-time information, beginning inventories, target inventories (safety stock), and economic (purchase) order quantities,
- Prepare a purchases budget given inventory budgets (raw materials and finished goods) and the costs of items to be purchased,
- Describe the benefits and costs associated with various levels of inventory,
- Define lead times and describe their effect upon the reordering process,
- Describe safety stocks, their purpose, the costs that they minimize, and their effect upon reorder points and overall inventory levels,
- Describe economic order quantities/lot sizes, their purpose, the costs that they minimize, and their effect upon overall inventory levels,
- Based on material included in the chapter appendix, calculate the economic order quantity/lot size for a particular item given data on:

> unit cost
> inventory carrying costs
> ordering costs
> annual usage

## NEW VOCABULARY AND CONCEPTS

| | |
|---|---|
| Target inventory/Safety stock | Minimum reorder point |
| Economic (manufacturing) lot size (ELS) | Reorder point |
| Economic (purchase) order quantity (EOQ) | Inventory carrying cost |
| Explode (requirements) | Bin minimum/Physical minimum |
| Stock-out | ABC Inventory Control |
| Lead time | Setup/Ordering cost |

- The function of target inventories or safety stocks
- Exploding requirements to lower inventory levels
- The effect of lead times on reordering
- Cost trade-offs in determining safety stocks and economic order quantities/lot sizes.

## REVIEW QUESTIONS

1. What are the two major purposes or intentions of budgeting inventory and purchases?
2. What are the differences in the steps involved in budgeting inventory and purchases between a merchandiser and a manufacturer?
3. Describe the informational content of the following budgets or schedules:
   a) The finished-goods inventory budget
   b) The production schedule
   c) The raw-materials inventory budget
   d) The purchases budget

4. For each budget/schedule cited in Question 3 above:
   a) List the necessary information inputs required to prepare it;
   b) For such information that is derived from a previous budgeting step, identify the budget/schedule that provides the source of such information.

5. What executive/manager is usually responsible for the preparation of the four budgets/schedules cited in Question 3 above?

6. What are at least four benefits (potential cost savings) resulting from planning for larger inventories?

7. What are at least three disadvantages (potential costs) resulting from planning for larger inventories?

8. a) What are lead times?
   b) How do they affect the planning/scheduling process?

9. a) What is the minimum reorder point?
   b) How is the minimum reorder point (quantity) determined? Give an example illustrating your reply.

10. a) What is safety stock or target inventory?
    b) What is its function?
    c) What two costs (involved in the trade-off) are minimized by the optimal safety stock quantity?

11. a) What is the reorder point (quantity)?
    b) How is the reorder point (quantity) determined? Give an example illustrating your reply.
    c) What is the difference between the reorder point and the minimum reorder point?

12. To what does the term ABC inventory control refer?
    b) What costs are minimized by the ABC inventory control approach?
    c) What underlying cost phenomena often provide the justification for using the ABC inventory control approach?

13. a) What is physical minimum or bin minimum inventory control?
    b) In what situations is it used?

14. a) What are economic order quantities/lot sizes?
    b) What is the reason for their use?
    c) What two costs (involved in the trade-off) are minimized by the use of the EOQ order quantity?
    d) What is the significance of the fact that the total unit cost curve of an item is often relatively flat for some distance above and below the EOQ lowest point?

## MINI-CASES AND QUESTIONS FOR DISCUSSION

MC 4.1 John Jenkins is concerned about economic order quantities and safety stocks. He says, "It seems to me that providing for both economic order quantities and safety stocks is just like overkill or double counting. They both involve planning for inventory in excess of immediate projected requirements. Therefore each provides protection against stock-outs. Why not just have one or the other?

Do you agree with John? Do EOQ's and safety stocks really serve the same function? Would a higher cost of stock-out lead to increased safety stocks, order quantities, or both? Discuss.

**MC 4.2** It would appear that a firm may face a very high cost in employee dissatisfaction and turnover if production workload is very uneven during the year. What are some of these costs, even if they are not readily measurable? Discuss.

**MC 4.3** If uneven production workload has a significant cost (see MC 4.2 above), why is this cost ignored in determining economic lot sizes? Doesn't the fact that ELS scheduling may have to be rescheduled to "uneconomic" timing to balance workload indicate that ELS scheduling ignores workload factors? And doesn't the knowledge that a factory is scheduled on an ELS basis (taking into account only costs of products) tend to reinforce the workers' belief that management considers them just another commodity? Discuss.

**MC 4.4** Suppose you were scheduling production for an item with an ELS of 5,000 units and you had a month with additional requirements of 7,000 units. Would you schedule only 5,000 units, or would you schedule 7,000 or perhaps 10,000? What would be the justification for your decision? Discuss.

**MC 4.5** As a consultant to a retail hardware store chain with four stores in a metropolitan area, you have been attempting to sell the management on the desirability of budgeting. At a recent meeting the chain's president told you, "I can see where budgeting would be important to a manufacturer of one of the items we sell, and possible even to our wholesale suppliers with long lead times in obtaining goods from manufacturers. But budgeting sure doesn't seem relevant to our firm.

"A firm with long lead times has to plan ahead. In our case, everything we buy comes from local wholesalers on a weekly basis. Once a week we check our stock and order whatever we need. It arrives within 48 hours. And if we have a critical stock-out, we can rush-order necessary replacements and have them in the stores within 24 hours. I can see no reason why we would ever need a purchases budget, even if it were only expressed in total dollars per month."

What will you respond at your next meeting with the president? Is there any reason for this firm in its situation to have any type of purchases budget? Can it have an overall budgeting system without a purchases budget? Discuss.

## ESSENTIAL PROBLEMS

**EP 4.1** Prepare a finished-goods inventory budget for the year, and determine the anticipated amount of sales, cost of goods sold, and year-end inventory in dollars for the year, given the following information:

Beginning inventory:      11,600 units
Target inventory:         Quantity equal to anticipated
 (Safety stock)            next month's sales
Economic order quantity:  15,000 units

Selling price per unit:       $7.00
Unit cost:                     $4.00

Sales budget in units (next two years):

| | | | |
|---|---|---|---|
| Jan. | 11,000 | Jul. | 2,000 |
| Feb. | 9,000 | Aug. | 4,000 |
| Mar. | 5,000 | Sep. | 6,000 |
| Apr. | 4,000 | Oct. | 12,000 |
| May | 3,000 | Nov. | 15,000 |
| Jun. | 2,000 | Dec. | 13,000 |

**EP 4.2** Prepare a finished-goods inventory budget for the year, and determine the anticipated amount of sales, cost of goods sold, and ending inventory in dollars for the year, given the following information:

Beginning inventory:       500 units
Target inventory:
(Safety stock)             50 percent of current month's sales
Economic order quantity:   2,000 units
Selling price per unit:    $75.00
Unit cost:                 $55.00

Sales budget in units (next two years):

| | | | |
|---|---|---|---|
| Jan. | 900 | Jul. | 1,300 |
| Feb. | 1,000 | Aug. | 1,200 |
| Mar. | 1,500 | Sep. | 1,400 |
| Apr. | 2,000 | Oct. | 1,700 |
| May | 1,800 | Nov. | 1,900 |
| Jun. | 1,600 | Dec. | 1,400 |

**EP 4.3** Given the following finished-goods minimum requirements from the finished-goods inventory budget and the following economic manufacturing lot sizes, prepare a production schedule indicating months in which orders must be started in production. You may assume product P production orders must go into production the month before they are needed in finished goods. Product Q requires two months' lead time. You need not be concerned with attempting to balance production workloads.

| | Product P | Product Q |
|---|---|---|
| Economic lot size | 6,000 | 9,000 |
| Finished goods requirements: | | |
| Jan. | 0 | 0 |
| Feb. | 0 | 0 |
| Mar. | 2,000 | 8,000 |
| Apr. | 4,000 | 2,000 |
| May | 3,000 | 3,000 |
| Jun. | 2,000 | 3,000 |
| Jul. | 3,000 | 1,000 |
| Aug. | 2,000 | 4,000 |
| Sep. | 2,000 | 5,000 |
| Oct. | 1,000 | 1,000 |
| Nov. | 500 | 2,000 |
| Dec. | 500 | 3,000 |

**EP 4.4** Based on the finished goods requirements given in Problem EP 4.3, prepare a production schedule indicating when orders must be started into production, given the following information. You need not be concerned with attempting to balance production workloads.

|  | Product P | Product Q |
|---|---|---|
| Economic lot size | 9,000 | 8,000 |
| Lead times | 2 months | 1 month |

**EP 4.5** Prepare a raw-materials inventory budget and a purchases budget, and determine the anticipated year-end inventory in dollars, given the following information.

|  | Material A | Material B | Material C |
|---|---|---|---|
| Beginning inventory: | 1,500 | 2,400 | 6,000 |
| Economic order quantity: | 8,000 ± 20% | 9,000 ± 20% | 30,000 ± 20% |
| Unit cost: | $0.11 | $0.16 | $0.04 |
| Units used (required) for one unit of product X: | 1 | 0 | 2 |
| Units used (required) for one unit of product Y: | 0 | 2 | 3 |

Target raw-materials inventory (Safety stock): 10 percent annual usage
Production schedule (Date shop orders start into production):

|  | Product X | Product Y |
|---|---|---|
| Jan. | 4,000 | 3,000 |
| Feb. | 0 | 0 |
| Mar. | 0 | 3,000 |
| Apr. | 4,000 | 0 |
| May | 0 | 3,000 |
| Jun. | 4,000 | 3,000 |
| Jul. | 0 | 0 |
| Aug. | 0 | 3,000 |
| Sep. | 4,000 | 0 |
| Oct. | 0 | 3,000 |
| Nov. | 0 | 0 |
| Dec. | 4,000 | 0 |

**EP 4.6** Prepare a raw-materials inventory budget and a purchases budget, and determine the anticipated year-end inventory in dollars, given the following information:

|  | Material X | Material Y | Material Z |
|---|---|---|---|
| Beginning inventory: | 600 | 300 | 1,000 |
| Economic order quantity: | 900 ± 20% | 700 ± 20% | 4,000 ± 20% |
| Unit cost: | $3.00 | $2.00 | $0.30 |
| Units required for one unit of product A: | 1 | 1 | 2 |
| Units required for one unit of product B: | 2 | 0 | 4 |

Target raw-materials inventory (Safety stock):   15 percent of annual usage
Production schedule (Date shop orders start into production):

|       | Product A | Product B |
|-------|-----------|-----------|
| Jan.  | 450       | 300       |
| Feb.  | 0         | 300       |
| Mar.  | 450       | 0         |
| Apr.  | 0         | 300       |
| May   | 0         | 0         |
| Jun.  | 900       | 0         |
| Jul.  | 0         | 300       |
| Aug.  | 450       | 0         |
| Sep.  | 0         | 300       |
| Oct.  | 0         | 300       |
| Nov.  | 450       | 0         |
| Dec.  | 0         | 0         |

**EP 4.7** From the following list of costs related to inventory, identify with a "TL" those associated with carrying too little inventory:

a) Volume discounts lost because of purchasing in small quantities,

b) Customer dissatisfaction resulting from past back orders (delayed deliveries),

c) State and local personal property taxes,

d) Excessive setup and ordering costs,

e) Sales loss through inability to supply customer requirements when needed,

f) Loss incurred when more efficient and lower-priced product is offered by competitor,

g) High costs of purchase order forms,

h) Insurance on inventory,

i) High order-scheduling costs in the production control department,

j) Costs of deterioration of finished products,

k) Interest costs on borrowed funds,

l) Overtime paid for a rush order in production,

m) Air-freight paid for a rush order of raw material.

**EP 4.8** From the list of inventory-related costs given in Problem EP 4.7, identify with a "TM" those costs associated with carrying too much inventory.

**EP 4.9** a) Given the following information, calculate the reorder points:

|              | Product X  | Product Y  |
|--------------|------------|------------|
| Safety stock | 400 units  | 200 units  |
| Lead time    | 4 weeks    | 9 weeks    |
| Usage        | 200/week   | 100/week   |

b) What would be the change in the reorder points calculated above if the lead times for both products increased by two weeks?

c) What would be the change in the reorder points originally calculated above if the usages of both products increased 50 percent?

EP 4.10 a) Given the following information, calculate the reorder points:

| | Product A | Product B |
|---|---|---|
| Economic lot size | 700 units | 2,000 units |
| Safety stock | 150 units | 400 units |
| Lead time | 11 weeks | 8 weeks |
| Usage | 500/week | 200/week |

What would be the change in the reorder points originally calculated above if:

b) Lead times for both products decreased by three weeks?

c) Usage of both products decreased by 25 percent?

d) Economic lot sizes doubled?

EP 4.11 A retail store with many different and changing merchandise items often cannot budget sales, inventory, and purchases by individual units. Instead, budgeting is done for a group of products under the control of a buyer (manager) in terms of total dollars. Planned purchases are determined for the department in terms of planned sales minus open stock (beginning inventory) plus closing stock (target inventory). At any point during the budget period, the buyers then make purchasing decisions on the basis of their "open to buy," which is equal to their planned purchases (budgeted purchases) less commitments to date.

Since unit requirements and unit costs are not developed in the retailer's system, sales data is converted to cost data through application of an average markup percentage for the product group or buyer's department. It is common to communicate open stock, closing stock, and planned purchases in terms of selling prices; and then translate planned purchases to cost via elimination of the average markup. In retailing, markup represents gross profit expressed as a percentage of selling price. An item costing $4 and selling for $10 would have a 60 percent markup. A retail department with an average markup of 40 percent and planned purchases at selling of $200,000 would be budgeting purchases at a cost of $120,000.

The sales budget for a particular department in the Giant Department Store projects sales for the second quarter (retailers usually have fiscal years beginning February first) as follows:

| May | $200,000 |
|---|---|
| June | $240,000 |
| July | $250,000 |

You may also assume the following data relevant to the department:

Average markup = 60 percent
Opening stock for May = $100,000 at selling
Closing stock for second quarter = $125,000 at selling
Second-quarter purchases and purchase commitments
as of 6/15 = $215,00 at cost

As buyer for the department,

a) What were your planned (budgeted) purchases at cost for the second quarter?

b) What was your "open to buy" at cost on June 15?

**EP 4.12** Refer to Problem EP 4.11. Answer the same two questions assuming the following different data:

> Second-quarter planned sales = $740,000
> Average markup = 45 percent
> May opening stock = $120,000 at selling
> Closing stock for second quarter = $110,000 at selling
> Second-quarter purchases and purchase commitments
>   as of 6/15 = $301,500 at cost

## SUPPLEMENTARY PROBLEMS

**SP 4.13** Given the data supplied for part (a) of Problem EP 4.9 and the following:

|  | Product X | Product Y |
|---|---|---|
| Economic lot size | 3,000 units | 1,000 units |
| Unit cost | $50 | $200 |

What would be, for each product, the:

a) Average number of production orders scheduled each year (round to one decimal)?

b) Average dollar investment in inventory?

c) Average inventory turnover?

**SP 4.14** Answer the same questions asked in Problem SP 4.13 for products A and B (refer to part (a) of problem EP 4.10 above) if they cost $20 and $5 apiece, respectively?

**SP 4.15** A firm has developed the following history on two of its raw-material items that are used continuously in production:

|  | Product A | Product B |
|---|---|---|
| Normal lead time (60% of time) | 8 weeks | 6 weeks |
| Extended lead time (20% of time) | 9 weeks | 7 weeks |
| Extended lead time (10% of time) | 10 weeks | 8 weeks |
| Extended lead time (10% of time) | 11 weeks | 9 weeks |
| Normal usage (80% of time) | 200 units per week | 300 units per week |
| Increased usage (10% of time) | 250 units per week | 350 units per week |
| Increased usage (10% of time) | 300 units per week | 400 units per week |

Assume that the firm wished to ignore variations of usage from normal, and was willing to risk being out of stock 20 percent of the time; for each item, what would be the planned:

a) Safety stock?

b) Reorder point?

**SP 4.16** Refer to the data given in Problem SP 4.15. If the firm did not wish to risk delivery delays more than ten percent of the time or stock-outs resulting from increased usage more than ten percent of the time, what should be (for each item) the planned:

a) Safety stock?

b) Reorder point?

*Note.* The following problems are based on material covered in the chapter appendix.

**SP 4.17** A firm has obtained the following data related to inventory costs on two of its products:

| | Product A | Product B |
|---|---|---|
| Setup costs in factory | $300 | $1,100 |
| Relevant product cost per unit* | $50 | $20 |
| Total product cost per unit | $70 | $30 |
| Annual usage | 6,000 units | 14,000 units |

| | |
|---|---|
| Costs of issuing production order | $15 |
| Space costs (% of relevant costs) | 2% |
| Personal property taxes (% total costs) | 6% |
| Insurance (% total costs) | 5% |
| Interest cost on invested capital | 12% |
| Deterioration and obsolescence risk | |
| (% total costs) | 2% |

\* Relevant cost for determining space costs is the variable cost per unit, which will be covered in Chapter 5.

For Product A, determine the total ordering cost (S) and the total inventory carrying cost per unit (RC).

**SP 4.18** Refer to the information given in Problem SP 4.17. Determine for product B the total ordering cost (S) and the total inventory carrying cost per unit (RC).

**SP 4.19** Calculate the economic manufacturing lot size for Product A from the data given in Problem SP. 4.17.

**SP 4.20** Calculate the economic manufacturing lot size for Product B from the data given in Problem SP 4.17.

**SP 4.21** What would be the change in the economic lot size for Product A calculated in Problem SP 4.19 if:

a) The costs of issuing a production order doubled?

b) Space, property tax, and cost of capital costs dropped to 1%, 4%, and 10%, respectively?

**SP 4.22** What would be the change in the economic lot size calculated for Product B in Problem SP 4.20 if:

a) Manufacturing setup costs were reduced to $400 per lot?

b) Space costs increased to seven percent?

## SUGGESTIONS FOR FURTHER READING

Horngren, C., *Cost Accounting: A Managerial Emphasis,* Fourth Edition. Englewood Cliffs, N.J.: Prentice-Hall, Inc., 1977; Chapter 14.

Morse, Wayne J., *Cost Accounting: Processing, Evaluating, and Using Cost Data.* Reading, Massachusetts: Addison-Wesley Publishing Company, 1978; Chapter 15.

Van Horne, James C., *Fundamentals of Financial Management,* Third Edition. Englewood Cliffs, N.J.: Prentice-Hall, Inc., 1977; Chapter 8.

Weston, J. Fred, and Eugene F. Brigham, *Essentials of Managerial Finance,* Fourth Edition. Hinsdale, Ill.: The Dryden Press, 1977; Chapter 8.

CHAPTER 4 APPENDIX
# Determination of Economic Order Quantity

### Factors Involved in EOQ/ELS Determination

As explained in this chapter, determination of economic order quantities for purchasing (EOQ) or economic lot sizes for manufacturing (ELS) involve minimizing ordering and inventory carrying costs. Ordering costs are the costs of placing an additional order regardless of the quantity of items ordered. Ordering costs per order ($S$) include:

- Making arrangements for the order (both purchasing and manufacturing),
- Paper work and personnel costs for preparing the order (both purchasing and manufacturing),
- Follow-up costs while the order is in progress to ensure on-time delivery/completion (both purchasing and manufacturing),
- Minimum transportation or freight-in costs (purchases only),
- Costs of recording receipt and making payment (purchases only),
- Costs of setting up machines and equipment in the factory to produce the particular item (manufacturing only).

Costs of carrying inventory are a function of the usage (demand) of the item. The higher the annual usage ($U$), the more rapidly the EOQ will be used up and the lower the inventory carrying cost. The annual inventory carrying costs per unit ($RC$) include:

- Space costs (costs of storage),
- Insurance,
- Property taxes,
- Risk of obsolescence (competition develops a more desirable product) and deterioration or spoilage,
- Interest cost on capital invested in inventory (cost of capital).

### Obtaining Necessary Data

Many of the particular components of both ordering or setup costs ($S$) and inventory carrying costs per unit ($RC$) may be difficult to measure precisely. Experience has shown, however, that even a reasonable estimate of these costs and the use of EOQ/ELS for scheduling will generally result in significant savings over wholly arbitrary order quantities. Often ordering costs for purchasing run between $15 and $200 per order. As mentioned in the chapter, inventory carrying costs often average 25 percent per year of the cost of the item. These costs can and should be calculated separately for items with special storage or deterioration/obsolescence risk characteristics. However, for most items, an annual percentage estimate applicable to all items $(R)$ applied to the item's cost $(C)$ is sufficient.

## Combined Costs

The total annual ordering expense for a given item is therefore:

$$S \times \frac{U}{EOQ} \quad \text{or} \quad \frac{SU}{EOQ}$$

where

$$S = \text{total order expense per order,}$$
$$U = \text{annual usage in units,}$$
$$EOQ = \text{economic order quantity or lot size.}$$

The total annual inventory cost for a given item is:

$$\frac{EOQ}{2} \times R \times C$$

where

$$\frac{EOQ}{2} = \text{Average amount of EOQ on hand during the year,}$$

$$R = \text{Inventory carrying cost per year expressed as a decimal fraction,}$$

$$C = \text{Cost per unit of the product or part.}$$

Therefore the total annual expense of ordering and carrying the item in stock equals:

$$\frac{SU}{EOQ} + \frac{EOQ(RC)}{2}.$$

These costs are illustrated in Fig. 4.6.

The lowest total cost point corresponds to the intersection of the two separate cost curves. Through application of differential calculus to the total cost of ordering and carrying the item, this point representing the EOQ/ELS can be shown to be:

$$EOQ/ELS = \sqrt{\frac{2\,SU}{RC}}.$$

In the Tripper Company example for 19X2, for purchased finished tow ropes,

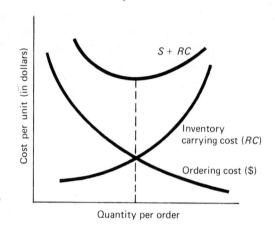

**Figure 4.6**

Quantity per order

$S$ = ordering cost:      Assume $125
$U$ = annual usage:      Budgeted at 6,000 units
$R$ = annual carrying charge rate:      Assume 25%
$C$ = unit cost:      Budgeted at $5

$$EOQ = \sqrt{\frac{2 \cdot \$125 \cdot 6{,}000}{0.25(\$5)}}$$

EOQ = 1095.45, which was rounded to 1,100 units for scheduling convenience (see below).

### Economic Range vs. Point

As cited earlier in this chapter, the EOQ total unit cost curve has a tendency for most items to be fairly flat over a range above and below the optimum (lowest) point. This "flatness" indicates that the actual order quantity may depart from the ideal, either higher or lower, often by as much as 20 percent, before substantial cost penalties are encountered. A firm may therefore choose any order quantity within this range that proves convenient for scheduling and controlling purposes.

You should remember that the EOQ/ELS range is still only a guideline for normal situations and should not be applied blindly. Two examples of where good business judgment should supersede blind adherence to the output of the formula follow. Suppose you are faced with January sales requirements for 3,000 units and no further uses throughout the balance of the year. If beginning inventory was 500 units and the EOQ was 3,500 units, how many would you order? Common sense would indicate you should order only 2,500 units. Even though you might be below the economic range, carrying costs for an entire year could more than make up for the larger per-unit ordering costs incurred. Remember ELS assumes a uniform usage throughout the year.

On the opposite end of the range, suppose you had immediate requirements for 6,000 units and the ELS was only 4,000. How many would you schedule into production? Obviously you should schedule the full 6,000 units, since they will all be used immediately and incur no inventory carrying cost.

### Limitations on Use of EOQ/ELS

Three situations indicating departure from the EOQ/ELS range have been mentioned so far:

1. Schedule modification to balance factory workload;
2. Radically uneven usage patterns;
3. Immediate demand in excess of EOQ/ELS range.

There are two other situations that may require a departure from the simple EOQ calculation. The EOQ formula assumes not only uniform usage but also:

- Constant per-unit inventory carrying charges (unlimited storage capacity and no increasing risk of spoilage or obsolescence with increased quantities);
- Constant per-unit purchased cost/price (no volume/quantity discounts).

Where either of these conditions is **not** met, the EOQ/ELS formula should **not** be used. Instead, total costs of various combinations may be arranged in a table, and the optimal EOQ chosen by inspection. More sophisticated mathematical approaches beyond the scope of this text may also be used in the solution of such a problem.

# 5

# COST BEHAVIOR
# AND THE
# PLANNING
# OF OPERATING COSTS:
# THE OPERATING
# BUDGETS

## CHAPTER PREVIEW

The purpose of this chapter is to acquaint you with costs, their behavior, and their predictability. It also covers the remaining steps involved in the preparation of operating budgets—the direct labor budget, the manufacturing overhead budget, and the general, selling, and administrative expense (GSA) budgets. In this chapter, you can:

- Become familiar with the actual preparation of direct labor, manufacturing overhead, and GSA budgets and with the data inputs upon which such budgets are based.
- Learn how budgets are initially prepared by and for each manager (responsibility center) in the firm, and the advantages of so-called participative budgeting over imposed budgeting.
- Learn the meaning of controllability as applied to costs and budget levels in which costs first appear.
- Learn how managers at higher levels of responsibility incorporate into their own budgets their subordinates' budgets and other elements unique to their own higher level of authority and responsibility.
- Become more aware of the relative importance to the firm of cost planning and control and of the distinction between direct and indirect costs.
- Learn how certain costs have certain inherent characteristics or attributes that are useful for planning and decision-making purposes.
- Discover that costs behave in one of three identifiable patterns, and that knowledge of each cost's pattern greatly facilitates prediction of its expected level within broad ranges of future activity.

In the appendix to this chapter, you can also learn:

- How to identify and determine the specific behavioral pattern of a particular cost from data relating to the amount incurred at different levels of activity or operations.

With this knowledge you will have a complete basic understanding of the steps necessary to prepare operating budgets. You will also have a necessary familiarity with the meaning and usefulness of fixed, variable, and mixed attributes of given costs; and you will be in a position to apply this knowledge to various aspects of profit planning, project decision-making, and capital budgeting, which are introduced in the next three chapters.

## WHAT WILL MY TOTAL OPERATING COSTS BE NEXT YEAR?

With completion of the sales budget and the production schedule and purchases budgets, Tripper Manufacturing Company has completed planning its actual physical activities (workload) for the forthcoming year. Managers now know:

- What items are expected to be purchased and when. This information provides the basis for planning activities in the purchasing, receiving, and accounts payable (part of accounting) departments.
- What items are expected to be manufactured and when—the basis for planning all manufacturing activities and costs, together with some of the general administrative and accounting workload.
- What items are expected to be sold and shipped to customers and when—the basis for planning distribution, selling, and the balance of general administrative activities.

Tripper is now in a position to prepare operating cost and expense budgets at each level of responsibility (for each responsibility center) within the firm. These budgets, when aggregated, will provide planned operating costs for the company as a whole. Combined with revenues from the sales and other revenue budgeting process (Chapter 3), and with purchases data (Chapter 4), they provide information for completing the firm's overall operating or operations budget.

Expected costs of inventory to be purchased from suppliers may represent a small portion of a firm's total expected costs. Recall from Chapters 1 and 2 that a manufacturer also has substantial conversion costs (labor and manufacturing overhead) that together often exceed material costs in arriving at the total cost of finished goods. And manufacturers, merchandisers, and even service companies all share substantial selling and administrative costs. Knowledge of **all** expected costs and revenues is essential to effective planning and control. Preparation of cost budgets (other than purchases) to complete the total operations picture is the central focus of this chapter.

You may have gained the impression from earlier chapters that budgets are prepared only in terms of the total firm and only by persons associated with top management. Overall sales, inventory, and purchases budgets do represent total company planning. But recall from Chapter 3 that total sales budgets are often constructed from inputs supplied by individual selling groups within the organization (territories, product lines, and so forth), and even from projections supplied by individual salespersons. Cost budgets in total for the firm are, of course, necessary; but many firms prepare cost budgets starting with individual managers. Each manager of each component (department) within the organization may have a separate budget covering costs in his or her own particular area of responsibility. The individual budgets are then aggregated into the total company budget.

The odds are very great that you will become involved in and be responsible for budgeting as soon as you become a supervisor or manager. To gain familiarity with the budgeting of costs in a particular area, you are asked to assume for a moment that you are the assembly foreman in the Tripper plant. Workers and equipment under your supervision and jurisdiction are used to complete shop orders for economy and deluxe skis. In assembly, the bindings and skegs (hardware sets) from the raw materials storeroom are attached to the ski frames completed by the molding department. You are naturally interested in, if not concerned with, what lies ahead for **you** and **your** department during the forthcoming year. Will you have more or less volume than this year? What problems may be anticipated (hiring and training more personnel, or possibly layoffs) and how can you plan now to take care of them?

It is late in October of 19X1 and, as assembly foreman, you have the responsibility to budget for your *controllable costs* for 19X2. Controllable in this sense means **both** those costs over which you have exclusive authority (for example, payroll costs of workers whom you can lay off and recall) and also those over which you have significant influence (for example, your proportionate share of total factory maintenance costs). Controllable costs **exclude** any part of costs over which you have little or no influence (as examples, a share of general office costs or depreciation on equipment in the assembly department).

Budgets may be prepared primarily for planning or primarily for subsequent control purposes. Some firms believe that planning and information considerations are paramount. They wish budgets to focus the individual manager's attention upon all items for which he or she is responsible. In the Tripper case, such an approach would result in including in your assembly department budget items such as anticipated expenses for depreciation on tools and equipment. It might even include an allocation for expenses of overall building depreciation and factory administration. Firms that believe in this approach feel that to exclude such items might lessen the manager's feelings of overall responsibility.

Other firms believe that individual managers' budgets should focus on immediate controllability rather than overall responsibility. For planning purposes, noncontrollable items such as depreciation are excluded from the operating manager's budget and are only included as part of completing the total firm's budgeted income statement (Chapter 10). Firms that focus on controllability believe that inclusion of noncontrollable items in operating budgets is more than just a waste of time and effort. In terms of your assembly department budget, such firms believe two counterproductive effects could result. First, to include in your budget items over which you have no control or influence could prove irritating and might dilute your sense of budget responsibility. How could you feel you "owned" a budget and feel personally responsible for its outcome when it included items completely beyond your control? Second, such information appearing during the control process could distract your attention, which should be focused exclusively on your controllable items.

There appears to exist no consensus with respect to these alternatives. You should be aware of their existence and the philosophies behind each approach. You may assume that Tripper believes in focusing upon controllable items and proceed with preparing your budget on that basis. As in previous examples, you will be asked to budget direct labor cost and manufacturing overhead only for the first three months of 19X2. Planning the remaining nine months will be essentially repetitive.

From the 19X2 final production schedule (Exhibit 4.10 in the previous chapter), you know that planned activity in your assembly department during the first three months of the year will involve completion of three separate shop orders:

> January: One order for 1,700 deluxe skis
> February: One order for 2,100 economy skis
> March: One order for 2,100 economy skis

You also have the following information with respect to your operations during the first quarter of 19X1:

> Final production schedule for first quarter of 19X1 (Exhibit 5.1)
> Direct labor budget for first quarter of 19X1 (Exhibit 5.2)
> Actual costs incurred during first quarter of 19X1 (Exhibit 5.3)
> Foreman's notes concerning cost variances during first quarter of 19X1 (Exhibit 5.4)
> Overhead budget for first quarter of 19X1 (Exhibit 5.5)

## Exhibit 5.1

### TRIPPER WATER SKI MANUFACTURING COMPANY

**Final Production Schedule (Units)**
**for First Quarter 19X1 (Units)**

|  | January | February | March | Total first quarter |
|---|---|---|---|---|
| *Economy ski* | | | | |
| Requirements | 1,035 | 1,225 | 1,440 | 3,700 |
| Carryover stock | 0 | 965 | 1,740 | |
| Current needs | 1,035 | 260 | 0 | |
| Scheduled production | 2,000 | 2,000 | 0 | 4,000 |
| | | | | |
| *Deluxe ski* | | | | |
| Requirements | 350 | 350 | 500 | 1,200 |
| Carryover stock | 0 | 1,250 | 900 | |
| Current needs | 350 | 0 | 0 | |
| Scheduled production | 1,600 | 0 | 0 | 1,600 |

**Exhibit 5.2**

TRIPPER WATER SKI MANUFACTURING COMPANY

**Direct Labor Budget—Assembly Department, First Quarter 19X1**

| | January | | February | | March | | Total First quarter | |
|---|---|---|---|---|---|---|---|---|
| | Units | Dollars | Units | Dollars | Units | Dollars | Units | Dollars |
| Economy skis ($1.25 V) | 2,000 | $2,500 | 2,000 | $2,500 | 0 | 0 | 4,000 | $5,000 |
| Deluxe skis ($1.50 V) | 1,600 | 2,400 | 0 | 0 | 0 | 0 | 1,600 | 2,400 |
| Total | | $4,900 | | $2,500 | | 0 | | $7,400 |

**Exhibit 5.3**

TRIPPER WATER SKI MANUFACTURING COMPANY

**Actual Costs Incurred—Assembly Department, First Quarter 19X1**

| | January | February | March | Total first quarter |
|---|---|---|---|---|
| Economy skis assembled (units) | 2,000 | 2,200 | 0 | 4,200 |
| Deluxe skis assembled (units) | 1,600 | 0 | 1,700 | 3,300 |
| Direct labor | $5,200 | $2,750 | $2,720 | $10,670 |
| Manufacturing overhead: | | | | |
|     Indirect labor | 1,720 | 1,440 | 1,340 | 4,500 |
|     Indirect materials | 1,200 | 990 | 540 | 2,730 |
|     Maintenance | 400 | 700 | 800 | 1,900 |
|     Total D.L. and M.O. | $8,520 | $5,880 | $5,400 | $19,800 |

**Exhibit 5.4**

TRIPPER WATER SKI MANUFACTURING COMPANY

**Foreman's Budget Performance Notes—Assembly Department, First Quarter 19X1**

Direct Labor:

Economy skis: Budget OK; most variance due to increased production, balance due slow skeg attachment corrected

Deluxe skis: Budget $0.10 too low; effectively all variance due to low budget and increased volume

Indirect labor: Budget OK; all variance due to increased production quantity

Indirect materials: Budget OK; $300 accidental loss of supplies in February, steps taken prevent recurrence; most of remaining variance due to increased production quantity

Maintenance: Budget OK; variance due to increased production volume and to delay in assembly tool overhaul from January to March

Exhibit 5.5

TRIPPER WATER SKI MANUFACTURING COMPANY

**Manufacturing Overhead Budget—Assembly Department**
**First Quarter 19X1**

|  | January | February | March | Total first quarter |
|---|---|---|---|---|
| Scheduled assembly: |  |  |  |  |
| Economy skis (units) | 2,000 | 2,000 | 0 | 4,000 |
| Deluxe skis (units) | 1,600 | 0 | 0 | 1,600 |
| Indirect labor<br>($1,000/Mo. F; $0.20 V)* | $1,720 | $1,400 | $1,000 | $4,120 |
| Indirect materials<br>($30/Mo. F; $0.30 V)* | 1,110 | 630 | 30 | 1,770 |
| Maintenance<br>($500/Mo. F; $0.05 V)* | 680 | 600 | 500 | 1,780 |
| Total | $3,510 | $2,630 | $1,530 | $7,670 |

* Indicates budgeting rate expressed as sum of a certain amount of constant or fixed dollars per month plus a certain amount of dollars that varies with the number of skis assembled regardless of model.

## Preparing the Direct Labor Budget

Study Exhibits 5.1, 5.2, and 5.3. See if you can determine on what basis the 19X1 direct labor budget was calculated, and why 19X1 costs exceeded the budget. Exhibit 5.2 indicates that assembly direct labor was budgeted at $1.25 per economy ski and $1.50 per deluxe ski. The letter V stands for variable cost, one which varies in direct proportion to the quantities of items produced. Variable costs will be discussed later in this chapter.

Actual assembly direct labor costs exceeded planned (budgeted) costs by $3,270 for the first quarter of 19X1 as can be seen by comparing Exhibits 5.2 and 5.3. However, if you compare the actual quantities assembled with the planned quantities, you will see that actual activity exceeded budget. Remember from Chapter 3 that 19X1 sales ran 5 percent ahead of budget, and production schedules would have been adjusted accordingly. If the assembly budget had been redetermined based on the higher level of activity, it would have provided for $5,250 for economy skis and $4,950 for deluxe skis for the quarter.[1] The difference between the budget revised for actual production levels and actual costs incurred would only be $470. The redetermined budget would have represented a fairly accurate plan and your costs were controlled so as to be reasonably close to this plan, especially for economy skis.

---

[1]   Economy skis:   4,200 × $1.25 = $5,250
     Deluxe skis:   3,300 × $1.50 = 4,950
                            $10,200

As part of the control process, which will be covered in Chapters 11 through 15, you, as foreman of the assembly department, will make notes, during each year, as to those items that significantly depart from budget. These notes will indicate what has been or should be done, so that you may plan more accurately on the next budget. Exhibit 5.4 contains your notes so far this year (19X1). Based on last year's experience, your observations, and available data, how much direct labor cost should you budget for January, February, and March of 19X2? Total direct labor each month will be the product of the units produced and the labor cost per unit. You have the schedule of units to be produced. What labor rate should you use?

Your expected labor rate per ski will, in turn, depend upon expected hourly wage rates and the labor efficiency (skis finished per hour). In this example, you may assume no anticipated wage rate increase. What labor rate per ski for each model should you use for budgeting 19X2?

You probably should budget $1.25 per ski for economy skis, since this amount proved accurate and you have no reason to anticipate change. Deluxe skis should probably be budgeted at $1.60, based on your experience and the results of your investigation during the first quarter of the year. Using Exhibit 5.2 as a model, prepare, on a separate sheet of paper, a direct labor budget for the assembly department for the first quarter of 19X2, before proceeding.

Exhibit 5.6 is an appropriate budget, given the foregoing information.

**Exhibit 5.6**

TRIPPER WATER SKI MANUFACTURING COMPANY

**Direct Labor Budget—Assembly Department, First Quarter 19X2**

|  | January | | February | | March | | Total first quarter | |
|---|---|---|---|---|---|---|---|---|
|  | Units | Dollars | Units | Dollars | Units | Dollars | Units | Dollars |
| Economy skis ($1.25 V) | 0 | 0 | 2,100 | $2,625 | 2,100 | $2,625 | 4,200 | $5,250 |
| Deluxe skis ($1.60 V) | 1,700 | $2,720 | 0 | 0 | 0 | 0 | 1,700 | 2,720 |
| Total | | $2,720 | | $2,625 | | $2,625 | | $7,970 |

## Preparing the Manufacturing Overhead Budget

Turn now to Exhibits 5.3, 5.4, and 5.5, which are related to manufacturing overhead items within your control. Can you determine the basis on which the 19X1 overhead budget was calculated? Were overhead costs reasonably planned and controlled, considering that the actual costs exceeded the budget by $1,460 ($9,130 minus $7,670)?

The overhead budget (Exhibit 5.5) indicates that projected costs for each item each month are determined by first calculating a variable rate times the total number of all models of skis to be assembled (similar to planning direct labor). Portions of indirect labor, indirect materials, and maintenance have been found by experience to vary in direct proportion to the number of skis assembled. This portion of each cost, like all direct labor, is known as variable. *Variable costs* will be discussed further below. To each variable cost portion is added a fixed monthly amount. A portion of each cost has been found to be constant or fixed each month, regardless of the number of skis assembled. *Fixed costs* will also be discussed later in this chapter.

To fully understand this computation, look at the budget for indirect labor for January, 19X1, when 3,600 skis were scheduled for assembly:   3,600 times $0.20 (variable rate for indirect labor) equals $720.   $720 plus $1,000 (monthly fixed amount of indirect labor) equals $1,720, which was the amount budgeted for indirect labor for that month. Costs of this type, which have both fixed and variable components, are known as *mixed costs*, and will be discussed further later in this chapter.

An examination of Exhibits 5.3, 5.4, and 5.5 indicates that assembly overhead costs were well planned and controlled during the first quarter of 19X1. Again, as in the case of direct labor, if the overhead budget had been recalculated on the basis of actual units assembled, the budget for the quarter would have been $8,715. Costs of $9,130 were actually incurred, and most of the $415 variance is explained by the accidental $300 loss of supplies in February of 19X1.

Since there appears to be no basis for a revision of the overhead budgeting rates, you may use the 19X1 rates for budgeting 19X2. You should complete the overhead budget for the first three months of 19X2 on a separate sheet of paper before proceeding to the next paragraph. Use Exhibit 5.5 as a model. This experience should assist you in becoming more familiar with the behavior of mixed costs and with the budgeting process.

### Exhibit 5.7
### TRIPPER WATER SKI MANUFACTURING COMPANY

**Manufacturing Overhead Budget—Assembly Department, First Quarter 19X2**

|  | Jan. | Feb. | March | Total first quarter |
|---|---|---|---|---|
| Scheduled assembly: |  |  |  |  |
| Economy skis (units) | 0 | 2,100 | 2,100 | 4,200 |
| Deluxe skis (units) | 1,700 | 0 | 0 | 1,700 |
| Indirect labor ($1,000/Mo. F; $0.20 V)* | $1,340 | $1,420 | $1,420 | $4,180 |
| Indirect materials ($30/Mo. F; $0.30 V)* | 540 | 660 | 660 | 1,860 |
| Maintenance ($500/Mo. F; ¢0.05 V)* | 585 | 605 | 605 | 1,795 |
| Total | $2,465 | $2,685 | $2,685 | $7,835 |

* F designates cost portion that is fixed. V designates that portion of cost that is variable per ski regardless of model.

You are correct, and you have an adequate initial understanding of the budgeting process at each responsibility level, if your overhead budget conforms to Exhibit 5.7.

## BUDGETING BY RESPONSIBILITY CENTERS

Continuing for a moment with the Tripper Company example, as foreman can you see the difference between working out your own budget and having one simply handed to you by your supervisor? As first mentioned in Chapter 2, if you have the responsibility for preparing your own budget, you can "own" it and may be more likely to support it (attempt to control costs within budgetary goals and/or to do an even better job of planning next year). As a foreman, you would not be expected to develop all the necessary budget rates by yourself. The budgeting section of the accounting department will assist you in this area. Regardless who prepares preliminary rates, you and your supervisor ultimately have to agree on the appropriate rate. Once the rates are established, the budget department may perform the extensions for you.[2]

The process of preparing budgets, starting with the lowest-level responsibility centers within the organization and involving participation of the supervisor, his or her manager, and the budgeting department, is known as *participatory budgeting.* When budgets are not prepared on a participatory basis, and instead are handed down from on high, the system may be described as one involving *imposed budgets.* As a foreman, would you support an imposed budget? Or would you be inclined to say to yourself, "No way!—that's **their** plan, not mine. **They** don't know what is really necessary in **my** department."

Just as there exists no consensus with respect to the total-responsibility-vs.-controllability content of operating budgets, as discussed above, no unanimity of agreement exists as to the desirability of participatory vs. imposed budgets. Firms that operate with imposed budgets believe them superior for many reasons, including:

1. They may be more accurate if prepared by expert budgeting personnel.

2. Individual managers may not have all necessary information or the "big picture" desirable for completing good budgets.

3. It is management's responsibility at all levels, starting with top management, to define objectives for subordinates to achieve. It would be inappropriate to ask a subordinate to participate in designing his or her own job.

---

[2]   Computers can be very helpful in performing all of the routine extensions and summarizations once the individual managers have agreed upon appropriate rates. Computers can also prove invaluable in providing data from which accurate rates may be derived.

4. Budgets established by subordinates may contain too much slack or padding, rather than attainable goals.

5. Budgets may need to be modified by top management. To consult over modifications with all managers may be too time-consuming. To make modifications without consultation will probably be viewed as imposing, anyway (see below). Therefore, attempting participatory budgets is a waste of time and effort.

Firms that believe in participatory budgets acknowledge that involvement of all concerned requires extra time and effort. They believe, however, that the benefits outweigh the additional costs. Benefits attributed to participatory budgeting by its supporters include:

1. Budgets may be more accurate if prepared by managers directly involved with and responsible for a given operation, rather than by remote experts not responsible for the eventual outcome.

2. Managers who participate in the development of their own budgets may be more highly motivated subsequently to control their operations to achieve budgeted goals. They may develop a feeling of ownership of their budgets, and thus act more responsibly.

Advocates of participatory budgets are aware that the motivational benefits may be fragile and easily lost if changes become necessary and are imposed without consultation. If original participatory budgets are subsequently slashed by a higher authority without consultation and participation, then they may become even less effective than originally imposed budgets would have been. Often a vicious game may then be started where, next year, the individual manager "pads" his budget, in anticipation of arbitrary cuts. In turn, the top management cuts even deeper, knowing that the preliminary budget is padded. Individual managers are further motivated to spend everything in the budget each year so that their budget will not be cut next year. Since the primary purpose of budgeting is planning, how accurate and dependable a plan do you think results from such a system?[3]

The choice between participatory and imposed budgets is also related to the basic philosophy of management in a given firm and management's assumptions with respect to subordinates. These issues will be further briefly explored in a discussion of approaches to control in Chapter 11. They are also more adequately covered in management courses devoted to organizations and human behavior. In the Tripper example, you may assume that Tripper follows a participatory system and that the budgeting rates used in your assembly department budget were the result of an agreement between you and your superior.

---

[3] Unfortunately, many institutional and governmental budgets have evolved to this sorry state. See Chapter 15.

## BUILDING THE COMPANY OPERATING EXPENDITURE BUDGET

Step 9 in the overall budgeting process for a manufacturer involves completing the company operating expenditure budget. This budget is made up from the manufacturing budget and the general selling and administrative (GSA) budget. The manufacturing budget is a composite of the direct labor and overhead budgets for each responsibility center. The GSA budget is a composite of the component budgets in each GSA responsibility center. Preparation of the manufacturing and GSA budgets and their components may be considered as Steps 7 and 8 in the overall budgeting process.

### Manufacturing Budget

Preparation of the company manufacturing budget is the responsibility of the vice-president for operations (or manufacturing). This budget combines information with respect to planned conversion costs (direct labor and overhead) from the lower-level responsibility budgets, together with additional items controllable only at the overall factory level.

In the Tripper Company there are three departments in the factory with jurisdiction over conversion costs:

Assembly Department:    where skis and hardware are assembled,

Moulding Department:    where ski frames are manufactured,

Maintenance Department:    a service department serving both assembly and moulding.

The direct labor and overhead budgets for these departments are combined with other budgeted items to make up the company manufacturing.

Note in Fig. 5.1 that the maintenance budget is connected to the overall company manufacturing budget with a dotted line. The purpose of the dotted line is to call your attention to the fact that the maintenance budget does not totally add into the overall company manufacturing or operating budgets. The maintenance department is a service department serving **both** assembly and moulding. Since maintenance in each department is a joint responsibility of the production department foreman and the maintenance supervisor, the common costs will appear on both their budgets. When budgets are combined into the manufacturing budget, only half of each duplicate pair is aggregated, in order to avoid double counting. Service department budgets will be discussed further in Chapter 11.

Exhibits 5.8 and 5.9 together comprise the Tripper manufacturing budget for 19X2. Total direct labor expense anticipated for 19X2 is budgeted separately on Exhibit 5.8 to maintain the labor-vs-overhead distinction that is maintained in Tripper's cost accounting system (Chapter 1). Note that all direct labor is "located" in one of the two production departments.

Exhibit 5.9 is the total manufacturing overhead cost budget for 19X2. To avoid presenting you with unnecessary detail, Exhibit 5.9 is presented in summary form, by quarters. Note that maintenance costs are distributed among

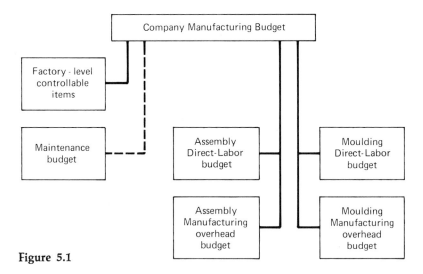

**Figure 5.1**

indirect labor, indirect materials, and supervision. Also note three additional items not budgeted at the departmental level—utilities, insurance, and property taxes. These items are not controllable at the departmental level and are there-

**Exhibit 5.8**

TRIPPER WATER SKI MANUFACTURING COMPANY

**Direct Labor Budget for the Year 19X2**

|  | Moulding department | Assembly department | Total company |
|---|---|---|---|
| Jan | $ 18,530 | $ 2,720 | $ 21,250 |
| Feb | 17,955 | 2,625 | 20,580 |
| Mar | 17,955 | 2,625 | 20,580 |
| First quarter | $ 54,440 | $ 7,970 | $ 62,410 |
| Apr | $ 18,530 | $ 2,720 | $ 21,250 |
| May | 36,485 | 5,345 | 41,830 |
| Jun | 17,955 | 2,625 | 20,580 |
| Second quarter | $ 72,970 | $10,690 | $ 83,660 |
| Jul | $ 36,485 | $ 5,345 | $ 41,830 |
| Aug | 0 | 0 | 0 |
| Sep | 0 | 0 | 0 |
| Third quarter | $ 36,485 | $ 5,345 | $ 41,830 |
| Oct | $ 17,955 | $ 2,625 | $ 20,580 |
| Nov | 0 | 0 | 0 |
| Dec | 0 | 0 | 0 |
| Fourth quarter | $ 17,955 | $ 2,625 | $ 20,580 |
| Total Year | $181,850 | $26,630 | $208,480 |

fore excluded from department budgets. And finally note that the budget is identified as an **expenditure** rather than as an expense budget. *Expenses* include such past-related items as depreciation and amortization of noncurrent assets that do not involve cash costs in the current (or immediately subsequent) period. Such items are not controllable in the current period, and therefore are irrelevant to operating budgets restricted to controllable items. *Expenditures* are defined as acts involving the payment of cash or the giving of a commitment to pay cash (debt). Expenditures occur and are often controllable in the current period, and therefore are the **only** items relevant to control-oriented operating budgets.

### Exhibit 5.9
### TRIPPER WATER SKI MANUFACTURING COMPANY

**Total Manufacturing Overhead Expenditure Budget[a]**
**for the Year 19X2**

|  | First Quarter | Second Quarter | Third Quarter | Fourth Quarter | Total Year |
|---|---|---|---|---|---|
| Scheduled production: |  |  |  |  |  |
| Economy skis | 4,200 | 4,200 | 2,100 | 2,100 | 12,600 |
| Deluxe skis | 1,700 | 3,400 | 1,700 |  | 6,800 |
|  | 5,900 | 7,600 | 3,800 | 2,100 | 19,400 |
| Indirect labor: |  |  |  |  |  |
| Moulding ($7,333/Mo F + 2.0 V)[b] | $ 33,800 | $37,200 | $29,600 | $26,200 | $126,800 |
| Assembly ($1,000/Mo F + .02 V) | 4,180 | 4,520 | 3,760 | 3,420 | 15,880 |
| Maintenance ($1,250/Mo F + 0.3 V) | 5,520 | 6,030 | 4,890 | 4,380 | 20,820 |
| Total ($9,583/Mo + 2.5 V) | $ 43,500 | $47,750 | $38,250 | $34,000 | $163,500 |
| Indirect materials: |  |  |  |  |  |
| Moulding ($160/Mo F + 0.4 V) | $  2,840 | $ 3,520 | $ 2,000 | $ 1,320 | $  9,680 |
| Assembly ($30/Mo F + 0.3 V) | 1,860 | 2,370 | 1,230 | 720 | 6,180 |
| Maintenance ($250/Mo F + 0.1 V) | 1,340 | 1,510 | 1,130 | 960 | 4,940 |
| Total ($440/Mo F + 0.8 V) | $  6,040 | $ 7,400 | $ 4,360 | $ 3,000 | $ 20,800 |
| Supervision ($5,417/Mo F) | 16,250 | 16,250 | 16,250 | 16,250 | 65,000 |
| Utilities ($600/Mo F + 0.6 V) | 5,340 | 6,360 | 4,080 | 3,060 | 18,840 |
| Insurance | 13,000 |  |  |  | 13,000 |
| Property taxes | 18,000 |  |  |  | 18,000 |
| Total ($18,623/Mo F + 3.9 V) | $102,130 | $77,760 | $62,940 | $56,310 | $299,140 |

[a] Does not include $52,000 of annual depreciation expense that does not involve current year expenditure.
[b] Budgeting rates include designations for fixed (F) and variable (V) components.

### General Selling and Administrative Budget

The remaining portion of the company's operating budget is the general selling and administrative expenditure (GSA) budget. In this budget the firm's period costs are projected for the forthcoming year. The GSA budget is once

**Exhibit 5.10**
TRIPPER WATER SKI MANUFACTURING COMPANY

**General, Selling, and Administrative Expenditure Budget**[a]
**for the Year 19X2**

| | First quarter | Second quarter | Third quarter | Fourth quarter | Total year |
|---|---|---|---|---|---|
| Sales | $244,000 | $512,000 | $377,000 | $131,000 | $1,264,000 |
| Wages and salaries[b] (27,350/Mo. F) | 82,050 | 82,050 | 82,050 | 82,050 | 328,200 |
| Distribution and marketing ($1,320/Mo. F + 0.008 V)[c] | 5,910 | 8,060 | 6,980 | 5,000 | 25,950 |
| Interest[d] ($330/Mo. F) | 3,960 | | | | 3,960 |
| Insurance ($1,160/Mo. F) | 6,960 | | 6,960 | | 13,920 |
| Property taxes ($500/Mo. F) | 6,000 | | | | 6,000 |
| Miscellaneous ($340/Mo. F) | 1,020 | 1,020 | 1,020 | 1,020 | 4,080 |
| Total ($32,000/Mo. F + $0.008 V[b]) | $105,900 | $ 91,130 | $ 97,010 | $ 88,070 | $ 382,110 |

[a] Does not include $12,000 of annual depreciation expense that does not involve current year expenditure.
[b] Includes salaries of all executives.
[c] Variable expenses vary per sales dollar.
[d] Does not yet include interest on any additional financing that may be planned for the year.

again a composite of separate budgets starting with the lowest level of responsibility in the separate GSA areas. In the Tripper Company, individual responsibility center budgets might be prepared for:

• Controller's Department,
• Distribution expenses (the shipping department),
• Separate geographic selling divisions,
• Home-office marketing expenses (market research, advertising, sales, management, and so forth).

Each of these budgets would be prepared in a similar manner to that for the individual foreman's departmental budget. Responsibility for preparation of the overall GSA budget may be divided between the vice-president for sales and the controller, with each accountable for one portion. Exhibit 5.10 presents the total GSA budget for 19X2.

## Operating Expenditure Budget

The 19X2 operating expenditure budget (not illustrated in this chapter) for the Tripper Company may be thought of as including:

- The direct labor budget (Exhibit 5.8)
- The manufacturing overhead budget (Exhibit 5.9)
- The GSA budget (Exhibit 5.10)

This composite budget predicts all operating costs anticipated during 19X2 from normal operations. Together with the firm's Sales budget (Chapter 3), Purchases budget (Chapter 4), Capital budget (Chapter 8), Cash budget (Chapter 9), and Financial budget (Chapter 10), it provides data for the firm's overall or master budget for the forthcoming year.

## THE IMPORTANCE OF COSTS AND THEIR PROPER BUDGETING AND CONTROL

From the Tripper example, you should have noticed that considerably more attention and detail planning is devoted to costs than to revenue. This disparity of attention is the natural consequence of two facts first mentioned in Chapter 3. Revenues are more difficult to predict accurately and are less controllable. Costs, on the other hand, are almost entirely controllable by the firm. Some costs may be committed for many years, such as costs related to capacity assets. Nevertheless, even these costs are a result of management decisions, and they are controllable by management in the long run.

Cost control in some ways can be considered as more significant than revenue control. Saving $1 of costs produces slightly more than $1 of profit (the matching revenue dollar plus interest savings on invested capital), whereas obtaining an additional $1 of revenue results in substantially less than $1 of profit (the additional revenue dollar is accompanied by related additional costs). You should also be careful not to confuse the term cost with the financial accountant's term expense. The term "cost" refers to the use of resources for some purpose. The term "expense" refers to the treatment of the cost as a reduction in income in a particular period. Although all costs eventually become expenses, in a particular year a cost may not be treated as an expense. A product cost may be capitalized and held in inventory as an asset if sale of the product does not occur until the following period. Also, some expenses, such as depreciation on office equipment, represent expirations of costs incurred in prior periods.

## TYPES OF COSTS

Costs may be thought of as being of one of two types, direct or indirect. Direct costs are those that are readily traceable to or identifiable with a specific activity or product **and** that are so traced and identified by the accountants in a particular firm. It is important to realize that directness is not an inherent characteristic of a particular cost. In essence a direct cost is merely a cost that accountants choose to treat (identify) as direct.

Manufacturing labor provides a good example. Where it is feasible and economical, the cost accountant may identify a portion of manufacturing labor that is specifically and exclusively related to working on particular products as direct labor. Other manufacturing labor (such as that related to materials handling) might feasibly be identified with specific products but it may not be economical to do so. Furthermore, some manufacturing labor cannot be traced to specific products or activities because it is common to several (maintenance and janitorial labor are examples) and therefore must be classified as indirect. Indirect costs are all costs that are not classified as direct. They are either common or joint to several products or activities and therefore not traceable, or they cannot be traced economically. As first discussed in Chapter 1, the identification of certain costs as direct makes the accountant's determination of product costs of a specific **unit** more accurate than if all costs were treated as indirect and arbitrarily allocated to different products.

## CHARACTERISTICS OF COSTS

Certain types of costs have inherent characteristics or attributes **regardless** of their treatment by accountants. For planning and control purposes, costs may be:

- Committed,
- Programmed or discretionary,
- Avoidable or escapable,
- Completely or partially variable,
- Nonvariable or fixed.

*Committed costs* are those that, except in emergencies, are "locked in" or not subject to change in the current period (year). Examples of committed costs would include those committed by contractural relationships (lease or purchase contracts stretching over several years) and those resulting from past expenditures (depreciation on buildings and equipment).

*Programmed* or *discretionary costs* are those that are committed or set for one particular period at the discretion of management. They are not committed for future periods and were not committed from prior periods. Examples of programmed costs include such items as advertising, charitable contributions, and employee training programs. Such costs are discretionary on the part of management. They may be readily and arbitrarily changed from year to year, and also may more easily be cut back in an emergency than longer-term committed cost.

*Avoidable* or *escapable costs* are those that are changeable with respect to a specific management decision. If Tripper were to discontinue manufacturing and selling its deluxe skis, certain costs could be avoided or escaped. It could avoid the costs of materials and direct labor used to produce the skis. It might also avoid some previous committed costs by selling equipment used exclusively to manufacture deluxe skis. Other committed costs such as executive salaries might not be avoidable. Avoidable costs will be explored more thoroughly in Chapter 7.

Costs may change in proportion to changes in the volume of activity within a specific time period, or they may not. These characteristics are a major consideration in the budgeting process and may be viewed as cost behavior.

## COST BEHAVIOR

Can you visualize the extreme difficulty, if not impossibility, of budgeting costs with any reasonable degree of accuracy if you had no idea how cost behaved with changes in activity? If you were anticipating a ten-percent increase in volume over the prior year's budget, as in the Tripper example, would you automatically plan for a ten-percent increase in each cost item? Intuitively you know that not all costs increase in direct proportion to increased volume. But which do and which do not? To answer this question, one first needs to know how different types of costs can behave in response to different activity (volume) levels. Then one would need to identify each cost within the firm as to its behavioral type or category.

Costs will be found to behave in one of three ways over a specific short-run period or within a specific short-term time horizon. Commonly, cost behavior is analyzed within a period of one year, to correspond to the usual budget time horizon. As introduced in the Tripper example, a particular cost may be fixed, variable, or mixed.

### Fixed Costs

Fixed costs include those that are unaffected by changes in the volume of activity. Examples of fixed costs would include certain committed and programmed costs such as:

> Rent or depreciation on buildings and equipment
> Property taxes and insurance on buildings and equipment[4]
> Salaries of managers and chief executives.

Note that the definition of a fixed cost specified that it did not change as a result of changes in volume. On a per-unit basis, a fixed cost would decline as it was "spread" over more and more units. See Fig. 5.2(a) and (b). Also note that while a fixed cost is one that does not change with changes in **volume,**

---

[4]   Property taxes and insurance on inventory may be variable, depending upon the amount of inventory on hand. See below.

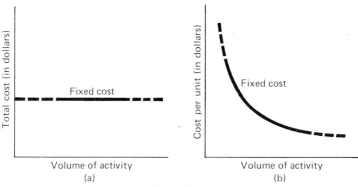

**Figure 5.2**

a fixed cost may change independently of changes in volume. The company president's salary or property taxes and insurance on building and equipment may change without any change in the volume of the firm's activities. Also, a fixed cost may change in **amount** from period to period. A fixed cost is unchanging **only** with respect to volume changes, and only within a limited time period.

A final qualification with respect to cost behavior in general, and fixed costs in particular, involves a *relevant range* of activity. Suppose Tripper were currently operating two factories, each with a capacity of 30,000 skis per year. The combined depreciation/rent would be fixed **only** over a relevant range of from 30,000 to 60,000 skis. At a volume below 30,000, Tripper could shut down and perhaps sell one factory. The previous fixed costs could be reduced. At a volume above 60,000 units, additional capacity, with attendant additional fixed costs, would have to be acquired.

Figure 5.3 illustrates the step-by-step nature of fixed costs, and the fact that a given **level** of fixed costs holds only over a specific relevant range. Look back at the first two earlier diagrams illustrating a fixed cost. Note that the relevant range is denoted by a solid line (curve). The dotted line extends to the axis for ease of reading values, but does **not** represent the level of cost to be expected at that low quantity level. It is beyond the relevant range.

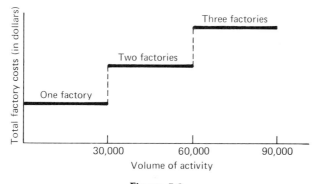

**Figure 5.3**

## Variable Costs

Some costs are just the opposite of fixed costs. They may vary directly **in exact proportion** to changes in volume, and are known as variable costs. Certain costs are usually wholly variable. Costs of material used in a product (direct material) and costs of labor specifically traceable to producing the product (direct labor) are usually wholly variable: 30 percent more products produced will require 30 percent more direct material and 30 percent more direct labor, and vice versa. Sales commissions are another example of wholly variable costs.

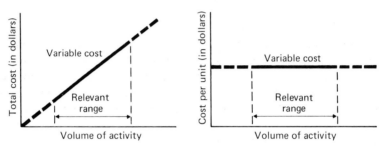

**Figure 5.4**

Note in Fig. 5.4 that a variable cost varies in total with changes in volume and is constant **per unit** at different volume levels. Note also that costs are variable in a specific amount only over a limited relevant range. Below the relevant range variable costs may be higher (automated equipment no longer feasible, or purchase volume discounts no longer applicable). Above the relevant range, variable costs could be higher (overload and loss of efficiency) or lower (use of more automated equipment or greater volume discounts on purchases).

## Linearity Assumptions

Some costs may be essentially variable but not in a completely linear manner. Figure 5.5(a) indicates a cost that changes with volume but not in constant proportion. The result is curvilinear. For simplification of computation, accountants usually will assume, again over a relevant range, that the curve is flat and the cost directly variable or mixed. They will use the dashed line as an adequate predictor of the cost's behavior. Figure 5.5(b) indicates what is known as a step-variable cost. In one sense, all salaried employees represent fixed costs. Therefore, in a strict sense, a firm with eight indirect labor employees on salary would have its relevant range for budgeting data purposes limited to the capacity of a single employee. At a level of volume requiring

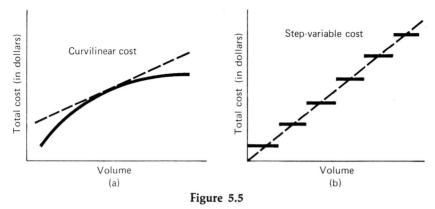

Figure 5.5

only seven employees, a lower range of fixed costs would exist. Beyond the capacity of the eighth employee, the ninth hired laborer would create a new relevant range. In larger firms, where the incremental step is proportionately very small, to classify such costs as fixed and be restricted to planning over very small relevant ranges would be counterproductive. Instead, in such situations, the step-variable costs are assumed to be variable, as shown by the dashed line drawn through the midpoints in Fig. 5.5(b).

## Mixed Costs

Some costs such as those illustrated for Tripper's assembly department are neither almost entirely fixed nor variable. They represent a combination or a mixture of both, and may be called mixed costs.[5] The best example of a mixed cost for an individual would be the cost of renting an automobile. Many cars are rented on the basis of a fixed fee per day ($20) and a variable charge per mile driven ($0.15 per mile). Your total cost per day of renting the car would increase with increased mileage, but not in exact proportion. Your total cost per day would be the sum of a purely fixed component ($20 per day whether the car is driven or not) and a purely variable component of $0.15 per mile actually driven.

Most different costs are of the mixed type shown in Fig. 5.6. Note that the cost has a fixed component and a variable component. Recall that several costs in the Tripper budget example were mixed. The budget rate was given as a certain number of dollars fixed per period plus a certain number of dollars varying with the amount of activity occurring during the period. Again, as is true for fixed and variable costs, the proportions of fixed and variable costs in a given mixed cost are constant only over a relevant range.

---

[5] Mixed costs are also known as either semivariable or semifixed. These two alternative terms will not be used, since mixed appears more descriptive for learning purposes.

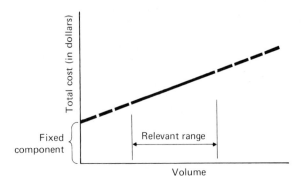

**Figure 5.6**

## DETERMINING SPECIFIC COST PATTERNS

It should be obvious to you that an effective budget system is dependent upon properly identifying the behavioral pattern of each cost, and determining its *budgeting rate* over a specific relevant range of activity. The budgeting rate is defined herein as the specific dollar factors to be used in budgeting the specific cost ($xxF or $yyV or $xxF + $yyV). Responsibility for the initial determination of budgeting rates is usually assigned to the budget section of a firm's accounting department. Final responsibility for approval and use of such rates must lie with the individual manager to whom they are applicable; otherwise an imposed budgeting system will effectively result. In determining appropriate budgeting rates, the first step is to obtain usable cost data. Various information sources may be used. The most obvious would be records of past costs incurred at different volume levels. Also, any contractual arrangements in existence pertaining to the costs under investigation would have to be checked (purchase commitments, wage contracts, and so forth). Where information on past costs and contractual arrangements is not available, or where it is deemed inadequate or inappropriate (a new process now being used), two other alternatives exist. A firm may rely on engineering estimates of how the costs may be expected to behave. And, in addition to or in place of engineering estimates, it may use test data derived from pilot or test runs.

Once usable information is available, it is first inspected to identify obvious wholly fixed costs. Most committed and programmed costs are usually found to be fixed in nature. Costs that are not identifiable as fixed will be wholly variable or mixed. Commonly, the data relevant to nonfixed costs is subject to regression analysis to determine the fixed variable components. (See Fig. 5.7).

As covered in Chapter 3 with respect to the determination of demand curves (lines), regression analysis involves determining the regression line (cost line in this case) that represents the best fit for the available data. The best-fit line would be the one that would have most closely (least amount of error) predicted in advance each of the events (observations) that occurred. Three techniques of applying linear regression analysis to such data were covered in Chapter 3. They were the visual-fit approach (simplest and often

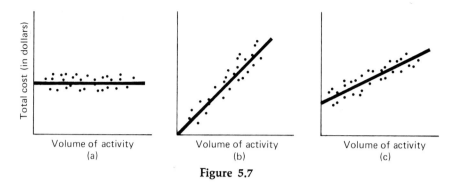

**Figure 5.7**

least reliable), the high–low point method (fairly simple and often more objective than the visual-fit approach), and the least-squares method (more complex and the most accurate, covered in the appendix to Chapter 3). The
appendix to this chapter reviews these approaches to the determination of the
fixed and variable cost components.

## Choosing the Activity Base

In regression analysis, an important step is choosing the most appropriate
measure of volume or the activity base. A particular variable cost (or variable
portion of a particular mixed cost) may correlate very well with one activity
(volume) measure and not at all with another measure. Which of the following
activity bases would you expect to best correlate with expenditures for salespersons' travel:

- Machine hours used in production?
- Direct labor hours expended in manufacturing?
- Direct labor cost dollars incurred?
- Number of separately invoiced shipments?
- Number of salesperson calls on potential/actual customers?
- Total dollar sales?

Probably regression analysis would reveal that sales travel expense would
most closely correlate with the number of customer calls, as shown in Fig.
5.8(b). Rarely would it be found to correlate with volume measures related
to production. Conversely, a manufacturer's indirect labor cost would probably be found to most closely correlate with machine hours, direct labor hours,
or some other measure of production activity. And cost in the shipping and
billing departments probably would vary with the number of separate shipments.

For budgeting purposes, each firm should select activity bases which:

1. Are readily measurable and available,
2. Correlate adequately with the costs being budgeted, and
3. Are few in number.

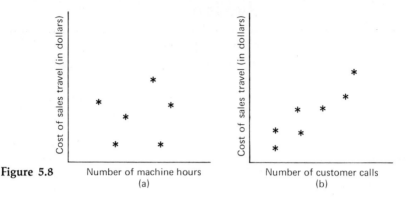

Figure 5.8      Number of machine hours         Number of customer calls
                                       (a)                              (b)

Note that there may be a tradeoff between many different activity measures each correlating very well with a particular cost and the need to employ a few simple measures to avoid excessive complexity in the budgeting process. Note that the second criteria suggests adequate correlation for prediction purposes as distinct from the very best. For example, indirect manufacturing costs may be found to correlate adequately with direct labor hours and avoid the necessity of tabulating machine hours. Similarly, shipping, billing, and sales travel costs may be adequately budgeted in terms of sales calls. Where a dollar measure of activity is employed (direct labor dollars, sales dollars, and so forth), care must be exercised to factor out the effects of wage rate and price inflation. An increase in total labor costs or sales revenue may not necessarily indicate an increase in the actual volume of activity.

## OPERATING EXPENDITURE BUDGETS FOR NONMANUFACTURERS AND NONPROFIT-DIRECTED ORGANIZATIONS

As first mentioned in Chapter 3, this text focuses primarily on problems and activities relevant to manufacturing firms. It does so because a manufacturer generally has all the problems of a nonmanufacturer and then some. A nonmanufacturing profit-directed firm (wholesale or retail merchandiser) budgets operating costs in the same manner as does a manufacturer. The essential difference is that the merchandiser does not have to prepare production schedules, raw material budgets, direct labor budgets, or manufacturing overhead budgets. A merchandiser's operating expenditure budget is made from or consists of only a finished-goods inventory budget, a purchases budget, and a GSA budget. Exhibit 5.11 lists for contrast the necessary steps in different types of businesses.

You should also note that the necessity of cost determination, accurate cost budgeting, and cost control is becoming increasingly more apparent for nonprofit-directed organizations. Operating budgets prepared on a similar

Exhibit 5.11

---

**Steps Involved in Preparation of Operating
Expenditure Budgets**

| | Service firms | Merchandisers | Manufacturers |
|---|---|---|---|
| 1. Sales budget | X | X | X |
| 2. Finished goods inventory budget | | X | X |
| 3. Production schedule | | | X |
| 4. Raw materials inventory budget | | | X |
| 5. Purchases budget | | X | X |
| 6. Direct labor budget | | | X |
| 7. Manufacturing overhead budget | | | X |
| 8. GSA budget | X | X | X |
| 9. Operating expenditure budget | X | X | X |

---

basis to those for profit-directed firms are both feasible and desirable in many not-for-profit organizations. This subject will be explored further in Chapter 15.

## USES OF COST INFORMATION

Data with respect to various costs of specific products or activities, the behavior of such costs in response to volume changes, and relevant ranges over which such behavior may reasonably be expected, have many important uses, primarily to nonaccountants. Cost data is, of course, used by managers in preparing budgets as demonstrated in the Tripper Company example. It is also necessary for analysis of cost–volume–profit relationships and for profit planning, both of which will be covered in Chapter 6. Its usefulness with respect to pricing decisions is also covered in the appendix to Chapter 6.

Cost data modified to reflect specific after-tax cash flows is one of the essential ingredients in both business project (nonroutine) decisions of all types and in the capital budgeting process. These two subjects will be covered in Chapters 6 and 7, respectively. For now it is important that you see the relevance and necessity of knowing costs in terms of fixed and variable components for the purpose of preparing operating expenditure budgets.

Recall from Chapter 2 that operating expenditure budgets are combined with sales budgets and with capital budgets in the preparation of the firm's cash budget. You have now been introduced to both sales and operating expenditure budgeting. The next three chapters will introduce business decisions and capital budgets. In Chapter 9, capital budgets, sales budgets, and operating expenditure budgets will be brought together in the preparation of the firm's overall cash budget.

## CHAPTER OVERVIEW

Based on the material covered in this chapter, you should be able to:

- Describe the purpose and content of operating expenditure budgets for a merchandising firm.
- Describe the differences in content and preparation of operating expenditure budgets between those prepared for merchandisers and for manufacturers.
- Prepare direct labor, manufacturing overhead, and GSA budgets, given budgetary rates and anticipated levels of activity.
- Prepare operating expenditure budgets at higher levels of responsibility, aggregating data from lower-level budgets and incorporating those costs controllable only at the higher level.
- Describe the advantages and disadvantages of participatory vs. imposed budgeting.
- Describe the input information necessary to prepare direct labor, manufacturing overhead, and GSA budgets.
- Explain the difference between a cost and an expense, and why budgeting focuses on costs rather than expenses.
- Describe the difference between direct and indirect costs, and identify which manufacturing costs are usually treated under each category.
- Define programmed, committed, and avoidable costs, and explain the usefulness of these categories.
- Define fixed, variable, and mixed costs; and explain whether these distinctions are similar to other cost categorizations such as direct, indirect, programmed, committed, avoidable, and so forth.
- Define the relevant range and explain its relevance in turn to the projection of costs.
- Describe the accountant's linearity assumption as it applies to cost behavior, and give two different examples of the application of the linearity assumption.
- Describe how one could determine the fixed and variable components of any given cost in terms of possible sources of data for analysis, and also describe several techniques useful for such analysis.

### NEW VOCABULARY AND CONCEPTS

| | |
|---|---|
| Controllable costs | Mixed costs |
| Variable cost | Participatory budgeting |
| Fixed costs | Imposed budgets |

Expenses
Expenditures
Cost
Direct costs
Indirect costs
Committed costs

Programmed/discretionary
   costs
Avoidable/escapable costs
Relevant range
Budgeting rate
Activity base

- Advantages of participatory budgeting over imposed budgeting
- Sources of data for determining budgeting rates

## REVIEW QUESTIONS

1. (a) What is a controllable cost?
   (b) Might the same cost for the same thing be budgeted on two distinct responsibility-center budgets? Explain.

2. (a) What is the difference in method of preparation between an imposed budget and a participatory budget?
   (b) What is often the difference in effectiveness as a planning and control device between imposed budgets and participatory budgets?

3. (a) Why is completion of the budgeted production schedule necessary before the direct labor budgets and manufacturing overhead budgets can be completed in each production department?
   (b) Why is completion of the budgeted production schedule and the sales budget necessary before the GSA budget can be completed?

4. (a) What budgets are normally included in the firm's manufacturing budget?
   (b) What are some of the budgets that may be included (depending upon the firm's size and organization) in a firm's GSA budget?

5. (a) What is the difference between a cost and an expense?
   (b) Even though both are important, why is successful cost control more productive than successful revenue control?

6. What is the difference between a direct and an indirect cost?

7. (a) What is a committed cost?
   (b) What is a programmed cost?
   (c) What is the difference between a committed cost and a programmed cost?
   (d) Can committed and programmed costs be variable or mixed? Explain.

8. (a) What are avoidable or escapable costs?
   (b) In what context are costs considered avoidable?

9. Describe in terms of the values (zero or positive) of each of their fixed and variable components:
   (a) Fixed costs,
   (b) Variable costs,
   (c) Mixed costs.

10. What is meant by the terms *fixed* and *variable* components of cost?

11. (a) What is the relevant range?
    (b) How is the relevant range applicable to the fixed and variable components of a particular cost?

12. What is the relationship between curvilinear costs, step-variable costs, and the accountant's linearity assumption? Explain with examples.

13. (a) Are most direct costs variable?
    (b) Are most indirect costs fixed? If not, give examples of variable and/or mixed costs that are classified as indirect.

14. (a) What is the budgeting rate?
    (b) How is it used in the budgeting process?

15. What are four possible sources of cost information potentially useful in determining a budgeting rate?

16. (a) What is regression analysis?
    (b) What is its relevance to the budgeting of costs? Explain with examples.

17. (a) What is an activity base?
    (b) List several possible activity bases that might be appropriate for budgeting:
      • Manufacturing overhead costs
      • Shipping and billing cost
      • Various sales-related costs

## MINI-CASES AND QUESTIONS FOR DISCUSSION

MC 5.1  Pat Bober and Diana Kennedy are approaching the subject of budgeting from two entirely different positions. Pat says, "I really don't think budgeting personnel should be involved in the setting of budgets. Budgeting personnel eventually would intimidate lower-level supervision. They would understand the inner workings of the budgeting process at all levels, would be probably more mathematically proficient, and would be in partnership with computers. How could a poor line foreman not be snowed and end up with an 'imposed budget'?"

Diana sees things quite differently. She replies, "I think if budget types want to play their budgeting games, they should do so without involving the foreman and pretending that the result is his/her budget. Foremen are supervisors of people and shouldn't have to waste time with paperwork. Foremen's jobs are to see that the human and material resources entrusted to them are used as efficiently and effectively as possible. They are responsible to the General Foreman/Plant Superintendent/Vice-President for Operations (manufacturing), **not** to the budget, the budgeting personnel, or the Controller. If a foreman gets the job done, fine. If not, a different foreman is required, not a revised budget! If the Controller needs to or wants to plan, let him do so without wasting the foreman's time."

Is it possible that both Pat and Diana may have a point? Discuss the issues involved and their resolution.

MC 5.2  John Trainor is confused. He understands that a primary function of organizations is to clearly delineate responsibility. To him the budgeting practice of showing service-center costs on both the budgets of the service center and of the using departments runs completely contrary to his concept of organizational responsibility. He is concerned that this practice may have several undesirable consequences:

1. Each manager could "let the other worry about it."

2. The service-using manager could become really frustrated. He would have no control over the efficiency of the services performed, and no way to control possible inefficiency costs.

Discuss John Trainor's concerns. Is the budgetary practice referred to appropriate? What other alternatives or modifications might be desirable?

**MC 5.3** How could a firm budget a cost that was not correlated with volume, such as a programmed cost? On whose budget should such a cost appear? Discuss in terms of specific examples.

**MC 5.4** What would you expect to find as the similarities and the differences between budgeting costs for a manufacturer and estimating costs as part of the bid preparation process for a general construction contractor? Discuss those techniques that might be used profitably by both.

**MC 5.5** It is possible that a cost that has always been completely variable could become fixed overnight as a result of a management decision/action. And fixed costs can be converted into mixed or variable costs. Discuss specific circumstances where such transformations could occur and the implication to budgeting for subsequent periods.

**MC 5.6** Many small firms cannot afford detailed cost records. The only past cost data readily available for budgeting purposes is aggregated in terms of line items on the firm's past income statements. Could operating expenditure budgets at the total firm level be prepared for such firms? How could the necessary budgeting rates be determined? Discuss, with specific examples.

**MC 5.7** Is the trend of business costs in the direction of becoming more fixed or more variable? What is the significance of this trend to the role (authority and discretion) of the manager? Discuss.

## ESSENTIAL PROBLEMS

**EP 5.1** Each of the following are general, selling, and administrative (GSA) costs:

1. Supplies for use in the shipping department
2. Supplies for use in the accounting department
3. Personnel (indirect labor) in the shipping department
4. Salary of secretary to sales vice-president
5. Depreciation on office building, furniture, and equipment
6. Travel and entertainment expense of salesmen working in a particular sales territory

7. Advertising expenses (firm has separate advertising department)
8. Sales commissions of salesmen working in a particular sales territory
9. Controller's salary

(a) Identify each cost as most probably fixed per budget period (F), variable in relation to some measure of sales volume (V), or mixed (M).

(b) Assume that the firm has only two levels of management in the GSA area. Identify each cost as most probably first included in a lower-level supervisory budget (SUP) or as included only at the sales vice-president or controller budget level (EXEC).

EP 5.2  Each of the following are manufacturing costs:

1. Direct labor
2. Depreciation on plant and equipment
3. Maintenance supplies
4. Rent on leased special purpose equipment
5. Indirect labor for maintenance
6. Factory supplies
7. Fire insurance on factory building and equipment
8. Supplies used in purchasing department
9. Property taxes on factory building and equipment
10. Salary of vice-president for operations (manufacuring)
11. Indirect labor for material handling
12. Direct materials used in production

(a) Identify each cost as most probably fixed per budget period (F), variable in relation to some measure of production volume (V), or mixed (M).

(b) Assume that the firm has only two levels of management in the factory. Identify each cost as most probably first included on the lower-level foreman/supervisor budget (FOR) or as only included at the operations vice-president level (EXEC).

EP 5.3  As foreman of the shipping department, you are required to budget the costs under your control (influence) for the third quarter of 19XX. You have the following information with respect to your costs:

| Cost | Budgeting rate |
| --- | --- |
| Indirect labor | $2,750/Month F + $0.03/Sales dollar V |
| Indirect materials (Supplies) | $0.004/Sales dollar V |
| Shipping (Freight out) | $0.013/Sales dollar V |

You also have a sales budget indicating the following sales for the quarter:

| Month | Quantity |
| --- | --- |
| July | $200,000 |
| Aug. | 120,000 |
| Sep. | 90,000 |
| Total | $410,000 |

Prepare the budget for your department for each month and in total for the quarter.

**EP 5.4** As the moulding department foreman, you are required to budget costs under your control (influence) for the second quarter of 19XX. You have the following information with respect to your costs:

| Cost | Budgeting rate |
| --- | --- |
| Indirect labor | $10,500/Quarter F + $2.00 V/unit produced |
| Indirect materials (Supplies) | $480/Quarter F + $0.40 V/unit produced |
| Maintenance | $7,500/Quarter F + $0.35 V/unit produced |

You also have a production schedule indicating the following total numbers of skis to be produced in your department during the quarter:

| Month | Quantity |
| --- | --- |
| April | 2,000 units |
| May | 3,000 units |
| June | 5,000 units |
| Total | 10,000 units |

Prepare the budget for your department for each month and in total for the quarter.

**EP 5.5** As vice-president for sales, you have the following budgets approved for the first quarter of 19XX for each of the responsibility centers within your area (two sales territories and the shipping department):

| Approved budgets | Jan. | Feb. | Mar. |
| --- | --- | --- | --- |
| Sales territory #1: | | | |
| Salaries ($1,800/Mo. F) | $1,800 | $1,800 | $1,800 |
| Commissions (0.02 V) | 1,600 | 1,800 | 2,200 |
| Travel ($600/Mo. F + 0.005 V) | 1,000 | 1,050 | 1,150 |
| Total ($2,400/Mo. F + 0.025 V) | $4,400 | $4,650 | $5,150 |
| Sales territory #2: | | | |
| Salaries ($600/Mo. F) | $ 600 | $ 600 | $ 600 |
| Commissions (0.02 V) | 1,600 | 1,800 | 2,200 |
| Travel ($300/Mo. F + 0.005 V) | 700 | 750 | 850 |
| Total ($900/Mo. F + 0.025 V) | $2,900 | $3,150 | $3,650 |
| Shipping department: | | | |
| Indirect labor ($690/Mo. F + 0.03 V) | $3,090 | $3,390 | $3,990 |
| Indirect materials (Supplies) ($0.004 V) | 320 | 360 | 440 |
| Shipping (Freight out) ($0.013 V) | 1,040 | 1,170 | 1,430 |
| Total (690/Mo. F + 0.047 V) | $4,450 | $4,920 | $5,860 |

You also have the following items with control residing at your level:

| Cost | Budgeting rate |
|------|----------------|
| Sales supervision wages and salaries | $4,000/Quarter F |
| Home office supplies | $500/Quarter F |
| Depreciation on sales office equipment | $1,500/Quarter F |
| Advertising and sales promotional materials | $2,125/Quarter F + $.008/Sales dol. V |

The sales budget reveals:

|  | Jan. | Feb. | Mar. | Total |
|--|------|------|------|-------|
| Budgeted sales | $80,000 | $90,000 | $110,000 | $280,000 |

Prepare your budget for the first quarter of 19XX by month and in total. Your budget should cover:

- Wages, salaries, and commissions
- Distribution and marketing (indirect shipping supplies, shipping costs, advertising, travel)
- Depreciation
- Miscellaneous (home office supplies)

**EP 5.6**  As vice-president for operations, you have the following budgets approved for the second quarter of 19XX for each of the responsibility centers within your area (assembly, moulding, and maintenance). Note that budgets for direct labor, purchasing, receiving and raw materials stores, and material control (scheduling) are omitted for problem simplification.

| Approved budgets | Apr. | May | June |
|------------------|------|-----|------|
| Assembly department: |  |  |  |
| Indirect labor ($1,000/Mo. F + 0.20 V) | $1,900 | $2,000 | $2,100 |
| Indirect materials ($30/Mo. F + 0.30 V) | 1,380 | 1,530 | 1,680 |
| Maintenance ($500/Mo. F + 0.05 V) | 725 | 750 | 775 |
| Supervision ($1,500/Mo. F) | 1,500 | 1,500 | 1,500 |
| Total ($3,030/Mo. F + 0.55 V) | $5,505 | $5,780 | $6,055 |
| Moulding department: |  |  |  |
| Indirect labor ($3,500/Mo. F + 2.00 V) | $12,500 | $13,500 | $14,500 |
| Indirect materials ($160/Mo. F + 0.40 V) | 1,960 | 2,160 | 2,360 |
| Maintenance ($2,500/Mo. F + 0.35 V) | 4,075 | 4,250 | 4,425 |
| Supervision ($2,415/Mo. F) | 2,415 | 2,415 | 2,415 |
| Total ($8,575/Mo. F + 2.75 V) | $20,950 | $22,325 | $23,700 |

| Approved budgets | Apr. | May | June |
|---|---|---|---|
| Maintenance department: | | | |
| Indirect labor | | | |
| ($1,250/Mo. F + 0.30 V) | $2,600 | $2,750 | $2,900 |
| Indirect materials | | | |
| ($250/Mo. F + 0.10 V) | 700 | 750 | 800 |
| Supervision | | | |
| ($1,500/Mo. F) | 1,500 | 1,500 | 1,500 |
| Total | | | |
| ($3,000/Mo. F + 0.40 V) | $4,800 | $5,000 | $5,200 |

You also have the following items with control residing at your level:

| Cost | Budgeting rate |
|---|---|
| Supervision | $5,000/Mo. F |
| Utilities | $1,040/Mo. F + $0.30 V |
| Insurance | $1,000/Mo. F |
| Property taxes | $1,500/Mo. F |
| Depreciation | $4,000/Mo. F |

The production schedule reveals:

| | Apr. | May | June | Total |
|---|---|---|---|---|
| Budgeted production units | 4,500 | 5,000 | 5,500 | 15,000 |

Prepare your budget for the second quarter of 19XX by month and in total. Your budget should cover:

- Indirect labor
- Indirect materials
- Supervision
- Utilities
- Insurance
- Property taxes
- Depreciation

EP 5.7 The Borroughs Company is a wholesaler of automotive parts. Income statements for the years 19X6 through 19X8 are given below (in thousands of dollars):

| | 19X8 | 19X7 | 19X6 |
|---|---|---|---|
| Sales | $1,400 | $1,100 | $900 |
| Cost of goods sold | 770 | 660 | 540 |
| Gross profit | $ 630 | $ 440 | $360 |
| Operating expenses: | | | |
| Wages and salaries | 189 | 140 | 120 |
| Supplies | 31 | 24 | 20 |
| Insurance | 11 | 10 | 10 |
| Utilities | 35 | 17 | 15 |
| Rent | 90 | 80 | 80 |
| Depreciation | 40 | 40 | 40 |
| Miscellaneous | 28 | 11 | 9 |
| Income from operations | $206 | $118 | $66 |
| Provision for income taxes | 72 | 41 | 23 |
| Net income | $134 | $ 77 | $43 |

Assume you were asked to budget 19X8 income early in 19X8 on the basis of 19X6 and 19X7 data (ignoring 19X8 actual data). You may assume that 19X8 sales were originally budgeted at $1,200,000, that fixed costs were not expected to change from those incurred in 19X7, and that income taxes averaged 35 percent of income from operations.

a) Determine budgeting rates for:

   Cost of goods sold

   Wages and salaries

   Supplies

   Insurance

   Utilities

   Rent

   Depreciation

   Miscellaneous

b) Prepare the 19X8 budgeted income statement.

**EP 5.8** Refer to the data given for the Borroughs Company in Problem EP 5.7. Assume that, early in 19X8, the company experienced major increases only in its fixed costs and increased its markup on sales. Ignoring 19X6 data except for identification of wholly fixed and wholly variable cost elements, prepare a budgeted income statement for 19X9, assuming that sales for 19X9 are expected to be $1,500,000. Round your budget to even thousands of dollars.

## SUPPLEMENTARY PROBLEMS

**SP 5.9** The following information is available to you relating to costs incurred for packing supplies, labor, and shipping (freight out) expenses during particular representative months:

| Units shipped | Costs incurred |
|---|---|
| 6,000 | $ 9,000 |
| 7,000 | 10,100 |
| 8,500 | 12,000 |
| 10,000 | 14,500 |
| 10,800 | 15,000 |

Using the high–low point method of regression analysis:

a) Determine the fixed and variable components of this cost for budgeting purposes—the budgeting rate.

b) Assuming the anticipated volume was still within the relevant range, what cost would you budget for 11,750 units to be shipped (using the budgetary rate derived by the high–low point method above)?

**SP 5.10** The following information is available to you relating to costs incurred for factory indirect materials (supplies) costs during certain representative months:

| Units manufactured | Costs incurred |
| --- | --- |
| 40,000 | $2,900 |
| 47,000 | 3,250 |
| 50,000 | 3,600 |
| 60,000 | 3,800 |
| 65,000 | 4,150 |
| 69,000 | 4,350 |

Using the high–low point method of regression analysis:

a) Determine the fixed and variable components of this cost for budgeting purposes—the budgeting rate.

b) How much cost would you budget for an activity level of 55,000 units?

*Note.* The following problems involve techniques covered in the chapter appendix.

**SP 5.11** Refer to the data given in Problem SP 5.9. Using the least-squares method:

a) Determine the fixed and variable components of the packing and shipping cost, rounding to the nearest cent.

b) Determine the standard error for the regression line obtained in (a) above.

c) If you desired 99 percent assurance in predicting this cost within the relevant range of the above data, between what limits would your forecast (budget) be made?

**SP 5.12** Answer questions (a), (b), and (c) from Problem SP 5.11 with respect to the data supplied as part of Problem SP 5.10.

**SP 5.13** In preparation for budgeting indirect labor for the forthcoming year, you have used a computer program (or hand calculator) to analyze past cost data, using the LSRA method. You have before you the following results:

| Correlated to: | a (Slope) | b (Intercept) | $\sigma$ (Std. Error) |
| --- | --- | --- | --- |
| Machine hours | $5.10 | $37,000 | $1,042 |
| Direct labor dollars | $0.85 | 27,000 | 920 |
| Direct labor hours | $5.00 | 30,000 | 730 |

Expected data with respect to each of the activity bases for the forthcoming period is given below:

| | |
| --- | --- |
| Machine hours | 18,000 hours |
| Direct labor dollars | $120,000 |
| Direct labor hours | 20,000 hours |

a) Determine the indirect labor budget for the period, using each of the three different activity bases.

b) If data pertaining to all three bases were readily available, which would you choose as the activity base for indirect labor budgeting and why?

c) Which of the three budgeted amounts in (a) above is the best predictor and should be used? Explain your reasoning.

**SP 5.14** Refer to Problem SP 5.13. Assume that, instead of indirect labor, you were budgeting packaging and shipping supplies for the forthcoming period. Your computer or hand calculator has given you the following results of LSRA analysis of available data:

| Correlated to: | a (Slope) | b (Intercept) | $\sigma$ (Std. Error) |
|---|---|---|---|
| Total dollar sales | $0.06 | $44,000 | $2,300 |
| Number customer orders | 7.00 | 17,000 | $3,200 |
| Number separate shipments | 7.50 | 15,000 | $2,100 |

(Orders and shipments differ, since several orders may be combined in a single shipment and some orders partially shipped with backordered items separately shipped later.)

Expected activity levels for the forthcoming period include:

| | |
|---|---|
| Sales | $1,600,000 |
| Number orders | 18,000 |
| Number shipments | 16,000 |

a) Determine the packaging and shipping supplies budget for the period, using each of the three alternative activity bases.

b) If data pertaining to all three bases were readily available, which base should you use for budgeting this item and why?

c) Since either number of orders or number of shipments might be difficult to obtain readily, could a budgeting rate based on total sales be used with reasonable confidence? Ninety-nine percent of the time, how much additional error might be expected using sales as compared to a more accurate base as a predictor?

## SUGGESTIONS FOR FURTHER READING

Benston, George J., "Multiple regression analysis of cost behavior," *Accounting Review*, **XLI**, No. 4.

Horngren, C., *Cost Accounting: A Managerial Emphasis*, Fourth Edition. Englewood Cliffs, N.J.: Prentice-Hall, Inc., 1977; Chapter 25.

Morse, Wayne J., *Cost Accounting: Processing, Evaluating, and Using Cost Data*. Reading, Massachusetts: Addison-Wesley, 1978; Chapters 3 and 5.

CHAPTER 5 APPENDIX

# Determining Fixed and Variable Cost Components Using Regression Analysis

As discussed in this chapter, in order to budget or predict future costs, you must first determine the behavior of each separate cost at different levels of activity. Using past, actual, or experimentally derived data or engineered estimates, the first step is to identify obvious fixed, programmed, and committed costs. Then the tools of regression analysis may be applied to all other cost data to determine variable and fixed cost components (a purely variable cost may be viewed as a mixed cost with a fixed component of zero).

This appendix will first review cost behavior as covered in this chapter. Regression analysis of cost data will then be covered. If you are not familiar with the techniques of regression analysis, you might first read the Appendix to Chapter 3 for additional reinforcement.

## Review of Cost Behavior

All costs may be viewed as having a fixed and variable component (either positive or zero). Some costs such as most committed and programmed costs[6] have a fixed positive amount and a variable component of zero.

When the variable component is zero (zero slope of the regression line), the cost is considered wholly fixed and often simply called "fixed." See Fig. 5.9.

Other costs have a positive variable component and a fixed component of zero (regression line passes through the origin); see Fig. 5.10. When the regression line intersects the Y (cost) axis at zero (at the origin), the fixed component is zero and the cost is wholly variable and often simply called "variable."

Most costs have both a positive fixed and a positive variable component and are known as mixed costs. A mixed cost can be viewed as the sum of a fixed cost and a variable cost (see dashed lines in Fig. 5.11). The fixed component intersects the Y (cost) axis at an amount equal to the fixed cost. The

---

[6]   Some variable costs may be committed such as a long-term purchase contract committing the firm to a price of so much per unit over several years. In practice, most programmed and committed costs are fixed in total over the budget period.

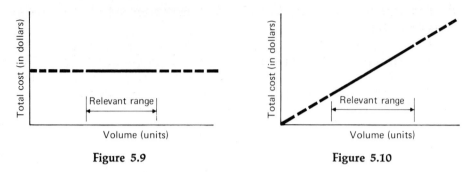

Figure 5.9                    Figure 5.10

variable component intersects the origin, and its slope equals the variable cost per unit of volume.[7]

To be able to predict the behavior (amount) of a particular cost at a particular level of volume, you must determine or estimate the regression line for the cost applicable or within the relevant range in which you wish to forecast. The techniques for finding or determining the line for a particular cost are known as cost regression analysis techniques.

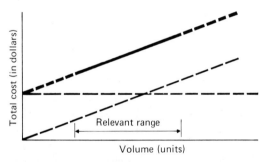

Figure 5.11

### Regression Analysis—Visual-Fit Approach

The simplest technique of regression analysis is known as the visual-fit method. Various cost–volume pairs (from experience or engineering estimates) are first plotted on a graph similar to those above. Then visually a line of best fit (regression line) is selected and drawn. The line of visual best fit is the one where the distance of all points representing valid combinations[8] from

---

[7]   Note that the cost regression line will intersect the Y-axis either at some positive fixed cost amount (the lines for both fixed costs and mixed costs) or at zero (the line for a variable cost). To intersect the X-axis at a positive amount and therefore the Y-axis below zero would be unreal. Such a line would indicate that some quantity was free (zero cost) and below this quantity the firm would receive revenue (negative cost).

[8]   Care must be taken to ignore points that represent abnormal readings and are not representative of future conditions.

the line appears least, where the line would have predicted all of the points with the least error.

Following the visual-fit method, future costs may be predicted from the graph in Fig. 5.12 by first locating the anticipated volume on the X-axis. Then the point on the cost line and its Y (cost) value is determined by inspection.

Where costs involved are sufficiently great that a forecasting error could be serious, the visual-fit method may prove too inaccurate.

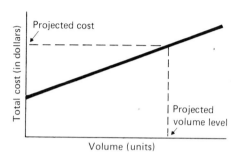

**Figure 5.12**

**Regression Analysis—High–Low Point Method**

A somewhat more accurate, and usually more rapid, approach to regression analysis than visual fit is the high–low point method. The essence of this method involves selecting two points (cost–volume pairs), one at a higher volume level and one at a lower level, which are considered to be representative. Then the regression line is "drawn" through these two points, but not on graph paper. Instead the line is drawn mathematically, using the equation for a straight line in the form:

$$Y = ax + b$$

where

$Y =$ Cost value in dollars,

$a =$ Slope, or variable cost per unit,

$X =$ Volume in units,

$b =$ Y-axis intersection point, or amount of fixed cost.

The two representative points are used to form two simultaneous equations with $a$ and $b$ as the unknowns (not yet determined values). The two equations are then solved simultaneously, and the variable and fixed components ($a$ and $b$) of the particular cost are thus determined.

The high–low point method of regression analysis is simple, quick, and more objective than the visual-fit approach. However, it may not result in the best predictive data. The points chosen may not be representative, and the information content or value of all other points is ignored.

Regression analysis for cost components applies to all costs, both manufacturing and nonmanufacturing. As an example, consider a nonmanufacturing cost such as selling cost. Intuitively you should expect selling cost to be mixed. With greater volume there would be more distribution cost, more travel and plane expense, more sales commissions, and so forth. Yet you should not expect selling cost to be wholly variable since, at the very least, it is unlikely that the sales manager and his staff would be willing to be paid entirely on commission, as opposed to having some base salary. Assume that for selling cost you have the following observations, each applicable to a particular representative month:

Sales volume (units) 8,000:    Total selling costs:   $47,000;
Sales volume (units) 2,000:    Total selling costs:   $17,000.

Substituting into two equations:

( I) $47,000 = a(8,000) + b$,
(II) $17,000 = a(2,000) + b$.

Subtracting Eq. (II) from Eq. (I):

$$30,000 = (6,000)a,$$
$$a = \$5.00.$$

Substituting $a$ equal to $5.00 into either Eq. (I) or (II) and solving for $b$ results in:

$$b = \$7,000.$$

You have verified that the selling cost in this particular firm is a mixed cost. If your selected high and low points were representative, then you can forecast selling costs on the basis of $7,000 fixed (F) per month and $5.00 per unit variable (V).

### Regression Analysis—Least-Squares Method

The third technique of linear (straight-line) regression analysis is known as the least-squares method or least-squares regression analysis (LSRA). This LSRA technique was covered in the appendix to Chapter 3 in an application relating to obtaining the demand curve (line) for a particular product. In this appendix, only an illustration of the LSRA technique applied to a cost curve will be covered. If you are unfamiliar with the mathematics or terminology of LSRA, you should first review the appendix to Chapter 3 before proceeding.

As an example of LSRA applied to the determination of the regression line for a particular cost, consider a situation involving factory indirect labor for the year. Assume you have the following historical data, which you believe representative:

| Volume of activity (units) | Indirect labor cost incurred per year |
|---|---|
| 13,000 | $102,000 |
| 16,000 | 108,000 |
| 17,000 | 112,000 |
| 19,000 | 117,000 |
| 20,000 | 118,000 |
| 23,000 | 127,000 |

Recall that you will be using the following two equations:

(A) $$\sum XY = b \sum X + a \sum X^2,$$

(B) $$\sum Y = nb + a \sum X,$$

where

$\sum XY =$ Costs times volumes summed,
$b =$ Constant representing amount of fixed cost per year,
$\sum X =$ Total volumes,
$\sum X^2 =$ Each volume squared, then summed,
$a =$ Slope representing variable cost per unit of annual production,
$\sum Y =$ Total costs,
$n =$ Number of observations of cost–volume pairs.

From the data available you can determine:

$\sum XY = 12,462$ million,
$b =$ Unknown fixed cost to be obtained via LSRA method,
$\sum X = 108,000$,
$\sum X^2 = 2,004$ million,
$a =$ Unknown variable cost per unit, to be obtained via LSRA method,
$\sum Y = \$684,000$,
$n = 6$.

Substituting into the two equations, you will have:

(A) $\quad 12,462$ million $= b(108,000) + a(2,004$ million$)$,
(B) $\quad 684,000 = b(6) + a(108,000)$.

Dividing Eq. (A) by 108,000 and Eq. (B) by 6:

(A₁)                          $115,389 = b + 18,556a,$
(B₁)                          $114,000 = b + 18,000a.$

Subtracting Eq. (B₁) from Eq. (A₁):

$$1,389 = 556a,$$
$$a = \$2.50 \text{ (rounded)}.$$

Substituting $a = \$2.50$ into Eq. B₁:

$$114,000 = b + 18,000(2.50),$$
$$b = \$69,000.$$

From the foregoing LSRA method, you have determined that factory indirect labor for the year may be budgeted on the basis of $69,000 fixed plus $2.50 per unit of activity variable.

### Estimated (Budgeting) Error

As covered in the appendix to Chapter 3, the LSRA method has the added advantage of making available a measure of the probability of error resulting from using the regression line as a forecasting (budgeting) tool. Recall that the standard error (of estimate) is calculated by the formula:

$$SE = \sqrt{\frac{\Sigma(Y - \overline{Y})^2}{n - 2}}$$

where

   $Y$ = observed cost at a particular volume,
   $\overline{Y}$ = predicted cost at the same volume from the regression line,
   $n$ = number of observations.

   Continuing with the above example, you can use the budgeting rates obtained above ($69,000 F + $2.50 V) to determine what costs would be predicted (budgeted) at the various observed volume levels given earlier.

| Volume of activity (units) | Indirect labor cost observed | Indirect labor cost predicted |
|---|---|---|
| 13,000 | $102,000 | $101,500 |
| 16,000 | 108,000 | 109,000 |
| 17,000 | 112,000 | 111,500 |
| 19,000 | 117,000 | 116,500 |
| 20,000 | 118,000 | 119,000 |
| 23,000 | 127,000 | 126,500 |

Visual inspection reveals that the regression line is a good predictor. The maximum error is only $1,000, or less than one percent. The standard error is obtained by first calculating the individual errors (variances)—$Y - \overline{Y}$. These variances are first each squared and then summed. Summation sign $(Y - \overline{Y})$ squared in this example equals three million. With $n$ equal to 6, solving the equation for the standard error reveals it to be $866.03, or $866.00 rounded. Since three standard errors occur less than one percent of the time, in using the budgeting rates obtained above for indirect labor, you may be confident of being within $2,600 ($866.00 times 3 rounded) of the actual yearly total, over 99 percent of the time.

As mentioned in the Appendix to Chapter 3, computation using the LSRA approach is vastly simplified by using existing computer programs or hand calculators programmed for trend or regression analysis. You might check to see whether you have access to equipment that can assist you with these computations. Unfortunately many calculators programmed for regression analysis are not also programmed for calculation of the standard error (of estimate).

### Regression Analysis—Nonlinear

Remember that the three techniques of regression analysis described above (visual fit, high–low point, and LSRA) all assume a linear or constant relationship between two items (the volume of activity and the cost incurred). As discussed in this chapter, if the relationship is not linear or if more than two variables are involved, then the accountant has two choices:

1. Assume linearity over a limited relevant range (most common practice).

2. Use multiple regression analysis for more than two variables or other techniques beyond the scope of this text.

# 6

---

# CONTRIBUTION
# AND
# PROFIT PLANNING

## CHAPTER PREVIEW

The intention of this chapter is to introduce you to profit planning and the important concepts of cost of capital and contribution as tools of profitability analysis. In this chapter you can learn:

- Why a satisfactory profit is necessary for a firm's survival and growth.
- That a firm's investors collectively demand a certain return on their investment, and that this return is measurable as the firm's cost of capital.
- That profits are usually the result of active planning and implementation, and various approaches used by management in planning profits.
- That a concept known as contribution provides both insight and a valuable tool for profitability analysis at different levels of business activity.
- How to apply contribution analysis to the solution of various business problems, and some of the common business problems for which the contribution-analysis technique is appropriate.

In the appendix to this chapter you can be introduced to the subject of pricing and several elements involved in pricing policy formation.

With this information you will be in a position to make appropriate decisions among certain alternative proposals. You will also have the conceptual foundation necessary for the next two chapters, which are devoted to business decision-making.

## HOW CAN I INCREASE MY PROFITABILITY?

Do you have the impression from the last three chapters that a business only:

- Plans to sell what it can of existing products,

- Plans its costs to be as low as reasonable, and then

- Hopes revenues will exceed expenses, but can only accept whatever happens?

If you have such an impression, it is only part of the picture. For most success-ful businesses, profit is not just a lucky accident. Profit results from deliberate and careful planning of both the routine, day-to-day decisions that are in-cluded in operating budgets and also the nonroutine decisions that involve choices from among thousands of alternative courses of action.

Profit-generating decisions cover the entire time horizon discussed in Chapter 2. Some involve long- and intermediate-range planning. They include both long-term commitment of new resources, such as additional plant and equipment, and also significant long-term reallocation of existing resources (disposing of existing facilities and acquiring others). Decisions of this type will be covered in Chapter 8. Other decisions with an intermediate- and short-range horizon involve alternative uses of existing resources. Decisions of this type are introduced in Chapter 7. Finally, there are nonroutine decisions that involve modifications or changes to the existing budget.

Managers require a framework for analyzing all such decisions. They also require guidelines, criteria, or decision rules, to facilitate their choosing of the alternative that will most benefit the firm. This chapter introduces the foun-dation or conceptual basis for such decision criteria. The following two chap-ters develop specific methods of analysis and specific decision rules applicable to particular types of decisions.

To experience the need for such criteria, once again imagine that you are the president and owner of the Tripper Water Ski Manufacturing Company, and that it is early in November of 19X1. You have before you for immediate action two proposals from your vice-president for sales. The first proposal involves a major change in marketing strategy, and is summarized in Exhibit 6.1. The second involves possible acceptance of a single special order at a price apparently below cost, and is set forth in Exhibit 6.2. Both proposals require immediate action (acceptance or rejection) on your part.

As the president and owner of Tripper, what would you do? You will benefit if you first analyze these proposals and arrive at a recommendation for each, before proceeding to the next paragraph. All necessary data for your analysis is available in Exhibits 3.8, 4.10, 4.12, 4.13, 5.8, 5.9, and 5.10 in the previous three chapters. Make a record, on a separate sheet of paper, of the basis for your decision, so that you can compare your analysis to the ones below.

## Exhibit 6.1

---

### Proposal for Change in Marketing Strategy

Actions recommended:
1. Immediately (effective 1/1/X2) reduce selling prices of all products 10 percent
2. Immediately (effective 1/1/X2) increase advertising budget by $75,000 per year

Result expected:
1. Within year achieve total unit sales increase of 25 percent
2. Overall increase in revenue of $157,964 or $82,964 more than increased advertising costs.

### Revenue Comparison

|  | Present plan | | | Proposed plan | | |
|---|---|---|---|---|---|---|
|  | Price | Quantity | Total | Price | Quantity | Total |
| Economy | $50 | 12,800 | $ 640,000 | $45 | 16,000 | $ 720,000 |
| Deluxe | 80 | 7,050 | 564,000 | 72 | 8,812 | 634,464 |
| Tow rope | 10 | 6,000 | 60,000 | 9 | 7,500 | 67,500 |
|  |  |  | $1,264,000 |  |  | $1,421,964 |

---

## Exhibit 6.2

---

### Proposal for Special Order

The Nippon Sports Company wishes to purchase 4,000 of our deluxe skis to sell in Japan for a price in equivalent U.S. dollars of $45 each. The skis will carry a Nippon decal (applied by them at their expense) and will not in any way be identified in customer's minds with our company.

The price offered by Nippon is $140,400 or $35.10 per ski. Our full product cost is $40 per ski, but this order will involve no additional selling or distribution costs on our part. This order should be accepted. The $19,600 "loss" is acceptable because it enables us to maintain production levels in our shop. We will thus avoid laying off skilled employees while we reduce our finished-goods inventory levels in accordance with the 19X2 budget.

---

## Analysis of Proposed Change in Marketing Strategy

Did you concur with the sales vice-president's recommendation for reduced prices and increased advertising? Assuming that your goal is to maintain or increase profits, you should reject this proposal. To adopt it would reduce profits by over $32,000 per year. Revenues would increase $157,964 but costs would increase $190,707. The sales vice-president's proposal neglects to consider the $115,707 of manufacturing costs of the additional products to be sold. Your sales vice-president should be concentrating on those factors within his

## Exhibit 6.3

### TRIPPER WATER SKI MANUFACTURING COMPANY

**Budgeted Income from Operations on Contribution Basis
for the Year 19X2**

|  |  | Dollars | Percentage |
|---|---|---|---|
| Sales[a] |  | $1,264,000 | 100.0 |
| Variable manufacturing expenses: |  |  |  |
| Direct materials[b] | $161,735 |  |  |
| Direct labor[c] | 213,565 |  |  |
| Variable manufacturing overhead[d] | 77,415 | 452,715 | 35.8 |
| Variable general, selling, and administrative expenses[e] |  | 10,112 | 0.8 |
| Total contribution |  | $ 801,173 | 63.4 |
| Less: Fixed manufacturing expenses[d] |  | 223,476 | 17.7 |
| Fixed general, selling and administrative expenses[e] |  | 384,000 | 30.4 |
| Income from operations |  | $ 193,697 | 15.3 |

[a] From Exhibit 3.8.
[b] $5.50 per economy ski, $8.70 per deluxe ski, $5.00 per tow rope.
[c] $9.80 per economy ski, $12.50 per deluxe ski.
[d] From Exhibit 5.9.
[e] From Exhibit 5.10.

control—revenue and marketing costs. It is your job to see to it that other costs are appropriately considered in a balanced perspective. To analyze this and similar proposals, it is not necessary to rebudget the entire company in detail.[1] Instead you can estimate the decision impact at the total firm level by using your knowledge of cost behavior developed in Chapter 5. Exhibit 6.3 presents the firm's anticipated 19X2 income from operations based on the sales and operating budgets prepared in previous chapters. Note that this exhibit is **not** a final budgeted income statement for the forthcoming year. Still to be incorporated are the effects of proposed capital and financial budgets, which will be developed in Chapters 8, 9, and 10.

Also note that Exhibit 6.3 is prepared in what is known as a *contribution format* or *classification*. Remember from Chapter 5 that, for a given period and within a relevant range of activity, costs behave in predictable fixed and variable patterns. Contribution is defined as the excess of revenues over vari-

---

[1] If a major change of this type were adopted however, rebudgeting would be desirable for two reasons. Revisions in cost estimated on a total firm basis might be different when worked out by individual responsibility centers. Secondly, at least a review of proposed budget revisions would be desirable to avoid moving into an imposed budgeting approach.

Exhibit 6.4

---

**Contribution Comparison**
**(Assuming Constant Product Mix)**

|  | Present budget | Proposed plan | | Differences |
|---|---|---|---|---|
| Sales | $1,264,000 | $1,421,964[a] | + | $157,964 |
| Variable manufacturing cost | 452,715 | 565,894[b] | − | 113,179[c] |
| Variable selling cost | 10,112 | 12,640[b] | − | 2,528[c] |
| Contribution | $ 801,173 | $ 843,430 | + | $ 42,257 |

[a] From Exhibit 6.1.
[b] 125 percent of presently budgeted costs.
[c] Cost increase denoted as negative (−).

---

able costs, or as the amount of revenues remaining after deducting variable costs.

$$\text{Profit (income)} = \text{Revenue} - \text{Expense},$$
$$\text{Profit} = \text{Revenue} - (\text{Variable costs} + \text{Fixed costs}),$$
$$\text{Profit} = \text{Revenue} - \text{Variable costs} - \text{Fixed costs},$$
$$\text{Profit} = \text{Contribution} - \text{Fixed costs},$$

where

$$\text{Contribution} = \text{Revenue} - \text{Variable costs}.$$

Exhibit 6.3 indicates that the firm expects a contribution next year of $801,173. This contribution must first cover fixed costs before there is any profit. Contribution in excess of fixed costs equals income. Contribution will be discussed more thoroughly later in this chapter.

Returning to the Tripper marketing proposal, Exhibit 6.4 illustrates an analysis of the proposal's effect upon the variable revenue and costs of the firm. It assumes that a 25-percent increase in sales volume is still within the relevant range of the budgeting rates. Note that the projected results of the proposal indicate an increased contribution, after allowing for **all** increased **variable** costs, of $42,257.[2] If there were no increases in fixed costs associated with the proposal, it should be accepted. However, an integral part of the

---

[2]   Students sometimes think that contribution is analogous to gross profit considering only variable cost of goods sold. This analogy can be dangerous and misleading as some cost of goods sold for a manufacturer may be fixed. Also, there may be variable period costs, as deliberately included in this example. Contribution is the net amount remaining after **all** variable costs, both variable product costs **and** variable period costs.

proposal to achieve the $42,257 of additional contribution was an increase in the annual advertising budget. Contribution analysis has enabled you to simply and efficiently identify the proposed benefits of the increased advertising and price reduction. The benefits are $42,257 of increased contribution. The costs, increased advertising, are $75,000. Benefits do not exceed costs, and the proposal should be rejected.

### Analysis of Proposed Special Order

Turning now to the proposed special order from the Nippon Sports Company, did you reject this order as below cost? Or did you assume (as did the sales vice-president) that a $19,600 "loss" would be involved which would have to be considered in the light of "costs" of uneven production schedules? If your response was "Yes" to either question, you need to reflect upon the differences between full product costs (Chapter 1) and fixed and variable costs (Chapter 5).

Assuming that the firm has the capacity, the Nippon special order should definitely be accepted. It involves no loss. Instead, it will produce an increased contribution of $40,000; and, since it involves no increased fixed costs, an increase in income from operations of $40,000.[3] The fact that the order may also assist in balancing workload in the factory, and thus reduce the costs (real dollars and psychological) of uneven production scheduling, is an **added** benefit.

In analyzing the Nippon special-order proposal, the most efficient approach is to once again focus on contribution. In this instance, you can focus on the contribution arising out of the order itself and ignore regular production (assuming adequate capacity[4]). The variable manufacturing cost of a deluxe model ski (obtainable from earlier budgeting data) is:

| | |
|---|---|
| Direct material | $ 8.70 |
| Direct labor | 12.50 |
| Variable manufacturing overhead | 3.90 |
| Total variable manufacturing cost | $25.10 |

Note that variable selling cost of $0.008 per sales dollar does not apply to this special order; see the vice-president's memo (Exhibit 6.2).

---

[3]   Increased net income before taxes will be somewhat less than $40,000 because of the interest cost on the additional inventory investment while the order is in process and until final payment is received. The necessity of considering changes in working capital requirements associated with business decisions will be further discussed in Chapters 7, 8, and 10.

[4]   If the order on top of regular business would exceed the firm's capacity, simple contribution analysis would be inappropriate. Capacity constraints will be explored in Chapter 7.

What is the *contribution per unit* (ski)[5] from each of the special order skis? And what is the total contribution from the entire order for 4,000 skis? You correctly understand the concept of contribution if you see that, on this order, the contribution per unit is $10 ($35.10 revenue minus $25.10 variable cost), and, for the order as a whole, is $40,000. In this instance, your choice as the president is between obtaining a $40,000 contribution (take the order) or obtaining none (reject the order).

If the Nippon special order were not independent in its effects, if it would impair or reduce expected sales of standard products, then of course these effects would have to be incorporated into the decision. Independence is stipulated in this example.

Do you feel there is something unfair or illegal about Tripper's selling deluxe skis under its own brand domestically for $80 and to the Nippon Company for $35.10?[6] Are you uneasy about business profits in general, and concerned that they might somehow be immoral? Ethical judgments are beyond the scope of this text. However, the next section will briefly discuss the role of profits within our economy. After reading the next section, you may be in a position to make more informed personal judgments about business profits, and be more comfortable using profitability as **one** of the criteria for business decisions.

## ROLE OF PROFIT

In all developed economies (whether so-called capitalistic, socialistic, or communistic), some measure of return on resources invested is used to measure the efficiency of resource usage, and to guide future resource allocations. In the United States, return on legally borrowed resources (debt) is defined as interest; and return on ownership investment is defined as profit or earnings. In the traditional economic model, it was assumed that, since owners bore ultimate risk, they should be entitled to and would seek maximum possible profits. Potentially unlimited profits were assumed necessary to motivate individuals to save and make ownership investments in businesses. At the other extreme are those who believe any profit is a rip-off of the consumer, or labor, or both.

Regardless of one's attitude toward profit, business requires capital invest-

---

[5]    Contribution per unit is often referred to as the contribution margin or the marginal contribution since:

Contribution            = Revenue − Variable cost,
Contribution margin = Marginal revenue − marginal cost.

Since a margin (difference) can also be thought of in total, the terms *contribution per unit* or *unit contribution* will be used throughout this text to avoid possible confusion.

[6]    It is assumed in this example that this special order does not fall within constraints of the Robinson–Patman Act. This act will be discussed in the appendix to this chapter.

ment. This capital ultimately can come only from the savings of society in the form of current consumption foregone or given up. Private individuals and government bureaus or corporations must be persuaded to forego current consumption so that new investable capital may be formed. Foregone consumption can either be forced (taxes) or can result from a sufficiently strong nongovernmental incentive (potential interest or profit). So long as private investment continues to be a factor in the United States (as opposed to all investment coming from government tax revenues), an adequate reward (incentive) must be provided for such investment. Whether adequate must mean potentially unlimited is open to question and is beyond the scope of this text. For your purposes it would seem appropriate to accept some amount of **reasonable** profit as justified within the business system.

## PROFIT MAXIMIZATION VS. SATISFACTORY PROFIT

Coexistent with the concept of necessary unlimited profits for the individual owner-investor was the assumption that the exclusive goal of the firm was to maximize net income (profit to the owners). The goal of profit maximization was a logical outgrowth of earlier economic models of single-owner firms. It was extended to corporations with the assumption that corporate directors and managers would always act in the best interests of the owners (stockholders), that their goals would be congruent. Whether or not individual stockholders' goals are solely to maximize profit, corporate managers' goals (and therefore those of the firm) can no longer be assumed to be pure profit maximization.

Suppose the president of a large corporation with head offices in New York City needed to attend a meeting in San Francisco. Assume a commercial jet plane was scheduled at a convenient time. Profit maximization for stockholders would dictate that the president forego the corporation jet as slower (less efficient use of his time) and much more costly. If the president were maximizing profits, he or she would take the commercial plane. Furthermore, the president should fly coach. How many large corporation presidents will you find flying commercial coach?

In addition to the separate interests of management and employees, society generally no longer supports maximum possible profit as an acceptable business goal. At some point profits are deemed excessive and may be subject to social and even governmental sanctions or constraints. Also, more and more, firms are expected to forego greater profits in deference to achieving other social objectives. Environmental cleanup and preservation, minority hiring and special training, and year-round employment stability are examples of parallel goals that may reduce maximum profit. In the Tripper example, the firm's choice to forego some profit in return for a more pleasant physical work environment would be another instance.

The concept of *satisfactory profit* has replaced maximum profit in most economic models that attempt to describe current business behavior. A business today is a composite of multiple goals. Sufficient profit to **satisfy** owners may be considered a necessary, but not the only, objective of business management.

## DETERMINING A SATISFACTORY PROFIT—THE COST OF CAPITAL

The amount or percentage of profit necessary to satisfy owners will vary depending upon the riskiness of the particular firm. In the market (or set of all investors and investments), investors demand and receive a higher return on more risky investments. Exhibit 6.5 illustrates the common pattern of greater return for greater risk. This exhibit can be viewed as the pattern for any one particular firm. The entire curve (line) would shift upwards for more risky firms. It might shift to the point where a high-risk firm's bonds might have to pay more return (interest) than a relatively risk-free corporation (like American Telephone and Telegraph Company) would have to earn on its common stock.

**Exhibit 6.5**

**Table of Investment Risk and Return**

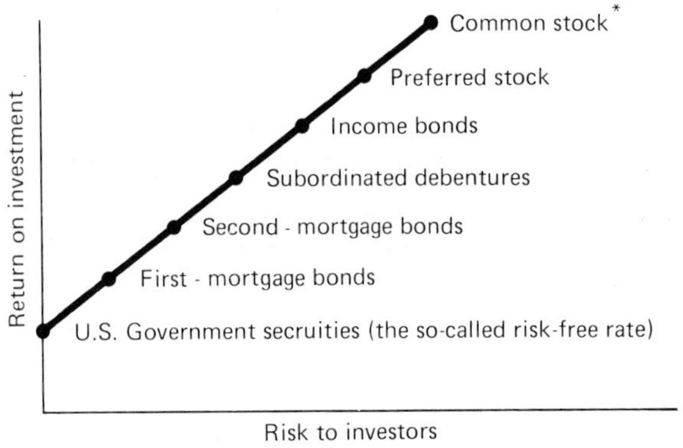

Return on investment / Risk to investors

- Common stock*
- Preferred stock
- Income bonds
- Subordinated debentures
- Second - mortgage bonds
- First - mortgage bonds
- U.S. Government securities (the so-called risk-free rate)

* Return measured in terms of earnings and growth, not just dividends.

Note that the required investment return on common equity is generally considered to include more than just dividends. In a hypothetical steady-state situation with no growth, no inflation, and dividends equal to 100 percent of earnings, perhaps dividends alone could be an adequate measure of return. In the usual situation with dividends less than earnings, the investor anticipates or requires growth in future dividends as a reward or return on current earnings withheld. The many considerations involved in measuring the return on common equity are more appropriately covered in finance courses and texts.

At this point the important ideas to understand are merely:

1. A firm must be able to raise new capital to survive and prosper. Additional capital is necessary not only for possible expansion, but to maintain a steady state in an inflationary economy.

2. There exists a limit to the firm's debt percentage or to its capacity to raise new capital exclusively through less costly debt securities. If a firm has too much debt (is too highly leveraged), the required interest payments, regardless of earnings, introduce too much risk.

3. A balanced proportion of new capital must therefore come from owners.

4. Owners will invest additional capital only if they can earn a satisfactory profit when compared with other firms of equal risk.

5. Therefore, in the long run, in order to survive, a firm must strive to earn a satisfactory profit as defined by the market (existing and potential investors). If it does not earn a satisfactory profit, it will eventually be unable to attract necessary new capital.

Since a corporation's profits are subject to income tax, and only after-tax profits are available to stockholders, the necessary overall investment return (cost of capital) is usually calculated on an after-tax basis. Necessary return to creditors (interest) is a tax-deductible expense. Therefore the effective after-tax cost of debt is reduced by the tax rate. For example, assume a corporation's creditors demanded eight percent on debt and its common stockholders demanded 15 percent for their greater risk. If the firm was subject to an income tax rate of 40 percent, the income before taxes would have to represent a 25 percent return on the owner's investment for the owners to benefit by 15 percent.[7]

On an after-tax basis, the necessary interest costs on debt would be 4.8 percent. The interest tax deduction offsets or shields an equal amount of otherwise taxable income; 40 percent tax on this income is saved. Therefore, the effective after-tax interest cost equals the interest amount minus 40 percent of the interest amount, or 60 percent of the before-tax interest cost.

New capital will be raised from both creditors and owners in proportions acceptable to the market. Assume only creditors (demanding 4.8 percent after taxes) and common stockholders (demanding 15 percent) were involved and the ideal long-term debt percentage (long-term debt ÷ sum of long-term debt and stockholders' equity) was 30 percent for a particular firm.[8] On average, over several years, for every $3 of new debt the firm would have to obtain $7 from common stockholders to maintain its desired debt percentage. The

---

[7]   Let $x$ equal desired before-tax earnings; then

$$x - 0.4x = 15\% \quad \text{(necessary after-tax earnings)},$$
$$x = 25\%.$$

[8]   A third source of capital could be preferred stock at a cost between that for debt and for common stock. More sophisticated cost of capital computations are covered in finance or financial management courses.

weighted average *cost of capital* for this firm on an after-tax basis would be 11.94, or 12 percent when rounded ($0.3 \times 4.8 + 0.7 \times 15$).

With a 12 percent cost of capital, the firm must earn on its assets invested an average of 12 percent on an after-tax basis to **survive** in the long run. In the next two chapters you will have the chance to learn how this required rate of return is used in evaluating business decision alternatives.

## ACHIEVING EARNINGS EQUIVALENT TO THE COST OF CAPITAL

With a firm's cost of capital a minimum average rate of return demanded by its particular mix of investors, and with a satisfactory profit defined as the level designed to satisfy owner expectations/demands, average target profit may become a range, as shown in Fig. 6.1.

The *target profit range* may be extremely narrow in very large firms where social and governmental pressures even question the validity of profits at the cost of capital level. It may be much broader for the small private firm with the only upper limits being the owner's conscience or ultimate customer boycott.

Independently of the breadth or narrowness of a particular firm's target profit range, the firm's management is concerned with making sure profits **average** out within its range. The concept of average profits is important to remember. In some years management knows profits may be below cost of capital as a direct result of economic recession, adverse competitor action, or unforeseen problems. It therefore must target other specific years' profits above or near the top of the range. Only in this way can the firm average out within the desired range, and at least above the necessary cost of capital minimum or floor.

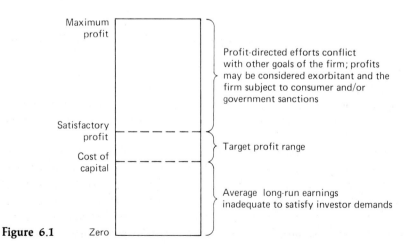

**Figure 6.1**

Maximum profit

Profit-directed efforts conflict with other goals of the firm; profits may be considered exorbitant and the firm subject to consumer and/or government sanctions

Satisfactory profit

Target profit range

Cost of capital

Average long-run earnings inadequate to satisfy investor demands

Zero

Target profit can be thought of as being achievable in one of five ways:

1. pure luck;
2. improving profitability of existing operations/activities;
3. adding new profitable operations/activities;
4. controlling new and existing operations/activities so that potentially available profits are not lost; and
5. discontinuing unprofitable operations.

Management cannot rely on lucky or fortuitous profits. Immediate or short-run attention and energy is focused upon obtaining higher revenues from existing products and reducing noncommitted costs. Product pricing and revenue maximization will be covered in the appendix to this chapter. Short-term cost minimization is primarily accomplished through the budgeting process.

At the time operating budgets are prepared, every effort is made to encourage planning for minimum costs while, at the same time, avoiding unrealistically low projections or the atmosphere of arbitrarily imposed cost cutting. If the overall master budget indicates inadequate profit, it is appropriate to review each part of the budget **with the affected manager** and make necessary and realistic cost reductions. Also, as part of the control process to be introduced in Chapters 10 through 14, areas of possible future cost reduction are identified and noted by managers throughout the year for incorporation in the following year's budget.

Profitability of existing operations/activities is also enhanced through nonroutine decisions designed to increase volume and/or reallocate existing resources to reduce costs. Unfortunately, as demonstrated with the Tripper proposals, it is easy to lose sight of costs and particularly their short-run behavior.

## COMMON ERRORS IN PROFIT PLANNING

The term profit planning is commonly used and should not be misunderstood as implying a specific activity. Profit planning encompasses all budgeting and decision-making activities within the firm having an effect upon profits (which covers most decisions). There are certain common errors in profit planning which should be avoided.

Two of the more common involve misunderstandings of unit costs. Short-run profit opportunities may be dismissed as being below cost when actually they provide a positive profit contribution. The Nippon special ski order demonstrated this pitfall. Conversely, the old adage "we lose money on each item, but we'll make it up in volume" may be false. If revenues are below variable costs (negative contribution), increased volume will only increase losses. And if revenues provide only a slight contribution, necessary volume to cover all fixed costs might exceed the firm's capacity.

Another very common profit-planning error involves a misunderstanding of the behavior of total costs. Refer to the Tripper operating income budget for 19X2 (Exhibit 6.3). Suppose your sales vice-president came up with a third proposal to spend an additional $100,000 each year in advertising and sales promotion with the expectation of increasing overall volume 15 percent. Assume the proposal would not affect unit prices or variable costs, and was within the relevant range (except for the $100,000 of additional advertising, other fixed costs would not change). Should you accept this proposal?

A common misconception is that income varies directly with volume. Such an assumption ignores the existence of fixed costs over a relevant range. With this misconception the proposal might be incorrectly rejected on the basis that $29,000 of benefits (15 percent increase over $193,697 of profits, rounded) do not exceed $100,000 of costs. Do you see that income should not be treated as a simple or direct variable? Income is affected by fixed costs. Do you also see that this third proposal should be adopted? The benefits would be in excess of $120,000. If unit prices and variable costs do not change, a 15 percent volume increase will increase total contribution by $120,176. With fixed costs (advertising) increasing only $100,000, a $20,000 additional profit would result.

## CONTRIBUTION AND PROFITABILITY ANALYSIS

Are you convinced of the value of *contribution analysis* as a convenient tool for use in profit planning? Contribution analysis relates costs, volumes, and resultant profits. It is sometimes known as CVP (for cost–volume–profit) analysis. It allows for the fact that, for most firms, there is never any certain profit on any item sold. There is only contribution. Each year an initial quantity of sales produces no profit. The resulting contribution first must cover fixed cost.

Until all fixed costs are completely covered (equalled), the firm is operating at a loss. Where the total contribution exactly equals total fixed costs, there is no loss or profit and the firm is said to be at *breakeven*. Above breakeven, and until the capacity of existing fixed costs is reached (within the relevant range), **all** contribution becomes pure before-tax profit. Figure 6.2 may help you remember this vital concept. Contribution first fills the fixed-costs container. When the fixed-costs container is full, the firm is at breakeven. Thereafter all contribution flows off the top and to profits.

The basic concept of breakeven can also be illustrated with profit equations:

$$\text{Profit} = \text{Revenue} - \text{Expense}$$
$$\text{Profit} = \text{Revenue} - (\text{Variable cost} + \text{Fixed cost})$$
$$\text{Profit} = (\text{Revenue} - \text{Variable cost}) - \text{Fixed cost}$$
$$\text{Profit} = \text{Contribution} - \text{Fixed Cost}$$

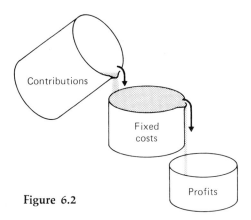

**Figure 6.2**

At breakeven where profit is equal to zero:

Zero = Contribution − Fixed cost     or     Contribution = Fixed cost.

Although breakeven is but one special case or particular point (where profit is zero) in overall CVP analysis, the terms CVP analysis and breakeven analysis are sometimes used interchangeably.

**Exhibit 6.6**
## TRIPPER WATER SKI MANUFACTURING COMPANY

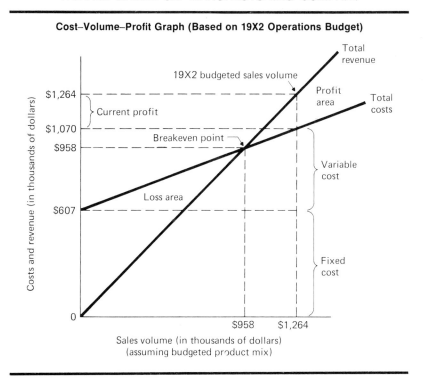

**Cost–Volume–Profit Graph (Based on 19X2 Operations Budget)**

**Exhibit 6.7**

TRIPPER WATER SKI MANUFACTURING COMPANY

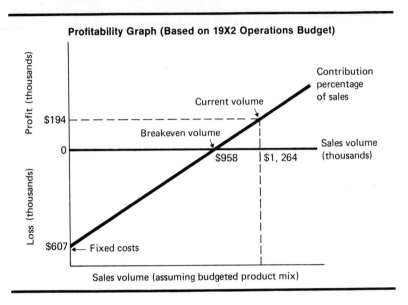

Profitability Graph (Based on 19X2 Operations Budget)

Exhibits 6.6 and 6.7 illustrate contribution analysis graphically. In the conventional CVP graph (Exhibit 6.6), the expected profit and loss for any level of sales is given by the vertical distance between the total cost line (sum of fixed and variable costs) and the total revenue line. Breakeven is shown as the point where the vertical distance is zero—the intersection point. Contribution analysis can be used to forecast profit or loss for any volume level within the relevant range. The analysis may be performed graphically (plotting the firm's factors and then reading off values at different alternative volume levels) or more simply and accurately using simple algebra, as will be described below.

Exhibit 6.7 is another form of a CVP graph that directly relates changes in volume to profits. This approach calls attention to resultant profit instead of highlighting changes in costs. It is often preferable in making visual presentations to groups of people relating various volume alternatives. Note that the profitability graph essentially compares contribution as a percentage of sales (see Section below) with revenue. Since total costs are mixed, at zero volume the contribution percentage line intersects the Y-axis at a point equivalent to the level of fixed costs. The vertical distance between the contribution and revenue lines equals profit (beyond breakeven) or loss (below breakeven volume).

## CONTRIBUTION PER UNIT VS. CONTRIBUTION PERCENTAGE

On both the CVP graph and the profitability graph, volume of activity may be expressed in units of profit or in sales dollars. Contribution analysis per unit is applicable when the product being evaluated is independent of all others (as in

### Exhibit 6.8

### TRIPPER WATER SKI MANUFACTURING COMPANY

**Product Contributions**

|  | Economy ski | Deluxe ski | Tow rope |
|---|---|---|---|
| Selling price | $50.00 | $80.00 | $10.00 |
| Variable material | 5.50 | 8.70 | 5.00 |
| Variable labor | 9.80 | 12.50 | 0 |
| Variable manufacturing overhead[a] | 3.90 | 3.90 | 0 |
| Variable selling costs[b] | 0.40 | 0.64 | 0.08 |
| Contribution per unit | $30.40 | $54.26 | $ 4.92 |

[a] Varies per ski regardless of type.
[b] Varies per sales dollar.

the example of the Nippon Sports Company special order for skis). Contribution per unit is also applicable at the total firm level where only one product is sold.

Where a firm has multiple products (the most common situation), it is rare that all products will have the same unit contribution.[9] When different products have different contributions, a change in the product mix (proportions of different products sold) can change the total contribution without, or together with, a change in sales volume. In the previous Tripper example, contribution (Exhibit 6.3) and breakeven (Exhibits 6.6 and 6.7) were based on the budgeted 19X2 product mix from Exhibit 3.8 of:

> 12,800  economy skis
> 7,050  deluxe skis
> 6,000  tow ropes

Exhibit 6.8 provides data on selling prices, costs, and contributions of each of Tripper's products based on 19X2 budgeting rates. The 19X2 budgeted sales, product mix, and anticipated contribution, would therefore be:

| Item | Sales quantity | Sales dollars | Sales mix % | Contribution |
|---|---|---|---|---|
| Economy skis | 12,800 | $ 640,000 | 50 | $389,120 |
| Deluxe skis | 7,050 | 564,000 | 45 | 382,533 |
| Tow ropes | 6,000 | 60,000 | 5 | 29,520 |
|  |  | $1,264,000 | 100% | $801,173 |

---

[9]   Many merchandising firms apply a uniform mark-on percentage to costs in establishing selling prices. In this situation, contribution is uniform per sales dollar but not per product unit.

Tripper could have the same $1,264,000 sales budget and a different contribution and projected income if the mix were different. For example, the sales mix could have been:

| Item | Sales quantity | Sales dollars | Sales mix % | Contribution |
|---|---|---|---|---|
| Economy skis | 9,950 | $ 497,500 | 39 | $302,480 |
| Deluxe skis | 8,800 | 704,000 | 56 | 477,488 |
| Tow ropes | 6,250 | 62,500 | 5 | 30,750 |
| | | $1,264,000 | 100% | $810,718 |

Note that, with this mix alternative, contribution and projected income would be increased by $9,545 with no change in expected total sales volume. More items with a higher unit contribution are being sold.

When a firm has more than one product, and when unit contributions are not uniform, then contribution analysis for the firm **must** be based on an assumed constant sales mix (a particular "package" with a particular weighted average mix of products). Different analyses and projections must be prepared for different sales mix packages. Product or sales mix will be discussed further in the appendix to this chapter and in Chapters 14 and 17.

In planning for multiproduct firms, the *contribution percentage* for the assumed mix package is used. In the third Tripper proposal (middle p. 234), the contribution percentage of 63.4 percent (Exhibit 6.3) that reflects the assumed weighted-average sales mix could be used. Recall that the proposal called for $100,000 of increased annual fixed advertising costs with an expected benefit of a 15 percent sales increase. 15 percent of 19X2 originally budgeted sales would be $189,600. At a contribution rate of 63.4 percent, additional resulting contribution would be $120,206 which is the same amount (except for a $30 rounding error) obtained earlier by projecting an entirely new total income statement. The contribution percentage (assuming a constant sales mix) must be used in situations involving multiple products with non-uniform unit contributions.

## SOME USES OF CONTRIBUTION ANALYSIS

Some common situations in which contribution analysis may prove useful include:

1. calculating breakeven and the margin of safety;
2. evaluating breakeven sensitivity to changes in prices, variable costs, or fixed costs;
3. projecting profit, given planned sales;
4. determining necessary sales, given costs and target profit;

5. selecting among products, given limited facilities; and

6. providing range limits for pricing decisions (to be covered in the appendix to this chapter).

## Breakeven and Margin of Safety

The determination of breakeven sales volume in dollars has been discussed above in the graphical form. Breakeven is defined as the level of activity at which total contribution equals total fixed costs. Therefore the *breakeven sales volume* (BSV) in dollars may be calculated by any of the following three formulas:

At breakeven:

**1.**

$$\text{Total contribution} = \text{Total fixed costs}$$
$$\text{Units sold} \times \text{Unit contribution} = \text{Total fixed costs}$$

$$\frac{\text{BSV}}{\text{Revenue per unit}} = \frac{\text{Total fixed costs}}{\text{Unit contribution}}$$

$$\text{BSV} = \frac{\left(\begin{array}{c}\text{Total fixed}\\\text{costs}\end{array}\right) \times \left(\begin{array}{c}\text{Revenue}\\\text{per unit}\end{array}\right)}{\text{Unit contribution}}$$

**2.**

$$\text{Total contribution} = \text{Total fixed costs}$$
$$\text{BSV} \times \text{Contribution rate} = \text{Total fixed costs}$$

$$\text{BSV} = \frac{\text{Total fixed costs}}{\text{Contribution rate}}$$

**3.**

$$\text{Since contribution rate} = 1 - \text{Variable cost rate}$$

$$\text{BSV} = \frac{\text{Total fixed costs}}{1 - \text{Variable cost rate}}$$

Note that the variable cost rate and the contribution rate are merely the variable cost and contribution percentages of sales expressed as a decimal.

The breakeven point is of interest to managers as a measure of the relative safety of the firm's current position. Assuming current sales volume is above the BSV, the difference is referred to as the *margin of safety*:

$$\text{Margin of safety} = \text{Current sales volume} - \text{BSV.}$$

The margin of safety indicates how far sales volume could fall before the firm would suffer losses. Tripper's budgeted 19X2 BSV was previously calculated as $974,000 (rounded). Therefore its margin of safety at 19X2 projected sales of $1,264,000 is $290,000 or 23 percent of projected sales. Sales could fall 23 percent before Tripper would suffer a loss.

In Chapter 8 you can learn that the effect on breakeven, or more precisely on the margin of safety, is an important consideration in accepting or rejecting proposals that involve additional fixed costs.

### Breakeven Sensitivity

Managers are also concerned with *breakeven sensitivity* or how the firm's BSV would be affected by changes in prices, variable costs, or fixed cost. Recall the first Tripper sales vice-president's proposal discussed earlier. It was rejected because the $42,257 contribution did not exceed the $75,000 incremental fixed advertising cost. What was the effect of the proposed ten-percent reduction in selling prices on the firm's BSV? From Exhibit 6.4 you can calculate the firm's new contribution percentage as 59.3 (down from 63.4 shown on Exhibit 6.3). Its BSV would therefore be $1,024,411 ($607,466 fixed costs divided by 0.593) or increased by $50,411 over the budgeted BSV. If the increase in breakeven were significant and the margin of safety were also substantially lower (not the case in this proposal), then the proposal might be rejected even if the incremental advertising costs were less than the contribution benefits. It might be exposing the firm to too much risk (losses resulting from slight sales volume decline). This risk would have to be separately examined against the proposal's net benefits.

### Profit Projections

Managers often wish to know what current profit levels may be expected to accompany different potential levels of sales. With this information they can better pick the best pricing policy or the best among alternative advertising/ marketing plans. In effect, the Tripper sales vice-president's first proposal was rejected because, although it projected revenue increases of $157,964, its effect would have been to reduce before-tax profit by $32,743.

### Necessary Sales Volume

Often in evaluating proposals for new activities or product lines that involve additional investment, managers want to know what revenue level must be attained before a satisfactory return (target profit) is being earned on the proposed investment. If the satisfactory sales volume appears not readily obtainable, the proposal may be rejected on such grounds. As an example, assume you are considering a proposal involving a contribution percent of 40 and fixed costs of $500,000. Your cost of capital is 15 percent, and you wish to earn **at least** this much return on your $500,000 investment. Can you calculate the *necessary sales volume* per year for this project to earn a barely satisfactory return?

In this type of situation you are using a "breakeven plus" approach. The necessary sales volume (NSV) equals that amount where the contribution will equal the sum of total fixed costs **plus** an adequate, or desired, investment return:

$$\text{NSV} = \frac{\text{Total fixed costs} + \text{Desired profit}}{\text{Contribution rate}}.$$

In the above problem, minimum necessary annual sales volume would be $1,437,500.

Several variations of the necessary sales volume analysis may also serve management. In certain instances a particular price may be set by the market or proposed as an alternative. Management might then wish to know what sales volume in **units** must be achieved to earn a satisfactory return. The analysis would proceed as above but with the additional step of dividing the NSV obtained by the established or proposed unit price.

$$\text{Necessary sales quantity (units)} = \frac{\text{NSV}}{\text{Unit price}}.$$

In the above example, if the price were to be $20 per unit, necessary sales volume in **units** would be 71,875 ($1,437,500 divided by $20). Alternatively, a target quantity might be considered reasonable for the market to absorb or for the firm's facilities to produce. Management might then desire to know what price must be obtained from customers in order for the project to earn a satisfactory return. In this instance, the NSV would be divided by the target quantity:

$$\text{Necessary unit price} = \frac{\text{NSV}}{\text{Expected sales quantity (units)}}.$$

## Product Selection

Managers may be forced to choose between two mutually exclusive products because of limited facilities. One approach to this decision is to calculate the total contribution per year from each alternative, and then select the one with the highest contribution. For example, a retailer may have to choose between two products to stock and sell because of limited shelf (display) space. Assume the choice were between product X with a unit contribution of $0.40 and product Y with a contribution of $0.55. To select product Y because it has the highest unit contribution may be inappropriate and may not maximize total annual contribution. Total contribution is the product of the unit contribution and the volume sold. Often retailers use inventory turnover as a ready measure of volume. Recall that:

$$\text{Inventory turnover} = \frac{\text{Cost of goods sold}}{\text{Average inventory}}.$$

In the above example, suppose projected turnovers were 7 for product X and 5 for product Y. Which product should the retailer stock and sell? Given these projections, product X will produce the greater total contribution. Enough more will be sold each year to more than offset Y's higher **unit** contribution.

## ASSUMPTIONS AND LIMITATIONS OF CONTRIBUTION (CVP) ANALYSIS

At this point it may appear to you that contribution analysis provides a short-cut approach to resolving most business problems. It is a simple, efficient, and reliable technique where applicable. Unfortunately, there are many business decisions where contribution analysis is inappropriate and may lead to incorrect evaluations. To understand the applicability of contribution analysis, you need to review and remember its underlying asumptions, which also act as its limitations. If **any** of the following assumptions are not correct for a particular problem, then contribution analysis is **invalid** and **inappropriate.**

The most important and critical assumption of contribution analysis is that **all alternatives under consideration are within the relevant range.** Contrbiution analysis assumes that fixed costs will **not** change with changes in volume within the relevant range. If volumes under consideration are above or below the relevant range, fixed costs and variable costs per unit or mix may change, and contribution analysis (using data applicable within the relevant range) is invalid.

Even within the relevant range, contribution analysis further assumes:

1. **Constant sales or product mix** (described above);
2. **Linearity of costs and revenue** (no changes with changes in volume of variable cost elements; no changes in productivity or efficiency, and no changes resulting from price breaks or volume discounts related to purchases or sales).[10]
3. **Constant inventory levels** (volume of production or purchasing equals volume of sales).[11]

In Chapter 7 you can learn more about those business decisions for which contribution analysis is appropriate.

## CONTRIBUTION (CVP) ANALYSIS FOR NONPROFIT-DIRECTED ORGANIZATIONS

Contribution analysis as an analytical tool is not limited to those situations involving the generation of profits. In nonprofit-directed organizations, service benefits may be quantified and used in lieu of revenue. The objective then

---

[10]   Recall from Chapter 5 that many variable costs that are not linear may be assumed to vary directly. If a linear relationship may be reasonably assumed, contribution analysis may be used.

[11]   When the volume of production or purchasing does not equal sales volume, contribution analysis may be modified so as to still be usable. In such cases total costs will reflect sales volume plus or minus costs of changes in inventory levels. The variable costs associated with planned inventory changes may be added to fixed costs to calculate breakeven when inventory levels are being reduced, and vice versa.

becomes achieving maximum benefits from a given level of funding (analogous to a relevant range of capital provided by investment).

Revenue surrogates may include such items as:

- Future fees and/or donations collected,
- Future tax revenue resulting from training and job placement programs or small business assistance programs,
- Future savings of such items as welfare costs or property losses and insurance costs (as a result of better police, fire, or flood protection).

Examples of contribution analysis applied to nonprofit-directed organizations will be included in Chapter 15.

## CONTRIBUTION AND PRODUCT COSTING ALTERNATIVES

Before leaving the discussion of contribution, you should be aware that many accountants advocate incorporating the concept of contribution into product costing or inventory costing under GAAP. Recall, from Chapter 1, that currently GAAP require that product costs reported in ending inventory and cost of goods sold be the full or total cost, including both direct and indirect costs. For a manufacturer, full product cost includes all manufacturing overhead and this overhead must be applied (allocated) to or absorbed by each product. Current GAAP is therefore described as requiring full costing or *absorption costing*.

Concern over the arbitrariness of indirect cost allocation, some theoretical questions concerning the propriety of treating fixed costs as product costs, and the fact that full product cost is usually not a useful figure for decision purposes, have together lent support to a proposed alternative. The major alternative to full costing is known as *direct costing*, or sometimes as *variable costing*.[12] Direct-costing supporters would include in product costs only variable costs. Fixed costs that are part of overhead (such as depreciation) would be excluded from product cost and treated as a period cost. All fixed costs would be expensed in the period when incurred.

Figure 6.3 shows the cost flows under the two alternatives, and Fig. 6.4 illustrates the cost distinctions for a manufacturer. Note that the only difference between direct and absorption costing is in the **timing** of expense recognition of fixed inventory-related costs. Under direct costing, inventory-related fixed costs are recognized as expense (expensed) immediately as they are incurred. Under absorption costing, expense recognition is deferred until the inventory has been sold to customers.

---

[12]   A third alternative known as *relevant costing*, which lies somewhere between full and direct costing, has also been advocated. Although possibly sounder theoretically than either of the other two, relevant costing has to date received little support.

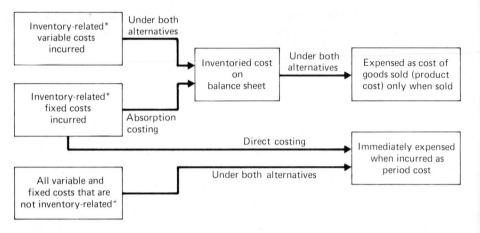

* Costs directly or indirectly associated with the
procurement and/or manufacture of products for
sale to customers.

**Figure 6.3**

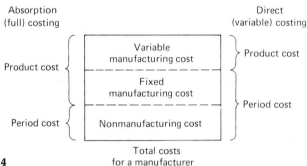

**Figure 6.4**

Although direct costing is not currently acceptable under GAAP, you
should be familiar with it as an alternative to full costing. Many firms currently employ direct costing for internal reporting purposes, and then convert
to full costing for financial statements. Exhibit 6.3 earlier in this chapter illustrates the direct costing or contribution approach to reporting income.

## CHAPTER OVERVIEW

**Based upon the material contained in this chapter, you should now be in
a position to:**

- **Define contribution and breakeven, and give examples of how each is
calculated.**

- Define a satisfactory profit and a target profit range, and describe how each may be an appropriate and necessary goal for business organizations in lieu of specific profit maximization.
- Define cost of capital and describe, with examples, how it may be determined for a particular firm, and its importance to that firm.
- Describe three of the most common errors made in profit planning.
- Draw a CVP graph and explain its information content and usefulness.
- Draw a profitability graph and explain its information content, usefulness, and difference from a CVP graph.
- Define contribution percentage and describe how it is obtained and in what circumstances it is appropriately used.
- Define contribution per unit and describe how it is obtained and in what circumstances it is appropriately used.
- Describe the margin of safety and its significance to management.
- Describe, with examples, various appropriate uses of contribution analysis for such areas as:

> Break-even sensitivity
> Profit projection
> Necessary sales volume (total)
> Necessary unit sales volume
> Necessary prices
> Product selection

- Describe the limitations of contribution analysis and give examples of where it would be inappropriate with respect to:

> Relevant range
> Product mix
> Cost and revenue linearity
> Changing inventory levels

- Describe direct costing as an alternative to the full costing approach currently required by GAAP, and explain the differences between these two approaches to product costing.

## NEW VOCABULARY AND CONCEPTS

| | |
|---|---|
| Contribution format (Income statement) | Margin of safety |
| Contribution per unit | Breakeven sales volume (BSV) |
| Satisfactory profit | Breakeven sensitivity |
| Cost of capital | Necessary sales volume |
| Target profit range | Absorption costing |
| Contribution/CVP analysis | Direct (variable) costing |
| Contribution percentage | |

- Profit level necessary for a firm's survival.
- Weighted-average cost of capital as a minimum return demanded by investors.

## REVIEW QUESTIONS

1. (a) What is meant by contribution? By contribution rate? By contribution per unit? By contribution analysis?
   (b) How is the contribution percentage or the contribution rate determined?
   (c) What is the variable cost rate, and how does it interrelate with the contribution rate and with revenue?
   (d) How is the contribution per unit (product) determined?

2. What is the relationship between total contribution, total fixed costs, and income from operations before taxes?

3. (a) What is the role of profit in our society?
   (b) What investment practices or patterns that may differ among various political-social-economic systems make profit necessary within the U.S. economy?
   (c) What is a satisfactory profit?
   (d) How does a satisfactory profit differ from maximum profit?

4: (a) What is a firm's cost of capital?
   (b) How is it determined? Explain, with examples.
   (c) Why is it important that a firm know, or be able to reasonably estimate, its own cost of capital?
   (d) How is the cost of capital rate used by the firm?

5. (a) If annual interest charges are $100,000 or 5 percent and the firm is subject to a 35-percent income tax rate, what is the effective after-tax interest cost in dollars and as a percent?
   (b) If a satisfactory annual net income to stockholders is $300,000 and the firm is subject to a 40-percent income tax rate, how much income should be earned from operations before taxes?

6. What is a target profit range and how is it relevant to profit planning?

7. Suppose this year a multiproduct firm had $50,000 of income and sales of $500,000 and was budgeting next year's sales at $800,000 (still within relevant range). What are two reasons, other than cost inflation, why a projection of $80,000 of income would most probably be incorrect?

8. (a) What is meant by breakeven dollar sales volume? Breakeven unit sales volume?
   (b) What is the margin of safety?
   (c) How are these concepts of interest and usefulness to managers?

9. (a) What is a CVP graph?
   (b) What information does it disclose?

10. (a) What is a profitability graph?
    (b) What information does it disclose?
    (c) What is the essential difference between a profitability graph and a CVP graph?

11. (a) What is meant by product mix?
    (b) How does product mix relate to contribution analysis in general and to the preparation of CVP graphs and profitability graphs in particular?
    (c) How does product mix relate to the choice between using unit contributions and contribution rates in contribution analysis?

12. (a) What is meant by breakeven sensitivity?
    (b) How may breakeven sensitivity analysis be of use to managers? Explain, with examples.

13. (a) What is meant by the concept of necessary sales volume?
    (b) How does it differ from breakeven sales volume?
    (c) How is it calculated? Explain, with examples.

14. How may contribution analysis serve in product selection decisions (choice between mutually exclusive products)?

15. (a) What are the major assumptions, and therefore limitations, of contribution analysis as a decision-making tool?
    (b) Give examples of business problems related to each of the above limitations where contribution analysis would be **inappropriate.**

16. (a) What is the difference between direct costing and full costing?
    (b) Which is currently required by GAAP?
    (c) How does direct costing relate to contribution analysis?

## MINI-CASES AND QUESTIONS FOR DISCUSSION

**MC 6.1** A firm, or more correctly its management, is not solely at the mercy of investors with respect to its cost of capital rate. Management can influence the firm's cost of capital in different ways. The following results of management activity considered independently may cause the firm's cost of capital to change (increase or decrease):

- Firm has too much debt
- Firm has too little debt (in proportion to industry averages)
- Firm grows in overall size, either internally or through acquisitions of other firms
- Firm has profits dramatically above industry averages and social norms
- Firm has highest acceptable profits even though erratic from year to year
- Firm has less than highest acceptable profits but earnings are steady and predictable
- Firm has earnings consistently below industry averages

Do you think the first statement is correct? Considering each of the listed items independently, if you believe it would influence the firm's cost of capital, describe how and in which direction. Discuss the issues involved.

**MC 6.2** Nonchanging inventory levels (production or purchasing equals sales) is given as an assumption and limit to the applicability of contribution analysis. What difference would changing inventory levels make? Why cannot contribution analysis be made by using appropriate variable costs associated with the current period's cost of goods sold, rather than with actual costs incurred? Discuss.

**MC 6.3** Is it fair to the consumer for a firm to establish its prices based on target profits? Discuss.

**MC 6.4** Assuming enough differences apply to avoid the constraints of the Robinson–Patman Act (see chapter appendix), is it fair for a firm to charge two different prices to two different customers for substantially the same item? Is it fair and ethical for a discount store to sell an appliance for less than the same appliance might be sold at a dealer's or at a department store? Discuss.

**MC 6.5** Can the contribution approach be applied to situations involving different relevant ranges so long as appropriate different fixed and variable costs are used for alternatives falling into different ranges? Discuss.

**MC 6.6** Opponents of full (absorption) costing claim that it enables management to hide losses in inventory, that under full costing a firm could report profits up until the day it became insolvent and failed. Proponents of full costing claim that all necessary costs (both fixed and variable) must be included in product costs. They point out that, in the long run, a firm that does not cover its full product costs will fail. Are either or both positions correct? What do you think would be a desirable solution to this dilemma? Discuss.

## ESSENTIAL PROBLEMS

**EP 6.1** The Sprat Company is a merchandiser with the following proforma income statement for the forthcoming year (amounts in thousands of dollars):

| | | |
|---|---:|---:|
| Sales | | $3,000 |
| Cost of goods sold[1] | | 1,500 |
| Gross margin | | $1,500 |
| Operating expenses: | | |
|   Wages and salaries[2] | $800 | |
|   Sales commissions[1] | 150 | |
|   Distribution expenses[3] | 40 | |
|   Depreciation[4] | 160 | |
|   Property taxes and | | |
|     insurance[4] | 40 | 1,190 |
| Income from operations | | $ 310 |
| Provision for income tax | | 124 |
| Net Income | | $ 186 |

*Notes.* (1) Completely variable
    (2) Mixed cost: $500 fixed and $300 variable
    (3) Mixed cost: $10 fixed and $30 variable
    (4) Fixed costs

Prepare an income statement for the Sprat Company, following the contribution format.

EP 6.2 Refer to the data given for problem EP 6.1 above.

    a) What was Sprat's total contribution at its currently projected sales level?

    b) What is the firm's contribution percentage?

    c) What is its breakeven sales volume in dollars?

    d) How much is the firm's safety margin in both dollars and percent of expected sales?

    e) Assuming a 20-percent sales increase would still be within the relevant range, how much profit before income taxes could be expected at such an increase in volume?

EP 6.3 The Zebra Company's long-term capital structure consists of 400 $1,000 bonds with an annual interest rate of 8 percent, and stockholders' equity of $600,000. Assume Zebra's stockholders could obtain a 16-percent return from other firms of similar risk. Determine the following for Zebra, assuming a 40-percent income tax rate:

    a) Necessary income from operations before taxes to satisfy stockholders;

    b) After-tax cost of debt as a percent and in dollars per year;

    c) Weighted average after-tax cost of capital rate rounded to one decimal.

EP 6.4 Refer to Problem EP 6.3.

    1. Answer the same three questions concerning Zebra, based on the same data **except** assume the firm had only 300 bonds outstanding and was subject to a 30-percent tax rate.

    2. What effect does a decrease in the long-term debt ratio have on a firm's cost of capital? Explain.

    3. What effect does an increase in the income-tax rate have on a firm's cost of capital? Explain.

EP 6.5 Each of the following sets of data (a)–(h) is independent of that in the other columns. Complete the missing amounts for columns (a) through (d).

| | a | b | c | d | e | f | g | h |
|---|---|---|---|---|---|---|---|---|
| Sales | $1,000 | $2,000 | $3,000 | ? | ? | $4,000 | $5,000 | $6,000 |
| Variable costs | $600 | ? | ? | $1,500 | ? | ? | ? | ? |
| Contribution | ? | ? | ? | ? | ? | ? | $2,000 | ? |
| Fixed costs | ? | $400 | $950 | ? | $2,000 | ? | ? | $400 |
| Net Income | $100 | $200 | ? | $400 | ? | $800 | $300 | ? |
| Units sold | ? | 200 | ? | ? | 400 | ? | ? | 1,000 |
| Selling price per unit | $5 | ? | $20 | ? | $12 | $80 | ? | ? |
| Variable cost per unit | ? | ? | $9 | $3 | ? | $62 | $6 | $5 |
| Contribution per unit | ? | ? | ? | $4 | $7 | ? | ? | ? |

EP 6.6 Refer to the data given in Problem 6.5. Complete the missing elements for columns (e) through (h).

**EP 6.7** The Ajax Corporation's 19X7 and 19X8 income statements are given below. You may assume that, for 19X7, 75 percent of Ajax's cost of goods sold was variable, 75 percent of its before-tax period costs were fixed, and income taxes were 30 percent of accounting income before taxes. Give the following information for Ajax for 19X7 (round to one decimal and to even thousands of dollars):

a) An income statement prepared on the contribution basis

b) Variable cost rate

c) Contribution rate

d) Breakeven sales volume

e) Margin of safety

f) Variable cost per unit, assuming the firm had only one product, selling for $20 each.

g) Contribution per unit under the same assumptions as given in (f) above.

|  | 19X8 | 19X7 |
|---|---|---|
| Sales | $420,000 | $400,000 |
| Less:  Cost of goods sold | 252,000 | 300,000 |
| Gross Profit | $168,000 | $100,000 |
| Less:  Operating expenses | 108,000 | 60,000 |
| Income from operations | $ 60,000 | $ 40,000 |
| Less:  Provision for income taxes | 18,000 | 12,000 |
| Net income | $ 42,000 | $ 28,000 |

**EP 6.8** Refer to the data for the Ajax Corporation given in Problem EP 6.7. You may assume that the same percentages for variable and fixed costs applied in 19X8 as in 19X7.

1. Answer the seven questions given in Problem EP 6.7 for Ajax for 19X8.

2. Three separate changes independently contributed to the difference in Ajax's margin of safety between 19X7 and 19X8. Identify these factors, their amounts, and how each would have affected the margin of safety had the others not existed.

**EP 6.9** The Babcock Company is considering the potential profitability of a new product line. The line would involve annual fixed costs of $500,000. Variable costs are estimated at 65 percent of sales.

a) What would be the breakeven dollar sales volume for this line (rounded to the nearest thousand dollars)?

b) What would be expected income (ignoring taxes) at the following projected annual sales volume?

1. $2,000,000 expected volume

2. $2,500,000 optimistic estimate

3. $1,000,000 pessimistic estimate

**EP 6.10** Refer to Problem EP 6.9. Answer the same questions assuming that fixed costs were estimated at $540,000 and variable costs at 55 percent of sales.

**EP 6.11** A supermarket manager has limited shelf space, and is forced to choose between two competing brands of spices—Super Spice and Tasty Spice. He can only afford space to carry one line, and he estimates his inventory turnover as nine times for the Tasty Spice line and eleven times for Super Spice.

a) If his cost was the same for both but selling prices differed—Tasty sold for $1.39 per container and Super sold for $1.10—which line should he stock and why?

b) Assume Tasty cost $0.83 and sold for $1.39 per container, and Super cost $0.61 and sold for $1.10; which line should he stock and why?

**EP 6.12** An all-night food store has space to display and sell only one brand of English muffins. Two brands are available: Prestige Muffins, which sell for $0.69 per package and cost $0.41; and Best Buy Muffins, which sell for $0.59 and cost $0.39.

a) If expected unit sales of both brands were the same, which should be carried and why?

b) If expected sales volume of the higher-priced muffin were lower (eight times monthly turnover as compared to ten for the less expensive brand), which should be carried and why?

c) Would your answer to (b) above differ if Best Buy Muffins could be purchased for $0.36? Explain.

**EP 6.13** Assume the following budgeted income statement was applicable to your firm (either merchandiser or manufacturer) for the year just starting:

| | |
|---|---:|
| Sales (625,000 units) | $5,000,000 |
| Cost of goods sold (100% variable) | 4,000,000 |
| Gross Profit | $1,000,000 |
| Operating expenses (80% fixed) | 700,000 |
| Income before taxes | $ 300,000 |

For **each** of the following events considered independently, indicate **both**:

1. The effect (amount of change and direction) on budgeted income before taxes, and

2. The new sales volume in units required to maintain the $300,000 budgeted income level.

a) Necessary warehouse and equipment are destroyed by fire. Depreciation/rental on replacements is $20,000 more each year than originally budgeted.

b) Competitors lower their price to $7 per unit and you follow suit.

c) Your supplier increases the cost of your product or material included in your product (by $0.30 per unit).

**EP 6.14** Refer to Problem EP 6.13. Assume the same budgeted data and answer the same two questions for each of the following events considered separately:

a) Suppliers increase your costs $0.53 per unit, representing an eight-percent cost inflation adjustment. You and your competitors are able to pass on only a five-percent (of selling price) increase to your customers.

b) You give your employees an eight-percent cost-of-living adjustment (wages and salaries expense is increased nine percent because of fringe costs). Wages and salaries represent 30 percent of cost of goods sold and 20 percent of total operating expenses.

c) Assume a different budgeted cost structure as follows:

| | |
|---|---:|
| Sales (625,000 units) | $5,000,000 |
| Cost of goods sold (100% variable) | 2,000,000 |
| Gross Profit | $3,000,000 |
| Operating expenses (80% fixed) | 2,700,000 |
| Income before taxes | $ 300,000 |

Suppliers increase your variable cost of goods sold by eight percent. You and your competitors are able to pass on cost increases in the form of a five-percent price increase to your customers.

**EP 6.15** The Meredith Company is considering various alternative prices for its new product, Zonkers. Its market research department has come up with the following projection of the product's demand curve (Chapter 3):

| Price | Expected unit sales |
|:---:|:---:|
| $1.00 | 200,000 |
| 2.00 | 100,000 |
| 3.00 | 75,000 |
| 4.00 | 50,000 |

Variable costs are $0.40 per unit plus a ten-percent sales commission. Fixed costs are $100,000 per year.

a) For each alternative price, calculate the breakeven sales volume in units, the margin of safety, and the expected earnings before taxes.

b) Which price should Meredith choose and why?

**EP 6.16** Your firm is considering operations at a different point on its demand curve. Its currently budgeted income statement is given below.

| | |
|---|---:|
| Sales (200,000 units) | $700,000 |
| Cost of goods sold (100% variable) | 490,000 |
| Gross profits | $210,000 |
| Operating expenses (90% fixed) | 100,000 |
| Income before taxes | $110,000 |

a) For each of the alternative points on the demand curve, determine **both** the amount and direction of change in breakeven dollar sales volume and also in earnings before taxes. Alternate demand curve points under consideration are:

| Unit price | Expected unit sales |
|:---:|:---:|
| $3.75 | 150,000 |
| 3.40 | 250,000 |
| 3.00 | 300,000 |

b) Would you recommend that your firm change its prices? If yes, to which price and why?

**EP 6.17** The Phillips Company's budgeted income statement for the current year is given below. Suppose the firm desired a target profit of $90,000 before taxes.

| | |
|---|---:|
| Sales (200,000 units ) | $900,000 |
| Cost of goods sold (100% variable) | 700,000 |
| Gross Profit | $200,000 |
| Operating expenses (80% fixed) | 160,000 |
| Income before taxes | $ 40,000 |

a) How many additional units would have to be sold at a price of $4.50 to achieve target profit?

b) Assume the price could be increased to $5.00. At this price, how many total units must be sold to achieve target profit?

c) Assume the firm's capacity was 225,000 annually. At capacity, what price would have to be obtained to achieve target profit?

**EP 6.18** Refer to Problem EP 6.17. Assume the same data **except** current budgeted selling price is $18 (50,000 budgeted unit sales), and the firm desires a target profit of $60,000.

a) How many additional units would have to be sold at $18 each to achieve target profit?

b) At a price of $20 each, how many total units must be sold to achieve target profit?

c) Assume the firm's annual capacity was 40,000 units. At capacity, what price would have to be obtained to:

1. Break even?
2. Achieve target profit?

**EP 6.19** The vice-president for operations of the Sprat Manufacturing Company is evaluating new automated processing equipment. The department into which the process would be introduced currently budgets manufacturing costs at $3 per unit variable and $20,000 per month fixed. The new equipment would reduce variable manufacturing costs to $1 per unit. The increased equipment rental cost (rental on new equipment less rental on existing equipment) would be $10,000 per month.

a) Above what average monthly activity level would the new machine be desirable?

b) What would be the net additional costs or savings resulting from the introduction of the new process if monthly activity averaged:

1. 4,000 units?
2. 12,000 units?

**EP 6.20** Refer to Problem EP 6.19. Answer the same two questions based on the same data **except** assume the new equipment would have a differential rental of $25,000 per month and would reduce variable costs to $0.50 per unit.

**EP 6.21** The Nelthrop Company's margin of profit **over minimum satisfactory profit** is currently 20 percent of total current sales. Demand for the firm's products is quite sensitive to changes in consumer expectations of disposable income, and the firm is, therefore, quite properly concerned with maintaining an adequate margin over minimum satisfactory profit volume. Assume the firm's fixed costs are $500,000 annually, variable costs are 70 percent of sales, and target profit is $100,000. Also assume the firm's product (or product mix) is selling at a price of $20.

a) What was the firm's current sales volume in dollars and in units?

b) What was the firm's current margin of profit over satisfactory profit volume in:

1. Total dollars of revenue?

2. Unit sales assuming no price change?

3. Proportion of unit price assuming no volume change?

c) Answer the same questions as in (b) above but with respect to the margin of safety (over breakeven).

EP 6.22 Refer to Problem EP 6.21. Assume the same data except that fixed costs were $620,000 annually.

a) What was the firm's breakeven sales volume in dollars and units?

b) What is the necessary sales volume in dollars and in units to just achieve minimum satisfactory profit?

c) What is current sales volume in dollars and in units?

d) If unit sales remain at the current level, by how much could unit prices decrease and:

1. Still result in a satisfactory profit?

2. Still result in breakeven?

e) If unit prices remained at $20, by how much could unit volume decrease and:

1. Still result in a satisfactory profit?

2. Still result in breakeven?

## SUPPLEMENTARY PROBLEMS

SP 6.23 The Armstrong Company is considering expanding its sales coverage to a new region (territory). Sales costs would involve salaries and commissions for additional sales personnel of $75,000 annually plus 10 percent sales commission. An additional regional sales office would cost $30,000 per year. As an alternative, the company could sell through manufacturers' representatives in the territory, giving them a straight 20 percent commission on sales. Incremental clerical costs in the home office under this arrangement would be $10,000 per year.

You work for Armstrong, and the sales vice-president has requested that you present him with an analysis of the profitability of each alternative at different expected unit sales volume levels corresponding to different proposed product prices. These different alternatives are:

|  | Price | Expected unit volume in new territory |
|---|---|---|
|  | $4.00 | 225,000 |
|  | 6.00 | 175,000 |
|  | 8.00 | 90,000 |

You know that variable manufacturing costs for the firm currently average $3.00 per unit.

a) Prepare the requested analysis.

b) Recommend which price should be chosen from among the alternatives, and why.

c) Recommend which course of action should be taken (do not expand, or expand by one method and at one price), and why. Alternatively, explain what data you would need to make an appropriate recommendation.

**SP 6.24** Refer to Problem SP 6.23. Make the same analysis and recommendations assuming: commissions could be reduced to 6 percent for sales personnel and to 15 percent for manufacturers' representatives, clerical expenses for manufacturers' representatives reduced to $5,000 per year, and variable manufacturing costs could be reduced to $2.50 per unit.

**SP 6.25** Each of the following sets of data (A)–(E) relates to a proposed new product line for a firm and is independent of the others. Determine the missing amounts, assuming, in each case, that the firm desired a minimum satisfactory profit. Except for unit prices, all dollar amounts given and required are rounded to even thousands.

|  | A | B | C | D | E |
|---|---|---|---|---|---|
| Given/necessary sales volume ($) | ? | ? | ? | ? | 2,000 |
| Given/necessary sales volume (units) | 100,000 | ? | 20,000 | 40,000 | 50,000 |
| Given/necessary unit price | ? | $40 | ? | $25 | ? |
| Given/necessary variable cost rate | 60% | 40% | 30% | ? | 80% |
| Given/maximum allowable fixed costs | $180 | $152 | $98 | $210 | ? |
| Given/necessary before-tax income | ? | ? | ? | ? | ? |
| Investment required | $500 | $400 | $300 | $600 | $700 |
| Cost of capital* | 12% | 13% | 14% | 15% | 16% |
| Variable costs ($) | ? | ? | ? | ? | ? |
| Breakeven sales volume ($) | ? | ? | ? | ? | ? |
| Breakeven sales volume (units) | ? | ? | ? | ? | ? |

* To simplify calculations, given on a before-tax basis.

**SP 6.26** Each of the following sets of data (P)–(T) relates to a proposed new product line for a firm and is independent of the others. Determine the missing amounts, assuming, in each case, that the firm desired a minimum satisfactory profit. Except for unit prices, all dollar amounts given and required are rounded to even thousands.

|  | P | Q | R | S | T |
|---|---|---|---|---|---|
| Given/necessary sales volume ($) | $500 | ? | ? | ? | ? |
| Given/necessary sales volume (units) | ? | 50,000 | 4,000 | ? | 10,000 |
| Given/necessary unit price | $40 | $8 | ? | $5 | ? |
| Given/necessary variable cost rate | 70% | ? | 65% | 35% | 75% |
| Given/maximum allowable fixed costs | ? | $125 | $52 | $148 | $124 |
| Given/necessary before-tax income | ? | ? | ? | ? | ? |
| Investment required | $400 | $500 | $300 | $600 | $700 |
| Cost of capital* | 14% | 15% | 16% | 17% | 18% |
| Variable costs ($) | ? | ? | ? | ? | ? |
| Breakeven sales volume ($) | ? | ? | ? | ? | ? |
| Breakeven sales volume (units) | ? | ? | ? | ? | ? |

**SP 6.27** From recent income statements of the Lochland Corporation, you have noted income from operations before taxes of $70,000 and $190,000 at sales levels of $300,000 and $500,000, respectively.

a) What are the firm's apparent fixed costs?

b) What is the firm's apparent variable cost rate?

c) What is the firm's variable cost per unit if the contribution is $9 per unit?

d) What is the firm's breakeven dollar sales volume?

e) What would profits before taxes be at a sales volume of $400,000?

f) What dollar sales volume would be required to earn a target profit of $100,000 **after taxes,** assuming a 35-percent tax rate?

**SP 6.28** Refer to Problem SP 6.27. Answer the same six questions, assuming that the income statements had disclosed, at the $300,000 and $500,000 sales volume levels, a net loss of $10,000 and a net profit of $80,000 respectively.

---

* To simplify calculations, given on a before-tax basis.

CHAPTER 6 APPENDIX
# Pricing and Product Mix

---

PRICING

The theory and practice of pricing is covered in micro-economics and marketing courses. The intention of this appendix is to introduce the various general approaches to making pricing decisions, and to the relevance of pricing to managerial accounting, and vice versa. In earlier chapters it was pointed out that, to date, business has invested more energy in the planning and control of costs rather than revenues or prices. You learned that revenues are less controllable than costs, and that an incremental dollar of cost savings is more significant to profit than an incremental dollar of additional revenue. From this information, you should **not** infer that revenue and prices are less important than costs.

### Importance of Pricing Decision

Making the *pricing decision* (what price to charge for a particular product) may involve considerable analysis for one firm and involve no effort for another. The pricing decision is trivial for those firms with products selling in perfect markets, where the market determines the price and the firm is a "price taker." In such situations, the firm has no pricing decision to make. There is no way it can price and sell above the market price, and no incentive to sell below the market price, since it can sell all it wants at the prevailing price. Its only real decision is whether to enter or to stay in the market. Can the item (product) be obtained (purchased or manufactured) at a cost low enough to produce a satisfactory profit? Farmers growing widely used commodities and miners of precious metals are in this situation. Most other businesses are not.

Where the market is somewhat elastic (Chapter 3) and the firm is a "price maker," the pricing decision can be critical. It will contribute to the determination of **both** the volume of the firm's activity and the total revenues that can be generated.[13]

---

[13]    Other elements than price can also influence demand. Demand may be influenced by quality, service, packaging, substitutability of and for other products, habit, advertising and sales promotion, and numerous other factors.

## Economic Model of Pricing

There is a traditional economic model for the pricing decision. It assumes demand elasticity and both a limited demand for the firm's products and also diminishing returns on the firm's resources (costs) invested. Diminishing returns merely recognizes that, at some point, with increasing volume within the firm's capacity, operations will become less efficient, from overcrowding and overutilization of resources. This pricing model may be shown graphically as in Fig. 6.5. In Fig. 6.5, TC is the total cost curve and TR is the total revenue curve. The optimal price and volume combination is at the point OPV where the difference between total cost and total revenue (the profit) is greatest.

This simple model is valuable in picturing the concept of pricing decision objectives. Beyond that it is limited in usefulnes. The model ignores competitor actions and reactions. It ignores the effect on demand of competing products, the cross-elasticity of demand. The model assumes that profit maximization, rather than **satisfactory** profit, is the goal of all firms. And, finally, it assumes that price is the sole determinant of demand.

Even if the model were relevant, the necessary data to accurately plot the curves is most often not available. If it were, management could merely look up the optimum point on the firm's demand curve and the pricing decision would be no problem. In marketing courses you can learn how considerable sums may be expended in market research activities, and how sophisticated mathematical techniques may be employed, in an attempt to approximate a firm's or product's demand curve.

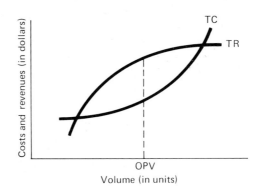

**Figure 6.5**

## Practical Economics of Pricing

Even though the manager is often flying blind with respect to the appropriate demand curve(s), he or she must remember some practical realities about most prices. If the price is set **too high,** it will either be absorbed or rejected by the market. If rejected, the firm has no revenue. If absorbed, short-term very high profits will result. This, in turn, will probably attract either increased competition or charges of price gouging and possible governmental regulation or both. If prices are set **too low,** the firm will be unable to earn a minimum necessary return on its investment (cost of capital). It will be unable to obtain additional capital to maintain its position in an inflationary economy, or to expand. It must eventually fail.

In this chapter, you had the opportunity to become familiar with and to understand the concept of contribution. You learned that, **in the short run,** prices should be accepted that **exceed variable costs** even if they do **not** cover an appropriate proportion of **fixed cost.** Some contribution is better than none. **In the long run,** however, if some combination of prices and volume (total revenue) does not cover **all** costs, both fixed and variable, **plus** provide an adequate profit, the firm will not survive. No amount of superior planning and cost control and no high levels of management efficiency and effectiveness can counterbalance inadequate long run revenue.

## Cost-Related Pricing

Managers, therefore, analyze prices in relationship to costs. The costs that management considers in making pricing decisions are **not** the past costs of financial accounting. Prices are set to cover future sales. They must take into account any expected modification in product design, and any expectations of future costs with allowance for changes due to productivity, different levels of volume, and, of course, inflation.

Prices often are not, and cannot, be based solely on costs. Nor are they often set exclusively in terms of what the market will bear regardless of costs. If you are looking for simple rules and formulas, you won't find them in business and especially in the area of pricing. You can only remember that most prices, if not *cost-based,* are *cost-related.*

Relating prices to costs proves useful in several ways. Cost data provides a reference point or base line for departure in the pricing decision. Costs give some indication of a floor under which competitors will not go (assuming competitors' costs are comparable). Costs indicate the floor below which the firm cannot set its long-term prices.[11] And costs are also an important factor in product design. A product will be designed so as to meet a cost target, enabling sale at a profit in a specific market. Subsequent sections briefly outline some of the more common approaches to cost-related pricing. They are all based upon some form of cost as an indicator but **not** a final determinant of selling price.

## Pricing New Products

The difficulty encountered in pricing new products depends upon their degree of "newness." Where a new product is very similar to existing products on

---

[11] There are some situations where a firm may desire or must tolerate one or more of many products being permanently priced below cost. Examples include items necessary to complete product lines and deliberate "loss leaders." These situations are beyond the scope of this appendix.

the market, the pricing decision is more like that for an established product (see below). Where a proposed new product is really new, a high degree of uncertainty may exist. Also there may be a very high cost of pricing error.

With an existing product with established customer demand, a price increase greater than customers will tolerate may be quickly rescinded and sales volume restored. However, if a new product is priced too high, it may be rejected and never be given another chance. No use pattern has been established. Also, an initial price that is too low may establish a price image in the customer's mind. It may thereafter be difficult, if not impossible, subsequently to raise a price that was initially set too low.

Because of the risks involved and their attendant costs (losses), it is cost-effective for managers to purchase "insurance" in the form of extensive market surveys and even test marketing. Both surveys and test marketing are designed to reduce uncertainty and risk. Surveys are primarily aimed at attempting to estimate the always elusive demand curve. Test marketing can not only validate consumer acceptance and various price–volume relationships; it can also validate cost projections (both product cost and distribution costs).

### Pricing Established Products

Established product prices are often reviewed and set in relationship to one of three bases:

- Contribution approach,
- Full cost approach,
- Full cost plus approach.

The contribution approach to pricing involves adding an established *markon* percentage to a product's variable cost.[15] For this reason, it is sometimes also known as *direct cost* (based) *pricing*. The markon should be sufficient to cover general selling and administrative expenses **and** provide a satisfactory profit. A deliberately higher markon may be applied to those items with a high risk of slow or limited "fad" sales, such as high-fashion clothing. A uniform contribution, or direct-cost-based, approach may be an inappropriate oversimplification in those situations where individual products' demand upon selling overhead (storage and display space costs, inventory investment, and so forth) was not reasonably uniform. Nevertheless, this approach is commonly used by merchandisers (wholesalers and retailers) because of trade practice (tradition) and because it may be too costly to develop anything but a few overall average markon percentages for different product groups.

The *full-cost* (based) *approach* is similar to the contribution approach, in that a markon percentage is applied to a cost. In this instance, the product's full-cost (variable cost plus an allocation of fixed cost) is used as a base. Since

---

[15]  Note that, in the language of selling, an individual item's gross profit expressed as a percentage of its cost is called "markon." The same difference expressed as a percentage of selling is known as a "markup." Thus an item costing $50 and selling for $100 would have a 100-percent markon and only a 50-percent markup.

markon on full product cost results in gross profit or gross margin on the income statement, this approach is also known as the *gross margin method*. It takes into account nonuniform products (assuming fixed cost allocations are appropriate). It also reflects particular assumed volume levels that may not be appropriate over an extended period of time.

Still another approach bases a markon upon variable cost plus an allowance for the particular resources used for the product. In effect it is a variation of full costing that incorporates engineering estimates providing for an adequate return on specific assets employed. This cost data may be very costly to compile, and therefore the method is usually limited to high-unit-cost, low-volume items such as airplanes, machine tools, large electric-power generators, and similar items.

In the last analysis, prices for established products must be set in terms of an educated and experienced "guesstimate" or feeling or intuition of what the market will tolerate.

## Pricing Special Orders

Special orders, by definition, are different from the marketing of new or established products. If the firm has adequate current capacity to accept the order, it usually involves a single one-time decision with no long-run consequences. Therefore, long-run satisfactory profit considerations are not relevant. However, if a special order exceeds the firm's capacity and other volume would have to be sacrificed if the order were accepted, then the order no longer may be considered to involve an independent one-shot decision.

Special orders are usually priced by following either the contribution method or on the basis of time and material. If the firm has adequate capacity, the order does not affect sales of regular products, and the Robinson–Patman Act (see below) is not relevant, then **any price** obtainable that exceeds variable cost makes the order desirable. As mentioned earlier in this chapter, in such a case the choice is simply between some contribution and none. The price may be established as a markon to variable costs or, where variable costs are unknown or uncertain, on the basis of time and material. Under *time and material pricing*, the sales contract does not involve a set price. Instead a price is agreed to for whatever direct labor hours and direct material units may be involved. The time price per hour (direct labor) and the material price per unit each include a markon designed to contribute to overhead and profit.

Where a special order still does not affect regular volume and Robinson–Patman does not apply but its acceptance exceeds the firm's capacity, then the order should **not** be accepted unless:

1. Its contribution exceeds the contribution loss on other work displaced, and

2. There are no long-term repercussions resulting from the cutback of other volume.

Situations of this type will be discussed further in Chapter 7.

Where a special order does affect the volume of regular business or Robinson–Patman applies, then it no longer may be considered as independent and special. It must be priced in terms of the effect on all revenues as if it involved an established product.

## Competitive Bids

Large-volume or high-cost contracts between firms or between a firm and the government are often awarded on a competitive bid basis. Bid prices may be made on several bases:

- Set price per unit
- Different set prices per unit, depending upon actual volume ordered— a tiered bid
- Time and material
- Actual cost plus a fixed fee
- Actual cost plus a percentage fee

Bid pricing is common in government contracting, construction, and in the oil and automobile industries. In government contracting the federal Cost Accounting Standards Board regulates cost classifications and methods of cost determination. Further examination of bid pricing is beyond the scope of this text.

## Regulated Prices

Some prices are established by government regulatory bodies. Public utilities (natural gas, water, electricity, and telephone) pricing is an example. For utilities, prices are usually established by regulatory commissions on the full-cost-plus basis previously described as one alternative approach for established products. The regulated price is set and periodically reviewed to allow recovery of full costs plus a minimum established satisfactory return on the owners' investment. Other examples of regulated prices include fares for air, train, taxi, and ocean travel and shipping rates (called tariffs) in interstate shipment. The intention of price regulation is to preclude excessive profits. It may also involve precluding price cutting to avoid encouraging consumption (alcohol) or to provide subsidy for the maintenance of otherwise unprofitable services (air service to small communities).

## Related Pricing Issues

Three related issues should be included in any consideration of pricing: credit policy, the Robinson–Patman Act, and transfer pricing. A firm's overall credit policy, or credit terms applicable to particular products or customers, is effectively an integral part of its price structure. When a firm extends credit to customers, it is temporarily investing resources in these customers. Prices must be set high enough to cover credit office and collection costs and the capital costs of such investments. Alternatively, the firm must at least realize that credit extension has the effect of reducing the net price obtained by the amount of credit costs. Credit policy was discussed in Chapter 3.

The Robinson–Patman Act (or specifically the Robinson–Patman Amendment to the Clayton Anti-Trust Act) applies to prices quoted or charged to **competing** customers for the **same** goods. Note that this law does not apply to competitive bids or to specially designed product situations. Nor does it apply to different customers who do not compete in the same markets, such as wholesalers and retailers, domestic and foreign customers, and so forth. Robinson–Patman, as interpreted by the courts, essentially forbids price discrimination (different prices charged or quoted for the same products to competing customers) unless the price difference can be shown to result from different actual full costs incurred, including the effects of volume of production. Also, many states have laws prohibiting "dumping," or the sale of goods or services to consumers below full cost. The existence of these regulations provides still further justification for a firm's keeping adequate cost records.

A final price-related issue involves the setting of *transfer prices* that are to be charged between divisions of the same firm. Ideally, a price would exist that would perfectly motivate both the supplying and acquiring divisions to behave in the best interests of the overall firm. When the company would be best served by internal transfer, both division managers would be motivated in that direction. And when the company would be best served (higher profit) by the supplying division using its capacity for outside customers and the acquiring division turning to outside suppliers, again both division managers would be so motivated. Unfortunately, it can be shown that, in many situations, no single price works in the ideal fashion. Establishing transfer prices and attendant company rules or policies can then become a real problem. The transfer pricing problem will be explored in Chapter 14.

## PRODUCT MIX

As you may have surmised from the discussion of product mix in this chapter, the common situation of a firm's selling two or more products may add much complexity to the pricing decision. Theoretically every permutation and combination of price of each product should be considered. In addition, interdependence or cross-elasticity may exist among products within a firm's own product line. Pricing a mix of products is a difficult subject usually considered only in advanced or graduate marketing courses. Where a product mix situation exists, even without demand interdependence, the existence of common fixed costs indicates the necessity of pricing all products together and not individually. The pricing objective is to maximize the contribution of all products together to cover common fixed costs and to provide a satisfactory profit.

In practice most firms find such far-reaching analysis impractical. For some, computer simulations of a wide range of alternatives have provided worthwhile clues indicating desirable price restructuring. However, since prices are to a great degree market-determined, managers often price individual products or product lines somewhere between full cost (floor) and what their feel, experience, or research tells them is the maximum the market will accept. Limited price–volume combinations of limited numbers of items may be analyzed for the optimum. Otherwise managers can only hope that interaction with the market will somehow lead to an optimal product pricing mix.

As mentioned in this chapter, managerial accounting in both planning and control must assume a single product mix for budgeting and control purposes. In evaluating the firm's overall performance as part of a control process, differences between planned revenue and actual revenue may result from differences in planned and actual sales mix. In Chapter 14 you can learn how this so-called *mix variance* may be isolated and measured. Identification of the mix variance serves not only to explain what has happened to revenue but also to provide an indication of a potential revised product mix for future budgeting purposes.

## SUGGESTIONS FOR FURTHER READING

Anthony, Robert N., and Glenn A. Welsch, *Fundamentals of Management Accounting*, Revised Edition. Homewood, Illinois: Richard D. Irwin, Inc., 1977. Chapter 2.

Horngren, C., *Cost Accounting: A Managerial Emphasis*, Fourth Edition. Englewood Cliffs, N.J.: Prentice-Hall, Inc., 1977; Chapter 11.

Morse, Wayne J., *Cost Accounting: Processing, Evaluating, and Using Cost Data*. Reading, Massachusetts: Addison-Wesley Publishing Company, 1978; Chapter 6.

Van Horne, James C., *Fundamentals of Financial Management*, Third Edition. Englewood Cliffs, N.J.: Prentice-Hall, Inc., 1977. Chapters 16–18.

Weston, J. Fred, and Eugene F. Brigham, *Essentials of Managerial Finance*, Fourth Edition. Hinsdale, Illinois: The Dryden Press, 1977; Chapters 4 and 20.

# 7

# RELEVANT COSTS AND BUSINESS DECISIONS

CHAPTER PREVIEW

This chapter is intended to provide you with an introduction to the making of nonroutine business decisions and to the data that are relevant to different types of decisions. In this chapter, you can learn:

- . That there are many business decisions that either involve costs and benefits extending beyond the current year or, for other reasons, are not part of normal budgeted operations.
- That these decisions involve planning considerations similar to yet different from the budgeting of normal operations.
- The importance of identifying and using only relevant costs (and benefits) in a particular decision, and how decision relevancy is defined.
- The relevance of avoidable costs, sunk costs, opportunity costs, and related fringe costs to business decisions, and how these costs may be obtained.
- The effort-saving distinction between investment decisions and non-investment decisions.
- Different decision rules applicable to different types of noninvestment decisions.
- The necessity of including considerations of taxes and the time value of money in noninvestment decisions if, and only if, anticipated flows of costs and benefits are uneven.
- The importance of nonquantifiable considerations in arriving at a final decision.

With this knowledge, you will be in a position to make appropriate nonroutine business decisions that do not involve investments. You will be aware of relevant data necessary for such decisions. And you will have a solid foundation of understanding upon which to build your knowledge of the elements involved in making investment decisions. The factors relevant to investment decision-making will be covered in Chapter 8.

## SHOULD I MAKE OR BUY THIS ITEM?

As the operations vice-president of Tripper, you occasionally are faced with decisions that are somewhat different from routine day-to-day planning, operating, and controlling decisions. These nonroutine decisions can be thought of as in a gray or overlap area between short-range planning (budgeting) and intermediate-range planning. They are short-range in that they often require immediate decision and may involve early implementation. And they may also be intermediate-range in that their effects may extend beyond the current period.

For example, assume that you have just been approached by a furniture maker—the Jones Company—that has excess capacity. Jones wants you to consider subcontracting to them the manufacturing (moulding) of your wooden economy skis. If you decide to work with Jones, the wooden ski would become a purchased part. It would then require only assembly of hardware to be a finished product.

Jones offers to supply skis to your specifications at a price of $23.00 per ski, in quantities of seven to ten thousand per year, and at $20.00 per ski in quantities of 10 to 15 thousand per year. You are interested in looking further into this idea. You could use the space and facilities that would be made available to produce the new line of water ski safety jackets and belts that is scheduled to start production next year. You have already estimated that it would be necessary to rent additional space in an adjoining building for belt and jacket production at a cost of $24,000 per year. After learning of the Jones offer, you have asked for and obtained from the controller the latest cost information related to economy skis:

### Current Unit Cost Data Related to Economy Skis

|                     | Moulding | Assembly | Total   |
|---------------------|----------|----------|---------|
| Material            | $3.00    | $2.50    | $5.50   |
| Direct labor        | 8.55     | 1.25     | 9.80    |
| Overhead (variable) | 2.75     | .55      | 3.30    |
| Overhead (fixed)    | 10.07    | 1.33     | 11.40   |
| Total Cost          | $24.37   | $5.63    | $30.00  |

For the moment, assume that there are no considerations other than minimizing cost. You may also assume that the anticipated volume of economy skis for the forthcoming year is approximately 13,000 units. On the basis of cost savings alone, would you choose to subcontract the moulding of wooden skis? Take the time to work out your decision with all supporting data on a separate sheet of paper, before you read the next paragraph. If you then find that you are correct, the experience should be rewarding and reinforcing. You will know you can proceed to more sophisticated decision problems with confidence. If you are incorrect, you will then have the opportunity to identify misunderstandings and misconceptions that require correction before you attempt more sophisticated problems.

On the basis of cost alone, you are correct if your decision is to continue the moulding of economy skis and to rent required space for next year's belt and jacket production. If you were to subcontract the skis to Jones at a price of $20 per ski and use the freed space for belt and jacket production, your annual costs would be $50,100 greater at a projected volume of 13,000 skis per year than if you made the correct decision. Annual costs "saved" through subcontracting would include:

|  |  |
|---|---|
| Variable moulding costs ($14.30 per ski) | $185,900 |
| Rent on additional space | 24,000 |
| Total | $209,900 |

In exchange for "saving" $209,900, you would be incurring an additional cost of $260,000 (13,000 skis at $20 each). Hardly a desirable choice to minimize costs.

If you were assuming you could save the full $30 cost per ski, you were not using data relevant to the decision. Only moulding costs could possibly be saved. And if you were assuming you could save the full $24.37 of costs allocated to moulding, you were not concentrating on the avoidable costs related to your decision. The $10.07 of fixed overhead could not be avoided in this example. Relevant and avoidable costs will be further explained below.

## INTERMEDIATE PLANNING AND DECISIONS INVOLVING A SEGMENT OR PORTION OF THE FIRM'S ACTIVITIES

In making nonroutine decisions, a manager must plan or budget the outcomes of each alternative and then compare the results. One approach would be to budget the entire firm through to a pro-forma income statement for each alternative. This approach would make sense if the alternatives under consideration were so far-reaching in their consequences that virtually all segments of the firm would be affected. It would make no sense, and be unnecessarily time-consuming and costly, for those decisions that involved only a small portion or subset of the firm's activities. In this and the following chapter, you can learn:

1. how to identify what portions of the firm's activities are affected by a particular decision (by so doing, you can limit your effort to a consideration of the alternative effects in this narrower area), and

2. what criteria or decision rules to apply to different kinds of decisions (with this knowledge you can both avoid unnecessary computation, and also be assured that your decision will ultimately maximize net income for the firm).

## RELEVANT COSTS

*Relevant costs* (and revenues) are those that are affected by or will change as a result of a particular decision; that is, costs (and revenues) that will change or be different in the future solely as a direct result of the decision alternative chosen. All relevant costs (and revenues) must be considered in making a particular decision. Irrelevant costs (or revenues) are those that are **not** affected by the decision. In the Tripper example above, the following costs were wholly irrelevant to the make-or-buy decision:

* $23 price from Jones,
* $5.63 portion of ski product cost identified with the assembly department,
* $10.07 of fixed overhead cost per ski in the moulding department currently allocated for financial accounting (inventory or product cost) purposes.

Can you see why each of these costs is irrelevant to this particular make-or-buy decision? The $23 price is not relevant to the quantities under consideration in the decision. The $5.64 assembly cost is irrelevant since the hardware will still have to be attached to the skis regardless of whether they are purchased or manufactured. Also, in this example, the $10.07 per ski of fixed overhead in the moulding department will continue whether or not the skis are manufactured. The overhead is fixed with respect to this decision.[1]

The emphasis on the relevancy of costs may seem obvious or even trivial to you. You would be well advised not to dismiss it or skip over it lightly. Most student and manager decision errors can be traced either to forgetting to include an item that is relevant, or to the inclusion of an item that is irrelevant. This latter error—including an irrelevant item—may not seem so bad. Most of the time the inclusion of an irrelevant item in each of the alternatives under consideration would merely result in extra and unnecessary computation. The extra data does, of course, increase the risk of computational error. Of more importance, however, is the fact that, some of the time, inclusion of irrelevant data will lead to an incorrect decision, as will be shown below.

You should note that relevancy is **not** an attribute of a particular cost. The identical cost may be relevant to one decision and irrelevant to another. You should remember that relevancy relates to **a particular decision.** Something is **only** relevant in terms of a particular decision and then **only** if it is affected (changes) by or as a result of, one of the decision alternatives.

In previous chapters you had the opportunity to learn certain terminology and concepts related to costs. Product vs. period costs and direct vs. indirect

---

[1]   If the skis were purchased, the fixed overhead previously allocated to economy skis would then be applied as additional cost to the deluxe skis. The deluxe skis would then be "required" to absorb all fixed cost in the moulding department. In some situations, some fixed costs can be reduced as part of a decision alternative. See below.

costs were associated with how accountants treat certain costs in the financial accounting system. Controllable vs. noncontrollable costs and discretionary (programmed) vs. committed costs related to useful concepts in the preparation of operating budgets. Fixed, mixed, and variable costs related to the behavior of particular costs within relevant ranges. The identification of these cost attributes is essential for budget preparation and for CVP analysis (Chapter 6). In this chapter you can learn of other cost characteristics useful in the decision-making process. Like the term "relevant cost," the terms "avoidable/escapable costs," "sunk costs," "opportunity costs," and "related fringe costs" all refer to concepts associated with a particular decision. The following table illustrates this important distinction:

| Cost concept: | Related to: |
| --- | --- |
| Product vs. period | GAAP and financial accounting system |
| Full absorption (product) cost vs. Direct (variable) cost | Alternatives within financial accounting system (Full cost only acceptable) |
| Direct vs. indirect | Accountant's choice within cost accounting system |
| Standard vs. actual | Accountant's choice within cost accounting system |
| Fixed, mixed, and variable | Attribute of cost behavior useful for budgeting and CVP |
| Discretionary (programmed) and committed | Variability for budgeting purposes |
| Controllable vs. noncontrollable | Appropriateness for inclusion in budget for particular responsibility center |
| Avoidable/escapable | Cost, but only for a particular decision |
| Sunk | Cost, but only for a particular decision |
| Opportunity | Cost, but only for a particular decision |
| Related fringe | Cost, but only for a particular decision |

## AVOIDABLE/ESCAPABLE COSTS (OR REVENUES)

The terms "avoidable cost" and "escapable cost" are used synonymously to identify costs that are affected by (change) or that result from a particular decision alternative. Note that this definition is almost the same as that for relevant costs. The **only** costs that are relevant to a particular decision are those that are avoidable or escapable. In the earlier Tripper example, the $10.07 per unit of fixed overhead allocated was not **relevant** because it would not have been **avoidable** if the moulding of economy skis had been subcontracted.

Do not make the mistake of assuming, based on the earlier simplified Tripper example, that only variable costs are avoidable. In many make-or-buy (or other) decisions involving potential discontinuation of activities, some fixed cost is avoidable. For example, with no further activity planned for a segment of the business related, fixed indirect labor costs such as a foreman's salary could be suspended. Fixed asset costs could likewise become avoidable if leased equipment was no longer required and could be returned to the lessor.[2]

Think back to Chapter 5 and the concept of relevant range. Essentially the concept of relevant range refers to a collection of fixed costs that provide operating capacity over a particular range of volume or activity.

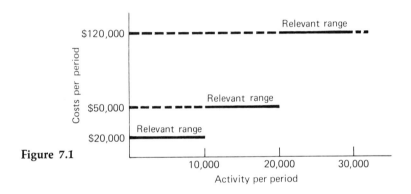

**Figure 7.1**

In Fig. 7.1, $50,000 of fixed costs provided capacity for the firm to operate economically at volume levels of from 10,000 to 20,000 units per year, the relevant range over which these costs were fixed. At a volume below 10,000 units, some fixed costs could be reduced (avoided) as the firm moved to a lower capacity level. A decision alternative involving volumes of less than 10,000 or more than 20,000 would involve results **beyond or outside of the relevant range.** You can review and reinforce these concepts with the following:

- When, and **only** when, all decision alternatives are within a relevant range of fixed cost, only variable costs will be avoidable.
- When decision alternatives extend to beyond a relevant range, both variable and some fixed costs are avoidable.

---

[2]   Note that asset ownership costs such as depreciation and insurance are not included at this time as examples of avoidable fixed costs. If the asset could not be sold, ownership costs would not be avoidable. If the asset could be sold, the decision would involve an investment (in this case, a disinvestment). Decisions that involve investments or disinvestments are more complex and will be covered in Chapter 8.

## SUNK COSTS

If a cost must be avoidable to be relevant to a decision, then all unavoidable (not escapable) costs must be irrelevant to that same decision. *Sunk costs* are past committed costs which, because of their having been committed in the past, are unavoidable today. Sunk costs are essentially irrelevant to a decision. Think of a situation where you were faced with the following facts:

**1.** Yesterday you committed your firm for five years to a new machine costing $100,000 (either purchase or noncancellable lease). Depreciation or lease payments will run $20,000 per year. You manufacture and sell for $2 each one million gizmos per year. Your new machine, which isn't even delivered, can produce gizmos at a cost of $0.50 apiece. Assume this $0.50 represents variable operating costs and does not include any allocation of depreciation or machine purchase cost.

**2.** Today a better machine becomes available, also with five years of useful life, at a cost of $200,000. It can make your gizmos for $0.30 each (variable cost). Should you purchase or lease the newer machine? Can you afford to ignore your brand new machine acquired yesterday?

If you decide yes, you will order the newer machine, you probably understand the concept of sunk cost. On the other hand, if you reason that you can't afford to "throw away" your new (now old) machine, you are making a very common, human error. You are allowing actions and decisions of the past to constrain your choices of today when it is not profitable to do so. If a past decision turns out to be a mistake, it does not serve you to continue the mistake into the present and the future.[3]

### Relevant Decision Costs at Annual Volume of One Million Gizmos[a]

|  | First (old) machine | Second (newer) machine |
|---|---|---|
| Operating costs per year | $500,000 | $300,000 |
| Machine depreciation/lease costs per year | zero[b] | 40,000[c] |
| Total future costs per year | $500,000 | $340,000 |

(a) Taxes are ignored in this illustration.
(b) No future costs, since machine is already paid for (purchase cost or lease payments irrevocably committed in the past).
(c) $200,000 cost pro-rated over five-year useful life.

In the above example, you cannot afford **not** to acquire the newer machine. It will save you $200,000 per year, will pay for itself within one year and then

---

[3]   There may, of course, be potential political consequences arising out of having to admit to a poor decision.

make you an additional $800,000. The fact that the newer machine will recover your past loss is nice and also wholly irrelevant to the decision as to whether it should be acquired. The $100,000 sunk-cost commitment yesterday is irrelevant to today's choice since it is not avoidable under either alternative (acquiring or not acquiring the newest machine).

Now suppose you could also sell the first "old" machine (or sublease it) for $10,000, and save an additional $36,000 in taxes because of the tax-loss write off (to be discussed in Chapter 8). Would this $46,000 cash benefit related to the old machine be irrelevant to your decision? Would the $100,000 still be a sunk cost, or would the sunk cost be only $54,000 of nonrecoverable loss?

You are correct if you see that, under these circumstances, your sunk cost (which doesn't change and which doesn't cost you anything today and tomorrow) is now only $54,000. The $46,000 of recoverable cash is relevant to your decision. It is a cash benefit that you will receive if you acquire the newest machine and that you will forego (not receive) if you stay with the first machine.

### Alternative Decision Costs at Annual Volume of One Million Gizmos[a]

| | First (old) machine | Second (newer) machine |
|---|---|---|
| Operating costs per year | $500,000 | $300,000 |
| Machine depreciation/lease costs per year | 9,200[b] | 40,000[c] |
| Total future costs per year | $509,200 | $340,000 |

(a) Taxes are ignored in this illustration.
(b) Assumes $46,000 potential cash recovery (sale + tax loss savings) if sold. This benefit foregone is pro-rated over five-year useful life.
(c) $200,000 cost pro-rated over five-year useful life.

## OPPORTUNITY COSTS

Note, in the above illustration, the inclusion of the $46,000 of cash recoverable on sale (pro-rated to $9,200 per year) as an additional cost of the old machine. By keeping the old machine you would be giving up $46,000 in cash you could otherwise obtain from resale and tax loss recovery. The $54,000 balance of unrecoverable original cost is a sunk cost and irrelevant. But the $46,000 after-tax recoverable cash becomes an *opportunity cost* of staying with the existing machine. An opportunity cost can be viewed as the benefits foregone of the best alternative use of resources that have been committed. The $46,000 of recoverable cash in the above equipment example, and the $24,000 of extra space rental that could be saved if economy ski moulding were subcontracted in the earlier problem, are both examples of opportunity costs or savings.

Real opportunity costs are always relevant and must be considered in a business decision. However, care must be exercised to ensure in each case that the opportunity cost is real. Note that, in the case of holding onto the already purchased machine, there is a very real flow of cash that is being foregone. Think back to the Tripper make-or-buy problem with slightly different data. Suppose the Jones Company's bid for 13,000 skis per year was $15 each. Given the other facts, the cost alternatives would be:

|  | Cost of manufacturing per year | Cost of buying per year |
|---|---|---|
| Avoidable variable product costs | $185,900 | $195,000 |
| Opportunity space cost | 24,000 | zero |
| Total | $209,900 | $195,000 |

Under these different circumstances, it would be advisable for the firm to purchase the skis from Jones for an annual savings of $14,900.

Suppose, however, that the $24,000 opportunity space costs are not real, that the belts and jackets were being purchased finished, and the space released by subcontracting had no other cash-saving use. It would be inappropriate to impute a savings to the released space that would not be realizable. Without a real opportunity cost savings, the released space becomes just another sunk cost. Relevant comparative data would be:

|  | Cost of manufacturing | Cost of subcontracting |
|---|---|---|
| Avoidable costs | $185,400 | $195,000 |
| Opportunity costs | zero | zero |
| Total | $185,400 | $195,000 |

And the appropriate decision would be to manufacture rather than subcontract the skis.

Opportunity costs are **not** recorded by accountants in the financial cost accounting system. They are, however, very necessary for inclusion in decision data whenever they are both **relevant** and **real.**


## RELATED FRINGE COSTS

A secondary and often overlooked type of cost should also be included in decision models. Many costs have associated or *related fringe costs*. Examples of such related costs would include:

- Transportation-in on purchased items (unless the price includes delivery).
- Insurance and taxes on owned property.
- Delivery costs on sales (unless sold FOB plant).
- Fringe benefits (Social Security, retirement, health, and so forth) related to wage and salary costs. These can often average 20 to 25 percent.

In decision problems where costs of different alternatives are reasonably close, you must be careful to include all relevant related fringe costs. Otherwise your data would be incomplete and could lead you to an erroneous conclusion.

## POSSIBLE RELATED INVESTMENTS

All business decisions may be arbitrarily divided into two groups. *Investment decisions* can be viewed as involving any decision where one or more of the alternatives under consideration in turn involves either:

1. An additional investment of resources with the benefits extending beyond one year, or
2. The disposition or release of previous investments.

Investment decisions must take into account the opportunity cost of capital invested and the recovery of this capital. Techniques for evaluating investment decisions will be covered in Chapter 8.

The second classification of business decisions may be called *noninvestment decisions*. Many business decisions fall into this group. Noninvestment decisions are those wherein **all** alternatives under consideration involve no change in invested capital—no new investments and no disposition or release of existing investments. The decision rules and the number of related factors that must be considered regarding noninvestment decisions are simpler than for those involving investments.

Noninvestment decisions, in turn, can be divided into subclassifications depending upon the factors that are relevant. The various types of noninvestment decisions include:

those that involve only revenue,
those that involve only variable costs,
those that involve uniform flows of expected benefits and costs,

and

those that involve uneven future flows of benefits and costs.

These subclassifications can be important since (in order) each classification involves a more complex analysis. For you to approach a simple revenue decision applying the tools necessary to analyze uneven future benefit and cost flows would be a great waste of your time and effort. For you to attempt to make a decision that involved uneven flows using the simple decision rule appropriate for revenue decisions could be disastrous. Each of the various classifications of noninvestment decisions will be discussed below.

## NONINVESTMENT DECISIONS INVOLVING ONLY REVENUES

Decisions involving purely revenues are uncommon. They would essentially be limited to pricing decisions involving no expected or desired change in cost or product sales mix. This type of decision was covered in Chapter 6. Remember that, in this limited type of problem where no costs are relevant, the decision rule can be simply to **maximize revenue** or choose the alternative that will yield the highest total revenue to the firm. This limited group of decisions is mentioned again in this chapter merely to present a complete picture of all types of noninvestment decisions.

## NONINVESTMENT DECISIONS INVOLVING ONLY VARIABLE COSTS

Some business decisions involve only variable costs. Where the only relevant variables in any of the decision alternatives are variable costs, then the decision rule can be simply to **minimize costs** or choose the alternative that will incur the lowest total cost.

The final modification of the previous make-or-buy problem, wherein there was no relevant change in fixed space costs, involved a simple cost-minimization decision. In all similar problems, total variable costs under each alternative are determined, and then the alternative with the least cost is chosen. Other examples of noninvestment decisions that involve only variable costs would include:

- choosing between two suppliers of the same item at different prices,
- choosing between two suppliers of the same service at different prices, and
- choosing between alternative engineering designs or manufacturing methods for the same product in those situations where no capital outlay would be involved.

## NONINVESTMENT DECISIONS INVOLVING UNIFORM FLOWS OF EXPECTED COSTS AND BENEFITS

Many noninvestment business decisions involve changes in expected costs (either fixed or variable or both) and possibly also changes in revenues. When all alternatives involve **uniform or even flows of** expected costs and of benefits, decision rules can be simplified. Examples of uniform benefits would include additional revenue or reduced costs of a specific amount per item (product) regardless of volume, or of a specific reduction per period in a fixed cost. Most situations where the flows are not all uniform involve some initial cost or savings that is not repeated for several periods. These situations involve investments and are covered in Chapter 8.

## Within Relevant Range and Below Capacity

When the decision alternatives do not involve changes in fixed costs (decision alternatives are all within the relevant range), and the firm is operating and would be operating below capacity, then the decision rule can be simply **maximize contribution.** Remember from Chapter 6 that a firm's or product's contribution is the difference between selling price and variable costs. If a decision does not affect total fixed costs, then maximum income will result from the choice that maximizes contribution.

Two examples of decisions of this type involve whether to accept special orders and whether to sell a product or process it further. Suppose a sweater manufacturer produces sweaters with a variable manufacturing cost of $9 each. Its productive capacity is 90,000 sweaters per year, and it is currently producing and selling nationally 60,000 sweaters per year. Sweaters are sold to wholesalers at a price of $15, and salesmen are paid a five-percent commission on all sales. All other period costs may be assumed to be fixed.

Assume that the firm has an opportunity to sell a special order of 10,000 sweaters to a foreign department-store chain at a price of $11 each. At no increase in manufacturing costs, the sweaters would carry the foreign firm's label, and they would be sold at retail for $20 as compared to the $35 retail price at which the manufacturer's own sweaters are sold in the U.S. No sales commission will be paid on this special order. Should the firm accept the order, and what costs are relevant to this decision?

You are correct if you see that the firm should accept the order. Assuming the market would be sufficiently differentiated (separated) so that the "cheaper" sweaters would not affect the firm's existing domestic business, the only data relevant would be:

- The order is within the firm's capacity (relevant range), and no changes in fixed costs are involved.
- The order provides a unit contribution of $2 per sweater ($11 selling price minus $9 variable cost) or a total contribution of $20,000.

The order should be accepted, since the choice is between a contribution of $20,000 and none.

Selling or processing further is a second example of this type of decision. Suppose a lumber sawmill was considering an alternative use for the sawdust that was a by-product of its sawing operations. It expects to have 40 tons of sawdust each year. Currently it is burning its sawdust as fuel for the mill and estimates this is saving $12,000 in fuel costs annually. It can sell its sawdust to a manufacturer of artificial fireplace logs for $400 a ton; or it can have its sawdust compacted into fireplace logs by a subcontractor. The subcontractor would charge $0.05 per log to compress the sawdust with kerosene and wrap it. The $0.05 would include costs of transportation, kerosene, and wrapping paper. Each log would require one-half pound of sawdust, and, when completed, could be sold to wholesalers for $0.25. Should the firm:

1. Continue to burn its sawdust?
2. Sell its sawdust?
3. Manufacture and sell fireplace logs?

You are correct if you see that the firm should manufacture and sell fireplace logs. As discussed in the appendix to Chapter 1, accountants would probably assign the joint cost of wood logs and sawing entirely to sawed lumber. Sawdust would be treated as a by-product with zero cost at the split-off point. However, the alternative fuel cost establishes an opportunity cost of $300 per ton for the sawdust. If the only choices were to continue burning or to sell, then the firm should sell the sawdust and buy fuel:

|  | Burn | Sell |
|---|---|---|
| Revenue | zero | $16,000 |
| Variable cost | zero | 12,000† |
| Contribution | zero | $ 4,000 |

**Exhibit 7.1**

**Computations Involved in Decision to Sell or Process Further**

|  | Total basis | | Per unit basis* | |
|---|---|---|---|---|
|  | Sell | Process further | Sell | Process further |
| Revenue | $16,000 | $40,000 | $0.10 | $0.25 |
| Variable costs: |  |  |  |  |
| Sawdust | 12,000 | 12,000 | 0.075 | 0.075 |
| Further processing | zero | 8,000 | zero | 0.05 |
| Contribution | $ 4,000 | $20,000 | $0.025 | $0.125 |

* All per unit data in terms of one-half pound of sawdust (4,000 half-pound units per ton).

Evaluating the sell-or-process-further decision can be done either on a per-unit basis or in total. Exhibit 7.1 illustrates both approaches, and indicates

---

†    Opportunity cost of replacement fuel.

the clear advantage of the firm's processing sawdust further into fireplace logs for sale.

## Within Relevant Range and at Capacity

When a firm is operating at the capacity of any part of its productive facilities, a decision rule to maximize contribution may **not** maximize net income to the firm. Suppose a firm had only two products, A and B. Assume data with respect to these products as follows:

|  | Product A | Product B |
|---|---|---|
| Unit selling price | $100 | $60 |
| Variable unit costs | 60 | 40 |
| Contribution per unit | $ 40 | $20 |
| Hours required to manufacture | 4 | 1 |

Also assume the firm has budgeted $50,000 for the period for advertising (a programmed cost). The advertising agency advises that, with such a low budget, most results can be expected by focusing the campaign on one item instead of attempting to cover both. Current sales are running 20,000 units of A and 40,000 units of B annually. It is expected that advertising A would result in a 25-percent increase it its sales, whereas advertising B would increase its sales by only 15 percent. As a first decision, should the firm advertise **either** of its products?

You should see that, based on projected sales increases, and assuming that the firm has adequate capacity to meet sales demand, the firm should advertise. Even the less attractive result of advertising product B would increase contribution by $120,000 (40,000 units times 0.15 times $20) for a cost of only $50,000 in advertising. If the firm has no capacity constraint and should advertise, which product should be promoted? If there is no capacity limit, product A should be selected for promotion. Expected additional contribution would be $200,000 from A and only $120,000 from B.

Now assume that both products are processed over a group of machines that have an effective combined annual capacity of 120,000 hours (after making an allowance for holidays and down time for repairs). In this situation, the firm's current sales are requiring all of its productive capacity. Should the firm still advertise, and if so, which product?

With the firm at capacity, the decision rule changes. The firm should advertise, but it should promote product B. At capacity, increased sales of one product will require forfeiting sales of the other. Since 5,000 additional units of product A will require 20,000 additional machine hours, production of B will have to be cut back 20,000 units; but 6,000 additional units of B cut back A production and sale by only 1,500 units.

|  | Promoting A | Promoting B |
|---|---|---|
| Possible added units | 5,000 units | 6,000 units |
| Increased contribution from increased sales | $200,000 | $120,000 |
| Lost contribution on forfeited sales | 400,000 | 60,000 |
| Advertising costs | 50,000 | 50,000 |
| Net benefit | ($250,000) Loss | $ 10,000 Gain |

A shortcut approach to analyzing such problems at capacity is to use the decision rule **maximize unit contribution per unit of constraining factor.** In this example, A's unit contribution per unit of constraining factor (hours of machine time) was $10, whereas B's was $20. The use of this criterion clearly signals preference for B over A at capacity. Where there exists more than one constraining factor, computations become more complex. A technique known as *linear programming* has been developed to assist in maximizing (or minimizing) an objective in terms of multiple constraints. Linear programming is introduced in Chapter 17.

## Beyond Relevant Range

When any alternative under consideration in a noninvestment decision involves a change in fixed cost per period, simply maximizing contribution (or contribution per unit of constraint) will not always suffice to maximize the firm's net income.

|  | Alternative 1 | Alternative 2 |
|---|---|---|
| Contribution | $100,000 | $160,000 |
| Fixed cost | 60,000 | 130,000 |
| Net decision benefit | $ 40,000 | $ 30,000 |

In the above illustration, Alternative 2 has the higher contribution. However, fixed costs of Alternative 2 are sufficiently great to offset the higher contribution. The *net decision benefit* is lower, and Alternative 1 is the preferred choice. The net decision benefit can be viewed as net income before taxes coming from the area or segment of the firm under consideration, or as net income from the decision alternative. When decision alternatives involve changes in fixed costs, a new relevant range is under consideration. The appropriate decision rule becomes **maximize the net decision benefit.**

There are many examples of noninvestment decisions that involve changes in fixed costs. The ones that will be reviewed below include:

overtime vs. additional shift
operation vs. shutdown

Others involving such areas as sales commission vs. salary, adding or dropping product lines, and maintaining or increasing the advertising budget will be illustrated in the chapter problems. Note also that those decisions previously illustrated (make-or-buy, special orders, and sell or process further) could also involve changes in fixed costs. If changes in fixed costs were involved, the decision would require analysis following the net decision benefit criterion or decision rule, and will also be illustrated in the chapter problems.

As you are aware, overtime pay for hours worked beyond the base per week (usually 40 hours per week) is at least 50 percent greater than the cost of employing additional personnel at regular base pay. In situations where workload exceeds 40 hours by a small amount, and especially when excess workloads are sporadic, it is usually most appropriate to schedule and pay for overtime with existing personnel. Employees often appreciate the additional earnings; within limits efficiency is not severely impaired by longer hours; and costs to the firm are less than hiring and training costs.[4] It should also be obvious to you that, at some point, overtime becomes counterproductive for both the firm and the employees.

Consider a situation of a firm with 100 hourly employees working a single shift. Average wage costs including fringe benefits are $6 per hour straight time and $9 per hour overtime. Each employee is averaging three hours of overtime per week, and this workload is expected to continue. First, assume that there exists adequate capacity (space and equipment) to add personnel to the present shift. Adding workers to the present shift would not involve additional fixed costs. This decision would then involve merely minimizing variable cost. What should the plant superintendent do?

In this simple example, it would probably be in the firm's best interest to hire seven more full-time employees. Their cost would be $1,680 per week and would be offset by $2,520 of overtime saved.[5] Now assume a slightly different situation. Employees are averaging eight hours of overtime per week. There is no additional space or equipment capacity for more employees on the present shift. An additional shift would cost $6,000 more per month for supervision, security, utilities, and higher insurance. Assuming 4.3 weeks per month, should an additional shift be considered, and how many hourly employees would be involved?

In this situation, a second shift with 20 hourly employees would be desirable and would save the firm $4,320 per month.

---

[4]   Training costs can be considered as including more than costs of formal training programs. Inefficiency cost (higher-than-normal cost per unit of output) while a new employee is learning the job and making interpersonal adjustments with fellow employees can be thought of as training costs.

[5]   Three hundred hours of existing overtime per week. Seven additional employees at 40 hours equals 280 hours of straight time with 20 hours of overtime still required.

|  | Single shift | Two shifts |
|---|---|---|
| Variable costs: |  |  |
| Straight time | $103,200 | $123,840 |
| Overtime | 30,960 | zero |
| Additional fixed costs | zero | 6,000 |
| Total costs | $134,160 | $129,840 |

Another type of decision involving changes in fixed costs involves whether to continue operations or to temporarily shut down. This decision is typically faced by an entertainment or service complex subject to seasonality of weather or located in a seasonal resort area. Assume you own a resort hotel with 500 rooms. Your variable cost of supplying a room per night (linens, maid service, incremental utilities, and maintenance) is $8. Fixed costs, if open all year, amount to $906,000. Rooms in season can rent for $50 per night whereas out-of-season maximum charges are $12. Your season runs for six months, and your room revenues average a total of $3,150,000 for the regular season (70 percent occupancy). During the off season your total expected room revenue would be $324,000 (30 percent occupancy). This $324,000 would still result in a contribution of $108,000 ($324,000 times 4/12). Should you stay open year-round?

At first glance it might appear that you should stay open as long as there was any contribution. If all your fixed costs were the same under either alternative, this would be the appropriate decision. However, usually when an operation is shut down, fixed costs can be reduced to a bare minimum level known as *standby costs*. There also may be *shutdown costs* such as protecting, "mothballing," or storing certain items, and severance pay for employees. There can be *startup costs*, also, such as removing items from mothballing or storage, cleanup, and hiring and training costs of new employees. All of these costs must be considered in arriving at an appropriate decision. Costs saved in shutdown may exceed contribution from remaining open. Conversely, costs of shutdown and startup may be so great that an operation should be continued in the short run even with a zero or negative contribution.

In the example of the resort hotel, assume the following additional facts:

|  | Remain open | Standby |
|---|---|---|
| Fixed costs per month: |  |  |
| Depreciation | $10,500 | $10,500 |
| Liability insurance | 500 | 0 |
| Property insurance | 1,000 | 1,500 |
| Utilities | 1,000 | 500 |
| Hotel operating staff | 48,000 | 6,000 |
| Hotel security staff | 2,000 | 4,000 |
| Maintenance | 12,000 | 3,000 |
|  | $75,000 | $25,500 |
| Shutdown costs |  | 40,000 |
| Startup costs |  | 90,000 |

Based on the information given, you should evaluate the alternatives and make a recommendation, before proceeding with the next paragraph.

You have a good grasp of net decision benefit analysis if you see that the hotel should be shut down during the off-season months despite the available $108,000 contribution. The only data relevant to the decision concerns the six-month off-season period:

|  | Remaining open | Shutdown |
|---|---|---|
| Fixed/standby costs | −$450,000 | −$153,000 |
| Contribution | + 108,000 | 0 |
| Shutdown cost | 0 | − 40,000 |
| Startup cost | 0 | − 90,000 |
| Net decision benefit (cost) | ($342,000) | ($283,000) |

It is more costly to remain open than to shut down.


## Summary of Decision Rules for Even Flows

To review the decision rules so far introduced for noninvestment decisions involving **even** flows of benefits and costs, they are as follows:

| Factors relevant to decision | Decision rule |
|---|---|
| Only revenues | Maximize revenue |
| Only variable costs | Minimize costs |
| Costs and benefits within relevant range and below capacity | Maximize total contribution |
| Costs and benefits within relevant range and at capacity | Maximize unit contribution per unit of constraining factor |
| Costs and benefits beyond relevant range | Maximize net decision benefit (or minimize net decision cost) |


## NONINVESTMENT DECISIONS INVOLVING UNEVEN FLOWS OF COSTS AND BENEFITS

Where the projected flow of costs and benefits relevant to a decision alternative extend over several years and are **not** uniform year by year, then the introduction of two additional considerations becomes necessary. The effects of income taxes and the time value of money must be included in the decision model. The decision rule becomes **maximize the net present value of net after-**

**tax benefits** or, if there are no net decision benefits, then **minimize the net present value of after-tax costs.**

(Note. If you are not already familiar with discounted net present value analysis, you should study the appendix to this chapter before proceeding.)

An example may assist you to see the necessity of adjusting for taxes and net present value (NPV) in the event of uneven flows of costs and/or benefits. Assume that you are considering which of two factories, P or Q, you should lease. Your opportunity cost of capital is 12 percent, and your firm is subject to a 40-percent income-tax rate. Data relevant to your decision is as follows (amounts shown are in thousands of dollars):

|              | Factory P | | Factory Q | |
|              | Savings | Lease costs | Savings | Lease costs |
|---|---|---|---|---|
| First year   | $ 235  | $1,200  | $ 300  | $ 400  |
| Second year  | 235    | 1,200   | 300    | 700    |
| Third year   | 235    | 1,200   | 300    | 1,000  |
| Fourth year  | 235    | 1,200   | 300    | 1,300  |
| Fifth year   | 235    | 1,200   | 300    | 1,600  |
| Sixth year   | 235    | 1,200   | 300    | 1,900  |
| Seventh year | 235    | 1,200   | 300    | 2,200  |
| Total        | $1,645 | $8,400  | $2,100 | $9,100 |

Note that factory Q lease payments are uneven. They are on an increasing schedule of $300,000 each year. Netting costs and savings, and ignoring both taxes and the present value of money, it appears that factory P is the least costly:

|                 | Factory P   | Factory Q   |
|---|---|---|
| Total net costs | $6,755,000  | $7,000,000  |

At a 40-percent income-tax rate, each year the effective *net after-tax cost* is $(1 - t)$ times the before-tax cost (where $t$ is the tax rate expressed as a decimal). Assuming that the firm has taxable income, any additional deductible cost offsets or shields an equal amount of taxable income, which otherwise would be subject to tax at 40 percent. Taxes saved are thus 40 percent of any additional deductible net costs. The effective after-tax cost (actual cost minus tax savings) at a 40-percent tax rate is, therefore, only 60 percent of the actual before-tax cost.

Adjusting net factory lease costs each year to effective after-tax flows and discounting at the 12-percent cost-of-capital rate, you can see that factory Q is clearly preferable:

| | Factory P | | | Factory Q | | |
|---|---|---|---|---|---|---|
| Year | After-tax net costs | 12% PV Factor[6] | NPV | After-tax net costs | 12% PV factor | NPV |
| 1 | $ 579 | — | — | $ 60 | 0.8929 | $ 54 |
| 2 | 579 | — | — | 240 | 0.7972 | 191 |
| 3 | 579 | — | — | 420 | 0.7118 | 299 |
| 4 | 579 | — | — | 600 | 0.6355 | 381 |
| 5 | 579 | — | — | 780 | 0.5674 | 443 |
| 6 | 579 | — | — | 960 | 0.5066 | 486 |
| 7 | 579 | — | — | 1,140 | 0.4523 | 516 |
| Total | $4,053 | 4.5638 | $2,642 | $4,200 | | $2,370 |

After considering tax effects and the present value of money, it turns out that factory Q is not $245,000 more costly. It is actually $272,000 **less** costly!

| | Factory P | Factory Q |
|---|---|---|
| NPV of net after-tax costs | $2,642,000 (rounded) | $2,370,000 (rounded) |

In solving uneven-flow problems, benefits (savings) are offset, or "netted," with costs to obtain a single net benefit (or cost) before-tax amount for each year. This amount is adjusted for tax effects, and then discounted to net present value. In the above example, each year involved incurrence of net cost. The net cost was adjusted to after-tax net cost by multiplying by 0.6 (1 -- t).

In other problems, one or more years may involve a net benefit. A net benefit in a given year may be assumed to result in additional taxable income at additional the tax rate $t$; tax costs must then be allowed for. *Net after-tax benefits* would be net benefits before taxes times $(1 - t)$; thus, in the case of a 40-percent tax rate, only 60 percent of net benefits remain after a 40-percent tax payment.

## REVIEW OF DECISION RULES

Exhibit 7.2 employs a *decision tree* or branching flow chart to illustrate all of the decision rules applicable to noninvestment decisions. Study this decision tree as a means of reviewing the different circumstances and appropriate rules

---

[6]   Net after-tax costs each period are lease costs less operating savings times 60 percent. For Factory P the stream of net costs is uniform over all seven years and therefore the cumulative PV factor from Table B may be used to simplify computation ($579,000 × 4.5638 and rounded).

**Exhibit 7.2**

**Noninvestment Decisions and Appropriate Decision Rules**

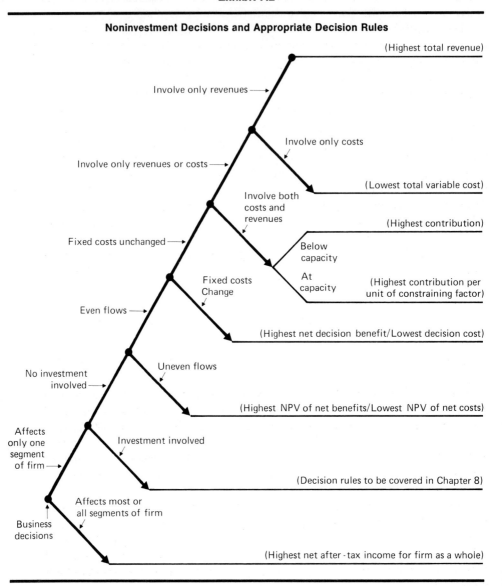

introduced in this chapter. Note especially that, as decision alternatives affect more and more items, the appropriate decision rule (with the related computations) becomes more complex, and vice versa.

## NONQUANTIFIED CONSIDERATIONS

The term "decision rule" has been used throughout this chapter since it is a commonly accepted business/mathematical term. It can be misleading unless you always remember that a **decision rule applies to all outcomes** of an alternative and **not just** to those that are **quantified** or quantifiable.[7]

Most business decision alternatives involve outcomes some of which are not readily quantifiable. Often **nonquantified considerations** weigh heavily in the final decision. Sometimes nonquantified considerations outweigh or overbalance quantified results, and the final decision may appropriately be the opposite of that indicated by the "numbers." Successful managers quantify as many aspects of a decision alternative as feasible. Having a partially quantified "signal" assists in judging the more subjective factors. As an example, suppose you were making two separate purchasing decisions, each involving the selection of one out of two suppliers (vendors). Vendors A and B could supply material P, and vendors C and D could supply material Q. Suppose that you were confident that all four vendors would maintain quality standards, but you were concerned that B and D might sometimes fail to keep their delivery promises by as much as two weeks. Would you automatically give the orders to A and C?

The readily quantifiable aspects of these two decisions involve the vendors' bids or prices. For convenience, they are given below in terms of annual costs (price times usage):

|  | Vendor A | Vendor B | Vendor C | Vendor D |
|---|---|---|---|---|
| Material P (10,000 units) | $400,000 | $300,000 | | |
| Material Q (40,000 units) | | | $200,000 | $199,500 |

Can you see how the quantifiable data assists you in evaluating the nonquantified aspects of the decision? You would probably give the order for material P to vendor B. The potential costs of occasional late delivery will probably not exceed $100,000, and you might even consider some additional safety stock, with a $100,000 cost differential. You also would probably order material Q from vendor C. In this case, the assurance of on-time delivery would probably be worth the extra $500.

Important nonquantified considerations may exist for each of the decision problems illustrated in this chapter. They were ignored when the problems were first presented, in order to focus your attention upon the readily quantifiable considerations. Exhibit 7.3 lists a few of the more obvious additional considerations that might be relevant to the final decision. You should study these lists to become more familiar with the various factors that can be relevant to business decisions. Awareness of all considerations relating to a par-

---

[7] Some considerations may not be quantified because they are not quantifiable. Others may be quantifiable but are not readily quantified because of the effort and cost involved. Although they are beyond the scope of this elementary text, on-going developments in applied probability and decision theory, together with ready economic access to computers, make possible the quantification of many previously nonquantified decision variables.

**Exhibit 7.3**

---

**Nonquantified Considerations Possibly Relevant to
Decision Problems Illustrated in This Chapter**

| Decision problem | Nonquantified considerations |
|---|---|
| 1. Tripper make/buy decision | a) Quality reliability<br>b) Delivery reliability<br>c) Certainty of future space needs for manufacture of ski belts and jackets<br>d) Reliability of Jones as continued source if their own furniture volume grows |
| 2. New vs. newer gizmo manufacturing machine | a) Date when newest announced machine could be delivered and installed<br>b) Any special arrangements required for newest announced machine relating to location/space, operator training, or maintenance |
| 3. Special order for sweaters | a) Risk of lost regular sales if customers or wholesalers learn of special selling prices |
| 4. Use of sawdust in sawmill | a) Availability of fuel<br>b) Potential marketing problems with different type of product<br>c) Reliability of subcontractor |
| 5. Allocating advertising budget | a) Availability of additional capacity directly or through product redesign<br>b) Customer dissatisfaction from backorders/unfilled demand for product A |
| 6. Overtime vs. additional shift | a) Quality of work on second shift<br>b) Training problems of new workers if all assigned to second shift<br>c) Balancing workers (total numbers and/or numbers of trained workers) between shifts |
| 7. Continue operations vs. temporary shutdown | a) Loss of trained personnel<br>b) Possible repeat business in-season or word-of-mouth advertising from off-season customers<br>c) Other alternatives to increase off-season business |

---

ticular business problem comes from knowledge about and experience with the particular problem area. You will have the opportunity to learn more about such considerations in other more advanced business core courses such as finance; marketing; organizations and human behavior; operations management; legal, political, and social environment of business; and business policy.

## CHAPTER OVERVIEW

Based upon the material covered in this chapter, you should now be able to:

• Define a noninvestment decision and a relevant cost or benefit.

- Explain the concepts of avoidable (escapable) costs, sunk costs, opportunity costs, and related fringe costs, as they relate to business decisions.
- Describe and give an example of different decision alternatives wherein each of the following decision rules might be appropriate, and explain why the rule is appropriate to the particular alternative:

> Maximize revenues
> Minimize costs
> Maximize contribution
> Maximize contribution per unit of constraining factor
> Maximize net decision benefit
> Maximize NPV of net after-tax benefits
> Maximize after-tax net income for the firm as a whole.

- Explain, with an example, the significance of whether or not a firm is at capacity, in making the appropriate choice of decision rule in a given situation.
- Explain the significance of whether costs and/or benefits extending beyond one year are uniform, to the appropriate choice of a decision rule in the particular circumstances.
- Define nonquantified considerations, and describe, with examples, how they might be relevant to a business decision.

## NEW VOCABULARY AND CONCEPTS

| | |
|---|---|
| Relevant costs | Net decision benefit |
| Sunk costs | Standby costs |
| Opportunity costs | Shutdown costs |
| Related fringe costs | Startup costs |
| Investment decisions | Net present value (NPV) |
| Noninvestment decisions | Net after-tax costs |
| Linear programming | Net after-tax benefits |

- Effect of available capacity upon decision rules
- Effect of uneven flows of benefits or costs over several years upon decision rules
- Relevance of NPV and after-tax costs and benefits to certain noninvestment decisions
- Potential significance of nonquantified considerations.

## REVIEW QUESTIONS

1. a) What are relevant costs? To what are they relevant?
   b) How can you determine whether a cost or benefit is relevant?
2. a) What are avoidable/escapable costs?
   b) How are they relevant to a decision? Explain with examples.

    c) Are all variable costs avoidable? If not, explain which variable costs are not avoidable.

    d) Are all fixed costs **not** avoidable? Describe any situations where some fixed costs could be avoidable.

3. a) What is a sunk cost?

    b) How do sunk costs relate to business decisions?

    c) Are all costs or benefits connected to a previously committed asset or contract sunk? If not, explain the circumstances when some of such committed costs are not treated as sunk costs.

4. a) What are opportunity costs?

    b) What is the difference between a real and an unreal opportunity cost? Give examples.

    c) What is the difference in the way real and unreal opportunity costs are treated in business decisions?

5. What are related fringe costs? Give examples.

6. a) What is a noninvestment decision?

    b) Can a decision involving no new investment but including the possible retirement of an existing investment be properly treated as a noninvestment decision?

7. For each of the following decision rules, describe:

    a) The characteristics of the decision problem for which the decision rule would be appropriate.

    b) An example of such a problem

    c) Why a decision rule appearing higher on the list (with a lower identification number) would not be appropriate.

    1. Maximize revenue

    2. Minimize cost

    3. Maximize contribution

    4. Maximize contribution per unit of constraining factor

    5. Maximize net decision benefit

    6. Maximize NPV of net after-tax benefits

    7. Maximize net after-tax income for the firm as a whole

8. What types of noninvestment problems require consideration of tax effects and the present value of money?

9. If a firm is subject to a 30-percent income tax rate, what would be the relevant after-tax amounts if:

    a) Net benefits (without considering tax effects) were projected as $40,000 for a particular year?

    b) Net costs (without considering tax effects) were projected as $30,000 for a particular year?

10. a) What are nonquantified considerations?

    b) How do nonquantified considerations relate to business decision problems? Give examples.

    c) Can a relevant consideration be quantifiable and yet deliberately **not** quantified as part of a decision-making process? Explain.

    d) If major considerations relating to a particular decision are not readily quantifiable, why should one bother to arrive at a tentative quantified decision using possibly less important data?

## MINI-CASES AND QUESTIONS FOR DISCUSSION

**MC 7.1** John is an economist. He states, "The reason that different decision rules apply at capacity from those used when the firm is below capacity is connected with opportunity costs. Below capacity there is no real opportunity cost to additional use of facilities. At capacity there suddenly is a very real opportunity cost." Is John correct? Discuss.

**MC 7.2** There is only one situation where irrelevant data, if included equally in all alternatives under consideration, may result in an incorrect signal. This situation is one in which there are nonuniform cost or benefit flows extending over future years and after-tax discounted flow computations are involved.

Is this statement correct? If yes, how can the inclusion of irrelevant data possibly result in an incorrect signal? Discuss.

**MC 7.3** The concept of sunk cost and its irrelevance to the present and the future extends far beyond the area of business decisions. It relates as well to personal choices, decisions, and actions whether or not they involve financial costs and benefits.

Is this statement correct? Discuss.

## ESSENTIAL PROBLEMS

**EP 7.1** The Carr Company currently manufactures and sells three joint products all made from common material costing $130,000 up to the split-off point when they are currently sold for:

| Product | Current sales |
|---------|---------------|
| A | $80,000 |
| B | 50,000 |
| C | 20,000 |

Each of the three products could be individually processed further with costs and revenues as follows:

| Product | Additional costs of processing | Expected sales if processed further |
|---------|-------------------------------|-------------------------------------|
| A | $40,000 | $110,000 |
| B | 90,000 | 150,000 |
| C | 40,000 | 30,000 |

Should any or all of these products be processed further? Explain.

**EP 7.2** The Smith Company currently manufactures and sells three joint products all made from common material costing $400,000 up to the split-off point.

They are then all processed further with resulting additional costs and revenues as follows:

| Product | Additional processing cost | Sales |
|---|---|---|
| X | $100,000 | $250,000 |
| Y | 90,000 | 180,000 |
| Z | 30,000 | 20,000 |

If the products could be sold at split-off for the following: X, $160,000; Y, $80,000; and Z, zero, which products would you recommend:

a) Continue to be processed further, and why?

b) Be sold at split-off, and why?

c) Be disposed of at split-off, and why?

**EP 7.3** A retailer has limited space for stocking, displaying, and selling different items. Currently there is no free or available space for additional items; 200 units of product A are currently stocked, and inventory turnover is five times per year. The manager is considering displacing product A with product B; 100 units of product B can be stocked and displayed in the same space. The manager estimates that product B will turn over seven times annually. Other data on these products include:

| | Product A | Product B |
|---|---|---|
| Unit selling price | $5.00 | $10.00 |
| Unit purchase cost | 3.00 | 7.50 |

a) Which product has the higher markup?

b) Which product is more profitable per unit sold?

c) Which product should be carried, and why?

**EP 7.4** A manufacturer has two products, P and Q, both of which require production time on the same machine. Data relevant to these products include:

| | Product P | Product Q |
|---|---|---|
| Unit selling price | $100 | $50 |
| Unit variable cost | 70 | 10 |
| Machine time required | 20 min. | 30 min. |

a) So long as there exist available (unused) machine hours, which product is preferable to sell? Explain.

b) If the machine is at capacity, which product is preferable to sell? Explain.

**EP 7.5** The Home Appliances Sales Company has been paying its twelve salespersons an average base salary of $12,000 per year plus a five-percent sales commission (based on sales). Average earnings of sales personnel have been running $18,000 annually. The firm, at the encouragement of its employees, is considering dropping sales commissions entirely and raising salaries to an average of $16,000. It believes that, if it follows through with this plan, sales may drop as much as three percent. Projected data under the existing plan indicate:

| | |
|---|---|
| Sales | $1,440,000 |
| Variable costs | 864,000 |
| Fixed costs | 400,000 |
| Net income | $ 176,000 |

a) Should the firm adopt the straight salary plan?

b) What other nonquantifiable considerations should be considered?

**EP 7.6** Refer to Problem EP 7.5. Assume that the firm is also considering a modified commission plan which would:

Decrease sales commissions to 2 percent
Increase salaries to an average of $15,500

Sales would not be expected to drop under this plan.

Which of the three plans (present salary and commissions, proposed salaries, or modified salary and commission) should the firm adopt, and why?

**EP 7.7** A wholesaler has no difficulty in obtaining additional salespersons who are all paid on a straight commission basis. It is concerned with whether to encourage its sales personnel to concentrate their calls on large retail customers, on smaller retailers, or serve both. Current experience indicates that calls on large retailers yield an average order of $350, whereas the average order from a small retailer is $250. Studies indicate that a salesperson can call on an average of seven large retailers or nine small retailers per day. Large retailers require visits with more personnel at each call. The average salesperson is currently calling upon twelve large and twenty-seven small retailers per week.

a) What would you recommend the wholesaler do to increase sales and why?

b) What other nonquantifiable considerations would you think should be relevant?

**EP 7.8** Refer to the information given in Problem EP 7.7. If sales personnel were salaried and the firm could not readily hire or afford additional personnel:

a) What would you recommend the firm do to increase sales and why?

b) What other considerations might be relevant?

**EP 7.9** The Warder Company is currently selling three products, P, Q, and R. Products Q and R are complementary (sales of one affect the sales of the other). The company estimates that discontinuing either product would reduce sales of the other by 50 percent. Current data with respect to these products are as follows:

| | Product P | Product Q | Product R |
|---|---|---|---|
| Sales | $3,600,000 | $1,800,000 | $600,000 |
| Unit sales price | 40 | 30 | 20 |
| Unit full product cost | 30 | 32 | 25 |
| Unit variable cost | 19 | 20 | 22 |

Should Warder discontinue product R? Explain.

**EP 7.10** Refer to Problem EP 7.9.

 a) What would be your recommendation and why, if products Q and R were not complementary?

 b) Assume that Q and R were complementary, as stated in Problem EP 7.9, but that costs were different, as follows:

| | Product Q | Product R |
|---|---|---|
| Full product cost | $31 | $25 |
| Unit variable cost | 28 | 23 |

 What would be your recommendation, and why?

**EP 7.11** The Thompson Company is currently manufacturing part K; currently 40,000 units are manufactured annually and used in assembly. Cost data are as follows:

| | Part K |
|---|---|
| Direct material | $160,000 |
| Direct labor | 400,000 |
| Overhead (variable) | 40,000 |
| Overhead (fixed) | 120,000 |
| Total costs | $720,000 |

The firm is considering an offer to subcontract this part. The subcontractor would supply the part delivered at a price of $14.

 a) Should part K be subcontracted? Explain.

 b) What other factors should Thompson consider in arriving at this decision?

**EP 7.12** Refer to the data given in Problem EP 7.11. Make your recommendation, with supporting data, for each of the following different situations, each considered independently:

 a) Subcontractor's price $16

 b) Subcontractor's price $16 and space freed by subcontracting is assigned a cost, on the basis of square footage, of $80,000 annually. The freed space would be used to relieve congestion in materials handling and storage.

 c) Subcontractor's price $17 and fixed costs amounting to $70,000 annually could be saved if the part were subcontracted.

 d) Subcontractor's price $16 and fixed costs amounting to $50,000 annually could be saved.

 e) Below what annual volume should subcontracting be considered, given the conditions in (c) above?

**EP 7.13** The Visgoth Company manufactures and sells fire extinguishers under its own brand. Data from the prior year's income statement, which should be approximately the same in the current year, reveals:

| Sales (average price $18) | $900,000 |
|---|---|
| Variable manufacturing and selling costs | 600,000 |
| Contribution | 300,000 |
| Fixed costs (manufacturing, selling, and administrative) | 250,000 |
| Net income | $ 50,000 |

Contributions may be assumed to be uniform over all present products. Visgoth has a manufacturing capacity of 80,000 average extinguishers annually.

A large mail-order firm has offered to purchase 20,000 extinguishers each year, to be sold under its own brand name. This extinguisher will be the same as an average extinguisher in the firm's current line. The price offered to Visgoth is $14 per extinguisher.

a) Should Visgoth accept the order if it would not affect sales of existing products? Explain.

b) Should Visgoth accept the order if it projects that a five-percent drop in its existing business would result? Explain.

**EP 7.14** Refer to Problem EP 7.13. Make and explain your recommendations for each of the following changed situations, considered independently:

a) Special order price is $17, and existing sales would be expected to drop ten percent.

b) How far could existing product sales drop (by what percentage) at a special order price of $17 before the special order became undesirable?

c) Special order price is $15; there is expected to be a five-percent drop in existing sales, and the firm must rent an additional machine to apply the mail-order brand label. The rental on the additional machine would be $10,000 annually.

d) If the special order price were $12.75, a five-percent drop in sales was expected to result from taking the order, and an additional machine would have to be rented at a cost of $15,000 annually, is there a quantity that could be special-ordered that would make this special-order arrangement attractive? If yes, would you recommend taking an order for such quantity?

**EP 7.15** The Suburban Pharmacy is planning to add a new department. It is considering both cosmetics and greeting cards, but can add only one. Based on a survey of other stores and trade association data:

• Cosmetics would probably generate $30,000 of sales annually. Variable costs would be 55 percent, and $6,000 of additional fixed part-time salaries and rented counter costs would be required per year. Sales of other items lost from reduced selling space (to make room for cosmetics) would equal sales gain from increased store traffic resulting from new department.

• Greeting cards would probably generate $20,000 of annual sales at a gross profit of 60 percent. Additional fixed costs would be only $2,000 annually. So much space would be lost to card racks that sales of existing items would drop two percent.

The pharmacy's annual income statement, projected without either department, would show:

| | |
|---|---|
| Sales | $400,000 |
| Variable costs | 260,000 |
| Fixed costs | 110,000 |
| Net income | $ 30,000 |

Which department should be added? Explain.

**EP 7.16** Refer to Problem EP 7.15. Make and explain your recommendations for each of the following different situations considered separately:

a) All of the projections are the same except that greeting cards will not affect the volume of existing sales.

b) Both departments can be added but sales of existing items will drop ten percent.

c) Only one department may be added. Greeting cards will not affect other sales. Cosmetics will require an $8,000 fixed annual cost and will increase sales of other items by four percent.

**EP 7.17** The Fantasyworld Amusement Park earns 90 percent of its revenues during the months of April through October. It is considering shutting down for the five off-season months (November through March). Shutdown costs would be $125,000 and startup costs would be $250,000. Its fixed costs on a standby basis would be $105,000 per month. Projected data for the forthcoming year, assuming no shutdown, are as follows:

| | |
|---|---|
| Sales | $8,000,000 |
| Variable costs | 4,800,000 |
| Fixed costs  ($240,000 per month) | 2,880,000 |
| Net income | $ 320,000 |

Should the park shut down during the off season? Explain.

**EP 7.18** Refer to Problem EP 7.17.

a) What would be your recommendation if shutdown and startup costs totaled $120,000?

b) What would be projected income for the next twelve months, following your recommendation in (a) above?

c) What could the firm do to improve its net income if shutdown and startup costs were zero?

## SUPPLEMENTARY PROBLEMS

(*Note.* Supplementary problems assume familiarity with net present value calculation. NPV is reviewed in the appendix to this chapter.)

**SP 7.19** As a result of detailed studies of the costs and benefits of two proposals, the following table of net costs is prepared. The firm is subject to a 40-

percent income-tax rate, and its cost of capital is 14 percent. Before-tax net costs are as follows:

| Year | Proposal #1 | Proposal #2 |
|------|-------------|-------------|
| 0 | 0 | 0 |
| 1 | $6,000 | $3,000 |
| 2 | 5,000 | 3,000 |
| 3 | 5,000 | 4,000 |
| 4 | 4,000 | 4,000 |
| 5 | 4,000 | 5,000 |
| 6 | 3,000 | 5,000 |
| 7 | 3,000 | 6,000 |
| | $30,000 | $30,000 |

a) Find the NPV of the total after-tax costs of each alternative.

b) Which proposal would you recommend, and why?

SP 7.20 Assume you have been asked by your firm to evaluate two alternative proposals for obtaining a needed machine under lease. Both leases run for five years. One lease provides for a $15,000 payment on signing, with two $5,000 payments at the end of the first and second years. Maintenance is the responsibility of the lessee. The second lease provides for ascending payments over the five years, with maintenance taken care of by the lessor. Expected operating costs also differ between the two machines, as shown below:

| | Lease Proposal #1 | | | Lease Proposal #2 | |
|------|---|---|---|---|---|
| Year | Annual operating costs | Annual lease payments | Annual maintenance costs | Annual operating costs | Annual lease payments |
| 0 | $ 0 | $15,000 | $ 0 | $ 0 | $ 0 |
| 1 | 2,000 | 5,000 | 500 | 3,000 | 500 |
| 2 | 2,000 | 5,000 | 500 | 3,000 | 2,000 |
| 3 | 2,000 | 0 | 500 | 3,000 | 5,000 |
| 4 | 2,000 | 0 | 500 | 3,000 | 10,000 |
| 5 | 2,000 | 0 | 500 | 3,000 | 15,000 |
| Totals | $10,000 | $25,000 | $2,500 | $15,000 | $32,500 |

a) What is the total cost (before allowing for tax effects and the present value of money) of each alternative?

b) If the firm's cost of capital is 12 percent and the firm is subject to a 40-percent tax rate, what is the NPV of the total after-tax costs of each lease?

c) Which lease should the firm choose, and why?

SP 7.21 The Crazy Growth Company has reached the capacity of its present facilities. It is considering moving into one of two factories on a five-year lease basis. Confusion costs are so great in the present factory that both new factories will offer substantial operating savings as compared with existing operations. Forecasted before-tax data with respect to the two plants are given below:

| | Factory 1 | | Factory 2 | |
| | Operating | Lease | Operating | Lease |
| Year | savings | costs | savings | costs |
|---|---|---|---|---|
| 0 | $ 0 | $ 0 | $ 0 | $ 0 |
| 1 | 13,000 | 40,000 | 9,000 | 70,000 |
| 2 | 15,000 | 60,000 | 10,000 | 70,000 |
| 3 | 17,000 | 80,000 | 10,000 | 70,000 |
| 4 | 17,000 | 100,000 | 10,000 | 70,000 |
| 5 | 17,000 | 120,000 | 10,000 | 70,000 |
| Totals | $79,000 | $400,000 | $49,000 | $350,000 |

The firm is subject to a 30-percent tax rate and its cost of capital is eight percent.

a) What is the NPV of the total net after-tax costs under each alternative?

b) Which factory should the firm move into, and why?

SP 7.22 Refer to Problem SP 7.21. Assume the same data except that the tax rate is 40 percent and the cost of capital is 14 percent.

a) What is the total net after-tax cost of each alternative (before allowing for the present value of money)?

b) What is the NPV of the total net after-tax costs under each alternative?

c) Which factory should the firm move into, and why?

d) If your recommendation differs from that made in Problem SP 7.21, what has caused this difference?

## SUGGESTIONS FOR FURTHER READING

Horngren, C., *Cost Accounting: A Managerial Emphasis*, Fourth Edition, Englewood Cliffs, N.J.: Prentice-Hall, Inc., 1977; Chapters 11 and 12.

Morse, Wayne J., *Cost Accounting: Processing, Evaluating, and Using Cost Data*. Reading, Mass.: Addison-Wesley Publishing Company, 1978; Chapters 6 and 7.

Van Horne, James C., *Fundamentals of Financial Management*, Third Edition. Englewood Cliffs, N.J.: Prentice-Hall, Inc., 1977; Chapters 12 and 13.

Weston, J. Fred, and Eugene F. Brigham, *Essentials of Managerial Finance*, Fourth Edition. Hinsdale, Illinois: The Dryden Press, 1977; Chapter 10.

CHAPTER 7 APPENDIX

# Review of Net Present Value (NPV)

The concept of present value and the techniques for calculating present value are often now covered in the first course in financial accounting. Present value calculation is necessary to determine the initial book value of a note with interest (real or imputed) included in the face value, and also to determine the initial value of property acquired under a capital lease.[8] If you are already familiar with present value calculations, this appendix can serve as a review.

Money has a time value. In an inflationary economy, a dollar today is worth more in terms of purchasing power (what it will buy) than a dollar five or ten years from today. Even if there were no inflation, money would have a time value related to the fact that it could be readily invested (in government bonds, savings accounts, and so forth) and earn compound interest.[9] In the balance of this appendix, it will be **assumed** that there is **no inflation.** Adjusting for the effects of inflation will be discused in Chapter 16. At this point your attention should be focused on the time value of money resulting solely from the opportunity to earn compound interest.

As an individual, you may earn different interest rates or "returns" on your investment, depending upon the risk you wish to assume. As discussed in Chapter 6, the opportunity interest rate or rate of return for a business is its cost-of-capital rate.

### Present Value of a Single Receipt (or Payment)

Assume that the cost-of-capital rate for your firm is 12 percent. If you have $1,000 today, you can "invest" these dollars in your firm and earn 12-percent compound interest. Five years from today (ignoring income taxes) you would have $1,762. Similarly, it can be shown that, if you had $567 today, you could

---

[8]  See the companion text *Financial Accounting Information: An Introduction to Its Preparation and Use,* Reading, Massachusetts, Addison-Wesley Publishing Company, 1978; Chapters 11 and 12.

[9]  Compound interest assumes that interest earned in each period is not withdrawn but remains invested. In future periods, interest is therefore earned on both the principal and the accumulating interest.

invest this amount at 12-percent compound interest and have $1,000 at the end of five years.

If you had a choice, and ignoring the effects of inflation and taxes, which would you rather have: $1,000 today or $1,000 five years from today? Would you be as well off either way? Can you see that receiving or having $1,000 today is better than having it in five years? You would not be as well off if you didn't have the $1,000 during the next five years. You would suffer an opportunity loss of $762 in interest. Cash on hand today is worth more than cash five years from today because of the opportunity to earn compound interest.

Now suppose you had a choice of receiving $567 today or $1,000 five years from today. Which would you prefer, ignoring all other factors except interest? Can you see that you would be indifferent (you wouldn't care either way)? In either case you would be equally well off at the end of five years. You would have $1,000. In this instance, it is customary to say that "$567 is the present (today's) value of $1,000 to be received in five years, discounted at 12 percent." The term "discounted present value," although redundant, is also occasionally used. This statement merely means that the compound-interest opportunity cost has been factored out. The present value or PV of any amount X at some point in the future is the number of dollars today that could be invested at compound interest to equal X at the future point:

PV ($X in y years) = Amount that, if invested today, would accumulate
    compound interest and be equal to $X after y
    years.
    PV $X = $X minus compound interest dollars that could
    be earned.

The PV of an amount $Z today is $Z. No interest difference is involved. The PV of an amount in the future is meaningful only when both the future period when the amount is available and the opportunity interest rate (discount rate) are known. The formula for the PV of any amount X is:

$$PV\ (X) = \frac{1}{(1 + i)^n} \times X$$

where

$i$ = Interest rate per period,
$n$ = Number of periods.

Many business calculators are programmed for PV. If you do not have such a calculator, Appendix A at the back of this book contains a table of present values (Table A). Table A gives the present value of one dollar for various combinations of periods and discount rates. For example, if you wished to find the present value of $890 to be received in five years at a 12-percent discount rate, you would:

• First look up or calculate the present value factor for 12 percent at five years, which is 0.5674.

- Multiply the factor per dollar times the number of dollars you are discounting ($890).
- Determine the PV to be $504.99, or $505 rounded (890 × 0.5674).

PV doesn't apply only to future cash inflows; it also applies equally to future outflows. The PV equivalent cost to you today of $1,000 to be paid out in five years is again only $567 ($1,000 × 0.5674 rounded). Assuming you could invest the $1,000 during the five years and earn compound interest at 12 percent, you would have the chance to earn and keep the $433 interest difference.

## Present Value of a Stream of Receipts (or Payments)

PV as a tool is quite helpful with problems involving streams of costs and/or benefits projected over future years. It allows all of these different amounts with different values to be combined in terms of a uniform measurement— their net present value (NPV) in today's dollars. Assume that you have the following information related to a particular project in a firm with a ten-percent cost-of-capital rate (taxes may be ignored):

| Year | Benefits (+) | Costs (−) | Net (±) |
|---|---|---|---|
| 0 | 0 | 0 | 0 |
| 1 | +$3,000 | −$8,000 | −$5,000 |
| 2 | +10,500 | −10,000 | +    500 |
| 3 | +17,000 | −12,000 | + 5,000 |
| 4 | +24,000 | −14,000 | +10,000 |

Obviously this project is improving with age, but what is the NPV of the costs and benefits for possible use in comparing to other projects? Using a PV programmed calculator, or Table A at the back of the book, determine the solution, before reading the next paragraph. This exercise will help you test your understanding of PV.

The NPV of this particular stream of costs and benefits, discounted at 10 percent, equals $6,454.

| Year | Net benefits (+) (Costs (−)) | PV factor at 10 percent | PV (rounded) |
|---|---|---|---|
| 0 | 0 | 1.0000 | 0 |
| 1 | −$5,000 | 0.9091 | −$4,545 |
| 2 | +    500 | 0.8264 | +    413 |
| 3 | + 5,000 | 0.7513 | + 3,756 |
| 4 | +10,000 | 0.6830 | + 6,830 |
| | | | NPV $6,454 |

Note that, in the above table, two conventional notations are used. Year 0 indicates today when the present value factor is 1.0000 (no compound interest involved). Year 1 indicates a cash outflow or inflow occurring one year from now, and therefore affected by one year's interest; and years 2, 3, and 4 similarly designate time in the future. Also note that a plus indicates a cash inflow or benefit, and a minus indicates a cash outflow or cost.

## Simplified Calculation When Payment Stream Uniform

Where a stream of future net costs or net benefits is uniform or nearly uniform, a simplified technique is available to reduce the number of calculations. Table B in Appendix A gives the present value of a stream of payments of $1 received or paid at the end of each period.

Suppose you wished to determine the NPV of the following project data discounted at 14 percent:

| Year | Net cost |
|------|----------|
| 0 | $1,000 |
| 1 | 1,000 |
| 2 | 1,000 |
| 3 | 1,000 |
| 4 | 1,000 |
| 5 | 1,000 |

The PV of the year zero (now or today) cost is $1,000, and you could apply the separate factors for each year from Table A for 14 percent to years one through five. Alternatively, you could obtain the factor for a stream of $1 payments for years one through five from Table B, which is 3.4331. With a single calculation you could determine the NPV of all future amounts as $3,433 ($1,000 times 3.4331 and rounded). Added to the $1,000 PV of the year zero (now) cost, the NPV of the costs of this project would be $4,433.

You can also convert nearly uniform data relating to a different project and use this technique as a time-saver. Suppose your data were as follows:

| Year | Original data | Restated data |
|------|---------------|----------------|
| 0 | 0 | 0 |
| 1 | +$1,500 | +$1,500 |
| 2 | + 1,500 | + 1,500 |
| 3 | + 1,500 | + 1,500 |
| 4 | + 1,500 | + 1,500 |
| 5 | − 2,000 | + 1,500 and −3,500 |
| 6 | + 1,500 | + 1,500 |
| 7 | + 1,500 | + 1,500 |
| 8 | + 1,500 | + 1,500 |

Note the nonuniform flow in the original data. Without uniform flows, Table B may **not** be used. Rather than use Table A and eight separate calculations, the original data is restated to a uniform flow and one additional single-period flow. Using a nine-percent rate that may be asumed appropriate to this different example, you will find in Table B that the PV factor for a $1 eight-year stream is 5.5348. The PV factor for a single payment in year five is 0.6499 (Table A). The NPV would be:

$$+1,500(5.5348) = \$+8,302 \quad \text{(rounded)}$$
$$-3,500(0.6499) = -2,275 \quad \text{(rounded)}$$
$$\text{NPV} = \quad \$6,027$$

The NPV approach may also be used as one method of evaluating or ranking investment decisions. NPV used for this purpose will be covered in Chapter 8 and in the appendix to Chapter 8.

## PRESENT VALUE REVIEW PROBLEMS

If you have not recently worked with present value calculations, the following review problems may be of assistance to you in strengthening your skills. Solutions to all of these problems will be found in Appendix C.

1. Present value of a single payment (Table A); what is the present value of:
   (a) $10,000 to be received next week?
   (b) $5,000 to be received in one year, discount rate eight percent?
   (c) $9,000 to be received in four years, discount rate 14 percent?
   (d) $7,000 to be paid in eleven years, discount rate seven percent?
   (e) $50,000 to be paid in thirty years, discount rate 12 percent?

2. Present value of a stream of equal payments (Table B); what is the present value of:
   (a) $500 per year for two years, discounted at ten percent?
   (b) $11,000 per year receivable for seven years, discounted at eight percent?
   (c) $3,000 per year payable for fourteen years, discounted at 12 percent?
   (d) $100,000 per year payable for forty years, discount rate 15 percent?

3. Present value of an uneven stream of payments (Tables A and B); what is the present value of:

(a) Discount rate 10%

| Year | Payment |
|---|---|
| 0 | $1,000 |
| 1 | 2,000 |
| 2 | 2,000 |
| 3 | 500 |
| 4 | 2,000 |
| 5 | 2,000 |

(b) Discount rate 12%

| Year | Receipt |
|---|---|
| 0 | 0 |
| 1 | $3,000 |
| 2 | 3,000 |
| 3 | 3,000 |
| 4 | 3,000 |
| 5 | 4,000 |

4. NPV of a stream including both costs (outflows) designated minus and benefits (inflows or savings) designated plus; what is the NPV of:

(a) Discount rate 12%

| Year | Flow |
|------|------|
| 0 | $-10,000 |
| 1 | + 2,500 |
| 2 | + 2,500 |
| 3 | + 2,500 |
| 4 | + 2,500 |

(b) Discount rate 14%

| Year | Flow |
|------|------|
| 0 | $+40,000 |
| 1 | -13,000 |
| 2 | -13,000 |
| 3 | -13,000 |
| 4 | -13,000 |

(c) Discount rate 8%

| Year | Flow |
|------|------|
| 0 | $-100,000 |
| 1 | + 24,000 |
| 2 | + 24,000 |
| 3 | + 24,000 |
| 4 | + 24,000 |
| 5 | + 40,000 |

(d) Discount rate 10%

| Year | Flow |
|------|------|
| 0 | $-50,000 |
| 1 | +25,000 |
| 2 | +25,000 |
| 3 | +25,000 |
| 4 | -40,000 |
| 5 | +25,000 |

# 8

# INVESTMENT DECISIONS— THE CAPITAL BUDGET

From Managerial Accounting Information by A. Thompson Montgomery. Revised February 1980. Copyright © 1979 by Addison-Wesley Publishing Company, Inc. Philippines copyright 1979 by Addison-Wesley Publishing Company, Inc. All rights reserved.

## CHAPTER PREVIEW

The purpose of this chapter is to extend your knowledge and skills related to business decisions to include those involving investments. In this chapter you can learn:

- The importance and risk associated with investment decisions as compared to noninvestment decisions.
- The unique characteristics of, and tax considerations related to, investment decisions.
- Various approaches to analyzing alternative investment proposals to determine their acceptability.
- Approaches used to select among acceptable proposals those that can be funded or implemented.
- How allowance for risk may be incorporated in the decision process.
- Certain other important considerations often relevant to investment decisions.
- How the results of investment decision analysis are eventually incorporated in the firm's capital budget.

In the chapter appendix, you may review your knowledge of capital leases, learn how to use the internal rate-of-return approach to investment analysis, and learn to analyze a lease-vs.-buy decision.

With this knowledge, you will have completed your introduction to the process of business decision making. You will have a basic understanding of how a firm's capital budget is prepared. And you will be ready to return to the overall budget preparation process and its completion in the following two chapters.

## WHICH TRUCK SHOULD I BUY?

As president of the Tripper Company, you are faced with the necessity of purchasing a new delivery truck. You use several delivery trucks to transport finished products to your major customers and to wholesalers. One of your present trucks has been wrecked. Since it was fairly old, you have made the decision not to attempt repair; instead, you have decided to purchase one of two possible new trucks.

The wrecked truck has an accounting book value of $3,000 (original cost $13,000 and accumulated depreciation of $10,000). For tax purposes it has already been depreciated to zero.

Truck A has a price of $18,000. You expect that its useful life to the firm will be five years, and that its salvage value after five years will be $2,000. The dealer will give you a $1,000 trade-in allowance on your wrecked truck towards the purchase of Truck A. You expect that effective operating costs (expenditures for fuel, oil, maintenance, license, and insurance) for Truck A will average $8,000 per year after adjustment for tax effects.

Your other alternative is Truck B, which has a higher price ($23,000) but will deliver better mileage and is expected to cost less to maintain. Truck B also has a more pleasing appearance than Truck A, but the appearance has no effect on the usefulness. Truck B has a useful life of five years, and it has an expected salvage value of $3,000 at the end of five years. A $2,000 trade-in allowance on the wrecked truck is available for Truck B. You estimate that Truck B's operating costs (after adjustments for tax effects) will average $7,400 per year. If your firm's cost-of-capital rate (Chapter 6) is 12 percent, which truck should you purchase, and why?

In arriving at your decision, you must first decide whether any data with respect to the wrecked truck is relevant to your choice between Truck A and Truck B. You correctly understand the concept of sunk cost if you see that the entire $3,000 of undepreciated accounting book value of the wrecked truck represents a sunk cost (Chapter 7) and is irrelevant to the choice between Truck A and Truck B.[1] Since the old truck is traded in under either alternative, you can ignore data relating to the old truck and start with net cash costs of A and B.

Ignoring the time value of money, it would appear that the two trucks are identically costly over the five years. Truck B initially costs $4,000 more than A, but it costs $600 less per year to operate and has a $1,000 greater salvage value after five years.

---

[1] A portion of the $3,000 book value of the old truck may be added to the balance sheet cost of the new truck for financial reporting purposes, but this should not affect your economic decision. Also, as will be discussed below, any undepreciated value, for tax purposes, of the old truck would be relevant to analyzing the investment cost of each truck but not relevant to the choice between them. In this example, it will be assumed, for simplification, that the old truck has already been depreciated to zero on the firm's tax returns.

|                                          | Truck A   | Truck B   |
|------------------------------------------|-----------|-----------|
| Cash price (after trade-in)              | −$17,000  | −$21,000  |
| Total operating costs (over five years)  | − 40,000  | − 37,000  |
| Salvage recovery                         | + 2,000   | + 3,000   |
|                                          | −$55,000  | −$55,000  |

Would you therefore pick B on the strength of its more pleasing appearance? Would you do this if it cost you an additional $1,271 cash (above the $21,000 net purchase price) today for this feature? If the more pleasing appearance is not worth paying a price (after trade-in) of $22,271 for Truck B, then A would be less costly than B. The $1,271 difference in effective cost will be explained below.

This decision problem is similar to the last category of noninvestment decisions described in Chapter 7. The essential difference is that it includes an investment and, therefore, involves a more complicated determination of after-tax costs. After-tax cost determination for investment problems will be covered later in this chapter. Remember from Chapter 7 that a problem with **uneven flows** of net costs or benefits over future years must be evaluated in terms of the NPV of these flows. In this chapter you can learn that proper analysis of all major investment decisions will include determining the NPV of all after-tax flows.

To reinforce your understanding of NPV calculations, you should determine the NPV of the total net after-tax costs of Truck A and Truck B, before proceeding to the next paragraph. To save your having to turn to Appendix A, discounted at 12 percent the *PVF* (present value factor) of a stream of payments of $1 over five years is $3.6048 and of a single payment of $1 at the end of five years is $0.5674.

The correct total NPV of the after-tax costs of Trucks A and B are $44,703 and $45,974, respectively. Truck B is $1,271 more costly than A in terms of present value (today's dollars):

|                                        | Truck A   | Truck B   |
|----------------------------------------|-----------|-----------|
| Year 0 (now) (PVF = 1.000)             | −$17,000  | −$21,000  |
| Five-year cost (PVF = 3.6048)          | − 28,838  | − 26,676  |
| Salvage value (PVF = 0.5674)           | + 1,135   | + 1,702   |
| NPV                                    | −$44,703  | −$45,974  |

Note that, in the above example, there is no tax effect associated with the investment itself or with the recovery of salvage value. In more realistic examples to be introduced below, an investment may earn an investment tax credit (ITC). Salvage value recovery may also have a tax effect if there is any gain or loss on sale compared to the tax book value.[2] In the above example, you may assume that the tax book values after five years were exactly $2,000 and $3,000, respectively. Also note that net operating costs (or net operating benefits) and depreciation deductions for tax purposes may always be assumed to have related tax effects, and therefore require adjustment to after-tax amounts.

In the remainder of this chapter, you can learn that some investment decisions involve choosing the least NPV cost (or most NPV benefit) where the investment is **necessary,** as in the above example. Where the investment is optional, then the NPV analysis is extended to evaluate the adequacy of a proposal's return on the capital invested.

## CHARACTERISTICS OF INVESTMENT DECISIONS

Investment decisions were defined in Chapter 7 as any decision involving a commitment of resources (or the elimination of a previous commitment) where the related benefits extended beyond the current year or period. Such decisions are also commonly referred to as *capital budgeting decisions*. The term "investment decision" will be used in this text for two reasons. Capital budgeting decisions are usually thought of as being optional; that is, they are implemented only if the return on investment is satisfactory. This chapter is focused upon both those investment decisions that are mandatory (must be made) and those that are optional (made only if expected to earn a satisfactory return). Secondly, the use of the term investment decision avoids potential confusion between the process of decision making (sometimes called capital budgeting) and the actual preparation of the firm's capital budget to reflect the **results** of the decision-making process.

Investment decisions may become quite complex and may involve knowledge and skills beyond the elementary level. Business majors will be exposed to a more thorough and more advanced coverage of this subject in finance or financial management courses that are often included in an undergraduate business core. The purpose of this chapter is to provide an introduction and overview of the process to enable you to grasp its significance and interrelationship with a firm's overall budgeting and control process.

As compared to noninvestment decisions (Chapter 7), investment decisions have the following distinctive characteristics:

- They involve a commitment of resources over future time periods, and are therefore related to intermediate or long-range planning (Chapter 2);

---

[2]   As covered in financial accounting, accounting book value and tax book value (undepreciated cost carried on tax returns) at the time of disposition may differ for the same depreciable asset. This difference may result from the different depreciation objectives of financial and tax accounting. Depreciation for financial accounting purposes is selected to best match asset costs with future revenues. Depreciation for tax purposes is often selected to maximize deductions allowable under the Internal Revenue Code, regardless of the expected pattern of associated earned revenues.

- They generally involve more risk of loss or error than do most non-investment decisions;
- They require attention to after-tax cash (or working capital) flows rather than to accounting net income;
- They involve additional investment-related tax considerations;
- They may be subject to different methods of analysis; and
- They may be subject to different criteria for acceptability (decision rules).

Each of these distinctive characteristics will be discussed in the following sections.

### Resource Commitments and Risk

Investment decisions involve the commitment of significant resources over extended time periods.[3] Usually investment decisions also involve future costs and benefits that are measurable, that is, may be estimated with reasonable confidence. Where benefits are believed certain but undefinable, as might be the case when investing in recreation facilities for employees, then a purely arbitrary judgment must be made.

Noninvestment decisions are usually readily reversible and, therefore, involve less risk. Price change and manufacture or purchase (subcontract) decisions can often be quickly reversed if they turn out to be a mistake. The costs of reversal may not be high. In contrast, the extended commitment of resources over time associated with an investment decision is not readily reversible. If an excessive or otherwise inappropriate commitment is made, the resulting carrying costs or losses are often quite high. For example the firm that builds a new special-purpose $50,000,000 factory to produce large quantities of a new product probably will have significant costs or losses if the product sells only in small quantities or not at all. A major technological breakthrough can also make an investment (either a product or equipment) obsolete and relatively worthless. Conversely, should a firm fail to commit necessary resources, inadequate capacity can result in lost customers to the competition, with very high costs of recovery. Inadequate commitment to modernization of capacity can also leave a firm with obsolete facilities and potential inability to compete.

There is still another risk related to investment decisions. Such decisions, by their nature, are dependent upon estimates or projections of costs and benefits, often extremely far into the future. In a rapidly changing world, long-term projections can have a significant risk of error. How certain are you

---

[3]    Some investments below a certain minimum amount that will vary with the materiality to a particular firm's size may be considered insignificant. They will arbitrarily be included as part of operating expenses in the short-term budgeting process. For example, complete investment analysis would be inappropriate in deciding upon the acquisition of a single chair or pencil sharpener.

of your earnings eight years from today? The matter of risk related to error in projected data will be discussed under "incorporating provision for risk" below.

### Focus upon After-Tax Cash Flows

As discussed in Chapter 7, many noninvestment decisions can be resolved in terms of contribution or of maximizing income from operations before taxes. All investment decisions, because of investment-related tax considerations, must be evaluated in terms of so-called *after-tax cash flows*.[4] After-tax cash flow measurement is essentially aimed at excluding depreciation or amortization charges, as such, from relevant costs. Since investment decision analysis already includes measurement of the amount of the investment, to include future depreciation or amortization costs in the analysis would result in double-counting.

To see the irrelevancy of depreciation and amortization charges, consider the following example. Assume you purchased as an investment a typewriter costing $500, which you planned to rent to others for a price of $30 per month. Assume the typewriter had a useful life of five years, zero salvage, and expected rentals of ten months per year. Ignoring, for the moment, both taxes and present value, what would be the gross return (benefit) from your investment? Your investment would be $500, and your return before taxes $1,500, or $1,000 more than the recovery of your investment. To include depreciation charges of $100 per year and thus compare benefits of only $1,000 against an investment cost of $500 would be inappropriate.

Depreciation or amortization would be completely irrelevant and could be totally ignored if it were not for the effect of depreciation on taxable income and the actual amount of cash flows involved in the payment of income taxes. Depreciation must therefore be considered as part of the determination of tax effects. The depreciation tax effect will be discussed in detail below.

You should recognize that cash flow costs for an investment decision should include **both** expenditures related to the decision and also any lost opportunity costs (benefits) that actually involved cash flows; that is, any cash inflows foregone as a result of the decision. For example, the cash flow costs of a new project that is to take over excess space currently rented to an outsider should include the "cost" of the rent given up.

Similarly, cash benefits from an investment would include not only possible increased revenues (for investments intended to increase revenues) but also cost savings. Often an investment is made with the intention (benefit) of reduced costs. Reduced cash operating expenditures and any real opportunity cost savings should all be included as cash benefits related to an investment

---

[4]   More precisely, benefits and costs are usually measured in terms of flows of working capital; the usually minor delays for receivables collections or funds expense payments are ignored. Thus, so-called net-after-tax cash flows are really measuring the after-tax effect upon funds from operations.

decision. For example, if new equipment freed space, and actual cash benefits (rents) could be realized from the freed space, then the added rent revenue would be part of the cash flow benefit relevant to the investment decision. Note that any opportunity costs or benefits must be **real**, to be included. They must involve changes in cash flows resulting from the investment.

## INVESTMENT-RELATED TAX CONSIDERATIONS

As in the case of noninvestment decisions with uneven cost/benefit flows extending over several years, all investment decisions must be evaluated in terms of **after-tax** cash flows. Any before-tax incremental cash inflows (but **not** including recovery of tax book value or tax basis) must be adjusted for tax. Remember, from Chapter 7, that the formula for such adjustment is:

$$\text{Before-tax benefits} \times (1 - t) = \text{After-tax realizable benefits,}$$

where $t$ is applicable income-tax rate expressed as a decimal. Similarly, any before-tax incremental cash outflows (**not** including the investment itself or depreciation charges) are adjusted by:

$$\text{Before-tax costs} \times (1 - t) = \text{After-tax effective costs.}$$

### Depreciation Tax Shield

Investment decisions also are affected by changes in the *tax shield* provided by depreciation. Although not a cash flow, allowable tax deductions for depreciation (or amortization) serve to offset or shield otherwise taxable income. An additional depreciation charge of $5,000 per year reduces taxable income by $5,000. At a 40-percent tax rate, $2,000 in taxes that would otherwise have to be paid are saved. Conversely, if a depreciable asset is disposed of as part of an investment proposal **and** *tax depreciation* (depreciation for tax purposes) of $3,000 would no longer be taken next year, then $1,200 of **additional taxes** would have to be paid that year (assuming a 40-percent rate). This $1,200 of additional cash outflow next year would have to be included as part of the cost of disposing of the asset.

Note that tax-shield effects are based on the amount of depreciation to be taken for tax purposes on the firm's **tax return** and **not necessarily** amounts appearing in the financial statements. Any gain or loss on an asset's disposition would be based on the difference between proceeds of sale and the *tax basis* (tax book value), **not** the accounting book value. In the earlier Tripper example, the tax basis (tax book value) was assumed to be zero (fully depreciated for tax purposes). If the wrecked truck had been **sold** for $500 scrap value, there would have been a taxable gain on disposition. Two cash flows would then be involved, a $500 inflow (sale proceeds) and a $200 additional tax payment (assuming an applicable 40-percent tax rate). The $2,500 accounting loss on disposition ($3,000 book value less $500 realized salvage) would not involve any cash flow. The $2,500 sunk cost would be irrelevant to any investment decision.

Gains or losses on the sale of depreciable assets are subject to ordinary income-tax rates.[5] Net realizable after-tax benefits of the $500 gain above at a 40-percent tax rate would be $300. In a different situation, had there been a taxable loss of $2,000 (proceeds $500, tax basis $2,500), then the net after-tax cash proceeds would have been $1,300. The $500 salvage, as such, is not subject to tax. The $2,000 tax loss shields $2,000 of otherwise taxable income, and thus saves $800 in taxes. The effect of the disposition would be:

- $1,300 cash inflow in current year,
- $800 cash outflow (lost depreciation deductions) in appropriate future years.

Where a depreciable asset is traded in on another asset performing substantially the same function, where there is a direct trade-in, no taxable gain or loss may be recognized in the year of disposition. Instead, any residual "gain" or "loss" on disposition is carried forward and modifies the initial tax basis of the new asset. Tax depreciation on the new asset is affected accordingly.

At this point a more comprehensive example may assist you to understand depreciation tax effects. Suppose you are considering replacing asset E with asset F. Asset E has a (tax) basis of $2,000, which would have been taken as tax depreciation over the next two years. It is sold for $2,500 and replaced with a similar asset F, which costs $10,000. Asset F has a five-year life and zero salvage value for tax purposes, and will be tax depreciated on a straight-line basis.[6] Assume a 40-percent tax rate. You should attempt to determine all of the incremental cash flows related to these actual or projected events, before proceeding.

You are correct if you identified the related incremental cash flows as follows:

|  | Before-tax data | | | | After-tax cash flows | | |
|  | E | | F | | E | F | Net |
| Year | Cash | Depr. | Cash | Depr. | | | |
|---|---|---|---|---|---|---|---|
| 0 | +$2,500 | 0 | −$10,000 | 0 | +$2,300 | −$10,000 | −$7,700 |
| 1 | 0 | −$1,000 |  | +$2,000 | − 400 | + 800 | + 400 |
| 2 | 0 | − 1,000 |  | + 2,000 | − 400 | + 800 | + 400 |
| 3 | 0 | 0 |  | + 2,000 | 0 | + 800 | + 800 |
| 4 | 0 | 0 |  | + 2,000 | 0 | + 800 | + 800 |
| 5 | 0 | 0 |  | + 2,000 | 0 | + 800 | + 800 |

[5]  Gains or losses on nondepreciable assets may be subject to more favorable capital gains tax treatment. Since capital gains tax rarely relates to capital budgeting decisions, it will not be covered in this text.

[6]  For financial accounting purposes it could have a ten-year life and be depreciated on a year's-digits basis, and this would be irrelevant.

In the above example, with no trade-in involved, the $500 gain on the sale of machine E is subject to tax. Also, in years one and two, $1,000 each year of depreciation tax shield is no longer available from machine E with resultant additional taxes—cash outflows—of $400 each year. For all five years there are additional depreciation tax deductions and resultant cash savings coming from machine F.

If, instead of being sold, machine E had been traded in for a credit of $2,500 on machine F, there would have been no tax effect related to the exchange. The initial basis of machine F for depreciation purposes would have been $9,500 ($7,500 cash cost plus basis of old machine); and tax depreciation on machine F taken on a straight-line basis would have been $1,900 each year.

Before leaving the subject of tax depreciation, you should note that it is very common to use 150 percent declining balance or double (200 percent) declining balance (DDB) tax depreciation.[7] This practice merely adds complexity to calculations, but otherwise does not affect the concept of tax shield. DDB tax depreciation will hereafter be used to familiarize you with its effects.

### Investment Tax Credit

An additional tax aspect peculiar to investment decisions involves the *investment tax credit* or ITC. To promote the growth or replacement of capital assets, the U.S. government provides a tax credit or subsidy at the time of purchase. Note that the ITC is not a tax deduction or shield; it is a direct credit against taxes payable, and, therefore, 100 percent of any ITC may be considered a cash savings.

The ITC applies to most new fixed assets with useful lives beyond three years. The rate may be periodically changed by Congress to stimulate or dampen economic growth. For ease of calculation, a rate of ten percent will be used throughout this text. The sole effect of the ITC is to reduce the initial cost of an investment by the entire ITC. Note that the ITC does **not** reduce initial asset basis for tax depreciation.[8] An example of the ITC effect, on after-tax cash flows related to some equipment costing $4,000 with a four-year life, zero salvage, DDB tax depreciation, and a 40 percent tax rate, follows:

| Year | | Without ITC | With 10% ITC |
|---|---|---|---|
| 0 | Initial cost | $4,000 | $3,600 |
| 1 | Depreciation tax savings | 800 | 800 |
| 2 | Depreciation tax savings | 400 | 400 |
| 3 | Depreciation tax savings | 200 | 200 |
| 4 | Depreciation tax savings | 200 | 200 |

---

[7]    Under DDB, twice the straight-line rate is taken based on the declining book value or tax basis each year. In the final year, the necessary amount to arrive at salvage value is taken. Also, under DDB a trade-in may involve a taxable gain in the year of trade instead of an adjustment of the new asset's basis. This "recapture" provision is beyond the scope of this text and will not be illustrated.

[8]    The ITC will also reduce initial financial accounting book value under the deferred method of accounting for the ITC. However, it will not reduce the initial financial accounting book value if the firm elects the flow-through method.

## Netting All Tax Effects into a Single Figure

Rather than adjust each separate cash cost or benefit within each year for tax effect, it is usually simpler to make a single determination of tax effect for each year. Exhibit 8.1 illustrates a table designed for such an approach. Note that Column E is reserved for possible tax effects pertaining to the investment or salvage recovery transactions only. For assets not entitled to the ITC, and where no part of salvage value represented taxable gain or loss (asset disposed of at tax basis or as part of a trade-in), then Column E would be blank.

Note that Column F is reserved for tax effects on annual operating items. For each year, cash flow benefits are netted against cash flow costs and depreciation. Net benefits times *t* would be recorded in Column F as a minus amount (additional tax costs). Net cost times *t* would be recorded as a plus (additional tax savings). Observe that Column H contains the net cash flow to be discounted, and specifically excludes Column D.

## Comprehensive Example of Tax Effects

Returning to the Tripper Company truck choice problem given at the beginning of the chapter, assume that the relevant facts were modified to be as follows:

> Applicable income-tax rate: 30 percent
> Applicable ITC: Ten percent
> Tax depreciation: DDB, assuming zero salvage
> Assume both trucks disposed of after five years, not as part of a trade-in.
> Tax basis of wrecked truck: $2,000
> Cash (or cash plus debt) cost of Truck A: $23,000
> Salvage value of Truck A after five years: $2,000
> Before-tax annual operating costs of A: $13,000
> Cash (or cash plus debt) cost of Truck B: $28,000
> Salvage value of Truck B after five years: $2,500
> Before-tax annual operating costs of B: $12,000

To test your understanding, you should determine the NPV of all after-tax cash flows (including the investment) for each truck, assuming a twelve-percent cost of capital.

You adequately understand tax effects if you determined that the NPV costs for A and B were $46,485 and $47,474, respectively. Exhibit 8.2 illustrates the calculations. Note, in Exhibit 8.2 for Truck A, that the ten-percent ITC produces a $2,300 tax savings in year zero, and the $2,000 gain on eventual disposition (asset depreciated to zero for tax purposes and no trade-in involved) results in a $600 additional tax. DDB tax depreciation (40-percent rate) was taken on an initial basis for depreciation of $25,000 (cash cost of $23,000 plus $2,000 carryover undepreciated tax basis from wrecked truck). Similar tax adjustments were made for Truck B.

**Exhibit 8.1**

**Suggested Table for Determining After Tax Cash Flows**

| Year | Relevant costs/benefits | | | | Tax effects | | | Net cash flow |
|---|---|---|---|---|---|---|---|---|
| | A | B | C | D | E | F | G | H |
| | Investment or salvage | Additional cash benefits | Additional cash costs | Tax depreciation or amortization | of investment or salvage (of A) | of net cash operating benefits— depreciation (or B, C, and D) | Net tax effect (E and F) | $(\pm A + B - C \pm G)$ |
| 0 | | | | | | | | |
| 1 | | | | | | | | |
| 2 | | | | | | | | |
| 3 | | | | | | | | |
| · | | | | | | | | |
| · | | | | | | | | |
| · | | | | | | | | |

**Exhibit 8.2**

## Comprehensive Example of Tax Effects

| Year | A Investment or salvage | B Additional cash benefits | C Additional cash costs | D Tax depreciation or amortization | E Tax effects of A | F Tax effects of B, C, and D | G Net tax effect (E and F) | H Net cash flow (A, B, C, and G) | I 12% PVF | J PV |
|---|---|---|---|---|---|---|---|---|---|---|
| **Truck A** | | | | | | | | | | |
| 0 | −$23,000 | 0 | 0 | 0 | +$2,300 | 0 | +$2,300 | −$20,700 | 1.000 | −$20,700 |
| 1 | 0 | 0 | −$13,000 | −$10,000 | 0 | +$6,900 | +6,900 | − 6,100 | 0.893 | − 5,447 |
| 2 | 0 | 0 | − 13,000 | − 6,000 | 0 | + 5,700 | + 5,700 | − 7,300 | 0.797 | − 5,818 |
| 3 | 0 | 0 | − 13,000 | − 3,600 | 0 | + 4,980 | + 4,980 | − 8,020 | 0.712 | − 5,710 |
| 4 | 0 | 0 | − 13,000 | − 2,160 | 0 | + 4,548 | + 4,548 | − 8,452 | 0.636 | − 5,375 |
| 5 | + 2,000 | 0 | − 13,000 | − 3,240 | − 600 | + 4,872 | + 4,272 | − 6,728 | 0.567 | − 3,815 |
| | | | | | | | | | NPV | −$46,865 |
| **Truck B** | | | | | | | | | | |
| 0 | −$28,000 | 0 | 0 | 0 | +$2,800 | 0 | +$2,800 | −$25,200 | 1.000 | −$25,200 |
| 1 | 0 | 0 | −$12,000 | −$12,000 | 0 | +$7,200 | + 7,200 | − 4,800 | 0.893 | − 4,286 |
| 2 | 0 | 0 | − 12,000 | − 7,200 | 0 | + 5,760 | + 5,760 | − 6,240 | 0.797 | − 4,973 |
| 3 | 0 | 0 | − 12,000 | − 4,320 | 0 | + 4,896 | + 4,896 | − 7,104 | 0.712 | − 5,058 |
| 4 | 0 | 0 | − 12,000 | − 2,592 | 0 | + 4,378 | + 4,378 | − 7,622 | 0.636 | − 4,848 |
| 5 | + 2,500 | 0 | − 12,000 | − 3,888 | − 750 | + 4,766 | + 4,016 | − 5,484 | 0.567 | − 3,109 |
| | | | | | | | | | NPV | −$47,474 |

## ALTERNATIVE APPROACHES TO ANALYZING
## INVESTMENT DECISIONS

Investment decisions may be considered as falling into one of three broad categories. Some investment decisions are **mandatory** and involve no measurable benefits. In such situations it is assumed that the investment is required in the context of overall firm operations; and the decision rule or acceptability criteria is merely **choose the alternative with the least NPV after-tax cost.** Other decisions are mandatory and involve measurable benefits. A third group may be viewed as **optional,** since investments in this group are accepted only when the benefits provide a satisfactory return on the investment. Where investment decisions (whether mandatory or optional) involve measurable benefits, various analysis approaches have been proposed and used. They include:

- Intuitive/judgmental/arbitrary
- Simple payback
- Time-adjusted payback
- Unadjusted rate of return
- Internal rate of return (IRR)
- NPV

Each of these approaches will be discussed below.

The *arbitrary approach* (also called judgmental or intuitive) is just what it sounds like. No formal analysis of investment costs or benefits is attempted. The decision is made on the basis of "feel," "hunch," or "experience." Where an investment is trivially small, or where future flows cannot be estimated with any reasonable accuracy, then this approach is the best available.

The *simple payback approach* is the easiest to calculate of the nonarbitrary methods. Usually, under this approach, net benefits before taxes are compared, on a cumulative basis, to the amount of initial investment. The object is to determine the number of years (periods) required before accumulated benefits equal original investment costs, or the number of years before the investment is paid back or recovered. A $25,000 investment with before-tax benefits of $7,500 per year would be said to have a simple payback of 3.3 years. Following this method, investments with an earlier payback are preferable to those with a longer payback. Acceptability might be stated in terms of "accept any investment with a payback of less than four years, and reject any over four." Note that this approach is simplistic in that:

- It ignores both taxes and the present value of money;
- It ignores any return (interest) on the investment by ignoring benefits beyond the payback cutoff.

The simple payback approach is **not** recommended as a desirable tool for investment evaluation. The approach can, however, be useful as a crude risk estimator when used together with one of the less simplistic approaches described below.

*Time-adjusted payback* is similar in intent to simple payback except that benefits accumulated are measured in after-tax dollars and are discounted at the firm's cost of capital. Time-adjusted payback does include the effects of both taxes and present value. It still does not measure any return (interest) **on** the investment; only the return **of** the investment is measured. Therefore, it is not recommended as the exclusive tool for investment analysis.

Time-adjusted payback might be appropriately used by those firms with extreme liquidity problems that are anticipated to extend over the next few years. Even then the approach would only be appropriate to choosing among mutually exclusive mandatory investments. In such applications, early recovery of cash would be made more important than any longer-run return on investment. Time-adjusted payback may also be a very valuable tool for assessing risk associated with an otherwise acceptable investment that has been evaluated by a more appropriate criterion. This use will be covered under "incorporating provision for risk," below.

A fourth alternative can be considered as a group of various approaches collectively known as *unadjusted rate-of-return methods*. These methods do provide for evaluating investment return, some on a before-tax and some on an after-tax basis. Since they ignore the time value of money and still involve calculations almost as complex as methods making allowance for present value, they will hereafter be ignored as impractical and obsolete approaches.

A fifth alternative is known as the *internal rate-of-return method (IRR)*. This method attempts to measure the return on a given investment in terms of after-tax cash flows. Present value is taken into account but, under the method, the discount rate ends up being the return rate of the investment itself rather than the firm's cost-of-capital rate. This difference can produce different acceptability signals than would the NPV approach, and it can be shown that the NPV signal is always more appropriate. IRR also involves more complicated calculations; it will be covered in the appendix to this chapter. IRR can be considered an acceptable but not preferred method.

The sixth and preferred alternative is the *net present value* or *NPV method*. This method measures investment return in terms of discounted after-tax cash flows. Essentially, it involves identifying all expected future after-tax net cash flows (excluding any interest or principal payments on borrowed funds) and then discounting these flows (benefits) at an appropriate rate. The discounted present value of the sums invested (no discount is involved if all investment is made initially) is then subtracted from the NPV of future benefits. A negative result (NPV investment > NPV benefits) indicates that the proposed investment's return is less than the discount rate used. A zero or positive NPV (NPV benefits ≥ NPV investment) indicates a return equal to or greater than the discount rate. For this reason, the method may also be referred to as the excess present value method.

Exhibit 8.3 illustrates the application of the NPV approach to the analysis of a proposed investment. Note that when an eight-percent discount rate is used, the NPV of the investment is a positive $16,545, indicating that the investment return exceeds eight percent. When a 12-percent discount rate is

## Exhibit 8.3

### Illustration of NPV Approach to Investment Analysis

| Year | After-tax cash flows | PV 8% discount | PV 10% discount | PV 12% discount |
|---|---|---|---|---|
| 0 | −$300,000 | −$300,000 | −$300,000 | −$300,000 |
| 1 | + 70,000 | + 64,813 | + 63,637 | + 62,503 |
| 2 | + 80,000 | + 68,584 | + 66,112 | + 63,776 |
| 3 | + 80,000 | + 63,504 | + 60,104 | + 56,944 |
| 4 | + 80,000 | + 58,800 | + 54,640 | + 50,840 |
| 5 | + 89,398* | + 60,844 | + 55,507 | + 50,724 |
| Total | +$ 99,398 | +$ 16,545 | $ zero | −$ 15,213 |

* Includes salvage recovery.

used, the NPV is negative, indicating a return of less than 12 percent. Note that the use of a ten-percent discount results in an NPV of exactly zero. A zero NPV indicates that the investment return is precisely ten percent and also that the investment's internal rate of return (IRR) is ten percent.

You may be wondering about two questions concerning the NPV method:

1. Why aren't interest and, possibly, principal payments included in the cash outflows, especially if they relate to a loan clearly identified with the proposal under consideration?

2. What discount rate should be used? If borrowed funds are to be used or invested, isn't the interest rate to be paid (the *incremental borrowing rate*) the most appropriate?

In answer to the first question, calculating the present value (discounting) removes or factors out an amount of interest at least equivalent to the discount rate used. To also include any interest expense in the cash flows would result in double-counting the cost of interest. The NPV of benefits or returns (after providing for interest) is compared to the investment to see whether the principal is adequately recovered. Again, to include any loan principal repayments in cash flows being discounted would involve double-counting the recovery of principal.

The appropriate discount rate to be used in most investment decisions is the firm's average cost-of-capital rate, first discussed in Chapter 6. If you do not recall what the cost-of-capital rate is or how it is determined, you should review Chapter 6 before proceeding. A firm's cost-of-capital rate is the **average** rate that must be paid to **all** suppliers of capital considered together. To accept some projects because they returned an amount equal to the lower incremental borrowing rate would mean that other projects would have to be rejected if they did not have a rate equal to the owner's equity rate (higher than the cost of capital). To apply different tests to different proposals, or to the same proposal in different years, depending on the current method that might be chosen for financing, would hardly make sense. Therefore the **average** cost-of-capital rate is used for most discounting.[9]

If you now understand which cash flows are relevant to investment analysis and the NPV approach to analyzing these flows, you are in a position to turn to the remaining parts of the investment decision or capital budgeting process. The next section will review the decision rules or criteria applicable to various types of investment decisions. After decision rules you will find specific techniques for applying and simplifying NPV analysis to specific decisions.

Even though an investment may satisfy simple NPV criteria, inflation, inherent risk, or lack of available capital may make it undesirable or impossible to implement. Each of these areas will be briefly discussed in turn. Finally, those investments that the firm chooses to implement must be incorporated in the capital budget. This chapter will close with an example of a final capital budget.

## ACCEPTABILITY CRITERIA (DECISION RULES) FOR INVESTMENT DECISIONS

Following the preferred NVP approach, acceptability for different types of investment decisions can be stated as follows:

- **Mandatory investments with no alternatives:** no decision involved; investment must be accepted and funded/implemented.

- **Mandatory investments with mutually exclusive alternatives:** choose alternative with lowest negative (or highest positive) NPV of after-tax cash flows, including investment flow. The Tripper truck choice would be an example of this type of decision.

- **Optional investments with no mutually exclusive alternatives:** accept any with zero or positive NPV of after-tax cash flows, including investment flow. Accepted investments might still not be funded/implemented; see below. Whether or not to invest in an entirely new additional product line would be an example of this type of decision.

- **Optional investments with mutually exclusive alternatives:** consider only alternatives with zero or higher NPV of after-tax cash flow, including investment flow. Among qualifying mutually exclusive alternatives, choose the one with the highest positive NPV. Again, acceptable

---

[9]   Where an investment proposal has already been accepted as meeting cost-of-capital criteria or as essential for other purposes, and where the decision merely involves the best method of financing the project, then the incremental borrowing rate may be more appropriate. This situation will be discussed in the chapter appendix in terms of the lease-vs.-buy alternative.

**Exhibit 8.4**

---

**Decision Rules for Various Types of Investment Decisions**

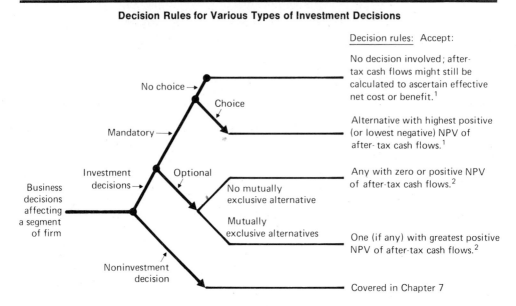

Decision rules: Accept:

No decision involved; after-tax cash flows might still be calculated to ascertain effective net cost or benefit.[1]

Alternative with highest positive (or lowest negative) NPV of after-tax cash flows.[1]

Any with zero or positive NPV of after-tax cash flows.[2]

One (if any) with greatest positive NPV of after-tax cash flows.[2]

Covered in Chapter 7

*Notes.*  1. By definition, these "Acceptable" proposals must be funded/implemented.
2. Acceptable proposals may be subject to capital rationing if number exceeds available capital resources.

---

investments may still not be funded/implemented; see below. Evaluating two new trucks as possible but not mandatory replacements for an existing truck would be an example of this type of decision.

Exhibit 8.4 illustrates the acceptance criteria for different types of investment decisions.

## TECHNIQUES OF INVESTMENT DECISION ANALYSIS

You should already have a good grasp of how to analyze and evaluate any investment decision. In this section you can learn how to:

1. Adjust for uneven lives among mutually exclusive alternatives.

2. Apply the *differential cost analysis* method to the analysis of mutually exclusive alternatives.

3. Perform a complete analysis of a sophisticated investment problem.

### Adjustment for Uneven Lives

In Chapter 2 you were introduced to the concept of a decision time horizon. Can you see that the data for two or more *mutually exclusive investment alternatives* (you can choose only one) cannot be properly compared unless all alternatives extend to the same time horizon? In the Tripper truck example, if Truck B's useful life had been seven instead of five years, and if seven years of costs for truck B had been compared to only five years of costs for truck A, a possibly desirable B wouldn't stand a chance. Or if, in some other comparison, twelve years of benefits on one investment were compared to six years on another, would you have comparable data?

When mutually exclusive alternatives under consideration have different investment lives, they **must** be made equivalent before a comparison is attempted. There are two ways in which comparability may be achieved. Generally, where the life of one investment alternative is less than half the life of another, an analysis should involve two or more sequential investments in the short-lived asset compared to the long-lived asset. For instance, if you are attempting to compare P with a nine-year life to Q with a three-year life, you should compare three sequential three-year investments in Q as against one nine-year investment in P. Or, if Q had a four-year life, then two sequential investments in Q could be compared against P cut off at eight years.

When the shorter-lived asset's life is more than half of the longer life (for instance, one alternative five years and the other seven), then it is acceptable to cut off the longer life to match the shorter. Cutting off a life merely means assuming disposition before the end of the investment's useful life, and estimating salvage recovery accordingly.

When estimating data in the future, an estimate of salvage value at a specific future date may be just as reliable as any estimates of future costs and benefits beyond that date. Assume a decision between two pieces of equipment and the following information:

*Equipment S:*   Cost:   $100,000
            Useful life:   Five years
            Net savings:   $30,000 per year
            Salvage:   $10,000 at end of five years

*Equipment T:*   Cost:   $130,000
            Useful life:   Seven years
            Net savings:   $38,000 per year
            Salvage:   $15,000 at end of five years
                  $10,000 at end of seven years

In this example, Equipment T would be compared using only five years of net savings and a salvage value after five years of $15,000. The remaining two years would be cut off or ignored for comparative analysis purposes.

## Using Differential Cost Analysis as a Shortcut

The term *differential costs* is sometimes used synonymously with avoidable or escapable costs. The term is also used to describe cost (or benefit) differences among two or more alternatives under consideration. To avoid confusion, hereafter in this text the term "differential costs" will be used **solely** to apply to cost or benefit differences among different sets of avoidable cost or benefit data. It will **not** be used interchangeably with avoidable or escapable costs.

The differential cost approach is a technique for reducing computation time in alternative choice decisions. To illustrate, suppose you were choosing among two alternatives, A and B, and you had the following data:

| | Alternative A | Alternative B | Differential costs (B − A) |
|---|---|---|---|
| Initial investment | $ −10,000 | $ −12,000 | $ −2,000 |
| First-year operating costs | −    900 | −    700 | +    200 |
| Second-year operating costs | −  1,000 | −    800 | +    200 |
| Third-year operating costs | −  1,100 | −    900 | +    200 |
| Third-year salvage value | +  4,000 | +  5,500 | +1,500 |

Note that differential costs (cost and benefit differences) have been calculated on the basis of B − A or, in other words, "How does B compare to A?" Plus signs indicate comparative benefits of the alternative being compared (B), and minus signs comparative costs (greater costs). B costs $2,000 more in year 0 but has a series of comparative benefits extending over the next four years.

In this example, assuming a 12-percent cost-of-capital rate and calculating the NPV of each alternative and of all differential costs and benefits, you can see that:

• The NPV's of the two alternatives determined separately were:

| | Alternative A | | Alternative B | |
|---|---|---|---|---|
| Year | Cash flow | 12% NPV | Cash flow | 12% NPV |
| 0 | −$10,000 | −$10,000 | −$12,000 | −$12,000 |
| 1 | −    900 | −    804 | −    750 | −    625 |
| 2 | −  1,000 | −    797 | −    800 | −    638 |
| 3 | −  1,100 | −    783 | −    900 | −    641 |
| 3 | +  4,000 | +  2,847 | +  5,500 | +  3,915 |
| Total | −$ 9,000 | −$ 9,537 | −$ 8,900 | −$ 9,989 |

The difference between their separately determined NPV's (−$9,989 and −$9,537) and the NPV of their differential costs and benefits both equal −$452:

| Year | Differential costs (B − A) | 12% NPV |
|---|---|---|
| 0 | −$2,000 | −$2,000 |
| 1 | +    200 | +    179 |
| 2 | +    200 | +    159 |
| 3 | +    200 | +    142 |
| 3 | +  1,500 | +  1,068 |
| Total | +$    100 | −$    452 |

The NPV differential cost −$452 indicates that, as compared to A, B is $452 more costly. Alternative B with a negative differential cost NPV is less desirable than A. A differential cost NPV of zero would indicate identical attractiveness; and a positive NPV of differential costs would indicate that alternative B was more attractive.

Where a decision involves mutually exclusive alternatives, differential analysis can indicate **relative** desirability with one less PV computation than the number of alternatives under consideration. NPV's of each alternative do not need to be independently calculated. Instead, any **one** alternative is chosen as the reference, and all others are compared to it. The highest positive NPV of differential costs will indicate the most attractive alternative. In a mandatory situation where one alternative must be chosen regardless of whatever return is acceptable, the alternative with the highest possible NPV differential costs is the one that should be accepted and implemented. For example, suppose you currently were using machine P and were considering Q and R as possible alternatives. You still have a mandatory investment situation. One investment, possibly continuing with the present machine, would have to result. In this case, you could determine differential NPV comparing separately Q to P (Q − P) and R to P (R − P). If neither differential was positive, then you would stay with P. If either or both were positive, you would choose the one with the highest positive NPV of differential costs.

Another time-saving feature of the differential cost approach is that differentials can be calculated on a before-tax basis. Tax effects are then calculated only once for the differentials. This procedure will be demonstrated in the following problem.

## SAMPLE ANALYSIS OF SOPHISTICATED INVESTMENT PROBLEM

To provide a sample analysis of an investment decision with several alternatives, assume the following situation. Your firm presently has machine P, which has eight more years of useful life and is used exclusively to manufacture "nerds." Anticipated nerd volume is 40,000 units annually. Two other machines, Q and R, are on the market, which may be so desirable that one should replace P. You must decide whether to stay with P or replace it with either Q or R. Your firm's cost of capital is 14 percent, and you may assume a 40-percent income-tax rate. Data relating to these three machines are given in Exhibit 8.5.

In making your analysis, remember that you must first determine a common decision time horizon. To cut off everything at five years (R's useful life) would be too short a time for evaluating Q, and would probably be unrealistic with respect to P. Eight years would appear a desirable time horizon. Eight years matches P's remaining life, Q can be reasonably cut off at eight years, and two R's can be projected with the second one cut off at the eight-year horizon. Note that, in estimating your second acquisition and use of R, you might wish to project different costs and benefits. For simplification in this problem you may assume that R's costs and benefits will remain the same.

## Exhibit 8.5

### Comparison of Costs for Three Machines (for Accounting and Tax Purposes)

| | Machine P | Machine Q | Machine R |
|---|---|---|---|
| Present accounting book value ($80,000 cost less $60,000 accumulated depreciation) | $20,000* | — | — |
| Cost | | $100,000ᵃ | $40,000ᵇ |
| Annual operating and maintenance cost | $ 4,000 | $ 3,000 | $ 2,000 |
| Unit cost of nerds made | $  1.10 | $  0.50 | $  0.85 |
| Tax basis | $ 5,000 | — | — |
| Future tax depreciation | $2,500/yr. for 2 years (two-year remaining life and zero salvage for tax purposes) | | |
| Estimated life for accounting purposes | 8 years (remaining)* | 12 years* | 5 years* |
| Salvage value after: | | | |
| 12 years | | $ 3,000* | |
| 8 years | $2,000 | $ 18,000 | $12,000ᶜ |
| 5 years | | | $ 2,000 |
| Salvage value today | $5,000 | | |
| Financial accounting depreciation method | | Straight-line* | Straight-line* |
| Estimated life for tax purposes | | 7 years | 4 years |
| Tax depreciation method | | DDB (29% rate) | DDB (50% rate) |
| ITC to apply | | 10% | 10% |

ᵃ $20,000 down and a four-year note at eight percent interest for the balance.
ᵇ $10,000 down and a four-year note at nine percent interest for the balance.
ᶜ If machine is purchased 5 years from now.

* Have you properly identified all data marked with an asterisk as being wholly irrelevant to this decision problem?

Using an eight-year decision time horizon, you would be well advised to invest your time at this point in attempting a solution to this problem before proceeding to the next paragraph. The effort (cost to you) should take about 30 minutes. The benefit will be either significant reinforcement (if you find you have already mastered the material so far introduced), or important feedback (if you identify areas of uncertainty requiring review). Exhibits 8.6, 8.7, and 8.8 illustrate appropriate NPV analysis of each machine. Both Q and R are preferable to continuing to use P, as both have lower NPV after-tax costs over the next eight years.

The same guidance could be obtained with less effort by using the differential cost approach. Exhibits 8.9 and 8.10 demonstrate this method with machines Q and R, each compared to P. The differential cost approach arrives at the same final NPV difference as could be obtained from comparing Exhibits 8.6, 8.7, and 8.8. The slight difference of two dollars is the result of rounding errors. You should study these five exhibits carefully until you understand fully how they are prepared. Note especially that, under the differential cost approach, a comparative cost savings ($25,000 per year on Exhibit 8.7) is treated as additional taxable income in the determination of differential tax effect.

You will have the opportunity to make similar analyses in the chapter-end problems. Once analysis of investment proposals is completed, and acceptable proposals are identified, there is sometimes the question as to whether they can all be funded or implemented.

## CAPITAL RATIONING

Investment decisions really involve two sequential steps:

1. Determination of acceptability of proposals (discussed above).
2. Deciding whether to fund or implement those proposals found acceptable.

The decision rules with respect to funding and implementation conceptually parallel the rules introduced in Chapter 7 for planning use of productive resources. Remember that, below capacity, all potential uses of productive resources providing a positive contribution should be taken. At capacity, choices must be made on the basis of uses maximizing contribution per unit of scarce resources.

In terms of acceptable investment opportunities, when the aggregated capital demands of all available acceptable investments (after selecting from mutually exclusive alternatives) is less than the amount of available capital (capital capacity), then **all** should be funded and implemented. No comparison among acceptable proposals (excluding selection from among mutually exclusive alternatives) needs to be made.

When aggregated investment demand exceeds readily available capital (capital scarcity), then the limited capital must be rationed among acceptable

**Exhibit 8.6**

**Separate NPV Analysis of Machine P**
**(All Amounts other than PV Factors in Dollars)**

| Year | Investment/ salvage | Operating and nerd costs | Investment/ salvage/ depreciation tax effects | Operating cost tax effects | Net tax effect | Net cash flow | 14% PV factors | PV cash flows |
|---|---|---|---|---|---|---|---|---|
| 0 | 0 | 0 | 0 | 0 | 0 | 0 | 1.000 | 0 |
| 1 | 0 | -$48,000[a] | +$1,000 | + 19,200 | +$20,200 | -$27,800 | 0.877 | -$ 24,381 |
| 2 | 0 | - 48,000 | + 1,000 | + 19,200 | + 20,200 | - 27,800 | 0.769 | - 21,378 |
| 3 | 0 | - 48,000 | 0 | + 19,200 | + 19,200 | - 28,800 | 0.675 | - 19,440 |
| 4 | 0 | - 48,000 | 0 | + 19,200 | + 19,200 | - 28,800 | 0.592 | - 17,050 |
| 5 | 0 | - 48,000 | 0 | + 19,200 | + 19,200 | - 28,800 | 0.519 | - 14,947 |
| 6 | 0 | - 48,000 | 0 | + 19,200 | + 19,200 | - 28,800 | 0.456 | - 13,133 |
| 7 | 0 | - 48,000 | 0 | + 19,200 | + 19,200 | - 28,800 | 0.400 | - 11,520 |
| 8 | + 2,000 | - 48,000 | - 800[b] | + 19,200 | + 18,400 | - 27,600 | 0.351 | - 9,688 |
| | | | | | | | NPV = | -$131,537 |

[a] 40,000 nerds times $1.10 plus $4,000.
[b] Assume sold and not replaced; therefore, $2,000 taxable gain.

**Exhibit 8.7**

## Separate NPV Analysis of Machine R
### (All Amounts other than PV Factors in Dollars)

| Year | Investment/ salvage | Operating and nerd costs | Investment/ salvage/ depreciation tax effects | Operating cost tax effects | Net tax effect | Net cash flow | 14% PV factors | PV cash flows |
|---|---|---|---|---|---|---|---|---|
| 0 | −$95,000ª | 0 | +$10,000[b] | 0 | +$10,000 | −$85,000 | 1.000 | −$ 85,000 |
| 1 | 0 | −$23,000 | + 10,600[c] | +$9,200 | + 19,800 | − 3,200 | 0.877 | − 2,806 |
| 2 | 0 | − 23,000 | + 7,236 | + 9,200 | + 16,436 | − 6,564 | 0.769 | − 5,048 |
| 3 | 0 | − 23,000 | + 5,848 | + 9,200 | + 15,048 | − 7,952 | 0.675 | − 5,368 |
| 4 | 0 | − 23,000 | + 4,152 | + 9,200 | + 13,352 | − 9,648 | 0.592 | − 5,712 |
| 5 | 0 | − 23,000 | + 2,948 | + 9,200 | + 12,148 | − 10,852 | 0.519 | − 5,632 |
| 6 | 0 | − 23,000 | + 2,093 | + 9,200 | + 11,293 | − 11,707 | 0.456 | − 5,338 |
| 7 | 0 | − 23,000 | + 5,124 | + 9,200 | + 14,324 | − 8,676 | 0.400 | − 3,470 |
| 8 | + 18,000 | − 23,000 | − 7,200[d] | + 9,200 | + 2,000 | − 3,000 | 0.351 | − 1,053 |
| | | | | | | | NPV = | −$119,427 |

ª $100,000 cost less proceeds sale of P.
[b] 10% ITC, no tax effect on sale of P.
[c] DDB tax depreciation (29% rate) on initial basis of $100,000, first two years offset by loss of deduction for P, shields income from 40% tax rate.
[d] Assume sold, therefore $18,000 taxable gain.

## Exhibit 8.8

### Separate NPV Analysis of Machine R
#### (All Amounts other than PV Factors in Dollars)

| Year | Investment/ salvage | Operating and nerd costs | Investment/ salvage/ depreciation tax effects | Operating cost tax effects | Net tax effect | Net cash flow | 14% PV factors | PV cash flows |
|---|---|---|---|---|---|---|---|---|
| 0 | −$35,000ᵃ | 0 | +$4,000ᵇ | 0 | +$ 4,000 | −$31,000 | 1.000 | −$ 31,000 |
| 1 | 0 | −$36,000 | + 7,000ᶜ | $14,400 | + 21,400 | − 14,600 | 0.877 | − 12,804 |
| 2 | 0 | − 36,000 | + 3,000 | $14,400 | + 17,400 | − 18,600 | 0.769 | − 14,303 |
| 3 | 0 | − 36,000 | + 2,000 | $14,400 | + 16,400 | − 19,600 | 0.675 | − 13,230 |
| 4 | 0 | − 36,000 | + 1,000 | $14,400 | + 15,400 | − 20,600 | 0.592 | − 12,195 |
| 5 | − 38,000ᵈ | − 36,000 | + 4,200ᵉ | $14,400 | + 18,600 | − 55,400 | 0.519 | − 28,753 |
| 6 | 0 | − 36,000 | + 8,000 | $14,400 | + 22,400 | − 13,600 | 0.456 | − 6,202 |
| 7 | 0 | − 36,000 | + 4,000 | $14,400 | + 18,400 | − 17,600 | 0.400 | − 7,040 |
| 8 | + 12,000 | − 36,000 | − 800ᶠ | $14,400 | + 13,600 | − 10,400 | 0.351 | − 3,650 |
| | | | | | | | NPV = | −$129,177 |

ᵃ $40,000 cost less proceeds sale of P.
ᵇ 10% ITC, no tax effect on sale of P.
ᶜ DDB tax depreciation (50% rate) on initial basis of $40,000, offset by loss of deduction for P in years one and two, shields income from 40% tax rate.
ᵈ $40,000 cost less proceeds sale of first R.
ᵉ $4,000 ITC plus tax savings on $500 fifth-year depreciation.
ᶠ No tax depreciation, tax on $2,000 gain on sale.

**Exhibit 8.9**

## NPV Differential Costs of Machine Q Compared to P (Q − P)
### (All Amounts other than PV Factors in Dollars)

Differential costs (Q − P)

| Year | Investment/salvage | Operating and nerd costs | Depr. tax shield | Tax effect[a] | Differential cash flow[b] | 14% PV factors | PV cash flows |
|---|---|---|---|---|---|---|---|
| 0 | −$95,000 | $0 | $0 | +$10,000 | −$85,000 | 1.000 | −$85,000 |
| 1 | 0 | + 25,000 | + 24,000[c] | − 400 | + 24,600 | 0.877 | + 21,574 |
| 2 | 0 | + 25,000 | + 15,590 | − 3,764 | + 21,236 | 0.769 | + 16,330 |
| 3 | 0 | + 25,000 | + 14,619 | − 4,152 | + 20,848 | 0.675 | + 14,072 |
| 4 | 0 | + 25,000 | + 10,379 | − 5,848 | + 19,152 | 0.592 | + 11,338 |
| 5 | 0 | + 25,000 | + 7,369 | − 7,052 | + 17,948 | 0.519 | + 9,315 |
| 6 | 0 | + 25,000 | + 5,232 | − 7,907 | + 17,093 | 0.456 | + 7,794 |
| 7 | 0 | + 25,000 | + 12,811 | − 4,876 | + 20,124 | 0.400 | + 8,050 |
| 8 | + 16,000 | + 25,000 | 0 | − 16,400 | + 24,600 | 0.351 | + 8,635 |
| | | | | | | NPV = | +$12,108 |

a Operating cost "savings" less differential tax shield are subject to additional tax of 40%. Also includes ITC and tax on disposition.
b Sum of investment/salvage, operating and nerd costs, and tax effect.
c Tax shield under alternative Q = $26,500 ($29,000 depreciation less $2,500 on P foregone). Tax shield under alternative P = $2,500. Difference = $24,000.

## Exhibit 8.10

### NPV Differential Costs of Machine R Compared to P (R − P)
#### (All Amounts other than PV Factors in Dollars)

Differential costs (R − P)

| Year | Investment/ salvage | Operating and nerd costs | Depr. tax shield | Tax effect[a] | Differential cash flow | 14% PV factors | PV cash flows |
|---|---|---|---|---|---|---|---|
| 0 | −$35,000 | $ 0 | $ 0 | +$4,000 | −$31,000 | 1.000 | −$31,000 |
| 1 | 0 | + 12,000 | + 15,000[b] | + 1,200 | + 13,200 | 0.877 | + 11,576 |
| 2 | 0 | + 12,000 | + 5,000 | − 2,800 | + 9,200 | 0.769 | + 7,075 |
| 3 | 0 | + 12,000 | + 5,000 | − 2,800 | + 9,200 | 0.675 | + 6,210 |
| 4 | 0 | + 12,000 | + 2,500 | − 3,800 | + 8,200 | 0.592 | + 4,854 |
| 5 | − 38,000 | + 12,000 | + 500 | − 600 | − 26,600 | 0.519 | − 13,805 |
| 6 | 0 | + 12,000 | + 20,000 | + 3,200 | + 15,200 | 0.456 | + 6,931 |
| 7 | 0 | + 12,000 | + 10,000 | + 800 | + 11,200 | 0.400 | + 4,480 |
| 8 | + 10,000 | + 12,000 | 0[c] | − 4,800 | + 17,200 | 0.351 | + 6,037 |
| | | | | | | NPV = | +$ 2,358 |

a Operating cost "savings" less differential tax shield are subject to additional tax of 40%. Also includes ITC and tax on disposition.
b Tax shield under alternative R = $17,500 ($20,000 depreciation less $2,500 depreciation on P foregone). Tax shield under alternative P = $2,500.
Difference = $15,000.
c Assume no depreciation taken on R in year 8. Then both P and R would be subject to a $2,000 taxable gain in year 8.

investments to ensure maximum benefit. *Capital rationing* applies only to optional investments. It may be assumed that mandatory investments have been made, and any excess available capital is being rationed.[10]

Many firms ration capital by ranking all acceptable proposals and choosing from the top as many as can be comfortably funded. The crudest ranking is merely in terms of NPV dollars. An investment opportunity with a positive $20,000 of NPV would have preference over one with only $19,000 of NPV. Can you see at least one potential fallacy in this approach? Although NPV dollars indicate the absolute amount of return on the specific investment, they do **not** take into account the **relative** return on the amount invested. For instance, consider two investments, A and B. A involves an investment of $20 million and has an NPV of $4,000. B involves an investment of $4,000 and has an NPV of $3,000. Simple ranking by dollars would indicate A more preferable than B. Do you see the fallacy of this approach? The relative amount invested is not considered.

To allow for ranking in terms of benefits compared to costs, a *profitability index*, or a benefit–cost ratio, is often used:

$$\text{Profitability index} = 1 + \frac{\text{NPV}}{\text{Required initial investment}}.$$

Ranking and selection based on a profitability index is at least preferable to ranking on the basis simply of NPV dollars alone.

Ranking by profitability index and working down from the top until available funds are exhausted still may not be optimal. Often distinct investment proposals (**not** mutually exclusive alternatives) are not wholly independent in their effects. Also, investments on ranked lists are rarely in even incremental quantities. For example, you have ranked acceptable proposals by NPV profitability index and have:

1. Investment required $49 million
2. Investment required $30 million
3. Investment required $6 million
4. Investment required $4 million

What would you do if you had only $40 million? Or $59 million? Or $83 million? Various combinations of proposals must be evaluated to see which combinations result in the highest **combined NPV.** Such combined analysis can become complex and time-consuming where more than a few possible combinations are involved. Computer simulation and linear programming techniques can be of great assistance with such problems.

Since capital rationing is more appropriately a finance subject, it will not be explored further at this time.

---

[10]  Where capital requirements for mandatory investments exceed the amount of available capital, the firm has a problem and may have to restrict or terminate operations. Resolution of this situation is beyond the scope of this text.

## INCORPORATING PROVISION FOR RISK

As mentioned earlier in this chapter (and as should be obvious to you), many business investments involve commitments of large sums of capital for many years before **any** return is realized. In a rapidly changing world, reliability of the very best forecasts of cash flows twenty, ten, or even five years from today is subject to question. Obviously, some investments are more risky than others, or are more sensitive to forecast errors. Managers would like to incorporate risk in their analysis, and several techniques have been employed to this end.

At the simplest level, an investment deemed acceptable using NPV analysis is subsequently also evaluated in conjuction with its simple payback. For example, suppose you could choose only two of the following apparently acceptable investments; which would you pick?

| Investment | Amount invested | NPV | Simple payback |
|---|---|---|---|
| A | $10 million | $40,000 | 5 years |
| B | 8 million | 39,000 | 11 years |
| C | 6 million | 35,000 | 3 years |

Ranking by profitability index and also considering simple payback would help:

| Investment | Profitability index | Simple payback |
|---|---|---|
| C | 1.006 | 3 years |
| B | 1.005 | 11 years |
| A | 1.004 | 5 years |

An investment that does not recover the original capital invested for many years can be more risky than one with an early payback. Forecasted data far into the future could prove very unreliable. Technological breakthroughs or changes in customer tastes could make a long-term project obsolete before it was paid off. Can you see how the use of even simple payback can serve as a crude indicator of possible risks from long-term commitment, and be better than ignoring such risks completely? In the above example, investment C would be an obvious first choice. It has the highest profitability index, and capital is recovered in about three years. You might reasonably expect that not too many changes will occur in three years. Choosing the second investment may not be routine by the index rank. Simple payback signals significant potential long-term commitment risk for B. Many firms would probably select A over B. At least simple payback has "flagged" a potentially risky situation for further analysis.

Preferable to simple payback as a risk indicator is time-adjusted payback, which was described earlier. Time-adjusted payback allows for tax effects and the time value of money. It would indicate how soon the firm could fully recover its investment and its **minimum** required return on capital. A previously mentioned source of risk is the potential obsolescence of equipment. Significantly more efficient or relatively less costly equipment may come on the market in a few years. Where an investment involves capital equipment or facilities (as most business investments do), the time-adjusted payback indicates the number of years management would have to "bet" a better machine would **not** come along, in order for them to "break even" on their investment. For investments with long paybacks, management might require special engineering studies of the probability of technological obsolescence, in order to assist it in evaluating relative risk.

Another method of incorporating risk is similar to one in use by press photographers for half a century. On the scene of a newsworthy event, the press photographer often does not have time to make accurate exposure readings. If he or she over- or underexposes, often the picture cannot be rephotographed after the film is developed and the error discovered. To avoid the risk of a poorly exposed picture, the photographer will usually shoot "one on, one over, and one under." He or she will bracket the target with what seems to be a high (over) exposure and a low (under) one.

Investment analysis may similarly incorporate additional estimates of the NPV, one at a higher or reasonably optimistic forecast level and another at a lower or reasonably pessimistic level. This approach is often called the *three-point estimate approach.* With three "pictures" to choose from, the investment analyst is in a better position to assess the sensitivity of the proposed investment to changes in future flows and, therefore, to its potential risk.

As an example, the after-tax net benefits of a ten-year investment of $345,000 might be evaluated as:

Conservative/pessimistic:   $60,000 per year
Most likely:   $100,000 per year
Hopeful/optimistic:   $150,000 per year

The corresponding NPV's at 12 percent would then be:

Conservative/pessimistic:   −$6,000
Most likely:   +$220,000
Hopeful/optimistic:   +$502,500

Another investment of a similar amount analyzed in this fashion might reveal NPV's of:

Conservative/pessimistic:   −$150,000
Most likely:   +$10,000
Hopeful/optimistic:   +$25,000

Can you see how this approach helps to identify the risk associated with an investment proposal? Clearly, in the examples above, the first investment appears acceptable and the second probably too risky.

Recent developments in mathematical probability measurements and the ready availability of computers have made possible much more sophisticated techniques of risk analysis. Various combinations of future possible flows can be assigned probabilities of occurrence. Then a great many alternatives may be simulated on the computer and, with the use of "Monte Carlo" techniques, investments may be ranked in terms of probabilistic outcomes. Management may then select those investments with the highest probability of earning at least the minimum required return.[11] Such advanced techniques are beyond the elementary level of this text. They are mentioned for your understanding and awareness.

Regardless of the approach used to assessing risk, what should a firm do with proposals that are determined to be more risky than others? To always reject high-risk investment opportunities may not always be a sound strategy. A general economic reality is that higher-risk investments demand (reward the investor with) a higher rate of return. A high-risk investment proposal might also have such a high return as to make it desirable.

An approach sometimes used is to apply a higher discount rate (thereby requiring a higher return) to all investment proposals having a time-adjusted (or simple) payback greater than a predetermined cutoff. For example, a firm whose cost of capital is 12 percent might require that all proposals with a payback of over six years be reevaluated at a 20-percent rate. Only those providing the additional eight-percent risk return would merit further consideration.

## Sensitivity Analysis

Still another approach to dealing with the significance of risk is known as *sensitivity analysis*. All different investment-related risks involve uncertainty, the possibility that actual future cash flows will differ from those that were projected. Sensitivity analysis involves studying the effect upon total NPV of potential changes in the various projected data inputs to the decision model. Each investment alternative can be recalculated under different assumed cash flows, to answer such questions as:

---

[11]  Probability ranking of two investments A and B might reveal:

| Investment | NPV | Probability |
|:---:|:---:|:---:|
| A | −$40,000 | 0.4 |
|   | +60,000 | 0.5 |
|   | +100,000 | 0.1 |
| B | −2,000 | 0.1 |
|   | +50,000 | 0.6 |
|   | +200,000 | 0.3 |

Investment B clearly has a higher probability of being successful.

There are also techniques for risk acceptance known as the *portfolio approach* that essentially involve spreading risks with different investments to minimize loss in case one or a few prove undesirable.

- How far can sales (price or quantity or both) or savings fall below projections before the investment becomes undesirable?
- By how much can costs exceed estimates and still have the investment be desirable?
- How sensitive is the investment return (NPV) to the timing of various projected inflows and outflows?
- Which of the different data inputs have the most significant impact on the alternative's NPV? Which inputs are most crucial to the success of the investment and, therefore, must be estimated with the greatest accuracy? How accurate must these estimates be? What is their margin for error?

As a simple example of sensitivity analysis, assume a proposed investment involving the following projected data:

| Year | Investment/ operating costs | Revenues | Tax effects* | Net cash flows | 14% PV |
|---|---|---|---|---|---|
| 0 | −$60,000 | $ 0 | $ 0 | −$60,000 | −$60,000 |
| 1 | −12,000 | +48,000 | −6,400 | +29,600 | +25,965 |
| 2 | −12,000 | +48,000 | −6,400 | +29,600 | +22,777 |
| 3 | −12,000 | +48,000 | −6,400 | +29,600 | +19,980 |
| | | | | NPV | +$ 8,722 |

How far could projected revenues fall before the investment would become undesirable (NPV below zero)? Net cash flows of $25,845 each year would result in a zero NPV ($25,845 times 2.3216 and rounded would result in exactly $60,000 in benefits). Sales could drop to $41,742 annually and still result in a $25,845 positive net cash flow.[12]

## PROVIDING FOR INFLATION

You have probably been wondering whether projections illustrated so far with no provision for inflation are worth the cost of the paper they are written on. Inflation is not so much a risk as a certainty. The difficulty or gamble is in predicting the appropriate inflation rate. Some reasonable estimates of inflationary effects need to be incorporated in decision analysis. You may also have

---

\* Assume 40-percent tax and straight-line depreciation.

[12] Each sales dollar adds $0.60 to net cash flow after taxes. Therefore, reduction in sales ($X$) times 0.6 equals reduction in cash flow:

$$0.6X = 3755$$
$$X = 6,258 \text{ (rounded).}$$

perceived that, if a constant inflation rate could be accurately assumed, then an additional application of the PV technique might be used to adjust future estimates before discounting for interest. The subject of adjusting for inflation will be explored in Chapter 16.

## OTHER CONSIDERATIONS

In Chapter 7, with respect to noninvestment decisions, you were alerted to the importance of nonquantified considerations. So called "other considerations" apply equally to investment decisions, and may possibly be of greater significance because of the more extended commitment of resources involved. The various risks discussed earlier may be considered as a nonquantified consideration, unless incorporated in the NPV analysis in more sophisticated computer programs. Factors (other than dollars invested and the return on the investment) that are relevant to investment decisions are numerous. Some examples include:

- future market trends related to both product sales and resource availability,
- future trends in employee relations,
- possibilities of changes in government regulations, and
- similar environmental factors.

Two other specific considerations that are relevant to many investment decisions, and which are readily quantifiable, may be overlooked. A net investment of resources, by definition, will usually increase the firm's fixed costs. Increased fixed costs will usually increase the firm's breakeven volume. The effect of an investment upon the firm's breakeven must be considered another element of risk. For example, consider a firm with:

Annual capacity = 100,000 units

Present sales volume = 90,000 units

Present breakeven = 60,000 units

If a proposed investment would raise this firm's breakeven volume to 89,000 units, it might be too risky regardless of its individual investment return. At a breakeven so close to current sales volume, the risk might be too great that a slight loss in volume could result in significant operating losses for the firm.

In addition to the effect upon breakeven, each potential investment's effect upon net working capital requirements must be considered.[13] Some investments

---

[13]   As discussed in the companion text, the term working capital is often used in the business world to mean only current assets. To avoid possible misinterpretation, the term net working capital will be used in this text to refer to the difference between current assets and current liabilities.

are intended to increase sales of existing products, or to add new products. Additional sales generate requirements for increased net working capital to finance both the additional receivables and also a portion of any necessary additional inventory. Any requirement for more net working capital must be included in any investment decision as a relevant part of the total resources to be invested. Similarly, any investment decision aimed at product cost reduction may reduce capital required in inventory; and a decision whether to discontinue a product line or a business segment must include an allowance for reduced net working capital requirements.

## CONTROL OVER INVESTMENT DECISIONS

Since many investment decisions involve long-term commitment of the firm's resources, approval of new investments is generally reserved to a *capital budgeting committee* reporting directly to top management or to the board of directors. All major investment proposals, including new plant and equipment, advertising budgets, research and development budgets, new employee training programs, and the like, are reviewed by such a committee. In addition to ensuring that approved new investments are expected to at least recover the firm's cost of capital, the capital budgeting committee is usually responsible to see that *follow-up audits* are carried out. Follow-up audits are intended to appraise the accuracy of original projections so that estimating included in future proposals may be even more accurate.

The capital budgeting committee may also be charged with recommending policies and procedures designed to minimize potential behavioral conflicts between capital budgeting and performance evaluation. Very desirable investments from the viewpoint of the firm may involve considerable planned losses in the early years. In evaluating the operating performance of individual managers directly responsible for the investment, allowance must be made for these planned losses. Otherwise, individual managers will be discouraged from proposing or taking the responsibility to implement otherwise desirable investments.

## THE FINAL CAPITAL BUDGET

Once an investment (or group of investments) has been selected for implementation, the next step is to include it in the capital budget. The firm's capital budget can be considered a detailed listing of those investments scheduled for implementation during the forthcoming budget period. Any planned asset retirements are also scheduled. Exhibit 8.11 illustrates the capital budget for 19X2 as prepared for the Tripper Company. It incorporates the results of the truck-replacement decision discussed earlier, together with some others added to provide a more realistic example.

**Exhibit 8.11**

TRIPPER WATER SKI MANUFACTURING COMPANY

---

**Capital Budget for 19X2**

January:   Acquire Truck A at cost $18,000 less $1,000 trade-in on existing wrecked truck. Truck A five-year useful life and $2,000 salvage. Wrecked truck cost $13,000, has accumulated depreciation of $10,000, and has a tax basis of zero.

July:   Acquire Machine P as a replacement for Machine Q. Machine P cost = $24,000, ten year life, $2,000 salvage. Machine Q cost $16,000, has accumulated depreciation of $10,000, has a tax basis of $3,000, and will be sold for $5,000.

---

The capital budget completes the planning or demand requirements being placed on the firm's financial capacity during a forthcoming budget year. Together with the operating budget(s), it provides the basis for the next step in the budgeting process, which involves preparing a preliminary cash budget. Cash budgeting and cash management will be covered in the next chapter.

## CHAPTER OVERVIEW

Based upon the material introduced in this chapter, you should now be in a position to:

- Explain why, in the analysis of investment decisions, incremental after-tax cash (or working capital) flows are evaluated, rather than simply incremental revenues and expenses.
- Explain why the firm's cost-of-capital discount rate is usually used in NPV analysis of an investment decision, in preference to the incremental borrowing rate.
- Describe, with examples, how cash flows may include actual and opportunity costs as benefits, and opportunity losses as costs.
- Describe and give examples of how both depreciation tax shields and the investment tax credit are relevant to investment decisions.
- Identify and evaluate the strengths and weaknesses of the six different approaches suggested for determining the acceptability of investment proposals.

- Describe the appropriate acceptability criteria when using NPV analysis for each of the following types of investments:
  - a) Mandatory with no alternatives
  - b) Mandatory with mutually exclusive alternatives
  - c) Optional with no alternatives
  - d) Optional with mutually exclusive alternatives
- Explain the significance of common decision time horizons to the analysis of investment alternatives, and describe appropriate adjustments to proposals with different lives.
- Describe and give examples of the use of the differential cost approach to investment analysis.
- Using the NPV approach, analyze for acceptability investment proposals by determining either the separate NPV's of each proposal or (where appropriate) the NPV's of the differential costs.
- Explain why capital rationing may be necessary, and describe the various approaches used.
- Describe both the relevance of different types of risk to investment decisions, and also several alternatives for incorporating an allowance for risk in the decision process.
- Identify two potentially significant "other considerations" that should always be investigated in conjunction with any investment proposal.
- Explain the role of a firm's capital budgeting committee.
- Explain how investment decision making relates to the preparation of the firm's capital budget; and how the capital budget, in turn, relates to the overall budgeting process.

## NEW VOCABULARY AND CONCEPTS

| | |
|---|---|
| Present value factor | Incremental borrowing rate |
| Capital budgeting decisions | Differential cost analysis |
| After-tax cash flows | Mutually exclusive |
| Tax shield | investments |
| Tax depreciation | Capital capacity |
| Tax basis | Capital rationing |
| Investment tax credit (ITC) | Profitability index |
| Arbitrary (method of investment | Three-point estimate approach |
| analysis) | Sensitivity analysis |
| Simple payback | Capital budgeting committee |
| Time-adjusted payback | Follow-up audits |

- Depreciation and tax shields
- NPV of future cash flows and investment desirability/acceptability
- Different types of risk related to investment decisions

## REVIEW QUESTIONS

1. a) What is a present value factor?
   b) How is it used?

2. What are six distinctive characteristics of investment decisions as compared with noninvestment decisions?

3. a) What are several different risks associated with investment decisions, and why are they significant?
   Explain how risk may relate to:
   b) Commitment and future losses?
   c) Data projection accuracy?
   d) Equipment obsolescence?

4. Why are after-tax cash flows used in investment decision analysis in preference to before-tax revenues and expenses?

5. a) Why is the cost-of-capital rate used for discounting most investment decisions, as opposed to the incremental borrowing rate?
   b) If all relevant cash flows are to be included in investment analysis, should you include payments of principal and interest on a loan identified exclusively with a particular investment? If not, explain.

6. Should any of the following items be included in the quantified part of an investment analysis as a relevant benefit? Explain.
   a) Incremental revenues or contribution associated with and resulting from the investment?
   b) All "opportunity expenses" saved as a result of the investment?
   c) All opportunity costs that involved cash flows and that are saved as a result of the investment?
   d) All operating costs involving cash flows that are reduced as a result of the investment?
   e) Any taxes saved as a result of the investment?

7. Should any of the following items be included in the quantified part of an investment analysis as a relevant cost? Explain:
   a) Incremental operating costs involving cash flows associated with the investment?
   b) All "opportunity benefits" lost as a result of the investment?
   c) All opportunity benefits that involve cash inflows and that will be terminated as a result of the investment?
   d) Any additional taxes owed as a direct or indirect result of the investment.

8. a) What is a tax shield? Explain, with examples.
   b) What is the cash flow benefit of an incremental amount of depreciation $X$ when the tax rate is $t$?

9. a) What is the investment tax credit?
   b) How does it relate to investment decision analysis?
   c) If an incremental investment $I$ is entitled to an ITC at a rate $c$, and the firm is subject to income tax at the rate $t$, what is the associated cash flow benefit of the ITC?

10. a) Can there be a difference in any year between accounting book value and depreciation expenses on the one hand, and the tax basis and the tax depreciation reductions on the other? If yes, explain.

b) What is the relevance of accounting book value and depreciation expenses to investment analysis?

c) What is the relevance of the tax basis and tax depreciation reductions to investment analysis?

11. For each of the following six approaches to determining the acceptability of an investment proposal:

a) Explain the intention of the approach (what it measures).

b) Describe, with an example, how the approach is applied to a particular decision.

c) Give a criterion of acceptability that might be used in conjunction with the approach.

d) Describe the strengths (advantages/usefulness) and weaknesses (disadvantages) of the approach.
   (1) Arbitrary
   (2) Simple payback
   (3) Time-adjusted payback
   (4) Unadjusted rate of return
   (5) Internal rate of return
   (6) Net present value

12. For each of the following four types of investment decisions being evaluated following the NPV method, give the appropriate criterion (decision rule) for determining acceptability:

a) Mandatory investment with no investment alternatives?

b) Mandatory investment with mutually exclusive investment alternatives?

c) Optional investment with no investment alternatives?

d) Optional investment with mutually exclusive investment alternatives?

13. a) How is the concept of decision time horizon relevant to the analysis of mutually exclusive investment alternatives?

b) How should one adjust for uneven lives in such a situation?

14. a) What is differential cost analysis?

b) What is the information content (what does it tell you) of an amount representing the NPV of differential costs (and benefits)?

c) How may the NPV of differential costs (and benefits) be used? Explain, with examples.

15. a) What is the relationship between capital capacity and capital rationing?

b) What is an investment proposal's profitability index, and how is it measured?

c) Describe and evaluate several alternatives intended to accomplish optimal capital rationing.

16. a) How may payback (simple or time-adjusted) be used to evaluate risk?

b) What does the time-adjusted payback period tell you with respect to any equipment included as part of the investment?

c) What is the three-point method of analysis? What information does it supply?

d) How can a discount rate different from the cost of capital be appropriately used in NPV investment analysis to incorporate risk? Explain.

e) What is meant by sensitivity analysis in the context of an investment decision? What kinds of information can result from sensitivity analysis, and how may it be useful? Explain, with examples.

17. How do the concepts of breakeven and of net working capital relate to the analysis of investment acceptability? Explain.

18. a) What is the role of the capital budgeting committee?
    b) What is meant by a follow-up audit? What is its purpose?
    c) Can desirable approaches to investment decisions and performance evaluation possibly introduce behavioral conflicts or lack of goal congruence? Explain.

## MINI-CASES AND QUESTIONS FOR DISCUSSION

**MC 8.1**  Mr. John Reinhart has been with the company for over 40 years, the last 20 of which have seen him as a member of the capital budget committee. He is arguing against a specific proposal for a new product line. "I don't give a —— if the so-called NPV is positive; the payback is too long. This firm prospered for many years, using payback, before anybody even heard of NPV.

"If NPV is so great, why don't we use it consistently? At our last meeting we approved for funding the new training program, which couldn't even show a positive NPV; and at the same meeting we rejected the new servo-controlled drill press that had a clearly positive NPV. If you business-school types want to play with your calculators and computers and compute NPV's or even XYZ's, that's fine. Just don't try to claim a project should . ? funded just because it has a positive NPV."

Could John be both right and wrong at the same time? Are there circumstances where a positive NPV should be rejected and a negative NPV accepted? If so, what good is NPV anyway? Discuss.

**MC 8.2**  Why isn't the practice of using different depreciation methods, and especially different useful life estimates, on balance sheets and tax returns illegal, improper, or at least unethical? Discuss.

**MC 8.3**  "If a firm today accepted and funded (implemented) all investment proposals with an NPV equal to or exceeding the firm's current incremental borrowing rate, eventually the firm's cost of capital rate could increase dramatically. And eventually the incremental borrowing rate itself could be greater than today's cost of capital rate." Is this statement correct? Discuss.

**MC 8.4**  Assume that a particular investment proposal has been evaluated by the NPV method using a cost-of-capital rate $r$ and is determined to have a negative NPV indicating nonacceptability. Could the identical investment have an internal rate of return greater than $r$ which **could** indicate acceptability? Discuss.

## ESSENTIAL PROBLEMS

**EP 8.1** Given the following information with respect to investment A, determine the after-tax cash flow for each separate year of the investment's life:

    Investment cost: $50,000

    Useful life: Five years

    Salvage value at end of useful life: Zero

    Tax depreciation: Straight-line, five-year life, zero salvage

    Income tax rate: 40 percent

    Additional contribution generated by investment: $17,700 per year

**EP 8.2** a) Given the following data with respect to investment B, determine the after-tax cash flows for each separate year of the investment's life:

    Investment: $40,000

    Useful life: Five years

    Salvage value at end of useful life: Zero

    Tax depreciation: Straight-line, five-year life, zero salvage

    Income tax rate: 40 percent

    Additional contribution generated by investment: $14,000 per year

    b) Refer also the Problem EP 8.1. If a firm's cost-of-capital rate is 14 percent, and investments A and B are mutually exclusive alternatives, which should be chosen and why? Use NPV analysis.

**EP 8.3** Given the following data relevant to a particular investment C, compute the after-tax cash flows for each separate year at a 40-percent tax rate:

    Asset cost: $100,000

    Useful life: Four years

    Salvage value at end of useful life: $3,000

    Tax depreciation: DDB, four-year life, zero salvage

    Contribution per year generated by investment: $42,000

**EP 8.4** Given the following data relevant to investment D, compute the after-tax cash flows for each separate year of the investment's five-year life at a 40-percent tax rate:

    Asset cost: $200,000

    Useful life: Five years

    Salvage value at end of useful life: $5,000

    Salvage value at end of four years: $20,000

    Tax depreciation: DDB, four-year life, zero salvage

    Contribution per year generated by investment: $80,000

**EP 8.5** Assuming a 12-percent cost of capital, determine the NPV of the after-tax cash flows of investment C described in Problem EP 8.3.

**EP 8.6** a) Assuming a 12-percent cost of capital, determine the NPV of the after-tax cash flows of investment D described in Problem EP 8.4.

b) Assuming that the investments described in Problems EP 8.3 and EP 8.4 were mutually exclusive alternatives, at a 12-percent cost-of-capital rate and at a 40-percent income-tax rate, which would you choose as having the higher return (NPV)?

c) What would be the amount of the NPV of the differential costs?

d) Which investment has the highest NPV index, and what is its index?

**EP 8.7** a) Assuming an eight-percent cost of capital and a 20-percent tax rate, determine the NPV of the after-tax cash flows of investments C and D described in Problems EP 8.3 and EP 8.4. Consider the two investments as mutually exclusive alternatives.

b) Which investment has the higher return (NPV)?

c) What is the amount of the NPV of the differential costs?

d) Which investment has the highest NPV index, and what is its index?

**EP 8.8** Answer the four questions contained in Problem EP 8.7, assuming a 14-percent cost of capital and a 30-percent income-tax rate.

**EP 8.9** Your firm must replace an existing old machine with either machine E or F. The old machine has been depreciated to zero for tax purposes, and will be traded in on either E or F. Data relevant to these two machines is as follows.

|  | E | F |
|---|---|---|
| Investment cost net of trade-in | $100,000 | $100,000 |
| Useful life | 5 years | 5 years |
| Salvage value at end of useful life | $4,000 | $4,000 |
| Tax depreciation:   Straight-line, five years | | |
| ITC applicable | 10% | 10% |
| Operating costs:   Year 1 | $10,000 | $20,000 |
| Operating costs:   Year 2 | 30,000 | 50,000 |
| Operating costs:   Year 3 | 40,000 | 50,000 |
| Operating costs:   Year 4 | 60,000 | 30,000 |
| Operating costs:   Year 5 | 50,000 | 20,000 |

a) Assume an applicable income-tax rate of 30 percent. Calculate the after-tax cash flows for each new machine for each year separately.

b) Calculate the NPV of after-tax cash flows for both machines, assuming an eight-percent cost of capital.

c) Which machine is the preferable investment, and why?

**EP 8.10** Refer to the data given for investments E and F in Problem EP 8.9.

a) What would be your recommended choice between these two machines for investment, assuming a cost-of-capital rate of 20 percent, and why?

b) If your recommendation immediately above differs from the one you would make in response to questions (b) and (c) in Problem EP 8.9, explain why the different discount rates could cause the difference.

**EP 8.11** a) Assume that a truck costs $20,000, has a useful life for tax purposes of ten years and zero salvage, will be depreciated for tax purposes using the straight-line method, and has an NPV of zero at a 15-percent cost-of-capital rate. If the applicable income-tax rate is 20 percent, what must be the annual before-tax benefits or cost savings?

b) Assume that a firm requires a 14-percent return on its investments. How much would it be willing to pay for new equipment which:

- Would qualify for a ten-percent ITC?
- Would have a 15-year life for tax purposes and zero salvage value?
- Would result in annual operating savings of $9,000 per year for 15 years?

You may assume that straight-line depreciation would be used for tax purposes, and that applicable taxes are 30 percent.

**EP 8.12** a) Assume that a piece of equipment costs $100,000 and has a useful life of six years and zero salvage. It will be depreciated for tax purposes following DDB, a four-year life, and zero salvage. The applicable income-tax rate is 30 percent. The NPV of all after-tax cash flows, including annual savings, discounted at 15 percent is zero. What must be the amount of annual before-tax operating benefits?

b) Assume that a firm requires a 12-percent return on its investments. How much would it be willing to pay for a new truck which:

- Would qualify for a 12-percent ITC?
- Would have a ten-year life and zero salvage?
- Would have a six-year life for tax purposes, with zero salvage?
- Would result in annual operating savings of $11,000 per year for ten years?

You may assume that DDB will be used for tax depreciation and that applicable income taxes are at 40 percent.

**EP 8.13** A firm is considering the following investment G. From the data given, and using the NPV method, make a recommendation as to whether the investment is acceptable, and support your recommendation.

Investment cost:   $400,000

Useful life:   Nine years

Salvage value at end of useful life:   $5,000

Tax depreciation:   Straight-line, six-year life, zero salvage

Income tax rate:   40 percent

Additional contribution generated by investment:   $86,000 yer year

Appropriate cost of capital:   14 percent

ITC allowable:   Ten percent

**EP 8.14** Refer to Problem EP 8.13. Assume all of the same facts, except assume that the firm was planning to depreciate the investment for tax purposes following DDB over six years, with zero salvage.

a) What would be your recommendation under these modified circumstances?

b) Can you see any benefit to a firm's electing DDB and minimum acceptable (to the Internal Revenue Service) useful life on its tax returns? Explain.

## SUPPLEMENTARY PROBLEMS

**SP 8.15** The Wexler Company is evaluating a potential new product line. Its financial, engineering, and market studies have produced the following information:

1. Necessary advertising costs to obtain target sales volume:

| Year | Amount |
| --- | --- |
| 1 | $500,000 |
| 2 | 300,000 |
| 3 | 100,000 |
| 4–10 | 50,000 each year |

2. Projected sales over the next ten years at a price of $20 each would be:

| Year | Amount |
| --- | --- |
| 1 | $1 million |
| 2 | 2 million |
| 3 | 6 million |
| 4–10 | 5 million each year |

3. Expected variable unit costs would be:

| | |
| --- | --- |
| Manufacturing | $6 |
| General selling and administrative | $3 |

4. Necessary new plant and equipment would cost $4 million, have a 20-year useful life, and salvage value of $40,000 at the end of 20 years. It was also estimated that the equipment could be sold for $900,000 after ten years. For tax purposes, DDB would be used, based on an eight-year life and zero salvage period, and the investment would qualify for a ten-percent ITC. Additional net working capital to finance increased receivables and inventory of $300,000 would also be required.

5. Fixed costs (other than depreciation) to be incurred in connection with the new product line would total $1,350,000 per year.

a) Using the NPV approach and assuming an applicable income-tax rate of 20 percent and a cost-of-capital rate of 12 percent, analyze this investment proposal and make your recommendation to Wexler's management as to whether they should proceed. Support your recommendation with relevant data.

b) Wexler's existing and projected (assuming the new product line is not added) income statement is as follows:

| | |
|---|---:|
| Sales | $16,000,000 |
| Variable manufacturing costs | 7,200,000 |
| Fixed manufacturing costs | 2,400,000 |
| Variable selling costs | 400,000 |
| Fixed general selling and administrative costs | $ 3,500,000 |
| Net income before taxes | $ 2,500,000 |
| Less income taxes | 1,000,000 |
| Net income | $ 1,500,000 |

Would this additional information make the proposed new product line more or less attractive? Explain.

**SP 8.16** Refer to the data given for the Wexler Company in Problem SP 8.15. Assume all of the same facts except the following:

Variable manufacturing costs would be $10 per unit.

Fixed costs (other than depreciation) would total $2 million per year.

Cost of capital would be 14 percent and the applicable income tax rate would be 40 percent.

Answer questions (a) and (b) from Problem SP 8.15 based on this revised information. Explain any changes in your recommendations arising out of the modified data.

**SP 8.17** The Fairfax Company is considering discontinuing one of its product lines known as the Boodles line. Data relevant to the firm is as follows:

| | Boodles | All other | Total |
|---|---:|---:|---:|
| Sales | $400,000 | $4,600,000 | $5,000,000 |
| Cost of goods sold | 380,000 | 1,840,000 | 2,220,000 |
| Gross margin | 20,000 | 2,760,000 | 2,780,000 |
| Variable selling expenses | 10,000 | 230,000 | 240,000 |
| Fixed GS&A expense | 104,000 | 1,196,000 | 1,300,000 |
| Net income (before taxes) | $ (94,000) | $1,334,000 | $1,240,000 |

The firm is subject to a 40-percent income-tax rate, and its cost of capital is 15 percent. If Boodles are discontinued, some sales loss of other products amounting to a maximum of 1 percent could be expected. Also, certain fixed assets used exclusively for Boodles could be disposed of. These assets have an accounting book value of $80,000. Their tax basis is $25,000, with $5,000 of tax depreciation to be taken in each of the next five years if Boodles are continued. These assets could be sold now for $30,000. Fixed charges, other than depreciation, amounting to $26,500 per year could also be eliminated if Boodles were discontinued.

What would you recommend to the Fairfax Company? Support your recommendation with relevant data.

**SP 8.18** The Muldoon Company is currently purchasing for $5 each, in quantities of 600,000 units per year, a component used in one of its assemblies. The firm requires a 12-percent return on its investments and is subject to an income-tax rate of 30 percent. It is considering manufacturing this part in the future rather than continuing to purchase it. If the part were to be manufactured, it is estimated that:

1. Manufacturing costs would be:

| | |
|---|---|
| Direct material | $1.50 |
| Direct labor | 2.00 |
| Variable overhead | 0.30 |
| Fixed overhead | 0.70* |
| Total | $4.50 |

2. Presently unused space and some equipment would be used. The depreciation, insurance, taxes, and maintenance costs on the space (allocated on the basis of square footage) amount to $11,000 per year. The unused equipment has an accounting book value of $30,000 and would be depreciated over ten years at $3,000 per year. It has already been fully depreciated to zero for tax purposes. If the part is not manufactured, the equipment will be sold for $5,000.

3. Manufacturing the part will require the following additional investments:

   • $100,000 net increase in inventory (new investment in raw materials and work-in-process, offset by a partial reduction in finished goods).

   • $2,500,000 in new equipment would be purchased. It would have a ten-year life and a salvage value of $25,000 at the end of ten years. For tax purposes the equipment will be depreciated to zero over eight years on a DDB basis.

Using NPV analysis, analyze the manufacturing alternative and make your recommendation to Muldoon, with supporting data.

**SP 8.19** Your firm has the following investment proposals which have been discounted at the firm's cost of capital:

| | Investment required | NPV |
|---|---|---|
| J | $10,000,000 | $40,000 |
| K | 2,000,000 | 30,000 |
| L | 16,000,000 | 20,000 |
| M | 400,000 | 10,000 |
| N | 900,000 | 5,000 |
| P | 3,000,000 | 500 |
| Q | 6,000,000 | −1,000 |
| R | 22,000,000 | −5,000 |

a) Calculate the profitability index for each acceptable investment.

b) If each investment were completely independent of the others, which investments would you exclude and why, if you had only $29,500,000 available?

c) Again assuming independence, which investments would you fund if you had only $4,000,000 available?

---

* Includes allocation of additional fixed costs given in (2) and (3).

**SP 8.20** Refer to Problem SP 8.19. Assume that time-adjusted paybacks for the above investments were as follows:

| | | | |
|---|---|---|---|
| J | 3 years | N | 1 year |
| K | 4.5 years | P | 14 years |
| L | 7.0 years | Q | never |
| M | 3.5 years | R | never |

Assuming that all proposals were independent of each other, which would you recommend for funding if the firm had only $11,500,000 available? Explain your reasoning.

**SP 8.21** The Danforth Company has approval for the acquisition of a new piece of equipment costing $40,000. It estimates the equipment will have a ten-year life and will have a salvage value after ten years of $4,000. It also estimates that maintenance costs will run $800 per year. Tax depreciation would be on a DDB basis, with a six-year life and zero salvage. The ITC would not apply, the firm's cost of capital is 12 percent, and the applicable tax rate is 30 percent. The firm can borrow $40,000 on a fully amortized ten-year loan at an interest cost of five percent.

Danforth can also lease the same machine for ten years at an annual rental of $5,300. Which alternative would you recommend for Danforth, and why?

**SP 8.22** Refer to Problem SP 8.21. Assume that all facts are the same except:

- Equipment would be depreciated for tax purposes on a straight-line basis over ten years, with the $4,000 salvage value.
- Lease payments would be $5,500 per year.

Which alternative would you recommend on the basis of the revised information? Explain your recommendation.

**SP 8.23** The Kennedy Wholesale Company is considering two distinct capital budgeting proposals. The first proposal is for a new product line, and the second involves investment in commercial real estate. Data relevant to these two investments is given below:

**First investment (new product line):**

| | |
|---|---|
| Additional special-purpose equipment | $300,000 |
| Useful life for tax purposes | 10 years |
| Salvage value after ten years | $ 40,000 |
| Additional annual revenue (all credit sales) | $245,000 |
| Expected contribution | 35 percent |
| Receivables turnover | 7 times |
| Inventory turnover | 5 times |

**Second investment (commercial real estate):**

| | |
|---|---|
| Cost of land and building | $350,000 |
| Appraised value of land | $ 50,000 |
| Building useful life for tax purposes | 30 years |
| Salvage value of building for tax purposes | Zero |
| Expected market value of land and building at end of ten years | $300,000 |

| | |
|---|---|
| Annual rentals | $117,500 |
| Annual maintenance and operating costs (expenditures) | $ 20,000 |

You may assume that invoices on purchases of merchandise are all paid within ten days to take advantage of the two-percent discount terms. The firm is subject to a 40-percent income-tax rate and depreciates new equipment using DDB for tax purposes. The equipment would qualify for a ten-percent investment tax credit. Real estate would be depreciated for tax purposes using 150-percent declining balance. The firm's after-tax cost of capital averages 12 percent.

a) Are either or both investments desirable? Explain.

b) If both investments are desirable and the firm can finance only one, which should it choose and why?

**SP 8.24** Refer to Problem SP 8.23. Answer the same two questions, assuming that all data were as given except:

| | |
|---|---|
| • Expected contribution from new product line | 45 percent |
| • Expected receivables turnover | 8 times |
| • Expected inventory turnover | 7 times |
| • Annual maintenance and operating costs (expenditures) | $30,000 |

## SUGGESTIONS FOR FURTHER READING

Bierman, H., and S. Smidt, *The Capital Budgeting Decision*, Fourth Edition. New York: The Macmillan Company, 1975.

Horngren, C., *Cost Accounting: A Managerial Emphasis*, Fourth Edition. Englewood Cliffs, N.J.: Prentice-Hall, Inc., 1977; Chapters 12 and 13.

Morse, Wayne J., *Cost Accounting: Processing, Evaluating, and Using Cost Data*. Reading, Mass.: Addison-Wesley Publishing Company, 1978; Chapters 16 and 17.

Van Horne, James C., *Fundamentals of Financial Management*, Third Edition. Englewood Cliffs, N.J.: Prentice-Hall, Inc., 1977, Chapters 13 and 14.

Weston, J. Fred, and Eugene F. Brigham, *Essentials of Managerial Finance*, Fourth Edition. Hinsdale, Illinois: The Dryden Press, 1977; Chapter 11.

CHAPTER 8 APPENDIX

# Review of Capital Leases, Lease/Buy Decisions, and Internal Rate of Return

## Accounting For Leased Property

Many firms have recently been engaged in what has been called *"off-balance-sheet financing."* This term has been applied to those cases where firms have elected to acquire the use of capital assets on a long-term lease basis rather than by purchase. Recall from financial accounting that, for accounting purposes, leases are divided into two classifications. Ordinary leases, which cover a period less than the asset's useful life, and which are often cancellable on short notice, are classified as *operating leases*. Accountants treat operating leases on the financial statements like any other executory contract. The lessee discloses no asset since it is not legally owned. Liabilities are recorded only for those amounts earned by the lessor, and owed by the lessee as of the balance sheet date, that have not been paid. Footnote disclosure is required where amounts involved are material, but executory amounts are not entered in the accounts.

All leases are treated as operating leases unless they qualify for treatment as *capital leases*. Capital leases (also called financing or purchase leases) differ from operating leases in that they generally cover the useful life of the asset, are noncancellable, and effectively are a purchase with a 100-percent mortgage.[14] Where a lease qualifies as a capital lease, the transaction is no longer off-balance sheet. Capital leases are treated as nonexecutory purchases.

Initially (upon signing), capital leases are recorded as both an asset and a liability in equal amounts. The asset value is the NPV of all lease payments discounted at the firm's incremental borrowing rate (the rate that would have been charged if the asset had been purchased with a mortgage). The identical total NPV of the lease payments is recorded as a liability and is classified into current and noncurrent portions, in accordance with the lease payment terms.

Determination of that portion of a particular lease payment that represents principal (NPV liability) repayment follows the method of distinguishing principal and interest in repayments under any fully amortized loan. Each year (or payment period) the interest is accrued on the entire unpaid principal (NPV) balance. The difference between this accrued interest and the total payment

---

[14]   GAAP provide specific tests to distinguish capital leases that are beyond the scope of this text.

represents the portion of principal being repaid that will reduce the unpaid balance. Early lease payments will therefore include a higher proportion of interest than later payments when the loan has been reduced.

After acquisition, the asset and liability "portions" of a capital lease are treated separately. The asset amount is amortized following some systematic method (straight-line, years' digits, declining balance, and so forth) over the life of the lease. The individual lease payments mature, accrue current interest (difference between principal repayment portion and full lease payment), and are paid in accordance with the payment schedule of the particular lease.

### The Lease-Vs.-Buy Decision

The lease-vs.-buy decision can represent a special case of investment decision making. Lease versus buy are two mutually exclusive alternatives involving the determination of the least effective cost of implementing a decision. Where the decision to either lease or buy either has previously qualified as an acceptable investment (via capital budgeting) or else is a mandatory investment, it can be assumed for comparison purposes that the **use** of the item is to be acquired, and that the **only choice** is the **method of financing.** In this situation, the cost-of-capital rate would not necessarily be relevant. Instead, the incremental borrowing rate may be used for discounting.[15]

The other difference in lease/buy analysis involves the inclusion of principal and interest repayments as part of the cost under the "buy" alternative. The comparison is assumed as between a capital lease on the one hand and a borrow-and-buy alternative on the other. On the buy side, no outlay is assumed in year zero. Instead, a 100-percent, fully amortized loan is assumed, with payments of principal and interest spreading over the useful life of the asset.

A worksheet of 11 columns is useful for making lease/buy comparisons:

*Column 1:* Years involved in the common time horizon of the alternatives.

*Column 2:* Portion of assumed 100-percent fully amortized mortgage representing principal repayment in each year.

*Column 3:* Portion of assumed 100-percent fully amortized mortgage representing interest payment in each year.

*Column 4:* Net differential operating costs associated **only** with buying (often only maintenance that can be ignored if maintenance is **not** included under lease and would then be the same under both alternatives).

*Column 5:* Tax depreciation deductions for each year.

---

[15] Where the asset acquisition by either lease or purchase has **not** previously been qualified as meeting the cost-of-capital return criterion, or where some differential risk may be reasonably assumed between the two alternatives, then the cost-of-capital rate would be more appropriate.

## Exhibit 8.12

### Worksheet to Accompany Lease-vs.-Buy Decision Problem SP 8.21

| (1) Year | (2) Assumed loan principal repayment | (3) Assumed loan interest repayment | (4) Maintenance cost | (5) Depreciation tax deductions | (6) Tax effects | (7) Cash outflow if owned | (8) After-tax lease cost | (9) Differential costs (7) − (8) | (10) PV factors at 5%* | (11) PV of differential costs |
|---|---|---|---|---|---|---|---|---|---|---|
| 0 | | | | | | | | | | |
| 1 | −$3,200 | −$2,000 | −$800 | $13,200 | +$4,800 | −$1,200 | −$3,710 | +$2,510 | 0.952 | +$2,390 |
| 2 | − 3,360 | − 1,840 | − 800 | 8,844 | + 3,445 | − 2,655 | − 3,710 | + 1,055 | 0.907 | + 957 |
| 3 | − 3,520 | − 1,680 | − 800 | 5,923 | + 2,521 | − 3,479 | − 3,710 | + 231 | 0.864 | + 200 |
| 4 | − 3,680 | − 1,520 | − 800 | 3,971 | + 1,887 | − 4,113 | − 3,710 | + 403 | 0.823 | + 332 |
| 5 | − 3,840 | − 1,360 | − 800 | 2,660 | + 1,446 | − 4,554 | − 3,710 | + 844 | 0.784 | + 662 |
| 6 | − 4,080 | − 1,120 | − 800 | 5,402 | + 2,197 | − 3,803 | − 3,710 | + 93 | 0.746 | + 69 |
| 7 | − 4,280 | − 920 | − 800 | 0 | + 516 | − 5,484 | − 3,710 | − 1,774 | 0.711 | − 1,261 |
| 8 | − 4,480 | − 720 | − 800 | 0 | + 456 | − 5,544 | − 3,710 | − 1,834 | 0.677 | − 1,242 |
| 9 | − 4,680 | − 520 | − 800 | 0 | + 396 | − 5,604 | − 3,710 | − 1,894 | 0.645 | − 1,222 |
| 10 | − 4,880 | − 320 | − 800 | 4,000 | 864 | − 2,864 | − 3,710 | + 846 | 0.614 | + 519 |
| | | | | | | | | | NPV | −$ 722 |

*(Handwritten annotations appear in the margins: "5% 4,000 800" and "4% 2,888 900" beside column (3); "1048" beside the +957 entry in column (11).)*

* Since acquisition already approved and only decision is method of acquisition, incremental borrowing rate is used in place of cost of capital.

*Column 6:*   Tax effects (resulting from costs in Columns 3, 4, and 5, and any tax effect associated with salvage value in the final year).

*Column 7:*   Cash outflow if owned (net of Columns 2, 3, 4, and 6, with possible inclusion of salvage recovery in the final year).

*Column 8:*   After-tax lease cost (lease payments $\times$ $(1 - t)$).

*Column 9:*   Differential cost (Column 7 $-$ Column 8) = benefits (+) or costs (−) associated with owning, as compared to leasing.

*Column 10:*   PV factors at incremental borrowing discount rate.

*Column 11:*   PV of different costs for each year.

*Sum of Column 11:*   NPV of differential costs

As in the case of any differential cost analysis, a negative NPV indicates the alternative selected as the comparison base (leasing, in this illustration) to be more desirable. A complete illustration of a lease-vs.-buy decision is included in this chapter as Problem SP 8.21. Exhibit 8.12 illustrates the worksheet used in the solution of this problem.

## Internal Rate of Return (IRR)

As mentioned in this chapter, the IRR of a particular investment alternative is that discount rate that will exactly equate all after-tax cash flow benefits with after-tax cash flow costs including investments or, in other words, where the NPV will be zero. Recall, from Exhibit 8.3, that using a discount rate of ten percent resulted in an NPV of zero. The investment given in that exhibit can therefore be said to have an IRR of ten percent. The IRR is also known as the time-adjusted rate of return, the discount rate, or the true rate of return.

Note that, under the NPV approach, you start with an assumed discount rate and then determine the residual NPV as some dollar amount positive, negative, or zero. In determining the IRR, you start with an assumed target residual NPV of zero dollars and search for the discount rate that will bring about this result. You are correct if you see that, if you were using the NPV approach and happened to arrive at an NPV of zero, you would have "stumbled upon" the investment's IRR.

Determining an investment's or project's IRR can involve complex and time-consuming calculations, especially where the flows are uneven. Should your calculator be programmed for IRR, you can merely properly enter the cash flows for each year and obtain the answer. Otherwise, you will probably require several passes or iterations using the tables. You would first arbitrarily choose an interest (discount) rate that you thought might be close, and then determine the investment's NPV using that rate.

If your NPV is zero, you guessed perfectly and have your answer. If your NPV is greater than zero, your assumed rate was too low. Remember, from the NPV approach, that an excess positive NPV amount indicates that the investment return is more than the discount rate (i.e., has a higher internal rate of return). Conversely, a negative NPV result would indicate that the initial rate was too high. If your first NPV is not zero, it would then be necessary to try again with a more appropriate rate until you have the exact rate or can estimate it as between two rates available in your tables.[16]

Where IRR is used as an instrument of capital rationing, projects with IRR's below the firm's cost of capital are rejected. Those above may then be ranked by their IRR's for further capital rationing selection.

In addition to involving time-consuming and complex calculations, the IRR approach has another disadvantage. As mentioned in the chapter, it is possible that an investment may have an IRR above the firm's cost-of-capital rate and still have an NPV discounted at the cost-of-capital rate that is slightly negative. This paradox results from the simple fact that each method assumes **reinvestment** of cash generated during the life of the investment at the discount rate. Where the internal rate of return (discount rate) is higher than the cost-of-capital rate, reinvestment benefits (in the form of compound interest earned) are assumed that may not be obtainable. For this reason, wherever NPV and IRR give different signals, the NPV conclusion should be accepted.

---

[16] Logarithms can be used, together with the formula for IRR, to precisely determine the internal rate of return. As the result is still an approximation, and is to be used only as a guideline, this precision will not be introduced in this text.

# 9

## CASH PLANNING– THE CASH BUDGET

## CHAPTER PREVIEW

The purpose of this chapter is to provide you with information about cash management or cash budgeting and the significance of this activity for a business. In this chapter you can learn:

- The objective or purpose of cash budgeting and its vital importance to all firms;
- How all expected cash inflows and outflows may be pinpointed either from formal budgets or from other sources for firms not having a formal budgeting system;
- How a firm may arrange in advance to maintain solvency and to put any excess cash to work;
- Why cash management must be viewed as a continuous rather than a periodic process.

With this knowledge you will be in a position both to appreciate the significance of cash management and to prepare cash budgets for your firm. You will have completed your understanding of all of the component elements of the budgeting process, and you will be in a position to learn about the final synthesis of all budgeting activity, known as the master budget, which will be covered in the following chapter.

# REVIEW OF PREVIOUS BUDGETING STEPS

Preparing the preliminary cash budget is Step 11 in the overall budgeting process as described for a manufacturer. Nonmanufacturers have fewer inputs to their operating expenditure budgets, and therefore fewer steps. Exhibit 9.1 summarizes the steps leading up to the preparation of a cash budget for different types of firms.

Recall that in Chapter 3 you were introduced to the preparation of the sales budget. For both merchandisers and manufacturers, the sales budget provides detailed information as to expected demand for products that will be required in merchandise or finished goods inventory. For all firms the sales budget provides the basis for planning selling and marketing expenditures and for anticipating cash to be received from customers.

In Chapter 4 you had the opportunity to learn about inventory planning and control. Inventory budgets were shown to indicate the level of investment required in this asset; and resulting purchases budgets were shown to provide the basis for planning cash outflows to suppliers. Chapter 5 covered the preparation of operating expenditure budgets that provide data for forecasting all other operating cash outflows expected during the forthcoming year.

Chapters 6, 7, and 8 dealt with various aspects of business decisions and with the preparation of the capital budget. The capital budget essentially schedules all anticipated acquisitions and dispositions of fixed capacity assets that are planned during the forthcoming year. It provides the basis for planning both expected cash needs to pay for acquisitions and also expected cash receipts from the sale of capacity assets. You may have skipped one or more of the last three chapters and be planning to return to them later. You can proceed with this chapter and the balance of the budgeting process with no

**Exhibit 9.1**

**Budgeting Steps Leading to Preparation of the Preliminary Cash Budget**

|  | Service firms | Merchandisers | Manufacturers |
|---|---|---|---|
| Sales budget | 1 | 1 | 1 |
| Finished goods inventory budget |  | 2 | 2 |
| Production schedule |  |  | 3 |
| Raw materials inventory budget |  |  | 4 |
| Purchases budget |  | 3 | 5 |
| Direct labor budget |  |  | 6 |
| Manufacturing overhead budget |  |  | 7 |
| GSA budget | 2 | 4 | 8 |
| Operating expenditure budget | 3 | 5 | 9 |
| Capital budget | 4 | 6 | 10 |
| Preliminary cash budget | 5 | 7 | 11 |

difficulty. You need only assume at this point that, in addition to the sales, inventory, purchases, and operating expenditure budgets, management has prepared a schedule of anticipated acquisitions and dispositions of fixed capacity assets.

So that the elements of cash budgeting are not too abstract and possibly confusing, you are now asked to return to the Tripper Company.

## WILL WE HAVE ENOUGH CASH IN JANUARY TO MEET THE PAYROLL?

As the new owner and president of the Tripper Company during the late fall of 19X1, you find that you are anxiously awaiting completion of the 19X2 budgeting process. Initially your real interest was only in the projection of next year's profits. However, you have just had luncheon with the president of your firm's bank, and now you are concerned. Your banker reminded (advised) you that Tripper was a seasonal business, and that it had usually required a short-term bank loan for the first six months of each year. He stated that he wished to know within a week whether you would need a loan for 19X2, and, if so, for how much.

You realize that the company customarily has heavy expenditures for purchasing and production in the early months of each calendar year. You also know that the bulk of sales come at mid-year, with collections of accounts receivable lagging sales by over a month. However, you had not previously connected these facts with the firm's cash position.

In response to your request, your controller supplies you with a memo abstracting data from the 19X1 cash budget. He explains that one year ago a preliminary cash forecast by month for 19X1 revealed the anticipated balances given in Exhibit 9.2. Note, in this exhibit, that preliminary projections of anticipated cash receipts and disbursements (not illustrated at this point) indicated cash shortages during the first six months of 19X1. Based upon the preliminary 19X1 projections, a $90,000 short-term bank loan had been arranged in late 19X0 to cover all cash needs and to maintain approximately $10,000 of cash on hand for unforeseen circumstances.

### Exhibit 9.2

**End-of-Month Cash Balances**
**before Short-Term Financing and Investments**
**(taken from 19X1 Preliminary Cash Budget)**

| | | | |
|---|---|---|---|
| January | $(16,065) | July | $ 21,520 |
| February | (57,715) | August | 83,800 |
| March | (78,540) | September | 61,410 |
| April | (77,820) | October | 89,635 |
| May | (71,960) | November | 101,785 |
| June | (55,040) | December | 84,860 |

*Note.* Amounts in parentheses indicate negative balances or shortages.

The controller explains that, since all necessary prior budgeting steps for 19X2 have been completed, he is now ready to prepare the new cash budget. He suggests that you work with him on budgeting the first quarter of 19X2 so that you can become familiar with this vital part of the budgeting process.

## IMPORTANCE OF CASH MANAGEMENT

Cash management or cash budgeting is probably the most essential part of a firm's planning and control process. More than half of all businesses that fail do so because of inadequate or nonexistent cash and financial management. Have you ever run out of cash and been unable to eat for a day or two, or can you at least imagine being in such a position? Or have you ever been forced to pass up an opportunity because you didn't have adequate cash on hand or adequate time to arrange for a loan?

If you can see the desirability of cash planning for yourself, you may be able to understand its absolute necessity for a business. If a business is to survive in the long run, it must be able to take advantage of new profit opportunities to offset unforeseen losses and to replace existing opportunities that expire. Of even greater significance is the immediate survival of a firm. Immediate survival is *solvency*, the ability to pay bills when due. A firm may have all kinds of other assets and great earnings, but if it does not have cash to pay employees on payday—to meet the payroll—it is in big trouble and may fail. If all assets are invested in receivables, inventory, and fixed capacity assets, and all earnings somehow end up in more of these assets, the firm will be insolvent. Vendors may occasionally extend payment due dates to accommodate a firm with a temporary cash shortage. Even the government, with accompanying high interest charges, may allow a firm to delay payment of income and property taxes. But employees do not have the personal resources to support delayed paychecks. They have to eat and pay their rent. Employees must be paid in cash on time, or they will leave and work where their paychecks are dependable.

Unless an individual can afford large excess casn reserves, he or she cannot blindly pay out cash and indiscriminately purchase on account without running into trouble. A business is no different. It cannot afford large reserves of excess cash. Because of its cost of capital and the necessity of earning satisfactory profits on the resources (assets) invested, a business cannot afford to have significant amounts of idle cash. The opportunity cost of idle cash can be too great.

## OVERVIEW OF CASH BUDGETING PROCESS

The objective of cash budgeting is to plan all cash receipts and disbursements with reasonable accuracy and detail. Then any necessary arrangements may be made in advance to ensure an adequate supply of cash on hand at all times. A secondary objective is to identify amounts of excess cash so that they may be invested, used to reduce debt, or distributed to owners.

The cash budgeting process may be thought of as having six distinct phases:

*Phase 1:*  Planning of cash from operations

*Phase 2:*  Incorporating other planned cash flows for capital, financial, and tax budgeting activities

*Phase 3:*  Making provisions for adequate cash

*Phase 4:*  Providing for use of excess cash

*Phase 5:*  Preparing the final cash budget

*Phase 6:*  Continuously revising and updating the cash budget as necessary throughout the year.

Information for preparing cash budgets can come from other budgets described in earlier chapters as parts of an overall budgeting and control system. Where a firm does not have a formal budgeting system, cash flows may still be estimated from financial statements. This process will also be briefly described at the end of this chapter. For a firm with a complete budgeting system, the sources of information for planning cash from operations are indicated in Fig. 9.1.

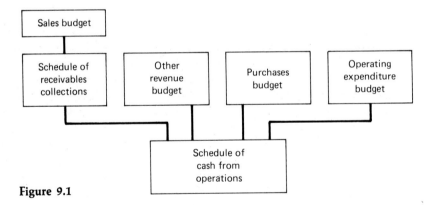

**Figure 9.1**

A format for the schedule of cash from operations is shown below:

Cash inflows from operations:

From sales
From other revenue

Total

Cash outflows for operations:

For purchases
For other operations

Total

Net cash inflow from operations

Cash inflows from operations come from cash sales, collections of accounts receivable for sales on account, and from other nonsales revenue. This information is obtained from the sales and the other revenue budgets (Chapter 3). Cash outflows for operations may be determined from the purchases budget (Chapter 4) and from the operating expenditure budget. Remember, from Chapter 5, that the operating expenditure budget is a composite of all the direct labor, manufacturing overhead, and GSA budgets for the various levels of responsibility within the firm. A preliminary cash budget can be prepared in Phase 2 by combining information from the schedule of cash from operations with information from the capital budget (Chapter 8) and from the tax and financial budgets. (See Fig. 9.2.)

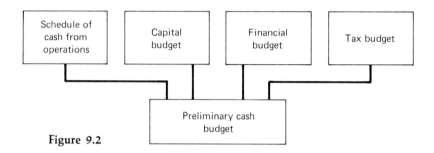

**Figure 9.2**

The financial budget contains information on plans for regular distributions to investors (interest and dividends), plans for acquisition of new capital (new long-term debt and/or new stock), and any plans for debt repayment or retirement. The tax budget contains estimates of quarterly income-tax payments due within the forthcoming year. Both the financial budget and the tax budget will be covered more explicitly in Chapter 10.

The *preliminary cash budget* contains the forecasted cash balance (positive or negative) by month for the forthcoming year. This forecasted balance for each month is obtained by starting with the anticipated opening balance (from the current year's updated cash budget or the preceding month's budgeted ending balance), and adjusting for projected cash flows related to operations, capital investments, financing activities, and taxes. Exhibit 9.3 illustrates a cash budget. Note that the preliminary balance for the first month indicates a negative $51,000, which is then covered by a short-term loan.

Phase 3 involves making arrangements for the provision of adequate cash. Note, on Exhibit 9.3, a requirement for $10,000 as a minimum cash balance. The best of cash budgets are still only estimates. Unanticipated expenses or delayed collections could result in a cash shortage if a firm budgeted for a zero cash balance. Recall the concept and purpose of a safety stock for inventory, discussed in Chapter 4. A minimum cash balance is a safety stock of cash. In the first months, the preliminary budget (Exhibit 9.3) indicated the need for $51,000 of cash. A loan of $61,000 is planned, and the final budget shows an adequate $10,000 minimum balance. In the second month the situation reverses. The preliminary balance indicates $120,000 above minimum. The

**Exhibit 9.3**

ILLUSTRATION OF CASH BUDGET—PRELIMINARY AND FINAL

| | First month | Second month |
|---|---|---|
| Net cash inflow from operations | $(50,000) | $ 80,000 |
| Capital investment flows: | | |
|   Outflows for acquisitions | (20,000) | 0 |
|   Inflows from dispositions | 5,000 | 0 |
| Financial activity flows: | | |
|   Routine outflows to investors: | | |
|     Interest payments | (2,000) | 0 |
|     Dividend payments | (4,000) | 0 |
|   Proceeds (inflows) from new financing: | | |
|     Additional long-term debt | 0 | 20,000 |
|     Additional stock | 0 | 30,000 |
|   Outflows for long-term debt retirement | 0 | (10,000) |
| Income tax payments | (10,000) | 0 |
| Beginning cash balance | 30,000 | 10,000 |
| Balance before short-term financing | $(51,000) | $130,000 |
| Plus:  Short-term loans | 61,000 | 0 |
| Less:  Short-term loan repayments and interest | 0 | 61,305 |
| Less:  Invested in marketable securities | 0 | 55,000 |
| Plus:  Proceeds including interest from marketable securities | 0 | |
| Budgeted cash balance | $ 10,000 | $ 13,695 |
| Desired minimum balance | $ 10,000 | $ 10,000 |

loan can be, and is, repaid, leaving a balance of $68,695 after allowing for the interest payments.

The fourth and final phase involves investing excess cash to earn interest. The budget indicates that $55,000 (assuming minimum $5,000 increments) can be invested in marketable securities for at least one month. Good cash management involves both ensuring adequate cash and also arranging for temporarily idle funds to earn interest. In a large corporation with perhaps $555,000,000 instead of only $55,000 of excess, one month's interest at a ten-percent annual interest rate would bring in over $458,000!

## BUDGETING THE FIRST QUARTER

Returning to the Tripper example, to budget the first quarter of 19X2 involves first preparing the *schedule of cash from operations*. In turn, the first step in this process involves preparation of the *schedule of receivables collections* from the 19X2 sales budget (Exhibit 3.8 in Chapter 3), which is repeated on page 367 as Exhibit 9.4.

**Exhibit 9.4**

**TRIPPER WATER SKI MANUFACTURING COMPANY**

## Sales Budget for the Year 19X2

| Percent | | Economy skis Units | Economy skis Dollars | Deluxe skis Units | Deluxe skis Dollars | Tow ropes Units | Tow ropes Dollars | Total Dollars |
|---|---|---|---|---|---|---|---|---|
| 30 | Jan. | 750 | $ 37,500 | 400 | $ 32,000 | 325 | $ 3,250 | $ 72,750 |
| 30 | Feb. | 750 | 37,500 | 400 | 32,000 | 325 | 3,250 | 72,750 |
| 40 | Mar. | 1,000 | 50,000 | 550 | 44,000 | 450 | 4,500 | 98,500 |
| 100 | 1st qtr. | 2,500 | $125,000 | 1,350 | $108,000 | 1,100 | $11,000 | $ 244,000 |
| 25 | Apr. | 1,250 | $ 62,500 | 750 | $ 60,000 | 550 | $ 5,500 | $ 128,000 |
| 35 | May | 1,750 | 87,500 | 1,050 | 84,000 | 770 | 7,700 | 179,200 |
| 40 | Jun. | 2,000 | 100,000 | 1,200 | 96,000 | 880 | 8,800 | 204,800 |
| 100 | 2nd qtr. | 5,000 | $250,000 | 3,000 | $240,000 | 2,200 | $22,000 | $ 512,000 |
| 50 | Jul. | 2,000 | $100,000 | 1,000 | $ 80,000 | 700 | 7,000 | $ 187,000 |
| 30 | Aug. | 1,200 | 60,000 | 600 | 48,000 | 600 | 6,000 | 114,000 |
| 20 | Sep. | 800 | 40,000 | 400 | 32,000 | 400 | 4,000 | 76,000 |
| 100 | 3rd qtr. | 4,000 | $200,000 | 2,000 | $160,000 | 1,700 | $17,000 | $ 377,000 |
| 50 | Oct. | 650 | $ 32,500 | 350 | $ 28,000 | 400 | $ 4,000 | $ 64,500 |
| 30 | Nov. | 400 | 20,000 | 200 | 16,000 | 350 | 3,500 | 39,500 |
| 20 | Dec. | 250 | 12,500 | 150 | 12,000 | 250 | 2,500 | 27,000 |
| 100 | 4th qtr. | 1,300 | $ 65,000 | 700 | $ 56,000 | 1,000 | $10,000 | $ 131,000 |
| | Total Year | 12,800 | $640,000 | 7,050 | $564,000 | 6,000 | $60,000 | $1,264,000 |

## Schedule of Receivables Collections

The sales budget discloses total expected sales, both cash and on account, for each month. It reports revenue expected to be earned from completed transactions for inclusion as a current asset (cash or accounts receivable) on the firm's balance sheet. This information must be converted to expected cash inflows from cash sales and from collections of current and prior month's receivables. To make this conversion you will need to know, based on the firm's unique experience, what proportion of each month's expected sales will be collected in cash in the current and subsequent months.

Tripper's collection pattern is as follows:

30%   during current month (includes both cash sales and accounts paid within the month),
40%   during first month following sale,
28%   during second month following sale,
2%    uncollectable accounts charged off to bad debt expense during third month following sale (no cash flow involved).

Suppose sales were as follows for a given period:

| Month | Sales |
|-------|-------|
| 1 | $1,000 |
| 2 | 2,000 |
| 3 | 3,000 |
| 4 | 4,000 |
| 5 | 5,000 |

Following the Tripper collection pattern, what would you project as cash inflows in months 3, 4, and 5? You should work out your solution on a separate piece of paper, before proceeding.

You are correct if you budgeted cash inflows from sales for months 3, 4, and 5 as $1,980, $2,960, and $3,940, respectively:

|  | Month 3 | Month 4 | Month 5 |
|--|---------|---------|---------|
| Budgeted sales | $3,000 | $4,000 | $5,000 |
| 30% current month | 900 | 1,200 | 1,500 |
| 40% prior month | 800 | 1,200 | 1,600 |
| 28% second prior month | 280 | 560 | 840 |
| Cash collections | $1,980 | $2,960 | $3,940 |

To familiarize yourself with the process, you should now practice by budgeting, on a separate sheet of paper, Tripper's receivable collections for the first quarter of 19X2. Relevant sales data from the current and future budget are as follows:

| Month | Budgeted sales |
|---|---|
| November, 19X1 | $37,500 |
| December, 19X1 | 25,000 |
| January, 19X2 | 72,750 |
| February, 19X2 | 72,750 |
| March, 19X2 | 98,500 |

You adequately understand the process of budgeting receivables collections if you determined expected cash inflows for the first quarter of 19X2 to be:

| | |
|---|---|
| January | $ 42,325 |
| February | 57,925 |
| March | 79,020 |
| Total | $179,270 |

Exhibit 9.5 is the completed schedule of collections for the entire year. Note the very real seasonality of Tripper's cash inflows. They are almost distributed normally (a bell curve) with the peak in July. If Tripper's pattern of cash requirements is not similarly distributed over the same months, then cash problems may arise.

For firms with other revenues such as rents, royalties, interest, dividends, and so forth, these would also have to be budgeted to complete the projection of cash inflows from all operations sources. Other revenue has been eliminated from the Tripper example for simplification.

## Schedule of Cash from Operations

The second and more involved portion of the schedule of cash from operations involves budgeted cash outflows. Cash outflows for operations are usually budgeted in at least two separate parts: payments for purchases of inventory and disbursement for all other operations (except interest). The distinction is convenient for several reasons. For a merchandiser, it parallels the distinction between product and period costs. For most firms, purchases are separately budgeted (Chapter 4). And finally, in a cash emergency a firm may wish to evaluate savings (delayed outflows) possible from postponing acquisitions or from stretching out payments to suppliers. Separate disclosure of purchase outflows provides a ready reference for such an evaluation.

Tripper's 19X2 purchases budget has been completed and was included as Exhibit 4.13 in Chapter 4. It appears again as Exhibit 9.6. Converting budgeted purchases to budgeted cash outflows for purchases is very similar to determining receivables collections. In both cases the cash flow lags the accrual (receivable or payable). Most firms take advantage of credit offered by suppliers. You may assume that Tripper's suppliers offer 30-day terms and no cash discount, and, therefore, that Tripper pays in full for all purchases in

**Exhibit 9.5**

TRIPPER WATER SKI MANUFACTURING COMPANY

**19X2 Schedule of Receivables Collections**

| | Jan | Feb | Mar | Apr | May | Jun | Jul | Aug | Sep | Oct | Nov | Dec |
|---|---|---|---|---|---|---|---|---|---|---|---|---|
| Budgeted sales | $72,750 | $72,750 | $98,500 | $128,000 | $179,200 | $204,800 | $187,000 | $114,000 | $ 76,000 | $64,500 | $39,500 | $27,000 |
| Cash collected: | | | | | | | | | | | | |
| 30% Current month | 21,825 | 21,825 | 29,550 | 38,400 | 53,760 | 61,440 | 56,100 | 34,200 | 22,800 | 19,350 | 11,850 | 8,100 |
| 40% Prior month | 10,000 | 29,100 | 29,100 | 39,400 | 51,200 | 71,680 | 81,920 | 74,800 | 45,600 | 30,400 | 25,800 | 15,800 |
| 28% Second prior month | 10,500 | 7,000 | 20,370 | 20,300 | 27,580 | 35,840 | 50,176 | 57,344 | 52,360 | 31,920 | 21,280 | 18,060 |
| Total cash collections | $42,325 | $57,925 | $79,020 | $ 98,100 | $132,540 | $168,960 | $188,196 | $166,344 | $120,760 | $81,670 | $58,930 | $41,960 |

Assumes cash collection pattern:

30% during month of sale (cash sales plus collections within month of sale).
40% during first month following sale.
28% during second month following sale.
2% uncollectable accounts written off during third month following sale.

**Exhibit 9.6**

## TRIPPER WATER SKI MANUFACTURING COMPANY

### Purchases Budget for the Year 19X2

| | Wood | | Resin and cloth | | Hardware sets | | Tow ropes | | Total dollars |
|-----|------|------|------|------|------|------|------|------|------|
| Jan | 0 | | 1,360 | $ 8,432 | 3,700 | $ 9,250 | 0 | 0 | $ 17,682 |
| Feb | 1,800 | $ 5,400 | 0 | 0 | 0 | 0 | 0 | 0 | 5,400 |
| Mar | 2,100 | 6,300 | 0 | 0 | 3,800 | 9,500 | 1,220 | $ 6,100 | 21,900 |
| Apr | 0 | | 1,640 | 10,168 | 0 | 0 | 0 | 0 | 10,168 |
| May | 2,100 | 6,300 | 1,700 | 10,540 | 3,800 | 9,500 | 880 | 4,400 | 30,740 |
| Jun | 2,100 | 6,300 | 0 | 0 | 3,000 | 7,500 | 1,300 | 6,500 | 20,300 |
| Jul | 2,100 | 6,300 | 1,700 | 10,540 | 3,000 | 7,500 | 0 | 0 | 24,340 |
| Aug | 0 | | 0 | 0 | 0 | 0 | 0 | 0 | 4,000 |
| Sep | 0 | | 0 | 0 | 0 | 0 | 800 | 4,000 | 4,000 |
| Oct | 2,100 | 6,300 | 0 | 0 | 3,000 | 7,500 | 960 | 4,800 | 18,600 |
| Nov | 0 | | 0 | 0 | 0 | 0 | 0 | 0 | 0 |
| Dec | 0 | | 0 | 0 | 0 | 0 | 0 | 0 | 0 |
| Total | 12,300 | $36,900 | 6,400 | $39,680 | 20,300 | $50,750 | 5,160 | $25,800 | $153,130 |

the month following acquisition. Where cash discounts are taken, determining expected cash outflows may be more involved. Planning for cash discounts will be discussed later in this chapter.

Based on the 19X2 purchases budget, and assuming no purchases were made in December of 19X1, you should be able easily to project cash outflows for purchases during the first quarter of 19X2 as:

| | |
|---|---|
| January | $ zero |
| February | 17,682 |
| March | 5,400 |
| Total | $23,082 |

Note that, in this chapter, the amounts used in the Tripper cash budget are **not** rounded except to even dollars. Detailed amounts are given so that you may track or reconcile any computation or summarization the source of which may not be clear.

Cash outflows for operations (other than purchases and interest) are determined from the budget for operating expenditures. Interest is excluded, even if shown in the firm's operations budget, since it is separately included in a later phase of the cash budgeting process. Tripper's operating budget for 19X2 is shown as Exhibit 9.7. It represents a composite of Tripper's direct labor, manufacturing overhead, and GSA budgets (included in Chapter 5 as Exhibits 5.8, 5.9, and 5.10). Note that, for convenience, all expenses for wages and salaries (direct labor, indirect labor, factory supervision, and GSA wages and salaries) are combined into a single amount designated as **payroll.** Also, for simplification, all payroll taxes and fringe benefits are ignored in this example.

Converting the operating expenditure budget to a cash flow basis is a bit more involved than converting sales or purchases. The timing of payments for various operating expenses is not always uniform. For Tripper you may assume:

1. All payroll is on a semimonthly basis. Therefore, 50 percent of each month's accrued payroll expense is paid out in that month, and the other half in the month following.

2. Property taxes and insurance are paid in the month indicated.

3. All other operating expenses (excluding interest) are paid in the month following accrual.

4. $24,220 of 12/31/X1 liabilities—accounts payable ($3,000) and wages and salaries payable ($21,220)—are to be paid in January, 19X2.

To achieve an adequate understanding of cash budgeting, it is necessary that you practice some of the more involved steps where you have available self-checking solutions and explanations. On a separate sheet of paper, before proceeding to the next paragraph, you should budget cash outflows for operations (other than purchasing) for the first quarter of 19X2. You should also

**Exhibit 9.7**

**TRIPPER WATER SKI MANUFACTURING COMPANY**

**19X2 Operating Expenditure Budget[a]**

| | Jan | Feb | Mar | Apr | May | Jun | Jul | Aug | Sep | Oct | Nov | Dec | Total |
|---|---|---|---|---|---|---|---|---|---|---|---|---|---|
| Purchases | $17,682 | $ 5,400 | $21,900 | $10,168 | $30,740 | $20,300 | $24,340 | $ 4,000 | 0 | $18,600 | 0 | 0 | $ 153,130 |
| Payroll[b] | 67,850 | 68,180 | 68,180 | 67,850 | 93,680 | 68,180 | 93,680 | 42,350 | $42,350 | 68,180 | $42,350 | $42,350 | 765,180 |
| Supplies | 1,800 | 2,120 | 2,120 | 1,800 | 3,480 | 2,120 | 3,480 | 440 | 440 | 2,120 | 440 | 440 | 20,800 |
| Utilities | 1,620 | 1,860 | 1,860 | 1,620 | 2,880 | 1,860 | 2,880 | 600 | 600 | 1,860 | 600 | 600 | 18,840 |
| Distribution and marketing | 1,902 | 1,902 | 2,108 | 2,344 | 2,756 | 2,958 | 2,815 | 2,232 | 1,928 | 1,835 | 1,635 | 1,535 | 25,950 |
| Miscellaneous | 340 | 340 | 340 | 340 | 340 | 340 | 340 | 340 | 340 | 340 | 340 | 340 | 4,080 |
| Interest | 6,960 | | | | | | 6,960 | | | | | | 13,920 |
| Insurance | 16,960 | | | | | | | | | | | | 16,960 |
| Property taxes | 24,000 | | | | | | | | | | | | 24,000 |
| Total | $139,114 | $79,802 | $96,508 | $84,122 | $133,876 | $95,758 | $134,495 | $49,962 | $45,658 | $92,935 | $45,365 | $45,265 | $1,042,860 |

Notes. a Combines budgeted expenditures from the following budgets:
- Purchases Budget
- Direct Labor Budget
- Manufacturing Overhead Budget
- GSA Budget

b Combines all budgeted expenditures for wages and salaries including:
- Direct Labor (Direct Labor Budget)
- Indirect Labor (Manufacturing Overhead Budget)
- Supervision (Manufacturing Overhead Budget)
- Wages and Salaries (GSA Budget)

complete the cash-from-operations schedule by determining net cash inflow from operations for each month and in total for the quarter. Net cash inflow is simply total cash inflows (sales and other revenues) minus total cash outflows (purchases and other operations). The amount for any month may be positive, indicating a cash contribution, or negative, indicating a drain on available cash.

Did you determine net cash flow from operations for the quarter as a net outflow (negative inflow) of $90,996? Exhibit 9.8 presents the complete schedule of expected cash from operations for 19X2. Note that Tripper's seasonality, the necessity of maintaining certain fixed expenditures throughout the year, and the necessity to invest in inventory in advance of sale and collection, all combine to create a nonuniform flow. Net negative cash flows occur in January, February, March, November, and December. Without additional cash, Tripper will be unable to meet payrolls starting in January, 19X2.

## COMPLETING THE PRELIMINARY CASH BUDGET

In addition to operations, a firm has other activities involving cash flows, both routine and nonroutine. They are all related to financing the business; to long-term investments by the firm in noncurrent assets; or to distributions of EBIT[1] to governments in taxes, to creditors in interest, or to owners in dividends. From Tripper's capital budget (Exhibit 8.9 in Chapter 8) and from its financial budget (to be covered in Chapter 10) you have the following expected cash flows other than from operations:

| | | |
|---|---|---|
| January | $17,000 | Payment for new truck |
| | 6,960 | Semiannual interest payment on long-term debt |
| | 11,000 | Fourth quarter 19X1 income taxes |
| March | 25,000 | Dividend payment |
| April | 10,000 | First quarter 19X2 income taxes |
| July | 19,800 | Net outflow from disposition of old equipment and acquisition of new[2] |
| | 6,960 | Semiannual interest payment on long-term debt |
| | 10,000 | Second quarter 19X2 income taxes |
| September | 25,000 | Dividend payment |
| October | 10,000 | Third quarter 19X2 income taxes |

---

[1]   EBIT is a common financial abbreviation for earnings before interest and taxes.

[2]   For simplicity, in this example it has been assumed that the tax effects of these transactions are immediate and are incorporated in the net flows rather than shown separately.

**Exhibit 9.8**

## TRIPPER WATER SKI MANUFACTURING COMPANY

### Schedule of Cash from Operations for the Year 19X2

| | Jan | Feb | Mar | Apr | May | Jun | Total year |
|---|---|---|---|---|---|---|---|
| Cash inflows from operations: | | | | | | | |
| From sales | $ 42,325 | $ 57,925 | $ 79,020 | $98,100 | $132,540 | $168,960 | $1,236,730 |
| From other revenues | 0 | 0 | 0 | 0 | 0 | 0 | 0 |
| Total | $ 42,325 | $ 57,925 | $ 79,020 | $98,100 | $132,540 | $168,960 | $1,236,730 |
| Cash outflows for operations: | | | | | | | |
| For purchases[a] | $ 0 | $ 17,682 | $ 5,400 | $21,900 | $ 10,168 | $ 30,740 | $ 153,130 |
| For other operations[b] | 99,105[c] | 73,677 | 74,402 | 74,443 | 86,869 | 90,386 | 875,940 |
| Total | $ 99,105 | $ 91,359 | $ 79,802 | $96,343 | $ 97,037 | $121,126 | $1,029,070 |
| Net cash inflow from operations | (56,780) | (33,434) | (782) | 1,757 | 35,503 | 47,834 | 207,660 |

| | Jul | Aug | Sep | Oct | Nov | Dec |
|---|---|---|---|---|---|---|
| Cash inflows from operations | | | | | | |
| From sales | $188,196 | $166,344 | $120,760 | $81,670 | $ 58,930 | $ 41,960 |
| From other revenues | 0 | 0 | 0 | 0 | 0 | 0 |
| Total | $188,196 | $166,344 | $120,760 | $81,670 | $ 58,930 | $ 41,960 |
| Cash outflows for operations: | | | | | | |
| For purchases[a] | $ 20,300 | $ 24,340 | $ 4,000 | 0 | $ 18,600 | 0 |
| For other operations[b] | 88,208 | 77,530 | 45,962 | 58,573 | 61,420 | 45,365 |
| Total | $108,508 | $101,870 | $ 49,962 | $58,573 | $ 80,020 | $ 45,365 |
| Net cash inflow from operations | 79,688 | 64,474 | 70,798 | 23,097 | (21,090) | (3,405) |

Notes. [a] Assumes no purchases in December, 19X1, and payment the month following.
[b] Excludes interest and income tax payments and assumes other payments:
- Payroll paid 50% current month and 50% month following.
- Insurance and property tax in month designated.
- All other expenses in month following.
[c] Includes $24,220 of 12/31/X1 accounts and wages payable.

Assuming a 1/1/X2 cash balance of $85,690, projected cash from operations as scheduled in Exhibit 9.8, and using the above data, determine preliminary forecasted cash balances for the end of the first three months of 19X2.

Exhibit 9.9 is a preliminary cash budget for the entire year of 19X2. It indicates that action must be taken during the first five months to avoid insolvency.

Before moving to various alternatives for arranging adequate cash, you should remember that other possible cash flows (nonoperational) may be included in a preliminary cash budget. In the Tripper example, only capital asset acquisition and disposition, interest, dividends, and taxes were illustrated. In addition to these items, a firm might also have included in its current financial budget plans for the retirement of long-term debt and/or an inflow of capital from the sale of new bonds or stock. When any of these events is anticipated, the related cash flow would have to be incorporated in the preliminary cash budget.

## MAKING PROVISIONS FOR ADEQUATE CASH

Returning to Tripper, as president and owner you (or your controller) need to make immediate arrangements for adequate cash for the first six months of 19X2. As mentioned above, adequate cash means more than some small positive amount. A firm will almost inevitably have unforeseen requirements during the year. Some payments may have to be made earlier than anticipated, and sales or receivables collections could also be slower than expected. For these reasons, Tripper desires a safety stock, or a minimum balance, of cash of $10,000.

Including the allowance for a $10,000 minimum cash balance, Exhibit 9.9 indicates that Tripper will face a cash shortage as high as $84,000 (rounded) by April of 19X2. The shortage will not be over until June. There are several **internal** alternatives for relieving a cash shortage that should be considered first. Can you guess them?

### Internal Sources

In order of descending feasibility, the internal alternatives for consideration usually include:

1. delay planned discretionary outflows such as acquisitions, or even possible dividend payments,
2. defer payments to suppliers,
3. accelerate collections of receivables, and
4. sell noncash assets.

The last two options should always be considered. However, they are rarely sensible unless there are no other feasible alternatives. Usually all noncash assets other than inventory are needed in the business. An inventory reduction

**Exhibit 9.9**

## TRIPPER WATER SKI MANUFACTURING COMPANY

**Preliminary Cash Budget for the Year 19X2**

| | Jan | Feb | Mar | Apr | May | Jun | Jul | Aug | Sep | Oct | Nov | Dec |
|---|---|---|---|---|---|---|---|---|---|---|---|---|
| Net cash inflow from operations | $(56,780) | $(33,434) | $ (782) | $ 1,757 | $ 35,503 | $47,834 | $79,688 | $ 64,474 | $ 70,798 | $ 23,097 | $ (21,090) | $ (3,405) |
| Capital investments | (17,000) | | | | | | (19,800) | | | | | |
| Interest | (6,960) | | | | | | (6,960) | | | | | |
| Dividends | | | (25,000) | | | | | | (25,000) | | | |
| Income taxes | (11,000) | | | (10,000) | | | (10,000) | | | (10,000) | | |
| Beginning cash balance | 85,690 | (6,050) | (39,484) | (65,266) | (73,509) | (38,006) | 9,828 | 52,756 | 117,230 | 163,028 | 176,125 | 155,025 |
| Budgeted ending cash balance | $ (6,050) | $(39,484) | $(65,266) | $(73,509) | $(38,006) | $ 9,828 | $52,756 | $117,230 | $163,028 | $176,125 | $155,035 | $151,630 |

can be accomplished through the first alternative. Also, reasonable efforts to ensure prompt collection of receivables should already be taking place; to accelerate collections further often proves more costly than other alternatives.

The first two options are usually more promising. The second draws down the firm's limited balance of supplier goodwill, and can only be used infrequently for very short periods. Established suppliers may be willing to forego immediate payment but only temporarily, and not if delayed payment were to become habitual. Therefore, the first alternative, delaying planned outflows, since it does not involve outsiders, may be the simplest. Refer to Exhibit 9.9. Can you identify those planned discretionary flows that could be subject to delay?

Interest payments and income tax payments are not discretionary. Dividends, while discretionary by definition, may not really be so for large corporations with many stockholders who count on regularly scheduled dividend payments. For such firms, to delay dividends could cause not only massive inconvenience but also significant loss in the market value of the firm's stock (if the move is interpreted as signaling adverse developments).

In the Tripper example, with few stockholders, perhaps the stockholders (principally yourself) could accept delayed dividends at less personal cost than the cost to the firm of borrowing funds. For illustrative purposes, assume that the first dividend payment can be rescheduled to July.

In many firms, the only truly discretionary outflows involve planned acquisitions. However, since acquisitions are rarely planned in advance of need, delay may be undesirable and costly. Postponements for very short periods may cause minimum disruption and should be investigated. In Tripper's case the only postponement that would help cash flow would be to delay the truck acquisition. The truck is needed immediately, and even a two- or three-month delay would provide relatively little cash benefit.

By first investigating internal sources, you have managed to reduce the size of the problem. The revised anticipated cash balances for the first six months are given below. Note that the delay of the first dividend payment until July will have no effect on the forecasted balances for the second six months.

| January | $( 6,050) | April | $(48,509) |
|---------|-----------|-------|-----------|
| February | (39,484) | May | (13,006) |
| March | (40,266) | June | 34,828. |

## External Sources

Having checked *internal sources* first, you can now turn to possible *external sources*. There are three possible external sources of additional cash for any firm:

Short-term loans or revolving credit arrangements
Long-term debt
Sale of additional stock (or additional owner investment)

The choice among these sources depends first upon the duration of need. If the preliminary cash budget indicates a chronic or continuous shortage, then a long-term investment of additional cash is required. The choice between long-term debt and owner's equity involves maintaining the appropriate long-term capital structure (proportion of debt) for the firm. Long-term financing will be discussed in Chapter 10.

In the Tripper example, the cash shortage is clearly seasonal. There is no apparent long-term cash shortage. For these situations, short-term bank financing is most appropriate. Advance arrangements should be made with the bank for a six-month loan of $60,000, which will provide coverage for the peak April shortage plus the desired minimum cash balance.[3] You may assume that interest on the loan is at a 6⅔ percent annual rate and is payable with the principal in June. The revised cash forecast for 19X2, including the loan and its interest payment of $2,000 will therefore be:

| | | | |
|---|---|---|---|
| January | $53,950 | July | $ 50,756 |
| February | 20,516 | August | 115,230 |
| March | 19,734 | September | 161,028 |
| April | 11,491 | October | 174,125 |
| May | 46,994 | November | 153,035 |
| June | 32,828 | December | 149,630 |

Note that the last six months' balances are now changed to reflect the $2,000 interest payment in June.

## PROVIDING FOR USE OF EXCESS CASH

Proper cash management primarily involves ensuring adequate cash on hand. It is secondarily concerned with appropriate use of excess cash. As pointed out earlier, any excess cash on hand is certainly not contributing to earning the cost of capital invested. If the existence of excess cash is chronic or continuous, the firm should seriously consider reducing its long-term debt and/or distributing some in dividends to stockholders. Where excess cash is seasonal, as in the Tripper example, it is properly temporarily invested in easily liquidated short-term marketable securities (usually short-term government "paper" or bank certificates of deposit).

For the sake of simplicity assume that:

• Cash on hand in excess of $30,000 is considered excess;

• Excess cash can be invested but only in $10,000 units and only for a minimum of two months;

• Such investments may be assumed to earn 0.5-percent interest per month.

---

[3]    In finance or financial management courses, you will learn about other methods of short-term financing, such as a $60,000 line of credit or revolving credit, which could provide adequate cash coverage at a lower interest cost than a full six-month loan.

Can you readily determine both the amounts and the timing of desirable short-term investments for Tripper and also the amount of interest to be earned? Tripper should invest:

|  |  | Interest |
|---|---|---|
| $20,000 | July through December | $ 600 |
| 60,000 | August through December | 1,500 |
| 40,000 | September through December | 800 |
| 10,000 | September through November | 150 |
|  |  | $3,050 |

Note that the $3,050 of interest to be earned more than offsets the $2,000 interest **cost** on the short-term loan. You may assume that the $3,050 is received when the investments are liquidated ($150 in November and $2,900 in December). Tripper will plan to convert all temporary investments into cash by year-end in anticipation of the high cash outflow occurring in January each year.

## THE FINAL CASH BUDGET

The *final cash budget* may now be prepared, and is given in Exhibit 9.10. Note that it incorporates the following arrangements made since the preliminary budget:

1. First dividend payment delayed to July

2. $60,000 short-term bank loan for first six months

3. $2,000 additional interest payment in June on short-term loan

4. $20,000 short-term investment (July through December)

5. Additional $60,000 short-term investment (August through December)

6. Additional $40,000 short-term investment (September through December)

7. Additional $10,000 short-term investment (September through November)

8. $150 of interest on investments to be received in November

9. $2,900 of interest on investments to be received in December

Note also that the final cash budget illustrated in Exhibit 9.10 includes, for clarification, subtotals for beginning and ending balances before short-term financing (borrowing and investing) activities and their associated principal and interest flows. This format is used to assist you to distinguish the effects

**Exhibit 9.10**

## TRIPPER WATER SKI MANUFACTURING COMPANY

**Final Cash Budget for the Year 19X2**

| | Jan | Feb | Mar | Apr | May | Jun | Jul | Aug | Sep | Oct | Nov | Dec |
|---|---|---|---|---|---|---|---|---|---|---|---|---|
| Net cash inflow from operations | $(56,780) | $(33,434) | $ (782) | $ 1,757 | $35,503 | $47,834 | $79,688 | $ 64,474 | $ 70,798 | $ 23,097 | $(21,090) | $ (3,405) |
| Capital investments | (17,000) | | | | | | (19,800) | | | | | |
| Interest | (6,960) | | | | | | (6,960) | | | | | |
| Dividends | | | | | | | (25,000) | | (25,000) | | | |
| Income taxes | (11,000) | | | (10,000) | | | (10,000) | | | (10,000) | | |
| Beginning balance | 85,690 | (6,050) | (39,484) | (40,266) | (48,509) | (13,006) | 34,828 | 52,756 | 117,230 | 163,028 | 176,125 | 155,035 |
| Balance before short-term financing | (6,050) | (39,484) | (40,266) | (48,509) | (13,006) | 34,828 | 52,756 | 117,230 | 163,028 | 176,125 | 155,035 | 151,630 |
| Beginning balance allowing for short-term borrowing | | 20,516 | 19,734 | 11,491 | 46,994 | 94,828 | 50,756 | 95,230 | 81,028 | 44,125 | 23,035 | 29,780 |
| Additional short-term loans[a] | 60,000 | | | | | | | | | | | |
| Short-term loan[b] repayment with interest | | | | | | (62,000) | | | | | | |
| Additional investments in marketable securities[a] | | | | | | | 20,000 | 60,000 | 50,000 | | | |
| Proceeds from sale of marketable securities including interest[c] | | | | | | | | | | | 10,150 | 122,900 |
| Budgeted cash balance | $ 53,950 | $ 20,516 | $19,734 | $11,491 | $46,994 | $32,828 | $30,756 | $ 35,230 | $ 31,028 | $ 44,125 | $ 33,185 | $152,680 |

[a] Assume borrowed/invested on first day of month
[b] Total interest costs $2,000
[c] Total interest revenues $3,050 assuming sold last day of month

of these activities. These subtotals will usually not be found on a firm's cash budget (see Exhibit 2.12 in Chapter 2).

The final cash budget supplies information to the master budget with respect to:

- ending cash balance for the balance sheet,
- anticipated interest expenses for the income statement, and
- changes with respect to marketable securities and short-term loans for use in determining the expected balances of these items.

## APPROPRIATE TIME SEGMENTS FOR CASH BUDGETING

The Tripper cash budget was prepared on a calendar-month basis. Flows were assumed as even throughout the month. In firms where cash flows are not reasonably uniform within a calendar month, to use a calendar month for cash budgeting purposes might be inappropriate. Had Tripper budgeted on only a total-year basis (see the total-year column of Exhibit 9.8), the cash-shortage months would not have been disclosed. Similarly, for a firm with large payments to suppliers on the tenth of each month because of discounts offered, a calendar-month budget might hide or fail to disclose severe cash shortages within the month. The cash budgeting interval should be timed to focus attention on the point of greatest cash outflow during the month. For example, with the semimonthly payrolls, Tripper might be better advised to budget from the close of business on the first of each month through the first day of the subsequent month. In this way it could measure cash the day semimonthly payroll checks were drawn.

## CASH BUDGETING WITHOUT A FORMAL BUDGETING AND CONTROL SYSTEM

Many firms, especially smaller ones, do not choose or cannot afford a formal budgeting system for purchases and other operating expenditures. These firms still must budget their cash flows. When a firm does not have purchases and operating expense budgets to draw upon, cash outflows can be estimated for each quarter (or even for each month) by working backwards from a sales budget and a budgeted income statement. The sales budget would be prepared in the usual manner (Chapter 3). The budgeted or projected income statement would be prepared starting with total budgeted sales and then including variable expenses as a percent of sales. Fixed costs are then added to complete the picture. This process was discussed in Chapter 6.

For example, assume that the Birch Company had prepared the following sales budget and projected income statement:

Sales:

| | | |
|---|---:|---:|
| First quarter | $ 50,000 | |
| Second quarter | 140,000 | |
| Third quarter | 90,000 | |
| Fourth quarter | 40,000 | $320,000 |
| Cost of goods sold (60% of sales) | | 192,000 |
| Gross Profit | | $128,000 |
| Less: Variable GSA expenses (10% of sales) | | 32,000 |
| Fixed GSA expenses | | 56,000 |
| Income from operations before taxes | | $ 40,000 |

Also assume that Birch had determined that, on the average:

- Manufacturing costs were 30 percent material, 25 percent direct labor, 30 percent variable overhead, and 15 percent fixed overhead.

- Fixed manufacturing costs requiring cash (excluding depreciation) were $20,000 per year.

- Fixed GSA expenses, other than interest and noncash items (depreciation and bad-debt expense), were $41,000 per year.

- 77 percent of sales were collected in the quarter sold, 22 percent in the subsequent quarter, and 1 percent proved uncollectable.

- Sales for the fourth quarter of the prior year were $40,000.

Can you readily estimate cash inflows from sales by quarter? You should have no difficulty estimating cash inflows as shown.

| | First quarter | Second quarter | Third quarter | Fourth quarter |
|---|---:|---:|---:|---:|
| Sales | $50,000 | $140,000 | $ 90,000 | $40,000 |
| Collections: | | | | |
| 77% current quarter | 38,500 | 107,800 | 69,300 | 30,800 |
| 22% prior quarter | 8,800 | 11,000 | 30,800 | 19,800 |
| Total cash collections | $47,300 | $118,800 | $100,100 | $50,600 |

A preliminary estimate of expenditures for purchases and other operating expenses can be made as follows:

|  | First quarter | Second quarter | Third quarter | Fourth quarter |
|---|---|---|---|---|
| **Basis for estimating expenditures:** | | | | |
| Sales | $50,000 | $140,000 | $90,000 | $40,000 |
| Cost of goods sold (60% of sales) | 30,000 | 84,000 | 54,000 | 24,000 |
| **Estimated expenditures:** | | | | |
| Variable selling costs (10% of sales) | 5,000 | 14,000 | 9,000 | 4,000 |
| Fixed GSA expenses | 10,250 | 10,250 | 10,250 | 10,250 |
| Purchases (30% of cost of goods sold) | 9,000 | 25,200 | 16,200 | 7,200 |
| Variable conversion costs (55% of cost of goods sold) | 16,500 | 46,200 | 29,700 | 13,200 |
| Fixed conversion cost | 5,000 | 5,000 | 5,000 | 5,000 |
| Total | $45,750 | $100,650 | $70,150 | $39,650 |

Note that this approach assumes constant inventory levels and no economic purchasing or manufacturing lot sizes. Also, fixed costs involving cash outflows have been assumed to be evenly distributed among quarters. Firms having uneven flows can adjust accordingly.

If lead times are insignificant (effectively zero), then payment lag times could be applied to the foregoing expenditure estimates. Cash outflows could be projected in the same manner as previously described for a full budgeting system.

If lead times are significant, projected expenditures would have to be adjusted accordingly. Suppose that the Birch Company's production lead time was two months and all manufacturing was completed by the beginning of the month of sale. Assuming that sales were equal each month within a single quarter, then 50 percent of conversion costs and 67 percent of materials costs would be incurred in the prior quarter.[4] Can you determine projected expenditures for purchases and for variable manufacturing costs for Birch for the first quarter, assuming the above lead times?

You are correct if you determined these amounts to be $19,800 and $31,350, respectively. Exhibit 9.11 indicates budgeted expenditures for operations for Birch, assuming the lead times and other facts given above. It assumes that the first quarter sales of the following year will be the same as the first quarter sales of the year being budgeted.

---

[4]   All first month's sales manufactured in the prior quarter. First month's production cost (one-half of total) of second month's sales also completed in prior quarter. Purchases of materials for first and second month's sales completed in prior quarter.

## Exhibit 9.11
### BIRCH COMPANY

#### Schedule of Expenditures for Operations

| | First quarter | Second quarter | Third quarter | Fourth quarter |
|---|---|---|---|---|
| Expenditures for operations: | | | | |
| Purchases (1/3 current qtr.)[a] | $ 3,000 | $ 8,400 | $ 5,400 | $ 2,400 |
| Purchases (2/3 following qtr.)[b] | 16,800 | 10,800 | 4,800 | 6,000 |
| Variable conversion costs | | | | |
| (50% current qtr.)[b] | 8,250 | 23,100 | 14,850 | 6,600 |
| Variable conversion costs | | | | |
| (50% following qtr.)[b] | 23,100 | 14,850 | 6,600 | 8,250 |
| Variable selling costs[c] | 5,000 | 14,000 | 9,000 | 4,000 |
| Fixed conversion costs[c] | 5,000 | 5,000 | 5,000 | 5,000 |
| Fixed GSA costs[c] | 10,250 | 10,250 | 10,250 | 10,250 |
| Total expenditures | $71,400 | $86,400 | $55,900 | $42,500 |

[a] Based upon materials cost of 18% of sales (cost of goods sold 60% of sales, material cost 30% of cost of goods sold).
[b] Based upon variable manufacturing cost (excluding material cost) of 33% of sales (cost of goods sold 60% of sales, conversion cost 55% of cost of goods sold).
[c] Previously determined and unaffected by lead times.

The data from Exhibit 9.11 may be converted to cash outflows by allowing for the time lag between expenditure incurrence (accrual) and payment. Assume that 80 percent of a quarter's expenditures are paid within the same quarter and 20 percent the following quarter, and that prior-year fourth-quarter expenditures were $42,500.[5] Prepare a schedule of cash from operations for the Birch Company, and compare it to the one shown in the tabulation below.

### Schedule of Cash from Operations

| | First quarter | Second quarter | Third quarter | Fourth quarter |
|---|---|---|---|---|
| Cash inflows from sales[a] | $47,300 | $118,800 | $100,100 | $50,600 |
| Cash outflows for operations:[b] | | | | |
| 80% of current quarter | 57,120 | 69,120 | 44,720 | 34,000 |
| 20% prior quarter | 8,500 | 14,280 | 17,280 | 11,180 |
| Total | $65,620 | $ 83,400 | $ 62,000 | $45,180 |
| Net cash inflows from operations | $(18,320) | $ 35,400 | $ 38,100 | $ 5,420 |

Notes. (a) From the schedule of receivables collections.
(b) Based on the schedule of operating expenditures.

---

[5]   The 80–20 split recognizes that all third-month expenses except payroll and some portion of the third-month payroll are paid in the following quarter.

The preliminary and final cash budgets for Birch can be prepared by following the procedures outlined earlier in this chapter. They will not be further illustrated for the Birch Company. This example has been included to demonstrate how cash from operations may be budgeted even without formal operating budgets to draw upon.

## UPDATING CASH BUDGETS THROUGHOUT THE YEAR

One final caution with respect to cash management or cash budgeting: Do **not** assume that cash budgeting can be completed once a year and then forgotten until next year's budgeting time rolls around. It should be obvious to you that most cash-forecasting errors or unanticipated cash flows will have a cumulative effect, continuing indefinitely into the future. For this reason, a firm's cash position and projected future cash position must be redetermined about once a month. In some very large firms it is even desirable to update the cash budgets daily. Obviously, such activity is greatly facilitated by the use of computers. Remember that cash management is a relatively continuous process, rather than a periodic one. Cash budgeting may be monthly, but cash management must be continuous, on a **day-to-day** basis.

## CHAPTER OVERVIEW

Based upon the material contained in this chapter, you should now be in a position to:

- Explain the importance of effective cash management and the significance of maintaining solvency;
- Describe the objectives of the cash budgeting process;
- Describe, with examples, how budgeted sales and other revenue are converted to expected cash inflows from operations and the function of the schedule of receivables collections;
- Explain, with examples, how expected cash outflows for purchases may be determined, both for firms having a formal budgeting system and for those that do not;
- Explain, with examples, how expected cash outflows for all operating expenses, except for purchases and interest, may be determined for firms having a formal budgeting system and for those that do not;
- Describe the elements included in a preliminary cash budget and the purpose of preparing such a budget;
- Describe the various internal and external adjustments and sources of cash that may be used to ensure adequate cash on hand;
- Explain the functions of the minimum cash balance and of short-term investments in marketable securities and their significance to cash management;
- Describe the significance of the proper selection by a given firm of its cash-budgeting planning interval or time segment;
- Explain why cash management must be considered a relatively continuous rather than a periodic process.

## NEW VOCABULARY AND CONCEPTS

Solvency
Preliminary cash budget
Schedule of cash from operations
Schedule of receivables collections
Internal sources   (for relieving cash shortage)
External sources   (of additional cash)
Final cash budget

• Possible time lag between expenditure (accrual) and cash flow.

## REVIEW QUESTIONS

1. a) What are the primary and secondary objectives of cash management?
   b) What is the risk/cost to the firm if the primary objective is not achieved?
   c) What is the loss/cost to the firm if the secondary objective is not achieved?

2. Can you describe the separate sequential parts or phases of the cash budgeting activity? Do so with examples. (You do not necessarily need to divide the activity into the same six parts as in the chapter.)

3. a) What different cash inflows are commonly part of cash from operations?
   b) What are the sources of expected data for these items, regardless of whether a firm has a complete formal budgeting system?
   c) What is the schedule of receivables collections and how does it relate to determining cash inflows from operations?
   d) Explain why budgeted sales and budgeted cash inflows from sales could differ for a given period.

4. Why are outflows for purchases often separately identified on a schedule of cash from operations?

5. a) Assuming a complete formal budgeting system, which budgets for a manufacturer would supply necessary information for the schedule of cash from operations?
   b) Which of the above would supply information for projecting cash inflows?
   c) Which of the above would supply information for projecting cash outflows?

6. What are the appropriate responses to questions (a), (b), and (c) (question 5 above) for a merchandiser (wholesaler or retailer) with a complete budgeting system?

7. a) What is the difference between an expense and an expenditure?
   b) Where there is a difference for a given item, which is budgeted and why?

8. In projecting cash outflows for purchases and other operations:
   a) Can the total amount of expenditure budgeted for a given period be assumed to represent cash outflow for that period? Explain, with an example.
   b) Is an expenditure budgeted in a prior period ever included as a projected cash outflow in the current period? Explain, with an example.

9. a) In preparing the preliminary cash budget, what common items, in addition to net cash inflow from operations, are included?
   b) Which of these items represent cash inflows, which outflows, and which represents neither?
   c) What are the sources of information for each of these items?

10. a) Can the preliminary cash budget ever project the ending cash balance for a period as being negative without being in error?
    b) Explain how a preliminary forecasted cash balance could ever be negative.
    c) What is the significance of a forecasted negative cash balance?

11. What is a minimum cash balance? Explain its function.

12. What are the common internal sources/activity changes that should be examined when attempting to eliminate a forecasted cash shortage?

13. a) What are the common external sources of additional cash to alleviate a cash shortage?
    b) Which are preferable for long-term shortages?
    c) Which are preferable for short-term shortages?

14. What items can make a difference between a preliminary cash budget and a final cash budget? Explain.

15. Can either of the following make a significant difference to the effectiveness of a cash budgeting system as an early warning device? Explain with examples.
    a) The length of the planning interval: month, quarter, year?
    b) The cutoff point: end of month, midway in month, and so forth?

16. How can a merchandiser estimate cash required each period for operations if the firm does not have a system of operating budgets? Explain, with examples.

17. How can a manufacturer estimate cash required each period for operations if the firm does not have a system of operating budgets? Explain, with examples.

18. Why is cash budgeting essentially a continuous rather than a periodic (once-a-year) process? Explain.

## MINI-CASES AND QUESTIONS FOR DISCUSSION

MC 9.1 Jessica Jackson is an aggressive young commercial loan officer with her bank. She has just presented her boss with a new plan, and he has taken it under consideration. Jessica's plan is to offer business customers (who would qualify for loans in the same amount) a standby overdraft plan as follows:

1. Firm and bank would estimate the future year's cash needs by quarter to establish maximum possible need for cash. This estimating could be done rapidly from financial statements, since much less accuracy and detail would be required than if the firm were to budget cash formally. The firm would also provide the bank with its future sales budget, and agree to deposit all sales receipts.

2. The bank would extend to the customer overdraft rights for the year in the amount determined, plus a margin of safety. A modest fee (see below) would be charged for this standby (overdraft) privilege.

3. The bank would honor checks throughout the year so long as the negative (overdraft) balance did not exceed the loan limit. Negative balances would earn regular commercial loan interest. The bank's computer would be programmed to flag for the bank and the firm's attention:

   a) Any significant departure from budgeted sales;

   b) Any overdrafts requiring use of the safety margin;

   c) The cash-use pattern as compared to the sales pattern for use in planning the following year.

The bank's computer would also generally forecast overdraft requirements so that the bank would not become dangerously committed.

   Jessica reasoned that:

1. The firm would benefit. It would save about half the cost of the detailed cash budgeting process throughout the year; the other half would go as a fee to the bank. It could forget about cash management, and let the professional cash manager (bank) do the "driving."

2. The bank, whose only real interest is in renting money to safe customers, would also benefit. "Overdrafts" under this system would be just as safe, and earn just as much interest, as regular commercial loans. Added to this, the standby service fees, which could run into many thousands of dollars per firm, would be almost pure profit to the bank.

What do you think of Jessica's proposal from the viewpoint of a firm? Of her bank? Why isn't this pattern widely in use? Discuss.

MC 9.2   Purchases, operating, capital, and cash budgets focus only upon expenditures, as distinct from expenses. You also learned that depreciation, amortization, and losses of past expenditures (sunk costs) are irrelevant to business decisions. Why do financial accountants include such items as depreciation and amortization in financial statements if they are irrelevant to both budgeting and decision-making? Could they merely be pointing out past mistakes? Discuss.

MC 9.3   Refer to MC 9.2. Would it be correct to say that managers, through budgeting and control systems and in making business decisions, really are concerned with maximizing funds from operations as distinct from net income? Does maximizing funds from operations in turn maximize net income? Is it possible that the statement of changes in financial position (funds flow statement) is a better overall measure of current management performance than is the income statement with its traditional "bottom line"? Discuss.

## ESSENTIAL PROBLEMS

**EP 9.1** The Allison Company's receivables collection experience is as follows:

25% of current month's sales either are cash or are collected within the month,

40% of each month's sales are collected during the first month following sale,

20% of each month's sales are collected during the second month following sale;

14% of each month's sales are collected during the third month following sale;

1% of each month's sales is uncollectable and is written off to bad debt expense in the fourth month following sale.

a) Prepare in good form a schedule of receivables collections for the third quarter of 19XX, given the following budgeted sales data:

| | | | |
|---|---|---|---|
| Jan | $200,000 | Jul | $ 30,000 |
| Feb | 150,000 | Aug | 90,000 |
| Mar | 100,000 | Sep | 160,000 |
| Apr | 80,000 | Oct | 250,000 |
| May | 60,000 | Nov | 300,000 |
| Jun | 40,000 | Dec | 400,000 |

b) Assume that the projected balance of accounts receivable on June 30th (after projected write-off of February uncollectables) was $64,000. Determine the projected balance of accounts receivable as of the end of the third quarter of 19XX.

**EP 9.2** a) Refer to Problem EP 9.1. Prepare in good form a schedule of receivables collections for the fourth quarter of 19XX.

b) Determine the projected balance of accounts receivable as of 12/31/XX.

**EP 9.3** The Allison Company's operating expenditure budget for the last seven months of 19XX is given in Exhibit 9.12. Prepare a schedule of cash outflows for operations for the third quarter of 19XX. Show projected disbursements for purchases and other operations (excluding interest) separately and in total by month. Assume that payroll is all paid in the current month, insurance and property taxes are paid in the month budgeted, and all other expenses are paid in the month following.

**EP 9.4** Refer to Problem EP 9.3. Prepare a schedule of cash outflows for operations by month on the same basis for the fourth quarter of 19XX.

**EP 9.5** Data with respect to the Barbara Company is given in Exhibit 9.13. Prepare a preliminary cash budget in good form (refer to Exhibit 9.8) for the third quarter of 19XX by month. You may assume that the cash balance as of June 30, 19XX, was budgeted at $35,000.

**EP 9.6** Refer to Problem EP 9.5. Assume that the preliminary budgeted cash balance as of September 30, 19XX, was $(150,000)—a projected negative cash balance or cash shortage. Prepare a preliminary cash budget by month for the fourth quarter of 19XX.

**Exhibit 9.12**
ALLISON COMPANY

### Portion of 19XX Operating Expenditure Budget[a]

| | June | July | August | September | October | November | December |
|---|---|---|---|---|---|---|---|
| Purchases | $18,000 | $32,000 | $50,000 | $60,000 | $80,000 | $40,000 | $30,000 |
| Payroll[b] | 16,000 | 28,000 | 42,000 | 60,000 | 70,000 | 90,000 | 50,000 |
| Supplies | 800 | 600 | 900 | 1,600 | 2,500 | 3,000 | 4,000 |
| Utilities | 300 | 900 | 1,600 | 2,500 | 3,000 | 4,000 | 2,000 |
| Distribution and marketing | 4,500 | 8,000 | 12,500 | 15,000 | 20,000 | 10,000 | 7,500 |
| Miscellaneous | 500 | 500 | 500 | 500 | 500 | 500 | 500 |
| Interest | 7,000 | | | 7,000 | | | 7,000 |
| Insurance | | 15,000 | 8,000 | | | | |
| Property taxes | | | | | | | |
| Total | $47,100 | $85,000 | $115,500 | $146,600 | $176,000 | $147,500 | $101,000 |

Notes.  a Combines budgeted expenditures from the following budgets:
  • Purchases budget
  • Direct labor budget
  • Manufacturing overhead budget
  • GSA budget
  b Combines all budgeted expenditures for wages and salaries including:
  • Direct labor (direct labor budget)
  • Indirect labor (manufacturing overhead budget)
  • Supervision (manufacturing overhead budget)
  • Wages and salaries (GSA budget)

**Exhibit 9.13**

BARBARA COMPANY

**Preliminary Schedule of Cash Flows
for Last Six Months of 19XX**

|  | July | August | September | October | November | December |
|---|---|---|---|---|---|---|
| Collections of receivables | $90,000 | $150,000 | $200,000 | $300,000 | $400,000 | $500,000 |
| Collections of other revenues |  |  | 20,000 |  |  | 20,000 |
| Disbursements for purchases | 40,000 | 60,000 | 80,000 | 100,000 | 75,000 | 50,000 |
| Disbursements for other operating expenditures | 80,000 | 120,000 | 160,000 | 200,000 | 150,000 | 100,000 |
| Capital investments |  | 50,000 |  |  | 30,000 |  |
| Proceeds from disposition of noncurrent assets |  | 20,000 |  |  | 10,000 |  |
| Interest payments |  |  | 5,000 |  |  | 5,000 |
| Dividend payments |  |  | 40,000 |  |  | 40,000 |
| Income tax payments | 30,000 |  |  | 30,000 |  |  |

**EP 9.7** The projected cash balance from the preliminary cash budget for the first six months of 19XX prepared by the Charlie Company is given below. You may assume that all reasonable internal sources of cash have been investigated. Charlie can borrow from the bank in $5,000 increments for minimum 30-day periods at an interest cost of eight percent per year, payable with principal at the termination of the loan. It may invest excess cash to earn six percent annually in $10,000 increments for a minimum of 60 days. Interest is received when the investment is liquidated. Charlie wishes to maintain a $15,000 minimum cash balance.

| Jan | $ 28,000 | Jul | $(14,000) |
|---|---|---|---|
| Feb | $ 37,000 | Aug | $ 3,000 |
| Mar | $ 27,000 | Sep | $ 29,000 |
| Apr | $ 16,000 | Oct | $ 37,000 |
| May | $(10,000) | Nov | $ 42,000 |
| Jun | $(25,000) | Dec | $ 27,000 |

Prepare a final cash budget for the first six months of 19XX.

**EP 9.8** Refer to Problem EP 9.7. Assume that the budgeted cash balance was $(25,284) as of June 30, 19XX. All loans had been repaid and all interest paid as of that date. The second six months' preliminary cash budget data does not yet reflect the $284 of net interest cost incurred during the first six months. Prepare a final cash budget for the Charlie Company for the second six months of 19XX.

**EP 9.9** The following data (A through H), in thousands of dollars, are taken from eight separate final cash budgets. Each firm has planned a minimum cash balance of $20,000. Determine the missing element for items A through D.

|  | A | B | C | D | E | F | G | H |
|---|---|---|---|---|---|---|---|---|
| Net cash inflow from operations + or (−) | ? | 101 | (60) | 200 | 20 | 83 | 16 | 22 |
| Capital investments − | 10 | 20 | 0 | 30 | 10 | 30 | 15 | ? |
| Interest (long-term financing) − | 6 | 5 | (9) | 10 | 7 | 6 | 8 | 5 |
| Dividends − | 3 | 15 | 0 | 40 | 15 | 12 | 0 | 10 |
| Income taxes − | 24 | 20 | 0 | 30 | 5 | 7 | 12 | 20 |
| Beginning balance + or (−) | 20 | 25 | 21 | 20 | 23 | 26 | ? | 22 |
| Additional short-term loans + | 0 | 0 | ? | 0 | 0 | 0 | 50 | 0 |
| Repay short-term loans plus interest − | 0 | 0 | 0 | ? | 0 | 31 | 0 | 0 |
| Additional investments in marketable securities − | 35 | ? | 0 | 0 | 0 | 0 | 0 | 0 |
| Proceeds from sale of marketable securities including interest + | 0 | 0 | 0 | 0 | ? | 0 | 0 | 41 |
| Budgeted cash balance + or (−) | 24 | 21 | 20 | 24 | 22 | ? | 23 | 25 |

**EP 9.10** Refer to Problem EP 9.9. Determine the missing element for items E through H, each considered independently.

**EP 9.11** The Darcy Company is a wholesaler. Its pro-forma (budgeted) income statement for 19XX is given below:

| | | |
|---|---:|---:|
| Sales | | $2,000,000 |
| Cost of goods sold | | 1,200,000 |
| Gross profit | | $ 800,000 |
| Operating expenses: | | |
| Payroll | $360,000 | |
| Interest | 10,000 | |
| Depreciation | 20,000 | |
| Other operating expenses | 210,000 | 600,000 |
| Income from operations | | 200,000 |
| Provision for income taxes | | 80,000 |
| Net Income | | $ 120,000 |

- Cost of goods sold is completely variable. The firm maintains $100,000 of inventory on hand. It purchases items for sale on a monthly basis one month in advance of sale, paying in the month after purchase.
- Payroll is all fixed salary, payable in the current month.
- Interest is payable quarterly in March, June, September, and December.
- Other operating expenses are $5,000 per month fixed, with the balance variable with sales. Other operating expenses are paid 50 percent in the month incurred and 50 percent in the following month.
- Income taxes are payable quarterly in equal installments the month following the end of the quarter.

• $80,000 in dividends are planned, half in March and the other half in September.

The sales budget for the forthcoming year is given below. 40 percent of sales are collected in the month of sale and 60 percent in the following month.

| Jan | $120,000 | Jul | $210,000 |
|-----|----------|-----|----------|
| Feb | 140,000 | Aug | 190,000 |
| Mar | 160,000 | Sep | 170,000 |
| Apr | 180,000 | Oct | 150,000 |
| May | 200,000 | Nov | 130,000 |
| Jun | 220,000 | Dec | 130,000 |

Prepare a preliminary cash budget for the third quarter of 19XX. You may assume that the cash balance as of June 30, 19XX, was budgeted as $18,000.

**EP 9.12**  Refer to Problem EP 9.11. Prepare a preliminary cash budget for the fourth quarter of 19XX for the Darcy Company. You may assume that the cash balance as of September 30, 19XX, was budgeted as $63,875.


## SUPPLEMENTARY PROBLEMS

**SP 9.13**  Refer to Problem EP 9.1. Assume the same budgeted sales but a different receivables collection experience with respect to each month's sales, as follows:

  10%   are cash sales;

  15%   are collected during the month of sale, with the customers taking a two-percent cash discount;

  40%   are collected during the following month; on one-fourth of these collections, customers take a two-percent cash discount;

  25%   are collected during the second month following sale;

  8%   are collected during the third month following sale;

  2%   are uncollectable and are written off to bad-debt expense in the fourth month following sale.

  a) Prepare, in good form, a schedule of receivables collections for the third quarter of 19XX.

  b) Assume that the projected balance of accounts receivable on June 30th (after write-off of February uncollectables) was $61,000. Determine the projected balance of accounts receivable as of the end of the third quarter of 19XX.

**SP 9.14**  Refer to Problem SP 9.13.

  a) Prepare, in good form, a schedule of receivables collections for the fourth quarter of 19XX.

  b) Determine the projected balance of accounts receivable as of 12/31/XX.

**SP 9.15**  Refer to Problem EP 9.3. Assume the same expenditure budget but a different payment pattern as follows:

- One-half of purchases paid in the current month, taking a two-percent cash discount;

- One-fourth of purchases paid in the following month, taking a two-percent cash discount;

- One-fourth of purchases paid in the following month, with no discount taken;

- Payroll paid in the current month;

- Property tax paid in the month budgeted;

- Insurance, distribution and marketing, and utilities paid in the month following, with no discount;

- Supplies and miscellaneous paid in the month following, taking a two-percent cash discount;

- Interest excluded from computation of cash outflow for operations.

Prepare a schedule of cash outflows for operations for the third quarter of 19XX. Show projected disbursements for purchases and other operations (excluding interest) separately and in total by month.

**SP 9.16**   Refer to Problem SP 9.15. Prepare a schedule of cash outflows for operations by month on the same basis for the fourth quarter of 19XX.

**SP 9.17**   The Ebbtide Company retails marine hardware. Pro-forma (budgeted) income statements for each quarter of 19XX are given below:

|  | First quarter | Second quarter | Third quarter | Fourth quarter | Total year |
|---|---|---|---|---|---|
| Sales | $500,000 | $1,050,000 | $1,050,000 | $600,000 | $3,200,000 |
| Cost of goods sold | 300,000 | 630,000 | 630,000 | 360,000 | 1,920,000 |
| Gross profit | $200,000 | $ 420,000 | $ 420,000 | $240,000 | $1,280,000 |
| Operating expenses: |  |  |  |  |  |
| Wages and salaries | 93,000 | 142,500 | 142,500 | 102,000 | 480,000 |
| Interest | 8,000 | 8,000 | 8,000 | 8,000 | 32,000 |
| Depreciation | 16,000 | 16,000 | 16,000 | 16,000 | 64,000 |
| Other | 44,000 | 66,000 | 66,000 | 48,000 | 224,000 |
| Income from operations | $ 39,000 | $ 187,500 | $ 187,500 | $ 66,000 | $ 480,000 |
| Provision for taxes | 16,000 | 75,000 | 75,000 | 26,000 | 192,000 |
| Net Income | $ 23,000 | $ 112,500 | $ 112,500 | $ 40,000 | $ 288,000 |

Mr. Roger Sloan is the newly hired treasurer of Ebbtide and has gathered the following information for cash budgeting purposes:

- Sales are 20 percent for cash and 80 percent on account; 50 percent of credit sales are collected during the first month following sale and the other half during the second month. On a quarterly basis Mr. Sloan estimates that collections include all receivables from the prior quarter and 60 percent of current quarter's sales. He reasons that 40 percent of the second month's and 80 percent of the third month's sales will not have been collected by the end of the quarter. And, assuming that each month equals one-third of the quarter,

$$0.4 \left(\frac{\text{quarter}}{3}\right) + 0.8 \left(\frac{\text{quarter}}{3}\right) = 0.4 \text{ quarter sales not yet collected.}$$

Receivables on January 1 totaled $120,000.

- The company has decided, for 19XX, to end each month with inventory sufficient to cover sales for the next two months. On a quarterly basis, Mr. Sloan therefore estimated quarter-ending target inventory at two-thirds of the following quarter's budgeted cost of goods sold. Merchandise inventory on hand on January 1 was $480,000, which was excessive for that time of year and would have to be sold off.

- Purchases of inventory are paid within 15 days to take advantage of discounts, and cost of goods sold and ending inventory amounts reflect the cost net of discount. On average this means that one-half of purchases are paid in the month of purchase and one-half the following month. Mr. Sloan estimates, on a quarterly basis, that each quarter's cash disbursements for purchases will include prior quarter's inventory payables plus 5/6 or 83 percent (rounded) of current quarter purchases. Accounts payable for inventory purchases as of January 1 amounted to $20,000.

- Wages and salaries and interest payments are all paid in the month or the quarter budgeted.

- Other operating expenses are paid in the month following incurrence. On a quarterly basis, Mr. Sloan estimates that disbursements for other operating expenses will include prior quarter's payables for these items plus two-thirds or 67 percent (rounded) of the current quarter's budgeted expenditures. Accounts payable for other operating expenses as of January 1 were $12,000.

- Income taxes are payable quarterly during the first month following the end of the quarter. Taxes payable on January 15 for last year's fourth quarter were $10,000.

- The firm is planning to pay four quarterly dividends of $40,000 each in March, June, September, and December.

- The firm desires a minimum cash balance of $20,000. Cash on hand on January 1 was $22,000.

a) Following Mr. Sloan's guidelines, prepare a preliminary cash budget for the Ebbtide Company for the first quarter of 19XX.

b) Does your preliminary budget indicate any need for short-term borrowings to maintain adequate cash? If yes, how much cash should be borrowed during the first quarter?

**SP 9.18** Refer to Problem SP 9.17 above.

a) Following Mr. Sloan's guidelines, prepare a preliminary cash budget for the second quarter of 19XX.

b) Does your preliminary budget indicate any need for short-term borrowings to maintain adequate cash? If yes, how much cash should be borrowed during the second quarter?

SP 9.19 Refer to problem SP 9.17. As the president and major stockholder of the Ebbtide Company, you are concerned over the competence and the reliability of your new treasurer, Mr. Sloan. You have noticed several instances where he has been inclined to take dangerous shortcuts to reduce his workload. You therefore decide to review his cash budget for 19XX. He has indicated that no short-term borrowings of cash are necessary during 19XX, and you know they have been in prior years.

Mr. Sloan somewhat resentfully turns over his budgeting data file to you as requested. You note that it includes the following detailed information apparently not used by Mr. Sloan in preparing his cash budget:

- Budgeted sales by month for the forthcoming year were:

| | | | | |
|---|---|---|---|---|
| Jan | $100,000 | Jul | $400,000 |
| Feb | 150,000 | Aug | 400,000 |
| Mar | 250,000 | Sep | 250,000 |
| Apr | 300,000 | Oct | 250,000 |
| May | 350,000 | Nov | 200,000 |
| Jun | 400,000 | Dec | 150,000 |

- Sales in the previous year were $100,000 in both November and December.
- Wages and salaries were $13,300 per month fixed, and the balance was variable with sales.
- Interest was payable in the third month of each quarter.
- Other operating expenses were $8,000 per month fixed, and the balance were variable with sales.

a) Prepare a preliminary cash budget by month for the first quarter of 19XX.

b) Does your preliminary cash budget indicate any need for short-term borrowings (in $5,000 increments) to maintain adequate cash? If yes, how much cash should be borrowed each month?

c) What are the sources of any significant differences between your budgeting by the month and Mr. Sloan's budgeting by the quarter? Could these differences cause problems in future quarters?

SP 9.20 Refer to Problems SP 9.17 and SP 9.19.

a) Prepare a preliminary cash budget by month for the second quarter of 19XX. You may assume that the preliminary cash budget for the first quarter indicated a cash balance of $88,000 as of March 31, 19XX.

b) Does your preliminary cash budget indicate any need for short-term borrowings (in $5,000 increments) to maintain adequate cash? If yes, how much cash should be borrowed each month?

c) What are the sources of any significant differences between your budgeting by the month and Mr. Sloan's budgeting by the quarter?

SP 9.21 Betty Muniz is planning to open a woman's-wear store in a recently built shopping center. She has been gathering information and experience for several years, working as an employee in similar stores. Betty projects that her sales (all cash) will reach $35,000 per quarter by the third quarter of operation. She expects $15,000 of sales the first quarter and $25,000 the next. Other projected data include:

- Minimum inventory equal to one-third of next quarter's sales. 85 percent of purchases paid in the quarter of purchase, with the balance paid in the following quarter. Cost of goods sold estimated at 55 percent of sales.

- Store rental per month of $700 or three percent of prior quarter's sales, whichever is greater. Rent payable in advance at the beginning of each month. $600 rental security deposit required, along with the first month's rent.

- Other operating expenses (excluding interest and depreciation) $1,000 per month fixed, plus four percent of sales variable, two-thirds payable in quarter when incurred and one-third in subsequent quarter.

- Assisting part-time salespersons costing an average of $2,000 per quarter, payable in the current quarter.

- Required investment in store fixtures and equipment $16,000, with annual depreciation of $4,000.

- Minimum desired cash balance $5,000.

- Bank interest charges are ten percent per annum on any loans. Interest is payable quarterly at the end of each quarter. Loans are received or repaid in $1,000 increments at the beginning or end of each quarter.

Betty wishes to borrow necessary funds from the bank on a short-term basis to get her new business started. She knows the bank will not be receptive to her loan request unless she demonstrates careful planning of her cash needs. She has asked you to prepare her cash budget by quarter for the first year of operations. Prepare such a cash budget, including necessary loans to maintain the desirable minimum cash balance.

**SP 9.22** Refer to Problem SP 9.21. Assume that Betty has $20,000 to invest in her business and that, until all loans are repaid with interest, she will withdraw only $500 per month for personal living expenses. Also assume that bank financing is available in $1,000 thirty-day increments.

a) Prepare a loan request for Betty to submit to her bank, indicating amounts required and intended payments of interest and principal by quarter, for the duration of the required financing.

b) Prepare pro-forma (budgeted) income statements for Betty for each of the first two years of operation, assuming that sales level off at $35,000 per quarter, starting in the third quarter of operation. Taxes may be ignored.

## SUGGESTIONS FOR FURTHER READING

Van Horne, James C., *Fundamentals of Financial Management*, Third Edition. Englewood Cliffs, N.J.: Prentice-Hall, Inc., 1977; Chapters 5, 6, 9, and 10.

Weston, J. Fred, and Eugene F. Brigham, *Essentials of Managerial Finance*, Fourth Edition. Hinsdale, Illinois: The Dryden Press, 1977. Chapters 6 through 9.

CHAPTER 9 APPENDIX
# Review of Funds Flow

•

(Note. If you have not recently completed a course in financial accounting, or if coverage of the statement of changes in financial position was minimal in your financial accounting course, you should first review Appendix D at the back of this book before proceeding with this chapter appendix.)

## VARIOUS DEFINITIONS AND USES OF THE TERM "FUNDS"

A very real and major source of confusion for most elementary accounting students is the fact that the term "funds" has many quite distinct meanings or usages. Seven of these different meanings are:

1. Cash
2. Readily available cash (cash plus marketable securities)
3. Quick assets (cash plus marketable securities plus receivables)
4. Net working capital[6]
5. All discretionary resources[7]
6. An amount of cash set aside (often in a trust or with an escrow agent) for a specific purpose, such as a pension fund to cover employee pension obligations or a sinking fund to retire bonds at maturity
7. In institutional or governmental accounting, an amount designated/ authorized to cover a particular type or group of expenditures

---

[6]   The term "working capital" is often used in business as a synonym for current assets. Net working capital will be used throughout this text to clearly delineate the amount of current assets not provided by short-term creditors. Arithmetically, net working capital equals total current assets minus total current liabilities.

[7]   The term "discretionary resources" or, more precisely, a discretionary resource flow, refers to an inflow or outflow of assets resulting from a management decision. The purchase or sale of an asset would involve a discretionary resource flow. Expiration of book value (depreciation, amortization, loss) would not be the result of a current management action, and would therefore not be considered a discretionary resource flow.

Unfortunately many books and reports use the term funds unaccompanied by further elaboration or definition. As the reader, you must determine which meaning is appropriate in the overall context of the presentation. This appendix will focus upon funds as cash, net working capital, or all discretionary resources. Hereafter, where the term is used without modification, it will be used to mean net working capital. Otherwise the terms "funds (cash)" or "funds (ADR)" will be employed.

The purpose of this appendix is to review the objectives, information content, and usefulness of three commonly prepared but different so-called "funds flow statements":

- The statement of changes in financial position (SCFP) (funds defined as including all discretionary resources)
- The working capital funds flow statement (funds defined as net working capital)
- The cash funds flow statement (funds defined as including only cash)

As part of this review, the distinction between funds from operations and either income from operations or net income will be clarified. You will also have the opportunity to learn the difference between funds from operations (determined either on a cash or on a net working capital basis) as developed on a so-called "funds flow statement" and cash from operations as previously used in this chapter. This appendix will **not** attempt to cover the procedures for preparation of various funds statements.[8]

## FUNCTION AND INFORMATION CONTENT OF FUNDS FLOW STATEMENTS

Funds flow statements, and specifically the statement of changes in financial position (SCFP), are outputs of the financial accounting system. As such, their content and function is prescribed by generally accepted accounting principles (GAAP). You may recall from financial accounting that the income statement is often referred to as the link between two balance sheets. This statement is only partially correct. The income statement articulates with successive balance sheets in that net income, after adjustment for dividends (cash and stock) and any prior period adjustments, does explain any change in retained earnings. Actually the statement disclosing all changes to retained earnings including income is the statement of retained earnings. It provides the link between successive balance sheets only with respect to retained earnings. What about all the other changes in other balance sheet items?

---

[8]   For details of statement preparation, refer to Chapter 14 in the companion text *Financial Accounting Information, An Introduction To Its Preparation and Use,* Addison-Wesley Publishing Company, 1978; or to appropriate chapters in other elementary financial accounting texts.

**Exhibit 9.14**

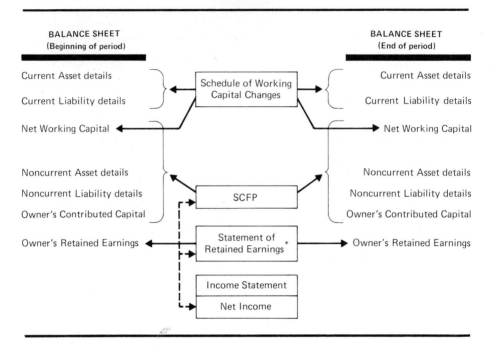

* For a proprietorship, the Statement of Owner's Capital reconciles all owner's capital, not just Retained Earnings.

The SCFP is the real link between balance sheets. It summarizes the various discretionary resource flows occurring during the period. Exhibit 9.14 illustrates this connection.

Most SCFP's are prepared with funds defined as net working capital (NWC) and also include other major resource flows not involving flows of working capital.[9] Exhibit 9.15 illustrates a SCFP prepared for the Ashdown Corporation on such a basis. Study this exhibit and see if you can readily translate/decode its meaning.

Exhibit 9.15 essentially focuses on the Ashdown Corporation's financial management activities occurring during the period. It discloses that the firm obtained $775,000 of additional NWC from operations. It also obtained another $350,000 of additional working capital from three other sources: sale of noncurrent assets ($50,000), new long-term borrowings ($100,000), and additional owner investment ($200,000).

The SCFP (Exhibit 9.15) also discloses what was done with the $1,125,000 of new working capital available for management's use or application: $400,000 was used to acquire additional noncurrent assets; $50,000 was applied to the

---

[9]   GAAP also allows for SCFP preparation on other bases such as cash, ready cash, or quick assets.

**Exhibit 9.15**

ASHDOWN CORPORATION

**Statement of Changes in Financial Position**
**(Prepared to highlight change in Net Working Capital for the Year 19XX)**
**(000 omitted)**

**Sources**

| | |
|---|---:|
| Net income | $ 650 |
| Adjustments for nonfund items[a] | 125 |
| Funds from operations | $ 775 |
| Proceeds from sale of noncurrent assets | 50 |
| Proceeds from additional long-term debt | 100 |
| Proceeds from sale fo additional stock (new owner investment) | 200 |
| Total | $1,125 |

**Applications**

| | |
|---|---:|
| Acquire additional noncurrent assets | $ 400 |
| Retire long-term debt | 50 |
| Dividends (owner withdrawals) | 300 |
| Total | $ 750 |
| | |
| Increase in balance of net working capital | $ 375 |

[a] See Exhibit 9.18.

retirement of existing long-term debt; $300,000 was expended in distributions to owners. And the remaining $375,000 was still on hand at the end of the period, in the form of additional NWC.

Exhibit 9.15 illustrates the most common possible sources and applications of NWC. To readily visualize and remember possible sources and uses of NWC, think of a balance sheet prepared on a net working capital basis, a balance sheet where total current liabilities have been subtracted from current assets and also eliminated from equities:

| | | | |
|---|---|---|---|
| Net working capital | $XXX | Long-term debt | $XXX |
| Noncurrent Assets | XXX | Owners' Equity | XXX |
| | $XXX | | $XXX |

You should note that the **only possible** nonextraordinary sources of additional NWC for any firm are:

- Operations,
- Sale of noncurrent assets,
- Additional long-term debt,
- Additional owner investment.

Similarly, the **only possible** nonextraordinary uses of NWC are:

- Loss in operations,
- Purchase of noncurrent assets,
- Retirement of long-term debt,
- Dividends (distributions to owners).

## BALANCED APPROACH

Exhibit 9.15 illustrated a format for the SCFP that highlighted changes in the balance of NWC. Exhibit 9.16 is an alternative acceptable approach to presentation of the SCFP. Note that the information contained in Exhibits 9.15 and 9.16 is identical. The only difference between them is that Exhibit 9.16 includes the $375,000 year-end increase in the balance of NWC as an application.

The balanced format has the logic of a closed system. It is logical to include an increase in NWC as an application since that amount of funds generated during the year ended up in the "working capital bank." A firm must have a minimum balance of NWC to operate, and often funds are raised from outside for the sole purpose of increasing the NWC balance on hand and available.

In the opposite situation, where the total of other applications exceeds outside sources, the corresponding reduction in the balance of NWC is shown as a source. To see the logic of this approach, think of a firm where the **only** event all year was the purchase of a fixed asset, costing $80,000, for cash. The

**Exhibit 9.16**
ASHDOWN CORPORATION

Statement of Changes in Financial Position
(Prepared on a Balanced Format Basis)
for the Year 19XX (000 omitted)

**Sources**

| | |
|---|---|
| Net income | $ 650 |
| Adjustments for nonfund items[a] | 125 |
| Funds from operations | $ 775 |
| Proceeds from sale of noncurrent assets | 50 |
| Proceeds from additional long-term debt | 100 |
| Proceeds from the sale of additional stock (new owner investment) | 200 |
| Total sources | $1,125 |

**Applications**

| | |
|---|---|
| Acquire additional noncurrent assets | $ 400 |
| Retire long-term debt | 50 |
| Dividends | 300 |
| Increase balance of net working capital | 375 |
| Total applications | $1,125 |

[a] See Exhibit 9.17.

application of the $80,000 of NWC to the purchase of additional noncurrent assets is obvious. But what was the source? Where did the $80,000 come from? In this example, the source was a reduction in the balance of NWC. $80,000 of working capital was taken from the NWC "bank" balance and used elsewhere.

A convenient way to remember and understand various sources and applications possibly appearing on a SCFP is to think of the balanced or closed-system format. Working capital that "moved around" during the year all came from somewhere, and all ended up somewhere. Following the balanced model, the various possible sources and applications or uses are mirror images of each other:

| Possible sources[10] | Possible applications[10] |
| --- | --- |
| Funds from operations | Funds lost in operations |
| Sale of noncurrent assets | Purchase of noncurrent assets |
| Additional long-term debt | Retire/extinguish existing long-term |
| Additional owner investment (addi- | debt |
| tional stock) | Distribution to owner(s) (dividends) |
| Decrease balance of NWC | Increase balance of NWC |

## FUNDS FROM OPERATIONS

One of the more difficult concepts for the elementary accounting student involves the distinction between funds from operations and either income from operations or net income. To grasp the distinction, you must first be able to visualize what is considered a flow of working capital and what is not.

Figure 9.3 illustrates the various parts of a balance sheet. Note that a wavy line separates current from noncurrent items. A flow of working capital is defined as an event that results in a change in the balance of **net** working capital. Recall the various transactions and adjustments that you learned in financial accounting and particularly their effect on the firm's balance sheet. Some transactions do **not** change the NWC balance. Examples would include:

• Purchasing a current asset on account,
• Paying a current liability,
• Collecting a receivable.

The effects of both parts of the transaction are **above** the wavy line.

---

[10] Does not include extraordinary funds flows, which would be separately disclosed on the SCEP. A firm having an extraordinary gain of $120,000 on noncurrent assets, a $70,000 extraordinary loss of inventory, and funds from operations including extraordinaries of $300,000, would disclose:

| | | |
| --- | --- | --- |
| Funds from operations | | $250,000 |
| Plus: Extraordinary gain on noncurrent assets | | 120,000 |
| Less: Extraordinary loss on inventory | | 70,000 |
| Funds provided | | $300,000 |

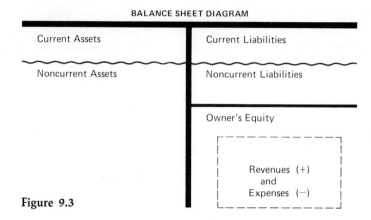

**Figure 9.3**

Certain adjustments also do **not** affect the firm's NWC balance. They include:

- Any write-down or write-off of noncurrent assets (depreciation, amortization, depletion, or loss),
- Amortization of investments premium or discount included as part of investments revenue,
- Recognition of income in another firm's undistributed earnings (equity method),
- Amortization of long-term liability premium or discount included in interest expense.

Note that, again, the effects of both parts of these adjustments are **below** the wavy line.

Transactions and adjustments that do affect the NWC balance, and therefore do represent flows of funds, **all** affect the balance sheet **both above** and **below** the wavy line. A line drawn connecting their effects will always cross the wavy line. Examples of transactions and adjustments affecting the NWC balance and "crossing" the wavy line include:

- Sales to customers for cash or on account,
- Other revenues earned and therefore resulting in an increase to cash or a current receivable,
- Any expenses involving use (decrease) of current assets (cash, inventory, supplies, prepaid items), or incurrence (increase) of a current liability,
- Other financial transactions previously discussed as sources or applications of NWC including:

> Purchase or sale of noncurrent assets,
> Additional long-term debt or retirements thereof,
> Additional owner investment or withdrawals.

The SCFP reports the effect of all events occurring during the year that changed the NWC balance[11]—which cross the wavy line. If you are unfamiliar with the balance sheet diagram or uncertain about visualizing events whose effect crosses the wavy line, an event that changes NWC can also be identified from an equation for NWC that is derived from the basic balance sheet equality.

$$
\begin{aligned}
\text{Assets} &= \text{Equities} \\
\text{Assets} &= \text{Liabilities} + \text{Owners' Equity} \\
(\text{CA} + \text{NCA}) &= (\text{CL} + \text{NCL}) + (\text{CC} + \text{RE}). \\
\text{CA} - \text{CL} &= \text{NCL} + \text{CC} + \text{RE} - \text{NCA} \\
\text{NWC} &= \text{NCL} + \text{CC} + \text{RE} - \text{NCA}
\end{aligned}
$$

where

$$
\begin{aligned}
\text{CA} &= \text{Current assets} \\
\text{NCA} &= \text{Noncurrent assets} \\
\text{CL} &= \text{Current liabilities} \\
\text{NCL} &= \text{Noncurrent liabilities} \\
\text{CC} &= \text{Contributed capital} \\
\text{RE} &= \text{Retained earnings.}
\end{aligned}
$$

Any transaction or adjustment resulting in a change in any item on the right-hand side of this equation that does not, at the same time, change another item by an equal and opposite amount will change the balance of NWC.[12]

For concise disclosure, all funds flows representing revenues or expenses are combined in the single net amount identified as funds from operations.

Exhibit 9.17 illustrates an income statement prepared for the Ashdown Corporation in a **nonconventional** format. Following this format, you can see that funds from operations is the net of all revenues and expenses that do involve flows of funds (NWC). You can also see that net income is the result of adjusting funds from operations for various revenues and expenses that did **not** involve NWC flows and for a fund inflow that was not part of operations ($20,000 gain on disposition of fixed assets). Note that **all** of the differences between net income and funds from operations involve either noncurrent assets or noncurrent liabilities. A firm with no noncurrent items would report funds from operations and net income as the same amount.

Still referring to Exhibit 9.17, if you started with the net income figure of $650,000, how could you arrive at the correct amount for funds from operations? Try working this out and arriving at $775,000, on a separate piece of paper, before proceeding.

You are correct if you started with $650,000 and:

1. **Added** all nonfund expenses, losses, and other income-reducing adjustments.

---

[11] Plus certain others—see "matched pairs," below.

[12] I am indebted to Professor Larry Tomassini at the University of Texas at Austin for suggesting the use of this equation to reinforce the concept of NWC changes.

**Exhibit 9.17**

ASHDOWN CORPORATION

**Income Statement—Unconventional Format—for the Year 19XX**
**(000′ omitted)**

| | | |
|---|---:|---:|
| Sales | | $5,170 |
| Other revenue involving fund inflows[a] | | 148 |
| Total fund revenue | | $5,318 |
| Less:  Expenses involving fund outflows: | | |
| Cost of goods sold | $3,360 | |
| Interest[b] | 49 | |
| Income taxes[b] | 444 | |
| All other[c] | 690 | 4,543 |
| Funds from operations | | $ 775 |
| Add:  Fund gain on asset disposition[d] | | 20 |
| Revenues not involving fund inflows[e] | | 50 |
| Revenue adjustments not involving funds[f] | | 2 |
| Subtract: | | |
| Expenses not involving fund outflows[g] | | 150 |
| Interest adjustments not involving funds[h] | | 1 |
| Loss on noncurrent asset | | 40 |
| Net tax deferral[i] | | 6 |
| Net income | | $ 650 |

[a] $148,000 interest and dividends received
[b] All paid or payable
[c] All involved cash outflow or incurrence of current liability
[d] Not included as part of funds from operations
[e] $50,000 share of significantly influenced investee's undistributed earnings (equity method)
[f] $7,000 amortization of investments' discount, and $(5,000) amortization of investment premium
[g] $130,000 of depreciation on fixed assets, and $20,000 of amortization of other noncurrent assets
[h] $4,000 of bond discount amortization, and $(3,000) of bond premium amortization
[i] $16,000 of current taxes deferred, and $(10,000) of taxes previously deferred now payable

2. **Subtracted** all nonfund revenues and income-increasing adjustments.
3. **Subtracted** fund gain on asset disposition as not part of operations.

Refer now to Exhibits 9.18 and 9.19. Exhibit 9.18 is an income statement for the Ashdown Corporation in a more conventional format. All revenues and expenses are the same as in Exhibit 9.17; only the format is different. Exhibit 9.19 reconciles net income and funds from operations in the same fashion as you did above.

Note that expenses such as depreciation are added to net income **not** because they are additional sources of funds, but in order to reverse their subtraction as part of income determination, since they do **not** represent funds outflows. Similarly, revenues such as the $50,000 share of not-yet-distributed

**Exhibit 9.18**

ASHDOWN CORPORATION

---

**Income Statement for the Year 19XX**
**(000 omitted)**

| | | |
|---|---:|---:|
| Sales | | $5,170 |
|    Cost of goods sold | | 3,360 |
| Gross profit | | $1,810 |
| Less:  Operating expenses | | |
|         Depreciation of fixed assets | $130 | |
|         Amortization of intangible assets | 20 | |
|         All other[a] | 690 | 840 |
| Operating income | | $ 970 |
| Add:  Investments income (revenue)[b] | $200 | |
|       Gain on noncurrent asset disposition | 20 | 220 |
| Subtract: | | |
|       Interest expense[c] | $ 50 | |
|       Loss on noncurrent asset disposition | 40 | 90 |
| Income from operations before taxes: | | $1,100 |
|    Provision for income taxes[d] | | 450 |
| Net income | | $ 650 |

[a] All involved cash outflow or incurrence of current liability
[b] Includes:  $148,000  interest and dividends received
               $ (5,000)  amortization of investment premium
               $ 7,000  amortization of investments' discount
               $ 50,000  share of significantly influenced investee's undistributed earn-
                      ings
[c] Includes:  $ 49,000  of interest paid and payable
               $ 4,000  of bond discount amortization
               $ (3,000)  of bond premium amortization
[d] Includes:  $444,000  of taxes paid and payable
               $ 16,000  of taxes being deferred
               $ (10,000)  of taxes previously deferred now payable

---

earnings are subtracted, to reverse their inclusion in income since they did **not** represent fund inflows. Gains on noncurrent asset dispositions (which did involve fund inflows) were also subtracted, as not being part of operations.

### Different Uses of the Term "Operations"

The terms "operations" and "operating," like "funds," have several different meanings or uses that may prove confusing. On the income statement, operations (as in income from operations) is precisely defined by GAAP to include all revenues, gains, expenses, and losses unless they qualify as extraordinary or relate to discontinued operations.[13] Operations on the SCFP (as in funds from operations) has the same meaning but it is always reported on an after-tax basis and any gains on noncurrent asset dispositions are excluded. These

---

[13]   Refer to the Glossary, or to a financial accounting text, for a description of the GAAP requirements for classification as either extraordinary or discontinued.

### Exhibit 9.19
### ASHDOWN CORPORATION

**Reconciliation of Funds from Operations and Net Income**
**for the Year 19XX**
**(000 omitted)**

| | | |
|---|---:|---:|
| Net income: | | $650 |
| Add: | | |
| (1) Depreciation on fixed assets | $130 | |
| (2) Amortization of other noncurrent assets | 20 | |
| (3) Amortization of premium on investments | 5 | |
| (4) Losses (not extraordinary) on disposition of noncurrent assets | 40 | |
| (5) Portion of provision for income taxes representing deferral | 16 | |
| (6) Amortization of liability discount | 4 | 215 |
| Subtract: | | |
| (7) Amortization of investments discount | $ 7 | |
| (8) Portion of investments income representing share of earnings from investee not yet received in dividends | 50 | |
| (9) Amortization of noncurrent liability premium | 3 | |
| (10) Portion of provision for income taxes representing previous deferral | 10 | |
| (11) Gains on disposition of noncurrent assets | 20 | 90 |
| Equals:   Funds from operations[a] | | $775 |

[a] Assuming no extraordinary items

gains are shown separately as part of the total proceeds of funds derived from the sale of noncurrent assets—a distinct, separate source of funds. If gains were also included in funds from operations, they would be double-counted.

The term "operating" (as in operating income) has a third meaning somewhat different from operations. An income statement will often include an additional subtotal for operating income as a part of income from operations. This practice is illustrated in Exhibit 9.18. In this sense, "operating" refers to the primary activities of the firm. It specifically **excludes** certain revenues and expenses, not only those classified as extraordinary or relating to discontinued operations, but also those related to financial activities. As illustrated, it excludes gains and losses on asset dispositions, interest costs, and other revenues.

## MATCHED PAIRS

The purpose behind the disclosure of operations data (funds from operations or income from operations) is to provide the reader with information about the results of normal or regular activities. Such data may then be used as a basis for forecasting the future, since it is potentially repeatable, in contrast to extraordinary or discontinued items.

Funds from operations, together with a reconciliation with net income, are disclosed on the SCFP along with other NWC flows related to nonoperations activities. The SCFP may also include other major resource flows that do not involve NWC. Examples of these additional items would include:

- Any noncurrent assets acquired in exchange for new long-term debt;
- Any noncurrent assets acquired in direct exchange for another noncurrent asset;
- Any noncurrent assets acquired in exchange for new long-term debt;
- Any noncurrent assets acquired in exchange for stock or as a direct owner investment;
- Any noncurrent debt retired in exchange for stock (an ownership interest) as part of a debt conversion.

None of these events involves a flow of net working capital, and yet all may represent major financial transactions with significant influence on the firm's financial position.

For example, assume that, in a given year, a firm experienced the following events:

1. Acquired fixed asset in direct trade (no cash or debt involved) for another with a book value of $30,000;
2. Acquired fixed asset costing $50,000, paying $10,000 down and giving a five-year, interest-bearing promissory note for the balance;
3. Acquired fixed asset with a fair market value of $60,000 in exchange for stock;
4. $70,000 of long-term debt was converted to stock.

Refer again to the balance sheet diagram introduced earlier. The effect of each of these events is illustrated in Fig. 9.4. Note that if the SCFP were restricted

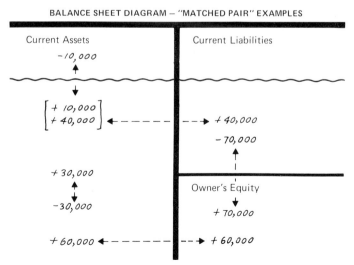

BALANCE SHEET DIAGRAM – "MATCHED PAIR" EXAMPLES

**Figure 9.4**

to reporting only NWC flows, only the $10,000 portion of the new asset would be disclosed. All of the other significant resource and/or financial structure changes would be ignored. Note also that each of these nonworking-capital flow events represents a "matched pair" of resource flows (source and application):

| Source | Application |
|---|---|
| $40,000 of new long-term debt | $40,000 of new noncurrent assets |
| $30,000 sale of noncurrent assets | $30,000 acquisition of noncurrent assets |
| $60,000 of additional stock (owner investment) | $60,000 of new noncurrent assets |
| $70,000 of additional stock (owner investment) | $70,000 reduction in long-term debt |

Also note that matched pairs all involve either **noncurrent** assets or **noncurrent** liabilities, or both. A firm having no noncurrent assets and no long-term debt could not have any matched pairs.

Matched pairs may also be identified in terms of the equation for NWC derived earlier:

$$NWC = NCL + CC + RE - NCA.$$

A matched pair will affect items on the right side of this equation in equal and opposite amounts, and therefore will **not** change the balance of NWC. Remember that not all matched pairs are reported on the SCFP. Matched pairs that do **not** involve discretionary resource flows with outsiders such as:

> depreciation or amortization of noncurrent assets,
> amortization of debt or investment premium or discount,
> equity in another firm's undistributed earnings,
> change in deferred income taxes, and
> stock dividends

are ignored on the SCFP. **Only** those matched pairs that involve discretionary resource flows are included on the SCFP.


## FUNDS FLOW STATEMENT—WORKING CAPITAL ONLY

For use in financial management, a second type of funds flow statement may be prepared. The working capital funds flow statement is the same as the SCFP (prepared on a NWC basis) **except** that it ignores or excludes any "matched pairs." It focuses exclusively on flows of NWC. Note that, for a firm having no noncurrent items, or for a firm having no matched pairs during a given period, a working capital funds flow statement and a SCFP will be identical. In such situations there are no matched pairs to make a difference.

# FUNDS FLOW STATEMENT—CASH ONLY

A third type of funds flow statement may be prepared that focuses on cash flows. Noncurrent asset, noncurrent debt, and owners' capital exchanges involving cash are included as sources and applications. Instead of funds (NWC) from operations completing the picture, it is necessary to include cash from operations. Funds from operations focuses upon only flows of NWC and not upon flows within NWC. Cash from operations focuses upon any revenues and expenses that involve flows of cash.

Funds from operations may be reconciled with cash from operations, or cash from operations may be determined, given funds from operations, in the following manner:

1. Start with: Funds from operations

2. Adjust for changes occurring during the period in the balance of net noncash current assets:

Add any net decrease, or<br>Subtract any net increase

3. Adjust for changes occurring during the period in the balance of total current liabilities:

Add any increase, or<br>Subtract any decrease

4. Equals: Cash generated (lost) in operations.

Exhibit 9.20 illustrates a reconciliation of funds from operations and cash generated in operations. It also includes a schedule of working capital changes, which is required by GAAP to accompany a SCFP as supplementary information. Note that the schedule of NWC changes reconciles with the change in the overall balance of NWC as reported for the Ashdown Corporation on Exhibits 9.20 and 9.21.

Also note that the $700,000 of cash generated in operations normally will **not** reconcile with the period's increase in the balance of cash. The $700,000 of cash from operations was just one of the sources of additional cash during the year. $350,000 of cash was also obtained from other sources, and a total of $750,000 was expended for new noncurrent assets, debt retirement, and dividends.

Exhibit 9.21 is a statement of cash flows for the Ashdown Corporation. Note that the $300,000 net increase in cash does reconcile with the changed cash position as reported on the schedule of working capital changes (Exhibit 9.20). Exhibit 9.21 assumes that all nonoperations sources and applications reported on the SCFP (prepared on a NWC basis) and illustrated in Exhibit 9.16 involved cash flows—no matched pairs of resource flows occurred. In such a situation, Exhibit 9.21 would also be acceptable under GAAP as a SCFP prepared on a cash rather than a working capital basis.

**Exhibit 9.20**

ASHDOWN CORPORATION

Schedule of Working Capital Changes and
Schedule of Cash Generated in Operations
for the Year 19XX
(000 omitted)

**Schedule of working capital changes:**

|  | Beginning of year | End of year | Change |
|---|---|---|---|
| Cash | $ 100 | $ 400 | +300 |
| Receivables | 900 | 875 | − 25 |
| Inventory | 500 | 700 | +200 |
| Total current assets | $1,500 | $1,975 | +475 |
| Accounts payable | $ 300 | $ 450 | +150 |
| Other current liabilities | 200 | 150 | − 50 |
| Total current liabilities | $ 500 | $ 600 | +100 |
| Net working capital | $1,000 | $1,375 | +375 |

**Schedule of cash generated in operations:**

|  |  |
|---|---|
| Funds from operations | $775 |
| Net increase in balance of noncash current assets—(subtract) | −175 |
| Net increase in balance of current liabilities—(add) | +100 |
| Cash generated in operations | $700 |

To see the distinction between a cash (funds) flow statement and a SCFP (cash basis) in other circumstances, merely assume the following with respect to Exhibit 9.16:

• Of the $400,000 of new noncurrent assets, $125,000 were acquired, paying $25,000 down and giving a $100,000 ten-year, interest-bearing note for the balance. $25,000 were acquired in even trade for other noncurrent assets. The remaining $250,000 of assets were purchased for cash.

• $50,000 of long-term debt was converted to stock during the year.

Under these different assumptions, there were three matched pairs of resource flows which did **not** involve cash flows:

| Sources | Application |
|---|---|
| $100,000 of new long-term debt | $100,000 of new noncurrent assets |
| $ 25,000 of noncurrent assets traded | $ 25,000 of noncurrent assets acquired in trade |
| $ 50,000 of additional stock | $ 50,000 of long-term debt retired |

**Exhibit 9.21**

ASHDOWN CORPORATION

---

**Statement of Cash Flows
for the Year 19XX
(000 omitted)**

| | |
|---|---:|
| **Sources of cash:** | |
| Net income | $ 650 |
| Adjustments for nonfund items[a] | +125 |
| Funds from operations | $ 775 |
| Adjustments for changes in noncash NWC items[b] | −75 |
| Cash generated in operations | $ 700 |
| Proceeds from sale of noncurrent assets | 50 |
| Proceeds from additional long-term debt | 100 |
| Proceeds from sale of stock (additional owner investment) | 200 |
| Total sources of cash | $1,050 |
| | |
| **Applications (uses) of cash:** | |
| Purchase additional noncurrent assets | $ 400 |
| Retire existing long-term debt | 50 |
| Dividends (owner withdrawals) | 300 |
| Total applications (uses) of cash | $ 750 |
| Increase in balance of cash on hand | $ 300 |

[a] See Exhibit 9.19.
[b] See Exhibit 9.20.

---

With these matched pairs, a cash flow statement for Ashdown (as distinct from a SCFP prepared on a cash basis) would report (000 omitted):

| | |
|---|---:|
| **Sources:** | |
| Cash from operations | $700 |
| Proceeds from sale of noncurrent assets | 25 |
| Proceeds from sale of stock | 150 |
| | $875 |
| | |
| **Applications:** | |
| Purchase of noncurrent assets | $275 |
| Dividends | 300 |
| | $575 |
| Increase in balance of cash on hand | $300 |

Once again, as illustrated in this modified example, the difference between the cash flow statement and the SCFP prepared on a cash basis is due merely to those matched pairs of resource flows that did **not** involve cash.

## CASH FLOW STATEMENTS AND CASH BUDGETS

A cash (funds) flow statement is not very common. It is historical and, as such, of little use for cash management. Cash budgets, as discussed in this chapter, differ from cash flow statements in several respects:

1. They are projections of future flows rather than reports of past flows. They thus have value for future decision guidance.

2. They usually are broken down into more detailed individual items, which are more readily subject to management control.

For firms, or more particularly outside investors, who desire a basis for estimating future cash flows, and who do not have or have access to cash budgets, a cash flow statement prepared on a pro-forma or projected basis may be a satisfactory alternative. Preparation of projected cash flows based on published financial statements is beyond the scope of this text. It is often covered in more advanced finance and investment courses.

# 10

# TOTAL RESOURCE PLANNING – THE MASTER BUDGET

## CHAPTER PREVIEW

The purpose of this chapter is to provide you with information about the final phase of the budgeting process—the preparation of the master budget. In this chapter you can:

- Learn how the various budgets with which you are already familiar may be combined at the total firm level to produce pro forma financial statements—a budgeted income statement, a budgeted SCFP, and a budgeted ending balance sheet.
- Discover the content and function of the firm's financial budget.
- Become aware of the function of preliminary budgeted financial statements and particularly their use as a basis for determining need for additional long-term financing.
- Learn the necessity of adequate capitalization (resources available) and the risks inherent in a firm's being under- or overcapitalized.
- Learn of the possible differences, and their sources, that may exist between preliminary and final budgeted financial statements.
- Develop awareness of several reasons why a firm might elect to revise previously prepared budgets, and of the potential difficulties connected with the process of budget revision.

With this chapter you will have completed your introduction to and basic understanding of the entire budgeting process for a business or profit-directed organization. You will have the necessary foundation to begin learning (in Chapters 11 through 14) how budgets may be used for management control. You will also have the foundation to be introduced to budgeting in nonprofit-directed institutions, in Chapter 15.

## WHAT WILL BE MY PROFIT AND FINANCIAL POSITION NEXT YEAR?

As the president of Tripper, involved in your first budgeting process, you are learning that planning involves more than having a hazy idea of what you would like to do and where you would like to go, and then operating on a day-to-day basis in the general direction of your goals. In Chapter 6 you were introduced to the fact that profits are usually the result of careful choices among alternatives rather than blind luck. In the cash budgeting process (Chapter 9), you experienced the need for careful cash planning to avoid insolvency. And from financial accounting, you should be aware that a certain minimal level of capital resources or assets is required if a firm is to operate successfully at any particular level of activity or volume.

The final stages of the budgeting process involve putting all the pieces together and seeing whether they will work satisfactorily. The budgeting process started with a projection of a desired and expected level of sales volume, the sales budget. The operating and purchases budgets have generated the expected level of costs associated with this target level of activity. The purchases, inventory, and capital budgets have made possible the projection of necessary noncash assets to sustain the target activity level. The cash budget has projected necessary and expected levels of cash, marketable securities, and short-term financing.

Completing the master budget involves projecting required and anticipated levels of all assets that are needed for the target activity level. This projection usually takes the form of a pro forma or projected lefthand side of a balance sheet. Anticipated sources of financing for these assets are similarly projected as the righthand side of the balance sheet. Projected sources would include:

- anticipated levels of current liabilities,
- existing and any already planned additional long-term debt,
- existing and any already planned additional owner's contributed capital, and
- existing and planned additional retained earnings (planned profits less planned dividends).

If adequate financing is already budgeted, the overall budgeting process can be considered as completed. If not, further plans must be made to obtain necessary additional financing. Should adequate financing not be available, the entire budget must then be reviewed and revised to a lower level of expenditure or activity.

The master budgeting activity has seven steps that are common to most firms, and manufacturers have an additional preliminary step. These steps are illustrated in Fig. 10.1 and will be described in this chapter.

Recall, from Chapter 2, that one of the two major objectives of the overall budgeting process is to plan for adequate resources to support the firm's

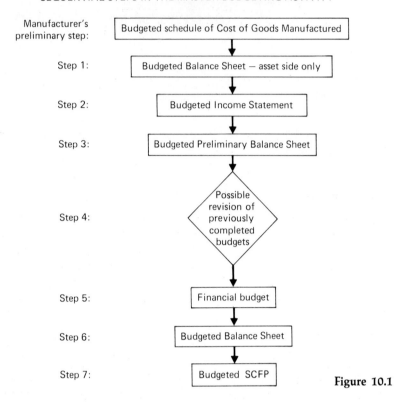

Figure 10.1

sales and profit goals. The master budgeting activity focuses upon and completes resource planning to ensure adequate capitalization. The need for adequate capitalization (having sufficient and appropriate resources or assets) is often covered in financial accounting. However, the subject will be briefly reviewed before discussing each master budgeting step.

## PLANNING OF REQUIRED RESOURCES

Overall resource planning has three objectives:

1. to ensure that an adequate but not excessive amount of resources are on hand available for use;

2. to ensure an appropriate composition or distribution of the adequate resources among cash, receivables, inventory, other current assets, and various noncurrent assets; and

3. to complete resource planning in sufficient time to provide, in turn, adequate lead time for obtaining any additional required financing in an orderly and efficient manner.

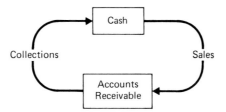

**Figure 10.2**

The first concern of resource planning is adequate working capital to finance the firm's *operating cycle.*

### The Operating Cycle and the Need for Working Capital

Recall, from financial accounting, the concept of a firm's operating cycle. A firm in the service business and operating on a cash basis would need only a minimum investment in working capital. If no supplies were required, only a small amount of cash on hand as a change fund might be all that would be required. A service firm on a cash basis, but needing supplies on hand for use when required (a secretarial or janitorial firm), would need both a change fund and a small investment in supplies. A service firm extending credit to customers would require an additional investment in order to finance receivables. (See Fig. 10.2.) Cash would be tied up in wages paid and supplies purchased and used until receivables were collected. The larger the volume of sales, and the longer the collection period (slower receivables turnover), the larger would be the requirement for continuous or long-term investment in working capital.

Exhibit 10.1 illustrates the operating cycles of a merchandiser and a manufacturer. Note that, as distinct from service firms, these businesses also require an investment in inventory. Again, the greater the volume and the longer the cycle (slower turnover of inventory and receivables), the larger will be the long-term need for investment in working capital. Note also that a manufacturer may have more invested in a slower inventory turnover than a merchandiser would have, because of the additional time and conversion costs required before products are available for sale.

### Requirements for Noncurrent Assets

In addition to long-term investment in working capital, many firms and especially manufacturers require long-term investment in plant and equipment or fixed capacity assets.[1] Recall from Chapter 5 that a given investment in plant and equipment can support only a given range of activity—the so-called rele-

---

[1]    Larger firms may also find it desirable or necessary to provide long-term financing to suppliers and/or distributors. In such situations, additional capital is tied up in noncurrent investments.

**Exhibit 10.1**

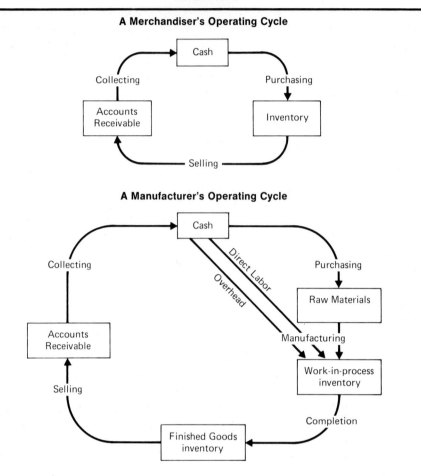

**A Merchanshiser's Operating Cycle**

**A Manufacturer's Operating Cycle**

vant range. As intended activity expands beyond a relevant range, further investment in expanded capacity will be required, along with additional working capital.

### Appropriate Amount of Total Assets—Adequate Capitalization

To fully grasp the significance of planning adequate resources, think of the consequences of having too little or too much. What happens to a firm that is *undercapitalized*, that has insufficient resources for its current level of operations? A firm that is undercapitalized cannot support its desired sales volume. At best it will be chronically out of stock or short of service personnel, equipment, and time. It will be continuously back-ordering or delaying its customer's demands. Often, in an attempt to make sales and to service customers, the undercapitalized firm will overpurchase inventory and capacity assets, become insolvent, and fail.

Being *overcapitalized*, having excessive and unneeded resources on hand, is equally undesirable, even if not potentially fatal in the short run. Excess or unnecessary *redundant assets* are unproductive; they do not "earn their keep." A firm with unnecessary redundant assets usually finds it impossible, in the long run, to earn a satisfactory return on its invested assets. As described in Chapter 6, a firm chronically unable to cover its cost of capital may eventually be unable to raise necessary additional capital for expansion when warranted, or just to survive in a rapidly changing world.

## Appropriate Composition of Assets

Not only must a firm be adequately capitalized, but the composition or distribution of its available resources must also be appropriate to its current and anticipated operations. A firm may require and have $10,000,000 of total assets, but if these assets are all in plant and equipment or even inventory, it may be unable to finance receivables and may become insolvent. Financial management involves the management (planning and control) of all assets, not just cash. The techniques of *asset management* are more properly covered in courses in financial management. The master-budgeting part of the overall budgeting process provides some of the information required for effective asset management.

## PREPARING THE BUDGETED BALANCE SHEET (ASSET SIDE)

Returning to the Tripper example, information is available in the late Fall of 19X1 to project the firm's balance sheet assets as of 12/31/X2. Assume that Tripper's projected 12/31/X2 assets would be of the same type as in 19X1 and would consist of:

> Cash
> Marketable securities
> Accounts receivable (net)
> Raw materials inventory
> Work-in-process inventory
> Finished goods inventory
> Supplies
> Prepaid items
> Land
> Buildings (net of accumulated depreciation)
> Equipment (net of accumulated depreciation)
> Office furniture and fixtures (net of accumulated depreciation)

Can you recall which of the already prepared budgets would supply the necessary information to project the balances for each of these items? Most of the necessary information has already been budgeted. Exhibit 10.2 illustrates the various sources of this data.

**Exhibit 10.2**

## SOURCES OF INFORMATION FOR BUDGETING BALANCE SHEET ASSETS

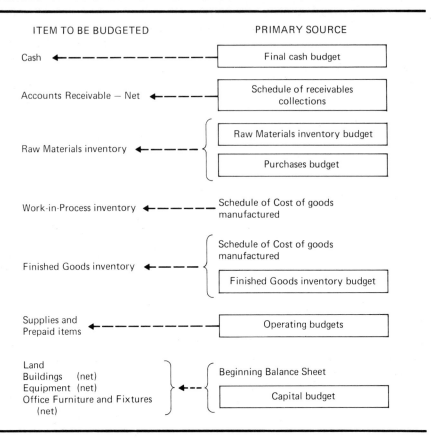

| ITEM TO BE BUDGETED | PRIMARY SOURCE |
| --- | --- |
| Cash | Final cash budget |
| Accounts Receivable — Net | Schedule of receivables collections |
| Raw Materials inventory | Raw Materials inventory budget / Purchases budget |
| Work-in-Process inventory | Schedule of Cost of goods manufactured |
| Finished Goods inventory | Schedule of Cost of goods manufactured / Finished Goods inventory budget |
| Supplies and Prepaid items | Operating budgets |
| Land / Buildings (net) / Equipment (net) / Office Furniture and Fixtures (net) | Beginning Balance Sheet / Capital budget |

### Budgeting Cash and Marketable Securities

Perhaps the easiest items to obtain for the balance sheet at this stage in the budgeting process are the projected balances for cash and marketable securities on 12/31/X2. Recall that these amounts have already been projected and are available as part of the cash budgeting process (Chapter 9). Tripper's final cash budget for 19X2 (Exhibit 9.10) projected ending cash as $152,680 or $153,000 (rounded). The ending balance of marketable securities was projected as zero.

### Budgeting Accounts Receivable

Data for budgeting Accounts receivable—net is available from the schedule of receivables collections (Exhibit 9.5) and from the firm's experience with uncollectable accounts. Recall that Tripper's average collection pattern with respect to a given month's sales was:

30%   collected same month (cash sales plus collections within the month of sale),
40%   during first month following sale,
28%   during second month following sale,
 2%   uncollectable and written off during the third month following sale.[2]

Therefore, 19X2 sales through September will have been collected or written off by 12/31/X2. From the 19X2 sales budget, remaining projected sales for the year were:

| | |
|---|---|
| October | $64,500 |
| November | $39,500 |
| December | $27,000 |

You should make your own projection, rounded to the nearest thousand dollars, of 12/31/X2 accounts receivable—net (accounts receivable less allowance for uncollectables), before proceeding.

The correct projection of ending accounts receivable—net is $29,000 based on the above data.[3] Accounts receivable—net can also be projected by simply using the firm's previous ratio for receivables turnover[4] and dividing it into budgeted sales for the year. In the Tripper example, assume that more accurate data were not available. If Tripper's receivables turnover had been averaging 41 times (indicating a seasonal business with most sales occurring and collected by year-end) and sales were budgeted at $1,264,000 (Exhibit 3.8), then average net receivables could be estimated at $30,829 or $31,000. $31,000 would be an adequate estimate of the $29,420 obtained by more accurate measurement. The error would result from using a historical cost ratio when changes in sales volume and timing could be occurring.

## Budgeting Inventories

A merchandiser can budget ending inventories by taking forecasted quantities on hand at year-end from the finished goods inventory budget (Exhibit 4.9) and extending by each item's cost. If price/cost changes have occurred during

---

[2]   Early write-off of uncollectables is assumed to simplify the Tripper example. Normally a firm might wait at least six to nine months or longer before giving up on a receivable and declaring it uncollectable.

[3]   Accounts receivable:

| | | |
|---|---|---|
| 2% | of October sales | $ 1,290 |
| 30% | of November sales | 11,850 |
| 70% | of December sales | 18,900 |
| | Total | $32,040 |
| Uncollectables allowance: | | |
| 2% | fourth-quarter sales | $ 2,620 |
| Accounts receivable net of uncollectables | | $29,420 or $29,000 rounded |

[4]   $$\text{Receivables turnover} = \frac{\text{Sales}}{\text{Average accounts receivable—net}}$$

the year or period, then costs selected for extension would have to follow the firm's choice of inventory method relating to cost flow assumptions (FIFO, LIFO, or average cost).

Alternatively, ending inventories may be approximated through the use of the firm's gross margin and inventory turnover ratios.[5] Projected cost of goods sold is first obtained by applying the complement of the firm's gross margin percentage (1 − Gross margin percentage) to budgeted sales. For in stance, Allway Stores, with $1,000,000 of budgeted sales and with a 60-percent gross margin percentage, projects $400,000 as cost of goods sold ($1,000,000 times 40 percent). Anticipated cost of goods sold will then be divided by the firm's average inventory turnover, to obtain average inventory on hand, which may then be used to estimate the ending inventory balance. Continuing with the above example, with an average inventory turnover of five times a year, Allway Stores could project $80,000 of ending merchandise inventory.

Budgeting a merchandiser's inventory on the basis of past cost and turn-over ratios can be reasonably accurate only if price-to-cost (markon) percentages, product mix, and inventory turnover can all be assumed to remain reasonably uniform from one year to the next. Furthermore, when data is not available from detailed inventory budgets, care must be exercised to make sure that budgeted ending inventory is adequate to meet the following period's expected demand.

### Completing the Budgeted Schedule of Cost of Goods Manufactured

A manufacturer with three distinct inventory levels and many different in-ventory costs is usually well advised to complete its budgeted cost of goods manufactured before attempting to complete its budget for ending inventories on the balance sheet. Beginning balances of raw materials and work-in-process inventories are obtainable from the prior year's projected ending balance sheet ($4,000 and $18,000, respectively, for Tripper). Raw materials purchases and ending raw materials inventory are obtainable from the purchases and raw materials inventory budgets (Exhibits 4.13 and 4.12). In Tripper's case, these amounts were $127,000 and $3,000, respectively.

Direct labor and manufacturing overhead for 19X2 for Tripper were al-ready budgeted as $208,000 and $352,000 (Exhibits 5.8 and 5.9). If deprecia-tion on manufacturing assets was not included in the overhead budget, it must be determined as part of the financial accounting system. Depreciation allo-cated to manufacturing overhead for 19X2 for Tripper was $52,000 and is included in the $352,000 of expected manufacturing overhead. The remaining item necessary to complete the budgeted schedule of cost of goods manufac-tured is the projection of ending work-in-process inventory. This amount may

---

[5]    Gross margin percent $= \dfrac{\text{Gross profit}}{\text{Sales}} \times 100$

   Inventory turnover $= \dfrac{\text{Cost of goods sold}}{\text{Average inventory}}$

be obtained by first comparing the budgeted final production schedule (Exhibit 4.10) and the finished goods inventory budget (Exhibit 4.9), and then costing those shop orders that were not expected to be completed by year-end. In the Tripper example, it has been assumed, for simplification, that the 19X2 expected ending work-in-process inventory was zero.

Using Exhibit 2.14 for format, and the above data, you should separately complete Tripper's 19X2 budgeted schedule of cost of goods manufactured, rounded to even thousands of dollars, before proceeding.

The correct projection of the cost of products that would be transferred into finished goods inventory during 19X2 is $706,000. Exhibit 10.3 is Tripper's 19X2 budgeted schedule of cost of goods manufactured. Note that this schedule also provides the expected amounts of ending inventory to be included in the budgeted balance sheet for raw materials and work-in-process. As covered in Chapter 9 under the budgeting of purchases and operating expenditures, a firm not having formal operating budgets can still approximate expected expenses for purchases, direct labor, and manufacturing overhead through using its average gross margin ratio to project cost of goods sold (as described above as an alternative for a merchandiser). With an esti-

**Exhibit 10.3**

TRIPPER WATER SKI MANUFACTURING COMPANY

**Budgeted Schedule of Cost of Goods Manufactured (in thousands) for the Year 19X2**

| | | |
|---|---:|---:|
| Direct materials: | | |
| Beginning raw materials inventory | $ 4 | |
| Add: Net purchases during 19X2 | 127 | |
| Total raw materials available | $131 | |
| Deduct: Ending raw materials inventory | 3 | |
| Direct materials used in manufacturing | | $128 |
| Direct labor | | 208 |
| Manufacturing overhead: | | |
| Indirect labor | $164 | |
| Indirect materials (supplies) | 21 | |
| Supervision | 65 | |
| Utilities | 19 | |
| Insurance | 13 | |
| Property taxes | 18 | |
| Depreciation | 52 | |
| Total overhead costs | | 352 |
| Total manufacturing costs | | $688 |
| Add: Beginning work-in-process inventory | | 18 |
| | | $706 |
| Deduct: Ending work-in-process inventory | | 0 |
| Cost of goods manufactured | | $706 |

mate of cost of goods sold, product cost percentages for material, labor, and overhead may then be used to estimate manufacturing expenses. Note that the accuracy of this approach is limited by all of the following assumptions:

- Gross profit (markon) and product mix will be unchanged;
- Inventory levels will be unchanged;
- Either overall volume of activity is unchanged or else all product costs are considered variable;[6]
- Unit costs and prices either do not change or else change in a proportional manner.

Completion of inventory budgeting involves determination of the expected balance of finished goods inventory. The opening balance is obtainable from the prior year's ending balance sheet ($70,000 in the Tripper example). Inputs of manufactured items during the year were budgeted in the schedule of cost of goods manufactured as $706,000. Any inputs of purchased finished products such as Tripper's tow ropes may be obtained from the purchases budget ($26,000 from Exhibit 4.13). Goods available for sale may then be projected as the sum of beginning inventory plus inputs. In the Tripper example, goods available for sale is projected as $802,000. Cost of goods sold may then be determined by costing shipments projected in the finished goods inventory budget (Exhibit 4.9).[7] In Tripper's case, 19X2 cost of goods sold determined by following this approach is $734,000. To reinforce your understanding of cost-of-goods-sold budgeting, you should project the ending finished goods inventory for Tripper based on the foregoing data, before proceeding.

You adequately understand budgeting of ending inventories for a manufacturer if you see how the following amounts were obtained:

| | |
|---|---|
| Raw materials | $ 3,000 |
| Work-in-process | zero |
| Finished goods | $68,000 |

If you do not have a clear picture of inventory budgeting, you should reread this inventory section carefully, tracing each amount through the related exhibits.

---

[6]   Since assuming all overhead to be variable is usually inappropriate, if a budgeting rate (separate fixed and variable components) can be determined for overhead, the use of such a rate is preferable to a simple percentage.

[7]   Again, as in the case of budgeting raw materials, in the event of cost changes occurring during the year, appropriate costs must be used in accordance with the firm's choice of accounting method (FIFO, LIFO, or average cost). Also, if a standard cost system is used (Chapter 1), then anticipated accounting variances should be estimated and included as part of cost of goods sold.

## Budgeting Other Working Capital Requirements

The remaining elements of working capital or current assets appearing on the balance sheet (supplies and prepaid items) are often insignificant in amount. A firm may merely project the same average amounts from year to year; or it may obtain more accurate amounts by comparing beginning figures from the prior year's balance sheet, and projected expenditures from the cash and operating budgets, and then estimating expirations or usage. In the Tripper example, you may assume that the 12/31/X2 expected balances of these items were $6,000 (supplies) and $2,000 (prepaid items).

## Budgeting Noncurrent Assets

Noncurrent assets are budgeted based on the previous balance sheet amounts, changes anticipated in the capital budget (Exhibit 8.9), and appropriate recognition of depreciation and amortization expense established as part of the financial accounting system.[8] Exhibit 10.4 illustrates how noncurrent asset 19X2 ending balances were budgeted for the Tripper Company.

With all assets now budgeted for 12/31/X2 as shown on Exhibit 10.5, the next step towards completion of the master budget involves budgeting the income statement.

### Exhibit 10.4
### TRIPPER WATER SKI MANUFACTURING COMPANY

**Budgeting of Noncurrent Assets**
**for the Year 19X2**
**(000 omitted)**

| Item | Balance[a] 12/31/X1 | From capital budget[b] | 19X2 Depreciation amortization | Balance 12/31/X2 |
|---|---|---|---|---|
| Land | $ 25 | 0 | 0 | $ 25 |
| Buildings | 700 | 0 | 0 | 700 |
| Accum. depr., bldgs. | (400) | 0 | 39 | (439) |
| Equipment | 200 | +41 | 0 | 212 |
|  |  | −29 |  |  |
| Accum. depr., equip. | (100) | −20 | 21 | (101) |
| Furniture and fixtures | 50 | 0 | 0 | 50 |
| Accum. depr., F. and F. | (25) | 0 | 4 | (29) |
| Total noncurrent assets | $450 |  |  | $418 |

[a] Exhibit 2.16.
[b] Exhibit 8.9.11

---

[8]   Other noncurrent asset changes (not illustrated in the Tripper example) could include changes in long-term investments and funds and in intangible assets. Such changes would be included in the capital budget, or could be anticipated from other sources within the financial accounting system.

## Exhibit 10.5

### TRIPPER WATER SKI MANUFACTURING COMPANY

**Budgeted Assets as of 12/31/X2**
**(000 omitted)**

| | | |
|---|---:|---:|
| Cash | | $153 |
| Accounts receivable—net | | 29 |
| Inventories: | | |
|    Raw materials | $ 3 | |
|    Work-in-process | 0 | |
|    Finished goods | 68 | 71 |
| Supplies | | 6 |
| Prepaid items | | 2 |
|    Total current assets | | $261 |
| Land | | 25 |
| Buildings | | 700 |
| Accum. depr. on bldg. | | (439) |
| Equipment | | 212 |
| Accum. depr. on equip. | | (101) |
| Office furniture and fixtures | | 50 |
| Accum. depr. on F. and F. | | (29) |
|    Total assets | | $679 |

## Exhibit 10.6

**Sources of Information for Preparing Budgeted Income Statement**

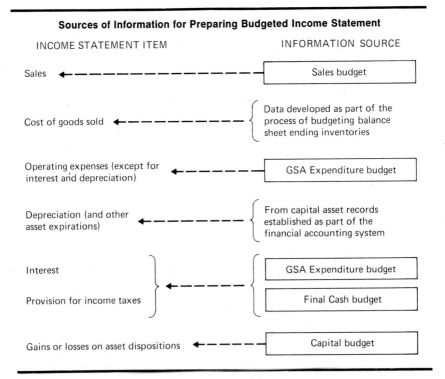

## PREPARING THE BUDGETED INCOME STATEMENT

All of the elements to be included in Tripper's 19X2 budgeted income statement have been projected in previous steps of the budgeting process. The only exception might be depreciation and amortization or other asset expirations ($12,000, in the Tripper example), which are classified as period costs and may not be included in a GSA budget prepared on an expenditure basis. In such situations, these amounts may be obtained from appropriate records established as part of the financial accounting system.

Exhibit 10.6 indicates the sources of necessary data used in preparing a budgeted income statement for those firms that have operating budgets. Exhibit 10.7 is Tripper's budgeted income statement for 19X2 as prepared from these sources.

For firms not having operating budgets for GSA expenditures, these items may be projected by estimating budgeting rates (fixed and variable components) based on various levels of sales volume from the prior year's income statements. These rates can then be applied, in conjunction with budgeted sales for the forthcoming year, to provide an estimate of various period cost expenses. Note that the accuracy of budgeting on this basis is subject to the same limitations previously cited for estimating product costs as part of the schedule of cost of goods manufactured.

**Exhibit 10.7**

TRIPPER WATER SKI MANUFACTURING COMPANY

**Pro Forma (Budgeted) Income Statement (in thousands) for the Year 19X2**

| | | |
|---|---:|---:|
| Sales | | $1,264 |
| Less cost of goods sold: | | |
| Beginning finished goods inventory | $ 70 | |
| Cost of goods manufactured | 706 | |
| Purchases of finished goods | 26 | |
| Goods available for sale | $802 | |
| Less:  Ending finished goods inventory | 68 | 734 |
| Gross profit | | $ 530 |
| Less:  Operating expenses: | | |
| Wages and salaries | $328 | |
| Marketing and distribution | 26 | |
| Interest | 13 | |
| Insurance | 4 | |
| Property taxes | 6 | |
| Miscellaneous | 4 | |
| Bad debt expense | 25 | |
| Depreciation | 12 | 418 |
| Loss on disposition of equipment | | 4 |
| Income from operations before taxes | | $ 108 |
| Provision for income taxes | | 41 |
| Net income | | $   67 |

## COMPLETING THE PRELIMINARY BUDGETED BALANCE SHEET

With the budgeted income statement completed, you can now return to the balance sheet and budget the expected equities for Tripper as of 12/31/X2. Recall, from financial accounting, that the equity side of a balance sheet may be viewed not only as representing claims against total assets, but also as representing **sources of total assets.** It is at this step in the budgeting process that the firm can determine whether it is or can be adequately capitalized to sustain its projected level of activities.

Anticipated current liabilities can be projected from the operating expenditures budget (Exhibit 9.7) and the final cash budget (Exhibit 9.10). Recall from Chapter 9 that, as part of projecting cash outflows, certain budgeted expenditures did not require payment until the following month. $65,000 of liabilities for purchases and current operations incurred during 19X2 were not expected to be paid by 12/31/X2. The final cash budget also indicated that no short-term borrowings of cash were anticipated at year-end.

A firm has one other budget that was first mentioned in Chapter 9. This budget is known as the financial budget. It includes anticipated financing activities during the forthcoming year, and can be thought of as a preliminary budgeted SCFP.

A firm prepares its preliminary financial budget from the capital budget, the budgeted income statement, and any already existing plans to raise addi-

**Exhibit 10.8**

TRIPPER WATER SKI MANUFACTURING COMPANY

**Pro Forma (Budgeted) SCFP
for the Year 19X2**

| | | |
|---|---:|---:|
| **Sources:** | | |
| Net income | | $ 67,000 |
| Add:  Depreciation on noncurrent assets | $64,000 | |
|           Loss on sale of noncurrent assets | 4,000 | 68,000 |
| Sale of fixed asset | | 5,000 |
|           Total sources | | $140,000 |
| | | |
| **Applications:** | | |
| Purchase of noncurrent assets | | $ 41,000 |
| Dividends | | 50,000 |
| | | 91,000 |
| Increase in balance of net working capital | | 49,000 |
| | | $140,000 |

tional capital through additional long-term debt or new owner investment (sale of stock), and any existing plans to retire long-term debt or to distribute dividends. Based on Tripper's capital budget (Exhibit 8.9), budgeted income statement (Exhibit 10.7), planned distribution of $50,000 in dividends (Chapter 9), and no other existing plans to acquire or retire long-term financing, prepare a preliminary capital budget, in even thousands of dollars, following the format of the SCFP (Exhibit 2.13).

Exhibit 10.8 is Tripper's pro-forma or budgeted SCFP for 19X2. Note that it indicates no planned changes in the amount of long-term debt or in owners' contributed capital. Tripper's noncurrent equities as of 12/31/X1 (Exhibit 2.16) were:

| | |
|---|---|
| Long-term debt | $185,000 |
| Capital stock | 300,000 |
| Paid-in capital | 50,000 |
| Retained earnings | 62,000 |

From the foregoing information you should project Tripper's equities as of 12/31/X2, before proceeding.

### Exhibit 10.9
### TRIPPER WATER SKI MANUFACTURING COMPANY

**Pro Forma (Budgeted) Balance Sheet (in thousands)**
**as of 12/31/X2**

| Assets | | | Equities | |
|---|---|---|---|---|
| Cash | | $153 | Accounts payable | $ 3 |
| Accounts receivable—net | | 29 | Wages and salaries payable | 21 |
| Inventories: | | | Interest payable | 6 |
| Raw materials | $ 3 | | Taxes payable | 32 |
| Work-in-process | 0 | | Other current liabilities | 3 |
| Finished goods | 68 | 71 | Total Current Liabilities | $ 65 |
| Supplies | | 6 | Long-term debt | 185 |
| Prepaid items | | 2 | Total Liabilities | $250 |
| Total Current Assets | | $261 | | |
| Land | | 25 | | |
| Buildings | | 700 | | |
| Accum. depr. on bldg. | | (439) | | |
| Equipment | | 212 | Stockholders' Equity: | |
| Accum. depr. on equip. | | (101) | Capital stock ($10 par) | $300 |
| Office furniture and fixtures | | 50 | Paid-in capital | 50 |
| Accum. depr. on F. and F. | | (29) | Retained earnings | 79 |
| Total Assets | | $679 | Total Equities | $679 |

Exhibit 10.9 is Tripper's budgeted balance sheet for the end of 19X2. Were you surprised that the projected equities of $679,000 balance previously projected assets in this same amount (Exhibit 10.5)? The balance sheet equation was maintained throughout the master-budgeting process through the other budget components (the cash budget, capital budget, income statement, and SCFP).

## DETERMINING NEED FOR ADDITIONAL LONG-TERM FINANCING

The preliminary budgeted balance sheet and the preliminary financial budget must be examined by the firm to ascertain whether projected sources are realistically obtainable and whether appropriate debt ratios are being maintained.[9] In the Tripper example, there is no current borrowing of funds indicated at year-end. The debt ratio[10] is projected at 36.8 percent, compared to 37.8 percent as of 12/31/X1 (Exhibit 2.16); and you can assume that this is appropriate for a firm in Tripper's industry. Therefore, with no further financing indicated, the Tripper budgeting process for 19X2 may be considered completed. The preliminary financial budget (Exhibit 10.8) and preliminary budgeted balance sheet (Exhibit 10.9) may be considered final.

The master budgeting process would not be completed for a firm where the preliminary balance sheet indicated the need for additional long-term financing. Suppose a preliminary budgeted balance sheet for another firm, the Beck Corporation, indicated (000 omitted):

| | | | | |
|---|---|---|---|---|
| Current assets | $300 | Current loans | | $250 |
| | | Other current liabilities | | 200 |
| Noncurrent assets | 500 | Total current liabilities | | $450 |
| | | Long-term debt | | 220 |
| | | Total owners' equity | | 130 |
| Total assets | $800 | Total equities | | $800 |

Obviously, even if the firm could obtain $250,000 in short-term financing (which is doubtful), it could not long maintain solvency with a current ratio of only 0.67 to 1.

Assume further that Beck and its creditors wished to maintain a minimum current ratio of 1.5 to 1 and a maximum debt ratio of .65 to 1. Based on $800,000 of required assets, can you determine the appropriate composition of Beck's equities within the above guidelines? A minimum (safe) composition for Beck in this example would be (000 omitted):

---

[9]   See the appendix to this chapter for a discussion of financial leverage.

[10]   Debt ratio $= \dfrac{\text{Total liabilities}}{\text{Total equities}}$

| | | |
|---|---|---|
| Current liabilities | $200 | (1.5 ratio with $300 of current assets) |
| Long-term debt | 320 | (.65 of total equities less current liabilities) |
| Owners' equity | 280 | |
| | $800 | |

To support its projected level of operations, Beck must be able to raise an additional $100,000 (or less) of long-term debt and an additional $150,000 (or more) of owners' investment to replace its projected short-term borrowings of $250,000. If such financing is feasible, it must be planned; and the firm's cash budget, budgeted income statement (for additional interest and financing costs), budgeted balance sheet, and budgeted SCFP must be modified accordingly. Considerations involved in the raising of additional capital are more properly included in texts in business finance and financial management. A brief overview of the subject is included in the appendix to this chapter, so that you may better understand the resource planning function of budgeting.

## POSSIBLE OVERALL BUDGET REVISION

Returning to the Beck Corporation introduced above, suppose that Beck's financial management did not believe that more than $150,000 in long-term debt and owners' capital could be obtained within the next year. What should Beck do? If any dividends had been planned, they might be passed. However, unless at least $100,000 of dividends had been planned and could be passed without undue hardship to the owners, Beck will have to scale down its operations to a level that can be financially supported. Scaling down operations might involve merely postponing capital asset purchases and other programmed or discretionary costs (Chapter 5). Or it might involve reducing the sales budget and rebudgeting the entire company.

Possible need for overall budget revision could also arise in situations where the preliminary master budget revealed a profit that was unsatisfactory to top management. Again rebudgeting of expenditures would be necessary to see which items might be reduced or eliminated without impairing operations or being otherwise counterproductive.

Recall from Chapter 2 the difference between an imposed and a participative budgeting system. Rebudgeting or budget revision may be viewed by employees just like the making of a new budget. Often the benefits of a budget carefully constructed from the lowest level of responsibility on a participative basis may be sacrificed by an arbitrary imposed cut occurring as part of the master budgeting process. Cost reduction may be essential for the firm; there may really be no choice in the matter; but managers at all levels should be made aware of such a reality **outside** of the budgeting system. From such awareness, revisions can be made by the individual managers, who will then have to live with them. The responsibility and resultant control benefits of a participative budget can then continue to exist.

The last four chapters and this chapter have all focused on budgeting decisions at the total firm or top management level. You should not make the mistake of looking at budgets only from the top down or from a top management perspective. As discussed in Chapters 2 and 5, and as will be explored further in the next four chapters on budgetary control, budgets are very important management tools at all levels within the organization and especially at the level of first-line supervision. First-line supervisors have primary responsibility to translate the firm's goals into action. The supervisor's budget, if properly prepared and understood, can serve as the single most important guideline communicating the specific objectives of the particular responsibility center in a form congruent with the firm's overall goals. In effect, the responsibility center budget may be viewed as a direct communication link between the supervisor or manager and the firm's president.

Budget revision may be necessary as part of determining the final budget for the forthcoming period. Thereafter, during the ensuing period, revisions of the budget are rare. Recall from Chapter 9 that cash budgeting is a continuous rather than a periodic process for financial managers. Cash budgets must be revised at least monthly to reflect the cumulative effects of various estimating errors. In contrast to cash budgeting, the balance of the budgeting system— the operating, capital, and financial budgets—are prepared periodically rather than continuously. To continuously revise the entire budget would be prohibitively costly in time and money.

Regardless of whether noncash budgets are revised, events simply do not always turn out as planned. Actual results will differ from those planned. Fortunately, in the noncash areas, budgeting is not cumulative. For example, assume that January and February sales were budgeted at $100,000 and $130,000, respectively; and assume that actual January sales were only $80,000. If this difference did not indicate an overall trend, the budgets for February and subsequent months, without revision, might still represent appropriate expectations. Techniques exist, and will be covered in Chapters 11 and 13, for modifying operating budgets (as performance-measuring devices) to reflect actual events as they occur. Major revision and rebudgeting is, therefore, unnecessary throughout the year unless there develops evidence of major planning error. If a major error or unforeseen development results in budgets being too far off target, the entire budget may have to be reviewed and revised. Such occasions are fortunately rare if budgets are prepared properly in the first place. Major budget revisions will therefore not be discussed further in this text. You can view them as essentially a repeat of the entire process.

## COMPLETING THE MASTER BUDGET

Whether or not minor or even major revision is necessary, a firm's budgeting process should continue until the result is something that all levels of management can live with. The result is then integrated into the final pro forma or budgeted financial statements, which provide at the same time both the core and the summarization of the firm's plans for the forthcoming year. The pro forma statements provide the tools with which top management and directors can evaluate the firm's overall performance during the coming year. The supporting components—the operating budgets and the cash budget—in turn provide the basis for performance evaluation and control in each area and at each level of responsibility. The process of performance measurement and control will be examined in the next five chapters.

## SIMPLIFIED MASTER BUDGETING

Many smaller firms do not have and often cannot afford formal or detailed operating budgets; yet these firms have the same need as others to plan adequate cash and appropriate overall capitalization. Pro forma or budgeted financial statements are essential to the adequate financial management of all but the smallest of firms. In Chapter 9 you were introduced to a simplified way of projecting an income statement and associated cash budget for a firm that did not have operating budgets. This same approach may be extended to projecting all of a firm's financial statements. Supplementary Problem 10.15 illustrates this process for a wholesaler.

Master budgets prepared by simple extrapolation may be less accurate than if they were prepared as the culminating step of an overall budgeting process. Nevertheless, they are usually preferable to none at all. Some indication of future capital needs at least may avoid unpleasant surprises. And some standard reflecting reasonable expectations against which to evaluate the firm's overall performance at year-end is preferable to a simple comparison to last year's data.

## CHAPTER OVERVIEW

Based on the material contained in this and the preceding nine chapters, you should have a good general understanding of the entire budgeting process for a firm, and of how cost accounting data and systems support the budgeting activity. From the material in this chapter you should be able to:

- Describe, with examples, how each of the major asset categories on the pro forma balance sheet may be budgeted, together with sources of information available in firms with and without operating budgets.

- Explain, for each line, how a manufacturer budgets its schedule of cost of goods manufactured and from what sources necessary information is obtained.
- Describe, for a manufacturer, the interrelationship between the budgeted schedule of cost of goods manufactured and both the balance sheet and the income statement.
- Explain, for each line, how a budgeted income statement may be prepared, together with the sources of necessary information in firms with and without operating budgets.
- Describe the information sources for preparing the firm's financial budget and for completing the equity portion of the firm's preliminary pro forma balance sheet.
- Describe the possible differences between preliminary budgeted balance sheets and preliminary financial budgets on the one hand and final budgeted balance sheets and SCFP's on the other, and explain the cause of any differences that might exist.
- Provide several reasons why a firm might decide to significantly revise already prepared budgets, or even to rebudget the entire company, based on data revealed by the preliminary budgeted balance sheet and by the budgeted income statement.
- Explain why it is usually undesirable for top management to simply make revisions that appear necessary in various budgets in the master-budget portion of the overall budgeting process.
- Explain why cash budgeting is a continuous process, whereas operating budgets are prepared periodically.

## NEW VOCABULARY AND CONCEPTS

| | |
|---|---|
| Operating cycle | Redundant assets |
| Undercapitalized | Asset management |
| Overcapitalized | |

- Possible need to revise financial budget, or even previously completed budgets, arising from data on preliminary pro forma financial statements.

## REVIEW QUESTIONS

1. a) What is meant by the fact that a firm is undercapitalized?
   b) What are the risks inherent in undercapitalization?
2. a) What is meant by the fact that a firm is overcapitalized, and how does this relate to so-called redundant assets?

b) What are the risks of overcapitalization? Are they as immediate and severe as those of being undercapitalized?

3. a) What is meant by the term adequate or appropriate composition of assets? Explain, with examples.

b) Can an inappropriate composition of assets be as risky to the firm as its being under- or overcapitalized? What are the risks? Explain, with examples.

4. What are the three objectives of resource planning within a firm?

5. How will changes in a firm's activity level or changes in the length of its operating cycle affect its need for long-term investment in net working capital? Explain, with examples.

6. a) What is the firm's financial budget?
   b) What information does it contain?
   c) How is it used in preparing budgeted financial statements?

7. For a firm having a complete budgeting system, explain, with examples, how each of the following items on the budgeted balance sheet are projected and the sources of information for such a projection:

   a) Cash
   b) Marketable securities
   c) Accounts receivable—net
   d) Inventories
   e) Other current assets
   f) Noncurrent assets

   g) Current borrowings
   h) Other current liabilities
   i) Long-term debt
   j) Owners' contributed capital
   k) Retained earnings

8. Refer to Question 6 above.
   a) How would your answers to questions (a) through (k) differ for a merchandiser without operating budgets?
   b) How would your answers differ for a manufacturer without operating budgets?

9. For a manufacturer having a complete budgeting system, explain, with examples, how each of the elements of a pro forma schedule of cost of goods manufactured is budgeted and the sources of information involved.

10. How would a manufacturer without operating budgets
    a) Budget a schedule of cost of goods manufactured?
    b) Budget its income statement? Explain, with examples.

11. How would a manufacturer with a complete budgeting system budget its income statement? What would be the sources of information for each line item? Explain, with examples.

12. How would a merchandiser budget its income statement, assuming that:
    a) It had a complete budgeting system?
    b) It did not have operating budgets? Explain, with examples.

13. Why is the budgeted balance sheet, when it is first completed, referred to as the preliminary budgeted balance sheet? What items could appear on the preliminary pro forma balance sheet or income statement, and where would they be disclosed, that could lead to a different balance sheet being the final budgeted balance sheet? Explain, with specific examples.

14. If, in the master-budgeting stage of the overall budgeting process, top management discovers items that are undesirable or unacceptable, why shouldn't they be changed by top management immediately? Explain, with an example.

## MINI-CASES AND QUESTIONS FOR DISCUSSION

**MC 10.1** Ms. Mary Jenkins is the president of the Galway Corporation. She is currently reviewing the operating budget for the accounting and budgeting department with Mr. John Snyder, the corporation's controller. She maintains, "John, the real purpose of the whole budgeting process is to prepare budgeted financial statements. From them we have our anticipated profit and a clear indication of any financing requirements.

"If we were to do away with all of our operating budgets, we could save $30,000 a year from your budget. With a good sales budget and adequate capital budgeting, either one of us could prepare pro-forma statements that would be sufficiently accurate to anticipate capital requirements. After all, we don't obtain financing in dollars and pennies. I think we should consider dropping the operating budgets and saving $30,000."

If you were John Snyder, how would you justify your budget requirement? Could Ms. Jenkins' statement that adequate pro forma financial statements could be prepared without operating budgets be correct? Even if it were, could there be other reasons for having operating budgets? Discuss.

**MC 10.2** At a budget meeting called to review the preliminary master budget for the Mills Corporation, Mr. Simon Legraw, the financial vice-president, is speaking: "Look, I don't see why we should have any more delay. We're all agreed that budgeted expenditures in the shipping department are too high. Why don't we just chop them to where they belong, run the totals, and sign off on the budget today?

"John (speaking to the operations vice-president), I realize that you want to discuss it with old George (shipping foreman) first, but he had his chance to come up with a budget. It's his padding of expenses or just plain dumb estimating that has us all tied up here today. Why should **we** await his pleasure? Who is running this plant anyway, George or us (referring to the president and the other executives sitting around the conference table)? And, John, who's running your show? I thought George worked for the plant superintendent, who works for you. Should I be sending your paycheck to George? I'm really up to **here** with all this consultation with underlings. The good old Marine Corps would never have won the war if we'd stopped and consulted with every dumb corporal before we dared move! I say we've got to show these people who's boss!" (By now, Simon is pounding the table and shouting.)

As the vice-president for operations, how would you reply to Simon? Do you really want to delay the whole budgeting process while you and your plant superintendent meet with George? Discuss.

## ESSENTIAL PROBLEMS

**EP 10.1** The Carter Company's receivables collection experience for each month's budgeted sales has been as follows:

30%  first month
40%  second month
20%  third month
8%  fourth month
2%  uncollectable

Uncollectable accounts are not written off until the sixth month following the sale.

Carter's sales budget for the second six months of 19X3 was as follows:

| | | | |
|---|---|---|---|
| July | $550,000 | October | $700,000 |
| August | 600,000 | November | 800,000 |
| September | 650,000 | December | 900,000 |

Determine Carter's 12/31/X3 accounts receivable and allowance for uncollectables as they should appear on its budgeted balance sheet for that year.

**EP 10.2** Refer to Problem EP 10.1. Determine the same two items as of 12/31/X4, given the following 19X4 sales budget data:

| | | | |
|---|---|---|---|
| July | $600,000 | October | $750,000 |
| August | 650,000 | November | 850,000 |
| September | 700,000 | December | 950,000 |

**EP 10.3** The Dillworth Sales Company is a wholesaler. Last year its gross profit ratio was 40 percent and it expects the same this year. Last year's ending inventory amounted to $140,000 at cost. Dillworth was targeting a reduced inventory this year as a hoped-for result of a new inventory planning and control system. The current year's sales were budgeted at $1,500,000, and total purchases were budgeted at $880,000. Based on the above information, determine Dillworth's budgeted inventory at the end of the current period.

**EP 10.4** Eggburt Stores sold products which, for control purposes, were divided by product line. Eggburt had a computerized inventory control system. A printout of product line 18 revealed the following expected balances on hand at year-end:

| Item | Stock balance (units) | Economic order quantity (units) |
|---|---|---|
| A | 400 | 500 |
| B | 7,000 | 10,000 |
| C | 1,100 | 2,000 |
| D | 40 | 100 |
| E | 900 | 1,000 |
| F | 3,600 | 5,000 |

The most recent purchase costs of these items, which are always acquired in economic order quantities, are as follows:

| Item | Most recent cost per unit |
|---|---|
| A | $1.00 |
| B | 0.50 |
| C | 0.80 |
| D | 5.00 |
| E | 0.90 |
| F | 0.75 |

Assuming that Eggburt has elected FIFO for inventory measurement purposes, determine its budgeted ending inventory for product line 18 for the current year.

**EP 10.5** The following information has been taken from various budgets for the Holly Corporation for the years 19X6 and 19X7 (000 omitted):

| | 19X7 | 19X6 |
|---|---|---|
| Raw materials—Beginning inventory | $15 | $10 |
| Raw materials—Ending inventory | 10 | 15 |
| Raw materials—Purchases | 120 | 90 |
| Direct labor | 250 | 170 |
| Manufacturing overhead | 385 | 255 |
| Work-in-process—Beginning and ending | 40 | 40 |
| Finished goods—Beginning inventory | ?75 | 65 |
| Cost of goods sold | 780 | 500 |

a) Prepare a budgeted schedule of cost of goods manufactured for the Holly Corporation for 19X6.

b) Determine budgeted ending finished goods inventory 12/31/X6.

**EP 10.6** Refer to Problem EP 10.5. Assume 12/31/X6 ending finished goods inventory was $75,000.

a) Prepare a budgeted schedule of cost of goods manufactured for the Holly Corporation for 19X7.

b) Determine budgeted ending finishing goods inventory as of 12/31/X7.

**EP 10.7** The Gregory Manufacturing Corporation's recent schedules of cost of goods manufactured have revealed the following information:

| Item | Percent of sales |
|---|---|
| Raw materials used | 20 variable |
| Direct labor | 20 variable |
| Manufacturing overhead | 25 variable + $40,000 Fixed |

During the forthcoming year, Gregory has budgeted sales at $1,500,000. Inventory levels are expected to remain constant at:

| | |
|---|---|
| Raw materials | $ 35,000 |
| Work-in-process | 45,000 |
| Finished goods | 125,000 |

Prepare, in good form, a budgeted schedule of cost of goods manufactured for Gregory for the forthcoming year.

**EP 10.8** The Frances Manufacturing Company's schedules of costs of goods manufactured from its financial statements for the years 19X2 and 19X3 are given in condensed form below.

|  | 19X3 | 19X2 |
|---|---|---|
| Raw materials used | $ 390,000 | $ 360,000 |
| Direct labor | 520,000 | 480,000 |
| Manufacturing overhead | 494,000 | 480,000 |
| Total manufacturing costs | $1,404,000 | $1,320,000 |
| Beginning WIP inventory | 120,000 | 120,000 |
|  | $1,524,000 | $1,440,000 |
| Ending WIP inventory | 120,000 | 120,000 |
| Cost of goods manufactured | $1,404,000 | $1,320,000 |

The following data for Frances is also relevant to budgeting inventories:

|  | Budgeted 19X4 | Actual 19X3 | Actual 19X2 |
|---|---|---|---|
| Sales | $3,000,000 | $2,600,000 | $2,400,000 |
| Ending finished goods inventory | 300,000 | 240,000 | 240,000 |
| Raw material purchases | 470,000 | 390,000 | 360,000 |
| Ending raw materials inventory | ? | 30,000 | 30,000 |
| Cost of goods sold | ? | 1,404,000 | 1,320,000 |

Note that the Frances Company is planning to increases its inventory levels with ending finished goods budgeted at $300,000. You may assume that Frances has no purchased finished items, that all products are manufactured. Also note that Frances' manufacturing overhead, as you might expect, is not completely variable.

Prepare a complete (everything but manufacturing overhead should be detailed) budgeted schedule of cost of goods manufactured for the Frances Company for 19X4. You may assume that ending work-in-process inventory will be $144,000 and that sufficient items will be manufactured to meet both sales demand and target ending finished goods inventory.

**EP 10.9** The income statements for the years 19X4 and 19X5 for the Jerry B Company are given below (000 omitted). 19X6 sales are budgeted at $800,000. Using the same techniques discussed in Chapter 5 for budgeting departmental costs, prepare a budgeted income statement for Jerry B for 19X6.

|  | 19X5 | 19X4 |
|---|---|---|
| Sales | $750,000 | $650,000 |
| Cost of goods sold | 450,000 | 390,000 |
| Operating expenses |  |  |
| Wages and salaries | 100,000 | 90,000 |
| Insurance | 10,000 | 10,000 |
| Supplies | 22,000 | 20,000 |
| Depreciation | 40,000 | 40,000 |
| Interest | 30,000 | 30,000 |
| Income from operations | $ 98,000 | $ 70,000 |
| Provision for income tax | 34,300 | 24,500 |
| Net income | $ 63,700 | $ 45,500 |

**EP 10.10** Refer to Problem 10.9. Prepare a budgeted income statement for 19X6 for the Jerry B Company, assuming that sales are budgeted at $900,000.

## SUPPLEMENTARY PROBLEMS

**SP 10.11** Data from the equity section of the preliminary budgeted balance sheet and preliminary financial budget for 19X9 for Kissler Hotel Supplies are given below (000 omitted). Also included is information concerning Kissler's target capital structure from the viewpoint of desirable leverage. Assuming that any type and amount of financing is feasible, prepare a final budgeted balance sheet equity section, and a budgeted SCFP, reflecting plans for appropriate financing to achieve desired leverage.

Preliminary Budgeted Balance Sheet—Equity Section

| | |
|---|---|
| Current borrowings | $200 |
| Other current liabilities | 50 |
| Long-term debt | 150 |
| Contributed capital | 200 |
| Retained earnings | 100 |

Preliminary Financial Budget

| | |
|---|---|
| **Sources** | |
| Funds from operations | $130 |
| Disposition of noncurrent assets | 10 |
| Total sources | $140 |
| | |
| **Applications** | |
| Purchase of noncurrent assets | $ 70 |
| Dividends | 40 |
| Increase in balance of net working capital | 30 |
| Total applications | $140 |

Desired Capital Structure

| Equity classification | Percentage of total equities |
|---|---|
| Current liabilities | 10 |
| Long-term debt | 30 |
| Owners' equity | 60 |

**SP 10.12** Refer to Problem SP 10.11. Prepare the same two statements for the Kissler Company, assuming all the same data except for a different desired capital structure. Instead of the structure given in Problem SP 10.11, assume that Kissler's desired structure was:

| Equity classification | Desired level |
|---|---|
| Current liabilities | 2:1 current ratio |
| Total debt | 30% of total equities |
| Preferred equity | 20% of total equities |
| Common equity | 50% of total equities |

You may assume that Kissler had just retired all of its earlier preferred stock, and that current assets as of 12/31/X9 were budgeted at $120,000.

**SP 10.13** From the following budgeted data (000 omitted) for the Lorrine Corporation, prepare budgeted financial statements (balance sheet, schedule of cost of goods manufactured, income statement, and statement of changes in financial position) for the year 19X6.

|  | 19X7 | 19X6 |
|---|---|---|
| Cash as of 12/31 | $ 160 | $ 200 |
| Marketable securities as of 12/31 | 0 | 400 |
| Annual net sales | 7,000 | 6,000 |
| Receivables turnover | 5 | 6 |
| Raw materials |  |  |
|   Inventory as of 1/1 | 50 | 60 |
|   Inventory as of 12/31 | 90 | 50 |
|   Purchases | 1,540 | 1,190 |
| Work-in-process: |  |  |
|   Inventory as of 1/1 | 100 | 75 |
|   Inventory as of 12/31 | 150 | 100 |
|   Direct labor | 2,200 | 2,000 |
|   Manufacturing overhead[a] | 1,750 | 1,375 |
| Finished goods: |  |  |
|   Inventory as of 1/1 | 400 | 350 |
|   Inventory as of 12/31 | 500 | 400 |
| Other current assets as of 12/31 | 35 | 25 |
| Fixed assets as of 1/1 | 2,900 | 2,690 |
| Accum. depr. on fixed assets as of 1/1 | 1,200 | 1,000 |
| Annual depr.—period cost[b] | 50 | 30 |
| Annual depr.—product cost[c] | 230 | 170 |
| Other period expenses[d] | 1,050 | 970 |
| Income taxes | 180 | 150 |
| Current borrowings as of 12/31 | 70 | 0 |
| Other current liabilities as of 12/31 | 1,380 | 1,150 |
| Long-term debt as of 1/1 | 200 | 600 |
| Contributed capital as of 1/1 | 2,000 | 1,800 |
| Retained earnings as of 1/1 | 525 | 315 |
| Dividends | 140 | 140 |

*Notes.* [a] Includes portion of depreciation allocated to product cost.
  [b] Revised to reflect acquisitions during the year.
  [c] Revised and updated: already included as part of manufacturing overhead above.
  [d] All except cost of goods sold, depreciation, and income taxes.

During 19X6, the Lorrine Corporation also planned to acquire additional fixed assets costing $210,000, to retire long-term debt in the amount of $400,000, and to obtain $200,000 in additional contributed capital through the sale of stock.

**SP 10.14** Refer to Problem SP 10.13. During 19X7, the Lorrine Corporation planned to acquire $400,000 of new fixed assets and to incur $100,000 of additional long-term debt. Prepare budgeted financial statements (balance sheet, schedule of cost of goods manufactured, income statement, and SCFP) for the year 19X7.

SP 10.15 John Anderson and Daughters is a hardware wholesaler. Although the firm is incorporated, all the stock is held by John and his family. It is early in January of 19X8 and John has just returned from the local bank. He went to obtain a good-sized personal loan to cover the family's proposed vacation in Russia in March, and was planning to repay the loan from 19X8 business profits.

Even though John's credit was good and the bank did not turn down the loan application, the bank loan officer recommended that John first obtain pro forma or budgeted financial statements for 19X8. The loan officer explained that, with these statements, both he and John would

**Exhibit 10.10**

## JOHN ANDERSON AND DAUGHTERS, INC.

### Balance Sheets as of 12/31/X6 and 12/31/X7

| Assets | 19X7 | 19X6 |
|---|---|---|
| Cash | $ 77,000 | $ 70,000 |
| Accounts receivable | 96,250 | 91,800 |
| Inventory | 80,500 | 73,500 |
| Supplies | 7,700 | 7,000 |
| Total current assets | $261,450 | $242,300 |
| Land | 20,000 | 20,000 |
| Building | 200,000 | 200,000 |
| Less:  Accumulated depreciation | (99,000) | (90,000) |
| Equipment and fixtures | 80,000 | 80,000 |
| Less:  Accumulated depreciation | (56,000) | (48,000) |
| Total assets | $406,450 | $404,300 |
| **Equities** | | |
| Current liabilities | $130,725 | $121,150 |
| Long-term debt | 40,570 | 40,570 |
| Total liabilities | $171,295 | $161,720 |
| Contributed capital | 200,000 | 200,000 |
| Retained earnings | 35,155 | 42,580 |
| Total equities | $406,450 | $404,300 |

### Income Statements for the Years 19X6 and 19X7

| | 19X7 | 19X6 |
|---|---|---|
| Sales | $770,000 | $700,000 |
| Cost of merchandise sold | 462,000 | 420,000 |
| Operating expenses: | | |
| Wages and salaries | 137,000 | 130,000 |
| Utilities | 10,850 | 10,500 |
| Insurance | 15,000 | 15,000 |
| Property taxes | 14,350 | 11,650 |
| Interest | 3,650 | 6,350 |
| Depreciation | 17,000 | 17,000 |
| Income from operations | $110,150 | $ 89,500 |
| Provision for income taxes (35%) | 38,552 | 31,325 |
| Net income | $ 71,598 | $ 58,175 |

**Exhibit 10.10 (continued)**

## JOHN ANDERSON AND DAUGHTERS, INC.

**Statements of Changes in Financial Position for 19X6 and 19X7**

| Sources | 19X7 | 19X6 |
|---|---|---|
| Net income | $ 71,598 | $ 58,175 |
| Add:  Depreciation | 17,000 | 17,000 |
| Funds from operations | $ 88,598 | $ 75,175 |
| Disposition of fixed assets | 0 | 15,000 |
| Total | $ 88,598 | $ 90,175 |
| **Applications** | | |
| Purchase of noncurrent assets | 0 | $ 20,000 |
| Retire noncurrent debt | 0 | 30,000 |
| Dividends | $ 79,023 | 39,000 |
| Increase in net working capital | 9,575 | 1,175 |
| Total | $ 88,598 | $ 90,175 |

be in a better position to estimate the extent of 19X8 profits and how much could be withdrawn from the business.

John Anderson has never prepared budgets or even complete financial statements. His accountant has merely maintained records that were adequate for the various taxing authorities. As a first step towards budgeting 19X8, John's accountant has prepared financial statements for 19X6 and 19X7. These statements are included in Exhibit 10.10. John has asked you to complete his 19X8 budgeted financial statements.

In completing your pro forma statements, you may make the following assumptions:

- Sales will increase 15 percent.
- Receivables and inventory turnover will remain constant.
- All variable costs vary with sales dollars.
- There will be no inflation of any costs during 19X8.
- The firm experiences no uncollectable accounts.
- There are no plans to acquire or dispose of noncurrent assets during 19X8.
- The firm does not intend to acquire any new long-term debt or retire any existing debt during 19X8.
- The 12/31/X7 ratio of current liabilities to 19X7 operating expenses (excluding depreciation) may be considered desirable.
- No dividends are planned as part of the current projection.

*Required:*

a) Prepare budgeted balance sheet, income statement, and SCFP for 19X8.

b) Prepare a brief memo to John Anderson indicating the maximum amount of dividends that could be withdrawn at the end of 19X8 without impairing the firm's solvency, together with the basis for your recommendation.

**SP 10.16** Refer to Problem SP 10.15. Complete the same requirements using all of the same information except for the assumptions stated. Instead of the assumptions given in Problem SP 10.15, you should prepare your budgeted financial statements incorporating the following different assumptions:

- Sales will increase 25 percent.
- Receivables turnover will remain constant, but inventory turnover is expected to increase by one time (complete turnover) per year as a result of using a new minicomputer for inventory control.
- Variable costs will vary with sales dollars.
- Operating costs are expected to increase an average of ten percent during 19X8. The ten-percent increase is applicable to all expenditures, both fixed and variable. The Anderson firm is on LIFO.
- On 1/1/X8, the firm expects to sell display fixtures originally costing $30,000 and with a 12/31/X7 book value of $10,000. Annual depreciation on these fixtures has been $3,000 and sale proceeds are expected to be $12,000.
- Anderson expects to replace the old display fixtures with new ones to be installed in late January, 19X8, at a cost of $24,000. These new fixtures have an expected useful life of 10 years, zero salvage, and are to be depreciated on a straight-line basis.
- Anderson expects to refinance its nine-percent, long-term debt on 7/1/X8 with a new eight-year loan at eight-percent interest.
- The 12/31/X7 capital structure and various balance sheet proportions may be considered desirable.
- Dividends of $20,000 are planned for 19X8.

## SUGGESTIONS FOR FURTHER READING

Morse, Wayne J., *Cost Accounting: Processing, Evaluating, and Using Cost Data.* Reading, Massachusetts: Addison-Wesley Publishing Company, 1978; Chapter 9.

Van Horne, James C., *Fundamentals of Financial Management,* Third Edition. Englewood Cliffs, N.J.: Prentice-Hall, Inc., 1977; Chapters 4, 10, and 11.

Weston, J. Fred, and Eugene F. Brigham, *Essentials of Managerial Finance,* Fourth Edition. Hinsdale, Illinois: The Dryden Press, 1977; Chapters 6, 19, 21 and 22.

APTER 10 APPENDIX

# Financing Desired Resources

The economic resources (assets) already invested in a particular firm, and any additional resources desired or required by the firm, come from three possible sources:

1. Customers (through profits on operations),
2. Creditors (through loans and resources supplied on account),
3. Owners (through additional owner investment—additional stock sold)

It is a part of the function and responsibility of a firm's financial management both to:

- Determine the amount of additional resources (capital) required, and
- Make arrangements to obtain these required additional resources at the least long-run cost to the firm and its owners.

Methods for determining the amount of resources required were introduced earlier in this chapter. Choosing sources of additional financing and making necessary arrangements to obtain additional resources are activities that are not part of managerial accounting. Many significant technical considerations and factors enter into these financial management decisions that are beyond the scope of this text. They are covered in courses devoted to business finance. It is the intention of this appendix merely to introduce you to various financing activities, together with a few of the issues relating to the choice among these alternatives.

Although clearly outside of the usual scope of managerial accounting texts, a brief introduction to the financing of a firm's resources has proved valuable to many students in reinforcing their understanding of the purpose and value of budgeting. It is unfortunately easy to become so immersed in managerial accounting, cost accounting, and budgeting concepts and procedures that one loses touch with the reasons that these activities exist. As introduced in Chapter 1 (and to be covered in some detail in the next four chapters), budgets do provide valuable bases for evaluating the firm's performance and that of its individual managers. But future performance evaluation is only one use of budgets, and it is only meaningful for those firms that prepare operating budgets by responsibility centers.

All successful firms, whether or not they have operating budgets, must plan for adequate and appropriate capitalization. The master budget is the basis for all such planning and, in one sense, for all of the financial management activities within the firm. To fully appreciate the importance of any tool, rather than just accept it because some authority tells you that it is important, you need to have some idea of its ultimate use. The master budget is a tool of financial management, and this appendix will cover some of the activities growing out of the use of this tool.

## OVERVIEW OF FINANCING ALTERNATIVES

The term *financing* refers to the process of obtaining resources desired by the firm. Financing can be classified by duration (short-term vs. long-term) and by the source from which capital can be acquired.

### Short-Term Financing

Short-term financing commonly refers to arrangements made for one year or less. There are eight separate common sources or approaches to short-term financing:

1. Purchasing on account
2. Delaying payments on accounts or converting accounts payable to notes payable
3. Factoring or borrowing against accounts receivable or inventory
4. Obtaining short-term loans
5. Renting assets
6. Obtaining advances from customers
7. Delaying planned acquisition of resources
8. Delaying planned distributions to owners

Whenever a firm purchases on account, it is being financed or obtaining financing from its suppliers. At a given level of activity, a firm normally is taking advantage of all credit of this type that is economical, and this area would not usually represent a source of additional financing. However, where additional financing is required for expanded operations, the incremental availability of supplier credit is a partial source.

Delaying or stretching out payments on existing accounts is another possible source of short-term financing. Additional resources are not added by this action, but cash that would otherwise be paid out is made temporarily available for other uses. As discussed in Chapter 9, most suppliers are not themselves adequately financed nor are they in the business of financing customers beyond customary trade time periods. Therefore, taking advantage of this source usually involves really taking involuntary advantage of suppliers, and may only be done infrequently if at all. Financing through delayed payments to creditors can be prohibitively costly if creditors retaliate by limiting the availability of future credit. Where delayed payment merely means missing a proffered discount and paying within normal terms, the supplier is not being abused or taken advantage of. But a missed discount can represent far more costly financing than that from almost any other source.[11] In some industries suppliers will, by custom, usually on a seasonal basis, extend additional credit. Often they may require that the delayed or extended account be converted to an interest-bearing, short-term note.

A firm may also factor (sell) or borrow against its accounts receivable. In a few industries factoring is a normal trade practice, essentially already part of the firm's long-term financing, and therefore not an available source of **additional** financing. In most others it is uncommon and not a preferred source. Where not commonly practiced, factoring may be interpreted by customers and suppliers as a "last-ditch" or "up-against-the-wall" maneuver to stave off insolvency. In such situations, factoring could be prohibitively costly (factoring cost plus lost customers plus reduction of otherwise available trade credit). Inventory may also be factored without the risks mentioned for factoring of receivables. The distinctions between factoring an asset and pledging it as security for a short-term loan are real but not important to your initial general understanding of possible financing sources.

The most common source of short-term financing is a short-term loan, either unsecured or secured by pledging receivables or inventory. A few large firms offer such financing to their suppliers, and commercial loans are a primary activity of most banks. As described and illustrated in Chapter 9, short-term loans are particularly appropriate to finance seasonal inventory buildups in advance of sales and receivables collections.

Another source of short-term financing is the rental of buildings or equipment. Rather than borrow funds and purchase assets needed for short periods, these resources may be rented or leased on a short-term basis. Rentals or short-term leases have the additional advantage of representing off-balance-sheet financing. The firm's debt ratio is not impaired since future short-term rent and lease obligations are executory and, as such, are excluded under GAAP from the firm's accounts.[12]

In certain circumstances, usually associated with special or custom products, short-term financing in the form of cash advances from customers is

---

[11]    For example, the effective annual interest cost of missing discounts and paying in 30 days when terms are 2/10, net 30 (a two-percent discount for payment within 10 days) is 36.7 percent!

$$\frac{2}{98} \times \frac{360}{20} = 36.73$$

[12]    GAAP does require that material future obligations, even though executory, must be disclosed in statement footnotes. Also, leases that are not short-term and readily cancellable may qualify under GAAP as capital leases, requiring different accounting treatment. See page 454.

possible. Typically, where an item to be manufactured or acquired for a particular customer is so unique as to have little possibility of sale to others (should the original customer not complete the purchase and make payment in full), partial or full payment in advance may be required. Advanced payments to at least finance materials costs are common in residential construction and remodeling.

Temporary financing (in the sense of retaining cash that would otherwise be disbursed) can be obtained from delaying planned acquisition of assets or scheduled distributions (dividends) to owners. Both of these alternatives were first discussed in Chapter 9. As mentioned, delaying asset acquisition probably would impair operations unless the asset was not really needed when originally scheduled. Also, delayed distributions to owners, although economically desirable for the owners, may prove difficult. As in the case of delayed payments to creditors, such financing is involuntary and could be very costly if the delay were interpreted as a sign of trouble or poor earnings.

Short-term financing is appropriate where the need is of short duration—seasonal financing of inventory or construction financing. It may also be appropriate in circumstances where desired and intended long-term financing can be accomplished more efficiently and at less cost if delayed for a short period. In other circumstances, where additional working capital or noncurrent assets are required for an extended period, long-term financing is indicated.

### Long-Term Financing—Equity Financing

Long-term financing can come from owners or creditors. Owner financing is commonly called equity financing. This term was developed when the term equity applied only to owner's shares in or claims against assets and creditor claims were known only as liabilities. Today the term equity financing is potentially confusing when all asset shares or claims, both creditors' and owners', are now collectively referred to as equities.

Equity financing or owner financing can be in one of two forms: long-term or permanent retention of earnings (profits from customers) or additional owner investment. Retained-earnings financing has been very prevalent in U.S. industry. It has several distinct advantages over the alternative of earnings distribution and sale of new stock. Simply withholding profit distributions is less costly and much less difficult for the firm. Approval for additional stock issue from owners, and sometimes from the state of incorporation, is not required. Filings with the Securities and Exchange Commission (SEC) are not involved. And the cost of printing and distributing (selling) additional stock is avoided.

Obtaining additional financing through the retention of earnings is also less costly to the owners. If profits available for distribution were to be distributed to owners and then reinvested through purchase of additional stock, owners would be required to invest additional cash just to maintain their interest. Distributed earnings would be subject to income tax, and only the after-tax balance would be available for reinvestment.

Retained-earnings financing has limitations. As mentioned above under delaying dividends, excessive withholding of dividends, even when most desirable for the firm and its owners, can be interpreted as necessitated by adverse or undesirable performance. Usually the payment of some portion of earnings in dividends is demanded by the market. Insufficient dividends can preclude or make very difficult the raising of additional capital through stock sale, and thus ultimately raise the firm's overall cost of capital (see Chapter 6). Also, unless earnings that are retained are frozen into contributed capital through stock dividends (see below), creditors will be less inclined to provide proportionate additional credit. Retained earnings could be withdrawn in the future, removing the creditors' cushion or safety factor, and drastically increasing the firm's debt ratio.

Recall, from financial accounting, that the vehicle for freezing or capitalizing retained earnings into contributed capital is the stock dividend. A stock dividend involves the distribution of additional shares of stock to owners in proportion to existing outstanding shares. The market value of the shares distributed is then transferred from retained earnings to the contributed capital account. This amount is thereafter never available for dividends. The retention of earnings and their capitalization via stock dividends is the least costly form of equity financing. It has all of the benefits to owners and creditors of an additional sale of stock with few of the complications and costs. This practice is therefore very common.

Where needs for equity capital exceed amounts available from some reasonable proportion of retained earnings, the firm obtains the financing through the sale of additional stock. Additional contributed capital can be obtained through the sale of either common or preferred stock. Recall, from financial accounting, that common stock represents voting ownership and control of a corporation. Existing stockholders, unless they waive them, have preemptive (first-refusal) rights to purchase additional shares of common stock in proportion to their existing ownership shares.

Preferred stock may also be sold as a means of obtaining long-term financing. Preferred stock differs from common stock in several important respects. It is preferred as to dividends in any given year. If common dividends are to be paid, preferred dividends must be paid first. It usually has a fixed dividend rate. It represents a preferred claim over the common in the event of liquidation of the firm. And it is generally nonvoting.

Preferred stock may also be:

1. Participating—entitled to additional dividends above the fixed rate in very profitable years.

2. Cumulative—entitled to any portion of prior years' passed (unpaid) preferred dividends before common dividends are paid.

3. Convertible—exchangeable at a fixed ratio for shares of common stock at the option of the preferred shareholder.

4. Callable—subject to retirement at a fixed price at the discretion of the firm.

As a source of financing, preferred stock represents a hybrid somewhere between debt and common stock. It is less costly over the long run than common stock, since common stockholders demand a high return for their greater risk. If nonparticipating, it provides a source of financial leverage along with debt (see discussion of leverage below). And it is more costly than debt, although, unlike interest on debt, preferred dividends do not have to be paid when insufficient profits are available.

### Long-Term Financing—Debt Financing

The remaining source of financing to the firm is from creditors in the form of long-term debt. Long-term debt may be in the form of long-term notes, bonds, debentures, or leases. Long-term notes, bonds, and debentures are fairly straightforward debt instruments, and are adequately described in financial accounting. Recall that some debentures, known as convertible or as CVD's, may be sold with the option of conversion (exchange) into preferred and/or common stock.

Long-term leases may be one of two different types, operating leases or capital leases. Operating leases are essentially long-term rental arrangements. Characteristically they:

- cover a time period significantly less than the useful life of the asset;
- are cancellable, often without significant penalty;
- provide that the owner (lessor) be responsible for most or all of the costs usually associated with ownership, such as maintenance and insurance.

Like short-term rentals or leases, longer-term operating leases have the additional advantage over other long-term financing alternatives of representing off-balance-sheet financing.

Capital leases differ from operating leases in that:

1. They generally cover a longer time period, usually approaching or equivalent to the useful life of the asset.

2. They are either noncancellable or else cancellable only with a high penalty payment.

3. They generally provide that the lessee (renter) assume most of the costs usually associated with ownership (taxes, maintenance, insurance, and so forth).

4. They usually provide that the lessee may continue to use the asset over its useful life by purchase at a nominal fee or lease renewal upon termination of the original capital lease.

5. Total lease payments significantly exceed the original cost of the asset.[13]

---

[13]   See Statement of Financial Accounting Standards No. 13, Accounting for Leases, Financial Accounting Standards Board, November, 1976; or refer to intermediate accounting or finance texts for the exact determinants of a capital lease.

Capital leases are essentially like a purchase with a 100-percent mortgage. The lease payments provide the lessor with the full cost of the asset plus interest. Where a firm wishes to finance a new capital asset, capital leasing offers an alternative to separately borrowing the funds and then purchasing the asset.

Capital leasing used to have the advantage over borrowing and purchasing of representing off-balance-sheet financing. Since capital leases still do not represent legal ownership, and since they are still theoretically executory, GAAP, until recently, allowed disclosure similar to that required for operating leases. The asset itself and future lease payment obligations were excluded from the accounts. Hence the term "off-balance-sheet." A firm used to be able to obtain significant long-term debt financing in such situations, and yet have its balance-sheet debt ratios disclose a low debt proportion.

Capital leases now must be disclosed on the balance sheet. The asset is included with fixed assets, is initially valued at the present value of total lease payments (discounted at the firm's incremental borrowing rate), and is subsequently amortized over the useful life as if it were owned. The liability is classified in current and noncurrent portions in the amount of the future lease payments, again discounted by the borrowing rate (thus excluding the future-interest cost component). Lease payments, including accruing interest, disappear from the balance sheet when paid per the terms of the lease.

The cost of long-term debt financing is lower than that of equity financing. Required interest payments on debt are lower because of less risk, since interest is payable in all years whether or not the firm is profitable, and since debt has a prior claim against the firm's assets in the event of liquidation. Also, interest payments are tax deductible. Recall, from Chapter 6, that the effective interest cost of debt is the interest required times $(1 - t)$, where $t$ is the tax rate expressed as a decimal. The effective cost of \$4,000 of annual interest when the firm is subject to a 40-percent tax rate is only \$2,400.

To determine the true or effective cost of debt financing, the stream, or all future interest or lease payments in after-tax-dollar costs, is discounted and compared to the amount borrowed. That discount rate, which equates the firm's outflows to the amount borrowed, is the internal rate of return (IRR—see Chapter 8 appendix) to the creditor and the effective interest cost to the borrower.[14] In the case of capital leases, that discount rate, which equates discounted total payments to the original cash cost of the asset, equals the effective annual interest cost of the financing.

## CHOICES BETWEEN DEBT AND EQUITY FINANCING— FINANCIAL LEVERAGE

As mentioned in this and earlier chapters, the ideal capital structure (proportions of debt and equity financing) varies for different industries. It is desirable, for most firms, to have some portion of long-term financing in the form of

---

[14]   The after-tax effective interest cost to the borrower and the effective after-tax interest benefit to the lender may differ if they are subject to different tax rates.

debt and/or preferred stock. There are two related reasons for not having all common equity financing. First, since preferred stock, and especially long-term debt, are less costly, the firm's overall cost of capital is reduced by having a mix or blend of sources. Secondly, lower-cost sources of financing can result in additional benefits to common stockholders. This amplification of profits is known as *trading on equity*, or *financial leverage*. Financial leverage describes the situation where, if capital can be obtained at a given cost and invested in the business to earn a higher return, then the difference goes to the owners as additional profit. In effect, the owners are making money on other investors' (creditors') money.

Sources of leverage are long-term debt (notes, bonds, and debentures) and preferred stock. Debt provides potentially greater leverage because of its low interest cost and because of the tax deductibility of debt interest. Preferred stock provides less leverage than debt but more safety since the preferred dividend payment is not required each year. To see the effects of leverage, consider three firms—A, B, and C—each with a total of $500,000 of long-term financing (capital structure). Assume that all firms have the same EBIT (earnings before interest and taxes) of $150,000 or a 30-percent return on long-term total investment; and that all are subject to a 40-percent tax rate. Firm A is financed exclusively with common stock. Firm B is financed with 60-percent common and 40-percent preferred stock having a ten-percent dividend rate. Firm C is financed with 60 percent common and 40-percent debt having an eight-percent annual interest rate.

|  | A | B | C |
|---|---|---|---|
| Long-term debt (8% interest) | 0 | 0 | $200,000 |
| Preferred stock (10% dividend) | 0 | $200,000 | 0 |
| Common equity | $500,000 | 300,000 | 300,000 |
| Total long-term invested capital | $500,000 | $500,000 | $500,000 |

Before proceeding, calculate the annual return both in dollars and as a percent of investment to the common stockholders of each firm.

The returns to stockholders in this example are $90,000 (18%), $70,000 (23.3%), and $80,400 (26.8%), respectively:

|  | A | B | C |
|---|---|---|---|
| Return on assets employed (EBIT/Long-term assets) | 30% | 30% | 30% |
| EBIT | $150,000 | $150,000 | $150,000 |
| Interest expense | 0 | 0 | 16,000 |
| Income taxes | 60,000 | 60,000 | 53,600 |
| Net income | $ 90,000 | $ 90,000 | $ 80,400 |
| Preferred dividends | 0 | 20,000 | 0 |
| Earnings available to common stockholders | $ 90,000 | $ 70,000 | $ 80,400 |
| Common equity | 500,000 | 300,000 | 300,000 |
| Return on common equity | 18% | 23.3% | 26.8% |

In this illustration, the advantages of trading on equity are obvious. But does this mean that a firm should have maximum possible leverage, as high a proportion of debt as creditors will allow? Leverage can cut both ways. Consider the same three firms with all factors the same except that EBIT, instead of being a 30-percent return, was only seven percent or $35,000. Once again, calculate income available to common shareholders in dollars and as a percentage of investment.

|  | A | B | C |
|---|---|---|---|
| Return on assets employed (EBIT/Long-term assets) | 7% | 7% | 7% |
| EBIT | $ 35,000 | $ 35,000 | $ 35,000 |
| Interest expense | 0 | 0 | 16,000 |
| Income taxes | 14,000 | 14,000 | 7,600 |
| Net income | $ 21,000 | $ 21,000 | 3 11,400 |
| Preferred dividends | 0 | 20,000 | 0 |
| Earnings available to common stockholders | $ 21,000 | $ 1,000 | $ 11,400 |
| Common equity | 500,000 | 300,000 | 300,000 |
| Return on common equity | 4.2% | 0.3% | 3.8% |

Note that when the earnings rate on total long-term assets is less than the effective cost of the leverage financing, the common stockholder is worse off. Financial leverage, especially involving debt, carries substantial risk as well as potential benefits.

Part of the responsibility of a firm's financial management is to determine, and to continually monitor, the desirable leverage ratio for the firm. Companies with high stable earnings in industries with the same pattern (such as public utilities) can afford to take advantage of greater leverage. Firms with volatile earnings in industries characterized by wide swings in earnings (for example, machine-tool manufacturers) can risk very little leverage and especially very little debt. Financial management is also responsible for arranging to obtain needed additional long-term financing for the firm in such proportions that, over the long run, the firm's desired capital structure is maintained.

# 11

# BUDGETARY CONTROL THROUGH RESPONSIBILITY CENTERS

CHAPTER PREVIEW

In Chapters 3 through 10 you had the opportunity to learn the various aspects of a firm's planning or budgeting system. The purpose of this chapter is to introduce you to the process of control and managerial accounting's role in this process. In this chapter you can learn about the following:

- In addition to providing the basis for financial planning, budgets and standards may be used as a basis for control of a firm's activities.

- The objectives and elements of control as the term is used in a business context and the role of managerial accounting in a firm's control system.

- Different styles or approaches to management based upon alternative assumptions about human behavior and philosophies of management.

- How a planning and control system must be adapted to the management style of the particular firm.

- Different ways in which a firm may be organized, and the need for planning and control systems to match the responsibility centers within the firm's current organization.

- Different types or classifications of responsibility centers and the different information requirements of each type.

- The steps in the control cycle and the appropriate information content of performance reports designed to facilitate control.

- How performance information, and particularly variances from plan, may be identified and analyzed.

- How control information may be effectively used by managers, and also how the information may be *misused* with possibly counterproductive results.

With this information you will have a good general overview of the budgetary control process. You will have the background necessary to learn, in the next three chapters, how specific performance reports may be prepared and used in different situations.

## HOW CAN MANAGERS' PERFORMANCE BE MEASURED?

As the new president of the Tripper Manufacturing Company, you have completed the firm's budget for 19X2. You and your managers can now concentrate on implementing the various plans incorporated in the budget. Because you arrived on the scene during 19X1, 19X2 will be the first complete year that the company is under your management. You are, therefore, especially interested both in achieving the 19X2 budget and also in the methods you and your managers will use to bring about that result.

Have you ever been a manager of a large number of people where you had other lower-level managers or supervisors who reported to you? If not, take a few moments to project yourself into such a situation. Aside from possible feelings of power and importance, do you also feel some uncertainty as to the best way to manage your managers? Can you perceive any difficulty in making sure your managers do what they are supposed to do with reasonable efficiency? After objectives have been mutually understood, you must have feedback information on each manager's performance in order to evaluate how well he or she is doing. Based on your evaluation of each manager's performance, you may wish to acknowledge a job well done or to attempt to induce a modification in a manager's future behavior.

Can you visualize the importance of feedback information and its evaluation to your success as a manager? Without it you could not manage effectively. Can you see that subordinate managers working for you, and superior managers to whom you report, both also need feedback information to evaluate their own performance and that of their subordinates? Necessary feedback information must cover more than simply "Did the job get done?" or "What was the number of units produced?" These effectiveness criteria can often be measured and evaluated informally or visually. What is also required is information relating to the efficiency of performance (least reasonable cost, or maximum reasonable revenue, or both). Before you could take appropriate action, you would need to evaluate **both** what or how much a manager had done, and how well or efficiently he or she had done whatever was accomplished. Just to know how much revenue a manager produced, or how much cost was incurred, by itself would be insufficient. You would also require some plan or standard against which to evaluate the actual result. Budgetary control is concerned with this required feedback information and performance evaluation.

Returning to your role as Tripper's president, you are interested in learning about and assessing the firm's control systems. To do this, you have decided personally to monitor performance (budget implementation) along a single path in your firm's chain of command. As you were personally involved in budget preparation for the assembly department (Chapter 5), you elect to follow closely the performance of that department throughout 19X2.

You know from your experience and from the introductory discussion in Chapter 2 that effective management involves both planning and control. With your attention now focused on control, you are first interested in finding out:

1. Exactly what is meant by the term control? What is control, what are its objectives, and what does it involve?

2. How is managerial accounting involved in the control process?

3. How do performance reports relate to the firm's organization and to its components?

4. What information should be contained on various performance reports?

5. How should this information be used by managers?

6. Are there ways that control information should **not** be used; that is, are there uses that could be counterproductive?

## CONTROL OBJECTIVES

Just as budgeting is a planning process, *control* is also a process. Control in a business is the process of ensuring, or attempting to ensure, that desired results are obtained. In Chapter 2, control was likened to the experience of driving or controlling a car as it proceeded along a highway. If you were driving from one place to another, you would first decide where you were going, when, and how you were going to get there (by what route). This would be your budget. As you were driving to your destination, to assure safe on-time arrival you would be continuously monitoring your progress visually. You would be alert for necessary changes in speed and direction, and would appropriately control your auto.

As the manager of a very small firm, where you could personally observe everything that was going on, you could monitor performance on a day-to-day basis and make necessary changes as indicated. If you could see that you were running short of merchandise, you could order more. Conversely, you would delay any existing orders or delay reordering if unsold merchandise was piling up in the back room. Similarly, you would hire or furlough personnel when you observed excessive customer service delays or employees standing around with nothing to do. You could adequately measure your progress towards sales and profit targets by keeping totals of daily cash register sales, watching your bank balance, and comparing these two with prior experience. You could personally see to it that desired results were being achieved.

In a larger firm, where the chief executive cannot personally supervise and observe all activities, responsibilities must be delegated to junior executives and managers. An information system must be devised to act as a surrogate for the personal observations of the various managers and of the chief executive. The control objective remains the same, to ensure desired results.

Desired results, as you have seen, are formalized in the larger firm and communicated in the form of a plan or budget. The budget is an expression of desired results but should not be assumed to be a substitute for them or the result itself. Where changed circumstances, or even a planning error, make a budget or other standard inappropriate, effective control will direct activity away from the inappropriate plan to a more desirable objective.

## ELEMENTS OF CONTROL

Extending your concept of control from the very small firm up to and including the giant multinational corporation, you should be able to see intuitively that control involves three major elements, as shown in Fig. 11.1.

ELEMENTS OF CONTROL

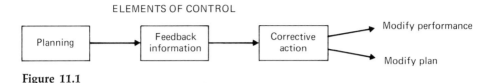

**Figure 11.1**

1. A plan or objective expressed in measurable terms.[1]

2. An information system, which provides feedback on actual performance as compared to planned performance, and highlights or calls attention to significant differences or variances from plan.

3. Appropriate remedial action on the part of management and employees, as indicated, to either:

   • Modify future performance to conform to plan, or

   • Revise plans in the current or future periods.

## ROLE OF MANAGERIAL ACCOUNTING

Control is exercised by line managers, those with responsibility for and authority over production and distribution activities. The line managers and their employees make the decisions and take the actions that bring the firm under control. Managerial accounting supports the control responsibilities of line managers through designing, implementing, and interpreting both a planning system (budget or other standard) and a feedback reporting system.

The design of a firm's managerial accounting system (MAS) for both budgeting and control must match the particular firm's management style or mode. Different styles or approaches to managing people necessitate different reporting systems. To appreciate these differences and their implications to reporting requires a rudimentary understanding of human and organizational motivation and behavior.

---

[1]  Note that *measurable* does not necessarily always mean measurable in financial terms. There are many instances where nonfinancial measures are less costly to obtain, simpler, more understandable, and more useful than financial measures. Examples would include physical measures such as the number of customers (served); units of product (produced and/or shipped); machine hours; labor hours; kilowatt-hours; units, pounds, gallons, or tons of material; and so forth.

## HUMAN AND ORGANIZATIONAL MOTIVATION
## AND BEHAVIOR

The study of the motivation and behavior of individuals and of organizations (groups) is an essential supplement to one's own intuition and experience if one is to become an effective manager. Business school requirements or cores generally contain one or more courses introducing the subject of organizational behavior, and many business majors concentrate or specialize in the area. This text cannot begin to cover all of the important related considerations. Nevertheless, a few of the relevant concepts will be introduced, so that you can begin to grasp the importance of the articulation between a firm's managerial approach or philosophy and its MAS.

Essentially, management approaches or styles may be viewed as on a spectrum. At one end is the firm whose management approach is characterized by the belief that responsibility is vested solely in managers and supervisors. Managers and supervisors in such firms are expected continuously and closely to motivate, monitor, and direct the behavior of subordinate managers, supervisors, and employees. Employees are not expected or allowed to have any significant interest, commitment, or involvement in the goals of the organization. Initiative may be discouraged. Employees are merely expected and required to do assigned tasks. The traditional management approach in the military provides a good example of this style.

At the opposite end of the spectrum are those organizations where responsibility is assumed by and vested in the individual employee. Employees are self-motivated, and monitoring and direction by superiors is minimal and usually takes the form of coordination. This pattern may be observed among rescue teams or small business partnerships, where each member is aware of and has confidence in his or her own and other members' roles and competencies.

Apparently these different management styles arise from two divergent views or assumptions concerning human motivation and behavior. In one view, it is assumed that most employees must be induced or motivated to work, and that most employees shun the assumption of responsibility. Douglas McGregor categorized these beliefs as Theory X.[2] They include assumptions that individuals primarily desire security, have little ambition, dislike work and responsibility and will avoid it if possible, prefer to be directed, must be coerced into working, and must be closely directed if their efforts are to be congruent with their employer's objectives.

The opposite view, which McGregor labeled Theory Y, assumes that most people:

• are potentially ambitious and have an unused creative capacity;

• find work natural and not inherently distasteful;

---

[2]   Douglas McGregor, *The Human Side of Enterprise*, McGraw-Hill Book Company, New York, 1960, pp. 33–34 and 47–48.

- under appropriate conditions will accept and even seek responsibility;

and

- need not be coerced or directed but will direct themselves towards objectives to which they are committed.

It appears that three conditions must be met if Theory Y is to be operational for an individual and the firm. First, an individual's basic needs for physiological and psychological security must be perceived by him or her as having been met.[3] Second, the individual must be committed to the same goals as those of the firm—there must be goal congruence. Third, the individual's environment must consist of Theory Y type expectations. It appears that most individuals will behave in the manner which their superiors and colleagues expect of them.[4]

For simplicity, the two styles of management cited above will hereafter be referred to as *authoritarian* and *participative*, and the two attitudes as *dependent* and *responsible*. Can you see how a firm's MAS for both budgeting and control would necessarily differ depending upon the dominant or intended style of the firm's management?

If the firm's approach is essentially authoritarian, then:

- The information system must be very detailed and must provide frequent feedback.

- The system must be highly standardized and uniform, so that it will be perceived as fair to all parties.

- Participation and planning will be minimal and possibly counterproductive.[5]

- Variations in performance from plan will be viewed as a cause for punishment or reward.

You should not conclude that authoritarian management is ineffective or undesirable. Where management experiences a high degree of uncertainty associated with a task, and where employees are not skilled or experienced in dealing with various possible eventualities, then authoritarian management may be perceived by both as the only reasonable choice. At the other extreme, when there is considerable certainty and tasks are routine and can be planned

---

[3]  See Maslow's hierarchy of human needs in Abraham H. Maslow, *Motivation and Personality*, Harper, New York, 1954.

[4]  See J. Sterling Livingston, "Pygmalion in Management," *Harvard Business Review*, July–August, 1969, pp. 81–89.

[5]  Even dependent (as defined) employees will resent having their input solicited if it is to be subsequently ignored by an authoritarian management.

in detail, and where a system of punishments and rewards to provide adequate motivation exists and is administered with fairness, then authoritarian management can be both effective and efficient. Also, although participation leads to greater employee satisfaction, it has yet to be shown necessarily to lead to higher levels of performance.

Where a firm's management style is essentially participative, then its MAS should be designed differently. Since goal congruence is essential, heavy emphasis must be placed on adequate and open communication of objectives so that they may be commonly shared. A high degree of participation is needed in the establishment of objectives, budgets, and standards. The system can be less detailed, more flexible, and tailored to the needs of particular individuals and groups, with only periodic, as compared to very frequent, feedback. Reported variances between performance and plan need not be perceived as sources of reward and punishment. Instead, they may be perceived as nothing more than a signal or a trigger for mutual problem-solving activity directed at modifying future performance or future plans. Budgets and standards, if participative, can be perceived by all involved as simply formal codifications of plans and objectives mutually agreed upon previously. Performance reports can then be perceived as simply feedback messages to facilitate the attainment of mutual objectives.

Rarely will **all** managers in an organization be either authoritative or participative in their approaches to management. Individuals differ in their assumptions and in their experience related to human behavior and desirable management philosophy. Furthermore, the relative degree of uncertainty of the task at hand can be different at different times and for different parts of the organization. Often a firm's management will evidence a dominant theme reflecting the style of the senior executive.

It is also probably even more rare to find an organization in which employees are essentially either all dependent or all capable and desirous of assuming responsibility. Most managements, therefore, reflect a blend of the two management styles, and an appropriate information system must therefore be blended to match.

One risk of participative systems, previously cited in Chapters 2 and 10, deserves emphasis. Especially in those firms where the management style is a blend of the participative and the authoritarian, employees can be very sensitive in their perceptions to even minor changes in the operation of a budgeting and control system. Where budgets or standards are even partially imposed, or where they are subsequently subject to arbitrary change or use, they may no longer be perceived as simply codifications of mutually agreed and committed objectives. Instead they may be viewed as devices to induce or force higher levels of output from workers and, as such, a target for resistance or sabotage. In such a climate of suspicion, performance reports may also take on the image of instruments employed to pinpoint and focus upon mistakes and errors. Many of the advantages of participative management may be nullified or lost.

## RELATING BUDGETS AND PERFORMANCE STANDARDS TO ORGANIZATIONAL STRUCTURE

Budgets and performance standards must not only be compatible with a firm's management style; they must also conform to the firm's organizational structure. If standards are not designed so as to be clearly applicable to a particular organizational unit, they are relatively valueless as a control device. One of the characteristics of an effective organization is the clear delineation of authority and responsibility among various organizational subsets or components. Plans and standards must be applicable to such responsibility centers so that it is the **individual center's** plan and performance that is being reported and not partially that of someone else.

### Patterns of Organization

Organizational structures are not all alike. Although they commonly involve delegation of authority and responsibility, the basis for, or pattern of, delegation can differ widely. There are at least four distinct bases for dividing an organization, which are illustrated in Exhibit 11.1 (see page 468).

1. *Function:* Separate organizational units may be delineated by type of activity performed—marketing, production, accounting, and so forth.
2. *Geographic location:* Distinct organizations may be established in different locations, with each responsible for all activities within certain geographic boundaries.
3. *Product line:* Firms with several distinct product lines may be organized so that most or all activities related to a particular product line are grouped in a single responsibility center. For example, home appliances may be in one division and industrial equipment in another.
4. *Customer:* Firms with just a few major customers may establish organizational units designed to satisfy the demands of a particular customer or group of customers. A defense contractor could have separate divisions for Army, Navy, and Air Force contracts.

Many firms combine elements of these four separate patterns. Manufacturing and administration may be divided along functional lines, with sales activities broken down by territory (see Exhibit 2.17). Or all activities may be distributed functionally, and then additional staff product-line managers may be assigned to monitor and coordinate all activities related to a particular group of products (Exhibit 11.2).

Regardless of the particular pattern of organization, the information system designed for planning and control must be compatible with the organization structure. Information concerning a particular activity must be available to all managers responsible for such activity. Remember, from Chapter 5, the concept or principle of controllability. Controllability requires that all managers having significant influence over a particular activity are jointly responsible for it, and must participate in its planning and control. Planning and

**Exhibit 11.1**
## DIFFERENT PATTERNS OF ORGANIZATION

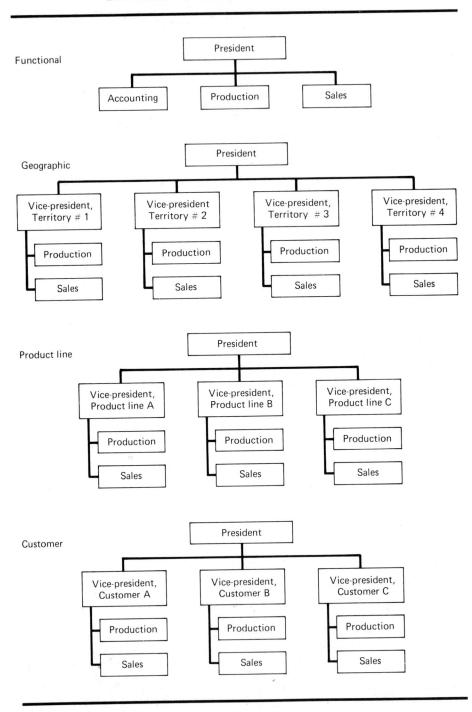

**Exhibit 11.2**
COMBINED FUNCTIONAL AND PRODUCT LINE ORGANIZATION

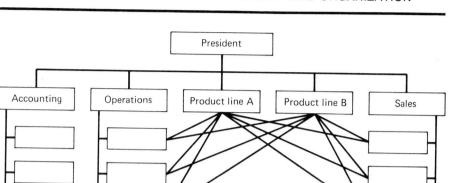

control information must be available to all. Service-center costs, introduced in Chapter 5 and to be discussed in more detail in Chapter 12, are prime examples of an area of joint responsibility.

As discussed in earlier chapters, controllability requires that information relating to items not under a manager's influence or control be **excluded** from planning and control reports designated for that manager's responsibility center. Inclusion of noncontrollable items may divert attention from important controllable items and/or may increase the responsible manager's feelings of frustration and helplessness.

## Types of Responsibility Centers

In any given organization there may be four different types of responsibility centers, depending upon the type of activity and the scope of authority and responsibility assigned. These four types of responsibility centers are:

1. Expenditure centers,[6]
2. Revenue centers,
3. Profit centers, and
4. Investment centers.

---

[6]   The term "expenditure center" is **not** in common use. It is deliberately chosen instead of the term "expense center" to focus your attention upon the controllability of expenditures as distinct from the timing of expenses, the latter being determined by financial accounting requirements. The term "cost center" is also widely used. Using cost center may be ambiguous, since the term also refers to a source or grouping of product cost data that may involve more than a single responsibility center.

*Expenditure centers* (see Fig. 11.2) are the most common and the simplest to understand. Within an expenditure center, the manager's primary authority and responsibility is restricted to the planning and control of expenditures or costs. In some cases, some revenue may also exist (sale of scrap or by-products by a manufacturing department), but such revenue is clearly incidental and of secondary importance. Figure 11.2 pictures the almost exclusive attention devoted to control of expenditures or costs. In an expenditure center there is no opportunity to measure profitability and no control over invested resources. Various departments within a factory (moulding, assembly, and maintenance in the Tripper example) are the most obvious examples of expenditure centers. The department foreman has no effective control over sales (assuming quality is maintained) and no authority to make major investment decisions.

EXPENDITURE CENTER

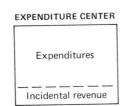

**Figure 11.2**

Planning and control for expenditure centers using financial measures may take the form of standard costs (Chapter 1) or of operating budgets (Chapter 5). Control of expenditure centers through the use of standard costs will be covered in Chapter 13. Control of expenditure centers where operating budgets are used as the performance standard will be discussed in Chapter 12.

A second and somewhat more involved type of responsibilty center is known as a *revenue center* (see Fig. 11.3). A revenue center is primarily responsible for marketing or selling products or services. Can you visualize and give an example of a revenue center? Could you generally describe the information content of planning and control reports for revenue centers, and contrast them with reports for expenditure centers?

REVENUE CENTER

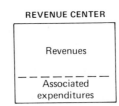

**Figure 11.3**

A given sales territory or geographic division might be easiest to visualize as a revenue center. As shown in the illustration above, the primary responsibility of the center's manager would be to raise revenue through sales. Administrative and selling costs could also be involved. However, such costs would be secondary, and would normally be expected to occur in proportion to revenue. Planning and control of revenue centers may be complicated by product-mix and receivables-collection considerations. Control of revenue centers and these related factors will be covered in Chapter 14.

The third less common type of responsibility center is the so-called *profit center* (see Fig. 11.4). A semiautonomous operating division in another part of the country or abroad could be controlled as a profit center. As illustrated above, a responsibility center classified as a profit center is charged with planning and controlling both revenues and most related expenditures. A profit center is similar to a distinct and independent business, except that discretion over invested resources and responsibility for financing and financial costs is not delegated by top management to profit centers. In a profit center, plans and performance with respect to revenues, expenditures, and also profits is formally monitored. Control of profit centers will also be discussed in Chapter 14.

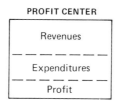

**PROFIT CENTER**

Revenues

Expenditures

Profit

**Figure 11.4**

The final classification of responsibility centers is the one for *investment centers*. As shown in Fig. 11.5, investment centers may be thought of as profit centers that have authority over and responsibility for investment decisions relating to capital assets. Managers of investment centers have control over a nearly autonomous business. Often the only element missing is control over long-term financing, which is reserved to the home office or parent corporation. Planning and control systems for these centers measure revenues, expenditures, capital budgets, profits, and return on investment. Control over investment centers will also be covered in Chapter 14.

**INVESTMENT CENTER**

Revenues

Expenditures

Profit

Capital investment

Return on investment

**Figure 11.5**

Control over responsibility centers in nonprofit-directed organizations is often handled differently than in business organizations. For this reason, control in nonprofit-directed organizations is segregated in a separate chapter (Chapter 15) devoted exclusively to this growing area of responsibility.

## THE CONTROL CYCLE

Operating management can be viewed as having two components—day-to-day activities and periodic review. Recall the activities of the proprietor of a very small firm, described earlier. Control was exercised on a continuous basis with periodic assessment of performance based on cumulative sales and cash balances. In larger firms with managers dependent upon the MAS for feedback, the manager's activities may be similarly divided into day-to-day decision making and periodic review. The process of periodic review can, in turn, be viewed as a *control cycle* following the three elements of control (plan, feedback, action) cited earlier. Periodic review starts with measures of performance.

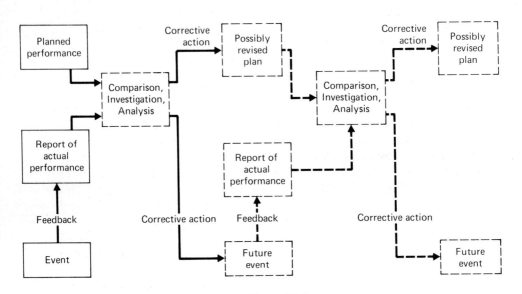

Figure 11.6

Note, in Fig. 11.6, that managers compare actual performance with plan, investigate and analyze any significant differences, and then take any indicated corrective action. Also note that corrective action may be limited to or include a revision of an inappropriate plan. Managerial accounting participates in the control cycle through providing performance reports,[7] and assisting managers in the identification, investigation, and analysis of significant variances from plan.

---

[7]   Performance reports are also known as "control reports." Since the word control has undesirable "Orwellian" or authoritarian connotations for many individuals, the term performance report is preferable.

You have seen how the MAS in a particular firm should be adapted to management styles and to the firm's organizational structure. You are now aware of the different types of responsibility centers that may exist within a firm and of the steps in the control cycle. Now you should consider different types of performance, the ways to interpret performance reports, and how control information may be used productively or misused.

## OBJECTIVES OF PERFORMANCE REPORTS

A manager of a responsibility center is charged with getting a job done at a reasonable cost. Note that **two distinct responsibilities** are involved. The manager must be *effective*. He or she is responsible for producing a desired level of input (customer orders) or output (products or services). Often the best measures of effectiveness are physical measures involving units of product or service. Control over the effectiveness of a responsibility center is often accomplished separately from the MAS. Information systems reporting on effectiveness are usually covered in marketing, production, and operations management courses and will not be the primary focus of this text.

The second major responsibility of a manager involves *efficiency*. For any actual level of activity (whether that level was as planned, greater than planned, or less than planned), a manager is responsible for controlling costs, spending the least cost reasonable or appropriate for the activity level attained. Performance reports that are part of the MAS focus on dollar measures of efficiency. In this chapter, performance measures will be introduced in terms of comparisons between planned revenue and expenditures and those actually occurring. It will be assumed in this chapter that actual levels of activity are the same as those originally planned in the budget. Chapters 12 and 13 will introduce control measures for those situations where actual activity levels differ from those originally planned.

The objective of performance reports is to provide necessary information with respect to each responsibility center, for comparison with planned, standard, or budgeted performance. Do you have some notion of what information should be included in performance reports and, more particularly, how it should be classified? Returning to the Tripper example, what information should be included in the performance report for the Tripper assembly department? Exhibit 11.3 is the Tripper assembly department's budget for the first six months of 19X2. Assume that it is now the end of June, 19X2; what information would you like to have in order to evaluate the department's performance during the first six months of the year?

Exhibit 11.4 is a performance report for the month of June. Note that actual performance has been recorded and classified to match the identical items of planned performance. Performance evaluation in comparison to budgets will be further discussed in Chapter 12.

## Exhibit 11.3
### TRIPPER WATER SKI MANUFACTURING COMPANY

**Operating Budget—Assembly Department**
**First Six Months 19X2**

|  | January | February | March | April | May | June | Total |
|---|---|---|---|---|---|---|---|
| Scheduled assembly: |  |  |  |  |  |  |  |
| Economy skis (units) | 0 | 2,100 | 2,100 | 0 | 2,100 | 2,100 | 8,400 |
| Deluxe skis (units) | 1,700 | 0 | 0 | 1,700 | 1,700 | 0 | 5,100 |
| Direct labor | $2,720 | $2,625 | $2,625 | $2,720 | $5,345 | $2,625 | $18,660 |
| Indirect labor ($1,000/Mo. F; $0.20 V) | 1,340 | 1,420 | 1,420 | 1,340 | 1,760 | 1,420 | 8,700 |
| Indirect materials ($30/Mo. F; $0.30 V) | 540 | 690 | 690 | 540 | 1,170 | 690 | 4,320 |
| Maintenance ($500/Mo. F; $0.05 V) | 585 | 605 | 605 | 585 | 690 | 605 | 3,675 |
| Total | $5,185 | $5,340 | $5,340 | $5,185 | $8,965 | $5,340 | $33,355 |

*Note.* Variable cost for overhead items is the same per ski regardless of model.

**Exhibit 11.4**

TRIPPER WATER SKI MANUFACTURING COMPANY

### Performance Report—Assembly Department

| | June 19X2 Current month | | | | Year-to-date | | | |
|---|---|---|---|---|---|---|---|---|
| | Budget | Actual | Variance | % | Budget | Actual | Variance | % |
| Direct labor | $2,625 | $2,575 | $ 50 F | 2 | $18,660 | $19,000 | $ 340 U | 2 |
| Indirect labor | 1,420 | 1,920 | 500 U | 35 | 8,700 | 9,700 | 1,000 U | 11.5 |
| Indirect materials | 690 | 600 | 90 F | 13 | 4,320 | 4,120 | 200 F | 5 |
| Maintenance | 605 | 1,665 | 1,060 U | 175 | 3,675 | 3,600 | 75 F | 2 |
| Total | $5,340 | $6,760 | $1,420 U | 27 | $35,355 | $36,420 | $1,065 U | 3 |

## CONTENT OF PERFORMANCE REPORTS

To be most effective, plans (standards or budgets) and performance should be measured and reported in the same way. As previously discussed, planning should be broken down to controllable levels and into controllable segments. Planning should start at the lowest organizational level of influence or controllability over a given item. Planning should also be in terms of readily controllable segments about which **performance data may be readily obtained.** To budget a single amount for conversion costs would be counterproductive, since the separately controllable elements (direct labor and various overhead items) are not identified. Moreover, it is futile to plan at a level of detail beyond the capacity of the accountant's information system (cost of power consumed on the west side of the building on sunny afternoons), because performance could not be readily reported.

With the planning system properly focused on **relevant, controllable,** and **measurable data,** the appropriate rule for the information content of performance reports is simply "match the detail in the standard or budget." Note that data recorded by the cost accounting system must be detailed at the lowest responsibility center—so-called responsibility accounting. Thereafter it may be classified and summarized in two quite different patterns, one for budget reports and the other for financial accounting.

Performance reports do more than just report what has actually happened. Recall that managerial accounting assists managers in identifying significant areas that may require corrective action. It does this by calculating variances (differences between planned and actual performance), expressing them both in dollars and as a percentage of plan, and by also including all information on a year-to-date basis.

Refer again to Exhibit 11.4. Note that variances are shown both in dollar amounts and as a percentage of budget. The absolute dollar amount is useful in estimating the potential benefits (in comparison to possible costs) of effective action. For instance, substantial investigative time would probably be counterproductive with reference to the indirect materials variance. Only $90 are involved and the variance is favorable. On the other hand, $500 of potential savings would probably merit some time being spent looking into the indirect labor variance.

Note also that variances are coded "F" for favorable or "U" for unfavorable. A *favorable variance* is merely one that could lead to a greater profit than originally planned. $5,000 more actual revenue than planned and $3,000 less expenditure than planned would **both** be identified as favorable variances. Conversely, less revenue or more expenditure than planned would represent an *unfavorable variance.* You should be careful **not** to interpret favorable as necessarily meaning "good" or "desirable," or unfavorable as necessarily implying "bad" or "undesirable." Remember that the plan itself could prove to be in error or to be inappropriate in unanticipated circumstances. Later in this and subsequent chapters, you will find examples where so-called favorable variances may be signals of distinctly undesirable performance, and vice versa.

Percentage variance provides useful information concerning the order of magnitude or significance of an item, and also about the potential for correction. For example, even if the direct labor variance on Exhibit 11.4 had been unfavorable, a two-percent variance could probably never be improved. On the other hand, the 35-percent unfavorable variance for indirect labor and the 175-percent variance for maintenance both strongly signal a need for investigation and the possibility for improvement.

Year-to-date information allows for balancing-out of variances over time, and also can provide trend information. Referring again to Exhibit 11.4, can you see examples of these information benefits? The current month's $1,060 unfavorable maintenance variance is more than offset by a $75 favorable variance over the first six months. The current month probably simply reflects the result of work scheduled in April and May being delayed and combined with scheduled maintenance in June. Returning once again to the indirect labor variance, note that year-to-date information indicates that the problem is not new and is getting worse (overall unfavorable variance of 11.5 percent, compared to current month's variance of 35 percent).

## THE CONTROL CHART

The availability of variances both in absolute amounts and as a percentage of plan facilitates determination of the significance of a variance and the desirability of attempted corrective action. However, you as a manager must still operate with a rule of thumb such as "Anything over $500 or 10 percent should be checked." Ideally you would like variances identified for you and your superior as either:

- Probably *random* and therefore not readily controllable,
- Probably nonrandom and therefore subject to more effective control.

Some expenditures have random characteristics; their causes are not completely predictable or controllable. Recall from Chapter 5 that, when a budgeting rate is established, it is based on a line of best fit for a series of different pairs of costs and activity levels.

The budgeting rate is essentially an average or mean expectation, and, at any one volume level, a cost may never be exactly on the regression line. Figure 11.7 illustrates a variable cost, and a similar illustration would apply

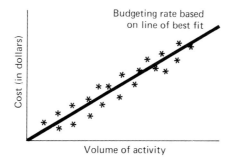

Figure 11.7

equally well for a mixed or even fixed cost.

Some costs are subject to little random variation (Fig. 11.8). Supplies cost or direct material costs may be quite uniform at any given level of volume. Other costs such as maintenance may vary considerably at the same volume level (Fig. 11.9) as a result of random equipment breakdowns not directly variable with the level of activity.

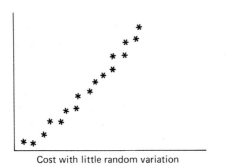

Cost with little random variation

**Figure 11.8**

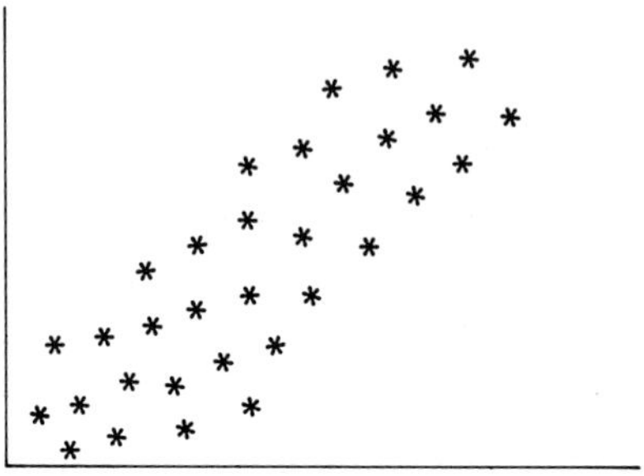

Cost with significant random variation

**Figure 11.9**

Fortunately, statistical analysis and the concept of the *control chart* provide a more precise way to identify variances that are most probably random and therefore still under control. Statistical analysis of variances is usually covered in those statistics courses that are part of a business-school common core. The technique will be briefly described in Chapter 17, along with other quantitative tools that are useful in planning and control.

Statistical analysis of variance results in defining limits within which a variance may be considered probably random and therefore still within control. This information can be used by managers to set their investigation limits more objectively in terms of dollars and percentages. Any variance outside of or beyond these limits (see Fig. 11.10) would be considered as out of control and requiring investigation and action. Those firms that have their budgeting and control systems on computers may readily incorporate control limits in the reporting of variances.

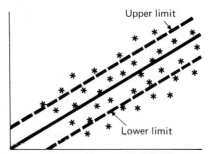

Figure 11.10

The control-chart concept has many more uses in management than just budget-variance analysis of expenditures. Control charts are used extensively in manufacturing quality control. In this application, "variances" in quality are being evaluated to distinguish those that can normally be expected from those requiring remedial action. The same concept is useful to marketing personnel in interpreting the results of market research, or patterns of variance in actual sales as compared to budgeted sales.

## USING CONTROL INFORMATION

Performance reports, by highlighting exceptions, assist managers in directing their efforts to those areas that are out of control. *Management by exception* is useful in periods of overload, and some people consider it the most efficient way for managers to operate all of the time. However, giving attention only to exceptions may not be the panacea that some claim. Possible adverse behavior resulting from this approach will be discussed below.

### Exhibit 11.5
### ILLUSTRATION OF MULTILEVEL PERFORMANCE REPORTING[a]

| President: | | | |
|---|---|---|---|
| Controller | $ 6,400 | $ 6,500 | $   100 U |
| Operations vice-president | → 42,000 | 42,450 | 450 U |
| Sales vice-president | 31,000 | 29,960 | 1,040 F |
| Other | 3,000 | 3,700 | 700 U |
| Total | $82,400 | $82,610 | $  210 U |
| **Operations vice-president:** | | | |
| Finished goods stores | $ 2,050 | $ 2,000 | $    50 F |
| Assembly | → 5,340 | 5,760 | 420 U |
| Moulding | 15,900 | 15,300 | 600 F |
| Receiving and room stores | 2,400 | 2,490 | 90 U |
| Purchasing | 4,800 | 4,650 | 150 F |
| Material control | 3,000 | 3,430 | 430 U |
| Maintenance | 2,010 | 2,420 | 410 U |
| Other | 6,500 | 6,400 | 100 F |
| Total | → $42,000 | $42,450 | $  450 U |
| **Assembly department foreman:** | | | |
| Direct labor | $ 2,625 | $ 2,575 | $    50 F |
| Indirect labor | 1,420 | 1,920 | 500 U |
| Indirect materials | 690 | 600 | 90 F |
| Maintenance | 605 | 665 | 60 U |
| Total | → $ 5,340 | $ 5,760 | $  420 U |

[a] June, 19X2, current-month accounts only are shown for illustration.

Actually, using control information as a basis for action is a management activity and is beyond the scope of this text. Nevertheless it should be obvious to you from Exhibit 11.4 that the assembly foreman and his superior should be concerned about the indirect labor variance and should investigate causes and possibilities for remedial action.

Remember, from Chapter 2, that performance reports are prepared for each level of responsibility within the organization; copies go to the responsible manager(s) and the immediate superior. The two most affected individuals then have the opportunity to confer on corrective action already taken or to be taken. Exhibit 11.5 illustrates how reports to higher levels can carry summaries of lower-level performance.

## MISUSING PLANNING AND CONTROL INFORMATION

Before moving to a discussion (in the next three chapters) of specific control systems and their uses, you should be aware of some of the ways in which budgets, standards, and performance reports may be **misused.** Two obvious misuses of budgets (or standards) involve their use by subordinates to gain favor with or appease superiors, and their use by superiors as an absolute performance requirement. Managers who include, or approve inclusion of, amounts in their budgets that are not realistic are serving neither themselves nor their firm. A superior may be pleased momentarily by a budget showing overly optimistic revenues or low costs; a superior making unrealistic demands for higher revenues or lower costs may be temporarily appeased with an unattainable budget. In both situations the firm will suffer the consequences of inaccurate planning, which may introduce many varied and serious problems. Also, the erroneous information will be revealed eventually when performance falls far short of budget, and the manager(s) involved may be disciplined for failure to meet goals.

To use budgets as an absolute performance requirement can be equally counterproductive. Budgets are simply plans made within a given set of future expectations. Where circumstances later vary from those that were anticipated, performance should be modified accordingly. A salesperson whose travel budget did not anticipate the arrival in the area of a new potentially large customer should not postpone calling until next year for fear of being over budget. Managers who find, at year-end, that they are under budget should not frantically spend to achieve the budgeted level of expenditures.[8]

---

[8]  Where budgets become ends in themselves rather than means, and especially where the next year's budget will be based on this year's expenditures, managers have a strong incentive to spend all that is in the budget. This situation has unfortunately been typical in governmental budgeting. Revised governmental budgeting approaches to remove the inappropriate incentives will be discussed in Chapter 15.

Excessive preoccupation with, or slavish adherence to, the budget may bring about so-called *budgetary slack*. Where a manager experiences criticism for going over budget, regardless of circumstances, he or she will be strongly motivated to pad or introduce slack into future budgets to cover all possible contingencies. The result can be both highly unrealistic planning and inefficient operation. The excessively loose standard can provide little guidance to either the manager or the superior concerning desirable performance.[9]

Control information included in performance reports may be similarly misused or abused. Where budgets or standards and performance reports are used as surrogates for interpersonal communication ("I don't want to waste time discussing the problem; just get out there and make your budget"), everyone loses. For the subordinate, the budget has been made an end in itself (see above). For the superior, possibly vital input relating to changing conditions has been effectively shut off. Budgets and performance reports should serve as triggers for effective communication and not as substitutes.

Unfavorable budget variances may be continuously used by managers as an excuse for abuse and criticism of employees, rather than as a signal for mutual exploration of a potential problem area. In such situations, effective communication and problem resolution may be blocked as, again, "meeting the budget" becomes an end in itself. Preoccupation with unfavorable variances can represent a serious oversight. A significant favorable variance could be signaling a serious planning error or a potentially dangerous lack of performance. Can you think of examples where significant "favorable" variances could be indications of problems equal to or even greater than problems signaled by unfavorable variances?

Repeated high "favorable" revenue variances could be an indication that budgeted activity levels have been set too low. Replanning for additional inventory, and possible additional financing, may be required, in order to avoid lost sales and customer dissatisfaction. Consistently high favorable cost variances could imply that actual costs are lower than expected, and additional profitable business might be obtainable with lower prices. Also consider the situations where a vital operation in the manufacture of a product was being omitted or equipment was not being serviced and properly maintained. Both would appear as "favorable" variances!

One final abuse of control information is worth noting. It relates to the continuous as compared to periodic use of management by exception. Most people have come to understand that, when parents communicate with children only about misbehavior, they will generate more misbehavior. The child will misbehave as the only way to get **attention.** Unfortunately some managers, and even some management theorists, neglect to apply the attention

---

[9]    This situation is unfortunately prevalent in governmental budgeting where the budget represents a legal expenditure ceiling that may not be exceeded. Governmental budgeting will be discussed in Chapter 15.

principle to adults. If a subordinate receives recognition and attention from a superior only in an exception situation where something has gone wrong (large budget variances), how do you think the subordinate will obtain desired attention and recognition in future periods?

## CHAPTER OVERVIEW

Based on the material contained in this chapter, you should now be able to:

✴ • Explain the concept of control as it applies to a business, and describe the objectives of control.

• Describe, with examples, the various elements of control and the control cycle.

• Explain the role of managerial accounting in the control process.

• Briefly explain the difference between two distinct styles or approaches to managing people, identified as "authoritarian" and "participative," and describe the assumptions regarding human behavior that are implicit to each style.

• Describe the methods of preparing and using planning and control information appropriate to each style of managing.

• Explain, with examples, the importance of relating budgets or standards and control reports to responsibility centers.

• Explain, with examples, the differences among the four patterns of organization based upon function, geographic location, product line, or customers.

• Describe the four types of responsibility centers, identified as expenditure, revenue, profit, and investment centers; and give the objectives and types of responsibility delegated to each type.

✴ { • Differentiate between measures of effectiveness and efficiency in control reporting.

• Describe the objective and information content of performance reports prepared as part of the MAS for planning and control.

• Explain, with examples, the usefulness of variances expressed in dollars, as a percentage, and in year-to-date terms.

• Explain, with an example, the concept of the control chart, and how this concept is applicable to the analysis of variances.

• Describe, with examples, some of the ways in which planning and control information can be misused.

## NEW VOCABULARY AND CONCEPTS

| | |
|---|---|
| Theory X (assumptions) | Profit centers |
| Theory Y (assumptions) | Investment centers |
| Authoritarian management | Control cycle |
| Participative management | Effective (performance) |
| Dependent (behavior) | Efficient (performance) |
| Responsible (behavior) | Favorable variance |
| Functional organization | Unfavorable variance |
| Geographic organization | Random (variance) |
| Product-line organization | Control chart |
| Organization by customer | Management by exception |
| Expenditure centers | Budgetary slack |
| Revenue centers | |

• Relating planning and control systems to management styles and to responsibility centers.

• Different types of responsibility centers.

• Management by exception and the principle of attention.

• Variance analysis; random vs. controllable variances.

## REVIEW QUESTIONS

1. a) What is meant by the term "control" as used with respect to business?
   b) What are the objectives of control in a business?
   c) Why is control not exclusively directed towards conformance with plan? Explain, with examples.

2. a) What are the three basic elements of control?
   b) How do these elements interrelate with budgets or standards and performance reports in the control cycle?
   c) What is the role of managerial accounting in the control cycle?

3. a) What is McGregor's Theory X and how does it relate to a style of managing?
   b) What is McGregor's Theory Y and how does it relate to a style of managing?
   c) What is the relationship between different styles of management and different systems of planning and control information? Explain, with examples.

4. a) What is meant by matching a planning and control system to the responsibility centers within a particular organization?
   b) Why is this matching necessary or at least desirable?

5. a) What are four distinct patterns of delineation of organizational responsibility?

    b) Can a given organization include more than one pattern? Explain your answer, with examples.

6. a) What four types of responsibility centers may be present in a given firm?
   b) What are the different objectives and areas of responsibility of each of the four types of centers?

7. a) Are effectiveness and efficiency both objectives of any manager? Explain the difference.
   b) Which objective is usually reported upon by a MAS in financial terms? Why are dollar measurements more appropriate to this objective than to the other?

8. a) What is the function of performance reports?
   b) What are the various items of information often appearing in a performance report?
   c) How do performance reports assist managers in comparing planned and actual performance and in evaluating the significance of departures from plan?
   d) How do performance reports at different levels of responsibility relate to each other? Explain, with examples.

9. a) What is meant by a random variance?
   b) Why is it useful to a manager to distinguish those performance variances that are probably random?
   c) What is a control chart, and how would it relate to the analysis of variances?

10. a) What are the advantages and dangers of management by exception?
    b) How do performance reports relate to management by exception?

11. a) Does a variance always indicate that the actual performance was undesirable? Explain.
    b) Can a favorable variance be just as undesirable as an unfavorable one? Explain, with examples.

12. a) What is budgetary slack? How may it arise and what are its consequences?
    b) What are some of the ways in which planning and control information can be misused?
    c) What are the potential consequences of such misuse?

## MINI-CASES AND QUESTIONS FOR DISCUSSION

MC 11.1 You have just been hired as the foreman of the assembly department in the Berlow Manufacturing Company. Berlow manufactures skateboards, and your department has 23 employees—12 women and 11 men. The plant superintendent (your immediate superior) and the firm's top executives all appear to strongly support a participative style of management. After a few days on the job, it becomes apparent that 18 of your employees are highly responsible and individualistic. They are hard workers, seem to delight in effectively handling minor problems as they arise, and were evidently somewhat resentful of your predecessor who was described as an ex-Marine drill sergeant who ran the assembly department like boot camp.

Your other five employees are different from the rest and are almost childlike. They seem to be constantly seeking the direction of others as to their actions, and to be confused and almost paralyzed by any minor problems or by anything that is nonroutine. They have told you several times how much they miss Hal, your predecessor. All five have good performance and attendance records, and are the senior employees in the department.

What management style should you adapt? Can you be authoritarian with some employees and in some situations, and not in others? Must your approach be consistent or the same with all of your workers? Discuss.

**MC 11.2** As a regional sales manager for the Sparky Corporation, you find that you have a problem. One of your district managers, Jean Tuttle, has been running consistently and significantly over budget for the past few months on travel and entertainment expenditures for her district sales personnel. Your superior, Margot Walker, as the corporate sales manager, is demanding that you do something about these excess costs. Margot's last communication on the subject ended with, "Look, I personally made up each of those district budgets, and I expect them to be followed!"

How should you proceed with Jean? Would your answer be different if the district budget had been prepared by Jean instead of Margot? Discuss.

**MC 11.3** As the general foreman of the Scott Manufacturing Corporation, you have just received the performance reports for the month of September. Indirect labor data are given below.

| Depart- | Current month | | Year-to-date | |
| ment | Budget | Actual | Budget | Actual |
|---|---|---|---|---|
| 1 | $200,000 | $203,500 | $1,800,000 | $1,830,000 |
| 2 | 180,000 | 183,000 | 1,440,000 | 1,439,000 |
| 3 | 60,000 | 62,000 | 600,000 | 605,000 |
| 4 | 230,000 | 234,500 | 1,840,000 | 1,836,000 |
| 5 | 140,000 | 143,000 | 980,000 | 995,000 |
| 6 | 110,000 | 112,000 | 880,000 | 875,000 |
| 7 | 10,000 | 10,200 | 90,000 | 92,000 |
| Total | $930,000 | $948,200 | $7,630,000 | $7,672,000 |

What should be your approach with respect to these indirect labor costs in your meetings with each of your foremen? Do you expect that you will have a problem explaining an $18,200 unfavorable variance to the vice-president for manufacturing? What should you tell the vice-president? Discuss.

MC 11.4  Some supporters of participative management believe that, if it is to work, the approach must be "pure" or complete, and must not be "diluted" with authoritarian actions. They reason that:

- In the past, most management has been authoritarian.
- Employees are therefore conditioned to expect authoritarian management and to be skeptical of any attempts at participative management, initially viewing such attempts as window dressing, or partially phony.
- Any evidence of the authoritarian approach will therefore be interpreted as proof of management's **real** intentions, and will result in nullifying the future benefits of participation.

Do you support this position? Discuss.

MC 11.5  Some people believe that descriptions of management styles as authoritarian or participative may be appropriate to describe tendencies or components of an individual manager's style. However, they believe that a manager's effectiveness stems from self-awareness—acceptance of self as a unique individual—and from a management style that is unique to the individual manager and accepts the uniqueness of each employee. If this were true, a given firm's management would be a constantly changing mix (as managers change), with each manager employing a different approach.

Can a management approach that is a blend of the authoritarian and the participative be effective? Can it be as effective as either the purely authoritarian or the purely participative? Discuss.

MC 11.6  Effective control in a firm includes not only effective control by each manager over his or her responsibility center, but effective coordination among the various centers. Coordination is accomplished through organizations and budgets. Isn't there a trade-off—a fine line between, on the one hand, encouraging individual managers **not** to adhere slavishly to budgets and to modify performance in circumstances where the plan proves inappropriate, and, on the other hand, losing coordination among different managers who depart from plan in different directions? How can or should a firm deal with this dilemma? Discuss.

MC 11.7  Some management by exception is necessary. Immediate "fires" must be given priority. And yet excessive management by exception may generate more exceptions. How can a manager efficiently budget his or her time (focus on problem areas and areas requiring the manager's expertise) and still avoid excessive management by exception? Discuss.

## ESSENTIAL PROBLEMS

EP 11.1  Assume that a firm is organized functionally into three divisions: operations, sales, and administrative. Purchasing, receiving, material and production control, manufacturing, factory personnel, inventory stores, and shipping activities are all under the control of the vice-president for operations. Advertising, market research, and sales are all the responsibility of the vice-president for sales. And accounting, budgeting, the firm's computer center, and general office management are all delegated to the controller.

For each of the following costs, indicate the appropriate division that should plan and control the cost, as one of the following:

ADM  The administrative division

OPS  The operations division

SLS  The sales division

XXX  None of the above, since the item is not controllable by any of the three officers.

a) Depreciation on factory equipment

b) Depreciation on office equipment

c) Depreciation on factory building

d) Advertising manager's salary

e) Assembly foreman's salary

f) Salespersons' salaries

g) Salespersons' travel expenses

h) Supplies used in factory machining department

i) Supplies used in administrative office

j) Advertising supplies used

k) Interest on debt

l) Electricity consumed in the assembly department

m) Lost material (scrap) in a machining department

n) Direct labor in the assembly department

o) Supplies used in the sales office

p) Sales commissions

q) Packing supplies

r) Cost of hiring new factory employees

s) Payroll "fringe" benefits for workers in the shipping department

t) Supplies used by production scheduling

u) Cost of repairing parts improperly manufactured in a machining department

v) Paint used in the assembly department

w) Cost of help-wanted advertising for factory employees

x) Cost of snow removal from the senior executives' parking lot

y) Heat, light and power in the factory

z) Rental for bookkeeping machines used in the accounting department

**EP 11.2** Refer to Problem EP 11.1. Assume that the firm's organization chart delineating reporting responsibility was as shown in Fig. 11.11.

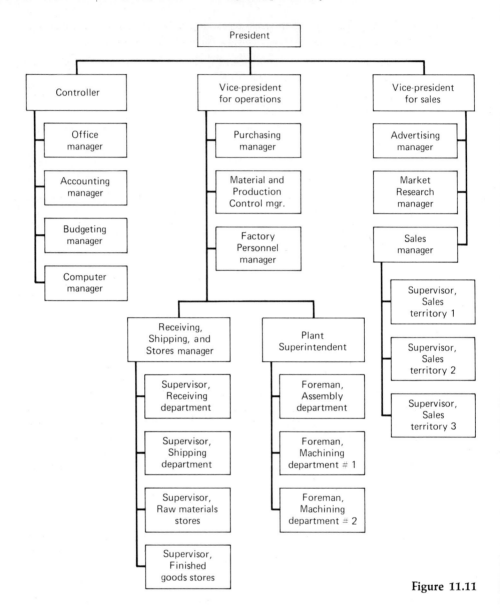

**Figure 11.11**

Assume that budget and control information is reported in detail to the responsible manager and his or her immediate superior, in summary form only at higher levels within a specific chain of authority, and not at all in the other chains.

For each of the items listed in Problem EP 11.1, indicate which foreman, supervisor, manager, or vice-president would be the responsible manager—the one on whose budget and control report the item would first appear.

**EP 11.3** For each of the following separate numbered situations, you may assume that the budget was appropriate; that is, was not in error.

a) Give examples of conditions where the reported variance could indicate superior or desirable performance.

b) Give examples or conditions where the same variance could indicate substandard or undesirable performance.

1. A $10,000 favorable sales revenue variance (more revenue than planned)

2. A $10,000 unfavorable sales revenue variance (less revenue than planned)

3. An $8,000 favorable material handling labor variance (less cost than planned)

4. An $8,000 unfavorable material handling labor variance (more cost than planned)

5. A $5,000 favorable heat, light, and power variance (less cost than planned)

6. A $5,000 unfavorable heat, light, and power variance (more cost than planned)

**EP 11.4** Assume that you are the general foreman of the Daisy Manufacturing Company and that the budget department forwards to you each month a copy of your budget performance report and a copy of the performance report for each of the foremen reporting to you. Each foreman also receives a copy of his or her report, and the vice-president for operations, who is your superior, receives a copy of yours. Your assembly foreman has bitterly complained to you that he thinks the system is unfair. He believes he should receive his own report first (at least a few days in advance) in order to have all his answers ready, and then review it with you. He doesn't believe it is fair for you to be advised of areas where he is over budget without the explanations accompanying the information.

a) Do you think this system should be changed to follow the foreman's recommendation? Explain.

b) What are the advantages of the present system? Assuming that it could not be changed, what could you tell or show your foreman that might allow him to accept the system?

**EP 11.5** As the supervisor of sales territory #3 for your firm, you have just received your performance report for the month of March. See Exhibit 11.6.

a) Considering the current month's data only, which variances would you consider serious enough to indicate a condition that may possibly require corrective action? Explain.

b) Does the year-to-date data modify your conclusions under (a) above? If yes, explain.

c) Is your territory considered an expenditure center, a revenue center, or a profit center? Explain.

**EP 11.6** As the foreman of machining department #2, you have just received your performance report for the month of August, as given in Exhibit 11.7.

**Exhibit 11.6**

PERFORMANCE REPORT, TERRITORY #3—March, 19XX

| | Current month | | | | Year-to-date | | | |
|---|---|---|---|---|---|---|---|---|
| | Budget | Actual | Variance | % | Budget | Actual | Variance | % |
| Gross sales | $900,000 | $870,000 | $30,000 U | 3.0 | $2,400,000 | $2,500,000 | $100,000 F | 4.0 |
| Sales returns and allowances (1%)* | 9,000 | 8,000 | 1,000 F | 11.0 | 24,000 | 22,000 | 2,000 F | 8.0 |
| Net sales (99%)* | $891,000 | $862,000 | $29,000 U | 3.0 | $2,376,000 | $2,478,000 | $102,000 F | 4.3 |
| Salaries ($18,000 F) | 18,000 | 18,000 | 0 | 0 | 54,000 | 54,000 | 0 | 0 |
| Commissions (3% V) | 26,730 | 25,860 | 870 F | 3.0 | 71,280 | 74,340 | 3,060 U | 4.3 |
| Travel (2% V + $5,000 F) | 22,820 | 26,240 | 3,420 U | 15.0 | 62,520 | 63,240 | 720 U | 1.2 |
| Total (5% V + $23,000 F) | $ 67,550 | $ 70,100 | $ 2,550 U | 3.7 | $ 187,800 | $ 191,580 | $ 3,780 U | 2.0 |

* Percent of gross sales; all other variable items based on net sales.

**Exhibit 11.7**

PERFORMANCE REPORT, MACHINING DEPARTMENT #2—AUGUST, 19XX

| | Current month | | | | Year-to-date | | | |
|---|---|---|---|---|---|---|---|---|
| | Budget | Actual | Variance | % | Budget | Actual | Variance | % |
| Units manufactured | 8,000 | 8,600 | 600 | 7.5 | 55,000 | 50,000 | 5,000 | 9.1 |
| Direct labor ($7 V) | $56,000 | $60,200 | $4,200 U | 7.5 | $385,000 | $353,200 | $31,800 F | 8.3 |
| Indirect labor ($0.5 V + $12,000 F) | 16,000 | 16,200 | 200 U | 1.3 | 123,500 | 122,000 | 1,500 F | 1.2 |
| Supplies ($0.1 V + $900 F) | 1,700 | 3,600 | 1,900 U | 111.8 | 12,700 | 19,800 | 7,100 U | 55.9 |
| Maintenance ($0.2V + $1,800 F) | 3,400 | 3,350 | 50 F | 1.5 | 25,400 | 25,720 | 320 U | 1.3 |
| Total ($7.8 V + $14,700 F) | $77,100 | $83,350 | $6,250 U | 8.1 | $546,600 | $520,720 | $25,880 F | 4.7 |

a) Considering the current month's data only, which variances would you consider serious enough to indicate a condition that may require corrective action? Explain.

b) Does the year-to-date data modify your conclusions under (a) above? If yes, explain.

c) Is your department considered an expenditure center, a revenue center, or a profit center? Explain.

d) From the above data, prepare the year-to-date section of the performance report for July, 19XX.

**EP 11.7** Mr. Trent Graves has been president of the Hardman Company for twelve years. He is totally devoted to his job, putting in an average of 70 hours per week with no vacations. He personally knows all 212 of the firm's employees, and usually makes the time to visit briefly with each one of them at least every other week. At each visit he checks up to see how well the individual is doing with reference to his "suggestion" made to the employee at the time of the previous visit. Mr. Graves carries a small notebook in which he notes "suggestions" that he makes for the employees' improvement. Mr. Graves is rather proud of both his "suggestion system" and the fact that he practices "management by objectives."

He also has a budgeting system that is his pride and joy. Each year he works every weekend for two months, preparing the budget for each of his managers. He then allows each manager one-half hour for questions at the time the manager is handed his or her annual budget. This way Mr. Graves hopes to avoid any misunderstanding on objectives. He wishes he could find more time so that he could make up budgets for each employee instead of just the managers. Hardman Company has been consistently profitable. Employees appeared satisfied. Many remark that there are never any surprises from the "old man."

a) Does Mr. Graves' suggestion system fit your understanding of the purposes of such systems and how they usually work? If not, explain how they differ.

b) Would you recommend that Mr. Graves attempt to invite more participation in the budgeting process at Hardman? Explain.

c) What are the risks, if any, in Mr. Graves' approach?

**EP 11.8** Refer to Problem EP 11.7. Mr. Graves has just read an article about another firm's MBO system. The article pointed out that a review often running two or three hours was held every six months with each manager. Mr. Graves tells you that he's going to start having such meetings in addition to the half-hour annual budget question session and the weekly visits. He tells you that, "Those reviews might really help those guys get clear on the objectives I set for them."

a) Would you classify Mr. Graves' style of management as authoritarian or participative?

b) Do you think Mr. Graves views his employees according to Theory X or Theory Y?

c) Does Mr. Graves really plan to have an MBO system in the usual sense? If not, describe the differences.

## SUPPLEMENTARY PROBLEMS

There are no supplementary problems in Chapter 11.

## SUGGESTIONS FOR FURTHER READING

Caplan, Edwin H., *Management Accounting and Behavioral Science*. Reading, Massachusetts: Addison-Wesley Publishing Company, 1975.

Hersey, Paul, and Kenneth Blanchard, *Management of Organization Behavior*, Second Edition. Englewood Cliffs, N.J., Prentice-Hall, Inc., 1972.

Hopewood, A., *Accounting and Human Behavior*. Englewood Cliffs, N.J.: Prentice-Hall, Inc., 1976.

Horngren, C., *Cost Accounting: A Managerial Emphasis*, Fourth Edition. Englewood Cliffs, N.J.: Prentice-Hall, Inc., 1977; Chapter 6.

Lawler, E., and J. Rhode, *Information Control in Organizations*. Pacific Palisades, California: Goodyear Publishing Co., Inc., 1976.

Likert, Rensis, *The Human Organization, Its Management and Value*. New York: McGraw-Hill Book Company, 1967.

Maslow, Abraham H., *Motivation and Personality*. New York: Harper, 1954.

Morse, Wayne J., *Cost Accounting: Processing, Evaluating, and Using Cost Data*. Reading, Massachusetts: Addison-Wesley Publishing Company, 1978; Chapter 10.

Schiff, M., and Y. Lewin, eds., *Behavioral Aspects of Accounting*. Englewood Cliffs, N.J.: Prentice-Hall, Inc., 1974.

# 12

## CONTROL OF EXPENDITURE CENTERS— COMPARISON WITH THE BUDGET

CHAPTER PREVIEW

The purpose of this chapter and the next is to provide you with additional information concerning performance control for expenditure centers. This chapter will focus upon performance measurement and variance analysis in terms of budgets, with which you are already familiar. You can learn:

- That variances result from both the effectiveness and the efficiency of performance.
- That certain variances may need to be divided further so that efficiency of cost control may be readily apparent.
- The difference between fixed and flexible budgets, and how flexible budgets facilitate the measurement of performance.
- The importance of selecting meaningful measures of activity, so that budgets used as performance standards will be as accurate as feasible.
- The desirability of segregating fixed and controllable costs in the reporting of performance.
- Special problems and techniques related to the budgeting and controlling of programmed and certain nonmanufacturing costs.
- How common costs may be allocated to responsibility centers for planning and control purposes, and the difficulties with and approaches to controlling expenditures in service centers.

In the appendix to this chapter, you can also learn how service-center and other indirect and fixed costs are allocated in the cost accounting system to arrive at full product costs; and how such allocations may make the analysis of manufacturing overhead variance more complex.

With this information you will have an adequate basic understanding of performance control over expenditure centers in those firms having operating budgets or budgeting rates. You will be in a position to complete the picture in the next chapter by learning about expenditure control in firms having standard cost systems.

## MEASURING EXPENDITURE CENTER PERFORMANCE IN UNPLANNED SITUATIONS

As president of the Tripper Company, you are continuing to monitor control of the assembly department. In July of 19X2, 2,100 economy skis and 1,700 deluxe skis were originally scheduled for production (Exhibit 4.10). The 3,000 hardware sets ordered for June delivery had arrived in June, and 2,100 of these were used in June as planned (Exhibit 4.12). In June, the employees of your hardware supplier went out on strike, and the labor contract impasse is still unresolved as of the end of July. As a consequence, the 3,000 hardware sets ordered for July have still not arrived.

With only 900 hardware sets available, they have been allocated proportionately to the two July assembly shop orders. 500 economy skis and 400 deluxe skis were assembled during July and delivered to finished goods stores. Expenditures during July in the assembly department were as follows:

| | |
|---|---|
| Direct labor | $1,455 |
| Indirect labor | 1,300 |
| Indirect materials | 1,000 |
| Maintenance | 540 |
| Total | $4,295 |

The original budget for July for the assembly department was based on the anticipated production of 2,100 economy skis and 1,700 deluxe skis. It is shown below. Remember, from Chapter 5, that variable overhead in the Tripper assembly department varies in proportion to skis assembled regardless of model.

Original July Budget—Assembly Department

| | |
|---|---|
| Direct labor: | |
| Economy skis ($1.25 V) | $2,625 |
| Deluxe skis ($1.60 V) | 2,720 |
| | $5,345 |
| Indirect labor ($1,000/Mo. F; $0.20 V) | 1,760 |
| Indirect materials ($30/Mo. F; $0.30 V) | 1,170 |
| Maintenance ($500/Mo. F; $0.05 V) | 690 |
| Total | $8,965 |

The assembly department in total for the month is $4,670, or 52.1 percent, under the original budget! Are you pleased with the performance of the assembly foreman? Has he kept all of his controllable expenditures under control during July? Remember that Tripper has been chosen as a fairly small firm so that the numbers will be more meaningful within your personal experience. Should you find a $9,000 budget and a $4,600 variance not too important, you might mentally add two zeros to all the figures in this example for more impact.

Chapter 11 introduced performance measurement in terms of comparison of actual expenditures to budgeted expenditures. Exhibit 12.1 illustrates a performance report prepared for July comparing the actual expenditures incurred with the original July budget. Note that when the original budget is used as the basis for measuring performance it is called a *fixed budget*.[1] In performance measurement a fixed budget means one that is **not** modified to reflect any differences in the level of actual activity (output) from the level originally planned.

Study Exhibit 12.1. Note that it reports all variance as favorable and in substantial percentages. Is your assembly foreman really the "hero" that is pictured by the fixed budget performance report? Does this report give you the information you need in order to evaluate the foreman's performance?

You correctly perceive one of the major problem areas of performance measurement covered in this chapter if your answer is "No, the variances in Exhibit 12.1 are misleading." They do not allow for the drastically reduced level of actual activity.

## FIXED VS. FLEXIBLE BUDGETS

Now turn to Exhibit 12.2 prepared for the same department for the same month. In Exhibit 12.2 the budget data has been recalculated on the basis of the actual level of activity. So long as the actual level of activity remains within the relevant range of the budgeting rates (assumed in this example), the revised budget amounts indicate what the foreman should have spent at his actually attained level of volume. Where a budget is revised based on different activity levels, it is known as a *flexible budget*.[2]

Can you see that the flexible budget (based) performance report is a far more desirable instrument of communication than is the fixed budget report whenever there is a significant change in activity levels? Remember that you may want to add two zeros to all dollar amounts in comparing Exhibits 12.1 and 12.2, to highlight the significance of the differences. In Exhibit 12.2, the whole issue of different volume levels has been effectively removed from the picture. The flexible budget reveals that the assembly foreman did not do such a good job of cost control, after all. Given the radical cutback in scheduling, the unfavorable direct and indirect labor variances are probably as good as could be reasonably expected, since it is difficult enough to furlough employees on short notice without attempting to cut off their pay in midday. However, note the over-200-percent unfavorable variance for indirect materials. The

---

[1]    The term *static budget* is sometimes used to connote the fact that the original budget is being used unchanged, regardless of changed circumstances.

[2]    Flexible budgets may also be called **variable budgets.** The term variable budget is not used in this text to avoid excessive identification with variable costs. A flexible budget may contain both variable and fixed costs.

**Exhibit 12.1**

TRIPPER WATER SKI MANUFACTURING COMPANY

**Fixed Budget Performance Report, Assembly Department—July, 19X2**

| | Current month | | | | Year-to-date | | | |
|---|---|---|---|---|---|---|---|---|
| | Budget | Actual | Variance | % | Budget | | Variance | % |
| Production: | | | | | | | | |
| Economy skis (units) | 2,100 | 500 | 1,600 | 76.2 | 10,500 | 8,900 | 1,600 | 15.2 |
| Deluxe skis (units) | 1,700 | 400 | 1,300 | 76.5 | 6,800 | 5,500 | 1,300 | 19.1 |
| Total skis (units) | 3,800 | 900 | 2,900 | 76.3 | 17,300 | 14,400 | 2,900 | 16.8 |
| Direct labor ($1.25 V Economy; $1.60 V Deluxe) | $5,345 | $1,455 | $3,890 F | 72.8 | $24,005 | $20,455 | $3,550 F | 14.8 |
| Indirect labor ($1,000/Mo. F; $0.20 V) | 1,760 | 1,300 | 460 F | 26.1 | 10,460 | 11,000 | 540 U | 5.2 |
| Indirect materials ($30/Mo. F; $0.30 V) | 1,170 | 1,000 | 170 F | 14.5 | 5,490 | 5,120 | 370 F | 6.7 |
| Maintenance ($500/Mo. F; $0.05 V) | 690 | 540 | 150 F | 21.7 | 4,365 | 4,140 | 225 F | 5.2 |
| Total | $8,965 | $4,295 | $4,670 F | 52.1 | $44,320 | $40,715 | $3,605 F | 8.1 |

Note. Variable overhead based on total skis assembled regardless of model.

**Exhibit 12.2**

TRIPPER WATER SKI MANUFACTURING COMPANY

**Flexible Budget Performance Report, Assembly Department—July 19X2**

| | Current month | | | | Year-to-date | | | |
|---|---|---|---|---|---|---|---|---|
| | Budget | Actual | Variance | % | Budget | Actual | Variance | % |
| Production: | | | | | | | | |
| Economy skis (units) | 2,100 | 500 | 1,600 | 76.2 | 10,500 | 8,900 | 1,600 | 15.2 |
| Deluxe skis (units) | 1,700 | 400 | 1,300 | 76.5 | 6,800 | 5,500 | 1,300 | 19.1 |
| Total skis (units) | 3,800 | 900 | 2,900 | 76.3 | 17,300 | 14,000 | 2,900 | 16.8 |
| Direct Labor ($1.25 V Economy; $1.60 V Deluxe) | $1,265 | $1,455 | $ 190 U | 15.0 | $19,925 | $20,455 | $ 530 U | 2.7 |
| Indirect labor ($1,000/Mo. F; $0.20 V) | 1,180 | 1,300 | 120 U | 10.2 | 9,880 | 11,000 | 1,120 U | 11.3 |
| Indirect materials ($30/Mo. F; $0.30 V) | 300 | 1,000 | 700 U | 233.3 | 4,620 | 5,120 | 500 U | 10.8 |
| Maintenance ($500/Mo. F; $0.05 V) | 545 | 540 | 5 F | 1.0 | 4,220 | 4,140 | 80 F | 1.9 |
| Total | $3,290 | $4,295 | $1,005 U | 30.5 | $38,645 | $40,715 | $2,070 U | 5.4 |

Note. Variable overhead based on total skis assembled regardless of model.

foreman and his supervisor should look into this situation in an attempt to ensure that it doesn't happen again.

Another example of the value of flexible budgeting can further demonstrate its value and give you an opportunity to test your understanding of the mechanics of the various computations involved. Assume that the situation at Tripper were reversed and, for some reason, two lot sizes (2,100 units each) of economy skis and one (1,700) of deluxe skis had been assembled during July. Exhibit 12.3 illustrates a fixed budget performance report for this different assumed situation (year-to-date data omitted, to focus your attention upon the current month). Note that this report portrays the foreman in an exceedingly unfavorable light, with an almost 40-percent overall unfavorable variance. If you were the foreman in this situation, would you like to have to explain and justify all of these very unfavorable variances?

To review the budgeting process and the details of flexible budget performance report preparation, you should prepare, on a separate sheet of paper, such a report for this revised situation. All necessary budgeting rates and volumes are given in Exhibit 12.3.

Your variable budget performance report should be the same as Exhibit 12.4. Note that Exhibit 12.4 indicates that the assembly foreman did an excellent job of staying on top of all expenditures, even with greatly increased volume.

**Exhibit 12.3**
### TRIPPER WATER SKI MANUFACTURING COMPANY

**Fixed Budget Performance Report—Current Month Only**
**Assembly Department**

| | Budget | Actual | Variance | % |
|---|---|---|---|---|
| Production: | | | | |
| Economy skis (units) | 2,100 | 4,200 | | |
| Deluxe skis (units) | 1,700 | 1,700 | | |
| Total skis (units) | 3,800 | 5,900 | | |
| Direct labor ($1.25 V Economy; $1.60 V Deluxe) | $5,345 | $ 8,000 | $2,655 U | 49.7 |
| Indirect labor ($1,000/Mo. F; $0.20 V) | 1,760 | 2,000 | 240 U | 13.6 |
| Indirect materials ($30/Mo. F; $0.30 V) | 1,170 | 1,820 | 650 U | 55.6 |
| Maintenance ($500/Mo. F; $0.05 V) | 690 | 710 | 20 U | 2.9 |
| Total | $8,965 | $12,530 | $3,565 U | 39.8 |

*Note.* Variable overhead based on total skis assembled regardless of model.

**Exhibit 12.4**

TRIPPER WATER SKI MANUFACTURING COMPANY

**Flexible Budget Performance Report—Current Month Only**
**Assembly Department**

| | Current month | | | |
|---|---|---|---|---|
| | Budget | Actual | Variance | % |
| Production: | | | | |
| Economy skis (units) | 2,100 | 4,200 | | |
| Deluxe skis (units) | 1,700 | 1,700 | | |
| Total skis (units) | 3,800 | 5,900 | | |
| Direct labor ($1.25 V Economy; $1.60 V Deluxe) | $ 7,970 | $ 8,000 | $ 30 U | 0.4 |
| Indirect labor ($1,000/Mo. F; $0.20 V) | 2,180 | 2,000 | 180 F | 8.3 |
| Indirect materials ($30/Mo. F; $0.30 V) | 1,800 | 1,820 | 20 U | 1.1 |
| Maintenance ($500/Mo. F; $0.05 V) | 795 | 710 | 85 F | 10.7 |
| Total | $12,745 | $12,530 | $215 F | 1.7 |

*Note.* Variable overhead based on total skis assembled regardless of model.

## PERFORMANCE REPORTING FOR EXPENDITURE CENTERS

The Tripper assembly department provides an example of an expenditure center. Remember, from Chapter 11, that performance reporting for expenditure centers focuses on cost control or cost efficiency—whether planned activities are accomplished within budgeted costs. As demonstrated in the Tripper example, changes in volume levels from those originally planned make performance evaluation more difficult. It is desirable, in such circumstances, to separate measures of effectiveness (units produced) from measures of efficiency (expenditures or cost incurred, in comparison to the actual volume of units produced).

The manager of an expenditure center may—or may not—be responsible for the different activity level. Often, as in the Tripper example, a manufacturing department is dependent upon other responsibility centers for its activity. Items cannot be manufactured or assembled until material or parts are available. Also, manufacturing departments are often required to produce at higher levels than planned, in order to make up for earlier delays, to meet increased demand, or to handle special orders for favored customers.[3] However,

---

[3]    Some firms break out, or separately identify, excess costs of rush activity (overtime, special deliveries, and so forth) and also report them on sales department budgets, since rush orders are jointly controllable by the sales and production departments.

ineffectiveness is not always someone else's responsibility. In some situations, an expenditure center could be responsible for its own lower volume. Poor planning and control within the center could result in not getting the job completed.

## Volume Variance

Regardless of the cause or source of the changed level of activity, it is desirable to segregate those cost elements that are directly attributable to the difference in activity levels. This difference in costs that would be expected between the different volume levels (originally budgeted volume and actual volume) is known as the *volume variance* or as the "effectiveness variance." With the volume variance eliminated, or at least identified, performance evaluation is made easier. In those situations where the responsibility center manager is **not** responsible for the changed activity level, noncontrollable items are appropriately eliminated from performance evaluation. Where the manager is partially or wholly responsible, the effectiveness problem may be dealt with independently. In this chapter you can learn how performance evaluation based on flexible budgets automatically eliminates or adjusts for any volume variance. In the following chapter you will see how a standard cost system accomplishes the same result.

The volume variance for a given item is simply the amount of dollars originally budgeted (OB) minus the dollars that would have been budgeted on a revised (flexible) budget (RB) for the actual activity level:

$$\text{Volume variance} = \text{OB} - \text{RB}$$

## Spending Variance

The difference between the costs indicated on the revised (flexible) budget and those actually incurred (ACT) represent the controllable or the *spending variance*:[4]

$$\text{Spending variance} = \text{RB} - \text{ACT}$$

Note that, whereas a volume variance is also known as an effectiveness variance, a spending variance is **not** the same as an efficiency variance. Although a spending variance may indicate overall efficiency in an abstract sense, it may result from noncontrollable factors. Chapter 13 will discuss further how to break down certain spending variances in order to identify those portions attributable to efficiency of performance.

Spending variances are identified as either favorable (F) or unfavorable (U). "Favorable" merely indicates less expenditure than budget, and "unfavorable" the opposite. Recall, from Chapter 11, that favorable does **not** necessarily mean desirable, or vice-versa.

---

[4]   The spending variance is also known as the flexible budget variance or sometimes simply as the budget variance.

The algebraic sum of both the volume and the spending variances for a given item equals the total fixed budget variance (the difference between actual expenditures and those budgeted in the original or fixed budget):

$$\text{Total fixed budget variance} = OB - ACT;$$

$$\text{Total fixed budget variance} = \left(\begin{array}{c}\text{Volume}\\\text{variance}\end{array}\right) + \left(\begin{array}{c}\text{Spending}\\\text{variance}\end{array}\right)$$

Exhibit 12.5 illustrates different combinations of volume and spending variances in different situations. Note, in Exhibit 12.5, that a volume variance may also be designated as favorable or unfavorable, and that such identification is essentially meaningless. The unfavorable/favorable designation merely indicates more/less budgeted expenditure than the amount originally budgeted. Study Exhibit 12.5 until you are comfortable with the three variances and could determine any one of them, given the other two or appropriate budget and actual cost data.

**Exhibit 12.5**

EXAMPLES OF VOLUME AND SPENDING VARIANCES

OB = amount originally budgeted
RB = amount which would be budgeted on a
 flexible or revised budget
ACT = costs actually incurred

**Higher activity levels than planned:**

OB = $5,000
  $2,000 U   Volume variance
RB = 7,000
  $1,000 U   Spending variance        $3,000 U   Fixed budget
ACT = 8,000                                       variance

OB = $4,000
  $2,000 U   Volume variance
RB = 6,000
  $  500 F   Spending variance        $1,500 U   Fixed budget
ACT = 5,500                                       variance

**Lower activity levels than planned:**

OB = $9,000
  $3,000 F   Volume variance
RB = 6,000
  $1,000 F   Spending variance        $4,000 F   Fixed budget
ACT = 5,000                                       variance

OB = $8,000
  $3,000 F   Volume variance
RB = 5,000
  $1,200 U   Spending variance        $1,800 F   Fixed budget
ACT = 6,200                                       variance

To reinforce your understanding of these three variances, you should determine the fixed budget variance, the volume variance, and the spending variance in total for the Tripper assembly department for July 19X2 (Exhibits 12.1 and 12.2) and for the other sample month (Exhibits 12.3 and 12.4). You should do this on a separate sheet of paper, before proceeding.

You adequately understand the concepts of volume and spending variances if you determined that the variances were as follows:

|  | July 19X2 | Other month |
|---|---|---|
| Volume variance (OB − RB) | $5,675  F | $3,780  U |
| Spending variance (RB − ACT) | 1,005  U | 215  F |
| Fixed budget variance (OB − ACT) | $4,670  F | $3,565  U |

In performance reports that are based on flexible budget data, the entire reported variance will be a spending variance as previously defined. The spending variance measures cost control at the level of volume actually experienced. The accuracy of the spending variance depends upon the accuracy of the budgeting rate used, which, in turn, depends on the appropriateness of the activity measure selected.

## IMPORTANCE OF SELECTING MEANINGFUL ACTIVITY MEASURE

The subject of appropriate selection of activity measures was first introduced in Chapter 5. The most appropriate activity or volume measure in a given situation is the one that most closely varies with cost changes, and vice versa (Fig. 12.1). It would be the measure in the closest clustering of observations around the line of best fit and would, therefore, be the best basis for predicting expenditures at different activity levels within the relevant range.[5]

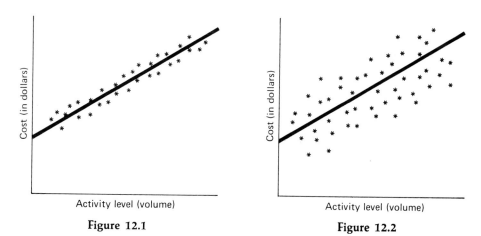

Figure 12.1                    Figure 12.2

---

[5]    Where the least-squares approach to regression analysis is employed (Appendices to Chapters 3 and 5), the best predictive measure can be identified as the one having the least standard error of estimate.

The desirability of choosing a meaningful activity measure is illustrated in Figs. 12.1 and 12.2. A better or more useful measure (more accurate predictor) was selected in Fig. 12.1. Any physical measure of activity or output should be considered in making a selection for budgeting and control purposes. The only constraint upon selection is that the measure chosen must be readily available at little cost.

Remember that the relationship between cost and volume does not necessarily correlate with sales. Changing inventory levels, prices, or product mix can preclude any direct relationship with sales or sales dollars. Common activity bases in use include:

- **Number of customer orders**—often the best base for budgeting packing, distribution, and billing costs.

- **Number of units purchased, produced, or shipped**—often used as the base for budgeting purchasing, receiving, and manufacturing overhead, and possibly for packing and distribution costs.

- **Number of labor hours or machine hours**—used as a base for budgeting various manufacturing overhead items.

Note that it is generally undesirable to use a dollar measure (sales, shipments, labor costs, purchases, and so forth) as an activity base. What is desired is a measure of **output,** and dollars are often not a stable output measure. Cost inflation or changing mix of prices, wage rates, or purchase costs may invalidate a dollar measure as a consistent measure of output. Even though the cost being budgeted is subject to inflation, to use another dollar cost as a base may introduce too much unreliability. Sometimes total sales dollars may be useful in budgeting some cost elements within a revenue center (Chapter 14). They were chosen as Tripper's base for GSA budgeting only for simplification of the example.

Also note that a nondollar-input measure is often used as a surrogate for an output measure at lower levels of operating budgeting and control. Direct labor hours and direct machine hours cited above are actually inputs. Nevertheless, they may closely correlate with output and be more readily measurable than units of product. In the Tripper example, products (skis) are reasonably homogeneous and readily counted. What about a center producing both small pocket AM radios and large console TV's? Would an output measure of 6,000 units be a meaningful measure of activity if one month it included 5,900 radios and 100 TV's and the next 6,000 TV's? In such cases an input measure such as labor or machine hours can better serve as a common denominator of work performed.

In practice an input measure is often used at the lower-level responsibility levels. At higher or total firm levels, an output measure, even expressed in dollars, may prove adequate and more useful. Also, in practice, the measure that is best for a given item may not be used. Having many different measures in use can be costly to keep track of and can introduce confusion. Usually one or perhaps two measures of activity for a given center are chosen, which have a high correlation with the behavior of total expenditures for the center.

## SEGREGATING FIXED AND NONCONTROLLABLE COSTS

The budgeting and control system illustrated for the Tripper Company is focused upon controllable expenditures. Expenses or costs that do not involve current expenditure (such as expirations of previously acquired assets) are omitted from all responsibility center reports and are incorporated only at the total firm level as part of budgeting net income. Some firms feel it desirable to show all related costs on a center's performance report even if some are not controllable. The intention is to expand the manager's awareness of all aspects of the business related to his or her area of responsibility.

Where noncontrollable items such as depreciation are included in budgets and performance reports, it is desirable that they be segregated and shown separately. They are included only for information purposes, and should be identified as noncontrollable. It should be clear to all using the performance report that such costs and any related variances are **not** controllable by the center manager.

Fixed items may also be disclosed separately from variable costs on performance reports. Fixed cost variances may be less controllable. If, early in a given year, an unanticipated increase in equipment rental occurred, or if it was decided to give a nonbudgeted raise to certain salaried employees, unfavorable fixed-cost variances would continue for each subsequent month throughout the current budgeting year. Disclosing fixed-cost components separately segregates such "noncontrollable" variances from measures of variable cost control.

Exhibit 12.6 illustrates a performance report providing separate disclosure of variable, fixed, and noncontrollable items. Note, under fixed expenditures, that it appears the foreman is stuck with a $300-per-month unfavorable indirect-labor variance and a $500-per-month unfavorable equipment-rental variance. Also note that the report deliberately avoids disclosure of noncontrollable cost variances. Noncontrollable costs in this example include depreciation on equipment used in the department and allocations of utilities and other costs not within the foreman's control. Fixed and noncontrollable costs usually involve overhead, and the analysis and interpretation of overhead variances may be more complex than for direct or variable costs.

## SPECIAL CONSIDERATIONS RELATED TO OVERHEAD VARIANCES

Firms that have operating budgets plan (budget) overhead costs using a budgeting rate. As first discussed in Chapter 5, this rate distinguishes between fixed and variable cost behavior. Therefore, as illustrated, when the actual level of activity is different from the planned level, a revised overhead allow-

**Exhibit 12.6**

ILLUSTRATION OF PERFORMANCE REPORT THAT SEPARATELY REPORTS VARIABLE, FIXED, AND NONCONTROLLABLE ITEMS—MONTH OF MARCH, 19XX

| | Current month | | | | Year-to-date | | | |
|---|---|---|---|---|---|---|---|---|
| | Budget | Actual | Variance | % | Budget | Actual | Variance | % |
| Production (units) | 20,000 | 25,000 | | | 60,000 | 55,000 | | |
| **Controllable expenditures for actual production** | | | | | | | | |
| **Variable:** | | | | | | | | |
| Direct labor ($4) | $100,000 | $ 99,200 | $800 F | 0.8 | $220,000 | $224,400 | $4,400 U | 2.0 |
| Indirect labor ($0.70) | 17,500 | 18,100 | 600 U | 3.4 | 38,500 | 37,350 | 1,150 F | 3.0 |
| Supplies ($0.10) | 2,500 | 2,600 | 100 U | 4.0 | 5,500 | 5,780 | 280 U | 5.0 |
| Maintenance ($0.05) | 1,250 | 1,100 | 150 F | 12.0 | 2,750 | 2,570 | 180 F | 6.5 |
| Total variable ($4.85) | $121,250 | $121,000 | 250 F | 0.2 | $266,750 | $270,100 | $3,350 U | 1.3 |
| **Fixed:** | | | | | | | | |
| Indirect labor | $ 4,000 | $ 4,300 | 300 U | 7.5 | $ 12,000 | $ 12,600 | $ 600 U | 5.0 |
| Equipment rental | 3,000 | 3,500 | 500 U | 16.7 | 9,000 | 10,500 | 1,500 U | 16.7 |
| Maintenance | 500 | 500 | 0 | 0 | 1,500 | 1,500 | 0 | 0 |
| Total fixed | $ 7,500 | $ 8,300 | $800 U | 10.7 | $ 22,500 | $ 24,600 | $2,100 U | 9.3 |
| **Total controllable** | $128,750 | $129,300 | $550 U | 0.4 | $289,250 | $294,700 | $5,450 U | 1.9 |
| **Noncontrollable costs:** | | | | | | | | |
| Depreciation | $ 5,000 | $ 5,000 | | | $ 15,000 | $ 15,000 | | |
| Utilities | 420 | 490 | | | 1,260 | 1,350 | | |
| Other | 210 | 210 | | | 630 | 630 | | |
| **Total noncontrollable** | $ 5,630 | $ 5,700 | | 0.4 | $ 16,890 | $ 16,980 | | |

ance may be readily calculated, which realistically provides for change only in any variable elements.

Firms that do not have operating budgets may still attempt to measure performance in terms of total overhead costs for the entire factory or by responsibility center. In such situations, the standard for performance comparison may be limited to the amount of overhead applied/absorbed into work-in-process inventory in the firm's accounts. Instead of having a variable budget variance (variable budget − actual expenditure) as a performance measure, these firms have only the amount of over- or underapplied overhead:

$$\begin{pmatrix} \text{Overhead} \\ \text{applied} \end{pmatrix} - \begin{pmatrix} \text{Actual} \\ \text{overhead} \end{pmatrix} = \begin{pmatrix} \text{Over- or under-} \\ \text{applied overhead} \end{pmatrix}.$$

Recall, from Chapter 1, that overhead may be applied to work-in-process inventory on the basis of a predetermined overhead rate. The predetermined overhead rate is similar to a budgeting rate but it has one critical difference. The predetermined overhead rate does **not** distinguish fixed and variable cost components. A single rate is used that effectively assumes all overhead to be variable:

$$\text{Predetermined overhead rate}^{6} = \frac{\text{Total expected overhead for the period}}{\text{Total of activity base expected for the period}}.$$

Where actual activity differs from planned activity for the period (the usual situation), overhead applied will not be the same as variable budgeted overhead. A portion of planned fixed costs will have been over- or underapplied regardless of actual expenditures.

As an example, consider the following situation. Assume that a firm known as the Ajax Corporation planned to produce 50,000 gadginators during the year and anticipated total manufacturing overhead of $600,000 ($400,000 variable and $200,000 fixed). The overhead application rate would be $12 per gadginator:

$$\frac{\$600,000}{50,000} = \$12.$$

If, at the end of the year, only 40,000 gadginators had been produced, $480,000 of overhead would have been applied to work-in-process inventory. Assuming that variable overhead varied per gadginator produced, the budgeting rate in this example would have been $200,000 fixed plus $8 variable. The flexible budgeted overhead for a volume of 40,000 units would have been $520,000. Can you identify the source of the $40,000 difference between the $520,000 flexible budget and the $480,000 of overhead applied to inventory?

---

[6] The base for determining the predetermined overhead rate is often referred to as the normal volume or standard volume. It represents the expected level of activity in the forthcoming year, or an average over the next few years. It may also be based on attainable capacity even though this is greater than currently anticipated volume. See the discussion on setting standards included in Chapter 13.

The overhead application rate of $12 per unit was essentially providing for $8 per unit variable cost and $4 per unit for fixed cost. With only 40,000 units produced, only $160,000 of fixed cost was applied to inventory. The remaining $40,000 ($4 × 10,000 units) would be underapplied even if overhead costs were perfectly planned and controlled and actual costs had been exactly $520,000.

Attempting to use an accounting overhead variance (over- or underapplied overhead) as a performance measure is often further complicated by the choice of activity base. Predetermined overhead rates are not usually established on a unit-of-output basis, as illustrated above. Instead, an input measure such as direct labor hours (DLH) or machine hours is generally used. In such situations a variation in the efficiency of input usage (more or less labor or machine hours per unit of output than planned) will also cause a difference between overhead applied and the amount of overhead that would have been budgeted under a flexible budgeting system.

As you can see, accounting variances for overhead (as distinct from budget variances) are of little usefulness in evaluating performance. The distortions introduced by treating fixed costs as variable and from efficiency in the use of the activity base can be isolated and identified. This process will be covered in the appendix to this chapter, since it can help to clarify your understanding of the differences between budgeting variances arising out of operating budgets and accounting variances developed in the cost accounting system. However, even when the total overhead spending variance for a particular center has been identified, it provides no information as to the source of the variance. The variance reflects a total for all overhead elements and does not pinpoint specific controllable expenditures that may require corrective action.[7]

## BUDGETING AND CONTROLLING PROGRAMMED AND NONMANUFACTURING COSTS

Return now to firms that have operating budgets; there are certain additional cost considerations with which you should be familiar. So far your attention has been directed primarily to manufacturing costs. Manufacturing costs generally have three characteristics: They relate to repetitive activities or operations; they can readily be identified with measurable units of activity (output); and they can often be planned or engineered with significant precision. Costs that are repetitive, readily identified with measurable output, and subject to

---

[7]   A further problem inherent in the attempted use of accounting variances for performance evaluation concerns the organizational unit being measured. Cost accounting records are established for cost centers that may differ from responsibility centers for control purposes. The distinction between cost and responsibility centers is not important at the elementary level. It is only important that you see that accounting variances may not be applicable to a specific responsibility center.

engineering standards or rates may be identified as engineered or *ratable costs.*[8]

Two obvious examples of ratable costs would be direct material and direct labor. These inputs may be readily correlated with output (units of product) for budgeting purposes. Assembly of one slalom ski requires one ski body, one hardware set, and a measurable amount of direct labor. A really measurable causal relationship exists between the input expenditure (material and labor) and the output (units of finished skis). In the following chapter, you can learn how some ratable costs may be controlled through the use of precisely engineered cost standards.

A few manufacturing overhead items and many nonmanufacturing costs have almost the opposite characteristics. They occur or are incurred infrequently; they are difficult if not impossible to relate to measurable output or benefit; and consequently they are not easily planned or engineered (see Fig. 12.3). Costs that are nonrepetitive, that cannot be readily related to measurable output or benefits, and that are not readily ratable have been previously identified (Chapter 5) as discretionary or *programmed costs.*[9] Examples of nonratable or programmed costs would include expenditures for an annual factory employees' picnic, institutional advertising (in contrast to product advertising), basic research, and donations to educational institutions, public TV, and charities.

Most costs fall on a continuum between the extremes of a readily ratable direct material cost and a completely programmed donation cost. Obviously the more ratable a particular cost, the more easily it can be budgeted and measured for performance control. A cost that is less ratable is more difficult to identify with an activity base (output measure). The efficiency of cost control in such instances is more difficult to measure in quantitative terms.

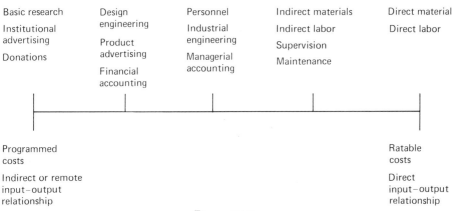

Figure 12.3

---

[8]   The term **engineered costs** is commonly used, but may imply that a cost has, in fact, been engineered or subject to estimate by an engineer. A cost may be inherently engineerable or ratable without having been engineered.

[9]   Programmed costs are also known as **managed costs** since they are determined primarily by somewhat arbitrary management decisions.

There are several approaches to managing costs that are not readily ratable:

1. They may be grouped and collectively evaluated in terms of a measurable output.
2. They may be broken down into smaller elements, some of which may be ratable.
3. They may be correlated with surrogate outputs.
4. Certain costs identifiable with project stages may be controlled with a technique known as PERT.
5. They may be treated as a purely programmed cost.

Often several different costs indirectly related to a measurable output may be identified collectively with that output. Certain sales and marketing costs may be grouped as *order-filling costs* and related to the number of customer orders shipped during a particular period. Order-filling costs could include:

- Costs of credit investigation and approval
- Warehousing costs
- Packaging and shipping costs
- Billing costs

*Order-getting costs* may also be collectively correlated with the number of orders received, units ordered, and so forth. Order-getting costs could include:

- Market research costs
- Product and packaging design costs
- Advertising
- Sales salaries, bonuses, and commissions
- Sales travel costs

Costs may also be broken down into portions identifiable with output measures. For example, the cost of a large accounting department could be divided into identifiable portions relating to payroll, billing, payables, disbursements, and all other activities. The first four subdivisions could then be associated with specific output measures, as follows:

|  |  |  |
|---:|:---:|:---|
| Payroll | to | number of employee checks |
| Billing | to | number of customer orders |
| Payables | to | number of purchase orders |
| Disbursements | to | number of checks drawn |

One of the sources of difficulty in identifying output measures for use in evaluating efficiency of expenditures may be the existence of a considerable time delay between the cost and the benefit. Benefits may be spread over the future and not be readily identifiable with a particular expenditure. When a direct laborer attaches hardware to a ski, the cost and the measurable benefit (result) are essentially simultaneous. When $200,000 is spent sponsoring a TV commercial on a Tuesday night, however, the benefits may be cumulative and may extend in small and measurable increments over several years. In such situations a solution might take the form of a surrogate measure. At relatively low cost, a polling organization could be commissioned to sample periodically customer recognition of the firm's products. Advertising expenditure could then be correlated with increase in the level of recognition.

Still another approach to managing nonratable costs is *PERT* or PERT–cost. Where significant costs are directly related to a particular project, and where the project has identifiable subset stages of completion, the PERT approach may be desirable. PERT was originally developed under the auspices of the Department of Defense for monitoring government contracts. Essentially it involves budgeting each phase or subset of a project as if it were a distinct output. PERT will be described more fully in Chapter 17.

Where costs are not ratable and not amenable to control through one of the four approaches described above, then they must be treated as pure programmed costs. The manager or management team with authority decides that benefits justify a particular amount and timing of expenditure. Performance reports can only disclose expenditures against the planned amount. Managers must separately assess benefits in comparison to costs.

## BUDGETING AND CONTROLLING COMMON COSTS AND SERVICE CENTERS

The last consideration involving expenditure control, to be introduced in this chapter, involves planning and control of common costs and service centers. The problems of budgeting common costs in service centers were first discussed in Chapter 5, relating to budgeting for Tripper's maintenance department. You may recall that Tripper budgets all maintenance costs in the maintenance supervisor's budget, and that it also budgets an allocation of maintenance costs in each using department. The duplication is deliberate and is removed when summarizing for higher-level reporting, in order to avoid double counting. Duplication is desirable since maintenance costs are controllable by both the maintenance supervisor and the service-using foreman.

Remember that budgets and performance reports should focus on controllable expenditures by responsibility center. Expenditures are considered controllable by each manager who has any significant influence over the amount of expenditure incurred or events leading to its incurrence. Service centers such as maintenance departments, cafeterias, computer facilities, and others are "problem centers," in that they involve common costs—costs that are jointly controllable by more than one responsibility-center manager.

There are five distinct, common approaches to the planning and control of service-center costs, all of which are in use and none of which provides an ideal solution:[10]

1. No separate budget; charge out all actual costs to the using departments, based on services used.

2. No separate budget; charge out all actual costs to the using departments, based on an allocation formula independent of current usage.

3. Control as an artificial profit center, with transfer prices for services used, based on equivalent outside market costs.

4. Establish a separate budget for the service center, and charge out for usage at full cost rate, based on budgeted costs, with the intention of breaking even.

5. Establish a separate budget, and charge the using department a rate based on only variable costs.

Each of these five approaches will be discussed below. To illustrate the alternatives and their effects, assume that your firm has a service center such as a maintenance department or a computer center. For simplification, assume that there are only two using departments, general office and manufacturing. Data for a particular period for the service center are as follows:

|  | Actual costs incurred | Budgeted costs* |
|---|---|---|
| Total variable costs | $ 79,600 | $ 60,000 |
| Total fixed costs | 50,000 | 40,000 |
| Total costs | $129,600 | $100,000 |
| Hours of service supplied | 1,800 hrs. | 2,000 hrs. |

\*    In those cases where a separate budget is prepared.

## Charging All Costs on the Basis of Usage

The first approach (charging out all actual costs based on usage) probably evolved from the cost accountant's need, for product-costing purposes, to allocate **all** costs into product inventory. Allocation of service-center costs for product-costing purposes is discussed in the appendix to this chapter. Such allocations are required under GAAP. Since they must be performed anyway, their use for performance reporting involves no additional work or cost.

From the above data, and assuming the 1,800 hours were used (800 by general office and 1,000 by manufacturing), $57,600 would be charged to the general office budget and $72,000 to manufacturing. Can you see where such a system would provide little effective control over service-center expendi-

---

[10]    There are, of course, many other possibilities that involve combinations of these five approaches. A more exhaustive discussion of service-center cost allocation may be found in intermediate cost accounting texts.

tures? If you were a using manager, what could you do about the $29,600 of excess (over budget) costs in the service center?

The approach of charging out all costs incurred based on usage can lead to several abuses. There is little effective control over total expenditures. The service-center manager can spend, or allow to be spent, unnecessary sums since they will all be charged out anyway. The using manager's defense is to cut back, and probably underuse the service facility. And such cutbacks produce the added disruptive effects of increasing the costs charged to other managers for the same usage! If, in the next period, actual costs were the same but manufacturing had cut back usage to only 800 hours (a 20-percent reduction in its usage), it would be charged $64,800, or 90 percent of its previous charge; and the general office would also be charged $64,800 or $7,200 more, for the same usage.

## Charging All Costs by Predetermined Formula

The second approach (allocating all costs by formula to users, regardless of current usage) can lead to even more undesirable results. Once again the service-center manager has no incentive to hold the line or to reduce costs. Furthermore, users may be motivated to increase usage (overusage). The costs of a single user's demands are divided among all users.

Under this approach, in the above example, all service-center actual costs ($129,600) could be divided, 44 percent ($57,024) to general office and 56 percent ($72,576) to manufacturing, regardless of actual usage. If, in the next period, manufacturing doubled its usage, assume that the increased workload exactly doubled the variable costs in the service center. The general office, with no increased usage, would be charged an additional $35,024, representing 44 percent of the additional $79,600 costs "caused" by manufacturing.

## Artificial Profit Center with Market-Based Transfer Prices

A third approach (artificial profit center with market-based transfer prices based on usage) avoids the problems of the first two approaches. The service center is separately budgeted and controlled. It charges out for services rendered to using departments, based on usage. The charge is set as a *transfer price* equivalent to the cost of the service if obtained from an outside supplier. The term transfer price applies to any charges or allocations for goods or services supplied between segments of a given organization. Any intersegment charge, such as the two types previously discussed, may be considered a transfer price. However, the term usually is applied only to charges between segments that are established as profit centers. Charges between expenditure or cost centers are generally referred to as simply cost allocations.

Transfer prices will be discussed more fully in Chapter 14, along with profit and investment centers. In Chapter 14 you can learn that transfer prices may be set on different bases, somewhat equivalent to the different alternatives under discussion for service-center costs. At this point, you should merely focus on a service charge based on the equivalent cost for obtaining the service from an outside supplier.

Under this alternative, the service-center manager is accountable for cost control and may be able to earn a "profit." However, charging service users a market-based transfer price can have three disadvantages:

1. The high cost (which will include fixed cost allocation and "profit") may tend to discourage use even though it may be to the firm's overall benefit to have greater usage. For instance, better computer-prepared scheduling control reports covering activities within one manufacturing department could reduce lead times and benefit the firm by reducing inventory carrying costs. However, these benefits would not appear on the individual foreman's report to offset costs that he or she is responsible for minimizing.

2. If the user has the freedom to choose an outside supplier at no additional cost, occasional scheduling bottlenecks in the service center may not be highlighted and resolved. Instead, the using manager may just go outside, with resultant underusage of the firm's fixed cost investment in its service center.

3. The service center might not be effectively managed to maximize "profit." The manager may have no incentive to control costs. Instead, the margin over budgeted costs may be viewed as budgetary slack and costs may be allowed to increase to the point of absorbing some or all potential profit.

To illustrate the profit-center approach in the context of the earlier example, assume that a transfer price of $75 per hour was realistic in terms of outside supplier charges; and assume that the general office and manufacturing were charged $60,000 (800 hours) and $75,000 (1,000 hours), respectively. The service-center performance report would be as follows:

|  | Budget | Actual | Variance |
|---|---|---|---|
| Charges to using departments | $150,000 | $135,000 | $15,000 U |
| Total variable costs | 60,000 | 79,600 | 19,600 U |
| Total fixed costs | 40,000 | 50,000 | 10,000 U |
| Profit | $ 50,000 | $ 5,400 | $44,600 U |

## Separate Budgeting with Full-Cost Usage-Based Charges

The fourth approach to service-center cost allocation is essentially similar to the third, except that the transfer prices or charges are established in a manner similar to that for a predetermined overhead absorption rate. If total usage and total service costs match the budget, the artificial profit center would break even at year-end.

Using the earlier data, service charges would be $50 per hour (budgeted total costs of $100,000 divided by 2,000 budgeted service hours). Charges to the using departments would be $40,000 (general office, 800 hours) and $50,000 (manufacturing, 1,000 hours). The service center's performance report would disclose:

|  | Budget | Actual | Variance |
|---|---|---|---|
| Charges to using departments | $100,000 | $90,000 | $10,000 U |
| Variable costs | 60,000 | 79,600 | 19,600 U |
| Fixed costs | 40,000 | 50,000 | 10,000 U |
| Total | 0 | −$39,600 | $39,600 U |

This approach provides for cost control by the service-center manager, and probably would not discourage usage as much as the first or third systems would. However, treating service-center budgeted fixed costs as variable for purposes of allocation can create the same distortions discussed earlier under predetermined overhead rates. When usage is below plan, the underutilized portion of fixed costs ($4,000, in the above example) is not charged to the using departments. From another viewpoint, allocating **any** portion of service-center fixed costs to user budgets may be considered inappropriate, since no part of such fixed costs is controllable by the using manager.

## Separate Budgeting and Variable-Cost-Based Usage Charges

The fifth, and final, approach offered for your consideration involves separate budgeting and control for the service center, with charges to using departments at a rate based upon budgeted variable costs. Under this approach, the service-center manager is fully responsible for controlling fixed costs and for keeping variable costs at the budgeted rate. The using manager is charged only for actual usage at the incremental cost rate.

Continuing with the above example, services would be charged to users at $30 per hour; and the service-center performance report would show:

|  | Budget | Actual | Variance |
|---|---|---|---|
| Charges to using departments | $60,000 | $54,000 | $ 6,000 U |
| Variable costs | 60,000 | 79,600 | 19,600 U |
| Fixed costs | 40,000 | 50,000 | 10,000 U |
| Total | −$40,000 | −$75,600 | $35,600 U |

This variable-cost-based approach, on balance, has probably the fewest drawbacks. It may be more costly to operate (accounting and report preparation cost) than the first two approaches. However, it provides for accountability and control by the service-center manager. Cost allocations ideally should reflect the underlying decision or "cause" and resulting benefit. The consuming department's cost should not be dependent upon either service department efficiency or short-run usage by other consumers. Where a high proportion of service-center costs are variable, charging for actual usage at a rate based on budgeted variable costs may be a nearly ideal solution. However, if service-center fixed costs are high, a variable-cost rate may lead to overusage. Some additional allocation of fixed cost may be desirable in order to reflect long-run expected usage costs.

## COST ALLOCATION FOR PLANNING AND CONTROL

Common costs may be allocated for different purposes. They may be allocated to motivate managers as part of the budgeting and control process, as in the service-center discussion above; or they may be allocated as part of asset valuation and income determination (to be discussed in the appendix to this chapter).[11] The distinction between allocation for planning and control purposes and for product costing is important, as the former may have motivational effects upon managers (for example, potential over- or underutilization of service centers, as discussed above). Common cost allocation problems are not limited to service-center costs. Wherever two responsibility centers share the use of a common facility, or where one department must spend time and/or materials reworking an item defectively manufactured or purchased by another, the common cost problem arises.

Solutions will vary in the circumstances peculiar to the firm, and often in adaptations to personalities of individual managers. An individual firm must weigh the costs (information and undesirable motivations) against the benefits (more effective planning and control) for each alternative. A particular system such as the first approach in the service-center example above could be optimal in a small firm like Tripper, where costs involved were not great and where all activities were highly visible to all involved persons. The same system could be disastrous in larger firms with millions of dollars involved and service centers in remote geographic locations. Moreover, charging rework costs back to other departments can impel managers to devote excessive time to disputing the appropriateness of such charges. Cost allocation presents perhaps the biggest headache in the design of accounting systems. There are no easy answers when one attempts to divide fixed or common costs, which, by their nature, are indivisible. The selection and implementation of managerial accounting systems for planning and control remains as much an art as a science.

---

[11]   Other terms used synonymously with allocate (as in cost allocation) include apportion, assign, distribute, load, and trace. The terms **absorb** and **apply** are generally restricted to product costing applications.

CHAPTER OVERVIEW

Based on the material covered in this chapter, you should now be in a position to:

- Describe, with examples, the difference between fixed and variable budgets and the results of their usage as instruments for measuring performance.
- Given a fixed budget, actual expenditures, and appropriate budgetary rates, calculate the flexible budget, and determine, for each separate expenditure and in total, the volume and spending variances.
- Define a volume variance as it pertains to operating budgets, and explain, with examples, how it may be determined.
- Define a spending variance, explain with examples how it may be determined, and describe its significance as a measure of performance.
- Explain the importance, for effective budgeting and control, of selecting appropriate activity measures or bases for different controllable costs.
- Describe, with examples, how the most appropriate activity measure for a controllable cost may be selected.
- Explain why it may be desirable to segregate variable, fixed, and non-controllable costs on a budget performance report.
- Describe the difference between a budget variance and an accounting variance.
- Explain how applied overhead may differ from flexible budgeted overhead, and why the over- or underapplied overhead accounting variance is not particularly useful as a performance measure.
- Describe the differences between so-called ratable or engineered costs and those described as programmed or managed costs.
- Describe several ways in which costs that are not readily ratable may be measured and reported for more effective control.
- Identify the problems associated with control of service centers and common costs.
- Explain and evaluate five common ways in which service-center costs may be reported for control purposes.

## NEW VOCABULARY AND CONCEPTS

| | |
|---|---|
| Fixed budget | Ratable cost |
| Flexible budget | Order-filling cost |
| Volume variance (budget) | Order-getting cost |
| Spending variance | PERT |
| Transfer price | |

## REVIEW QUESTIONS

1. a) What is the difference between a performance report prepared with a fixed budget and one prepared using a flexible budget?
   b) How is a flexible budget prepared? Explain with an example.

2. a) What is the management objective in an expenditure center?
   b) What is the objective of a performance report or of a performance measurement for an expenditure center?

3. a) Is an expenditure center always responsible for levels of activity actually achieved?
   b) If not, explain, with examples, circumstances where an expenditure center manager would and would not be responsible.

4. a) What is a volume variance in connection with operating budgets?
   b) How is a volume variance determined?
   c) How is a volume variance related to the performance variance in a report prepared using a flexible budget?

5. a) What is a spending variance?
   b) How is a spending variance determined?
   c) How is a spending variance related to the performance variance in a report prepared using a flexible budget?

6. Which of the following is a more useful measure of cost efficiency or cost control?
   Total variance between fixed budget and actual
   Volume variance
   Spending variance

7. a) How is the selection of an activity base for budgeting and performance evaluation related to the dispersion of observations around a line of best fit?
   b) Of several possible activity bases all readily available at little cost, what criteria would you use to choose the optimal?
   c) Why is a dollar measure such as direct material or direct labor dollars generally an undesirable activity base for budgeting and control?

8. What are the advantages of segregating variable, fixed, and noncontrollable costs on a performance report?

9. a) What is the difference between a budget variance and an accounting variance?
   b) When an attempt is made to use the overhead accounting variance as a performance measure, what two factors may cause a difference between over- or underapplied overhead and the total overhead spending variance that would be developed under a budget system?
   c) Even if the spending variance can be isolated from over- or underapplied overhead, why is this amount not particularly useful for cost control?

10. a) What is a ratable cost?
    b) How does it differ from a programmed cost?
    c) How do output measurements relate to this difference?

11. What are five approaches that may be used to control costs that are not readily ratable?

12. a) What are order-filling and order-getting costs?
    b) How do they differ?
    c) How may these concepts be applied to the control of selling and marketing costs?

13. What are the control (responsibility) problems associated with service-center and other common costs?

14. a) Describe, with examples, the five common systems for controlling service-center costs.
    b) Describe the strengths and weaknesses of each of the five systems.

## MINI-CASES AND QUESTIONS FOR DISCUSSION

**MC 12.1** As plant superintendent for the Waco Company, this year you are looking forward to operating with the new flexible budgeting system. In the past, your performance reports for your foremen were prepared on a fixed budget basis. Each month's meeting with each foreman had been a hassle, with the foreman claiming nonresponsibility and inability to control costs because volumes of activity were different from those planned. This year you believe the reports will pinpoint responsibility, now that volume variances will have been eliminated.

Your first monthly meeting with your first foreman is a surprise. The monthly report shows significant unfavorable variances for labor, both direct and indirect. Your foreman opens the meeting with, "Boss, there's not a —— thing I can do about those —— labor variances; it's all overtime. Some of it comes from that delayed material. You remember Joe (purchasing agent) screwed up on those castings, and they were two weeks late in getting here. And you remember how you were all over me to make up for lost production. Well, I'm on schedule now but it took a lot of overtime to do it.

"The rest of the overtime is for the Albertson order. Remember Mary (sales manager) got the order with no lead time on the basis that we'd get it out in a week. My men had to practically work day and night to rush that one through."

It all sounds to you something like last year. Should your foreman be responsible and held accountable for these overtime costs? Or should they be charged to Joe and Mary? What can/should you, as superintendent, do about the current situation? Discuss.

**MC 12.2** The Super Control Company has a system where costs in one department caused by another are charged to the "causing department," and they appear on that department's budget. You are plant superintendent, and one of your foremen is back in your office for the fourth time in the same morning. He is angry and exasperated and says, "I finally tracked down that $900 charge from assembly. We goofed last month and made the holes too deep in the therbogs. The inspectors who report to you didn't catch the error when the therbogs left our shop. They didn't catch it through five subsequent machining operations and even in assembly.

It was only discovered after final assembly when the therbuggers wouldn't work.

"The $900 is for disassembly labor on overtime. Why should I pay Sally's (assembly foreman) overtime? If she ran her shop right, there would have been time to disassemble on straight time. And if those jerks she has working for her had their eyes open, they'd never have assembled the deep-holed therbogs to begin with. We had to scrap them. I don't mind eating the costs up to when we finished the therbogs. I don't see why I should absorb the costs of all those later operations when others could have caught the defective parts."

You are aware that almost half of each of your days is spent attempting to deal with such problems. And you know your foremen spend 80 percent of their time going over charge-backs and arguing with each other. Everyone is sure the other is using the charge-back system as a dumping ground for excess cost.

Does the system, and the way that it is being handled, seem to serve you and your foremen well? If not, what changes would you recommend and why? Discuss.

MC 12.3  Operating budgets cost time and money. What are some of the costs necessary to establish and maintain a system of operating budgets, in addition to the cost already being incurred for inventory (product cost) accounting? What are some of the benefits of operating budgets? Discuss.

MC 12.4  As the controller of the Everclear Company, you are feeling somewhat defeated. Prior to the current year, for both product cost and planning and control purposes, your department was allocating actual costs incurred in the maintenance department on the basis of service hours. For years it seemed that nobody except the maintenance foreman was happy with the resultant charges that appeared on user operating budgets. This past year you changed the allocation basis for planning and control purposes. Currently, based on an average usage proportion over the past three years, you are allocating maintenance costs to using departments by a flat percentage of total budgeted costs for the maintenance department. Now it seems that everyone, including the maintenance foreman, is unhappy.

The most recent incident involved your own data processing supervisor, Mary Lambert. Mary has just left your office after an extremely unpleasant meeting that degenerated to the point where Mary was shouting and threatening to resign. The new system had resulted in a quarterly allocation to Mary's budget of $8,000. The prior year's allocations were all around $5,000 based on usage, but overall maintenance costs had jumped 60 percent.

In the previous week, Mary's budget had been charged $4,000, representing a major damage-repair bill from an outside service firm. A piece of Mary's equipment had broken down and could be repaired only by outside experts. The repairman had advised Mary that the breakdown resulted from inadequate routine maintenance. Mary's budget for the week also included $2,000 of unplanned overtime charges incurred when her department had to catch up for time lost while the machine was down.

Mary was furious, and demanded that the entire $8,000 allocated maintenance charge be removed from her budget, and also that the $6,000 of breakdown-related costs be charged to maintenance. She maintained that the $3,000 increase in maintenance charges was unfair because the increase in overall maintenance costs was involved in an extensive two-year project refurbishing all factory equipment. She didn't think the basic $5,000 was fair for the last quarter since no maintenance had been performed in her department. Maintenance personnel had been working full time on the factory equipment.

As controller, what should you do? Should you allocate costs differently? How should you handle the $3,000 quarterly maintenance allocation increase? The $5,000 (or $8,000) quarterly charge? The $6,000 of repair-related charges? Discuss.

## ESSENTIAL PROBLEMS

**EP 12.1**  Identify each of the following costs as:

| | |
|---|---|
| RR | Readily ratable |
| PR | Probably ratable but difficult to measure output |
| PP | Probably programmed since output is too difficult to identify and measure |

a) Salaries of purchasing agents

b) Secretarial and clerical costs in the purchasing department

c) Personnel and supplies in the receiving department

d) Personnel and supplies in production scheduling and control

e) Personnel and supplies in inventory storerooms

f) Direct material

g) Direct labor

h) Indirect material

i) Indirect labor

j) Factory supervision

k) Factory and equipment maintenance

l) Personnel training programs

m) Hiring costs

n) Personnel and supplies in industrial engineering

o) Personnel and supplies in packing and shipping

p) Personnel and supplies in the accounting department

q) Personnel and supplies in the advertising department

r) Personnel and supplies in market research

s) Personnel and supplies in product design engineering

t) Cost of product advertising

u) Cost of institutional advertising

v) Basic research

w) Charitable donations

x) Dues to trade association

**EP 12.2** Refer to Problem EP 12.1. For each of the costs that are readily ratable (RR), select from the following list the activity base or bases that probably would correlate as an output measure or surrogate for budgeting and control purposes.

- Number of purchase orders placed per month
- Pounds, gallons, and so forth, of items purchased per month
- Number of production shop orders active per month
- Number of machine hours per month
- Number of direct labor hours per month
- Number of units manufactured per month
- Number of employees hired per month
- Number of customer orders shipped per month
- Dollar volume of sales per month

**EP 12.3** Given the following data with respect to a firm's machine department, which of the first two activity measures—units produced or direct labor hours—appears to be a better predictor of the department's costs for budgeting purposes?

| Units produced | Direct labor hours | Machine hours | Units of raw material used | Machining department expenditures |
|---|---|---|---|---|
| 8,400 | 24,900 | 16,500 | 13,600 | $143,000 |
| 6,400 | 19,400 | 13,300 | 10,900 | 118,000 |
| 5,800 | 17,500 | 11,100 | 9,600 | 103,000 |
| 3,200 | 10,600 | 6,800 | 5,900 | 68,000 |
| 2,800 | 9,200 | 5,500 | 5,100 | 58,000 |

Least-squares regression analysis (Chapter 5 Appendix) results in the following additional data:

| | Units produced | Direct labor hours | Machine hours | Units raw material used |
|---|---|---|---|---|
| Slope | 15.05 | 5.42 | 7.73 | 9.95 |
| Y-axis intercept | 17,936 | 9,556 | 15,751 | 8,248 |

**EP 12.4** Refer to the data given in Problem EP 12.3.

a) Which of the four measures of activity available appears to be the best predictor of the department's costs for budgeting purposes?

b) Why is the measurement you selected in (a) above better than any of the others?

**EP 12.5** The following historical data is available relating to expenditures incurred in production department B in your firm during the previous year:

| | Direct labor hours | Department B expenditures |
|---|---|---|
| First quarter | 7,000 | 188,000 |
| Second quarter | 9,000 | 235,000 |
| Third quarter | 10,000 | 265,000 |
| Fourth quarter | 6,000 | 165,000 |

Using the high–low-point method of regression analysis (Chapter 5), determine the flexible budgeting rate for the department for the current year, assuming no cost inflation.

**EP 12.6** The following historical data is available relating to expenditures incurred in production department D in your firm last year:

| | Direct labor hours | Department D expenditures |
|---|---|---|
| First quarter | 1,800 | $ 73,100 |
| Second quarter | 2,700 | 106,050 |
| Third quarter | 3,100 | 120,700 |
| Fourth quarter | 3,500 | 136,000 |

a) Using the high–low-point method of regression analysis (Chapter 5), determine the flexible budgeting rate for the department for the current year, assuming no cost inflation.

b) What rate should be used in the current year if costs have increased an average of eight percent?

**EP 12.7** Your firm uses a fixed budget based performance reporting system. As plant superintendent, you are about to meet with the supervisor of the assembly department to review her performance for the month of March. The performance report for March is given in Exhibit 12.7.

Although all variances appear unfavorable, you know that assembly processed an additional order in March which had not been originally scheduled.

a) Calculate the volume variance, both current month and year-to-date, for the department in total and for each of the four separately budgeted expenditures.

b) Is your supervisor doing a good job of cost control? Which variances might merit further investigation?

**EP 12.8** The Krampton Company uses a fixed budgeting performance system. As foreman of the machine department, you are about to meet with the plant superintendent to review your performance report for April. The report is given in Exhibit 12.8.

Although all variances appear favorable, you realize that a delay in an incoming steel shipment significantly reduced your production from that originally planned.

**Exhibit 12.7**

FIXED BUDGET PERFORMANCE REPORT, ASSEMBLY DEPARTMENT—MARCH, 19XX

| | Current month | | | | Year-to-Date | | | |
|---|---|---|---|---|---|---|---|---|
| | Budget | Actual | Variance | % | Budget | Actual | Variance | % |
| Units assembled | 4,000 | 5,000 | | | 9,000 | 10,000 | | |
| Direct labor ($7 V) | $28,000 | $34,900 | $6,900 U | 24.6 | $63,000 | $ 70,100 | $7,100 U | 11.3 |
| Indirect labor ($3,000 F + $2 V) | 11,000 | 12,100 | 1,100 U | 10.0 | 27,000 | 28,500 | 1,500 U | 5.6 |
| Indirect materials ($500 F + 0.50 V) | 2,500 | 3,200 | 700 U | 28.0 | 6,000 | 6,550 | 550 U | 9.2 |
| Maintenance ($900 F + 0.10 V) | 1,300 | 1,400 | 100 U | 7.7 | 3,600 | 3,750 | 150 U | 4.2 |
| Total ($4,400 F + 9.60 V) | $42,800 | $51,600 | $8,800 U | 20.6 | $99,600 | $108,900 | 9,300 U | 9.3 |

**Exhibit 12.8**
KRAMPTON COMPANY

**Performance Report, Machining Department—April, 19XX**

| | Current month | | | | Year-to-date | | | |
|---|---|---|---|---|---|---|---|---|
| | Budget | Actual | Variance | % | Budget | Actual | Variance | % |
| Units completed | 55,000 | 30,000 | | | 220,000 | 195,000 | | |
| Direct labor ($0.50 V) | $27,500 | $15,400 | $12,100 F | 44.0 | $110,000 | $ 98,000 | $12,000 F | 10.9 |
| Indirect labor ($2,000 F + 0.05 V) | 4,750 | 4,500 | 250 F | 5.3 | 19,000 | 18,900 | 100 F | 0.5 |
| Indirect materials ($600 F + 0.01 V) | 1,150 | 890 | 260 F | 22.6 | 4,600 | 4,400 | 200 F | 4.3 |
| Maintenance ($2,800 F + 0.08 V) | 7,200 | 5,200 | 2,000 F | 27.8 | 28,800 | 25,900 | 2,900 F | 10.1 |
| Total ($5,400 F + $0.64 V) | $40,600 | $25,990 | $14,610 F | 36.0 | $162,400 | $147,200 | $15,200 F | 9.4 |

a) Calculate the volume variance, both current month and year-to-date, for the department in total and for each of the four separately budgeted items.

b) Do you have all expenditures reasonably under control? Which variances will your superintendent probably wish to discuss?

**EP 12.9** Refer to the data given in Problem EP 12.7. Assuming no volume variances through February, prepare a performance report for the month of March and year-to-date, on a flexible budgeting basis.

**EP 12.10** Refer to the data given in Problem EP 12.8. Assuming no volume variances through March, prepare a performance report for the month of April and year-to-date, on a flexible budgeting basis.

**EP 12.11** Factory overhead for June, 19XX for the Laribee Company had been originally budgeted at $240,000 ($180,000 variable and $60,000 fixed), assuming 12,000 units would be produced. Each unit was expected to require five direct labor hours. The current overhead absorption rate was $4 per direct labor hour. Actual production in June was 15,000 units, and actual direct labor hours expended were 73,000. Actual overhead costs incurred were $320,000. Determine the following items for June, 19XX:

a) Overhead applied or absorbed

b) Over- or underapplied overhead

c) Budgeted overhead on a flexible budgeting basis

d) Overhead spending variance

**EP 12.12** Determine the same four items required in Problem EP 12.11 for the Murphy Corporation for August, 19XX. August production was originally planned to require 6,000 direct labor hours with each unit expected to require one-half hour to complete. Overhead (including $6,000 of budgeted fixed overhead) was being applied at the rate of $6.00 per direct labor hour. Actual production in August was 10,000 units, and 5,300 direct labor hours were expended. Actual overhead costs incurred were $32,000.

**EP 12.13** The following data are available for the Trident Company's computer center for a recent period:

| | Budget | Actual |
|---|---|---|
| Total variable costs | $25,000 | $34,000 |
| Total fixed costs | $50,000 | $50,000 |
| Total chargeable hours | 500 hrs | 480 hrs |
| Hours of usage: | | |
| Department A | 100 | 60 |
| Department B | 150 | 180 |
| Department C | 250 | 240 |

You may assume that computer services were available from outside service bureaus for $185 per hour.

a) Calculate the charges to Department A under the following systems:
   (1) Actual costs charged on the basis of actual usage
   (2) Actual costs charged on the basis of planned usage formula

(3) Charges based on market-based transfer price

(4) Charges based on full budgeted costs and actual usage

(5) Charges based on budgeted variable costs and actual usage

b) Prepare the computer center's budget performance report under:

(1) Profit center, with market-based transfer prices for actual usage

(2) Expenditure center, with charges based on full budgeted costs and actual usage

(3) Expenditure center, with charges based on budgeted variable costs and actual usage

**EP 12.14** Refer to Problem EP 12.13. Answer the same questions for the firm's maintenance department, based on the following data:

|  | Budget | Actual |
|---|---|---|
| Total variable costs | $125,000 | $135,000 |
| Total fixed costs | $ 25,000 | $ 27,000 |
| Total chargeable hours | 5,000 | 5,400 |
| Hours of usage: |  |  |
| Department A | 1,000 | 900 |
| Department B | 1,500 | 1,800 |
| Department C | 2,500 | 2,700 |

Assume that the outside rate for maintenance services was $40 per hour.

## SUPPLEMENTARY PROBLEMS

(*Note.* These supplementary problems are based on material contained in the Appendices to Chapters 5 and 12.)

**SP 12.15** Refer to the data given in Problem EP 12.3.

a) Calculate the standard error of the estimate for the two regression lines relating units produced and direct labor hours to department expenditures.

b) If these two activity measures were the only ones readily available, which should be chosen for budgeting purposes? Explain the reason for your choice.

**SP 12.16** Refer to the data given in Problem EP 12.3.

a) Calculate the standard error of the estimate for the two regression lines relating machine hours and units of raw material used to department expenditures.

b) If these activity measures were the only ones readily available, which should be chosen for budgeting purposes? Explain the reasons for your choice.

c) Considering all four activity measures, which would be the best for budgeting purposes? Explain.

**SP 12.17** The Morgan Company had one service center, two producing departments, and three products. Service-center costs were allocated to the producing departments by formula, ⅔ to producing department #1 and ⅓ to department #2. Indirect costs in producing departments were allocated to products on the basis of direct labor hours. Note that product C is completed in production center #1. Cost data accumulated for a recent period by responsibility center is as follows:

| | |
|---|---|
| Service center | $ 90,000 |
| **Production center #1:** | |
| Product A: | |
| Direct material | $140,000 |
| Direct labor | $ 60,000 |
| Direct labor hours | 6,000 |
| Product B: | |
| Direct material | $ 50,000 |
| Direct labor | $ 24,000 |
| Direct labor hours | 4,000 |
| Product C: | |
| Direct material | $ 20,000 |
| Direct labor | $ 30,000 |
| Direct labor hours | 5,000 |
| Indirect costs | $120,000 |
| Total costs | $444,000 |
| **Production center #2:** | |
| Product A: | |
| Direct material | $    0 |
| Direct labor | $ 35,000 |
| Direct labor hours | 7,000 |
| Product B: | |
| Direct material | $ 20,000 |
| Direct labor | $ 45,000 |
| Direct labor hours | 9,000 |
| Indirect costs | $ 66,000 |
| Total costs | $166,000 |
| Total manufacturing costs | $700,000 |

a) Determine total costs for each production center after allocation of service-center costs.

b) Determine total costs of each product.

**SP 12.18** The Nike Corporation had two service centers, two producing departments, and two products. Service-center costs were allocated to producing departments in two separate ways. Costs in service center (a) were allocated in proportion to direct labor hours in the producing department. Costs in service center (b) were allocated by formula, ⅔ to producing department #2 and ⅓ to producing department #1. Indirect costs in production centers were absorbed into product cost at a predetermined rate of $10 per direct labor hour.

Actual costs incurred for the period were:

| | |
|---|---|
| Service center (a) | $150,000 |
| Service center (b) | 30,000 |
| Production center #1  ⅓ | |
| Direct material: | |
| Product A | $ 40,000 |
| Product B | 12,000 |
| Direct labor: | |
| Product A (12,000 DLH) | 72,000 |
| Product B ( 4,000 DLH) | 24,000 |
| Indirect costs: | 66,000  10 (hr |
| Total | $214,000 |
| Production center #2 | |
| Direct material:  ⅔ | |
| Product A | 0 |
| Product B | 6,000 |
| Direct labor: | |
| Product A (5,000 DLH) | 35,000 |
| Product B (3,000 DLH) | 21,000 |
| Indirect costs: | 18,000  10/hr |
| Total | $ 80,000 |
| Total manufacturing cost | $474,000 |

a) Determine total costs for each production center after allocation of service-center costs.

b) Determine total costs allocated to product A and to product B.

c) Define any unallocated cost, and describe how it will affect the firm's year-end financial statements.

**SP 12.19** Refer to Problem EP 12.11. Calculate for the Laribee Company for June, 19XX:

a) Over- or underapplied overhead

b) Overhead volume variance

c) Overhead efficiency variance

d) Overhead spending variance

**SP 12.20** Refer to Problem SP 12.19. Calculate the same four items for the Murphy Corporation for August, 19XX, based on the data given in Problem EP 12.12.

## SUGGESTIONS FOR FURTHER READING

Horngren, C., *Cost Accounting: A Managerial Emphasis,* Fourth Edition. Englewood Cliffs, N.J.: Prentice-Hall, Inc., 1977; Chapters 8, 15, and 16.

Morse, Wayne J., *Cost Accounting: Processing, Evaluating, and Using Cost Data.* Reading, Massachusetts: Addison-Wesley Publishing Company, 1978; Chapters 10 and 12.

CHAPTER 12 APPENDIX
# Allocating Costs to Products and Overhead Variance Analysis

GAAP require that all manufacturing-related costs be included in product costs. Chapter 1 introduced you to cost accounting for product costs. As described in that chapter, direct costs may be accumulated by individual product, and all indirect costs may be accumulated on a total factory basis in a single account for manufacturing overhead. Manufacturing overhead may then be allocated[12] to various products at actual (all actual overhead is applied) or on the basis of a predetermined rate. A system such as the one described in Chapter 1, and in this chapter under predetermined overhead rates, adequately fulfills GAAP requirements.

A firm may have several production and service centers not all equally involved with each product, and a firm may also wish to accumulate indirect cost by responsibility center for operating budget and control purposes. In such situations, as will be described in this appendix, allocation of costs to products may involve several distinct sequential steps.

Where a more detailed cost breakdown is desired for product costing or operating budgets, both direct and indirect costs are first accumulated by responsibility center. For illustration, think of a hypothetical firm known as the Virgo Manufacturing Company, which has five responsibility centers within the manufacturing division, as follows:

Service center (a)
Service center (b)

Production (cost) center #1
Production (cost) center #2
Production (cost) center #3

Note that, although Virgo has five responsibility centers, it has only three production or cost centers actually involved in the manufacturing process. The

---

[12]   Costs may also be allocated in attempting to arrive at a total cost for pricing determination where competitive market prices are not available as a reference. They may also be allocated as part of the intermediate and long-range planning process to assess potential probability. Where such cost allocation involves government contracts, it is subject to guidelines promulgated by the Cost Accounting Standards Board (CASB).

other two centers are service centers, much like the maintenance department in the Tripper Company.

Assume that Virgo manufactures three separate products—A, B, and C—and that actual costs incurred during a given period were as shown in Exhibit 12.9. Note that only product B is processed in all three production centers. Product A is not involved with Cost center #3, and product C is not involved with Cost center #1. Also note that, whereas indirect costs would be sepa-

**Exhibit 12.9**

## VIRGO MANUFACTURING COMPANY

| Costs as Accumulated by Responsibility Center | | |
|---|---:|---:|
| **Service center (a):**  Indirect costs | | $ 21,000 |
| **Service center (b):**  Indirect costs | | $ 40,000 |
| **Production center #1:** | | |
| Direct material: | | |
| Product A | $ 40,000 | |
| Product B | 65,000 | $105,000 |
| Direct labor: | | |
| Product A | $ 60,000 | |
| Product B | 120,000 | 180,000 |
| Indirect costs: | | 61,000 |
| Total | | $346,000 |
| **Production center #2:** | | |
| Direct material: | | |
| Product A | $ 20,000 | |
| Product B | 15,000 | |
| Product C | 80,000 | $115,000 |
| Direct labor: | | |
| Product A | $ 30,000 | |
| Product B | 60,000 | |
| Product C | 90,000 | 180,000 |
| Indirect costs: | | 123,000 |
| Total | | $418,000 |
| **Production center #3:** | | |
| Direct material: | | |
| Product B | $ 5,000 | |
| Product C | 30,000 | $ 35,000 |
| Direct labor: | | |
| Product B | $ 30,000 | |
| Product C | 10,000 | 40,000 |
| Indirect costs: | | 11,000 |
| Total | | 86,000 |
| Total manufacturing costs | | $911,000 |

rately accumulated by type (indirect labor, indirect materials, supervision, and so forth) within each center, they are shown only in total, to simplify the illustration.

The first cost-allocation step involves assigning all service-center costs to production or cost centers. You may assume that costs are assigned on the basis of usage, with the costs of service center (a) being divided equally among all three production centers. Center (b)'s costs are allocated one-half to production center #2 and one-fourth each to centers #1 and 3. Exhibit 12.10 illustrates this assignment, and Exhibit 12.11 discloses the results of such allocation.

Final product cost data is obtained by allocating costs from production centers to individual products, as illustrated in Exhibit 12.12. For simplification it will be assumed that total indirect costs accumulated in a production center are allocated to products in proportion to direct labor dollars. Results of such an allocation are shown in Exhibit 12.13. You should study Exhibits 12.9 through 12.13 carefully, until you are completely familiar with the cost allocations illustrated. Note that total manufacturing costs were $911,000 on Exhibits 12.9, 12.11, and 12.13. The $911,000 has merely been allocated and reallocated to different classifications in this example.

If predetermined overhead rates (or standard costs, to be described in Chapter 13) were employed, then accounting variances could exist between total costs incurred and allocated to production (cost) centers and those costs applied to product cost inventory.

**Exhibit 12.10**

VIRGO MANUFACTURING COMPANY

**Cost Allocation to Production (Cost) Centers**

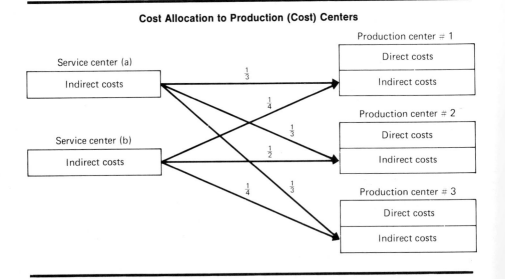

**Exhibit 12.11**

VIRGO MANUFACTURING COMPANY

**Costs Allocated by Production (Cost) Center**

**Production center #1:**

Direct material:

| | | |
|---|---|---|
| Product A | $ 40,000 | |
| Product B | 65,000 | $105,000 |

Direct labor:

| | | |
|---|---|---|
| Product A | $ 60,000 | |
| Product B | 120,000 | 180,000 |

Indirect costs:

| | | |
|---|---|---|
| Center #1 | $ 61,000 | |
| Center (a) | 7,000 | |
| Center (b) | 10,000 | 78,000 |
| Total | | $363,000 |

**Production center #2:**

Direct material:

| | | |
|---|---|---|
| Product A | $ 20,000 | |
| Product B | 15,000 | |
| Product C | 80,000 | $115,000 |

Direct labor:

| | | |
|---|---|---|
| Product A | $ 30,000 | |
| Product B | 60,000 | |
| Product C | 90,000 | 180,000 |

Indirect costs:

| | | |
|---|---|---|
| Center #2 | $123,000 | |
| Center (a) | 7,000 | |
| Center (b) | 20,000 | 150,000 |
| Total | | $445,000 |

**Production center #3:**

Direct material:

| | | |
|---|---|---|
| Product B | $ 5,000 | |
| Product C | 30,000 | $ 35,000 |

Direct labor:

| | | |
|---|---|---|
| Product B | $ 30,000 | |
| Product C | 10,000 | $ 40,000 |

Indirect costs:

| | | |
|---|---|---|
| Center #3 | $ 11,000 | |
| Center (a) | 7,000 | |
| Center (b) | 10,000 | 28,000 |
| Total | | $103,000 |
| Total manufacturing costs | | $911,000 |

**Exhibit 12.12**
## COST ALLOCATION TO PRODUCTS

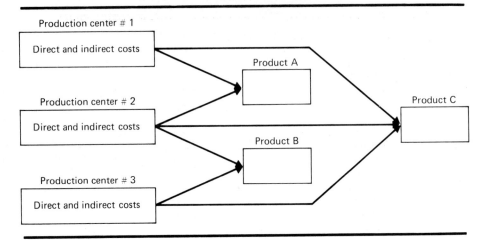

## Special Problems Related to Service Centers

The difficulties of budgeting and controlling service-center costs were discussed earlier in this chapter. Service centers can also involve more difficult allocation decisions than those illustrated above. A firm may have many service centers, involving such activities as:

- Maintenance
- Industrial engineering
- Factory personnel
- Computer center (factory portion)
- Production and inventory control
- Employees' cafeteria
- Materials handling
- Cost accounting

Problems arise when service centers provide service to each other. The cafeteria may use the computer facilities for food inventory control and may also provide service to computer-center employees. To avoid interservice or reciprocal allocations, reallocations, and re-reallocations, a step-down sequential approach is followed.

All service centers are first ranked in terms of service value added, the excess of costs of **services rendered** over **services received.** For example, a firm might have a maintenance department, a computer center, and a cafeteria, all established as independent service centers. Ranking these centers on the

**Exhibit 12.13**

VIRGO MANUFACTURING COMPANY

---

**Costs Allocated by Product**

**Product A:**
Direct material:
| | | |
|---|---|---|
| Center 1 | $ 40,000 | |
| Center 2 | 20,000 | $ 60,000 |

Direct labor:
| | | |
|---|---|---|
| Center 1 | $ 60,000 | |
| Center 2 | 30,000 | 90,000 |

Indirect costs:
| | | |
|---|---|---|
| Center 1 | $ 26,000 | |
| Center 2 | 25,000 | 51,000 |
| Total | | $201,000 |

**Product B:**
Direct material:
| | | |
|---|---|---|
| Center 1 | $ 65,000 | |
| Center 2 | 15,000 | |
| Center 3 | 5,000 | $ 85,000 |

Direct labor:
| | | |
|---|---|---|
| Center 1 | $120,000 | |
| Center 2 | 60,000 | |
| Center 3 | 30,000 | $210,000 |

Indirect costs:
| | | |
|---|---|---|
| Center 1 | $ 52,000 | |
| Center 2 | 50,000 | |
| Center 3 | 21,000 | 123,000 |
| Total | | $418,000 |

**Product C:**
Direct material:
| | | |
|---|---|---|
| Center 2 | $ 80,000 | |
| Center 3 | 30,000 | $110,000 |

Direct labor:
| | | |
|---|---|---|
| Center 2 | $ 90,000 | |
| Center 3 | 10,000 | 100,000 |

Indirect costs:
| | | |
|---|---|---|
| Center 2 | 75,000 | |
| Center 3 | 7,000 | 82,000 |
| Total | | $292,000 |
| Total manufacturing costs | | $911,000 |

## Exhibit 12.14
### SEQUENTIAL COST ALLOCATION

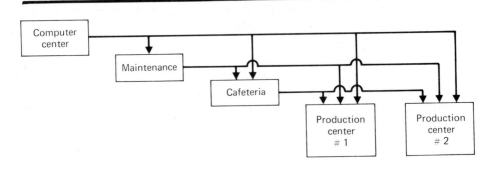

basis of value added results in:

| Service center | Costs of services rendered | Costs of services received | Net service value added |
|---|---|---|---|
| Computer center | $800,000 | $140,000 | $660,000 |
| Maintenance | 200,000 | 160,000 | 40,000 |
| Cafeteria | 100,000 | 120,000 | (20,000) |

Service-center costs are then allocated to other service centers and to producing departments, starting with the center having the highest value added (the computer center, in the above example) and proceeding sequentially down the list until all service costs are allocated. Exhibit 12.14 illustrates such sequential allocation.

The sequential allocation method is not as accurate as when simultaneous linear equations are used for more precise resolution of interdependent cross-allocations. These more sophisticated approaches are properly covered in intermediate cost accounting courses.

## OVERHEAD VARIANCE ANALYSIS

As first mentioned in this chapter, the attempted use of the accounting overhead variance (over- or underapplied overhead) as a performance measure can involve some complexity in isolating the overhead spending variance. As previously mentioned, the use of a single predetermined overhead rate (which treats all overhead as variable) and the use of an input measure (such as direct labor hours or machine hours) as the activity base can introduce two additional sources of variance. A difference between planned and actual activity levels will generate an accounting variance for the fixed overhead over- or underabsorbed. A difference between planned and actual usage of the activity base **per unit of output** can introduce a variance attributable to the efficiency of usage of the activity base.

Earlier in this chapter, the Ajax Corporation example demonstrated the variance attributable to fixed overhead. To also illustrate the variance attributable to the efficiency of usage of the activity base, turn again to the Ajax Corporation with different data. Assume that, at the beginning of a particular year, the Ajax Corporation planned to produce 50,000 gadginators during that year. It planned four hours of direct labor to make each gadginator, and expected total manufacturing overhead to be $600,000 ($400,000 variable and $200,000 fixed) for the year. Its predetermined overhead application (absorption) rate would then be $3 per direct labor hour:

$$\text{Predetermined overhead rate} = \frac{\$600,000}{200,000 \text{ hours}}.$$

Assume that, at year-end, actual data revealed:

| | |
|---|---|
| Actual production | 40,000 units |
| Actual direct labor hours | 170,000 hours |
| Actual total overhead | $590,000 |
| Overhead applied | $510,000 |
| Underapplied overhead | $ 80,000 |

What meaningful variance information, for performance purposes, may be derived from the above data?

## Three-Way Overhead Variance Analysis

With the introduction of another variable (the efficiency of labor usage) we have four overhead related elements, and therefore three variances. The four elements are:

| | |
|---|---|
| Actual overhead costs (ACT) | $590,000 |
| Revised budgeted overhead costs (RB) | 520,000[13] |
| Overhead applied or absorbed (OA) | 510,000 |
| Standard overhead (SOH) | 480,000 |

Note that the *standard overhead* represents the amount of overhead that would have been applied (absorbed) if there had been no labor variance, or if overhead had been applied on the basis of labor hours that should have been expended for the actual output. Note that 40,000 units of output should have been produced with 160,000 hours of labor. At the predetermined overhead

---

[13]   This is the same amount that would appear under a flexible budgeting system based on output measurements. With $400,000 of variable and $200,000 of fixed overhead budgeted in anticipation of 50,000 units of output, the budgeting rate would be $8 variable per unit plus $200,000 fixed. The flexible or revised budget based on 40,000 units of actual output would be $520,000.

rate of $3 per labor hour, $480,000 would have been absorbed if there had been no labor efficiency variance.

The total variance being explained by this three-way analysis is the difference between the actual overhead incurred (ACT) and the standard overhead (SOH), or a difference of $110,000, in this example. Three distinct variances contribute to this total variance:

1. The *overhead spending variance* (ACT − RB), with which you are already familiar.

2. The *overhead volume variance* (RB − OA), which, in this analysis, measures the difference between overhead applied and the revised or flexible budgeted overhead.

3. The *overhead efficiency variance* (OA − SOH), which measures the difference between overhead that was actually applied (absorbed) and the amount that would have been applied had there been no labor variance, the standard overhead.[14]

For practice and for understanding, you should calculate, on a separate sheet of paper, the three overhead variances for the Ajax Corporation from the data given, before proceeding.

The correct variance components are shown below:

| | | |
|---|---|---|
| Actual overhead (ACT) | $590,000 | |
| | | Spending variance +$70,000 |
| Revised budgeted overhead (RB) | 520,000 | |
| | | Volume variance    +10,000 |
| Overhead applied (OA) | 510,000 | |
| | | Efficiency variance +30,000 |
| Standard overhead (SOH) | 480,000 | |
| | | Total variance    +$110,000 |

Overhead volume and efficiency variances have little practical usefulness. They are introduced here because they are usually included in managerial accounting courses and literature, and are thought to be helpful in understanding the interrelationships of budgeting and cost accounting data. The volume variance does not involve amounts actually spent and is, therefore, irrelevant to performance evaluation. Where the overhead absorption rate is based upon the firm's practical capacity, as opposed to the expected level of activity, then the volume variance could serve as a measure of the cost of idle capacity (the amount of cost that would have been absorbed had the firm been operating at

---

[14]  The overhead efficiency variance may also be calculated by factoring the predetermined overhead rate out of the (OA − SOH) equation. Then:

$$\begin{pmatrix} \text{Overhead} \\ \text{efficiency} \\ \text{variance} \end{pmatrix} = \begin{pmatrix} \text{Standard units} \\ - \text{Actual units} \end{pmatrix} \times \begin{pmatrix} \text{Predetermined} \\ \text{overhead} \\ \text{rate} \end{pmatrix}.$$

effective capacity).[15] Furthermore, if absorption rates are based on normal activity and the firm is currently operating below the normal level, the volume variance might be an indication of the cost of below-normal operations.

Even the use of an accounting overhead volume variance is of questionable value. A far better measure of the opportunity cost of unused capacity would be lost contribution—the contribution that **could** have been earned by the additional products necessary to achieve full capacity operations.

The overhead efficiency variance, like the overhead volume variance, is independent of spending activity. It essentially reflects the efficiency of labor usage (assuming that overhead is applied on the basis of direct labor hours). If direct labor used were the same as direct labor that **should** have been used at the actual activity level (per the flexible budget), then the overhead efficiency variance would be zero. As a measure of the efficiency of labor usage, the overhead efficiency variance is less desirable than the variance readily obtainable for direct labor itself.

The only possibly meaningful variance is the overhead spending variance; and it is more readily obtainable by ignoring over- or underapplied overhead and first determining total flexible budgeted overhead. As discussed earlier in this chapter, the total spending variance provides limited information. It does not identify which overhead elements require attention. Also, if the product cost center differs from responsibility centers, then the accounting spending variance may not be identifiable with a responsible manager.

---

[15]  Where overhead application is based upon capacity, and volume variances (underapplied overhead) are written off to cost of goods sold, the effect on the firm's financial statements is to approach the result of a direct (variable) cost system. Remember, from Chapter 5, that a complete direct cost system (not acceptable under GAAP) would write off all fixed manufacturing costs as incurred.

# 13

# EXPENDITURE CONTROL AND STANDARD COSTS

## CHAPTER PREVIEW

Chapter 1 introduced the use of standard costs as one alternative available for accumulating product costs within a firm's accounts. The purpose of this chapter is to provide you with additional knowledge of standard costs, both as they are used in cost accounting and as they may provide information for budgeting and control. In this chapter you can:

- Learn the similarity and differences between budgeting rates and standards.
- Discover the two commonly used alternative bases for setting standards, the claimed strengths and weaknesses of each, and the people involved in standard setting within the firm.
- Learn how standard costs provide additional information further pinpointing responsibility for variances, and how to derive this information through variance analysis.
- Develop an understanding of which responsibility centers may be responsible for different variances, and how responsibility may be diffused by the interdependence of certain variances.
- Learn how standard costs are incorporated in the firm's accounts.
- Become familiar with the use of standards in place of or in conjunction with operating budgets.
- Explore the application of standards to nonmanufacturing activities and some of the issues involved.

In the appendix to this chapter, you may learn the recording procedures used by accountants for product costs.

With this knowledge you will have completed your introduction to alternatives for budgeting and controlling expenditure centers. You will have the essential foundation to proceed to a discussion of control of revenue, profit, and investment centers in the following chapter.

## WHO IS RESPONSIBLE FOR THESE VARIANCES?

Tripper's assembly department was not the only one with problems in July of 19X2. In reviewing overall performance with the operations vice-president, you discover significant unfavorable materials variances and also significant labor variances in the moulding department. Exhibit 13.1 indicates that the cost of raw materials used in the moulding department exceeded budget by $5,150, or 34.7 percent. Also, direct labor costs exceeded budget by $2,265, or 9.8 percent. There seems to be some difficulty pinpointing responsibility for corrective action.

The purchasing manager is blaming the moulding department foreman for materials variances, claiming that raw material is being inefficiently used. With so much material being wasted by the foreman, additional quantities over budget must be purchased in order to maintain production schedules. At least, that is the claim of the purchasing manager.

### Exhibit 13.1
### TRIPPER WATER SKI MANUFACTURING COMPANY

**Performance Report—Moulding Department[a]**
**for the Month of July, 19X2**

| | Original fixed budget | Revised flexible budget | Actual expenditure | Spending variance | Percent |
|---|---|---|---|---|---|
| **Production:** | | | | | |
| Economy skis | 2,100 | 2,700 | | | |
| Deluxe skis | 1,700 | 0 | | | |
| **Controllable expenditures:** | | | | | |
| Raw materials[b] | $26,340 | $14,850 | $20,000 | $5,150 U | 34.7 |
| Direct labor[c] | $34,485 | $23,085 | $25,350 | $2,265 U | 9.8 |
| Indirect labor[d] ($7,333 F + 2.0 V) | $14,933 | $12,733 | $12,143 | $ 590 F | 4.6 |
| Indirect materials[d] ($160 F + 0.4 V) | $1,680 | $ 1,240 | $ 1,290 | $ 50 U | 4.0 |
| Maintenance[d] ($1,000 F + 0.35 V) | $ 2,330 | $ 1,945 | $ 2,050 | $ 105 U | 5.4 |
| Total | $79,768 | $53,853 | $60,833 | $6,980 | 13.0 |

*Notes.* [a] Year-to-date information omitted to focus attention to current month.
[b] Budgeting rates $5.50 per economy ski and $8.70 per deluxe ski.
[c] Budgeting rates $8.55 per economy ski and $10.90 per deluxe ski.
[d] Variable cost per ski regardless of model.

The moulding foreman denies excess wastage. He points out that a certain amount of spoilage is normal and should be expected. Suppose that wood could only be purchased in six-foot lengths, and skis are designed to be five feet long; one foot of wood will be wasted. The moulding foreman also claims that the quality of raw material is deteriorating. This deterioration, in turn, requires additional labor costs and results in increased spoilage. Finally, with respect to materials, the moulding foreman suggests that the unfavorable variance may simply be the result of higher-than-planned prices. Purchasing desired quantity and quality at the lowest price is the responsibility of the purchasing department. So either or both the purchasing manager and the moulding foreman may be responsible for the unfavorable materials variance, depending upon the specific underlying facts.

The dispute over the unfavorable labor variance is equally circular. The variance appears on the moulding foreman's performance report but he protests that he cannot do anything about it. He claims the unfavorable labor variance results principally from a combination of two factors beyond his control—high wage rates and overtime. The foreman has different employees with different skills and seniority and different wage rates. Different operations within the department and on different skis require different skill levels. Normally, the foreman is responsible for matching workers to jobs, and his budget assumed such a balanced mix.

The moulding foreman claims that a large portion of the current unfavorable labor variance represents overtime or assignment of high-priced workers to less-skilled work, all resulting from rush orders. He states that, if the sales manager would allow adequate lead time, especially on special orders, and if the purchasing manager would just arrange for on-time delivery of materials, then the major part of the unfavorable labor variance could be eliminated. He claims the balance is the responsibility of the personnel manager for hiring too many "high-priced" workers and for supporting excessive wage increases.

As you might expect, the sales, purchasing, and personnel managers are reluctant to accept full responsibility for the unfavorable labor variance in the moulding department. They maintain that rush orders, late deliveries, and wage rates are at a practical minimum, and that budgets should provide for such costs. They also suggest that the real source of the problem might be poor productivity or lack of efficiency on the part of the workers in the moulding department. Labor efficiency is the foreman's responsibility.

As the owner–manager of Tripper, what can you do about these two impasses? In addition to apparently excessive expenditures, the bitterness developing between the purchasing manager, the personnel manager, the sales manager, and the moulding foreman is certainly neither conducive to efficient operations nor in keeping with your goal of a pleasant, supportive environment at Tripper. It would be very helpful if you could break down the materials and labor variances in some way that could further pinpoint responsibility. Your controller has suggested the development of explicit standards, and possibly even a standard cost system, as a solution.

## BUDGETING RATES AND STANDARDS

Can you see that some kind of standard for both material and labor must have been used at the time the Tripper budget was prepared? For planned production in the moulding department, a certain quantity of raw material at a certain price was budgeted. Also, a certain quantity (hours) of labor at a certain labor rate was implicit in the moulding department's budget for direct labor. In Tripper's case, it appears that these implicit standards should be made more explicit, so that they may also be incorporated into performance evaluation.

A standard is merely a norm by which performance (output) may be planned and later evaluated. Standards for effectiveness are designed to measure whether or not a job gets done. They are output measures and are usually established in physical, rather than dollar, terms. For instance, an effectiveness standard for the moulding department could simply be units of products scheduled for completion during a given period. As mentioned in earlier chapters, effectiveness measures are generally separate from budget performance reports that are designed to measure efficiency.

Recall, from Chapter 12, that, in measuring performance, the original fixed budget variance (originally budgeted amount less actual expenditure) may be divided into a volume variance and a spending variance:

Original budget − Flexible budget   = Volume variance;
Flexible budget − Actual expenditure = Spending variance.

Recall that the volume variance may be viewed as a measure of effectiveness (accomplishing designated tasks). Spending variance may be considered one measure of overall efficiency, but this view may be less than realistic. Often a portion of a spending variance may not be immediately controllable.

Efficiency refers to resources used (inputs) in obtaining outputs, and the resources used represent a **quantity** of goods or services times a **price:**

| | | |
|---|---|---|
| Units of raw material | × | Price per unit, |
| Hours of labor | × | Price (rate) per hour, |
| Units of supplies | × | Price per unit, |
| Years of insurance coverage | × | Price per year, |

and so forth. Since most prices are determined by market factors external to the firm and often beyond a manager's immediate control, efficiency, in the controllable sense, relates primarily to the quantity of resources used and only secondarily to price.

The distinction between quantity and price is not too significant in budgeting and controlling overhead costs. One supervisor at $1,000 per month or one insurance policy at $12,000 per year do not lend themselves to any meaningful further breakdown. However, a distinction between price and quantity can be very meaningful for revenue (to be discussed in Chapter 14) and for two costs that are often significant in amount—direct material and direct labor.

The budgeting rate for material used in the moulding department was $5.50 per economy ski and $8.70 per deluxe ski (Exhibit 13.1). You may assume that these rates, in turn, resulted from the expectations that:

One economy ski requires 5.5 feet of wood costing $1.00 per foot, and

One deluxe ski requires one batch of fiberglass and resin costing $8.70 per batch.[1]

In business it is often desirable to establish, where feasible, an efficiency standard for use in guiding and measuring performance. Since most efficiency standards are related to the **costs** incurred in making a unit of output, they are known as *standard costs*. Standard costs are similar to, but not necessarily the same as, budgeting rates for variable items. A budgeting rate and a standard cost for planning and controlling materials requirements incorporate **both** a quantity of material needed for a unit of output (production) and a price to be paid for each unit of material.

A standard cost for material, or a *material standard*, specifies the quantity of material that **should be used** and the price that **should be paid** for the material required to manufacture one unit of product. For example, the economy ski requires 5.5 feet of a particular width, thickness, and quality of wood, at $1 per foot. Here 5.5 feet would be known as the *standard quantity*, and $1 would be the *standard price*. The product of the standard quantity and the standard price would be the standard material cost, or material standard—$5.50 for each economy ski.[2]

$$\text{Standard cost} = \text{Standard quantity} \times \text{Standard price.}$$

A standard cost for labor, or a *labor standard*, similarly specifies the quantity (hours) of labor that **should be required** and the price or rate per hour that **should be paid** to complete an operation in the manufacture of one unit of product. For example, to complete the manufacture of an economy (wood) ski in the moulding department (a ski without hardware, which will be added later in assembly) might require 1.5 hours at $5.70 per hour, for a total of $8.55.[3]

What is the difference between a standard cost and a budgeting rate? There are three possible differences:

**1.** Budgeting rates may be used for fixed, mixed, or variable costs; and the activity base may be any output measure or even an input measure such as direct labor or machine hours. Standard costs in manufacturing are meaning-

---

[1]   An actual rate or standard would specify a number of feet or inches of glass cloth and a number of ounces of resin. Such detail would unnecessarily complicate the Tripper example.

[2]   Note that in accounting the term price usually refers to a number of dollars per unit ($1 per foot or the selling price of $50 per economy ski). The term cost often refers to an aggregate per batch or per order, or to some other combination of quantity times price.

[3]   A standard could also be set for each separate operation within the moulding department.

ful only for variable costs; and they are always based on outputs in terms of units of product. A standard cost is therefore a budgeting rate based on output units.[4]

**2.** Budgeting rates are used in the budgeting and control system separately from the cost accounting system. Standard costs are generally incorporated in the firm's cost accounting system and then also used as the budgeting rates in the budgeting and control system.

**3.** Budgeting rates represent reasonable expectations of what will probably happen. Standard costs represent targets of what **should** happen.

Note also that standards or standard costs and budgeting rates are unit concepts, whereas budgets are a total concept. Budgets express amounts of expected total costs for a given quantity of units.

## SETTING STANDARDS AND STANDARD COSTS

Standards are norms of what costs should be. They are desirable for control purposes in facilitating, as will be described below, the making of a distinction as to the cause of a variance—too much/too little quantity, or too high/too low price, or a combination of both. Thus they assist in identifying responsibility for corrective action, which could otherwise be difficult, as was demonstrated in the Tripper example. Standards are particularly applicable to situations involving continuous or repeated production of uniform or homogeneous products. Their use in a firm's cost accounting system may reduce inventory record-keeping costs. In these circumstances, the potential savings from better control and reduced clerical costs may exceed the costs of establishing and maintaining standards, and a standard cost system becomes desirable.

Since standards are really meaningful only for purely variable costs (the allocation of the fixed cost would be relevant only to precisely one quantity of output), they are most commonly used for direct material and direct labor. Standards for overhead items or in total (like a predetermined overhead rate) may be used within the cost accounting system for product costing. However, as you can discover later in this chapter, they have little value for control purposes.

Standards may be established on different bases. Four such different bases would be:

**1.** *Ideal standards:* inputs required at a level of maximum efficiency with no allowance for error—no mistakes, no delays, no decrease (even temporary) in worker efficiency, no breakdown of machines or tools, and so forth.

---

[4]   Note that a manufacturer may also establish a standard cost for overhead based on an assumed volume level (similar to a predetermined overhead rate based on units of output). Also, standards may be used for nonmanufacturing activities. Both of these subjects will be discussed further below.

2. *Attainable standards:* inputs required at a practical or realistic level of high but attainable performance.

3. *Expected standards:* inputs required at an average level of performance.

4. *Historical standards:* inputs that were required in the past, regardless of inefficiencies and any changes in methods that may have subsequently occurred.

Only one of the first two bases, **ideal** or **attainable,** are commonly used. Some managements choose ideal standards. Their objective is to avoid building in any inefficiencies that might be incorporated in attainable standards. Instead, they desire to have the standard serve as a constant reminder/indicator of what could be done—as a goal to strive for. Note that, when standards are set on an ideal basis, the budgeting process, which should always be aimed at realistic expectations, must incorporate a planned unfavorable variance. The planned unfavorable variance may, in turn, be viewed as incorporating the very slack that the ideal standard was intended to avoid.

Other managements choose attainable standards. Ideal standards may reduce worker motivation if they induce a feeling of hopelessness, whereas attainable standards can be accepted as possible. Attainable standards usually include an allowance for reasonable material spoilage and waste (in material standards) and for allowable and expected worker rest periods and machine down time (in labor standards).[5] For instance, the Tripper economy ski might ideally require only 5.0 feet of wood. If it was reasonable to expect cutting errors, imperfect but best obtainable pieces of wood, and so forth, to result in the loss of one out of every eleven skis cut, the standard of 5.5 feet of wood required would be appropriate.

Standards usually are the result of *work measurement.* Work measurement involves the careful analysis of a particular task to determine the most efficient manner in which it can be performed. The ultimate objective of work measurement is to develop a best way to perform a task and to determine the labor hours required. Several individuals are necessarily involved in establishing a standard. Usually an industrial engineer initially determines the physical measurement (quantity or time and skill level required). The engineer will also estimate an adequate allowance for reasonable "inefficency," for use in setting an attainable standard. The price component will be reviewed with the purchasing manager for materials and with the personnel or industrial relations manager for labor wage rates. The complete standard (price times quantity) is then reviewed with the managerial accountant in terms of similar recorded expense, to verify that the standard is attainable. Finally, the standard is fully reviewed and approved by the manager responsible for achieving the standard.

---

[5]   Some systems exclude from the standard an allowance for costs of spoilage and/or reworking or salvaging defective items. Such items are then budgeted and controlled through a separate overhead account.

## Maintaining or Revising Standards

One of the costs of incorporating standards that must be included in assessing their desirability is the additional cost of maintaining (revising) standards once they are established. A standard that is obsolete or inappropriate because of subsequent changes in material specifications, manufacturing processes or tooling, or prices can be more dangerous than no standard to begin with. Usually standards are only adjusted annually, or when there is a major change in specifications or processes. Annual changes often take the form of percentage adjustments to reflect price and wage changes.

One difficulty related to the use of standards also requires attention. This difficulty is known as the "creeping change problem." It is common for a series of minor changes to occur over a period of several years with respect to a particular standard. A slightly improved quality of material, which reduces manufacturing time, may be substituted by the supplier. A minor engineering change to the product can have the same effect. A slightly better tool may come into use. None of these changes appears by itself to merit a revision of the standard. Cumulatively they can result in the standard becoming too "loose." A firm must develop systems to protect itself against the effect of creeping changes.

Moreover, a new standard that does not provide for the *learning-curve effect* may be obsolete shortly after it is established. In your own experience you have found that practice or successive repetition of the same task will improve your skill and will usually reduce the time necessary to complete the activity. Research has shown that often a specific rate of improvement is constant over doubled quantities. Suppose that, for a particular task, the improvement rate was 80 percent (the average percentage found applicable to airplane manufacture during World War II). If the first attempt required 100 minutes, the second should require 80 minutes, the fourth 64 minutes, the eighth approximately 51 minutes, and so forth. Plotting such observations will result in a curve sloping down and to the right (see Fig. 13.1). The slope of the so-called learning curve is steep during the early trials and gradually flattens out.

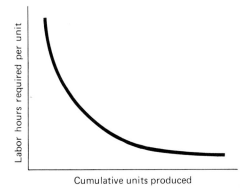

**Figure 13.1**

Cumulative units produced

A standard that is developed based on early production observations of a new operation must be adjusted for the learning-curve effect, or it will become too loose as the cumulative volume of production increases. Different tasks or operations have different learning curves that can only be developed by empirical observation.

## STANDARD COST VARIANCES

Properly established and maintained standards can be very useful in helping to pinpoint the cause or source of variances. Returning to the earlier Tripper moulding-department example (Exhibit 13.1), assume that the fixed and flexible budgeting rates for materials had been based on engineered standard costs. The material standard for economy skis was $5.50 per ski (5.5 feet of wood at $1.00 per foot). Actual July production was 2,700 skis, so the variable budget allowance for materials was $14,850. Actual costs were $20,000; and the resulting $5,150 unfavorable spending variance is in dispute between the purchasing manager and the foreman. The $20,000 of actual costs represented 16,000 feet of wood costing $1.25 per foot. Can you see how the standard cost for materials can assist in identifying the cause of the unfavorable variance?

### Direct Material Variances

Where a material standard exists, the total material spending variance is the sum of the *material price variance* and the *material usage (quantity) variance*.

$$\begin{pmatrix} \text{Total material} \\ \text{spending variance} \end{pmatrix} = \begin{pmatrix} \text{Material price} \\ \text{variance} \end{pmatrix} + \begin{pmatrix} \text{Material usage} \\ \text{variance} \end{pmatrix}.$$

The material price variance may be determined by multiplying the actual quantity purchased/consumed by the difference between the actual price paid and the standard price allowed:

$$\begin{pmatrix} \text{Material} \\ \text{price} \\ \text{variance} \end{pmatrix} = \begin{pmatrix} \text{Actual price} - \\ \text{Standard price} \end{pmatrix} \times \begin{pmatrix} \text{Actual} \\ \text{quantity} \end{pmatrix}.$$

Substituting for the actual costs in this example (16,000 feet at $1.25 per foot), the material price variance would be $4,000 unfavorable:

$$\$4,000 = (\$1.25 - \$1.00) \times 16,000.$$

Note that the equations are set up so that a positive result indicates a cost in excess of plan, which is then designated as unfavorable.

Can you grasp intuitively the significance or meaning of the material price variance? The 16,000 feet of lumber used in July cost $0.25 per foot more than the standard. Thus $4,000 of unplanned or excess costs resulted from the price differential and is identified as the material price variance.

The material usage variance may be determined by multiplying the standard price allowed by the difference between the actual quantity used and the standard quantity allowed:

$$\left(\begin{array}{c}\text{Material}\\\text{usage}\\\text{variance}\end{array}\right)=\left(\begin{array}{c}\text{Actual quantity}-\\\text{Standard quantity}\end{array}\right)\times\left(\begin{array}{c}\text{Standard}\\\text{price}\end{array}\right).$$

In this example, 2,700 skis were produced. At 5.5 feet of lumber allowed per ski, 14,850 feet should have been used; 16,000 feet were actually used and, therefore, the material usage variance was $1,150 unfavorable:

$$\$1,150 = (16,000 - 14,850) \times \$1.00.$$

Again, a positive result indicates usage in excess of that planned and is designated unfavorable. The $1,150 unfavorable material usage variance indicates that, even if there had been no price variance, $1,150 of unplanned or excess cost was the direct result of excess material usage in production.

The distinction between price and usage variances may also be illustrated graphically. Exhibit 13.2 illustrates the total $5,150 unfavorable material spending variance and its components. Note the small area in the upper right-hand corner. You may consider $287.50 of unfavorable variance as a **joint** price–usage variance. If the extra 1,150 feet had not been used, the extra $0.25 per foot price might not have been required. The joint variance has no usefulness and the price difference applies regardless of the quantity. Therefore, conventionally, the joint variance is included as part of the overall price variance and was so included in the above formulas.

**Exhibit 13.2**

ILLUSTRATION OF MATERIAL VARIANCES

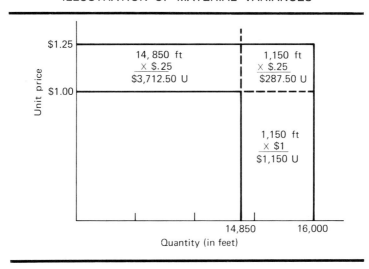

The $5,150 unfavorable material spending variance has now been explained:

| | |
|---|---|
| $4,000 U | Material price variance |
| 1,150 U | Material usage variance |
| $5,150 U | Total material spending variance |

Both the moulding foreman and the purchasing manager are responsible, with the major source of the problem identified as being with purchasing, which has been paying higher prices than the standard.

As mentioned earlier, price is often market-determined and not immediately controllable by the purchasing manager. Therefore, the unfavorable material price variance may be more properly viewed as probably a failure to properly forecast prices (and have the appropriate prices incorporated in the budgeting rates or standards). The purchasing manager may have been unable to buy at a price of $1.00 per foot. In some situations, poor planning by sales, production, or even purchasing might result in premium prices or transportation charges being paid for rush orders of material. A material price variance by itself cannot pinpoint responsibility; it can only identify a path for further investigation.

The material usage variance is often a more appropriate measure of efficiency. In fact, this variance is often identified as the material efficiency variance rather than as the usage or quantity variance. The quantity of resources used is a direct measure of efficiency and is more controllable than price. However, although excess material usage may be inefficient, the cause or source of the inefficient use is not necessarily the using foreman. Inefficient usage could result from an incorrect standard to begin with, inferior material, rush work, or other factors beyond the foreman's immediate control. As with all variances, the material usage variance does not in itself fix responsibility. It can only identify a factor that may require further investigation.

You may also be wondering why the entire material spending variance appears on the moulding foreman's budget. Several alternative disclosure practices are in common use. Some firms, such as Tripper, budget all material on the using department's budget, and break out the entire material spending variance at the time of actual usage. This system may be the simplest, but it results in including the price variance on the user's budget although the user has no control over it.

Other firms segregate the price and usage components for control purposes. The using department budgets material at standard. "Actual" material costs on the user's budget are then reported in terms of actual quantities used times standard prices. Any resulting variance will then be entirely a material usage variance, possibly controllable by the user. The material price variance component is separately identified with the purchasing department on its budget, either at time of purchase or, in some firms, at the time the purchase order is first placed.

The advantages of splitting material variances for control purposes should be obvious:

- Variances appear only where they are possibly controllable.
- The price variance will be reported in a more timely (earlier) manner for corrective action, especially if measured at the time the purchase order is placed. Remember that materials are often purchased in economic order quantities. If the price variance does not appear until the time of usage, it could be many months after the fact before a variance would be reported.

### Direct Labor Variances

A direct labor spending variance parallels a material spending variance. Both have price and usage or efficiency components. They differ in that often the components are given different names and also that the price and efficiency components may not be determined at different points in time. The price component, since it results from different wage rates paid, is often called the *labor rate variance:*

$$\begin{pmatrix} \text{Labor} \\ \text{rate} \\ \text{variance} \end{pmatrix} = \begin{pmatrix} \text{Actual rate} - \\ \text{Standard rate} \end{pmatrix} \times \begin{pmatrix} \text{Actual} \\ \text{hours} \\ \text{worked} \end{pmatrix}.$$

Furthermore, the quantity or usage component, since it results from worker efficiency, is usually known as the *labor efficiency variance:*

$$\begin{pmatrix} \text{Labor} \\ \text{efficiency} \\ \text{variance} \end{pmatrix} = \begin{pmatrix} \text{Actual hours} - \\ \text{Standard hours} \end{pmatrix} \times \begin{pmatrix} \text{Standard} \\ \text{rate} \end{pmatrix}.$$

As with the material variance, the total labor spending variance is the sum of the two components:

$$\begin{pmatrix} \text{Total direct labor} \\ \text{spending variance} \end{pmatrix} = \begin{pmatrix} \text{Labor rate} \\ \text{variance} \end{pmatrix} + \begin{pmatrix} \text{Labor efficiency} \\ \text{variance} \end{pmatrix}.$$

For an example of the calculation of direct labor variances, return to the Tripper case, where the standard for the moulding operations was $8.55 per economy ski, or 1.5 hours at $5.70 per hour. Assume an original budget for the period of 3,000 skis, with 2,700 actually produced. Actual direct labor costs were $25,350, representing 3,900 hours at an average cost of $6.50 per hour. Before proceeding you should attempt to determine, on a separate sheet of paper, the following variances with respect to direct labor and decide whether each was favorable or unfavorable:

- The total fixed budget variance
- The volume variance
- The spending variance
- The labor rate variance
- The labor efficiency variance.

The correct labor variances in this example are:

Total fixed budget variance = \$300 F (\$25,650 − \$25,350)
Volume variance         = 2,565 F (\$25,650 − \$23,085)
Spending variance       = 2,265 U (\$23,085 − \$25,350)
Labor rate variance      = \$3,120 U (\$6.50 − \$5.70) × 3,900 hours
Labor efficiency variance = \$855 F (3,900 − 4,050) × \$5.70

Note that, in this example, there was a \$3,120 unfavorable labor rate variance, indicating that employees earning a higher wage rate than provided for in the standard had been assigned to various jobs. The efficiency variance was \$855 favorable. Only 3,900 actual hours were incurred to produce 2,700 skis, for which the standard was 4,050 hours (2,700 × 1.5). This could be the result of more highly skilled (higher paid) workers taking less time per ski. Note that the component variances can offset each other—one favorable and the other unfavorable. This offsetting could also occur for material, where a lower-quality (cheaper) material can result in a higher usage (wastage) factor. Exhibit 13.3 illustrates the different variances that may be generated from standard costs.

What is your evaluation of the moulding foreman's performance with respect to direct labor for July? Does the breakdown of the labor spending variance substantiate his claim of noncontrollability over the \$2,265 unfavorable variance? Assuming the standard to be accurate, the \$855 favorable

**Exhibit 13.3**

ILLUSTRATION OF DIFFERENT VARIANCES POSSIBLE
WITH STANDARD COSTS

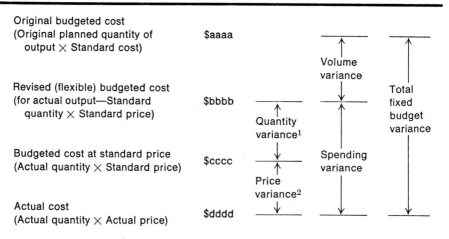

Notes. [1] Material usage variance or direct labor efficiency variance.
     [2] Material price variance or direct labor rate variance.

efficiency variance appears to back up the foreman's claim that excess costs arose from higher wage rates and overtime. Some firms separately report over-time premium on performance reports, in order to highlight this cost.

### Interdependence and Responsibility for Variances

Direct labor variance is generally reported on the individual production fore-man's budget, since it is usually controllable at that level. However, as mentioned, there may be exceptions to controllability that must be identified outside the budgeting system and with which you should be familiar. A labor efficiency variance could result from nonstandard materials, delayed materials, or rush orders, none of which would be the foreman's responsibility. A labor rate variance could result from wage increases not yet incorporated in stan-dards, or from overtime premiums incurred in filling rush orders or making up for material delivery delays, both of which again would be beyond the fore-man's immediate control.

You should also remember that labor variances can be interdependent. A higher-skilled (higher-paid) worker than planned in the standard may complete an item in less than the standard time, and vice versa.

As also cited above, a material usage variance could result from a purchas-ing deviation in materials quality. A materials price variance could result from rush buying, supplier rush premiums, or expediting incoming transportation premiums (air vs. truck), all resulting from rush orders beyond the purchasing department's control. And higher-cost material, if the cost represented better quality, could result in lower usage, and vice versa. Standard costs and stan-dard cost variances do provide more detailed information to assist in identify-ing responsibility. However, they cannot replace the necessity for management investigation and interpretation.

## STANDARDS AND DIFFERENT COST ACCOUNTING SYSTEMS

When a firm decides to go to the expense of setting engineered standards, it will usually do more with them than just use them as more sophisticated budgeting rates. As first described in Chapter 1, standard costs are usually incorporated in the firm's product cost accounts. In fact, some firms use stan-dard costs in lieu of operating budgets.

The use of standard costs for product costing has several advantages. Cost data for pricing decisions is uniform and is not subject to the vagaries of actual costs. Actual costs incurred during a given year for the same product could vary dramatically as a result of significant inefficiencies, severe winters, and so forth. Data reflecting a unit cost of $30.00 one quarter, $50.00 the next, and $35.00 for a third would not provide a good basis for making a tight pricing decision. A uniform standard cost would provide a much better and more reliable basis.

Perhaps a greater advantage is the fact that standard costs eliminate the necessity of cost-flow assumptions (LIFO, FIFO, average cost) and the necessity of maintaining records of different inventory cost layers (batches) for each product throughout the year.[6] Under a standard cost system, inventories are all priced at standard, and variances may be closed to cost of goods sold.[7]

To illustrate how standard costs are carried in a firm's accounts, return to the Tripper example given as part of the introduction to variance analysis. Tripper purchased 16,000 feet of wood at a price of $1.25. The standard price was $1.00. Therefore, of the $20,000 of purchases, only $16,000 (the standard cost of the actual quantity purchased) would be entered in raw materials inventory. The $4,000 unfavorable price variance will be written off as an addition to cost of goods sold.

The following illustrations show the cost flows through T-accounts. You need not be familiar with the debit/credit bookkeeping language to follow these diagrams. Just visualize each separate T as a distinct account or record; in the case of inventory and cost of goods sold accounts, these are increased on the left and decreased on the right.

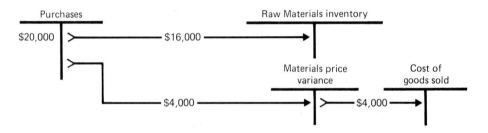

When the 16,000 feet was used to manufacture only 2,700 economy skis, the usage variance would also be broken out:

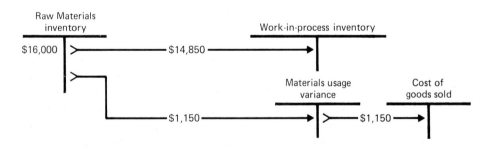

[6]   Where standards are changed annually, layers may be maintained on an annual basis.

[7]   As described in Chapter 1, where material price variance is not identified until usage (materials transferred to work-in-process), raw materials inventory would be carried at actual cost rather than at standard. Also, recall that material or significant variances may be prorated between ending inventory and cost of goods sold rather than entirely written off.

Direct labor costing $25,350 was incurred in the manufacture of 2,700 skis. Both the labor rate variance and the labor efficiency variance are broken out at this point:

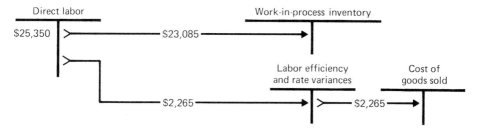

Note that, in this example, raw materials inventory was carried at standard cost (16,000 feet at $1.00 per foot). Also note that material and direct labor were added to work-in-process inventory at standard (2,700 units at $5.50 plus 2,700 units at $8.55).

In Chapter 1 you learned that there were essentially two different types of cost systems, depending upon the type of manufacturing in a particular firm. Where a firm manufactures only a single homogenous product at one time, the process cost system with only a single work-in-process account is used. For the firm that consistently manufactures different or nonhomogeneous products, separate work-in-process inventory accounts are established for each separate product or job order under the job-order cost system. The standard cost system is not so much a third distinct system as it is a possible variation of the other two.

Standard costs are commonly found in process cost systems because of the standardized product and continuous processing. Under a standard cost process system, variances are accumulated by expenditure center periodically and on the basis of equivalent units completed. They are then used for control reporting purposes, as well as being subsequently closed to cost of goods sold.

Standard costs may also be used in conjunction with a job-order system, although this practice is less common. Since a firm with a job-order system has many different products or batches, each requiring separate standards, the cost of establishing and maintaining different standards may exceed the control benefits. Accounting under a job-order system with standard costs is similar to that under a process system. Material and labor are charged to different work-in-process accounts for different jobs at standard. Any over- or underapplied amount represents an accounting variance. This variance may be used for control purposes and may be eventually closed to cost of goods sold.

## STANDARDS FOR OVERHEAD

Standard costs for overhead may appear confusing since many overhead items represent either fixed or mixed costs. Recall that a standard per unit of output for a fixed cost, and especially a programmed cost, is essentially meaningless.

Nevertheless, to comply with GAAP, which require that full product costs be included in inventory, overhead must be allocated to products. Recall, from Chapters 1 and 12, that overhead is often applied or assigned to work-in-process inventory on the basis of a predetermined overhead rate. In nonstandard cost systems, overhead is often applied for convenience in terms of an input activity measure, such as actual direct labor hours or actual machine hours incurred. As described in Chapter 12, this practice can lead to an overhead efficiency variance, in addition to overhead volume and overhead spending variances.

Under a standard cost system, the overhead standard is merely a predetermined overhead rate, with the activity measure being units of output.[8] With overhead applied at standard, based on actual output, no variance arising out of inefficient utilization of an input measure can occur. Nevertheless, an overhead accounting variance (over- or underapplied overhead) will **always** occur unless the actual number of units produced exactly equals the standard volume (normal volume or practical capacity) used as a base for determining the standard overhead rate:

$$\left(\begin{array}{c}\text{Standard overhead}\\ \text{rate}\end{array}\right) = \frac{\text{Total expected (budgeted) overhead costs}}{\text{Standard volume}}.$$

Remember, from Chapter 12, that the variance caused by different levels of activity than those anticipated is identified as the overhead volume variance. It consists of that portion of fixed overhead cost not allocated to inventory (or overallocated) because of the difference between actual and standard volume.

To see clearly the source of the overhead volume variance, assume a situation where there was no overhead spending variance. At the beginning of a year the firm anticipated total overhead costs during the coming year as $200,000 variable and $100,000 fixed. Standard volume was 50,000 units, and therefore standard overhead was set at $6 per unit. Assume that, at year-end, the actual output was 40,000 units and actual overhead was $260,000. Variable overhead had been perfectly controlled to the new activity level. Overhead applied at standard would be $240,000, leaving a variance of underapplied overhead of $20,000. This $20,000 represents 20 percent (or $2 per unit) of the fixed overhead allocation that could not be applied to the 10,000 "missing"

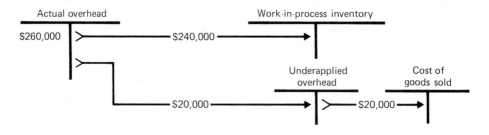

---

[8]   Standard direct labor (an input measure) may be used, but since **standard** direct labor correlates perfectly with output units, the effect is identical to using units of output.

units. It would be closed to cost of goods sold (or prorated to inventory and cost of goods).

## STANDARDS AND OPERATING BUDGETS

Because of fixed cost components, overhead costs are more readily budgeted and controlled through the flexible budgeting system than through standard costs. Purely variable overhead items can, of course, be readily subject to separate standard costs. In practice, however, for product cost purposes, all overhead is generally treated uniformly as a single aggregate amount.

Standard costs are **not** an alternative to operating budgets. They are complementary. In essence, a standard is simply a flexible budget (budgeting rate) for a cost item expressed per unit of output. Standards enhance the accuracy of budgeting and controlling direct materials and direct labor. Remaining manufacturing and nonmanufacturing costs are often more effectively controlled through variable budgets distinct from the cost accounting system.

## STANDARDS FOR NONMANUFACTURING ACTIVITIES

So far standard costs have been discussed only in terms of direct material, direct labor, and overhead in a manufacturing firm. These applications are quite common. The principle of developing and using standard costs is equally applicable to other areas. However, standard costs are much less prevalent for nonmanufacturing activities, and those that do exist were developed many years after manufacturing standards had become quite common.

Several factors could explain the delayed and limited application of standards to nonmanufacturing activities. Often nonmanufacturing activities are less standardized, have a higher proportion of fixed costs, and may be accompanied by a psychological resistance to standards.

To be meaningful and effective, a standard must relate to identifiable and homogeneous units of output (products). Most nonmanufacturing activities are not involved with readily measurable homogeneous outputs. For example, typists in a steno pool or word-processing center could have standards set per page of output, but the mix of material (routine and simple letters vs. statistical tables) may be too diverse to accommodate standardization.

Standards are also only meaningful with respect to variable costs, and most nonmanufacturing costs are mixed or fixed. Even clerical and filing personnel are usually salaried. Therefore, in the word-processing center example, the only real variable cost would be the paper consumed. Since the most homogeneous output measure would be pages typed, to decide that one typed page required one sheet of paper would not provide particularly valuable control information.

The final reason for the limited and slow growth of standards outside of the manufacturing area may be considered psychological. Belief systems exist that tend to associate standards with fact_, or "blue-collar" production, and construe them as "not O.K." or demeaning in the office or "white-collar" situation. Standards are therefore generally resisted by nonmanufacturing employees. In many instances, the imposition of standards in an office has been closely followed by office unions, and this prospect has not made standards appealing to management. Output quotas have been sometimes used successfully. However, a quota is essentially similar to a budget rather than an engineered standard. Nonmanufacturing activities therefore continue to be most effectively controlled by formal or informal budgets.

Despite the limitations cited above, work measurement and the use of standards have made recent inroads outside of the factory. Major users of work measurement are the government and government-related agencies. Where there are large-volume, repetitive tasks such as check processing, mail sorting, and other routine paperwork handling activities, work measurement has proved valuable.

## CHAPTER OVERVIEW

Based on the material contained in this chapter, you should now be in a position to:

- Describe, with examples, a standard cost and how it may differ from a budgeting rate.
- Distinguish between the price and quantity components of a standard, and describe, with examples, how each relates to a standard for material and a standard for labor.
- Distinguish between the two commonly used alternative bases for establishing standards, and cite the alleged advantages and disadvantages of each.
- Describe work measurement and explain its objectives.
- Describe the individuals often involved in setting standards for material and labor, and the role of each.
- Explain, with examples, how standards may be useful in the control process to further define responsibility for departures from budget.
- Describe the two variance components of material and labor standards, how each is calculated, and what each means.
- Describe, with examples, who is usually responsible for material price, material usage, labor rate, and labor efficiency variances; and describe what inefficiencies cause such variances.
- Explain how variances may be interdependent and how responsibility may still not be pinpointed by the use of standard costs.

- Describe how standard costs may be incorporated in a firm's cost accounting system, which variances are generated, and how these variances are disposed of.
- Explain the difference between a predetermined overhead rate used in a nonstandard cost system and a standard overhead rate used as part of a standard cost system.
- Identify the accounting variance that may exist with predetermined overhead rates that cannot exist with the use of an overhead standard.
- Explain why standards are complements rather than alternatives to operating budgets.
- Explain why budgets are preferable to standards for control of overhead.
- Describe several factors that inhibit the spread or use of standards beyond manufacturing activities.

## NEW VOCABULARY AND CONCEPTS

| | |
|---|---|
| Standard cost | Work measurement |
| Material standard | Creeping change problem |
| Standard quantity | Learning-curve effect |
| Standard price | Material spending variance |
| Labor standard | Material price variance |
| Ideal standard | Material usage variance |
| Attainable standard | Labor spending variance |
| Expected standard | Labor rate variance |
| Historical standard | Labor efficiency variance |

## REVIEW QUESTIONS

1. What is the difference between:
   a) A budgeted cost for a given item and a standard cost for that item?
   b) A budgeting rate and a standard cost?
2. Can standards be developed and meaningfully applied for all budgeted costs? Explain.
3. Are standard costs primarily measures of efficiency or of effectiveness? Explain.
4. a) What is an example of a material standard?
   b) What are the components of a material standard?
5. a) What is an example of a labor standard?
   b) What are the components of a labor standard?
6. a) What individuals are normally involved in setting a material standard and a labor standard?
   b) What is the role of each?

7. What are each of the following types of standards:
   a) Ideal standards?
   b) Attainable standards?
   c) Expected standards?
   d) Historical standards?

8. Which two of the types of standards listed in Question 7 above are commonly in use?

9. a) Why and when is it desirable to revise standards that have previously been established?
   b) What is the creeping change problem, and what is its effect upon standard costs?
   c) What is a learning curve and how does it relate to standard setting?

10. a) What is a material price variance?
    b) What is its cause?
    c) How is it determined?
    d) When may it be determined?
    e) What is its significance; what does it mean?
    f) What manager is normally responsible for a material price variance?
    g) What other managers may have indirect control over a material price variance? Explain, with examples.

11. Answer the seven questions listed as part of Question 10 for a materials usage variance.

12. Answer the same seven questions listed in Question 10 for a labor rate variance.

13. Answer the same seven questions listed in Question 10 for a labor efficiency variance.

14. a) What is meant by the interdependence of variances?
    b) How can the interdependency of certain variances diffuse responsibility? Give examples.

15. a) What accounting variances are usually generated within the accounts for a firm having a full standard cost system?
    b) Do all of these accounting variances represent specifically controllable items? Explain.

16. Why are standard costs more readily applicable to firms employing process costing than to those with job-order costing?

17. What is the essential difference between an overhead absorption (application) rate and a standard overhead rate?

18. What three factors have probably precluded significant application of standard costs to nonmanufacturing activities?

## MINI-CASES AND QUESTIONS FOR DISCUSSION

MC 13.1 The Arkus Manufacturing Company has a standard cost system with standards for material, labor, and overhead for each product. The controller had several times suggested that the firm also develop and use operating budgets for the factory's machining and assembly departments. The factory manager each time rejects such suggestions as representing unnecessary paperwork. He maintains, "Each month, from the cost accounting department I get the three important figures, the materials variance (raw material inventory is carried at actual cost), the labor variance, and the amount of under- or overapplied overhead. These tell me whether or not the shop is in control. I have all the information I need."

Do you believe the general foreman has all the information he needs? How meaningful is a single figure for material, labor, or overhead variance for the entire factory? Discuss.

**MC 13.2** The advocates of ideal standards object to the use of attainable standards because they may be construed as sanctioning substandard performance. The implication is that a standard that allows for error or for rest periods will reinforce their occurence.

The advocates of attainable standards maintain that a standard must be realistic. They believe the standards should be something that a responsible employee could adopt and internalize as a target of excellence. Do you believe one of these positions to be correct and the other incorrect, or do they represent distinctly different approaches or philosophies of managament? Do you see any correlation between these positions and McGregor's Theory X and Theory Y, introduced in Chapter 11? Discuss.

**MC 13.3** Whether ideal or attainable, doesn't a standard still represent rigid behavior imposed on an employee? Would standards tend to encourage or discourage initiative and innovation on the part of production workers? Would standards, even if set at an attainable level, be compatible with a Theory Y (McGregor) atmosphere or environment? Discuss.

**MC 13.4** Assume a situation where a labor standard is also used as a basis for incentive pay (piece rate) to employees. In such a situation, would workers be motivated to suggest revisions that would increase efficiency and lower standards? Would creeping changes result in continuously increasing production, or might workers hold back (controlled production), fearing a cut in the rate? Discuss.

## ESSENTIAL PROBLEMS

**EP 13.1** The Wombat Company is in the process of establishing material and labor standards for one of its products called win. A win is made from plastic tubing (with a particular thickness, diameter, and quality specification). Wombat's engineers have specified that 2.7 feet of tubing will be required for each win, including an allowance for the width of each cut. The lowest cost at which the tubing can possibly be purchased is $0.16 per foot.

The operations of cutting the tubing and completing its conversion to a finished win have been studied by engineers. They conclude that they should require a total of 1.85 hours, and that the work can be satisfactorily performed by a semi-skilled worker earning $4.20 per hour. Determine the following for Wombat, assuming its standards are set on an ideal basis:

a) Material price standard

d) Labor rate standard

b) Material quantity standard

e) Labor time standard

c) Material standard per unit

f) Labor standard per unit

**EP 13.2** Refer to the information given for the Wombat Company in Problem EP 13.1. Assume that Wombat wished to establish attainable standards and that you had the following additional information:

- Although occasionally a roll of tubing (135 feet) is available for $21.60, generally, to obtain necessary quantities, the firm must purchase the tubing necessary in precut lengths. The desired tubing is available only in 10-, 12-, or 14-foot lengths, and there is no use (or salvage value) for short pieces remaining after cutoff. The best possible prices for precut tubing are $1.65 (10-foot), $1.95 (12-foot), and $2.24 (14-foot). However the market is seasonal and volatile, and the best average year-round price for cut tubing would be $1.70 (10-foot), $2.00 (12-foot), and $2.25 (14-foot).

- Although a worker can produce a win from tubing in 1.85 hours non-stop, company practice is to allow a paid rest break of 15 minutes at mid-morning and mid-afternoon, and an unpaid half-hour lunch break at mid-day. An average of another 18 minutes per day (eight-hour shift) are generally lost in machine down time, tooling replacement, and other interruptions.

  The mix of work scheduled in the production department requires mostly highly skilled and unskilled labor. Therefore very few semi-skilled workers at $4.20 per hour are available. Over the year, assuming excellent scheduling by the foreman, an average labor rate of $4.50 per hour would be optimal for the manufacturing of wins.

  a) Determine the following for Wombat on an attainable basis:

  - Material price standard
  - Labor rate standard
  - Material quantity standard
  - Labor time standard
  - Material standard per unit
  - Labor standard per unit

  b) For each of the above six items and in total per win, determine the difference between the attainable standard and the ideal standard.

**EP 13.3** The Purvis Company employs standard costs based on attainable standards for all of its products. The following events took place during 19X7:

1. An engineering change eliminated an operation in the manufacture of a product.

2. All foremen were given a 10-percent salary increase.

3. Utility brown-outs during several severe winter storms cut production by 20 percent, for a total of six weeks.

4. A supplier's strike for two months necessitated the purchasing of materials from distant sources, with higher incoming freight charges.

5. New materials handling equipment has reduced the average time required to move products from one department to another.

6. Hourly wage rates have been increased for all workers.

7. Utility rates and property taxes for the plant have increased.

8. A material previously used is no longer available. The replacement is more expensive but reduces wastage in production.

9. A slowdown of the firm's employees caused substantial negative efficiency variances during the first three months of the year.

10. During the last three quarters, labor efficiency variances were consistently at least five percent favorable. Workers were paid a straight hourly wage without production incentives.

11. A shortage of materials in the fall caused temporary layoffs of some lower-paid workers, and resulted in high rate variances.

12. The firm's higher level of production has resulted in a re-estimation of the useful life of its equipment. Annual depreciation expenses therefore have been increased.

   a) Which of the first six events should be reflected in a revision of material or labor standards?

   b) Which of the first six events will probably result in material or labor variances (assuming no change in standards), which variances will be affected, and which will be favorable or unfavorable?

   c) Which of the first six events will probably result in material or labor variances even after standards have been appropriately revised, which variances will be affected, and which will be favorable or unfavorable?

   d) Which of the first six events should result in modification of budgets for total manufacturing costs or expenses for 19X8?

**EP 13.4** Refer to Problem EP 13.3. Answer the same four questions (a), (b), (c), and (d), for events 7 through 12.

**EP 13.5** The Tulare Company manufactures merps. In conjunction with cost accounting, purchasing, personnel, and the affected foreman, the company's industrial engineer has determined that one merp should require three pounds of glub costing $4.00 per pound and two and one-quarter hours of semi-skilled labor costing $5.60 per hour. The firm keeps its raw material inventory at standard.

In February of 19X2, Tulare had planned to purchase one economic order quantity of four tons (8,000 pounds) of glub. In March the production department was scheduled to manufacture one economic lot size of merps, consisting of 1,500 units.

The February shipment was damaged in transit, and only 7,500 pounds were acceptable to Tulare. The supplier invoice, including freight-in, was settled by paying $29,250.

In March the production department completed 1,400 merps, using 4,400 pounds of glub and incurring $18,400 in direct labor costs for 3,200 hours.

Determine the following items for the Tulare Company, assuming no other activity had been planned or did occur. Identify all variances as favorable (F) or unfavorable (U).

a) Original purchases budget

b) Revised (flexible) purchases budget

c) Original direct labor budget

d) Revised (flexible) direct labor budget

e) Material volume variance (purchasing)

f) Material spending variance (purchasing)

g) Material price variance

h) Material volume variance (production)

i) Material spending variance (production)

j) Material usage variance

k) Labor volume variance

l) Labor spending variance

m) Labor rate variance

n) Labor efficiency variance

**EP 13.6**  Refer to the data given for the Tulare Company in Problem EP 13.5. Answer the same 14 questions for the months of July and August, given the following additional information:

- Quantity of glub ordered:  5 tons
- Quantity received in good condition:  9,900 pounds
- Total price and freight paid:  $40,095
- Production originally scheduled:  3,000 units
- Merps produced:  2,800
- Glub used:  8,300 pounds
- Direct labor cost incurred:  $34,770 for 6,100 hours

**EP 13.7**  Each of the eight columns of the matrix in Exhibit 13.4 represents a completely independent situation. Complete the missing items in columns A through D. Assume Raw Materials Inventory carried at standard cost.

**EP 13.8**  Refer to Problem EP 13.7. Complete the missing items in columns E through H. Consider each column independently. Assume Raw Materials Inventory carried at standard cost.

**EP 13.9**  The Lightfoot Company manufactures a single product with the following cost standards:

| | | |
|---|---|---|
| Material | $12.00 | (6 pounds at $2.00 per pound) |
| Labor | 10.00 | (2 hours at $5.00 per hour) |
| Overhead | 20.00 | (Rate of $10.00 per standard |
| Total | $42.00 | labor hour) |

During 19X8, Lightfoot purchased and used 32,000 pounds of material costing $62,400. Direct labor costing $56,100 was incurred (11,000 hours).

## Exhibit 13.4

| | A | B | C | D | E | F | G | H |
|---|---|---|---|---|---|---|---|---|
| Actual material purchased (lbs.) | 1,000 | ? | 3,000 | 2,000 | 2,500 | ? | 4,000 | 5,000 |
| Cost of order including freight-in | $1,900 | $3,900 | ? | $6,500 | $12,125 | $13,200 | ? | $33,350 |
| Standard material cost per unit | $6.00 | $5.00 | ? | $18.00 | $100 | $32 | ? | $280 |
| Standard price | ? | $2.50 | $1.00 | $3.00 | ? | $2.00 | ? | ? |
| Standard quantity (lbs) | 3 | ? | 10 | 2? | ? | ? | 9 | 40 |
| Material price variance | ? | $150 U | $150 F | ? | ? | $1,200 U | $2,000 U | ? |
| Actual units product completed | 200 | ? | ? | ? | 100 | 325 | 400 | 75 |
| Actual materials used | ? | 700 | 2,900 | 2,100 | 2,100 | ? | 3,800 | 3,000 |
| Actual labor costs incurred | $4,875 | ? | $8,690 | $17,690 | $1,890 | ? | $159,500 | $37,700 |
| Standard labor cost per unit | $24.00 | ? | $30 | ? | $20 | $28 | ? | $560 |
| Standard rate | $6.00 | $5.00 | ? | $6 | ? | $7 | $5 | ? |
| Standard hours | ? | 3.0 | 7.5 | 10 | 4 | ? | 70 | ? |
| Material usage variance | $100 U | ? | ? | $900 U | $500 U | $400 F | $3,000 U | ? |
| Labor rate variance | ? | $130 U | $110 F | $290 U | ? | $1,100 U | $14,500 U | $2,900 F |
| Labor efficiency variance | ? | $500 U | $200 F | $600 F | ? | $700 F | $5,000 U | $1,400 F |
| Actual labor hours | 750 | 1,300 | 2,200 | ? | 420 | 1,200 | ? | 5,800 |

Factory overhead was $101,300 for the year, during which 5,000 units were completed and 4,500 shipped to customers. You may assume that all beginning inventories were zero, and that ending raw materials and work-in-process inventories were zero. Determine for 19X8:

a) Material price variance

b) Material usage variance

c) Labor rate variance

d) Labor usage variance

e) Cost of goods sold appearing on the 19X8 income statement

**EP 13.10**   Refer to the data given for the Lightfoot Company in Problem EP 13.9. Determine the same five items (a), (b), (c), (d), and (e), for 19X9, assuming no standard cost changes and the following events:

During 19X9, Lightfoot purchased and used 47,000 pounds of material costing $98,700. Direct labor of 15,500 hours costing $80,600 was incurred. Factory overhead amounted to $150,000. A total of 8,000 units was completed, and 8,200 units were shipped to customers (depleting last year's carryover stock). You may assume that beginning and ending raw materials and work-in-process inventories were zero.

## SUPPLEMENTARY PROBLEMS

(*Note.* Part (b) of each supplementary problem is related to the material contained in the appendix to this chapter.)

**SP 13.11**   The following data (all amounts rounded to even thousands of dollars) is taken from the records of the Klute Company for the years 19X5 and 19X6. The Klute Company recorded all inventory at actual cost following a periodic system. Factory overhead was applied using a predetermined overhead rate based on direct labor hours (DLH).

|  | 19X5 | 19X6 |
|---|---|---|
| Beginning raw materials inventory | $15 | $? |
| Ending raw materials inventory | 20 | ? |
| Gross purchases | 215 | 275 |
| Freight-in | ? | 15 |
| Purchase returns | 15 | 10 |
| Purchase discounts | 5 | ? |
| Net purchases | ? | 250 |
| Raw materials used | ? | ? |
| Originally planned DLH | 45,000 hrs. | 45,000 hrs. |
| Actual DLH | 40,000 hrs. | ? |
| Actual direct labor cost per hour | $7 | $7.20 |
| Total direct labor | ? | 342 |
| Originally planned overhead | 360 | 396 |
| Under-(over-)applied overhead | 25 | ? |
| Actual overhead | ? | 410 |
| Beginning WIP inventory | 60 | ? |

|                                    | 19X5 | 19X6 |
|------------------------------------|------|------|
| Ending WIP inventory               | 50   | 70   |
| Cost of goods manufactured         | ?    | ?    |
| Beginning finished goods inventory | 140  | ?    |
| Ending finished goods inventory    | 155  | 160  |
| Cost of products sold to customers | ?    | 980  |
| Reported cost of goods sold        | 820  | ?    |

a) Determine each of the missing items (identified with ?) for 19X5.

b) Assume that actual costs had already been journalized to:

> Gross purchases
> Freight-in
> Purchase returns
> Purchase discounts
> Beginning inventory balances
> Direct labor
> Manufacturing overhead

Prepare all necessary journal entries to close the cost accounts, record ending inventory, and determine cost of goods sold.

**SP 13.12** Refer to Problem SP 13.11. Complete the same two requirements (a) and (b) for the year 19X6.

**SP 13.13** The Jaygo Company used a full standard cost system with raw materials inventory carried at standard. The following data (rounded to even thousands of dollars) was taken from the company's records for 19X2 and 19X3:

|                                                  | 19X2   | 19X3  |
|--------------------------------------------------|--------|-------|
| Beginning raw materials inventory                | $300   | $ ?   |
| Ending raw materials inventory                   | 250    | 265   |
| Net purchases                                    | 410    | 480   |
| Unfavorable (favorable) material price variance  | 10     | (20)  |
| Unfavorable (favorable) material usage variance  | 20     | 10    |
| Raw materials used                               | ?      | ?     |
| Actual direct labor                              | 900    | 915   |
| Direct labor applied                             | 840    | 928   |
| Unfavorable (favorable) labor variance           | ?      | ?     |
| Actual overhead                                  | 875    | 1,055 |
| Under-(over-)applied overhead                    | (45)   | ?     |
| Overhead applied                                 | ?      | 1,025 |
| Beginning WIP inventory                          | 120    | ?     |
| Ending WIP inventory                             | 140    | 128   |
| Cost of goods manufactured                       | ?      | ?     |
| Beginning finished goods inventory               | 360    | 335   |
| Ending finished goods inventory                  | ?      | 345   |
| Cost of products sold to customers               | ?      | 2,430 |
| Reported cost of goods sold                      | 2,240  | ?     |

a) Determine each of the missing (identified with ?) items for 19X2.

b) Assume that actual costs had already been posted to:

Net purchases
Beginning inventory balances
Direct labor
Manufacturing overhead

Prepare all necessary journal entries to close the cost accounts, record ending inventory, and determine cost of goods sold.

SP 13.14   Refer to Problem SP 13.13 above. Complete the same two requirements (a) and (b) for the year 19X3.


## SUGGESTIONS FOR FURTHER READING

Horngren, C., *Cost Accounting: A Managerial Emphasis*, Fourth Edition. Englewood Cliffs, N.J.: Prentice-Hall, Inc., 1977; Chapters 7 and 9.

Morse, Wayne J., *Cost Accounting: Processing, Evaluating, and Using Cost Data*. Reading, Massachusetts: Addison-Wesley Publishing Company, 1978; Chapter 13.

CHAPTER 13 APPENDIX

# Review of Recording Procedures for Product Costs

(*Note.* If you have not recently completed a course in elementary financial accounting, you should read Appendices D and E at the back of this book before proceeding.)

In this appendix it will be assumed that all product-related costs have already been recorded by a debit to the appropriate cost account and a credit to cash, accounts payable, or an expiring asset. Recall that a cost account accumulates costs that are part of inventory costs (product costs). Cost accounts differ from expense accounts. Expense accounts accumulate costs that are to be written off or expensed in the current period (period costs).

## Merchandiser's Inventory

A merchandiser (wholesaler or retailer of products) has only a single inventory account appearing on the balance sheet and often identified as merchandise inventory.[9] Usually acquisitions, and acquisition-related adjustments, are **not** recorded directly into the merchandise inventory account. Instead entries involve one or more of four inventory cost accounts:

> Gross Purchases
> Freight-In
> Purchase Returns
> Purchase Discounts

These accounts comprise net purchases, and may be closed to such an account at year-(period-)end (see Fig. 13.2).

---

[9]   Merchandise inventory is the control (summary) account appearing on the balance sheet. A retailer following the retail accounting method (see below) will usually maintain separate subsidiary or detail inventory accounts for each product group or department. Merchandisers not following the retail inventory method must maintain separate subsidiary accounts for each product or homogeneous product group in order to properly identify cost changes occurring during the year.

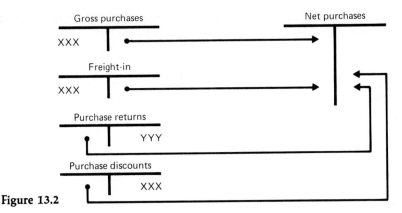

**Figure 13.2**

As an example, assume the following four events eventually resulting in net purchases of $91,200:

- Merchandise purchased at invoice price of $100,000
- Related incoming freight bill of $3,000
- Merchandise costing $10,000 found to be defective and returned
- Invoice paid in full, within discount period, with $88,200

The related journal entries would be:

|  | DR | CR |
|---|---|---|
| Gross purchases | $100,000 | |
|    Accounts payable | | $100,000 |
| Freight-in | 3,000 | |
|    Accounts payable | | 3,000 |
| Accounts payable (or receivable) | 10,000 | |
|    Purchase returns | | 10,000 |
| Accounts payable | 90,000 | |
|    Cash | | 88,200 |
| | | 1,800 |

Closing to net purchases would involve:

|  | DR | CR |
|---|---|---|
| Net purchases | $91,200 | |
| Purchase returns | 10,000 | |
| Purchase discounts | 1,800 | |
|    Gross purchases | | $100,000 |
|    Freight-in | | 3,000 |

Following the periodic inventory method, at year-(period-)end purchases and beginning inventory are first closed to cost of goods sold. The amount of ending inventory determined actually to be on hand as a result of a physical inventory is then recorded as a "correction" or adjustment to the original one-hundred-percent write-off.[10]

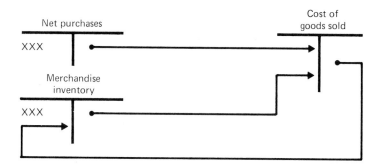

Continuing with the same illustration, and assuming beginning inventory of $11,000 and ending inventory of $12,000, cost of goods sold would be $90,200:

|  | DR | CR |
|---|---|---|
| Cost of goods sold | $102,200 | |
|    Net purchases | | $91,200 |
|    Merchandise inventory | | 11,000 |
| Merchandise inventory | 12,000 | |
|    Cost of goods sold | | 12,000 |

Under a perpetual inventory system, merchandise shipments would be recorded throughout the year. The year- or period-end inventory balance would then be adjusted to the actual amount determined by physical count. This would correct the ending inventory data for clerical errors and merchandise shrinkage (deterioration and theft).

In the above illustration, assume that recorded shipments throughout the year had been $87,000. A shrinkage adjustment of $3,200 would be required in order to arrive at ending inventory of $12,000:

---

[10] Ending inventory cost would be determined from an actual physical count, with dollars assigned as a result of applying the  retail inventory method and/or appropriate cost flow assumptions (LIFO, FIFO, average cost) discussed in Appendix D at the back of this book.

|  | DR | CR |
|---|---|---|
| Merchandise inventory | $91,200 | |
| Net purchases | | $91,200 |
| Cost of good sold | 87,000 | |
| Merchandise inventory | | 87,000 |
| Cost of goods sold | 3,200 | |
| Merchandise inventory | | 3,200 |

## Retail Inventory Method

Where cost records for each separate product may be economically maintained, determining the cost of ending inventory from a physical count is merely a matter of extension and totalling. Many retailers find that they cannot afford either cost records by item or a perpetual inventory system.[11] These firms must estimate the cost of their ending inventory by using selling price as a basis. The retail inventory method involves obtaining an average ratio between the cost and the selling price of all merchandise (goods) available for sale. A physical inventory is then taken, and extended at selling price (selling price for each item is readily available at the time of the physical count). The cost of ending inventory is then estimated by applying the goods-available ratio.

A specific example should assist you in understanding the retail inventory method. Assume that a firm had a beginning inventory of merchandise costing $300,000 and priced at selling at $550,000. During the year, additional merchandise costing $1,800,000 is acquired and priced or marked to sell for $3,000,000. Also, during the year certain slow-moving merchandise was marked down (reduction of originally planned selling price) $50,000 to encourage sales. Can you determine the goods available for sale ratio? If ending physical inventory were $450,000 at selling (priced in terms of selling prices), what would be a reasonable estimate of ending inventory at cost?

|  | Cost | Selling |
|---|---|---|
| Beginning inventory | $ 300,000 | $ 550,000 |
| Net purchases | 1,800,000 | 3,000,000 |
| Markdowns | — | (50,000) |
| Goods available for sale | $2,100,000 | $3,500,000 |
| Ending inventory | ? | $450,000 |

From the above table, of all merchandise available for sale, the average gross profit was 40 percent; that is, the average cost is 60 percent of selling price. Assuming that ending inventory was a representative sample of this entire quantity, $270,000 (60 percent of $450,000) would be a reasonable estimate of its cost.

---

[11]   The growing use of computers for unit stock control makes perpetual inventory more feasible, especially for retailers.

Note that the retail method is merely a device for estimating the cost of ending inventory.[12] It is not incorporated in the accounts. Only the final estimate of ending inventory is journalized. Since a single average for all merchandise in a store may be misleading, many firms separately calculate the goods available ratio and estimate ending inventory for each different product group (department). In this way, groups of items with significantly different markups are separately recorded. A change in sales mix among groups with widely differing markups will then not be buried in an overall average.

In its simplest form, when costs are changing, the retail method results in a moving-average approach to inventory measurement similar to the weighted-average method you learned in financial accounting. A method known as retail LIFO may also be used. Retail LIFO is more complicated and is beyond the scope of this text. It is covered in intermediate accounting texts.

## Manufacturer's Inventories

The flow of product costs for a manufacturer was illustrated in Exhibits 1.4, 1.7, 1.8, and 1.9 in Chapter 1 and in various illustrations contained in this chapter. Net purchases are determined in the same manner as for a merchandiser described above. You may also assume that all other manufacturing costs have been journalized to either the direct labor account or to manufacturing overhead.

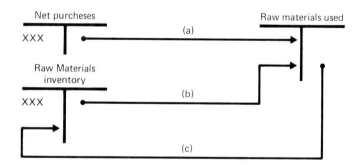

Raw materials used is like cost of goods sold for the raw materials storeroom. All purchases and beginning inventory are first closed to raw materials used. Then ending raw materials inventory (based on a physical count) is reversed to the raw materials inventory account. Assume purchases of $800,000, beginning inventory of $100,000, and ending inventory of $70,000. Entries to determine the $830,000 cost of materials used would be:

---

|                                  | DR        | CR        |
| -------------------------------- | --------- | --------- |
| (a) Raw materials used           | $800,000  |           |
|       Net purchases              |           | $800,000  |
| (b) Raw materials used           | $100,000  |           |
|       Raw materials inventory    |           | $100,000  |
| (c) Raw materials inventory      | 70,000    |           |
|       Raw materials used         |           | 70,000    |

If the firm were on a standard cost system, wished to isolate materials price variance at the time of purchase, and carried raw materials inventory at standard, entries (a), (b), and (c), above would all be made at standard (actual quantity times standard price). Any balance in the net purchases account would represent a material price variance (debit = unfavorable), and would be closed to cost of goods sold.

The same cycle is repeated for work-in-process. The only difference is that there are three inputs. Cost of goods manufactured (goods transferred to finished goods inventory) is like cost of goods sold for the factory floor. Beginning work-in-process inventory ($200,000), materials used ($830,000), direct labor ($1,600,000), and manufacturing overhead ($3,200,000) are all first closed to cost of goods manufactured. Ending work-in-process inventory ($330,000) is then reversed to the work-in-process inventory account.

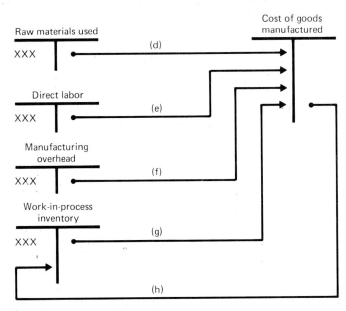

|                                       | DR          | CR          |
| ------------------------------------- | ----------- | ----------- |
| (d) Cost of goods manufactured        | $830,000    |             |
|       Raw materials used              |             | $830,000    |
| (e) Cost of goods manufactured        | 1,600,000   |             |
|       Direct labor                    |             | 1,600,000   |
| (f) Cost of goods manufactured        | 3,200,000   |             |
|       Manufacturing overhead          |             | 3,200,000   |

|  | DR | CR |
|---|---|---|
| (g) Cost of goods manufactured | 200,000 | |
| Work-in-process inventory | | 200,000 |
| (h) Work-in-process inventory | 330,000 | |
| Cost of goods manufactured | | 330,000 |

Where a firm uses a predetermined overhead rate or an overhead standard, entry (f) will be at a standard amount. Any remaining balance (over- or underapplied overhead) will then be closed to cost of goods sold or prorated to inventories and cost of goods sold.

Where a firm uses standard costs, entries (d) through (h) will all be made at standard. Accounting variances remaining in materials used, direct labor, and manufacturing overhead will be closed to cost of goods sold or prorated.

Cost of goods sold is finally determined in a third cycle. It will not be illustrated, since it is the same cycle first described above for a merchandiser. For a manufacturer, the account cost of goods manufactured inputs finished goods rather than net purchases. If beginning finished goods had been $570,000, cost of goods manufactured $5,500,000, and ending finished goods $510,000, then cost of goods sold would be $5,560,000:

|  | DR | CR |
|---|---|---|
| Cost of goods sold | $6,070,000 | |
| Cost of goods manufactured | | $5,500,000 |
| Finished goods inventory | | 570,000 |
| Finished goods inventory | 510,000 | |
| Cost of goods sold | | 510,000 |

# 14

---

# CONTROL OF REVENUE,
# PROFIT,
# AND
# INVESTMENT CENTERS

CHAPTER PREVIEW

The goal of this chapter is to complete your introduction to budgetary control for business firms. Chapters 12 and 13 were devoted to control of expenditure centers. This chapter is devoted to performance reporting for other types of responsibility centers including revenue, profit, and investment centers. In this chapter you can:

- Learn the characteristics of a so-called revenue center, and how performance reports for revenue centers may include information on both revenue earned and expenditures incurred to generate revenue.

- Discover that budgeting and control of expenditures is essentially the same whether part of a revenue center or an expenditure center.

- Develop an understanding that the analysis of overall revenue variance is parallel to the analysis of direct material and direct labor variances under a standard cost system. They all three involve separately identifying the effects of changes in price and quantity (volume).

- Learn that revenue variances, in addition to price and quantity changes, may be caused by changes in planned product (sales) mix, and develop the ability to determine and properly interpret sales price, sales quantity and sales mix variances.

- Discover that revenue and expenditure variance analysis techniques may also be used to analyze a firm's overall performance as reported in its income statement.

- Discover a third type of responsibility center known as a profit center, and learn some of the benefits of using profit centers as control instruments.

- Explore the problems involving cost allocations and transfer prices in the context of profit centers.

- Discover that the fourth type of responsibility center for budgeting and control purposes is known as an investment center, and that investment centers are simply further logical extensions of the profit center concept.

- Learn that, in parallel to cost allocation difficulties for profit centers, there are several alternatives for allocating investment to investment centers, each with strengths and weaknesses.

- Develop an understanding of the various approaches to evaluating the performance of profit and investment centers and the informational benefits and limitations of each.

- Explore some of the undesirable behavior that may result from certain control measures and from current (GAAP) financial reporting requirements, and develop an appreciation for the continuing need for appropriate management judgment in specific circumstances.

In the appendix to this chapter you may learn how several current GAAP requirements for external financial reporting may have an adverse or undesirable effect upon internal management decisions.

When you have assimilated the material contained in this chapter, you will have completed your introduction to business cost accounting, budgeting, and control. In subsequent chapters you may expand this knowledge to include budgeting and control in nonprofit-directed organizations, proposals for accounting and decision making in periods of inflation, and more sophisticated quantitative techniques applicable to managerial accounting activities.

## HOW GOOD A JOB IS THE SALES VICE-PRESIDENT DOING?

To this point, discussion of budgetary control has focused upon control of expenditures within expenditure centers. Revenue center reports require slightly different analysis. Recall from Chapter 11 that, whereas expenditure centers essentially have only expenditures,[1] revenue centers have both revenues and expenditures, revenues being the primary focus of attention and control.

The Tripper sales department budget performance report for June, 19X2, is given in Exhibit 14.1. Study this exhibit carefully and note the significant differences between a sales performance report and those expenditure-center reports with which you are already familiar (Chapters 12 and 13). In addition to a subsection for sales and marketing expenditures, the report discloses sales revenue and also has a separate subsection for sales-related data based upon but not normally included in the firm's accounting system. Note that budgeted sales are shown as the amount originally budgeted in the fixed budget. Revenue variance therefore is analogous to total fixed budget variance (spending variance plus volume variance) for an expenditure.

Expenditures for sales and marketing are reported in the pattern with which you are already familiar. Budgeted figures represent flexible budget amounts based on actual sales; and the variance is a spending variance. Note that the information disclosed for contribution is different from either the pattern for revenue or that for expenditure. Budgeted contribution represents the total contribution (sales revenue less all sales, marketing, manufacturing, purchasing, and general administrative variable costs) planned in the original (fixed) budget. The $103,610 shown in the "actual" column does **not** represent actual contribution earned in July. Instead it represents the variable budgeted contribution, the contribution that would be earned from actual sales if there were no variable cost spending variances. The $28,270 unfavorable contribution variance is analogous to a volume variance. It discloses the amount of original planned contribution that is expected to be lost because of actual sales being different from what was originally budgeted. Note that total expected contribution variance can result both from lower volume and also from change in product/sales mix, as will be discussed below. It represents that portion of contribution controllable by the sales and marketing department. Actual contribution for the period (**not** shown on the sales performance report) may still differ from the $103,610 of variable budget expected contribution, as a result of variable cost spending variances throughout the organization.

Observe, in Exhibit 14.1, that total sales revenue for the year is running substantially below budget ($88,750 unfavorable), and that June was a particularly disappointing month. How significant to the firm is the current month's $72,920 unfavorable revenue variance? Does this represent $72,920 of lost profit?

---

[1]   Recall that expenditure centers may have minor secondary revenue, such as the proceeds from the sale of scrap material.

**Exhibit 14.1**

TRIPPER WATER SKI MANUFACTURING COMPANY

**Budget Performance Report, Sales Department—June, 19X2**

| | Current month | | | | Year-to-date | | | |
|---|---|---|---|---|---|---|---|---|
| | Fixed/ flexible budget | Actual/ flexible budget | Variance | % | Fixed/ flexible budget | Actual/ flexible budget | Variance | % |
| Sales[1] | $204,800 | $131,880 | $72,920 U | 35.6 | $756,000 | $667,250 | $88,750 U | 11.7 |
| Sales and marketing expenditures:[2] | | | | | | | | |
| Wages and salaries | 10,350 | 10,350 | 0 | 0 | 62,100 | 62,100 | 0 | 0 |
| Distribution | 790 | 940 | 150 U | 19.0 | 4,000 | 4,400 | 400 U | 10.0 |
| Advertising | 800 | 700 | 100 F | 12.5 | 4,800 | 5,000 | 200 U | 4.2 |
| Travel | 685 | 725 | 40 U | 5.8 | 2,595 | 2,730 | 135 U | 5.2 |
| Miscellaneous | 100 | 80 | 20 F | 20.0 | 300 | 350 | 50 U | 16.7 |
| Total expenditures | $ 12,725 | $ 12,725 | $    70 U | 0.6 | $ 73,795 | $ 74,580 | 785 U | 1.1 |
| Sales-related data: | | | | | | | | |
| Total expected contribution[3] | $131,880 | $103,610 | $28,270 U | 21.4 | $486,315 | $419,085 | $67,230 U | 13.8 |
| Past-due order backlog[4] | 0 | $ 14,300 | $14,300 U | 1.5 | — | — | — | — |
| Average collection period (days) | 45 | 44 | — | — | 45 | 45 | — | — |
| Market share (%) | 4.5 | 4.2 | 0.3 U | — | 4.5 | 4.1 | 0.4 U | — |

[1] Amount shown in first column is original (fixed) budgeted amount.
[2] Amounts shown in first column are revised (flexible) budgeted expenditures.
[3] Amount shown in first column is based on original (fixed) sales budget. Amounts shown in actual and variance columns are flexible budgeted contribution and contribution volume variance, respectively.
[4] Amount shown in percent column is average days' budgeted sales (assuming 21.5 shipping days per month).

Also, note that sales and marketing expenditures appear to be well under control. There is no need for you to review the process of expenditure control within revenue centers because the elements are similar to those found in expenditure centers. Revenue center expenditures may be readily controlled through variable budgets, and they differ from manufacturing expenditures in only two ways. First, revenue-generating expenditures usually involve a higher proportion of programmed and fixed costs. Second, the analysis of expenditure variances within revenue centers may require more judgment. Where possible, manufacturing, general, and administrative expenditures should be decreased with lower-than-planned activity levels. However, when sales volume is declining or is lower than expected, it may be in the best interest of a firm to **increase** certain expenditures designated to generate future revenue. For instance, additional travel costs, or even expenditures for market research, might be warranted, in order to determine why expected sales are not materializing.

## ELEMENTS OF REVENUE CONTROL

Returning to the control of revenues and Tripper's unfavorable overall revenue variance, there are two distinct elements or objectives of revenue control. The first objective is to ensure that total revenue meets budget, or that any significant variance is explained so that corrective action or rebudgeting may be undertaken. The second objective is to identify any significant variation in sales mix that might also alter eventual profit. And, finally, there are several revenue-related factors where control information may be useful. Such factors include market share, order backlog, and average collection period. You can now proceed to become familiar with the significance of each of the elements associated with revenue control.

### Revenue Variance

The total revenue variance ($88,750 unfavorable year-to-date in Exhibit 14.1) may result from either or both a change in price or a change in quantity. The analysis of revenue variance follows the same pattern used for materials or labor variances within a standard cost system. You should already be familiar with these patterns from your study of the material in Chapter 13.

Actual revenue can vary from budget as a result of a *sales price variance.* In many firms the sales department is authorized to make price changes during the year, where such changes are believed necessary or desirable to maximize revenue.[2] Price changes may take the form of an increase or decrease in posted

---

[2]   Care must be exercised to ensure that price changes do not result in discrimination among customers of the same type, in violation of the Robinson–Patman Act (Chapter 6 Appendix).

or listed prices from those incorporated in the original budget. They may also take the form of special discounts and allowances on certain items.

The sales price variance is calculated by multiplying the actual quantity sold by the difference between the actual price obtained and the standard or budgeted price:

$$\begin{pmatrix} \text{Sales} \\ \text{price} \\ \text{variance} \end{pmatrix} = \begin{pmatrix} \text{Actual price} - \\ \text{Standard price} \end{pmatrix} \times \begin{pmatrix} \text{Actual} \\ \text{quantity} \\ \text{sold} \end{pmatrix}.$$

This computation must be performed for each separate product. Year-to-date detailed information for Tripper is:

|  | Actual price | Standard price | Actual quantity sold | Sales price variance |
|---|---|---|---|---|
| Economy skis | $50 | $50 | 8,000 | ? |
| Deluxe skis | 75 | 80 | 3,150 | ? |
| Tow ropes | 10 | 10 | 3,100 | ? |

Calculate the sales price variance, before proceeding.

In this Tripper example, the only price change from budgeted prices occurred for deluxe skis; possibly discounts were being offered to spur lagging sales. The sales price variance was $15,750 unfavorable, all coming from deluxe skis and indicating that, of the year-to-date's $88,750 of revenue reduction, $15,750 resulted from lower-than planned prices or from price discounts. Note that the term reduction is used instead of loss. Assuming that the skis could not have been sold for more than their actual selling price, the $15,750 represents a reduction in overly optimistic expectations, as differentiated from a loss of something actually possessed by the firm.

Also note that, in the case of revenue performance, a negative variance represents less-than-planned inflow, and is, therefore, denoted as unfavorable (reduction in income). This is the opposite of the case for expenditure variances, where a negative variance represents less-than-planned expense, more-than-planned income, and, therefore, a favorable variance.

The sales price variance is as important to monitor as a spending variance in an expenditure center. Sales price variance is controllable by the sales department and, dollar for dollar, an unfavorable sales price variance has the same effect as an unfavorable spending variance: they both reduce net income. In the Tripper example, assuming that some unplanned expenditure or price cut was essential to achieve planned sales quantity, management should be confident that a price cut represented the least costly approach. Perhaps a different outlay (additional promotion expenditure) could achieve the same result at less cost.

Total revenue is also affected by the volume of units sold. The *sales volume variance* is calculated by multiplying the standard or budgeted price by the difference between the actual quantity sold and the budgeted quantity:

$$\begin{pmatrix} \text{Sales} \\ \text{volume} \\ \text{variance} \end{pmatrix} = \begin{pmatrix} \text{Actual quantity} - \\ \text{Budgeted quantity} \end{pmatrix} \times \begin{pmatrix} \text{Standard} \\ \text{price} \end{pmatrix}.$$

Again, the computation must be performed for each separate product. For Tripper, for the first half of 19X2:

|  | Actual quantity sold | Budgeted quantity to be sold | Standard or budgeted price |
|---|---|---|---|
| Economy skis | 8,000 | 7,500 | $50 |
| Deluxe skis | 3,150 | 4,350 | 80 |
| Tow ropes | 3,100 | 3,300 | 10 |

From the above data, you should calculate the year-to-date sales volume variance, before proceeding.

The correct volume variances on a year-to-date basis are:

| | | |
|---|---|---|
| Economy skis | $25,000 | F |
| Deluxe skis | 96,000 | U |
| Tow ropes | 2,000 | U |
| | $73,000 | U |

Note that greater-than-planned sales of economy skis partially offset the lower sales of deluxe skis and tow ropes for a **net** unfavorable variance of $73,000. The $73,000 unfavorable sales volume variance represents the revenue shortfall from budget that may be attributed to lower quantities of units sold. Together with the $15,750 unfavorable price variance, it explains the total $88,750 unfavorable year-to-date revenue variance shown in Exhibit 14.1:

| | | |
|---|---|---|
| Sales price variance | $15,750 | U |
| Sales volume variance | 73,000 | U |
| Total revenue variance | $88,750 | U |

Before leaving sales price and sales volume variances, you should note that, for variety, they were both illustrated on a year-to-date basis. Of course management would also desire this information for the current month. The calculations (not illustrated) would be identical but based on data for monthly unit sales and prices.

## Contribution Variance

For a firm with only a single product, assuming variable costs could be controlled, an $88,750 unfavorable revenue variance would only result in reduced income equal to the contribution loss resulting from reduced sales of the one product. Can you see where, in the multiproduct firm, the contribution loss could be less, or even **greater?**

Assume the following facts for Tripper:

|  | Economy ski | Deluxe ski | Tow rope |
|---|---|---|---|
| Selling price | $50.00 | $80.00 | $10.00 |
| Variable cost | 19.20 | 25.10 | 5.00 |
| Unit contribution | $30.80 | $54.90 | $ 5.00 |
| Unit contribution percent | 61.6 | 68.6 | 50 |

Recall, from the initial discussion of contribution in Chapter 6, that a change in product mix may result in a change in total contribution, even with no change in total revenue. The *contribution mix variance,* together with the sales price variance, measure the total *expected contribution variance* (the difference between expected variable budgeted contribution and the originally budgeted contribution).

The contribution mix variance measures the change in contribution resulting from variation in sales volume, assuming no change in unit selling prices or unit variable costs.[3] It is calculated for each separate product by multiplying the budgeted contribution per unit by the difference between actual and budgeted unit sales:

$$\begin{pmatrix} \text{Contribution} \\ \text{mix variance} \end{pmatrix} = \begin{pmatrix} \text{Actual unit sales} - \\ \text{Budgeted unit sales} \end{pmatrix} \times \begin{pmatrix} \text{Budgeted unit} \\ \text{contribution} \end{pmatrix}.$$

From the data supplied both above and earlier for use in calculating the sales volume variance, you should determine Tripper's contribution mix variance for the first half of 19X2, before proceeding.

You are correct if you determine the contribution mix variance to be $51,480 unfavorable:

|  | Actual unit sales | Budgeted unit sales | Budgeted unit contribution | Contribution mix variance |
|---|---|---|---|---|
| Economy skis | 8,000 | 7,500 | $30.80 | $15,400 F |
| Deluxe skis | 3,150 | 4,350 | 54.90 | 65,880 U |
| Tow ropes | 3,100 | 3,300 | 5.00 | 1,000 U |
| Total |  |  |  | $51,480 U |

The $51,480 unfavorable contribution mix variance discloses the potential seriousness of the revenue sales variance with respect to budgeted profit. It assumes no price variances and no spending variances affecting variable prod-

---

[3]  Changes in variable costs are controlled and reported on expenditure budgets for both revenue and expenditure centers.

uct costs. Together with the sales price variance, it reflects the total unfavorable year-to-date expected contribution variance of $67,230, as reported in Exhibit 14.1:

| | |
|---|---|
| Contribution mix variance | $51,480  U |
| Sales price variance | 15,750  U |
| Total expected contribution variance | $67,230  U |

The total expected contribution variance is also known as the marketing variance, since it pinpoints potential change in budgeted net income resulting from sales and marketing activity. Note that the two components provide information for use in separate investigations by the sales department relating to remedial action. As mentioned above, the sales price variance should be investigated to ensure that it did not result from:

- unrealistic prices included in the original budget,
- unnecessary price changes or discounts, or
- price changes or discounts that could have been more efficiently replaced at less cost with other types of sales promotion expenditure.

The contribution mix variance similarly may be further investigated to ensure that:

- budgeted sales mix is realistic, and
- sales and promotional activities are properly balanced to achieve the desired sales mix.

### Other Sales-Related Data

Revenue, sales, or marketing control may also involve budgeting and reporting other data, including such items as order backlog, average collection period, market share, and even units shipped. *Order backlog* represents the dollar value of orders received but not yet shipped to customers. In some firms such as machine-tool manufacturers, orders may precede production, and be scheduled for future delivery. In such instances, reported backlog information may be split into not-yet-due and past-due amounts. The size of the firm's not-yet-due order backlog may serve as a valuable measure of sales performance. (Not-yet-due backlog is not illustrated, since it is not applicable to Tripper.) For most firms, customer orders received are for immediate delivery.

For all firms, past-due backlog (backorders) serves as an indicator of delays in the order-filling and shipping activity, or in production. Past-due backlog information is important for sales and production management as an indication of potential customer dissatisfaction and possible lost future orders. In Exhibit 14.1 for Tripper, past-due order backlog amounts to $11,500. Significance may be measured by average days' sales ordered but not yet shipped, which in Tripper's case was only 1.5 days. This small delay may be considered as normal order processing, packing, and shipping time for Tripper.

*Average collection period* (days) for accounts receivable may also be included on the sale department's performance report. Even though primary responsibility for collections may be assigned to the credit department under the controller, the sales department has influence. Sales may be pushed too hard to slow-paying customers, or in such large amounts that individual customers are no longer able to pay on time. Abuses of credit as a sales and marketing tool can lead to costs (costs of capital tied up in receivables and uncollectible accounts) exceeding the benefits of additional sales. Since average receivables (or average collection period) are affected by sales activity, the item meets the test of controllability. It can provide a useful measure of the effectiveness of the firm's credit policy as a sales tool, when considered in conjunction with revenue performance.

*Market share,* or the percentage of the entire market represented by the particular firm's sales, can also be a meaningful performance measure. A firm will often budget a target share of the overall market. Viewed in conjunction with revenue, market share may provide an indication of the cause of a sales variance. In Tripper's case (Exhibit 14.1) both revenue and market share are off budget in approximately equal proportions. This would indicate a clear failure by Tripper to achieve the budget, or perhaps excessively optimistic budgeting. Had the market share been constant or increasing at the same time as sales were below budget, this fact would provide an indication that any problem was industry-wide and not necessarily within the firm's immediate control.

One other item of information (not previously illustrated for Tripper) is often included on sales performance reports for those firms having a single or perhaps a very few products. Budgeted and actual amounts may be more meaningful if they are expressed in terms of units of product. The measure may be less abstract than aggregate dollars. For example, Tripper's current unfavorable sales variance may be readily perceived when June performance is reported as:

|  | Units budgeted | Units actually sold | Variance in units |
|---|---|---|---|
| Economy skis | 2,000 | 2,100 | 100 F |
| Deluxe skis | 1,200 | 700 | 500 U |
| Tow ropes | 880 | 800 | 80 U |

Note that reporting activity in units of product clearly identifies the volume variance. However, it cannot replace total revenue reporting, as otherwise a possible price variance would not be disclosed.

## Revenue Reports by Responsibility Center

Reporting performance in measures other than dollars (units sold, number of orders received, number of customer calls/visits, and so forth) can be especially effective at first-level responsibility centers. Dollar aggregates are more meaningful at the higher levels of management reporting, since they serve as a common denominator for diverse activities. In firms larger than Tripper, revenue-center reporting may be divided by individual responsibility centers following the same pattern as previously illustrated for individual manufacturing departments. Depending upon the firm's marketing organization, revenue-center reporting could be by geographic selling territories, product groups, customer groups, or some combination of these.

## HOW WELL IS THE FIRM DOING OVERALL?

In Chapters 12 and 13 you have been introduced to control reporting at the level of first-line supervision. Aggregation to the vice-presidential level within the Tripper organization has been demonstrated above for revenue-center reporting. The obvious next step is budgetary control at the total firm level.

In your role as the owner and president of Tripper, assume that it is January of 19X3. You have completed the 19X3 budget, and you are awaiting the final results for 19X2. In late January, your controller delivers two reports that are significant to operations control at your level—the master operating budget performance report for December, 19X2, and the 19X2 budgeted and actual income statements.[4]

The master operating budget performance report for the month (Exhibit 14.2) indicates that, in December, all three vice-presidents had their individual centers reasonably under control. For the total year, variances by functional area were:

| | |
|---|---:|
| Sales vice-president: | |
| Sales | $31,600  U |
| Revenue generating expenditures | 1,251  U |
| Operations vice-president: | |
| Manufacturing costs | 1,000  U |
| Controller: | |
| Accounting and administrative costs | 9,010  U |

You may also assume that sales for the year were comprised of:

> 13,000  economy skis sold at $50 each
> 6,970  deluxe skis sold at $75 each
> 5,925  tow ropes sold at $10 each

Applying tools of revenue analysis introduced earlier in this chapter, together with Tripper's data for budgeted quantities, selling prices, and unit

---

[4]   You would also be interested in the effectiveness and efficiency of the firm's financial management, and would probably start with a comparison between the firm's budgeted and actual SCFP and balance sheet. Control and analysis of this type is more appropriately covered in courses in Finance and Financial Management. It will not be illustrated or covered in this text.

**Exhibit 14.2**

TRIPPER WATER SKI MANUFACTURING COMPANY

**Master Operating Budget Performance Report—December, 19X2**

| | Current month | | | | Year-to-date | | | |
|---|---|---|---|---|---|---|---|---|
| | Budget | Actual | Variance | % | Budget | Actual | Variance | % |
| **Manufacturing:** | | | | | | | | |
| Purchases | $      0 | $      0 | $      0 | 0 | $ 153,000 | $ 155,000 | $ 2,000 U | 1.3 |
| Direct labor | 0 | 0 | 0 | 0 | 208,000 | 209,000 | 1,000 U | 0.5 |
| Indirect labor | $ 9,583 | $10,000 | 417 U | 4.4 | 164,000 | 162,000 | 2,000 F | 1.2 |
| Indirect materials | 440 | 210 | 230 F | 52.3 | 21,000 | 19,000 | 2,000 F | 9.5 |
| Supervision | 5,415 | 5,500 | 85 U | 1.6 | 65,000 | 66,000 | 1,000 U | 1.5 |
| Utilities | 600 | 500 | 100 F | 16.7 | 19,000 | 20,000 | 1,000 U | 5.3 |
| Insurance | 0 | 0 | 0 | 0 | 13,000 | 13,000 | 0 | 0 |
| Property taxes | 0 | 0 | 0 | 0 | 18,000 | 18,000 | 0 | 0 |
| Total expenditures | $16,038 | $16,210 | $ 172 U | 0.01 | $ 661,000 | $ 662,000 | $ 1,000 U | 1.6 |
| **Sales and marketing:** | | | | | | | | |
| Sales | $27,000 | $28,000 | $1,000 F | 3.7 | $1,264,000 | $1,232,000 | $32,000 U | 2.5 |
| Wages and salaries | 10,350 | 10,350 | 0 | 0 | 124,200 | 124,200 | 0 | 0 |
| Distribution | 168 | 175 | 7 U | 4.2 | 7,394 | 7,600 | 206 U | 2.8 |
| Advertising | 800 | 600 | 200 F | 25.0 | 9,600 | 9,900 | 300 U | 3.1 |
| Travel | 476 | 412 | 64 F | 13.4 | 7,505 | 8,400 | 895 U | 11.9 |
| Miscellaneous | 100 | 125 | 25 U | 25.0 | 1,200 | 1,050 | 150 F | 12.5 |
| Total expenditures | $11,894 | $11,662 | $ 232 F | 2.0 | $ 149,899 | $ 151,150 | $ 1,251 U | 1.0 |
| **Accounting and administrative:** | | | | | | | | |
| Wages and salaries | $17,000 | $18,000 | $1,000 U | 5.9 | $ 204,000 | $ 212,000 | $ 8,000 U | 3.9 |
| Insurance | — | — | — | | 3,960 | 4,000 | 40 U | 1.0 |
| Interest | — | — | — | | 13,920 | 14,750 | 830 U | 6.0 |
| Property taxes | — | — | — | | 6,000 | 6,000 | 0 | 0 |
| Miscellaneous | 240 | 210 | 30 F | 12.5 | 2,880 | 3,020 | 140 U | 4.9 |
| Total expenditures | $17,240 | $18,210 | $9,700 U | 5.6 | $ 230,760 | $ 239,770 | $ 9,010 U | 3.9 |

contributions, you should determine the following for the Tripper Company for 19X2, before proceeding:

1. The sales price and sales volume components of Tripper's $32,000 unfavorable revenue variance.

2. The expected contribution variance.

3. The expected unfavorable gross profit variance.

4. The expected unfavorable variance for income from operations before taxes.

You correctly understand the calculation and use of revenue-related variances if you anticipate that income from operations before taxes will be reported as $44,000 lower than originally budgeted. This new expected income figure results from several sequential analytical steps. Exhibit 14.3 indicates that the $32,000 reduction in anticipated revenue resulted from a $2,850 favorable volume variance being offset by a $34,850 unfavorable price variance.

Total expected contribution will, therefore, be reduced by approximately $33,000 ($34,850 unfavorable price variance and $1,393 favorable mix vari-

**Exhibit 14.3**

**TRIPPER WATER SKI MANUFACTURING COMPANY**

| Revenue Related Variances for 19X2 | | | |
|---|---|---|---|
| **Sales price variance** | Actual price | Standard price | Actual quantity | Sales variance |
| Economy skis | $50 | $50 | 13,000 | 0 |
| Deluxe skis | 75 | 80 | 6,970 | $34,850 U |
| Tow ropes | 10 | 10 | 5,925 | 0 |
| Total price variance | | | | $34,850 U |

| **Sales volume variance** | Actual quantity | Budgeted quantity | Standard price | Sales volume variance |
|---|---|---|---|---|
| Economy skis | 13,000 | 12,800 | $50 | $10,000 F |
| Deluxe skis | 6,970 | 7,050 | 80 | 6,400 U |
| Tow ropes | 5,925 | 6,000 | 10 | 750 U |
| Total volume variance | | | | $ 2,850 F |

| **Contribution mix variance** | Actual quantity | Budgeted Quantity | Budgeted unit contribution | Contribution mix variance |
|---|---|---|---|---|
| Economy skis | 13,000 | 12,800 | $30.80 | $ 6,160 F |
| Deluxe skis | 6,970 | 7,050 | 54.90 | 4,392 U |
| Tow ropes | 5,925 | 6,000 | 5.00 | 375 U |
| Total mix variance | | | | $ 1,393 F |

ance). Remember that this expected reduction in contribution assumes no variable cost spending variance. Together with the $1,000 unfavorable manufacturing spending variance (Exhibit 14.2), and assuming that all variable costs used in the calculation of contribution mix are manufacturing costs,[5] expected gross profit would be $34,000 less than originally budgeted.

Exhibits 14.4 and 14.5 present the firm's performance in terms of the financial statements for cost of goods manufactured and for net income. Note how the $1,000 of unfavorable manufacturing spending variance increases cost of goods manufactured and cost of goods sold. Gross profit is $34,000 less than budgeted as a result of the price, mix, and spending variances. The approximately $10,000 of unfavorable spending variance in the general, selling, and administrative areas further reduces expected profit. $44,000 of income shortfall (Exhibit 14.5) is then partially offset by lower-than-planned income tax liability. Net income is, therefore, off by only $29,000. This $29,000 variance still represents 43.3 percent of the revised budgeted amount, with the source of the reduction being almost entirely in the sales price variance.

### Exhibit 14.4
#### TRIPPER WATER SKI MANUFACTURING COMPANY

**Performance Report—Cost of Goods Manufactured, 19X2 (Thousands of Dollars)**

|  | Budget | Actual | Variance | % |
|---|---|---|---|---|
| Direct materials: |  |  |  |  |
| Beginning raw material inventory | $ 4 | $ 4 | 0 | 0 |
| Add: Net purchases | 127 | 130 | $3 U | 2.4 |
| Total raw materials available | $131 | $134 | $3 U | 2.3 |
| Deduct: Ending inventory | 3 | 4 | 1 U | 33.3 |
| Direct materials used | $128 | $130 | $2 U | 1.6 |
| Direct labor | 208 | 209 | 1 | 0.5 |
| Manufacturing overhead |  |  |  |  |
| Indirect labor | 164 | 162 | 2 F | 1.2 |
| Indirect materials | 21 | 19 | 2 F | 9.5 |
| Supervision | 65 | 66 | 1 U | 1.5 |
| Utilities | 19 | 20 | 1 U | 5.3 |
| Insurance | 13 | 13 | 0 | 0 |
| Property taxes | 18 | 18 | 0 | 0 |
| Depreciation | 52 | 52 | 0 | 0 |
| Total overhead | $352 | $350 | 2 F | .6 |
| Total manufacturing costs | 688 | 689 | 1 U | 0.2 |
| Add: Begin. WIP inventory | 18 | 18 | 0 | 0 |
|  | $706 | $707 | $1 U | 0.2 |
| Deduct: Ending WIP inventory | 0 | 0 | 0 | 0 |
| Cost of goods manufactured | $706 | $707 | $1 U | 0.2 |

[5]  Assumed for simplification in this example.

**Exhibit 14.5**

## TRIPPER WATER SKI MANUFACTURING COMPANY

**Performance Report—Income Statement,
19X2 (Thousands of Dollars)**

| | Budget | Actual | Variance | % |
|---|---|---|---|---|
| Sales | $1,264 | $1,232 | $32 U | 2.5 |
| Less cost of goods sold: | | | | |
| Begin. F. G. inventory | 70 | 70 | — | — |
| Cost of goods manufactured | 706 | 707 | 1 U | 0.2 |
| Purchases of finished goods | 26 | 25 | 1 F | 3.8 |
| Goods available for sale | $ 802 | $ 802 | 0 | 0 |
| Less ending inventory | 68 | 66 | 2 U | 2.9 |
| Cost of goods sold | $ 734 | $ 736 | 2 U | 0.3 |
| Gross profit | $ 530 | $ 496 | 34 U | 6.4 |
| Less operating expenses: | | | | |
| Wages and salaries | 328 | 336 | 8 U | 2.4 |
| Marketing and distribution | 26 | 26 | 0 | 0 |
| Interest | 13 | 15 | 2 U | 15.4 |
| Insurance | 4 | 4 | 0 | 0 |
| Property taxes | 6 | 6 | 0 | 0 |
| Miscellaneous | 4 | 4 | 0 | 0 |
| Bad debt expenses | 25 | 26 | 1 U | 4.0 |
| Depreciation | 12 | 12 | 0 | 0 |
| Total operating expenses | $ 418 | $ 429 | $11 U | 2.6 |
| Loss on equipment disp. | 4 | 3 | 1 F | 25.0 |
| Income from operations | $ 108 | $ 64 | $44 U | 40.7 |
| Provision for income tax | 41 | 26 | 15 F | 36.6 |
| Net income | $  67 | $  38 | 29 U | 43.3 |

Many of the techniques for analyzing the overall performance of a firm such as Tripper are also applicable to budgetary control of a segment of a larger firm that is established as a profit center.

## PROFIT CENTERS FOR CONTROL

Many business decisions must take into account certain trade-off considerations involving both cost and revenue. An improvement in product quality (higher cost) might make possible an even greater price increase with a resultant higher contribution. Or a slight price reduction (reduced unit contribution) could so increase volume that total contribution would increase significantly. The necessary close coordination between cost, price, revenue, and contribution-related decisions may be impaired in larger firms if responsibilities continue to be divided solely by separate expenditure and revenue centers. Therefore, many firms establish profit centers for control purposes.

A profit center is an entity for accounting and control purposes that is responsible for a particular group of products and all revenue and most or all expenses associated with these products. Profit centers may be divisions of a large firm that are separately incorporated, and have their own "books" and financial statements. Profit centers may also represent merely artificial accounting entities within the same firm. Profit centers are essentially established for one or more of three reasons:

1. Cost/benefit decisions and trade-offs are delegated to managers close to the sources of necessary information. These managers can often make better decisions than their superiors, who are more remote from necessary information sources.
2. It is believed that managers will do a better job (be more highly motivated) if they can identify their own responsibility centers as having some of the characteristics of their own personal business, and that there will be a greater goal congruence with the profit objectives of top management.
3. A profit center will provide good experience and act as a training ground for future top management.

These reasons are considered to be the benefits of *decentralization* or decentralized authority over decisions. However, decentralization is in itself a distinct concept from profit centers. Each can exist without the other. An expenditure or revenue-center manager may be granted a high degree of autonomy in decision making. Conversely, a profit-center manager may be delegated very little decision authority.

Note that, where decision authority is decentralized (with or without profit centers), advantages may be accompanied by corresponding disadvantages. Managers may tend to establish local service centers that might be more economically centralized (data processing, personnel, and accounting might be examples). Also, managers may make decisions that are undesirable (from the firm's viewpoint) as a result of not having data relevant to the "big picture," or because they may be motivated to improve their own center's performance at the expense of the overall firm's performance (see suboptimization below).

Where profit centers for budgeting and control purposes are used to facilitate decentralization, certain difficulties can arise. These difficulties primarily involve cost allocation and transfer pricing. In Chapter 12, some of the problems related to control of service centers were introduced. Recall the advantages and disadvantages of allocating service-center costs to using departments. Similar advantages and disadvantages exist with respect to common costs involving profit centers. For instance, should a near-autonomous division be charged with a portion of the common cost (with other profit centers) of the central or home office? When two profit centers may be physically located in the same building, should the building costs (depreciation, insurance, taxes, and so forth) be allocated? If so, how?

The arguments against common cost allocation rest on controllability. For example, the salary of the profit-center manager and all of the costs of the home office are not controllable by the manager. Proponents of controllability argue that inclusion of common costs in the profit center's income statement will, at best, divert attention from truly controllable items, and may induce feelings of frustration and defeat in the manager.

The arguments for inclusion are based on the manager's needs for adequate information in order to make optimal pricing decisions. Even though uncontrollable at the level of the profit-center manager, **all** necessary costs must be covered in the long run by revenue before any profit can result. The exclusion of part of the total cost picture on the grounds of controllability could result in a manager targeting inadequate revenue. Also, the manager might not be adequately motivated to tightly control costs in the context of (artificially) high reported profits. Perhaps the best solution is for profit-center performance reports to carry all related costs, and to segregate clearly noncontrollable direct and indirect items. Also, as illustrated below in Exhibit 14.6, controllable segment margins may be developed and noncontrollable allocations shown thereafter.[6]

## Transfer Prices

Related to the common cost and service-center problem, and perhaps even more difficult to resolve in the case of profit centers, is the issue of transfer price. A transfer price is the amount charged by one profit center to another for goods or services provided. Where the providing and receiving managers have no choice in the transfer decision, the problem is simply one of appropriate cost allocation as described above and discussed in Chapter 12.[7] On the other hand, where the providing manager may refuse to supply the using manager in preference to outside customers, or where the using manager has the choice of going to an outside vendor, then the transfer pricing problem exists.

If profit centers did not exist, the decision congruent with overall goals of the firm would be to simply:

- Supply internally if the incremental cost (including opportunity costs) to the supplying division is equal to or less than the purchase cost to the receiving division of the same good or service acquired from an outside source.
- Do not supply internally if incremental costs (including opportunity costs) to the supplying division is greater than the outside purchase cost for the using division.

With profit centers having decision autonomy, and with possible opportunity costs involved, what price could be established that would **always** motivate

---

[6]   Note also that GAAP now requires segment reporting as supplementary disclosure to a firm's external financial statements.

[7]   Such centralization of decision authority and possibly arbitrary cost allocation could be a source of frustration to the managers involved and could also be inconsistent with profit-center decentralization objectives.

**Exhibit 14.6**
PROFIT CENTER PERFORMANCE REPORT
PREPARED ON A NET INCOME BASIS

|  | Budget | Actual | Variance | % |
|---|---|---|---|---|
| Revenue | $485,000 | $470,000 | $15,000 U | 3.1 |
| Variable costs: |  |  |  |  |
| Wages | 120,000 | 115,000 | 5,000 F | 4.2 |
| Materials | 90,000 | 83,000 | 7,000 F | 7.8 |
| Equipment rentals | 30,000 | 29,000 | 1,000 F | 3.3 |
| Utilities | 5,000 | 5,000 | 0 | 0 |
| Miscellaneous | 1,000 | 1,200 | 200 U | 20.0 |
| Total | $246,000 | $233,200 | $12,800 F | 5.2 |
| Contribution to fixed costs and profit | $239,000 | $236,800 | $ 2,200 U | 0.1 |
| Percent of sales | 49.3% | 50.4% | — | — |
| Identifiable/controllable fixed costs: |  |  |  |  |
| Salaries | $ 60,000 | $ 55,000 | $ 5,000 F | 8.3 |
| Depreciation | 20,000 | 20,000 | 0 | 0 |
| Insurance | 15,000 | 16,000 | 1,000 U | 6.7 |
| Property tax | 10,000 | 12,000 | 2,000 U | 20.0 |
| Total | $105,000 | $103,000 | $ 2,000 F | 1.9 |
| Net contribution to common costs and to profit | $134,000 | $133,800 | 200 U | 0.1 |
| Percent of sales | 27.6% | 28.5% | — | — |
| Common costs allocated: |  |  |  |  |
| Home office costs | $ 38,100 | $ 41,000 |  |  |
| Interest | 10,000 | 11,000 |  |  |
| Income taxes | 18,000 | 16,000 |  |  |
| Total | $ 66,100 | $ 68,000 |  |  |
| Divisional net income | $ 67,900 | $ 65,800 |  |  |
| Percent of sales | 14.0% | 14.0% |  |  |

**both** managers to the decision that is in the firm's best interest? Consider a situation with the following facts pertaining to a given interdivisional product or service:

- Incremental cost of providing product or service in supplying division $15,000
- Cost to the using division of obtaining same product or service from outside supplier $20,000
- Revenue obtainable by the supplying division if product or service is sold to outside customers $21,000
- Additional costs in using division $ 5,000
- Revenue obtained by using division $26,000

In this example, so long as the supplying division has excess capacity, the item should be provided internally. The $5,000 difference between supplier cost and the firm's incremental cost would be retained internally to cover fixed costs and profit rather than given to outsiders. What transfer price should be used in this solution so as to motivate **both** managers to seek internal transfer as a way of maximizing their individual profits?

A transfer price set at variable or incremental cost ($15,000) would provide no incentive to the supplying division manager.[8] Although it would motivate desirable internal procurement on the part of the using manager, the variable cost price would provide misleading information to the using manager for use in making pricing decisions. In the long run the using manager must obtain revenue adequate to cover all costs, including the fixed costs in the supplying division.

A transfer price set at the supplying division's full standard cost ($19,000, for example) would provide adequate motivation (so long as it did not exceed outside supplier price) and pricing information to the using manager. However, although the supplying manager would be obtaining some contribution from internal sales, there would not be motivation to provide equal or preferential treatment, as compared to outside sales.

To establish the transfer price at outside customer price would properly motivate the supplying manager. But note that in a condition of imperfect markets (difference between supplying division outside price and cost to using division of going outside the firm) as illustrated, this transfer price ($21,000) could improperly motivate outside procurement by the using division. Even in the case of perfect markets, unless the transfer price was set slightly below the market price (reflecting savings in selling, credit, and distribution costs), the buying division would have no incentive to purchase internally.

Note that, so far in this illustration it has been assumed that the supplying division has excess capacity. At capacity (with respect to possible outside sales), it is in the firm's overall interest to motivate outside procurement by the using division. Only a price at or above the outside supplier's price would automatically accomplish this desired result; and you have seen that such a price is inappropriate when the supplying division is operating below capacity.

Can you see that a single transfer price, depending upon the circumstances, can lead to *suboptimization*? Suboptimization describes the situation where each manager, maximizing his or her own self-interest (profit), does **not** provide the overall firm with maximum profit.

Where a reasonably "perfect" external market exists for the good or service in question, the maximum outside price obtainable by the providing division and the outside alternative purchase price to the using division will tend to be equal. The transfer price in such circumstances may best be set at

---

[8]   Recall, from Chapter 7, that the incremental cost may differ from purely variable cost by the amount of any related avoidable fixed costs. For simplification in this discussion, both incremental and variable costs will be presumed the same.

the outside market price (adjusted for savings in selling, credit, and distribution costs); and desirable decisions will usually result."

Where the external market is imperfect or nonexistent, probably the best transfer pricing arrangement would be the the use of an equivalent to a full standard cost with several restrictions. The using division could go outside only at a price below the standard variable cost; and the supplying division would be required to accept and process all orders from the using division. With the same restrictions, the transfer price could also be set at variable cost. However, it would be inadequate for the using manager's pricing decisions.

Do you feel that you have completed a full circle and are back where you started? The conditions suggested above do restrict the decision freedom of the managers, and may mitigate some of the intended benefits of having profit centers. Many other approaches to solving the transfer pricing dilemma without the use of restrictions have been suggested and tried. These other approaches include:

- actual-cost-based prices,
- negotiated prices,
- dual prices or dual allocation, and
- introduction of artificial profit.

As discussed in Chapter 12 for service-center cost allocation, all transfer prices based on actual costs incurred should be considered as undesirable. They provide for passing through inefficiencies to the user. To avoid using actual-cost-based prices in the absence of usable external market data, many firms have attempted to use *negotiated prices*, arrived at between the divisions in an attempt to be fair to both sides. There are two significant drawbacks to the use of negotiated prices. With changing costs (inflation), they require relatively frequent renegotiation, which can be inefficiently time-consuming. Moreover, the result of negotiations may more often reflect the relative negotiating skill and political power of the managers involved, instead of an economically desirable signaling device (price).

Dual price or dual allocation methods have also been proposed, wherein transfer prices are set at standard variable cost and are supplemented by a periodic charge or allocation of a lump sum of fixed costs. The objective of such a system is to appropriately focus short-run buy–sell decisions upon variable costs and contribution while maintaining awareness, for pricing purposes, of the long-run necessity of covering fixed costs. The dual allocation approach may not be well received when the supplying division is at capacity and should or does choose to sell outside.

Still another alternative involves setting the transfer price at standard cost (either variable or full) and adding an artificial profit margin to the supplying

---

⁹  Suboptimality can still result if the supplying division chooses to sell outside, and the using division cannot obtain timely alternative service from outside suppliers.

division's reports. This artificial profit does not appear as a cost to the using division. It merely is designed to properly motivate the selling division manager, and is eliminated from the total firm's records when the divisions are aggregated.

Transfer pricing problems can be further complicated if the divisions are separate legal entities and separate tax considerations become involved. Also, in such cases, provisions of the Robinson–Patman Act (Chapter 6 Appendix) or even antidumping legislation and international trade agreements may be relevant factors. In the last analysis, transfer pricing is essentially another form of cost allocation. As first cited in Chapter 1, cost allocations of common costs must, of necessity, be arbitrary. They cannot always provide the optimal basis for business decisions.

## INVESTMENT CENTERS

Profit centers, by definition, are really not quite like independent firms. Profit centers do not incorporate allocations of invested capital and the appropriate costs of such capital. Where the profit-center concept for control purposes is extended to include such items, the result is known as an investment center. Investment centers may be thought of as profit centers with the addition of an asset base. However, the selection of the appropriate asset base can present difficulties.

Three fundamental questions must be resolved in arriving at an asset base appropriate for a particular investment center:

1. Which assets should be included?
2. How should the assets selected be measured?
3. Should the base be assets or net assets (assets − liabilities)?

Essentially, the issue of which assets should be included involves the choice between all assets directly and indirectly involved in the investment center's activities and only those productive assets that are currently in use. Once again the issues related to common costs and controllability are involved. Firms that establish investment centers for control purposes rarely decentralize the management of cash and marketable securities. Receivables and receivables collections may also be centralized. Also, certain fixed or capacity assets may be commonly or jointly used with other investment centers and therefore not really be controllable. Cost of the corporate headquarters (home office) building would be an example.

Advocates emphasizing controllability would exclude such items from the asset base. Those desiring comparability with other divisions or firms urge the necessity of including a reasonable allocation of all assets employed. Perhaps the most common solution is to include all directly identifiable nonmonetary assets (inventory and capacity assets) plus an allocation of common assets including working capital. This approach serves as a constant reminder to the manager that the center's objective is to earn an adequate return on **both** the readily separable and the common assets.

Assuming that you have determined which assets you wish to include in the center's base, you still must decide how they will be measured (that is, have dollars assigned). Before you say "book value, of course," you might consider the result in performance reporting. Assume an investment center with the following:

> Income stream for six years = $5,000 per year (after depreciation)
> Initial cost of assets = $50,000
> Depreciation of $8,000 per year for six years

In such a situation, over the six-year period, the firm is earning a constant profit and its assets are wearing out. Performance-control reporting of return on investment using book value for the asset base would present a different and unreal picture:

| Year | Income | Asset book value | ROI |
|------|--------|------------------|------|
| 1 | $5,000 | $50,000 | 10% |
| 2 | 5,000 | 42,000 | 12% |
| 3 | 5,000 | 34,000 | 14.7% |
| 4 | 5,000 | 26,000 | 19.2% |
| 5 | 5,000 | 18,000 | 27.8% |
| 6 | 5,000 | 10,000 | 50% |

The first year's return would be 10 percent. Thereafter the return would continue climbing until it was reported as 50 percent after six years! The use of asset book value results in increasing returns. Its use could also deter the manager from acquiring additional assets or from modernizing existing assets. Such action would be reported as an increase in the base (denominator) and thus a **decrease** in earned return. The use of book value, therefore, provides little incentive for additional investment. It can also impair comparability among investment centers where different depreciation methods are employed, or where the investment bases are noncomparable with respect to age or size.

Using the undepreciated original cost as the asset base avoids the problems of automatically increasing return and of noncomparable depreciation methods. However, it could still result in potential noncomparability between centers having relatively old and relatively new assets, especially in periods of inflation.

Two other alternative measurements have been proposed as solutions to this problem. The first involves a modification of book value, with all centers employing an increasing charge depreciation method.[10] This system would

---

[10] An example of an increasing charge method would be years' digits without reversal of the digits. For instance, a three-year asset would have $\frac{1}{6}$ depreciation in the first year, $\frac{1}{3}$ in the second, $\frac{1}{2}$ in the final year.

minimize the increasing-return effect of using conventional book value. An otherwise constant income stream would be progressively reduced by increasing depreciation charges. Therefore a declining asset base would be matched with a declining income stream, leading to a more nearly constant ROI. In the past this alternative has been unpopular because many people assumed that the same depreciation method used under GAAP for financial reporting should be used for investment-center measurement. With an increasing awareness that accounting methods for managerial reporting need not (except for reduced calculation and paperwork costs) match those used for external reporting, the modified book value method may become more acceptable.

Still another alternative for measuring an investment center's asset base is the use of replacement cost. For these purposes, replacement cost would be defined as the current cost of replacing equivalent productive capacity. The use of replacement costs would avoid the previously cited disadvantages of simple book value or unadjusted original cost. Replacement cost would be preferable to modified book value in those instances where past mistakes (sunk costs) were being carried into the present ROI computation. Remember, from Chapter 8, that a depreciable assets book (or even modified book) value may include substantial unrealized sunk-cost losses. Where such sunk costs are included in the asset base for ROI calculation, the **current** investment return will be understated.

Past objections to the use of replacement costs have been that they did not reflect the amount actually invested, and that they were too difficult to determine. As managements turn more to measuring performance in terms of current realities and opportunity costs, replacement costs should gain wider acceptance. Also, recent SEC requirements for supplementary disclosure of replacement costs in financial reporting for very large firms has forced the development of techniques for economically estimating the necessary amounts. Although beyond the scope of this text, these techniques should minimize the problem of the feasibility of making the replacement-cost measurement.[11] As replacement costs are perceived as both desirable and feasible, their use as perhaps the most appropriate asset base should increase.

The third cited problem involving the asset base was "Should the base be assets or net assets?" Financial accountants have traditionally been oriented to the return on owners' investment (net assets). It is, therefore, not surprising that this same approach should have been proposed for investment centers. In application, the net assets approach can be difficult if not impossible to apply to investment centers. Except for trade credit, responsibility for incurrence of liabilities (short-term borrowings, taxes, and long-term debt) is generally centralized in top management. Identification or assignment of liabilities

---

[11]   One example of the simplifying techniques that are now in common use involves index adjustment. An index applicable to a representative asset subject to a particular rate of specific inflation/deflation is developed, and then used for all similar assets as a group. Calculations and engineering estimates for each separate asset are thus avoided.

to investment centers is therefore, in effect, wholly arbitrary and relatively meaningless.

As you may have learned in financial accounting, the efficiency of operating management, as distinct from financial management, is often best measured by EBIT (earnings before interest and taxes) as a percent of average assets employed. Since neither financial nor tax management is generally delegated to an investment center, efficient employment of assets remains the objective of the center. Assets employed (not net assets) are, therefore, the more appropriate base for evaluating an investment center's performance.

## PERFORMANCE EVALUATION

Performance of a profit center may be focused upon one of two measures: net income, or contribution toward the firm's income. The choice is linked to the decision relating to the allocation of costs from outside the profit center, as discussed earlier in this chapter. Where a share of all related operating and financial expense (including all home office expense) is allocated to each profit center, as illustrated in Exhibit 14.6, a net income focus is the result. Essentially, performance measurement is in terms of the center's *operating ratio* of income as a percent of sales:

$$\text{Operating ratio} = \frac{\text{Income}}{\text{Sales}}.$$

Where costs, and especially fixed costs, which are out of the center's control, are **not** allocated, evaluation is in terms of the center's (segment's) contribution, or the *segment margin*. Exhibit 14.7 illustrates a profit-center report prepared on a contribution basis. Note how pure contribution and the net contribution after covering the center's fixed costs are separately identified. Also, note that this approach restricts costs identified with the profit center to those that are controllable by or at least solely identified with the center.

Two distinct approaches also exist for evaluating the performance of an investment center: return on investment (ROI) and *residual income*. A center's ROI is simply its income expressed as a percentage of its investment (asset base or average total assets employed):

$$\text{ROI} = \frac{\text{Income}}{\text{Investment}}.$$

Actually a center's ROI is affected by two somewhat distinct ratios, the operating ratio and the *investment turnover:*

$$\text{ROI} = \text{Operating ratio} \times \text{Investment turnover,}$$

$$\text{ROI} = \frac{\text{Income}}{\text{Sales}} \times \frac{\text{Sales}}{\text{Investment}}.$$

The operating ratio is the same one previously discussed as a measure for profit centers. The investment turnover measures the efficiency of asset usage in

**Exhibit 14.7**

PROFIT CENTER PERFORMANCE REPORT
PREPARED ON CONTRIBUTION (SEGMENT MARGIN) BASIS

|  | Budget | Actual | Variance | % |
|---|---|---|---|---|
| Revenue | $485,000 | $470,000 | $15,000 U | 3.1 |
| Variable costs: |  |  |  |  |
| Wages | 120,000 | 115,000 | 5,000 F | 4.2 |
| Materials | 90,000 | 83,000 | 7,000 F | 7.8 |
| Equipment rentals | 30,000 | 29,000 | 1,000 F | 3.3 |
| Utilities | 5,000 | 5,000 | 0 F | 0 |
| Miscellaneous | 1,000 | 1,200 | 200 U | 20.0 |
| Total variable costs | $246,000 | $233,200 | $12,800 F | 5.2 |
| Contribution to fixed costs and profit | $239,000 | $236,800 | $ 2,200 U | 0.1 |
| Percent of sales | 49.3% | 50.4% | — | — |
| Identifiable/Controllable fixed costs: |  |  |  |  |
| Salaries | $ 60,000 | $ 55,000 | $ 5,000 F | 8.3 |
| Depreciation | 20,000 | 20,000 | 0 | 0 |
| Insurance | 15,000 | 16,000 | 1,000 U | 6.7 |
| Property tax | 10,000 | 12,000 | 2,000 U | 20.0 |
| Total | $105,000 | $103,000 | $ 2,000 F | 1.9 |
| Net contribution to common costs and to profit | $134,000 | $133,800 | 200 U | 0.1 |
| Percent of sales | 27.6% | 28.5% | — | — |

generating sales. It reflects sales dollars generated per dollar of assets. It is important that an investment-center manager strive to improve each ratio, and necessary actions differ for each. Reduction of operating expense in relation to sales will improve the operating ratio. Excessive preoccupation with this ratio can lead to excessive investment in "cost-saving" equipment. A one-million-dollar machine with savings equal to its depreciation plus $100 per year would appear worthwhile if only the operating ratio were to be considered. The Dupont Corporation is credited with being the first large firm to direct its managers' attention to investment turnover as well as to the operating ratio. Investment turnover may be improved through increasing sales with the same investment, decreasing investment for the same sales volume, or both.

Return on investment as a performance measure has several attributes. It is intended to motivate the optimal utilization of assets. It provides a common measure among widely divergent types of activities. A professional baseball team and an automobile manufacturer may be compared in terms of ROI. As a concept, ROI is simple and readily understood.

ROI as a performance measure, however, has several shortcomings. As cited above, the asset base generally must include arbitrary allocations, and it also presents measurement problems. ROI emphasis may also lead to suboptimization through negative incentive for investment. If you were a manager being measured by a single fraction, how could you more quickly improve your "measured performance"? Which would have a more significant effect on your fraction: a dollar of increased income (numerator) or a dollar of decreased investment (denominator)?

In an attempt to avoid some of the ROI pitfalls, the General Electric Company developed an alternative performance measure known as *residual income*. The residual income approach involves charging an investment center with an interest or capital charge for the assets employed. The charge may be set in terms of the firm's cost of capital or at an even greater amount, which might be deemed necessary to adjust for high-risk operations or divisions. Performance is then evaluated in terms of income earned in excess of the minimum desired rate of return:

$$\text{Residual income} = \begin{pmatrix} \text{Investment} \\ \text{center} \\ \text{income} \end{pmatrix} - \begin{pmatrix} \text{Capital} \\ \text{charge} \end{pmatrix}.$$

Residual income measures performance in terms of absolute dollars, rather than in terms of a simple rate. To see how the use of residual income can avoid the possible negative incentives inherent in ROI measurement, consider the following example: The Consumer Products Division of the Mammoth Manufacturing Corporation currently is reporting income of $2,000,000, with average invested capital of $10,000,000. The corporation's cost of capital is 12 percent. The Consumer Products Division manager is considering an additional investment of $300,000, which will increase divisional income by $45,000. If the manager is being evaluated by ROI, will he be inclined to push for this investment?

$$\text{ROI without new investment} = \frac{\$2,000,000}{\$10,000,000} = 20\% \, ;$$

$$\text{ROI with new investment} \quad = \frac{\$2,045,000}{\$10,300,000} = 19.6\%.$$

The additional investment will lower the manager's ROI-measured performance and, therefore, he will be motivated to reject it. The reduction results from the investment's return (15 percent) being less than the division's current ROI (20 percent). However, the investment is clearly desirable for the corporation (15 percent return exceeds corporation's 12 percent cost of capital). In this example, ROI performance measurement could lead to suboptimization.

Use of the residual-income approach could **prevent** suboptimization in this example. Assume that the division was not considered high-risk, and that the corporation's capital charge was calculated at 12 percent on average assets invested:[12]

---

[12]   The capital charge rate may also be called the imputed interest rate, since it represents a desired rate of return not necessarily correlated with actual interest costs paid by the corporation or even with the corporation's cost of capital.

608   Chapter 14 | Control of Revenue, Profit, and Investment Centers

Without new investment:

| | |
|---|---|
| Divisional income | $2,000,000 |
| Less: Capital charge | 1,200,000 |
| Equals: Residual income | $ 800,000 |

With new investment:

| | |
|---|---|
| Divisional income | $2,045,000 |
| Less: Capital charge | 1,236,000 |
| Equals: Residual income | $ 809,000 |

Since the proposed investment's return exceeds the corporation's capital charge, residual income signals its desirability, and goal congruence between the division manager and the corporation is maintained.

Regardless of the performance measure chosen, it should by now be obvious to you that no **single** measure can replace intelligent budgeting and comprehensive evaluation of performance in terms of the unique characteristics of the individual responsibility center and of the individual manager. Congruence of behavior between the manager's actions and the goals of the firm is the desired end. Various performance measures may lead to goal congruence in certain circumstances and not in others. In Chapter 12 you were introduced to the fact that no single method for budgeting and controlling service-center costs will always preclude suboptimal behavior. Earlier in this chapter you had the opportunity to see that the same problem exists with respect to transfer prices among profit centers or investment centers. Preoccupation with any one performance measure can lead to suboptimization in certain situations. The measure or measures chosen must be adapted to specific current circumstances. Exhibit 14.8 reviews the investment-center measures introduced in this chapter.

**Exhibit 14.8**

## SUMMARY OF ALTERNATIVE MEASURES FOR INVESTMENT CENTERS

| Measure | Characteristics |
|---|---|
| 1. Only operating ratio or $\dfrac{\text{Income}}{\text{Sales}}$ | Good measure of current operating performance but ignores investment return. |
| 2. Only investment turnover or $\dfrac{\text{Sales}}{\text{Investment}}$ | Good measure of efficient asset usage but ignores efficiency of current operating cost control. |
| 3. Simple ROI or $\dfrac{\text{Income}}{\text{Investment}}$ | Combines operating ratio and investment turnover and is commonly understood generalized measure applicable to widely dissimilar activities. May involve arbitrary asset base allocations and may act as negative incentive for investment. |
| 4. Residual income or Divisional income less Capital charge | Similar to ROI but avoids pitfalls of measuring by a unique rate. Less readily understood and cannot be subdivided to operating ratio and investment turnover. |

You should also be aware that several financial accounting standards (GAAP) for external reporting can lead to inappropriate or suboptimal behavior on the part of managers. Whether GAAP standards are incorporated in internal reports, or whether managers are simply anticipating the way their decisions will be reported to creditors and stockholders, the dampening effect on otherwise sound economic decisions may occur. In the appendix to this chapter you will find a brief discussion of these GAAP-related considerations.

Managerial accounting can only provide management with limited information for budgeting and performance evaluation purposes. It is not designed to nor can it provide answers. It cannot replace good judgment applied to each distinct situation. As a future manager, you must be continually aware of the limitations and of the benefits of managerial accounting information and of related analytical techniques. You need to be cognizant of the risks inherent in overdependency on particular measurements. And, at the same time, you should now be familiar with many of the tools that the managerial accountant can make available to simplify your job of managing.

## CHAPTER OVERVIEW

Based on the material contained in this chapter, you should now be able to:

- Calculate sales price, sales volume, and contribution mix variances, and explain their significance to the analysis of revenue variances.
- Explain why price, volume, and mix variances must be calculated by product and how they may offset each other.
- Describe at least three revenue-related performance measures, other than revenue and contribution variances, that may be useful in evaluating revenue centers.
- Analyze and explain a firm, investment, or profit center's income variance in terms of sales, volume, mix, and spending variances.
- Describe at least three benefits attributed to profit centers and investment centers.
- Distinguish between decentralization and the use of profit centers, and describe several potential disadvantages of decentralization of authority.
- Explain the concept of suboptimization as it relates to decision making by managers in investment and profit centers, and give examples in terms of transfer prices and investment decisions.
- Describe three different considerations or problems related to the establishment of the asset base for an investment center.

- Explain the difference between the net income and the segment-margin approach to performance evaluation for profit centers, together with the advantages and disadvantages of each.
- Define investment turnover and operating ratio, and explain their significance to the management of an investment center.
- Explain, with examples, the difference between the ROI and residual-income measures for investment centers, and the advantages and disadvantages ascribed to each.

## NEW VOCABULARY AND CONCEPTS

Sales price variance                      Decentralization
Sales volume variance                     Suboptimization
Contribution mix variance                 Negotiated prices
Expected contribution variance            Investment center
Order backlog                             Operating ratio
Average collection period                 Segment margin
Market share                              Residual income
Profit centers                            Investment turnover

- Performance measurement and suboptimization.

## REVIEW QUESTIONS

1. What are at least two characteristics of revenue-center expenditures and their behavior that may be different from usual attributes of expenditures in an expenditure center?

2. a) What are the two components of a total revenue variance?
   b) How is each determined?

3. a) What is the significance (meaning) of a favorable sales price variance? Of an unfavorable one?
   b) What is the significance (meaning) of a favorable sales volume variance? Of an unfavorable one?

4. a) What are the two components of a total contribution variance?
   b) How is the contribution mix variance determined?
   c) What is the significance (meaning) of a favorable contribution mix variance? Of an unfavorable one?

5. Why must price, volume, and mix variances be separately determined for each product in a multiproduct firm?

6. a) What is order backlog, and how may it relate to performance measurement of a revenue center?
   b) What is an average collection period, and how may it relate to performance measurement for a revenue center?

c) What is market share and how may it relate to performance measurement for a revenue center?

7. How may the following items be combined in analyzing a profit or investment center's net income variance? Explain with an example.

   • Sales price variance

   • Sales volume variance

   • Contribution mix variance

   • Various spending variances

8. What are three reasons for establishing profit centers within the firm?

9. What is meant by suboptimization in the context of profit and investment centers? How does suboptimization relate to goal congruence? Explain with examples.

10. a) What is the transfer pricing problem?

    b) Where an active external market exists for the product or service in question, is the transfer pricing problem made easier or more difficult? Explain.

    c) Where there is no active external market for a particular good or service, will any one transfer price, in conjunction with divisional autonomy, always act to preclude suboptimization? Explain.

11. What is the difference between an investment center and a profit center?

12. In establishing investment centers, what considerations (problems) exist with respect to:

    a) Choice of assets to be included?

    b) Measurement of assets that are to be included?

    c) Choice between assets and net assets?

13. a) Describe two overall performance measurements for each of the following:
       1. Profit centers
       2. Investment centers

    b) Describe how each of the four measures in (a) above is calculated.

14. a) What is an operating ratio? Describe, with an example.

    b) What is investment turnover? Describe, with an example.

    c) How do the operating ratio and the investment turnover relate to ROI? Explain.

15. Is it possible that an investment desirable for the firm as a whole might be undesirable for a particular division that is being measured by ROI or residual income? Explain.

## MINI-CASES AND QUESTIONS FOR DISCUSSION

MC 14.1 Ms. Suzanne Jackson is the manager of the sporting goods division, an investment center in the Monroe Corporation. Monroe ranks its divisions by their ROI, and Ms. Jackson is near the bottom of the list. In a meeting with the corporate controller, she objects strongly to the performance measurement basis used. Referring to other divisions reporting higher ROI than hers, she states, "I think that, if we are going to be compared, let alone ranked, we should all have our performance measured in the same way. There are at at least five ways in which my division's performance is being unfairly measured for comparison purposes:

1. "My division is on LIFO for financial reporting since you decided we wanted LIFO for tax purposes, and LIFO tax must be matched by LIFO financial. The other divisions are on FIFO, and report higher earnings in periods of inflation.

2. "My division has a lot of very expensive assets acquired by my predecessor and still on the books at a ridiculously high cost. Their current value is less than one-third of their undepreciated book value.

3. "My newer assets are all on DBB depreciation, whereas the other divisions are on straight-line.

4. "In my end of the business, we have very high promotional expense to repair our goodwill bridges that were almost completely burned by my predecessor. None of these costs are treated as assets with future value. All they do is reduce my reported earnings now.

5. "And I object to the working capital allocation included in my asset base. You are allocating central receivables in proportion to annual sales dollars. This does not take into account receivables turnover. I bet my average receivables are less than 30 days, as almost all my customers take the discount. The firm's average is 45 days, which means I'm being charged for other divisions' receivables investment.

"I really think you ought to change your system."

What do you think is Suzanne Jackson's position? Is her reasoning correct? Do each of the five items comparatively place her at an inappropriate disadvantage? What would you recommend the controller do? Discuss.

**MC 14.2** John Shremp is another division manager dissatisfied with his performance measurement. His firm follows the practice of revaluing depreciable assets to current replacement cost at the time a new manager is appointed. Thereafter they are normally depreciated so long as the individual stays with that division. John has been the manager of his division for seven years. He feels the newer managers receive an unfair comparative advantage over him under the periodic revision system.

Betty Volckman, another division manager in the same firm, believes that, if anything, the system favors the longer-term managers. She says, "John, with inflation your assets are much more valuable than your old book values. If they were revalued to replacement cost today, your ROI would take a substantial drop."

Who is more nearly correct, John or Betty? Can any revaluation system be equitable? Discuss.

**MC 14.3** Another dimension of the transfer price problem involves reciprocity. Top management wants division A to use its capacity to supply part P to customer X at a lower profit than could be earned by A making other products for other customers. The reasoning is that customer X buys 20 percent of the output of division B, and would probably go elsewhere if it could not buy advantageously from division A. The manager of division A objects to having his earnings penalized for the benefit of division B.

Should the division manager have the right to refuse to supply customer X at the lower profit margin? If the firm wished to continue the present arrangement, how could it more equitably measure A's performance? Discuss.

**MC 14.4**  It has been suggested (and tried by many firms) that a division manager's pay be augmented by a bonus tied to the division profit or ROI. Proponents of such plans argue that a bonus keyed to profit performance would act to increase the commitment of managers to their division's performance. And it would also allow them to personally share in the firm's benefits from superior performance by the division.

Opponents cite the many possibilities for suboptimal behavior when a manager has focused too much on a single performance measure. They can visualize, among other aspects:

- Noncooperation or reluctant cooperation in the matter of transfer prices to other divisions or with respect to customer reciprocity.

- A definite incentive **not** to invest in modernized equipment, employee training, and even adequate maintenance; and possibly a motive to cut back on existing activities.

- An excessive preoccupation and time investment with "fairness" of the system which, by its very nature, must in some areas be arbitrary.

Do you think the advantages of division performance bonuses outweigh the disadvantages, or vice versa? Discuss.

**MC 14.5**  Some advocates of management and control through profit and investment centers argue that full-cost allocation is necessary. It not only provides essential pricing information but it also provides comparability among divisions, and between divisions and similar business entities outside of the firm. Others that support a decentralized control system maintain that effective management and such comparability are, in themselves, inherently incompatible, and, thus, unattainable objectives. They maintain that a divisional control system is just that. They feel measurements should be those that reflect and pinpoint the reality of responsibility in each particular situation. They see no real need to have divisional statements articulate with each other or with the firm's financial reporting accounts. They believe that a division having little autonomy over financing and overall strategic planning cannot be compared to an independent company to begin with.

What do you believe should be the objectives of divisional performance measurement and control? Are comparability and consistency, as defined above, necessary or even desirable objectives? Discuss.

**MC 14.6**  You are the vice-president for operations of the Beale Manufacturing Company. A transfer pricing dispute between the Industrial Products

Division and the Components Division was submitted to your Transfer Price Arbitration Committee. The committee recommended a price of $90 per unit, which was turned down by both division managers. The problem is now in your hands.

Essential facts related to the disputed component part are as follows:

- Variable cost of disputed part to Components Division    $ 40
- Full cost of disputed part to Components Division    $75
- Price that would provide Components Division with equivalent of average gross margin earned on all sales    $90
- Price that Components Division could get for disputed part from outside customers    $100
- Price that Industrial Products Division can get for completed assembly    $580
- Total variable cost of assembly, excluding cost of disputed part    $208
- Normal overhead allocation in Industrial Products Division to completed assembly    $100
- The Components Division is presently working at capacity.
- The disputed part can be produced only by the Components Division. It is not available from outside suppliers.
- The annual volume under dispute involves 10,000 disputed parts going into 10,000 assemblies.

In a meeting Betty Tyler, the Components Division manager, maintains "My division is evaluated on my ROI, and my salary is tied to my earnings as an incentive. I don't have any extra capacity, and I can sell all the disputed parts to outsiders for $100 each. At that price the Industrial Division will still make a profit. Why should my division and my paycheck take a licking just so they can make more profit?"

Mike Reich, the Industrial Products Division manager, was equally adamant. He claimed, "My division invented and marketed the assembly and we expect volume to grow substantially over the next few years. Why should we have to give up part of the profit on our item so that Ms. Tyler can make a profit off of us? If we pay her the variable cost of $40, we would make our average normal profit of 40 percent. It might be fair to give her full cost and drop our profit to 33 percent, but this would drag down my division's performance and my paycheck. Any price over $75 is pure ripoff!"

As vice-president for operations, what should you do? What transfer price should be used? How will you explain your choice to each manager? Discuss.

### ESSENTIAL PROBLEMS

**EP 14.1** The Cady Corporation planned to sell 40,000 units of product P during 19XX at a price of $14. During 19XX it actually sold only 38,000 units at an average price of $13. If the variable cost of P was $9, determine for 19XX:

a) Total revenue variance

b) Sales price variance

c) Sales volume variance

d) Contribution mix variance

e) Total contribution variance

**EP 14.2** The Drake Corporation sold two products, P and Q. It had budgeted sales for the period of 6,000 units of P at a price of $9 and 2,500 units of Q at a price of $20. Actual sales were 5,000 units of P at $10 each and 3,000 units of Q at $15 each. Assume that variable costs were $7 for P and $12 for Q. Determine the following for the period:

a) Budgeted revenue from P

b) Budgeted revenue from Q

c) Budgeted total revenue

d) Budgeted contribution from P

e) Budgeted contribution from Q

f) Budgeted total contribution

g) Total revenue variance

h) Total contribution variance

i) Sales price variance for P

j) Sales price variance for Q

k) Total price variance

l) Sales volume variance for P

m) Sales volume variance for Q

n) Total sales volume variance

o) Contribution mix variance for P

p) Contribution mix variance for Q

q) Total contribution mix variance

**EP 14.3** a) Complete the missing data for columns A, B, and C in Table 14.1, each considered independently.

### Table 14.1

|  | A | B | C | D | E | F |
|---|---|---|---|---|---|---|
| Sales price variance | $500 U | $300 F | ? | ? | $400 U | ? |
| Sales volume variance | $300 F | ? | $200 U | $600 U | ? | ? |
| Contribution mix variance | $100 F | ? | ? | ? | ? | $200 U |
| Total sales variance | ? | $800 U | $900 F | $800 U | $300 U | $300 F |
| Total contribution variance | ? | $600 U | $800 F | $300 U | $350 U | $500 F |

b) Match each variance in columns A, B, and C with the most appropriate explanation (by number) from those listed below:

1. Selling prices were lower (or discounts were higher) than budgeted.

2. Selling prices were higher (or discounts were lower) than budgeted.

3. Unit sales volume was greater than budgeted.

4. Unit sales volume was less than budgeted.

5. Higher prices more than offset the effect of lower unit sales volumes.

6. Lower unit sales volume was partially offset by higher prices.

7. More items were sold at higher prices.

8. Higher unit sales volume more than offset the effect of lower prices.

9. Lower prices were partially offset by higher unit sales volume.

10. Fewer items were sold at lower prices.

**EP 14.4** Refer to Problem EP 14.3.

a) Complete the missing data for columns D, E, and F in Table 14.1, each considered independently.

b) Match each variance in columns D, E, and F with the most appropriate explanation (by number) given as part of Problem EP 14.3.

**EP 14.5** Compute the missing data in Table 14.2 for products A through D.

**EP 14.6** Compute the missing data in Table 14.3 for products E through H.

**EP 14.7** Exhibit 14.9 is a performance report for the Filbert Manufacturing Division (a profit center) of the Gregory Corporation for the year 19XX. Assume the following additional data:

Budgeted sales and production 50,000 units
Actual sales and production    45,000 units

Determine the sources underlying the division's $219,000 unfavorable net

### Exhibit 14.9
### FILBERT DIVISION

| Performance Report 19XX | Budgeted | Actual |
|---|---|---|
| Revenue | $1,800,000 | $1,440,000 |
| Variable expenses: | | |
| Materials | 150,000 | 141,750 |
| Labor | 500,000 | 425,250 |
| Overhead | 400,000 | 337,500 |
| Selling | 100,000 | 94,500 |
| Contribution to fixed expense and profit | $ 650,000 | $ 441,000 |
| Fixed expenses: | | |
| Overhead | 125,000 | 130,000 |
| Selling | 250,000 | 240,000 |
| Administrative | 75,000 | 90,000 |
| Net contribution to firm's fixed expenses and profit | $ 200,000 | $ (19,000) |

Table 14.2

| | Product A Budgeted | Product A Actual | Product B Budgeted | Product B Actual | Product C Budgeted | Product C Actual | Product D Budgeted | Product D Actual |
|---|---|---|---|---|---|---|---|---|
| Sales revenue | $3,000 | ? | $2,400 | ? | ? | ? | ? | ? |
| Unit sales | 500 | 400 | ? | ? | ? | 50 | ? | ? |
| Selling price | ? | $7 | $8 | $6 | ? | $25 | $4 | ? |
| Unit variable cost * | $4 | ? | ? | ? | ? | ? | ? | ? |
| Unit contribution | ? | ? | ? | ? | $13 | $15 | ? | ? |
| Total contribution | ? | ? | ? | ? | ? | ? | $200 | ? |
| Sales price variance | | ? | | $1,000 U | | ? | | $600 F |
| Sales volume variance | | ? | | ? | | ? | | $1,600 F |
| Contribution mix variance | | ? | | $800 F | | $325 U | | $400 F |

Table 14.3

| | Product E Budgeted | Product E Actual | Product F Budgeted | Product F Actual | Product G Budgeted | Product G Actual | Product H Budgeted | Product H Actual |
|---|---|---|---|---|---|---|---|---|
| Sales revenue | ? | ? | ? | ? | ? | ? | ? | ? |
| Unit sales | ? | ? | ? | 600 | 700 | 600 | ? | 900 |
| Selling price | ? | $2 | ? | ? | ? | ? | ? | $10 |
| Unit variance cost * | ? | ? | $3 | ? | $1 | ? | ? | ? |
| Unit contribution | $2 | ? | $1 | ? | ? | ? | $2 | $5 |
| Total contribution | ? | ? | ? | ? | $1,400 | $600 | ? | ? |
| Sales price variance | | $200 U | | $600 U | | ? | | ? |
| Sales volume variance | | $300 U | | $400 F | | ? | | ? |
| Contribution mix variance | | $200 U | | ? | | ? | | $600 F |

* Budgeted and actual assumed same.

contribution variance in terms of:

a) Sales price variance
b) Sales volume variance
c) Contribution mix variance
d) Spending variances for various expenses

**EP 14.8** Refer to Exhibit 14.9 above. Assume that budgeted sales and production had been 40,000 units, and that actual sales and production had been 45,000 units. Explain the $219,000 unfavorable net contribution variance in terms of:

a) Sales price variance
b) Sales volume variance
c) Contribution mix variances
d) Spending variances for various expenses

**EP 14.9** Complete the missing data for columns A through D in Table 14.4, each considered independently.

**EP 14.10** Refer to Problem EP 14.9. Complete the missing data for columns E through H in Table 14.4, each considered independently.

**EP 14.11** The asset base assigned to a particular investment center consisted of depreciable assets costing $300,000 (acquired on 1/1/X4 and determined to have a useful life of five years with zero salvage) and an additional $200,000 of working capital. Operating income for 19X5, before depreciation charges, amounted to $128,000. Assume that the firm uses book value of operating assets as its asset base, and has a minimum required rate of return on assigned assets equal to its costs of capital of 15 percent. Evaluate the center's 19X5 performance in terms of both ROI and residual income under each of the following alternatives:

a) The firm uses straight-line depreciation.
b) The firm uses years' digits depreciation.
c) The firm uses double-declining balance depreciation.

**EP 14.12** The Hereford Corporation has three operating divisions, all established for control purposes as investment centers. Data for each of the divisions for the year 19X9 is given below. You may assume that each division acquired all of its assets on 1/1/X7, and that they were all estimated to have four-year lives with zero salvage. Divisional performance is measured with operating ratios, residual income, and ROI, with the asset base being the book value of assigned assets as determined by the division. The firm desires a minimum 12-percent return on assets invested.

| | Division X | Division Y | Division Z |
|---|---|---|---|
| Sales | $275,000 | $330,000 | $950,000 |
| Operating income before depreciation expense | 47,000 | 113,000 | 169,500 |
| Original cost of assigned depreciable assets | 100,000 | 400,000 | 900,000 |
| Depreciation method used | Straight-line | Years' digits | DDB |
| Nondepreciable assets assigned | 150,000 | 200,000 | 300,000 |

Table 14.4

| | A | B | C | D | E | F | G | H |
|---|---|---|---|---|---|---|---|---|
| Sales | $80,000 | ? | ? | $60,000 | ? | $50,000 | $100,000 | ? |
| Operating income | ? | ? | $9,000 | ? | ? | $7,500 | ? | ? |
| Asset base (Investment) | ? | ? | ? | ? | ? | $30,000 | ? | $28,000 |
| Operating ratio (%) | 12.5% | 20% | ? | ? | ? | ? | ? | ? |
| Investment turnover (Times) | ? | 0.60 | 1.50 | ? | 2.00 | ? | ? | 2.5 |
| ROI | 25% | ? | 15% | ? | 10% | ? | ? | 25% |
| Minimum required return: | | | | | | | | |
| Percentage | 20% | 15% | ? | 14% | ? | ? | 16% | ? |
| Dollars | ? | $7,500 | ? | $2,100 | $2,400 | $3,900 | $8,000 | $4,200 |
| Residual income | ? | ? | zero | $300 | $(400) | ? | $500 | ? |

a) Determine the operating ratio, ROI, and residual income for each division, and rank the divisions by each performance measurement.
b) Assume that each division used straight-line depreciation for comparability. Determine the operating ratio, ROI, and residual income for each division, assuming straight-line depreciation. Rank the divisions by each of these measures.

EP 14.13 The Kenwood Corporation has two operating divisions, both established as investment centers. Budgeted data for both divisions for the year 19X7 are given below. The manager of division A is considering acquiring additional equipment effective 1/1/X7. The equipment would cost $120,000, would have annual depreciation of $20,000 (six-year life, zero salvage), and would result in annual cash operating savings of $30,000. The company's required rate of return is 12 percent, and income taxes may be ignored.

|  | Division A | Division B |
|---|---|---|
| Sales | $500,000 | $900,000 |
| Operating expenses | 460,000 | 852,000 |
| Asset base (determined as average book value of assets in use during the year) | 200,000 | 600,000 |

a) Ignoring tax effects, what would be the NPV, discounted at the required rate of return, of the proposed equipment?
b) Assuming funds were available, should Kenwood acquire the equipment for use in division A?
c) If the manager of division A did not acquire the equipment, what would be the division's expected ROI and residual income?
d) What would be the division's expected ROI and residual income if the equipment were acquired?
e) Is there congruence between the firm's interest and the division manager's interest with respect to the potential acquisition of the equipment? Explain.

EP 14.14 Refer to Problem EP 14.13. Assume that the manager of division B was also considering acquiring some new equipment effective 1/1/X7. The equipment would cost $300,000, would have annual depreciation of $60,000 (five-year life, zero salvage), and would result in annual operating savings of $83,000. Answer the same five questions, (a) through (e), as in Problem EP 14.13 with respect to this equipment and division B.

## SUPPLEMENTARY PROBLEMS

SP 14.15 Refer to Problem EP 14.7 and to Exhibit 14.9 above. In addition to the data given in that problem, assume the following information:

• Budgeted (standard) materials cost = $0.50 per pound
• Actual material used = 315,000 pounds

- Budgeted (standard) direct labor per unit = 2 hours
- Actual direct labor cost per hour = $5.25

As part of the analysis of the division's performance, determine the component variances for material and for labor.

**SP 14.16** Refer to Problem EP 14.8 and to Exhibit 14.9 above. In addition to the data given in that problem, assume the following information:

- Budgeted (standard) material per unit = 5 pounds
- Actual material price paid = $0.63 per pound
- Budgeted (standard) direct labor rate = $5 per DLH
- Actual direct labor incurred = 94,500 hours

As part of the analysis of the division's performance, determine the component variances for material and for labor. Also, determine the firm's breakeven sales volume in units and in dollars.

**SP 14.17** The following data is available with respect to the Narker Company's Nark Division:

| | Product P | Product Q | Total |
|---|---|---|---|
| Selling price | $30 | $40 | — |
| Direct labor | 2 | 6 | $8 |
| Direct material | 4 | 2 | 6 |
| Variable manufacturing overhead | 5 | 7 | 12 |
| Variable selling expense | 3 | 4 | 7 |
| Fixed manufacturing overhead | — | — | $100,000 |
| Fixed GSA expense | — | — | 59,000 |
| Investment | — | — | 530,000 |

a) Assuming a sales mix of two P's for each Q, how many P's and Q's must be sold in order for the division to break even?

b) Assuming a sales mix of two P's for each Q, how many P's and Q's must be sold in order for the division to earn a 15-percent ROI before taxes?

c) What would be the Nark Division's ROI at a volume of 10,000 P's and 5,000 Q's?

d) If Narker charged a 15-percent minimum return capital charge, what would be the Nark Division's residual income at a volume of 12,000 P's and 6,000 Q's?

e) Assume that the current volume of the division was 10,000 P's and 5,000 Q's. The division is considering a special order of 10,000 P's at a reduced price. The order would not impair existing sales or sales prospects. Adequate capacity exists, and the overall firm's cost of capital is 15 percent. Acceptance of the order would entail $20,000 of additional annual fixed costs and an investment of $50,000 in additional equipment. What would be the lowest price (in even dollars) that the division could accept which would still benefit the corporation?

f) Referring to the special order in (e) above, what would be the lowest price the division could accept without reducing its present ROI?

**SP 14.18** Refer to Problem SP 14.17. You may assume that revised price and cost data for the Narker Company's Nark Division is as follows:

|  | Product P | Product Q | Total |
|---|---|---|---|
| Selling price | $45 | $30 | — |
| Variable cost | 24 | 17 | $31 |
| Fixed cost | — | — | $165,000 |
| Investment | — | — | 795,000 |

Answer the same six questions, (a) through (f), as given in Problem SP 14.17.

**SP 14.19** The Friendly Corporation retails garden supplies with two separate chains of stores—the do-it-yourself discount chain and the country garden group. Each chain of stores is operated as a separate division.

One particular fertilizer is purchased in large quantities by the discount division in plain bags. Some is then transferred (resold) to the garden division which, in turn, rebags it in a more elaborate package for sale to customers. The transfer price has been set at $1.00 per bag, which represents the wholesale cost in quantities of 500 tons (10,000 bags). Annual sales for the garden division of this one type of fertilizer have averaged about 490 tons per year. Rebagging has cost $0.10 per bag.

The discount division, with much larger volume, has purchased the fertilizer on an annual contract for 2,000 tons. At this volume it has been able to obtain a 10-percent quantity discount ($0.90 per bag). The discount would be only five percent for annual purchases between 1,250 and 1,750 tons.

The garden division manager has been offered an equivalent fertilizer packaged in the more elaborate bag by another wholesaler, at a price of $1.05 per bag.

a) What action would be in the best interests of the corporation?

b) As division manager of the garden stores, what would you do?

c) As division manager of the discount stores, what would you do?

d) What transfer price should be used? Explain.

**SP 14.20** The Everclear TV Corporation originally manufactured only picture tubes in its tube division. More recently it added a video division that manufactures completed TV chassis for sale to other television set manufacturers. Video division customers buy the chassis, install them in various cabinets, and sell the finished TV sets to customers. The corporation has established each division as a distinct investment center, and each division manager's salary is significantly dependent on the division's ROI.

Available data are as follows:

| Sales volume | Internal tube cost | Additional chassis cost | Sales price | External tube cost |
|---|---|---|---|---|
| 200,000 | $48.00 | $67 | $140 | $60 |
| 500,000 | 37.20 | 63 | 125 | 50 |
| 800,000 | 34.50 | 60 | 110 | 45 |
| 1,100,000 | 33.25 | 58 | 100 | 43 |

The variable portion of the internal tube cost is approximately $30.00.

a) Assuming that the tubes were acquired internally, what would be the chassis income for the corporation at each level of activity?

b) What is the most profitable level of operations for the corporation?

c) If the external tube cost (market price) is used as the transfer price, what is the most profitable level of operations for the tube division?

d) If the market price for tubes is the transfer price, what is the most profitable level of operations for the video division?

e) What transfer price should the firm use?

## SUGGESTIONS FOR FURTHER READING

Anthony, R.N., and J. Dearden, *Management Control Systems: Cases and Readings,* Third Edition. Homewood, Illinois Richard D. Irwin, Inc., 1976.

Davidson, Sidney, James S. Schindler, Clyde P. Stickney, and Roman L. Weil, *Managerial Accounting: An Introduction to Concepts, Methods, and Uses.* Hinsdale, Illinois: The Dryden Press, 1978; Chapter 14.

Horngren, C., *Cost Accounting: A Managerial Emphasis,* Fourth Edition. Englewood Cliffs, N.J.: Prentice-Hall, Inc., 1977; Chapters 6, 22, and 23.

Morse, Wayne J., *Cost Accounting: Processing, Evaluating and Using Cost Data.* Reading, Massachusetts: Addison-Wesley Publishing Company, 1978; Chapters 11 and 18.

Solomons, David, *Divisional Performance: Measurement and Control.* New York: Financial Executives Research Foundation, 1965.

CHAPTER 14 APPENDIX
# GAAP and Dysfunctional Management Decisions

*Dysfunctional behavior* (dysfunctional decisions) is defined as behavior that is not in the best economic interests of the firm. In this and previous chapters you have been introduced to several types of managerial accounting data (sunk costs, cost allocations, transfer prices, ROI measurements) that, when used blindly, can lead to dysfunctional behavior. The central focus of this text has been upon managerial accounting information as the primary basis for managers' decisions. Managers are also concerned with the way external financial statements prepared following GAAP will report the results of their actions to creditors and owners.

In this appendix, you can learn that several financial accounting standards (GAAP) for external reporting can lead to inappropriate or dysfunctional behavior on the part of managers. Three significant problem areas are worth noting that involve intangible assets, tangible fixed assets, and inventories.

### Intangible Assets

As a division manager, assume that you are considering a proposal for the investment of $20,000,000 over a three-year period in research and development. Benefits are expected, starting five years from now, to eventually total $50 to $60 million. The NPV of this project, discounted at the firm's cost of capital, is +$10,000,000. Even discounted at your division's current higher ROI, the NPV is positive. During the next two years without the R & D expenditure, you expect divisional net income of $20,000,000 each year and an average investment of $90,000,000. You are currently paid $100,000-a-year salary, plus a bonus equal to twice your division's ROI rate times your base salary. Your division also has the highest ROI in the company; and you are reasonably certain that, if you stay at the top, you will be promoted to executive vice-president in three years. Will you be inclined to accept or reject the R & D proposal?

Recall, from financial accounting, that GAAP requires immediate write-off (period cost treatment) of most investments in intangible assets that do not result in a legal right or claim. It may clearly be in the best interest of the firm to:

- Invest in the research and development of new products to stay competitive in the rapidly changing world.
- Invest in market research and advertising to develop present and continuing customer goodwill.
- Invest in the training of employees and managers to augment their skills and value to the firm.

In these and similar cases, where the benefits may accrue over a period of many years (and where some may not even **appear** for several years), GAAP prohibits capitalization and matching. A manager being evaluated by conventional standards of profitability, or even a firm's directors being evaluated by outside investors, may be hesitant to make a desirable investment that will be reported as an immediate loss. The same reservations would apply to tangible investments with gradually accruing benefits, unless they were to be depreciated on a decelerating basis (uncommon). All developmental projects with delayed or spread-out payoffs run up against this problem. In the long run, assuming that they are worthwhile to begin with, their value will be recognized. Too often, however, the responsible manager will have moved to a different position, or the payoff will be unidentifiable in an aggregation of other benefits. No currently proposed GAAP alternative is designed to cope with this timing problem.

A solution might be to disregard GAAP guidelines in preparing internal performance evaluation reports. For ROI or residual income determination, all developmental projects could be capitalized and subsequently amortized or depreciated on a basis designed to match expected benefits. However, this approach would not remove the potential negative incentive for top management whose performance would still be subject to evaluation under GAAP.

### Sunk Costs

Current GAAP also introduces a different problem with respect to past expenditures that may have been capitalized as assets. Recall, from Chapters 7 and 8, that sunk costs are irrelevant to investment decisions. A past mistake that is still capitalized in the form of undepreciated or unamortized book value should not be allowed to preclude action designed to obtain future net benefits. Yet a manager may properly be reluctant to make a necessary and desirable investment in modernization of capacity when faced with a large write-off of sunk cost as a loss in the year of the investment. The source of this problem is the failure of GAAP to recognize properly partial obsolescence of capacity assets as it occurs. Conventionally, such obsolescence is often not recognized until the time of sale. Some proposals for current-value accounting would alleviate this problem of capitalized sunk costs. However, such proposals may also involve a questionable redefinition of income. Current-value accounting will be discussed further in Chapter 16.

The possible elimination of any undepreciated sunk costs from the asset base at the time a new division manager is appointed has been suggested for

ROI or residual income internal measurement purposes. Such a practice could also eliminate the possible negative incentive to new investment for the division manager. However, once again top management may disapprove investments that could trigger large write-offs.

### Inventory Accumulation

A final consideration relevant to GAAP and managerial decision-making involves inventory. Under GAAP a firm with production continually in excess of sales may continue to report high profits, up to the point of insolvency and failure. Recall, from Chapter 1, the difference between product costs and period costs, and the difference between direct costing and full (absorption) costing as applied to product costs (inventory). GAAP requires full costing, and this practice has the effect of capitalizing fixed manufacturing costs into inventory. The recognition of such costs as an expense is, thus, deferred until sale. A manager who builds inventory, therefore, increases current profitability (by postponing recognition of fixed manufacturing costs) at the expense of decreased solvency.

Proposals to modify GAAP to provide for direct costing of inventory and period-cost treatment of fixed manufacturing cost, if adopted, would eliminate this contradictory situation.[13] Until then, management must carefully monitor solvency, along with reported income, at both the division and total firm level.

---

[13]   Another alternative, known as relevant costing, would have the same salutary effect. The relevant costing approach is a hybrid of direct and full costing. Fixed manufacturing cost, or some portion thereof, is capitalized only if there is a demonstrable future benefit (savings); otherwise it is expensed. For instance, a firm with an annual capacity of 100 units, current annual sales of 50 units, expected sales next year of 150 units, and current production of 100 units, could capitalize 50 percent of fixed manufacturing cost. The rationale would be that the inventory buildup was essential to sales in the subsequent period.

# 15

## CONTROL
## IN ORGANIZATIONS
## THAT ARE NOT
## PROFIT DIRECTED

## CHAPTER PREVIEW

The purpose of this chapter is to provide you with a brief introduction to budgeting and accounting systems and control problems in organizations that are not profit-directed. In this chapter, you can learn, for nonbusiness organizations:

- That goals, traditions, and many of the decision variables differ from those in business.
- That budgeting and control applications also differ, even though the underlying concepts and objectives of budgeting and control are common to all organizations.
- How control objectives currently differ from those in a business.
- That budgets are often prepared solely in terms of inputs (expenditures), and accounting systems are designed to measure only commitments for and actual cash outlays.
- That different approaches to budgeting are being introduced that more closely parallel business budgeting as described in earlier chapters.
- How the so-called fund accounting system used by most nonprofit-directed organizations differs from conventional business accrual accounting.
- That input budgeting and fund accounting provide inadequate information for measuring the effectiveness and the efficiency of an organization (as those terms have been previously defined for business firms).
- That the absence of accrual accounting inhibits the effectiveness of the newer forms of budgeting as control instruments.

In the appendix to this chapter, you will find an illustration of the fund accounting system used by most nonbusiness organizations.

With the information contained in this chapter, you should be in a better position to understand the current behavior of governments and other nonbusiness institutions. You will be able to appreciate some of the issues and problems faced by those attempting to improve managerial control in the public sector. You may also enhance and reinforce your understanding of the advantages of business "output" budgeting coupled with accrual accounting as described in previous chapters.

## CENTRAL THEME

Organizations that are not profit-directed, such as governments, public schools, colleges, universities, most hospitals, and charitable organizations, have traditionally been viewed as being distinctly different from business firms. In fact, the study of nonbusiness organizations, and especially their accounting and control systems, has, in the past, been almost entirely omitted from most business school curricula.[1] Today there exists a growing awareness that the differences are not that great. Managers of nonbusiness organizations face many of the same problems and decisions as do their counterparts in business. With perhaps 30 percent of the nation's human and financial resources committed to the nonbusiness sector, this area no longer can be ignored.

This text views budgeting and control in the broad sense of a process used by all managers. The process is designed to ensure that existing and additional resources have been and are obtained and used to accomplish the organization's objectives in an efficient and effective manner. In Chapter 2 you were introduced to the many common characteristics of all organizations, whether business or nonbusiness. This chapter will assume the same theme of commonality: that business budgeting and control concepts can and should be similar in both profit and nonprofit-directed organizations. It will offer you a brief initial exposure to a few of the differences in the way these concepts are applied in nonprofit-directed organizations, and it will also present some of the reasons for these differences.[2]

Before proceeding, a minor matter of terminology requires clarification. The term *nonbusiness organizations* can be interpreted as excluding hospitals, government-owned utilities, and the like, since they may be run as businesses. In this text, nonbusiness will be used to include **any** government or private endeavor not established with the intention of earning a profit for the owner(s). The terms not-for-profit and nonprofit-directed have also been used to emphasize this distinction. However, these terms are awkward to read or speak. Therefore, in the balance of this chapter, the simpler term *nonprofit* will be used as synonymous with nonbusiness as defined above.[3]

---

[1]  At the undergraduate level, senior accounting majors have usually had the option of taking a single elective course in governmental or fund accounting. Advanced accounting courses also often include some exposure to the mechanics of fund accounting. Such courses are effectively closed to nonaccounting students, since they require the intermediate accounting course sequence as a prerequisite. At the graduate level in business and economics schools, programs in public administration or public management are becoming more prevalent.

[2]  For a truly excellent and comprehensive introduction to this area, you should read *Management Control in Nonprofit Organizations* by Robert N. Anthony and Regina Herzlinger (Homewood, Illinois: Richard D. Irwin, Inc., 1975).

[3]  You should be aware that the term nonprofit may also be used outside of this text in referring to a business that currently is unprofitable.

## HOW MUCH SHOULD WE BUDGET FOR NEXT YEAR?

In all previous chapters, the central focus has been upon business firms orga-nized to make profit. To illustrate managerial accounting in a profit-directed setting, the Tripper Water Ski Manufacturing Company has been used. In this chapter, you are asked to assume that you are a member of your local district school board.[4] The school superintendent has just presented the next year's budget for possible modification and approval. A condensed form of the budget proposal is given in Exhibit 15.1.

Your board must approve the overall level of spending for operations, since the total funds requirements for operations will provide the basis for determining next year's district property tax rate. Your board must also determine the desirability and the level of proposed major capital expenditures, since any that are approved will require additional financing through new school bonds. An additional bond issue will be subject to voter approval at the next election.

In making your evaluation you are very aware that most taxpayers in your district already feel that their property taxes are too high. Any substantial tax increase may trigger a taxpayers' revolt similar to the one in California that cut existing property taxes and limited future increases. You also are concerned over your chances for reelection if you cannot convince the voters of the necessity and desirability of the final budget. Finally, you are aware that many recent school bond issues have been turned down by voters in your state. You therefore wish to approve only those major capital expenditures which you are certain are absolutely necessary, and which you can sincerely defend to the voters.

Study Exhibit 15.1 with the understanding that, in an actual situation, you would have much more supporting detail. You may assume that the superin-tendent provided the board with personal assurance that his proposal was a "bare-bones" budget, and that any cuts would result in disaster. How would you proceed to answer, or to obtain the answer to, the following questions:

- How much taxpayer money should be spent on education?

- Are the schools in your district presently doing a good or at least an adequate job? How do you measure the schools' output, other than simply as bodies graduated? How can the quality of education be measured and evaluated?

- Was this year's expenditure level appropriate? Is there any evidence of padding or slack in the budget? Is there so-called "fat" that could be "trimmed," and how could you identify it?

- Are the proposed increases for next year really necessary and desirable? Would your answer be different if all salary increases represented raises

---

[4]   You could also experience the problems peculiar to nonprofit organizations if you imagined yourself involved with a hospital, a symphony orchestra, a university, a charitable organization, or any branch of federal, state, or local government.

**Exhibit 15.1**
ILLUSTRATION OF PROPOSED SCHOOL BUDGET—SUMMARY
DATA ONLY

| | Current year | Next year | Percent change |
|---|---|---|---|
| **Instruction:** | | | |
| Salaries and benefits | $2,500,000 | $2,875,000 | +15.0 |
| Supplies | 140,000 | 151,000 | + 7.9 |
| Total | $2,640,000 | $3,026,000 | +14.6 |
| **Transportation:** | | | |
| Salaries and benefits | $ 500,000 | $ 560,000 | +12.0 |
| Fuel, maintenance, and insurance | 214,000 | 233,000 | + 8.9 |
| Total | $ 714,000 | $ 793,000 | + 4.9 |
| **Facilities:** | | | |
| Maintenance and repair—Buildings | $ 205,000 | $ 215,000 | + 4.9 |
| Maintenance and repair—Equipment | 97,000 | 92,000 | − 5.2 |
| Maintenance and repair—Grounds | 64,000 | 69,000 | + 7.8 |
| Utilities and insurance | 58,000 | 60,000 | + 3.4 |
| Total | $ 424,000 | $ 436,000 | + 2.8 |
| **Administration:** | | | |
| Salaries and benefits | $ 800,000 | $ 944,000 | +18.0 |
| Supplies | 40,000 | 42,000 | + 5.0 |
| Additional equipment—Instructional | 214,000 | 171,000 | −20.1 |
| Additional equipment—Office | 79,000 | 95,000 | +16.8 |
| Total | $1,133,000 | $1,252,000 | +10.5 |
| **Total operations** | $4,911,000 | $5,507,000 | +12.1 |
| **Capital outlays:** | | | |
| New gymnasium | | $1,840,000 | |
| Renovate junior high class building | | 2,310,000 | |
| Replace administration building | | 2,950,000 | |
| Total | | $7,100,000 | |

and cost-of-living adjustments, and overall enrollment was increasing? Declining? Should administrative personnel receive more than teachers? How could the benefits alleged to result from these increases be measured for comparison to costs?

• What are the benefits to be derived from each of the proposed major capital outlays? Can these be adequately quantified for inclusion in the conventional capital budgeting decision model (Chapter 8)? If not, how could you decide whether the outlays were really necessary?

Do not expect answers to be provided to the foregoing questions. If you really considered how the questions might be answered, the school board model served its purpose: to draw your attention to the unique aspects of non-profit organizations. You may hold strong personal attitudes or opinions with respect to these questions, but opinions usually are different from the results of rational businesslike decisions.

The balance of this chapter will be devoted both to clarifying the similarities and differences between business and nonbusiness organizations, and also to describing budgets and control systems for nonprofit organizations. You will grasp the essentials of the nonprofit situation more readily if you will first take the time to think about and identify why the above questions might be easier to answer for Tripper than for a school district. As a first step, you should consider the different purposes and characteristics between profit and nonprofit organizations.

## PURPOSE AND IMPORTANT CHARACTERISTICS OF BUSINESS ORGANIZATIONS

In trying to appreciate the similarities and differences between business and nonbusiness planning and control systems, it is desirable first to review the purpose and certain characteristics common to business firms. Some were stated and some were implicit in earlier chapters. As discussed in Chapters 2 and 6, the central purpose or objective of all business firms is to make an adequate profit or return on the owners' capital invested in the entity—to earn at least the firm's cost of capital. A business may provide goods and/or services but they are not considered objectives or ends in themselves. Goods or services are merely the means to the end of making a profit.

With its central objective defined in monetary terms, a business is in a unique position. Its primary outputs can be readily quantified and measured (dollars and revenue). Effectiveness can be evaluated in terms of quantified outputs obtained (actual revenue or market share in comparison to budget). A firm's efficiency expressed as a benefit/cost ratio is also easily measured: $X$ dollars of revenue (output) resulting from $Y$ dollars of expense (input).

Two other characteristics of a business are worth noting. First, most firms operate in the marketplace with some competition. The market, and whatever competition exists, serve to provide standards or comparative measures for evaluating the individual firm's or manager's performance. Second, many firms are fairly flexible in adapting to change. As customers' tastes evolve, and as different materials and processes become available, a business will modify product lines or even move into or out of whole industries, in order to survive and to profit. Most businesses are therefore characterized by:

1. readily measurable objectives and outputs,

2. available market standards, and

3. flexibility.

## PURPOSE AND IMPORTANT CHARACTERISTICS
## OF NONPROFIT ORGANIZATIONS

Nonprofit organizations may be just the opposite. Their purpose is to supply socially desirable services (or goods) without attempting to earn a profit. The services (or goods, such as water or electric power) may be ends in themselves. Where revenue or fees are involved (hospital fees, tuitions, fines, and so forth), the profit objective is limited to minimizing loss or, possibly, to breaking even. In unusual cases where revenues exceed costs of services provided, the excess is used to expand upon or improve future services or to reduce future service fees. Without revenue and profit measurement, there exists no single performance criterion. In fact, many nonprofit organizations have multiple goals that are not necessarily compatible. For example, a hospital may wish to provide medical care at low cost and, simultaneously, to support medical research and also provide training for future doctors.

In most nonprofit organizations, no direct relationship between costs and benefits may exist. Service outputs and benefit/cost ratios may be difficult to measure in quantitative terms. How does one measure the benefit of having a navy of a particular size?

Often marketplace standards are nonexistent or are irrelevant to an evaluation of either effectiveness or efficiency. What comparative standard is available for assessing the performance of the Red Cross or the FBI? Furthermore, nonbusiness organizations are often fairly inflexible and subject to severe political pressures. How easily and quickly can an obsolescent or obsolete military base be closed? How rapidly do innovative educational techniques that have been proven in a classroom become uniformly adopted throughout the education "industry"?

You are probably having difficulty perceiving **all** nonprofit organizations as characterized by few measurable outputs and few comparative outside standards, or being relatively political and inflexible. *Not* all nonprofit organizations are so characterized. It may be helpful to imagine a continuum with businesses on one extreme end and welfare organizations and churches at the other.

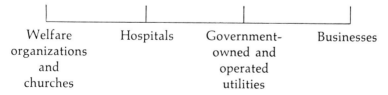

| Welfare organizations and churches | Hospitals | Government-owned and operated utilities | Businesses |

Between the two extremes would lie nonprofit organizations that may be more or less like a business, such as hospitals and government-owned and operated utilities. An in-depth study would require grouping nonprofit organizations along the continuum, and then examining each group separately. In this introduction you will be asked to ignore the *borderline cases* such as government corporations and authorities, and to think instead in terms of a distinctly nonbusiness type of operation. A public university will be used to illustrate various concepts introduced in this chapter, since a university may be more familiar to you than any other nonprofit organization.

## CONTROL OBJECTIVES: SIMILARITIES AND DIFFERENCES

Returning to similarities for the moment, all organizations share certain planning and control objectives. The goals or objectives of each organization need to be defined and communicated to all members, in order to at least make goal congruence a possibility. Specific short-run objectives or activities should be made explicit, to serve as a basis for assessing the desirability of planned resource commitments, and also for the later evaluation of performance effectiveness. Control must exist over resource commitments (expenditures) to ensure that both the quantity and the type are consistent with organizational objectives and also that they do not exceed available sources of funds. Finally, some measurement of resources actually used (inputs) is desirable, so that they can be compared with objectives attained (outputs) to provide evidence of efficiency.

You have had the opportunity in the first fourteen chapters of this text to learn how these objectives are accomplished for businesses with readily measurable outputs. Objectives are established in terms of both expected outputs (sales budgets) and also the matching resources to be used and/or obtained (inputs). Business budgets are broken down by those centers responsible for obtaining outputs and for using inputs.

In business firms, performance is then evaluated by comparing actual results to the budget. A cost accounting system established on an accrual basis measures outputs (resources obtained) and inputs (resources used) for various responsibility centers. Note that accrual accounting provides measurements of inputs by the resource **user** and at the time and in terms of those resources actually **used** or consumed. Inputs acquired and not used or expiring in the current period are carried forward to future periods as assets. In each period, accrual accounting measures and reports resources used (expenses) regardless of whether obtained in prior periods or in the current period. (See chart at top of page 635.)

In many nonprofit organizations, two factors mentioned earlier have led to a modification of control objectives. First, there may be multiple objectives, which may be inherently noncongruent. A city government may desire to provide certain services efficiently. It may also desire to be the "employer of last resort," and to provide work for the otherwise unemployable. Efficiency with respect to one objective may preclude efficiency in another. Second, the objectives or the outputs may not be readily measurable. "Adequate police protection" or "adequate fire fighting capability" is not sufficiently precise to serve as a standard against which the desirability of a given level of input (expenditure) may be objectively evaluated. Given these two factors, budgets

**Under Accrual Accounting**

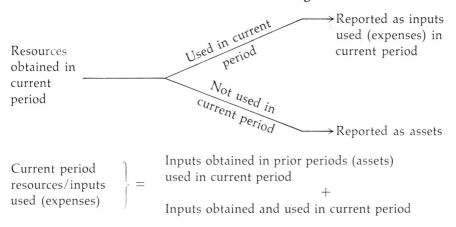

Resources obtained in current period — Used in current period → Reported as inputs used (expenses) in current period

Not used in current period → Reported as assets

$$\left.\begin{array}{l}\text{Current period}\\\text{resources/inputs}\\\text{used (expenses)}\end{array}\right\} = \begin{array}{l}\text{Inputs obtained in prior periods (assets)}\\\text{used in current period}\\\qquad\qquad +\\\text{Inputs obtained and used in current period}\end{array}$$

frequently are somewhat arbitrarily established in terms of generalized objectives. An entire organization's costs may be budgeted in much the same way as a programmed cost is budgeted within a business. Control must, therefore, often be exercised in terms of inputs alone—an absolute ceiling of expenditure in a particular area for a given period. Control emphasis is upon assurance that expenditures or obligations incurred in a particular period do not exceed a predetermined or budgeted level.

## BUDGETING INPUTS—DEFINING LIMITS TO OBLIGATIONS

In various governmental responsibility centers, and in many other nonbusiness activities, budgets are fixed for the period in terms of maximum allowable expenditures. Note the difference in the intention of the budgeted amount. In budgeting for businesses, as you have learned, a budgeted expenditure is a reasonable expectation of what will occur, given an expected level of output (activity). During the ensuing budgeted period, a responsibility center may exceed the budget and is encouraged to do so when warranted by changed or nonanticipated circumstances. In governments and many other nonprofit organizations, the intention of the budget is to serve as a ceiling (in government the amount legally available) for the period, beyond which expenditures cannot be incurred **regardless** of circumstances.[5]

In establishing nonbusiness budgets, the organization's objectives and expected outputs are taken into account. However, in traditional nonprofit systems, they are **not** made explicit in terms that can be used effectively to

---

[5]    In governments a supplementary budget appropriation must first be enacted to provide authorization for additional expenditure.

assess the desirability of proposed expenditures.[6] Instead, the basis for budgeting this year's expenditures generally becomes the amount used last year, together with necessary adjustments. Adjustments are almost always upwards.

Before proceeding, stop and consider the motivational aspects of such a system. If you were a manager, especially of a governmental unit, would your intention at the time of budget preparation be to request a budget amount equal to a reasonable expectation of your needs? If next year you find that you underestimated your needs, or even in the event of totally unexpected circumstances, you could still not exceed your budget. An additional budget appropriation is often difficult, if not impossible, to obtain, especially on short notice. Without a protective cushion (slack or padding) in your budget, you might end up literally unable to do your job. The more conscientious you were about meeting your job responsibilities, the more you would be motivated to pad your budget to provide for contingencies.

To compound the problem, what would be your motivation at year-end if you had unexpended funds? Suppose your current budget for office supplies was $5,000, and that it was one month before the end of the fiscal year. You have already spent $4,000, and have adequate supplies on hand to last for several months. At year-end, uncommitted funds are lost forever, and, in budgeting next year, your base used this year would be only $4,000. You would probably be foolish not to purchase totally unneeded supplies both to justify this year's request and also to establish a better negotiating base for next year. The system does not induce goal congruence between the manager and the taxpayer.

The process for establishing nonbusiness budgets is similar to the preliminary and final budget phases in a business. A budgetary request is developed starting at the lowest levels of responsibility. The overall budget request (in government known as the *legislative* or *executive budget*) is then submitted to the legislature or board, as appropriate. The budget request is reviewed and modified (usually downwards) by the authoritative body. The final approved (authorized) budget results from this process. In governments it takes the form of an *appropriation*, which represents the legally authorized expenditure ceiling.

The *authorized budget*, or appropriation, specifies expenditure amounts for each separate type of activity. It generally does not provide permission for transfers from one category to another. Such budgets are known as line-item budgets, since each line on a page becomes in itself a minibudget (a ceiling of expenditure for the particular item).

The aim of input budgeting (and of the matching fund accounting system that will be described below) is absolute control over expenditure. It is not targeted at providing useful information for assessing effectiveness or efficiency in terms of organizational objectives. You also should not underestimate the importance of legal constraints upon the system. Practices and procedures

---

6   In hospitals, government-owned utilities, various authorities, and other borderline cases, outputs are explicitly budgeted, and expenditures planned in terms of anticipated activity levels.

that may seem unnecessarily complex are necessitated by legal requirements applicable to many nonbusiness organizations as well as to government. The restrictions upon transfers between categories in a line-item budget are often mandated by legislation.

In response to legal limitations, maximizing the budget may become the primary objective of the organizational unit. Status, recognition, and power may be defined in terms of budget size and growth rate. And considerable energy may be expended in developing strategies and in gamesmanship designed to result in budget increases for the following year.

Since input budgets are not intended to provide output-related control information, they have limited value:

- Outputs or achievements are not specified;
- Inputs are specified in terms of quantities to be acquired currently, independent of usage;
- Inputs are identified with the acquiring rather than the using responsibility center; and
- Input amounts do not represent reasonable expectations of need. Instead they can best be described as some amount arbitrarily resulting from maximum justifiable request, subject to imposed cuts.

You should see that budgets of this type are relatively worthless for control in the business sense. No basis is provided for measuring either the effectiveness or the efficiency of resource usage. Input budgets can only serve as a basis for controlling expenditures in terms of fixed planned levels. All items become analogous to programmed costs in a business under a fixed budgeting system.

## BUDGETING OUTPUTS AND RELATED INPUTS— PPBS, MBO, AND ZBB

With the continuously growing significance of the nonprofit segment of the U.S. economy, the need for more effective control is becoming greater. Obviously in response to this need, several systems focused on outputs, effectiveness, and efficiency have been developed. Four approaches to the problem will be outlined below. They are known as:

PPBS (Planning–Programming–Budgeting System),
MBO (Management by Objectives),
ZBB (Zero-Based Budgeting), and
Sunset Legislation.

### PPBS

PPBS involves the establishment of a segment or program as an entity having a coherent objective. A program can be thought of as being like an element of a strategic or intermediate-range plan (Chapter 2). In the broadest sense, a program may be defined as an intention to modify or maintain some situation in a specific desirable manner. An example of a program would be "improvement of English reading and writing skills among college students."

The PPBS system starts with the statement of a coherent objective (the planning portion). Under PPBS, the objective or benefit of a program need not be measurable in financial terms (dollars of revenue), but it can be. The objectives of a job training program for the unemployed and underemployed could be set forth in terms of welfare costs (payments plus costs of services) saved, plus additional income tax revenue on resulting added employee earnings. Examples of nonfinancial measures would include number of students educated (possibly defined in terms of test achievement) for an educational program, or percentage reduction in violent crimes for a police-related program. At lower levels of responsibility within a program, surrogate measures such as student–faculty contact hours or number of arrests leading to conviction may prove useful to middle managers in evaluating performance.

The programming part of PPBS involves determination of the specific activities deemed desirable as means toward accomplishing the program plan or objective. Desirable equipment, types of instruction, student–faculty ratios, number of police per 1,000 population, and so forth, would be examples of implementing programs.

Under PPBS, budgeting would then proceed in terms of the costs of resources to be used in achieving the programmed objectives. Performance could then be measured in terms of cost effectiveness such as cost per student educated or cost of violent crime averted.

A *program budget* might cut across several established responsibility centers. Recall that, in business, a product-line manager has responsibility for dealing with various levels and with different functional subdivisions within the firm. Exhibit 15.2 illustrates the similar interface between an English reading and writing improvement program and a university structure.

Note, in Exhibit 15.2, that the English Skills Improvement Program cuts across several universities (distinct responsibility centers). Within each university, it may be involved in several distinct line items within the budgets for several different colleges. Also note that when program costs are assigned to specific responsibility centers, adequate planning and control may be achieved in terms of direct costs only. However, full costs are desirable for planning and controlling the program itself. Only with full costs available can the cost effectiveness of the overall program be properly evaluated.

Programmed budgeting is quite similar to business budgeting. There are five major differences:

1. The output activity may not always be budgeted in financial terms.

2. The programmed budget may be more like a service-center budget. The program entity may not correspond to a single organizational component or structure.

3. A programmed budget focuses on overall objectives and is normally generated at the top of an organization and then integrated among lower levels.

**Exhibit 15.2**
ILLUSTRATION OF PROGRAM BUDGET

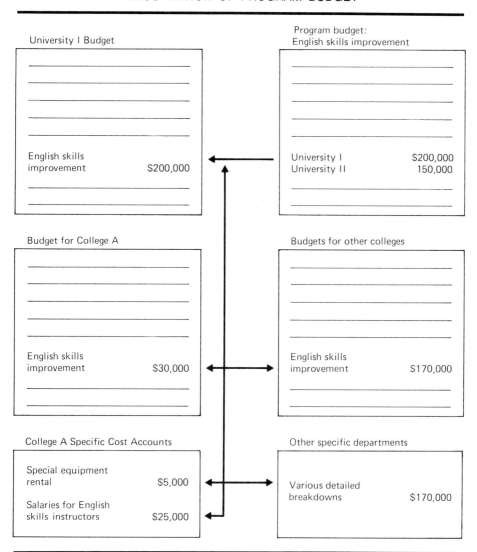

4. The approved programmed budget represents an **estimate** of what will happen rather than an **agreement** between a supervisor and a subordinate as to what will happen.

5. PPBS concentrates on major programs and objectives and therefore may not cover all of the activities within the organization.

Programmed budgeting was considered to have great promise in the 1960s. It was installed in the Department of Defense in 1961. Attempts were made to expand the use of PPBS into other branches of the federal government during the middle and late 60's. However it was not accepted and has not been required since 1971. It has been claimed that PPBS failed because it generated too much paperwork. Other reasons that may have contributed to its demise include:

- Input budgeting has been very prevalent for over forty years, and inertia is a powerful force, especially in nonprofit organizations.
- Since it does provide output-based measures for effectiveness and efficiency, PPBS can prove a threat to nonbusiness employees who currently have no such standard by which they may be evaluated.
- In any governmental or other nonbusiness organization, knowledge represents political power and, therefore, may be withheld to a manager's advantage. PPBS would require and provide more open communication, thus reducing political power.
- Many existing PPBS systems have not yet proved to enhance effective control. One apparent reason for this failure is the failure of the accounting system to provide adequate data for effective performance measurement. This subject will be explored more fully later in this chapter.

## MBO

MBO or Management by Objectives is more of an approach to budgeting rather than a system in itself. MBO was discussed in Chapter 2 as the underlying rationale for business budgeting. In nonbusiness budgeting, MBO has been primarily used as a tool for resource allocation within established budgetary limits, rather than as a basis or foundation for budgeting. It was introduced into the federal government in 1973 as a replacement for PPBS, and has subsequently apparently disappeared through inattention.[7]

## ZBB

Although not new in concept, Zero-Based Budgeting (ZBB) seems recently to be an idea whose time has come. The current version of ZBB was developed at Texas Instruments, Inc., in 1969 by Peter A. Pyhrr. It has been used extensively in the private sector in the past few years as a supplement to regular budgeting, and appears to be an effective instrument for identifying potential savings in programmed cost areas. ZBB has also been mandated by presidential directive to be the basis for preparing the federal governmental (executive) budget, commencing with the 1979 fiscal year.

As previously mentioned, current budgeting practice in much of the nonbusiness sector (and possibly in some areas of large private corporations) may be thought of as *incremental budgeting*. Under incremental budgeting, atten-

---

[7]   Note, however, that whereas MBO may have quietly disappeared from the nonprofit scene it is alive, well, and prospering in business organizations.

tion is directed to additions to the prior year's budget. The existing level of activity is assumed to carry forward and, customarily, only increases over the prior year's appropriations are considered or need to be justified.

In contrast to incremental budgeting, ZBB does not differentiate "old" and "new" dollars. All budget dollars each year must be justified. In theory each responsibility center starts from zero each year; hence the name ZBB. In application the required justification each year would generate an unacceptable level of energy and paperwork. Therefore, ZBB includes a comprehensive review approximately every six years. In other years, the starting point of the budgeting process can be thought of as zero increments above the minimum activity level for each decision package, as these terms will be defined below.

ZBB, as distinct from PPBS and MBO, focuses on activities, starting at the lowest responsibility center within the organization and moving upwards. Managers at the lowest cost or expenditure centers must:

1. Identify separate basic service or overhead units which are controlled (known as "decision packages").

2. Identify for each package, the minimum activity level and the related levels of benefits and costs. The minimum activity level is defined as that level below which the operation should be entirely eliminated as no longer viable.

3. Identify for each package, expanded activity increments, with their attendant benefits and costs.

4. Identify available alternatives and costs for achieving comparable benefits at each activity level.

5. Rank decision packages by priority.

Packages with ranking are then aggregated at successively higher levels within the organization.

The intention of ZBB is to generate consideration as part of the budget preparation process, and to provide data for consideration in the budget review process, of the following questions:

• Are current activities both effective and efficient?

• Can and should present activities/levels be reached or eliminated to accomplish overall budget reduction or in favor of more desirable alternative activities?

Supporters of ZBB cite five major benefits:

1. ZBB is total in scope. Everything is examined impartially, old money, new money, and even so-called uncontrollable commitments such as interest on debt.

2. ZBB forces identification and measurement of objectives.

3. It forces consideration of alternative methods for accomplishing objectives.

4. It provides for comparative rankings among old and new, rather than just among new budget increments; and

5. It encourages involvement by lower-level management personnel in the blending of operating decisions with the budget.

Opponents of ZBB are more skeptical of its feasibility and value than they are hostile to its concepts. Opponents point to the increased workload involved in ZBB, as contrasted to incremental budgeting. They cite the 1962 experience at the Department of Agriculture when the department experimented with an earlier version of ZBB. At that time, so much paperwork (tens of thousands of pages of justifications and alternatives) was generated that it swamped the budget personnel and killed the experiment. ZBB opponents are skeptical with respect to the alleged advantages of focusing on objectives. They believe that, in a great many cases, meaningful output measures cannot be found. Also, even with meaningful measures of output, the association of desirable costs with various activity levels or "decision packages" may be extremely difficult and mostly arbitrary. Therefore, ZBB would involve meaningless measures and would be reduced to a mere paperwork exercise.

Opponents of ZBB also feel that the system will encourage just as much gamesmanship as at present. For example, more essential projects may be ranked below those that are less essential for tradeoff bargaining purposes. Those who oppose ZBB also cite its track record. Apparently, in the public sector to date (state and local governments), ZBB has resulted in no significant cost savings.[8]

In the private sector, ZBB has apparently proved to be a valuable adjunct to conventional budgeting when used periodically (once every five to ten years). In the public sector its feasibility may still need to be proved. As mentioned, its use is currently mandated for the executive branch of the federal government, and it has been receiving the active personal backing of the President. However, ZBB poses the same threats cited above under PPBS.[9] The established bureaucracy might follow the Agriculture Department model and respond with an impossibly overwhelming torrent of paper. The progress of ZBB in the federal government should prove interesting to observe.

## Sunset Legislation

Easily confused with ZBB is so-called **Sunset Legislation.** Neither are new ideas but they are both experiencing more current attention. They both require reexamination of established activities instead of allowing the incremental budgeting approach described earlier.

---

[8]    See the article "Zero-based budgeting is a fraud," Robert N. Anthony. *Wall Street Journal*, April 27, 1977.

[9]    Even the title is considered so threatening that the State of California uses "Zero-Based Analysis" and the Xerox Corporation harks back to PPBS with their "Program-Base Budgeting" title for ZBB.

Sunset legislation does not involve ZBB but is conceptually similar. It involves automatic termination dates for specific programs or segments unless they are re-authorized by the legislature. Such enforced review generates analysis similar to that under ZBB. Since a common pattern for sunset laws is to require re-authorization over staggered six-year terms, the potential confusion with ZBB and its six-year comprehensive review provision is obvious. Sunset laws exist in Colorado, Florida, and Louisiana, and are pending in other states.

Sunset legislation, ZBB, MBO, and PPBS are still all aimed at establishing input-based budgets. Where output plans are developed as part of the budgeting process, effective performance measurement and control is still dependent upon the availability of appropriate accounting data. Information on actual performance must be available in terms of the measured objectives.

## RESPONSIBILITY ACCOUNTING FOR EFFECTIVE CONTROL

Effective control of operations in an organization is dependent upon having an attainable plan, and then adequate feedback to enable evaluation of performance in terms of the plan. The feedback of information must be in the same terms or language as the plan; otherwise comparison becomes relatively meaningless. Effectiveness of control is also predicated on the existence of freedom to deviate deliberately from a plan (or revise the plan) when circumstances change or do not develop as originally expected.

Unfortunately, most budgeting and control systems in nonprofit organizations preclude effective control as described in earlier chapters for business organizations. To understand the situation, it is desirable first to focus on the information prerequisite to effective control. One way to describe these prerequisites is to say simply that three information systems/conditions must exist:

1. A plan or budget focused upon outputs and inputs in relation to outputs.
2. A cost accounting system able to supply data in these same terms, outputs obtained and inputs used.
3. Freedom to deviate from plan as appropriate.

Many nonbusiness budgets are input-based, as has been described above. With only an input-based plan, only inputs (resources obtained) can be controlled.

What about those institutions that do establish output-based budgets employing PPBS, MBO, or ZBB? Can the institution's cost accounting system deliver compatible data for comparison to such a budget? The answer is, "Yes, it can," and, to anticipate the obvious next question, the answer is that in many cases "No, it does not currently."

As you learned in financial accounting and in Chapter 1 of this text, business uses the accrual system of accounting. The accrual system is designed specifically to measure revenues earned and resources actually used (expenses), regardless of when these resources were ordered (their purchase was committed or obligated). Where an output-based budget can be combined with an accrual accounting system, the first two information prerequisites to effective control have been met. However, even though accrual accounting is ubiquitous in the business world, its use is highly limited among nonprofit-directed institutions. As a group, only hospitals and other borderline organizations use a full accrual system.

Most nonprofit organizations employ the so-called *fund* or *obligation accounting* system.[10] The purpose of the fund accounting system is to account for funds (monetary assets) assigned to a particular fund. Fund accounting is **not** intended to account for the care and disposition of non-monetary assets once they have been acquired by the fund. Most fund accounting systems, therefore, essentially follow a modified cash basis, under which only monetary assets and liabilities are measured and recorded.[11] Since a fund is not involved in the concept of ownership, owners' equity accounts are replaced with a single account for fund balance.

Recall, from your study of financial accounting, that the basic equation of accrual accounting is:

$$\text{Assets} = \text{Equities (creditors' and owners' claims or shares)}$$

or

$$\text{Assets} = \text{Liabilities} + \text{Owners' Equity}.$$

During any given period (before closing), under accrual accounting, this equation may be expanded to include:

$$\text{Assets} = \text{Liabilities} + \text{Owners' Equity} + \text{Revenue} - \text{Expenses}$$

or

$$\text{Assets} + \text{Expenses} = \text{Liabilities} + \text{Owners' Equity} + \text{Revenue}.$$

The basic equation in fund accounting is:

$$\text{Assets} = \text{Liabilities} + \text{Fund balance};$$

and during a period, this equation is expanded to include:

$$\text{Assets} + \text{Expenditures} = \text{Liabilities} + \text{Revenue} + \text{Fund balance}$$

---

[10]   GAAP primarily cover profit-directed or accrual accounting. There exist two major sources of principles or guidelines for fund accounting. The first is GAAFR (for Government Accounting, Auditing, and Financial Reporting), promulgated by the National Council on Government Accounting (NCGA). The NCGA is a 1974 successor to several previous organizations starting in 1934. More recently the AICPA has also become a source of authoritative guidance for state and local governments.

[11]   As previously explained, some nonprofit organizations are close to borderline. The fund accounting systems in these organizations use a form of modified accrual accounting, wherein some nonmonetary assets such as inventory and supplies, and even fixed assets, may be included.

Since a single organization may have more than one fund, with transfers from one fund to another, the equation may be further expanded to include:

$$\begin{array}{l} \text{Assets} + \text{Expenditures} \\ + \text{ Interfund claims} \end{array} = \begin{array}{l} \text{Liabilities} + \text{Revenue} \\ + \text{ Fund balance} \\ + \text{ Interfund obligations} \end{array}$$

Interfund claims are essentially similar to accounts receivable, and interfund obligations to accounts payable. Note that, in application, this expanded equation differs from the accrual equation in the following ways:

- Assets may be restricted to include only monetary assets and often exclude revenue receivable;
- Since no accruals are involved, expenses are limited to actual expenditures;
- Liabilities also include commitments or obligations; and
- Fund balance replaces Owners' Equity

Fund accounting also differs from accrual accounting in that, during a period (before closing), budget information is actually included in the accounts. Nominal accounts are established for anticipated revenues and authorized expenditures. During a period, the fund accounting system itself may be thought of as providing a continuous budget performance report. The difference between anticipated and actual revenues, and the difference between authorized and actual expenditures (including commitments) is constantly available in the fund's accounts.[12]

When an organization has more than one fund—for instance, a fund for operations, one for new construction, one for bonded indebtedness, and so forth—the fund designated to cover operations is known as the *general fund*. Funds other than the general fund will not be discussed in this text. A further discussion of fund accounting, together with a simplified illustration of the accounts and entries involved, is included in the appendix to this chapter.

As part of acquiring an overview of control in nonbusiness organizations, it is particularly important that you see clearly that:

1. Where the control objective is limited to controlling the commitment and actual expenditure of funds, input-based budgets incorporated in the fund accounting system provide an adequate and inherently coherent system.
2. Where a control objective also includes the effective and efficient use of existing and acquired resources, even if an output-based budget exists, a fund accounting system is not designed to and therefore cannot provide adequate control information. Specifically, it **cannot** provide data relating to:
   - Nonmonetary assets available for future use,

---

[12]  Fund accounts and their balances are illustrated in the appendix to this chapter.

- Actual use of nonmonetary assets previously and currently acquired,
- Which responsibility centers were the users of these nonmonetary assets.

Effective control, as defined in the business sense, requires a responsibility accounting system that can report the costs of operating a particular responsibility center for a given period. Operating costs of a particular center are the expenses of that center, and some form of accrual accounting is necessary to generate adequate expense data. Note that a fund accounting system can be modified to incorporate desirable accruals and deferrals, as is currently done in previously identified borderline organizations. Inclusion of accruals need not hinder desirable expenditure and commitment control. Nominal accounts for authorization (appropriations) and commitments (encumbrances or obligations) may be readily incorporated in any double-entry accounting system.

The introduction of accruals is gradually occurring within the federal government, other government units, and nongovernmental institutions. In addition to the elements of tradition, inertia, and fear of effectiveness and efficiency measures previously cited, delays in desirable modifications of fund accounting systems may be attributed to lack of consensus with respect to accounting for capital (fixed) assets.

## CAPITAL BUDGETING IN THE NONBUSINESS SECTOR

So far in this chapter, discussion has been focused upon the control of operations. Control over expenditure for capital or fixed assets, so-called *capital costs*,[13] must also exist. Two dimensions of capital costs, capital budgeting and accounting for cost expiration (depreciation), both may differ between business firms and nonbusiness institutions and governments.

### Benefit/Cost Analysis

As you had the opportunity to learn in Chapters 7 and 8, capital budgeting decisions in a business are based on benefit/cost analysis in terms of discounted cash flows. In nonprofit-directed organizations, the analysis involves determining whether discounted *social benefits* exceed discounted *social costs*. Social benefits may include actual revenues (such as fees collected), additional

---

[13]   The terms capital cost and cost of capital are potentially confusing since they refer to two distinctly different concepts. Capital cost is widely used and can be thought of as synonymous with nonmonetary asset cost. It refers to expenditures or outlays for the acquisition of capital assets (future service potentials). Capital cost does **not** refer to interest or return to investors. It is independent of the method or costs of financing.

Cost of capital, on the other hand, refers to equities in the organization. Cost of capital generally refers to a mix of necessary interest charges and adequate earnings to satisfy investors. It is discussed in Chapter 6.

taxes collected (resulting from a higher tax base, as cited for job training programs), and reduced operating costs. They may also include opportunity cost savings or positive *externalities*, such as lower cost of crime loss or property insurance, of fire loss or fire insurance, of illness loss or medical insurance, of flood loss or catastrophe insurance, and so forth. Note that expected benefits may be received by many separate individuals, groups, and organizations, and that they may not be readily measurable in monetary terms.

Social costs would include both incremental cash outflows and also the opportunity costs of any negative externalities. Examples of negative externalities would include the cost to individuals and firms of being displaced by construction (or even by flooding, in the case of a dam) and any environmental damage. Social benefit/social cost analysis may be observed in the environmental impact studies now required for many business and public projects.

Benefit/cost analysis in nonprofit-directed organizations may be thought of as a counterpart of CVP analysis for a business firm, as first discussed in Chapter 6. Evaluation should be based on a clear distinction between variable and fixed costs. Relevant costs should include variable costs and those fixed costs that are not committed. Assume the following facts with respect to a new course offered by a college:

| | |
|---|---|
| Setup costs (course and course materials preparation) | $20,000 |
| Instructor's salary, first semester (portion) | 3,500 |
| Other operating expenses, per semester | 500 |
| | $24,000 |
| Number of students enrolled first semester | 24 |

Evaluation of the cost effectiveness of the new course in terms of $1,000 per student would be inappropriate and misleading.

A more appropriate analysis might first involve identifying and, if possible, quantifying the benefits to the student and possibly to the college (recognition) of offering the new course. A reasonable expected **future** enrollment per semester should then be determined. Benefits and costs per student could then be estimated, ignoring setup costs, with any net profit considered as a contribution toward recovery of initial startup cost:

| | | |
|---|---|---|
| Anticipated yearly benefits of new course | | $35,000 |
| Instructors' annual salary | $28,000 | |
| Other operating costs | 2,000 | |
| Net annual benefit | | $5,000 |
| Expected annual enrollment | | 250 students |
| Net benefit per student | | $20 |

## Accounting For Capital Costs

Once a capital budgeting decision is approved and implemented, the expenditures involved must be accounted for. The accounting differs between the accrual and the fund systems. The difference occurs with respect to capitalization and subsequent depreciation expense. At issue is the question as to who should pay for capital assets and their eventual replacement in nonprofit organizations.

The underlying assumption of business financial accounting (the accrual system) is that existing users and owners of capital assets must bear not only costs of maintenance but also the costs of replacement. Income available for distribution to owners does not exist until capital has been maintained.[14] A portion of the capital expenditure of prior periods is allocated as a cost in the current period via depreciation. Depreciation serves to advise management and owners that a portion of funds generated in operations must be accumulated in the firm (even without specific funding of depreciation) in order to maintain invested capital.

What about institutions where capital assets are acquired by donation (hospital and university buildings and equipment) or by specific appropriation (government assets)? In these situations, it may be assumed that future donors or taxpayers will bear the cost of replacement. Should depreciation expense be charged when there is no intention of accumulating replacement funds?

It is argued that, in nonprofit institutions and governments, since there is no profit intention and no need to measure distributable income, depreciation is irrelevant and meaningless. An opposing view holds that capitalization and subsequent depreciation is still meaningful in these situations, for one or more of four reasons:

**1.** Even if not allocated to each responsibility center using a particular capital asset, depreciation is essential at the total program level in order to measure adequately the effective total annual cost of the program. To treat all capital assets as 100-percent sunk costs, just because they were donated or appropriated in prior periods, can distort benefit/cost analysis.

**2.** Depreciation, as part of total cost, is necessary where pricing decisions related to fees to be charged are involved. Knowing full costs (including depreciation) would still be relevant in those cases where the intention was to set fees without aiming at recovery of full costs. The fee-setting body should be aware of the annual loss (subsidy) involved in any proposed fee structure.

**3.** Depreciation should be taken into account when comparing the relative economies of public vs. private provision of desired services. For instance, to compare costs of municipal operation of trash collection with bids from private firms would be misleading unless depreciation was included or excluded from both alternatives.

**4.** Developing and maintaining book value of capital assets entrusted to

---

[14]   Capital to be maintained under current GAAP is defined as only historical dollars invested. The effects of inflation on dollar purchasing power and replacement costs will be discussed in Chapter 16.

individual responsibility centers could provide the basis for increased accountability of the center manager. The rapidly escalating cost of capital assets places much greater responsibility of stewardship in the public interest upon managers, supervisors, and even workers using such assets. With no effective attention currently being given to the cost of capital assets once acquired,[15] an individual using an asset has little incentive, other than convenience, to protect it from loss or destruction. Currently, employee remuneration in nonprofit organizations rarely recognizes the value of assets controlled; and retention and promotion decisions rarely consider the individual's "track record" in preserving capital assets.

At present, there appears to exist little consensus with respect to the desirability of depreciation accounting in nonprofit organizations, except for the borderline institutions.[16] Comparative data is, therefore, distorted between centers where one has acquired assets by donation or appropriation and the other through the issuance of debt (bonds). Expenditure accounting shows no financing charge for one, and interest as part of operating cost for the other. Where a sinking fund is involved, the distortion can be even greater. The organization with donated or appropriated assets still reports no capital costs (interest or depreciation) as part of operations. The other reports as operating costs (expenditure) both interest and principal repayment contribution to its sinking fund. At least the latter may be compared to a business firm, as principal repayment contributions may approximate depreciation.

To recapitulate, the traditional approach to fund accounting in many nonprofit organizations may be considered as having two weaknesses in relation to performance evaluation and control:

1. The exclusive preoccupation with expenditure control restricts attention to procurement rather than use. In a business, this approach might be analogous to cash-basis accounting, with budgeting and control focused on the current activities of the purchasing (procurement) and personnel (hiring) departments.

2. The failure to accrue (or defer) costs, especially of capital assets, precludes effective matching with benefits even if such benefits were made explicit. Also the failure to allocate capital costs makes it relatively difficult to prepare meaningful comparisons to other nonprofit organizations or to business firms.

---

[15]  Inventories of capital assets may be periodically taken which treat, at the user responsibility level, $50 desks and $5,000,000 pieces of equipment equally, as merely items with serial numbers.

[16]  Those borderline institutions that may be given their initial asset base, and thereafter are expected to maintain their operations and operating capacity (government corporations), are, of course, different. Depreciation accounting is appropriate and is used in these cases.

## OTHER ISSUES

Of the many other control-related subjects applicable to nonprofit organizations, two deserve mention as part of this introductory discussion. One involves **pricing** and the other **flexibility.** Just as there is little consensus and uniformity within the nonbusiness sector with respect to the appropriate reporting of depreciation and capital assets, there is also no uniform approach to either pricing or charging for services rendered. The pricing issue involves both the decision as to which services should be subject to fee, and also, where a fee is to be charged, the appropriate amount or size of the fee.

Services performed by governments and other nonbusiness organizations fall on a spectrum. At one extreme are those that directly and indirectly benefit the entire public—so-called **public goods,** like national defense or public health. And at the other end are services where most or all of the benefit accrues to a specific individual or group. Examples of services benefiting specific users would include police personnel assigned to cordon off areas for shooting movies and TV films on location, Coast Guard towing of disabled private pleasure craft, and so forth. Public policy would probably be best served by providing so-called public goods at no fee or on an ability-to-pay basis. Other services would then be charged to the user(s) at full cost. Such a policy is rarely followed consistently in current practice.

Where fees are charged with an intention of cost recovery, there exists considerable diversity of practice. Nonborderline institutions rarely include recovery of capital costs as previously discussed. The result is that cost-recovery fees are inappropriately low, and excess or unnecessary usage may be encouraged. At another extreme are those service fees that represent full reimbursement of actual costs. As with service centers within a firm, full actual cost reimbursement provides no incentive for cost control.

It would appear that services that are not public goods should not be given away. Where benefits are not reasonably uniform to all, then the users of the service should pay. The users should be charged an amount that would at least cover full standard costs. Fees should be high enough to discourage excess usage and, at the same time, not so high as to provide a pass-through cover for inefficiency.

The final issue involves flexibility. Recall that early in this chapter it was stated that effective control requires three elements—output-based budgeting, output-based responsibility accounting, and the flexibility to deviate from budget in unanticipated circumstances. Many current control systems in the nonbusiness sector are so completely oriented to absolute control over expenditures that they become counterproductive. Where a budget revision in light of unanticipated circumstances becomes effectively impossible to obtain, there is strong motivation for excessive padding. At the other extreme, narrowly defined appropriations provide the basis for practically unlimited "changed circumstances" and "reimbursable cost overruns" on the part of those providing goods and services to the government.

Management control in nonprofit organizations is often not as effective as in the private sector. Since the need for effective management in this segment of the economy is great and becoming greater, you may anticipate the possibility of more change than in the business segment over the next few years. The problems are complex and often political. The intention of this chapter has been merely to increase your awareness of the influence of various budgeting and accounting systems upon the control issues.

## CHAPTER OVERVIEW

Based upon the material contained in this chapter, you should now be in a position to:

- Describe the differences in purpose and characteristics between business and nonbusiness organizations, and explain how these differences have led to different control objectives.

- Explain the difference between input-based and output-based budgets.

- Describe the control objective of systems where input-based budgets are incorporated in the fund accounting system.

- Discuss possibly counterproductive incentives intrinsic to the input-based approach, and explain why many such systems are not particularly useful for evaluating the effectiveness and efficiency of organizations.

- Describe the roles of PPBS, MBO, ZBB, and sunset legislation, and outline the essential elements of each.

- Describe some of the factors that may explain the slow growth/ acceptance of PPBS, MBO, ZBB, and accrual accounting in nonprofit organizations.

- Explain the differences between capital budgeting for business firms and for nonprofit organizations, and give examples of benefit/cost analysis applied to a capital budgeting proposal in a nonprofit organization.

- Describe the arguments for and against inclusion of depreciation charges in nonbusiness accounting.

- Distinguish between those goods and services for which a full-cost fee may be inappropriate and those where it would be desirable; and describe a desirable basis for the establishment of such fees.

## NEW VOCABULARY AND CONCEPTS

| | |
|---|---|
| Borderline cases (organizations) | Sunset legislation |
| Legislative budget | Fund (obligation) accounting |
| Authorized budget/appropriation | General-fund |
| Program budget | Capital costs |
| PPBS | Social benefits |
| MBO | Externalities |
| ZBB | |
| Incremental budgeting | |

- The distinction between budgets that are output-based and those that are focused on inputs.
- The differences between accrual accounting and fund accounting.

## REVIEW QUESTIONS

1. a) What is the purpose of a business that differs from that of a nonprofit organization?
   b) What are three important characteristics of business firms that are not, or may not be, present in most nonprofit organizations?

2. a) What is the central purpose of most nonprofit organizations?
   b) How does this purpose affect the measurement of the effectiveness and efficiency of performance of such organizations? Explain, with examples.
   c) How may effectiveness and efficiency be measured in at least partially nonfinancial terms? Give examples.

3. a) What are "borderline organizations," as defined in this chapter? Give examples.
   b) What are the characteristics of such organizations and their budgeting and control systems that make them "borderline"?

4. a) What control objectives are common to business and nonbusiness organizations?
   b) Which control objectives are unique to business firms?
   c) What two factors may lead nonbusiness organizations to have different control objectives than business firms?
   d) Which control objectives are unique to nonbusiness organizations?

5. a) What is the difference between an input-oriented budget and one which is output-based?
   b) What is the difference in intention between a given figure included in an input-based budget and that of a similar figure appearing on a business budget?
   c) What potentially counterproductive (from the viewpoint of social interest) motivations may be inherent in the input-based budgeting process?

6. a) What is an appropriation?

   b) What is its purpose?

   c) How does it differ from a finally approved budget in a business firm?

7. What aspects or characteristics of an input-based budget make it unsuitable as an instrument for measuring the effectiveness and efficiency of an organization's performance (other than with respect to limiting expenditures)?

8. a) What is the Planning–Programming–Budgeting System (PPBS)?

   b) How does it differ from more traditional input-based budgeting systems?

   c) What parallel exists between PPBS and budgeting for a product-line manager within a business firm?

   d) What three major differences exist between a business budget for a responsibility center and a programmed budget following PPBS?

9. a) What is MBO?

   b) How has it been used in nonbusiness budgeting?

10. a) What is zero-based budgeting (ZBB)?

    b) How does zero-based budgeting differ from incremental budgeting as commonly practiced in many governments and other nonbusiness organizations?

11. a) What is sunset legislation?

    b) What is its purpose and how does it relate to ZBB?

12. What factors may be responsible for the slow acceptance of PPBS, MBO, and ZBB, as part of the governmental budgeting process?

13. What are the three essential system prerequisites for effective control as defined in a business context?

14. What differences exist between accrual accounting and fund accounting with respect to:

    a) Cost responsibility?

    b) Cost timing?

    c) Executory agreements?

    d) Earned but not received revenue?

    e) Capitalization of nonmonetary assets?

    f) Depreciation?

    g) Inclusion of budget data in the accounts?

    h) Identification of the balance of assets minus liabilities?

15. a) Does the fund accounting system, as generally designed and operated, provide information concerning the full costs of operating a particular responsibility center? Explain.

    b) Can a particular organization have more than one fund? If yes, explain with examples.

    c) What is the general fund within an organization? What is its purpose?

16. a) How does capital budgeting differ between business and nonbusiness organizations?

    b) What type of report required of business (and nonbusiness organizations) is related to social benefit/social cost (including externalities) analysis in a nonprofit organization?

17. a) What is the justification for excluding depreciation from operating costs for certain nonprofit organizations?

    b) What are some of the problems introduced by the exclusion of depreciation charges?

    c) What are some of the arguments that can be used to support inclusion of capitalization of assets and depreciation charges in most nonprofit organizations' accounting?

**18.** In nonprofit organizations, what standards appear desirable with respect to pricing?

    a) What types of items should be subject to user fees?

    b) What cost data should provide the basis for setting user fees?

    c) Is full-actual-cost reimbursement a desirable basis for charging service fees? Explain.

## MINI-CASES AND QUESTIONS FOR DISCUSSION

**MC 15.1** Mr. Trent Jones, an owner and manager of a small mid-western manufacturing firm, is addressing members of the local Chamber of Commerce. He states in part, "A bill is before our state legislature which is, in effect, a 'sunset law,' just like Colorado's. It provides that all government agencies each ten years must justify their continuation or else automatically go out of existence, a kind of zero-based programmed budgeting approach to the problem. I heartily support this legislation, and suggest that you do also.

    "These laws don't go far enough, but we taxpayers have to make a start somewhere. There's no excuse for not having zero-based budgeting each year. All of our operating budgets are zero-based, and so are all of yours. We have no difficulty building from zero each year; why should the government?

    "And while we're at it, we should all push for 100-percent programmed budgeting to take effect within the next few years. (*Warming to his subject and pounding the lectern*) Every government agency should be required to justify its existence each year, not only once every ten!"

    Do you concur with Mr. Jones? Does Mr. Jones correctly understand the concepts of PPBS and ZBB? Would it be practical to require each governmental responsibility center to justify its existence each year? Would zero-based input budgeting each year be the same as business budgeting? Would zero-based programmed budgeting be the same as business budgeting? Discuss.

**MC 15.2** Capital budgeting decisions in the public sector involve benefit/cost analysis in terms of discounted social cost. But what discount rate should be used? Is the low incremental borrowing rate on government or municipal bonds an appropriate measure, or would a rate approximating an average cost-of-capital rate for private business in the same industry be more appropriate? Where government is effectively competing against private enterprise, wouldn't the use of the low government interest rate represent unfair competition? Wouldn't it allow for socially undesirable inefficiency, or inappropriately low prices, or both?

What about those situations where there is no private-sector activity? Should organizations with no private-sector equivalents have a different discount rate than others in competition with business? Discuss.

MC 15.3 Within input budgeting and fund accounting, what could realistically be done to remove the incentives to spend up to the budget by year-end? What might be done that could realistically lower the motivation to pad or include slack in the budget for contingencies? Would businesses that currently supply goods and services to governments support such changes? Discuss.

MC 15.4 There appears to be some risk that, if ZBB replaces PPBS, overall objectives may not be adequately coordinated or even emphasized. Preoccupation with ranking and justification at the lowest level of responsibility may foster lack of goal congruence with overall goals. Or arbitrary re-ranking at higher organizational levels to achieve congruence could offset the advantages of starting at the bottom. Should ZBB be combined with PPBS? Should decision-package benefits be correlated and measured in terms of overall objectives? Discuss.

## ESSENTIAL AND SUPPLEMENTARY PROBLEMS

There are no essential or supplementary problems for Chapter 15.

## SUGGESTIONS FOR FURTHER READING

Anthony, Robert N., and Regina Herzlinger, *Management Control in Nonprofit Organizations.* Homewood, Illinois: Richard D. Irwin, Inc., 1975.

Henke, Emerson, *Accounting for Nonprofit Organizations.* Belmont, California: Wadsworth Publishing Corporation, Inc., 1966.

Lynn, Edward S., and Robert J. Freeman, *Fund Accounting: Theory and Practice.* Englewood Cliffs, N.J.: Prentice-Hall, Inc., 1974.

Phyrr, Peter A., "Zero-base budgeting," *Harvard Business Review,* November–December, 1970.

CHAPTER 15 APPENDIX
# An Introduction to Fund Accounting

(*Note.* This appendix is intended for those students familiar with financial accounting procedures who desire a brief exposure to the essential differences in fund accounting. If you are not already familiar with conventional journal entries and T-account posting for businesses, this appendix may be confusing and of little value for you.)

Many nonprofit organizations, and all governments, use some form of the so-called *fund accounting system.* Fund accounting differs from the accrual accounting system used by businesses in several ways:

**1.** The legal or business organizational entity under business accounting is treated as a single unit. Under fund accounting, an organization may be divided into different components, each accounted for by a separate fund. A fund is a distinct accounting entity established to account for certain resources designated for accomplishing specific activities or objectives. For instance, a hospital might have separate funds for operations, new building construction, government sponsored research, and so forth. Governments and many other organizations using fund accounting each have a general fund covering operating activities. Other funds may exist for special projects, capital asset acquisitions, and so forth. Where more than one fund exists within a given organization, transfers of resources among funds is accomplished through interfund clearing accounts (interfund claims and interfund obligations) which operate like receivables and payables between separate business entities.

**2.** The focus of fund accounting is on reporting upon the custodianship and expenditure of monetary resources. Attention is directed toward whether monetary resources have been expended in the desired or prescribed manner and amount. There is no attempt to evaluate the results of such expenditure.

**3.** Within each fund there exist separate accounts for assets and liabilities, with a single account for "fund balance" replacing the Owner's Equity accounts found in a business firm. Most fund accounting systems operate on a modified cash, rather than an accrual, basis. Noncurrent (capital) assets are expensed when acquired, rather than being capitalized. Depreciation is usually ignored, except for those organizations involved in self-sustaining activities, or where depreciation is actually funded (monies earmarked and set aside for asset replacement). Current assets with future value (inventories, supplies, prepaid items) are similarly expensed in the period acquired.

**4.** Government and many other fund accounting systems incorporate within each fund accounts for anticipated revenues and for budgeted appropriations. Appropriations are those amounts that the fund is authorized to spend for designated purposes within the year. The system is designed, as will be illustrated below, to continuously provide information on the amounts of funds still available in each category for commitment or expenditure. Within business accounting, executory agreements are not recorded. Under fund accounting, commitments or obligations to expend resources are generally recorded at the time of commitment. Commitments are known as *encumbrances* (or as *obligations*, in the federal government). The amounts still available (appropriation less the sum of expenditures and open encumbrances to date) is known as the *unencumbered balance*.

**5.** Where a fund may be subdivided (have separate subsidiary accounts) into responsibility centers, the basis for division is the center responsible for the *expenditure* of funds to acquire goods or services. Segregation on this basis ignores whether the center is responsible for the use or disposition of the items acquired.

**6.** The usual sequence of recording is:
  a) Record authorization (appropriation),
  b) Record encumbrance,
  c) Record expenditure (first step in a business accounting system),
  d) Possibly, record accrual or deferral.[17]

### Illustration of Fund Accounting

To give you some familiarity with a fund accounting system and how it operates, a highly simplified example of a public university will be illustrated. Assume that, at the beginning of a period, the balance sheet for the university's general fund was as follows:

| Assets | | Liabilities and fund balance | |
|---|---|---|---|
| Cash | $100,000 | Payables | $ 30,000 |
| | | Fund balance | 70,000 |
| | $100,000 | | $100,000 |

During the period, you may assume that the following six events took place, in the sequence given:

---

[17] As mentioned above, most fund accounting is on a modified cash basis. Some funds follow a modified accrual system, wherein inventory, supplies, and occasionally capital assets are deferred; but accrued revenues and prepaid expenses are not included. Hospitals and government-owned utilities generally follow a full accrual system.

1. Revenue for the forthcoming period (tuition, fees, and other financial support) is estimated at $600,000. Also the university's governing body (state legislature, board of trustees, or regents, as appropriate) has approved appropriations for the coming period of $580,000, including, for the College of Business, $60,000 for equipment, $30,000 for salaries, and $20,000 for other items.

2. Equipment costing $100,000 is ordered by the university. Included in this group of orders is $35,000 of equipment for the College of Business.

3. The equipment on order for the College of Business, together with an invoice for $35,000, is received.

4. Invoices totalling $45,000 are paid by the university.

5. Throughout the period, $585,000 of anticipated revenue is actually collected.

6. During the period, additional expenditures totalling $530,000 are incurred and paid. Included in this group are $30,000 for salaries and $20,000 for other items identified with the College of Business. You may assume that only $55,000 had previously been encumbered with these encumbrances in other (nonbusiness) colleges.

The following entries would record these events. Exhibit 15.3 illustrates the record of these entries in the university general fund account, expressed in T-account form. Exhibit 15.4 includes the record of entries in a subsidiary ledger for a segment of the university identified as the College of Business. Note that other operating segments (other colleges) have not been illustrated.

1. Budgeted revenue and appropriations are recorded at the start of the period.

|  | DR | CR |
|---|---|---|
| Estimated revenue | $600,000 | |
| Appropriations | | $580,000 |
| Fund balance | | 20,000 |

Note that appropriations are broken down in detail on subsidiary ledgers by responsibility center.

2. The university commits (obligates) itself to the purchase of $100,000 of equipment.

|  | DR | CR |
|---|---|---|
| Encumbrances | $100,000 | |
| Reserve for encumbrances | | $100,000 |

Note that encumbrances are also detailed on subsidiary ledgers as **both** encumbrances and reductions of appropriations. The subsidiary ledger for the College of Business now reveals (balance in equipment appropriations account) only $15,000 available for future encumbrance/expenditure. The general-ledger control accounts for appropriations, encumbrances, and expenditures, together reveal an all-university balance of $480,000 still available for encumbrance/expenditure.

**Exhibit 15.3**

## UNIVERSITY GENERAL FUND (CONTROL) ACCOUNTS

| Cash | | | |
|---|---|---|---|
| (BB) $100,000 | | (4) | $ 45,000 |
| (5) | 585,000 | (6) | 530,000 |
| (EB) $110,000 | | | |

| Payables | | | |
|---|---|---|---|
| | | (BB) $ 30,000 | |
| (4) | $ 45,000 | (3a) | 35,000 |
| | | (EB) $ 20,000 | |

| Estimated revenue | | | |
|---|---|---|---|
| (1) | $600,000 | (7) | $600,000 |

| Reserve for encumbrances | | | |
|---|---|---|---|
| (3b) | $ 35,000 | (2) | $100,000 |
| (6b) | 55,000 | | |
| | | (EB) | 10,000 |

| Encumbrances* | | | |
|---|---|---|---|
| (2) | $100,000 | (3b) | $ 35,000 |
| | | (6b) | 55,000 |
| | | (8) | 10,000 |

| Fund balance | | | |
|---|---|---|---|
| | | (BB) $ 70,000 | |
| (7) | $ 15,000 | (1) | 20,000 |
| | | (8) | 5,000 |
| | | (EB) | 80,000 |

| Expenditures* | | | |
|---|---|---|---|
| (3a) | $ 35,000 | | |
| (6) | 530,000 | (8) | $565,000 |

| Revenue | | | |
|---|---|---|---|
| (7) | $585,000 | (5) | $585,000 |

*Notes.* BB = Beginning balance
EB = Ending balance
\* = Items broken down in
subsidiary ledgers by
responsibility center
(Exhibit 15.4).

| Appropriations* | | | |
|---|---|---|---|
| (8) | $580,000 | (1) | $580,000 |

**Exhibit 15.4**

## SUBSIDIARY APPROPRIATIONS LEDGER, COLLEGE OF BUSINESS

| Encumbrances | | Expenditures | | Equipment appropriations | |
|---|---|---|---|---|---|
| (2) $45,000 | (3b) $35,000 | (3a) $35,000 | | (a) $45,000 | (1) $60,000 |
| | | | | (3a) $35,000 | (3b) $35,000 |

| Encumbrances | Expenditures | | Salary appropriations | |
|---|---|---|---|---|
| | (6a) $35,000 | | (6a) $30,000 | (1) $30,000 |

| Encumbrances | Expenditures | | Other item appropriations | |
|---|---|---|---|---|
| | (6a) $20,000 | | (6a) $20,000 | (1) $20,000 |

**3(a).** Receipt of equipment and invoice for $35,000 for College of Business equipment is recorded.

| | | |
|---|---|---|
| Expenditures | $35,000 | |
| Payables | | $35,000 |

This entry parallels the usual entry in business accounting. The expenditure is also recorded in the subsidiary ledger to *both* the equipment expenditure and appropriations accounts.

**3(b).** The encumbrance associated with the goods or services received is now reversed.

| | | |
|---|---|---|
| Reserve for encumbrances | $35,000 | |
| Encumbrances | | $35,000 |

Reversal is also recorded in the subsidiary ledger. Note that, if the actual expenditure ended up as less than originally encumbered (not illustrated in this example), the entire original encumbrance would be reversed, "opening up" additional unencumbered funds. In this example you may assume that the encumbrance and the expenditure were the same, and that the College of Business still had $10,000 of equipment on order and $15,000 of unencumbered funds for additional equipment. Had the cost been greater than originally encumbered, entries 3(a) and 3(b) would result in a reduction of available (not encumbered or expended) funds.

**4.** Payment of $45,000 of payables is recorded.

| | | |
|---|---|---|
| Payables | $45,000 | |
| Cash | | $45,000 |

**5.** Collection of $585,000 of anticipated revenue is recorded.

| | | |
|---|---|---|
| Cash | $585,000 | |
| Revenue | | $585,000 |

Separate general fund (and possibly subsidiary ledger) revenue accounts for different major sources would usually be used, in place of the single revenue account illustrated.

**6(a).** Other expenditures totalling $530,000 are paid.

| | | |
|---|---|---|
| Expenditures | $530,000 | |
| Cash | | $530,000 |

**6(b).** Associated encumbrances are reversed.

| | | |
|---|---|---|
| Reserve for encumbrances | $55,000 | |
| Encumbrances | | $55,000 |

For simplification of this illustration it has been assumed that a large sum was unencumbered. Not all expenditures need be encumbered before incurrence. Encumbrance is used whenever a significant lead time is anticipated between commitment and expenditure.

At the end of the period, the normal accounts are closed to fund balance:

7. To close the nominal revenue accounts:

| | | |
|---|---|---|
| Revenue | $585,000 | |
| Fund balance | 15,000 | |
| Estimated revenue | | $600,000 |

The revenue shortfall reduces the fund carryover balance.

8. To close the nominal expenditure and appropriations accounts:

| | | |
|---|---|---|
| Appropriations | $580,000 | |
| Expenditures | | $565,000 |
| Encumbrances | | 10,000 |
| Fund balance | | 5,000 |

Expenditures and remaining commitments were $5,000 less than planned (appropriated). The fund carryover balance is therefore increased by this amount.

After closing, the ending balance sheet for the university's general fund would appear as follows:

| Assets | | Liabilities and fund balance | |
|---|---|---|---|
| Cash | $110,000 | Payables | $ 20,000 |
| | | Reserve for encumbrances | 10,000 |
| | | Fund balance | 80,000 |
| | $110,000 | | $110,000 |

Note that the outstanding commitment or obligation for $10,000 of equipment for the College of Business is reported as a liability.

The foregoing illustration is designed to provide you with a general understanding of the operation of a fund accounting system. For a good basic introduction that is more complete, you might refer to either Henke or Lynn and Freeman listed under Suggested Readings immediately preceding this appendix.

# 16

## ADJUSTING FOR INFLATION

## CHAPTER PREVIEW

The intention of this chapter is to introduce you to the necessity of adjusting decision information for inflation, and to the desirability of making similar adjustments to financial accounting data prior to its use as a basis for management decisions. This chapter also covers various approaches to making such adjustments. In this chapter you can learn:

- That dysfunctional behavior (decisions) may result from using data that is not properly adjusted for the effects of inflation.
- That different types of adjustment are necessary for short-run and long-run decision data.
- How, in periods of inflation, present GAAP may preclude appropriate timely reporting of certain economic realities.
- That conventional financial reporting may mislead the user as to the individuals responsible for certain events, and therefore can result in deterring managers from taking economically desirable actions.
- That several basic unresolved issues currently preclude consensus as to both the need for change in GAAP and the direction any change should take.
- How the major alternatives to conventional financial reporting that are under consideration would work, together with the strengths and weaknesses of each alternative.

In the appendix to this chapter, you can learn four different techniques for adjusting a firm's financial statements to reflect more current information.

Based on the material contained in this chapter, you should be in a better position to determine when inflation adjustments to any data you are using may be desirable or necessary, and to make the indicated adjustments.

## HOW COULD INFLATION AFFECT MY DECISION?

Continuing with the Tripper Water Ski Manufacturing Company, and with your role as president and controlling stockholder, you are currently looking over an investment proposal that has been turned down by your firm's capital budgeting committee. Even though rejected by a majority vote of the committee, the proposal has been forwarded for your review at the insistence of your vice-president for sales. As a committee member, he alone voted for accepting the proposal; and his accompanying memo states in part:

> The projected costs and benefits in the attached proposal are all stated in terms of current costs and prices. It is obvious that, using the data as given, the proposal has a negative NPV discounted at our 12-percent cost of capital.

> However, I think we are making a mistake in not accepting and implementing this proposal, for two reasons. First, the use of the moulding machine in making our deluxe ski will significantly improve the quality of our product. Not only will the ski look better, but a good skier will be able to feel the difference in improved performance. The proposal already incorporates an anticipated 10-percent increase in sales volume reflecting this better quality. The proposal also notes, as a nonquantifiable benefit, the improvement that I am sure will also result in our firm's overall image of quality. We cannot be sufficiently certain to incorporate a numerical increase in sales quantities at this time, but I am sure sales of the economy ski will also increase. Customers are bound to associate the higher quality across our entire product line and therefore, feel the economy ski is an even better bargain. I believe this factor alone justifies accepting the proposal even with a negative NPV.

> The second consideration may have even more far-reaching implications to our overall decision process. The data included in the proposal does not provide for future inflation. You will note that, in this proposal, costs are not subject to inflation. The machine itself is to be leased for five years at a fixed annual rental. The machine supplier, as part of the package, will also supply our projected requirements of improved raw material (cloth and resin) on a long-term purchase contract at a constant price. Potential cost inflation can only occur with respect to our in-house operating costs (labor, utilities, and so forth) and, in this instance, cost inflation will represent additional savings (higher costs would otherwise have to be paid).

> I believe we can expect an average annual inflation rate of eight percent over the next five years. Based on our past market experience we should have no trouble increasing our prices, with no loss in sales, at least in step with inflation. Therefore, with outflows constant and cost savings and prices increasing, we expect greater dollar net benefits than projected in the proposal. The payout will be quicker, and the NPV might even turn out to be positive.

> Finally, if my thinking makes sense, and I think it does, perhaps we should revise our capital budgeting guidelines for all proposals. Maybe we should require that all proposals identify individual costs and benefits as either subject to inflation or not. And perhaps we should somehow incorporate adjustment in all of our capital budgeting decisions.

As Tripper's president, what would you do with respect to the proposed moulding machine? The original proposal is included in Exhibit 16.1. You may assume an expected eight-percent annual inflation rate. Before starting to read the next paragraph, you should attempt to adjust the data in Exhibit 16.1 for inflation where applicable, and to calculate a revised NPV. Attempting to develop your own approach without the benefit of a "text solution" should open up the various problem dimensions for you, and should make the remainder of this chapter more meaningful and relevant.

One approach applicable to this specific proposal involves first increasing, by eight percent per year, the projected cash flows for those items that are subject to inflation. You may assume, for simplification, that inflation occurs evenly throughout the year; and therefore, on average, total first year figures should be increased by four percent. In effect, using the average rate is just like assuming that the full eight-percent jump occurred at midyear. For example, take the first year's internal operating benefits of $47,940. By year-end the cost being saved would have been running at a rate of $51,775 annually ($47,940 × 1.08). During the year, total savings adjusted for inflation would be $49,858; that is, either

- $47,940 × 1.04   (average increase for year)        = $49,858

or

- $23,970 × 1.00   (first six months, no increase)      = $23,970
  $23,970 × 1.08   (second six months, full increase) = $25,888
                            $49,858

Note also that inflation is like compound interest. Data for the second year, since it has not already been adjusted for the first year's eight-percent inflation rate, must be adjusted by 12.32 percent (1.08 for the first full year × 1.04 for the second-year average). The third and subsequent years are similarly adjusted for the compound effect of inflation. Exhibit 16.2 shows the data adjusted by this method. Note that the NPV is now substantially positive.

Does a $22,914 positive NPV intuitively appear realistically when the NPV before adjustment was a negative $618? Or is the process of adjusting for inflation still not completed? What is the underlying difference between the net after-tax cash flows appearing on Exhibits 16.1 and 16.2 (ignoring present value for the moment)? The data given in Exhibit 16.1 was inappropriate because it did not portray the actual cash flows that could be expected in an inflationary economy. Exhibit 16.2 does project the actual cash flows (in dollars) that may be expected.

But are the dollars in different years comparable? Are they common units of measurement? Ignoring interest and the time value of money temporarily, think of your own experience over the past few years. Is a single dollar as valuable to you today as, say, a dollar four years ago? Isn't today's dollar less valuable, in that it has less *purchasing power* or command over goods and services?

**Exhibit 16.1**

**TRIPPER WATER SKI MANUFACTURING COMPANY**

**Moulding-Machine Investment Proposal (Quantitative Summary)**
**(not adjusted for inflation)**

| Year | Incremental costs (external)[a] | Incremental benefits (internal)[b] | Net cash flows | Tax effects[c] | Net after-tax cash flows | 12% PV factor | PV |
|---|---|---|---|---|---|---|---|
| 0 | −$36,000 | 0 | −$36,000 | +$14,400 | −$21,600 | 1.0000 | −$21,650 |
| 1 | − 41,215 | +$47,940 | + 6,725 | − 2,690 | + 4,035 | 0.8929 | + 3,603 |
| 2 | − 42,020 | + 50,320 | + 8,300 | − 3,320 | + 4,980 | 0.7972 | + 3,970 |
| 3 | − 42,900 | + 53,030 | + 10,130 | − 4,050 | + 6,080 | 0.7118 | + 4,328 |
| 4 | − 43,760 | + 55,420 | + 11,660 | − 4,665 | + 6,995 | 0.6355 | + 4,445 |
| 5 | − 44,690 | + 58,150 | + 13,460 | − 5,385 | + 8,075 | 0.5674 | + 4,582 |
| | | | | | | Total NPV | −$ 618 |

Notes: [a] $36,000 of setup cost; lease payments of $25,000 per year; increased material costs of $1.30 per ski.
[b] Unit sales increase of 15% per year instead of originally forecasted 5%; unit variable cost reduction of $0.40 per ski.
[c] Tax rate 40%. Assume setup cost tax deductible in first year.

## Exhibit 16.2

### TRIPPER WATER SKI MANUFACTURING COMPANY

**Moulding Machine Investment Proposal (Quantitative Summary) (adjusted to reflect expected cash flows)**

| Year | Incremental costs (external)[a] | Incremental benefits (internal)[b] | Net cash flows | Tax effects[c] | Net after-tax cash flows | 12% PV factor | PV |
|---|---|---|---|---|---|---|---|
| 0 | -$36,000 | 0 | -$36,000 | +$14,400 | -$21,600 | 1.0000 | -$21,600 |
| 1 | - 41,215 | +$49,858 | + 8,643 | - 3,457 | + 5,186 | 0.8929 | + 4,631 |
| 2 | - 42,020 | + 56,519 | + 14,499 | - 5,800 | + 8,699 | 0.7972 | + 6,935 |
| 3 | - 42,900 | + 64,331 | + 21,431 | - 8,572 | + 12,859 | 0.7118 | + 9,153 |
| 4 | - 43,760 | + 72,606 | + 28,846 | - 11,538 | + 17,308 | 0.6355 | + 10,999 |
| 5 | - 44,690 | + 82,276 | + 37,586 | - 15,034 | + 22,552 | 0.5674 | + 12,796 |
| | | | | | | Total NPV | +$22,914 |

Notes: [a] 36,000 of setup costs, lease payments of $25,000 per year, increased material costs of $1.30 per ski, no inflation adjustment as constant costs under long-term contract.
[b] Unit sales increase of 15% per year instead of originally forecasted 5%. Unit variable cost reduction of $0.40 per ski. Benefits adjusted for average inflation rate of 8% per year.
[c] Tax rate 40%. Assume setup cost tax deductible in first year.

To complete the analysis of the moulding machine proposal, all such cash flows need to be expressed in the same or common purchasing-power equivalents. Conversion to equivalent purchasing-power units will be discussed more thoroughly later in this chapter. For example, you may reason as follows:

- Net after-tax cash flows shown in Exhibit 16.2 represent total dollars at the end of each year.
- With an annual inflation rate of eight percent, each year each dollar loses approximately eight percent in purchasing power.[1] To equate all cash flows in terms of year zero's (today's) dollars of purchasing power, eight percent per year must be discounted to compensate for purchasing-power loss.
- Allowance for both purchasing-power loss and a 12-percent required interest (cost of capital) return may be accomplished by discounting projected net cash flows at 20 percent.

Exhibit 16.3 shows the final analysis of the moulding machine proposal, adjusted both for actual cash flows and for common purchasing-power units. Note that the NPV is still a positive $13,616. With a large positive NPV, and also with the nonquantified benefit, you should overrule your capital budgeting committee and accept the investment proposal.

Can you see that ignoring inflation can lead to dysfunctional behavior? Remember that dysfunctional behavior was defined in terms of management decisions that were not in the economic best interests of the firm. In the Tripper example, without adjustment for inflation, the very advantageous investment in the moulding machine might have been missed. The sales vice-president's recommendation for revised capital budgeting guidelines would certainly appear in order for Tripper. Note also that the investment decision is not the only one requiring allowance for inflation, nor is the technique illustrated the only method of reflecting the effects of inflation. There are many others.

## INFLATION AND POTENTIALLY DYSFUNCTIONAL DECISIONS

Ignoring the potential effects of inflation can adversely affect almost any business decision. The impact of inflation can, of course, be more serious on intermediate-range and long-range decisions, where the cumulative effect of infla-

---

[1]    The actual loss in purchasing power could be considered as only 7.4 percent if the new inflated price were considered as the base. If, after one year, it would take $1.08 to purchase what $1.00 could have purchased at the beginning of the year (8 percent annual inflation), then 8/108 or 7.4 percent has been lost. To avoid confusion between bases, both inflation and purchasing-power loss are commonly expressed in terms of prices at the beginning of the year. Therefore, with an eight-percent inflation rate, the loss in purchasing power will also be considered to be eight percent.

**Exhibit 16.3**

TRIPPER WATER SKI MANUFACTURING COMPANY

**Moulding Machine Investment Proposal (Quantitative Summary)**
**(adjusted for inflation)**

| Year | Incremental costs (external)[a] | Incremental benefits (internal)[b] | Net cash flows | Tax effects[c] | Net after-tax cash flows | 20% PV factor | PV |
|---|---|---|---|---|---|---|---|
| 0 | −$36,000 | 0 | −$36,000 | +$14,400 | −$21,600 | 1.0000 | −$21,600 |
| 1 | − 41,215 | +$49,858 | + 8,643 | − 3,457 | + 5,186 | 0.8333 | + 4,321 |
| 2 | − 42,020 | + 56,519 | + 14,499 | − 5,800 | + 8,699 | 0.6944 | + 6,041 |
| 3 | − 42,900 | + 64,331 | + 21,431 | − 8,572 | + 12,859 | 0.5787 | + 7,442 |
| 4 | − 43,760 | + 72,606 | + 28,846 | − 11,538 | + 17,308 | 0.4823 | + 8,348 |
| 5 | − 44,690 | + 82,276 | + 37,546 | − 15,034 | + 22,552 | 0.4019 | + 9,064 |
| | | | | | | Total NPV | +$13,616 |

*Notes.* [a] $36,000 of setup cost, lease payments of $25,000 per year, increased material costs of $1.30 per ski, no inflation adjustment as constant costs under long-term contract.
[b] Unit sales increase of 15% per year instead of originally forecasted 5%. Unit variable cost reduction of $0.40 per ski. Benefits adjusted for average inflation rate of 8% per year.
[c] Tax rate 40%. Assume setup cost tax deductible in first year.

tion becomes significant. In addition to investment decisions, the long-run impact of inflation must be considered with respect to:

- performance evaluation of investment centers,
- determining dividend policy,
- choosing among alternative sources of financing, and
- analyzing a firm's financial statements.

In evaluating the performance of investment centers (or of entire firms), care must be exercised not to compare inflated current income dollars with noncurrent (and therefore understated) investment dollars. Where a division's asset base is carried at historical cost, both ROI and residual income may be overstated. As an example, consider a division with an asset base acquired five years ago at a cost of $100,000. Assume that five years ago the division's income was $15,000 and, therefore, its ROI was 15 percent. Assume, further, that inflation has averaged nine percent per year over the past five years, and that revenues and expenditures have risen in proportion. If the division was still operating at the same actual level of activity, current income could be reported as $22,125.[2] The $22,125 of income could have no more purchasing power than the original $15,000. The division has not improved its performance. Yet, unless the asset base were adjusted, the division's ROI would appear to be up, from 15 percent to 22 percent.

Can you see that this problem can be even more serious in making comparisons among divisions (or firms)? Where different divisions have acquired their assets at different times, and where the asset bases are not adjusted to current dollars, comparisons of ROI or residual income would be distorted and effectively meaningless.

Failure to consider the long-run effects of inflation in making dividend decisions can be equally dysfunctional. Since depreciation allowances under GAAP are not adjusted to reflect inflated asset costs, a firm that distributes all or most of its reported income in dividends may not retain adequate funds to replace its capacity assets. In periods of inflation, reported income may be overstated in the distributable sense.[3]

Another management decision affected by the long-range impact of inflation concerns desirable capital structure (Chapter 10 Appendix). Without inflation, a firm's desirable debt ratio might be 0.4. Having more than 40 percent debt might be incurring too great a risk of possible default. However, in peri-

---

[2]  $15,000 times 1.475 ($1.09 \times 1.09 \times 1.09 \times 1.09 \times 1.045$) equals $22,125. Note that fixed charges such as depreciation would not increase as a result of inflation, and other contractual costs such as interest and rent might also not increase proportionally with inflation. Therefore, reported income would probably be even greater than $22,125.

[3]  The concept of distributable income is discussed further below and in the chapter appendix.

ods of significant inflation, debt with fixed dollar interest and principal payments becomes significantly "cheaper" with the passage of time. Interest and principal can be paid with inflationary dollars, each having less cost in terms of purchasing power. In periods of inflation, it may be appropriate for a firm to incur more debt than might otherwise be considered desirable.

Significant long-run inflation can, of course, also seriously impair the usefulness of a firm's external financial statements that are prepared on a historical cost basis following GAAP. Several alternative reporting systems will be briefly described later in this chapter. They will also be covered in more detail in the chapter appendix.

## Short-Run Decisions

Even in the short run (within one year), to ignore inflation can result in serious problems. Three areas—CVP analysis, standard costs, and cash budgeting—will serve to illustrate this point. Can you predict the effects, if any, of inflation on a firm's breakeven volume? Often, in periods of inflation, the distinction between contribution and fixed costs becomes even more significant. Many fixed costs may not only be fixed in terms of activity level, but also "fixed" in the context of inflation. A proposed course of action that might otherwise be rejected as not even breaking even might be acceptable where contribution was increasing as a result of inflation and fixed costs were remaining relatively constant. Or an investment that appeared too risky in increasing the firm's breakeven to too high a level of volume might appear safer in light of inflated contribution. Remember that, in any situation where contribution keeps pace with inflation and fixed costs do not, breakeven volume will drop with the passage of time.

Standard costs or budgeting rates must also reflect the anticipated effects of inflation. An annual inflation rate of only six percent could have a significant effect on $1,000,000 of budgeted costs. Over the year, the budget would understate expected costs by $30,000. Spending variances would be overstated as a result of inadequate budgetary provision for cost inflation.

Failure to adequately provide for inflation in the budgeting process can have more serious repercussions than merely reducing the credibility of performance reports. Where prices are based on budgeted or standard costs that do not reflect **anticipated** inflation, price adjustments may be inadequate to compensate for cost inflation. The most serious result of inadequate allowance for cost inflation in the budgeting process will be the effect upon cash management. If the cash budget inadequately anticipates inflation-caused growth in expenditures, a cash shortage, with the attendant risk of insolvency, may develop.

From the foregoing discussion, you should be well aware of the need to incorporate provisions for anticipated inflation in managerial accounting data. The next obvious question is how to do this. What techniques may be useful to reflect the effects of inflation?

# TECHNIQUES FOR INCORPORATING INFLATION ADJUSTMENTS

As first demonstrated in the Tripper moulding machine example, the objectives of inflation adjustment of decision data are twofold:

- To ensure that all data reflect expected actual dollar cash flows, and
- To ensure that all data is converted to common purchasing-power units.


## Short-Term Decisions

For short-term decisions (all relevant data within one year), it is only necessary to make sure that all data represent actual dollar expected flows. Unless current inflation is extreme (double-digit), it may be presumed that dollars flowing throughout the year all have the same purchasing power. Examples of short-term adjustments were previously discussed in terms of standard costs and budgets. If a budgeted expenditure for the year would be $10,000 without inflation, and if a six-percent annual inflation rate were anticipated, then the adjusted cash flow would be $10,300, reflecting the average inflation rate of three percent.


## Intermediate and Long-Range Decisions

Where relevant cash flows extend beyond one year, additional adjustment for equivalent purchasing power is desirable. Necessary adjustments may be accomplished using one of two ways, hereafter referred to as the two-step and one-step approaches. And, in certain special circumstances, adjustment may be bypassed entirely—the zero-step approach.

Following the two-step approach as demonstrated in the earlier Tripper example, future cash flows are first adjusted to reflect inflationary increases. Then the adjusted cash flows are discounted at a rate that combines **both** an allowance for desired investment return and also an allowance for lost purchasing power.

To understand the one-step or shortcut approach, consider unadjusted cash flows subject to inflation as follows:

| Year | Cash flows |
|------|------------|
| 0 | −$10,000 |
| 1 | + 4,000 |
| 2 | + 4,000 |
| 3 | + 4,000 |
| Net | +$ 2,000 |

With an eight-percent inflation rate and assuming, for simplification, that all flows occurred at year-end, adjusted cash flows would be:

| Year | Adjusted cash flows |
|------|---------------------|
| 0 | −$10,000 |
| 1 | +  4,320   ($4,000 × 1.08) |
| 2 | +  4,666   ($4,000 × 1.08 × 1.08) |
| 3 | +  5,039   (4,000 × 1.08 × 1.08 × 1.08) |
| Net | +$  4,025 |

Now adjusting for an eight-percent loss in purchasing power:

| Year | 8 percent PV adjusted cash flows |
|------|----------------------------------|
| 0 | −$10,000   (10,000 × 1.000) |
| 1 | +  4,000   ($4,320 × 0.9259) |
| 2 | +  4,000   ($4,666 × 0.8573) |
| 3 | +  4,000   ($5,039 × 0.7938) |
| Net | +$  2,000 |

Can you see that you have completed a full cycle? By adding eight percent, and then factoring out eight percent, you are back to the original unadjusted flows.

Where **all** future cash flows are unadjusted, and where **all** are expected to be affected by general inflation in the same manner, then a "zero-step" adjustment is appropriate.[4] In this particular situation, unadjusted cash flows may be used without adjustment. They may be assumed to represent flows that have been adjusted upwards for augmented cash flow and then back down again to reflect loss of purchasing power.

In the more usual case, some future cash flows may be affected by inflation and some may not, as illustrated in the Tripper moulding machine example. Again, assuming no flows have already been adjusted to reflect inflation, the single-step approach may be used. All future cash flows that will be affected by inflation are discounted only for interest or investment return. All future cash flows that will **not** be affected by inflation (fixed and contractual charges) must be discounted for **both** interest and loss in purchasing power. Be careful to note the "opposites" in the one-step rule. Following the one-step approach, cash flows are **not** first adjusted upwards to reflect inflation. The first step of the two-step approach is omitted. In the discounting step, flows that **are** subject to inflation are **not** adjusted for purchasing power loss. Flows that **are not** subject to inflation **are** subject to discounting for lost purchasing power.

If these rules are still a bit confusing, perhaps the illustration in Exhibit 16.4 will help. Note, in Exhibit 16.4, that to adjust flows subject to inflation

---

4   Note that if **any** projected flows have already been adjusted to reflect inflation, or if different flows are expected to have different rates of inflation (see discussion of specific vs. general inflation below), then separate discounting of different flows would be required.

**Exhibit 16.4**

DIFFERENT APPROACHES TO ADJUSTING DECISION DATA
FOR INFLATION

| Step 0: Cash flow before adjustment | Step 1: Adjusted for increased cash flow (multiplied by 1.26)[a] | Step 2: Adjusted for Decreased purchasing power (multiplied by 0.7938)[b] |
|---|---|---|

**All** future flows affected equally by inflation — any adjustment circular — therefore no inflation adjustment necessary (zero-step approach).

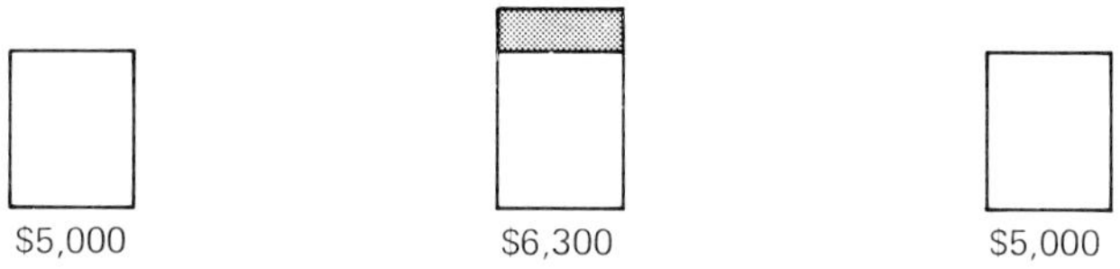

$5,000    $6,300    $5,000

**No** future flows affected by inflation (all frozen by contract) — Step 1 may be omitted and original data simply adjusted for declining purchasing power (one-step approach).

$5,000    $5,000    $3,969

Some flows affected and some not — Step 1 may be omitted and only constant flows discounted in Step 2 (one-step approach).

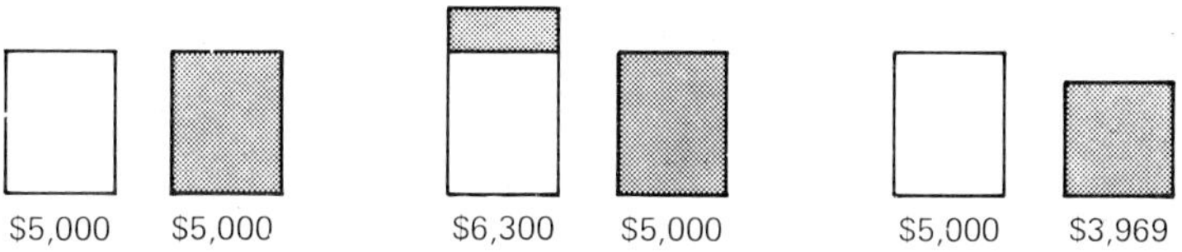

$5,000    $5,000        $6,300    $5,000        $5,000    $3,969

*Notes.* [a] Assume data projected 3 years into future with inflation of 8 percent per year. 1.08 × 1.08 × 1.08 = 1.26 rounded.
[b] PV factor for $1 at the end of 3 years discounted at 8 percent.

upwards (step one) and then back down for lost purchasing power (step two) is circular and may be omitted. And note that flows not subject to inflation (fixed or contractual) are not adjusted for inflation but **must** be discounted for loss in purchasing power.

To review inflation adjustment in the capital budgeting or investment context, consider the two cases presented in Exhibit 16.5. In the first case, assume that the firm is deciding whether or not to acquire equipment costing $100,000 with a ten-year life and zero salvage. Once acquired, the equipment would then be leased to the ultimate user for ten years at a fixed contract price. After-tax benefits would be $18,500 per year for ten years. If the firm's cost

**Exhibit 16.5**

CAPITAL BUDGETING DECISIONS

| Year | Case 1 Costs | Case 1 Benefits | Case 2 Costs | Case 2 Benefits |
|---|---|---|---|---|
| 0 | $100,000 | | | |
| 1 | | $18,500 | $20,000 | $40,000 |
| 2 | | 18,500 | 20,000 | 35,000 |
| 3 | | 18,500 | 20,000 | 30,000 |
| 4 | | 18,500 | 20,000 | 25,000 |
| 5 | | 18,500 | 20,000 | 15,000 |
| 6 | | 18,500 | 20,000 | 0 |
| 7 | | 18,500 | 20,000 | 0 |
| 8 | | 18,500 | 20,000 | 0 |
| 9 | | 18,500 | 20,000 | 0 |
| 10 | | 18,500 | 20,000 | 0 |

Case 1: NPV discounted at 12% = −$100,000 + $104,525 = +$ 4,525;
NPV discounted at 20% = −$100,000 + $77,561 = −$22,439.

Case 2: NPV discounted at 12% = −$113,000 + $109,370 = −$3,630;
NPV discounted at 20% = −$ 83,850 + $ 93,082 = +$9,232.

of capital was 12 percent, and if there was no anticipated general inflation, the equipment purchase and lease would be desirable, since the net cash flows would have a positive NPV of $4,525.

Now consider Case 1 in a situation where general inflation was expected to average eight percent annually over the next ten years. The fixed incoming payments (benefits) would have progressively less real purchasing power. Following the one-step approach to inflation adjustment, the fixed payments must be discounted for both the desired interest return and also to reflect declining purchasing power of the dollars to be received. In essence, the inflation loss is treated as an additional cost that must be recoverable before the investment is adjudged acceptable. Discounting at 20 percent (twelve percent cost of capital plus eight percent anticipated annual inflation) reveals a negative NPV of $22,439. The equipment purchase and lease investment is clearly undesirable when anticipated inflation is taken into account.

The opposite situation is illustrated in Case 2. Assume that a firm can lease equipment for its own use for ten years with fixed lease payments having an after-tax cost of $20,000 per year. The equipment will be used for a product expected to have only a five-year sales life, with diminishing benefits, as shown in after-tax dollars. Ignoring inflation and discounting at the firm's 12-percent cost of capital, the project has a negative NPV of $3,630 and might be rejected.

Making the same allowance for an anticipated eight-percent annual inflation rate, as was done for the first case, the project has a $9,232 positive NPV and probably should be undertaken. And in Case 2 the positive NPV assuming eight-percent annual inflation could be as great as $25,250, since the expected net revenues are not limited by price contract. If it were assumed that prices could be continually increased to provide for zero after-tax inflation loss, then cost would be discounted at 20 percent and benefits at only 12 percent.

It can be shown that the above approach is not precisely accurate. Also, inflation rates are extremely difficult to forecast, and will rarely, if ever, be linear. Nevertheless, although the method is somewhat crude, the discounted present value approach to adjust for fixed-dollar future cash flows can prove a satisfactory tool for estimating inflationary effects upon capital budgeting decisions.

## POTENTIAL FINANCIAL STATEMENT DISTORTIONS RESULTING FROM INFLATION

In Chapter 14 you had the opportunity to become familiar with several problems or distortions arising out of current Generally Accepted Accounting Principles (GAAP) applicable to financial accounting. Several examples were introduced wherein GAAP measurement of management's performance could provide a distorted picture of economic reality. Financial statements were shown to be relevant to management decisions in that they serve as a performance report on overall management. Where financial statements depart from economic reality, managers may be motivated to behave dysfunctionally in order to achieve a better-appearing report. These problems and others can result, during periods of significant inflation, from GAAP's adherence to both historical-cost-based measurement and also to the realization principle.

Recall, from your study of financial accounting, that, under current GAAP, a firm's assets are initially measured at their fair market value at the time of acquisition (historical cost). Thereafter, until such assets are used up, sold, or otherwise disposed of, they are carried at cost or at some lower amount reflecting cost expiration or decline in realizable value. Under GAAP, assets may be written **down** in recognition of deflation in market prices (for example, current market if below cost for marketable securities, and LOCM for inventories). However, the realization principle requires that they may not be written up above their original fair market value at the time of acquisition.[5] Where an asset's net realizable value (selling price, less cost of disposition) is greater because of inflation than its original book value, this *holding gain* is not recognized until the point where it is realized through sale. In those cases where obsolescence has radically reduced the net realizable value of fixed or capacity assets below current book value, the loss may not be im-

---

[5]   Note that increasing the investments account to reflect the firm's share of an investee's unremitted earnings following the equity method is **not** a write-up as such. Instead such an adjustment reflects the accrual of future expected dividends combined, for convenience, in the investment accounts rather than being separately disclosed.

mediately recognized. Loss recognition may be deferred through gradual depreciation or until realized at the time of disposition.

In an economy without inflation (or deflation) these accounting conventions may be accepted as adequately serving both managers and investors. However, in periods of significant inflation, one may question whether current GAAP do not result in inadequate if not misleading information.[6] Areas of possible distortion relate to the recognition of gains or losses on monetary items, the recognition and timing of holding gains or losses on nonmonetary assets, and the appropriateness of current GAAP measurement of assets and net income. Each of these problem areas will be clarified below.

## Monetary Gains or Losses

Recall from financial accounting that a *monetary item* is defined as cash or a claim for a specific amount of cash at a specific time. Typical monetary assets include cash, accounts receivable, notes receivable, funds, and bonds or other similar investments (certificates of deposit, mortgage notes, and short-term government "paper") held as either temporary investments of excess cash or for long-term investment purposes. Monetary liabilities include all current payables and most items classified as long-term debt.[7]

During a period of general inflation, a firm holding monetary assets will suffer a loss in the general purchasing power of these assets. Conversely, holding monetary liabilities will result in a gain in general purchasing power, since the liabilities are stated in simple dollars and may be settled in the future with dollars having less purchasing power. Losses on monetary assets are counterbalanced by gains on monetary debt. Only a firm with net monetary assets (monetary assets greater than monetary debt) will experience a net *monetary loss* in periods of general inflation. Most firms have net monetary debt (monetary debt greater than monetary assets), and therefore experience *monetary gains.*

Consider the simple case where a firm throughout the year, in addition to other items, has an average of $1,000 cash, $500 of accounts payable, and $600 of long-term debt. Assume a general inflation rate of eight percent for the year. What would be the firm's monetary gain or loss for the year?

The firm would lose $80 (0.08 × $1,000) in general purchasing power on its monetary asset holdings (cash). It would require $1,080 at year-end to purchase what $1,000 could buy at the beginning of the year. The firm would gain $88 (0.08 × $1,100) on the monetary debt, which could be settled in

---

[6]    Similar questions arise in periods of significant deflation. Only the case of inflation will be explored in this chapter.

[7]    Note that preferred stock (having no stated liquidation value) and common stock represent no certain claim against cash and are not considered monetary items. Similarly, estimated warranty cost, unearned revenue, and deferred income taxes are not considered monetary liabilities.

"cheaper" (less purchasing power) dollars. Overall the firm would have an $8 net monetary gain on its $100 of net monetary debt.

Currently GAAP make no provision for ever recognizing net monetary gain or loss. In a large firm, where net monetary debt may amount to millions, or even hundreds of millions, of dollars, this omission can be very significant. The firm's management may be carefully maintaining a high net debt position for the benefit of the owners. To maintain this position, additional costs may be incurred for debt interest and in the form of salaries and expenses to operate effectively with minimum cash. GAAP will recognize the costs but not the offsetting benefits. Therefore, the effectiveness and efficiency of management in maximizing monetary gain, or in minimizing monetary losses, is not reported. Management could dysfunctionally improve its apparent performance by sacrificing monetary gain, reducing reported costs, and thus increasing reported earnings.

## Holding Gains on Nonmonetary Items

Whereas distortion may result from the failure to report gains or losses in the case of monetary items, a different problem can occur with respect to reported gains on nonmonetary items. GAAP does report any holding gains on non-monetary assets at the time of their disposition. This practice may result in distortion or misleading information in several ways. First, any holding gains on inventory are not reported separately from normal trading margin. In periods of inflation, gross profit may include both normal markup (repeatable in terms of current costs and prices) and also recognition of a holding gain (not repeatable) on older, lower-cost inventory. GAAP do not provide for distinguishing these distinctly different types of revenue. Both are included in income from operations, which supposedly represents a "repeatable" amount.

Consider a firm with three units of product in inventory as follows:

One unit purchased last year for $3,
Two units purchased this year for $5 each.

Assume that in the current year two units are sold to customers for $7 apiece. FIFO cost of goods sold would be $8, and FIFO gross profit would be $6. Is the $6 a good measure of repeatable profit on the next two items sold? Or is the repeatable gross profit $4 with an additional $2 of nonrecurring (one-time) holding gain on the older, less costly inventory? To budget next year's gross profit at 43 percent ($\frac{6}{14}$ rounded) would be inappropriate. Only 28 percent ($\frac{4}{14}$ rounded) can be reasonably expected.

The above example may also be used to illustrate another problem related to holding gains on nonmonetary items. Current GAAP do not provide for comparability among different firms with respect to the timing of recognition of holding gains. The firm on FIFO will be reporting holding gains as part of income each year. The firm on LIFO may delay recognition of holding gains forever, or until it happens to use up some of its basic older stock of inventory.

Deferral of holding gain recognition on investments may also adversely motivate management performance. Deferred reporting could motivate management to unload assets in the current period, when such assets should properly be held into future periods. Where current management has previously acquired assets as a speculation in anticipation of inflation, and the inflation has occurred, it may be tempted to sell now to obtain personal credit for the gain. Even if probabilities favored future gains, to hold might result in any gain being credited to future (successor) managers rather than those currently in power. The converse may also be true. If current management expects to be in power for several more years, it might be tempted to hold appreciated assets with only a slight probability of future gain. For continuing management in such a situation, GAAP provides a "no loss" game. If additional appreciation occurs, assets may be sold with continuing management then getting the total credit. If no further appreciation occurs, continuing management still gets the credit for past gains. If a price drop occurs, so long as sale is made before prices drop below original cost, no loss is reported, because the original gain was never recognized and reported.

Finally, holding gains on nonmonetary assets, as reported under GAAP, may be partially or wholly illusory in terms of general purchasing power. Assume the following facts:

- Equipment costing $10,000 with a four-year life and zero salvage is being depreciated on a straight-line basis.
- General inflation during the first three years totals 20 percent.
- The equipment prices change to match general inflation so that, after three years, new equipment costs $12,000 ($10,000 × 1.2) and three-year-old equipment sells for $3,000 ($2,500 × 1.2).
- After three years, the firm sells its equipment with a GAAP book value of $2,500 for $3,000, and reports a gain of $500.

In this case does the firm really have a $500 gain (profit), or has it just happened to keep up with general inflation?

### Holding Losses on Nonmonetary Items

Holding losses may occur infrequently in periods of general inflation. Their discussion may seem out of place in a chapter on inflation. Nevertheless they are included as a good example of potentially dysfunctional behavior arising out of GAAP.

Treatment of holding losses on nonmonetary items under current GAAP may be even more inconsistent and potentially misleading than the treatment of holding gains. Under the LOCM rule, negative inflation (deflation) affecting inventory costs may trigger immediate loss recognition via a write-down to replacement cost if lower than original cost. Market value losses on a firm's portfolio of marketable securities must also be recognized in the current period. But recognition of deflation, or loss in net realizable value resulting from obsolescence, related to plant and equipment, or other noncurrent assets, may be treated differently. The loss recognition may be deferred either over the useful life of the asset (by sticking to original depreciation/amortization schedules), or else until realized at the time of disposition. As first discussed in Chapter 14, delayed recognition of holding loss on plant and equipment can have serious consequences.

Assume that a firm has equipment originally costing $100,000 with a ten-year life and zero salvage, and being depreciated on a straight-line basis. Over four years, technological developments make successively better equipment available. Resulting obsolescence of the old equipment reduces its resale value to $50,000, $30,000, $10,000, and finally $5,000, over the four years. GAAP do not require that the accumulating $55,000 of sunk costs over the four years be immediately recognized and written off. Instead, this sunk cost may be carried as an asset and systematically reduced over the remaining years of use through normal depreciation.

One of two serious consequences may result. Assume that, at the beginning of the fifth year, management determines (properly ignoring sunk costs in the decision) that it is economically desirable to replace the equipment. The equipment's GAAP book value is $60,000, including $55,000 of not-yet-recognized holding loss resulting from obsolescence. If the equipment is replaced, the economically desirable action will be accompanied by a reported $55,000 loss in the year of replacement, hardly an appropriate measure of performance. Even worse, management could be deterred from going through with the desirable replacement by the fact that it would trigger recognition of the previously deferred holding loss. Note, from the facts given in this illustration, that $50,000 out of the total of $55,000 was "lost" prior to the current year, and not reported in the years when the loss occurred.

## Asset Measurement

It should also be obvious that, in periods of general inflation, current GAAP may result in the understatement of total assets on a firm's balance sheet. This understatement will not be uniform among different firms; thus comparability will be destroyed. Firms on LIFO will have greater understatement than those on FIFO. Firms using accelerated depreciation, or with older capacity assets, may have greater understatement than those using straight-line or with more recently acquired assets.

Not only may comparability be destroyed, but also measures of return on investment may be distorted. As described earlier for investment centers, return on assets employed may be inappropriately overstated when based on understated assets.[x] Since understated assets are matched by understated owners' equity (since liabilities are usually appropriately measured), measures of return on owners' investment may be similarly overstated.

---

[x]    The overstatement of return may be further augmented in cases where a firm has significant real investment in intangible assets not reported as such under GAAP.

### Income Measurement

Under current GAAP, in periods of inflation all of the foregoing potential distortions affect the income statement and reported income.

1. Holding gains or losses on net monetary items are not reported.

2. Holding gains on nonmonetary items will not be reported currently unless realized through sale.

3. Reported holding gains on nonmonetary assets are not all segregated, and they may be illusory in terms of general purchasing power.

4. Holding losses on nonmonetary assets may not be reported currently unless realized through disposition.

5. Depreciation charges may be radically understated in terms of the appreciated cost of the expiring assets.

For some firms, it can be shown that these factors offset each other, and that current income reported under GAAP closely approximates income measured in terms of general purchasing power. But for many others it can be shown that conventionally reported income substantially differs from real income defined in terms of general purchasing power.

## DIFFERENT TYPES OF INFLATION

So far in this chapter it has been assumed that all inflation is uniform for all items. This, of course, is not realistic. During any period, prices of some items will rise more than others, some prices will remain the same, and some may actually decrease (hand calculators, for example). Where prices of most items are increasing, *general inflation* measured in terms of averages is said to exist. Individual items during the same period may be subject to *specific inflation* at greater, equal, or lesser rates, or even to price movement in the opposite direction (specific deflation). Inflation is often measured and reported in terms of *price indices*. To review the construction of a composite (average) index may assist you to clarify the distinction between general and specific inflation.

For simplicity, consider a composite index including only four products—A, B, C, and D. Exhibit 16.6 illustrates the price changes occurring for these items during a particular period, and the construction of a general inflation index for that period. Note that the new index is 108, indicating a **general** inflation rate of eight percent for the year. Also note that product A was the only item whose specific inflation rate coincided with the general inflation rate.

## DIFFERENT DEFINITIONS AND MEASURES OF INCOME

For many years accountants have been well aware of inflation and the potential distortions resulting from adherence to historical cost measurement and the realization principle. Various alternative modifications to GAAP have been

**Exhibit 16.6**

ILLUSTRATION OF PRICE CHANGES AND DETERMINATION
OF GENERAL PRICE INDEX

| Product | Price 1/1 | Price 12/31 | Percentage price change |
|---------|-----------|-------------|-------------------------|
| A | $10.00 | $10.80 | + 8 |
| B | 5.00 | 5.15 | + 3 |
| C | 3.00 | 3.90 | +30 |
| D | 2.00 | 1.75 | −12 |
| | $20.00 | $21.60 | |
| Price index | 100 | 108* | |

* 1/1 price assumed equal to 100; 21.60/20.00 = 108.

proposed, and the most widely supported alternatives will be presented below. To date, formal modification of GAAP has not occurred.

Simple custom and inertia, plus an absence of strong demand for change by statement users, have certainly contributed to the maintenance of the status quo. Also, the fact that present GAAP measurement is incorporated in legal contracts and in legislation makes change more difficult.[9] The problems of converting U.S. industry to metric measurement may be considered analogous, and probably less difficult.

Perhaps an equally important factor inhibiting change is the absence of consensus or agreement on a precise definition of income. There appears to exist general agreement if not intuitive acceptance that positive income involves an increase in well-offness of the firm, independent of owner investment or withdrawals. Income is not present until capital in existence at the beginning of the period has been first maintained. Any excess of net revenues and gains beyond that necessary to maintain the firm's capital is considered to be income.

The problem arises with respect to a definition of what capital is to be maintained and how it is to be measured. A related issue concerns whether any increase in well-offness must be realized and/or distributable to owners before being classified as income. Three distinct concepts of capital to be maintained are prevalent, and each has support.

## Simple Dollars Invested

One approach to defining the invested capital to be maintained is to consider that it merely represents dollars, regardless of their purchasing power. This

---

[9] For example, many contracts and bond indentures make reference to working capital as currently defined and measured. Also legislation constraining corporate dividend distributions for the protection of creditors cites retained earnings as currently measured and defined.

concept is the one that currently underlies today's GAAP. A firm with only cash and no liabilities, which starts the year with $1,000 and ends with $1,050, is reported as having $50 of income (assuming no additional owner investment and no owner withdrawals during the year). This $50 of income is to be reported even if general inflation were nine percent and the $1,050 could not purchase as much as the original $1,000. The simple dollar concept of income does not have widespread theoretical support. Nevertheless, it has many backers because it is at the same time both the most objective and also the easiest to measure.

### General Purchasing Power

A second income concept defines capital to be maintained in terms of the general purchasing power of the dollars invested. The specifics of an accounting system built upon this concept will be illustrated in the appendix to this chapter. In essence, the purchasing-power concept provides for no recognition of income unless the general purchasing power of net assets at the beginning of a period has first been maintained. It provides for recognition of loss where the general purchasing power of dollars invested has not been maintained. In the simple example cited above, *price-level-adjusted* accounting would report a loss of $40 rather than a profit of $50. With a general inflation rate of nine percent, the firm would require $1,090 ($1,000 × 1.09) at year-end to be as well off as it was at the beginning of the year in terms of purchasing power. A $90 increase would be necessary just to maintain the purchasing power of net assets (capital) invested. With only a $50 increase, the firm suffered a $40 loss (measured in terms of end-of-year dollars of purchasing power).

Supporters of the general purchasing-power approach stress both the need for reporting monetary gains or losses in periods of significant inflation, and also the relative objectivity of the system. Adjustment for changes in general price level merely requires applying a single objective national price index [such as the government-prepared Consumer Price Index (CPI)] to existing objectively verifiable cost data. General price-level adjustment will be illustrated below.

Opponents of general price-level adjustment question the appropriateness of applying a broad general index to specific situations. They question the accuracy and up-to-date validity of available indices. They question both the understandability and the real need for the resulting data.

### Current Productive Capacity

A third income concept is based upon the assumption that a firm does not have income until it has first maintained its capacity to continue in the same line of business. Under this approach, asset acquisition cost is replaced, as the measurement basis, by the current replacement cost of equivalent capacity or else, under an alternative proposal, the current net realizable value of existing assets. Note that these two approaches abandon general price-level adjustment for nonmonetary assets, and substitute the use of specific price changes.

Supporters of *replacement-cost accounting* for nonmonetary items, and those who would also include adjustment for **specific** purchasing-power gains or losses on net monetary items, claim it is more realistic and meaningful to deal with specific rather than general price changes. They maintain that it is more reasonable to recognize immediately specific gains and losses in specific situations, rather than first recognize unrealized gains or losses in terms of general price levels and adjust for specifics only at the point of realization.

Opponents of replacement-cost accounting have primarily stressed the loss of objectivity inherent in such systems. They point out that many replacement costs, especially for special-purpose equipment, could only be estimated; and that these estimates would be highly subjective and nonverifiable, especially where technological improvement has made actual replacement undesirable or impossible. They also point out that net realizable values would be even more subjective in the many cases where a special-purpose asset might have no market value (except scrap) and yet a very real usefulness value to the particular firm.

Another argument against approaches involving replacement cost or the maintenance of current productive capacity is more theoretical. In those situations where specific inflation exceeds general inflation for certain capacity assets, the cost of participating in the particular business has, in effect, gone up for all. New firms entering the industry would be required to have a greater initial capital investment. It does not seem reasonable that an older firm would not be judged as having earned income until it had set aside, through depreciation, enough net revenue to cover the cost of playing in a more expensive game.

A simple gambling analogy might clarify this point. Assume that you were playing at a crap table that had a minimum bet during the week of $1. The minimum bet was raised to $5 at 6 P.M. Friday for the weekend customers. If you started playing Friday afternoon at 5:30 with $1 (just enough to play the game) and stopped at 6:15 with $10, what would be your profit? To say that you had a profit of $9, but that your distributable or spendable profit was only $5, if you wished to continue playing the same game, would seem more reasonable than to claim your profit was only $5. Had there not been the $4 specific price increase (increase in minimum bet to $5), your profit would clearly be $9. If you wish to retain or reinvest $4 of this profit to continue playing a now more expensive game, or to expand your operations (playing five different $1 minimum games concurrently), that is your decision. It is difficult to see how, with no loss of general purchasing power, the $4 can be viewed as necessary to maintain capital.

## DIFFERENT TYPES OR CATEGORIES OF INCOME

The gambling analogy also serves to introduce the other income-related problem arising from inflation. A firm may have measurable *economic income* (increased well-offness) without that income being realized through sale. And, of that portion of income that is *realized income,* not all may be *distributable income* if the firm wishes to continue in business. The apparent original intention of current GAAP was to report as income only increases in well-offness that have been realized and could theoretically be distributed, at least by the end of the current operating cycle (receivables are collected). With inflation, realized income based on historical costs may be overstated (inadequate depreciation charges); and all realized income is rarely distributable if the firm wishes to continue operations in an inflated environment. Current financial statements prepared under GAAP do not report economic income, and do not distinguish between realized and distributable income. A system including such information will be described as part of the illustration of replacement cost accounting included in the appendix to this chapter.

The foregoing discussion has been intended to provide you with a brief introduction to the many unresolved issues surrounding the problem of accounting for inflation. You should now have some appreciation of why consensus with respect to an appropriate modification of current GAAP, or even with respect to the desirability of any modification, is difficult to achieve. In the balance of this chapter you will be introduced to various existing and proposed supplements and alternatives to historical cost accounting.

## ALTERNATIVES TO HISTORICAL COST REPORTING

The person who does not understand financial accounting and its attempt to provide objective and verifiable data may initially assume that financial statements disclose current values. "Value" is a very subjective term. You can easily think of things that would be very valuable to one person or firm and of little value to another. Value also implies a sale or output price, which may be difficult if not impossible to measure objectively. There may be no ready market for special-purpose equipment that may have significant future usefulness to a particular firm but only scrap value to others. Therefore, although there have been several proposals at the theoretical level that accounting measures be in terms of output prices, the need for objectivity has so far restricted serious consideration to various forms of input (cost) measurement.[10]

Current GAAP, with which you should already be familiar, require measurement or valuation in terms of historical cost **reduced** for expiration of proportionate usefulness or potential realizable value. There are four other input-(cost-)based measurement alternatives that have significant support:

---

[10]   Note, however, that some output measures are currently used in conjunction with input costs under current GAAP. In special cases (precious metals, agricultural products, and marketable securities held for resale by securities dealers), inventories may currently be measured in terms of net realizable value even if above cost. More generally, output prices may serve as upper or lower limits to cost valuation (lower of cost or current market for securities, LOCM for inventory, and salvage value as a floor for nonmonetary assets).

1. Historical cost combined with mandatory LIFO,
2. Price-level-adjusted historical cost,
3. Replacement cost,
4. Replacement cost adjusted for price-level changes.

Detailed illustrations of each of these alternatives will be found in the appendix to this chapter. The general characteristics and the alleged advantages and disadvantages of each will be discussed briefly below.

## Historical Cost and Mandatory LIFO

Many advocates of change from current GAAP believe that changes should be limited to allowing for and requiring LIFO measurement of inventories. They argue that:

- LIFO as an option has general acceptance and is understood by financial statement users;
- LIFO is objectively measurable (actual invoice prices);
- Conservatism is maintained (holding gains are not recognized until realized through sale);
- For many firms, the major share of inflation-related measurement distortion involves inventory; and
- LIFO results in the income statement being expressed in mostly current costs (depreciation is often a relatively less significant cost item).

Proponents of LIFO–GAAP acknowledge that balance sheets may understate assets in terms of current costs. However, they maintain that the balance sheet is of secondary importance to creditors and investors, and that asset adjustment for internal performance evaluation (as discussed in Chapter 14) may exist without requiring any modification of GAAP.

Advocates of historical cost and mandatory LIFO believe that LIFO inventory measurement should be mandatory for all firms in order to provide comparability of current-cost measurement of cost of goods sold. They object to restatement of other noncurrent asset usage or expiration to current costs because this would require subjective estimates. They oppose any asset write-up on the balance sheet as unconservative recognition of unrealized holding gain. And they also oppose any price-level adjustment as potentially confusing to statement readers and possibly inappropriate (should an inventory of hand calculators with decreasing market prices be nevertheless written up to reflect general inflation?).

Historical cost with mandatory LIFO would result in income measurement in terms of simple dollars (unadjusted for changes in general purchasing power). It would allow for maintenance of capital as measured by historical dollars invested, except for inventory investment, which would be measured in terms of most recent acquisition costs.

### Price-Level-Adjusted Historical Costs

Advocates of price-level-adjusted historical costs (or *PLAC*) maintain that such an approach:

- Does not depart from the objectivity and conservatism of historical cost based measurement (a uniform adjustment is made to data obtained from objectively verifiable transactions);
- Does recognize the change in the general purchasing power of the measuring unit (dollar) that occurs independently of the ups and downs of specific inflation; and
- Does allow for recognition of monetary gains or losses.

PLAC supporters argue that conservatism is maintained in that any holding gains resulting from trading profit (buying low and selling high) are not recognized until realized through sale. They maintain that the dominant distortion inherent in historical cost statements results from failure to recognize the effects of general vs. specific inflation. And they believe that PLAC represents the best compromise or trade-off between the two extremes of historical cost (most objective and relatively meaningless) and replacement cost (less objective and more meaningful).

PLAC would result in income measurement in terms of units of current general purchasing power (price-level-adjusted dollars). It would reflect maintenance of capital measured in terms of the current general purchasing power of the dollars originally invested.

### Replacement Cost

Advocates of replacement-cost accounting question the desirability and objectivity of any attempt to impute changes in the purchasing power of the measuring unit (dollar). They maintain that any attempt to adjust historical cost dollars is caught between two dilemmas. To use different indices to reflect the purchasing intentions (specific inflation) of a particular firm at a particular time would be entirely too subjective. To use a single average index applicable to all firms, as under PLAC, could be misleading. A firm's purchasing intentions might very well be centered in a segment of the economy where specific inflation (or even deflation) was substantially different from overall average inflation.

Replacement-cost supporters focus on measuring specific dollar costs currently related to specific assets, regardless of the alternative purchasing power of these dollars. They believe holding gains (or losses) measured in terms of specific inflation (or deflation) should be currently reported even if not yet realized through sale or cost expiration. They advocate separate disclosure of unrealized gains, and the distinction between trading profit (repeatable) and realized holding gain (nonrepeatable), both of which are presently combined as gross profit under GAAP.

Replacement-cost advocates do not agree with their opponents that replacement costs necessarily involve too many costly, difficult, and subjective estimates. They cite other nations, such as the Netherlands, where replacement-cost accounting has been commonly and successfully used for over 30 years. They also cite recent U.S. experience in developing supplementary replacement-cost data required by the SEC (see below).

Replacement-cost accounting, like current GAAP and GAAP with mandatory LIFO, results in income measured in terms of simple dollars (unadjusted for changes in general purchasing power). It differs in that the capital maintained is a combination of current productive capacity (nonmonetary assets at current replacement cost) and historical dollars invested (monetary assets).

### Replacement Cost Adjusted for Price-Level Changes

Perhaps not as widely supported as any of the three previously cited alternatives to simple historical cost measurement is the combination of replacement cost and price-level adjustment. Price-level-adjusted replacement cost, hereafter referred to as *PLARC*, may appear to you as most logical. It involves first adjusting specific nonmonetary items to reflect the effect on costs of specific inflation (or deflation). The resulting statements are then further adjusted to reflect the changes in general purchasing power of the dollar. The resulting statements thus would reflect both current costs in a specific industry and also measurement in terms of units of common current general purchasing power.

PLARC has had little widespread support, probably because it combines all of the alleged "evils" of departure from historical cost. PLARC requires estimates of replacement costs that are not purely objective; and unfamiliar and potentially confusing overall price-level adjustments are also involved. The two-step adjustment and the actual meaning or significance of resulting data can be complicated for the uninitiate. Finally, PLARC may involve an unacceptable redefinition of income.

Under PLARC, income is measured in terms of units of current general purchasing power **after** capital maintenance (defined as maintenance of current productive capacity of nonmonetary assets). As previously discussed, maintaining specific capacity as opposed to general investment power represents a radical departure from current income concepts.

## COMPARISON OF ALTERNATIVES

Perhaps the most effective way for you to grasp the difference among the various alternatives discussed is to compare actual statements prepared by following each different alternative. The point of reference will be the conventionally prepared statements for the ABC Corporation for the year 19X3. You may assume that ABC uses LIFO, and you should be familiar with this approach either from a recent exposure to financial accounting or from reviewing Appendix D at the back of this book.

Exhibit 16.7 illustrates the firm's 19X3 income statement and balance sheet prepared under FIFO, LIFO, PLAC, replacement cost, and PLARC. The details of the various adjustments involved in arriving at the data included in this exhibit are covered in the appendix to this chapter. For the moment you need only realize that an annual inflation rate of eight percent has been assumed, and that specific replacement costs of nonmonetary assets have not increased as rapidly as the general inflation rate.

## Income Statement

From the comparative income statements included in Exhibit 16.7(a) you can observe a wide range of possible "income" figures, from $141,000 to $269,000, for a range of $128,000. Before becoming too alarmed, note that, for the data assumed in this example, GAAP already allows a range of $104,000 ($251,000 under FIFO, less $147,000 under LIFO).

### Exhibit 16.7(a)
### ABC CORPORATION

**Comparison of FIFO, LIFO, PLAC, Replacement Cost, and PLARC Income Statements**
**For the Year 19X3 (000 omitted)**

|  | Conventional FIFO | Conventional LIFO | PLAC | Replacement cost | PLARC |
|---|---|---|---|---|---|
| Sales | $3,150 | $3,150 | $3,344 | $3,150 | $3,344 |
| Cost of goods sold | 1,736 | 1,840 | 1,990 | 1,881 | 1,956 |
| Gross profit | $1,414 | $1,310 | $1,354 | $1,269 | $1,388 |
| Operating expenses: |  |  |  |  |  |
| Depreciation | 25 | 25 | 40 | 37 | 37 |
| Other expenses and taxes | 1,140 | 1,140 | 1,186 | 1,140 | 1,186 |
| Distributable income | — | — | — | $ 92 | $ 165 |
| Realized holding gains (losses): |  |  |  |  |  |
| Inventory sold | — | — | — | 145 | 36 |
| Fixed assets depreciated | — | — | — | 12 | 9 |
| Fixed assets sold | 2 | 2 | (3) | 2 | (3) |
| Gain on net monetary items | — | — | 16 | — | 16 |
| Realized income | $ 251 | $ 147 | $ 141 | $ 251 | $ 223 |
| Unrealized holding gains (losses): |  |  |  |  |  |
| Inventory | — | — | — | 0 | 0 |
| Fixed assets | — | — | — | 18 | (61) |
| Economic income | — | — | — | $ 269 | $ 162 |

The major points that you should observe relating to the income statements in Exhibit 16.7(a) are the following:

- Only PLAC and PLARC attempt to disclose data in terms of current common purchasing-power units;

- Conventional FIFO and replacement-cost income reporting are essentially similar, with two major exceptions: FIFO does **not** distinguish realized holding gains and does **not** indicate unrealized holding gains;

- With most inventory holding gains deferred, gross profit under conventional LIFO closely approximates gross profit under replacement cost, but reported income may differ significantly;

- Although appearing to report similar overall results, conventional LIFO and PLAC report in **different measuring units** and similar numbers may be coincidental;

- PLARC is the only method attempting to measure current specific costs in terms of common current measuring units, and it is the only system reflecting holding losses of purchasing power resulting from investments in assets that do not keep pace with general inflation.

## Exhibit 16.7(b)
### ABC CORPORATION

**Comparison of FIFO, LIFO, PLAC, Replacement Cost, and PLARC Balance Sheets
As of 12/31/X3 (000 omitted)**

|  | FIFO | LIFO | PLAC | Replacement cost | PLARC |
|---|---|---|---|---|---|
| **Assets** | | | | | |
| Cash | $ 150 | $ 150 | $ 150 | $ 150 | $ 150 |
| Accounts receivable (net) | 300 | 300 | 300 | 300 | 300 |
| Inventory | 400 | 296 | 408 | 404 | 404 |
| Fixed assets | 800 | 800 | 1,167 | 980 | 980 |
| Less: Accumulated depreciation | (300) | (300) | (438) | (368) | (368) |
| Total assets | $1,350 | $1,246 | $1,587 | $1,466 | $1,466 |
| **Equities** | | | | | |
| Current liabilities | $ 250 | $ 250 | $ 250 | $ 250 | $ 250 |
| Long-term debt | 370 | 370 | 370 | 370 | 370 |
| Contributed capital | 450 | 450 | 814 | 450 | 814 |
| Holding gains | — | — | — | 116 | (121) |
| Retained earnings | 280 | 176 | 153 | 280 | 153 |
| Total equities | $1,350 | $1,246 | $1,587 | $1,466 | $1,446 |

## Balance Sheet

From the comparative balance sheets included in Exhibit 16.7(b) you can also observe a range of asset measurements. You should note the following major points:

- Conventional LIFO may radically understate assets by carrying inventories at old and unrealistically low costs (in terms of current prices);
- PLAC can overstate assets by assuming a general inflation rate that may be greater than the specific rate for particular assets (as in this example), or vice versa (not illustrated);
- Replacement cost and PLARC involve the same measurement of total assets in terms of current dollar costs, with PLARC disclosing both "real" retained earnings (after allowing for maintenance of general purchasing power of contributed capital) and also purchasing-power losses on investment in assets whose costs do not keep pace with inflation, or purchasing-power gains on those investments with specific inflation exceeding general inflation (not illustrated); and
- None of the alternatives involves any adjustment to the measurement of monetary assets and liabilities.


## SEC REQUIREMENTS

Before concluding this introduction to financial-statement adjustment for inflation, you should become aware of recent SEC requirements. Starting in 1977, the Securities and Exchange Commission (SEC) has required supplementary disclosure of certain special information in terms of replacement costs. This requirement is intended to make data available to financial-statement users who might like to calculate income on a replacement-cost basis. The supplementary disclosure is currently required only for very large firms (those nonfinancial corporations with more than $100,000,000 of inventory and fixed assets).

Disclosure is required of:

1. Replacement cost of inventory at the beginning and end of each period;
2. Replacement cost at the time of sale of all goods sold during the period;
3. Replacement cost of fixed (plant) assets, or equivalent productive capacity, at the beginning and end of each period; and
4. Depreciation cost of fixed (plant) assets based on average replacement costs throughout the period for the assets or their equivalent productive capacity and calculated on a straight-line basis.

Note that the SEC requires this information to be included in footnotes to statements as purely supplementary information. It does **not** require that assets and income be restated.

In the appendix to this chapter, you can learn how such replacement-cost data may be used to adjust conventionally prepared financial statements to reflect current replacement costs in the measurement of assets and income.

---

## CHAPTER OVERVIEW

Based upon the material contained in this chapter, you should now be able to:

- Explain how prospective inflation may affect both future cash flows and their purchasing power.

- Identify four long-run decisions, other than the capital budgeting decision, where the impact of inflation must be considered, and explain why and how it should be considered.

- Describe how inflation may adversely affect short-run planning and control with respect to CVP analysis, standard costs, budget performance reporting, and cash management.

- Describe, with examples, the two-step, one-step, and zero-step techniques for incorporating the effects of inflation into business decision data, and explain the peculiar circumstances under which the use of each different technique is appropriate.

- Explain how a failure to incorporate adjustments for inflation in a firm's *external* financial statements may lead to dysfunctional *internal* decisions by managers.

- Describe potential GAAP-related distortions resulting from inflation and involving monetary gains or losses, holding gains and losses on nonmonetary items, and overall asset and income measurement.

- Explain, with examples, the difference between general and specific inflation.

- Describe how a general price index may be prepared, and prepare one, given a representative sample of items and prices.

- Identify three different capital maintenance concepts of income, and explain their differences.

- Describe three different types or categories of current income that could exist concurrently, and explain their differences.

- Explain the concept of general purchasing power holding gains or losses on net monetary items, and calculate such an amount for a particular period, given average monetary assets, average monetary debt, and the general inflation rate applicable to the period.

- Identify four alternative approaches to adjusting conventional historical-cost financial statements to reflect inflation.
- Describe the essential differences between price-level-adjusted and replacement-cost-adjusted statements.
- Describe the replacement-cost information required by the SEC, what firms must disclose it, and how it is to be disclosed.

## NEW VOCABULARY AND CONCEPTS

| | |
|---|---|
| Purchasing power | Price-level adjustment |
| Holding gain | Replacement-cost accounting |
| Monetary item | Economic income |
| Monetary loss/gain | Realized income |
| General inflation | Distributable income |
| Specific inflation | PLAC |
| Price index | PLARC |

- Specific vs. general inflation
- Income and the maintenance of capital
- Output- vs. input-based asset measurement

## REVIEW QUESTIONS

1. How can inflation affect each of the following decision areas:
   a) Performance evaluation of investment centers?
   b) Determination of dividend policy?
   c) Choice among alternative sources of financing—desired capital structure?
   d) Overall financial-statement analysis?
   e) Capital budgeting (investment) decisions?
   f) CVP analysis?

2. a) In evaluating intermediate and long-range decision data extending over several years, if projected cash flows already reflect anticipated inflation, why is a further adjustment for inflationary effect necessary?
   b) What is this additional adjustment?

3. What are each of the following inflation-adjustment techniques and in what situations is each appropriate? Explain, with examples.
   a) Zero-step
   b) One-step
   c) Two-step

4. Are all expected future cash flows in a capital budgeting decision the same with respect to requiring adjustment for anticipated inflation? Explain, with examples.

5. How may external financial statements be the source of dysfunctional internal behavior by managers? Explain, with examples.

6. a) What is a holding gain?
   b) What is the difference between realized and unrealized holding gains?
   c) Regardless of their accounting treatment, how may holding gains (losses) on monetary items differ from those on nonmonetary assets?
   d) When are holding gains on monetary assets recognized and reported in:
      1. Conventional statements (current GAAP)?
      2. Price-level-adjusted statements?
      3. Replacement-cost-adjusted statements?
   e) When are holding gains on nonmonetary items recognized and reported in:
      1. Conventional statements (current GAAP)?
      2. Price-level-adjusted statements?
      3. Replacement-cost-adjusted statements?

7. What structure/conditions within a firm give rise to monetary gains in periods of inflation? Explain with examples.

8. a) What is a price index?
   b) How is it constructed?
   c) How is it applied to financial-statement adjustment?

9. What is the difference between specific and general inflation? Explain, with examples.

10. In adjusting conventionally reported amounts for ending inventory in periods of inflation, for either general or specific inflation or both, in which situation (FIFO or LIFO) will a **larger** amount of adjustment usually be required?

11. Answer Question 10 above with respect to cost of goods sold.

12. a) How does maintenance of capital relate to the determination or measurement of income?
   b) What three different definitions of capital to be maintained underlie conventional, price-level-adjusted, and replacement-cost-adjusted income?

13. a) What are the differences among distributable, realized, and economic income?
   b) In each of the following statements, which type or types of income are readily available and in what units is each type measured:
      1. Conventional statements?
      2. Price-level-adjusted statements?
      3. Replacement-cost-adjusted statements?
      4. Replacement-cost and price-level-adjusted statements?

14. As compared to conventional financial statements, what are the arguments for and against:
   a) Price-level-adjusted statements?
   b) Replacement-cost-adjusted statements?
   c) Statements which are adjusted both for replacement costs and for changes in general price levels?

15. a) What supplementary information related to replacement costs must currently be disclosed by certain firms as required by the SEC?
   b) Which firms must disclose this information?

## MINI-CASES AND QUESTIONS FOR DISCUSSION

**MC 16.1**   Mrs. Becky Goldfarb is addressing the board of directors at the annual stockholders' meeting of a corporation in which she is an investor. She says, in part, "I hope that, as our board, you will not support any move toward current-value accounting. The audited financial statements currently represent the one and only bit of objective information we stockholders receive with which we can evaluate the firm's, and especially your, performance. If we move to price-level or replacement-cost accounting, the objectivity is lost. We will then have only someone's estimate of values rather than the hard facts. I'd rather have the facts and do my own estimating if necessary.

"Please don't misunderstand my position. I support your need for current estimates for internal decision making. And I would welcome your sharing these estimates with the stockholders. I just don't believe they should replace objective data in the financial statements."

Is Mrs. Goldfarb correct in all of her perceptions of current-value accounting? Do you agree with her essential position? Discuss.

**MC 16.2**   Mr. Sammy Yee is a strong advocate of moving away from historical-cost financial statements. In a speech to a group of accountants and investment analysts, he says, in part, "The time is long past when we should have moved away from the archaic notion that historical-cost accounting best serves management and the investor. In all financial reporting there unfortunately must be a trade-off, and therefore, a balance, between objectivity and relevance. The only completely objective financial statements would report only past cash flows. These have so little relevance to the user's needs that we have already moved away from complete objectivity through the use of accrual accounting. Currently accruals and deferrals, and especially the measurement and reporting of long-lived assets, involve many kinds of nonobjective estimates. Why are we afraid to take the next logical step, and acknowledge the reality of inflation, instead of pretending that it does not exist?

"I have heard accountants say that they could not audit and give an opinion on current-value statements. I don't understand this position. Price-level adjustment requires no estimating. And even in the case of replacement cost adjustment, if accountants can certify useful lives and salvage values many years into the future, why can't they certify replacement costs as of today?

"There is no purely objective reality or truth with respect to a firm's current economic position. Each day we all must deal with our best approximations of economic reality. Accountants should provide us with their best approximation. Sure, judgment is involved, but isn't professional judgment what an accountant is paid for? In periods of inflation, conventional accounting reports are almost wholly irrelevant. It is time that we all had meaningful information that we can use!"

Do you support Mr. Yee's position? What are the arguments on the other side? Discuss.

MC 16.3 One of the arguments against moving accounting away from historical cost is that many conventional accounting concepts have been borrowed and incorporated in existing legal contracts. It is maintained that to change the basis of acounting would generate chaos in the business world with respect to such contracts. For example, a loan agreement may provide for maintenance of a given dollar amount of net working capital, a maximum debt ratio, or a minimum amount of retained earnings. The agreement would make the loan immediately payable if the constraints were not maintained.

Would change-over to price-level or to replacement-cost accounting affect such agreements? Would any such effects violate the spirit or the intention of the agreements? How could such agreements be modified, or what could be done, to allow an accounting change without causing chaos? Discuss.

## ESSENTIAL PROBLEMS

EP 16.1 Your firm has asked you to recommend based solely on financial considerations, whether a particular capital budgeting proposal should be accepted or rejected. The proposal involves an initial net cash outlay of $200,000 and expected after-tax benefits (cash flows) of $53,000 in terms of current prices per year for eight years. Your firm's average after-tax cost of capital is 15 percent.

a) What would be your recommendation if you assumed no inflation for the next eight years? Explain.

b) If the cash flow benefits were fixed in terms of dollars by contract, and you anticipated an average general inflation of five percent per year for the eight years, would your initial recommendation differ? Explain.

c) If your cash flow benefits were fixed, and you anticipated general inflation of ten percent per year, would your initial recommendation differ? Explain.

d) If you anticipated a ten-percent annual inflation rate and the future benefits were not fixed by contract (they could be expected to increase as a result of price increases closely matching annual price inflation), what would be your recommendation? Explain.

EP 16.2 Your firm has asked you to recommend, based solely on financial considerations, whether it should undertake a project with fixed contract payments of $20,000 per year net of tax savings for six years. Your firm's after-tax cost of capital is 12 percent, and the expected annual benefits are $17,000. Future benefits are not fixed by contract and, if there is general inflation, you may assume that the benefits will increase annually in exact proportion to general inflation.

a) What would be your recommendation if you assumed no inflation over the next six years? Explain.

b) If you anticipated an average general inflation rate of three percent over the next six years, would your initial recommendation differ? Explain.

c) If you anticipated an average general inflation rate of eight percent over the next six years, would your initial recommendation differ? Explain.

## SUPPLEMENTARY PROBLEMS

(*Note.* The supplementary problems are based on material covered in the chapter appendix.)

**SP 16.3** Data on prices of four items comprising a representative sample of a general group of prices is given below:

| Item | Price 12/31/X5 | Price 12/31/X6 | Price 12/31/X7 |
|------|------|------|------|
| 1 | $ 3.00 | $ 3.60 | $ 4.00 |
| 2 | $ 7.00 | $ 7.10 | $ 9.50 |
| 3 | $ 9.00 | $ 8.00 | $ 7.00 |
| 4 | $ 1.00 | $ 3.30 | $ 3.70 |
| Total | $20.00 | $22.00 | $24.20 |

Using 19X5 as a base year equal to an index of 100, construct general price-level indices as of:

a) 12/31/X6
b) 12/31/X7

Using these indices, adjust the following data appearing on the 12/31/X7 conventional financial statements for the change in general purchasing power:

c) Inventory originally costing $400,000 purchased in uniform quantities since mid-19X7.

d) Fixed capacity assets totalled $900,000 ($400,000 purchased on 1/1/X6 and $500,000 purchased on 1/1/X7).

e) Cost of goods sold of $2,400,000 representing inventory purchased uniformly between 7/1/X6 and 7/1/X7.

f) Sales, occurring uniformly throughout 19X7, of $3,000,000.

**SP 16.4** Data on the prices for five items comprising a representative sample of a general group of prices is given below:

| Item | Price 12/31/X1 | Price 12/31/X2 | Price 12/31/X3 |
|------|------|------|------|
| 1 | $0.40 | $0.44 | $0.49 |
| 2 | 2.12 | 2.20 | 2.26 |
| 3 | 1.43 | 1.36 | 1.20 |
| 4 | 0.60 | 0.60 | 0.60 |
| 5 | 0.45 | 0.80 | 1.28 |
| Total | $5.00 | $5.40 | $5.83 |

Using 19X1 as a base year equal to an index of 100, construct general price level indices as of:

a) 12/31/X2

b) 12/31/X3

Using these indices, adjust the following data appearing on the 12/31/X3 conventional financial statements for the change in general purchasing power:

c) Inventory originally costing $300,000 was purchased evenly between 7/1/X1 and 6/30/X2.

d) Fixed capacity assets total $700,000 ($200,000 purchased on 1/1/X2, $400,000 purchased on 1/1/X3, and $100,000 purchased on 12/31/X3).

e) Cost of goods sold of $1,200,000 reflects inventory purchased evenly throughout 19X3.

f) Sales occur uniformly throughout 19X3 and totalled $2,000,000.

**SP 16.5** Assume that the GNP Implicit Price Deflator was 138.0 on 12/31/X5 and 150 on 12/31/6. During 19X6 a certain corporation had the following average balances in the following accounts:

| | |
|---|---|
| Cash | $ 50,000 |
| Marketable securities (government paper) | 30,000 |
| Accounts and notes receivable | 180,000 |
| Investments (bonds) | 40,000 |
| Current liabilities | 120,000 |
| Long-term debt (bonds) | 180,000 |

Determine, as of 12/31/X6:

a) Gain or loss on monetary assets

b) Gain or loss on monetary debt

c) Net gain or loss on monetary items

**SP 16.6** Assume that the general price index was 164 on 12/31/X7 and 173 on 12/31/X8. During 19X8 a certain corporation had the following average balances in the following accounts:

| | |
|---|---|
| Cash | $300,000 |
| Marketable securities ($300,000 stocks and $100,000 bonds) | 400,000 |
| Accounts and notes receivable | 700,000 |
| Investments (all common and preferred stock) | 300,000 |
| Current liabilities | 600,000 |
| Long-term note payable | 900,000 |

Determine, as of 12/31/X8:

a) Gain or loss on monetary assets

b) Gain or loss on monetary debt

c) Net gain or loss on monetary items

**SP 16.7** Assume the following facts with respect to the Beck Corporation:

• General price index 130 on 12/31/X4 and 146 on 12/31/X5.

- Beck followed LIFO. Ending inventory was acquired evenly between 1/1/X4 and 6/30/X5. Goods sold had been acquired evenly between 7/1/X5 and 12/31/X5.
- Fixed capacity assets were acquired on average when the general price index was 110 and were being depreciated on a straight-line basis.
- All stock was sold when the index was 105.

Data from the 12/31/X5 balance sheet and income statement for the Beck Corporation prepared on a conventional basis were as follows (000 omitted):

| Assets | | Equities | |
|---|---|---|---|
| Cash | $ 50 | Current liabilities | $ 280 |
| Marketable securities (bonds) | 40 | Bonds payable | 200 |
| Accounts receivable | 200 | Contributed capital | 200 |
| Inventory | 300* | Retained earnings | 360 |
| Fixed assets | 600 | | |
| Accumulated depreciation | (150) | | |
| Total | $1,040 | Total | $1,040 |

* $260 on 12/31/X4.

| Income and Expenses | |
|---|---|
| Sales | $1,600 |
| Cost of goods sold | 880 |
| Depreciation expense | 50 |
| Other operating expenses and taxes | 520 |
| Net income | $ 150 |

Prepare, in good form, the Beck Corporation's 12/31/X5 balance sheet and income statement adjusted for general price-level changes. Round all amounts to even dollars.

**SP 16.8** Assume that the Beck Corporation's financial-statement data for 19X5 was the same as given in Problem EP 16.7. Prepare, in good form, rounded to even dollars, the year-end balance sheet and income statement, adjusted for changes in general price levels and assuming the following information:

- General price index 160 on 12/31/X4 and 172 on 12/31/X5.
- Beck followed FIFO. Ending inventory had been acquired evenly between 7/1/X5 and 12/31/X5. Goods sold had been acquired evenly between 7/1/X4 and 6/30/X5.
- Fixed capacity assets were acquired on average when the general price index was 120, and these assets were being depreciated on a straight-line basis.
- All stock was sold when the index was 110.

**SP 16.9** Refer to the conventionally prepared financial-statement data for the Beck Corporation for 19X5 as given in Problem EP 16.7. Assume that the following additional information (similar to SEC supplementary-disclosure data required of larger firms) was available:

- Ending inventory replacement cost was $290,000 on 12/31/X4 and $340,000 on 12/31/X5.
- The firm followed LIFO, and the replacement cost of goods sold at the time of sale was $880,000.
- Replacement cost of fixed assets was $700,000 on 12/31/X4 and $850,000 on 12/31/X5.
- Replacement cost of that portion of fixed assets depreciated during the year was $58,000.

Prepare, in good form, the 19X5 balance sheet and income statement for the Beck Corporation on a replacement-cost basis. Indicate on the income statement subtotals for distributable and realized income.

**SP 16.10** Refer to Problem EP 16.7. Prepare, in good form, the replacement-cost-adjusted balance sheet and income statement for the Beck Corporation for 19X5, assuming supplementary replacement cost data were as follows:

- Ending inventory replacement cost was $265,000 on 12/31/X4 and $310,00 on 12/31/X5.
- The firm followed FIFO, and the replacement cost of goods sold at the time of sale was $985,000.
- Replacement cost of fixed assets was $720,000 on 12/31/X4 and $860,000 on 12/31/X5. Replacement cost of that portion of fixed assets depreciated during the year was $80,000.

## SUGGESTIONS FOR FURTHER READING

Davidson, Sidney, James S. Schindler, Clyde P. Stickney, and Roman L. Weil, *Managerial Accounting: An Introduction to Concepts, Methods, and Uses.* Hinsdale, Illinois: The Dryden Press, 1978; Chapter 15.

CHAPTER 16 APPENDIX

# Illustrations of Various Inflation Adjusted Statements

In this appendix you may become familiar with some of the details involved in adjusting financial statements to reflect:

1. Adjustment for LIFO,
2. General price-level adjustment (PLAC),
3. Replacement-cost adjustment, and
4. Adjustment for both price level and replacement cost (PLARC).

The starting point will be the 19X3 financial statements for the ABC Corporation, which you may assume follow the FIFO inventory cost flow assumption acceptable under GAAP. The 19X2 and 19X3 balance sheets and the 19X3 income statement prepared conventionally are included in Exhibit 16.8.[11]

## ADJUSTMENT TO REFLECT LIFO COST FLOW ASSUMPTION

Adjustment from FIFO to LIFO merely involves the timing of the recognition of cost expirations in cost of goods sold. Exhibit 16.8 discloses that, during 19X3, the ABC Company had a total of $2,136,000 of goods available for sale (cost of goods sold plus ending inventory). To dramatize the disparity between alternative methods, assume that the goods available for sale consisted of:

8,000  units acquired four years ago at a cost of $37 each,
30,000  units acquired during the first six months of 19X3 at a cost of $48 each, and
8,000  units acquired during the last six months of 19X3 at a cost of $50 each.

Under FIFO, the 8,000 units in ending inventory were assumed to be those most recently acquired, and they would be assigned the $50 unit cost. The remaining $1,736,000 of goods available would be reported as cost of goods sold.

---

[11]   Statements of retained earnings and changes in financial position are not illustrated. The intention of this appendix is to focus your attention upon balance sheet and income statement effects. To include the other statements could involve confusing detail and divert your attention from important differences.

**Exhibit 16.8**

ABC CORPORATION

**Balance Sheets as of 12/31/X2 and 12/31/X3 and
Income Statement for the Year Ending 12/31/X3
(000 omitted)**

| Assets | 19X3 | 19X2 |
|---|---|---|
| Cash | $ 150 | $ 130 |
| Accounts receivable—net | 300 | 260 |
| Inventory* | 400 | 370 |
| Fixed assets | 800 | 850 |
| Less:  Accumulated depreciation | (300) | (318) |
| Total assets | $1,350 | $1,292 |

| Equities | | |
|---|---|---|
| Current liabilities | $ 250 | $ 235 |
| Long-term debt | 370 | 390 |
| Contributed capital | 450 | 450 |
| Retained earnings | 280 | 217 |
| Total equities | $1,350 | $1,292 |

| Income | |
|---|---|
| Sales | $3,150 |
| Cost of goods sold* | 1,736 |
| Depreciation expense | 25 |
| Other operating expenses and taxes | 1,140 |
| Gain on fixed asset disposition | 2 |
| Net income | $ 251 |

* Company uses FIFO.

In this example, assuming LIFO cost flow, the situation would be reversed. The 8,000 units of ending inventory would be assigned the oldest ($37) cost, and the $1,840,000 balance of goods available would be reported as sold. Exhibit 16.9 illustrates 19X3 statements prepared under FIFO and LIFO.

Note that under FIFO, in this example, all holding gain is recognized in income. The holding gains were:

$104,000  on the oldest inventory (8,000 × $13)
  60,000  on the early 19X3 inventory (30,000 × $2)
$164,000

FIFO income includes and does **not** separately identify this $164,000 of potentially nonrepeatable holding gain. LIFO reporting excludes recognition of $104,000 of holding gain from asset, income, and retained earnings measurement. LIFO reporting therefore provides a better measure of current costs on

**Exhibit 16.9**

ABC CORPORATION

Balance Sheet as of 12/31/X3 and
Income Statement for the Year Ending 12/31/X3
(000 omitted)

| Assets | Under FIFO | Under LIFO |
|---|---|---|
| Cash | $ 150 | $ 150 |
| Accounts receivable—net | 300 | 300 |
| Inventory | 400 | 296 |
| Fixed assets | 800 | 800 |
| Less: Accumulated depreciation | (300) | (300) |
| Total assets | $1,350 | $1,246 |

| Equities | | |
|---|---|---|
| Current liabilities | $ 250 | $ 250 |
| Long-term debt | 370 | 370 |
| Contributed capital | 450 | 450 |
| Retained earnings | 280 | 176 |
| Total equities | $1,350 | $1,246 |

| Income | | |
|---|---|---|
| Sales | $3,150 | $3,150 |
| Cost of goods sold | 1,736 | 1,840 |
| Depreciation expense | 25 | 25 |
| Other operating expenses and taxes | 1,140 | 1,140 |
| Gain on fixed asset disposition | 2 | 2 |
| Net income | $ 251 | $ 147 |

the income statement and therefore of potentially repeatable income. However, income measured under LIFO still includes $60,000 of nonidentifiable holding gain in income; and the balance sheet measurement of inventory under LIFO is understated by $104,000 (8,000 × $13) in terms of current costs.

## GENERAL PRICE-LEVEL ADJUSTMENT

Exhibit 16.10 includes the 19X3 statements before and after adjustment for changes in the general price level, together with lettered references to the explanations that follow. You may assume that during 19X3 the Consumer Price Index increased eight percent, and that this increase has been used to adjust the statements.

Before proceeding to study the details of the various adjustments involved, take a moment to study the overall results as shown in Exhibit 16.10. Note

**Exhibit 16.10**

## ABC CORPORATION

**19X3 Balance Sheet and Income Statement**
**Conventional and Price-Level Adjusted**
**(000 omitted)**

| Assets | Conventional* | Reference | Price level adjusted |
|---|---|---|---|
| Cash | $ 150 | (a) | $ 150 |
| Accounts receivable—net | 300 | (a) | 300 |
| Inventory | 400 | (b) | 408 |
| Fixed assets | 800 | (c) | 1,167 |
| Less: Accumulated depreciation | (300) | (c) | (438) |
| Total assets | $1,350 | | $1,587 |
| | | | |
| **Equities** | | | |
| Current liabilities | $ 250 | (a) | $ 250 |
| Long-term debt | 370 | (a) | 370 |
| Contributed capital | 450 | (d) | 814 |
| Retained earnings | 280 | (e) | 153 |
| Total equities | $1,350 | | $1,587 |
| | | | |
| **Income** | | | |
| Sales | $3,150 | (f) | $3,344 |
| Cost of goods sold | 1,736 | (b) | 1,990 |
| Depreciation expense | 25 | (c) | 40 |
| Other operating expenses and taxes | 1,140 | (f) | 1,186 |
| Gains (+) and losses (−) on fixed asset disposition | +2 | (g) | −3 |
| Gain on net monetary items | 0 | (a) | 16 |
| Net income | $ 251 | | $ 141 |

* Assuming FIFO.

that restatement of assets for general inflation has resulted in an increase of $237,000, or approximately 15 percent. Note that price-level-adjusted income is down $110,000, or approximately 44 percent; and that it would have been down $126,000, or over 50 percent, if it had not been for the $16,000 gain on net monetary debt. The management's maintenance of a net monetary debt position has partially offset the erosion of noncurrent asset holding gains (when restated to reflect current purchasing power). In terms of general purchasing power, conventional reporting overstates income in this example by $110,000. Now refer to the lettered adjustments in Exhibit 16.10, and the discussion below.

## (a) Monetary Items

No adjustment is necessary for monetary assets or liabilities. They are already stated in terms of dollars that may be assumed to represent dollars of purchasing power as of the end of the year. However, as explained earlier in this chapter, holding monetary assets and monetary liabilities during periods of inflation results in monetary gains and losses. Average monetary assets during 19X3 amounted to $420,000 (the sum of $450,000 and $390,000, divided by 2), and average monetary debt amounted to $620,000 (the sum of $615,000 and $625,000, divided by 2). Therefore, on average, the firm held net monetary debt of $200,000 during 19X3. A monetary gain of $16,000 ($200,000 × 0.08) is therefore reported.[12]

## (b) Inventory and Cost of Goods Sold

Adjustment for ending inventory and for cost of goods sold will differ significantly depending upon which inventory cost flow assumption has been used for conventional reporting purposes. In Exhibit 16.8 it was assumed that the ABC Corporation used FIFO. Ending inventory will have to be adjusted to reflect increased general price levels since the inventory was acquired. You may assume that an inspection of the firm's detailed inventory records reveals that ending inventory has been assumed under FIFO to have been on hand for an average of three months.

If the general price level had increased uniformly throughout 19X3, then the average rate of increase for the most recent six months may be assumed

---

[12]   In this example for simplicity, the net monetary gain has been calculated assuming the average monetary assets and debt existed from the beginning of the year. Instead, assume, more realistically:

- Ending long-term debt had been in existence since the beginning of the year when the index was 1.00,
- Ending cash had been acquired uniformly throughout the year (average index 1.04), and
- Current receivables and payables had been acquired on average when the index was 1.06.

The net monetary gain would then be calculated:

| | | Gain (loss) |
|---|---|---|
| Long-term debt | ($370,000 × 1.08/1.00) − $370,000 | $29,000 |
| Current debt | ($250,000 × 1.08/1.06) − $250,000 | 4,717 |
| Cash | ($150,000 × 1.08/1.04) − $150,000 | (5,769) |
| Current Receivables | ($300,000 × 1.08/1.06) − $300,000 | (5,660) |
| | Net | $22,888 |

Also note that monetary loss on net working capital and monetary gain on long-term debt may be separately disclosed on the income statement, the loss being classified with operating items and the gain with financial items such as interest.

as two percent.[13] Ending FIFO inventory is therefore adjusted for the two-percent price-level change of $8,000 (400,000 × 0.02). Note that the resulting $408,000 of general purchasing power is currently required in order to acquire the same inventory that cost $400,000 an average of three months ago. Note that there is **no intention** of reflecting current inventory replacement costs, which could be higher or lower. General price-level adjustment merely involves restatement of all nonmonetary costs into common current purchasing-power units.

The cost of goods sold under FIFO represented the cost of two batches that had been separately acquired, one (30,000 units) on average nine months before year-end and the other four years previously. The 30,000 units must be adjusted for six-percent inflation occurring since acquisition, and the 8,000 units must be adjusted for four years of inflation which you may assume, for illustration, to total 35 percent. The necessary adjustment would then be $190,000:

$$30,000 \times 48 \times 0.06 = \$\ 86,400$$
$$8,000 \times 37 \times 0.35 = \underline{103,600}$$
$$\$190,000$$

Had the ABC Corporation been using LIFO (see Exhibit 16.9), the adjustments would have been quite different. Cost of goods sold would require an adjustment increasing the reported amount by $94,000.[14] Note that this differs materially from the $190,000 adjustment to cost of goods sold under FIFO, and reflects the fact that LIFO cost of goods sold more closely reflects current costs. The ending inventory adjustment to the balance sheet originally prepared following LIFO would be significantly greater than under FIFO. The required ending inventory adjustment (not illustrated) would then be $103,600 ($296,000 × 0.35), reflecting four years of accumulated inflation.

### (c) Fixed Assets and Depreciation

Fixed or capacity assets must be adjusted for inflation since the dates of their original acquisition. For simplification assume that all 12/31/X3 fixed assets had been acquired in three lots, with appropriate indices as follows:

| Lot | Original cost | Index at date of acquisition |
|---|---|---|
| 1 | $400,000 | 115 |
| 2 | 300,000 | 140 |
| 3 | 100,000 | 150 |

---

[13] Note that although the subject is beyond the scope of this introductory-level presentation, assuming a two-percent average may be inappropriate. Remember that inflation is like compound interest. If inflation averaged two percent each quarter, then the annual rate would have been 8.24 percent (1.02 × 1.02 × 1.02 × 1.02).

[14] (30,000 × 48 × 0.06) + (8,000 × 50 × 0.02).

You may also assume that the same index for 12/31/X3 was 190. The appropriate adjustments would therefore be:

| Lot | Original cost | Multiplier | Price-level adjusted cost |
|-----|---------------|------------|---------------------------|
| 1 | $400,000 | 190/115 | $ 660,870 |
| 2 | 300,000 | 190/140 | 380,000 |
| 3 | 100,000 | 190/150 | 126,667 |
| | $800,000 | | $1,167,537 |

The cost of fixed assets on the price-level-adjusted balance sheet would then be shown at $1,168,000 (rounded). This amount would reflect the general purchasing power that would be sacrificed currently to be the equivalent of that sacrificed at the time of original acquisition.

Depreciation expense for the current period is similarly adjusted to reflect the additional current purchasing power that is expiring. Assume, on average, that depreciable assets have been subject to a general inflation rate of 60 percent. Depreciation expense would therefore be adjusted to $40,000 ($25,000 × 1.6).

Accumulated depreciation on the balance sheet is adjusted in a manner similar to that for the original cost of the assets. In any given year, the increase in accumulated depreciation may exceed the current year's depreciation expense. The difference represents an amount of retroactive or catch-up depreciation on prior years' expiration of usefulness, restated to current purchasing-power equivalence. Note that, after adjustment, accumulated depreciation will represent the same proportion of depreciable assets as that based on original acquisition cost. In this illustration, accumulated depreciation remains 37.5 percent of the restated cost, or $438,000 (rounded).

## (d) Contributed Capital

Contributed capital as a nonmonetary item is also adjusted to the current purchasing-power equivalent. Assume that all contributed capital was invested when the general inflation index was 105. Contributed capital of $450,000 is therefore adjusted to $814,000 (450,000 times 190/105, rounded).

## (e) Retained Earnings

Retained earnings of $153,000 in this illustration is adjusted to make total equities equal total assets. It can be reconciled by restating 12/31/X2 adjusted retained earnings to 12/31/X3 dollars ($119,000), adding adjusted net income ($141,000), and subtracting $107,000 of dividends distributed at year-end.

Retained earnings included in price-level-adjusted balance sheets may be viewed as including net differences in adjustments to nonmonetary assets and equities. Under more sophisticated reporting systems beyond the scope of this appendix, these amounts may be separately disclosed within owners' equity.

## (f) Revenues and Other Operating Expenses

In nonseasonal businesses it may be assumed that operating revenues and operating expenses (other than cost of goods sold and depreciation) occur evenly throughout the year. The average adjustment is therefore for six months of inflation or four percent.

## (g) Gain/Loss on Fixed Asset Disposition

On July 1, 19X3, the ABC Corporation sold equipment originally costing $50,000 for $9,000. Accumulated depreciation through 7/1/X3 amounted to $43,000 on a conventional basis. A gain of $2,000 on disposition over depreciated historical cost was therefore originally reported. If investigation revealed that general inflation had been 70 percent between the dates of acquisition and disposition of this asset, its adjusted book value at the point of sale would have been $12,000 rounded ($50,000 times 1.7, less 86 percent accumulated depreciation). The sale for $9,000 would have resulted in a $3,000 loss instead of a $2,000 gain.

## Summary

Price-level-adjusted financial statements eliminate some but not all of the inflation-related problems with conventional statements cited earlier in this chapter. Holding gains and losses on net monetary items are disclosed. With all costs and benefits reported, the efficiency of the management of monetary items may be evaluated. In terms of general purchasing power, the illusory portion of realized holding gains is eliminated, and a more realistic disclosure of any amount of realized holding losses is reported. Insofar as specific price changes parallel general inflation, unrealized holding gains are currently recognized, assets are more realistically reported in terms of current costs, and depreciation charges are similarly more realistic.

Price-level-adjusted statements do not, however, provide for distinguishing real holding gains from trading profit on inventory sold. They do not reflect any specific price changes that may differ substantially from changes in the general price level. Also, they may increase the distortion resulting from failure to currently recognize significant obsolescence of specific fixed assets by recording appreciation of assets that should be written down.[15]

## REPLACEMENT COST ADJUSTMENT

Another proposed alternative to historical-cost-based accounting is one that incorporates specific price changes related to nonmonetary assets. Under strict

---

[15] Although sometimes difficult to implement for assets not having a ready used market, a required extension of the LOCM rule to fixed assets could resolve the delayed obsolescence realization problem under either conventional or price-level accounting.

replacement cost accounting, general purchasing-power changes, along with attendant monetary gains and losses, are ignored. Individual nonmonetary assets, or asset groups, are valued at their current replacement cost at the balance sheet date, or at the current cost of equivalent productive capacity of the same age and condition. Differences in values over a period are recognized and treated as holding gains or losses, and are reported on the income statement. Asset expirations (depreciation and amortization) are stated in terms of the specific current replacement cost of the asset portion used. Where active markets exist for specific assets, current replacement costs that are fairly objective may be readily obtained. Where active markets do not exist, where the asset is specialized, or where technological change has made equivalent assets unobtainable, then engineering estimates or specific indices for specific asset groups must be employed. It is the subjectivity of such estimates and the expected difficulty and cost to obtain them, that form the basis for rejection of replacement-cost accounting by many accountants.

To illustrate replacement-cost accounting, the same 19X2/19X3 statements for the ABC Corporation (Exhibit 16.8) that served as a basis earlier for price-level adjustment will be used. You may assume the following data relevant to the ABC Corporation for 19X3:

- Replacement cost of inventory as of 12/31/X2 and 12/31/X3 was $374,000 and $404,000, respectively.
- Replacement cost of goods sold during 19X3 at the time of sale was $1,881,000.
- Replacement cost of fixed assets as of 12/31/X2 and 12/31/X3 was $1,000,000 and $980,000, respectively.
- Depreciation of fixed assets based on the average replacement cost of similar productive capacity was $37,000.

Exhibit 16.11 includes the ABC Corporation's financial statements prepared on a conventional and on a replacement-cost basis. Note on Exhibit 16.11 that only nonmonetary assets and expenses are adjusted. Restatement to replacement cost has resulted in an increase of $116,000 in the valuation of reported assets (disclosed as unrealized holding gains), and an increase of $18,000 in income, reflecting the current year's net unrealized asset appreciation. Necessary adjustments are explained below, and are referenced to Exhibit 16.11.

### (a) Inventory and Cost of Goods Sold

Recall that it was assumed that the ABC Corporation's conventional statements were prepared on a FIFO basis. Since ending inventory under FIFO is usually stated in near-current costs, only a minor adjustment of $4,000 is required to reflect specific cost increases between most recent acquisitions and year-end. Cost of goods sold requires a larger adjustment of $145,000 to reflect the cost increases between the earlier purchase and the resale dates.

**Exhibit 16.11**

## ABC CORPORATION

**19X3 Balance Sheet and Income Statement**
**Conventional and Replacement Cost Adjusted**
**(000 omitted)**

| Assets | Conventional* | Referenced | Replacement cost adjusted |
|---|---|---|---|
| Cash | $ 150 | | $ 150 |
| Accounts receivable—net | 300 | | 300 |
| Inventory | 400 | (a) | 404 |
| Fixed assets | 800 | (b) | 980 |
| Less: Accumulated depreciation | (300) | (b) | (368) |
| Total assets | $1,350 | | $1,466 |
| | | | |
| **Equities** | | | |
| Current liabilities | $ 250 | | $ 250 |
| Long-term debt | 370 | | 370 |
| Contributed capital | 450 | | 450 |
| Unrealized holding gains | 0 | (c) | 116 |
| Retained earnings | 280 | | 280 |
| Total equities | $1,350 | | $1,466 |
| | | | |
| **Income** | | | |
| Sales | $3,150 | | $3,150 |
| Cost of goods sold | 1,736 | (a) | 1,881 |
| Current depreciation expense | 25 | (b) | 37 |
| Other operatng expenses | | | |
| and taxes | 1,140 | | 1,140 |
| Gain on fixed asset disposition | 2 | (d) | 2 |
| Other realized holding gains | 0 | (d) | 157 |
| Realized income | $ 251 | | $ 251 |
| Unrealized holding gains—net | 0 | (c) | 18 |
| Total income and gains | $ 251 | | $ 269 |

* Prepared using FIFO.

Had ABC been on LIFO, the situation would have been reversed. Unless significant time had elapsed between recent acquisitions and sales, little or no adjustment would be required for cost of goods sold. But a major adjustment might be required to bring costs of "old" balance sheet inventory up to current replacement costs.

## (b) Fixed Capacity Assets and Depreciation

Fixed assets are written up to year-end replacement costs, and accumulated depreciation is increased proportionately. Depreciation expense is increased to reflect depreciation in terms of current replacement costs rather than lower original costs. Note that current depreciation charges do *not* equal the entire $68,000 increase in adjusted accumulated depreciation for the year. The $31,000 difference will be explained under unrealized holding gains below.

### (c) Unrealized Holding Gains

Total assets on the balance sheet have been increased by $116,000 to reflect unrealized appreciation as measured by current replacement costs. This unrealized holding gain is included under owners' equity as a distinct item. Reported retained earnings therefore remains "realized."

From replacement-cost data at the beginning of the year, and from conventional data included in Exhibit 16.8, you can determine that the unrealized holding gain appearing on the 12/31/X2 balance sheet (adjusted for replacement cost) would have been $98,000. During 19X3 an additional $18,000 ($116,000 − $98,000) of net unrealized gain is accrued, and this is reported as the last item on the replacement-cost-adjusted income statement. This $18,000 represents a $61,000 increase in the net unrealized holding gain on fixed assets, less the $12,000 of currently increased depreciation charges and less the $31,000 of additional accumulated depreciation previously cited. This $31,000 represents retroactive or catch-up depreciation for prior years, reflecting current higher asset replacement costs.

### (d) Realized Holding Gains

The $2,000 gain on disposition of fixed assets is reported as realized under both the conventional and replacement-cost systems (within replacement-cost accounts this amount would be transferred from unrealized to realized gain). The $157,000 other realized gain represents the sum of $145,000 (adjustment to cost of goods sold) and $12,000 (adjustment to appreciation) realized as part of adjusted expenses above.

### Summary

Replacement-cost-adjusted statements also eliminate some but not all of the inflation-caused problems with conventional statements. Holding gains and losses on nonmonetary assets in terms of specific price changes are recognized currently; and depreciation charges are realistically stated in terms of current replacement costs. Inventory holding gains are distinguished from trading profit. Obsolescence of fixed assets is currently recognized, and balance sheet assets are reported in terms of current cost. Strict replacement-cost-adjusted statements do not, however, disclose holding gains and losses on net monetary items; nor do they distinguish between real and illusory holding gains in terms of dollar general purchasing power. Also, as discussed earlier in the chapter under different measures of income, depreciation charges that may vary from general price-level adjustments may be inappropriate for income measurement purposes.

**Exhibit 16.12**

ABC CORPORATION

**Replacement-Cost-Adjusted Income Statement**
**For the Year Ending 12/31/X3**

| | | |
|---|---|---|
| Sales | | $3,150,000 |
| Cost of goods sold | | 1,881,000 |
| Gross profit | | $1,269,000 |
| Operating expenses: | | |
| Depreciation | $ 37,000 | |
| Other expenses and taxes | 1,140,000 | 1,177,000 |
| **Distributable Income** | | $ 92,000 |
| Realized holding gains: | | |
| Inventory sold | $ 145,000 | |
| Fixed assets depreciated | 12,000 | |
| Fixed assets sold | 2,000 | 159,000 |
| **Realized Income** | | $ 251,000 |
| Unrealized holding gains: | | |
| Inventory | $ 0 | |
| Fixed assets | 18,000 | 18,000 |
| **Economic Income** | | $ 269,000 |

## Reporting Three Types of Income Concurrently

A further benefit of replacement-cost accounting is that it makes possible concurrent disclosure of all three types of income discussed in this chapter. Exhibit 16.12 contains the same replacement-cost-adjusted 19X3 income information for the ABC Corporation that is included in Exhibit 16.11. Exhibit 16.12 differs in that it illustrates the concurrent reporting of the three types of income.

Note, on Exhibit 16.12, that the elimination of holding gains from gross profit, and the charging of depreciation based on replacement cost, result in an income from operations after taxes of only $92,000. This amount is identified as distributable income, or the amount that could be distributed to owners without jeopardizing operations at current prices and levels of activity.[16] Distributable income may also be viewed as the amount that is repeatable in the future at the same level of activity if there are no further price changes.

Distributable income plus realized holding gains equal realized income, and this amount is also disclosed in Exhibit 16.12. Note that realized income

---

[16] It can be argued that distributable income should be net of retroactive depreciation, and that the ABC Corporation actually had distributable income of only $61,000 ($92,000 reported less $31,000 retroactive depreciation) during 19X3. This issue is beyond the scope of this text.

under replacement-cost accounting equals net income under conventional accounting. It represents that portion of the firm's overall increase in well-offness that has been validated through exchanges with outside individuals and markets.

Realized income plus unrealized holding gain equals the firm's economic income, as measured by an overall increase in well-offness whether or not realized. GAAP standards of realization and conservatism currently preclude the measurement and reporting of unrealized gain on conventional financial statements. Although economic income may include fortuitous events as well as the results of astute management planning and action, it would appear a desirable additional measurement of management performance. As previously mentioned, realized income usually is like a delayed report. If only realized income is available for evaluation, credit for gains may be attributed to the wrong individuals, and lost opportunity gains will never be disclosed.

## ADJUSTMENT FOR BOTH REPLACEMENT COST AND GENERAL PRICE-LEVEL CHANGES

Exhibit 16.13 includes conventional disclosure and the financial statements adjusted to reflect **both** adjustment of nonmonetary assets and expenses to reflect replacement costs and also adjustment for changes in general purchasing power. Note, in Exhibit 16.13, that the balance sheet adjusted for PLARC is similar to that for simple replacement cost (Exhibit 16.11). Monetary assets and liabilities are **not** adjusted, since they already express current dollars. Nonmonetary assets have been adjusted to reflect replacement costs also in terms of current (year-end) dollars. Contributed capital is adjusted to reflect price-level change. Unrealized holding gains reflect replacement cost adjustment to current dollars.[17] Retained earnings reflects both revenue and expense adjustments to current dollars and gains on net monetary debt.

Note that, in Exhibit 16.13, revenue and expense items reflecting flows throughout the year (sales, cost of goods sold, and other operating expenses and taxes) are first adjusted to reflect replacement costs where applicable. These amounts are then further adjusted to reflect average general inflation of four percent. And note that the disposition of the fixed asset is disclosed as a loss in terms of purchasing power (see discussion above under PLAC).

Exhibit 16.13 reveals current year's and accumulated negative holding gains related to nonmonetary assets. The negative holding gain reflects the loss of purchasing power through investment in assets whose replacement

---

[17]   Note that when replacement costs are rising at a lower rate than general inflation, PLARC will report an unrealized holding loss representing the loss in general purchasing power attributable to holding an asset where the value is not keeping up with inflation.

## Exhibit 16.13

## ABC CORPORATION

**19X3 Balance Sheet and Income Statement
Conventional and Both Replacement Cost and Price-Level Adjusted
(000 omitted)**

| Assets | Conventional[a] | Adjustment for replacement cost | Adjustment for price level | PLARC adjusted |
|---|---|---|---|---|
| Cash | $ 150 | — | — | $ 150 |
| Accounts receivable—Net | 300 | — | — | 300 |
| Inventory | 400 | + 4 | — | 404 |
| Fixed assets | 800 | +180 | — | 980 |
| Less: Accumulated depreciation | (300) | − 68 | — | (368) |
| Total assets | $1,350 | | | $1,466 |
| | | | | |
| **Equities** | | | | |
| Current liabilities | $ 250 | — | — | $ 250 |
| Long-term debt | 370 | — | — | 370 |
| Contributed capital | 450 | — | +364 | 814 |
| Holding gains | 0 | +116 | −237 | (121) |
| Retained earnings | 280 | — | — | (153) |
| Total equities | $1,350 | | | $1,466 |
| | | | | |
| **Income** | | | | |
| Sales | $3,150 | — | +194 | $3,344 |
| Cost of goods sold | 1,736 | +145 | + 75 | 1,956 |
| Current depreciation expense | 25 | + 12 | — | 37 |
| Other operating expenses and taxes | 1,140 | — | + 46 | 1,186 |
| Gain on fixed asset disposition | 2 | — | − 5 | (3) |
| Other realized holding gains | 0 | +157 | − 96[b] | 61 |
| Realized income | $ 251 | | | $ 223 |
| Unrealized holding gains— Net | 0 | + 18 | − 79[c] | (61) |
| Total income and gains | $ 251 | | | $ 162 |

[a] Prepared following FIFO.
[b] Net of $112,000 holding loss on assets used and $16,000 gain on monetary debt.
[c] Holding loss on fixed assets.

cost is not keeping pace with inflation. Note also that realized and economic income are lower than under historical-cost FIFO, reflecting erosion of current purchasing power.

## COMPARISON OF ALTERNATIVES

Exhibit 16.7 in this chapter compares financial statements prepared under all of the preceding alternatives. Accompanying this exhibit is a discussion of the differences, which will not be repeated here. The purpose of this appendix has been to introduce you to the basis for determining a firm's financial statements under each of the four alternatives to conventional FIFO.

# 17

# QUANTITATIVE TECHNIQUES RELEVANT TO MANAGERIAL ACCOUNTING

## CHAPTER PREVIEW

The purpose of this chapter is to introduce several concepts and techniques applicable to constrained business decisions, to decisions under uncertainty, and to the control of projects and programmed costs. In this chapter, you can learn:

- That a technique known as linear programming (LP) may be useful in making decisions involving many combinations of different resource usage with multiple constraints.
- How to formulate an LP model and to interpret its solution without having to develop the mathematical skills necessary to obtain the solution.
- How to recognize the problems that can be solved with linear programming.
- That decisions involving significant uncertainty can be subject to rational solution, provided the probabilities of possible outcomes are known or may be estimated.
- That a systematic approach called decision analysis exists for dealing with decisions under uncertainty.
- How so-called decision trees can assist managers to visualize complex decisions involving many alternatives and to identify the most desirable course of action.
- That a systematic approach exists for planning and controlling multiple-step projects and programmed costs, and how you may use this approach in certain situations.

With the information contained in this and earlier chapters, you will have completed your introduction to some of the more important quantitative tools applicable to many business decisions. You should be in a position both to appreciate the wide-ranging usefulness of these tools and to develop confidence in the solutions that can be derived from quantitative models.

## WHAT IS THE BEST PRODUCT MIX IN THIS SITUATION?

As president of the Tripper Company, you are trying to resolve a problem brought to you by your operations vice-president. Your sales vice-president is also vitally concerned in its solution. The problem involves the moulding department, which now is, and in the near future will be, operating at capacity. The issue is what mix of economy and deluxe skis should be produced that will maximize the firm's profits.

In Chapter 7, you learned to seek maximum contribution and, in the face of a capacity constraint, to seek maximum contribution per unit of constraining factor. Unfortunately, your current problem is more complex. In addition to the constraint of the moulding department's productive capacity, there are other constraints. There is an upper limit on how many of each ski you can sell. This limit makes concentrating all resources on the production and sale of only one ski not a *feasible alternative*. A feasible alternative is one that satisfies all practical constraints. It may be possible to concentrate all production on one ski, but, since so much production could not be sold, it would not represent a feasible solution in a practical sense.

Availability of raw materials further constrains the number of possible alternatives. Given appropriate data, how could you determine the optimal (best possible) product mix? With more than one constraint operating, the simple rule that you learned in Chapter 7 is no longer applicable.

Before dealing with actual numbers, you should try to visualize that one possible approach to a solution would involve:

**First:** Identify all feasible solutions—those combinations that could be produced:
- from available raw material,
- within the department's capacity, and
- that could be sold;

**Second:** Determine the total contribution provided by each feasible solution; and

**Third:** Select the solution with the highest total contribution.

This approach would work; but it is not practical, for most real-life problems have too many feasible solutions. Even with the availability of computers, to check out the results of each feasible solution would be too costly and time-consuming.

What **would** be helpful would be a technique that would:

- Help you identify a single feasible solution,

- Advise you whether it was the best possible (optimal) solution, or whether you should try another, and in what direction (for instance, more of one product and less of another) you should go, and

- Let you perform the process iteratively so that, in a very few trials, you would find the optimal solution.

It would also be extremely valuable if such a technique could provide you with the **opportunity cost** of each of the constraints—the benefit available from introducing one additional unit of scarce resource.

## LINEAR PROGRAMMING

The tool or technique having all of these features exists. It is known as linear programming (LP). In the following paragraphs you may learn:

- how to set up an LP problem,
- how to solve the Tripper product mix problem using the LP method,
- how to identify problems amenable to LP solution,
- how to interpret the results you can obtain.

### Formulating the Problem

The first step in applying linear programming analysis to a particular situation is to formulate the problem and set up the LP *model.* A model is a representation of various factors involved and their interrelationships in a particular situation. You should already be familiar with various models, from model planes and cars to accounting systems and reports. Many decision models are expressed in algebraic form, and you have already been introduced in earlier chapters to the breakeven model, the EOQ/ELS model, the reorder-point model, the discounted cash flow or NPV model, and others.

The LP model consists of two parts, the *objective function* and the *constraints.* Where the objective is to maximize contribution or profit, the objective function will be in the form of an equation summarizing the various components of total contribution or profit. Where the objective is to minimize cost, the objective function will be an equation summarizing all of the relevant cost elements.

For example, assume that a firm had three products—A, B, and C—and that their unit contributions were \$3, \$7, and \$10, respectively. Allowing the letters to represent the quantities of each respective product produced and sold, the objective function for maximizing contribution (K) would be:

$$\text{Maximize: } K = 3A + 7B + 10C.$$

If this same firm, instead, were attempting to **minimize** total costs (T), and the products cost \$8, \$15, and \$25, respectively, the objective function would be:

$$\text{Minimize: } T = 8A + 15B + 25C.$$

Note that the unit values (\$3, \$7, and \$10 of contribution, and \$8, \$15, and \$25 of cost) are known as "coefficients."

Formulating the LP problem and setting up the model has three phases. The first phase involves identifying **all** of the relevant decision variables— those factors that can significantly affect the outcome. The second phase involves constructing the objective function as illustrated. The third phase involves stating **all** the constraints upon possible solutions. Constraints may be both physical (capacity limitations) and practical (market limitations).

The constraints separately depict each resource limitation relevant to the objective function. For example, in maximizing contribution, one of the constraints might be productive capacity. If the three products required 2, 5, and 6 hours, respectively, to produce, and if productive capacity totalled 2,000 hours for the period, then this one constraint would be expressed:

$$2A + 5B + 6C \leq 2,000.$$

Again, 2, 5, and 6 are the coefficients of this capacity constraint. Note that constraints usually involve inequalities. Most constraints in a maximization model involve upper limits. The above inequality, therefore, indicates that any feasible product mix will require 2,000 or less hours of productive capacity.

Note that, for models with the objective of minimizing costs, most of the inequalities in the various constraint equations would be the other way. If the firm's direct-labor costs (cost coefficients) were \$4, \$8, and \$11 per unit, respectively, and if it wished to minimize total cost while maintaining a payroll of at least \$500, then the labor-cost constraint would be:

$$\$4A + \$8B + \$11C \geq \$500.$$

It would indicate that any feasible product mix would have to result in total direct labor cost of \$500 or more.

## Computing the Optimal Solution

Once the objective function and all of the various constraints have been determined, solution involves manipulating the many simultaneous equations involved. Where there are only two variable (two products in a product-mix problem), a graphic solution is possible and will be illustrated below. Where three **or more** variables are involved, a graphic solution is no longer feasible and a mathematical technique known as the *simplex method* must be used.

The simplex method is a mathematical approach that follows the iterative steps described earlier. It is beyond the scope of this text and unnecessary to your basic understanding of LP usefulness, problem formulation, and solution interpretation. Since working the simplex method with paper and pencil can be tedious and complex, most LP problems are solved on a computer. Your computer center undoubtedly has an available simplex program, and you should have the opportunity to solve LP problems in quantitative methods courses.

## Product Mix Illustration

Returning to the Tripper situation, you now have a tool to resolve your ski-mix dilemma. To use the actual costs, unit contributions, and sales quantities developed for Tripper in earlier chapters would involve large numbers that could interfere with your initial grasp of LP analysis. Therefore, simplified data will be assumed as follows:

- Let $X$ equal the quantity of economy skis that are to be produced and sold. Each economy ski has a unit contribution of $30. Each ski requires six hours of production time in the moulding department and consumes two pounds of common raw material.
- Let $Y$ equal the quantity of deluxe skis that are to be produced and sold (unit contribution of $50). Each deluxe ski requires only four hours of production time but consumes a total of four pounds of common raw material.
- Only 2,400 hours of production time and only 1,600 pounds of common raw material are available each period.
- No more than 300 economy skis and no more than 350 deluxe skis can be sold in any one period.

From the foregoing data you should attempt to determine the objective function (let $Z$ equal total contribution) and **all** relevant constraint equations on a separate piece of paper, before proceeding.

Compare your model with the one shown in Exhibit 17.1. Did you determine correctly the objective function and the **six** relevant constraint equations? If each $X$ has a unit contribution of $30, and each $Y$ $50, the objective function stating the total contribution ($Z$) to be maximized will be:

(I)
$$Z = 30X + 50Y$$

There are six separate constraints. With each economy ski requiring six hours, and each deluxe ski requiring four hours, and with only 2,400 hours of capacity, the production capacity constraints may be expressed as:

(II)
$$6X + 4Y \leq 2,400 \text{ hours.}$$

### Exhibit 17.1
### TRIPPER WATER SKI MANUFACTURING COMPANY

**Product Mix Linear Programming Model**

| | |
|---|---|
| (I) | Maximize: $Z = 30X + 50Y$ |
| (II) | Subject to the constraints: $6X + 4Y \leq 2,400$ |
| (III) | $2X + 4Y \leq 1,600$ |
| (IV) | $X \leq 300$ |
| (V) | $Y \leq 350$ |
| (VI) | $X \geq 0$ |
| (VII) | $Y \geq 0$ |

With each economy ski using two pounds of raw material, and each deluxe ski using four, and with only 1,600 pounds of material available, the material constraint is expressed by:

(III)                              $2X + 4Y \leq 1,600$ pounds.

Since no more than 300 economy skis or 350 deluxe skis may be sold in a period, these two market constraints are expressed by:

(IV)                              $X \leq 300$ units

(V)                               $Y \leq 350$ units

Finally, since **negative** production is impossible, the following two constraints must also be included:

(VI)                              $X \geq$ zero

(VII)                             $Y \geq$ zero

Without these nonnegativity constraints, a mathematical solution could exist indicating negative production of one item, making additional material available to the other. Such a "solution" would of course be absurd. Therefore, the model must include these realistic limitations.

Note that Exhibit 17.2 indicates all six constraints (the two axes serve as negative production limits), and that each reduces or limits the area of possible solutions. The shaded area represents the set of all feasible solutions. Tripper can produce any combination within this area. However, you wish to maximize total contribution, and to find the one combination that will produce this result.

**Exhibit 17.2**

TRIPPER WATER SKI MANUFACTURING COMPANY

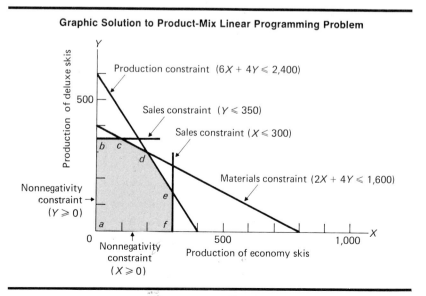

Graphic Solution to Product-Mix Linear Programming Problem

It can be shown that the optimal solution will always lie at one corner of the shaded area.[1] To find the optimal product mix, you have only to determine the total contribution at each corner point (identified as (a) through (f) on Exhibit 17.2). Substituting the production quantities at each corner point into the objective function (Eq. (I)) you can compute the following table:

| Corner | Unit contribution $\times$ Product mix | | Total contribution |
|---|---|---|---|
| (a) | 30(zero) + 50(zero) | = | $ (zero) |
| (b) | 30(zero) + 50(350) | = | $17,500 |
| (c) | 30(100) + 50(350) | = | $20,500 |
| (d) | 30(200) + 50(300) | = | $21,000 |
| (e) | 30(300) + 50(150) | = | $19,500 |
| (f) | 30(300) + 50(zero) | = | $12,000 |

Note that corner point (d), representing a product mix of 200 economy skis and 300 deluxe skis, represents the optimal solution for Tripper. This mix results in the greatest total contribution, $21,000 per period. Now that you have seen how LP can be used to solve a product-mix problem, you should generalize upon this example and learn how to identify those problems that lend themselves readily to an LP solution.

## GENERAL CHARACTERISTICS OF PROBLEMS AMENABLE TO LP SOLUTIONS

Many complex business problems are amenable to solution by LP. In order for LP to be applicable, a problem must have four general characteristics:

1. The problem must involve maximizing or minimizing some value that can be expressed in terms of a linear objective function. For example, a firm may wish to maximize profit or contribution or utilization of capacity. Or it may wish to minimize a specific cost, machine time used, labor hours, travel time, and so forth.

2. The solutions must be subject to constraints on available resources (funds, machine capacity, labor hours, storage space, number of shipping or distribution channels and their costs, and so forth); or, if necessary, resources that must be consumed (crude oil already in the pipeline that must be used, services under contract that cannot be stored, and so forth).

---

[1]    If the objective function were superimposed as a series of parallel lines, all having the slope of the objective function, the optimal contribution would occur at a point on one of the lines farthest from the origin and still touching the feasible (shaded) area. This point will always be a corner unless the objective function is parallel to one of the constraint lines (has the same slope). In such situations, known as degenerate solutions, all points between the two corners of the constraint line will result in the same maximum contribution, and there will be no single optimum point.

3. The relationships involved in both the objective function and the constraints must either be linear or be such that an assumption of linearity will not materially distort the solution.

4. The objective function and all relevant constraints must be capable of being quantified and formulated algebraically into the LP model.

## COMMON LP APPLICATIONS

Many business problems have these four characteristics, and LP is regularly used in their solution. The following list of applications is intended to illustrate the versatility of LP and the scope of its applications. LP has been used in:

- Investment portfolio management to select an optimal mix of investments,
- Blending the ingredients in gasoline, sausage, and animal feed with the objective of producing saleable product at least cost,
- Routing salespersons, shipments, and railroad boxcars to maximize results at least cost, and
- Production planning to achieve optimal use of personnel and to reduce stockouts and inventory carrying charges to lowest feasible levels.

## SHADOW PRICES

As mentioned earlier, LP can not only provide an optimal solution to a problem; it can also provide valuable additional information with respect to the opportunity costs of various constraints. In essence, you can think of **sensitivity analysis** of the optimal solution directed towards answering such questions as:

- What would be the benefits of more capacity (less constraint) arising out of a new optimal solution? These benefits can then be compared to estimated costs of additional capacity, to determine desirability.

and

- What would be the costs of additional constraints or lost capacity?

One instrument of LP sensitivity analysis involves the so-called *shadow prices* or marginal values of additional units of scarce resources. Shadow prices are readily available as outputs of most LP computer programs. Where the LP problem has been solved graphically without using the simplex method, you can best visualize what a shadow price would represent by:

First:    Expanding one constraint by one unit,

Second:   Recalculating the new optimal mix volume, and

Third:    Determining the difference between the old objective function value (for example, contribution) and the new.

The difference will represent the opportunity cost (benefit) of the marginal unit of the scarce resource.

Returning to the Tripper example, if the material constraint were relaxed by one unit (1,601 pounds instead of 1,600), the $X$ and $Y$ values at the new optimal point could be determined as 199.75 and 300.75, respectively. Recalculating total contribution for the new values of $X$ and $Y$:

$$30(199.75) + 50(300.375) = \$21,011.25$$

Thus one additional pound of raw material would enable the firm to increase its contribution by $11.25 ($21,011.25 − $21,000). This $11.25 is the marginal value (shadow price) of the raw material. If Tripper can purchase an additional pound of common raw material for less than $11.25, it should do so. Total contribution and profit would increase by the difference between the price paid and the $11.25 shadow price.

Can you see the value and usefulness of shadow prices? In a constrained situation, shadow prices can tell you whether additional resources would enable you to increase profits, when additional resources would add to profits, and how much additional profit could be earned. The simplex solution method produces shadow prices of all constraints (called dual variables) as a by-product of the optimal solution. In fact, probably more LP applications are undertaken to obtain the shadow prices than to obtain the optimal solution.

The foregoing discussion has been intended merely to acquaint you with LP and its usefulness. Next you can explore ways to approach decision making under uncertainty.

## HOW MANY TOW ROPES SHOULD WE ORDER?

The various decision models introduced so far in this text (including the LP model) have been *deterministic;* that is, the coefficients of the variables have been assumed to be known with certainty. How often can you predict the future with certainty? Virtually all business decisions must be made in an environment of relative uncertainty. Where the degree of uncertainty is very low (for example, the investment return on a U.S. government bond), or where the degree of uncertainty cannot readily be measured or estimated (see below), then a deterministic model is the practical or only alternative. However, where uncertainty is relatively high, and is associated with significant possible losses or lost profits, then it is logical that provision for uncertainty should be incorporated in business decisions if sufficient data is available.

Assume that Tripper was planning to introduce a new model of tow rope next year, and that already-planned advance publicity would mean that no "old" tow ropes could be sold after this year. Any "old" tow ropes in stock at year-end could be disposed of only through discount outlets, without the Tripper brand name and below cost.[2] The sales budget for this year originally

---

[2]   For simplification, you may assume that Tripper's wholesale and retail customers would experience no loss during the changeover; and therefore would not be reducing their orders this year in anticipation of the new model.

totalled 6,100 units to be sold for $10 each, and you may assume that the expected beginning inventory (carry-over stock from last year) was 500 units.

In determining the budgeted total annual contribution from tow ropes that are purchased finished at a unit cost of $5 and that are sold for $10, the equation (objective function) is simply:

$$\$5X = \$30,500.$$

The coefficient of expected sales (quantity $X$) is multiplied by the unit contribution ($5). Note that this coefficient is deterministic; it is stated as a single anticipated quantity. In recognition of the fact that the actual sales quantity may vary, the quantity coefficient may be expressed as a *probability distribution*. In a probability distribution, the various possible values of the coefficient are separately identified. Each separate value (quantity) is assigned a probability, or likelihood of occurrence. Probabilities are expressed as decimal fractions, so that the total for all different possibilities—the sum of the probabilities of all the separate possible outcomes—will equal 1.0.

In this example, assume that there are only three possible outcomes, with the following associated probabilities:[3]

> 0.2   chance (or likelihood) of sales demand for 5,000 tow ropes
> 0.5   chance of sales demand for 6,000 ropes
> 0.3   chance of sales demand for 7,000 ropes
> 1.0 = total of probabilities of sales quantity coefficient

You may also assume that a $5 contribution will be obtained from each unit purchased and sold during the year. Since stock on hand of old-model tow ropes at year-end can be disposed of for only $0.50 each, there will be a $4.50 loss for each unsold tow rope. Based on the foregoing information, can you determine how many tow ropes Tripper should purchase this year to maximize total net contribution? You should ignore inventory carrying charges and economic order quantities in this illustration.

## STATISTICAL DECISION MODELS

*Statistical decision models* are valuable in resolving this and similar problems. These models commonly involve five sequential steps.

### Alternative Actions

The first step is to identify all *alternative actions* (ideally all possible actions) available to the decision-maker. Realistically the alternatives must be both possible and reasonable. For example, purchasing 10,000 tow ropes is a possible alternative, but clearly not reasonable, since no more than 7,000 can be

---

[3]   In situations with many more possible outcomes, so-called continuous as opposed to discrete probability distributions may be involved. Mathematical techniques beyond the scope of this text exist for working with continuous distributions.

profitably sold. Alternative courses of action must be readily available to and under the control of the decision maker, and must be mutually exclusive.

In the tow rope example, with beginning inventory of 500 units, there are three alternative actions: ordering 4,500, 5,500, or 6,500 tow ropes. To order more or less than could possibly be sold would be foolish.

### Events or Occurrences

The next step is to identify all possible future *events* (also known as states of nature) that can occur. These events are beyond the direct control of the decision maker, and represent the situations about which he or she is uncertain. The set of events identified at this stage must be exhaustive or complete (all possible occurrences) and mutually exclusive (not redundant or overlapping). They must also be identified in such a way that probabilities may be assigned to them. In the Tripper illustration, the three events identified were possible sales demand of 5,000, 6,000, and 7,000 tow ropes.

### Probabilities of Each Event

The third step involves assigning *probabilities* to each previously identified event. Note that probabilities may be objective. *Objective probabilities* may be derived from historical data for similar past events. Or probabilities may be *subjective* or *estimated* based on surveys or even on the intuition of an experienced manager.

In the Tripper example, the probabilities were assigned as:

> 0.2   for the event of 5,000 sales demand,
> 0.5   for the event of 6,000 sales demand, and
> 0.3   for the event of 7,000 sales demand.

### Payoff Table

The next step involves identifying the criterion or objective, and then calculating a *payoff table*. Each combination of an action and an event results in an *outcome:*

$$\text{Action} + \text{Event} = \text{Outcome.}$$

The criterion is the measure or value of the outcome (net contribution, in this example). A payoff table merely indicates the value of the outcome or final result of taking each alternative action in combination with each alternative possible event or occurrence. The payoff (or outcome) is measured in terms of the criterion (net contribution, net revenue, net cost, and so forth).

The payoff table for the tow-rope decision problem is given in Exhibit 17.3. Note that the outcomes in each box give the **net contribution** (total contribution less any loss on excess stock) resulting from each combination of action and event. For instance, all outcomes are $25,000 for the action of

**Exhibit 17.3**

ILLUSTRATION OF PAYOFF TABLE

| Events / Actions | Sell 5,000 | Sell 6,000 | Sell 7,000 |
|---|---|---|---|
| Order 4,500 | $25,000 | $25,000 | $25,000 |
| Order 5,500 | $20,500 | $30,000 | $30,000 |
| Order 6,500 | $16,000 | $25,500 | $35,000 |

Note. Payoffs assume initial stock of 500 units, contribution of $5 per unit sold, and loss of $4.50 each on any unsold units at the end of the period.

ordering 4,500 units. With 500 units already in stock, only 5,000 units, with a unit contribution of $5, can be sold, regardless of sales demand. Note that if 6,500 units are ordered, and if sales demand turns out to be only 5,000 units, 2,000 units (1,500 excess ordered plus 500 beginning stock) must be disposed of, at a loss of $9,000.[4]

## Choosing the Best Alternative

With the payoff table complete, the decision-maker can now proceed to the fifth and final step, selecting the most desirable course of action. Perhaps the most widely used decision rule in such situations is to select the alternative with the highest *expected value*.[5] Expected value (or expected net contribution, in this example) is determined by first multiplying each possible payoff (each item in the payoff table) by the probability that it will occur. The probability-adjusted payoffs are then summed for each separate action, to result in the expected value of each alternative action.

To familiarize yourself with expected value, before proceeding you should calculate the expected values of each of the three alternative actions shown in Exhibit 17.3 using the probabilities given above.

---

[4]   The 500 units of initial stock technically are not part of the decision problem. They are not subject to future action and their cost is sunk. Therefore, in theory, they should be excluded from the payoff table. They are included in this simplified example to demonstrate incorporation of possible losses.

[5]   Highest expected value may not always signal the most desirable alternative since it does not take into account relative risk and possible risk aversion on the part of the decision-maker. See discussion of relative uncertainty and risk aversion below.

The expected values or expected net contributions are determined as follows:

| Act | Payoff × Probability | Expected value |
|---|---|---|
| Order 4,500 | $25,000(0.2) + $25,000(0.5) + $25,000(0.3) | $25,000 |
| Order 5,500 | $20,500(0.2) + $30,000(0.5) + $30,000(0.3) | $28,100 |
| Order 6,500 | $16,000(0.2) + $25,500(0.5) + $35,000(0.3) | $26,450 |

Following the maximum-expected-value decision rule, Tripper should order 5,500 tow ropes for an expected net contribution of $28,100. To order only 4,500 units would reduce the expected contribution by $3,100 ($28,100 − $25,000). The risk of loss if 6,500 units were ordered also reduces the expected contribution $1,650 below the $28,100 optimum. Note that a net expected contribution of $28,100 is not certain if Tripper orders 5,500 units. It is the most probable average outcome. Contribution from this action could be as low as $20,500 or as high as $30,000. Ordering 5,500 units results in Tripper having the best chance of making a contribution approximating $28,100.

### Relative Uncertainty and Risk Aversion

The action with the highest expected value may not, in all cases, be the preferred choice for the business decision-maker. Either or both of two interrelated considerations might dictate rejection of an alternative having the highest expected value. These two considerations involve relative uncertainty and the decision-maker's degree of risk aversion.

Expected value by itself does not provide a measure of the relative uncertainty in a given situation. Probability distribution can cover a wide range of alternatives or a very narrow range. Consider the following two independent actions:

| Action | Payoff | Probability | Expected value |
|---|---|---|---|
| 1 | Win (+) $ 10,000 | 0.55 | $+   5,500 |
|   | Lose (−) $  8,000 | 0.45 | −    3,600 |
|   |   |   | $+   1,900 |
| 2 | Win (+) $581,000 | 0.1 | $+  58,100 |
|   | Win (+) $200,000 | 0.3 | +   60,000 |
|   | Lose (−) $ 50,000 | 0.4 | −   20,000 |
|   | Lose (−) $500,000 | 0.2 | −100,000 |
|   |   |   | $+   1,900 |

Both actions have the same expected value, yet action 2 has a more widely dispersed probability distribution and might therefore be considered more risky.

To provide more complete information to the decision-maker, in addition to expected value, it is usually desirable to also have a *measure of dispersion* of the underlying probability distribution. The conventional measure of dispersion for a single variable is the *standard deviation*—the square root of the mean of the deviations from the expected value squared.[6] A commonly used measure of the relative dispersion is the *coefficient of variation*, which is the standard deviation divided by the expected value:

$$\text{Coefficient of variation} = \frac{\text{Standard deviation}}{\text{Expected value}}.$$

In the above example, the coefficients of variation would be:

| Action | Coefficient of variation |
|--------|--------------------------|
| 1 | 3.82 |
| 2 | 162.95 |

Note the much higher coefficient for action 2, indicating a much wider relative dispersion of possible outcomes.

The decision-maker's degree of *risk aversion* may also preclude choosing the alternative with the highest expected value. Suppose you personally had two possible bets with the following payoffs, probabilities, and expected values:

| Bet | Payoffs | Probabilities | Expected values |
|-----|---------|---------------|-----------------|
| 1 | Win $100 | 0.6 | $+ 60 |
|   | Lose $100 | 0.4 | − 40 |
|   |          |     | $+ 20 |
| 2 | Win $100,000 | 0.51 | $+51,000 |
|   | Lose $100,000 | 0.49 | −49,000 |
|   |          |     | $+ 2,000 |

Would you always choose the second bet with the higher expected value? Or might the second bet, with its almost equal chance that you could **lose** $100,-000, be too risky for you to consider? Would you be averse to this much risk?

Risk aversion is often both the result of an individual's past experience and also subject to the individual's current circumstances. Even though it may be difficult to measure, risk aversion cannot be ignored when making decisions. Incorporating allowances for relative dispersion and degree of risk aversion into statistical decision theory is beyond the scope of this text. Never-

---

[6]  The formula for the standard deviation applicable to these models is:

$$\sqrt{\sum_{x=1}^{n} (Ax - \bar{A})^2 Px}$$

where
      $Ax$ = each possible event,
      $\bar{A}$ = expected value,
      $Px$ = probability of each event.

theless, you should be familiar with the concepts and understand that they represent several reasons why highest expected value might not be the desirable choice in all situations.

## APPLYING PROBABILITIES TO BUDGETARY CONTROL

Since many budgeted amounts, and especially those for revenues, mixed costs, and variable costs, represent future estimates and are not really certain, you may be wondering why the overall budgeting process is essentially deterministic. There are probably two major reasons why, to date, there have been few instances of probabilities being incorporated in the budgeting process. In many cases it has been impossible or prohibitively expensive to develop dependable probability measures and to perform the necessary calculations to incorporate available probabilities into activity measures and budgeting rates. Also, some managers do not yet feel comfortable using probability analysis.

Probabilities are being more widely used in arriving at the deterministic budget for sales. For example, the 6,100 unit overall sales budget for tow ropes in the above example was the mean or expected sales quantity of the given sales probability distribution:

$$0.2(5,000) + 0.5(6,000) + 0.3(7,000) = 6,100.$$

Also, in Chapter 8 you had the opportunity to learn that probabilities may be incorporated into capital budgeting decisions, even if only by using the crude three-point basis for estimating data. In the near future, with the ready availability of computers to handle the involved calculations, and with the growing quantitative sophistication of managers, you may look forward to an increasing formal use of probabilities in business decision making and in budgetary control.

Probabilities are also being more widely used as part of performance evaluation and control. Recall from Chapter 11 the concept of the control chart and the establishment of ranges within which variances could be assumed to be normal or random and under control. The concept of a control chart (as originally developed for manufacturing quality control) is based upon the assumption that a standard or budgeted amount is realistically a mean of a range of acceptable amounts; that a certain amount of variance is normal, should be expected, and should **not** indicate any need for investigation and possible corrective action. The acceptable range is delineated by upper and lower control limits. Only those variances that exceed the control limits (lie outside of the acceptable range) are considered to be abnormal or nonrandom and requiring investigation.

Control limits are established by a process known as *statistical estimation theory*. The first step involves developing estimates of the population mean, $\mu$, and standard deviation, $\sigma$, of the particular data (cost or revenue) being budgeted and controlled. Random samples are drawn from the population (available past data) and the mean of the sample data ($X$) is presumed to estimate the population mean, $\mu$.[7]

The standard deviation of the population ($\sigma$) is estimated by the formula:

$$\hat{\sigma} = \sqrt{\frac{\sum_{j=1}^{n} (X_j - \overline{X})^2}{n - 1}},$$

where:

$\hat{\sigma}$ = estimate of population standard deviation,
$X_j$ = jth observation,
$\overline{X}$ = mean of all observations in the sample, and
$n$ = number of observations.

The next step is to establish control limits. A common basis is to use a 95-percent *confidence interval* calculated as:

$$\text{Control limits} = \overline{X} \pm 1.96\sigma.$$

With a 95-percent confidence interval, the probability that an observation falling within the range will be randomly caused (within control) is 95 percent. Only five percent of the time will a nonrandom (out-of-control) observation or variance fall within the acceptable range and not be investigated.[8]

For example, assume a particular budgeted cost with a mean ($X$) of $3,000 and a standard deviation of $400. Would an unfavorable variance of $700 be considered as within control if control limits were established at 95 percent?

The answer would be **yes,** since the upper control limit would be $3,784.00 and, therefore, an unfavorable variance up to $784 (1.96 × $400) would be considered as still being within control. Exhibit 17.4 illustrates this example. Note, in this exhibit, that variances of $1,000 unfavorable (cost of $4,000) and $800 favorable (cost of $2,200) are both considered abnormal and targets for investigation.

The foregoing discussion is intended merely to introduce several applications of the use of probabilities in making business decisions. Applications of statistical decision theory, along with the use of computers are undoubtedly the two most significant developments in business management over the past twenty years. As a business or as an accounting major, you may expect to be exposed to two or more courses devoted specifically to these areas.

---

[7]    If sufficient data are available, a sample size of at least thirty observations (cost or revenue amounts) should be taken. Ideally, numerous such samples should be taken with the population mean estimated as the mean of the various sample means. Techniques beyond the scope of this book, and covered in elementary statistics courses and texts, are available for smaller sample sizes.

[8]    Probability intervals other than 95 percent, such as two standard deviations (95.45 percent) or three standard deviations (99.73 percent), are also commonly selected.

**Exhibit 17.4**

SAMPLE STATISTICAL CONTROL CHART

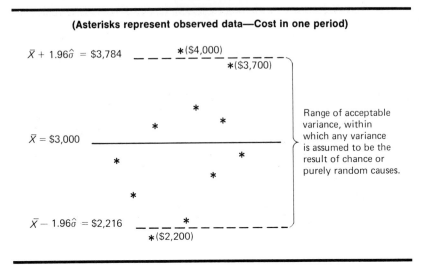

Can you begin to visualize how managers may incorporate probabilities into their decisions on other than a purely subjective (intuitive) basis? Business courses in statistics and quantitative methods are intended to help you develop facility in the selection and application of these tools. The foregoing discussion has been intended merely to introduce a few of the possible applications of statistics to budgeting and control. Next you can become acquainted with some techniques for organizing complex decision data, and for planning and controlling complex projects.

## DECISION TREES AND SEQUENTIAL EVENTS

The data from the previous tow-rope example for alternative actions, events, probabilities, payoffs, and expected values may all be incorporated into a *decision tree* A decision tree is a diagram of all possible actions, in the order in which the action is chosen, together with the possible events that may subsequently occur. Exhibit 17.5 illustrates a decision tree for the previously cited tow-rope-ordering problem. Note how each event branch is labeled on the upper side with the probability of its occurrence and on the bottom with the payoffs of the event. Note also that each action alternative has its expected value indicated below the line. The expected value is arrived at by working backwards from the branches (events) to the trunk (alternative actions). For instance, the $26,450 expected value for the alternative "order 6,500" is the sum of the branch payoffs times their respective probabilities,

$$\$16,000(0.2) + \$25,500(0.5) + \$35,000(0.3).$$

**Exhibit 17.5**

ILLUSTRATION OF SINGLE-STEP DECISION TABLE

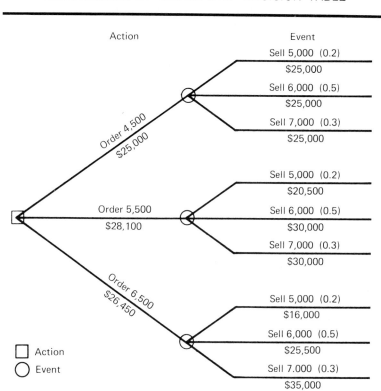

A decision tree may be more useful in depicting clearly alternatives and consequences than a simple table of data would be. Decision trees become almost essential as problems become more complex. They are especially helpful with decisions involving sequential events.

A decision is said to involve sequential events when subsequent decisions depend on prior decisions and their outcomes. For example, suppose the final year's supply of old-style tow ropes was to be ordered in two batches, one for each six-month period. And suppose sales demand was anticipated as follows:

| Period | Unit sales demand | Probability |
| --- | --- | --- |
| First six months | 2,700 ropes | 0.6 |
| | 2,200 ropes | 0.4 |
| Second six months | 3,900 ropes | 0.3 |
| | 3,500 ropes | 0.7 |

**Exhibit 17.6**

ILLUSTRATION OF SEQUENTIAL STEP DECISION TREE

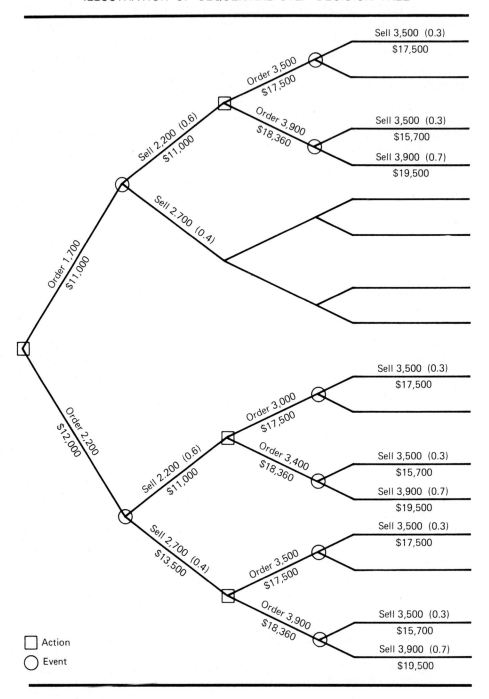

Assuming the same beginning inventory of 500 units, how much should be ordered in each period to optimize net contribution? You will more readily grasp the discussion that follows if you first attempt to complete a decision tree and calculate expected values, before proceeding to the next paragraph.

Exhibit 17.6 illustrates a sequential-event decision tree for this sample problem. Study this exhibit carefully until you see clearly how the tree was constructed. Note that, for the first six-month period, the tree (with the event payoffs) is constructed in essentially the same way as was the earlier tree in Exhibit 17.5. Alternative actions in the second six months depend upon outcomes of the first six months. If 2,200 units were ordered during the first six months, and only 2,200 units were sold, then the original carry-over stock of 500 units would be available for the second six months. It then would be foolish to order more than 3,400 additional tow ropes. Also, note on Exhibit 17.6 that data is not shown for "impossible" or unrealistic branches. Where only 1,700 units are ordered during the first period, no more than 2,200 units can be sold in that period.

Expected values are calculated moving backwards in time, starting at the right side with possible events and outcomes in the second six months. In the second six months, if stock on hand totals 3,900 units and all are sold, contribution will be $19,500 (3,900 times $5). If only 3,500 units are sold, net contribution will be only $15,700 reflecting the $17,500 contribution less the $1,800 loss on the 400 unsold units. Exhibit 17.6 indicates that the preferred choice is to order 2,200 units for the first six months. This decision should appear logical to you for all situations where any excess stock can always be sold in the following period. Also note that Exhibit 17.6 indicates preferred courses of action in the second six months depending upon the outcomes of the first period.

## PROJECT NETWORK ANALYSIS

A network approach similar to that for decision trees can be helpful in the planning and control of projects and programmed costs having multiple steps or stages, especially when the various stages are interdependent and sequential. Budgets are valuable tools for planning overall costs; but they do not contain the necessary information for scheduling a specific sequence of steps necessary to complete a particular project.

Different component steps in a particular task or project usually have different lead times for their completion.[9] Even in the simplest case where the

---

[9]   The term "lead time" as applied to a particular item can have two distinct meanings. Lead time may be used to refer only to procurement (purchasing) lead time. In this discussion, lead time will refer to the total time (ordering, procurement, and manufacturing) between the initial order and the completion of the finished item.

component steps are not sequential, the different lead times must be considered in planning and control. For illustration, consider a simple assembly made from three parts—A, B, and C—and recall the discussion of scheduling lead times contained in Chapter 4. Assume that final assembly operations were expected to take one month, and that the three component parts were all purchased finished. Procurement lead times for parts A, B, and C were one, two, and three months, respectively. Assuming that procurement lead times included an adequate allowance for the time necessary to schedule and place purchase orders, how far in advance of availability in finished-goods stores must these assemblies be ordered?

You correctly grasp the concept of multiple lead times if you see that these assemblies must be planned or ordered four months prior to availability. The scheduling is controlled by the *longest lead-time item* (part C takes three months for procurement and one month for assembly). Should all three parts be ordered four months in advance of target completion? Although scheduling (planning) must be completed four months in advance, to order all three parts four months in advance of target completion would result in unnecessary inventory carrying charge for parts A and B. The appropriate plan should provide for ordering part C at the beginning of the first month, part B at the beginning of the second month, part C at the beginning of the third, and finally for scheduling assembly to begin in the fourth month.

|  | Month 1 | Month 2 | Month 3 | Month 4 | Month 5 |
|---|---|---|---|---|---|
| Part C | | | | | |
| Part B | | | | | |
| Part A | | | | | |
| Assembly | | | | | |

Most business projects, like assemblies, have many component activities, and usually some of the activities are sequential; that is, one or more must be completed before the next can begin. Examples with which you should be familiar would include house construction (foundation before structure, before electrical, before finishing, and so forth) and the annual budgeting process (sales budget, then inventory budget, then operating expenditure budgets, and so forth).

Assume that you were scheduling the manufacturing and delivery to the customer of special product Z. Product Z is assembled from subassembly Q and part E. Subassembly Q, in turn, is assembled from parts C and D and subassembly P. Subassembly P is made from parts A and B. Parts A and C are manufactured parts made respectively from raw material A and C. Parts B, D, and E are purchased finished. These various components and their manufacturing/assembly sequence are shown in Exhibit 17.7.

You may assume that the various activities and their lead times involved in the scheduling and completion of this order were as follows:

**Exhibit 17.7**

DIAGRAM OF PRODUCT Z BILL OF MATERIALS AND
MANUFACTURING/ASSEMBLY SEQUENCE

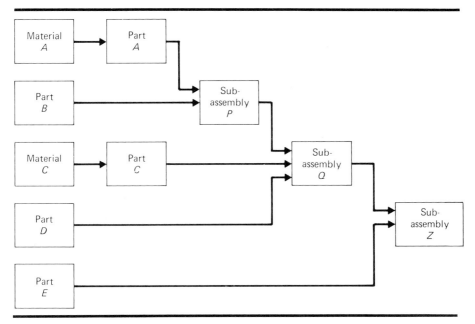

| Activity number | Activity description | Preceding activity number | Lead time in weeks |
|---|---|---|---|
| 1 | Scheduling all activities and issuing purchase orders | — | 1 |
| 2 | Procurement material A | 1 | 3 |
| 3 | Procurement part B | 1 | 1 |
| 4 | Procurement material C | 1 | 5 |
| 5 | Procurement part D | 1 | 3 |
| 6 | Procurement part E | 1 | 10 |
| 7 | Manufacture part A | 2 | 5 |
| 8 | Manufacture part C | 4 | 4 |
| 9 | Complete subassembly P | 3, 7 | 2 |
| 10 | Complete subassembly Q | 5, 8, 9 | 3 |
| 11 | Complete final assembly Z | 6, 10 | 4 |
| 12 | Packing, shipping and installation | 11 | 7 |

Can you determine, before proceeding:

• The minimum time required to complete this project?

• The sequence of critical activity that, if component lead times were to reduced, could lead to a reduction in overall project lead time?

*Network analysis* assists in providing the answers to these and other complex project-related questions. The minimum total lead time required for the above project is 25 weeks. Exhibit 17.8 illustrates the use of a network diagram. Note that each activity or operation is denoted by a circle. The numbers within the circle designate the activity reference number (sequence not important) and the minimum number of weeks necessary to complete the activity once it is started.

Necessary sequencing of activities is denoted by arrows. Note that one particular sequence or path connecting the first and last activities is denoted by a broken line. This broken line designates the *critical path*—the sequence with the longest lead time. Note that the critical path through a network is directly analogous to the longest lead-time item in the earlier nonsequential assembly example.

## Usefulness of Network Analysis

Identification of the critical path through network analysis has facilitated the determination of the project completion time. The critical path represents the sequence of activities to which management may wish to allocate additional resources should it be desirable to shorten overall completion time. The critical path is also the one requiring most follow-up, since any delays along this path will automatically delay the entire project.

Also note that network analysis facilitates identification of secondary critical paths. A secondary critical path is one that could become primary or controlling if total completion time of the original critical path were to be significantly reduced. If additional resources applied to activity 7 were to reduce its lead time by two weeks (from five to three), then sequence 1–4–8–10–11–12 would become the new critical path. Unless this sequence could also be shortened, only one week's savings of overall time could be accomplished.

Network analysis can also provide other useful information for scheduling and control purposes. In Exhibit 17.8 the numbers in parentheses above each activity indicate the **earliest** possible start and completion times (assuming that preceding activities are completed according to plan). For the critical path, the numbers indicate:

| Activity reference number | Earliest start (beginning of week) | Earliest completion (end of week) |
|:---:|:---:|:---:|
| 1 | 0 | 1 |
| 2 | 2 | 4 |
| 7 | 5 | 9 |
| 9 | 10 | 11 |
| 10 | 12 | 14 |
| 11 | 15 | 18 |
| 12 | 19 | 25 |

**Exhibit 17.8**
PROJECT NETWORK DIAGRAM

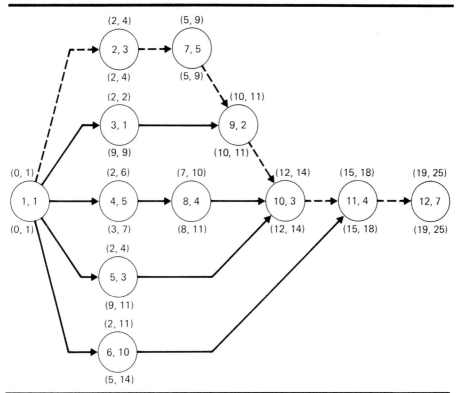

From this information, the project manager knows that, even if all resources are available, work cannot commence on a particular operation until the designated earliest start date. Work cannot be completed until the earliest completion date unless the network data is incorrect or additional resources are applied.

The numbers in parentheses below each activity identify the **latest** start and completion times without delaying the entire project. The manager knows that all resources must be available no later than the latest start date for each operation. The difference between the earlist and the latest start in completion dates indicates the available slack in the schedule. For example, part B could be scheduled to arrive (activity reference number 3) at any time between the end of week 2 and the end of week 9 without impairing the overall schedule. Note that, by definition, there is no slack along the critical path.

### CPM and PERT

Two popular approaches to network analysis and project management are known as CPM, for critical path method, and PERT, for program evaluation and review technique. CPM is deterministic, in that a single-point estimate of lead time is used (as in the above example). CPM also allows for a trade-off of time required and resources employed (not illustrated). It therefore provides a useful tool for budgeting the programmed costs associated with the project.

PERT involves the inclusion of probabilistic estimates of lead times, usually in the form of three-point estimates (optimistic, most likely, and pessimistic). PERT therefore allows for determination of probabilities of over-all completion time. Generally, PERT is more applicable to first-time and/or only-time (research and development) projects, where a high degree of un-certainty exists in the estimation of component lead times. CPM, on the other hand, is more appropriate for recurring projects where past experience allows for a deterministic (single-point) lead-time estimate that can be reason-ably accurate.

Network analysis can become very complex for projects with hundreds or thousands of separate activities. Fortunately, programs have been developed that enable the critical path and associated data to be developed by computers. Computers also facilitate allowing for weekends and holidays, and developing schedules in terms of calendar dates. Also, complete reschedules, reflecting earlier- or later-than-planned completion, are not so formidable where the network analysis is performed by computers. Computer network analysis is widely used in military procurement and large-scale construction projects.

## GENERAL DESIRABILITY OF MATHEMATICAL MODELS

Before completing this brief introduction to various quantitative techniques applicable to managerial accounting, you should consider the general advan-tages of building, where possible, mathematical models for all business deci-sions. In those situations where managers use their experience to make decisions that prove to be effective, it might appear that models would be superfluous. Nevertheless, every time a decision is made, at least implicitly:

- relative variables are being included or excluded,
- probabilities are being assigned,
- a criterion exists, and
- alternatives are being evaluated (ignoring or dismissing a variable or alternative is assigning it a low or zero probability).

Modern quantitative techniques merely take all implicit factors as explicit. They replace traditional responses, hunches, and rules of thumb. There are at least three advantages of building mathematical models:

1. The decision-maker is encouraged to make a systematic and thorough analysis of the decision situation.

2. The resulting model can be solved mathematically, or can at least facilitate simulating the outcomes of various alternatives.

3. The model can provide for sensitivity analysis. The decision-maker may obtain information on the effects of changes in all relevant variables without the necessity of experimentation with actual resource commitments.

Effective models do not complicate; they simplify. In the developing world of business decision-making, the future manager who does not appreciate and feel comfortable with the use of quantitative techniques may be at a serious disadvantage.

---

CHAPTER OVERVIEW

Based on the material contained in this chapter, you should now be in a position to:

- Identify, with examples, the types of problems that are amenable to solu-solution using linear programming analysis.
- Describe the four characteristics of a problem that make it amenable to solution via linear programming techniques.
- Describe the intention or outputs of linear programming and their information content.
- Describe the process of formulating an LP model in terms of the objective function and the constraint inequalities or equations; and explain the formulation of each equation/inequality in the model.
- Solve a product-mix problem using LP analysis, given appropriate data.
- Describe the economic significance and usefulness of shadow prices.
- Explain how control limits (the confidence interval) on a control chart are selected.
- Describe, with an example, how a control chart may be prepared and how the standard deviation is used in the preparation.
- Distinguish, with examples, the difference between deterministic and probabilistic decision models.
- Define and describe a probability distribution.
- Describe, with examples, the five sequential steps involved in decision making using statistical decision models.

- Distinguish between objective and subjective probabilities, and describe situations where each might be appropriate.

- Describe two considerations that might make the alternative action with the highest expected value not the preferred alternative.

- Explain, with examples, the usefulness of the decision tree in decision making, especially when sequential events are involved.

- Define network analysis as it applies to project management, and explain the information content and usefulness of a completed network diagram.

- Explain the similarities between a critical path in a network and the longest lead-time part for an assembly.

- Explain three major advantages of mathematical model building in a business decision situation.


## NEW VOCABULARY AND CONCEPTS

| | |
|---|---|
| Feasible alternative | Outcome |
| Linear programming (LP) | Expected value |
| Model | Measure of dispersion |
| Objective function | Standard deviation |
| Constraints | Coefficient of variation |
| Simplex method | Risk aversion |
| Shadow price | Statistical information theory |
| Deterministic | Confidence interval |
| Probability distribution | Decision tree |
| Statistical decision models | Longest lead-time item |
| Alternative actions | Network analysis |
| Events/states of nature | Critical path |
| Probabilities | CPM |
| Objective probabilities | PERT |
| Subjective/estimated probabilities | |
| Payoff table | |

- Most likely outcome and expected value


## REVIEW QUESTIONS

1. What is a feasible solution (alternative)?

2. What are the four essential characteristics of problems that lend themselves to solution via linear programming analysis?

3. a) What is a model?
   b) In the LP model, what is the role of the objective function? What is its purpose?

c) In the LP model, what are the constraint equations/inequalities, and what is their purpose?

d) What is nonnegativity constraint and what is its function?

4. What are two methods for computing the optimal solution LP model depending upon the number of variables involved?

5. a) What is a shadow price?
   b) What is its usefulness?

6. In relation to a control chart:
   a) What is the function or usefulness of control limits?
   b) Given the estimated standard deviation of the available data, how are control limits (the confidence interval) selected and established?

7. a) What is the difference between a deterministic and a probabilistic model?
   b) If most business decisions involve uncertainty, why are many decision models such as budgets, CVP analysis, EOQ/ELS, LP, and others usually deterministic?

8. a) What is a probability distribution?
   b) What is the sum of the probabilities of all possible occurrences included in a probability distribution?
   c) What is meant by a measure of dispersion of a probability distribution?
   d) What is the usefulness of a measure of dispersion?

9. a) What are the five sequential steps that are normally a part of applying a statistical decision model to a business decision?
   b) What is the difference between an alternative action and an event (state of nature)?
   c) What is the difference between objective and subjective probabilities, and where might each be appropriate?
   d) What is a payoff, and what is a payoff table?

10. a) What is an expected value?
    b) How does an expected value differ from an outcome or payoff?
    c) Could there be any situations where a decision-maker might appropriately reject an alternative course of action that has the highest expected value? Explain.

11. a) What is a decision tree?
    b) How may a decision tree be useful, especially with sequential events?

12. a) What is a project network analysis?
    b) What is the information content of a completed network diagram?
    c) What is a critical path?
    d) How is a critical path similar to a longest lead-time part?
    e) What is meant by the earliest start and completion times on a network diagram, and what is the usefulness of this information?
    f) What is mean by the latest start and completion times on a network diagram, and what is the usefulness of this information?
    g) What is meant by slack for a particular activity in a network diagram?
    h) Why is there no slack for any of the activities that are part of the critical path?

13. a) What is CPM?
    b) What is PERT?
    c) What is the essential difference between CPM and PERT?

14. How may computers facilitate network analysis?

15. What are three advantages of using mathematical models in business decisions?


## MINI-CASES AND QUESTIONS FOR DISCUSSION

**MC 17.1** John Corey is a business major. He is complaining to his friend Dawn Scott: "I don't see why all these business courses have to get so involved with far-out mathematics! I've never really liked math, and it even scares me a little.

"I have no trouble with the simple math of accounting or with calculating interest or percent or present value or things like that. What really turns me off are these mathematical models like linear programming, or especially those that include probability and statistics. I don't see why we can't just learn what to do in a given situation and let it go at that. Mathematical models make everything so complicated."

Do mathematical models really make business decisions more complicated? Could your education for business be complete without a thorough exposure to these tools? Discuss.

**MC 17.2** Gwen Zircher has been thinking about statistical decision models. She has just finished solving a decision-tree model, using the criterion of highest expected value. She can also see from the model that, if she had perfect information, she could obtain more profit than the expected value. With perfect information, there would be no uncertainty. All probabilities would be either 1.0 or zero.

Gwen is wondering whether the dollar difference between the expected values based on present information and the expected value based on perfect information might, in itself, be a useful piece of information. She knows that there might be situations where she would consider obtaining more information prior to making a decision (trial runs, market research, and so forth). She reasons that having the dollar-value incremental benefit of perfect information could serve as an upper limit on what she should consider spending for more information.

What do you think of Gwen's idea? Is it workable? Discuss.

**MC 17.3** As first discussed in Chapters 5 and 6, so-called programmed costs are difficult to budget and control since they have little correlation with measurable output. Could the detailed activity components (their completion) under either CPM or PERT serve as "outputs" for budgeting and controlling project costs? Under CPM could different activities each be assigned various combinations of lead times and costs (for example, three weeks without overtime and two weeks with), so that analysis could involve balancing between minimum cost and minimum completion times? Under PERT, could probabilities also be assigned to activity cost estimates? Discuss.

MC 17.4 LP is a deterministic model. Could probabilities be incorporated into the model in any way? For example, could the coefficients represent the mean of their underlying probability distributions? Discuss.

MC 17.5 How could probabilities be incorporated in budgeting and control? If a firm's budgeting and control reporting system were on a computer to facilitate computation, would it be desirable for a budgeted amount to be expressed as a three-point estimate (optimistic, most likely, pessimistic)? If it were, then variances from the most likely estimate could be divided between that portion within the range of the optimistic and pessimistic boundaries and any portion beyond this range.

Would budgets prepared on such a basis be useful, especially for final cash and financial budgeting? What would be the relationship, from a control standpoint, of such a system and the idea of the control chart? Discuss.

## ESSENTIAL PROBLEMS

EP 17.1 A firm has two products, P and Q. Product P requires seven pounds of material S and four pounds of material T. Product Q requires three pounds of S and eight pounds of T. Only 21,000 lbs. S and 16,000 lbs. of T are available during the current period. The unit contributions of P and Q are $22 and $14, respectively. Any quantity of P or Q produced can be sold. The firm wishes to maximize its profit in the current period.

a) Formulate the objective function to be maximized, identifying C as equal to the total contribution.

b) Give all necessary constraint equations/inequalities.

EP 17.2 A farmer is interested in applying fertilizer to his crops at minimum cost. He estimates that, to be effective, he should apply at least 20,000 pounds of one chemical and 30,000 pounds of a mineral.

These ingredients in combination are available in two commercially available mixed fertilizers. Fertilizer A contains a mixture of 30 percent chemical and 70 percent mineral. It is available at $40 per ton (2,000 pounds) in minimum quantities of one ton.

Fertilizer B is a mixture of 80 percent chemical and 20 percent mineral. It is available at a cost of $4 per hundred pounds, in minimum quantities of 100 pounds.

How many pounds of each mix should the farmer purchase and apply to his crops?

a) Formulate the objective function to be minimized.

b) Formulate all necessary constraint equations/inequalities.

c) Solve, using the graphic approach.

**EP 17.3** The Bobby Company has two products, A and B. The unit contribution of product A is $40 and of B is $50. The optimal product mix, as determined by a LP solution, is for Bobby to manufacture and sell $10,000 units of A and 30,000 units of B each period.

a) What is the objective function in the LP model used to obtain the optimal solution?

b) What is the contribution per period expected from the optimal product mix?

c) If the shadow price of one of the material constraints was $20 per pound, and if additional material could be acquired for $5 per pound, how much total contribution per period could Bobby expect if it were to acquire one additional pound of the material?

**EP 17.4** Refer to Problem EP 17.3. Answer the same three questions based upon revised data as follows:

|  | A | B |
|---|---|---|
| Unit contributions | $30 | $10 |
| Optimal product mix | 40,000 units | 15,000 units |
| Material shadow price | $10 | |
| Material cost | $ 2 | |

**EP 17.5** The Cox Manufacturing Company is planning to use the control-chart approach to budgetary control over maintenance costs. During one year the maintenance budget was established at $40,000 per month. The estimated standard deviation of past variances has been determined to be $900, and the company has selected a 95-percent confidence interval. Variances during the year were as follows:

| | | | | | |
|---|---|---|---|---|---|
| Jan. | $1,000 | U | Jul. | $2,000 | U |
| Feb. | 1,500 | F | Aug. | 600 | U |
| Mar. | 400 | F | Sep. | 1,100 | F |
| Apr. | 1,900 | F | Oct. | 2,400 | F |
| May | 1,200 | U | Nov. | 800 | F |
| Jun. | 1,700 | U | Dec. | 1,600 | U |

In applying the control-chart approach, which variances would **not** be investigated and why?

**EP 17.6** Refer to Problem EP 17.5. Assuming the same data except that the standard deviation was $1,000, which variances should be actively investigated and why?

**EP 17.7** A supermarket sells cut flowers. The flowers are purchased fresh each day at a cost of $0.50 per bunch, and are sold for $1.50 per bunch. Any flowers unsold at the end of each day are donated to a nearby hospital.
The demand distribution for flowers is as follows:

| Demand<br>(Bunches) | Probability |
|:---:|:---:|
| 0 | 0.02 |
| 10 | 0.18 |
| 20 | 0.40 |
| 30 | 0.30 |
| 40 | 0.10 |
| | 1.00 |

How many bunches should the store purchase each day in order to maximize profit on the flowers?

**EP 17.8** A sports shop at a resort hotel is ordering tennis balls for sale to visitors staying at the hotel. The hotel is located in a remote location and only two orders may be shipped and received during the season, one at the start and one half-way through the season. The shop owner is closing the shop and retiring at the end of the season. Any cans of tennis balls unsold at this time will have to be thrown away.

Estimated demand is as follows:

| | Demand<br>(Cans) | Probability |
|:---|:---:|:---:|
| First half of season | 150 | 0.6 |
| | 200 | 0.4 |
| Second half of season | 250 | 0.7 |
| | 300 | 0.3 |

Cans of tennis balls cost $1.25 and are sold for $3.00 each. The shop owner has 20 cans left over from the previous season, and wishes to maximize his profits on the sale of tennis balls.

a) Construct a decision tree for use in solving this problem.

b) How many cans should be ordered at the beginning of the season?

c) How many cans, and under what circumstances, should be ordered at midseason?

**EP 17.9** The controller of the XYZ Corporation is responsible for overseeing the preparation of the firm's annual budget. The budgeting process in the XYZ company is divided into the following distinct component activities:

| Activity<br>number | Activity description | Immediately<br>preceding<br>activity | Activity<br>lead time<br>(Days) |
|:---:|:---|:---:|:---:|
| 1 | Sales budget | — | 20 |
| 2 | Inventory budget | 1 | 15 |
| 3 | Purchases budget | 2 | 10 |
| 4 | Operating budget | 1 | 30 |
| 5 | Capital budget | — | 15 |
| 6 | Cash budget | 3, 4, 5 | 10 |
| 7 | Master budget and budgeted<br>financial statements | 6 | 5 |

a) Complete a network diagram for the budgeting process, including identification, for each activity, of the earliest and latest start and completion dates (expressed in working days).

b) Identify the critical path.

c) What is the minimum number of days that the controller should allow for completing the budgeting processes?

**EP 17.10** Refer to Problem EP 17.9. How and why would each of the following events, considered independently, change or not change the total project lead time?

a) Capital budgeting lead time reduced five days

b) Capital budgeting lead time increased to 40 days

c) Capital budgeting activity not started until 40 days after sales budget started

d) Operating budget lead time reduced to 25 days

e) Operating budget lead time reduced to 24 days

f) Cash budgeting takes three days more than planned

g) Inventory budget not started until 25 days after the start of the sales budget

## SUPPLEMENTARY PROBLEMS

*Note.* There are no Supplementary Problems in Chapter 17.

## SUGGESTIONS FOR FURTHER READING

Demski, Joel S., *Information Analysis.* Reading, Massachusetts: Addison-Wesley Publishing Company, 1972.

Grant, Eugene L., and Richard S. Leavenworth, *Statistical Quality Control,* 4th Ed. New York City: McGraw-Hill Book Company, 1972.

Horngren, C., *Cost Accounting: A Managerial Emphasis,* 4th Ed. Englewood Cliffs, N.J.: Prentice-Hall, Inc., 1977, Chapters 24 and 27.

Livingstone, John Leslie, ed., *Management Planning and Control: Mathematical Models.* New York: McGraw-Hill Book Company, 1970.

Miller, D.W., and M.K. Starr, *Executive Decisions and Operations Research,* 2nd Ed. Englewood Cliffs, N.J.: Prentice-Hall Inc., 1969.

Morse, Wayne J., *Cost Accounting: Processing and Using Cost Data.* Reading, Mass.: Addison-Wesley Publishing Company, 1978, Chapters 12, 14, and 15.

Schlaifer, Robert, *Analysis of Decisions under Uncertainty.* New York: McGraw-Hill Book Company, 1969.

Stockton, R. Stansbury, *Introduction to Linear Programming.* Homewood, Illinois: Richard D. Irwin, Inc., 1971.

Wagner, Harvey M., *Principles of Operations Research with Applications to Managerial Decisions,* 2nd Ed. Englewood Cliffs, N.J.: Prentice-Hall, Inc., 1975.

# APPENDIXES

# A

## PRESENT-VALUE TABLES

**Table A:**   Present Value of a Single Payment/Receipt of $1,

$$PV_A = \frac{1}{(1 + i)^n}$$

where $i$ = interest rate per period and $n$ = number of periods.

$i = 01$ to $06$; $N = 01$ to $50$

| N | 1% | 1.25% | 1.5% | 2% | 3% | 4% | 5% | 6% |
|---|------|-------|------|------|------|------|------|------|
| 1 | 0.9901 | 0.9877 | 0.9852 | 0.9804 | 0.9709 | 0.9615 | 0.9524 | 0.9434 |
| 2 | 0.9803 | 0.9755 | 0.9707 | 0.9612 | 0.9426 | 0.9246 | 0.9070 | 0.8900 |
| 3. | 0.9706 | 0.9634 | 0.9563 | 0.9423 | 0.9151 | 0.8890 | 0.8638 | 0.8396 |
| 4 | 0.9610 | 0.9515 | 0.9422 | 0.9238 | 0.8885 | 0.8548 | 0.8227 | 0.7921 |
| 5 | 0.9515 | 0.9398 | 0.9283 | 0.9057 | 0.8626 | 0.8219 | 0.7835 | 0.7473 |
| 6 | 0.9420 | 0.9282 | 0.9145 | 0.8880 | 0.8375 | 0.7903 | 0.7462 | 0.7050 |
| 7 | 0.9327 | 0.9167 | 0.9010 | 0.8706 | 0.8131 | 0.7599 | 0.7107 | 0.6651 |
| 8 | 0.9235 | 0.9054 | 0.8877 | 0.8535 | 0.7894 | 0.7307 | 0.6768 | 0.6274 |
| 9 | 0.9143 | 0.8942 | 0.8746 | 0.8368 | 0.7664 | 0.7026 | 0.6446 | 0.5919 |
| 10 | 0.9053 | 0.8832 | 0.8617 | 0.8203 | 0.7441 | 0.6756 | 0.6139 | 0.5584 |
| 11 | 0.8963 | 0.8723 | 0.8489 | 0.8043 | 0.7224 | 0.6496 | 0.5847 | 0.5268 |
| 12 | 0.8874 | 0.8615 | 0.8364 | 0.7885 | 0.7014 | 0.6246 | 0.5568 | 0.4970 |
| 13 | 0.8787 | 0.8509 | 0.8240 | 0.7730 | 0.6810 | 0.6006 | 0.5303 | 0.4688 |
| 14 | 0.8700 | 0.8404 | 0.8119 | 0.7579 | 0.6611 | 0.5775 | 0.5051 | 0.4423 |
| 15 | 0.8614 | 0.8300 | 0.7999 | 0.7430 | 0.6419 | 0.5553 | 0.4810 | 0.4173 |
| 16 | 0.8528 | 0.8197 | 0.7880 | 0.7284 | 0.6232 | 0.5339 | 0.4581 | 0.3936 |
| 17 | 0.8444 | 0.8096 | 0.7764 | 0.7142 | 0.6050 | 0.5134 | 0.4363 | 0.3714 |
| 18 | 0.8360 | 0.7996 | 0.7649 | 0.7002 | 0.5874 | 0.4936 | 0.4155 | 0.3503 |
| 19 | 0.8277 | 0.7898 | 0.7536 | 0.6864 | 0.5703 | 0.4746 | 0.3957 | 0.3305 |
| 20 | 0.8195 | 0.7800 | 0.7425 | 0.6730 | 0.5537 | 0.4564 | 0.3769 | 0.3118 |
| 21 | 0.8114 | 0.7704 | 0.7315 | 0.6598 | 0.5375 | 0.4388 | 0.3589 | 0.2942 |
| 22 | 0.8034 | 0.7609 | 0.7207 | 0.6468 | 0.5219 | 0.4220 | 0.3419 | 0.2775 |
| 23 | 0.7954 | 0.7515 | 0.7100 | 0.6342 | 0.5067 | 0.4057 | 0.3256 | 0.2618 |
| 24 | 0.7876 | 0.7422 | 0.6995 | 0.6217 | 0.4919 | 0.3901 | 0.3101 | 0.2470 |
| 25 | 0.7798 | 0.7330 | 0.6892 | 0.6095 | 0.4776 | 0.3751 | 0.2953 | 0.2330 |
| 26 | 0.7720 | 0.7240 | 0.6790 | 0.5976 | 0.4637 | 0.3607 | 0.2812 | 0.2198 |
| 27 | 0.7644 | 0.7150 | 0.6690 | 0.5859 | 0.4502 | 0.3468 | 0.2678 | 0.2074 |
| 28 | 0.7568 | 0.7062 | 0.6591 | 0.5744 | 0.4371 | 0.3335 | 0.2551 | 0.1956 |
| 29 | 0.7493 | 0.6975 | 0.6494 | 0.5631 | 0.4243 | 0.3207 | 0.2429 | 0.1846 |
| 30 | 0.7419 | 0.6889 | 0.6398 | 0.5521 | 0.4120 | 0.3083 | 0.2314 | 0.1741 |
| 31 | 0.7346 | 0.6804 | 0.6303 | 0.5412 | 0.4000 | 0.2965 | 0.2204 | 0.1643 |
| 32 | 0.7273 | 0.6720 | 0.6210 | 0.5306 | 0.3883 | 0.2851 | 0.2099 | 0.1550 |
| 33 | 0.7201 | 0.6637 | 0.6118 | 0.5202 | 0.3770 | 0.2741 | 0.1999 | 0.1462 |
| 34 | 0.7130 | 0.6555 | 0.6028 | 0.5100 | 0.3660 | 0.2636 | 0.1904 | 0.1379 |
| 35 | 0.7059 | 0.6474 | 0.5939 | 0.5000 | 0.3554 | 0.2534 | 0.1813 | 0.1301 |
| 36 | 0.6989 | 0.6394 | 0.5851 | 0.4902 | 0.3450 | 0.2437 | 0.1727 | 0.1227 |
| 37 | 0.6920 | 0.6315 | 0.5764 | 0.4806 | 0.3350 | 0.2343 | 0.1644 | 0.1158 |
| 38 | 0.6852 | 0.6237 | 0.5679 | 0.4712 | 0.3252 | 0.2253 | 0.1566 | 0.1092 |
| 39 | 0.6784 | 0.6160 | 0.5595 | 0.4619 | 0.3158 | 0.2166 | 0.1491 | 0.1031 |
| 40 | 0.6717 | 0.6084 | 0.5513 | 0.4529 | 0.3066 | 0.2083 | 0.1420 | 0.0972 |
| 41 | 0.6650 | 0.6009 | 0.5431 | 0.4440 | 0.2976 | 0.2003 | 0.1353 | 0.0917 |
| 42 | 0.6584 | 0.5935 | 0.5351 | 0.4353 | 0.2890 | 0.1926 | 0.1288 | 0.0865 |
| 43 | 0.6519 | 0.5862 | 0.5272 | 0.4268 | 0.2805 | 0.1852 | 0.1227 | 0.0816 |
| 44 | 0.6454 | 0.5789 | 0.5194 | 0.4184 | 0.2724 | 0.1780 | 0.1169 | 0.0770 |
| 45 | 0.6391 | 0.5718 | 0.5117 | 0.4102 | 0.2644 | 0.1712 | 0.1113 | 0.0727 |
| 46 | 0.6327 | 0.5647 | 0.5042 | 0.4022 | 0.2567 | 0.1646 | 0.1060 | 0.0685 |
| 47 | 0.6265 | 0.5577 | 0.4967 | 0.3943 | 0.2493 | 0.1583 | 0.1010 | 0.0647 |
| 48 | 0.6203 | 0.5509 | 0.4894 | 0.3865 | 0.2420 | 0.1522 | 0.0961 | 0.0610 |
| 49 | 0.6141 | 0.5441 | 0.4821 | 0.3790 | 0.2350 | 0.1463 | 0.0916 | 0.0575 |
| 50 | 0.6080 | 0.5373 | 0.4750 | 0.3715 | 0.2281 | 0.1407 | 0.0872 | 0.0543 |

$$i = 07 \text{ to } 14; N = 01 \text{ to } 50$$

| N | 7% | 8% | 9% | 10% | 11% | 12% | 13% | 14% |
|---|------|------|------|------|------|------|------|------|
| 1 | 0.9346 | 0.9259 | 0.9174 | 0.9091 | 0.9009 | 0.8929 | 0.8850 | 0.8772 |
| 2 | 0.8734 | 0.8573 | 0.8417 | 0.8264 | 0.8116 | 0.7972 | 0.7831 | 0.7695 |
| 3 | 0.8163 | 0.7938 | 0.7722 | 0.7513 | 0.7312 | 0.7118 | 0.6931 | 0.6750 |
| 4 | 0.7629 | 0.7350 | 0.7084 | 0.6830 | 0.6587 | 0.6355 | 0.6133 | 0.5921 |
| 5 | 0.7130 | 0.6806 | 0.6499 | 0.6209 | 0.5935 | 0.5674 | 0.5428 | 0.5194 |
| 6 | 0.6663 | 0.6302 | 0.5963 | 0.5645 | 0.5346 | 0.5066 | 0.4803 | 0.4556 |
| 7 | 0.6228 | 0.5835 | 0.5470 | 0.5132 | 0.4817 | 0.4523 | 0.4251 | 0.3996 |
| 8 | 0.5820 | 0.5403 | 0.5019 | 0.4665 | 0.4339 | 0.4039 | 0.3762 | 0.3506 |
| 9 | 0.5439 | 0.5002 | 0.4604 | 0.4241 | 0.3909 | 0.3606 | 0.3329 | 0.3075 |
| 10 | 0.5083 | 0.4632 | 0.4224 | 0.3855 | 0.3522 | 0.3220 | 0.2946 | 0.2697 |
| 11 | 0.4751 | 0.4289 | 0.3875 | 0.3505 | 0.3173 | 0.2875 | 0.2607 | 0.2366 |
| 12 | 0.4440 | 0.3971 | 0.3555 | 0.3186 | 0.2858 | 0.2567 | 0.2307 | 0.2076 |
| 13 | 0.4150 | 0.3677 | 0.3262 | 0.2897 | 0.2575 | 0.2292 | 0.2042 | 0.1821 |
| 14 | 0.3878 | 0.3405 | 0.2992 | 0.2633 | 0.2320 | 0.2046 | 0.1807 | 0.1597 |
| 15 | 0.3624 | 0.3152 | 0.2745 | 0.2394 | 0.2090 | 0.1827 | 0.1599 | 0.1401 |
| 16 | 0.3387 | 0.2919 | 0.2519 | 0.2176 | 0.1883 | 0.1631 | 0.1415 | 0.1229 |
| 17 | 0.3166 | 0.2703 | 0.2311 | 0.1978 | 0.1696 | 0.1456 | 0.1252 | 0.1078 |
| 18 | 0.2959 | 0.2502 | 0.2120 | 0.1799 | 0.1528 | 0.1300 | 0.1108 | 0.0946 |
| 19 | 0.2765 | 0.2317 | 0.1945 | 0.1635 | 0.1377 | 0.1161 | 0.0981 | 0.0829 |
| 20 | 0.2584 | 0.2145 | 0.1784 | 0.1486 | 0.1240 | 0.1037 | 0.0868 | 0.0728 |
| 21 | 0.2415 | 0.1987 | 0.1637 | 0.1351 | 0.1117 | 0.0926 | 0.0768 | 0.0638 |
| 22 | 0.2257 | 0.1839 | 0.1502 | 0.1228 | 0.1007 | 0.0826 | 0.0680 | 0.0560 |
| 23 | 0.2109 | 0.1703 | 0.1378 | 0.1117 | 0.0907 | 0.0738 | 0.0601 | 0.0491 |
| 24 | 0.1971 | 0.1577 | 0.1264 | 0.1015 | 0.0817 | 0.0659 | 0.0532 | 0.0431 |
| 25 | 0.1842 | 0.1460 | 0.1160 | 0.0923 | 0.0736 | 0.0588 | 0.0471 | 0.0378 |
| 26 | 0.1722 | 0.1352 | 0.1064 | 0.0839 | 0.0663 | 0.0525 | 0.0417 | 0.0331 |
| 27 | 0.1609 | 0.1252 | 0.0976 | 0.0763 | 0.0597 | 0.0469 | 0.0369 | 0.0291 |
| 28 | 0.1504 | 0.1159 | 0.0895 | 0.0693 | 0.0538 | 0.0419 | 0.0326 | 0.0255 |
| 29 | 0.1406 | 0.1073 | 0.0822 | 0.0630 | 0.0485 | 0.0374 | 0.0289 | 0.0224 |
| 30 | 0.1314 | 0.0994 | 0.0754 | 0.0573 | 0.0437 | 0.0334 | 0.0256 | 0.0196 |
| 31 | 0.1228 | 0.0920 | 0.0691 | 0.0521 | 0.0394 | 0.0298 | 0.0226 | 0.0172 |
| 32 | 0.1147 | 0.0852 | 0.0634 | 0.0474 | 0.0355 | 0.0266 | 0.0200 | 0.0151 |
| 33 | 0.1072 | 0.0789 | 0.0582 | 0.0431 | 0.0319 | 0.0238 | 0.0177 | 0.0132 |
| 34 | 0.1002 | 0.0730 | 0.0534 | 0.0391 | 0.0288 | 0.0212 | 0.0157 | 0.0116 |
| 35 | 0.0937 | 0.0676 | 0.0490 | 0.0356 | 0.0259 | 0.0189 | 0.0139 | 0.0102 |
| 36 | 0.0875 | 0.0626 | 0.0449 | 0.0323 | 0.0234 | 0.0169 | 0.0123 | 0.0089 |
| 37 | 0.0818 | 0.0580 | 0.0412 | 0.0294 | 0.0210 | 0.0151 | 0.0109 | 0.0078 |
| 38 | 0.0765 | 0.0537 | 0.0378 | 0.0267 | 0.0190 | 0.0135 | 0.0096 | 0.0069 |
| 39 | 0.0715 | 0.0497 | 0.0347 | 0.0243 | 0.0171 | 0.0120 | 0.0085 | 0.0060 |
| 40 | 0.0668 | 0.0460 | 0.0318 | 0.0221 | 0.0154 | 0.0107 | 0.0075 | 0.0053 |
| 41 | 0.0624 | 0.0426 | 0.0292 | 0.0201 | 0.0139 | 0.0096 | 0.0067 | 0.0046 |
| 42 | 0.0583 | 0.0395 | 0.0268 | 0.0183 | 0.0125 | 0.0086 | 0.0059 | 0.0041 |
| 43 | 0.0545 | 0.0365 | 0.0246 | 0.0166 | 0.0112 | 0.0076 | 0.0052 | 0.0036 |
| 44 | 0.0509 | 0.0338 | 0.0226 | 0.0151 | 0.0101 | 0.0068 | 0.0046 | 0.0031 |
| 45 | 0.0476 | 0.0313 | 0.0207 | 0.0137 | 0.0091 | 0.0061 | 0.0041 | 0.0027 |
| 46 | 0.0445 | 0.0290 | 0.0190 | 0.0125 | 0.0082 | 0.0054 | 0.0036 | 0.0024 |
| 47 | 0.0416 | 0.0269 | 0.0174 | 0.0113 | 0.0074 | 0.0049 | 0.0032 | 0.0021 |
| 48 | 0.0389 | 0.0249 | 0.0160 | 0.0103 | 0.0067 | 0.0043 | 0.0028 | 0.0019 |
| 49 | 0.0363 | 0.0230 | 0.0147 | 0.0094 | 0.0060 | 0.0039 | 0.0025 | 0.0016 |
| 50 | 0.0339 | 0.0213 | 0.0134 | 0.0085 | 0.0054 | 0.0035 | 0.0022 | 0.0014 |

$i = 15$ to $50 : N = 01$ to $50$

| N | 15% | 20% | 25% | 30% | 35% | 40% | 45% | 50% |
|---|-----|-----|-----|-----|-----|-----|-----|-----|
| 1 | 0.8696 | 0.8333 | 0.8000 | 0.7692 | 0.7407 | 0.7143 | 0.6897 | 0.6667 |
| 2 | 0.7561 | 0.6944 | 0.6400 | 0.5917 | 0.5487 | 0.5102 | 0.4756 | 0.4444 |
| 3 | 0.6575 | 0.5787 | 0.5120 | 0.4552 | 0.4064 | 0.3644 | 0.3280 | 0.2963 |
| 4 | 0.5718 | 0.4823 | 0.4096 | 0.3501 | 0.3011 | 0.2603 | 0.2262 | 0.1975 |
| 5 | 0.4972 | 0.4019 | 0.3277 | 0.2693 | 0.2230 | 0.1859 | 0.1560 | 0.1317 |
| 6 | 0.4323 | 0.3349 | 0.2621 | 0.2072 | 0.1652 | 0.1328 | 0.1076 | 0.0878 |
| 7 | 0.3759 | 0.2791 | 0.2097 | 0.1594 | 0.1224 | 0.0949 | 0.0742 | 0.0585 |
| 8 | 0.3269 | 0.2326 | 0.1678 | 0.1226 | 0.0906 | 0.0678 | 0.0512 | 0.0390 |
| 9 | 0.2843 | 0.1938 | 0.1342 | 0.0943 | 0.0671 | 0.0484 | 0.0353 | 0.0260 |
| 10 | 0.2472 | 0.1615 | 0.1074 | 0.0725 | 0.0497 | 0.0346 | 0.0243 | 0.0173 |
| 11 | 0.2149 | 0.1346 | 0.0859 | 0.0558 | 0.0368 | 0.0247 | 0.0168 | 0.0116 |
| 12 | 0.1869 | 0.1122 | 0.0687 | 0.0429 | 0.0273 | 0.0176 | 0.0116 | 0.0077 |
| 13 | 0.1625 | 0.0935 | 0.0550 | 0.0330 | 0.0202 | 0.0126 | 0.0080 | 0.0051 |
| 14 | 0.1413 | 0.0779 | 0.0440 | 0.0254 | 0.0150 | 0.0090 | 0.0055 | 0.0034 |
| 15 | 0.1229 | 0.0649 | 0.0352 | 0.0195 | 0.0111 | 0.0064 | 0.0038 | 0.0023 |
| 16 | 0.1069 | 0.0541 | 0.0281 | 0.0150 | 0.0082 | 0.0046 | 0.0026 | 0.0015 |
| 17 | 0.0929 | 0.0451 | 0.0225 | 0.0116 | 0.0061 | 0.0033 | 0.0018 | 0.0010 |
| 18 | 0.0808 | 0.0376 | 0.0180 | 0.0089 | 0.0045 | 0.0023 | 0.0012 | 0.0007 |
| 19 | 0.0703 | 0.0313 | 0.0144 | 0.0068 | 0.0033 | 0.0017 | 0.0009 | 0.0005 |
| 20 | 0.0611 | 0.0261 | 0.0115 | 0.0053 | 0.0025 | 0.0012 | 0.0006 | 0.0003 |
| 21 | 0.0531 | 0.0217 | 0.0092 | 0.0040 | 0.0018 | 0.0009 | 0.0004 | 0.0002 |
| 22 | 0.0462 | 0.0181 | 0.0074 | 0.0031 | 0.0014 | 0.0006 | 0.0003 | 0.0001 |
| 23 | 0.0402 | 0.0151 | 0.0059 | 0.0024 | 0.0010 | 0.0004 | 0.0002 | 0.0001 |
| 24 | 0.0349 | 0.0126 | 0.0047 | 0.0018 | 0.0007 | 0.0003 | 0.0001 | 0.0001 |
| 25 | 0.0304 | 0.0105 | 0.0038 | 0.0014 | 0.0006 | 0.0002 | 0.0001 | 0.0000 |
| 26 | 0.0264 | 0.0087 | 0.0030 | 0.0011 | 0.0004 | 0.0002 | 0.0001 | 0.0000 |
| 27 | 0.0230 | 0.0073 | 0.0024 | 0.0008 | 0.0003 | 0.0001 | 0.0000 | 0.0000 |
| 28 | 0.0200 | 0.0061 | 0.0019 | 0.0006 | 0.0002 | 0.0001 | 0.0000 | 0.0000 |
| 29 | 0.0174 | 0.0051 | 0.0015 | 0.0005 | 0.0002 | 0.0001 | 0.0000 | 0.0000 |
| 30 | 0.0151 | 0.0042 | 0.0012 | 0.0004 | 0.0001 | 0.0000 | 0.0000 | 0.0000 |
| 31 | 0.0131 | 0.0035 | 0.0010 | 0.0003 | 0.0001 | 0.0000 | 0.0000 | 0.0000 |
| 32 | 0.0114 | 0.0029 | 0.0008 | 0.0002 | 0.0001 | 0.0000 | 0.0000 | 0.0000 |
| 33 | 0.0099 | 0.0024 | 0.0006 | 0.0002 | 0.0001 | 0.0000 | 0.0000 | 0.0000 |
| 34 | 0.0086 | 0.0020 | 0.0005 | 0.0001 | 0.0000 | 0.0000 | 0.0000 | 0.0000 |
| 35 | 0.0075 | 0.0017 | 0.0004 | 0.0001 | 0.0000 | 0.0000 | 0.0000 | 0.0000 |
| 36 | 0.0065 | 0.0014 | 0.0003 | 0.0001 | 0.0000 | 0.0000 | 0.0000 | 0.0000 |
| 37 | 0.0057 | 0.0012 | 0.0003 | 0.0001 | 0.0000 | 0.0000 | 0.0000 | 0.0000 |
| 38 | 0.0049 | 0.0010 | 0.0002 | 0.0000 | 0.0000 | 0.0000 | 0.0000 | 0.0000 |
| 39 | 0.0043 | 0.0008 | 0.0002 | 0.0000 | 0.0000 | 0.0000 | 0.0000 | 0.0000 |
| 40 | 0.0037 | 0.0007 | 0.0001 | 0.0000 | 0.0000 | 0.0000 | 0.0000 | 0.0000 |
| 41 | 0.0032 | 0.0006 | 0.0001 | 0.0000 | 0.0000 | 0.0000 | 0.0000 | 0.0000 |
| 42 | 0.0028 | 0.0005 | 0.0001 | 0.0000 | 0.0000 | 0.0000 | 0.0000 | 0.0000 |
| 43 | 0.0025 | 0.0004 | 0.0001 | 0.0000 | 0.0000 | 0.0000 | 0.0000 | 0.0000 |
| 44 | 0.0021 | 0.0003 | 0.0001 | 0.0000 | 0.0000 | 0.0000 | 0.0000 | 0.0000 |
| 45 | 0.0019 | 0.0003 | 0.0000 | 0.0000 | 0.0000 | 0.0000 | 0.0000 | 0.0000 |
| 46 | 0.0016 | 0.0002 | 0.0000 | 0.0000 | 0.0000 | 0.0000 | 0.0000 | 0.0000 |
| 47 | 0.0014 | 0.0002 | 0.0000 | 0.0000 | 0.0000 | 0.0000 | 0.0000 | 0.0000 |
| 48 | 0.0012 | 0.0002 | 0.0000 | 0.0000 | 0.0000 | 0.0000 | 0.0000 | 0.0000 |
| 49 | 0.0011 | 0.0001 | 0.0000 | 0.0000 | 0.0000 | 0.0000 | 0.0000 | 0.0000 |
| 50 | 0.0009 | 0.0001 | 0.0000 | 0.0000 | 0.0000 | 0.0000 | 0.0000 | 0.0000 |

**Table B:**   Present Value of a Stream of Payments/Receipts
of $1 Each Period,*

$$PV_{\text{R}} = \frac{1 - \dfrac{1}{(1 + i)^n}}{i}$$

where $i$ = interest rate per period and $n$ = number of periods.

―――――――――――――

* Also known as present value of ordinary annuity of one dollar.

# Table B: Stream of Payments|Receipts

$i = 01$ to $06$; $N = 01$ to $50$

| N | 1% | 1.25% | 1.5% | 2% | 3% | 4% | 5% | 6% |
|----|---------|---------|---------|---------|---------|---------|---------|---------|
| 1 | 0.9901 | 0.9877 | 0.9852 | 0.9804 | 0.9709 | 0.9615 | 0.9524 | 0.9434 |
| 2 | 1.9704 | 1.9631 | 1.9559 | 1.9416 | 1.9135 | 1.8861 | 1.8594 | 1.8334 |
| 3 | 2.9410 | 2.9266 | 2.9122 | 2.8839 | 2.8286 | 2.7751 | 2.7233 | 2.6730 |
| 4 | 3.9020 | 3.8781 | 3.8544 | 3.8077 | 3.7171 | 3.6299 | 3.5460 | 3.4651 |
| 5 | 4.8534 | 4.8179 | 4.7826 | 4.7135 | 4.5797 | 4.4518 | 4.3295 | 4.2124 |
| 6 | 5.7955 | 5.7460 | 5.6972 | 5.6014 | 5.4172 | 5.2421 | 5.0757 | 4.9173 |
| 7 | 6.7282 | 6.6628 | 6.5982 | 6.4720 | 6.2303 | 6.0021 | 5.7864 | 5.5824 |
| 8 | 7.6517 | 7.5682 | 7.4859 | 7.3255 | 7.0197 | 6.7327 | 6.4632 | 6.2098 |
| 9 | 8.5660 | 8.4624 | 8.3605 | 8.1622 | 7.7861 | 7.4353 | 7.1078 | 6.8017 |
| 10 | 9.4713 | 9.3456 | 9.2222 | 8.9826 | 8.5302 | 8.1109 | 7.7217 | 7.3601 |
| 11 | 10.3676 | 10.2179 | 10.0711 | 9.7868 | 9.2526 | 8.7605 | 8.3064 | 7.8869 |
| 12 | 11.2551 | 11.0794 | 10.9075 | 10.5753 | 9.9540 | 9.3851 | 8.8632 | 8.3838 |
| 13 | 12.1337 | 11.9302 | 11.7315 | 11.3484 | 10.6350 | 9.9856 | 9.3936 | 8.8527 |
| 14 | 13.0037 | 12.7706 | 12.5433 | 12.1062 | 11.2961 | 10.5631 | 9.8986 | 9.2950 |
| 15 | 13.8650 | 13.6006 | 13.3432 | 12.8492 | 11.9379 | 11.1184 | 10.3796 | 9.7122 |
| 16 | 14.7179 | 14.4204 | 14.1312 | 13.5777 | 12.5611 | 11.6523 | 10.8378 | 10.1059 |
| 17 | 15.5622 | 15.2300 | 14.9076 | 14.2918 | 13.1661 | 12.1657 | 11.2741 | 10.4773 |
| 18 | 16.3983 | 16.0296 | 15.6725 | 14.9920 | 13.7535 | 12.6593 | 11.6896 | 10.8276 |
| 19 | 17.2260 | 16.8194 | 16.4261 | 15.6784 | 14.3238 | 13.1339 | 12.0853 | 11.1581 |
| 20 | 18.0455 | 17.5994 | 17.1686 | 16.3514 | 14.8775 | 13.5903 | 12.4622 | 11.4699 |
| 21 | 18.8570 | 18.3698 | 17.9001 | 17.0112 | 15.4150 | 14.0292 | 12.8211 | 11.7641 |
| 22 | 19.6604 | 19.1307 | 18.6208 | 17.6580 | 15.9369 | 14.4511 | 13.1630 | 12.0416 |
| 23 | 20.4558 | 19.8821 | 19.3308 | 18.2922 | 16.4436 | 14.8568 | 13.4886 | 12.3034 |
| 24 | 21.2434 | 20.6243 | 20.0304 | 18.9139 | 16.9355 | 15.2470 | 13.7986 | 12.5504 |
| 25 | 22.0232 | 21.3574 | 20.7196 | 19.5234 | 17.4131 | 15.6221 | 14.0939 | 12.7834 |
| 26 | 22.7952 | 22.0814 | 21.3986 | 20.1210 | 17.8768 | 15.9828 | 14.3752 | 13.0032 |
| 27 | 23.5596 | 22.7964 | 22.0676 | 20.7069 | 18.3270 | 16.3296 | 14.6430 | 13.2105 |
| 28 | 24.3164 | 23.5026 | 22.7267 | 21.2812 | 18.7641 | 16.6631 | 14.8981 | 13.4062 |
| 29 | 25.0658 | 24.2001 | 23.3760 | 21.8443 | 19.1885 | 16.9837 | 15.1411 | 13.5907 |
| 30 | 25.8077 | 24.8890 | 24.0158 | 22.3964 | 19.6004 | 17.2920 | 15.3724 | 13.7648 |
| 31 | 26.5423 | 25.5694 | 24.6461 | 22.9377 | 20.0004 | 17.5885 | 15.5928 | 13.9291 |
| 32 | 27.2696 | 26.2415 | 25.2671 | 23.4683 | 20.3888 | 17.8735 | 15.8027 | 14.0840 |
| 33 | 27.9897 | 26.9052 | 25.8789 | 23.9886 | 20.7658 | 18.1476 | 16.0025 | 14.2302 |
| 34 | 28.7027 | 27.5606 | 26.4817 | 24.4986 | 21.1318 | 18.4112 | 16.1929 | 14.3681 |
| 35 | 29.4086 | 28.2080 | 27.0756 | 24.9986 | 21.4872 | 18.6646 | 16.3742 | 14.4982 |
| 36 | 30.1075 | 28.8475 | 27.6607 | 25.4888 | 21.8322 | 18.9083 | 16.5468 | 14.6210 |
| 37 | 30.7995 | 29.4790 | 28.2371 | 25.9695 | 22.1672 | 19.1426 | 16.7113 | 14.7368 |
| 38 | 31.4847 | 30.1027 | 28.8050 | 26.4406 | 22.4925 | 19.3679 | 16.8679 | 14.8460 |
| 39 | 32.1631 | 30.7187 | 29.3645 | 26.9026 | 22.8082 | 19.5845 | 17.0170 | 14.9491 |
| 40 | 32.8347 | 31.3271 | 29.9158 | 27.3555 | 23.1148 | 19.7928 | 17.1591 | 15.0463 |
| 41 | 33.4997 | 31.9280 | 30.4589 | 27.7995 | 23.4124 | 19.9930 | 17.2944 | 15.1380 |
| 42 | 34.1581 | 32.5215 | 30.9940 | 28.2348 | 23.7014 | 20.1856 | 17.4232 | 15.2245 |
| 43 | 34.8100 | 33.1077 | 31.5212 | 28.6616 | 23.9819 | 20.3708 | 17.5459 | 15.3062 |
| 44 | 35.4555 | 33.6866 | 32.0406 | 29.0800 | 24.2543 | 20.5488 | 17.6628 | 15.3832 |
| 45 | 36.0945 | 34.2584 | 32.5523 | 29.4902 | 24.5187 | 20.7200 | 17.7741 | 15.4558 |
| 46 | 36.7273 | 34.8231 | 33.0565 | 29.8923 | 24.7754 | 20.8847 | 17.8801 | 15.5244 |
| 47 | 37.3537 | 35.3808 | 33.5532 | 30.2866 | 25.0247 | 21.0429 | 17.9810 | 15.5890 |
| 48 | 37.9740 | 35.9317 | 34.0425 | 30.6731 | 25.2667 | 21.1951 | 18.0772 | 15.6500 |
| 49 | 38.5881 | 36.4758 | 34.5246 | 31.0521 | 25.5017 | 21.3415 | 18.1687 | 15.7076 |
| 50 | 39.1962 | 37.0131 | 34.9997 | 31.4236 | 25.7298 | 21.4822 | 18.2559 | 15.7619 |

$i = 07$ to $14$; $N = 01$ to $50$

| N | 7% | 8% | 9% | 10% | 11% | 12% | 13% | 14% |
|---|---|---|---|---|---|---|---|---|
| 1 | 0.9346 | 0.9259 | 0.9174 | 0.9091 | 0.9009 | 0.8929 | 0.8850 | 0.8772 |
| 2 | 1.8080 | 1.7833 | 1.7591 | 1.7355 | 1.7125 | 1.6901 | 1.6681 | 1.6467 |
| 3 | 2.6243 | 2.5771 | 2.5313 | 2.4869 | 2.4437 | 2.4018 | 2.3612 | 2.3216 |
| 4 | 3.3872 | 3.3121 | 3.2397 | 3.1699 | 3.1025 | 3.0374 | 2.9745 | 2.9137 |
| 5 | 4.1002 | 3.9927 | 3.8897 | 3.7908 | 3.6959 | 3.6048 | 3.5172 | 3.4331 |
| 6 | 4.7665 | 4.6229 | 4.4859 | 4.3553 | 4.2305 | 4.1114 | 3.9976 | 3.8887 |
| 7 | 5.3893 | 5.2064 | 5.0330 | 4.8684 | 4.7122 | 4.5638 | 4.4226 | 4.2883 |
| 8 | 5.9713 | 5.7466 | 5.5348 | 5.3349 | 5.1461 | 4.9676 | 4.7988 | 4.6389 |
| 9 | 6.5152 | 6.2469 | 5.9953 | 5.7590 | 5.5371 | 5.3283 | 5.1317 | 4.9464 |
| 10 | 7.0236 | 6.7101 | 6.4177 | 6.1446 | 5.8892 | 5.6502 | 5.4262 | 5.2161 |
| 11 | 7.4987 | 7.1390 | 6.8052 | 6.4951 | 6.2065 | 5.9377 | 5.6869 | 5.4527 |
| 12 | 7.9427 | 7.5361 | 7.1607 | 6.8137 | 6.4924 | 6.1944 | 5.9177 | 5.6603 |
| 13 | 8.3577 | 7.9038 | 7.4869 | 7.1034 | 6.7499 | 6.4236 | 6.1218 | 5.8424 |
| 14 | 8.7455 | 8.2442 | 7.7862 | 7.3667 | 6.9819 | 6.6282 | 6.3025 | 6.0021 |
| 15 | 9.1079 | 8.5595 | 8.0607 | 7.6061 | 7.1909 | 6.8109 | 6.4624 | 6.1422 |
| 16 | 9.4467 | 8.8514 | 8.3126 | 7.8237 | 7.3792 | 6.9740 | 6.6039 | 6.2651 |
| 17 | 9.7632 | 9.1216 | 8.5436 | 8.0216 | 7.5488 | 7.1196 | 6.7291 | 6.3729 |
| 18 | 10.0591 | 9.3719 | 8.7556 | 8.2014 | 7.7016 | 7.2497 | 6.8399 | 6.4674 |
| 19 | 10.3356 | 9.6036 | 8.9501 | 8.3649 | 7.8393 | 7.3658 | 6.9380 | 6.5504 |
| 20 | 10.5940 | 9.8182 | 9.1286 | 8.5136 | 7.9633 | 7.4694 | 7.0248 | 6.6231 |
| 21 | 10.8355 | 10.0168 | 9.2923 | 8.6487 | 8.0751 | 7.5620 | 7.1016 | 6.6870 |
| 22 | 11.0612 | 10.2007 | 9.4424 | 8.7715 | 8.1757 | 7.6447 | 7.1695 | 6.7429 |
| 23 | 11.2722 | 10.3711 | 9.5802 | 8.8832 | 8.2664 | 7.7184 | 7.2297 | 6.7921 |
| 24 | 11.4693 | 10.5288 | 9.7066 | 8.9847 | 8.3481 | 7.7843 | 7.2829 | 6.8351 |
| 25 | 11.6536 | 10.6748 | 9.8226 | 9.0770 | 8.4218 | 7.8431 | 7.3300 | 6.8729 |
| 26 | 11.8258 | 10.8100 | 9.9290 | 9.1610 | 8.4881 | 7.8957 | 7.3717 | 6.9061 |
| 27 | 11.9867 | 10.9352 | 10.0266 | 9.2372 | 8.5478 | 7.9426 | 7.4086 | 6.9352 |
| 28 | 12.1371 | 11.0511 | 10.1161 | 9.3066 | 8.6016 | 7.9844 | 7.4412 | 6.9607 |
| 29 | 12.2777 | 11.1584 | 10.1983 | 9.3696 | 8.6501 | 8.0218 | 7.4701 | 6.9830 |
| 30 | 12.4090 | 11.2578 | 10.2737 | 9.4269 | 8.6938 | 8.0552 | 7.4957 | 7.0027 |
| 31 | 12.5318 | 11.3498 | 10.3428 | 9.4790 | 8.7332 | 8.0850 | 7.5183 | 7.0199 |
| 32 | 12.6466 | 11.4350 | 10.4062 | 9.5264 | 8.7686 | 8.1116 | 7.5383 | 7.0350 |
| 33 | 12.7538 | 11.5139 | 10.4644 | 9.5694 | 8.8005 | 8.1354 | 7.5560 | 7.0482 |
| 34 | 12.8540 | 11.5869 | 10.5178 | 9.6086 | 8.8293 | 8.1566 | 7.5717 | 7.0599 |
| 35 | 12.9477 | 11.6546 | 10.5668 | 9.6442 | 8.8552 | 8.1755 | 7.5856 | 7.0701 |
| 36 | 13.0352 | 11.7172 | 10.6118 | 9.6765 | 8.8786 | 8.1924 | 7.5979 | 7.0790 |
| 37 | 13.1170 | 11.7752 | 10.6530 | 9.7059 | 8.8996 | 8.2075 | 7.6087 | 7.0868 |
| 38 | 13.1935 | 11.8289 | 10.6908 | 9.7327 | 8.9186 | 8.2210 | 7.6183 | 7.0937 |
| 39 | 13.2649 | 11.8786 | 10.7255 | 9.7570 | 8.9357 | 8.2330 | 7.6269 | 7.0998 |
| 40 | 13.3317 | 11.9246 | 10.7574 | 9.7791 | 8.9511 | 8.2438 | 7.6344 | 7.1050 |
| 41 | 13.3941 | 11.9672 | 10.7866 | 9.7991 | 8.9649 | 8.2534 | 7.6410 | 7.1097 |
| 42 | 13.4525 | 12.0067 | 10.8134 | 9.8174 | 8.9774 | 8.2619 | 7.6469 | 7.1138 |
| 43 | 13.5070 | 12.0432 | 10.8380 | 9.8340 | 8.9887 | 8.2696 | 7.6522 | 7.1173 |
| 44 | 13.5579 | 12.0771 | 10.8605 | 9.8491 | 8.9988 | 8.2764 | 7.6568 | 7.1205 |
| 45 | 13.6055 | 12.1084 | 10.8812 | 9.8628 | 9.0079 | 8.2825 | 7.6609 | 7.1232 |
| 46 | 13.6500 | 12.1374 | 10.9002 | 9.8753 | 9.0161 | 8.2880 | 7.6645 | 7.1256 |
| 47 | 13.6916 | 12.1643 | 10.9176 | 9.8866 | 9.0236 | 8.2928 | 7.6677 | 7.1277 |
| 48 | 13.7305 | 12.1891 | 10.9336 | 9.8969 | 9.0302 | 8.2972 | 7.6705 | 7.1296 |
| 49 | 13.7668 | 12.2122 | 10.9482 | 9.9063 | 9.0362 | 8.3010 | 7.6730 | 7.1312 |
| 50 | 13.8007 | 12.2335 | 10.9617 | 9.9148 | 9.0417 | 8.3045 | 7.6752 | 7.1327 |

$i = 15$ to $50; N = 01$ to $50$

| N | 15% | 20% | 25% | 30% | 35% | 40% | 45% | 50% |
|---|-----|-----|-----|-----|-----|-----|-----|-----|
| 1 | 0.8696 | 0.8333 | 0.8000 | 0.7692 | 0.7407 | 0.7143 | 0.6897 | 0.6667 |
| 2 | 1.6257 | 1.5278 | 1.4400 | 1.3610 | 1.2894 | 1.2245 | 1.1653 | 1.1111 |
| 3 | 2.2832 | 2.1065 | 1.9520 | 1.8161 | 1.6959 | 1.5889 | 1.4933 | 1.4074 |
| 4 | 2.8550 | 2.5887 | 2.3616 | 2.1662 | 1.9970 | 1.8492 | 1.7195 | 1.6049 |
| 5 | 3.3522 | 2.9906 | 2.6893 | 2.4356 | 2.2200 | 2.0352 | 1.8755 | 1.7366 |
| 6 | 3.7845 | 3.3255 | 2.9514 | 2.6428 | 2.3852 | 2.1680 | 1.9831 | 1.8244 |
| 7 | 4.1604 | 3.6046 | 3.1611 | 2.8021 | 2.5075 | 2.2628 | 2.0573 | 1.8829 |
| 8 | 4.4873 | 3.8372 | 3.3289 | 2.9247 | 2.5982 | 2.3306 | 2.1085 | 1.9220 |
| 9 | 4.7716 | 4.0310 | 3.4631 | 3.0190 | 2.6653 | 2.3790 | 2.1438 | 1.9480 |
| 10 | 5.0188 | 4.1925 | 3.5705 | 3.0915 | 2.7150 | 2.4136 | 2.1681 | 1.9653 |
| 11 | 5.2337 | 4.3271 | 3.6564 | 3.1473 | 2.7519 | 2.4383 | 2.1849 | 1.9769 |
| 12 | 5.4206 | 4.4392 | 3.7251 | 3.1903 | 2.7792 | 2.4559 | 2.1965 | 1.9846 |
| 13 | 5.5832 | 4.5327 | 3.7801 | 3.2233 | 2.7994 | 2.4685 | 2.2045 | 1.9897 |
| 14 | 5.7245 | 4.6106 | 3.8241 | 3.2487 | 2.8144 | 2.4775 | 2.2100 | 1.9932 |
| 15 | 5.8474 | 4.6755 | 3.8593 | 3.2682 | 2.8255 | 2.4839 | 2.2138 | 1.9954 |
| 16 | 5.9542 | 4.7296 | 3.8874 | 3.2832 | 2.8337 | 2.4885 | 2.2164 | 1.9970 |
| 17 | 6.0472 | 4.7746 | 3.9099 | 3.2948 | 2.8398 | 2.4918 | 2.2182 | 1.9980 |
| 18 | 6.1280 | 4.8122 | 3.9279 | 3.3037 | 2.8443 | 2.4941 | 2.2195 | 1.9987 |
| 19 | 6.1982 | 4.8435 | 3.9424 | 3.3105 | 2.8476 | 2.4958 | 2.2203 | 1.9991 |
| 20 | 6.2593 | 4.8696 | 3.9539 | 3.3158 | 2.8501 | 2.4970 | 2.2209 | 1.9994 |
| 21 | 6.3125 | 4.8913 | 3.9631 | 3.3198 | 2.8519 | 2.4979 | 2.2213 | 1.9996 |
| 22 | 6.3587 | 4.9094 | 3.9705 | 3.3230 | 2.8533 | 2.4985 | 2.2216 | 1.9997 |
| 23 | 6.3988 | 4.9245 | 3.9764 | 3.3254 | 2.8543 | 2.4989 | 2.2218 | 1.9998 |
| 24 | 6.4338 | 4.9371 | 3.9811 | 3.3272 | 2.8550 | 2.4992 | 2.2219 | 1.9999 |
| 25 | 6.4642 | 4.9476 | 3.9849 | 3.3286 | 2.8556 | 2.4994 | 2.2220 | 1.9999 |
| 26 | 6.4906 | 4.9563 | 3.9879 | 3.3297 | 2.8560 | 2.4996 | 2.2221 | 2.0000 |
| 27 | 6.5135 | 4.9636 | 3.9903 | 3.3305 | 2.8563 | 2.4997 | 2.2221 | 2.0000 |
| 28 | 6.5335 | 4.9697 | 3.9923 | 3.3312 | 2.8565 | 2.4998 | 2.2222 | 2.0000 |
| 29 | 6.5509 | 4.9747 | 3.9938 | 3.3317 | 2.8567 | 2.4999 | 2.2222 | 2.0000 |
| 30 | 6.5660 | 4.9789 | 3.9951 | 3.3321 | 2.8568 | 2.4999 | 2.2222 | 2.0000 |
| 31 | 6.5791 | 4.9825 | 3.9960 | 3.3324 | 2.8569 | 2.4999 | 2.2222 | 2.0000 |
| 32 | 6.5905 | 4.9854 | 3.9968 | 3.3326 | 2.8570 | 2.5000 | 2.2222 | 2.0000 |
| 33 | 6.6006 | 4.9878 | 3.9975 | 3.3328 | 2.8570 | 2.5000 | 2.2222 | 2.0000 |
| 34 | 6.6091 | 4.9898 | 3.9980 | 3.3329 | 2.8570 | 2.5000 | 2.2222 | 2.0000 |
| 35 | 6.6166 | 4.9915 | 3.9984 | 3.3330 | 2.8571 | 2.5000 | 2.2222 | 2.0000 |
| 36 | 6.6231 | 4.9930 | 3.9987 | 3.3331 | 2.8571 | 2.5000 | 2.2222 | 2.0000 |
| 37 | 6.6288 | 4.9941 | 3.9990 | 3.3331 | 2.8571 | 2.5000 | 2.2222 | 2.0000 |
| 38 | 6.6338 | 4.9951 | 3.9992 | 3.3332 | 2.8571 | 2.5000 | 2.2222 | 2.0000 |
| 39 | 6.6381 | 4.9959 | 3.9993 | 3.3332 | 2.8571 | 2.5000 | 2.2222 | 2.0000 |
| 40 | 6.6418 | 4.9966 | 3.9995 | 3.3332 | 2.8571 | 2.5000 | 2.2222 | 2.0000 |
| 41 | 6.6450 | 4.9972 | 3.9996 | 3.3333 | 2.8571 | 2.5000 | 2.2222 | 2.0000 |
| 42 | 6.6479 | 4.9976 | 3.9997 | 3.3333 | 2.8571 | 2.5000 | 2.2222 | 2.0000 |
| 43 | 6.6503 | 4.9980 | 3.9997 | 3.3333 | 2.8571 | 2.5000 | 2.2222 | 2.0000 |
| 44 | 6.6524 | 4.9984 | 3.9998 | 3.3333 | 2.8571 | 2.5000 | 2.2222 | 2.0000 |
| 45 | 6.6543 | 4.9986 | 3.9998 | 3.3333 | 2.8571 | 2.5000 | 2.2222 | 2.0000 |
| 46 | 6.6559 | 4.9989 | 3.9999 | 3.3333 | 2.8571 | 2.5000 | 2.2222 | 2.0000 |
| 47 | 6.6573 | 4.9991 | 3.9999 | 3.3333 | 2.8571 | 2.5000 | 2.2222 | 2.0000 |
| 48 | 6.6585 | 4.9992 | 3.9999 | 3.3333 | 2.8571 | 2.5000 | 2.2222 | 2.0000 |
| 49 | 6.6596 | 4.9993 | 3.9999 | 3.3333 | 2.8571 | 2.5000 | 2.2222 | 2.0000 |
| 50 | 6.6605 | 4.9995 | 3.9999 | 3.3333 | 2.8571 | 2.5000 | 2.2222 | 2.0000 |

# B

## GLOSSARY OF BUSINESS AND ACCOUNTING TERMS

[*Note:* For those terms discussed in greater depth in the text or appendixes, the number of the chapter—(1), (2), and so forth—or the designation of the appendix—(A2), (A3), for chapter appendices, and (AD, (AE), for book appendices—that contains further discussion is shown in parenthesis.]

**AAA**    American Accounting Association.

**ABC inventory control** (4)    A system for unit inventory control wherein items are segregated into three groups for control purposes. Group A items with the highest costs receive close scheduling attention to minimize the need for costly *safety stock*. Less costly Group B items receive less attention and have some safety stock. Least costly Group C items are controlled informally, and stockout is avoided with large safety stocks.

**Absorption costing** (1)    See **Full costing.**

**Accelerated depreciation** (AD)    Any method of calculating *depreciation* where the charges become progressively smaller. *See* **Double-declining-balance** and **Years' digits** methods.

**Account**    A file for the accumulation of data on an item or group of similar items.

**Accounting changes**    Changes in *accounting method, accounting estimate,* or the *accounting entity.*

**Accounting cycle** (AE)    The sequence of steps followed by accountants, throughout the year (period).

**Accounting entity**    *See* **Entity.**

**Accounting estimate**    An estimate incorporated in a particular accounting measurement such as the period of *useful life* and the *salvage value* for a fixed asset.

**Accounting method** (AD)    A procedure for measuring and reporting financial information in conformance with *GAAP.*

**Accounting variance** (1)    The difference between the actual cost incurred and the predetermined or standard amount applied to the work-in-process inventory account(s). Any remaining balance in a direct labor, direct material, or manufacturing overhead account after product costs have been applied to inventory. Accounting variances are closed at the end of each fiscal year to cost of goods sold or, if material, are allocated among work-in-process, finished goods, and cost of goods sold accounts. Contrast with **Budget variance.**

**Accounts payable** (AD)    A *current liability* representing obligations to creditors for goods and services purchased on account.

**Accounts receivable** (AD)    A *current asset* representing claims against customers for goods or services sold on account.

**Accrual**   An amount recorded by an *adjusting entry* in recognition of a claim earned or obligation owed for which formal invoicing or payment has not occurred.

**Accrual basis (accounting)** (AD)   Income measured on the basis of revenues earned less expenses incurred, matched to related revenues independent of the timing of cash receipts and payments.

**Accumulated depreciation** (AD)   A *contra-asset* reporting the sum of all depreciation charges since an asset was acquired.

**Acid-test ratio**   *See* **Quick ratio.**

**Acquisition** (of a firm)   *See* **Business combination.**

**Activity base** (1)   The measure of production or sales volume selected for purposes of budgeting or applying costs. Can be direct-labor hours, machine hours, units completed, direct-labor dollars, sales dollars, or other measures, as appropriate.

**Activity budget** (2)   *See* **Sales budget.**

**Adjusted original cost** (AD)   A description of the current GAAP basis for measuring and reporting nonmonetary assets. These assets are originally recorded at cost and subsequently adjusted downwards to reflect expiration of usefulness or loss of recoverable value.

**Adjusted trial balance** (AE)   The *trial balance* taken after completion of adjustments and before closing.

**Adjusting entry**   An *entry* made at the end of an accounting period to record an event not previously recorded or recorded improperly. Examples include accruals, asset expirations, loss of recoverable values, discount or premium amortizations, revenue deferrals, and so forth.

**Adjustment** (AD)   The change in account balances resulting from an adjusting entry.

**Affirmatively misleading detail**   Reported amounts with such detail that an expression of accuracy that is not realistic is given to the reader. An example would be depreciation calculated and reported to the *nearest cent.*

**After-tax cash flows** (8)   Cash expenditures, investments, and revenues or cash savings in each period, after allowance for related tax savings or increased taxes.

**AICPA**   American Institute of Certified Public Accountants.

**Allowance for depreciation.**   *See* **Accumulated depreciation.**

**Allowance for uncollectibles** (AD)   A *contra-asset* indicating the amount of active *receivables* that are expected to prove uncollectible.

**Alternative actions** (17)   Alternative decisions available to management. Represented as the rows in a payoff table.

**Amortization** (AD)   The general process of systematically reducing an account balance to reflect asset expiration or the allocation of premiums and discounts to time periods. Known as *depletion* for wasting assets, and as *depreciation* for tangible fixed assets.

**Annual report** (AD)    A report prepared once a year by a corporation for its stockholders and other interested parties. It contains the year's financial statements, footnotes, auditor's opinion, and such other nonaudited information as management desires to disseminate.

**Application of funds** (A9)    Five possible uses of additional *working capital* other than funds lost in operations may be considered *applications*. They include working capital lost as an extraordinary loss, working capital used to acquire noncurrent assets, working capital used to retire noncurrent debt, dividends declared, and, finally, working capital generated elsewhere and used to increase the year-end balance of net working capital on hand.

**Appropriation**    In financial accounting, the segregation of a portion of *retained earnings* by action of the Board of Directors, to reflect a legal restriction of retained earnings available for dividends, or to reflect an intention to withhold future dividends. In government accounting, the authorization for a specific expenditure.

**Appropriation** (15)    *See* **Authorized budget.**

**Arbitrary** (method of investment analysis) (8)    Choosing an investment alternative by hunch or experience without analysis of related costs and benefits.

**"Arm's length"**    Refers to transactions between unrelated parties which may be used as evidence of *fair market value.*

**Asset** (AD)    A property, right, or claim owned or effectively controlled by the firm and having future objectively measurable value.

**Asset expiration**    The decline in future service potential of an asset as a result of deterioration and obsolescence. *See* **Depreciation** *and* **Amortization.**

**Asset management** (10)    Ensuring that amounts invested in cash, receivables, inventory, and capacity assets and their proportions are adequate, but not excessive, given a firm's level of activity and goals.

**Asset turnover** (A2)    The ratio of *net sales* to average total assets.

**Attainable standard** (13)    A work or performance measure reflecting expected results under conditions of high efficiency (as distinct from ideal, average, or historical efficiency). Includes allowance for normal machine breakdowns, waste, and material shrinkage.

**Audit** (AD)    An examination of accounting records, procedures, and controls to ensure their adequacy in conformance with GAAP and company objectives.

**Audit trail** (AE)    A system of cross-referencing information throughout accounting records, from original source document to final account posting.

**Auditor's opinion** (AD)   The auditor's statement accompanying the financial statements, indicating the extent of the audit and giving an evaluation of the adequacy and fairness of the financial statements in conformance with *GAAP*.

**Authoritarian management** (11)   An attitude or approach to managing people that assumes that responsibility can rest only with the superior or supervisor and that tends to centralize decision making. Consistent with McGregor's **Theory X.**

**Authorized budget** (15)   A budget that has been formally approved by the appropriate governing body. In government, represents an authority and upper limit for expenditure. Also known in government as an *appropriation.*

**Authorized stock**   The maximum number of shares of stock that a corporation may issue without obtaining further authorization from the state in which it is incorporated.

**Average collection period** (14)   *See* **Average days' receivables.**

**Average cost (inventory)** (AD)   One of several possible *inventory cost-flow assumptions.* Weighted average cost assumes that the cost of items shipped represented a proportional sample of the cost of all items available for sale. Ending inventory and cost of goods sold are priced at the same average cost per unit under this method. The average cost per unit is calculated by taking the sum of the products of [quantity times cost] for beginning inventory and net purchases, and then dividing by the quantity of items available for sale.

**Average days' receivables** (A2)   A measure of the average time necessary to collect *accounts receivable.* Calculated by dividing *receivables turnover* into 365.

**Average days' sales in inventory** (A2)   A measure of inventory turnover, or the average amount of inventory on hand in terms of sales. Calculated by dividing *inventory turnover* into 365.

**Avoidable costs** (5)   Those identifiable and measurable variable and fixed costs that, in the context of a specific decision alternative, may be saved. Also known as *escapable costs.*

**Bad debt**   An account receivable that is not deemed collectible.

**Bad-debt expense**   The sum of all accounts receivable determined to be uncollectible during the year, plus an allowance for still-active receivables at year-end expected to become uncollectible.

**Balance sheet** (AD)   The financial statement reporting assets and equities as of a specific date. Also known as a Statement of Financial Position.

**"Basket-purchase"**   The acquisition of a group of assets for a single price where the cost must be allocated to different members of the group for accounting purposes

**Beginning inventory**   The amount of inventory on hand at the start of the accounting period.

**Betterment**   An improvement to a capacity asset which is properly capitalized as an additional asset.

**Bin minimum** (4)   An informal system of unit inventory control wherein an item's recorder quantity is physically separated in the storage area in lieu of maintaining a stock record. Reorder activity is initiated when items from the reorder quantity stock are first used. Often used for low-cost items or for Group C items under *ABC inventory control*. Also known as *physical minimum*.

**Board of directors**   A group of individuals elected by the voting stockholders of a corporation to govern the company.

**Bond**   A negotiable certificate as evidence of debt.

**Bond conversion**   *See* **Debt conversion**.

**Bond discount**   A *contra-account* representing the amount of interest capitalized into the face value of a bond and not yet earned/owed.

**Bond premium**   An account representing the amount of cash given by the bond buyer in excess of face value for the privilege of receiving greater-"normal" future interest payments.

**Bond sinking fund**   *See* **Sinking fund**.

**Bonds payable** (AD)   A *liability* reporting the face value of outstanding bond indebtedness.

**Book value** (AD)   The amount recorded in the firm's accounts. For particular assets and liabilities, refers to the item **net** of valuation accounts. For common stock, refers to share of total assets not claimed by creditors and preferred stockholders. For the firm as a whole, equals net assets (total assets **minus** total liabilities).

**Book value of common stock** (A2)   The amount of assets not claimed by creditors or preferred stockholders—common shareholders' equity. *See* **Book value per share**.

**Book value per share** (of common stock) (A2)   Total stockholders' equity less preferred claims, divided by number of common shares outstanding.

**"Booked"**   Slang for "recorded in the firm's accounts."

**Borderline cases (organizations)** (15)   Term used to describe nonprofit organizations such as hospitals or government utilities wherein the budgeting, control, and accounting systems closely parallel those used by business firms.

**"Bottom line"**   Commonly used term referring to reported net income, the bottom line of the income statement.

**Breakeven**   *See* **Breakeven sales volume**.

**Breakeven analysis**   *See* **Contribution analysis**.

**Breakeven chart** (6)   A graph relating dollars of revenue or cost (Y-axis) to volume of activity (X-axis). Includes lines representing total costs and total revenues, with their intersection representing the *breakeven sales volume*. Also known as a cost–volume–profit (**CVP**) graph.

**Breakeven sales volume (BSV)** (6)   The volume of sales that will result in exactly zero net income for the firm. The activity level where the contribution equals the fixed costs. May be expressed in dollars or units.

**Breakeven sensitivity** (6)   The process of analyzing the effect upon a firm's *breakeven sales volume* of changes in relevant factors such as price, product mix, variable costs, and fixed costs.

**BSV**   *See* **Breakeven sales volume.**

**Budget** (2)   A plan for a firm or segment thereof, expressing in financial terms the expected results of future operations or activities. In government, a legal expenditure ceiling for a fiscal period.

**Budget variance** (2)   A difference between an actual cost or revenue and a budgeted amount. Not incorporated in product cost accounting. Contrast with **Accounting variance.** *See also* **Volume variance** *and* **Spending variance.**

**Budgetary slack** (11)   The difference between a budgeted amount and the amount that can be reasonably expected to occur. May be perceived as desirable safety factor by individual responsibility-center manager but is generally undesirable for the firm because of cumulative distorting effect upon overall master budget.

**Budgetary control** (11)   Control over a firm or responsibility center using *budgets* as a basis for performance evaluation.

**Budgeting** (2)   The process of planning expected revenues and costs for a particular firm or responsibility center for a particular period. In government, refers to planning expenditure ceilings for the forthcoming fiscal period. *See also* **Short-range planning.**

**Budgeting rate** (5)   The amount of variable cost per unit of activity and/or the amount of fixed cost for a particular expenditure category that may be expected within a *relevant range*. Used, together with a given activity level, to determine a total budgeted amount. Particularly applicable to *variable budgeting.*

**Business combination** (AD)   The joining of two previously separate firms into a single accounting entity, whether by consolidation or statutory merger. Will be accounted for by following either the pooling or the purchase method.

**Business entities**   *See* **Entity.**

**Business firm**   A privately owned organization existing to provide products and/or services to customers and to earn a profit in so doing. May be legally constituted as a proprietorship, partnership, or corporation.

**By-product**   A *joint product* that has such a small value in relation to its other joint product(s) that it is allocated or assigned a cost of zero at the *split-off point.*

**Call premium**   The amount of excess over par which a firm will pay if it elects to retire debt before maturity.

**Callable bonds**   Bonds that may be called (or *retired*) in advance of maturity.

**Capacity assets**   *See* **Fixed assets.**

**Capacity variance**   *See* **Overhead volume variance.**

**Capital budget** (2)   The plan for capital asset acquisitions and dispositions during the forthcoming period. May take the form of the budgeted SCFP.

**Capital budgeting committee** (8)   Those managers designated as responsible for accepting or rejecting capital budgeting (investment) proposals on behalf of the firm within the constraints of available financing.

**Capital budgeting** (2, 8)   Refers to the process of evaluating, selecting, and scheduling acquisition of long-term assets, and of planning the financing of such acquisitions.

**Capital budgeting decisions** (8)   The choices to accept or reject investment proposals or to make alternative choices among mutually exclusive proposals. May also include choices as to means of financing desired acquisitions.

**Capital capacity** (8)   The practical or chosen limit to available resources for use in asset acquisitions during a given period. Acts as a constraint upon the number of otherwise acceptable capital budgeting proposals that may be funded. May necessitate *capital rationing.*

**Capital charge** (14)   A charge allocated/assigned to an *investment center* representing the desired income (rate of return) that the center should earn on its assets employed. *See also* **Residual income.**

**Capital costs** (15)   Costs associated with the ownership of fixed assets. Usually refers to the difference between acquisition and disposition costs that is reported as depreciation expense in business accounting, but may also include interest costs on debt used to finance the asset(s).

**Capital invested**   Refers to resources (assets) invested in a firm by creditors and owners.

**Capital lease** (A8)   A lease which, in substance, is effectively a purchase with 100-percent financing. Leases which qualify as capital leases under specific FASB criteria are capitalized and shown as fixed assets and as debt.

**Capital-lease obligations** (A8)   A *liability.* The *present value* of remaining obligations under leases qualifying as capital leases. Capital-lease obligations may be both current and noncurrent.

**Capital markets** (A10)   Refers to various markets to which a firm may turn to raise additional invested capital. Examples would be the bond markets and the stock markets.

**Capital rationing** (8)   The process of assigning priorities and selecting among acceptable capital budgeting proposals a limited number for funding in a circumstance of limited funds or *capital capacity.*

**Capital stock** (AD)   The ownership shares of a corporation.

**Capital structure** (A10)   The composition of a firm's *equities.* The mix of current debt, noncurrent debt, and owners' equity.

**Capital surplus**   An inferior term for *paid-in capital.*

**Capitalize**   To record the effect of an *expenditure* as an asset rather than as an *expense.*

**Capitalized interest**   Interest incorporated into the face value of a debt instrument (note or bond).

**CASB**   Cost Accounting Standards Board.

**Cash** (AD)   Currency, checks, and bank-account balances.

**Cash-basis (accounting)** (AD)   Income measured on the basis of cash revenues received less cash expenditures occurring in the same period.

**Cash budget** (2)   A plan detailing for forthcoming periods all expected cash receipts from all sources and all expected cash disbursements for all purposes, together with resultant cash balances.

**Cash budgeting** (9)   *See* **Cash management.**

**Cash discount**   A reduction in sales or purchase price provided for prompt payment.

**Cash from operations** (9)   The amount of cash generated from ordinary business revenues, less expenses for the period, and including any changes within net working capital involving cash flows.

**Cash funds-flow statement** (A9)   *See* **Statement of cash flow.**

**Cash management** (9)   The planning and control of cash receipts and disbursements within the firm. The objective is to avoid cash shortage and to temporarily invest excess cash.

**Cash sales**   Sales to customers for cash. Customer pays cash at time of purchase.

**Certified financial statements** (AD)   Statements which are accompanied by an independent auditor's (CPA's) certificate or opinion.

**Change in accounting method**   *See* **Accounting method.**

**Change of accounting estimate**   *See* **Accounting estimate.**

**Charge** (AE)   Generally used to mean purchase on account. In accounting, also used synonymously with *debit.*

**Close/closing** (accounts) (AE)   The process, at year end, of transferring the balance in all *nominal* or *temporary accounts* to the real or permanent balance-sheet accounts. For example, all revenue, gain, expense, and loss accounts at year-end are closed to retained earnings (owner's capital).

**CMA**   Certificate in Management Accounting awarded by the National Association of Accountants.

**Coefficient of variation** (17)   For decision making under uncertainty, a commonly used measure of the relative dispersion of the underlying probability distribution. Determined by dividing the distribution's standard deviation by the expected value of all outcomes. A high coefficient of variation would indicate a greater chance that actual values may differ significantly from expected values.

**Collection of receivable** (9)   The receipt of cash in partial or full settlement of a claim that is evidenced by a receivable.

**Committed costs** (5)   Those costs that have been set by management action or contract in prior periods and therefore are not avoidable in the current period.

**Common book value** (stock) (A2)   *See* **Book value.**

**Common cost**   *See* **Joint cost.**

**Common stock** (AD)   Shares in a corporation, usually voting shares, and representing a residual claim against assets after settlement of creditors' and preferred stockholders' prior claims.

**Comparative analysis**   In financial-statement analysis, the comparison of one firm's statements with those of other firms or with industry norms.

**Completed-contract method**   Refers to the timing of revenue and expense recognition for a particular job order. Under completed-contract recognition, revenues and expenses are normally included in income determination only after the job is finished. Alternative to *percentage completion* method.

**Compound entry** (AE)   A *journal entry* affecting more than two accounts concurrently.

**Compound interest**   Interest based on principal and accumulated prior-period interest.

**Comptroller**   *See* **Controller.**

**Conglomerate**   A *parent corporation* with subsidiaries in different and dissimilar lines of business.

**Congruence** (2)   As used in the context of the objectives or goals of a firm, refers to agreements, conformity, or harmony among the goals of the firm and those of its employees.

**Conservatism** (AD)   A measurement principle under GAAP, wherein expenses and losses are recognized and reported when incurred or expected, but revenues and gains are not recognized and reported until they are realized or earned.

**Consignment**   Refers to inventory transferred from the owner (consignor) to another (consignee) for sale to third parties.

**Consistency** (AE)   A measurement principle under GAAP providing for continued use by a firm of the same accounting method or procedure once adopted. Consistency requires that changes in accounting method be infrequent and be justified by changing circumstances.

**Consolidated financial statements** (AD)   Statements prepared for an economic entity comprised of several legal entities—a *parent* and its *subsidiaries.*

**Constraint equations, or constraint inequalities** (17)   Those equations or inequalities included in a *linear programming model* that express the feasible limits to possible alternative solutions based upon physical, resource, or demand limitations.

**Contingent liability**   A potential liability, such as a pending lawsuit, which is dependent upon a future event (an adverse judgment being rendered) before becoming definite.

**Contra**   Opposite to, offsetting, subtracting. *See* **Contra-account.**

**Contra-account**   Any *valuation account* whose balance is subtracted from another account on the balance sheet. Examples include allowance for uncollectibles, accumulated depreciation, and receivables discount or bond discount.

**Contra-asset** (AE)   A negative *valuation account* related to an asset account.

**Contributed capital** (AE)   The amount of capital permanently invested or contributed by the owners. Normally, the sum of *capital stock* and *paid-in capital* accounts.

**Contribution** (6)   The amount remaining after all variable costs are subtracted from revenue. The portion of revenue available to contribute toward fixed costs and profit.

**Contribution analysis** (6)   The process of evaluating problems in terms of revenue, variable costs, contribution, fixed cost, and income components. Evaluating alternatives in terms of the contribution of each component. Also known as *breakeven analysis* or *CVP analysis.*

**Contribution format (income statement)** (6)   An acceptable alternative for classifying information in a firm's or segment's income statement where revenues are first followed by only variable costs and a subtotal is calculated for *contribution.* Fixed costs are shown below contribution in arriving at income.

**Contribution margin**   *See* **Contribution per unit.**

**Contribution mix variance** (14)   A measure of the variance between budgeted and actual contribution attributable solely to changes in sales volume (selling prices and variable costs are assumed constant). Calculated by taking the difference between actual and budgeted unit sales and multiplying by budgeted unit contribution for each product and then summing the mix variance for all products. Taken together with the *sales price variance*, it measures/explains the total *expected contribution variance*.

**Contribution per unit** (6)   The difference between sales price and variable cost for one specific product or service. Also referred to as *contribution margin*.

**Contribution percentage** (6)   The proportion of sales revenue representing contribution, expressed as a percentage. The complement of total variable costs as a percent of sales.

**Control account** (AE)   An account in the general ledger that shows the sum of the balances in individual *subsidiary accounts* kept in a *subsidiary ledger*.

**Control chart** (11)   A device for or approach to analyzing variances wherein specific variances are plotted/evaluated as being within or beyond control limits. Control limits are established in terms of standard deviations or data representing the process. Variances within control limits are considered random and not meriting investigation or subject to corrective action. Variances beyond limits are deemed controllable and requiring investigation.

**Control cycle** (11)   The repeated cycle in the control process involving planning, evaluating results, and taking appropriate corrective action.

**Controllable costs** (5)   Those costs over which a manager has significant influence. Controllable costs exclude those over which the particular manager has little or no influence, such as committed costs or costs that are under the control of senior executives.

**Controller** (2)   The title often used for the officer responsible for all accounting and sometimes all information-systems activities within a firm.

**Conversion costs** (1)   For a manufacturer, those costs involved in converting raw materials to finished goods. Conversion costs normally include direct labor and manufacturing overhead.

**Conversion index** (16)   An index constructed from two representative prices, used to adjust groups of assets for changing price levels or replacement costs.

**Convertible debenture**   A *bond* that may be exchanged by the bondholder for a given number of shares of capital stock.

**Corporation**   A legal entity authorized by a state to conduct business or perform some other function.

**Cost** (5)   The amount paid, or to be paid, for the acquisition of goods or services. Also the amount of cost allocated by accountants to a particular product, service, or activity.

**Cost accounting** (1)   The activity encompassing the recording, classifying, allocating, summarizing, and reporting of costs as incurred. Cost accounting contributes data to both financial accounting and managerial accounting. Contrast with **Financial accounting** and **Managerial accounting.**

**Cost allocation**   The process of spreading a *common cost* over several products, cost centers, or accounting periods. *See also* **Joint costs.**

**Cost of capital** (6)   The average rate of return a firm should earn on its assets and pay on its equities. A composite (usually calculated as a weighted average) of the interest rate required by creditors and the earnings rate required by owners.

**Cost center**   An organizational subset or activity for which expenses or expenditures are accumulated and reported. May be the same as an *expenditure* or *expense center* for budgeting and control, or may exist for a different activity.

**Cost expiration** (AD)   The recognition by accountants of a decline in future usefulness or eventual recoverable value of an asset. *See* **Amortization, Depreciation,** and **Depletion.**

**Cost of goods sold** (1)   The cost of *inventory* that has been sold to customers or that has otherwise disappeared—inventory expense.

**Cost or market, whichever is lower**   *See* **LOCM.**

**Cost method** (for investments)   The measurement normally applied to all investments except for voting common stock representing more than 20 percent of outstanding shares. The investment is carried at acquisition cost, and revenue is recognized only when received or receivable—interest earned or dividends declared. Alternative to *equity method.*

**Cost principle**   The measurement principle under GAAP which requires assets to be reported at *adjusted original cost.*

**Cost of sales**   *See* **Cost of goods sold.**

**CPA** (AD)   Certified Public Accountant.

**CPM** (17)   Critical path method. A deterministic network approach to scheduling and controlling activities/projects involving multiple operations, wherein single-point estimates of required lead times are employed. May incorporate trade-offs between resources employed and time required. *See also* **Critical path, Network analysis,** *and* **PERT.**

**CR** (or **Cr**) (AE)   Abbreviation for **Credit.**

**Credit** (AE)   In general business usage, refers to the privilege of purchasing or borrowing, with payment or repayment at a later date. In accounting, refers to the right side of an account or to record an amount on the right side of an account.

**Credit policy** (3)   A firm's policy concerning the amount and duration of credit extension to existing and potential customers, including discount and interest terms. When used appropriately, it is an effective tool of sales promotion.

**Credit sales**   Sales to customers on account.

**Creditor**   Someone who has a legal claim against the firm's assets resulting from supplying the firm with goods or services, lending funds, or some other commitment (customer claim for warranty, government claim for taxes, plaintiff claim for legally awarded judgment, or stockholder claim for dividends previously declared).

**Creeping change problem** (13)   In the context of maintenance of work-measurement standards, refers to a succession of minor improvements in efficiency that individually do not merit standard revision and that cumulatively result in inappropriate slack or looseness in the standard.

**Critical path** (17)   In *network analysis*, the particular series of sequential operations (connecting the first and last operations) that cumulatively has the longest total lead time as compared to any other series/sequence/path.

**Current assets** (AD)   Cash and any other assets that are expected to be converted into cash or consumed within a year or within the firm's normal *operating cycle*.

**Current marketable securities**   *See* **Marketable securities.**

**Current capital-lease obligations** (AD)   The *present value* of amounts owed within one year under leases qualifying as capital leases.

**Current liabilities** (AD)   Those liabilities that are payable within one year or the firm's normal *operating cycle*, and which will require *current assets* in settlement.

**Current ratio** (A2)   Total *current assets* divided by total *current liabilities*.

**CVD**   *See* **Convertible debenture.**

**CVP analysis** (6)   *See* **Contribution analysis.**

**DDB** (AD)   *See* **Double-declining-balance depreciation.**

**Debenture**   A bond that is not secured by a prior claim against specific assets or income.

**Debt** (AE)   Refers to the left side of an *account*, or to the recording of an amount on the left side of an account.

**Debt**   Any money owed.

**Debt conversion**   The exchange of a creditor claim for an ownership claim. Usually the result of bondholders exchanging their convertible bonds for stock.

**Debt ratio** (A2)   Total *liabilities* divided by total *equities*. Often referred to as the debt-equity ratio.

**Debt refinancing**   Arranging for the exchange of new debt for existing debt, with the new debt usually having a later maturity. In the case of bonds, may be called a *refunding*.

**Decentralization** (14)   The situation in a particular firm where a significant degree of authority over decisions has been delegated by top management to the managers of segments of the business.

**Decision tree** (17)   A diagram useful for indicating alternative courses of action, outcomes, their probabilities, and their expected values.

**Declining-balance depreciation** (AD)   A method of calculating depreciation or amortization by applying a constant percentage to the declining *book value* in successive periods.

**Deferral**   The carrying forward to a subsequent period of appropriate matching purposes of any item which will ultimately be recognized as *revenue* or *expense*.

**Deferred charges** (AD)   A *noncurrent asset. Expenditures* capitalized as assets to be amortized over future years. Similar to *prepaid items* but having a useful life beyond that which would qualify for current classification.

**Deferred income tax** (AD)   A liability (or asset) of indeterminate term (and, possibly, amount) representing taxes postponed (or paid in advance) through timing differences resulting from the use of different income accounting methods in tax returns and financial statements.

**Deferred method**   One of the methods acceptable for accounting for the *investment tax credit*. Following the deferred method, the tax savings are taken as a reduction of fixed asset cost. The benefit is thus deferred and picked up in higher income over the asset's useful life through lower depreciation charges.

**Deferred revenue** (AD)   A *liability* representing advances from customers. *See* **Revenue collected in advance,** *and* **Unearned revenue.**

**Deficit**   Negative *retained earnings* shown as contra to stockholders' equity.

**Demand curve** (3)   A curve or line connecting various combinations of specific prices (*Y*-axis) and expected sales volumes (*X*-axis) for a firm's product(s). Usually slopes downwards to the right, indicating higher customer demand at lower prices.

**Dependent (behavior)** (11)   Individual behavior characterized by unwillingness to accept responsibility and a desire to be led by authority. Childlike behavior. Consistent with McGregor's **Theory X** assumptions.

**Depletion** (AD)   The *amortization* reflecting use of wasting assets—natural resources such as oil, minerals, and timber.

**Depreciable asset**   A *tangible noncurrent asset* subject to expiration of usefulness and therefore requiring *depreciation*. Sometimes used to refer also to *intangible assets* requiring *amortization*.

**Depreciable base** (cost)    The cost of a tangible fixed asset to be depreciated over the asset's useful life—the cost less estimated salvage value.

**Depreciate/depreciation** (AD)    The *amortization* of *tangible fixed assets* to allocate cost expiration over their useful life.

**Deterministic** (17)    Certain or assumed to be certain. Characterized by single-point estimate of probable outcome.

**Differential cost analysis** (8)    An approach to analyzing business decisions between two alternatives under which only the incremental investment, revenue, and cost differences are considered.

**Dilution**    The actual or potential reduction in proportionate voting rights or share of earnings for a common stockholder, resulting from the issuance by a corporation of additional shares of stock.

**Direct cost** (1)    A cost that the accountant determines appropriate to be treated as direct (to identify and accumulate with respect to a particular material or product). Usually applies to direct material, direct labor, and certain variable overhead items.

**Direct costing** (6)    A costing alternative that includes only direct material, direct labor, and direct or variable manufacturing overhead in product cost. Indirect or fixed overhead is then treated as a period cost. Also called variable costing. Alternative to *full (absorption) costing* and to *relevant costing*. Direct costing is not acceptable under GAAP or to the IRS but is often useful in managerial analysis.

**Direct labor** (1)    Cost of labor identifiable with and assigned to production cost of specific product(s). Contrast with **Indirect labor.**

**Direct labor budget** (2)    The plan, usually by department, of expected costs of direct labor in forthcoming periods.

**Direct material** (1)    Cost of raw material identified with and assigned to production cost of specific product(s). Contrast with **Indirect materials (supplies).**

**Disbursement**    A payment or distribution of cash in currency or by check.

**Discontinued operations**    Activities or segments of a business which are being phased out. Revenues, gains, expenses, and losses related to discontinued operations are required by GAAP to be classified on the income statement, together with *extraordinary items* following *income from operations.*

**Discount**    When referring to purchases or sales, applies to amount of price reduction granted for prompt payment. When referring to receivables and payables, applies to interest (stated or imputed) that is included in the face value but has not yet been earned—the difference between an item's face value and its *present value.*

**Discount on notes receivable**    A *contra asset* representing interest capitalized into the face amount of the receivable but not yet earned.

**Discount on payables**   A *contra liability* representing interest capitalized into the face amount of the liability but not yet owed.

**Discount on purchases or sales**   A price reduction granted for prompt payment.

**Discount rate** (A7)   The interest rate assumed in the calculation of *discounted present value.*

**Discount rate**   The interest rate being used to convert future cash flows to *present values.*

**Discounted present value** (A7)   The value today of a future stream of cash flows with the assumed interest cost or benefit eliminated.

**Discounting a receivable**   The practice of borrowing funds in exchange for a receivable or with the receivable essentially serving as collateral for the loan.

**Discretionary costs** (5)   See **Programmed costs.**

**Discretionary resource exchanges** (A9)   A term used to apply to flows of resources into and out of a firm which occur as a result of management decisions. Discretionary resource exchanges are reported on the SCFP. Resource losses and expirations not resulting from discretionary action are not reported on the SCFP.

**Distributable income** (16)   The portion of realized (accounting) income that may be withdrawn by owners (assuming adequate liquidity) without impairing the firm's capacity to continue its present activities indefinitely at its present level of operations. Information that is readily available under *replacement cost accounting.*

**Distributable income** (16)   The amount of current income which, assuming adequate solvency, could be withdrawn by owners while still maintaining the firm's capital as variously defined.

**Dividend** (AD)   A distribution of income to corporate stockholders.

**Dividends per share**   The amount of dividends accruing to the benefit of the holder of a single share of the firm's currently outstanding stock.

**Donated capital**   Assets or claims against assets which are given or bequeathed to a corporation by an individual(s) or firm retaining no claim. Reflected as part of a corporation's *contributed capital.*

**Double-declining-balance depreciation** (AD)   A method of calculating depreciation or amortization using the declining-balance approach and using a fixed percentage equivalent to twice the straight-line percentage (the percentage that would be used following straight-line depreciation).

**Double entry** (AE)   Any bookkeeping system where transactions and adjustments are recorded in such a way as to constantly maintain the balance equality.

**DR** (or **Dr**) (AE)   Abbreviations for **Debit.**

**Drawing account**    A *nominal* or *temporary account* used in *partnerships* and *proprietorships* to record individual owner withdrawals during the year (period).

**Drawings**    Assets withdrawn by an owner during the year.

**Dual-column statements**    Financial statements prepared showing two measurements for the same items. For example, statements prepared on an historical-cost (GAAP) basis and also on a current-cost basis could disclose the two measurements in two adjoining colunms. Suggested as a means to facilitate changeover to a new measurement system if and when adopted.

**Dysfunctional behavior** (A14)    Behavior by managers or employees that, for any reason, is not consistent with the long-run economic objectives of the firm. Behavior that is not *goal-congruent*.

**Early debt retirement**    The repayment or other extinguishment of debt prior to scheduled maturity.

**Earned surplus**    An archaic and now improper term for *retained earnings*.

**Earnings.**    *See* **Income.**

**Earnings multiple**    Stock prices are often expressed as a multiple of earnings per share; for example, "The XYZ Company is selling at ten times earnings."

**Earnings per share** (common stock) (A2)    Net income available for common stockholders (net income minus preferred dividend) divided by the average number of common shares outstanding.

**EBIT** (A2)    Earnings before interest and taxes. Used as the best earnings measure for calculating earnings on average assets employed. In use, means earnings before interest, taxes, and any extraordinary or discontinued-operation items.

**Economic income** (16)    A measure of a firm's income (not currently reported under GAAP) that reflects all changes in well-offness including both realized income and any unrealized holding gains and losses as measured by current costs. Information readily available under *replacement cost accounting*.

**Economic life**    *See* **Useful life.**

**Economic lot size** (manufacturing) (4)    The optimal order quantity to schedule for production. Directly analogous to *economic order quantity* for purchases. *See* **Economic order quantity.**

**Economic order quantity** (purchasing) (4)    The optimal quantity of merchandise or material to order when actual or projected stock falls below the *reorder point*. The optimal trade-off between reordering (setup) costs and inventory-carrying costs including obsolescence. Calculated as $\sqrt{2SU/RC}$, where

$S =$ Cost of ordering or scheduling and set up,

$U =$ Annual usage (demand) quantity,

$R =$ Annual inventory-carrying cost rate (space, obsolescence, and interest), and

$C =$ Item's direct (variable) cost.

See also **Inventory carrying cost** and **Setup cost.**

**Effective (performance)** (11)   Effective performance is that which accomplishes the goals of the firm or segment but not necessarily in an economically *efficient* manner. Contrast with **Dysfunctional behavior.** See also **Efficient (performance).**

**Efficiency variance**   See both **Labor efficiency variance** and **Overhead efficiency variance.**

**Efficient (performance)** (11)   Efficient performance is that which maximizes results obtained from the resources expended regardless of whether the result achieved met or was congruent with the goals of the firm or segment.

**Efficient market hypothesis**   The supposition that market prices of securities react immediately and objectively to new information and that, at all times, they incorporate (reflect) all available information.

**Eliminations in consolidation** (AD)   As part of the preparation of *consolidated financial statements,* the amounts which are subtracted in the consolidated working papers from combined-statement totals. Eliminations are made to avoid duplication and to eliminate claims and transactions within the "consolidated family."

**ELS**   See **Economic lot size.**

**Encumbrance** (A15)   A commitment to expend funds, such as would result from issuing a purchase order. Recorded at the time of commitment under the fund accounting system but excluded from financial accounting while executory. In the federal government it is known as an "obligation."

**Ending inventory**   The amount of inventory on hand at the end of the year (period) which will be carried forward on the balance sheet to the following year.

**Engineered cost**   See **Ratable cost.**

**Entity**   The economic organization or business unit being reported upon in the financial statement. May correspond to a legal entity in the case of a corporation, or represent an artificial legal entity in the cases of segments, proprietorships, partnerships, and consolidations.

**Entry**   An instruction to change the balances in two or more accounts to reflect the effect of a transaction or adjustment. See **Journal entry.**

**EOQ**   See **Economic order quantity.**

**EPS** (A2)   See **Earnings per share.**

**Equities** (AD)    Claims against or sources of assets. The sum of all *liabilities* and *owners equity* on a *balance sheet*.

**Equity method** (investments)    A measurement principle required under GAAP for common-stock investments where the stock held (more than 20 percent) represents significant influence over the other firm. Following the equity method, the investor records, as an increase to investments and as revenue, its proportionate share of the investee's earnings each year. Any dividends are then treated as a collection of "future dividends receivable included in investments." Alternative to *cost method.*

**Equivalent units** (1)    As used in *process costing,* the number of units of completed product that could have been produced with the same product costs as were incurred during the period. Sometimes referred to as *equivalent production.*

**ERISA**    The federal law setting pension-plan requirements; identified as the Employee Retirement Income Security Act.

**Escapable costs** (5)    *See* **Avoidable costs.**

**Estimated liabilities** (AD)    Those liabilities where the precise amount and/or the specific creditor may not be known with certainty, but where the liability is not contingent. Examples would be accruals of service costs and estimated warranty repair or replacement costs.

**Estimated probabilities** (17)    Probabilities comprising a *probability distribution* that have been estimated based upon experience or intuition rather than derived formally from past data or sampling. Often useful when more formally derived probabilities are unavailable. Also known as *subjective probabilities.*

**Estimated warranty costs** (AD)    *See* **Estimated liabilities.**

**Events** (17)    In the context of statistical decision models, all those future occurrences that might take place that are beyond the direct control of the decision maker, are the situations about which the decision maker is uncertain, are mutually exclusive and exhaustive, and are capable of being assigned probabilities. Also known as *states of nature.*

**Excess present value**    In the context of *capital budgeting* decisions, the difference between the *present values* of anticipated cash inflows and outflows. Also known as *net present value* or *NPV.*

**Excess present value index** (8)    Used in *capital rationing,* the NPV of future cash flows divided by the initial cash investment.

**Executory agreement**    An agreement where neither party has completed any (or some portion) of intended performance, and therefore no claim arising out of past performance exists.

**Exogenous**    Outside of or resulting from occurrences beyond the control of the firm.

**Expected contribution variance** (14)    The difference between the variable budgeted contribution and the originally budgeted (fixed budget) contribution. Can be thought of as a volume variance for budgeted contribution.

**Expected standard** (13)   A standard of work measurement established on the basis of those inputs required at an average (as distinct from ideal, attainable, or historical) level of performance.

**Expected value** (17)   The mean or average of a probability distribution or of other data. In the context of statistical decision theory, refers to the product of each distinct payoff for a particular action times its individual probability of occurrence, summed. Often a decision rule is stated as, "Choose the action with the highest expected value."

**Expenditure**   As distinct from an *expense,* an expenditure always involves the outflow of cash or the incurrence of a liability. An expenditure results in either an asset or an expense. May be used in a narrower sense to apply only to cash outflow.

**Expenditure** (5)   The disbursement of cash to obtain goods or services.

**Expenditure center** (11)   A *responsibility center* wherein the primary controllable items are expenditures even though incidental revenue items may also exist and be controllable. Where cost expirations such as depreciation are also included, it is known as an *expense center.* Contrast with **Revenue center, Profit center, Investment center,** and **Cost center.**

**Expense** (5, AD)   Any reduction in *net assets* (total assets minus total liabilities) not involving a distribution to owners. The use, expiration, or loss of an asset, or the incurrence of a liability, not matched by a new reportable asset. Unusual expenses are often referred to as losses.

**Expense center** (11)   A responsibility center wherein the primary controllable items are expenses even though incidental revenue items may also exist and be controllable. Contrast with **Cost center, Expenditure center, Revenue center, Profit center,** and **Investment center.**

**Explode** (requirements( (4)   To extend the component or material requirements for a particular product by the number of products required, in order to establish total requirements for the components or materials.

**External** (outside) **source** (funds) (A9)   A place or group from which a firm might obtain additional invested working capital or other resources. The two external sources are long-term creditors and owners (stockholders).

**External sources** (of additional cash) (9)   Potential suppliers of cash to the firm including creditors and owners. Contrast with **Internal sources.**

**Externalities** (15)   In the context of cost/benefit analysis, indirect social benefits or social costs representing both measurable and nonmeasurable opportunity cost savings and opportunity costs.

**Extraordinary items**   An *expense* (loss) or *revenue* (gain) which is characterized as being both unusual in nature for the particular business and also not expected to recur in the foreseeable future. Extraordinary items are classified on the income statement following *income from operations.*

**Face value**    The stated amount due at *maturity* on a bond or note exclusive of any separately stated interest.

**Fair market value**    A price or cost arrived at in an arm's-length transaction or exchange, where both parties may be assumed to be acting in their rational self-interest.

**FASB** (AD)    Financial Accounting Standards Board.

**Favorable variance** (11)    For revenue items, an excess of actual revenue over budgeted revenue. For expense or expenditure items, an excess of budgeted costs over actual costs incurred. In both cases, where a variance leads to greater income than budgeted it is designated as favorable.

**Feasible alternative** (17)    In the context of *linear-programming* analysis, an alternative or option that satisfies all practical constraints. One that, in a practical sense, is a viable alternative for consideration.

**FICA**    Federal Insurance Contributions Act. FICA employee and employer taxes are more commonly known as "Social Security."

**FIFO** (AD)    First-in, first-out. One of several possible *inventory cost-flow assumptions*. FIFO assumes that earliest costs apply to inventory sold (cost of goods sold) and most recent costs apply to ending inventory on hand.

**Final cash budget** (9)    A *cash budget* that incorporates all expected cash inflows and outflows including arrangements for short- and long-term financing and plans for temporary investment of excess cash. Contrast with **Preliminary cash budget.**

**Financial accounting** (AD)    The accounting system for reporting a firm's financial position, income, and changes in financial position to outside investors and other interested parties. GAAP applies to financial accounting. Contrast with **Cost accounting** and **Managerial accounting.**

**Financial activities** (A2, A10)    Those activities of the firm primarily involved in the raising of new capital and the acquisition of noncurrent assets. Used to distinguish certain events from those involved in short-term operations of the business.

**Financial budget** (2)    The budget indicating all planned changes with respect to long-term debt, any planned additional owner investment, and all planned dividends. May take the form of a budgeted SCFP.

**Financial leverage** (A10)    Refers to the degree to which the firm is *trading on equity;* that is, the degree to which the firm is using "less costly" creditor and preferred stockholder-invested capital to generate earnings for the benefit of the common stockholder.

**Financial management** (2)    The management of *financial activities* as distinguished from operations (*operating management*) and tax liabilities (*tax management*).

**Financial position**    The condition of the firm at any one point in time expressed in financial terms as a statement of assets and equities in a balance sheet.

**Financial statements** (AD)   Those accounting reports required by GAAP—the *balance sheet*, the *income statement*, the *SCFP*, the *statement of retained earnings* (owner's capital), and the necessary footnotes thereto.

**Financial structure,**   *See* **Capital structure.**

**Financing activities**   *See* **Financial activities.**

**Financing lease**   *See* **Capital lease.**

**Finished goods** (1)   An *inventory account* for a *manufacturer* representing the cost of products completed and ready for sale.

**First-in, first-out**   *See* **FIFO.**

**Fiscal year**   A twelve-month reporting period for a firm. May or may not correspond to the calendar year.

**Fixed assets** (AD)   *Noncurrent assets* including such items as land, natural resources, buildings, machinery, equipment, office furniture and fixtures, and property held under capital lease.

**Fixed budget** (12)   A plan incorporating specific revenue and expenditures with no allowance for actual activity levels different from those originally anticipated. Also known as an *original budget*. Contrast with **Flexible budget.**

**Fixed cost** (5)   An expense or expenditure that does not or is not expected to vary during the planning period with different levels of activity within the *relevant range*. See also **Programmed costs, Committed costs,** and **Standby costs.**

**Flexible budget** (12)   A plan that incorporates specific revenue and expenditures with allowance for different activity levels that have been or may be experienced. Also known as a *revised budget* as distinct from an *original budget*. Contrast with **Fixed budget.**

**Flow of costs** (1)   The manner in which various costs are accumulated and transferred or allocated to and through the various cost classifications within the firm.

**Flow of working capital** (A9)   A change in the balance of *net working capital*.

**Flow-through method**   One method of accounting for the *investment tax credit*, which reports all benefits of the credit in the year such benefifits are realized.

**Follow-up audits** (8)   The review of actual costs incurred and actual benefits derived relating to implemented capital budgeting projects, for comparison with planned flows at the time the proposal was accepted.

**Foreign operations**   Operations of a firm or of (one of its) subsidiaries conducted outside of the United States. If foreign operations are significant, certain supplementary information concerning same must be disclosed along with the financial statements.

**Franchise**   A legal right or privilege to use a name or to sell certain brand products or services.

**Freight-in**   *See* **Transportation-in.**

**Freight-out**   The cost of shipping inventory to customers as part of a sale. Freight-out is treated as a period cost (selling expense) as incurred.

**Full costing** (1)   The method of determining product cost that includes all variable and fixed manufacturing costs (material, labor, and overhead), both direct and indirect. Required by GAAP. Contrast with **Direct costing** and with **Relevant costing.**

**Full disclosure**   A GAAP requirement that all material and relevant information to the investor concerning the firm be included in the financial statements or footnotes thereto.

**Full-acquisition cost**   A term used to reflect the GAAP initial measurement basis for assets. All normal costs of acquisition, except for any interest cost, are properly capitalized for the asset.

**Fully depreciated**   Refers to a *depreciable asset* whose *book value* is equal to its estimated *salvage value*, and for which no further expiration (depreciation) will be recorded.

**Fully diluted EPS**   The smallest possible EPS figure that would have occurred had all possible outstanding potential *dilution* (convertible securities, warrants, and options) taken place.

**Functional organization** (11)   An organization in which responsibilities are assigned and grouped in terms of functional activities (sales, production, personnel, and so forth) regardless of differing product lines or span of geographic operations. Contrast with **Product-line organization** and **Geographic organization.**

**Fund**   In financial accounting, an asset or group of assets set aside for a specific purpose and classified as noncurrent. In governmental accounting, a designated accounting entity for a specific purpose.

**Fund accounting** (15)   An accounting system different from financial accounting, used for government, governmental institutions, and many not-for-profit orgaizations.

**Funds**   Usually used synonymously with *working capital.* May also refer to cash or cash plus marketable securities.

**Funds from operations** (A9)   *Working capital* generated in operations—the difference between fund revenue (revenue involving an inflow of working capital) and fund expense (expense involving a reduction of net working capital).

**Funds statement**   Used to describe the SCFP.

**FUTA**   Federal Unemployment Tax Act. Provides for employer payroll taxes to cover costs of worker unemployment compensation.

**GAAP** (AD)   Generally Accepted Accounting Principles.

**Gain**   Excess of proceeds over costs for a specific transaction. Usually applied to financial, as opposed to operating, transactions.

**General fund** (15)   In accounting for nonprofit organizations, the primary or central fund established for operations.

**General inflation** (16)   The average overall increase in prices over a wide range of goods and services within an economy. Measured by a *general price index*. Contrast with **Specific inflation.**

**General ledger** (AE)   The collection of all active nonsubsidiary accounts in the firm.

**General partner**   An owner in a partnership who has unlimited personal liability for the debts of the partnership.

**General price index** (16)   A measure of current prices covering a wide range of goods and services within an economy, in comparison to the prices for the same goods and services during a base period. An indicator of **general inflation.** Examples include the consumer price index, the wholesale price index, and the GNP implicit price deflator. Contrast with **Specific price index.**

**General price-level-adjusted statements**   *See* **Price-level-adjusted statements.**

**General selling and administrative expense budget** (2)   The budget for all operations other than manufacturing.   The budget that includes all period costs.

**Generally Accepted Accounting Principles** (AD)   Standards for financial accounting and reporting currently promulgated by the Financial Accounting Standards Board. Not applicable to managerial accounting.

**Geographic organization** (11)   An organization in which responsibility is first assigned and grouped by geographical territories rather than by function or by product line.

**GNP implicit price deflator** (16)   A general price index, issued by the federal government, that attempts to reflect general price-level chaanges of all goods and services included in the gross national product (GNP).

**Goal congruence** (2)   A situation wherein the goals of the firm and those of its employees are in agreement, conformity, or harmony.

**Going-concern assumption** (AD)   The measurement assumption underlying financial statements prepared in accordance with GAAP. It is assumed that the firm will continue in business at least as long as the longest of its debt maturities or the remaining useful lives of its existing assets.

**Goods in process**   *See* **Work in process.**

**Goods available for sale** (1)   The sum of beginning inventory and net purchases (gross purchases plus transportation-in minus purchase returns minus purchase discounts) during an accounting period.

**Goodwill** (AD)   The excess of the cost over the fair market value of the net assets acquired in a purchase of control of another firm.

**Gross margin**   Net sales minus cost of goods sold.

**Gross profit**   *See* **Gross margin.**

**Gross-profit method**   A method used for estimating ending inventory and cost of goods sold for interim reports and in the event of destruction of accounting records. Cost of goods sold is estimated as a percentage of sales, using prior period's gross-profit percentage. The gross-profit method is not acceptable for measuring inventory and cost of goods sold in the annual financial statements.

**Gross-profit ratio** (1)   *Gross profit* devided by *net sales.*

**Gross purchases** (1)   The total of all invoice prices for inventory purchased during the period, not including transportation in and before recognizing purchase discounts and purchase returns.

**Gross sales**   Total of all sales at invoiced price before deductions for returns and allowances, and discounts.

**GSA**   *See* **General selling and administrative expense budget.**

**High–low point method** (3)   A method of *linear regression analysis* wherein one representative high and one representative low point (combination of volume and cost/price) are assumed to lie on the regression line. The slope (*a*) and intercept (*b*) of this line are determined by solving two simultaneous equations for the two points, in the form $Y = aX + b$. In analysis of cost data, the slope (*a*) equals the variable cost per unit of activity, and the intercept (*b*) equals the amount of fixed cost.

**Historical cost**   *See* **Original cost.**

**Historical cost accounting**   A term used to describe the current financial accounting system required by GAAP wherein *holding gains* are not recognized until realized. Contrast with **PLAC, PLARC,** and **Replacement-cost accounting.**

**Historical standard** (13)   A standard of work measurement established on the basis of those inputs previously required (as distinct from those required in the future for ideal, attainable, or average performance).

**Holding company**   A firm whose primary activity consists of holding the controlling stock of other operating companies.

**Holding gain (or loss)** (16)   Difference between price or replacement cost of an asset at the beginning and end of a period. Only realized (through sale) holding gains included in income reported under GAAP and amount not differentiated. Both realized and unrealized holding gains included in *economic income* and separately identified under *replacement-cost accounting.*

**Ideal standard** (13)   A standard of work measurement established on the basis of the absolute minimum inputs required to complete a task using existing facilities and specifications, with no allowance for machine breakdown, spoilage, normal shrinkage, or other inefficiency. Sometimes called a *perfection standard.* Contrast to **Attainable standards, Expected standards,** and **Historical standards.**

**Imposed budgets** (5)   Budgets that are established or modified by higher-level management for a responsibility center without participation/consultation with the affected center manager.

**Imputed interest**   The difference between the face amount of an obligation and its present value discounted at an appropriate interest rate—the amount of interest that may be inferred as capitalized into the face value of an obligation.

**Income** (AD)   *Revenue* minus *expenses* for a given period. Negative income is known as a loss.

**Income from (continuing) operations**   All revenues and gains minus all expenses and losses during a particular period except those specifically qualifying as *extraordinary*, or related to *discontinued operations*, or the effect of *accounting changes*.

**Income statement** (AD)   The final statement reporting all revenues, gains, expenses, and losses for the period, together with EPS data.

**Incremental borrowing rate** (8)   The interest rate which would need to be paid by the firm for its next material long-term secured loan. The lessee's incremental borrowing rate is used as the discount rate in the original determination of the present value of a lessee's capital-lease obligations.

**Incremental budgeting** (15)   A budgeting system in which attention is directed during budget preparation merely to additions to the prior period's budget (or actual expenditure level). The prior budget is the assumed starting point. Contrast to **ZBB.** Sometimes also used to describe the practice of allocating costs of a service center to users.

**Independent accountant**   The CPA engaged to audit and give a professional opinion on the firm's financial statements and supporting systems.

**Indirect cost** (1)   Any cost that is not recorded and accumulated as *direct cost* (identified with specific product or service) by accountants. Many costs are not readily identifiable with specific production or provision of service, and are treated as indirect costs. Indirect costs collectively are often referred to as *overhead costs. See also* **Indirect labor** *and* **Indirect material.**

**Indirect labor** (1)   All labor costs not identified as *direct labor,* such as costs for material handling and supervision. Indirect manufacturing labor is included in *manufacturing overhead* cost.

**Indirect materials** (1)   All materials costs not identified as *direct material;* also referred to as *supplies.* Indirect materials used in manufacturing are included as part of *manufacturing overhead* cost.

**Insolvent**   Unable to pay obligations when they are due.

**Installment (sales) method**   A method of revenue and expense recognition where gross profit is recognized in proportion to collection of the related receivable.

**Installment sales**    *Credit sales* where payments are scheduled in specific amounts over a specific period.

**Intangible assets** (AD)    Nonphysical *noncurrent assets* which are rights, claims, or other deferred expenditures. Examples include leasehold improvement, patents, trademarks, copyrights, franchises and goodwill.

**Intangible and other assets** (AD)    A category of *noncurrent assets* including intangible assets, deferred charges, assets involved in discontinued operations, goodwill, and miscellaneous noncurrent assets.

**Intercompany debt** (AD)    Refers to obligations between a parent and a subsidiary, which are eliminated in *consolidation*.

**Intercompany investment** (AD)    The controlling interest of a *parent* (included in the parent's investments account) in the *common stock* of the *subsidiary* (included in the subsidiary's stockholders' equity) which must be eliminated in *consolidation*. Any intercompany ownership of preferred stock or bonds would also be eliminated.

**Intercompany transactions**    Transactions occurring between a *parent* and a *subsidiary* that are eliminated from income statements and SCFP's in *consolidation*.

**Interest**    The cost or rent for use of money.

**Interest-bearing notes**    *Promissory notes* with interest explicitly stated separately from the principal of the note.

**Interim reports** (statements)    *Financial statements*, often abbreviated, which are issued covering periods shorter than the firm's *fiscal year* or normal *operating cycle*.

**Intermediate (-range) planning** (2)    Plans or objectives for implementation over the next two to five years that are realistic and achievable, and that are specific as to result but not as to method of implementation/accomplishment.

**Internal rate of return (IRR)** (A8)    The discount rate that will result in the NPV of all cash inflows (or savings) and all cash outflows related to a specific project or investment being equal to zero. May be used in capital budgeting to compare with an established minimum acceptable rate of return.

**Internal source** (funds) (A9)    Assets or activities from which a firm's management may obtain working capital or cash for nonoperational applications, without having to seek additional capital from long-term creditors or owners. Internal sources may be thought of as including funds from operations, sale of noncurrent assets, and reduction of net working capital balance.

**Internal sources** (for relieving cash shortage) (9)    Those possible sources of additional cash not involving borrowings or new owner investment. Include sale of noncurrent assets and cash generated in operations. Also temporarily could include accelerated collection of receivables, delayed payment of liabilities, or delayed profit distributions to owners.

**Inventoriable costs**   All costs that are properly included among product costs in inventory. *Product costs* as contrasted with *period costs.*

**Inventory** (AD)   A *current asset* representing goods and materials on hand ready for sale or which will be manufactured for sale to customers. "To inventory" means to physically count items in stock or to calculate the cost of items on hand.

**Inventory budget** (4)   The plan for the forthcoming period expressed in units for all products or balances of stock on hand, expected demand, and expected acquisitions. In manufacturing, separate inventory budgets may exist for different inventory levels. In retailing, may be limited to merchandise groups and expressed in sales price dollars.

**Inventory turnover** (A2)   A measure of the rapidity of movement of average inventory through the *operating cycle.* The *cost of goods sold* for a period, divided by the *average inventory* on hand during the period.

**Inventory-carrying cost** (4)   The product of the firm's annual inventory-carrying cost rate ($R$) and the product's direct cost per unit ($C$). Used in the calculation of *economic lot size* and *economic order quantity.* The carrying-cost rate includes *space,* interest (investment), and obsolescence risk costs. *See* **ELS** and **EOQ.**

**Inventory-flow assumption** (AD)   An assumption or arbitrary assignment relating specific purchase costs to specific items purchased. Necessary when specific identification of each unit in inventory with its purchase cost is not economically feasible. *See* **Average cost, FIFO,** *and* **LIFO.**

**Investing activities** (7)   *See* **Financial activities.**

**Investment centers** (11)   A segment or division of a business established as a distinct responsibility center with authority over revenues, costs, and noncurrent assets invested. Contrast to **Expenditure** or **Expense centers, Revenue centers,** and **Profit centers.**

**Investment decisions** (7)   A term used to distinguish those business decision alternatives that involve either a commitment of resources extending beyond one year into additional assets or the liquidation of existing long-term assets.

**Investment tax credit** (8)   A reduction in business income tax granted by the government in the year of acquisition of the qualifying assets to firms to subsidize replacement (modernization) of *capacity assets.*

**Investment turnover** (14)   The ratio of sales to amount of investment. Expresses the number of sales dollars generated during the period per dollar of investment intended to generate sales. Multiplied by the *operating ratio,* equals the return on investment (ROI).

**Investments** (AD)   The noncurrent asset account disclosing those assets held for long-term investment return rather than for use in business operations.

**Investors**    All those who commit goods or services to a firm. Investors include creditors, specifically including suppliers and employees, and owners.

**Invoice**    A document registering a claim for payment as part of a sales transaction—a "bill."

**IRR**    *See* **Internal rate of return.**

**IRS**    Internal Revenue Service.

**Issued shares**    Shares of a corporation's *authorized stock* that have been distributed to *stockholders.*

**ITC (9)**    *See* **Investment tax credit.**

**Job-order costing (1)**    A cost system in which work-in-process inventory costs (and possibly even raw-materials inventory costs) are accumulated under separate job orders identified with a particular product or batch of products in production. Contrast with **Process costing.**

**Joint cost (1)**    The single cost of two or more products that must be acquired or produced together. Examples would include *basket purchases,* the cost of beef and hides of cattle, and overhead for a center in which several different products are produced. Also referred to as *common cost. See also* **By-product, Cost allocation,** and **Split-off point.**

**Joint product (1)**    One of two or more products that must be acquired or produced together (simultaneously). *See* **Joint cost.**

**Journal (AE)**    A record in which entries reflecting transactions and adjustments are originally recorded in the order in which they occur.

**Journal entry (AE)**    An instruction to change balances in certain accounts which is recorded in a *journal* to reflect the effect of *transactions* and *adjustments.*

**Journalize (AE)**    To record an *entry* in a *journal.*

**Labor cost**    *See* **Direct labor cost.**

**Labor (cost)**    The cost of *direct labor* (hours worked in actual production) capitalized as part of *product cost* by a *manufacturer.*

**Labor efficiency variance (13)**    That portion of direct *labor spending variance* attributable to efficiency of time expended regardless of labor rate. Equals the standard labor rate times the difference between actual and standard (actual − standard) hours worked. A positive amount indicates excessive cost and is identified as unfavorable. *See also* **Labor spending variance.**

**Labor rate variance (13)**    That portion of direct *labor spending variance* attributable to the wage rate paid regardless of the relative efficiency of the hours worked. Equals the actual hours worked times the difference between the actual wage rate paid and the standard wage rate (actual −

standard). A positive amount indicates excessive cost and is identified as unfavorable. *See also* **Labor spending variance.**

**Labor spending variance** (13)   The difference (actual − budget) between actual direct labor cost incurred and the amount that should have been incurred given the actual volume produced (variable budget for direct labor). A positive amount indicates excessive cost and is identified as unfavorable. The algebraic sum of the direct *labor rate variance* and the direct *labor efficiency variance*.

**Labor standard** (13)   A work measurement standard used in a *standard cost system* indicating the desirable or expected direct labor cost per unit of product output. A labor standard is the product of two parts: a standard labor (wage) rate per hour and a standard time (hours required to complete each unit). *See also* **Standard cost.**

**Labor volume variance** (12)   The difference (variable budget − fixed budget) between the amount of direct labor cost that should have been incurred, given the actual level of production, and the amount of cost originally budgeted. Together with the *labor spending variance*, equals the difference between actual labor cost incurred and the amount originally budgeted.

**Land** (AD)   A *noncurrent asset* recorded at full acquisition cost and not depreciated.

**Last-in, first-out**   *See* **LIFO.**

**Lead time** (4)   The total time necessary (including procurement of materials and manufacturing) to complete an item once it is ordered. In a more restricted sense, may be used to refer only to purchasing lead time (from purchase order to delivery from supplier).

**Learning curve effect** (13)   The observable and predictable result that on successive performances of the same task the time required for completion diminishes.

**Leasehold improvement** (AD)   An improvement or betterment to property under *operating lease,* which is attached to the property and reverts to the lessor upon expiration of the lease.

**Least-squares regression analysis** (3A)   A mathematical method for calculating the slope and intercept of a *regression line* for a given set of data. The regression line so obtained is the one where the sum of the squares of the distances of all data from the line is less than for any other line. Hence the LSRA regression line is known to be the line of best fit as contrasted to one obtained by either the *visual fit* or *high-low-point methods. See* **Regression analysis** *and* **Regression line.**

**Ledger** (AE)   A group or collection of *accounts.*

**Legal capital**   The amount of *contributed capital* which is required by law to be retained in a corporation for the protection of creditors.

**Legislative budget** (15)   In government, represents the overall budget request submitted to the final authorization body (Congress, state legislature, board of supervisors, city council, and so forth).

**Lessee**   One who leases (uses) property belonging to another.

**Lessor**   One who owns the property (landlord) under lease to another.

**Leverage**   *See* **Financial leverage.**

**Liability** (AD)   A legal obligation to provide resources to another as the consequence of a past event.

**LIFO** (AD)   Last-in, first-out. One of several possible *inventory cost-flow assumptions.* LIFO assumes that most recent costs apply to inventory sold (cost of goods sold), and earliest costs apply to ending inventory on hand. Under LIFO, balance sheet inventory amounts may reflect very old, unrealistic low costs.

**Limited liability**   Refers to the fact that corporate stockholders (owners) are not personally liable for the debts of the company, whereas proprietors and general partners, as owners of their companies, have unlimited personal liability.

**Limited partner**   An owner in a partnership who has limited liability; he or she is not personally liable for the debts of the partnership.

**Linear programming** (7)   A mathematical technique of analysis facilitating the determination of the best alternative action(s), given multiple constraints upon necessary resources or opportunities for use. *See also* **Linear-programming model.**

**Linear-programming (LP) model** (17)   A mathematical model of a linear-programming problem. The LP model contains the *objective function* and the applicable *constraint equations/inequalities,* all of which are treated as simultaneous equations and solved by the *simplex method.*

**Linear regression (analysis)** (A3, A5)   A mathematical technique for determining a line (known as a *regression line*) that may be used as a predictor of linear relationships of two variables. For cost behavior, linear regression is used to differentiate fixed- and variable-cost components of a particular cost, given data on the cost incurred at different levels of activity. *See also* **Visual fit method, High-low-point method,** *and* **Least-squares regression analysis.**

**Liquidation**   The payment of an obligation. Also the sale of all noncash assets and cash distribution to creditors and owners as part of terminating a segment or an entire business.

**Liquidity**   A firm's ability to raise additional cash. Sometimes liquidity is used interchangeably with *solvency.*

**Loss**   The excess of expense or cost over revenue (proceeds) for a particular transaction; or an expiration, extinction, or disappearance of an asset with no matching revenue; or negative income for a period.

**LOCM**   A GAAP requirement for *inventory* measurement and reporting, where inventory must be written down below acquisition cost if eventual net recoverable value is lower than cost.

**Long-range planning** (2)   *See* **Strategic planning.**

**Long-term**   Noncurrent; ordinarily due beyond one year.

**Long-term debt**   A *noncurrent liability* or the total of all noncurrent liabilities.

**Long-term debt ratio** (A2)   The ratio of long-term debt to the sum of long-term debt and owners' equity.

**Long-term investments and funds** (AD)   A category of *noncurrent assets* including both noncurrent investments and also various special funds such as sinking funds.

**Longest lead-time item** (17)   In the context of a particular product or project comprised of several components, the component having the greatest *lead time*, which therefore controls the overall lead time for the completed product or project.

**Lower of cost or market**   *See* **LOCM.**

**LP** (17)   *See* **Linear programming.**

**LSRA** (A3, A5)   *See* **Least-squares regression analysis.**

**Major customer**   A term designating a single customer (individual, firm, or government agency) responsible for 10 percent or more of a firm's revenue. GAAP requires supplementary disclosure, in the financial statements, of data related to any major customers.

**Management by exception** (11)   An approach to managing wherein attention is focused only on events or performance that differ significantly from expectations or plans.

**Management information system**   A term used to describe all of the data files (the data base) and reports available within the firm for management decisions. The accounting system would thus be one part of the overall management information system.

**Management accounting**   *See* **Managerial accounting.**

**Managerial accounting**   A reporting system operating within a firm that is intended to facilitate management decision making, planning, and control. Also referred to as *management accounting.* Contrast with **Cost accounting** and **Financial accounting.**

**Manufacturer**   A firm that purchases raw materials/component parts and produces/assembles finished goods for sale to customers.

**Manufacturing cost**   All costs related to the production of goods, *material cost, labor cost,* and *manufacturing overhead cost.*

**Manufacturing cost** (1)   Factory costs—*direct material, direct labor,* and *manufacturing overhead*—included in arriving at full *product costs* for a manufacturer.

**Manufacturing overhead** (1)   All those *manufacturing costs* that are not treated as *direct material* or *direct labor* costs, that are not recorded and accumulated by readily identifiable units or batches of specific products. Manufacturing overhead is separately accumulated, and then allocated to individual product cost in some systematic and rational manner. Where the overhead allocation is based upon a predetermined rate or standard, more or less overhead may be allocated to individual product costs than was actually incurred for the period. The difference is known as over-applied or underapplied overhead. *See also* **Overapplied overhead** *and* **Underapplied overhead.** Included as part of full product cost by a manufacturer.

**Margin of safety** (6)   The difference (excess) between actual sales earned or projected and the firm's *breakeven sales volume.*

**Marginal cost**   The cost that would be incurred if one more unit of product is produced or sold or if a particular project is undertaken.

**Markdown**   The amount of reduction of a retail selling price below that which was originally established.

**Market price** (of stock)   The price per share at which stock of a given firm may be traded.

**Market share** (3)   The proportion of overall customer demand for a product or product line represented by the individual firm's sales.

**Market value** (of stock)   The current sale value of stock owned in a particular firm. The product of the number of shares owned times the *market price* per share.

**Marketable securities** (AD)   A *current asset* classification for readily salable securities held as temporary investments of excess cash (will normally be sold as cash is needed). Most current marketable securities are in the form of short-term government paper and certificates of deposit. The term is also used to apply to stocks and bonds of other firms and governments which are readily salable. In this context, where marketable securities are held with no intention of selling within one year (period), they are classified as *noncurrent*, under investments.

**Market-based (macro) forecasts** (3)   Sales projections that are based upon economic or industry forecasts of demand, supply, and/or funds available to potential customers. Contrast with **Sales-based (micro) forecasts.**

**Markup**   The difference between cost and the originally intended retail selling price. Usually expressed as a percentage of *selling price* rather than of cost.

**Master budget** (2)   The overall summary budget for the firm; includes budgeted financial statements and supporting budgets including the *master operating budget*, the *cash budget*, and the *capital budget.*

**Master operating budget** (2)   The budget for the overall firm that projects all expected revenue and expenditures (or expense) related to the firm's operations as distinct from its financing and investing activities.

"Matched pair" (A9)   A term used in this text to identify pairs (matching sources and applications) of material resource flows required by GAAP to be included in the SCFP and not involving flows of *working capital*. The most common "matched pairs" involve a portion of a new noncurrent asset (application) obtained in exchange for new noncurrent debt (source); new noncurrent assets (application) acquired as a direct owner investment (source); or conversion of noncurrent debt (application) to new stock (source).

Matching   The GAAP income-measurement principle involving the recognition of expenses on the income statement in the same period as that in which the related revenues are recognized (reported).

Material   As a noun, refers to a manufacturer's *raw material*. As an adjective, is used synonymously with "significant."

Material cost (1)   The cost of *direct materials,* as distinguished from *indirect materials* (supplies), used in the manufacture of a product.

Material (cost) (1)   The *direct cost* of raw material included by a manufacturer as part of full *product cost*.

Material price variance (13)   The difference between the actual cost incurred for a quantity of purchased material and the planned or standard cost of the same quantity:

(Actual price − Standard price) × Actual quantity.

A positive variance represents excessive cost and is therefore identified as unfavorable. May be identified either at the time of purchase (if raw-material inventory is carried at standard cost) or at the time material is used in production. Together with the *material usage variance*, explains the total *material spending variance.*

Material spending variance (13)   The difference between the actual cost incurred for *direct material* used and the variable budget cost for the period (actual − budget). A positive variance represents additional cost and is identified as unfavorable. The algebraic sum of the *material price variance* and the *material usage variance*. Together with the *material volume variance*, explains the difference between originally budgeted materials cost and actual costs incurred.

Material standard (13)   The standard cost per unit of product of the *direct material* incorporated therein. The product of a standard quantity of material required per product and a standard price per unit of material. *See also* **Standard cost.**

Material usage variance (13)   That portion of the *material spending variance* for a period attributable to actual usage of *direct material* being different from the planned or standard quantity that should have been used for the products actually produced:

(Actual quantity used − Standard quantity) × Standard price.

A positive variance indicates excessive cost and is identified as unfavorable. Together with the *material price variance*, equals the *material spending variance*.

**Material volume variance** (13)    The difference between variable budgeted direct material costs for the period and the amount originally budgeted (variable budget − fixed budget). Indicates difference in total planned direct material costs between original and actual levels of production. Together with *material spending variance*, explains the difference between originally planned direct material costs and those actually incurred.

**Materiality** (AD)    The GAAP disclosure principle involving separate identification of only those events or statement effects where the result is significant in terms of total assets or net income.

**Mathematical models** (3, 17)    A representation, in mathematical terms and notation, of all of the significant relevant factors in a particular situation or decision and of their interrelationships.

**Mature**    Having reached the date established for payment. *See* **Maturity.**

**Maturity**    The date when the principal of an obligation is due and payable. An obligation is said to "mature" when it becomes payable.

**MBO** (2)    Management by Objectives. An approach to the management of individuals and groups wherein periodically the progress towards achieving specific performance objectives is jointly evaluated by the superior and subordinate, and explicit objectives for the forthcoming period are set forth by mutual agreement. In business, a *participatory budget* and *budgetary control* system would be an example of MBO. MBO has also been attempted in government, particularly in the Department of Defense.

**Measure of dispersion** (17)    An indication of the degree of the spread of values around the mean of a *probability distribution*. *See also* **Standard deviation** *and* **Cofficient of variation.**

**"Meeting the payroll"**    Slang for maintaining solvency.

**Merchandising firm**    As distinct from a service business or manufacturer, one that acquires products (finished goods) and sells them to customers.

**Merge/merger**    The joining of two firms into a single economic entity. *See* **Business combination.**

**Minimum reorder point** (4)    As items are used, reserved for use, or sold, the quantity of stock on hand at which an order of replacement stock must be placed to avoid *stockout*, assuming no variation in normal usage or in procurement and/or manufacturing lead time. The product of the item's normal usage per period (day, week, or month) times the reorder lead time in periods. Includes no *safety stock* for variations in demand or reorder lead time. *See also* **Reorder point.**

**Minority**   *See* **Minority stockholders.**

**Minority interest**   An *equity* account appearing on a consolidated balance sheet representing the share in total assets attributable to stockholders who do not hold stock in the *parent corporation. (See* **Minority stockholders.**) Minority interests or claims against combined income are subtracted on a *consolidated income statement* so that the bottom line will represent income available to the parent's stockholders.

**Minority stockholders**   Stockholders in a corporation where another individual or firm has controlling interest (more than 50 percent of the voting stock). Usually considered in the context of a *subsidiary corporation* which is not wholly owned. *See* **Minority interest.**

**Mixed cost** (5)   A cost that increases in a linear relationship to increases in activity but where a portion exists even at an activity level of zero. A cost that has both *fixed cost* and *variable cost* components that can be ascertained through the use of *regression analysis.* Many *indirect costs* are found to be mixed costs. Also referred to as *semifixed costs* or *semivariable costs.*

**Model** (17)   A representation of something. *See* **Mathematical model, Decision tree,** *and* **Network model.**

**Monetary gain or loss** (16)   A firm's gain or loss in *general purchasing power* resulting from holding *net monetary debt* or *net monetary assets* during a period of general inflation (deflation). Monetary gain or loss is currently not measured and reported in financial statements.

**Monetary gain or loss** (16)   The increase or decrease in the general purchasing power of *monetary items* resulting from inflation. Holding monetary assets during a period of inflation results in a monetary loss. Holding monetary debt conversely results in a gain. Net monetary gain or loss on net monetary assets is readily identifiable and reported under *price-level adjusted accounting.*

**Monetary items**   Cash and other assets and liabilities where claims (receivable and payable) are definite and fixed as to both amount and time. The distinction between monetary and nonmonetary items is necessary for computations of foreign exchange gain or loss and for *monetary gain* or *loss* in general purchasing power as part of *price-level adjusted financial statements.*

**Multiple-step format**   One acceptable approach to classifying revenues and expenses on an income statement, involving subtotals for such items as gross profit and operating income (as distinct from income from operations).

**Mutually exclusive alternatives** (8)   Competing alternatives (investments, projects, or activities) where the implementation of one precludes the possibility of undertaking any of the others.

**NAA**   National Association of Accountants.

**National Association of Accountants (NAA)**   A national organization whose members share an interest in managerial and cost accounting. Oversees the CMA examination.

**Negotiated price** (14)   In the context of *transfer pricing*, a transfer price between two divisions, established on the basis of negotiations and resulting agreement on the part of the buying and selling division managers.

**Net after-tax benefits** (7)   The benefits (revenues, interest, dividends, or cost savings) of a particular undertaking less applicable income taxes, expressed as a net cash inflow for each period affected.

**Net after-tax costs** (7)   The costs (expenditures or lost benefits) of a particular undertaking less applicable income-tax savings, expressed as a net cash outflow for each period affected.

**Net assets**   Total *assets* minus total *liabilities*, or the share of total assets claimed or contributed by owners.

**Net current assets**   Another term for *net working capital*. Both equal current assets minus current liabilities.

**Net decision benefit** (7)   For noninvestment decision alternatives having even flows of benefits and costs over future periods, the sum of the benefits for a period less the sum of the relevant costs for that period. For decisions having uneven flows or involving investments or disinvestments, the net decision benefit can be misleading, and the NPV of after-tax cash flows over the life of the project or activity should be used for evaluation. *See also* **NPV.**

**Net income**   The difference between the total of all *revenue* and *gains* and the total of all *expenses* and *losses* for a period.

**Net loss**   Negative *net income*.

**Net present value** (or simply **present value**) (7)   The algebraic sum of the cash inflows from an investment, discounted at a given discount rate, less the associated cash outflows similarly discounted at the same rate. A positive NPV indicates an internal rate of return on investment (*IRR*) greater than the discount rate used; a negative NPV indicates a lower rate. An NPV of zero indicates that the IRR is equal to the discount rate used.

**Net purchases** (1)   Equals gross purchases plus freight-in less any purchase returns and less any purchase (cash) discounts taken. The amount relating to purchases that is added to inventory for the period.

**Net purchases** (1)   The net total acquisition cost of all merchandise or material acquired and accepted during the year. Gross purchases plus transportation-in minus purchase returns minus purchase discounts.

**Net quick assets**   *Quick assets* (cash, marketable securities, and net receivables) minus current liabilities.

**Net realizable value**   The amount of net cash that could result from disposition of an item. The selling price less costs of completion for sale and of selling.

**Net sales**   Gross sales less sales returns, allowances, and sales discounts.

**Net working capital** (AD)   The amount of working capital in the firm representing a necessary long-term investment by creditors and owners. Equals *current assets* minus *current liabilities. See also* **Working capital.**

**Net worth**   A potentially misleading term sometimes used in place of *net assets* or *owners' equity.*

**Network analysis** (17)   An approach to scheduling and controlling projects involving many different steps in different sequences or paths. Through using a *network model,* the *critical path* may be identified; and the effect on total project lead time or completion time of expediting various individual steps may be ascertained. *See also* **Critical path, Network model, CPM,** and **PERT.**

**Network model** (17)   A diagram used in *network analysis* indicating all distinct operations in a project and each step's preceding and subsequent step.

**Nominal account** (AE)   A temporary account opened each year (or period) to accumulate desired detailed information. Nominal accounts are closed at year-end to real or balance-sheet accounts.

**Noncurrent assets** (AD)   All assets that do **not** qualify for classification as *current assets.*

**Noncurrent capital-lease obligations** (AD)   The *present value* of amounts owed beyond one year under leases qualifying as *capital leases.*

**Noncurrent liabilities** (AD)   All liabilities that do **not** qualify for classification as *current liabilities;* long-term debt.

**Noninterest-bearing note**   A *promissory note* with all interest capitalized in the face or maturity value. A note with no explicitly stated interest separate from principal.

**Noninvestment decisions** (7)   Decision alternatives that involve neither investment of funds over several periods nor the disposition of an existing investment. A category of decisions that may simplify analysis since, if benefit and cost flows are uniform over future periods, tax consequences and present value may be ignored in the decision process. Contrast with **Investment decisions.**

**Nonmanufacturing cost** (1)   All costs for a service firm. For a merchandising firm, all costs except inventory (product) costs. For a manufacturer, all costs not involved with production of goods. Also known as general, selling, and administrative costs (expenses); treated as period cost. Contrast with **Manufacturing cost** and **Product cost.**

**Nonmonetary item**   Any asset or equity which is **not** a *monetary item.*

**Nonoperating revenue**   Revenue which is not derived from the firm's principal line(s) of business. Often designated as "other revenue."

**Note payable** (AD)   An unconditional obligation in writing to pay a specific amount of cash at either a specific time or else on demand.

**Non-profit-directed organizations** (2, 15)   Organizations such as hospitals, schools, charities, and governments, that are not established to earn a profit for the owners. Contrast with **Business firms.** Also simply known as *nonprofit organizations.*

**Nonprofit organizations** (15)   See **Non-profit-directed organizations.**

**Note receivable** (AD)   An unconditional obligation in writing by another to pay to the firm a specific amount of cash at either a specific time or else on demand.

**NPV**   *See* **Net present value.**

**NWC**   *See* **Net working capital.**

**Objective function** (17)   In *linear programming,* the equation that expresses the values and relationships to be maximized or minimized. *See also* **Linear programming** (LP).

**Objective probabilities** (17)   Probabilities that are formally derived from representative past operating or experimental data. Contrast with **Subjective probabilities.**

**Objectivity**   A GAAP measurement principle, which defers (perhaps indefinitely) recognition and recording of events and items until they can be reasonably measured in monetary terms, and the measurement is capable of independent verification.

**Obligation** (A15)   *See* **Encumbrance.**

**Obligations under capital leases** (AD)   May appear as both a current and a noncurrent liability. The noncurrent portion represents the *present value* of all payments due *beyond* one year under capital-lease contracts. The current portion represents the present value of the currently maturing payment(s) plus accrued interest charges (incorporated in the payment) which have been earned.

**Off-balance-sheet financing** (A8)   Refers to the practice of acquiring property under a long-term noncancellable lease, which may be (in substance) a purchase but which is accounted for as an *operating lease.*

**On account**   Term referring to a purchase or sale where the privilege is extended of delayed payment and no promissory note as evidence of the debt is required.

**On credit**   *See* **On account.**

**On consignment**   *See* **Consignment.**

**Operating**   Refers to revenues and expenses related to the firm's primary line(s) of business.

**Operating budget** (2)   A plan for a firm or a subdivision thereof that sets forth expected expenditures and/or revenue for the forthcoming period. A budget related to a firm's operations as distinct from its capital, cash, and financial budgeting activities. Applies to budgets for sales, inventory, production, purchases, factory operations, and general, selling and administrative expenditures.

**Operating cycle** (10)   The average time period involved for completion of the following series of events: Cash is converted into goods and services; goods and services are converted into receivables by a sale; and cash is collected on receivables. Also known as the *earnings cycle.*

**Operating earnings**   *See* **Operating income.**

**Operating expenses**   All expenses and losses for the period except *extraordinary items* and those related to *discontinued operations.* Often more narrowly defined to exclude also cost of goods sold, interest expense, provision for income taxes, and losses on financial activities.

**Operating income**   Used interchangeably with *income from operations,* or often more narrowly defined to include only revenues and expenses directly related to the firm's primary line(s) of business and specifically excluding other revenue, gains and losses on financial activities, interest expense, and provision for income taxes (income tax expense). *See also* **Income from operations.**

**Operating lease** (A8)   Any lease **not** meeting FASB criteria for identification as a *capital lease.* Operating leases are accounted for as executory contracts, no asset is recorded, and the liability and expense is only recognized *as earned* by the lessor.

**Operating management** (2)   Those managers concerned with overseeing the activities that make up the firm's main line(s) of business. Contrast with **Financial management** and **Tax management.**

**Operating profit**   *See* **Operating income.**

**Operating ratio** (A2, 14)   Net income (or alternatively, income from operations) divided by net sales and usually expressed as a percentage.

**Operational assets**   *See* **Fixed assets.**

**Opinion** (auditor's) (AD)   The auditor's report attesting to the financial statements, or disclaiming attestation.

**Opportunity cost** (7)   The income that could have been earned or the cost that could have been saved, by using an asset in its next-best alternative use. Opportunity cost is not measured and reported in financial statements.

**Order backlog** (14)   The number or value of existing and unfilled customer orders for goods and services.

**Order-filling cost** (12)   The sum of those costs directly related to filling customers' orders once received. Can include order pulling, packing, shipping, and billing costs. Contrast with **Order-getting cost.**

**Order-getting cost** (12)   The sum of those costs directly relating to obtaining customers' orders. Can include market research, advertising, and sales promotion costs. Contrast with **Order-filling cost.**

**Ordering cost** (4)   *See* **Setup cost.**

**Organization by customer** (11)   One form of business organization wherein major responsibilities are first divided into segments to match specific customers or groups of customers rather than by function or geographic territory. Contrast with **Functional organization, Geographic organization,** and **Product-line organization.**

**Organization chart** (2)   A diagram indicating all responsibility centers within the firm and the primary reporting (authority) relationships among them.

**Original budget** (13)   *See* **Fixed budget.**

**Original cost**   The initial (historical) cost(s) of an asset.

**Other revenue** (income)   *See* **Nonoperating revenue.**

**Outstanding** (stock)   Number of shares issued less any shares held as *treasury stock.*

**Overabsorbed overhead**   *See* **Overapplied overhead.**

**Overapplied overhead** (1)   An *accounting variance.* An amount of manufacturing overhead that, by using a *predetermined* or *standard overhead rate*, has been applied/absorbed/allocated to product cost(s) in work-in-process inventory in excess of the amount actually incurred. The excess of cost applied. Overapplied overhead at year-end is closed to (subtracted from) cost of goods sold or, if material, to work-in-process inventory, finished goods inventory, and cost of goods sold, in proportion to current location of goods manufactured during the year. Also known as *overabsorbed overhead.*

**Overcapitalized** (10)   In the context of a particular firm, refers to the situation where the firm has excessive/unneeded/redundant assets for its current or anticipated level of operations.

**Overhead (costs)** (1)   Any cost not identified or identifiable with the production or the sale of specific goods or services. In connection with manufacturing cost, known as *manufacturing overhead, factory overhead,* or *burden.* May also be used in referring to indirect general, selling, and administrative cost.

**Overhead absorbed**   *See* **Overhead applied.**

**Overhead applied**   The amount of *manufacturing overhead* assigned or allocated to product cost(s) in work-in-process inventory. Where a predetermined or standard overhead rate is used, overhead applied may differ from the actual amount of overhead incurred. *See also* **Underapplied overhead** *and* **Overapplied overhead.**

**Overhead efficiency variance** (A12)   The difference between the *standard overhead* that would have been applied had there been no *labor efficiency* *variance* and the overhead applied (applied overhead − standard overhead). The variance attributable to labor efficiency. A positive amount indicates excessive cost and is identified as unfavorable.

**Overhead rate**   A standard or other predetermined rate used as the basis for applying overhead to products or services. *See also* **Predetermined overhead rate** *and* **Standard overhead rate.**

**Overhead spending variance** (A12)   A *budget variance*. The difference between the actual amount of manufacturing overhead incurred and the variable budgeted overhead that should have been incurred at the actual level of activity (actual overhead − variable budgeted overhead). A positive variance indicates excessive cost and is identified as unfavorable.

**Overhead volume variance** (A12)   The difference between variable budgeted overhead and overhead applied (variable budgeted overhead − overhead applied). The result of fixed overhead applied at a predetermined rate per unit based on a number of units different from the actual activity level. A positive variance is identified as unfavorable.

**Owner withdrawal** (AD)   The transfer of assets (usually cash) from the firm to the owner(s). In a corporation, referred to as a *dividend.*

**Owner's capital**   Refers to that portion of total assets in a firm contributed (claimed) by owners. *See* **Owner's equity.**

**Owner's equity** (AD)   That share of total assets not claimed by creditors; total assets minus total liabilities. Same as *net assets.*

**Paid-in capital**   That portion of *contributed capital* in excess of amounts shown as par or stated value. Also may be used to refer to total contributed capital less *donated capital.*

**Parent** (company) (AD)   A firm owning voting control (over 50 percent of voting common stock) of another firm which is known as a *subsidiary.*

**Participative management** (11)   A style or approach to managing people under which subordinate managers are encouraged to participate in the establishment of performance objectives and to assume (rather than be assigned) responsibility for their implementation. Consonant with McGregor's **Theory Y.** Contrast with **Authoritarian management.**

**Participatory budget** (5)   A budget prepared under a system of *participative management* wherein subordinate managers participate in budget preparation, agree to the budget's reasonableness, and assume (rather than be assigned) responsibility for its implementation. Contrast with **Imposed budget.** *See also* **MBO.**

**Partnership**   A firm with two or more owners (general or limited partners) which is not incorporated. A partnership must have at least one *general partner.*

**Partnership agreement**   The agreement among partners specifying the division of earnings, division of net assets upon dissolution, and procedures to be followed upon death or disability of a partner.

**Par value**    The face value or the face amount of a *security* (bond, note, or stock).

**Payable**    Owed; past due, currently, or in the future.

**Payoff table** (17)    In the context of statistical decision models, a tabulation of the outcomes (values) of each alternative action in combination with each alternative possible event or occurrence.

**Period cost** (1)    An expenditure, asset expiration, or incurrence of a liability regularly expensed in the period when incurred rather than being capitalized as an *asset* or included as part of *product cost*.

**Periodic inventory** (system)    A system wherein *cost of goods sold* is **not** recorded perpetually throughout the year (period). Instead, it is calculated at year-end by taking a *physical inventory* to obtain ending inventory, and then subtracting ending inventory from *goods available for sale*.

**Periodic LIFO**    LIFO determined under the periodic-inventory method, wherein all shipments are presumed to have occurred at year-end.

**Permanent holding loss** (investments)    A loss of recoverable value on investments which is deemed permanent and is therefore recognized as a loss on the income statement.

**Permanent investment**    A term referring to the long-term invested capital in a business, the sum of noncurrent liabilities and owners' equity or, equivalently, the sum of net working capital and noncurrent assets.

**Perpetual inventory** (system)    A system in which inventory accounts are regularly updated to reflect purchases and shipments.

**Perpetual LIFO**    LIFO determined under the perpetual-inventory method, wherein purchases and shipments are recorded as they occur. Strict perpetual LIFO maintains records of LIFO "layers" as far back as the last stockout. Modified perpetual LIFO begins each period with a single opening "layer" at average cost, and only "layers" purchases during the year.

**PERT** (12, 17)    Program Evaluation and Review Technique. An approach to *network analysis* that may include probabilistic estimates of lead times (usually in the form of three-point estimates—optimistic, most likely, pessimistic), therefore allowing for determination of probabilities of overall completion time.

**Physical inventory**    Refers to physically counting and determining the cost of inventory on hand.

**Physical minimum** (4)    *See* **Bin minimum.**

**PLAC** (16)    *See* **Price-level-adjusted cost.**

**PLARC** (16)    An acronym used in this text for price-level-adjusted replacement-cost (statements). Under PLARC, statements are first adjusted for current replacement costs of nonmonetary assets and then adjusted for changes in general purchasing power.

**PPBS** (15)   Planning–Programming–Budgeting System. A formal system of *program budgeting* attempted in nonprofit organizations. Budgeting based on coherent objectives whether or not measurable in financial terms.

**Planning horizon** (2)   The limit or span of time into the future of a particular planning period or activity. The planning horizon of a budget is often one year. For a capital budgeting decision involving equipment with a useful life of 15 years, the decision time (planning) horizon would necessarily extend to cover 15 years.

**Pooling of interests** (AD)   A *business combination* wherein two firms of similar size join together and operate as a single economic entity, with the original owners maintaining their proportionate voting shares in the new entity.

**Pooling treatment** (method) (AD)   Accounting for a *business combination* which qualifies as a pooling by adding together the book values of assets and equities of the separate firms. Under the pooling method, there are no asset revaluations or *purchased goodwill*.

**Posting** (AE)   Recording entries in the accounts.

**Predetermined overhead rate** (1)   An *overhead rate* used as a basis for applying manufacturing overhead cost to work-in-process inventory when a *standard cost* system is not used. Calculated at the beginning of a period as the ratio of budgeted total manufacturing overhead to a budgeted activity measure such as expected total direct-labor hours.

**Preferred stock**   Stock with preference over *common stock* as to dividends and assets in dissolution. Preferred stock is usually nonvoting.

**Preliminary cash budget** (9)   A *cash budget* that does not yet incorporate either provisions for short-term investments of excess cash in marketable securities or provisions for borrowings to relieve anticipated cash shortages. May show negative balances of cash on hand. Contrast with **Final cash budget.**

**Prepaid items** (AD)   *Current assets* that represent past expenditures for future benefits. Prepaid items can be thought of as current receivables for services rather than for cash.

**Present value**   *See* **Discounted present value.**

**Present value factor** (8)   A discount factor for one dollar relevant to a single time period and a particular rate of interest (discount rate). Used to multiply by a given dollar cash flow to obtain the *present value* of that particular flow.

**Price elasticity** (3)   The degree to which customer demand will respond to (vary with) changes in the price of goods or services. Measured by the slope of the *demand curve*.

**Price–earnings ratio**   The *market price* per share of the firm's *common stock*, divided by the previous year's EPS.

**Price index** (16)   A ratio for a given period of the average prices during that period to the average prices for the same items existing during an earlier period designated as a base (or reference) period.

**Price level** (16)   The ratio for a particular period as measured by a particular *price index* series.

**Price level adjustment** (16)   The amount of change (adjustment) to a particular revenue, expense, or nonmonetary asset necessary to reflect the change in the purchasing power of the dollar occurring between the date the item was recorded (or previously adjusted) and the current date.

**Price-level-adjusted accounting** (statements) (16)   *Financial statements* containing measurements in dollars of uniform *general purchasing power.* Historical costs are adjusted to current amounts via general price-level indices.

**Price-level-adjusted cost** (16)   The valuation basis for *nonmonetary assets* in price-level-adjusted financial statements. Under price-level-adjusted cost, historical cost is adjusted to current purchasing power equivalence through the use of a *general price index.*

**Price variance**   *See* **Material price variance.**

**Pricing decision** (A6)   The decision as to what price to set for a particular good or service.

**Primary EPS**   Earnings per share calculated under the assumption that, out of all possible dilutions, the more probable dilutions have occurred. Primary EPS will usually be less than simple EPS, and will always be equal to or greater than *fully diluted EPS.*

**Prime cost** (1)   The sum of *direct material* and *direct labor* costs identified with a product or all products. A portion of full product cost. May be viewed as the *direct cost* of the product or products.

**Prior-period adjustment**   Certain balance sheet adjustments for errors in earlier periods made directly to the ending balance sheet and bypassing the income statement. GAAP narrowly restricts items that may qualify for treatment as a prior-period adjustment.

**Probabilities** (17)   Decimal values assigned to different events included in a *probability distribution* reflecting the likelihood of occurrence of each event. The sum of all probabilities in a given distribution will equal 1.0. May be objectively or subjectively derived. *See also* **Objective probabilities, Subjective probabilities,** *and* **Probability distribution.**

**Probability distribution** (17)   A set of mutually exclusive and exhaustive events or occurrences of a particular type, together with their individual *probabilities* of occurrence. The sum of all probabilities in a given distribution will total 1.0.

**Process costing** (1)   A system for accumulating product costs applicable to production of a single product or homogeneous products under which *direct material, direct labor,* and *manufacturing overhead* are all assigned to a single work-in-process inventory account. Unit costs are determined by dividing total manufacturing cost by *equivalent units.*

**Product**   Used to refer to either goods or services produced.

**Product cost** (1, AD)   As distinct from *period costs,* which are expensed in the period incurred, product costs are all costs that are included (capitalized) in inventory and not expensed until sale occurs.

**Product mix** (3)   A particular combination of products sold wherein different products have different prices and/or costs. Any other product mix will therefore result in different total revenue, total cost, or total contribution.

**Product-line organization** (11)   An organization wherein responsibility is primarily delegated to centers responsible for particular products rather than by function, customer, or geographic territory. Contrast with **Functional organization, Organization by customer,** and **Geographic organization.**

**Production schedule** (2)   A plan (schedule) of production work orders to be started/completed during a forthcoming period.

**Profit**   *See* **Income.**

**Profit centers** (11)   Responsibility centers within a firm responsible for both revenue and principal costs (or all costs) relating to such revenue, but not responsible for the asset investment involved/employed. Contrast with **Cost centers, Expenditure (expense) centers, Revenue centers,** and **Investment centers.**

**Profit-directed organizations** (2)   Businesses. Organizations existing for the purpose of earning a profit for the owners. Contrast with governments and other **non-profit-directed organizations.**

**Profitability graph**   A variation of a *breakeven graph* with the Y-axis showing dollars of profit and of loss and the X-axis showing unit sales volume. Sales revenue is plotted as a horizontal line intersecting the Y-axis at zero profit. Total costs are plotted separately, with the intersection at *breakeven sales volume. See also* **Breakeven graph.**

**Profitability index** (8)   A measure, used for ranking alternatives in capital rationing, that relates the net benefits accruing from a particular investment alternative to the investment required:

$$\text{Profitability index} = 1 + \frac{\text{NPV}}{\text{Required investment}}.$$

**Pro-forma**   Hypothetical or projected.

**Pro-forma financial statements** (2)   Projected statements. Financial statements projected on the basis of assumed events. Budgeted financial statements as part of the *master budget* are one example of pro-forma statements.

**Program budget(ing)** (3, 15)   In the context of governments and other non-profit organizations, a system under which budgets are established based upon explicit service objectives (programs) that may or may not be measurable in financial terms. *See also* **PPBS.**

**Programmed cost** (5)   A *fixed cost* committed for each period by management action and not usually easily identified with measurable units of output. Expenditures for advertising, employee training programs, and research and development are examples of programmed costs. Also known as *discretionary costs* or *managed costs.* Contrast with **Ratable cost.**

**Promissory note**   *See* **Note payable** *and* **Note receivable.**

**Property under capital lease** (AD)   A *fixed asset* indicating the unamortized balance of the *present value* of all payments required for property effectively controlled under a long-term, noncancelable lease, which qualifies as a capital lease.

**Proprietor**   The owner of a one-owner business or **proprietorship.**

**Proprietorship**   A one-owner business, or the owner's equity of a one-owner business.

**Purchase** (of another company) (AD)   A *business combination* where one firm acquires control of a *subsidiary* through giving subsidiary stockholders cash or debt instruments in exchange for their voting stock. Proportionate voting interest in the new economic entity is not maintained by the original owners.

**Purchase discount**   *See* **Cash discount.**

**Purchase method** (treatment) (AD)   Accounting for a *business combination* which does **not** qualify as a *pooling,* by recording the acquired firm's assets at the amounts effectively paid for them, with any payment in excess of fair market value of assets acquired being classified as *goodwill.*

**Purchase returns** (1)   Merchandise or material purchased from a supplier and recorded in the accounts, which are subsequently returned to the supplier for any reason.

**Purchased goodwill** (AD)   *See* **Goodwill.**

**Purchases budget** (2)   The plan or schedule for the forthcoming period of products or materials to be procured from outside suppliers and their expected costs.

**Purchasing power** (16)   The command of the dollar over goods and services. Purchasing power declines in periods of inflation. *Price-level-adjusted financial statements* attempt to report assets, equities, revenues, expenses, and resource flows in current dollars (common purchasing-power units).

**Quick assets**   Assets which are cash or can quickly become cash. Includes cash, marketable securities, and receivables.

**Quick ratio** (A2)   *Quick assets* divided by *total current liabilities.* Also known as the *acid-test ratio.*

**Random (variance)** (11)   In the context of *budgetary control* and the use of *control charts,* a variance that is assumed to be normal or subject to chance, and therefore not controllable or correctible through investigation and remedial action.

**Ratable cost** (12)   A cost that is repetitive, readily identifiable with measurable output, and subject to engineering standards or rates. Also known as an *engineered cost.*

**Rate variance**   *See* **Labor rate variance.**

**Raw material** (1)   A *current asset* representing inventory on hand and not yet used of material purchased by a *manufacturer* for use in manufacturing its product.

**Real account** (AE)   Permanent or balance sheet account, as distinct from *nominal* or *temporary account.*

**Realized holding gain** (16)   Gains on asset dispositions attributable to inflation rather than repeatable trading profit (difference between current prices and costs). Included in *realized income* under both GAAP and *replacement-cost accounting,* but only separately identifiable and identified under replacement cost accounting. Contrast with **Unrealized holding gain.**

**Realized income** (16)   Income that has been realized through exchange with persons or organizations distinct from the firm. Excludes holding gains (and possibly holding losses) that have not been realized. May not all be *distributable income.* Equal to *net income* as currently reported under GAAP.

**Receivables turnover** (A2)   Net credit sales (or, alternatively, net sales) divided by average net accounts receivable during the period.

**Reconcile**   Explain how one amount is derived from another.

**Redundant assets** (10)   Assets that are excessive or not required for current and anticipated levels of operation. *See also* **Overcapitalized.**

**Refunding**   Refers to refinancing *bonds payable* with new bonds.

**Regression analysis** (3)   *See* **Linear regression analysis.**

**Regression line** (A3, A5)   A line projecting or expressing a linear relationship between two variables, such as level of activity and cost incurred. *See also* **Regression analysis.**

**Related fringe costs** (7)   Associated costs that may vary directly with a particular cost under consideration. Labor fringe benefits such as employer payroll taxes, health plans, pension plans, and so forth are common examples.

**Relevant costing**   A product-costing alternative to direct and full (absorption) costing, under which fixed manufacturing costs are included in product costs when there exists demonstrable future benefit, and otherwise are excluded.

**Relevant costs** (7)   Those costs that are affected by an alternative under consideration and therefore are relevant to the particular decision involving that alternative. Include both *escapable* costs and real, measurable *opportunity costs.*

**Relevant range** (5)　A range of activity over which costs remain linear—fixed costs and variable cost rates remain constant. A range over which particular *budgeting rates* and *CVP analysis* remain valid.

**Reorder point** (4)　As units of inventory are used or reserved, the quantity of available stock that, when reached, must be accompanied by an order for replacement stock to avoid future *stockout*. The sum of the *minimum reorder point* (quantity) and the *safety stock* (quantity).

**Replacement cost** (16)　For an asset, the current cost of acquiring an asset of equivalent usefulness or productive capacity and in the same condition.

**Replacement-cost accounting** (16)　An alternative to *historical-cost accounting* (currently required under GAAP), in which nonmonetary assets are measured and reported at their current replacement costs and in which income and owners' equity include unrealized holding gain. Under simple replacement-cost accounting, changes in general purchasing power are ignored. Contrast with **PLAC** and **PLARC**.

**Reserve**　As properly used in accounting, refers only to an *appropriation* of *retained earnings*. In accounting, a reserve is not a fund nor does it imply that assets have been set aside.

**Reserve for depreciation**　An inferior term for *accumulated depreciation*.

**Residual income** (14)　In managerial accounting, refers to any excess of income in an *investment center* over the *capital charge* allocated/assessed to the center, representing the desired return on assets employed. A measure of investment-center performance. In financial accounting, refers to net income available to common stockholders (net income − preferred dividends).

**Responsibility accounting** (2)　Recording, classifying, and summarizing data within the firm by *responsibility center* to facilitate budgeting and performance evaluation.

**Responsibility center** (2)　A segment of an organization having responsibility for control of certain identifiable revenues and/or costs that is established as a distinct reporting entity for budgeting and control purposes.

**Responsible (behavior)** (11)　A term used in this text to denote employee behavior/attitude that is consonant with *McGregor's* **Theory Y**. Behavior characterized by assumption of responsibility for performance. Contrast with **Dependent (behavior).**

**Restriction** (of retained earnings) (10)　An amount of retained earnings not legally available for dividends as a result of contractual agreement with creditors or as a result of treasury stock acquired and not yet resold.

**Retail inventory method**　A method commonly used by retail firms for determining the cost of year-end inventory, and for estimating interim cost of goods sold. Inventory costs are estimated by using a percentage of selling price. The percentage is the weighted-moving-average percentage of goods available for sale at cost, to goods available at selling.

**Retained earnings** (AD)   *Net income* not yet distributed to owners. The sum of net income since the start of the corporation, less all dividends declared (cash and stock). At any given time, equal to total *stockholders' equity* less *contributed capital*.

**Retained earnings restrictions**   *See* **Restriction.**

**Retained earnings statement**   *See* **Statement of retained earnings.**

**Retroactive depreciation** (16)   In current-value accounting, applies to the amount of additional depreciation for prior years resulting from an increase in asset valuation in the current year. Also known as "catch-up depreciation."

**Return on assets employed** (A2)   EBIT divided by average total assets for the period.

**Return on common equity** (A2)   *Net income* (or income from operations after taxes) minus preferred dividend, divided by average common equity (total stockholders' equity minus preferred shares) for the period.

**Return on investment**   The net earnings on any investment (rent, interest, dividends) for a period, divided by the average amount invested during the period.

**Return on owners' equity** (A2)   *Net income* (or income from operations after income taxes) divided by average total owners' equity for the period.

**Revenue (AD)**   An inflow of *net assets* not donated, or resulting from additional owner investment. Assets received from the sale of goods or services to customers and from investments, or net assets received from the sale of noncurrent assets.

**Revenue centers** (11)   Organizational units having primary responsibility for revenue generated. May also be responsible for costs of generating revenue but not for costs of goods or services sold. Contrast with **Cost centers, Expenditure (expense) centers, Profit centers,** and **Investment centers.**

**Revenue collected in advance** (AD)   Advances of cash from customers, where the goods or services purchased have not as yet been delivered.

**Reversing entry** (AE)   An *entry* which is the opposite of a previous entry, and which therefore cancels the effect of the previous entry.

**Revised budget** (13)   *See* **Flexible budget.**

**Risk aversion** (17)   Refers to the fact that different individuals or firms may perceive (have) different capacities for sustaining losses, and therefore be more or less willing to undertake activities with given risks.

**Safety stock** (4)   A quantity of product or material on hand deemed desirable to provide insurance against *stockout* in the event of unanticipated increases in demand or delays in delivery between the time of reorder and the time of receipt of new stock. Together with the *minimum reorder-point* quantity, equals the *reorder-point* quantity. *See also* **Target inventory.**

**Sale**   A *revenue transaction* wherein goods or services are supplied to a customer in exchange for cash or a receivable.

**Sales budget** (3)   A plan (expressed both in dollars and in units) of sales expected for each product during the forthcoming period. Contrast with **Sales forecast.**

**Sales discount**   *See* **Cash discount.**

**Sales forecast**   A forecast or projection of sales demand that has not been modified/reaffirmed as the most reasonable/likely expectation of forthcoming sales—the *sales budget. See also* **Market-based (macro) forecasts** *and* **Sales-based (micro) forecasts.**

**Sales price variance** (14)   That portion of *total revenue variance* attributable to differences between actual price obtained and budgeted price:

(Actual price − Budgeted price) × Actual quantity sold.

Determined separately for each product and then summed. A positive variance indicates greater revenue and is identified as favorable. Together with the *contribution-mix variance,* equals the *total expected contribution variance.*

**Sales returns and allowance**   A *contra* revenue item including merchandise returned for credit by a customer and reductions of previously invoiced prices made to compensate for damaged, defective, or otherwise undesirable items sold to and retained by the customer.

**Sales volume variance** (14)   That portion of *total revenue variance* attributable to the difference between actual unit sales volume and budgeted unit sales volume:

(Actual quantity − Budgeted quantity) × Standard or budgeted price.

Determined separately for each product and then summed. A positive variance indicates greater revenue and is identified as favorable. The difference between variable budget sales and original (fixed) budget sales.

**Sales-based (micro) forecasts** (3)   A *sales forecast* based upon extrapolation of the firm's past experience and input from its own sales personnel. Contrast with **Market-based (macro) forecasts.**

**Salvage value** (AD)   The net recoverable cost (actual or estimated) of tangible fixed assets.

**Satisfactory profit** (6)   An amount of net income after taxes that is satisfactory to the firm's investors. An amount equivalent to the firm's cost of capital. May be less than the maximum profit that could be earned, especially in the short run.

**SCFP** (AD)   *See* **Statement of changes in financial position.**

**SCFP worksheet** (A9)   A working paper used in the preparation of a SCFP from other financial statements.

**Schedule of cash from operations** (9)   A detailed listing by time period (quarter, month, or shorter period) of all expected cash inflows (collections) and all expected cash outflows (expenditures) and their difference, related to the firm's operations. Does not include cash flows related to capital budgeting acquisitions and dispositions or financing activities (borrowings, debt repayments, interest, new owner investment, or dividends). A major input to the **preliminary cash budget.**

**Schedule of receivables collections** (9)  A detailed listing by time period (quarter, month, or shorter period) of expected cash inflows from cash sales and from collection of accounts receivable. A major input to the *schedule of cash from operations.*

**Schedule of working capital changes** (A9)  A supplementary listing of the changes in the balance of all current asset and current liability items during the period, which must accompany the SCFP as part of the financial statements.

**SEC** (AD)  Securities and Exchange Commission.

**Security**  A document evidencing ownership or indebtedness.

**Segment** (of a business)  A portion of a business representing a line of business or type of activity distinct from others.

**Segment margin** (14)  An amount of profit earned by a segment of the firm (profit or investment center) that contributes to the firm's profit. Equals the segment's *contribution* less those fixed costs/expenses exclusive to the segment less any additional fixed cost allocations that may be made to the segment.

**Semifixed cost**  *See* **Mixed cost.**

**Semivariable cost**  *See* **Mixed cost.**

**Sensitivity analysis** (8)  The process of analyzing a particular function/project/activity involving several variables, wherein a single variable at a time is given different values and the net effect upon the overall function is determined.

**Service center** (12)  A *responsibility center* that provides services to other responsibility centers rather than being directly involved in procurement, production, or sales activities. Maintenance, personnel, and computer departments are examples of service centers.

**Service firm**  A business that provides only services to customers, such as a financial institution. A service firm does not sell merchandise or products to customers. Contrast with a **Manufacturer** and a **Merchandising firm.**

**Service life**  *See* **Useful life.**

**Setup (cost)** (4)  The costs incurred for processing a single production shop order or purchasing order. For production orders, includes order scheduling, machine preparation (setup), and order follow-up costs. For purchasing includes costs of locating source of supply, issuing purchase order, order follow-up, receiving, and invoice processing and payment. An important element in the calculation of *economic lot size* or *economic reorder quantity. See also* **Ordering cost.**

**Shadow price** (17)    In *linear-programming* analysis, an important output of the optimal solution obtained by the *simplex method*. Discloses the marginal value or opportunity cost of one additional unit of a scarce resource.

**Shareholder**    One who owns shares of a corporation's common or preferred stock. *See* **Stockholder.**

**Short-range planning** (2)    *See* **Budgeting.**

**Short-term**    Current: due within one year.

**Shrinkage**    The difference between the balance of inventory shown after all transactions have been recorded and the *actual* quantity *on hand*. May result from theft, deterioration, loss, or clerical error.

**Shutdown costs** (7)    The costs that would be incurred to close down/suspend a particular operation or activity for a predetermined period. Distinct from costs of terminating or liquidating the operation or activity. Sometimes referred to as "mothballing" costs.

**Simple payback** (8)    A simple approach to evaluating an investment alternative, wherein the amount of investment is divided by the net annual benefits/savings to determine the time period before the initial investment is recovered. Ignores both tax effects and the time value (cost) of money, and therefore may be misleading for investments where either or both of these factors are significant. May be useful in *capital budgeting* as an additional tool of evaluation indicating the degree of time-commitment risk involved.

**Simplex method** (17)    A mathematical technique for use in the solution of a *linear-programming* problem. Involves a sequence of iterative steps designed to lead quickly to the optimal solution(s). Since calculations can be tedious, the solution is commonly performed by computer. Yields both optimal solution(s) and *shadow prices.*

**Sinking fund**    A *noncurrent asset.* A fund established to accumulate funds for the retirement of *long-term debt* or for other purposes.

**Social benefits** (15)    In the context of budgeting and controlling nonprofit organizations, the direct and indirect benefits including *externalities* (whether or not readily measurable) of a particular activity, project, or program.

**Social costs** (15)    In the context of budgeting and controlling nonprofit organizations, the direct and indirect costs including *externalities* (whether or not readily measurable) of a particular activity, project, or program.

**Solvency** (9, AD)    The ability to pay obligations when due.

**Sources of funds** (A9)    The places, activities, individuals, or groups from which a firm may obtain *working capital* for application elsewhere. Sources include operations, extraordinary gains, sale of noncurrent assets, new noncurrent debt, new owner investment, and reduction of balance of net working capital already on hand.

**Space costs**    The costs for a particular product or activity related to the occupancy of physical floor space or shelf space—storage costs for inventory. Includes such costs as rent or depreciation, utilities, insurance, and property taxes. One component of total *inventory-carrying cost* used in the calculation of economic lot size or *economic order quantity*.

**Specific** (cost) **identification** (AD)    One of the methods of measuring inventory costs, wherein items are each identified with their acquisition cost and an *inventory cost-flow assumption* becomes unnecessary.

**Specific inflation/specific price changes** (16)    Changes in the prices of certain specific goods or services as distinguished from general price-level changes averaged for all goods and services. Specific price changes move independently, and can even move in the opposite direction to general inflation.

**Specific price index**    A *price index* for a specific good or service or similar category. Useful in estimating replacement costs of assets, such as inventory, or specific groups of fixed assets. Contrast with **General price index.**

**Spending variance** (12)    The difference for any cost between the variable budgeted amount and the actual cost incurred (actual − variable budget). The amount spent in excess of the amount that should have been spent at the actual level of activity experienced. A positive amount indicates excessive cost and is identified as unfavorable.

**Split-off point** (1)    That point in the purchasing or production process involving *joint products* where one or more are separated and thereafter can be treated as (costs can be specifically identified with) a separate distinct product(s).

**Spoilage**    The cost of those materials or products rendered useless (except for possible scrap recovery value) in the production process. Spoilage that is considered to be ordinary and inevitable is identified as "normal spoilage" and included in product cost. Spoilage in excess of normal is known as "abnormal spoilage" and is preferably treated as a period cost.

**Standard cost** (13)    The planned cost of a unit of material or finished product that is predetermined and assigned to items procured or produced under a system of *standard costing* regardless of the actual costs incurred.

**Standard costing** (1)    A system applicable to both *job-order* and *process costing* of products, wherein the inventory cost of items purchased or manufactured is assigned their *standard cost* regardless of the actual costs incurred. Differences between actual and standard costs are known as *accounting variances* and are closed each period to cost of goods sold or, if material, may be allocated between ending inventory and cost of goods sold. *See also* **Job-order costing** *and* **Process costing.**

**Standard deviation** (17)    A measure of the dispersion around the mean of a *probability distribution* that is considered to be a normal distribution. Calculated as $\sqrt{(\sum(X - \overline{X})^2)/(n - 1)}$, where

$(X - \overline{X})$ = distance of each value from the mean,
$n$ = number of values (observations) in the distribution.

**Standard error (of the estimate)** (A3, A5)   A measure of the accuracy of a regression line as a predictor of relationships between two variables, that can be obtained as part of *least-squares regression analysis*. The higher the standard error, the greater the likelihood of estimating error through using the regression line. Calculated as $\sqrt{(\Sigma(Y - \overline{Y})^2)/(n - 2)}$, where

$(Y - \overline{Y})$ = deviations of available observed values of Y from regression-line values for the same X,

$n$ = number of observations.

*See also* **Regression analysis.**

**Standard overhead** (A12)   A term used in this text in connection with overhead variance analysis. Equals the amount of overhead at standard that would have been applied to inventory had there been no labor *efficiency variance*.

**Standard overhead rate** (13)   That portion of a product's *standard cost* representing overhead. The amount of overhead that will be applied to work-in-process inventory per unit of activity. *See also* **Predetermined overhead rate.**

**Standard price** (13)   The price component of a standard cost for material. The price that should be paid for one unit of raw material. Multiplied by the *standard quantity*, equals the material-cost component of a product's *standard cost*.

**Standard quantity** (13)   The usage component of a standard cost for material. The amount of material that should be used (consumed) in the manufacture of one unit of product. Multiplied by the *standard price*, equals the material-cost component of a product's standard cost.

**Standard rate** (13)   The wage-rate component of a standard cost for labor. The hourly rate that should be paid to (earned by) an employee having the requisite skill level to complete one unit of product within the prescribed *standard time*. Multiplied by the standard time, equals the labor-cost component of a product's *standard cost*.

**Standard time**   The time component of a standard cost for labor. The labor hours that should be expended to complete one unit of product. Multiplied by the *standard rate*, equals the labor-cost component of a product's *standard cost*.

**Standby costs** (7)   Those costs necessary to maintain the condition of a facility while in a shutdown or standby basis. Includes such costs as maintenance, insurance, security, and property taxes.

**Startup costs** (7)   Those costs necessary to restore a facility that has been shut down or on a standby basis to full operating capacity. Can include such costs as removal of protective covering, cleaning, painting, hiring personnel, and training.

**Stated value** (stock)   *See* **Par value.**

**Statement of cash flow** (A9)   A statement indicating cash generated from operations during the period, together with all other sources and applications of cash during the period.

**Statement of changes in financial position** (AD)   One of the four required financial statements under GAAP. A statement which discloses sources and applications of *working capital* (or cash), together with other major resource changes ("matched pairs") occurring during the year.

**Statement of financial position**   Another term for *balance sheet*.

**Statement of owner's capital** (AD)   One of the four financial statements required for a proprietorship or a partnership. Reconciles *owner's equity* at the beginning and the end of the period.

**Statement of retained earnings** (AD)   One of the four financial statements required for a corporation. Reconciles *retained earnings* at the beginning and the end of the period.

**States of nature** (17)   *See* **Events.**

**Statistical decision models** (17)   Mathematical models or techniques to facilitate decisions among alternative actions where probabilities of various *events* (outcomes) are known or may be estimated. Commonly involve five sequential steps:

1. identifying alternative available actions;
2. identifying possible future events or occurrences;
3. assigning probabilities to each event;
4. identifying the decision criterion and calculating a *payoff table;*
5. choosing the best alternative.

**Statutory merger**   A *business combination* resulting from either a *purchase* or a *pooling*, when the resulting economic entity is organized as a single legal entity and the parent–subsidiary relationship no longer exists.

**Stock**   In managerial accounting, the amount of inventory on hand at a given time. In financial accounting, also refers to ownership shares in a corporation.

**Stock dividend**   A pro-rata issuance and distribution of additional stock at no cost to existing stockholders. Usually limited to less than 20 percent of the shares previously outstanding.

**Stock split**   An issuance and distribution of additional shares of common stock on a pro-rata basis, to existing stockholders, at no cost to them. Generally limited to distributions in excess of 20 percent of shares previously outstanding.

**Stockholder**   An owner of the capital stock of a corporation.

**Stockholders' equity**   The *owners' equity* of a corporation.

**Stockout** (4)   The state or condition where the balance of inventory on hand and available for sale or use is zero.

**Straight-line (depreciation) method** (AD)   A method of determining depreciation or amortization wherein the *depreciable base* (cost less salvage value) is expensed in equal amounts over the asset's useful life.

**Strategic planning** (2)   Long-range planning or goal setting for the firm. Policy determination. Strategic plans usually extend beyond the intermediate range of two to five years and are expressed in terms of general objectives that are not necessarily measurable. Strategic plans usually do not address specific means of implementation. Also known as *long-range planning.* Contrast with **Intermediate-range plans** and **Budgets.**

**Subjective probabilities** (17)   See **Estimated probabilities.**

**Suboptimization** (14)   The condition where maximization of some value for a segment (division) precludes maximization of this same value for the firm or organization as a whole because of the existence of scarce resources or joint costs.

**Subsidiary** (AD)   A corporation legally owned or controlled by another corporation (*parent*) which owns more than 50 percent of the subsidiary's voting common stock.

**Subsidiary account**   A detail account carried in a subsidiary ledger. The subsidiary account's balance is combined with other like balances in a *control account* carried in the *general ledger.*

**Subsidiary ledger** (AE)   A ledger combining like subsidiary accounts whose combined total is carried in a corresponding control account in the general ledger.

**Sum-of-the-years' digits method** (AD)   *See* **Years' digits method.**

**Sunk costs** (7)   Past costs that are not *escapable* in terms of a particular decision alternative. Costs of past errors. Some sunk costs may be partially offset by income-tax savings, in which case the true sunk cost is the amount net of such savings. Contrast with **Escapable cost.**

**Sunset legislation** (15)   Legislation that provides for automatic termination dates for specific government programs, agencies, or other segments unless such activities are specifically reauthorized by separate legislative action.

**Supplies** (AD)   A current asset representing the cost of items acquired for consumption within one year as part of normal operating business activities. Supplies consumed in nonmanufacturing activities are disclosed as supplies expense, a period cost. Supplies consumed in manufacturing are included in *manufacturing overhead* as *indirect materials,* a product cost.

**SYD** (AD)   *See* **Years' digits method.**

**"T account"** (AE)   A symbol used as an instructional device to portray an account. Debits and credits are shown on the two sides, and the account title across the top.

**Take-home pay**   Employee earnings less taxes withheld and other payroll deductions. The portion of total pay actually received in cash by the employee.

**Tangible fixed assets** (AD)   Assets with future usefulness to the firm exceeding one year (noncurrent) which have physical form, such as land, buildings, equipment, and office furniture and fixtures.

**Target inventory** (4)   A minimum quantity of inventory desired at a specific future time. May be the same as *safety stock* or may exceed safety stock in anticipation of increased demand/usage.

**Target profit range** (6)   A term used in this book to describe a short-run range of acceptable/desirable profit, the use of which is intended to ensure long-range *satisfactory profit*.

**Tax accounting**   The accounting necessary to satisfy the IRS. The maintenance of adequate supporting records and the preparation and filing of necessary tax returns.

**Tax basis** (8)   The tax book value of a depreciable asset. The asset's cost less tax deductions taken to date. The basis for computing taxable gain or loss on disposition. Often lower than book value reported in financial statements.

**Tax credit**   A direct reduction of actual tax dollar liability, as distinct from a tax deduction.

**Tax deduction**   An amount specifically allowable as a deduction from taxable revenue and gain in the determination of taxable income. Similar to an expense in accounting; however, something that may logically be an expense may not be allowable under the tax code as a tax deduction.

**Tax depreciation** (8)   The amount of depreciation deduction taken for tax purposes, as distinct from depreciation expense used in financial accounting for income measurement.

**Tax management** (2)   A term used in this book to identify those business activities and decisions designed to reduce/minimize tax impact. Contrast with **Operating management** and **Financial management.**

**Tax management** (2)   The inclusion of "tax-consequence thinking" in the planning and execution of operating and financial decisions; and the preparation of required tax returns in such a manner as to minimize the firm's tax liability within the law.

**Tax shield** (8)   A tax deduction that reduces otherwise taxable income and therefore saves taxes. Often more narrowly defined to refer only to deductions not requiring outflow of net working capital. A depreciable asset providing future depreciation deductions is a common example of a potential tax shield.

**Taxable income**   The amount of income used as the basis for computing income-tax liability. Taxable revenue and gains less tax deductions. Rarely the same as accounting income before taxes because of both permanent differences and timing differences in the measurement of income between the two systems.

**Temporary holding loss** (investments)   A loss in recoverable (market) value of a noncurrent investment which is deemed temporary; that is, it will be recovered at or before the intended time when the specific invstment is to be liquidated.

**Temporary revaluations of long-term investments**   When a market loss is considered temporary, the asset "investment" is revalued (written down and written up but not *above* original cost) in the same manner as for *current marketable securities*. However, the corresponding temporary loss or gain is not included in the determination of net income. Instead it is reflected in a special valuation contra account included within owners' equity, which may be called "temporary loss on investments," or "temporary investments revaluation," or a similar title.

**Terms of sale**   Any conditions relating to payment connected with a particular sale transaction. For example, the terms "2/10, N/30" offer a two-percent cash discount if payment is made within ten days, and indicate full (net) payment is due within thirty days.

**Theory X (assumptions)** (11)   A group of assumptions regarding human motivation, identified by Douglas McGregor. Essentially, the group identified as Theory X postulates that individuals are dependent, needing motivation and direction, and desirous of avoiding responsibility. Contrast with **Theory Y** assumptions.

**Theory Y (assumptions)** (11)   A group of assumptions regarding human motivation, identified by Douglas McGregor. Essentially, the group identified as Theory Y postulates that individuals are self-motivated, creative, and desirous of assuming responsibility. Contrast with **Theory X** assumptions.

**Three-point estimate approach** (8)   A simplified method of incorporating probability into business decision analysis that involves projecting results under three different assumptions: the most likely outcome, a pessimistic forecast, and an optimistic forecast.

**Time-adjusted payback** (8)   A more sophisticated version of *simple payback* investment-decision analysis. Time-adjusted payback involves the determination of the number of years required for recovery of initial investment from benefits/cost savings that have been discounted to allow for the time value of money. Tax effects preferably are also taken into account. Contrast with **Simple payback.**

**Time-adjusted rate of return**   *See* **Internal rate of return** (IRR).

**Times interest earned** (A2)   Suggested as a measure of a firm's potential ability to cover interest payments in the future. EBIT divided by annual interest expense.

**Total assets**   The sum of all assets less all contra assets appearing on the balance sheet.

**Total revenue variance**   The difference between actual sales and originally budgeted sales. The sum of the *sales volume variance* (difference attributable to change in unit volume) and the *sales price variance* (difference attributable to change in prices of units sold).

**Trade discount**   A reduction from a list price offered or given to customers of a given type, such as a wholesale discount. Note that trade discounts are not recorded in the accounting system. Sales are initially recorded **net** of trade discounts.

**Trading on equity** (A10)   As an owner, earning money on the capital invested by others (noncurrent creditors and preferred stockholders). The objective of desirable debt financing. (*See also* **Financial leverage.**)

**Transaction** (AD)   Any exchange between the firm and another entity that affects the firm's financial position as reported on its balance sheet.

**Transfer price** (12)   A price assigned within the firm to goods or services provided by one responsibility center to another. Appropriate selection of transfer prices can be important, since inaccurate or carelessly calculated transfer prices might motivate *dysfunctional behavior* on the part of managers and lead to *suboptimization*.

**Transportation-in** (1)   The cost of delivering inventory from the supplier to the firm's selling locations (including to consignee's). If this cost is not already included in the invoice price for the inventory items, it is accumulated for inclusion in inventory-acquisition cost as part of net purchases.

**Treasury stock**   A small portion of a firm's own stock previously outstanding which has been reacquired—repurchased—and is being held for some purpose. A firm's own treasury stock is not shown as an asset on the balance sheet. Instead it is classified *contra* within *owners' equity*.

**Trial balance** (AE)   A summarization of all acccount balances with debits and credits separately totaled.

**Turnover**   The average number of times a particular *asset*, group of assets, or even total assets may be thought of as having been replaced during the year or period.

**Unappropriated retained earnings**   The amount of retained earnings which the directors indicate may serve as a basis for future dividends, subject to any footnoted restrictions, and subject to adequate solvency to allow declaration of a dividend.

**Unamortized cost**   The amount of the original cost of an *intangible asset* which has not yet been amortized to reflect expiration.

**Unaudited financial statements**   Financial statements which have not been subjected to an independent audit by a CPA.

**Uncertainty**   In the context of business decisions, often used synonymously with risk, referring to the variability of outcomes. More precisely, the term "risk" is applicable to those situations where various probabilities are known from experience, and "uncertainty" applies to those situations where probabilities can only be estimated.

**Undepreciated cost**    The current *book value* of a *tangible fixed asset.*

**Underabsorbed overhead**    *See* **Underapplied overhead.**

**Underapplied overhead** (1)    An *accounting variance.* An amount of manufacturing overhead incurred during the period in excess of that applied/absorbed/allocated (by using a *predetermined* or *standard overhead rate*) to product cost(s) in work-in-process inventory. The excess of cost incurred over cost applied. Underapplied overhead at year-end is closed to (added to) cost of goods sold or, if material, to work-in-process inventory, finished-goods inventory, and cost of goods sold in proportion to the location of goods manufactured during the year. Also known as *underabsorbed overhead.*

**Undercapitalized** (10)    Refers to a state wherein a firm has insufficient invested assets to support its current or intended level of activity.

**Unearned revenue** (AD)    *See* **Revenue collected in advance.**

**Unencumbered balance** (A15)    In *fund accounting,* the amount of a budget appropriation in a particular fund (or for a particular line item) that has not yet been spent or committed by contract.

**Unfavorable variance** (11)    A variance that has the effect of reducing income. A variance representing less revenue or more cost (expense) than planned.

**Units-of-production method** (AD)    One method of allocating *depreciation* over the useful life of a *tangible fixed asset.* The useful life is determined in terms of a usage measurement (e.g., a truck may have 200,000 miles of useful life). Annual depreciation is based on the proportion of current year's usage to useful life, times the depreciable base.

**Units-of-service method** (AD)    *See* **Units-of-production method.**

**Unlimited liability**    The legal status of *proprietors* and *general partners* (not true for limited partners or stockholders). Refers to full personal liability for all of the debts of the firm.

**Unrealized holding gain**    The appreciation of an asset above its fair market value at the time of acquisition, that has not yet been validated in the market by exchange with an outsider. Unrealized holding gains are not recognized in financial statements prepared under current GAAP. They are recognized in statements prepared following *replacement-cost accounting.*

**Useful life**    The period of time during which an *asset* is expected to provide benefit to the firm. The time period between date of acquisition and intended date of disposal.

**Use of funds**    *See* **Application of funds.**

**Valuation account**   An account, usually contra, which is used to modify the book value of another account. Examples include allowance for uncollectibles, discount on notes and bonds receivable and payable, accumulated depreciation, and treasury stock.

**Variable cost** (5)   A cost that changes in direct proportion to changes in activity levels, and that may be assumed to be zero at a zero activity level. Contrast with **Fixed cost** and **Mixed cost.**

**Variable costing**   *See* **Direct costing.**

**Variance**   In managerial accounting, the difference between two budgeted amounts (such as a volume variance between a fixed and a variable budget) or between a budgeted revenue or cost and the actual amount experienced or incurred. A *budget variance.*

In cost accounting, the difference between a cost incurred and the amount applied to product cost in work-in-process inventory. An *accounting variance.*

In statistics, a measure of dispersion of a distribution.

**Verifiability**   A principle of GAAP supporting the goal of objectivity in financial reporting. Verifiability requires that the transactions recognized in the financial statements must be supported by physical evidence such as receipts, cancelled checks, and so forth.

**Visual fit** (3)   An approach to *regression analysis* wherein the values are first plotted on a graph, and then a regression line is drawn so as to appear visually to approximate a line of best fit (variables above and below line are approximately equal). The slope and intercept of the line are then measured from the graph. Contrast with **High–low point method** and **Least-squares regression analysis.**

**Volume variance (budget)** (12)   The difference between a variable budget amount and the amount originally budgeted (fixed budget amount). That portion of the total variance between original budget and actual that is attributable to changes in the level of volume or activity. *See also* **Overhead volume variance.**

**Voting stock**   The capital stock of a corporation (usually only the common stock) which entitles the holder to vote for the election of directors and make other ownership decisions.

**Warranty**   A commitment by a seller to repair or replace products sold which proved defective within some stated time limit following sale.

**Wasting asset**   A natural resource which is limited in amount and is therefore depleted as used. Examples include oil and gas, minerals, and timber.

**Weighted average cost** (inventory) (AD)   *See* **Average cost.**

**Wholly owned subsidiary**   A corporation 100 percent of whose voting stock is owned by another corporation (parent), where there are no minority stockholders.

**Withdrawals**   Assets transferred from a firm to its owners.

**Work measurement** (13)   The analysis of tasks or activities to determine a standard or expected time or cost for their performance.

**Work in process** (1)   A *current asset* representing, for a *manufacturer*, inventory on hand at year-end in various astates of partial completion. The cost of such items will therefore be greater than their material cost but less than the full cost of a finished good.

**Working capital** (AD)   In general business use and in this text, refers only to *current assets*. Current assets less current liabilities are then known as *net working capital*. Possibly because accountants are accustomed to using the term current assets, many accounting texts define working capital as current assets minus current liabilities, and therefore discard net working capital as redundant. Unfortunately, both definitions are in use, and you must be careful to identify the meaning of this term in each situation.

**Working capital balance sheet**   An abbreviated balance sheet convenient in financial analysis for focusing attention on the permanent or long-term capital structure of the firm. A working capital balance sheet has total current liabilities eliminated from the assets and equities. It therefore consists of net working capital and noncurrent assets balanced by noncurrent debt and owners' equity.

**Working capital funds from operations** (A9)   A partially redundant term focusing attention on funds as being *net working capital* and not cash or all resources. *See* **Funds from operations.**

**Working capital funds-flow statement** (A9)   A statement of sources and applications of *net working capital* during the period. Would not include "matched pairs"; therefore, if any "matched pairs" existed during the year, a working capital statement would require the addition of the matched pairs, in order to qualify as a SCFP.

**Worksheet** (accounting) (AE)   A multicolumn working paper for convenient and rapid completion of the process of adjustment, closing, and statement preparation.

**Write off (down)**   To reduce an asset account balance, and charge to either expense or loss.

**Write up**   To increase an asset account balance not reflecting an actual transaction involving a flow of funds. GAAP currently allow write-ups in only three situations. Investments representing significant influence are written up to recognize proportional share of the other's earnings in advance of dividends. Current marketable securities may be written up, but not above original cost, to reflect market-value recovery of a previous write-down. Noncurrent investments previously written down to reflect a temporary loss may be written back up, but *not* above cost, to reflect recovery of market value.

**Years' digits method** (AD)   One of the common methods of *accelerated depreciation* or amortization. The digits representing the useful life are summed and divided into the *depreciable base* to obtain a single portion. The asset is then depreciated each year by an amount equal to the year's digit times one portion, in inverse order—the highest digit is used the first year.

**Yield method**   A method of amortizing *bond discount* or *premium* involving maintenance of the *book value* of the liability at present value each year to maturity. The yield method is preferred under GAAP, but straight-line amortization is allowed where the differences are not material. Also known as the *interest method*.

**ZBB** (15)   Zero-Base(d) Budgeting. An approach to establishing budgets wherein the entire activity and budget must be scrutinized and justified (starting from "ground zero"), rather than focusing on the rationale for changes from the prior period's budget or actual expenditure level. Contrast with **Incremental budgeting.**

# C

---

# SOLUTIONS TO
# ODD-NUMBERED
# ESSENTIAL AND
# SUPPLEMENTARY
# PROBLEMS

## Chapter 1

**EP 1.1**    a) Additional product costs = Net purchases = Gross purchases + Freight in − Purchase returns − Purchase discounts = $190,000.

b) Beginning inventory + Net purchases = Goods available for sale = $250,000. Goods available for sale − Ending inventory = Cost of goods sold = $180,000.

c)
| | |
|---|---|
| Space costs | $20,000 |
| Wages and salaries | 30,000 |
| Operating expenses | $50,000 |

**EP 1.3**    a)
| | | | |
|---|---|---|---|
| Beginning inventory, Raw Materials | $15,000 | | |
| Net purchases, Raw materials | 20,000 | | |
| Raw materials available | $35,000 | | |
| Less: Ending inventory, Raw materials | 10,000 | | |
| Raw materials used | | $ 25,000 | |
| Direct labor | | 50,000 | |
| Manufacturing overhead: | | | |
|    Indirect labor | $10,000 | | |
|    Factory supervision | 5,000 | | |
|    Factory space cost | 7,000 | | |
|    Factory supplies | 3,000 | 25,000 | |
| Total manufacturing costs | | $100,000 | |

b)
| | |
|---|---|
| Provision for income taxes | $10,000 |
| Salaries—Administrative and sales | 15,000 |
| Space cost—General and sales offices | 3,000 |
| Supplies—General office | 2,000 |
| Supplies—Shipping | 10,000 |
| Transportation-out | 5,000 |
| Total nonmanufacturing costs | $45,000 |

**EP 1.5**    a)
| | |
|---|---|
| Beginning work-in-process inventory | $ 10,000 |
| Total manufacturing costs (EP 1.3(a) above) | 100,000 |
| | $110,000 |
| Less: Ending work-in-process inventory | 5,000 |
| Cost of goods manufactured | $105,000 |

b) Nonmanufacturing costs = Period costs =   $ 45,000
(See EP1.3(b) above)

**EP 1.7**    A)
| | | |
|---|---|---|
| Total manufacturing costs | $15 | [3 + 4 + 8] |
| Cost of goods manufactured | $14 | [5 + 15 − 6] |
| Ending finished goods | $ 2 | [3 + 14 − 15] |

B)
| | | |
|---|---|---|
| Direct materials | $ 6 | [20 − 7 − 7] |
| Ending work-in-process | $ 3 | [4 + 20 − 21] |
| Beginning finished goods | $ 4 | [20 + 5 − 21] |

C) Total manufacturing costs          $45   [45 − 4 + 4]
   Manufacturing overhead              $10   [45 − 15 − 20]
   Cost of goods sold                  $44   [45 + 5 − 6]

D) Direct labor                        $ 6   [29 − 15 − 8]
   Beginning work in process           $ 4   [28 + 5 − 29]
   Ending finished goods               $ 4   [28 + 6 − 30]

EP 1.9                        ABCO COMPANY

### Schedule of Cost of Goods Manufactured
### for February 19X2

| | | |
|---|---:|---:|
| Direct materials | | |
| Beginning raw materials inventory | $15,000 | |
| Add: February net purchases | 20,000 | |
| Total raw materials available | $35,000 | |
| Less: Ending raw materials inventory | 10,000 | |
| Direct materials used in manufacturing | | $ 25,000 |
| Direct labor | | 50,000 |
| Manufacturing overhead | | |
| Indirect labor | $10,000 | |
| Factory supervision | 5,000 | |
| Factory space cost | 7,000 | |
| Factory supplies | 3,000 | 25,000 |
| Total manufacturing costs | | $100,000 |
| Add: Beginning work-in-process inventory | | 10,000 |
| | | $110,000 |
| Deduct: Ending work-in-process inventory | | 5,000 |
| Cost of goods manufactured | | $105,000 |

EP 1.11                        ABCO COMPANY

### Income Statement
### for Month of February, 19X2

| | | |
|---|---:|---:|
| Sales | | $160,000 |
| Less: Cost of goods sold | | |
| Beginning finished goods inventory | $ 30,000 | |
| Add: Cost of goods manufactured | 105,000 | |
| Goods available for sale | $135,000 | |
| Less: Ending finished goods inventory | 40,000 | 95,000 |
| Gross profit | | $ 65,000 |
| Less: Operating expenses | | |
| Salaries—Administrative and sales | $ 15,000 | |
| Space cost—General and sales offices | 3,000 | |
| Supplies—General office | 2,000 | |
| Supplies—Shipping | 10,000 | |
| Transportation-out | 5,000 | 35,000 |
| Income from operations before taxes | | $ 30,000 |
| Less: Provision for income taxes | | 10,000 |
| Net income | | $ 20,000 |

**SP 1.13**

| Direct material | $ 70,000 |
|---|---|
| Direct labor | 120,000 |
| Manufacturing overhead | 230,000 |
| Total manufacturing cost | $420,000 ÷ 60,000 units |
| Equals $7 per equivalent unit | |

**SP 1.15**

| | Units | | Material | | Equivalents |
|---|---|---|---|---|---|
| a) Transferred to finished goods: | 12,000 | × | 1.00 | = | 12,000 |
| Partially completed | 3,000 | × | 1.00 | = | 3,000 |
| Total equivalent units–Material | | | | | 15,000 |

| | Units | | Conversion | | Equivalents |
|---|---|---|---|---|---|
| Transferred to finished goods | 12,000 | × | 1.00 | = | 12,000 |
| Partially completed | 3,000 | × | 0.60 | = | 1,800 |
| Total equivalent units–Conversion | | | | | 13,800 |

b) Material cost per unit:
   Direct material cost $33,600 ÷ 15,000 equivalent units (−Material) equals $2.24
   Conversion cost per unit:
   Direct labor cost    $101,200
   Overhead applied    $202,400    ($101,200 × $2.00)
   Total conversion cost    $303,600 ÷ 13,800 equivalent units (−Conversion) equals $22.00
   Total product cost per unit:

| Material | $ 2.24 |
|---|---|
| Conversion | 22.00 |
| | $24.24 |

Note: A unit cost of $24.43 rounded ($337,000 ÷ 13,800) is incorrect since all material is added at start of production.

c) Ending WIP Inventory:

| | Equivalent units | Cost | Extension |
|---|---|---|---|
| Material cost | 3,000 | $ 2.24 | $ 6,720 |
| Conversion cost | 1,800 | 22.00 | 39,600 |
| Total | | | $46,320 |

d) 12,000 completed widgets less 2,000 in Ending finished goods = 10,000 widgets sold × $24.24 = $242,400 Cost of goods sold (not including accounting variances).

**SP 1.17**   a) Predetermined overhead rate,

$$\frac{\$40{,}000}{\$80{,}000} \frac{\text{Estimated overhead}}{\text{Estimated direct labor}},$$

equals $0.50 per Direct labor dollar.

b) Overhead applied = $85,000 Actual direct labor × $0.50 = $42,500 of overhead applied.

c)
| | |
|---|---|
| Actual overhead incurred | $45,000 |
| Overhead applied | 42,500 |
| Overhead accounting variance | $ 2,500   Underapplied |

d) Predetermined overhead rate,

$$\frac{\$\ 50{,}000}{\$125{,}000} \frac{\text{Estimated overhead}}{\text{Estimated prime cost}},$$

equals $0.40 per prime cost dollar.

e) Overhead applied = $120,000 Actual prime cost × $0.40 = $48,000 of overhead applied.

f)
| | |
|---|---|
| Actual overhead incurred | $40,000 |
| Overhead applied | 48,000 |
| Overhead accounting variance | $ 8,000   Overapplied |

**SP 1.19**   a) Overhead absorption rate = $4.00 per DLH $\left(\dfrac{\$120{,}000}{\$30{,}000}\right)$

Total manufacturing cost

| | Product A | Product P |
|---|---|---|
| Direct material | $100,000 | $ 50,000 |
| Direct labor | 60,000 | 150,000 |
| Applied overhead | 40,000 | 100,000 |
| | $200,000 | $300,000 |
| Total units manufactured | 100,000 | 5,000 |
| Unit manufacturing cost | $2.00 | $60.00 |

| | |
|---|---|
| Overhead incurred | $150,000 |
| Overhead applied | 140,000 |
| Underapplied overhead | $ 10,000 |

|                          | Product A          | Product B        |
|--------------------------|--------------------|------------------|
| Beginning finished goods | 20,000 @ $1.50     | 1,000 @ 50       |
| Goods manufactured       | 100,000 @ $2.00    | 5,000 @ 60       |
| Available units          | 120,000            | 6,000            |
| Ending units             | 25,000             | 800              |
| Units shipped            | 95,000             | 5,200            |
| LIFO shipments           | $190,000*          | $310,000†        |

\* 95,000 × $2.00
† (5,000 × $60.00) + (200 × $50.00)

| | |
|---|---|
| Shipments—Product A | $190,000 |
| Shipments—Product B | 310,000 |
| Underapplied overhead | 10,000 |
| LIFO Cost of goods sold | $510,000 |

b) Weighted average cost—Product A,

20,000 @ $1.50 = $ 30,000
100,000 @ $2.00 = 200,000
$230,000 ÷ 120,000,

equals $1.917 per unit (rounded).

Weighted average cost—Product B,

1,000 @ $50 = $ 50,000
5,000 @ $60 = 300,000
$350,000 ÷ 6,000,

equals $58.333 per unit (rounded).

| | |
|---|---|
| Shipments—Product A | $182,115 (95,000 × $1.917) |
| Shipments—Product B | 303,332 ( 5,200 × $58.333) |
| Underapplied overhead | 10,000 |
| Weighted average cost of goods sold | $495,447 (rounded) |

c)
| | |
|---|---|
| Shipments—Product A | $180,000 * |
| Shipments—Product B | 302,000 † |
| Underapplied overhead | 10,000 |
| FIFO Cost of goods sold | $492,000 |

\* (20,000 × $1.50)  + (75,000 × $2.00).
† ( 1,000 × $50.00) + ( 4,200 × $60.00).

## Chapter 2

EP 2.1    Steps in budgeting process for a nonmanufacturing (merchandising) firm:

Step 1: Preparation of sales budget—provides expected level of sales activity, unit demand for finished goods inventory, and expected dollar revenue.

Step 2: Preparation of finished goods inventory budget—provides unit demand for purchases and expected inventory levels (investment).

Step 3: Preparation of purchases budget—provides schedule of product acquisitions and one of the demands upon cash.

Step 4: Preparation of general, selling, and administrative expense budget—provides schedule of activities in the GS&A area, and provides another of the demands upon cash.

Step 5: Preparation of the capital budget—provides schedule of noncurrent asset acquisitions and retirements, and provides another of the demands upon cash (and possible debt financing).

Step 6: Preparation of the schedule of receivables collections—provides details of cash receipts to be expected from sales.

Step 7: Preparation of the cash budget—provides details of all expected cash receipts and disbursements and information of any requirements for additional cash investment and/or excess cash.

Step 8: Preparation of the master budget—incorporates all other budgets together with the final financial and cash budgets; provides pro-forma or expected financial statements for the forthcoming year.

* *Note:* For a merchandiser, the GSA budget is the operating budget. The GSA budget may first be prepared by responsibility centers and then aggregated to an all-company GSA budget.

**EP 2.3**   a) (1) Pro-forma statement of changes in financial position
   (2) Pro-forma income statement
   (3) Pro-forma balance sheet
   (4) Cash budget
   (5) Capital budget
   (6) Operating budgets


b) (1) Expected sources and applications of working capital
   (2) Expected revenues, expenses, and earnings
   (3) Expected financial position at year-end
   (4) Expected cash receipts and disbursements
   (5) Scheduled noncurrent asset acquisitions and dispositions
   (6) Expected costs and revenue by category by responsibility center


c) (1) Acts as budget of financing activities
   (2) Acts as budget of overall earnings for total firm performance measurement purposes
   (3) Purpose: to verify accuracy of capital investment, capital structure, solvency, and liquidity
   (4) Acts as basis for forthcoming year's cash management
   (5) Acts as budget for capital asset acquisitions and retirements
   (6) Serves as basis for evaluating performance during forthcoming year

**EP 2.5**   a) Uses unit sales demand from the sales budget to determine necessary acquisition of finished goods

b) Uses requirements from finished goods inventory budget to determine necessary production shop orders

c) Uses requirements for scheduled shop orders from production schedule to determine necessary acquisitions of raw material

d) Uses requirements from raw materials budget (and possibly from finished goods inventory budget for purchased finished products) to schedule purchases

e) Uses requirements for scheduled shop orders from production schedule to establish direct labor requirements

f) Uses requirements for scheduled shop orders from production schedule to establish manufacturing overhead requirements

g) Uses activity, as indicated in the sales budget and production schedule, to establish GSA expense requirements

**SP 2.7**   a) Current ratio = 1.8:1 $\left(\dfrac{\$300}{\$164}\right)$

b) Quick ratio = 1.2:1 $\left(\dfrac{\$190}{\$164}\right)$

c) Debt ratio = 0.47:1 $\left(\dfrac{\$194}{\$410}\right)$

d) Receivables turnover = 5 times $\left(\dfrac{\$800}{(\$165 + \$155)/2}\right)$

e) Inventory turnover = 4.4 times $\left(\dfrac{\$480}{(\$115 + \$105)/2}\right)$

f) Asset turnover = 1.97 times $\left(\dfrac{\$800}{(\$401 + \$410)/2}\right)$

g) Gross margin percentage = 40% $\left(\dfrac{\$320}{\$800} \times 100\right)$

h) Operating ratio = 9.75% $\left(\dfrac{\$78}{\$800} \times 100\right)$

i) Times interest earned = 27 times $\left(\dfrac{\$78 + \$3}{\$3}\right)$

j) Return on assets employed = 19.98% $\left(\dfrac{\$78 + \$3}{(\$401 + \$410)/2}\right)$

k) Return on owner's investment = 14.9% $\left(\dfrac{\$31}{(\$200 + \$216)/2}\right)$

**SP 2.9**   a) 1.8:1   b) 1.4:1   c) 0.52:1

d) 4 times   e) 5 times   f) 1.49 times

g) 60%   h) 16.7%   i) 13.5 times

j) 26.8%   k) 33.9%

**Chapter 3**

**EP 3.1**   a) Fully controllable items:   (8), (9), (10), (11), (12), and (13)

b) Partially controllable or influenceable items:   (14) and (15)

c) Items not controllable or influenceable:   (1), (2), (3), (4), (5), (6), and (7)

**EP 3.3**   The firm's demand curve might be expected to shift up and to the right (increased customer demand) in response to:

Price decrease (8)
Increased advertising (9)
Greater promotion (10)
More, more highly trained, or better paid sales personnel (11)
Improved product quality and appearance (12)
Improved product availability and service (13)
Improved customer experience with product (14)
Increased positive word-of-mouth advertising (15)

The opposite change in any of these factors taken separately might be expected to shift the firm's demand curve down and to the left (decreased customer demand).

**EP 3.5**   Potential water ski market:

| Age group | Population | Total market | Potential market* |
|---|---|---|---|
| 0–10 | 20,000,000 | 60,000 | 36,000 |
| 10–20 | 40,000,000 | 900,000 | 540,000 |
| 20–30 | 50,000,000 | 900,000 | 540,000 |
| 30–40 | 20,000,000 | 660,000 | 396,000 |
| 40–50 | 30,000,000 | 450,000 | 270,000 |
| Over 50 | 40,000,000 | 30,000 | 18,000 |
| | 200,000,000 | 3,000,000 | 1,800,000 |

\* 60 percent of total market not yet saturated.

**EP 3.7**   a)   $36 = 16{,}000a + b$
$\underline{76 = \phantom{1}6{,}000a + b}$
$-40 = 10{,}000a$
$a = -0.004$
$36 = 16{,}000(-0.004) + b$
$b = 100$

Demand curve: $Y = 100 - 0.004X$

b) At price of $40:
$40 = 100 - 0.004X$
$X = 15{,}000$ units of forecasted sales demand

At price of $65:
$65 = 100 - 0.004X$
$X = 8{,}750$ units forecasted sales demand

**EP 3.9**   a)   $50 = 350{,}000a + b$
$\underline{300 = 100{,}000a + b}$
$-250 = 250{,}000a$
$a = -0.001$
$b = 400$

b) At price of $60:
$60 = 400 - 0.001X$
$X = 340{,}000$ units of forecasted sales demand

At price of $225:
$225 = 400 - 0.001X$
$X = 175{,}000$ units of forecasted sales demand

c) Problem EP3.9 demand curve more elastic (sales demand less sensitive to price change) than Problem EP3.7 demand curve, since slope $(-0.001)$ is less steep than $(-0.004)$.

**EP 3.11**

| Total year forecast: | Product P | Product Q |
|---|---|---|
| Market-based | 13,120 | 35,700 |
| Sales-based | 11,880 | 32,300 |
| Midpoint | 12,500 | 34,000 |

| 19X9 sales budget: | Product P | | ProductQ | |
|---|---|---|---|---|
| First quarter | 1,875 | (15%) | 10,200 | (30%) |
| Second quarter | 3,125 | (25%) | 10,200 | (30%) |
| Third quarter | 3,750 | (30%) | 5,100 | (15%) |
| Fourth quarter | 3,750 | (30%) | 8,500 | (25%) |
| Total year | 12,500 | 100 % | 34,000 | 100% |

**SP 3.13**   a)

| Price, Y | Quantity, X | XY | $X^2$ |
|---|---|---|---|
| $ 36 | 16,000 | $ 576,000 | 256,000,000 |
| 43 | 14,000 | 602,000 | 196,000,000 |
| 53 | 12,000 | 636,000 | 144,000,000 |
| 59 | 10,000 | 590,000 | 100,000,000 |
| 69 | 8,000 | 552,000 | 64,000,000 |
| 76 | 6,000 | 456,000 | 36,000,000 |

Totals:

| | | | |
|---|---|---|---|
| $n$ | 6 | | |
| $\Sigma Y$ | $336 | | |
| $\Sigma X$ | | 66,000 | |
| $\Sigma XY$ | | | $3,412,000 |
| $\Sigma X^2$ | | | 796,000,000 |

A.   $\Sigma XY = b \Sigma X + a \Sigma X^2$
B.   $\Sigma Y = nb + a \Sigma X$

A.   $3,412,000 = 66,000b + 796,000,000a$
B.   $336 = 6b + 66,000a$

Let $B_1 = B \times 11,000$

A.   $3,412,000 = 66,000b + 796,000,000a$
$B_1$   $3,696,000 = 66,000b + 726,000,000a$

A. $- B_1 - 284,000 = 70,000,000a$
$a = -0.0041$ (rounded)
$b = 101.1$

*Demand curve equation:* $Y = 101.1 - 0.0041X$

b)

| Quantity, X | Price, Y | Estimated price, $\overline{Y}$ | $Y - \overline{Y}$ | $(Y - \overline{Y})^2$ |
|---|---|---|---|---|
| 16,000 | $36 | $35.5 | 0.5 | 0.25 |
| 14,000 | 43 | 43.7 | -0.7 | 0.49 |
| 12,000 | 53 | 51.9 | 1.1 | 1.21 |
| 10,000 | 59 | 60.1 | -1.1 | 1.21 |
| 8,000 | 69 | 68.3 | 0.7 | 0.49 |
| 6,000 | 76 | 76.5 | -0.5 | 0.25 |
| | | | $\Sigma (Y - \overline{Y})^2$ | = 3.9 |

Standard error $= \sqrt{\dfrac{\Sigma(Y - \overline{Y})^2}{n-2}} = \sqrt{\dfrac{3.9}{4}} = 0.9874$ (rounded).

SP 3.15    a)

| | Price, Y | Quantity, X | XY | $X^2$ |
|---|---|---|---|---|
| | $ 50 | 350,000 | $ 17,500,000 | 122,500,000,000 |
| | 100 | 297,000 | 29,700,000 | 88,209,000,000 |
| | 150 | 252,000 | 37,800,000 | 63,504,000,000 |
| | 200 | 198,000 | 39,600,000 | 39,204,000,000 |
| | 250 | 152,000 | 38,000,000 | 23,104,000,000 |
| | 300 | 100,000 | 30,000,000 | 10,000,000,000 |

Totals:

| | | | | |
|---|---|---|---|---|
| $n$ | 6 | | | |
| $\Sigma Y$ | $1,050 | | | |
| $\Sigma X$ | | 1,349,000 | | |
| $\Sigma XY$ | | | $192,600,000 | |
| $\Sigma X^2$ | | | | 346,521,000,000 |

A. $192,600,000 = 1,349,000b + 346,521,000,000a$
B.     $1,050 = 6b + 1,349,000a$

Let $B_1 = B \times 224,833.3$

$B_1$         $236,070,000 = 1,349,000b + 303,300,000,000a$
A. $- B_1$     $-43,470,000 = 43,221,000,000a$
                    $a = -0.001$  (rounded)
                    $b = 401$  (rounded)

*Regression line:*   $Y = 401.1 - 0.001X$

| Quantity X | Price Y | Estimated price, $\overline{Y}$ | $Y - \overline{Y}$ | $(Y - \overline{Y})^2$ |
|---|---|---|---|---|
| 350,000 | $ 50 | $ 51 | −1 | 1 |
| 297,000 | 100 | 104 | −4 | 16 |
| 252,000 | 150 | 149 | 1 | 1 |
| 198,000 | 200 | 203 | −3 | 9 |
| 152,000 | 250 | 249 | 1 | 1 |
| 100,000 | 300 | 301 | −1 | 1 |
| | | | | $\Sigma(Y - \overline{Y})^2 = 29$ |

$$\text{Standard error} = \sqrt{\frac{\Sigma(Y - \overline{Y})^2}{n - 2}} = \sqrt{7.25} = 2.69 \quad \text{(rounded)}$$

b) The regression line derived in this problem is a **less** precise forecasting tool than the one derived in Problem SP3.13, since it has a higher standard error ($2.69 as compared to $0.99).

c) The regression line derived in this problem indicates greater elasticity of demand than the one derived in Problem SP3.13, since the slope is less steep (−0.001 as compared to −0.004).

## Chapter 4

### EP 4.1 Finished Goods Inventory Budget (units)

| Month | Budgeted sales | Target inven-tory | Total require-ments | Less: Planned stock* | Necessary acqui-sitions | EOQ | Excess |
|---|---|---|---|---|---|---|---|
| Jan | 11,000 | 9,000 | 20,000 | 11,600 | 8,400 | 15,000 | 6,600 |
| Feb | 9,000 | 5,000 | 14,000 | 15,600 | 0 | 0 | 1,600 |
| Mar | 5,000 | 4,000 | 9,000 | 6,600 | 2,400 | 15,000 | 12,600 |
| Apr | 4,000 | 3,000 | 7,000 | 16,600 | 0 | 0 | 9,600 |
| May | 3,000 | 2,000 | 5,000 | 12,600 | 0 | 0 | 7,600 |
| Jun | 2,000 | 2,000 | 4,000 | 9,600 | 0 | 0 | 5,600 |
| Jul | 2,000 | 4,000 | 6,000 | 7,600 | 0 | 0 | 1,600 |
| Aug | 4,000 | 6,000 | 10,000 | 5,600 | 4,400 | 15,000 | 10,600 |
| Sep | 6,000 | 12,000 | 18,000 | 16,600 | 1,400 | 15,000 | 13,600 |
| Oct | 12,000 | 15,000 | 27,000 | 25,600 | 1,400 | 15,000 | 13,600 |
| Nov | 15,000 | 13,000 | 28,000 | 28,600 | 0 | 0 | 600 |
| Dec | 13,000 | 11,000 | 24,000 | 13,600 | 10,400 | 15,000 | 4,600 |
| Total | 86,000 | | | | | | |

* Planned stock equals prior month's target inventory plus excess.

Budgeted sales                $602,000 (86,000 × $7.00)
Budgeted cost of goods sold   $344,000 (86,000 × $4.00)
Budgeted year-end inventory   $ 62,400 (15,600 × $4.00)

### EP 4.3 Production Schedule

Product P

| Start month | Requirements[1] | Carryover[2] | Net requirements | Scheduled production |
|---|---|---|---|---|
| Jan | 0 | 0 | 0 | 0 |
| Feb | 2,000 | 0 | 2,000 | 6,000 |
| Mar | 4,000 | 4,000 | 0 | 0 |
| Apr | 3,000 | 0 | 3,000 | 6,000 |
| May | 2,000 | 3,000 | 0 | 0 |
| Jun | 3,000 | 1,000 | 2,000 | 6,000 |
| Jul | 2,000 | 4,000 | 0 | 0 |
| Aug | 2,000 | 2,000 | 0 | 0 |
| Sep | 1,000 | 0 | 1,000 | 6,000 |
| Oct | 500 | 5,000 | 0 | 0 |
| Nov | 500 | 4,500 | 0 | 0 |
| Dec | 0 | 4,000 | 0 | 0 |

*(See notes on next page.)*

Product Q

| Start month | Require-ments[1] | Carry-over[2] | Net require-ments | Scheduled produc-tion |
|---|---|---|---|---|
| Jan | 8,000 | 0 | 8,000 | 9,000 |
| Feb | 2,000 | 1,000 | 1,000 | 9,000 |
| Mar | 3,000 | 8,000 | 0 | 0 |
| Apr | 3,000 | 5,000 | 0 | 0 |
| May | 1,000 | 2,000 | 0 | 0 |
| Jun | 4,000 | 1,000 | 3,000 | 9,000 |
| Jul | 5,000 | 6,000 | 0 | 0 |
| Aug | 1,000 | 1,000 | 0 | 0 |
| Sep | 2,000 | 0 | 2,000 | 9,000 |
| Oct | 3,000 | 7,000 | 0 | 0 |
| Nov | 0 | 4,000 | 0 | 0 |
| Dec | 0 | 4,000 | 0 | 0 |

Notes: (1) Allowing for manufacturing lead times.
        (2) Excess ELS production from prior month.

**EP 4.5**            Raw Materials Inventory Budget (units)

Material A

| Month | Production require-ments | Safety stock | Total require-ments | Less: Planned stock* | Needed purchases | EOQ | Excess |
|---|---|---|---|---|---|---|---|
| Jan | 4,000 | 2,000 | 6,000 | 1,500 | 4,500 | 6,400 | 1,900 |
| Feb | 0 | 2,000 | 2,000 | 3,900 | 0 | 0 | 1,900 |
| Mar | 0 | 2,000 | 2,000 | 3,900 | 0 | 0 | 1,900 |
| Apr | 4,000 | 2,000 | 6,000 | 3,900 | 2,100 | 6,400 | 4,300 |
| May | 0 | 2,000 | 2,000 | 6,300 | 0 | 0 | 4,300 |
| Jun | 4,000 | 2,000 | 6,000 | 6,300 | 0 | 0 | 300 |
| Jul | 0 | 2,000 | 2,000 | 2,300 | 0 | 0 | 300 |
| Aug | 0 | 2,000 | 2,000 | 2,300 | 0 | 0 | 300 |
| Sep | 4,000 | 2,000 | 6,000 | 2,300 | 3,700 | 7,700 | 4,000 |
| Oct | 0 | 2,000 | 2,000 | 6,000 | 0 | 0 | 4,000 |
| Nov | 0 | 2,000 | 2,000 | 6,000 | 0 | 0 | 4,000 |
| Dec | 4,000 | 2,000 | 6,000 | 6,000 | 0 | 0 | 0 |

Material B

| Month | Production require-ments | Safety stock | Total require-ments | Less: Planned stock* | Needed purchases | EOQ | Excess |
|---|---|---|---|---|---|---|---|
| Jan | 6,000 | 3,600 | 9,600 | 2,400 | 7,200 | 7,200 | 0 |
| Feb | 0 | 3,600 | 3,600 | 3,600 | 0 | 0 | 0 |
| Mar | 6,000 | 3,600 | 9,600 | 3,600 | 6,000 | 7,200 | 1,200 |
| Apr | 0 | 3,600 | 3,600 | 4,800 | 0 | 0 | 1,200 |
| May | 6,000 | 3,600 | 9,600 | 4,800 | 4,800 | 10,800 | 6,000 |
| Jun | 6,000 | 3,600 | 9,600 | 9,600 | 0 | 0 | 0 |
| Jul | 0 | 3,600 | 3,600 | 3,600 | 0 | 0 | 0 |
| Aug | 6,000 | 3,600 | 9,600 | 3,600 | 6,000 | 7,200 | 1,200 |
| Sep | 0 | 3,600 | 3,600 | 4,800 | 0 | 0 | 1,200 |
| Oct | 6,000 | 3,600 | 9,600 | 4,800 | 4,800 | 7,200 | 2,400 |
| Nov | 0 | 3,600 | 3,600 | 6,000 | 0 | 0 | 2,400 |
| Dec | 0 | 3,600 | 3,600 | 6,000 | 0 | 0 | 2,400 |

Material C

| Month | Production require- ments | Safety stock | Total require- ments | Less: Planned stock* | Needed purchases | EOQ | Excess |
|---|---|---|---|---|---|---|---|
| Jan | 17,000 | 9,400 | 26,400 | 6,000 | 20,400 | 29,400 | 9,000 |
| Feb | 0 | 9,400 | 9,400 | 18,400 | 0 | 0 | 9,000 |
| Mar | 9,000 | 9,400 | 18,400 | 18,400 | 0 | 0 | 0 |
| Apr | 8,000 | 9,400 | 17,400 | 9,400 | 8,000 | 34,000 | 26,000 |
| May | 9,000 | 9,400 | 18,400 | 35,400 | 0 | 0 | 17,000 |
| Jun | 17,000 | 9,400 | 26,400 | 26,400 | 0 | 0 | 0 |
| Jul | 0 | 9,400 | 9,400 | 9,400 | 0 | 0 | 0 |
| Aug | 9,000 | 9,400 | 18,400 | 9,400 | 9,000 | 34,000 | 25,000 |
| Sep | 8,000 | 9,400 | 17,400 | 34,400 | 0 | 0 | 17,000 |
| Oct | 9,000 | 9,400 | 18,400 | 26,400 | 0 | 0 | 8,000 |
| Nov | 0 | 9,400 | 9,400 | 17,400 | 0 | 0 | 8,000 |
| Dec | 8,000 | 9,400 | 17,400 | 17,400 | 0 | 0 | 0 |

* Planned stock equals safety stock plus excess EOQ acquisition from prior month.

Purchases Budget (dollars)

| Month arriving | Material A | Material B | Material C | Total |
|---|---|---|---|---|
| Jan | $704 | $1,152 | $1,176 | $3,032 |
| Feb | 0 | 0 | 0 | 0 |
| Mar | 0 | 1,152 | 0 | 1,152 |
| Apr | 704 | 0 | 1,360 | 2,064 |
| May | 0 | 1,728 | 0 | 1,728 |
| Jun | 0 | 0 | 0 | 0 |
| Jul | 0 | 0 | 0 | 0 |
| Aug | 0 | 1,152 | 1,360 | 2,512 |
| Sep | 847 | 0 | 0 | 847 |
| Oct | 0 | 1,152 | 0 | 1,152 |
| Nov | 0 | 0 | 0 | 0 |
| Dec | 0 | 0 | 0 | 0 |
| Total | $2,255 | $6,336 | $3,896 | $12,487 |

Anticipated year-end inventory:

| Material | Units | Unit cost | Total |
|---|---|---|---|
| A | 2,000 | $0.11 | $220 |
| B | 6,000 | 0.16 | 960 |
| C | 9,400 | 0.04 | 376 |
| Total | | | $1,556 |

**EP 4.7**   Costs related or associated with carrying too little inventory: (a), (b), (d), (e), (g), (i), (l), and (m).

**EP 4.9**   a) (Lead time × Usage) + Safety stock = Reorder point
   Product X (    4    ×   200   ) +     400      = 1,200 units
   Product Y (    9    ×   100   ) +     200      = 1,100 units

b)

| | Old reorder point | New reorder point | Change |
|---|---|---|---|
| Product X | 1,200 | 1,600 | + 400 units |
| Product Y | 1,100 | 1,300 | + 200 units |

c)

| | Old reorder point | New reorder point | Change |
|---|---|---|---|
| Product X | 1,200 | 1,600 | + 400 units |
| Product Y | 1,100 | 1,550 | + 450 units |

**EP 4.11**   a) Budgeted sales − Open stock + Closing stock = Planned purchases
        $690,000     −     100,000   +     125,000    = $715,000 (selling)

       $715,000 × 0.4 = $286,000 Purchases at cost

b) Planned purchases − Commitments = Open to buy
      $286,000       − $215,000      = $71,000

**SP 4.13**   a)

| | Product X | Product Y |
|---|---|---|
| Annual usage | 10,400 units | 5,200 units |
| ELS | 3,000 | 1,000 |
| Average number of orders | 3.4 | 5.2 |

b) Average units on hand equal $\dfrac{ELS}{2}$ + Safety stock

| | Product X | Product Y | Total |
|---|---|---|---|
| Average units on hand | 1,900 | 700 | |
| Average inventory investment | $95,000 | $140,000 | $235,000 |

c) Inventory turnover equals $\dfrac{\text{Cost of goods sold}}{\text{Average inventory}}$

| | Product X | Product Y | Total |
|---|---|---|---|
| Cost of goods sold | $520,000 | $1,040,000 | $1,560,000 |
| Inventory turnover | 5.5 times | 7.4 times | 6.6 times |

**SP 4.15**

| | Product A | Product B |
|---|---|---|
| a) Safety stock for usage increase—20% risk | 0 | 0 |
| Safety stock reorder delay—20% risk | 1 wk usage | 1 wk. usage |
| Total safety stock | 200 units | 300 units |
| b) Reorder point* | 1,800 units | 2,100 units |

* (Normal lead time × normal usage) + Safety stock

**SP 4.17**  Product A:

| | |
|---|---:|
| Factory set-up cost | $300.00 |
| Order issuing cost | 15.00 |
| Total ordering cost ($S$) | $315.00 |
| | |
| Space cost per unit | $1.00 |
| Property tax cost per unit | 4.20 |
| Insurance cost per unit | 3.50 |
| Interest cost per unit | 8.40 |
| Deterioration risk per unit | 1.40 |
| Unit inventory carrying cost ($RC$) | $18.50 |

**SP 4.19**

$$\text{ELS} = \sqrt{\frac{2\,SU}{RC}} = \sqrt{\frac{2 \times 315 \times 6{,}000}{18.50}} = \sqrt{204{,}324} = 452 \text{ units}$$

**SP 4.21**

a) $\text{ELS} = \sqrt{\dfrac{2 \times 330 \times 6{,}000}{18.50}} = \sqrt{214{,}054} = 463 \text{ units}$

old ELS (452); new ELS (463); change = 11 units, or 2 percent increase

b) $\text{ELS} = \sqrt{\dfrac{2 \times 315 \times 6{,}000}{15.20^*}} = \sqrt{248{,}684} = 499 \text{ units}$

old ELS (452); new ELS (499); change = 47 units, or 10 percent increase

| | |
|---|---:|
| * Space | $0.50 |
| Property tax | 2.80 |
| Insurance | 3.50 |
| Interest | 7.00 |
| Deterioration/obsolescence | 1.40 |
| Unit inventory carrying cost ($RC$) | $15.20 |

**Chapter 5**

**EP 5.1**  a) and b)

| Cost | Probable identification | Mgmt. level |
|:---:|:---:|:---:|
| (1) | V | Sup. |
| (2) | M | Sup. |
| (3) | M | Sup. |
| (4) | F | Exec. |
| (5) | F | Exec. |
| (6) | M | Sup. |
| (7) | F | Exec. |
| (8) | V | Sup. |
| (9) | F | Exec. |

**EP 5.3**                Shipping Department Budget for Third Quarter 19XX

| Item | July budget | August budget | September budget | Third-quarter budget |
|------|------------|--------------|-----------------|----------------------|
| Indirect labor | $8,750 | $6,350 | $5,450 | $20,550 |
| Indirect materials | 800 | 480 | 360 | 1,640 |
| Shipping | 2,600 | 1,560 | 1,170 | 5,330 |
| Total | $12,150 | $8,390 | $6,980 | $27,520 |

**EP 5.5**                Sales Division Budget for First Quarter 19XX

| Item | Jan. budget | Feb. budget | Mar. budget | First-quarter budget |
|------|------------|------------|------------|----------------------|
| Wages, salaries and commissions | $10,023 | $10,723 | $12,124 | $32,870 |
| Distribution and marketing | 4,408* | 4,758 | 5,459 | 14,625 |
| Depreciation | 500 | 500 | 500 | 1,500 |
| Miscellaneous | 166 | 167 | 167 | 500 |
| Total | $15,097 | $16,148 | $18,250 | $49,495 |

* January distribution and marketing budget:

| | |
|---|---|
| Travel (Sales territory #1) | $1,000 |
| Travel (Sales territory #2) | 700 |
| Indirect materials (shipping) | 320 |
| Freight-out (shipping) | 1,040 |
| Advertising/promotional–Fixed | 708 |
| Advertising/promotional—Variable | 640 |
| Total | $4,408 |

**EP 5.7**   a) Budgeting rates:

| | |
|---|---|
| Cost of goods sold | $0.6 sales dollars V |
| Wages and salaries* | $30,000 F + $0.1 sales dollar V |
| Supplies | $0.022 sales dollar V |
| Insurance | $10,000 F |
| Utilities* | $6,000 F + $.01 sales dollar V |
| Rent | $80,000 F |
| Depreciation | $40,000 F |
| Miscellaneous | $0.01 sales dollar V |

* Mixed costs determined by high-low-point analysis.

b)

### Burroughs Company

#### 19X8 Budgeted Income Statement

| | | |
|---|---:|---:|
| Sales | | $1,200,000 |
| Cost of goods sold | | 720,000 |
| Gross profit | | $480,000 |
| Operating expenses | | |
| Wages and salaries | $150,000 | |
| Supplies | 26,400 | |
| Insurance | 10,000 | |
| Utilities | 18,000 | |
| Rent | 80,000 | |
| Depreciation | 40,000 | |
| Miscellaneous | 12,000 | 336,400 |
| Income from operations | | $ 143,600 |
| Provision for income taxes (35%) | | 50,260 |
| Net income | | $   99,340 |

**SP 5.9**

a)
$$\$15,000 = 10,800a + b$$
$$9,000 = 6,000a + b$$
$$\$ 6,000 = 4,800a$$
$$a = 1.25$$
$$b = 1,500$$

Budgeting rate = $1,500 F + $1.25 per unit V

b) $1,500 + $1.25(11,750) = $16,187.50   budgeted cost

**SP 5.11**

a)

| Cost, Y | Quantity, X | XY | X² |
|---:|---:|---:|---:|
| $ 9,000 | 6,000 | $ 54,000,000 | 36,000,000 |
| 10,100 | 7,000 | 70,700,000 | 49,000,000 |
| 12,000 | 8,500 | 102,000,000 | 72,250,000 |
| 14,500 | 10,000 | 145,000,000 | 100,000,000 |
| 15,000 | 10,800 | 162,000,000 | 116,640,000 |

Totals

| | | | | |
|---|---|---|---|---|
| $n$ | 5 | | | |
| $\Sigma Y$ | $60,600 | | | |
| $\Sigma X$ | | 42,300 | | |
| $\Sigma XY$ | | | $533,700,000 | |
| $\Sigma X^2$ | | | | 373,890,000 |

A.      533,700,000 = 42,300b + 373,890,000a
B.          60,600 =     5b +      42,300a
B. × 8,460   512,680,000 = 42,300b + 357,860,000a
              21,020,000 =              16,030,000a
                    a = $1.31   (rounded)
                    b = $1,037  (rounded)

Regression line: $Y = \$1.31X + \$1,037$

| b) | Quantity, $X$ | Cost, $Y$ | Estimated cost, $\bar{Y}$ | $Y - \bar{Y}$ | $(Y - \bar{Y})^2$ |
|---|---|---|---|---|---|
| | 6,000 | $ 9,000 | $ 8,897 | 103 | 10,609 |
| | 7,000 | 10,100 | 10,207 | −107 | 11,449 |
| | 8,500 | 12,000 | 12,172 | −172 | 29,584 |
| | 10,000 | 14,500 | 14,137 | 363 | 131,769 |
| | 10,800 | 15,000 | 15,185 | −185 | 34,225 |
| | | | | $\Sigma(Y - \bar{Y})^2 =$ | 217,636 |

$$SE = \sqrt{\frac{\Sigma(Y - \bar{Y})^2}{n - 2}} = \sqrt{72,545} = 269 \text{ (rounded)}$$

c) 99 percent = 3 standard errors (S.E.)
   3 (S.E.) = $807

Therefore, 99 percent of the time you would expect the cost to fall within the range equal to:

Cost per regression line $(Y = \$1.31X + \$1,037) \pm 807$

**SP 5.13**

| a) | Activity base | Budgetary rate | Budgeted indirect labor |
|---|---|---|---|
| | Machine hours | $5.10 V + $37,000 F | $128,800 |
| | Direct labor dollars | $0.85 V + $27,000 F | 130,000 |
| | Direct labor hours | $5.00 V + $30,000 F | 129,000 |

b) Direct labor hours is the best choice since it is a good surrogate measure of output (not affected by changes in wage rates) and, in this instance, correlates most closely with indirect labor cost (has lowest standard error).

c) Direct labor hours is the best predictor since it has the lowest standard error.

# Chapter 6

## EP 6.1

SPRAT COMPANY

Income Statement
(Contribution Format—000 omitted)

| | | |
|---|---:|---:|
| Sales | | $3,000 |
| Variable product costs | | 1,500 |
| Variable GS and A expenses | | |
| Wages and salaries | $300 | |
| Sales commissions | 150 | |
| Distribution | 30 | 480 |
| Total contribution | | $1,020 |
| Less: Fixed GS and A expense | | |
| Wages and salaries | $500 | |
| Distribution | 10 | |
| Depreciation | 160 | |
| Prop. tax and insurance | 40 | 710 |
| Income from operations | | $310 |
| Provision for income tax | | 124 |
| Net income | | $186 |

## EP 6.3

a) Necessary income from operations ($X$):

$$X - 0.4X = \text{Necessary net income} = 0.6X$$
$$\$600,000 \times 0.16 = \$96,000 \text{ necessary net income}$$
$$0.6X = \$96,000$$
$$X = \$160,000$$

b) After-tax cost of debt ($Y$):

$$Y = 8 \text{ percent less interest tax-shield savings}$$
$$= 0.08 - 0.4(0.08) = 0.6(0.08)$$
$$= 4.8 \text{ percent}$$
$$= 0.048 \times \$400,000 = \$19,200$$

c)

| | | |
|---|---:|---|
| Debt | $400,000 | 40 percent |
| Stockholders' equity | 600,000 | 60 percent |
| Total | $1,000,000 | 100 percent |

Weighted average after-tax cost of capital:
$$0.4(0.048) + 0.6(0.16) = 0.1152$$
$$= 11.52 \text{ percent}$$

## EP 6.5

| | (a) | (b) | (c) | (d) |
|---|---:|---:|---:|---:|
| Sales | $1,000 | $2,000 | $3,000 | $3,500 |
| Variable costs | $600 | $1,400 | $1,350 | $1,500 |
| Contribution | $400 | $600 | $1,650 | $2,000 |
| Fixed costs | $300 | $400 | $950 | $1,600 |
| Net income | $100 | $200 | $700 | $400 |
| Units sold | 200 | 200 | 150 | 500 |
| Unit selling price | $5 | $10 | $20 | $7 |
| Unit variable cost | $3 | $7 | $9 | $3 |
| Unit contribution | $2 | $3 | $11 | $4 |

EP 6.7   a)

## AJAX CORPORATION

### 19X7 Income Statement
### (Contribution format—000 omitted)

| | | |
|---|---|---|
| Sales | | $400 |
| Variable product costs | | 225 |
| Variable operating expenses | | 15 |
| Total contribution | | $160 |
| Less: Fixed product costs | $75 | |
|      Fixed operating expenses | 45 | 120 |
| Income from operations | | $ 40 |
| Provision for income taxes | | 12 |
| Net income | | $ 28 |

b) Variable cost rate $= \dfrac{240}{400} \times 100 = 60$ percent

c) Contribution rate $= 1 -$ Variable cost rate $= 40$ percent

d) B.E. Sales $= X$
At breakeven: $0.4X = \$120,000$,   $X = \$300,000$

e) Margin of safety $= \$400,000 - \$300,000 = \$100,000$, or 25 percent
of current sales

f) Variable cost per unit $= 0.6 \times \$20 = \$12$

g) Contribution per unit $= 0.4 \times \$20 = \$8$

EP 6.9   a) Breakeven dollar sales volume $(X)$:
At breakeven: $0.35X = \$500,000$,   $X = \$1,429,000$ (rounded)

b) Income $(Y) = 0.35X - \$500,000$
    (1) $Y = 0.35(2,000,000) - 500,000 = \$200,000$
    (2) $Y = 0.35(2,500,000) - 500,000 = \$375,000$
    (3) $Y = 0.35(1,000,000) - 500,000 = \$(150,000)$ (loss)

EP 6.11   a) With costs equal, objective is simply to maximize revenue.

Tasty revenue $= 9$ times basic inventory (units) times $\$1.39 = \$12.51$
Super revenue $= 11$ times basic inventory (units) times $\$1.10$
         $= \$12.10$

Therefore should stock Tasty Spices as they return $0.41 more per
unit of basic inventory.

b) With different contributions and limited space, objective to maximize annual contribution per unit of basic inventory:

$$\text{Tasty} = 9 \times (\$1.39 - \$0.83) = \$5.04$$
$$\text{Super} = 11 \times (\$1.10 - \$0.61) = \$5.39$$

Therefore Super Spices should be chosen.

EP 6.13   a) (1)  $20,000 income reduction
   (2) · Present selling price per unit  = $8.00
       · Present variable cost per unit  = $6.624
       · Present contribution per unit   = $1.376
       · Need additional contribution    = $20,000
       · Therefore need sell 14,535 more units for total of 639,535, to maintain $300,000 budgeted income.

   b) (1)  $625,000 revenue and income reduction
      (2) · New contribution per unit = $0.376
          · To cover $560,000 fixed costs and earn $300,000 income, must sell 2,287,234 units.

   c) (1)  $187,500 income reduction
      (2) · New contribution per unit = $1.076
          · To cover $560,000 fixed costs and earn $300,000 income, must sell 799,257 units.

EP 6.15   a)

| Price | Breakeven unit sales volume | Sales | Margin of safety | Earnings before taxes |
|---|---|---|---|---|
| $1.00 | 200,000* | $200,000 | $    0 | $    0 |
| $2.00 | 71,429 | $200,000 | $57,142 | $39,999† |
| $3.00 | 43,479 | $225,000 | $94,563 | $72,498 |
| $4.00 | 31,250 | $200,000 | $75,000 | $60,000 |

  * $0.50 unit contribution ($1.00 − $0.40 − $0.10)
    $0.5X = \$100,000$,   $X = 200,000$ units
  † $1.40 unit contribution ($2.00 − $0.40 − $0.20)
    28,571 units above breakeven × $1.40 = $39,999 income

   b) Meredith should choose the $3.00 price that maximizes income.

EP 6.17   a) · Unit variable cost = $3.66
           · Unit contribution = $0.84
           · To earn an additional $50,000 of income, 59,524 additional units would have to be sold.

b) · New unit contribution + $1.34
    · To cover $128,000 of fixed costs and earn $90,000 of target profit, 162,687 units would have to be sold.

c) · Let $X$ = unit contribution.
    · Then $225,000X = \$128,000 + \$90,000$,   $X = 0.97$ (rounded)
    · $3.66 (variable cost) + 0.97 (necessary unit contribution) = $4.63 necessary price to achieve target profit.

**EP 6.19**   a) · New machine desirable above activity level where incremental savings equal incremental costs.
    · Incremental savings ($2 per unit) equal incremental costs ($10,000 per month) at an activity level (volume) of 5,000 units produced per month.

b) (1) At level of 4,000 units:

| | |
|---|---:|
| Monthly costs increased | $10,000 |
| Monthly savings | 8,000 |
| Monthly net loss | $ 2,000 |

   (2) At level of 12,000 units:

| | |
|---|---:|
| Monthly savings | $24,000 |
| Monthly costs increase | 10,000 |
| Monthly net savings | $14,000 |

**EP 6.21**   a) · Let $X$ = current sales volume in dollars
    · Then $(0.8X)0.3 = \$500,000 + \$100,000$,
              $X = \$2,500,000$ or 125,000 units

b) (1) $500,000 ($2,500,000 × 0.2)
   (2) 25,000 units ($500,000 ÷ $20)
   (3) · Current contribution = $750,000 ($2,500,000 × 0.3)
     · Less fixed costs    = 500,000
     · Current income    = $250,000
     · Current income in excess target profit = $150,000
     · Price reduction still maintaining target profit = (150,000/125,000) = $1.20
     · Therefore 6 percent price reduction would still enable firm to earn target profit assuming no change in volume.

c) (1) · Current volume = $2,500,000
     · Let $X$ = breakeven volume.
     · At breakeven: $0.3X = \$500,000$,   $X = 1,666,667$
     · Safety factor over breakeven = $833,333

(2)   41,666 units ($833,333 ÷ 20 and rounded down)

(3) • Current income (excess over breakeven) = $250,000
    • Price reduction to breakeven = (250,000/125,000) = $2.00
    • Therefore 10 percent price reduction would still enable firm to
     breakeven, assuming no change in volume.

**SP 6.23**   a)

| | Additional regional office | Using manufacturer's representatives |
|---|---|---|
| *At price of $4.00:* | | |
| Sales | $900,000 | $900,000 |
| Variable manufacturing costs | 675,000 | 675,000 |
| Sales salaries | 75,000 | 0 |
| Sales commissions | 90,000 | 180,000 |
| Sales office | 30,000 | 0 |
| Clerical costs | 0 | 10,000 |
| Income | $ 30,000 | $ 35,000 |
| *At price of $6.00:* | | |
| Sales | $1,050,000 | $1,050,000 |
| Variable manufacturing costs | 525,000 | 525,000 |
| Sales salaries | 75,000 | 0 |
| Sales commissions | 105,000 | 210,000 |
| Sales office | 30,000 | 0 |
| Clerical costs | 0 | 10,000 |
| Income | $ 315,000 | $ 305,000 |
| *At price of $8.00:* | | |
| Sales | $720,000 | $720,000 |
| Variable manufacturing costs | 270,000 | 270,000 |
| Sales salaries | 75,000 | 0 |
| Sales commissions | 72,000 | 144,000 |
| Sales office | 30,000 | 0 |
| Clerical costs | 0 | 10,000 |
| Income | $273,000 | $296,000 |

b) Given the demand elasticity, the price of $6.00 should be chosen,
since it maximizes the total contribution in excess of manufacturing
costs.

c) Armstrong should expand. It should do so by establishing a regional
office rather than using manufacturer's representatives. At a price of
$6.00, this approach maximizes immediate income (see (a) above).
Since it involves mostly fixed costs, more income would be available
with expanded volume than with manufacturer's representatives.

| SP 6.25 | A | B | C | D | E |
|---|---|---|---|---|---|
| Sales volume | $600,000* | $340,000 | $200,000 | $1,000,000 | $2,000,000 |
| Unit sales volume | 100,000 | 8,500 | 20,000 | 40,000 | 50,000 |
| Unit price | $6 | $40 | $10 | $25 | $40 |
| Variable cost rate | 60% | 40% | 30% | 70% | 80% |
| Fixed costs | $180,000 | $152,000 | $98,000 | $210,000 | $288,000 |
| Income | $60,000 | $52,000 | $42,000 | $90,000 | $112,000 |
| Investment | $500,000 | $400,000 | $300,000 | $600,000 | $700,000 |
| Cost of capital | 12% | 13% | 14% | 15% | 16% |
| Variable costs | $360,000 | $136,000 | $60,000 | $700,000 | $1,600,000 |
| Breakeven volume | $450,000 | $253,334 | $140,000 | $700,000 | $1,440,000 |
| Breakeven units | 75,000 | 6,334 | 14,000 | 28,000 | 36,000 |

\* Necessary income = $60,000   ($500,000 × 0.12)
  Contribution = $240,000   ($180,000 + $60,000) = 40 percent of sales
  Sales = $600,000   ($240,000 ÷ 0.4)

**SP 6.27**   a) Sales  $300,000  $500,000
      Income  70,000  190,000
      Operating expenses  $230,000  $310,000

$$310,000 = 500,000a + b$$
$$230,000 = 300,000a + b$$
$$80,000 = 200,000a$$
$$a = 0.4$$
$$b = \$110,000 = \text{apparent fixed costs}$$

b) $0.40 per sales dollar = apparent variable cost rate

c) *At volume of $300,000:*
   Contribution = $180,000 ($70,000 income + $110,000 fixed cost)
   Therefore 20,000 units sold ($180,000 ÷ $9)
   Total variable costs = $120,000 ($300,000 × 0.4)
   Therefore variable cost per unit = $6.00.

d) *At breakeven:*
   0.6 (sales) = $110,000
   Breakeven volume = $183,334 (rounded)

e) *At volume of $400,000:*
   Contribution = $240,000 ($400,000 × 0.6)
   Fixed costs = 110,000
   Income  $130,000

f) $100,000 after-tax profit = 0.65 (before-tax profit)
   Before-tax profit = $153,846 (rounded)
   Required contribution = $263,846 ($110,000 fixed + $153,846 profit
   Required sales volume = $439,743 ($263,846 ÷ 0.6 and rounded)

## Chapter 7

**EP 7.1**

| Product A: | Additional processing costs | $ 40,000 |
|---|---|---|
| | Additional revenue | 30,000 |
| | Net benefit (loss) | $ (10,000) |
| | Decision | Do *not* process further. |

| Product B: | Additional processing costs | $ 90,000 |
|---|---|---|
| | Additional revenue | 100,000 |
| | Net benefit (loss) | $ 10,000 |
| | Decision | Process further. |

| Product C: | Additional processing costs | $ 40,000 |
|---|---|---|
| | Additional revenue | 10,000 |
| | Net benefit (loss) | $ (30,000) |
| | Decision | Do *not* process further. |

**EP 7.3**

a) Product A has higher markup [($5.00 − $3.00)/$5.00 × 100 = 40%] than Product B [($10.00 − $7.50)/$10.00) × 100 = 25%].

b) Product B is more profitable (has higher contribution) per unit sold since its unit contribution is $2.50 as compared with A's $2.00.

c) Annual sales:

| | Product A | Product B |
|---|---|---|
| Inventory turnover | 5 | 7 |
| Average inventory (units) | 200 | 100 |
| Expected sales (units) | 1,000 | 700 |
| Annual total contribution | $2,000 | $1,750 |

Product A should be carried since it generates the highest contribution from the limited selling space.

**EP 7.5**

a)

| | Present plan | Proposed plan |
|---|---|---|
| Sales | $1,440,000 | $1,396,800[1] |
| Variable costs | 864,000 | 768,240[2] |
| Fixed costs | 400,000 | 448,000[3] |
| Net income | $ 176,000 | $ 180,560 |

*Decision:* Adopt new plan since it both increases net income and meets employee desires.

*Notes:*
1. $1,440,000 × 0.97 = $1,396,800.
2. Present plan variable costs ($864,000) include 5% sales commission ($72,000). Variable costs unrelated to sales commissions ($792,000) × 0.97 = $768,240.
3. Present fixed costs ($400,000) plus $4,000 increased salary per salesperson times 12.

b) Salesforce's apparent desire for earnings security is sufficient to accept average $2,000 annual decrease in remuneration. Firm might consider making third alternative proposal providing more security than at present and still maintaining some incentive.

**EP 7.7**  a) Wholesaler might simply recruit more sales personnel, since all are paid on straight commission. There is no reason to sacrifice existing small-retailer volume for additional large-retailer business unless there is some limit (cost or availability) to size of sales force.

b) Present straight commission system should motivate highest return. Since concentrating on small retailers yields slightly lower daily sales (9 × $250 = $2,250) and commissions than on large retailers (7 × $350 = $2,450), either the sales force has achieved optimum personal mix trade-off (more visiting vs. less earnings), or perhaps all large retailers within the territory are already covered.

**EP 7.9**  No. Warder should not discontinue Product R despite its negative contribution.

|  | Product Q | Product R | Total |
|---|---|---|---|
| Unit sales | 60,000 | 30,000 | — |
| Unit contribution | $10 | $(2) | — |
| Present contribution | $600,000 | $(60,000) | $540,000 |
| Contribution if R is discontinued | $300,000* | 0 | $300,000 |

\* 50 percent loss in sales volume.

**EP 7.11**  a) Yes. Part K should be subcontracted if there are no significant nonquantifiable negative considerations.

| | | |
|---|---|---|
| Annual subcontracting costs | $560,000 | (40,000 × $14) |
| Avoidable costs | 600,000 | ($720,000 − $120,000) |
| Annual savings | $ 40,000 | |

b) Pro subcontracting:  More space
   Reduced production scheduling problems
   Con subcontracting:  Loss of direct control over quality and delivery
   Possible employee reaction

**EP 7.13**  a) Yes. Visgoth should accept the order for 20,000 units per year. It presently has 30,000 units available capacity.[1] The order would result in an additional contribution of $40,000 per year.[2]

*Notes:*
(1)  Present volume ($900,000/$18)    50,000 average units
     Total capacity    80,000 average units
     Available capacity    30,000

(2)  Unit variable cost ($600,000/50,000) = $12
     Unit mail-order contribution    = $ 2 ($14 − $12)
     Total mail-order contribution    = $40,000 (20,000 × $2)

b) Visgoth should still accept the order. Five-percent loss of existing contribution ($15,000) would be more than offset by the $40,000 additional mail-order contribution.

**EP 7.15**    Suburban should add cosmetics.

| Cosmetics: | | |
|---|---|---|
| | Additional sales | $30,000 |
| | Variable costs (55%) | 16,500 |
| | Additional contribution | $13,500 |
| | Additional fixed costs | 6,000 |
| | Addition to income | $ 7,500 |

| Greeting cards: | | |
|---|---|---|
| | Additional sales | $20,000 |
| | Variable costs (40%) | 8,000 |
| | Additional contribution | 12,000 |
| | Additional fixed costs | 2,000 |
| | Lost present contribution | 2,800[1] |
| | Addition to income | $ 7,200 |

*Note:* (1) 2% of ($400,000 − $260,000)

**EP 7.17**    Fantasyworld Amusement Park should not shut down in its off-season since it would lose $20,000.

*Gross benefits of shutdown:*

• Save fixed costs of $135,000 per month = $675,000

*Costs of shutdown:*

| • Shutdown and startup expenditures | $375,000 |
|---|---|
| • Lost contribution during closed months[1] | 320,000 |
| | $695,000 |

*Note:* (1) Ten percent of $3,200,000 annual contribution.

**SP 7.19**    a)

| Year | After-tax costs proposal #1 | After-tax costs proposal #2 | 14% Present value factor | PV proposal #1 | PV proposal #2 |
|---|---|---|---|---|---|
| 1 | $ 3,600 | $ 1,800 | 0.8772 | $ 3,158 | $ 1,579 |
| 2 | 3,000 | 1,800 | 0.7695 | 2,308 | 1,385 |
| 3 | 3,000 | 2,400 | 0.6750 | 2,025 | 1,620 |
| 4 | 2,400 | 2,400 | 0.5921 | 1,421 | 1,421 |
| 5 | 2,400 | 3,000 | 0.5194 | 1,247 | 1,558 |
| 6 | 1,800 | 3,000 | 0.4556 | 820 | 1,367 |
| 7 | 1,800 | 3,600 | 0.3996 | 719 | 1,439 |
| Total | $18,000 | $18,000 | | $11,698 | $10,369 |

b) Recommend proposal #2, since it is $1,329 less costly in NPV dollars than proposal #1.

**SP 7.21**   a)

| Year | After-tax net costs Factory 1 | After-tax net costs Factory 2 | 8% present value factor | PV cost Factory 1 | PV cost Factory 2 |
|------|------|------|------|------|------|
| 1 | $ 18,900[1] | $ 42,700 | 0.9259 | $ 17,500 | $ 39,536 |
| 2 | 31,500 | 42,000 | 0.8573 | 27,005 | 36,007 |
| 3 | 44,100 | 42,000 | 0.7938 | 35,007 | 33,340 |
| 4 | 58,100 | 42,000 | 0.7350 | 42,704 | 30,870 |
| 5 | 72,100 | 42,000 | 0.6806 | 49,071 | 28,585 |
| Total | $224,700 | $210,700 | | $171,287 | $168,338 |

Note (1): 0.7($40,000 − 13,000)

b) The Crazy Growth Company should move into factory number 2 since it will be $2,949 less costly than factory number 1.

## Chapter 7 Appendix

1. a)   $10,000   (time period too short for discount)
   b)   $4,629   ($5,000 × 0.9259)
   c)   $5,329   ($9,000 × 0.5921)
   d)   $3,326   ($7,000 × 0.4751)
   e)   $1,670   ($50,000 × 0.0334)

2. a)   $868   ($500 × 1.7355)
   b)   $57,270   ($11,000 × 5.2064)
   c)   $19,885   ($3,000 × 6.6282)
   d)   $664,180   ($100,000 × 6.6418)

3. a)

| Year | Payments |
|------|------|
| 1 | 2,000 |
| 2 | 2,000 |
| 3 | 2,000 − 1,500 |
| 4 | 2,000 |
| 5 | 2,000 |

PV stream of $2,000 equal future payments    $7,582   ($2,000 × 3.7908)

Less: Year 3 adjustment    1,127   ($1,500 × 0.7513)

PV of given future payments    $6,455
PV of Year zero payment    1,000   ($1,000 × 1.0000)

Total NPV    $7,455

b)

| Year | Receipts |
|------|------|
| 1 | 3,000 |
| 2 | 3,000 |
| 3 | 3,000 |
| 4 | 3,000 |
| 5 | 3,000 + 1,000 |

|  |  |  |
|---|---|---|
| PV stream of $3,000 equal future payments | $10,814 | ($3,000 × 3.6048) |
| Plus year 5 adjustment | 567 | ($1,000 × 0.5674) |
| Total NPV | $11,381 | |

4. a) 

|  |  |  |
|---|---|---|
| PV of year-zero outflow | $ −10,000 | ($10,000 × 1.0000) |
| PV of four-year stream of equal payments | +7,593 | ($2,500 × 3.0374) |
| NPV (net outflow) | $ −2,407 | |

b) 

|  |  |  |
|---|---|---|
| PV of year-zero inflow | $ +40,000 | ($40,000 × 1.0000) |
| PV of four-year stream of equal outflows | −37,878 | ($13,000 × 2.9137) |
| NPV (net inflow) | $ +2,122 | |

c) 

|  |  |  |
|---|---|---|
| PV of year-zero outflow | $−100,000 | ($100,000 × 1.0000) |
| PV of five-year stream of equal $24,000 inflows | +95,825 | ($24,000 × 3.9927) |
| PV of five-year single additional inflow of $16,000 | +10,890 | ($16,000 × 0.6806) |
| NPV (net inflow) | $ +6,715 | |

d) 

|  |  |  |
|---|---|---|
| PV of year-zero outflow | $ −50,000 | ($50,000 × 1.0000) |
| PV of five-year stream of equal $25,000 inflows | +94,770 | ($25,000 × 3.7908) |
| PV of year-four adjustment of $65,000 | −44,395 | ($65,000 × 0.6830) |
|  | $ +375 | |

# Chapter 8

## EP 8.1

| Year | Before-tax cash flow | Depreciation tax shield[1] | Incremental taxable income | Tax effect[2] | Net after-tax cash flow |
|---|---|---|---|---|---|
| 0 | −$50,000 | $ 0 | $ 0 | $ 0 | −$50,000 |
| 1 | +17,700 | 10,000 | +7,700 | −3,080 | +14,620 |
| 2 | +17,700 | 10,000 | +7,700 | −3,080 | +14,620 |
| 3 | +17,700 | 10,000 | +7,700 | −3,080 | +14,620 |
| 4 | +17,700 | 10,000 | +7,700 | −3,080 | +14,620 |
| 5 | +17,700 | 10,000 | +7,700 | −3,080 | +14,620 |

Notes:
(1) Each year's depreciation tax deduction shields otherwise taxable income in the same amount from income tax.
(2) Tax payable on incremental taxable income.

## EP 8.3

| Year | Before-tax cash flow | Depreciation tax shield | Incremental taxable income | Tax effect | Net after-tax cash flow |
|---|---|---|---|---|---|
| 0 | −$100,000 | $ 0 | $ 0 | $ 0 | −$100,000 |
| 1 | +42,000 | 50,000 | −8,000 | +3,200 | +45,200 |
| 2 | +42,000 | 25,000 | +17,000 | −6,800 | +35,200 |
| 3 | +42,000 | 12,500 | +29,500 | −11,800 | +30,200 |
| 4 | +42,000 | 12,500 | +29,500 | −11,800 | +30,200 |
| 4 | +3,000 | 0 | +3,000* | −1,200 | +1,800 |

* Since tax basis is zero, $3,000 salvage subject to income tax.

## EP 8.5

| Year | After-tax cash flow* | 12% PV factor | PV |
|---|---|---|---|
| 0 | −$100,000 | 1.0000 | −$100,000 |
| 1 | +45,200 | 0.8929 | +40,359 |
| 2 | +35,200 | 0.7972 | +28,061 |
| 3 | +30,200 | 0.7118 | +21,496 |
| 4 | +32,000 | 0.6355 | +20,336 |
| | | NPV | +$ 10,252 |

* From solution to Problem EP8.3.

## EP 8.7   a) Investment C:

| Year | Before-tax cash flow | Depreciation tax shield | Incremental taxable income | Tax effect | Net after-tax cash flow |
|---|---|---|---|---|---|
| 0 | −$100,000 | $ 0 | $ 0 | $ 0 | −$100,000 |
| 1 | +42,000 | 50,000 | −8,000 | +1,600 | +43,600 |
| 2 | +42,000 | 25,000 | +17,000 | −3,400 | +38,600 |
| 3 | +42,000 | 12,500 | +29,500 | −5,900 | +36,100 |
| 4 | +42,000 | 12,500 | +29,500 | −5,900 | +36,100 |
| 4 | +3,000 | 0 | +3,000 | −600 | +2,400 |

| Year | After-tax cash flow | 8% PV factor | PV |
|---|---|---|---|
| 0 | −$100,000 | 1.0000 | −$100,000 |
| 1 | +43,600 | 0.9259 | + 40,369 |
| 2 | +38,600 | 0.8573 | + 33,092 |
| 3 | +36,100 | 0.7938 | + 28,656 |
| 4 | +38,500 | 0.7350 | + 28,297 |
| | | NPV | +$ 30,414 |

Investment D:

| Year | Before-tax cash flow | Depreciation tax shield | Incremental taxable income | Tax effect | Net after-tax cash flow |
|------|------|------|------|------|------|
| 0 | −$200,000 | $    0 | $    0 | $    0 | −$200,000 |
| 1 | +   80,000 | 100,000 | −20,000 | +  4,000 | +   84,000 |
| 2 | +   80,000 | 50,000 | +30,000 | −  6,000 | +   74,000 |
| 3 | +   80,000 | 25,000 | +55,000 | −11,000 | +   69,000 |
| 4 | +   80,000 | 25,000 | +55,000 | −11,000 | +   69,000 |
| 4* | +   20,000 | 0 | +20,000 | −  4,000 | +   16,000 |

\* Investment D is assumed to have only a four-year life for purposes of comparison with Investment C.

| Year | After-tax cash flow | 8% PV factor | PV |
|------|------|------|------|
| 0 | −$200,000 | 1.0000 | −$200,000 |
| 1 | +   84,000 | 0.9259 | +   77,776 |
| 2 | +   74,000 | 0.8573 | +   63,440 |
| 3 | +   69,000 | 0.7938 | +   54,772 |
| 4 | +   85,000 | 0.7350 | +   62,475 |
| | | NPV | +$ 58,463 |

b) Investment D has a higher return in absolute NPV dollars ($58,463 as compared with $30,414 for Investment C).

c) Comparing Investment D to Investment C.

| Year | Differential after-tax cash flows D − C | 8% PV factor | PV differential costs |
|------|------|------|------|
| 0 | −$100,000 | 1.0000 | −$100,000 |
| 1 | +   40,400 | 0.9259 | +   37,406 |
| 2 | +   35,400 | 0.8573 | +   30,348 |
| 3 | +   32,900 | 0.7938 | +   26,116 |
| 4 | +   46,500 | 0.7350 | +   34,177 |
| | NPV Differential Costs | | +$ 28,047 |

d) Investment C has the highest profitability index.

$$\text{Profitability index} = 1 + \frac{\text{NPV}}{\text{Investment}}$$

For C:    $1 + \dfrac{30,414}{100,000} = 1.30$   (rounded)

For D:    $1 + \dfrac{58,463}{200,000} = 1.29$   (rounded)

**EP 8.9**   a) Machine E:

| Year | Before-tax cash flow | Depreciation tax shield [1] | Incremental taxable income | Tax effect | Net after-tax cash flow |
|------|---------------------|-----------------------------|----------------------------|------------|-------------------------|
| 0 | −$100,000 | $      0 | $      0 | +$10,000 [2] | −$90,000 |
| 1 | −   10,000 | 19,200 | −29,200 | +   8,760 | −   1,240 |
| 2 | −   30,000 | 19,200 | −49,200 | +  14,760 | −  15,240 |
| 3 | −   40,000 | 19,200 | −59,200 | +  17,760 | −  22,240 |
| 4 | −   60,000 | 19,200 | −79,200 | +  23,760 | −  36,240 |
| 5 | −   46,000 | 19,200 | −69,200 [3] | +  20,760 | −  25,240 |

Notes:
(1) $100,000 cost less $4,000 salvage equals $96,000 to be depreciated over five years.
(2) 10 percent ITC      (3) $4,000 salvage value has no tax effect.

Machine F:

| Year | Before-tax cash flow | Depreciation tax shield | Incremental taxable income | Tax effect | Net after-tax cash flow |
|------|---------------------|-------------------------|----------------------------|------------|-------------------------|
| 0 | −$100,000 | $      0 | $      0 | +$10,000 | −$90,000 |
| 1 | −   20,000 | 19,200 | −39,200 | +  11,760 | −   8,240 |
| 2 | −   50,000 | 19,200 | −69,200 | +  20,760 | −  29,240 |
| 3 | −   50,000 | 19,200 | −69,200 | +  20,760 | −  29,240 |
| 4 | −   30,000 | 19,200 | −49,200 | +  14,760 | −  15,240 |
| 5 | −   16,000 | 19,200 | −39,200 | +  11,760 | −   4,240 |

b) Machine E:

| Year | After-tax cash flow | 8% PV factor | PV |
|------|---------------------|--------------|-----|
| 0 | −$90,000 | 1.0000 | −$ 90,000 |
| 1 | −   1,240 | 0.9259 | −    1,148 |
| 2 | −  15,240 | 0.8573 | −   13,065 |
| 3 | −  22,240 | 0.7938 | −   17,654 |
| 4 | −  36,240 | 0.7350 | −   26,636 |
| 5 | −  25,240 | 0.6806 | −   17,178 |
| | | NPV | −$165,681 |

Machine F:

| Year | After-tax cash flow | 8% PV factor | PV |
|------|---------------------|--------------|-----|
| 0 | −$90,000 | 1.0000 | −$ 90,000 |
| 1 | −   8,240 | 0.9259 | −    7,629 |
| 2 | −  29,240 | 0.8573 | −   25,067 |
| 3 | −  29,240 | 0.7938 | −   23,211 |
| 4 | −  15,240 | 0.7350 | −   11,201 |
| 5 | −   4,240 | 0.6806 | −    2,886 |
| | | NPV | −$159,994 |

c) Machine F is the preferable investment since its effective NPV cost over its useful life is $5,687 less than the cost of Machine E.

**EP 8.11**   a) • Let $X$ = annual before-tax savings.
  • Depreciation tax shield = $2,000 each year
  • Tax shield effect = $400 tax savings each year
  • Net after-tax cash flow = $0.8X + \$400$ each year
  • NPV of stream of net after-tax cash-flow savings over ten years discounted at 15 percent = $5.0188(0.8X + 400)$
  • If NPV of costs and savings equal zero (given), then

$$5.0188(0.8X + 400) = \$20,000,$$
$$X = \$\ 4,481 \text{ (rounded).}$$

b) • Let $X$ = maximum cost of new equipment
  • Depreciation tax shield = $X/15$.
  • Tax shield effect = $0.3(X/15)$ tax savings each year.
  • Net after-tax cash savings each year = $0.7(\$9,000) + 0.3(X/15)$.
  • NPV of stream of net after-tax cash-flow savings over 15 years discounted at 14 percent =

$$6.1422\left[0.7(\$9,000) + 0.3\left(\frac{X}{15}\right)\right].$$

If the investment earns exactly 14 percent and the year-zero cash outflow is $0.9X$ (after allowing for ten percent ITC), then:

$$0.9X = \ 6.1422\left[0.7(\$9,000) + 0.3\left(\frac{X}{15}\right)\right],$$

$$X = \$49,790 \text{ (rounded).}$$

**EP 8.13**   Investment G:

| Year | Before-tax cash flow | Depreciation tax shield | Incremental taxable income | Tax effect | Net after-tax cash flow |
|---|---|---|---|---|---|
| 0 | −$400,000 | $     0 | $     0 | +$40,000 | −$360,000 |
| 1 | +   86,000 | 66,667 | 19,333 | −   7,733 | +   78,267 |
| 2 | +   86,000 | 66,667 | 19,333 | −   7,733 | +   78,267 |
| 3 | +   86,000 | 66,667 | 19,333 | −   7,733 | +   78,267 |
| 4 | +   86,000 | 66,667 | 19,333 | −   7,733 | +   78,267 |
| 5 | +   86,000 | 66,667 | 19,333 | −   7,733 | +   78,267 |
| 6 | +   86,000 | 66,667 | 19,333 | −   7,733 | +   78,267 |
| 7 | +   86,000 | 0 | 86,000 | −  34,400 | +   51,600 |
| 8 | +   86,000 | 0 | 86,000 | −  34,400 | +   51,600 |
| 9 | +   86,000 | 0 | 86,000 | −  34,400 | +   51,600 |
| 9 | +     5,000 | 0 | 5,000 | −   2,000 | +     3,000 |

| Year(s) | After-tax cash flow | 14% PV factor | PV |
|---|---|---|---|
| 0 | −$360,000 | 1.0000 | −$360,000 |
| 1–6 | + 78,267 | 3.8887 | + 304,357 |
| 7 | + 51,600 | 0.3996 | 20,619 |
| 8 | + 51,600 | 0.3506 | 18,091 |
| 9 | + 54,600 | 0.3075 | 16,789 |
| | | NPV | −$ 144 |

Do *not* invest, since the return will be less than the required 14 percent.

**SP 8.15**   a) Annual net savings:

| Years(s) | Contribution* | Incremental advertising | Incremental fixed costs | Net savings or (losses) |
|---|---|---|---|---|
| 1 | $ 550,000 | $500,000 | $1,350,000 | $(1,300,000) |
| 2 | 1,100,000 | 300,000 | 1,350,000 | (550,000) |
| 3 | 3,300,000 | 100,000 | 1,350,000 | 1,850,000 |
| 4–10 | 2,750,000 | 50,000 | 1,350,000 | 1,350,000 |

\* Variable unit costs ($9) = 45 percent [(9/20) × 100] of sales. Contribution rate is therefore 55 percent.

| Year | Before-tax cash flow | Depreciation tax shield | Incremental taxable income | Tax effect | Net after-tax cash flow |
|---|---|---|---|---|---|
| 0 | −$4,000,000 | $ 0 | $ 0 | +$400,000 | −$3,600,000 |
| 0 | − 300,000[1] | 0 | 0 | 0 | − 300,000 |
| 1 | − 1,300,000 | 1,000,000 | −2,300,000 | + 460,000 | − 840,000 |
| 2 | − 550,000 | 750,000 | −1,300,000 | + 260,000 | − 290,000 |
| 3 | + 1,850,000 | 562,500 | +1,287,500 | − 257,500 | + 1,592,500 |
| 4 | + 1,350,000 | 421,875 | + 928,125 | − 185,625 | + 1,164,375 |
| 5 | + 1,350,000 | 316,406 | +1,033,594 | − 206,719 | + 1,143,281 |
| 6 | + 1,350,000 | 237,305 | +1,112,695 | − 222,539 | + 1,127,461 |
| 7 | + 1,350,000 | 177,978 | +1,172,022 | − 234,404 | + 1,115,596 |
| 8 | + 1,350,000 | 533,939 | + 816,061 | − 163,212 | + 1,186,788 |
| 9 | + 1,350,000 | 0 | +1,350,000 | − 270,000 | + 1,080,000 |
| 10 | + 1,350,000 | 0 | +1,350,000 | − 270,000 | + 1,080,000 |
| 10 | + 900,000[2] | 0 | + 900,000 | − 180,000 | + 720,000 |
| 10 | + 300,000[3] | 0 | 0 | 0 | + 300,000 |

*Notes:*
(1) Investment in net working capital
(2) Analysis terminated after ten years representing limit of forecasted operating data. Ten-year salvage value given as $900,000.
(3) Recovery of net working capital

| Year | After-tax cash flow | 12% PV factor | PV |
|------|------------------|--------------|-----|
| 0 | −$3,900,000 | 1.0000 | −$3,900,000 |
| 1 | −   840,000 | 0.8929 | −   750,036 |
| 2 | −   290,000 | 0.7972 | −   231,188 |
| 3 | + 1,592,500 | 0.7118 | + 1,133,541 |
| 4 | + 1,164,375 | 0.6355 | +   739,960 |
| 5 | + 1,143,281 | 0.5674 | +   648,698 |
| 6 | + 1,127,461 | 0.5066 | +   571,172 |
| 7 | + 1,115,596 | 0.4523 | +   504,584 |
| 8 | + 1,186,788 | 0.4039 | +   479,344 |
| 9 | + 1,080,000 | 0.3606 | +   389,448 |
| 10 | + 2,100,000 | 0.3220 | +   676,200 |
| | | NPV | +$   261,723 |

Wexler should invest in the new product line since the proposal has a positive after-tax NPV of $261,723.

b) • Wexler's existing contribution rate is 52.5 percent:
($16,000,000 − $7,200,000 − $400,000) ÷ $16,000,000 × 100.
• Wexler's existing fixed costs total $5,900,000.
• Therefore the current breakeven sales volume is $11,238,000 ($5,900,000 ÷ 0.525 and rounded), or 70 percent of existing sales.
• After startup time with new line (beginning with the fourth year), the contribution rate would be 53.1 percent ($8,400,000 of existing annual contribution + $2,750,000 of additional annual contribution, divided by total annual sales of $21,000,000).
• Total fixed costs would be $7,300,000 (present $5,900,000 + $50,000 + $1,350,000).
• Therefore new breakeven sales volume will be $13,748,000 ($7,300,000 ÷ 0.531 and rounded), or 65 percent of annual sales.
• The new product line is additionally attractive in that it will increase the firm's margin of safety over breakeven.

**SP 8.17**   Pro-forma income statement, assuming Boodles are discontinued:

| | | |
|---|---|---|
| Sales | $4,554,000 | ($4,600,000 × 0.99) |
| Cost of goods sold | 1,821,600 | ($1,840,000 × 0.99) |
| Gross margin | $2,732,400 | |
| Variable selling | 227,700 | ($230,000 × 0.99) |
| Fixed GS and A | 1,257,500* | |
| Net income before taxes | $1,247,200 | |
| Provision for taxes | 498,880 | |
| Net income | $  748,320 | |

* $1,300,000 fixed GS and A less $26,500 savings less $16,000 depreciation.

PV of asset disposal:

| | | |
|---|---:|---|
| Cash inflow | $30,000 | |
| Less: Tax on gain | 2,000 | ($5,000 × 0.4) |
| Less: PV of future tax | | |
|   savings foregone | 6,704* | |
| Net | $21,296 | |

* Annual tax shield of $5,000 would have meant five-year stream of $2,000 annual savings discounted at 15 percent.

Fairfax should discontinue Boodles. After-tax income would be increased by $4,320 ($748,320 − $744,000); and there would be an additional net cash benefit of $21,296.

**SP 8.19**   a) Investments ranked by profitability (PR) index:

| Investment | NPV | PR index | Amount | Cumulative amount |
|:---:|---:|:---:|---:|---:|
| M | $10,000 | 1.025 | $ 400,000 | $ 400,000 |
| K | 30,000 | 1.015 | 2,000,000 | 2,400,000 |
| N | 5,000 | 1.00555 | 900,000 | 3,300,000 |
| J | 40,000 | 1.004 | 10,000,000 | 13,300,000 |
| L | 20,000 | 1.00125 | 16,000,000 | 29,300,000 |
| P | 500 | 1.00016 | 3,000,000 | 32,300,000 |
| Q | Negative | Negative | 6,000,000 | 38,300,000 |
| R | Negative | Negative | 22,000,000 | 60,300,000 |

b) Exclude Q and R as not earning minimum satisfactory return. Also exclude P, since others with higher index can use available capital.

c) Investments M, K, and N should be funded.

**SP 8.21**   See Exhibit 8.12 in Chapter 8 Appendix. NPV differential cost of owning, as compared to leasing, equals −$722, indicating that leasing is more beneficial (less costly) in this situation.

**SP 8.23**   a) New product line:
    • Necessary investment in net working capital:

| | | |
|---|---:|---|
| Expected cost of goods sold | $159,250 | ($245,000 × 0.65) |
| Average inventory at five times turnover | $ 31,850 | |
| Average receivables at seven times turnover | $ 35,000 | |
| Additional investment in NWC | $ 67,000 | (rounded) |

| Year | Before-tax cash flow | Depreciation tax shield | Incremental taxable income | Tax effect | Net after-tax cash flow |
|------|---------|---------|---------|---------|---------|
| 0 | −$300,000 | $   0 | $   0 | +$30,000 | −$270,000 |
| 0 | −   67,000 | 0 | 0 | 0 | −   67,000 |
| 1 | +   85,750 | 60,000 | +25,750 | +  10,300 | +   75,450 |
| 2 | +   85,750 | 48,000 | +37,750 | −  15,100 | +   70,650 |
| 3 | +   85,750 | 38,400 | +47,350 | −  18,940 | +   66,810 |
| 4 | +   85,750 | 30,720 | +55,030 | −  22,012 | +   63,738 |
| 5 | +   85,750 | 24,576 | +61,174 | −  24,470 | +   61,280 |
| 6 | +   85,750 | 19,661 | +66,089 | −  26,436 | +   59,314 |
| 7 | +   85,750 | 15,729 | +70,021 | −  28,008 | +   57,742 |
| 8 | +   85,750 | 12,583 | +73,167 | −  29,267 | +   56,483 |
| 9 | +   85,750 | 10,066 | +75,684 | −  30,274 | +   55,476 |
| 10 | +   85,750 | 40,265 | +45,485 | −  18,194 | +   67,556 |
| 10 | +   40,000 | 0 | +40,000 | −  16,000 | +   24,000 |
| 10 | +   67,000 | 0 | 0 | 0 | +   67,000 |

| Year | After-tax cash flow | 12% PV factor | PV |
|------|---------|---------|---------|
| 0 | −$337,000 | 1.0000 | −$337,000 |
| 1 | +   75,450 | 0.8929 | +   67,369 |
| 2 | +   70,650 | 0.7972 | +   56,332 |
| 3 | +   66,810 | 0.7118 | +   47,555 |
| 4 | +   63,738 | 0.6355 | +   40,505 |
| 5 | +   61,280 | 0.5674 | +   34,770 |
| 6 | +   59,314 | 0.5066 | +   30,048 |
| 7 | +   57,742 | 0.4523 | +   26,117 |
| 8 | +   56,483 | 0.4039 | +   22,813 |
| 9 | +   55,476 | 0.3606 | +   20,005 |
| 10 | + 158,556 | 0.3220 | +   51,055 |
| | | NPV | +$  59,569 |

b) Commercial real estate:

| Year | Before-tax cash flow | Depreciation tax shield[1] | Incremental taxable income | Tax effect | Net after-tax cash flow |
|------|---------|---------|---------|---------|---------|
| 0 | −$350,000 | $   0 | $   0 | $   0 | −$350,000 |
| 1 | +  97,500 | 15,000 | +82,500 | −33,000 | +   64,500 |
| 2 | +  97,500 | 14,250 | +83,250 | −33,300 | +   64,200 |
| 3 | +  97,500 | 13,540 | +83,960 | −33,584 | +   63,916 |
| 4 | +  97,500 | 12,860 | +84,640 | −33,856 | +   63,644 |
| 5 | +  97,500 | 12,210 | +85,290 | −34,116 | +   63,384 |
| 6 | +  97,500 | 11,610 | +85,890 | −34,356 | +   63,144 |
| 7 | +  97,500 | 11,030 | +86,470 | −34,588 | +   62,912 |
| 8 | +  97,500 | 10,480 | +87,020 | −34,808 | +   62,692 |
| 9 | +  97,500 | 9,950 | +87,550 | −35,020 | +   62,480 |
| 10 | +  97,500 | 9,450 | +88,050 | −35,220 | +   62,280 |
| 10 | + 300,000 | 0 | +70,380 | −28,152[2] | + 271,848 |

(See notes on following page.)

*Notes:*
(1) 150-percent declining balance on 30-year life, rounded to 5 percent per year. Depreciation deduction rounded to nearest $10.
(2) Assume no land appreciation. Building sale proceeds then $250,000, with tax basis of $179,620, resulting in $70,380 taxable gain.

| Year | After-tax cash flow | 12% PV factor | PV |
|---|---|---|---|
| 0 | −$350,000 | 1.0000 | −$350,000 |
| 1 | +   64,500 | 0.8929 | +   57,592 |
| 2 | +   64,200 | 0.7972 | +   51,180 |
| 3 | +   63,916 | 0.7118 | +   45,495 |
| 4 | +   63,644 | 0.6355 | +   40,446 |
| 5 | +   63,384 | 0.5674 | +   35,964 |
| 6 | +   63,144 | 0.5066 | +   31,989 |
| 7 | +   62,912 | 0.4523 | +   28,455 |
| 8 | +   62,692 | 0.4039 | +   25,321 |
| 9 | +   62,480 | 0.3606 | +   25,530 |
| 10 | + 334,128 | 0.3220 | + 107,589 |

NPV +$ 99,561

a) Both investments appear desirable since both have a positive NPV.

b) New product line profitability index          1.154   (rounded)
   Commercial real estate profitability index     1.284   (rounded)

If the firm can finance only one alternative, the commercial real estate with the higher profitability index would appear more desirable in providing a higher yield per dollar invested.

## Chapter 9

**EP 9.1**

a) Collections:

| | July | August | September |
|---|---|---|---|
| 25% current month | $ 7,500 | $22,500 | $40,000 |
| 40% prior month | 16,000 | 12,000 | 36,000 |
| 20% second prior month | 12,000 | 8,000 | 6,000 |
| 14% third prior month | 11,200 | 8,400 | 5,600 |
| Total | $46,700 | $50,900 | $87,600 |

b) Accounts receivable 6/30 .......... $ 64,000
   Add: Sales 7/1–9/30 .......... 280,000
   Deduct: Collections 7/1–9/30 .......... 185,200
   Write-offs for Mar., Apr., May .......... 2,400
   Accounts receivable 9/30 .......... $156,400

**EP 9.3**

### ALLISON COMPANY

#### Schedule of Cash Outflows for Operations, Third Quarter, 19XX

|  | July | August | September |
|---|---|---|---|
| Purchases | $18,000 | $32,000 | $ 50,000 |
| Other operations: |  |  |  |
| Payroll | 28,000 | 42,000 | 60,000 |
| Insurance | 15,000 | 0 | 0 |
| Property taxes | 0 | 8,000 | 0 |
| All other | 6,100 | 10,000 | 15,500 |
| Total | $67,100 | $92,000 | $125,500 |

**EP 9.5**

### BARBARA COMPANY

#### Preliminary Cash Budget Third Quarter, 19XX

|  | July | August | September |
|---|---|---|---|
| Net cash inflow from operations | (30,000) | (30,000) | (20,000) |
| Capital investments | 0 | (50,000) | 0 |
| Proceeds of disposition of noncurrent assets | 0 | 20,000 | 0 |
| Interest | 0 | 0 | (5,000) |
| Dividends | 0 | 0 | (40,000) |
| Income taxes | (30,000) | 0 | 0 |
| Beginning cash | 35,000 | (25,000) | (85,000) |
| Forecasted preliminary budget | $(25,000) | $(85,000) | $(150,000) |

**EP 9.7**

### CHARLIE COMPANY

#### Abbreviated Final Cash Budget, First Six Months, 19XX

|  | Jan. | Feb. | Mar. | Apr. | May | Jun. |
|---|---|---|---|---|---|---|
| Opening balance without short-term financing | $28,000 | $37,000 | $27,000 | $16,000 | $(10,000) | $(25,000) |
| Opening balance reflecting prior short-term financing | 28,000 | 27,000 | 17,000 | 6,000 | (9,850) | 150 |
| Additional short-term loans, loan repayments with interest |  |  |  |  | 25,000 | 15,000 |
| Additional investment in marketable securities | 10,000 |  |  |  |  |  |
| Sell securities, receive interest |  |  |  | 10,150 |  |  |
| Budgeted cash balance reflecting prior and current short-term financing | $18,000 | $27,000 | $17,000 | $16,150 | $15,150 | $15,150 |

EP 9.9      A)  $82      C)  $68
            B)  $45      D)  $86

EP 9.11

# DARCY COMPANY

Preliminary Cash Budget,
Third Quarter 19XX

|                                    | Jul.     | Aug.     | Sep.     |
|------------------------------------|----------|----------|----------|
| Cash inflow from operations        | $38,875  | $38,000  | $31,500  |
| Interest                           | 0        | 0        | (2,500)  |
| Income taxes                       | (20,000) | 0        | 0        |
| Dividends                          | 0        | 0        | (40,000) |
| Beginning cash balance             | 18,000   | 36,875   | 74,875   |
| Preliminary ending balance         | $36,875  | $74,875  | $63,875  |

### Schedule of Receivables Collections and Cash from Operations

|                                       | Jun.      | Jul.      | Aug.      | Sep.      |
|---------------------------------------|-----------|-----------|-----------|-----------|
| Budgeted sales                        | $220,000  | $210,000  | $190,000  | $170,000  |
| Collections:                          |           |           |           |           |
| 40% Current month                     |           | $ 84,000  | $ 76,000  | $ 68,000  |
| 60% Prior month                       |           | 132,000   | 126,000   | 114,000   |
| Purchases                             |           | 126,000   | 114,000   | 102,000   |
| Payroll                               |           | 30,000    | 30,000    | 30,000    |
| Other operating expense               |           |           |           |           |
| (see schedule below)                  |           | 21,125    | 20,000    | 18,500    |
| Cash inflow from operations           |           | $ 38,875  | $ 38,000  | $ 31,500  |

### Schedule of Cash Outflow for Other Operating Expense

|                                       | Jun.      | Jul.      | Aug.      | Sep.      |
|---------------------------------------|-----------|-----------|-----------|-----------|
| Budgeted sales                        | $220,000  | $210,000  | $190,000  | $170,000  |
| Fixed other operating expense         | $ 5,000   | $ 5,000   | $ 5,000   | $ 5,000   |
| Variable other operating expense*     | 16,500    | 15,750    | 14,250    | 12,750    |
| Total other operating expense         | $21,500   | $20,750   | $19,250   | $17,750   |
| Cash outflow required:                |           |           |           |           |
| 50% Current month                     |           | 10,375    | 9,625     | 8,875     |
| 50% Prior month                       |           | 10,750    | 10,375    | 9,625     |
| Total                                 |           | $21,125   | $20,000   | $18,500   |

\* Annual $210,000 less $60,000 fixed equals $150,000, or 7.5% variable.

**SP 9.13**   a)

## ALLISON COMPANY

### Schedule of Receivables Collections, Third Quarter, 19XX

|  | Jul. | Aug. | Sep. |
|---|---|---|---|
| 10% Current month (Cash sales) | $ 3,000 | $ 9,000 | $16,000 |
| 15% Current month × 98% (discounted) | 4,410 | 13,230 | 23,520 |
| 10% Prior month × 98% (discounted) | 3,920 | 2,940 | 8,820 |
| 30% Prior month | 12,000 | 9,000 | 27,000 |
| 25% Second prior month | 15,000 | 10,000 | 7,500 |
| 8% Third prior month | 6,400 | 4,800 | 3,200 |
| Total receivables collections | $44,730 | $48,970 | $86,040 |

b)

| | |
|---|---|
| Accounts receivable 6/30/XX | $ 61,000 |
| Credit sales 7/1–9/30[1] | 252,000 |
| | $313,000 |
| Collections of receivables 7/1–9/30[2] | 151,740 |
| Discounts allowed[3] | 1,160 |
| Uncollectables written off[4] | 4,800 |
| Accounts receivable 9/30 | $155,300 |

*Notes:*
(1) Total sales of $280,000 less 10 percent cash sales.
(2) Total collections less those representing cash sales.
(3) $58,000 of sales subject to discount × 2%.
(4) March, April, and May sales × 2%.

**SP 9.15**

## ALLISON COMPANY

### Schedule of Cash Outflows for Operations, Third Quarter, 19XX

|  | Jul. | Aug. | Sep. |
|---|---|---|---|
| 50% Current month's purchases (discounted) | $15,680 | $ 24,500 | $ 29,400 |
| 25% Prior month's purchases (discounted) | 4,410 | 7,840 | 12,250 |
| 25% Prior month's purchases not discounted | 4,500 | 8,000 | 12,500 |
| Total outflows for purchases | $24,590 | 40,340 | 54,150 |
| Payroll and property tax (current month) | 28,000 | 50,000 | 60,000 |
| Insurance, distribution, and marketing (prior month) | 4,500 | 23,000 | 12,500 |
| Supplies and miscellaneous (prior month discounted) | 1,274 | 1,078 | 1,372 |
| Total outflows for operations | $58,364 | $114,418 | $128,022 |

**SP 9.17**    a)

### EBBTIDE COMPANY

Preliminary Quarterly Cash Budget,
First Quarter, 19XX

| | |
|---|---|
| Cash inflow from operations | $66,320 |
| Interest | (8,000) |
| Income taxes | (10,000) |
| Dividends | (40,000) |
| Beginning cash balance | 22,000 |
| Preliminary forecasted ending balance | $30,320 |

Schedule of Receivable Collections and Cash from Operations,
First Quarter, 19XX

| | |
|---|---|
| Cash sales and receivables collections[1] | $420,000 |
| Purchases[2] | 219,200 |
| Wages and salaries | 93,000 |
| Other operating expenses[3] | 41,480 |
| Cash inflow from operations | $ 66,320 |

Notes:
(1) $120,000 + 0.6($500,000)$.
(2) 

| Cost of goods sold | $300,000 | |
|---|---|---|
| Target ending inventory | 420,000 | (2/3 × $630,000) |
| Inventory requirements | $720,000 | |
| Less: Beginning inventory | 480,000 | |
| Necessary purchases | $240,000 | |

83% Purchases + $20,000 = Cash outflow for purchases = $220,000
(3) $12,000 + 0.67($44,000)$.

b) Preliminary budget prepared on a quarterly basis following Mr. Sloan's method indicates no need for short-term borrowings during first quarter.

**SP 9.19**

### EBBTIDE COMPANY

Preliminary Cash Budget,
First Quarter, 19XX

| | Jan. | Feb. | March |
|---|---|---|---|
| Cash inflow from operations | $64,080 | $68,770 | $(8,850) |
| Interest | 0 | 0 | (8,000) |
| Income taxes | (10,000) | 0 | 0 |
| Dividends | 0 | 0 | (40,000) |
| Beginning cash balance | 22,000 | 76,080 | 144,850 |
| Preliminary forecasted ending balance | $76,080 | $144,850 | $ 88,000 |

Schedule of Receivables Collections and Cash from Operations

|  | Jan. | Feb. | March |
|---|---|---|---|
| 20% Current month (cash sales) | $20,000 | $30,000 | $50,000 |
| 40% Prior month | 40,000 | 40,000 | 60,000 |
| 40% Second prior month | 40,000 | 40,000 | 40,000 |
| Total collections | $100,000 | $110,000 | $150,000 |
| Purchases | 0 | 0 | 105,000 |
| Wages and salaries[1] | 23,920 | 29,230 | 39,850 |
| Other operating expenses | 12,000 | 12,000 | 14,000[2] |
| Cash inflow from operations | $64,080 | $68,770 | $(8,850) |

Schedule of Purchases

|  | Jan. | Feb. | March |
|---|---|---|---|
| Cost of goods sold (60% sales) | $60,000 | $90,000 | $150,000 |
| Target inventory | 240,000 | 330,000 | 390,000 |
| Inventory requirements | $300,000 | $420,000 | $540,000 |
| Less: Beginning inventory | 480,000 | 420,000 | 330,000 |
| Purchases required | $(180,000) | zero | $210,000 |

Notes:
(1) $13,300 fixed plus 10.62% sales variable
(2) $8,000 fixed plus 4% sales variable paid month following incurrence

b) No need to borrow during first three months.

|  | Quarterly basis | Sum of monthly projections |
|---|---|---|
| c) Cash sales and receivables collections | $420,000 | $360,000 |
| Purchases | 219,200 | 105,000 |
| Wages and salaries | 93,000 | 93,000 |
| Other operating expenses | 41,480 | 38,000 |
| Cash inflow from operations | $ 66,320 | $124,000 |

Average sales does not allow for collection time lags when sales are rapidly increasing.

SP 9.21                  BETTY MUNIZ WOMEN'S WEAR STORE

Preliminary Quarterly Cash Budget,
First Year of Operations

|  | First quarter | Second quarter | Third quarter | Fourth quarter |
|---|---|---|---|---|
| Cash inflow from operations | $(1,675) | $3,855 | $9,790 | $8,200 |
| Investment—Fixtures and equipment | (16,000) | 0 | 0 | 0 |
| Beginning cash balance | 0 | 5,725 | 5,980 | 5,245 |
| Balance before financing | $(17,675) | $9,580 | $15,770 | $13,445 |
| Additional short-term borrowing | 24,000 | 0 | 0 | 0 |
| Reduction in short-term borrowing | 0 | (3,000) | (10,000) | (8,000) |
| Interest | (600) | (600) | (525) | (275) |
| Budgeted ending cash balance | $5,725 | $5,980 | $5,245 | $5,170 |

Schedule of Cash Sales and Net Cash Inflow from Operations

|  | First quarter | Second quarter | Third quarter | Fourth quarter |
|---|---|---|---|---|
| Budgeted sales (= Collections) | $15,000 | $25,000 | $35,000 | $35,000 |
| Purchases of inventory | 10,905* | 15,175 | 18,700 | 19,250 |
| Store rental | 2,700 | 2,100 | 2,250 | 3,150 |
| Salespersons | 2,000 | 2,000 | 2,000 | 2,000 |
| Other operating expense | 1,070 | 1,870 | 2,260 | 2,400 |
| Cash inflow from operations | $(1,675) | $3,855 | $9,790 | $8,200 |

* Inventory requirements:

|  |  |  |
|---|---|---|
| Current quarter | $8,250 | ($15,000 × 0.55) |
| Minimum | 4,580 | ($25,000 × 0.55 ÷ 3) |
| Total | $12,830 |  |
| Paid current quarter | 10,905 | ($12,830 × 0.85) |
| Paid following quarter | $ 1,925 |  |

## Chapter 10

EP 10.1   12/31/X3  Accounts receivable will include:

| 70% December budgeted sales | = | $630,000 |
|---|---|---|
| 30% November budgeted sales | = | 240,000 |
| 10% October budgeted sales | = | 70,000 |
| 2% Third-quarter budgeted sales | = | 36,000 |
|  |  | $976,000 |

12/31/X3  Allowance for uncollectibles will include:
    2% Past 6 months' sales        =     $84,000

EP 10.3   Beginning inventory + Purchases − Cost of goods sold = Ending Inventory
Cost of goods sold = 60% of sales
$140,000 + 880,000 − $900,000 = $120,000

**EP 10.5**   a)

## HOLLY CORPORATION

Budgeted Schedule of Cost of Goods Manufactured
for the Year 19X6
(000 omitted)

| | | |
|---|---:|---:|
| Beginning raw materials | $ 10 | |
| Purchases | 90 | |
| Materials available | $100 | |
| Less: Ending raw materials | 15 | |
| Materials used | | $ 85 |
| Direct labor | | 170 |
| Manufacturing overhead | | 255 |
| Total manufacturing cost | | $510 |
| Beginning WIP inventory | | 40 |
| | | $550 |
| Less: Ending WIP inventory | | 40 |
| Cost of goods manufactured | | $510 |

b)

| | | |
|---|---:|---|
| Beginning finished goods inventory | $ 65 | (12/31/X5) |
| Cost of goods manufactured | 510 | |
| Goods available for sale | $575 | |
| Less: Cost of goods sold | 500 | |
| Ending finished goods inventory | $ 75 | (12/31/X6) |

**EP 10.7**

| | |
|---|---:|
| Raw materials used (20% sales) | $300,000 |
| Direct labor (20% sales) | 300,000 |
| Manufacturing overhead (25% sales + $40,000) | 415,000 |

## GREGORY MANUFACTURING CORPORATION

Budgeted Schedule of Cost of Goods Manufactured
for the Year 19X6

| | | |
|---|---:|---:|
| Beginning raw materials | $ 35,000 | |
| Purchases | 300,000 | |
| Materials available | $335,000 | |
| Less: Ending raw materials | 35,000 | |
| Materials used | | $300,000 |
| Direct labor | | 300,000 |
| Manufacturing overhead | | 415,000 |
| Total manufacturing cost | | $1,015,000 |
| Beginning WIP inventory | | 45,000 |
| | | $1,060,000 |
| Less: Ending WIP inventory | | 45,000 |
| Cost of goods manufactured | | $1,015,000 |

EP 10.9  
| Cost of goods sold (variable) | 60% |
|---|---|
| Wages and salaries (mixed)* | 10% + $25,000 |
| Insurance (fixed) | $10,000 |
| Supplies (mixed)* | 2% + $7,000 |
| Depreciation (fixed) | $40,000 |
| Interest (fixed) | $30,000 |

Provision for taxes (35% of income from operations)

* Obtained by high-low-point regression analysis.

## JERRY B COMPANY

### Budgeted Income Statement for 19X6

| | |
|---|---|
| Sales | $800,000 |
| Cost of goods sold | 480,000 |
| Operating expenses | |
| Wages and salaries | 105,000 |
| Insurance | 10,000 |
| Supplies | 23,000 |
| Depreciation | 40,000 |
| Interest | 30,000 |
| Income from operations | $112,000 |
| Provision for tax | 39,200 |
| Net income | $ 72,800 |

SP 10.11

| | Preliminary budgeted equities | | Desired structure | | | Necessary changes |
|---|---|---|---|---|---|---|
| | $ | $ | % | $ | $ | $ |
| Current borrowings | 200 | | | 20 | | −180 |
| Other current liabilities* | 50 | | | 50 | | none |
| Total current liabilities | | 250 | 10 | | 70 | −180 |
| Long-term debt | | 150 | 30 | | 210 | + 60 |
| Contributed capital | 200 | | | 320 | | +120 |
| Retained earnings* | 100 | | | 100 | | none |
| Total Stockholders' Equity | | 300 | 60 | | 420 | +120 |
| Total Equities | | $700 | 100% | | $700 | none |

* Not result of financing activities.

## KISSLER HOTEL SUPPLIES

### Budgeted Balance Sheet, Equity Section, As of 12/31/X9 (000 omitted)

| | |
|---|---|
| Current borrowings | $20 |
| Other current liabilities | 50 |
| Total current liabilities | $ 70 |
| Long-term debt | 210 |
| Contributed capital | 320 |
| Retained earnings | 100 |
| Total Equities | $700 |

## KISSLER HOTEL SUPPLIES

### Budgeted SCFP (Financial Budget)
### for the Year 19X9 (000 omitted)

*Sources:*

| | |
|---|---|
| Funds from operations | $130 |
| Disposition of noncurrent assets | 10 |
| New long-term debt | 60 |
| New stock | .120 |
| Total sources | $320 |

*Applications:*

| | |
|---|---|
| Purchase of noncurrent assets | $ 70 |
| Dividends | 40 |
| Increase in balance of net working capital* | 210 |
| Total applications | $320 |

* Additional $180,000 used to reduce current borrowings.

**SP 10.13**

## LORRINE CORPORATION

### 19X6 Budgeted Financial Statements (000 omitted)

#### Schedule of Cost of Goods Manufactured

| | | |
|---|---|---|
| Beginning raw materials | $   60 | |
| Purchases | 1,190 | |
| Materials available | $1,250 | |
| Ending raw materials | 50 | |
| Materials used | | $1,200 |
| Direct labor | | 2,000 |
| Manufacturing overhead | | 1,375 |
| Total manufacturing cost | | $4,575 |
| Beginning WIP inventory | | 75 |
| | | $4,650 |
| Less: Ending WIP Inventory | | 100 |
| Cost of goods manufactured | | $4,550 |

#### Income Statement

| | | |
|---|---|---|
| Sales | | $6,000 |
| Cost of goods sold: | | |
| Beginning finished goods inventory | $ 350 | |
| Cost of goods manufactured | 4,550 | |
| Goods available for sale | $4,900 | |
| Less: Ending finished goods inventory | 400 | 4,500 |
| Gross profit | | $1,500 |
| Depreciation expense | | 30 |
| Other period expenses | | 970 |
| Income from operations | | $ 500 |
| Provision for income taxes | | 150 |
| Net income | | $ 350 |

## BALANCE SHEET

| | | | |
|---|---|---|---|
| Cash | $ 200 | Current borrowings | $ 0 |
| Marketable securities | 400 | Other current liabilities | 1,150 |
| Accounts receivable—net | 1,000 | Total current liabilities | $1,150 |
| Inventories | | | |
|   Raw materials  $ 50 | | | |
|   Work-in-process  100 | | | |
|   Finished goods   400 | 550 | | |
| Other current assets | 25 | | |
| Total current assets | $2,175 | Long-term debt | $ 200 |
| Fixed assets | 2,900 | Contributed capital | 2,000 |
| Accumulated depreciation | (1,200) | Retained earnings | 525 |
| Total Assets | $3,875 | Total Equities | $3,875 |

## STATEMENT OF CHANGES IN FINANCIAL POSITION

*Sources:*

| | |
|---|---|
| Net income | $350 |
| Add: Depreciation | 200 |
| Funds from operations | $550 |
| New stock | 200 |
| Total sources | $750 |

*Applications:*

| | |
|---|---|
| Acquire fixed assets | $210 |
| Retire long-term debt | 400 |
| Dividends | 140 |
| Total applications | $750 |

**SP 10.15**    a)

### JOHN ANDERSON AND DAUGHTERS

Budgeted Income Statement
for the Year 19X8

| | | | |
|---|---|---|---|
| Sales | | $885,500 | ($770,000 × 1.15) |
| Cost of merchandise sold | | 531,300 | (60% variable) |
| Gross margin | | $354,200 | |
| Less: Operating Expenses | | | |
|   Wages and salaries | $148,550 | | (mixed $0.1 V + $60,000 F)* |
|   Utilities | 11,430 | | (mixed $0.005 V + $7,000 F)* |
|   Insurance | 15,000 | | ($15,000 fixed) |
|   Property taxes | 14,350 | | (assume fixed at 19X7 level) |
|   Interest | 3,650 | | (assume fixed at 19X7 level) |
|   Depreciation | 17,000 | $209,980 | ($17,000 fixed) |
| Income from operations | | $144,220 | |
| Provision for income taxes | | 50,477 | |
| Net Income | | $ 93,743 | |

* Budgeting rate determined by using high-low-point regression analysis.

Budgeted Balance Sheet
as of 12/31/X8

| Assets | | Equities | |
|---|---|---|---|
| Cash[6] | $155,263 | Current liabilities[4] | $138,950 |
| Accounts receivable[1] | 119,730 | Long-term debt | 40,570 |
| Inventory[2] | 96,570 | Total liabilities | $179,520 |
| Supplies[3] | 8,855 | | |
| Total current assets[5] | $380,418 | | |
| Land | 20,000 | | |
| Building | 200,000 | | |
| Equipment and Fixtures | 80,000 | | |
| Less Accumulated | | Contributed Capital | $200,000 |
| Depreciation[7] | (172,000) | Retained earnings[8] | 128,898 |
| Total Assets | $508,418 | Total Equities | $508,418 |

Notes:

(1) 19X7 Receivables turnover $= \dfrac{\$770,000}{(\$91,800 + 96,250)/2} = 8.2$

19X8 Budgeted receivables turnover $= 8.2$

$$\frac{\$885,500}{X} = 8.2,$$

$X \quad = \$107,990 \quad \text{(rounded)} = \text{Average receivables}$

$$\$107,990 = \frac{\$96,250 + Y}{2},$$

$Y = \$119,730 = 12/31/X8 \text{ Receivables}$

(2) 19X7 Inventory turnover $= \dfrac{\$462,000}{(\$73,500 + 80,500)/2} = 6$

19X8 Budgeted inventory turnover $= 6$

$$\frac{\$531,200}{X} = 6,$$

$X \quad = \$88,533 = \text{Average inventory}$

$$\$88,533 = \frac{80,500 + Y}{2},$$

$Y \quad = \$96,570 \text{ (rounded)} = 12/31/X8 \text{ Inventory}$

(3) Assume supplies increase in proportion to sales increase, as occurred from 19X6 to 19X7:

$$\$7,700 \times 1.15 = \$8,855$$

(4) Ratio of 12/31/X7 current liabilities to 19X7 operating expenses (excluding depreciation) = 0.72 to 1.

0.72 × $192,980 (19X8 Budgeted operating expenses excluding depreciation) = $138,950 (rounded).

(5) Budgeted funds from operations = $110,743   ($93,743 + $17,000)

| | |
|---|---|
| 12/31/X7 Net working capital | = 130,725 |
| 12/31/X8 Budgeted net working capital | = $241,468 |
| Add: 12/31/X8 Budgeted current liabilities | = 138,950 |
| 12/31/X8 Budgeted current assets | $380,418 |

(6) To reconcile budgeted total current assets.

(7)
| | |
|---|---|
| 12/31/X7 Accumulated depreciation | $155,000 |
| 19X8 Budgeted depreciation expense | 17,000 |
| 12/31/X8 Budgeted accumulated depreciation | $172,000 |

(8)
| | |
|---|---|
| 12/31/X7 Retained earnings | $ 35,155 |
| 19X8 Budgeted net income | 93,743 |
| 12/31/X8 Retained earnings | $128,898 |

### Budgeted SCFP for the Year 19X8

*Sources:*
Funds from operations                     $110,743

*Applications:*
Increase balance of net working capital   $110,743

b) Memorandum to John Anderson:

During 1978, you should be able to withdraw at least $102,518 in cash dividends without impairing solvency. A withdrawal of this amount would still leave $277,900 of current assets, thus maintaining the previous 2:1 current ratio and resulting in a quick ratio of 1.24:1.

An additional withdrawal of the $26,380 remaining retained earnings in cash would still leave a quick ratio of 1.05:1. This would be lower than the 12/31/X7 quick ratio of 1.33:1, but could still be safe if verified by a more detailed cash budget.

## Chapter 11

**EP 11.1**

| | | | |
|---|---|---|---|
| a) XXX | b) XXX | c) XXX | d) SLS |
| e) OPS | f) SLS | g) SLS | h) OPS |
| i) ADM | j) SLS | k) ADM | l) OPS |
| m) OPS | n) OPS | o) SLS | p) SLS |
| q) SLS | r) OPS | s) OPS | t) OPS |
| u) OPS | v) OPS | w) OPS | x) ADM |
| y) OPS | z) ADM | | |

**EP 11.3**   a) (1) Normal conditions with no price changes—favorable revenue variance would indicate superior performance.

(2) Abnormal conditions (weather, unanticipated economic recession, and so forth)—unfavorable revenue variance could be much less than expected under the circumstances and therefore represents a superior performance.

(3) Normal conditions—favorable variance could indicate increased efficiency.

(4) Nonanticipated situation (wage increase, large volume of rush orders, and so forth)—unfavorable variance could represent less excessive cost than might be expected in the circumstances and therefore superior performance.

(5) Normal conditions—favorable variance could indicate increased efficiency.

(6) Abnormal conditions (weather, rush orders with much overtime, and so forth)—unfavorable variance could represent less extra cost than might be expected in the circumstances and therefore superior performance.

b) (1) Price increases or nonanticipated significant upsurge in economy where a greater favorable variance could have been expected.

(2) Normal circumstances where unfavorable revenue variance would indicate substandard performance.

(3) Undesirable production delays resulting from less-than-timely movement of materials would indicate that material-handling cost savings were both illusory and undesirable.

(4) Normal circumstances where unfavorable variance would indicate inefficiency.

(5) Adverse working conditions resulting from overzealous cutbacks of utility costs would make such "savings" undesirable.

(6) Normal circumstances where unfavorable variance would indicate inefficient usage.

EP 11.5   a) • Sales drop could be significant and should be investigated.
   • Travel excess should require investigation.
   • Reduced sales returns and allowances might indicate inappropriate rejection of legitimate customer claims with long-run negative consequences.
   • Other variances relatively inconsequential.

   b) • Sales drop in current month could be simple result of poor monthly allocation of sales demand and therefore inconsequential. It also could be a reversal of previous favorable trend.

   c) Territory #3 is not an expenditure center since it includes significant revenue. It is not a profit center since only a small portion of costs necessary to generate revenue are included (costs of goods or services provided are omitted). Therefore it would be classified as a revenue center.

EP 11.7   a) No. A suggestion system is usually understood to encourage suggestions from employees to management.

b) Probably not for two reasons. The evidence indicates that the existing authoritarian system appears to be working well. It is also doubtful that Mr. Graves would really listen to or act upon more participation.

c) Mr. Graves' approach does risk missing out on potentially significant employee feedback. Also the existing acceptance of Mr. Graves' authoritarian approach may be connected to his personality and could disintegrate if a new manager were to replace him.

## Chapter 12

**EP 12.1**

| | | | | |
|---|---|---|---|---|
| a) PP | b) PR | c) RR | d) PR | e) PR |
| f) RR | g) RR | h) PR | i) PR | j) PP |
| k) PR | l) PR | m) RR | n) PR | o) RR |
| p) PP | q) PP | r) PP | s) PP | t) PP |
| u) PP | v) PP | w) PP | x) PP | |

**EP 12.3**

Units Produced as Activity Base:

| Units | Budget | Actual | Variance | Variance % |
|---|---|---|---|---|
| 8,400 | $144,356* | $143,000 | $1,356 F | 0.9 F |
| 6,400 | 114,256 | 118,000 | 3,744 U | 3.3 U |
| 5,800 | 105,226 | 103,000 | 2,226 F | 2.1 F |
| 3,200 | 66,096 | 68,000 | 1,904 U | 2.9 U |
| 2,800 | 60,076 | 58,000 | 2,076 F | 3.5 F |

Direct Labor Hours as Activity Base:

| DLH | Budget | Actual | Variance | Variance % |
|---|---|---|---|---|
| 24,900 | $144,514 | $143,000 | $1,514 F | 1.0 F |
| 19,400 | 114,704 | 118,000 | 3,296 U | 1.9 U |
| 17,500 | 104,406 | 103,000 | 1,406 F | 1.3 F |
| 10,600 | 67,008 | 68,000 | 992 U | 1.4 U |
| 9,200 | 59,420 | 58,000 | 1,420 F | 2.4 F |

* From data given, slope = variable cost and $Y$ intercept = fixed cost.

Using direct labor hours as the activity base appears to be the better predictor of the two measures. The variances are smaller.

Also, calculating the standard error of estimate (Chapter 5 Appendix and solution to Problem SP12.15), the standard error resulting from using direct labor hours is only $2,459 (rounded), as compared to the standard error for units produced of $3,095 (rounded), again indicating direct labor hours to be the better predictor.

**EP 12.5**

$$Y = aX + b$$
$$\$265,000 = a(10,000) + b$$
$$\$165,000 = a(\ 6,000) + b$$
$$\$100,000 = 4,000a,$$
$$a = \$25 \quad = \text{variable cost per DLH,}$$
$$b = \$15,000 = \text{fixed cost.}$$

**EP 12.7**    a)

|  | Current month | | |
| | Fixed budget | Flexible budget | Volume variance |
| --- | --- | --- | --- |
| Direct labor | $28,000 | $35,000 | $7,000 U |
| Indirect labor | 11,000 | 13,000 | 2,000 U |
| Indirect materials | 2,500 | 3,000 | 500 U |
| Maintenance | 1,300 | 1,400 | 100 U |
| Total | $42,800 | $52,400 | $9,600 U |

|  | Year-to-date | | |
| | Fixed budget | Flexible budget | Volume variance |
| --- | --- | --- | --- |
| Direct labor | $63,000 | $ 70,000 | $7,000 U |
| Indirect labor | 27,000 | 29,000 | 2,000 U |
| Indirect materials | 6,000 | 6,500 | 500 U |
| Maintenance | 3,600 | 3,700 | 100 U |
| Total | $99,600 | $109,200 | $9,600 U |

b)

|  | Current month | | | |
| | Flexible budget | Actual | Spending variance | % |
| --- | --- | --- | --- | --- |
| Direct labor | $35,000 | $34,900 | $100 F | 0.3 |
| Indirect labor | 13,000 | 12,100 | 900 F | 6.9 |
| Indirect materials | 3,000 | 3,200 | 200 U | 6.6 |
| Maintenance | 1,400 | 1,400 | 0 | 0.0 |
| Total | $52,400 | $51,600 | $800 F | 1.5 |

|  | Year-to-date | | | |
| | Flexible budget | Actual | Spending variance | % |
| --- | --- | --- | --- | --- |
| Direct labor | $ 70,000 | $ 70,100 | $100 U | 0.1 |
| Indirect labor | 29,000 | 28,500 | 500 F | 1.7 |
| Indirect materials | 6,500 | 6,550 | 50 U | 0.8 |
| Maintenance | 3,700 | 3,750 | 50 U | 1.4 |
| Total | $109,200 | $108,900 | $300 F | 0.3 |

Supervisor appears to be doing an excellent job of cost control. Only the current-month variance for indirect materials might merit further investigation.

**EP 12.9**    See solution to EP12.7(b).

**EP 12.11**  a) 73,000 hours × \$4 per hour absorption rate = \$292,000 of overhead applied.

b)
| | |
|---|---|
| Actual overhead incurred | \$320,000 |
| Overhead applied | 292,000 |
| Underapplied overhead | \$ 28,000 |

c) Budgeting rate = \$15 per unit variable plus \$60,000 fixed at volume of 15,000 units; flexible budgeted overhead = \$285,000.

d)
| | |
|---|---|
| Flexible budgeted overhead | \$285,000 |
| Actual overhead costs | 320,000 |
| Overhead spending variance | \$ 35,000 U |

**EP 12.13**  a)  1)
| | | |
|---|---|---|
| Actual total costs | \$84,000 | |
| Actual total hours of usage | 480 | hours |
| Actual cost per hour | \$175 | |
| Charged to Department A | \$10,500 | (based on 60 hours) |

2)
| | | |
|---|---|---|
| Actual total cost | \$84,000 | |
| Budget total hours of usage | 500 | hours |
| Budgeted hours for A | 100 | hours |
| Charged to Department A | \$16,800 | (based on 20%) |

3)
| | |
|---|---|
| Charged to Department A | \$11,100 |
| (60 hours at \$185 per hour) | |

4)
| | | |
|---|---|---|
| Budgeted total costs | \$75,000 | |
| Actual total usage | 480 | hours |
| Cost per hour | \$150 | |
| Charges to Department A | \$ 9,000 | (based on 60 hours) |

5)
| | | |
|---|---|---|
| Budgeted variable costs | \$25,000 | |
| Actual total usage | 480 | hours |
| Rate per hour | \$50 | (rounded) |
| Charges to Department A | \$ 3,000 | (based on 60 hours) |

b) 1)

| | Budget | Actual | Variance | Variance % |
|---|---|---|---|---|
| Chargeable hours | 500 hrs. | 480 hrs. | | |
| Revenue (charges) | \$92,500 | \$88,800 | \$ 3,700 U | 4.0 |
| Variable costs | 25,000 | 34,000 | 9,000 U | 36.0 |
| Fixed costs | 50,000 | 50,000 | 0 | 0.0 |
| Profit | \$17,500 | \$ 4,800 | \$12,700 U | 72.6 |

2)

| | Budget | Actual | Variance | Variance % |
|---|---|---|---|---|
| Chargeable hours | 500 hrs. | 480 hrs. | | |
| Variable costs | \$25,000 | \$34,000 | \$9,000 U | 36.0 |
| Fixed costs | 50,000 | 50,000 | 0 | 0.0 |
| Charges | 75,000 | 75,000 | 0 | 0.0 |
| Net costs | 0 | \$ 9,000 | \$9,000 U | — |

3)

| | Budget | Actual | Variance | Variance % |
|---|---|---|---|---|
| Chargeable hours | 500 hrs. | 480 hrs. | | |
| Variable costs | $25,000 | $34,000 | $9,000 U | 36.0 |
| Fixed costs | 50,000 | 50,000 | 0 | 0.0 |
| Charges | 25,000 | 25,000 | 0 | 0.0 |
| Net costs | $50,000 | $59,000 | $9,000 U | 18.0 |

**SP 12.15**  a)

$$SE = \sqrt{\frac{\Sigma(Y-\bar{Y})^2}{n-2}}$$

| Units produced | | Direct labor hours | |
|---|---|---|---|
| Variance* | $(Y-\bar{Y})^2$ | Variance* | $(Y-\bar{Y})^2$ |
| $1,356 F | 1,838,736 | $1,514 F | 2,292,196 |
| 3,744 U | 14,017,536 | 3,296 U | 10,863,616 |
| 2,266 F | 4,955,076 | 1,406 F | 1,976,836 |
| 1,904 U | 3,625,216 | 992 U | 984,064 |
| 2,076 F | 4,309,776 | 1,420 F | 2,016,400 |
| $\Sigma(Y-\bar{Y})^2$ | 28,744,340 | $\Sigma(Y-\bar{Y})^2$ | 18,133,112 |
| | SE = $3,095 (rounded) | | SE = $2,459 (rounded) |

b) Of the two activity measures, direct labor hours should be chosen for budgeting purposes since it has the lowest standard error of estimate (prediction).

* See solution to Problem EP12.3.

**SP 12.17**  a)

| | Production center #1 | Production center #2 | Totals |
|---|---|---|---|
| Product A: | | | |
| Direct material | $140,000 | $     0 | $140,000 |
| Direct labor | 60,000 | 35,000 | 95,000 |
| | | | $235,000 |
| Product B: | | | |
| Direct material | 50,000 | 20,000 | $ 70,000 |
| Direct labor | 24,000 | 45,000 | 69,000 |
| | | | $139,000 |
| Product C: | | | |
| Direct material | 20,000 | 0 | $ 20,000 |
| Direct labor | 30,000 | 0 | 30,000 |
| | | | $ 50,000 |
| Indirect costs | 120,000 | 66,000 | |
| Service center costs | 60,000 | 30,000 | $276,000 |
| Total | $504,000 | $196,000 | $700,000 |

b)

|  | Product A | Product B | Product C |
|---|---|---|---|
| Total direct costs | $235,000 | $139,000 | $ 50,000 |
| Indirect costs Prod. Ctr. #1* | 72,000 | 48,000 | 60,000 |
| Indirect costs Prod. Ctr. #2 | 42,000 | 54,000 | 0 |
| Total product costs | $349,000 | $241,000 | $110,000 |

| * Total indirect costs | $180,000 |
|---|---|
| Total direct labor hours | 15,000 |
| Indirect cost per direct labor hour | $12 |
| DLH Product A | 6,000 |
| Indirect costs allocated to Product A | $ 72,000 |

**SP 12.19**

a)
| Actual overhead | $320,000 |
|---|---|
| Flexible budgeted overhead | 285,000 |
| Overhead applied | 292,000 |
| Standard overhead | 300,000 |
| Underapplied overhead | 28,000 |

b)
| Flexible budgeted overhead | $285,000 |
|---|---|
| Less: Overhead applied | −292,000 |
| Overhead volume variance | $  7,000 F |

c)
| Overhead applied | $292,000 |
|---|---|
| Less: Standard overhead | −300,000 |
| Overhead efficiency variance | $  8,000 F |

d)
| Actual overhead | $320,000 |
|---|---|
| Less: Flexible budgeted overhead | −285,000 |
| Overhead spending variance | $ 35,000 U |

## Chapter 13

**EP 13.1**   a) $0.16      b) 2.7 feet       c) $0.432 per unit
        d) $4.20      e) 1.85 hours      f) $7.77 per unit

**EP 13.3**   a) Events that should be reflected in a revision of standards = (1) and (6).

b) Events probably resulting in material or labor variances:
   (1) Favorable direct labor variance
   (3) Unfavorable direct labor variance
   (4) Unfavorable material price variance
   (6) Unfavorable direct labor variance

    c) (3) Unfavorable direct labor variance
       (4) Unfavorable material price variance

    d) Events that should generate 19X8 budget revisions: (1), (2), (5), and (6).

**EP 13.5**    a) $32,000   original purchases budget ($4 $\times$ 8,000)
             b) $30,000   flexible purchases budget ($4 $\times$ 7,500)
             c) $18,900   original direct labor budget (2.25 $\times$ $5.60 $\times$ 1,500)
             d) $17,640   flexible direct labor budget (2.25 $\times$ $5.60 $\times$ 1,400)
             e) $2,000 F  materials volume variance [$4(7,500 − 8,000)]
             f) $750 F   materials spending variance [7,500($3.90 − $4.00)]
             g) $750 F   materials price variance [7,500($3.90 − $4.00)]
             h) $1,200 F  materials volume variance [$12(1,400 − 1,500)]
             i) $800 U   materials spending variance ($17,600 − $16,800)
             j) $800 U   materials usage variance [$4(4,400 − 4,200)]
             k) $1,260 F  labor volume variance ($17,640 − $18,900)
             l) $760 U   labor spending variance ($18,400 − $17,640)
             m) $480 U   labor rate variance [3,200($5.75 − $5.60)]
             n) $280 U   labor efficiency variance [$5.60(3,200 − 3,150)]

**EP 13.7**   A. $\dfrac{\text{Standard material cost}}{\text{Standard quantity}} = \dfrac{\$6.00}{3} = \$2.00$  per pound, standard price

        $1,900 − (1,000 pounds $\times$ $2) = $100 F  material price variance
        $100 U  material usage variance ÷ $2 = 50  pounds excess usage
        200  units $\times$ 3  pounds = 600  pounds standard usage
        600 + 50 = 650  pounds actual usage

        $\dfrac{\text{Standard labor cost}}{\text{Standard rate}} = \dfrac{\$24}{\$6} = 4$ standard hours

        $\dfrac{\text{Actual labor costs}}{\text{Actual labor hours}} = \dfrac{\$4,875}{750} = \$6.50$ per hour actual rate

        ($6.50 − $6.00)750 = $375 U  labor rate variance
        200 units $\times$ 4 hours = 800  standard hours
        (750 − 800)$6 = $300 F  labor efficiency variance

    B. Let $X$ = actual quantity purchased in pounds and ($3,900/$X$) = actual price paid per pound; then

$$\left(\frac{3,900}{X} - \$2.50\right) X = \$150 \quad \text{unfavorable material price variance,}$$
$$X = 1,500 \quad \text{pounds actually purchased.}$$

      Standard quantity = 2 pounds ($5.00 ÷ $2.50)

      Let $Y$ = actual units completed; then

$$[1,300 - (3Y)]5.00 = \$500 \quad \text{unfavorable efficiency variance;}$$
$$Y = 400 \quad \text{units completed.}$$

Let $Z$ = actual labor rate; then $1,300(Z - \$5) = \$130$   unfavorable rate variance,

$Z = \$5.10$   actual labor rate incurred;

$\$5.10 \times 1,300 = \$6,630$   actual labor costs incurred.

Standard labor cost per unit = $15 ($5.00 × 3); then

$400 \times 2 \times \$2.50 = \$2,000$   standard material usage
$700 \times \$2.50 = \underline{\$1,750}$   actual material usage
Material usage variance =   $\$250$ F.

C. Cost of ordering including freight = $2,850
   Standard material cost per unit   =    $10
   Actual units completed            =    300
   Standard labor rate               =    $4
   Material usage variance           =    $100 F

D. Standard quantity (pounds)        =    6
   Material price variance           =    $500 U
   Actual units completed            =    300
   Standard labor cost per unit      =    $60
   Actual labor hours                =    2,900

**EP 13.9**   a) $62,400 ÷ 32,000 = $1.95   actual price per pound
($1.95 − $2.00)32,000 = $1,600 F   materials price variance

b) (32,000 − 30,000)$2 = $4,000 U   materials usage variance

c) $56,100 ÷ 11,000 = $5.10   actual labor rate paid
($5.10 − $5.00)11,000 = $1,100 U   labor rate variance

d) (11,000 − 10,000)$5 = $5,000 U   labor efficiency variance

e) Actual overhead        = $101,300
   Standard overhead       =  100,000   ($20 × 5,000)
   Underapplied overhead  = $   1,300

Cost of goods sold:

| | |
|---|---:|
| Units shipped at standard | $189,000 |
| Favorable price variance | (1,600) |
| Unfavorable usage variance | 4,000 |
| Unfavorable rate variance | 1,100 |
| Unfavorable efficiency variance | 5,000 |
| Underapplied overhead | 1,300 |
| Total | $198,800 |

$ (thousands)

SP 13.11   a) 

| | | |
|---|---|---|
| Cost of products sold | 795 | (820 − 25) |
| Cost of goods manufactured | 810 | (140 + x − 155 = 795) |
| Applied overhead | 320 | (360/45 × 40) |
| Actual overhead | 345 | (320 + 25) |
| Direct labor | 280 | (7 × 40) |
| Raw materials used | 200 | (60 + x + 280 + 320 − 50 = 810) |
| Net purchases | 205 | (15 + x − 20 = 200) |
| Freight-in | 10 | (215 + x − 15 − 5 = 205) |

b)

| | DR | CR |
|---|---|---|
| Net purchases | $205,000 | $ |
| Purchase returns | 15,000 | |
| Purchase discounts | 5,000 | |
|    Gross purchases | | 215,000 |
|    Freight-in | | 10,000 |
| | | |
| Raw materials used | 220,000 | |
|    Net purchases | | 205,000 |
|    Raw materials inventory | | 15,000 |
| | | |
| Raw materials inventory | 20,000 | |
|    Raw materials used | | 20,000 |
| | | |
| Cost of goods manufactured | 860,000 | |
|    Raw materials used | | 200,000 |
|    Direct labor | | 280,000 |
|    Manufacturing overhead | | 320,000 |
|    WIP Inventory | | 60,000 |
| | | |
| WIP Inventory | 50,000 | |
|    Cost of goods manufactured | | 50,000 |
| | | |
| Cost of goods sold | 25,000 | |
|    Manufacturing overhead | | 25,000 |
| | | |
| Cost of goods sold | 950,000 | |
|    Cost of goods manufactured | | 810,000 |
|    Finished goods inventory | | 140,000 |
| | | |
| Finished goods inventory | 155,000 | |
|    Cost of goods sold | | 155,000 |

$ (thousands)

SP 13.13   a)

| | | |
|---|---|---|
| Raw materials purchases (standard) | 400 | (410 − 10) |
| Raw materials used (actual) | 450 | (300 + 400 − 250) |
| Raw materials used (standard) | 430 | (450 − 20) |
| Unfavorable labor variance | 60 | (900 − 840) |
| Overhead applied (standard) | 920 | (875 + 45) |
| Total manufacturing cost (standard) | 2,190 | (430 + 840 + 920) |
| Cost of goods manufactured | 2,170 | (120 + 2,190 − 140) |
| Cost of products sold to customers | 2,195 | (X + 10 + 20 + 60 − 45 = 2,240) |
| Ending finished goods inventory | 335 | (360 + 2,170 − 2,195) |

|  | DR | CR |
|---|---|---|
| b) Unfavorable price variance | $   10,000 | $ |
| Net purchases | | 10,000 |
| | | |
| Raw materials used | 700,000 | |
| Raw materials inventory | | 300,000 |
| Net purchases | | 400,000 |
| | | |
| Raw materials inventory | 250,000 | |
| Raw materials used | | 250,000 |
| | | |
| Unfavorable usage variance | 20,000 | |
| Raw materials used | | 20,000 |
| | | |
| Unfavorable labor variance | 60,000 | |
| Direct labor | | 60,000 |
| | | |
| Manufacturing overhead | 45,000 | |
| Overapplied overhead | | 45,000 |
| | | |
| Cost of goods manufactured | 2,310,000 | |
| Raw materials used | | 430,000 |
| Direct labor | | 840,000 |
| Manufacturing overhead | | 920,000 |
| WIP Inventory | | 120,000 |
| | | |
| WIP Inventory | 140,000 | |
| Cost of goods manufactured | | 140,000 |
| | | |
| Cost of goods sold | 90,000 | |
| Unfavorable price variance | | 10,000 |
| Unfavorable usage variance | | 20,000 |
| Unfavorable labor variance | | 60,000 |
| | | |
| Overapplied overhead | 45,000 | |
| Cost of goods sold | | 45,000 |
| | | |
| Cost of goods sold | 2,670,000 | |
| Cost of goods manufactured | | 2,310,000 |
| Finished goods inventory | | 360,000 |
| | | |
| Finished goods inventory | 335,000 | |
| Cost of goods sold | | 335,000 |

## Chapter 14

**EP 14.1**  a) Budgeted revenue      $560,000   (40,000 × $14)
        Actual revenue        494,000   (38,000 × $13)
        Total revenue variance   $ 66,000 U

b) Sales price variance $38,000 U   [($13 − $14)38,000]

c) Sales volume variance $28,000 U   [(38,000 − 40,000)$14]

d) Contribution mix variance $10,000 U   [(38,000 − 40,000)($14 − $9]

**EP 14.3**   a) A:  Total sales variance $200 U   (500 U + 300 F)
Total contribution variance 400 U   (100 F + 500 U)

B:  Sales volume variance 1,100 U   (800 U − 300 F)
Contribution mix variance 900 U   (600 U − 300 F)

C:  Sales price variance 1,100 F   (900 F − 200 U)
Contribution mix variance 300 U   (800 F − 1,100 F)

|  | A | B | C |
|---|---|---|---|
| b) Sales price variance | (1) | (2) | (2) |
| Sales volume variance | (3) | (4) | (4) |
| Contribution mix variance | (3) | (4) | (4) |
| Total sales variance | (9) | (6) | (5) |
| Total contribution variance | (9) | (6) | (5) |

**EP 14.5**

|  | Budget |  | Actual |  |
|---|---|---|---|---|
| **Product A:** | | | | |
| Sales revenue | $3,000 | | $2,800 | (400 × $7) |
| Unit sales | 500 | | 400 | |
| Selling price | $6 | (3,000 ÷ 500) | $7 | |
| Unit contribution | $2 | ($6 − $4) | $3 | ($7 − $4) |
| Total contribution | $1,000 | (500 × $2) | $1,200 | (400 × $3) |
| Sales price variance | | | $400 F | [($7 − $6)400] |
| Sales volume variance | | | $600 U | [(400 − 500)$6] |
| Contribution mix variance | | | $200 U | [(400 − 500)$2] |
| **Product B:** | | | | |
| Sales revenue | $2,400 | | $3,000 | (500 × $6) |
| Unit sales | 300 | ($2,400 ÷ 8) | 500 | [($6 − $8) ÷ $1,000] |
| Selling price | $8 | | $6 | |
| Unit variable cost | $4 | ($8 − $4) | | |
| Unit contribution | $4 | [(500 − 300) ÷ 800] | $2 | ($6 − $4) |
| Total contribution | 1,200 | (300 × $4) | $1,000 | (500 × $2) |
| Sales price variance | | | $1,000 U | |
| Sales volume variance | | | $1,600 F | [(500 − 300)$8] |
| Contribution mix variance | | | $800 F | |

|  | Product C | | Product D | |
|---|---|---|---|---|
|  | Budget | Actual | Budget | Actual |
| Sales revenue | $575 | $1,250 | $800 | $3,000 |
| Unit sales | 25 | 50 | 200* | 600* |
| Selling price | $23 | $25 | $4 | $5 |
| Unit variable cost | $10 | $10 | $3 | $3 |
| Unit contribution | $13 | $15 | $1 | $2 |
| Total contribution | $325 | $750 | $200 | $1,200 |
| Sales price variance |  | $100 F |  | 500 F |
| Sales volume variance |  | $575 F |  | $1,500 F |
| Contribution mix variance |  | $325 U |  | $400 F |

\* Let $X$ = Budgeted sales quantity,
$\quad Y$ = Actual sales quantity,
$\quad Z$ = Budgeted unit contribution.

Then $\qquad X \cdot Z = \$200$ Total contribution,
$$Z = \frac{200}{X};$$
$\quad (Y - X)Z = \$400$ Contribution mix variance,
$$(Y - X)\left(\frac{200}{X}\right) = 400,$$
$$Y = 3X;$$
$\quad (Y - X)\$4 = 1{,}600$ Sales volume variance,
$$(3X - X)4 = 1{,}600,$$
$$X = 200;$$
$$(Y - 200)4 = 1{,}600,$$
$$Y = 600;$$
$$200\, Z = \$200,$$
$$Z = \$1.$$

**EP 14.7**  a) Actual price $32   ($1,440,000 ÷ 45,000)
Standard price $36   ($1,800,000 ÷ 50,000)
Sales price variance $180,000 U   [($32 − $36)45,000]

b) Sales volume variance $180,000 U   [(45,000 − 50,000)$36]

c) Budgeted unit contribution $13   (650,000 ÷ 50,000)
Contribution mix variance $65,000 U   [(45,000 − 50,000)$13]

d)

|  | Variable cost per unit sold | Flexible budget | Actual | Spending variance |
|---|---|---|---|---|
| Materials | $ 3 | $ 135,000 | $141,750 | $ 6,750 U |
| Labor | 10 | 450,000 | 425,250 | 24,750 F |
| Overhead | 8 | 360,000 | 337,500 | 22,500 F |
| Selling | 2 | 90,000 | 94,500 | 4,500 U |
| Total | $23 | $1,035,000 | $999,000 | $36,000 F |

|  | Flexible budget | Actual | Spending variance |
|---|---|---|---|
| Fixed overhead | $125,000 | $130,000 | $ 5,000 U |
| Fixed selling expense | 250,000 | 240,000 | 10,000 F |
| Fixed administrative exp. | 75,000 | 90,000 | 15,000 U |
| Total | $450,000 | $460,000 | $10,000 U |
| Contribution mix variance |  |  | $ 65,000 U |
| Sales price variance |  |  | 180,000 U |
| Total Expected contribution variance |  |  | $245,000 U |
| Net variable cost variances |  |  | 36,000 F |
| Net fixed cost variances |  |  | 10,000 U |
| Net contribution |  |  | $219,000 U |

**EP 14.9**

|  | A | B | C | D |
|---|---|---|---|---|
| Sales | $80,000 | $30,000 | $90,000 | $60,000 |
| Operating income | $10,000[1] | $ 6,000 | $ 9,000 | $ 2,400 |
| Asset base | $40,000[2] | $50,000 | $60,000 | $15,000 |
| Operating ratio | 12.5% | 20% | 10% | 4% |
| Investment turnover | 2[3] | 0.60 | 1.50 | 4.00 |
| ROI | 25% | 12% | 15% | 16% |
| Minimum return: |  |  |  |  |
| Percentage | 20% | 15% | 10% | 14% |
| Dollars | $ 8,000[4] | $ 7,500 | $ 9,000 | $ 2,100 |
| Residual income | $ 2,000[5] | $(1,500) | Zero | $  300 |

Notes:
1. $80,000 × 0.125
2. $10,000 ÷ 0.25
3. $80,000 ÷ $40,000
4. $40,000 × 0.2
5. $10,000 − $8,000

**EP 14.11**

|  | (a) | (b) | (c) |
|---|---|---|---|
| Book value depreciable assets 12/31/X4 | $240,000 | $200,000 | $180,000 |
| Working capital allocation | 200,000 | 200,000 | 200,000 |
| Asset base 12/31/X4 | $440,000 | $400,000 | $380,000 |
| Book value depreciable assets 12/31/X5 | $180,000 | $120,000 | $108,000 |
| Working capital allocation | 200,000 | 200,000 | 200,000 |
| Asset base 12/31/X5 | $380,000 | $320,000 | $308,000 |
| 19X5 Asset base (average) | $410,000 | $360,000 | $344,000 |
| 19X5 Operating income | $128,000 | $128,000 | $128,000 |
| 19X5 ROI | 31.2% | 35.6% | 37.2% |
| 19X5 Capital charge (15% required return) | $ 61,500 | $ 54,000 | $ 51,600 |
| 19X5 Residual income | $ 66,500 | $ 74,000 | $ 76,400 |

**EP 14.13**   a)

| Year | Cash flow | 12% PV Factor | PV |
|------|-----------|---------------|-----|
| 0 | −$120,000 | 1.0000 | −$120,000 |
| 1 | + 30,000 | | |
| 2 | + 30,000 | | |
| 3 | + 30,000 | 4.1114 | + 123,342 |
| 4 | + 30,000 | | |
| 5 | + 30,000 | | |
| 6 | + 30,000 | | |

NPV  +   3,342

b) Yes; return exceeds firm's required rate.

c) *Without equipment:*

| | | |
|---|---|---|
| Operating income | $40,000 | ($500,000 − $460,000) |
| ROI | 20% | ($ 40,000 ÷ $200,000) |
| Capital charge | $24,000 | ($200,000 × 0.12) |
| Residual income | $16,000 | ($ 40,000 − $ 24,000) |

d) *With equipment:*

Addition to average asset base    $110,000    $\left(\dfrac{\$120,000 + \$100,000}{2}\right)$

| | | |
|---|---|---|
| Previous base | 200,000 | |
| New average asset base | $310,000 | |
| New operating income | $ 50,000 | ($40,000 + $30,000 − $20,000) |
| ROI | 16.1% | |
| Capital charge | $ 37,200 | |
| Residual income | $ 12,800 | |

e) No. Acquisition of machine would reduce divisional performance measures.

**SP 14.15**   Material standard $3.00 per unit   ($150,000 ÷ 50,000)
Material price standard $0.50 per pound
Materials usage standard 6 pounds per unit   ($3.00 ÷ $0.50)
Flexible materials budget $135,000   (45,000 × $3.00)
Actual costs incurred $141,750
Total materials spending variance $6,750 U
Materials usage variance $22,500 U   [(315,000 − 270,000)$0.50]
Actual materials price $0.45 per pound ($141,750 ÷ 315,000)
Materials price variance $15,750 F   [($0.45 − $0.50)315,000]

Labor standard $10 per unit   ($500,000 ÷ 50,000)
Labor rate standard $5   ($10 ÷ 2)
Labor hours standard 2 hours per unit
Flexible labor budget $450,000   (45,000 × $10)
Actual costs incurred $425,250
Total labor spending variance $24,750 F
Actual hours worked 81,000 hours   ($425,250 ÷ $5.25)
Labor efficiency variance $45,000 F   [(81,000 − 90,000)$5]
Labor rate variance $20,250 U   [($5.25 − $5.00)81,000]

**SP 14.17**   a) Unit contribution of P = \$16
Unit contribution of Q = \$21
Let $X$ = quantity of Q's sold
Then at breakeven:

$$\$16(2X) + \$21(X) = \$159{,}000,$$
$$X = 3{,}000 \text{ units of Q sold at breakeven,}$$
$$2X = 6{,}000 \text{ units of P sold at breakeven.}$$

b) 15 percent ROI    \$  79,500
Fixed costs              159,000
                         \$238,500

$$\$16(2X) + \$21(X) = \$238{,}500,$$
$$X = 4{,}500 \text{ units of Q;}$$
$$2X = 9{,}000 \text{ units of P.}$$

c) Total contribution    \$265,000   [10,000(\$16) + 5,000(\$21)]
   Less: Fixed costs       159,000
   Income                 \$106,000
   ROI                        20%

d) Total contribution    \$318,000   [12,000(\$16) + 6,000(\$21)]
   Less: Fixed costs       159,000
   Less: Capital charge     79,500
   Residual income       \$  79,500

e) Necessary additional contribution:
   15 percent return on additional investment    \$  7,500
   Return of investment                            50,000*
   Additional fixed costs                          20,000
          Total                                   \$77,500

f) Necessary additional contribution:
   20 percent return on additional investment    \$10,000
   Return of investment                            50,000
   Additional fixed costs                          20,000
$$10{,}000(X - \$14) = \$80{,}000,$$
$$X = \$22.00.$$

\* Could be allocated to several years if proposal were not for single special order.

Let $X$ = P selling price to break even. Then unit contribution from special order = $X - \$14$;

$$10{,}000(X - \$14) = \$77{,}500,$$
$$X = \$21.75.$$

SP 14.19   a)  Total annual costs to firm under present plan:

| Purchase cost | $36,000 | (2,000 × 20 × $0.90) |
|---|---|---|
| Rebagging | 980 | (490 × 20 × $0.10) |
| | $36,980 | |

Total annual costs if garden division buys separately:

| Discount division purchases | $28,690 | (1,510 × 20 × $0.95) |
|---|---|---|
| Garden division purchases | 10,290 | (490 × 20 × $1.05) |
| | $38,980 | |

The firm should not allow outside procurement by the Garden Division since this action would increase annual costs by $2,000.

b)  As Garden Stores Division manager, you should procure separately unless the transfer price is reduced. Your outside purchase costs ($10,290) would be less than your present transfer costs ($9,800) plus rebagging costs ($980).

c)  As division manager of the Discount Division, you should consider reducing your transfer price; otherwise the costs of your own sales would increase from $27,180 to $28,690.

d)  A transfer price of $0.95 might be most appropriate. It would represent the Discount Division's alternative cost and would provide the Garden Division manager with no incentive to procure outside unless the item were obtainable for less than $1.05. If the Garden Division could obtain appropriately bagged fertilizer for under $1.05, it would be in the best interests of the firm for him or her to do so.

**Chapter 15**   There are no Essential or Supplementary Problems in Chapter 15.

**Chapter 16**

EP 16.1   a)

| PV of cash outlay | −$200,000 | (−$200,000 × 1.0000) |
|---|---|---|
| PV of cash inflows over eight years | + 237,827 | ($53,000 × 4.4873) |
| NPV | +$ 37,827 | |

You should recommend acceptance with an NPV of $37,827.

b)

| PV of cash outlay | −$200,000 | (−$200,000 × 1.0000) |
|---|---|---|
| PV of cash inflows over eight years | + 203,372 | ($53,000 × 3.8372*) |
| NPV | +$ 3,372 | |

No. You should still recommend acceptance with an NPV of $3,372.

c) PV of cash outlay            −$200,000   (−$200,000 × 1.0000)
PV of cash inflows over eight
years                        + 176,432   ($53,000 × 3.3289†)
        NPV                    −$ 23,568

Yes. You should recommend against acceptance since the NPV adjusted for inflation is $23,568 negative.

d) You should recommend acceptance. Even with 10 percent anticipated inflation, since future benefits are not fixed by contract, you could assume they will increase to offset inflation. Therefore your original NPV determination of $32,827 could be assumed valid.

* Discounted by 20 percent (15% cost of capital plus 5% inflation adjustment).
† Discounted by 25 percent (15% cost of capital plus 10% inflation adjustment).

**SP 16.3**    a) 12/31/X6 index = 110 (22 ÷ 20)

b) 12/31/X7 index = 121 (24.20 ÷ 20)

c) • Assume that the index on 9/30/X7 = 118, or that three percent inflation occurred within the last three months.
   • Ending inventory adjusted for price-level changes = $412,000 = $400,000 × 1.03.

d) $400,000 × (121/100) = $484,000
    500,000 × (121/110) =   550,000

Total adjusted capacity assets = $1,034,000

e) $2,400,000 × $\left(\dfrac{121}{110}\right)$ = $2,640,000

f) • Assume midpoint index = 115:

$$\$3,000,000 \times \left(\frac{121}{115}\right) = \$3,156,522$$

**SP 16.5**    a) Assume midyear index = 144.0
     Cash* [$50,000 × (150/144)]                   = $ 52,083
     Marketable Securities† [$30,000 × (150/138)]    =    32,609

Accounts and Notes Receivable* $\left(\$180,000 \times \dfrac{150}{144}\right)$ = 187,500

     Investments† [$40,000 × (150/138)]           =    43,478
                                              $315,670

       Monetary assets adjusted for inflation     $315,670
       Monetary assets at cost                    300,000
       Loss on monetary assets                $ 15,670

* Assume acquired uniformly throughout year.
† Assume in existence at beginning of year.

b)  Current liabilities* $\left( \$120{,}000 \times \dfrac{150}{144} \right)$ = $125,000

Long-term debt† $\left( \$180{,}000 \times \dfrac{150}{138} \right)$  =  195,652

$320,652

| | |
|---|---|
| Monetary debt adjusted for inflation | $320,652 |
| Fixed amount of monetary debt | 300,000 |
| Gain on monetary debt | $ 20,652 |

c)  
| | |
|---|---|
| Gain on monetary debt | $ 20,652 |
| Loss on monetary assets | 15,670 |
| Net gain on net monetary debt | $  4,982 |

\* Assume acquired uniformly throughout the year.
† Assume in existence at the beginning of the year.

SP 16.7

## BECK CORPORATION

### Balance Sheet as of 12/31/X5
### Price-level adjusted (000 omitted)

| Assets | | Equities | |
|---|---|---|---|
| Cash | $ 50 | Total current liabilities | $280 |
| Marketable securities | 40 | Bonds payable | 200 |
| Accounts receivable | 200 | Total Liabilities | $480 |
| Inventory | 337[1] | | |
| Total Current Assets | $627 | Contributed capital | 278[4] |
| Fixed assets | 796[2] | Retained earnings | 68[5] |
| Less: Accumulated | | | |
| depreciation | (597)[3] | Total Stockholders' Equity | $346 |
| Total Assets | $826 | Total Equities | $826 |

## BECK CORPORATION

### Income Statement
### for the year 19X5,
### Price-level adjusted (000 omitted)

| | |
|---|---|
| Sales | $1,693[6] |
| Cost of goods sold | 905[7] |
| Gross Profit | $788 |
| Less Operating Expenses: | |
| Depreciation Expense | 66[8] |
| Other operating expenses and taxes | 550[6] |
| Income before adjustment for monetary items | $ 172 |
| Gain on net monetary debt | 24[9] |
| Net income | $ 196 |

*See notes on following page.*

*Notes:*

1. $300 \times \dfrac{146}{130} = 337$ rounded

2. $600 \times \dfrac{146}{110} = 796$ rounded

3. $796 \times 0.25 = 597$ to maintain proportional expiration

4. $200 \times \dfrac{146}{105} = 278$

5. To balance

6. Assume index at 138 on 7/1/X5 and at 142 on 10/1/X5. Assume flow throughout year therefore adjusted from midyear by 146/138.

7. $880 \times \dfrac{146}{142}.$

8. $50 \times \dfrac{146}{110}.$

9. Assume that all monetary assets and current liabilities were acquired evenly throughout year and that bonds payable existed at 1/1/X5.

$290 \times \dfrac{146}{138} = 307,$

$307 - 290 = 17$   Loss on monetary assets.

$280 \times \dfrac{146}{138} = 296;$

$296 - 280 = 16$   Gain on current monetary debt.

$200 \times \dfrac{146}{130} = 225$

$225 - 200 = 25$   Gain on noncurrent monetary debt.

**SP 16.9**

BECK CORPORATION

Balance Sheet as of 12/31/X5
Replacement-cost adjusted (000 omitted)

| Assets | | Equities | |
|---|---|---|---|
| Cash | $ 50 | Total current liabilities | $280 |
| Marketable securities | 40 | Bonds payable | 200 |
| Accounts receivable | 200 | Total Liabilities | $480 |
| Inventory | 340 | | |
| Total current assets | $630 | Contributed capital | $200 |
| Fixed assets | 850 | Unrealized holding gains | 228[1] |
| Less: Accumulated | | Retained earnings | 360 |
| depreciation | (212) | Total Stockholder's Equity | $788 |
| Total Assets | $1,268 | Total Equities | $1,268 |

Income Statement
for the year 19X5
Replacement-cost adjusted (000 omitted)

| | | |
|---|---:|---:|
| Sales | | $1,600 |
| Cost of goods sold | | 880 |
| Gross profit | | $ 720 |
| Less Operating Expenses: | | |
| Depreciation | $ 58 | |
| Other operating expenses and taxes | 520 | 578 |
| Distributable income | | $ 142 |
| Realized holding gains: | | |
| Inventory sold | $ 0[2] | |
| Fixed assets depreciated | 8[3] | 8 |
| Realized income | | $ 150 |
| Unrealized holding gains: | | |
| Inventory | $ 10[4] | |
| Fixed assets | 105[5] | 115 |
| Economic income | | $ 265 |

*Notes:*
1. To balance.
2. No adjustment was necessary for LIFO cost of goods sold.
3. $8,000 adjustment to current year's depreciation expense.
4. Unrealized holding gain as of 12/31/X4     $290 − $260 = $30
   Unrealized holding gain as of 12/31/X5     $340 − $300 = $40
   Increment during 19X5     $10
5. Assume fixed assets as of 12/31/X4 $600 (no acquisitions or dispositions).
   Unrealized holding gain as of 12/31/X4     $ 83($583 − $500)
   Unrealized holding gain as of 12/31/X5     $188($638 − $450)
   Increment during 19X5     $105

**EP 17.1**

Let $C$ = total contribution;
$P$ = quantity of Product P produced and sold;
$Q$ = quantity of Product Q produced and sold.
Then $7P$ = quantity of Material S consumed
$3Q$ = quantity of Material S consumed
$4P$ = quantity of Material T consumed
$8Q$ = quantity of Material T consumed

a) Maximize:   $C = 22P + 14Q$,
   subject to:   $7P + 3Q \leq 21{,}000$,
   $4P + 8Q \leq 16{,}000$,
   $P \geq 0$,
   $Q \geq 0$.

**EP 17.3**   Let $C$ = total contribution;
$A$ = quantity of Product A produced and sold;
$B$ = quantity of Product B produced and sold.

a) Maximize:   $C = 40A + 50B$

b) $1,900,000   [($40 \times 10,000) + (50 \times 30,000)]$

c) $15   ($20 incremental contribution less $5 incremental cost).

**EP 17.5**   Control limits at 95-percent confidence interval equal $\pm$ $1,764 (1.96 $\times$ $900). Therefore all variances, favorable or unfavorable, that are $\leq$ $1,764 would be considered random or within normal limits and would not be investigated. Specifically, variances for Jan., Feb., Mar., May, Jun., Aug., Sep., Nov., and Dec. would be considered as indicating that maintenance costs were under control. Only variances for Apr., July, and Oct. would be investigated.

**EP 17.7**

Payoff table

| Events Actions | Sell 0 | Sell 10 | Sell 20 | Sell 30 | Sell 40 |
|---|---|---|---|---|---|
| Order 0 | 0 | 0 | 0 | 0 | 0 |
| Order 10 | − 5 | +10 | +10 | +10 | +10 |
| Order 20 | −10 | + 5 | +20 | +20 | +20 |
| Order 30 | −15 | 0 | +15 | +30 | +30 |
| Order 40 | −20 | − 5 | +10 | +25 | +40 |

Expected value computation

| | Sell 0 Payoff × .02 | Sell 10 Payoff × .18 | Sell 20 Payoff × .40 | Sell 30 Payoff × .30 | Sell 40 Payoff × .10 | Total expected value |
|---|---|---|---|---|---|---|
| Order 0 | 0 | 0 | 0 | 0 | 0 | $ 0 |
| Order 10 | −0.10 | +1.80 | +4.00 | +3.00 | +1.00 | 9.70 |
| Order 20 | −0.20 | +0.90 | +8.00 | +6.00 | +2.00 | 16.70 |
| Order 30 | −0.30 | 0 | +6.00 | +9.00 | +3.00 | 17.70 |
| Order 40 | −0.40 | −0.90 | +4.00 | +7.50 | +4.00 | 14.20 |

The store should purchase (order) 30 bunches of flowers each day to maximize profit over the long run.

**EP 17.9**   a)   Budgeting Network Diagram ( — — — — — = critical path)

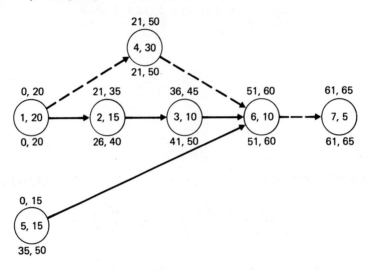

b) Critical path is sequence of operations:
   (1) Sales budget
   (4) Operating budget
   (6) Cash budget
   (7) Master budget and Budgeted financial statements

c) The controller should allow 65 working days for completion of the budgeting process.

# D

# REVIEW OF FINANCIAL ACCOUNTING

The intention of this Appendix is to review briefly the main ideas of financial accounting. If you have already studied the subject, much or all of the material contained herein will be familiar, will stimulate recall, or will identify areas requiring further study or in-depth review in a financial accounting text.[1] If you have **not** previously studied financial accounting, the material in this Appendix should provide you with adequate background of information for you to understand managerial accounting. However, by itself, the material is insufficient to provide you either with an adequate in-depth understanding of financial accounting as a distinct business function or with a sufficient grasp of the content of financial statements to be in a position to use them effectively.

## PURPOSE OF FINANCIAL ACCOUNTING

Whereas managerial accounting provides decision-making information for use by the internal managers of a firm, financial accounting is aimed at outsiders. Financial accounting provides information to existing and potential investors in a firm concerning the firm's **position** and its (or its management's) recent **performance.** A firm's investors, herein defined to include both creditors and owners, have invested or are contemplating investing resources in the firm. They are therefore interested both in the safety of their investment and in present and prospective returns (interest or earnings) on their investment.

Managerial accounting has only evolved in the past fifty years in response to the information needs of large complex organizations. Financial accounting, on the other hand, has been around for many centuries. Most people, therefore, identify the term "accounting" with financial accounting. Where they realize that there is more than one facet to accounting, they commonly identify all internal accounting as "cost accounting." As explained in Chapter 1, cost accounting encompasses the collection and summarization of cost data. Cost accounting data serves both financial and managerial accounting.

It will assist your understanding of all three areas if you keep in mind their distinct roles:

• Financial accounting provides position and performance reports to outside investors;

• Managerial accounting provides information for decision-making, planning, and control to internal managers; and

• Cost accounting provides cost data incorporated in both systems.

---

[1]    See this text's companion volume *Financial Accounting Information, An Introduction To Its Preparation and Use,* A. T. Montgomery (Reading, Mass.: Addison-Wesley Publishing Company, 1978), or any other financial accounting text.

## FINANCIAL STATEMENTS, GAAP, AND THE AUDITOR'S OPINION

Financial accounting information, the output of the system, may be found in the firm's *annual report*. The information is presented in four *financial statements* and accompanying footnotes.[2] One of the financial statements reports the firm's financial position or financial condition at the end of its business year. This statement is commonly referred to as the *balance sheet*. The other three statements report different aspects of the firm's performance for the year ending with the balance sheet date. They are known as:

- *The statement of changes in financial position (SCFP),*
- *The statement of owners' capital or retained earnings, and*
- *The income statement.*

Each of the four statements will be illustrated and described below.

The only standard or criterion relevant to managerial accounting data is whether it is cost-effective **for the specific firm.** For internal purposes, **any** type of information measured and reported in **any** fashion is satisfactory so long as the decision benefits of the information exceed the information costs. Since persons outside the firm do not use (or even have access to) managerial accounting information, there is no need for any uniformity or standardization of measurement and reporting practices among different firms.

In contrast, financial statements are used by outsiders to make comparative investment evaluations among different firms—"Is this firm a better credit risk than others?" or "Is this firm a better investment than others?" Some degree of standardization is therefore essential for ready understanding by the outside reader of a statement's information content and for comparability. In the United States, standards for measurements and reporting on financial statements are known as *generally accepted accounting principles* or *GAAP*. The study of financial accounting essentially involves learning GAAP and their applications to particular situations in particular firms.

You might expect GAAP to be a simple set of rules available in a rule book; unfortunately this is not the case. Business activities differ widely, and GAAP consist mostly of general approaches applicable across a broad range of activities. Also, most financial accounting measurement and reporting practices were developed independently by different firms over many years before there was any attempt at standardization. Attempts at standardization were only begun in the 1930's, and have had limited success. Consequently, GAAP may be better perceived as generally accepted accounting **practice,** with considerable divergence permitted in some areas with respect to the measurement

---

[2]   Annual reports, in addition to the financial statements for the current period, often contain data from prior years for trend comparison, together with descriptions of company activities and a letter from the firm's president summarizing recent activities and goals.

and reporting of the same underlying event. Those alternatives that have significant potential for noncomparability will be discussed below.

GAAP are not law in the United States. Instead, GAAP have evolved in practice and/or have been codified by private, professional authoritative bodies. Seven individuals comprise the *Financial Accounting Standards Board (FASB)*, which currently is the authoritative body for promulgating financial accounting standards or GAAP. In the United States, each firm prepares its own financial statements and is **not** required to follow GAAP. How then is any uniformity or comparability achieved? Firms with many owners (publicly traded firms) are required by the *U.S. Securities and Exchange Commission (SEC)*, or by state regulatory agencies, to have their financial statements (and supporting data and procedures) audited or examined by independent professional accountants who are licensed as *certified public accountants (CPA's)*. The purpose of the independent audit is to determine the degree of conformance with GAAP; and the annual report of such firms will include a copy of the *auditor's opinion*. The auditor's opinion will state that the statements fully conform with GAAP and fairly report the firm's position and performance, or else it will specify any areas of nonconformance. The fact that an independent professional attests to their fairness and GAAP conformance (and can be personally sued for damages if the opinion is in error) lends credibility to the statements. For the majority of medium- and small-sized firms not required to publish audited financial statements, owners or creditors may still require an audit before investing. You should be aware that you can reasonably expect financial statements to conform to GAAP only when they are accompanied by an auditor's opinion so stating.

## THE BALANCE SHEET—A POSITION STATEMENT

The financial statement that discloses the firm's financial position, or condition, as of the close of business on the statement date—the balance sheet—is like a photograph. It pictures the position at a specific point in time, and contains **no** data with respect to changes that have occurred since the last balance sheet; only the cumulative effect of all changes is shown. A firm's financial position can be understood as meaning "the resources it has (owns or effectively controls) and the existing claims against such resources." A firm's resources are identified as *assets*, and assets are customarily shown first or on the left side of a balance sheet. Claims against resources are identified as *equities*, and are commonly disclosed on the right side of the balance sheet.[3]

Assets may be defined as property, rights, or claims owned or effectively controlled by the firm, having significant future value or usefulness to the firm as of the balance sheet date, and capable of objective identification and mea-

---

[3]   It is easier to visualize a balance sheet in the so-called horizontal format with assets on the left and equities on the right. For printing layout convenience, some balance sheets have a vertical format, with equities shown below assets.

surement. Note that certain assets, such as the value of the firm's human capital (pool of trained and experienced managers and employees), or the value of brand- and firm-name recognition as a result of advertising, are not considered to be objectively measurable and therefore are not reported as assets. Those assets with insignificantly small values (staplers, wastebaskets, and so forth) are excluded, following the accounting principle of *materiality*. The accountant uses the word "material" as synonymous with "significant." Also note that assets are reported under the accounting principle of the *going concern*. Unless there is evidence to the contrary, the accountant assumes that the firm will continue in business indefinitely and thus be in a position to avail itself of the future usefulness of assets.

Commonly, assets and equities on the balance sheet are each grouped or classified into conventionally ordered subclassifications, and individual items are conventionally ordered within each subclassification. Exhibit D.1 illustrates items commonly found on balance sheets for merchandising firms.[4] Note in Exhibit D.1 that the first subclassification of assets is identified as *current assets*.

## Current Assets

Current assets can be defined as:

> Cash or other assets that will be converted into cash or consumed within the normal operating cycle of the business or within one year from the balance sheet date.

For *cash*, you will find listed the current balance of all cash on hand and in banks. Under *marketable securities* will be shown the current market value (or original cost, if lower) of those securities owned by the firm that are being held as temporary investments of excess cash, and that are readily available for conversion into cash as needed in the normal course of the firm's operations. *Current notes receivable* represents claims for cash due within one year and evidenced by promissory notes. The balance of *accounts receivable* represents current claims against customers for payment for merchandise purchased on account (charge accounts).[5] *Allowance for uncollectables* is a valuation account indicating the portion of existing receivables that, based on the

---

[4]   Merchandising firms (wholesalers and retailers) buy and resell merchandise inventory. Firms providing only services to customers would have balance sheets similar to those of merchandisers but would have no stock or merchandise on hand to sell and therefore no merchandise inventory (asset) account. Manufacturers' balance sheets are also similar to those for merchandisers, except that a manufacturer will disclose inventory in three different accounts depending upon the state of completion. Manufacturers' inventory accounts are described more fully in Chapter 1.

[5]   Installment sales receivables may extend beyond one year, that is, not all installment payments may be due within one year. Nevertheless it is customary to classify such receivables as current. Sometimes you will find installment accounts receivable separately identified, to distinguish them from other receivables.

## Exhibit D.1

### Sample Balance Sheet As of 12/31/X1   (000 omitted)

**Assets**

| | | |
|---|---:|---:|
| Cash | | $ 50 |
| Marketable securities | | 100 |
| Notes receivable | | 9 |
| Accounts receivable | $400 | |
| Less: Allowance for uncollectables | 12 | 388 |
| Inventory | | 500 |
| Supplies | | 30 |
| Prepaid items | | 40 |
| Total Current Assets | | $1,117 |
| | | |
| Investments | | 90 |
| Fixed assets: | | |
| Land | $ 60 | |
| Buildings and equipment | 390 | |
| Office furniture and fixtures | 87 | |
| Less: Accumulated depreciation | (190) | |
| Property held under capital lease | 65 | 412 |
| | | |
| Intangible and other assets: | | |
| Leasehold improvements | $ 20 | |
| Deferred charges | 35 | |
| Franchises | 50 | |
| Patents | 45 | |
| Trademarks | 25 | |
| Copyrights | 15 | |
| Purchased goodwill | 180 | 370 |
| Total Assets | | $1,989 |

**Equities**

| | | |
|---|---:|---:|
| Current notes payable | | $ 40 |
| Accounts payable | | 300 |
| Wages payable | | 100 |
| Taxes payable | | 52 |
| Interest payable | | 12 |
| Unearned revenue | | 6 |
| Estimated warranty costs | | 19 |
| Current obligations under capital lease | | 21 |
| Total Current Liabilities | | $ 550 |
| | | |
| Noncurrent notes payable | | 30 |
| Noncurrent obligations under capital lease | | 80 |
| Bonds payable | | 200 |
| Less: Bond discount | | (25) |
| Deferred income taxes | | 60 |
| Total Liabilities | | $ 895 |
| | | |
| Contributed capital | $600 | |
| Retained earnings | 494 | |
| Total Owners' Equity | | 1,094 |
| | | |
| Total Equities | | $1,989 |

firm's experience, are expected to prove uncollectable. Cash, marketable securities, and receivables (net of allowance for uncollectables) are collectively referred to as current *monetary assets* since they represent money or claims for a specific amount of money at a specific time.

*Inventory* represents the stock on hand of merchandise available for sale to customers. The amount of dollars shown represents a measure of the cost (or realizable value, if lower), and, in periods of inflation, is subject to different measurement assumptions that can result in widely divergent amounts for the same items (see discussion below under measurement alternatives). Under *supplies* is shown the cost of items on hand that will be consumed as part of normal operations within the year. The last current asset illustrated is identified as *prepaid items*, and represents the cost of services to be consumed that have already been paid for. Common prepaid items include prepaid rent and prepaid insurance.

## Noncurrent Assets

All assets not qualifying as current assets are considered to be noncurrent. The first *noncurrent asset* subclassification is identified as *investments*. Included in investments would be the cost of securities that are intended to be held beyond one year, any special funds (like savings accounts) set aside for specific purposes and not normally available to pay current bills, other assets acquired as investments rather than for use in the business, and potential receipts of distributions of previously earned profits from other firms that are controlled or significantly influenced by the reporting firm.[6]

Following investments in Exhibit D.1 is the second noncurrent asset subclassification, identified as *fixed assets.* Fixed assets may be both *tangible* (touchable) and *intangible* (a legal right or claim). Tangible fixed assets include such items as *land, buildings and equipment, and office furniture and fixtures,* all reported at their original costs or fair market value at the date of their acquisition.

Following tangible fixed assets is another valuation account identified as *accumulated depreciation.* The amount of accumulated depreciation is subtracted from the cost of tangible fixed assets. It is a cost reduction representing the accountant's estimate of the expiration that has occurred in the assets' usefulness, reflecting age, obsolescence, and wear and tear.[7] GAAP allows for

---

[6]   As in the case of marketable securities and inventory, investments will be carried below original cost if the current market value or expected realizable value is lower than original cost.

[7]   Measurement of depreciation differs from the valuation of uncollectable accounts. Allowance for uncollectables is estimated each year, based upon current conditions and recent experience. Depreciation, on the other hand, is usually a systematic cumulative reduction each year, projected over the useful life of the asset at the time of its original acquisition. Only if the originally anticipated useful life, or estimated resale value at the time of future disposition, proves to be significantliy in error, is the preplanned annual depreciation amount re-estimated.

widely differing rates of depreciation, and these will be covered below under measurement alternatives. Also, note that land is usually not depreciated, since its usefulness normally does not expire. In those cases where the value of acquired resources is used up (timber cut or minerals extracted), land cost is reduced and the expiration is identified as *depletion*.

Also included under fixed assets is *property held under capital lease*. This asset may be considered intangible in that the firm does not own the touchable building or equipment under lease. It merely has a legal right to use the taxable asset under a long-term, noncancellable lease qualifying as a capital lease.[8] Capital leases are originally recorded at the present value of all future lease payments (total lease payments less that portion of payments representing interest). Thereafter the cost is systematically reduced in a manner similar to depreciation but known as *amortization*. An account being amortized is reduced directly rather than being offset by a valuation account. After the first year, therefore, the amount shown for property held under capital lease will be the unamortized (not yet amortized) balance of the original present-value cost.

The final subclassification within noncurrent assets is identified as *intangible and other assets*. Included in this group are such items as: *leasehold improvements, deferred charges, franchises, patents, trademarks, copyrights*, and *purchased goodwill*. Leasehold improvements represent the cost of improvements to leased property (carpeting, lighting, painting, and so forth) that are attached and cannot be removed at the end of a lease. Deferred charges represent costs of services to be received, where their useful life extends significantly beyond one year. Deferred charges can be considered long-term prepaid items. Franchises, patents, trademarks, and copyrights represent the cost of acquiring these legal rights. All of these intangible assets are systematically amortized over their useful life, and the unamortized balance of original cost is reported on the balance sheet (see amortization of capital leases, above).

A final possible intangible asset is purchased goodwill. Goodwill, or the value of good customer, employee, supplier, and creditor relations, is established over time, and is a very real asset for most firms. However, since it is relatively impossible for a firm to measure objectively the value of its own goodwill, GAAP prohibits a firm from identifying its own goodwill as an asset. An exception exists when goodwill has been purchased as part of the acquisition of another firm. Where the cost of the purchased firm exceeds the current fair market value of the net assets acquired, the excess is presumed to represent purchased goodwill, and may be shown as an asset. GAAP require that purchased goodwill, because of its indefinite and immeasurable

---

8    Ordinary leases, known as operating leases, do not commit the firm to possession and use of property over most or all of its useful life, and therefore are not included as assets. Certain leases that are essentially similar to purchases with 100 percent mortgages, and which meet technical accounting criteria beyond the scope of this text, qualify as capital leases and are included as assets.

nature over time, be systematically amortized to zero over a period of not less than ten nor more than forty years.

## Asset Measurement and Accruals

Before leaving the discussion of balance sheet assets, you should note several fundamental accounting principles. Financial accountants, since their product may be used by individuals having an inherent conflict of interest, strive for unbiased objective presentation. You may wonder why assets are measured and reported in terms of historical costs rather than current dollars. The answer is that objective verifiable evidence exists of an asset's original cost, whereas current values are often subjective estimates. Asset measurement and reporting also reflects the accounting principle of *conservatism*. Accountants recognize losses (decline in market value) as soon as they are known. They do not recognize gains above cost until such gains are realized through sale.

You should also note that financial accounting operates on the *accrual* system rather than on a *cash basis*. Receivables are recognized as assets as soon as they are earned. The accountant generally does not wait until the cash has been collected before recognizing the sale and resultant asset. Other examples of accrued assets would include such items as accrued rent receivable, accrued interest receivable, and so forth. Accruals also apply to liabilities, as will be discussed below.

## BALANCE SHEET EQUALITY

In Exhibit D.1 you can observe that total assets of $1,989,000 are equalled by total equities of $1,989,000; the balance sheet **balances.** This balance is not mysterious. *Equities* are defined as claims by creditors and by owners, with the owners having the residual claim against total assets. If total assets equal $10,000, and total creditors' claims (*liabilities*) equal $8,000, then owners' equity will be exactly $2,000. If creditor's claims were to exceed $10,000 in this example, the firm would be legally bankrupt, and a balance sheet would not be prepared. Note that all equities are claims against the firm's total assets and **not** matching claims against any specific assets. The balance sheet equality can be expressed in two ways:

$$\text{Total Assets} = \text{Total Equities}$$

or

$$\text{Total Assets} = \text{Creditors' Equities (liabilities)} + \text{Owners' Equity.}$$

## Liabilities

On the right side of Exhibit D.1 there first appear creditors' equities or liabilities. Like assets, liabilities are subclassified as current and noncurrent. *Current liabilities* include all those amounts owed by the firm, as of the balance sheet date, that will require current assets in settlement within one year.[9] Current liabilities are often subdivided by type of creditor:

> *Current notes payable* to financial creditors,
> *Accounts payable* to trade creditors or suppliers,
> *Wages payable* to employees,
> *Taxes payable* to governments,

and so forth.

Note that one firm's current liabilities are another individual's or firm's current **receivables,** and vice versa.

Three other current liabilities shown in Exhibit D.1 might require further explanation. *Unearned revenue* does not represent a commitment to pay cash within a year. Instead it represents a liability to provide goods or services. Unearned revenue arises when a customer pays in advance for a good or service that has not been delivered by the balance sheet date. The unearned revenue liability is to provide the good or service paid for, or else return the cash. One firm's unearned revenue is another's prepaid item. *Estimated warranty repairs* represent another service liability in existence as of the balance sheet date on products already sold and still under warranty. *Current obligations under capital leases* represent the principle portion of currently due lease payments plus the interest portion earned by the lessor as of the balance sheet date.

Current liabilities will also include accruals for those items earned by creditors and unpaid as of the balance sheet date, such as wages and salaries since the last payday, utilities consumed since the last billing date, interest, rent, and so forth. Note that future obligations not yet earned (such as next month's rent under an operating lease) are **not** included on the balance sheet.

All liabilities not qualifying as current are classified as noncurrent. *Noncurrent* or *long-term liabilities* include such as *noncurrent notes payable, noncurrent obligations under capital leases, bonds payable,* and *deferred income taxes.* Notes, capital-lease obligations, and bonds all represent obligations to pay specific amounts of cash at specific future dates beyond one year from the date of the balance sheet. They are reported at their present value (principle only, future interest excluded). Often bonds payable, and sometimes noncurrent notes payable, will be accompanied by valuation accounts to adjust for any unearned future interest payments included in the face value of the debt instrument.

Deferred income taxes represent tax obligations that have been postponed for an indefinite period as a result of differences in the timing of ex-

---

[9]    Note that a current liability must both be payable in one year and also require current assets in settlement. A liability that is due within one year but that will be refinanced (replaced) with a new long-term liability would be classified as noncurrent. Also note that contingent liabilities, those that are dependent upon some future event (like a pending lawsuit) are not reported on the balance sheet.

pense recognition between that reported under GAAP and that allowed by the Internal Revenue Service. All liabilities, both current and noncurrent, are known as monetary except unearned revenue, estimated warranty repairs, and deferred income taxes. Recall that monetary items represent commitments for cash flows in specific amounts at specific dates. The first two exceptions represent product or service rather than cash obligations, and the third is indefinite as to the due date.

Before leaving the discussion of liabilities, you should become familiar with the concept of *net working capital (NWC)*.[10] NWC is simply total current assets less total current liabilities, or the amount by which current assets exceed current liabilities. NWC is a measure of the firm's *solvency*, or its ability to pay its current obligations when due. Insofar as all current assets are not in the form of cash with which to pay bills, an excess of current assets over current liabilities is required in order to maintain solvency.

## Owners' or Stockholders' Equity

As mentioned earlier, total owners' equity represents a residual claim against the firm's total assets by the firm's owners (total assets minus total liabilities equal total owners' equity). Exhibit D.2 illustrates owners' equity for the bal-

**Exhibit D.2**

### Balance Sheet Owners' Equity For Different Types of Firms As of 12/31/X1   (000 omitted)

**For a Proprietorship**

| | | |
|---|---|---|
| | John Doe, Capital | $1,094 |

**For a Partnership**

| | | |
|---|---|---|
| | John Doe, Capital | $  425 |
| | Mary Smith, Capital | 382 |
| | Ricardo Gonzalez, Capital | 287 |
| | Total Partners' Equity | $1,094 |

**For a Corporation**

| | | |
|---|---|---|
| Contributed capital | Preferred stock | $  100 |
| | Paid-in capital on preferred stock | 30 |
| | Capital stock | 300 |
| | Paid-in capital on common stock | 170 |
| Retained earnings | Reserve for contingencies | 140 |
| | Reserve for loan restriction | 100 |
| | Unappropriated retained earnings | 254 |
| | Total Stockholders' Equity | $1,094 |

---

[10]  Many accountants and accounting texts use the term "working capital" to mean current assets minus current liabilities, and they would consider "net working capital" to be redundant. Since many business persons and financial executives use working capital to mean only current assets, this text will use the term net working capital to reinforce the meaning "current assets **minus** current liabilities."

ance sheet given in Exhibit D.1. Note that the differences result from the legal form of the business, and that, regardless of the type of business, total owners' equity is still equal to total assets minus total liabilities.

In the case of a proprietorship or single-owner business, a single amount is reported as the owner's claim. For a partnership, each partner's share is separately shown. For a corporation with stockholders, stockholders' equity is essentially divided into two parts, *contributed capital* and *retained earnings*. Contributed capital reports the amount of assets permanently invested in (committed to) the firm by the stockholders. It, in turn, is usually broken down under such headings as preferred stock, capital stock, and paid-in capital, which are beyond the scope of this Appendix.

Retained earnings represents that share of total assets claimed by stockholders in excess of their permanent contribution. Where profits have been earned by the company and not all distributed in *dividends* to the stockholders, the cumulative undistributed profits will be identified as retained earnings. Retained earnings, in turn, may be subdivided into different reserves, to indicate the intention of the firm to withhold such profits from distribution to owners (dividends to stockholders). Note that in the situation where total stockholders' equity (total assets minus total liabilities) is less than the amount of the contributed capital, retained earnings will be reported as a negative amount, to balance and to reflect accumulated losses instead of profits.

## CHANGES AFFECTING THE BALANCE SHEET AND PERFORMANCE MEASUREMENT

Even though the balance sheet is prepared only once each accounting period or year, the supporting records (accounts) are continuously updated. Changes affecting the balance sheet can be thought of as being of two types, *transactions* or *adjustments*. Transactions are completed exchanges with individuals or organizations separate from the firm, and they are usually evidenced by formal paperwork such as an invoice or check (cash) issued or received. The effect of transactions are recorded in the accounts as the transactions occur. Adjustments represent necessary modifications of account balances to reflect accruals or expirations, are usually initiated by the accountant, and generally are made only at the end of the period, to "fine tune" the statement. Changes affecting the balance sheet are summarized in the three other financial statements—the SCFP, the statement of owner's capital, and the income statement. Exhibit D.3 illustrates the relationship among the four financial statements. Note that, as distinct from a balance sheet, these three statements each cover activity over a period of time.

### The Statement of Changes in Financial Position (SCFP)

The single financial statement that summarizes all changes occurring between successive balance sheets is the SCFP; Exhibit D.4 illustrates a SCFP. Note

**Exhibit D.3**

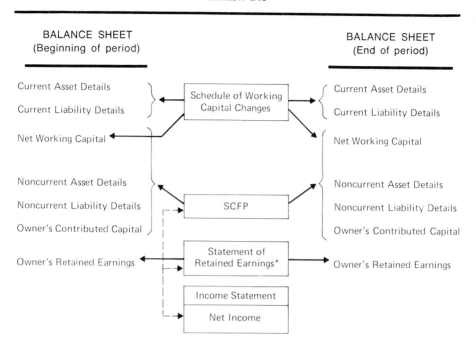

* For a proprietorship, the Statement of Owner's Capital reconciles all owner's capital, not just Retained Earnings.

that this statement usually summarizes resource flows in terms of NWC, as described earlier.

To understand the SCFP it is important that you refer again to Exhibit D.1 and observe that equities are not only claims against total assets; they also represent the **sources of assets**—that is, which groups have capital (assets) invested in the firm, and how much. Exhibit D.1 reveals that various current creditors have $550,000 invested in the business on a short-term basis; that noncurrent creditors have $345,000 invested on a long-term basis; and that the balance of the resources ($1,094,000) have been invested by the owners ($600,000 permanently invested and $494,000 of accumulated profits retained in the business).

The SCFP ignores detail changes within NWC, and instead focuses on major resource changes. Exhibit D.4 indicates that during the year 19X1:

• $325,000 of additional NWC was generated in operations,
• $15,000 was realized on the sale of a noncurrent asset,

**Exhibit D.4**

---

**Sample Abbreviated Statement of Changes in Financial Position
For the Year Ending 12/31/XX   (000 omitted)**

*Net Working Capital was Provided by:*

| | |
|---|---|
| Funds from operations | $325 |
| Disposition of fixed assets | 15 |
| Additional long-term debt | 30 |
| Additional owner investment | 100 |
| Total Funds Obtained | $470 |

*Net Working Capital was Used to:*

| | |
|---|---|
| Acquire new fixed assets | $150 |
| Retire old long-term debt | 120 |
| Provide distribution (dividends) to owners | 35 |
| Total Uses | $305 |
| Increase in the balance of Net Working Capital | $165 |

---

- $30,000 was borrowed on a long-term basis, and
- $100,000 was contributed as an additional investment by the owners.

The $470,000 of additional NWC was used as follows:

- $150,000 was used to acquire new fixed assets,
- $120,000 was used to retire old long-term debt,
- $35,000 was distributed to owners as a share of current profits, and
- $165,000 remained to increase the firm's NWC balance.

The Appendix to Chapter 9 contains a more detailed review of the SCFP.

**Balance Sheet Changes having no Effect on Owners' Equity**

Since the balance sheet equality must be maintained, all transactions and adjustments must ultimately affect **at least two** balance sheet accounts (hence the double-entry bookkeeping system, which will be reviewed in Appendix E). Some transactions result in changes in the balance sheet without changing the balance of owners' equity. A few examples would be:

- Firm borrows $1,000 from bank on short-term promissory note. (Cash increased $1,000, Current notes payable increased $1,000.)
- Firm pays current liability in the amount of $250. (Cash decreased $250, appropriate current liability decreased $250.)
- Noncurrent asset costing $10,000 is purchased for cash. (Cash decreased $10,000, appropriate noncurrent asset increased $10,000.)

- Noncurrent asset costing $200,000 acquired in exchange for $40,000 cash, a note payable within one year for $50,000, and a five-year promissory note for the balance. (Appropriate noncurrent asset increased $200,000, Cash decreased $40,000, Current notes payable increased $50,000, and Long-term note payable increased $110,000.)
- $20,000 is collected from customers on their accounts. (Cash increased $20,000, Accounts receivable decreased $20,000.)
- Merchandise costing $50,000 is purchased on account. (Inventory increased $50,000, Accounts payable increased $50,000.)

## Balance Sheet Changes Affecting Owners' Equity

Many transactions and most adjustments affect the balance of owners' equity. Examples of transactions affecting owners' equity include:

- Owners invest $100,000 of assets in the business. (Appropriate assets increased $100,000, Contributed capital increased $100,000.)
- Owners withdraw $35,000 cash as profit distribution (dividends). (Cash decreased $35,000, Retained earnings decreased $35,000.)
- Merchandise or services at a price of $60,000 are sold to customers for $10,000 cash and the balance on account. (Cash increased $10,000, Accounts receivable increased $50,000, and Owners' equity increased $60,000.)
- A utility bill for $400 is received and the service has been consumed. (Accounts payable increased $400, Owners' equity decreased $400.)

Examples of adjustments affecting owners' equity include:

- Interest amounting to $700 is earned on a promissory note receivable, has not yet been recorded, and an accrual is necessary. (Interest receivable is increased $700, Owners' Equity is increased $700.)
- $4,000 of accounts receivable are determined to be uncollectable. (Accounts receivable decreased $4,000, Owners' Equity decreased $4,000.)
- Merchandise costing $30,000 is determined to have been shipped (sold) to customers during the year. (Inventory decreased $30,000, Owners' Equity decreased $30,000.)
- Depreciation of $20,000 is determined to be appropriate for the year. (Accumulated depreciation negative balance is increased $20,000, Owners' Equity is decreased $20,000.)
- At year-end, wages amounting to $8,000 have been earned by employees since the last payday and must be accrued. (Wages payable increased $8,000, Owners' Equity decreased $8,000.)

Note that two types of transactions affecting owners' equity involve the owners—owner investment of assets and owner withdrawals (dividends).

Other transactions and adjustments affecting owners' equity are not owner-related. Nonowner transactions and adjustments that increase owners' equity are known as *revenue* items.[11] Nonowner transactions that decrease owners' equity are known as *expense* items. Revenue minus expense is defined as *income*. Income is an increase in owners' equity other than that resulting from an owner investment and before deducting owner withdrawals. For example, if nonowner events increasing owners' equity (revenue) totalled $2,445,000 during the year, and if nonowner events decreasing owners' equity (expenses) totalled $2,405,000 for the same period, the firm's net income for the year would be $40,000.

### The Statement of Owner's Capital or Retained Earnings

Balance sheet changes affecting owner's equity during the period are summarized and reported on the third financial statement, called the Statement of Owner's Capital. This simple statement is self explanatory, and is illustrated in Exhibit D.5. Note that the statement of owner's capital for a proprietorship includes all changes to owner's equity affecting both contributed capital and retained earnings.

**Exhibit D.5**

**Sample Statements of Changes in Owners' Capital and Retained Earnings
For the Year Ending 12/31/X1   (000 omitted)**

Statement of Owner's Capital (Proprietorship)

| | |
|---|---|
| Owner's Capital 12/31/X0 | $  989 |
| Additional owner investment | 100 |
| Net Income | 40 |
| Owner withdrawals | 35 |
| Owner's Capital 12/31/X1 | $1,094 |

Statement of Retained Earnings (Corporation)

| | |
|---|---|
| Retained earnings 12/31/X0 | $  489 |
| Net Income | 40 |
| Dividends | 35 |
| Retained earnings 12/31/X1 | $  494 |

Exhibit D.5 also illustrates the similar statement that is prepared for a corporation, and is known as the Statement of Retained Earnings. Note that the retained earnings statement is similar to the statement of owner's capital but excludes changes to contributed capital.

---

[11]  Donations to the firm by nonowners would be an exception. They are rare, and are excluded from this discussion.

# THE INCOME STATEMENT—A PERFORMANCE REPORT

The fourth financial statement is known as the income statement. Investors and managers may be gratified to learn that their firm had net income of $40,000 (as reported on the owner's capital or retained earnings statements), but they demand more detailed information about the various revenue and expense items resulting in net income. This detail is provided on the income statement as illustrated in Exhibit D.6. Note on Exhibit D.6 that all nonowner transactions and adjustments affecting owners' equity have been summarized by various categories and reported as revenue and expense.[12]

**Exhibit D.6**

---

### Sample Income Statement
### For the Year Ending 12/31/X1    (000 omitted)

| | | |
|---|---:|---:|
| Sales | | $2,400 |
| Less: Cost of goods sold | | 1,500 |
| Gross Profit | | $ 900 |
| Operating Expenses: | | |
| Wages and salaries | $300 | |
| Supplies | 90 | |
| Utilities | 10 | |
| Property taxes | 15 | |
| Interest | 25 | |
| Depreciation | 40 | |
| Amortization | 45 | |
| Bad debts | 30 | 555 |
| Gain on fixed asset disposition | | 45 |
| Income from operations before taxes | | $ 390 |
| Provision for income taxes | | 150 |
| Extraordinary flood loss | | 200 |
| Net Income | | $ 40 |

---

Two revenue items are reported, sales of $2,400,000 and gain on fixed asset disposition of $45,000. Revenue inflow that is not a normal part of operations is often defined as a "gain." Except for the subtotals for gross profit, income from operations, and net income, all other items on Exhibit D.6 represent expenses. Note that unusual expense is identified as a "loss."

---

[12]  For recording convenience, accountants will establish each year separate temporary records (accounts) for the desired revenue and expense categories. During the year, nonowner transactions and adjustments having an eventual effect upon owners' equity are first recorded in the temporary revenue and expense accounts. These accounts accumulate necessary data for income-statement preparation. At year-end, these temporary revenue and expense accounts are closed, and their balances transferred to owner's equity (retained earnings) to make the balance sheet balance.

Revenue, expense, gain, or loss may be part of operations or may be classified as extraordinary. Those items that are unusual in nature, not anticipated, and not expected to recur are separately classified as extraordinary. This practice enables the reader to identify an amount that might reasonably be expected to recur, for forecasting purposes. Referring to Exhibit D.6, if next year you could expect the sales and cost mixture to be about the same as this year, you could anticipate income from operations of $390,000 and net income of $240,000 (after taxes). This year's "bottom-line" net income of only $40,000 was the unique result of the $200,000 extraordinary flood loss.

The foregoing paragraphs have briefly covered the financial statements and their content. To complete your general understanding of financial accounting, you also need to be aware of the measurement alternatives within GAAP that may result in significantly differing results in reported assets and income.

## POTENTIALLY SIGNIFICANT MEASUREMENT ALTERNATIVES WITHIN GAAP

As mentioned earlier, GAAP allow a firm to measure (value) certain items or events in different ways in the financial statements. These different alternatives are known as different acceptable *accounting methods*. Once an accounting method is adopted for a particular item, it must be used consistently in the future. Measuring and reporting in a *consistent* manner is a fundamental principle of GAAP. Should a firm elect to change an accounting method, you will find the change noted as a departure from consistency in the auditor's opinion for the year in which the change occurred.

Significant alternative accounting methods exist in three major areas:

• Inventory measurement,

• Depreciation or amortization measurement, and

• Accounting for business combinations.

The major alternatives in each of these three areas will be briefly described below, together with their financial-statement effects.

### Inventory Measurement Alternatives

For firms that sell products to customers (all businesses except those that exclusively provide services), you already know that accountants first record the *product costs* of inventory as an asset. Inventory is then reduced when the items are actually sold to customers, with the balancing reduction to owners' equity reported as the expense "cost of goods sold" on the income statement. If there were no changes from year to year in the price/cost of products acquired for sale, then various alternative inventory accounting methods would all yield identical results. In reality, inflation continues to be a significant factor.

Even during periods of inflation, if the accountant always knew both:

the actual product cost of each item in inventory,

and

exactly which items were shipped to customers and which remained,

then no problem would exist in allocating total product costs each year between cost of goods sold and ending inventory.

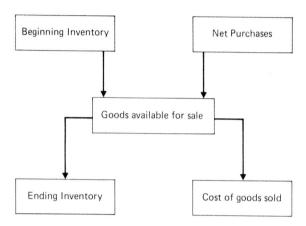

**Figure D.1**

When inventory is specifically *identifiable,* and where it is economical to do so, **no assumptions** are necessary. Where specific identification is not possible or economical (for example, different truckloads of gasoline at different costs discharged into the same service-station underground tank), an *inventory flow assumption* must be made by the accountant. Any of three common inventory flow assumptions are permitted under GAAP.

The accountant may **assume** that the costs of all items in inventory somehow blend or mix together, and that each item therefore has the *weighted average cost* of all items. For example, if a firm had:

- Beginning inventory of 500 units costing $1 each,
- Purchases early in the year of 300 units costing $2 each,
- Purchases later in the year of 200 units costing $3 each, and
- Total shipments to customers during the year of 800 units,

what would be the amounts reported for ending balance-sheet inventory and for cost of goods sold on the income statement, using the average-cost inventory method? Under average cost, the 200 units in ending inventory would be reported at $340, and the 800 units sold at $1,360.[13]

A second cost flow assumption that matches most common actual physical flows is first-in-first-out or *FIFO*. Under the *FIFO* method, the accountant assumes that items moved through inventory as if on a conveyer: the first items to arrive are the first shipped to customers and the last to arrive are still in stock. Under FIFO, the same situation given above would be reported as: ending inventory $600 and cost of goods sold $1,100.[14]

The third cost flow assumption, commonly used to minimize taxable and reported income in periods of inflation, is known as last-in-first-out or LIFO. Under LIFO, the accountant assumes that incoming products are added in layers to the top of a storage barrel, and that shipments are taken off the top. The same situation cited above would be reported following a LIFO flow assumption as ending inventory $200 and cost of goods sold $1,500.[15]

Note that, under GAAP, the same ending inventory can be reported at $200, or $340, or even $600. Corresponding cost of goods sold can be reported as $1,500 or $1,360, or even only $1,100. In a large firm with many products, these amounts could easily represent millions of dollars. In one year, the difference in reported cost of goods sold (and therefore reported net income) could be $400,000,000 between FIFO and LIFO. Can you see that, in periods of inflation, it could be inappropriate to directly compare reported performance of two firms following different inventory accounting methods? GAAP merely requires that the method being followed be followed consistently from year to year, and that it be identified for you in the financial-statement footnotes.

### Depreciation/Amortization Alternatives

In the same way that assumptions may be necessary or desirable for inventory cost flows, they are also often necessary in measuring and reporting the expiration of the cost of tangible and intangible noncurrent assets. Recall that cost expiration of tangible fixed assets is identified as depreciation, and that of an intangible asset as amortization. Permitted alternative assumptions are the same for both. Therefore, the remainder of this discussion will focus upon depreciation, with your understanding that it applies equally to intangible-asset amortization.

Recall that the cost of most fixed and intangible assets (other than land) expires over time and with use; that is, the resale value (*salvage value*) of the asset is less than its original asset value or cost. Depreciation is the process for **allocating** the anticipated cost expiration or loss over the asset's useful

---

[13] Total cost ($1,700) divided by total units (1,000) equal weighted average cost of $1.70 per unit.
[14] Last purchase of 200 units costing $3 each assumed to be still in stock; all others assumed shipped.
[15] The 200 units remaining at the bottom of the barrel are assumed to be the oldest units, costing $1 each; all others assumed shipped.

life in an attempt to match costs with the revenues earned in each period. GAAP allow for the use of any systematic and rational allocation method consistently applied to the same asset. Four different methods are well known and in common use. They are known as *units of production, straight-line, years' digits,* and *declining balance methods,* respectively.

Where an asset's cost expiration is primarily a function of its usage rather than the passage of time, and where the usage can be readily and economically measured, then the units-of-production or service method may be appropriate. Under this method, depreciation each year is measured as that portion of total expected depreciation represented by the proportion of total expected usefulness actually used in the current year. For example, assume an asset originally costing $110,000 with an estimated useful life to the firm of five years and an estimated salvage value of $10,000. A total of $100,000 of depreciation should be allocated to the five years of useful life. Where the primary cause of the depreciation is use, such as miles driven (rather than the passage of years), and where the useful life can be measured in units of use such as 200,000 miles, then depreciation can readily be based on usage—miles driven. If, in the third year, this truck was driven 45,000 miles for a total of 130,000 miles so far, then accumulated depreciation at year-end would be reported as $65,000, and the current year's depreciation as $22,500, under the units-of-production method.[16]

In parallel to the inventory situation with respect to specific identification, for many depreciable assets, units of production is either impossible or uneconomical to measure. In such cases, an assumption must be made as to the timing pattern of cost expiration. The most common alternatives are to assume equal usefulness and therefore equal cost expiration over the asset's useful life; or to assume that a high proportion of usefulness expires in the early years.

Where usefulness is assumed equal each year, the straight-line depreciation method is used. Straight-line depreciation merely involves allocating equal portions of the total amount to be depreciated to each year of the useful life. Continuing with the same truck example given earlier, under the straight-line method, the $100,000 of total depreciation would be allocated on the basis of $20,000 each year for the five years. For the third year, depreciation expense would be $20,000 and accumulated depreciation would be $60,000.

Where a high proportion of usefulness is assumed to expire in the first few years, one of two common *accelerated depreciation* methods is employed. The sum-of-the-years'-digits or *SYD* method involves first dividing the total amount to be depreciated by the sum of the digits representing the useful life, and then deducting the product of this share times the year of useful life in inverse order. For the $110,000 truck with $100,000 to be depreciated,

---

[16] $100,000 to depreciate divided by 200,000 units of usage (miles) equals depreciation rate of $0.50 per mile driven.

during the first year $33,300 (rounded) would be depreciated.[17] For the third year, $20,000 (3/15 times $100,000) would be depreciated, and accumulated depreciation would be $80,000 (5/15 + 4/15 + 3/15 of $100,000).

The second common accelerated depreciation method is known as declining balance depreciation. The *book value* of an asset is its original value less accumulated depreciation. Following declining balance depreciation, a fixed percentage of the remaining book value of the asset is deducted each year, with the final year's deduction being whatever is necessary to make book value equal to salvage value. A common declining balance rate is **twice** the straight-line rate; and the use of 200 percent of the straight-line rate is known as double-declining-balance depreciation or *DDB*. Continuing with the same truck example, the straight-line rate would be 20 percent per year for five years. The DDB rate would be 40 percent. In the first year, depreciation expense would be $44,000.[18] For the second year, depreciation expense would be $26,400 ($66,000 initial book value times 40 percent). For the third year, $15,800 (rounded) would be depreciated, and accumulated depreciation at the end of the third year would be $86,200 ($44,000 plus $26,400 plus $15,800).

As in the case of differing inventory flow assumptions, electing different depreciation methods can have a significant effect upon reported net income. In the truck example, for the first year, depreciation expense would be $20,000 under straight-line and $44,000 under DDB. And in the fifth year the situation would reversed, with $20,000 for straight-line and only $4,280 under DDB. As in the case of the inventory method, you may ascertain the depreciation method(s) being used from the financial-statement footnotes.

The third area within GAAP where allowable alternatives may produce significantly different balance sheet and income measurements involves accounting for business combinations. This subject will be introduced next.

## BUSINESS COMBINATIONS

When one firm acquires control of another, a *business combination* has occurred. The two firms may continue to operate as a single legal entity (a statutory merger), or they may continue as separate legal entities (a parent–subsidiary relationship). In both cases, a single combined set of financial statements is prepared for the combination, as required by GAAP.

Two different methods, depending upon the circumstances of the combination, are allowed under GAAP for valuing the acquired company's assets in the combination. Under the *pooling treatment*, no new basis of accounting is allowed. The combined balance sheet will essentially reflect the simple ad-

---

[17]   Sum of the digits 1 through 5 equals 15. First-year depreciation equals 5/15 of total depreciation.
[18]   Forty percent of the initial book value of $110,000. Note that the rate is applied to the book value and not to the total amount to be depreciated.

dition of the distinct, unrelated assets and equities of both firms.[19] The combined income statement will report the sum of both firm's incomes.

Under the *purchase treatment*, a new basis for accounting for the acquired firm's assets is deemed to exist at the time of the combination. The acquiring company will often be required to pay more than the book value of the acquired firm's net assets (total assets less total liabilities). This excess may reflect compensation for currently valued assets being higher than depreciated historical cost, and for the acquired firm's customer–creditor–employee goodwill. Under the purchase treatment, combined assets are written up to reflect current-cost revaluation of the acquired assets; and any remaining excess payment is included in combined assets as "purchased goodwill." Most or all of the entire excess payment (asset write-up plus goodwill) must be depreciated or amortized in the years following acquisition. Therefore, under the purchase treatment, future reported combined income may be substantially less than the sum of the two firm's separate incomes by the amount of the necessary depreciation and amortization charges covering the excess payment.

## READING, ANALYZING, AND UNDERSTANDING FINANCIAL STATEMENTS

The foregoing discussion should enable you to read financial statements and to understand their information content. Analyzing and interpreting financial statements in comparison to industry standards or to other firms often is facilitated by the use of ratio analysis. You will find simple ratio analysis covered in the Appendix to Chapter 2.

GAAP measurement standards, reporting conventions, and allowable alternatives can lead the statement user to make dysfunctional (not economically desirable) decisions. This problem area is explored in the Appendix to Chapter 14.

Finally, asset and income measurement in terms of historical costs as currently mandated by GAAP may provide less than completely relevant information in periods of continuing inflation. The later portion of Chapter 16 and the Appendix to Chapter 16 contain a brief discussion of alternative measurement systems under consideration, which are intended to reflect more current costs/values/dollars.

---

[19]   Items that are related (within the combined "family") will be omitted, to avoid double-counting. The amount reported as intercompany investment (from parent's assets) and as intercompany ownership (from subsidiary's contributed capital) will be eliminated. Also, any intercompany debt is eliminated from both assets and liabilities since, in terms of the combined entity, it is neither receivable from nor payable to outsiders.

# E

# DOUBLE-ENTRY BOOKKEEPING PROCEDURES

In Appendix D you learned the basic balance sheet equality—total assets balance (equal) total equities—that is the foundation of the financial accounting system. You also learned that transactions and adjustments affecting the balance sheet resulted in changes to the accounts which maintained the balance sheet equality. Back in the fifteenth century, a system was developed with the objective of maintaining this equality, even when thousands of changes (entries) needed to be recorded.

The debit/credit convention or coding system is very simple. Do not make it difficult merely because you cannot accept its simplicity. "*Debit*" comes from Latin and merely stands for "left" as on the left side. "*Credit*," also from Latin, merely stands for "right," as on the right side. Debit is usually abbreviated "Dr" (or "DR") and credit as "Cr" (or "CR"). One form of portraying a balance sheet is to show assets on the left side of the page and equities on the right. The debit/credit system arbitrarily assumes that all asset accounts will have left-side balances and all equity accounts will have right-side balances. Given this assumption (or convention), total *debits*, which mean only left-side balances, will always equal total *credits*, which mean only right-side balances.

A common way of portraying this idea in textbooks is to show accounts in the form of a "T" or "*T accounts.*" Each "T" account then has space for left-side amounts and right-side amounts. Note the similarity of a "T" account to the balance sheet, which has left-side items (assets) and right-side items (equities). For example:

ASSET ACCOUNT

| DR | CR |
|---|---|
| $100(+) | $40(−) |
| 70(+) | |

Note that debit or left-side is abbreviated "DR," and the credit, or right-side, is abbreviated "CR." Note also that the balance in the above account is "130 debit"; 170 debit offset by 40 credit equals 130 debit. An account can also have a credit balance. For example:

EQUITY ACCOUNT

| DR | CR |
|---|---|
| $100(−) | $200(+) |
| | 50(+) |

The above balance would be "150 credit."

An example of the operation of this system will serve to show its simplicity and beauty. Suppose a new firm, the AJAX Company, had just been started, and its only transaction so far was the owner investing $50,000 cash and merchandise costing $20,000 in the business. The balance sheet should then show:

| ASSETS | | EQUITIES | |
|---|---|---|---|
| Cash | $50,000 | Liabilities | 0 |
| Inventory | 20,000 | Owner's Equity | $70,000 |
| Total Assets | $70,000 | Total Equities | $70,000 |

The three accounts in "T"-account form would show:

```
            CASH
     _____
$50,000(+) |
```

```
          INVENTORY                          OWNERS' EQUITY
     _____                   _____
$20,000(+) |                                    | $70,000(+)
```

Note that total debits—left-side balances—of $70,000 equal total credits—right-side balances—of $70,000.

Now practice recording a few transactions following the debit/credit convention in "T"-account form. Suppose AJAX purchased an additional $5,000 of merchandise on account. To record the balance sheet effect, one would need to increase the inventory account by $5,000 and increase accounts payable by the same amount. Following the debit/credit coding, the journal entry for recording this transaction would be:

| | DR | CR |
|---|---|---|
| Inventory | $5,000 | |
| Accounts Payable | | $5,000 |

Note that debit/credit positioning is similar to a programming language. This entry can be decoded as instructing: "Post $5,000 to the debit (left) side of the Inventory account (increasing this asset by $5,000), and post $5,000 to the credit (right) side of the Accounts Payable account (increasing this liability by $5,000)."

Before proceeding, try setting up the four necessary "T" accounts involved on a separate sheet of paper. Record the original owner investment as shown above. Now record the purchase on account of merchandise costing $5,000.

You are correct and are well along the road to understanding the debit/credit system if your "T" accounts show:

```
            CASH                        ACCOUNTS PAYABLE
     _____                   _____
$50,000    |                                    | $5,000
```

```
          INVENTORY                        OWNER'S EQUITY
     _____                   _____
$20,000    |                                    | $70,000
  5,000    |
```

Note that the entry itself is balanced—$5,000 in debits equal $5,000 in credits. And, after posting, the "T"-account balances still reflect the equality. Seventy-five thousand dollars of total debits equals $75,000 of total credits.

Another example involving decreases should help you get a grasp of the overall system. Suppose AJAX paid $2,000 to suppliers on its Accounts Payable. The effect would be to reduce Cash by $2,000 and reduce Accounts Payable by the same amount. What would be the journal entry to record this transaction? Write down the journal entry and follow its instructions by posting to your "T" accounts before proceeding.

The journal entry would be:

|  | DR | CR |
|---|---|---|
| Accounts Payable | $2,000 | |
| Cash | | $2,000 |

Immediately after posting, the accounts would show:

| CASH | | ACCOUNTS PAYABLE | |
|---|---|---|---|
| $50,000 | $ 2,000 | $ 2,000 | $ 5,000 |

| INVENTORY | | OWNER'S EQUITY | |
|---|---|---|---|
| $20,000 | | | $70,000 |
| $ 5,000 | | | |

Note that the balance continues to be maintained in several forms. The entry itself is balanced. The total of the net balances in each of the accounts balances—$73,000 of net debits and credits. The total of all debits and credits in the system before netting each account still balances—$77,000 each of debits and credits.

## THE DEBIT/CREDIT CODE

In all, there are six possible different types of accounts:

- Asset accounts
- Contra-asset accounts
- Equity accounts
- Contra-equity accounts
- Revenue and gain accounts
- Expense and loss accounts

Asset accounts normally have debit balances. To increase an asset account, you would debit it, or post to the left side. To *decrease* an asset account, you would credit it.

| ASSET ACCOUNTS | |
|---|---|
| DR | CR |
| (Increase) | (Decrease) |

Contra-asset accounts, such as Accumulated Depreciation, are negative valuation accounts. They are shown on the balance sheet along with assets, but each subtracts from its related asset. They are therefore contra, or opposite to assets, and normally have a credit balance. To increase a contra-asset account you would credit, or post on the right side. To decrease a contra-asset account, you would debit it.

CONTRA-ASSET ACCOUNT

| DR | CR |
|---|---|
| (Decrease) | (Increase) |

Equity accounts normally have credit balances. How would you increase the balance in an equity account? How would you decrease it? Equity accounts are the opposite of asset accounts. They are increased by crediting and decreased by debiting or *charging*. "Charge" is often used synonymously for debit.

EQUITY ACCOUNTS

| DR | CR |
|---|---|
| (Decrease) | (Increase) |

Contra-equity accounts are shown on the balance sheet along with equities, but they subtract from their related equity accounts.[1] They are therefore contra, or opposite to, equity accounts, and normally have a debit balance. Contra-equity accounts are increased by charging (debiting) and decreased by crediting.

CONTRA-EQUITY ACCOUNTS

| DR | CR |
|---|---|
| (Increase) | (Decrease) |

To review, asset accounts normally have debit balances and equity accounts credit balances. Contra accounts are opposites. Remember, from Appendix D, that revenue increases owner's equity and that accountants store revenue information in temporary revenue accounts during the year. If revenue accounts are to increase owner's equity, what must be their normal balance, debit or credit? A positive balance in owner's equity is a credit. Therefore, a positive balance in a revenue account must also be a credit. Revenue accounts are increased by crediting, and decreased by debiting.

REVENUE ACCOUNTS

| DR | CR |
|---|---|
| (Decrease) | (Increase) |

---

[1]   Contra-equity accounts are equity valuation items and include such accounts as Discount on Notes (or bonds) Payable and Treasury Stock.

Expense accounts are temporary accounts to store specific types of expenses during the year. At the end of the year their balance is transferred to owner's equity as a reduction. Expense accounts, therefore, normally have a debit balance. They are increased by debiting and reduced by crediting.

EXPENSE ACCOUNTS

| DR | CR |
|---|---|
| (Increase) | (Decrease) |

An easy way to remember the debit/credit code is to think of the accounts in terms of the balance sheet. Exhibit E.1 is a visual summary of the various "T" accounts and the debit/credit code. All you really have to remember on the balance sheet is:

a) Asset accounts are on the left side of the balance sheet and have left-side (debit) normal or positive balances;

**Exhibit E.1**
VISUAL SUMMARY OF THE DEBIT/CREDIT CODE
(PROGRAMMING LANGUAGE)

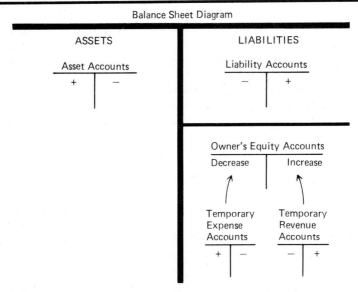

*Note.* Not shown are various contra-accounts which are exact opposites. For example, a contra-asset account:

ACCUMULATED DEPRECIATION

| − | + |
|---|---|

b) Equity accounts (liabilities and owner's equity) are on the right side of the balance sheet and have right-side (credit) normal or positive balances.

c) An increase to owner's equity is a credit; therefore revenue or gain, which increases owner's equity, must be a credit;

d) A decrease in owner's equity is a debit; therefore expense or loss, which decreases owner's equity, must be a debit;

e) Any contra accounts are just opposite.

## THE JOURNAL(S) AND THE AUDIT TRAIL

Transactions and adjustments are first recorded in a journal. The journal is like a diary of instructions. All transactions and adjustments are first recorded or *journalized* as an instruction, advising which accounts are to be changed and by how much. This instruction, which is made for each separate event (transaction or adjustment), is known as a *journal entry*. The journal entry will be accompanied by a brief written explanation such as "record purchase of inventory," "to record collection of a receivable," and so forth.

It may be desirable to check back through the accounts to the original source. Therefore, a journal entry is dated with the day journalized and also with a cross-reference code to the source document from which the accountant obtained information about the event. Thus an *audit trail* is created. If one wishes to check back on a given entry, one can go to the journal and be referred to the source document.

In larger firms with many transactions, more than one journal may be required in order to handle the volume of work. In such cases, it is common to have special journals for certain types of high-volume transactions, such as an Accounts Payable Journal or a Sales Journal.

## THE LEDGER(S) AND POSTING

Separate accounts are maintained for each type of information appropriate to the particular company. For example, all firms will have a cash account, but only those firms owning equipment would have an equipment account. All open or active accounts—those having or expected to have any balance—are kept together in a combined file known as the *ledger*. Journal entry instructions are periodically followed by posting to the individual accounts in the ledger. When posting is completed, the entry in the journal is marked as having been posted (to avoid double recording). The amount posted to the account in the ledger is also indexed back to the original entry by date of the journal entry, thus maintaining the audit trail.

## INTERIM TRIAL BALANCES

Periodically, and usually at least once a month, a *trial balance* is taken of all the accounts in the ledger. A trial balance involves totaling all the debit and credit amounts separately to see whether the totals agree. If the ledger is in balance, there could still be errors such as an amount posted to the wrong account. But if the ledger is not in balance, an error must exist. The purpose of frequent trial balances is like insurance. If an out-of-balance condition is discovered, then often only those entries and postings since the last trial balance need to be reviewed in order to locate the error.

## THE WORKSHEET AND THE PRE-ADJUSTING TRIAL BALANCE

At the end of the year or accounting period when statements are to be prepared, the net balance in each account is recorded on a *worksheet*. Exhibit E.2 shows a partially completed worksheet for the Potted Planter Company, with the pre-adjustment account balances recorded.

- Items are classified as debts or credits according to the debit/credit code, and
- The effects of revenue and expense transactions for the month are shown in temporary revenue and expense accounts and have not yet been combined (closed) with the $10,000 of beginning owner's equity.

Also note that debits and credits are totaled to make sure that the amounts are in balance before making adjustments.

Exhibit E.3 shows the records in the information flow or processing stream from the source document to the final statements.

## ADJUSTMENTS AND THE ADJUSTED TRIAL BALANCE

To speed up the process of completing the preparation of financial statements, year-end adjustments are first recorded directly on the worksheet. After the statements have been prepared, these adjustments are journalized and posted to the appropriate accounts. Exhibit E.4 shows the Potted Planter worksheet after the adjustments have been recorded. Note that all the account balances, adjusted where required, have been carried forward to the adjusted columns. Debits and credits are again totaled to make sure that no adjustment error has destroyed the ledger balance.

## CLOSING AND THE POST-CLOSING TRIAL BALANCE

Balance sheet accounts are permanent or *real accounts*. Their balances carry forward from year to year. To cite two examples, the amount of cash on hand, or the amount of debts owed to others, at year-end are the beginning balances

**Exhibit E.2**

**POTTED PLANTER**

| Sample worksheet | Before adjusting | | Adjustments | | Adjusted | | Income statement | | Balance sheet | |
|---|---|---|---|---|---|---|---|---|---|---|
| Accounts | DR | CR | DR | CR | DR | CR | DR | CR | DR | CR |
| Cash | $ 7,900 | $ | | | | | | | | |
| Accounts receivable | 350 | | | | | | | | | |
| Inventory | 3,900 | | | | | | | | | |
| Supplies | 200 | | | | | | | | | |
| Prepaid rent | 1,000 | | | | | | | | | |
| Equipment | 2,500 | | | | | | | | | |
| Accumulated depreciation | | 1,400 | | | | | | | | |
| Accounts payable | | 2,000 | | | | | | | | |
| Noncurrent note payable | | 10,000 | | | | | | | | |
| Owner's Equity | | | | | | | | | | |
| Sales revenue | | 2,500 | | | | | | | | |
| Cleanup expense | 50 | | | | | | | | | |
| Cost of goods sold | | | | | | | | | | |
| Supplies expense | | | | | | | | | | |
| Rent expense | | | | | | | | | | |
| Equipment depreciation | | | | | | | | | | |
| Utilities expense | | | | | | | | | | |
| Net Income | | | | | | | | | | |
| Totals | $15,900 | $15,900 | | | | | | | | |

**Exhibit E.3**
## RECORDS IN THE FLOW OF ACCOUNTING INFORMATION

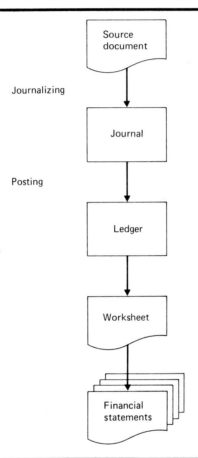

of the next year. Other accounts are temporary or *nominal accounts.* They are used to temporarily store specific information needed for certain reports and are then "emptied" at year-end. The process of emptying these temporary accounts by transferring their balances to the appropriate permanent accounts is called *closing.*

Exhibit E.5 shows the complete worksheet for the Potted Planter. Note that nominal accounts had been set up for all the revenue and expense items to appear on the income statement. In closing, the balance in each of these accounts has been transferred to owner's equity.[2] Note that, once again, debits

---

[2]    In practice, revenue and expense accounts are first closed to a new account called Income Summary. Income Summary then is closed to Owner's Equity for a proprietorship. For a partnership, income is distributed among individual partners' shares of ownership equity according to the partnership agreement. For a corporation, Income Summary is closed to a subaccount within corporate owners' equity known as Retained Earnings.

**Exhibit E.4**
POTTED PLANTER

| Sample worksheet | Before adjusting | | Adjustments | | Adjusted | | Income statement | | Balance sheet | |
|---|---|---|---|---|---|---|---|---|---|---|
| Accounts | DR | CR | DR | CR | DR | CR | DR | CR | DR | CR |
| Cash | $ 7,900 | $ | $ | $ | $ 7,900 | $ | | | | |
| Accounts receivable | 350 | | | | 350 | | | | | |
| Inventory | 3,900 | | | 1,050 | 2,850 | | | | | |
| Supplies | 200 | | | 125 | 75 | | | | | |
| Prepaid rent | 1,000 | | | 500 | 500 | | | | | |
| Equipment | 2,500 | | | | 2,500 | | | | | |
| Accumulated depreciation | | | | 50 | | 50 | | | | |
| Accounts payable | | 1,400 | | 140 | | 1,540 | | | | |
| Noncurrent note payable | | 2,000 | | | | 2,000 | | | | |
| Owner's Equity | | 10,000 | | | | 10,000 | | | | |
| Sales revenue | | 2,500 | | | | 2,500 | | | | |
| Cleanup expense | 50 | | | | 50 | | | | | |
| Cost of goods sold | | | 1,050 | | 1,050 | | | | | |
| Supplies expense | | | 125 | | 125 | | | | | |
| Rent expense | | | 500 | | 500 | | | | | |
| Equipment depreciation | | | 50 | | 50 | | | | | |
| Utilities expense | | | 140 | | 140 | | | | | |
| Net Income | | | | | | | | | | |
| Totals | $15,900 | $15,900 | $ 1,865 | $ 1,865 | $16,090 | $16,090 | | | | |

**Exhibit E.5**
POTTED PLANTER

| Sample worksheet | Before adjusting | | Adjustments | | Adjusted | | Income statement | | Balance sheet | |
|---|---|---|---|---|---|---|---|---|---|---|
| Accounts | DR | CR | DR | CR | DR | CR | DR | CR | DR | CR |
| Cash | $ 7,900 | $ | $ | $ | $ 7,900 | $ | $ | $ | $ 7,900 | $ |
| Accounts receivable | 350 | | | | 350 | | | | 350 | |
| Inventory | 3,900 | | | 1,050 | 2,850 | | | | 2,850 | |
| Supplies | 200 | | | 125 | 75 | | | | 75 | |
| Prepaid rent | 1,000 | | | 500 | 500 | | | | 500 | |
| Equipment | 2,500 | | | | 2,500 | | | | 2,500 | |
| Accumulated depreciation | | | | 50 | | 50 | | | | 50 |
| Accounts payable | | 1,400 | | 140 | | 1,540 | | | | 1,540 |
| Noncurrent note payable | | 2,000 | | | | 2,000 | | | | 2,000 |
| Owner's Equity | | 10,000 | | | | 10,000 | | | | 10,000 +585 |
| Sales revenue | | 2,500 | | | | 2,500 | | 2,500 | | |
| Cleanup expense | 50 | | | | 50 | | 50 | | | |
| Cost of goods sold | | | 1,050 | | 1,050 | | 1,050 | | | |
| Supplies expense | | | 125 | | 125 | | 125 | | | |
| Rent expense | | | 500 | | 500 | | 500 | | | |
| Equipment depreciation | | | 50 | | 50 | | 50 | | | |
| Utilities expense | | | 140 | | 140 | | 140 | | | |
| | | | | | | | | | | |
| Net Income | | | | | | | $ 585 | | | |
| Totals | $15,900 | $15,900 | $ 1,865 | $ 1,865 | $16,090 | $16,090 | $ 2,500 | $ 2,500 | $14,175 | $14,175 |

and credits have been totaled to ensure that the ledger is in balance after closing.

Compare the last columns of Exhibit E.5 with the actual Potted Planter ending balance sheet shown as Exhibit E.6. Can you see why the balance sheet reports $14,125 of total assets whereas the worksheet shows $14,175 of total debits? The answer is in the contra account, Accumulated Depreciation; $50 of accumulated depreciation is included with other credits on the worksheet. On the balance sheet it is shown contra to equipment and therefore subtracts in determining total assets. Also note on the worksheet that income is closed to owner's equity for a total of $10,585.

**Exhibit E.6**
POTTED PLANTER ADJUSTED BALANCE SHEET
AT END OF FIRST MONTH

| Assets | | Equities | |
|---|---|---|---|
| Cash | $7,900 | Accounts payable | $1,540 |
| Accounts receivable | 350 | Total Current Liabilities | $1,540 |
| Inventory | 2,850 | Noncurrent Note Payable | 2,000 |
| Supplies | 75 | | |
| Prepaid rent | 500 | Total Liabilities | 3,540 |
| Total Current Assets | $11,675 | | |
| Equipment | 2,500 | | |
| Less accumulated depreciation | (50) | Owner's Equity | $10,585 |
| Total Assets | $14,125 | Total Equities | $14,125 |

## ERROR CORRECTIONS AND OPENING REVERSALS

Because of the risks of additional errors and of the possibility that someone might be able to manipulate the firm's accounting records, accountants are careful to preserve the audit trail even when an error has been made. If an incorrect journal entry is discovered, or if an entry has been incorrectly posted, accountants do not use an eraser. Instead they will make the correction through two additional entries identified as error-correcting entries. The first entry will be a *reversing entry*. It will be designed to eliminate the incorrect posting by reversing it, or backing it out. For example, suppose the original entry had been:

| | DR | CR |
|---|---|---|
| Accounts Payable | $100 | |
| Cash | | $100 |

To record payment of account

Suppose that posting had been really fouled up and that accounts **receivable** had been debited $75 and cash credited $100. The wrong **account** was posted and with the wrong **amount,** so the ledger is out of balance. The error-correcting reversing entry would be:

|  | DR | CR |
|---|---|---|
| Cash | $100 | |
| Accounts Receivable | | $75 |

To reverse entry of X/X/XX posted in error

Note that this reversing entry is not balanced, but is necessary to cancel the original posting error.

After reversing out the error, the correction is completed with an additional entry in the form that should have been posted to begin with.

In some accounting systems, reversing entries are also used at the beginning of the year, to reverse the prior year's temporary year-end accrual adjustments. This is done to avoid the possibility of double-counting, when the item which was accrued subsequently arrives and is recorded normally.

For example, in the case of the Potted Planter, $140 of utilities expense was accrued at month end and is shown as a liability. The accrual was anticipating the invoice, which had not been received and journalized by the closing date. Assume that, in the following month, invoices arrived totalling $300, $140 of which represented costs of prior month's services. If the full $300 is normally recorded as a liability and as utilities expense, $140 will have been double-counted. Rather than record only part of the new invoice, the accountant will reverse the previous accrual at the start of the new accounting period. After reversal, no liability for this service will be in the accounts, and utilities expense will start with a credit (negative) balance of $140.

The $300 invoice is then recorded normally:

|  | DR | CR |
|---|---|---|
| Utilities Expense | $300 | |
| Accounts Payable | | $300 |

Note that the firm's total liability for these services is now correctly shown as $300. Also, the balance in Utilities Expense will be $160 ($300 debit less $140 credit), which is the correct portion applicable to the new period.

## THE ACCOUNTING CYCLE

The term *accounting cycle* is used to describe the several steps or stages of the accountant's activities during the year. The accounting cycle may be viewed as having eight sequential steps or phases:

1. Possible opening reversals (see above);
2. Journalizing and posting transactions throughout the year;
3. Interim trial balances;
4. Initial worksheet preparation, and the pre-adjusting trial balance;
5. Adjustments on the worksheet, and the adjusted trial balance;
6. Closing on the worksheet, and the post-closing trial balance;
7. Financial statement preparation;
8. Journalizing and posting adjusting and closing entries.

## SUBSIDIARY AND SPECIAL JOURNALS, LEDGERS, AND ACCOUNTS

The financial accounting bookkeeping system can be fully understood in terms of a single journal and ledger, and with accounts only for balance sheet and income statement items. In practice, most companies keep many more detailed accounts as components of a single balance sheet account. An obvious example would be accounts receivable. If a store had several thousand charge customers, to keep all of their separate balances on one record would be impossible. In such a case, a *subsidiary ledger* is maintained with *subsidiary accounts*, one for each separate customer. The total of all of the subsidiary-account balances is carried in the single balance sheet account, which is then known as the *control account*. Some other areas where detailed accounts are often maintained include subsidiary accounts for different types of inventory, fixed assets, and accounts payable.

## MACHINE AND COMPUTER SYSTEMS

In many firms, accounting records are maintained on machine or computer systems. Some smaller firms subcontract most of their bookkeeping to computer service bureaus. Regardless of the physical means employed to record, store, summarize, and report accounting information, the essential concepts are maintained, even though debit/credit programming language may not be used (as mentioned above). A discussion of the details of various machine and computer accounting systems is beyond the scope of this text.

# INDEX

(Italicized figures refer to pages in the Glossary, Appendix B.)